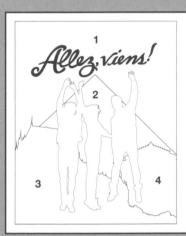

Front cover:

1 Pattern from a 17th century textile from Lyons which features a stylized pineapple – first brought to Europe from the West Indies, it was a favorite fruit of European royalty

2 Pyramid of glass designed by I.M. Pei as part of President François Mitterrand's renovation of the Louvre museum in Paris in the 1980s

3 The majestic Château Frontenac in Quebec City, a world-renowned hotel built in 1893

4 The famous Fort-de-France landmark Bibliothèque Schœlcher, named for the man who abolished slavery in Martinique in 1848

Back cover:
Young woman in traditional costume of Brittany, an area of France known for its intricate lacework

Give your students a window to the world!

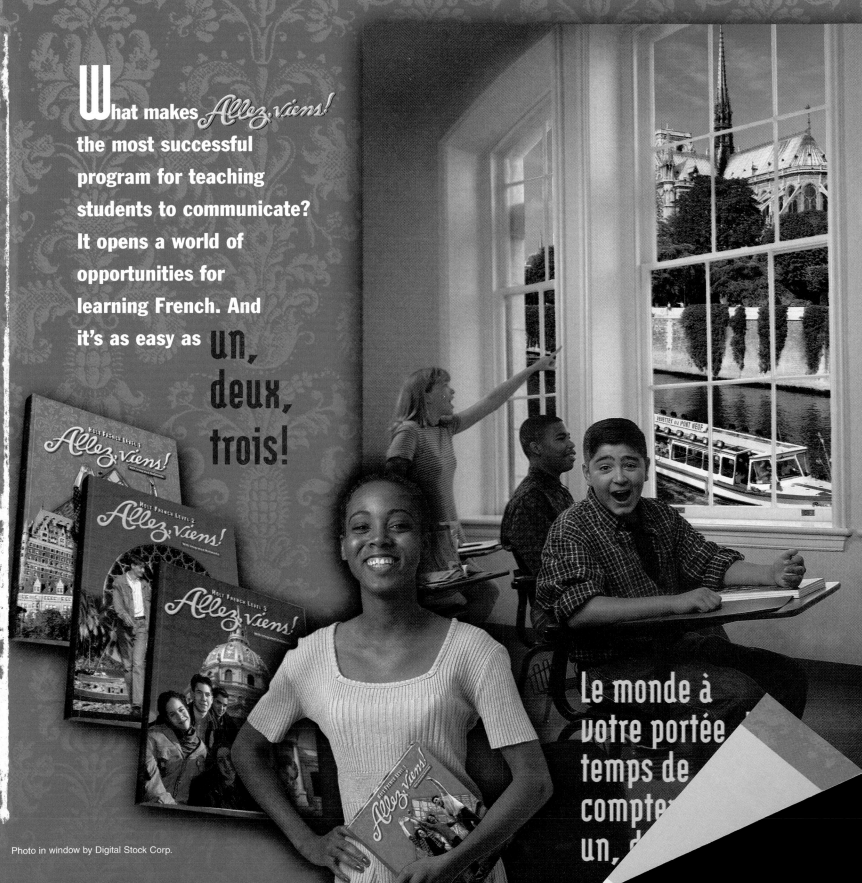

What makes *Allez, viens!* the most successful program for teaching students to communicate? It opens a world of opportunities for learning French. And it's as easy as **un, deux, trois!**

Le monde à votre portée temps de compte un,

Un

Easy-to-use teaching materials make a world of difference for you and your students.

Teacher Resources include:

- **Annotated Teacher's Edition**
- **Lesson Planner**
- **TPR Storytelling Book**
- **Exploratory Guide**
- **Listening Activities**
- **Activities For Communication**
- **Testing Program**
- **Alternative Assessment Guide**

"I'm going back to school rejuvenated! The resources in *Allez, viens!* make me feel like I'm opening a treasure chest of materials every day!"

Fred Pratt
San Marcos High School
San Marcos, Texas

As your student population grows increasingly diverse and you face more and more complex teaching situations, **Allez, viens!** offers all the support you need to be an effective French teacher.

The **Annotated Teacher's Edition** presents easy-to-read planning charts so you can integrate print and media resources into each lesson. It also helps you address the different learners in your classroom by providing games and projects, teaching strategies for kinesthetic, visual, and auditory learners, and suggestions for students with special needs.

The **Lesson Planner** gives you in-depth lesson plans for every chapter section and shows you how each plan meets the Standards for Foreign Language Learning.

In addition, the **TPR Storytelling Book** helps you engage every learner with motivating, active-learning activities correlated to each section of the textbook.

Especially for the middle grades...

- The 360-page **Middle School Teaching Resources** and audio CDs give you listening activities, interdisciplinary projects and games, critical thinking activities, and midterm and final exams geared to the middle school learner. A bridging instrument shows you how to use **Allez, viens!** over two years of instruction.
- An **Exploratory Guide** provides theme-centered lesson plans and resources to help you use **Allez, viens!** in an exploratory class.

Deux

The outlook for student language learning has never been better.

"We are very happy with the communicative approach of the Holt series, and our students are performing more and earlier than ever before."

Judith Speiller
Supervisor, World Languages and ESL
Edison, New Jersey Public Schools

Allez, viens! builds a proven communicative approach on a solid foundation of grammar and vocabulary to turn your students into proficient readers, writers, and speakers of French.

Every chapter section revolves around a different communicative goal, and the grammar and vocabulary lessons give students the tools they need to achieve this goal. ❶ Grammar and vocabulary are modeled in the communicative expressions. ❷ Grammar and vocabulary presentations explain each concept. ❸ Concepts learned in previous chapters are continually recycled.

Pupil Resources include:

- **Pupil's Edition**
- **Grammar and Vocabulary Workbook**
- **Practice and Activity Book**

 Listening activities are integrated into every presentation so students are continually practicing their listening skills.

 Writing is emphasized in every section of each chapter.

 Speaking activities in partners and groups build confidence and promote active learning.

 CD-ROM activities give students practice with vocabulary, grammar, and culture.

Trois

The most extensive multimedia package available brings the French-speaking world into view.

Allez, viens! brings the language and culture of French-speaking countries into your classroom with unparalleled video, CD-ROM, and Internet resources.

The *Video and Videodisc Programs* take students to each location in the textbook. Footage shot on location models the language learned in every chapter with dramatic episodes, commercials, songs, and excerpts from documentaries. Students also watch interviews with native speakers who talk about their culture and way of life.

Interactive, multisensory activities in the award-winning *CD-ROM Programs* reinforce and enrich textbook lessons with grammar, vocabulary, listening, speaking, reading, and writing activities.

The *HRW World Languages Web Site* puts the world literally at students' fingertips. Language comes alive as students explore each geographic location and practice their language and cultural skills in a completely authentic environment.

www.hrw.com

Multimedia Resources include:

- Video Program and Guide
- Videodisc Program and Guide
- CD-ROM Program and Guide
- World Languages Web Site
- Audio Compact Discs
- Teaching Transparencies
- Test Generator

Un, deux, trois, ça y est!
Le monde est à vos pieds!

Holt French Level 1

Allez, viens!®

With Integrated Multimedia

Annotated Teacher's Edition

John DeMado
Emmanuel Rongiéras d'Usseau

HOLT, RINEHART AND **WINSTON**
Harcourt Brace & Company

Austin • New York • Orlando • Atlanta • San Francisco • Boston • Dallas • Toronto • London

For permission to reprint copyrighted material in the *Annotated Teacher's Edition,* grateful acknowledgment is made to the following sources:

Editions Estel, Blois, France: Front and back of postcard, "Arènes d'Arles," no. 10033 Z.

France Miniature: Cover from brochure, *Le Pays France Miniature.*

National Standards in Foreign Language Education Project: "National Standards Report" from *Standards for Foreign Language Learning: Preparing for the 21st Century.* Copyright © 1996 by National Standards in Foreign Language Education Project.

Parc Astérix: Cover of brochure, *Parc Astérix,* 1992.

Photo Credits

Photo of compact discs that appear throughout the interleaf pages: ©1996 Photo Disc, Inc.; Pages T30, T37, T43(bl), HRW Photo/Marty Granger/Edge Productions; T43(br), HRW Photo/Sam Dudgeon; T62(l), Liaison International, Inc.; T62(cr), Kathy Willens/Wide World; T62(cl), Benainous-Scorcelletti/Liaison International, Inc. 65H(br), © European Communities; 93H(t), HRW Photo/Marty Granger/Edge Productions; 93H, Photo Edit.

Art Credits

All art, unless otherwise noted, by Holt, Rinehart & Winston.

Preliminary Chapter: Page T65, Guy Maestracci. **Chapter One:** Page 15I, Yves Lavor; 15J, Jocelyne Bouchard. **Chapter Two:** Page 41J, Guy Maestracci. **Chapter Three:** Page 65I, Michel Loppé, 65J, Michel Loppé. **Chapter Five:** Page 123H, Jocelyne Bouchard. **Chapter Six:** Page 147J, Guy Maestracci. **Chapter Seven:** Page 173H, Vincent Rio, 173J, Guy Maestracci. **Chapter Nine:** Page 231J, Michel Loppé. **Chapter Ten:** Page 255J, Michel Loppé. **Chapter Eleven:** Page 281I, Michel Loppé, 281J, Brian Stevens. **Chapter Twelve:** Page 309G, Brian Stevens; 309H, Anne de Masson; 309I, Anne Stanley.

COVER PHOTOGRAPHY CREDITS

FRONT COVER: (bl), Schœlcher Library, Fort-de-France, Martinique, HRW Photo/Marty Granger; (br), Château Frontenac, Quebec City, Canada, Miwako Ikeda/International Stock; (c), Louvre, Paris, France, Photo AKG London; (c), students jumping, Telegraph Colour Library/FPG International Corp.

BACK COVER: France, Brittany, young woman in regional costume, Steve Vidler/Leo de Wys, Inc.

FRONT AND BACK COVER: (bckgd pattern), Copyright ©1992 by Dover Publications, Inc.

ACKNOWLEDGMENTS continued on page R83, which is an extension of the copyright page.

Annotated Teacher's Edition

Contributing Writers

Jennie Bowser Chao
Consultant
East Lansing, MI

Ms. Chao was the principal writer of the Level 1 *Annotated Teacher's Edition.*

Jayne Abrate
The University of Missouri
Rolla Campus
Rolla, MO

Dr. Abrate contributed teaching suggestions, notes, and background information for the Location Openers of the Level 1 *Annotated Teacher's Edition.*

Margaret Sellstrom
Consultant
Austin, TX

Ms. Sellstrom contributed answers to activities of the Level 1 *Annotated Teacher's Edition.*

Field Test Participants

Marie Allison
New Hanover High School
Wilmington, NC

Gabrielle Applequist
Capital High School
Boise, ID

Jana Brinton
Bingham High School
Riverton, UT

Nancy J. Cook
Sam Houston High School
Lake Charles, LA

Rachael Gray
Williams High School
Plano, TX

Katherine Kohler
Nathan Hale Middle School
Norwalk, CT

Nancy Mirsky
Museum Junior High School
Yonkers, NY

Myrna S. Nie
Whetstone High School
Columbus, OH

Jacqueline Reid
Union High School
Tulsa, OK

Judith Ryser
San Marcos High School
San Marcos, TX

Erin Hahn Sass
Lincoln Southeast High School
Lincoln, NE

Linda Sherwin
Sandy Creek High School
Tyrone, GA

Norma Joplin Sivers
Arlington Heights High School
Fort Worth, TX

Lorabeth Stroup
Lovejoy High School
Lovejoy, GA

Robert Vizena
W.W. Lewis Middle School
Sulphur, LA

Gladys Wade
New Hanover High School
Wilmington, NC

Kathy White
Grimsley High School
Greensboro, NC

Reviewers

Jane Canales
Dripping Springs High School
Dripping Springs, TX

Jennifer Jones
U.S. Peace Corps volunteer
Côte d'Ivoire 1991–1993
Austin, TX

Jo Anne Jones
Peet Junior High School
525 East Seerley Blvd.
Cedar Falls, IA 50613

Kristin Kajer-Cline
Consultant
Kirkland, WA

Theresa Kobak
St. Patrick-St. Vincent High School
1500 Benicia
Vallejo, CA 94951

Diane Larson
Southeast Polk High School
2325 NE University Avenue
Runnells, IA 50237

Jo Anne S. Wilson
Consultant
Glen Arbor, MI

Professional Essays

*Standards for Foreign
Language Learning*
Robert LaBouve
Board of National Standards in
Foreign Language Education
Austin, TX

*Technology in the Language
Classroom*
Cindy A. Kendall
Williamston High School
Williamston, MI

Teaching Culture
Nancy A. Humbach
Miami University
Oxford, OH

Dorothea Brushke
Parkway School District
Chesterfield, MO

*Learning Styles and
Multi-Modality Teaching*
Mary B. McGehee
Louisiana State University
Baton Rouge, LA

Higher-Order Thinking Skills
Audrey L. Heining-Boynton
The University of North Carolina
Chapel Hill, NC

*Using Portfolios in the
Language Classroom*
Jo Anne S. Wilson
J. Wilson Associates
Glen Arbor, MI

Pupil's Edition

Authors

John DeMado
Washington, CT

Mr. DeMado helped form the general philosophy of the French program and wrote activities to practice basic material, functions, grammar, and vocabulary.

Emmanuel Rongiéras d'Usseau
Le Kremlin-Bicêtre, France

Mr. Rongiéras d'Usseau contributed to the development of the scope and sequence for the chapters, created the basic material and listening scripts, selected realia, and wrote activities.

Contributing Writers

Jayne Abrate
The University of Missouri
Rolla Campus
Rolla, MO

Sally Adamson Taylor
Publishers Weekly
San Francisco, CA

Linda Bistodeau
Saint Mary's University
Halifax, Nova Scotia

Betty Peltier
Consultant
Batz-sur-Mer, France

Reviewers

Dominique Bach
Rio Linda Senior High School
Rio Linda, CA

Jeannette Caviness
Mount Tabor High School
Winston-Salem, NC

Jennie Bowser Chao
Consultant
Oak Park, IL

Pierre F. Cintas
Penn State University
Abington College
Abington, PA

Donna Clementi
Appleton West High School
Appleton, WI

Cathy Cramer
Homewood High School
Birmingham, AL

Robert H. Didsbury
Consultant
Raleigh, NC

Jennifer Jones
U.S. Peace Corps volunteer
Côte d'Ivoire 1991–1993
Austin, TX

Joan H. Manley
The University of Texas at El Paso
El Paso, TX

Jill Markert
Pflugerville High School
Pflugerville, TX

Inge McCoy
Southwest Texas State University
San Marcos, TX

Gail Montgomery
Foreign Language Program
Administrator
Greenwich, CT Public Schools

Agathe Norman
Consultant
Austin, TX

Audrey O'Keefe
Jordan High School
Los Angeles, CA

Sherry Parker
Selvidge Middle School
Ballwin, MO

Sherron N. Porter
Robert E. Lee High School
Baton Rouge, LA

Marc Prévost
Austin Community College
Austin, TX

Norbert Rouquet
Consultant
La Roche-sur-Yon, France

Michèle Shockey
Gunn High School
Palo Alto, CA

Ashley Shumaker
Central High School West
Tuscaloosa, AL

Antonia Stergiades
Washington High School
Massillon, OH

Frederic L. Toner
Texas Christian University
Fort Worth, TX

Jeannine Waters
Harrisonburg High School
Harrisonburg, VA

Jo Anne S. Wilson
Consultant
Glen Arbor, MI

Field Test Participants

Marie Allison
New Hanover High School
Wilmington, NC

Gabrielle Applequist
Capital High School
Boise, ID

Jana Brinton
Bingham High School
Riverton, UT

Nancy J. Cook
Sam Houston High School
Lake Charles, LA

Rachael Gray
Williams High School
Plano, TX

Katherine Kohler
Nathan Hale Middle School
Norwalk, CT

Nancy Mirsky
Museum Junior High School
Yonkers, NY

Myrna S. Nie
Whetstone High School
Columbus, OH

Jacqueline Reid
Union High School
Tulsa, OK

Judith Ryser
San Marcos High School
San Marcos, TX

Erin Hahn Sass
Lincoln Southeast High School
Lincoln, NE

Linda Sherwin
Sandy Creek High School
Tyrone, GA

Norma Joplin Sivers
Arlington Heights High School
Fort Worth, TX

Lorabeth Stroup
Lovejoy High School
Lovejoy, GA

Robert Vizena
W.W. Lewis Middle School
Sulphur, LA

Gladys Wade
New Hanover High School
Wilmington, NC

Kathy White
Grimsley High School
Greensboro, NC

To the Student

Some people have the opportunity to learn a new language by living in another country. Most of us, however, begin learning another language and getting acquainted with a foreign culture in a classroom with the help of a teacher, classmates, and a textbook. To use your book effectively, you need to know how it works.

Allez, viens! *(Come along!)* is organized to help you learn French and become familiar with the cultures of people who speak French. The Preliminary Chapter presents basic concepts in French and strategies for learning a new language. This chapter is followed by six Location Openers and twelve chapters.

Location Opener You'll find six four–page photo essays called Location Openers that introduce different French-speaking places.

Chapter Opener The Chapter Opener pages tell you the chapter theme and goals, and outline what you learn to do in each section of the chapter.

Mise en train *(Getting started)* This illustrated story, which is also on video, shows you French-speaking people in real-life situations, using the language you'll learn in the chapter.

Première, Deuxième, and **Troisième étape** *(First, Second, Third Part)* After the **Mise en train,** the chapter is divided into three sections called **étapes.** At the beginning of each **étape,** there is a reminder of the goals for this part of the chapter. Within the **étape,** are **Comment dit-on?** *(How do you say . . . ?)* boxes that contain the French expressions you'll need to communicate and **Vocabulaire** and **Grammaire/Note de Grammaire** boxes that give you the French words and grammatical structures you'll need to know. Activities in each **étape** enable you to practice the new expressions, vocabulary, and structures and thereby develop your skills in listening, reading, speaking, and writing.

iv

Panorama Culturel *(Cultural Panorama)* On this page are interviews with French-speaking people from around the world. They talk about themselves and their lives, and you can compare their culture to yours. You can watch these interviews on video or listen to them on audio CD. You can also watch them using the CD-ROM program, then check to see how well you understood by answering some questions about what the people say.

Rencontre Culturelle *(Cultural Encounter)* This section, found in six of the chapters, gives you a firsthand encounter with some aspect of a French-speaking culture.

Note Culturelle *(Culture Note)* In each chapter, there are notes with more information about the cultures of French-speaking people. These notes might tell you interesting facts, describe common customs, or offer other information that will help you learn more about the French-speaking world.

Lisons! *(Let's read!)* The reading section follows the three **étapes.** The selections are related to the chapter themes and help you develop your reading skills in French. The **De bons conseils** *(Helpful advice)* boxes in this section are strategies to improve your reading comprehension.

Mise en pratique *(Review)* The activities on these pages practice what you've learned in the chapter and help you improve your listening, reading, and communication skills. You'll also review what you've learned about culture. A section called **Ecrivons!** *(Let's write!)* in Chapters 3–12 will help develop your writing skills.

Que sais-je? *(Let's see if I can . . .)* This page at the end of each chapter contains a series of questions and short activities to help you see if you've achieved the chapter goals. Page numbers beside each section will tell you where to go for help if you need it.

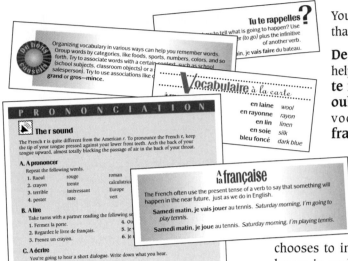

You'll also find special features in each chapter that provide extra tips and reminders.

De bons conseils *(advice)* offers study hints to help you succeed in a foreign language class. **Tu te rappelles?** *(Do you remember?)* and **Si tu as oublié** remind you of expressions, grammar, and vocabulary you may have forgotten. **A la française** *(The French way)* gives you additional expressions to add more color to your speech. **Vocabulaire à la carte** *(Additional Vocabulary)* lists extra words you might find helpful. These words will not appear on the quizzes and tests unless your teacher chooses to include them. **Prononciation** boxes in each chapter will help your pronunciation in French.

Si tu as oublié the verb *aller* va à la page 154.

Vocabulaire *(Vocabulary)* On the French-English vocabulary list on the last page of the chapter, the words are grouped by **étape**. These words and expressions will be on the quizzes and tests.

You'll also find French-English and English-French vocabulary lists at the end of the book. The words you'll need to know for the quizzes and tests are in boldface type.

At the end of your book, you'll find more helpful material, such as:
* a summary of the expressions you'll learn in the **Comment dit**-on... **?** boxes
* additional vocabulary words you might want to use
* a summary of the grammar you'll study
* a section of additional activities to practice the structures you'll learn
* a grammar index to help you find where structures are presented

Allez, viens! Come along on an exciting trip to new cultures and a new language!

Bon voyage!

Explanation of Icons in *Allez, viens!*

Throughout *Allez, viens!,* you'll see these symbols, or icons, next to activities. They'll tell you what you'll do with that activity. Here's a key to help you understand the icons.

 Listening Activities This icon indicates a listening activity. You'll need to listen to the CD or your teacher to complete the activity.

 CD-ROM Activities Whenever this icon appears, you know there's a related activity on the *Allez, viens! Interactive CD-ROM Program.*

 Writing Activities You'll see this icon next to writing activities. The directions may ask you to write words, sentences, paragraphs, or a whole composition.

 Pair Work Activities Activities with this icon are to be done with a partner. Both you and your partner are responsible for completing the activity.

 Group Work Activities If an activity has this icon next to it, you'll complete it with a small group of classmates. Each person in the group is responsible for a share of the work.

ANNOTATED TEACHER'S EDITION

Contents

Allez, viens! Contents

Come along—to a world of new experiences!

Allez, viens! offers you the opportunity to learn the language spoken by millions of people in countries in Europe, Africa, Asia, and around the world. Let's find out what those countries are.

CHAPITRE PRELIMINAIRE

Allez, viens! 1

T13

ALLEZ, VIENS

à Poitiers!

VISIT THE FRENCH CITY OF POITIERS AND—

Introduce yourself to some
French-speaking students • CHAPITRE 1
Talk about school activities • CHAPITRE 2
Shop for school supplies and clothes • CHAPITRE 3

CHAPITRE 1

Faisons connaissance! 16

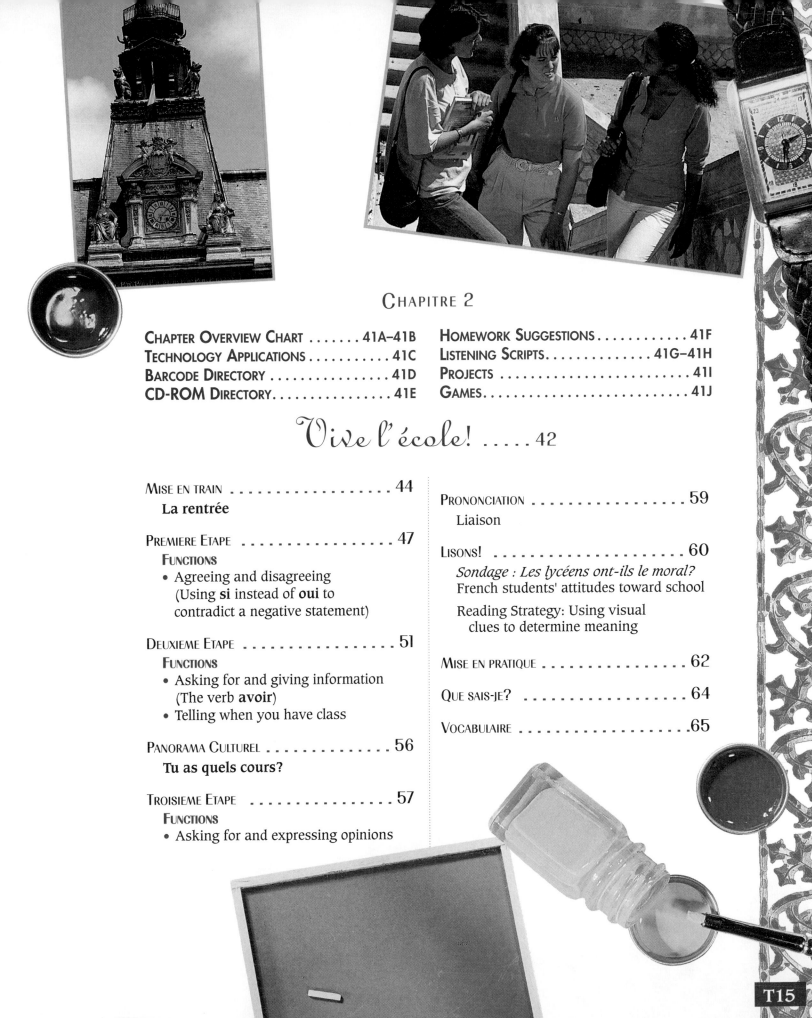

Chapitre 2

Vive l'école! 42

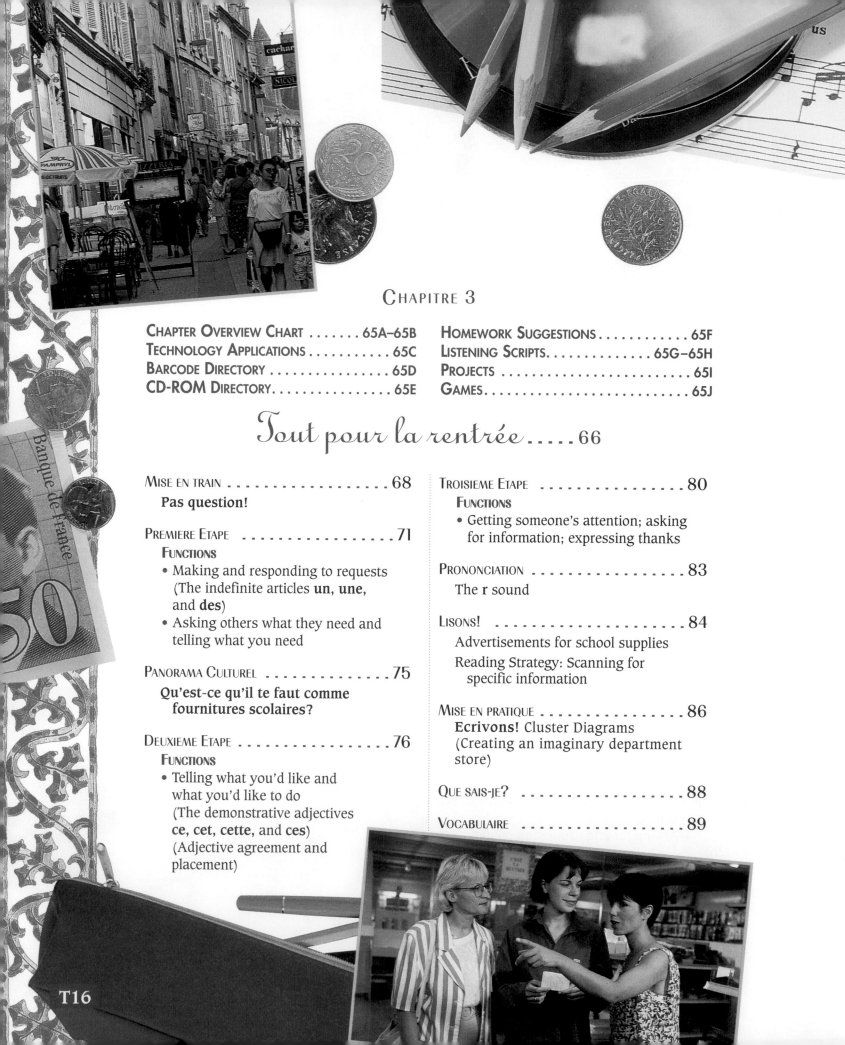

CHAPITRE 3

Tout pour la rentrée 66

ALLEZ, VIENS

à Québec!

VISIT THE CANADIAN CITY OF QUEBEC AND—

Find out about sports and hobbies in
francophone countries • **CHAPITRE 4**

CHAPITRE 4

Sports et passe-temps 94

ALLEZ, VIENS

à Paris!

CHAPITRE 5

On va au café? 124

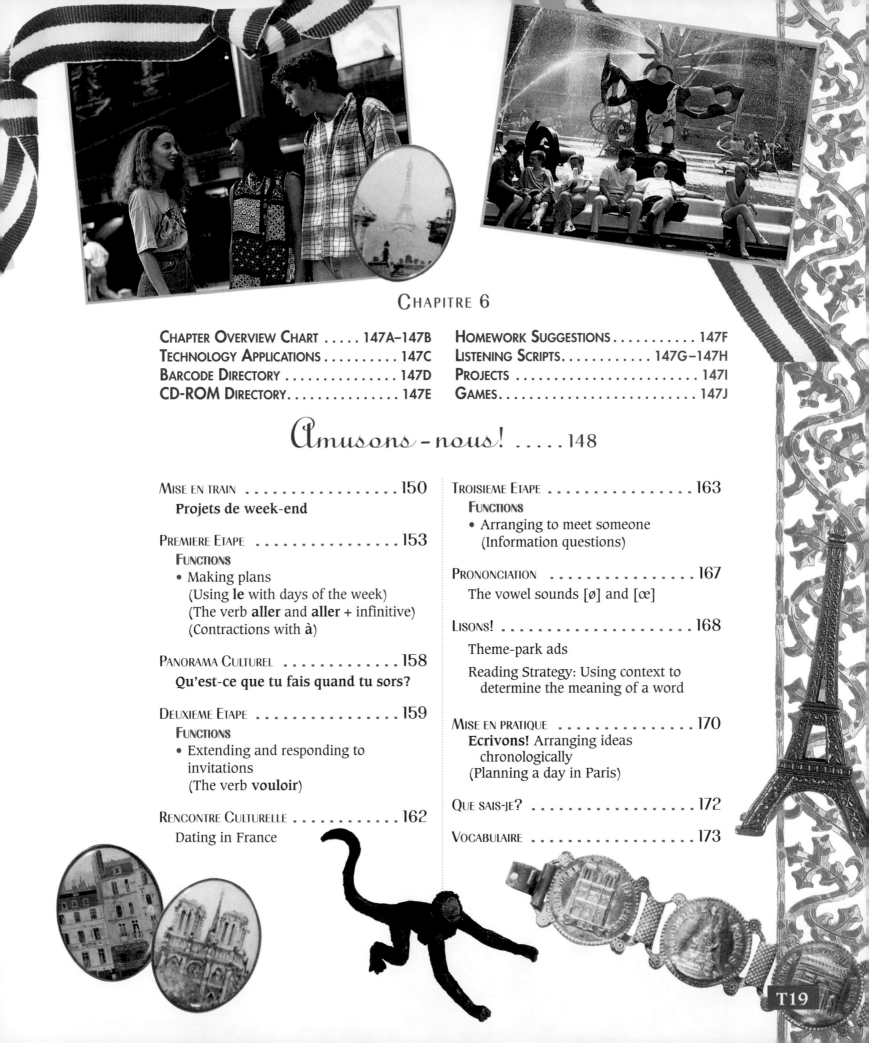

CHAPITRE 6

Amusons-nous! 148

CHAPITRE 7

La famille 174

ALLEZ, VIENS

à Abidjan!

CHAPITRE 8

Au marché 202

ALLEZ, VIENS

en Arles!

VISIT THE FRENCH CITY OF ARLES AND—

Talk about weekend activities • CHAPITRE 9
Find out how French-speaking teenagers
feel about fashion • CHAPITRE 10
Make vacation plans • CHAPITRE 11

CHAPITRE 9

Au téléphone 232

CHAPITRE 10

Dans un magasin de vêtements 256

CHAPITRE 11

Vive les vacances! 282

ALLEZ, VIENS

à Fort-de-France!

LOCATION • CHAPITRE 12 306

VISIT THE CAPITAL OF MARTINIQUE AND—

Ask directions
around town • CHAPITRE 12

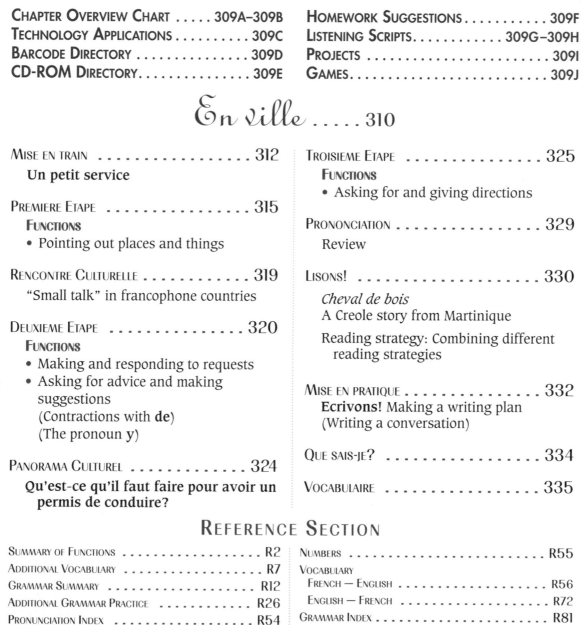

CHAPITRE 12

En ville 310

REFERENCE SECTION

Cultural References

Page numbers referring to material in the Pupil's Edition *appear in regular type. When the material referenced is located in the* Annotated Teacher's Edition, *page numbers appear in **boldface type**.* ◆

La France

ANGLETERRE

Mer du Nord

PAYS-BAS

ALLEMAGNE

Dunkerque
Calais
Lille

BELGIQUE

La Manche

LUXEMBOURG

Le Havre · Rouen
Caen

Reims

Meuse

Nancy · Strasbourg

Seine · Paris

Brest

Chartres

Colmar

Rennes

Orléans

Dijon

Saône

SUISSE

Nantes

Loire · Tours

F R A N C E

Poitiers

Vichy

Lyon

Limoges · Clermont-Ferrand

Grenoble

ITALIE

Océan Atlantique

LE MASSIF CENTRAL

Bordeaux

Garonne

Rhône

Avignon

Nice

Arles

Cannes

Montpellier

Aix-en-Provence

MONACO

Toulouse

Marseille

Biarritz

LES PYRÉNÉES

LE JURA · LES VOSGES · LES ALPES

N
O — E
S

ANDORRE

Mer Méditerranée

ESPAGNE

Corse

Ajaccio

L'Afrique francophone

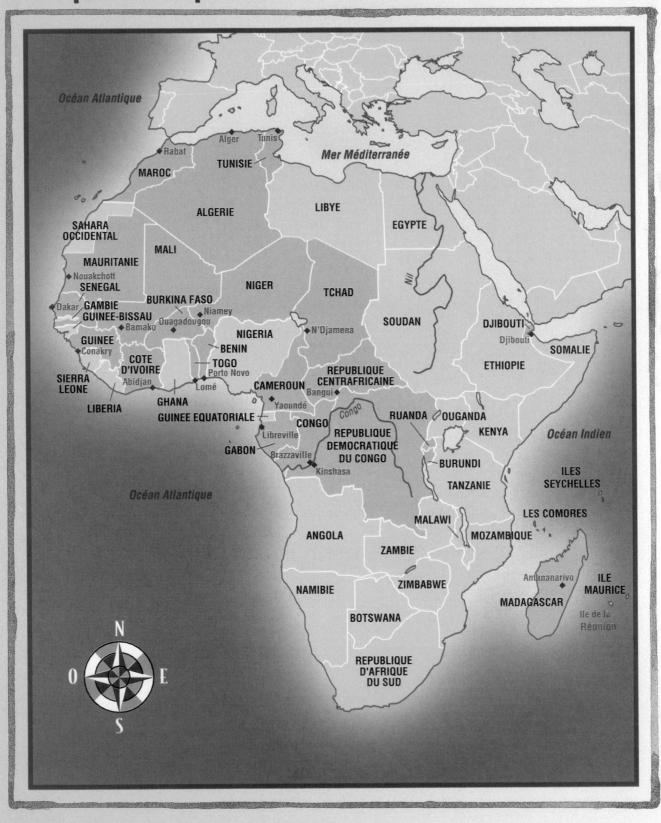

Océan Atlantique

Alger   Tunis
Rabat
TUNISIE
MAROC
Mer Méditerranée

ALGERIE
LIBYE
EGYPTE

SAHARA
OCCIDENTAL
MALI
MAURITANIE
Nouakchott
SENEGAL
NIGER
TCHAD
SOUDAN
DJIBOUTI
Djibouti
BURKINA FASO
Dakar GAMBIE
GUINEE-BISSAU   Niamey
Ouagadougou
Bamako   N'Djamena
SOMALIE
NIGERIA
GUINEE   BENIN   ETHIOPIE
Conakry
COTE   TOGO
D'IVOIRE   Porto Novo
REPUBLIQUE
CENTRAFRICAINE
SIERRA   Abidjan   Lomé
LEONE   CAMEROUN
Bangui
LIBERIA   Yaoundé
GHANA   RUANDA   OUGANDA
GUINEE EQUATORIALE   KENYA
Congo
CONGO
Océan Indien
Libreville   REPUBLIQUE
DEMOCRATIQUE
GABON   DU CONGO
Brazzaville   BURUNDI
Kinshasa   ILES
SEYCHELLES
TANZANIE
LES COMORES
MALAWI
ANGOLA   MOZAMBIQUE
ZAMBIE
Antananarivo   ILE
MAURICE
NAMIBIE   ZIMBABWE
MADAGASCAR
Ile de la
Réunion
BOTSWANA

REPUBLIQUE
D'AFRIQUE
DU SUD

N
O   E
S

Nil

xxiv

T30

L'Amérique francophone

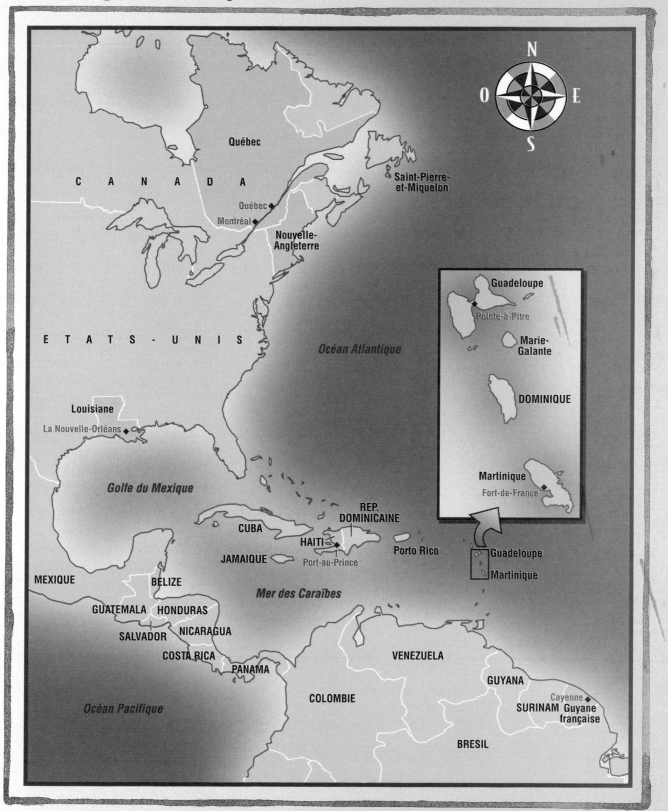

Québec

C A N A D A

Saint-Pierre-
et-Miquelon

Québec ◆
Montréal ◆

Nouvelle-
Angleterre

E T A T S - U N I S

Océan Atlantique

Louisiane
La Nouvelle-Orléans ◆

Golfe du Mexique

CUBA

REP.
DOMINICAINE

HAITI ◆
Port-au-Prince

Porto Rico

JAMAIQUE

MEXIQUE

BELIZE

Mer des Caraïbes

GUATEMALA   HONDURAS

SALVADOR   NICARAGUA

COSTA RICA

PANAMA

VENEZUELA

GUYANA

Cayenne ◆

Océan Pacifique

COLOMBIE

SURINAM Guyane
française

BRESIL

N
O   E
S

Guadeloupe

Pointe-à-Pitre ◆

Marie-
Galante

DOMINIQUE

Martinique

Fort-de-France ◆

Guadeloupe

Martinique

XXV

Since the early eighties, we have seen significant advances in modern language curriculum practices:

(1) a redefinition of the objectives of foreign language study involving a commitment to the development of proficiency in the four skills and in cultural awareness;

(2) a recognition of the need for longer sequences of study;

(3) a new student-centered approach that redefines the role of the teacher as facilitator and encourages students to take a more active role in their learning;

(4) the inclusion of students of all learning abilities.

The new Holt, Rinehart and Winston world language programs take into account not only these advances in the field of foreign language education, but also the input of teachers and students around the country. ◆

PRINCIPLES AND PRACTICES

As nations become increasingly interdependent, the need for effective communication and sensitivity to other cultures becomes more important. Today's youth must be culturally and linguistically prepared to participate in a global society. At Holt, Rinehart and Winston, we believe that proficiency in more than one language is essential to meeting this need.

The primary goal of the Holt, Rinehart and Winston world language programs is to help students develop linguistic proficiency and cultural sensitivity. By interweaving language and culture, our programs seek to broaden students' communication skills while at the same time deepening their appreciation of other cultures.

◆◆

We believe that all students can benefit from foreign language instruction. We recognize that not everyone learns at the same rate or in the same way; nevertheless, we believe that all students should have the opportunity to acquire language proficiency to a degree commensurate with their individual abilities.

Holt, Rinehart and Winston's world language programs are designed to accommodate all students by appealing to a variety of learning styles.

◆◆

We believe that effective language programs should motivate students. Students deserve an answer to the question they often ask: "Why are we doing this?" They need to have goals that are interesting, practical, clearly stated, and attainable.

Holt, Rinehart and Winston's world language programs promote success. They present relevant content in manageable increments that encourage students to attain achievable functional objectives.

We believe that proficiency in another language is best nurtured by programs that encourage students to think critically and to take risks when expressing themselves in the language. We also recognize that students should strive for accuracy in communication. While it is imperative that students have a knowledge of the basic structures of the language, it is also important that they go beyond the simple manipulation of forms.

Holt, Rinehart and Winston's world language program reflects a careful progression of activities that guides students from comprehensible input of authentic language through structured practice to creative, personalized expression. This progression, accompanied by consistent re-entry and spiraling of functions, vocabulary, and structures, provides students with the tools and the confidence to express themselves in their new language.

◆◆

Finally, we believe that a complete program of language instruction should take into account the needs of teachers in today's increasingly demanding classrooms.

At Holt, Rinehart and Winston, we have designed programs that offer practical teacher support and provide resources to meet individual learning and teaching styles.

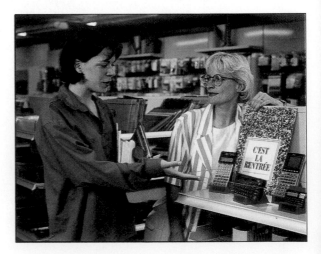

Using the Pupil's Edition of Allez, viens!

Allez, viens! *offers an integrated approach to language learning. Presentation and practice of functional expressions, vocabulary, and grammar structures are interwoven with cultural information, language learning tips, and realia to facilitate both learning and teaching. The technology, audiovisual materials, and additional print resources integrated throughout each chapter allow instruction to be adapted to a variety of teaching and learning styles.* ◆

ALLEZ, VIENS! LEVEL 1

Allez, viens! Level 1 consists of a preliminary chapter that introduces students to French and the French-speaking world followed by twelve instructional chapters. To ensure successful completion of the book and to facilitate articulation from one level to the next, Chapter 11 introduces minimal new material and Chapter 12 is a review chapter.

Following is a description of the various features in *Allez, viens!* and suggestions on how to use them in the classroom.

While it is not crucial for students to cover all material and do all activities to achieve the goals listed at the beginning of each chapter, the material within each chapter has been carefully sequenced to enable students to progress steadily at a realistic pace to the ultimate goal of linguistic and cultural proficiency. You, the teacher, as presenter, facilitator, and guide, will determine the precise depth of coverage, taking into account the individual needs of each class and the amount and type of alternative instructional material to be used from the *Allez, viens!* program.

STARTING OUT...

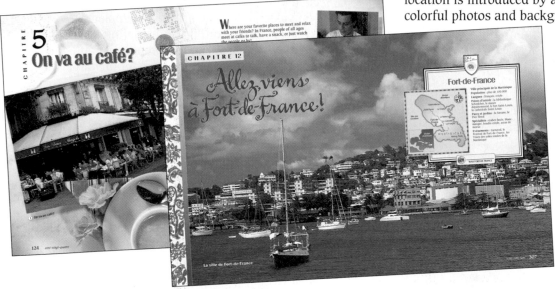

In *Allez, viens!*, chapters are arranged by location. Each new location is introduced by a **Location Opener,** four pages of colorful photos and background information that can be used to introduce the region and help motivate students. Students see an HRW Web site address (go.hrw.com) and a keyword for accessing location-specific resources.

The two-page **Chapter Opener** is intended to pique students' interest and focus their attention on the task at hand. It is a visual introduction to the theme of the chapter and includes a brief description of the topic and situations students will encounter, as well as a list of objectives they will be expected to achieve.

SETTING THE SCENE...

Language instruction begins with the **Mise en train,** the comprehensible input that models language in a culturally authentic setting. Whether presented on video or as a reading accompanied by the audio compact disc recording, the highly visual presentation—frequently in **roman-photo** format in the textbook—ensures success as students practice their receptive skills and begin to recognize some of the new functions and vocabulary they will encounter in the chapter. Following the **Mise en train** is a series of activities that can be used to help guide students through the story and check comprehension.

BUILDING PROFICIENCY STEP BY STEP...

Première, Deuxième, and **Troisième étape** are the three core instructional sections where the greater part of language acquisition will take place. The communicative goals in each chapter center on the functional expressions presented in **Comment dit-on... ?** boxes. These expressions are supported and expanded by material in the **Vocabulaire, Grammaire,** and **Note de grammaire** sections. Activities immediately following the above features are designed to practice recognition or to provide closed-ended practice with the new material. Activities then progress from controlled to open-ended practice where students are able to express themselves in meaningful communication. Depending on class size, general ability level, and class dynamics, you may wish to proceed sequentially through all activities in a chapter, supplementing presentation or practice at various points with additional materials from *Allez, viens!,* or to proceed more quickly to open-ended pair and group work.

DISCOVERING THE PEOPLE AND THE CULTURE...

Cultural information has been incorporated into activities wherever possible. There are also two major cultural features to help students develop an appreciation and understanding of the cultures of French-speaking countries.

Panorama Culturel presents spontaneous interviews conducted in various countries in the French-speaking world on a topic related to the chapter theme. The interviews may be presented on video or done as a reading supplemented by the audio compact disc recording. Culminating activities on this page may be used to verify comprehension and encourage students to think critically about the target culture as well as their own.

Rencontre Culturelle presents a cultural encounter that invites students to compare and contrast the foreign culture with their own.

Note Culturelle helps students gain knowledge and understanding of other cultures and can be used to enrich and enliven activities and presentations at various places throughout each chapter.

UNDERSTANDING AUTHENTIC DOCUMENTS...

Lisons! presents reading strategies that help students understand authentic French documents. The reading selections vary from advertisements to letters to short stories in order to accommodate different interests and familiarize students with different styles and formats. The accompanying activities progress from prereading to reading to postreading tasks and are designed to develop students' overall reading skills and challenge their critical thinking abilities.

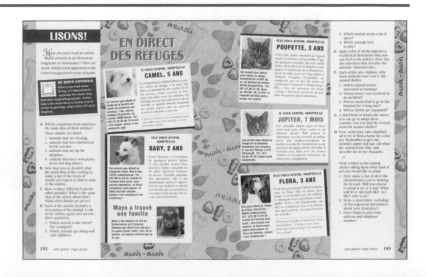

*T*ARGETING STUDENTS' NEEDS...

In each **étape** several special features may be used to enhance language learning and cultural appreciation.

De bons conseils suggests effective ways for students to learn a foreign language.

A la française provides students with tips for speaking more natural-sounding French.

Vocabulaire à la carte presents optional vocabulary related to the chapter theme. These words are provided to help students personalize activities; students will not be required to produce this vocabulary on the Chapter Quizzes and Test.

Tu te rappelles? is a re-entry feature that lists and briefly explains previously-learned vocabulary, functions, and grammar that students might need to review at the moment.

Si tu as oublié is a handy page reference to either an earlier chapter where material was presented or to a reference section in the back of the book that includes such aids as the Summary of Functions and the Grammar Summary.

PRONONCIATION

At the end of each **Troisième étape** is **Prononciation**, which explains certain sounds and spelling rules. Pronunciation is practiced using vocabulary words that contain the targeted sounds. In a dictation exercise that follows, students hear and write sentences using the targeted sounds and letters.

---

*W*RAPPING IT ALL UP...

Mise en pratique gives students the opportunity to review what they have learned and to apply their skills in new communicative contexts. Focusing on all four language skills as well as cultural awareness, the **Mise en pratique** can help you determine whether students are ready for the Chapter Test.

Ecrivons! helps students develop their writing skills by focusing on the writing process. Each **Ecrivons!** gives students a topic related to the theme and functions of the chapter and has students progress through the steps of prewriting, writing, and revising.

Que sais-je? is a checklist that students can use on their own to see if they have achieved the goals stated on the Chapter Opener. Each communicative function is paired with one or more activities for students to use as a self-check. Page references are given for students who need to return to the chapter for review.

Vocabulaire presents the chapter vocabulary grouped by **étape** and arranged according to function or theme. This list represents the active words and expressions that students will be expected to know for the Chapter Quizzes and Test.

*The **Allez, viens!** Video Program brings the textbook to life and introduces your students to people they will encounter in every chapter of the Pupil's Edition. Filmed entirely on location in French-speaking countries around the world, the video program features native speakers of French in realistic, interesting situations.*

Video is an ideal medium for providing the authentic input needed to increase proficiency in French. Both informative and entertaining, the episodes of the Video Program provide rich visual clues to aid comprehension and motivate students to learn more. ◆

*A*LLEZ, VIENS! VIDEO PROGRAM

The *Video Program* is fully integrated and correlates directly with the **Allez, viens!** *Pupil's Edition:*

LOCATION OPENER A narrated, full-motion collage of images from regions of French-speaking countries expands students' acquaintance with the geography and people of the places presented in each Location Opener. The *Video Program* provides additional images and cultural information about the locations visited in **Allez, viens!**

MISE EN TRAIN The introductory dialogue or story in each chapter is a videotaped dramatic episode based on the chapter theme. It introduces the targeted functions, vocabulary, and grammar of the chapter. **Mise en train** also re-enters material from previous chapters in new contexts. Since this video episode corresponds directly with the **Mise en train** in the textbook, it can be used as a general introduction to the chapter, as a chapter review, and as a visual support for presenting the elements of the lesson.

MISE EN TRAIN (SUITE) These continuations of the dramatic episodes provide high-interest input that helps motivate students and offers additional opportunities to expand on what they have learned. The **Mise en train (suite)** continues the story and resolves the dramatic conflict that was created in the **Mise en train.** Designed to facilitate proficiency by providing additional comprehensible input, this episode offers an extended presentation of the chapter material as well as re-entering functions, vocabulary, and structures from previous chapters.

PANORAMA CULTUREL Authentic interviews with native speakers of French bring the French-speaking world to life as real people talk about themselves, their country, and their way of life. Each interview topic is thematically related to the chapter. The interviews feature a wide variety of native speakers from around the world and introduce students to regional variations in speech, cultural diversity, and varying points of view. This assortment of interviews from around the French-speaking world enriches students' appreciation of French-speaking cultures and helps them better understand their own.

VIDEOCLIPS Students will enjoy the authentic footage from French television: music videos, commercials, and more. These short segments of video give students confidence as they realize that they can understand and enjoy material that was produced for native speakers of French. The **Vidéoclips** can also be used as challenge activities.

***ALLEZ, VIENS!* CAPTIONED VIDEO** The dramatic episodes for each chapter —**Mise en train** and **Suite**— are available with French captions on Videocassette 5. Target-language captions give students another opportunity to comprehend the language in the story and offer teachers additional possibilities for presenting and practicing new material in class. Suggestions for incorporating the captioned video into lessons are provided in the *Annotated Teacher's Edition.*

*A*LLEZ, VIENS! VIDEO GUIDE

The **Allez, viens!** *Video Guide* provides background information together with suggestions for presentation and pre-viewing, viewing, and post-viewing activities for all portions of the *Video Program.* In addition, the *Video Guide* contains a transcript and synopsis of each episode, supplementary vocabulary lists, and reproducible student activity sheets. The scripts for all portions of the *Video Program,* as well as a comprehensive answer key for student activities, are included in the *Video Guide.*

*A*LLEZ, VIENS! VIDEODISC PROGRAM AND GUIDE

The **Allez, viens!** *Videodisc Program* presents in videodisc format all the authentic footage, interviews, and dramatic episodes presented in the *Video Program,* plus additional cultural and geographic material to further enrich your students' experience. Barcodes provide instant access to all material and facilitate efficient integration of video resources into each lesson. Key barcodes are provided in the *Annotated Teacher's Edition.* Teaching suggestions, activity masters, and a complete barcode directory are provided in the *Videodisc Guide.*

Allez, viens! *CD-ROM and Resources*

*T*he **Allez, viens!** Interactive CD-ROM Program *brings together print, graphics, video, and audio to provide an enjoyable and instructional language experience. Simulated real-life tasks provide a realistic context for language learning and will appeal to students with a wide variety of learning styles. The program's student-driven approach motivates learners to explore the target language at their own pace.*

The *CD-ROM Program* is correlated with the core curriculum of *Allez, viens!* and is easy to integrate with your lesson plans. Correlations to the textbook are outlined both in the *CD-ROM Teacher's Guide* and in the *Annotated Teacher's Edition.*

The **Location Openers (Allez, viens à... !)** present a wealth of cultural information about locations around the French-speaking world. Students view a map and travelogue of each location as a native speaker describes the scenes in French. An on-screen transcript is also available. After students have watched the presentation, they use what they learned to complete a related activity.

En contexte lets students participate in a lifelike conversation with a video character. Students select the best response to a series of audio and video prompts to complete a task, such as ordering a meal.

Six kinds of **supporting activities** reinforce listening comprehension, speaking, reading, and writing skills, and knowledge of francophone culture. Items are pulled at random from a data bank so that students receive a different selection of items each time they practice an activity.

- **Chacun à sa place**   Students demonstrate comprehension by sorting words or phrases according to two or more categories.
- **Le bon choix**   This multiple-choice activity allows students to practice vocabulary, grammar, functional expressions, or culture.
- **Chasse au trésor**   Students click on an interactive image and hear a native speaker pronounce the corresponding word or phrase. Learners can record and listen to themselves, then check their comprehension of the new material.
- **Les mots qui manquent**   Students play Tic Tac Toe in pairs or against the computer by typing fill-in-the-blank items.
- **Jeu des paires**   When students correctly match all the pairs in this Concentration®-style game, they are rewarded with a videoclip.
- **Méli-mélo**   This text-sequencing activity allows students to construct and listen to sentences or conversations.

The **Panorama Culturel** features six unrehearsed interviews with people from around the French-speaking world. Students answer multiple-choice questions about the interviews. The on-screen transcript (in French or English at your discretion) helps students decipher spontaneous native speech.

In **A toi de parler** students are prompted by video or text to record part of a conversation. In **A toi d'écrire** students use the word processor to write about one of several scenarios. Student work can be saved to disk for record-keeping and evaluation.

A vos micros! and **A vos plumes!** provide students with tools that allow them to write or record original projects. You may also want to use the suggestions for assignments found in each chapter of the *CD-ROM Teacher's Guide.*

Users can access several **online support tools** as needed. The **Vocabulaire** reference section provides an extensive glossary of French-English and English-French words and expressions. The **Grammaire** section provides a summary of the grammar concepts presented in *Allez, viens!* The **Help** section guides users through the mechanics of the program.

The **Teacher Management System (TMS)** allows you to view and assess your students' work, manage passwords and records, and track students' progress as they complete CD-ROM activities. The TMS also allows you to activate optional English translation features for the **Location Opener** and **Panorama Culturel.**

Allez, viens! INTERACTIVE CD-ROM PROGRAM TEACHER'S GUIDE

The *CD-ROM Teacher's Guide* is designed to help you use the *CD-ROM Program.* It offers technical support, teaching suggestions, correlations, and copying masters. The opening pages detail all pertinent technical information. They also include professional essays about using CD-ROM and the Internet in the language classroom.

The guide provides specific information about integrating the *CD-ROM Program's* features into your lessons. For every chapter of **Allez, viens!,** the guide includes the instructional objectives of the CD-ROM activities and references to the corresponding *Pupil's Edition* pages. This section also features teaching suggestions and synopses of several CD-ROM features.

Finally, the guide includes copying masters for you and your students. These include checklists for tracking students' progress, evaluation rubrics, and information on typing accents and special characters.

Allez, viens! *Ancillaries*

The **Allez, viens!** *French program offers a comprehensive ancillary package that addresses the concerns of today's teachers. Because language teachers work with all types of students, the activities in our ancillaries accommodate all learning styles. The activities provided in the* **Allez, viens!** *ancillary materials are both innovative and relevant to students' experiences.* ◆

LESSON PLANNER

The *Lesson Planner* contains chapter-by-chapter suggestions on how to structure the daily lesson for optimal pacing and effectiveness.

- Each **Lesson Plan** guides you through the program's cycle of presentation, practice, and assessment.
- **Block scheduling suggestions** give the option of expanding the material as needed. Sample block scheduling lesson plans integrate the ancillary materials into lessons.
- **Correlations** to the Standards for Foreign Language Learning can be readily adapted to document weekly or monthly progress.
- A **homework calendar** copying master helps students track their assignments.

GRAMMAR AND VOCABULARY WORKBOOKS

The *Grammar and Vocabulary Workbook* reintroduces all major grammar points and offers additional focused practice with the structures, words, and phrases targeted in each **étape.**

- **Suggestions** for using these activities as homework can be found in the Chapter Interleaf pages of the *Annotated Teacher's Edition.*
- The *Grammar and Vocabulary Workbook Teacher's Edition* contains the same pages as the student workbook plus a convenient answer key at the end of the book.

PRACTICE AND ACTIVITY BOOKS

The *Practice and Activity Book* is filled with a variety of activities that provide practice with the functions, grammar, and vocabulary presented in each **étape.**

- Additional reading, culture, and journal activities for each chapter give students the opportunity to apply the reading and writing strategies they've learned in relevant, personalized contexts.
- The *Practice and Activity Book* reinforces many of the same concepts practiced in the *Grammar and Vocabulary Workbook* and provides opportunities to use them in more open-ended, creative contexts.
- The *Practice and Activity Book Teacher's Edition* contains the same pages as the student edition, and has overprinted answers for convenient use.

TPR STORYTELLING

Total Physical Response Storytelling (TPRS) is a communicative-based teaching method to which students respond enthusiastically. TPRS allows them to acquire, internalize, and produce language quickly. The *TPR Storytelling Book* begins with a thorough explanation of the TPR Storytelling method and how to implement this method in the classroom. The material is correlated with each chapter **étape** and may be used at any point during the study of that **étape.**

- **Vocabulary lists** include several active vocabulary words, as well as additional vocabulary words helpful for telling the corresponding mini-stories.
- **Teaching suggestions** help you teach the mini-stories, assist students in customizing their stories, and integrate TPRS into your lessons.
- **Explanations of gestures** help you teach concepts and words.
- **Illustrations** and the **text of each ministory** are provided and may be copied for the students or used to make overhead transparencies.

LISTENING ACTIVITIES

This component contains all print material associated with the *Audio Program.*

- **Student Response Forms,** as well as scripts and answers for all listening activities in the *Pupil's Edition,* appear here for convenient use.
- **Additional Listening Activities** provide students with a unique opportunity to develop their listening skills in a variety of authentic contexts. They appear here as activity masters with scripts and answers.
- At least one **song** that is culturally and thematically related to the chapter or location is recorded on each chapter's CD. The lyrics for that chapter's song(s) are provided with each chapter's listening material.
- **Scripts and answers** for the listening activities in the *Testing Program* (quizzes and chapter tests) also appear in this book.

TEACHING TRANSPARENCIES

Colorful teaching transparencies benefit all students, and the visual learner in particular, by adding variety to the daily lesson. To help you present and practice vocabulary, culture, and a variety of communicative functions, the *Teaching Transparencies* package includes:

- **Directory** of transparencies and **Planning Guide** to help integrate the transparencies into your lessons.
- **Situation transparencies**
- **Vocabulary transparencies** and overlays
- **Map transparencies** and overlays
- **Copying masters**
- Each transparency comes with **suggestions** for practicing the four skills and expanding the students' knowledge of culture.

T38

- Additional activities, projects, and games using the transparencies can be found throughout the *Annotated Teacher's Edition.*

ACTIVITIES FOR COMMUNICATION

Oral communication is the most challenging language skill to develop and test. The *Allez, viens! Activities for Communication* facilitates students' development of listening and speaking skills through pair-work activities that provide lifelike situations and contexts.

- **Communicative Activities** offer information-gap tasks in which students rely on a partner to supply information.
- **Situation Cards** offer opportunities for interviews and role-playing.
- **Realia** pages contain reproductions of authentic documents that provide students with additional reading and language practice. Included with the Realia are teaching suggestions and student activities.

TESTING PROGRAM

The *Testing Program* encourages students to work toward realistic communicative goals.

- One **Grammar and Vocabulary Quiz** per **étape** targets the structures and vocabulary within each **étape**.
- Each **Etape** Quiz includes a listening, reading, and writing section, and very often a culture section.
- Each **Chapter Test** includes listening, reading, writing, and culture sections and a score sheet for easy grading. Selected sections of each Chapter Test can be corrected on ScanTron®.
- There is one **Speaking Test** per chapter.
- One **Midterm** is provided and may be given upon completion of Chapter 6.
- A **Final Exam** is provided and may be given upon completion of Chapter 12.
- Also included in the *Testing Program* are **scripts, answers, and score sheets** for the **Etape** quizzes, Chapter Tests, Midterm Exam, and Final Exam.

ALTERNATIVE ASSESSMENT GUIDE

The *Alternative Assessment Guide* outlines various testing and scoring methods.

- Written and oral portfolio **assessment forms** include rubrics and progress reports.
- **Peer editing rubrics** provide suggested guidelines and standards for students.
- **Portfolio checklists** give you and the students a clear idea of what their portfolios should include.
- **Portfolio evaluation forms** help you assess student portfolios.

- **Teaching suggestions** provide ideas for performance assessment and portfolios.
- **Suggestions for using the CD-ROM for assessment** provide insight into teaching with the *CD-ROM Program.*

TEST GENERATOR

The **Allez, viens!** *Test Generator's* user-friendly CD-ROM format enables you to create customized practice sheets, quizzes, and tests for each chapter. Because the CD-ROM contains all three levels of *Allez, viens!,* you will find it a valuable aid in preparing reviews of material presented in previous levels. The *Test Generator* is available for IBM® PC and compatibles and Macintosh® computers.

EXPLORATORY GUIDE

The *Exploratory Guide* provides suggestions and techniques for teaching an exploratory class using a wealth of materials from the **Allez, viens!** program, such as the *Video* and *Audio Programs,* the *Interactive CD-ROM Program,* the *Teaching Transparencies,* and many workbook materials. Each unit contains:

- Lessons with **activity masters**
- **Vocabulary lists**
- **Review** and **assessment options**

The Annotated Teacher's Edition

The *Allez, viens!* Annotated Teacher's Edition *is designed to help you meet the increasingly varied needs of today's students by providing an abundance of suggestions and strategies. The* Annotated Teacher's Edition *includes the reduced pages of the* Pupil's Edition *with teacher annotations, wrap-around teacher text with video references and barcodes, notes, suggestions, answers, and additional activities, as well as interleafed pages of correlation charts, technology applications, barcode and CD-ROM directories, homework suggestions, scripts, projects, and games before each chapter.* ◆

USING THE LOCATION OPENER

Each reduced student page is wrapped with background information for you about the photographs and settings. In addition, teaching suggestions help you motivate students to learn more about the history, geography, and culture of French-speaking countries. You will also find the address for location-specific student resources on the HRW Web site (go.hrw.com).

USING THE CHAPTER INTERLEAF

The chapter interleaf includes a chapter overview correlation chart for teaching resources, technology applications, barcode and CD-ROM directories, homework suggestions, *Pupil's Edition* listening scripts, and suggestions for projects and games.

The **Chapter Overview** chart outlines at a glance the functions, grammar, culture, and re-entry items featured in each **étape**. A list of corresponding print and audiovisual resource materials for each section of the chapter is provided to help integrate video and ancillaries into your lessons. The pronunciation, reading, and review features for each chapter are also referenced, as well as a variety of assessment and portfolio options.

In every chapter, there are helpful resources to assist you in integrating technology into your lesson plans. The **Technology Applications** page provides a detailed list of audio, video, videodisc, transparencies, and CD-ROM technology resources, correlated by chapter section. After the Technology Applications, you will find a **Barcode Directory**, organized by chapter section, to help facilitate using videodiscs in your lesson. The **CD-ROM Directory** lists and describes the activities available in the *CD-ROM*

Program. This chart correlates CD-ROM activities for each section of the chapter.

Homework Suggestions propose a number of suitable homework activities taken from the *Pupil's Edition,* the *Practice and Activity Book,* the *Grammar and Vocabulary Workbook,* and the *CD-ROM Program.* Suggestions are organized by **étape.**

Textbook Listening Activities Scripts provide the scripts of the chapter listening activities for reference or for use in class. The answers to each activity are provided below each script for easy reference.

Projects propose extended four-skills activities based on the chapter theme and content. **Projects** suggestions are provided to give students the opportunity to personalize the information they've learned in the chapter. Individual projects offer students the chance to explore topics related to the chapter theme that are of personal interest to them. Group and cooperative learning projects encourage students to work together to apply what they've learned in the chapter by creating a poster, brochure, or report, often accompanied by an oral presentation.

Games provide students with informal, entertaining activities in which they can apply and reinforce the functions, structures, vocabulary, and culture of the chapter. **Games** appeal to a variety of learners and encourage teamwork and cooperation among students of different levels and learning styles.

USING THE WRAP-AROUND TEACHER TEXT

Wrap-around teacher text gives point-of-use suggestions and information to help you make the most of class time. The wrap-around style of the *Annotated Teacher's Edition* conveniently presents

barcodes, video references, teacher notes, suggestions, and activity answers together on the same page with the reduced *Pupil's Edition* page.

TEACHING CYCLE

For each **étape,** a logical instructional sequence includes the following steps to enable you to:

• **Jump Start!** your students with an individual activity that focuses their attention on previously-learned material while they wait for class to begin.

• **Motivate** students by introducing the topic in a personalized and contextualized way.

• **Teach** the functions, vocabulary, structures, and culture with a variety of approaches.

• **Close** each **étape** with activities that review and confirm the communicative goals.

• **Assess** students' progress with a quiz and/or performance assessment activity. **Performance Assessment** suggestions provide an alternative to pen and paper tests and give you the option of evaluating students' progress by having them perform communicative, competency-based tasks. These may include teacher-student interviews, conversations, dialogues, or skits that students perform for the entire class. These tasks can also be recorded or videotaped for evaluation at a later time.

• **Portfolio** icons signal activities that are appropriate for students' oral or written portfolios. They may include lists, posters, letters, journal entries, or taped conversations or skits. A variety of suggestions are provided within each chapter so that you can work with your students to select the activities that would best document their strengths and progress in the language. Portfolio information, including checklists and suggestions for evaluation, is provided in the *Alternative Assessment Guide,* pages iv–17. For a discussion of portfolio creation and use, see *Using Portfolios in the Language Classroom,* page T52.

*F*OR INDIVIDUAL NEEDS

Suggestions under the following categories provide alternate approaches to help you address students' diverse learning styles.

- **Visual, Auditory, Tactile,** and **Kinesthetic Learners** benefit from activities that accommodate their unique learning styles.
- **Slower Pace** provides ideas for presenting material in smaller steps to facilitate comprehension.
- **Challenge** extends activities into more challenging tasks that encourage students to expand their communicative skills.

*M*AKING CONNECTIONS

To help students appreciate their membership in a global society, suggestions for linking French with other disciplines, their community, and other cultures appear under the following categories:

- **Math... Art... Geography... Health... Science... History... Language Arts... Music...** and other links that relate the chapter topic to other subject areas, making French relevant to the students' overall academic experience.
- **Multicultural Links** provide students the opportunity to compare and contrast their culture with cultures of French-speaking countries and other parts of the world.

- **Community... Family Links** encourage students to seek opportunities for learning outside of the classroom by interacting with neighbors and family members. These suggestions also call on students to share their learning with their family and community.
- **Language-to-Language** suggestions compare French words, phrases, and structures with other languages and present relationships among them. These notes examine such things as word origins, syntax patterns, and similarities or differences in grammar.
- **Career Path** suggestions ask students to explore how the knowledge of another language may enhance career opportunities. Students have a chance to see how developing their skills in French will give them advantages in the job market.
- Annotations and icons are point-of-use references to the *Allez, viens!* ancillaries, *Pupil's Edition* grammar supplement, and suggested homework assignments.

*D*EVELOPING THINKING SKILLS

Thinking Critically helps students develop their higher-order thinking skills.

    Drawing Inferences, Comparing and Contrasting, Analyzing, Observing, and **Synthesizing** offer suggestions to extend activities beyond an informational level. They increase comprehension of language and culture, and they help students exercise and develop higher-order thinking skills.

    The game **Le mot juste** teaches students to use **circumlocution** by encouraging them to talk around unknown French terms in contextualized

situations. In addition, there are suggestions for circumlocution in the teacher's text in every chapter. These suggestions are thematically related to the chapter and give students an opportunity to practice the vocabulary in a creative way.

*E*STABLISHING COLLABORATIVE LEARNING

Cooperative Learning allows students to work together in small groups to attain common goals by sharing responsibilities. Students are accountable for setting the group objectives, completing the assignment, and ensuring that all group members master the material. Working together in cooperative groups allows students to take an active role in the classroom, to develop more self-esteem, and to experience less anxiety by working in and contributing to the success of small groups. Cooperative learning enables students to improve interpersonal communication skills by encouraging them to listen to and respect other opinions, and to share their own.

    Total Physical Response (TPR) techniques visually and kinesthetically reinforce structures and vocabulary. They are active learning exercises that encourage students to focus on class interaction while learning French.

*T*EACHING LISONS!

Teacher's notes and suggestions in **Lisons!** offer prereading, reading, and postreading activities to help students develop reading skills. Background information and useful terms related to the reading are provided as well.

Standards for Foreign Language Learning

BY ROBERT LaBOUVE

STANDARDS AND SCHOOL REFORM

In 1989 educational reform in the United States took on an entirely different look when state and national leaders reached consensus on six national educational goals for public schools. In 1994 a new law, *Goals 2000: Educate America Act,* endorsed these six goals and added two more. The most important national goal in the law for foreign language educators is Goal Three, which establishes a core curriculum and places foreign languages in that core. As a result of this consensus on national goals, the Federal government encouraged the development of high standards in the core disciplines.

We must first define "standards" in order to fully understand the rationale for their development. Content standards ask: What should students know and be able to do? Content standards have recently been developed by the foreign language profession as a collaborative project of the American Council on the Teaching of Foreign Languages, the American Association of Teachers of French, the American Association of Teachers of German, and the American Association of Teachers of Spanish and Portuguese. Performance standards ask: How good is good enough? Opportunity-to-learn standards ask: Did the school prepare all students to perform well? There is a growing consensus that states and local districts should address the last two types of standards.

DEVELOPMENT OF FOREIGN LANGUAGE STANDARDS

A task force of foreign language educators began work on the standards in 1993 by establishing specific foreign language goals. They then set content standards for each goal. The task force sought feedback from the foreign language profession through an extensive dissemination program and produced a draft of the standards document for introduction at a number of sites around the United States during the 1994–1995 school year. The final version, published in 1996, incorporated suggestions from the sites where the standards were introduced and reaction from volunteer reviewers and the field in general.

While the standards are world class, they are realistic and attainable by most students. The task force also realizes that the general set of goals and standards would have to be made language specific in a curriculum development process and that continuing staff development would be essential.

FOREIGN LANGUAGE GOALS AND STANDARDS

Communication Communicate in Languages Other than English	**Standard 1.1**	Students engage in conversations, provide and obtain information, express feelings and emotions, and exchange opinions.
	Standard 1.2	Students understand and interpret written and spoken language on a variety of topics.
	Standard 1.3	Students present information, concepts, and ideas to an audience of listeners or readers on a variety of topics.
Cultures Gain knowledge and understanding of Other Cultures	**Standard 2.1**	Students demonstrate an understanding of the relationship between the practices and perspectives of the culture studied.
	Standard 2.2	Students demonstrate an understanding of the relationship between the products and perspectives of the culture studied.
Connections Connect with other disciplines and Acquire Information	**Standard 3.1**	Students reinforce and further their knowledge of other disciplines through the foreign language.
	Standard 3.2	Students acquire information and recognize the distinctive viewpoints that are only available through the foreign language and its cultures.
Comparisons Develop Insight into the Nature of Language and Culture	**Standard 4.1**	Students demonstrate understanding of the nature of language through comparisons of the language studied and their own.
	Standard 4.2	Students demonstrate understanding of the concept of culture through comparisons of the cultures studied and their own.
Communities Participate in Multilingual Communities at Home and Around the World	**Standard 5.1**	Students use the language both within and beyond the school setting.
	Standard 5.2	Students show evidence of becoming life-long learners by using the language for personal enjoyment and enrichment.

FOREIGN LANGUAGE GOALS AND STANDARDS

The goals and standards describe a K–12 foreign language program for *all* students, presenting languages, both modern and classical, as part of the core curriculum for every student, including those whose native language is not English. Broad goals establish the basic framework of the language program. The proposed content standards set for these goals describe what students should know and be able to do in a language. The chart on page T42 shows how the standards are arrayed alongside the goals.

The first two goals in this expanded language program describe today's typical school language program. The last three are often identified by teachers as important, but are not always implemented. The standards-based program moves beyond an emphasis on skills to a redefinition of the content of a language program itself.

Sample progress indicators are provided for Grades 4, 8, and 12 as examples of what students can do to meet the standards and accomplish the goals of the language program. A higher level of performance will be expected as students progress from one benchmark grade to another. For example, Standard 1.1 at Grade 4 suggests that students can "ask and answer questions about such things as family, school events, and celebrations in person or via letters, e-mail, or audio and video tapes," but Standard 1.1 at Grade 12 suggests that students can "exchange, support, and discuss their opinions and individual perspectives with peers and/or speakers of the target language on a variety of topics dealing with contemporary and historical issues."

IMPACT OF THE STANDARDS

While there is an assumption that foreign language goals and standards will have a great impact upon the states and local districts, the national standards themselves are voluntary. Clearly, the standards will influence instruction and curriculum development in districts that choose to align their language programs with the national standards. Assessment programs will most likely begin to reflect the influence of the standards. The standards will also have an impact on the preparation of future teachers and on staff development for teachers now in the classroom.

A curriculum based on the standards will encourage students to take responsibility for their learning by making the language curriculum coherent and transparent to them. Students will know from the beginning what they should be able to do when they exit the program and they will be able to judge for themselves how they are progressing, especially at Grades 4, 8, and 12.

The standards will direct instruction in the classroom by providing curriculum developers and teachers with a broad framework upon which to construct the expanded language program. Standards for each goal will ensure that no goal is treated informally or left to chance. Teachers who use the content standards should play a critical role in their district by deciding how good is good enough for students who exit the program.

The standards will also have a significant impact on the demand for sequential, cross-disciplinary instructional materials for a K–12 language program. Another challenge will be the development of new technologies that increase learning in order to meet high standards.

Probably the greatest benefit that national standards may bring will be in the area of making possible articulation that is horizontal (linking languages to other disciplines) and vertical (grade to grade, school to school, and school to college). Language teachers will join their English and social studies colleagues in helping students become language-competent, literate citizens of the world. A language program that is at once coherent and transparent to students and others will provide all language educators a basis for reaching consensus about their expectations on what students should know and do. To those of us who feel that foreign language education is basic education for all students, the national standards document should become a strong advocate for languages in the curriculum of every school and for the extended sequences of study presented by the goals and standards. The standards document will make it easier for language educators to present a solid rationale for including foreign languages in the curriculum.

To receive information on ordering the standards document, *Standards for Foreign Language Learning: Preparing for the 21st Century,* please contact the project office:

National Standards Report
P.O. Box 1897
Lawrence, KS 66044
(800) 627-0629
FAX: (913) 843-1274

Allez, viens!

supports the Foreign Language Goals and Standards in the following ways:

THE PUPIL'S EDITION

- Encourages students to take responsibility for their learning by providing clearly defined objectives at the beginning of each chapter.

- Provides a variety of pair- and group-work activities to give students an opportunity to use the target language in a wide range of settings and contexts.

- Offers culture-related activities and poses questions that develop students' insight and encourage them to develop observational and analytical skills.

THE ANNOTATED TEACHER'S EDITION

- Provides a broad framework for developing a foreign language program and offers specific classroom suggestions for reaching students with various learning styles.

- Offers ideas for multicultural and multidisciplinary projects as well as community and family links that encourage students to gain access to information both at school and in the community.

THE ANCILLARY PROGRAM

- Provides students with on-location video footage of native speakers interacting in their own cultural and geographic context.

- Includes multiple options for practicing new skills and assessing performance, including situation cards, portfolio suggestions, speaking tests, and other alternatives.

- Familiarizes students with the types of tasks they will be expected to perform on exit exams.

Technology in the Language Classroom

BY CINDY A. KENDALL

Many remember when overhead projectors and audiocassettes were on the cutting edge. Today's foreign language teachers and their students are discovering new technological applications that make teaching and learning more exciting and effective. Teachers are integrating these technologies into their classes and fundamentally changing the way students learn languages.

The wealth of technological possibilities available to foreign language teachers, such as multimedia computer software, videodiscs, and the Internet, is more sophisticated than ever. This wider range of technological possibilities offers new challenges. In order to use technology effectively, teachers must become familiar with the resources available and understand how the use of technology can enhance language learning. ◆

WHAT ROLE DOES TECHNOLOGY PLAY IN THE FOREIGN LANGUAGE CLASSROOM?

Technology is a powerful tool in the foreign language classroom because it combines visual, auditory, and cultural input and allows for the simultaneous practice of listening, speaking, reading, and writing skills. It can help the instructor reach the five goals of the Standards for Foreign Language Learning: Communication, Culture, Connections, Comparisons, and Community.

The versatility, immediacy, and interactive nature of technology make studying a foreign language more relevant and meaningful to students. Through technology, students can "visit" countries where the target language is spoken and listen to and interact with native speakers. On the Internet, students can perform tasks in the target language at World Wide Web sites created in target-language countries. Technology makes the notion of the global village a reality for today's foreign language students.

In addition, technology helps the teacher work with students of differing skills and learning styles. Technology-based instruction offers teachers and students the flexibility of working as a class, in small groups, or as individuals.

WHAT TECHNOLOGICAL RESOURCES ARE AVAILABLE?

Overhead Projection

The overhead projector, a long-time companion in the classroom, provides a way to effectively combine visual and auditory practice. Transparencies can be an alternative to writing on the chalkboard, and have the added advantage of permitting the teacher to write presentations in advance that can be used over and over.

Audio

Foreign language instructors are familiar with the use of audiocassettes as part of students' listening comprehension practice, and know all too well some common problems with this format: the loss of time in cueing the appropriate segment and wear and tear on the audiocassette. Audio compact discs enable the teacher to cue the desired track quickly and deliver the same content with much greater ease. Other benefits of compact discs include higher-quality recordings and longer product shelf life.

Video and Videodisc

Video technology offers multiple benefits to teachers and is increasingly becoming a standard part of the curriculum system. Videos that are shot on location and feature native speakers in real settings can supply linguistically and culturally authentic input and facilitate comprehension with richer contexts, while at the same time reinforcing new language and structures. The use of video has progressed beyond simply watching. Videos and the guides that often accompany them give teachers ideas to motivate students, to provide comprehensible input, and to review material. By watching videoclips of interviews, ads, music performances, and other authentic target-language programming, students get a taste of the "real" foreign language. Videodiscs have brought a new and welcome dimension of video technology into the classroom. Like audio compact discs, videodiscs provide superior sound and images, a more durable physical medium, and quick random access using a barcode scanner.

Multimedia Software

Interactive CD-ROM programs are easy-to-use computer software programs that deliver large amounts of sound and images along with text. In the most effective CD-ROM programs, students not only hear and see language in action, but interact with it as well. This powerful learning tool weaves listening, reading, speaking, writing, and culture into a tapestry of realistic situations that motivates students to practice and communicate in the foreign language. As an added benefit for busy teachers, CD-ROM technology requires little or no training and is virtually foolproof. No matter how many students use the disc, it is impossible to erase the program or write over it.

CD-ROM technology gives teachers flexibility in several areas. They can work with students as a whole class, in small groups, or individually; they can use the program at any phase of the lesson cycle; and they can easily help students with varied learning strengths and styles.

Internet

The Internet is an electronic resource that offers unmatched potential for connecting the foreign language classroom to the outside world. The World Wide Web (WWW) is a treasure trove of authentic materials that can bring target-language cultures into the classroom on a daily basis. By connecting to the Internet and using WWW resources, teachers can overcome the difficulties inherent in teaching a foreign language in an English-speaking country and provide students with experiences they would otherwise not have. Students can find out what is playing at the movies in Paris or what the hours of operation are at the Louvre; they might read the latest headlines in Abidjan; or they can scan weather reports in Quebec or soccer scores in France. They can also download audio now; thanks to this new resource, accessing international music and broadcasts is easier than ever.

WHAT IMPLICATIONS DOES INCREASED USE OF TECHNOLOGY HAVE FOR TEACHERS AND STUDENTS?

Both teachers and students benefit in many ways from the growing variety of technological tools available for use in and out of the classroom. Students are more motivated to learn, and motivated students are easier to teach. The variety of formats the teacher can now offer makes it much easier to address individual learning styles in classrooms that have grown increasingly diverse.

New technologies also facilitate classroom management in many ways. Software programs can help the teacher build more effective presentations using less time and energy. Multimedia programs can often give students immedi-

ate feedback, track their progress through different types of assignments, and make accurate records management much easier for the teacher.

Along with their many benefits, teachers will find that new technologies also bring new responsibilities. Teachers who have used magazine articles and books understand the need to review such materials to be sure content is appropriate and will naturally apply similar standards to CD-ROM programs and to Internet activities. In addition, activities that put students in contact with the public on the Internet make it imperative that teachers set standards and communicate clearly with both parents and students about what is acceptable and safe.

As students move into working more independently with creative technologies both as individuals and in groups, teachers may also need to modify their strategies for monitoring students' work to maintain accountability and to make sure students are getting the most out of their time with each medium. Teachers may want to re-examine how they assess students; performance assessment and portfolio assessment offer opportunities for students to demonstrate their increasing skill in the language and can help prepare them for the kinds of proficiency tests that are becoming more common at checkpoints or as exit requirements.

Properly used, new technology tools can bring the language to life for students and make teachers' work easier and more effective. Teachers are learning new skills and adapting their approaches to classroom management and assessment. Students are also learning "how to learn" with these new resources, and the rewards can be great.

You can instruct your students to go to **http://go.hrw.com** for Internet resources designed specifically for them. For a wider range of material, including curriculum resources and access to a variety of Web sites, visit Holt, Rinehart and Winston's homepage at **http://www.hrw.com**. We recommend that you check the HRW Web site periodically for updated resources.

ALLEZ, VIENS!

The technology package for *Allez, viens!* facilitates presentation, practice, review, and assessment in the following ways:

The Pupil's Edition

◆ The *Pupil's Edition* indicates to both teacher and student when CD-ROM activities are available.

The Annotated Teacher's Edition

◆ The *Annotated Teacher's Edition* contains barcodes for use with the *Videodisc Program* and a quick guide to technology resources for each chapter. It also includes comprehensive lists and descriptions of the technology components that are available for every chapter as well as suggestions on how and when to incorporate technology components into the lessons.

The Ancillary Program

◆ The *Interactive CD-ROM Program* includes numerous activities that practice the chapter's functions, vocabulary, grammar, and culture. The CD-ROM also offers an online teacher management system to ensure student accountability. A *CD-ROM Teacher's Guide* is also provided.

◆ The *Video* and *Videodisc Programs* provide stories, interviews, and travelogues shot on location. A teacher's guide is provided for each component.

◆ The *Audio Program* allows students to practice listening to native speakers of French. The *Listening Activities* book, with suggestions and transcripts, is also helpful for these activities.

◆ The *Test Generator* allows teachers to create and print alternate tests and quizzes and review material.

◆ The *Lesson Planner* suggests appropriate places to integrate technology.

◆ The HRW Web site contains links to the World Wide Web and curriculum-appropriate material for teachers and students.

Teaching Culture

BY NANCY HUMBACH AND DOROTHEA BRUSCHKE

Ask students what they like best about studying a foreign language. Chances are that learning about culture, the way people live, is one of their favorite aspects. Years after language study has ended, adults remember with fondness the customs of the target culture, even pictures in their language texts. It is this interest in the people and their way of life that is the great motivator and helps us sustain students' interest in language study.

We must integrate culture and language in a way that encourages curiosity, stimulates analysis, and teaches students to hypothesize and seek answers to questions about the people whose language they are studying. Teaching isolated facts about how people in other cultures live is not enough. This information is soon dated and quickly forgotten. We must go a step beyond and teach students that all behavior, values, and traditions exist because of certain aspects of history, geography, and socio-economic conditions.

There are many ways to help students become culturally knowledgeable and to assist them in developing an awareness of differences and similarities between the target culture and their own. Two of these approaches involve critical thinking, that is, trying to find reasons for a certain behavior through observation and analysis, and putting individual observations into larger cultural patterns. ◆

> We must integrate culture and language in a way that encourages curiosity, stimulates analysis, and teaches students to hypothesize.

FIRST APPROACH: QUESTIONING

The first approach involves questioning as the key strategy. At the earliest stages of language learning, students begin to learn ways to greet peers, elders, and strangers, as well as the use of **tu** and **vous**. Students need to consider questions such as: "How do French-speaking people greet each other? Are there different levels of formality? Who initiates a handshake? When is a handshake or kisses on the cheeks **(la bise)** appropriate?" Each of these questions leads students to think about the values that are expressed through word and gesture. They start to "feel" the other culture, and at the same time, understand how much of their own behavior is rooted in their cultural background.

Magazines, newspapers, advertisements, and television commercials are all excellent sources of cultural material. For example, browsing through a French magazine, one finds a number of advertisements for food items and bottled water. Could this indicate a great interest in eating and preparing healthy food? Reading advertisements can be followed up with viewing videos and films, or with interviewing native speakers or people who have lived in French-speaking countries to learn about customs involving food selection and preparation.

Students might want to find answers to questions such as: "How much time do French people spend shopping for and preparing a meal? How long does a typical meal **en famille** last? What types of food and beverages does it involve?" This type of questioning might lead students to discover different attitudes toward food and mealtimes.

An advertisement for a refrigerator or a picture of a French kitchen can provide an insight into practices of shopping for food. Students first need to think about the refrigerator at home, take an inventory of what is kept in it, and consider when and where their family shops. Next, students should look closely at a French refrigerator. What is its size? What could that mean? (Shopping takes place more often, stores are within walking distance, and people eat more fresh foods.)

Food wrappers and containers also provide good clues to cultural insight. For example, since bread is often purchased fresh from a **boulangerie,** it is usually carried in one's hand or tote bag, with no packaging at all. Since most people shop daily and carry their own groceries home, heavier items like sodas often come in bottles no larger than one and one-half liters.

SECOND APPROACH: ASSOCIATING WORDS WITH IMAGES

The second approach for developing cultural understanding involves forming associations of words with the cultural images they suggest. Language and culture are so closely related that one might actually say that language *is* culture. Most words, especially nouns, carry a cultural connotation. Knowing the literal equivalent of a word in another language is of little use to students in understanding this connotation. For example, **ami** cannot be translated simply as *friend*, **pain** as *bread*, or **rue** as *street*. The French word **pain**, for instance, carries with it the image of a small local bakery stocked with twenty or thirty different varieties of freshly-baked bread, all warm from a brick oven. At breakfast, bread is sliced, covered with butter and jam, and eaten as a **tartine**; it is eaten throughout the afternoon and evening meals, in particular as an accompaniment to the cheese course. In French-speaking countries, "bread" is more than a grocery item; it is an essential part of every meal.

When students have acquired some sense of the cultural connotation of words—not only through teachers' explanations but, more importantly, through observation of visual images—they start to discover the larger underlying cultural themes, or what is often called deep culture.

These larger cultural themes serve as organizing categories into which individual cultural phenomena fit to form a pattern. Students might discover, for example, that French speakers, because they live in much more crowded conditions, have a great need for privacy (cultural theme), as reflected in such phenomena as closed doors, fences or walls around property, and sheers on windows. Students might also discover that love of nature and the outdoors is an important cultural theme, as indicated by such phenomena as flower boxes and planters in public places—even on small traffic islands—well-kept public parks in every town, and people going for a walk or going hiking.

As we teach culture, students learn not only to recognize elements of the target culture but also of their American cultural heritage. They see how elements of culture reflect larger themes or patterns. Learning what constitutes American culture and how that information relates to other people throughout the world can be an exciting journey for a young person.

As language teachers, we are able to facilitate that journey into another culture and into our own, to find our similarities as well as our differences from others. We do not encourage value judgments about others and their culture, nor do we recommend adopting other ways. We simply say to students, "Other ways exist. They exist for many reasons, just as our ways exist due to what our ancestors have bequeathed us through history, traditions, values, and geography."

Allez, viens!

develops cultural understanding and awareness in the following ways:

THE PUPIL'S EDITION

- Informs students about francophone countries through photo essays, maps, almanac boxes, and **Notes Culturelles** that invite comparison with the students' own cultural experiences.
- Engages students in analysis and comparison of live, personal interviews with native speakers in the **Panorama Culturel** sections.
- Uses the **Rencontre Culturelle** section to expose students to cross-cultural situations that require observation, analysis, and problem-solving.
- Helps students integrate the language with its cultural connotations through a wealth of authentic documents.

THE ANNOTATED TEACHER'S EDITION

- Provides teachers with additional culture, history, and language notes, background information on photos and almanac boxes, and multicultural links.
- Suggests problem-solving activities and critical thinking questions that allow students to hypothesize, analyze, and discover larger underlying cultural themes.

THE ANCILLARY PROGRAM

- Includes additional realia to develop cultural insight by serving as a catalyst for questioning and direct discovery.
- Offers activities that require students to compare and contrast cultures.
- Provides songs, short readings, and poems, as well as many opportunities for students to experience regional variation and idioms in the video, audio, and CD-ROM programs.

Learning Styles and Multi-Modality Teaching

BY MARY B. MCGEHEE

The larger and broader population of students who are enrolling in foreign language classes brings a new challenge to foreign language educators, calling forth an evolution in teaching methods to enhance learning for all our students. Educational experts now recognize that every student has a preferred sense for learning and retrieving information: visual, auditory, or kinesthetic. Incorporating a greater variety of activities to accommodate the learning styles of all students can make the difference between struggle and pleasure in the foreign language classroom. ◆

Incorporating a greater variety of activities to accommodate the learning styles of all students can make the difference between struggle and pleasure in the foreign language classroom.

ACCOMMODATING DIFFERENT LEARNING STYLES

A modified arrangement of the classroom is one way to provide more effective and enjoyable learning for all students. Rows of chairs and desks must give way at times to circles, semicircles, or small clusters. Students may be grouped in fours or in pairs for cooperative work or peer teaching. It is important to find a balance of arrangements, thereby providing the most comfort in varied situations.

Since visual, auditory, and kinesthetic learners will be in the class, and because every student's learning will be enhanced by a multi-sensory approach, lessons must be directed toward all three learning styles. Any language lesson content may be presented visually, aurally, and kinesthetically.

Visual presentations and practice may include the chalkboard, charts, posters, television, overhead projectors, books, magazines, picture diagrams, flashcards, bulletin boards, films, slides, or videos. Visual learners need to see what they are to learn. Lest the teacher think he or she will never have the time to prepare all those visuals, Dickel and Slak (1983) found that visual aids generated by students are more effective than ready-made ones.

Auditory presentations and practice may include stating aloud the requirements of the lesson, oral questions and answers, paired or group work on a progression of oral exercises from repetition to communication, tapes, CDs, dialogues, and role-playing. Jingles, catchy stories, and memory devices using songs and rhymes are good learning aids. Having students record themselves and then listen as they play back the cassette allows them to practice in the auditory mode.

Kinesthetic presentations entail the students' use of manipulatives, chart materials, gestures, signals, typing, songs, games, and role-playing. These lead the students to associate sentence constructions with meaningful movements.

A SAMPLE LESSON USING MULTI-MODALITY TEACHING

A multi-sensory presentation on greetings might proceed as follows.

FOR VISUAL LEARNERS

As the teacher begins oral presentation of greetings and introductions, he or she simultaneously shows the written forms on transparencies, with the formal expressions marked with an adult's hat, and the informal expressions marked with a baseball cap.

The teacher then distributes cards with the hat and cap symbols representing the formal or informal expressions. As the students hear taped mini-dialogues, they hold up the appropriate card to indicate whether the dialogues are formal or informal. On the next listening, the students repeat the sentences they hear.

FOR AUDITORY LEARNERS

A longer taped dialogue follows, allowing the students to hear the new expressions a number of times. They write from dictation several sentences containing the new expressions. They may work in pairs, correcting each other's work as they "test" their own understanding of the lesson at hand. Finally, students respond to simple questions using the appropriate formal and informal responses cued by the cards they hold.

FOR KINESTHETIC LEARNERS

For additional kinesthetic input, members of the class come to the front of the room, each holding a hat or cap symbol. As the teacher calls out situations, the students play the roles, using gestures and props appropriate to the age group they are portraying. Non-cued, communicative role-playing with props further enables the students to "feel" the differences between formal and informal expressions.

*H*ELPING STUDENTS LEARN HOW TO USE THEIR PREFERRED MODE

Since we require all students to perform in all language skills, part of the assistance we must render is to help them develop strategies within their preferred learning modes to carry out an assignment in another mode. For example, visual students hear the teacher assign an oral exercise and visualize what they must do. They must see themselves carrying out the assignment, in effect watching themselves as if there were a movie going on in their heads. Only then can they also hear themselves saying the right things. Thus, this assignment will be much easier for the visual learners who have been taught this process, if

they have not already figured it out for themselves. Likewise, true auditory students, confronted with a reading/ writing assignment, must talk themselves through it, converting the entire process into sound as they plan and prepare their work. Kinesthetic students presented with a visual or auditory task must first break the assignment into tasks and then work their way through them.

Students who experience difficulty because of a strong preference for one mode of learning are often unaware of the degree of preference. In working with these students, I prefer the simple and direct assessment of learning styles offered by Richard Bandler and John Grinder in their book *Frogs into Princes*, which allows the teacher and student to quickly determine how the student learns. In an interview with the student, I follow the assessment with certain specific recommendations of techniques to make the student's study time more effective.

It is important to note here that teaching students to maximize their study does not require that the teacher give each student an individualized assignment. It does require that each student who needs it be taught how to prepare the assignment using his or her own talents and strengths. This communication between teacher and student, combined with teaching techniques that

reinforce learning in all modes, can only maximize pleasure and success in learning a foreign language.

▶ REFERENCES

Dickel, M.J. and S. Slak. "Imaging Vividness and Memory for Verbal Material." *Journal of Mental Imagery* 7, i (1983):121–6.

Bandler, Richard, and John Grinder. *Frogs into Princes*. Real People Press, Moab, UT. 1978.

Allez, viens!
accommodates different learning styles in the following ways:

THE PUPIL'S EDITION

- Presents basic material in audio, video, and print formats.
- Includes role-playing activities and a variety of multi-modal activities, including an extensive listening strand and many art-based activities.

THE ANNOTATED TEACHER'S EDITION

- Provides suggested activities for visual, auditory, and kinesthetic learners, as well as suggestions for slower-paced learning and challenge activities.
- Includes Total Physical Response activities.

THE ANCILLARY PROGRAM

- Provides additional reinforcement activites for a variety of learning styles.
- Presents a rich blend of audiovisual input through the video program, audio program, CD-ROM program, transparencies, and blackline masters.

The following is an example of an art-based activity from *Allez, viens!*

15 Ils ont quels cours?

Some students are day-dreaming about the future. What classes are they taking to prepare for these careers?

Ils ont géométrie, physique et géographie.

Possible answers:

1. Elle a chimie et biologie.

2. Il a histoire et géographie.

3. Ils ont informatique et espagnol.

4. Il a danse et musique.

Higher-Order Thinking Skills

BY AUDREY L. HEINING-BOYNTON

Our profession loves acronyms! TPR, ALM, OBI, and now the HOTS! HOTS stands for higher-order thinking skills. These thinking skills help our students listen, speak, write, and learn about culture in a creative, meaningful way while providing them with necessary life skills. ◆

Introduce students to the life skills they need to become successful, productive citizens in our society.

WHAT ARE HIGHER-ORDER THINKING SKILLS?

Higher-order thinking skills are not a new phenomenon on the educational scene. In 1956, Benjamin Bloom published a book that listed a taxonomy of educational objectives in the form of a pyramid similar to the one in the following illustration:

Bloom's Taxonomy of Educational Objectives

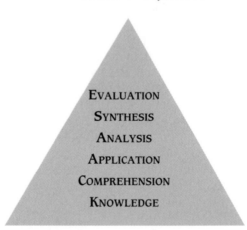

EVALUATION
SYNTHESIS
ANALYSIS
APPLICATION
COMPREHENSION
KNOWLEDGE

Knowledge is the simplest level of educational objectives and is not considered a higher-order thinking skill. It requires the learner to remember information without having to fully understand it. Tasks that students perform to demonstrate knowledge are recalling, identifying, recognizing, citing, labeling, listing, reciting, and stating.

Comprehension is not considered a higher-order thinking skill either. Learners demonstrate comprehension when they paraphrase, describe, summarize, illustrate, restate, or translate.

Foreign language teachers tend to focus the most on knowledge and comprehension. The tasks performed at these levels are important because they provide a solid foundation for the more complex tasks at the higher levels of Bloom's pyramid. However, offering our students the opportunity to perform at still higher cognitive levels provides them with more meaningful contexts in which to use the target language.

When teachers incorporate **application, analysis, synthesis,** and **evaluation** as objectives, they allow students to utilize **higher-order thinking skills.**

- **Application** involves solving, transforming, determining, demonstrating, and preparing.

- **Analysis** includes classifying, comparing, making associations, verifying, seeing cause-and-effect relationships, and determining sequences, patterns, and consequences.

- **Synthesis** requires generalizing, predicting, imagining, creating, making inferences, hypothesizing, making decisions, and drawing conclusions.

- Finally, **evaluation** involves assessing, persuading, determining value, judging, validating, and solving problems.

Most foreign language classes focus little on higher-order thinking skills. Some foreign language educators mistakenly think that all higher-order thinking skills require an advanced level of language ability. Not so! Students can demonstrate these skills by using very simple language available even to beginning students. Also, higher-order thinking tasks about the target culture or language can be conducted in English. The use of some English in the foreign language class in order to utilize higher cognitive skills does not jeopardize progress in the target language.

Higher-order thinking skills prepare our students for more than using a foreign language. They introduce students to the life skills they need to become successful, productive citizens in our society. When we think about it, that *is* the underlying purpose of education.

WHY TEACH HIGHER-ORDER THINKING SKILLS?

There is already so much to cover and so little time that some teachers may question the worth of adding these types of activities to an already full schedule. Yet we know from experience that simply "covering" the material does not help our students acquire another language. Incorporating higher-order thinking skills in the foreign language classroom can help guide students toward language acquisition by providing meaningful experiences in a setting that can otherwise often feel artificial.

Also, we now know that employing higher-order thinking skills assists all students, including those who are at risk of failing. In the past, we felt that at-risk students were incapable of higher-order thinking, but we have since discovered that we have been denying them the opportunity to experience what they are capable of doing and what they need to do in order to be successful adults.

SAMPLE ACTIVITIES EMPLOYING HIGHER-ORDER THINKING SKILLS

There are no limitations on incorporating higher-order thinking skills in the foreign language classroom. What follows are a few sample activities, some of which you might already be familiar with. Use *your* higher-order thinking skills to develop other possibilities!

▶ LISTENING

HOTS:	Analysis
TASKS:	Patterning and sequencing
VOCABULARY NEEDED:	Three colors
MATERIALS REQUIRED:	Three colored-paper squares for each student

After reviewing the colors, call out a pattern of colors and have the students show their comprehension by arranging their colored pieces of paper from left to right in the order you give. Then have them finish the pattern for you. For example, you say: **rouge, vert, bleu, rouge, vert, bleu...** now what color follows? And then what color?

This is not only a HOTS activity, it also crosses disciplines. It reviews the mathematical concept of patterning and sequencing. You can have the students form patterns and sequences using any type of vocabulary.

▶ READING

HOTS:	Synthesis
TASKS:	Hypothesizing and imagining
VOCABULARY NEEDED:	Determined by level of students
MATERIALS REQUIRED:	Legend or short story

After the students have read the first part of the story, have them imagine how the story would end, based on the values of the target culture.

▶ SPEAKING

HOTS:	Evaluation
TASKS:	Assessing and determining value
VOCABULARY NEEDED:	Numbers 0-25, five objects students would need for school
MATERIALS REQUIRED:	Visuals of five school-related objects with prices beneath them

Tell students that they each have twenty-five dollars to spend on back-to-school supplies. They each need to tell you what they would buy with their money.

▶ WRITING

HOTS:	Analysis
TASKS:	Classifying
VOCABULARY NEEDED:	Leisure activities
MATERIALS REQUIRED:	Drawings of leisure activities on a handout

From the list of activities they have before them, students should write the ones that they like to do on the weekend. Then they should write those that a family member likes to do. Finally, students should write a comparison of the two lists.

COMMITMENT TO HIGHER-ORDER THINKING SKILLS

Teaching higher-order thinking skills takes no extra time from classroom instruction since language skills are reinforced during thinking skills activities. What teaching higher-order thinking skills does require of teachers is a commitment to classroom activities that go beyond the objectives of Bloom's knowledge and comprehension levels. Having students name objects and recite verb forms is not enough. Employing HOTS gives students the opportunity to experience a second language as a useful device for meaningful communication.

▶ REFERENCES

Bloom, Benjamin. *Taxonomy of Educational Objectives. Handbook 1: Cognitive Domain.* New York: David McKay Company, 1956.

Allez, viens!

encourages higher-order thinking skills in the following ways:

THE PUPIL'S EDITION

- Develops critical thinking skills through a variety of activities, including interpretation of the visually presented **Mise en train**, journal writing, interviews, **Rencontre Culturelle** presentations, application of reading strategies, and situational role-plays.

THE ANNOTATED TEACHER'S EDITION

- Includes Thinking Critically and Multicultural Links features that provide the teacher with suggestions for activities requiring students to draw inferences, compare and contrast, evaluate, and synthesize.

THE ANCILLARY PROGRAM

- Incorporates higher-order thinking skills in Communicative Activities, Additional Listening Activities, and the chapter-related realia. In the *Practice and Activity Book,* students are guided carefully from structured practice to open-ended tasks that require higher-order thinking.

Using Portfolios in the Language Classroom

BY JO ANNE S. WILSON

The communicative, whole-language approach of today's language instruction requires assessment methods that parallel the teaching and learning strategies in the proficiency-oriented classroom. We know that language acquisition is a process. Portfolios are designed to assess the steps in that process. ◆

Portfolios offer a more realistic and accurate way to assess the process of language teaching and learning.

WHAT IS A PORTFOLIO?

A portfolio is a purposeful, systematic collection of a student's work. A useful tool in developing a student profile, the portfolio shows the student's efforts, progress, and achievements for a given period of time. It may be used for periodic evaluation, as the basis for overall evaluation, or for placement. It may also be used to enhance or provide alternatives to traditional assessment measures, such as formal tests, quizzes, class participation, and homework.

WHY USE PORTFOLIOS?

Portfolios benefit both students and teachers because they

- **Are ongoing and systematic.** A portfolio reflects the real-world process of production, assessment, revision, and reassessment. It parallels the natural rhythm of learning.
- **Offer an incentive to learn.** Students have a vested interest in creating the portfolios through which they can showcase their ongoing efforts and tangible achievements. Students select the works to be included and have a chance to revise, improve, evaluate, and explain the contents.
- **Are sensitive to individual needs.** Language learners bring varied abilities to the classroom and do not acquire skills in a uniformly neat and orderly fashion. The personalized, individualized assessment offered by portfolios responds to this diversity.
- **Provide documentation of language development.** The material in a portfolio is evidence of student progress in the language learning process. The contents of the portfolio make it easier to discuss student progress with the students as well as with parents and others interested in the student's progress.

- **Offer multiple sources of information.** A portfolio presents a way to collect and analyze information from multiple sources that reflect a student's efforts, progress, and achievements in the language.

PORTFOLIO COMPONENTS

The language portfolio should include both oral and written work, student self-evaluation, and teacher observation, usually in the form of brief, non-evaluative comments about various aspects of the student's performance.

THE ORAL COMPONENT

The oral component of a portfolio might be an audio- or videocassette. It may contain both rehearsed and extemporaneous monologues and conversations. For a rehearsed speaking activity, give a specific communicative task that students can personalize according to their individual interests (for example, ordering a favorite meal in a restaurant). If the speaking activity is extemporaneous, first acquaint students with possible topics for discussion or even the specific task they will be expected to perform. (For example, tell them they will be asked to discuss a picture showing a sports activity or a restaurant scene.)

THE WRITTEN COMPONENT

Portfolios are excellent tools for incorporating process writing strategies into the language classroom. Documentation of various stages of the writing process—brainstorming, multiple drafts, and peer comments—may be included with the finished product.

Involve students in selecting writing tasks for the portfolio. At the beginning levels, the tasks might include some structured writing, such as labeling or listing. As students become more proficient, journals, letters, and other more complicated writing tasks are valuable ways for them to monitor their progress in using the written language.

STUDENT SELF-EVALUATION

Students should be actively involved in critiquing and evaluating their portfolios and monitoring their own progress. The process and procedure for student self-evaluation should be considered in planning the contents of the portfolio. Students should work with you and their peers to design the exact format. Self-evaluation encourages them to think about what they are learning (content), how they learn (process), why they are learning (purpose), and where they are going in their learning (goals).

TEACHER OBSERVATION

Systematic, regular, and ongoing observations should be placed in the portfolio after they have been discussed with the student. These observations provide feedback on the student's progress in the language learning process.

Teacher observations should be based on an established set of criteria that has been developed earlier with input from the student. Observation techniques may include the following:

- Jotting notes in a journal to be discussed with the student and then placed in the portfolio
- Using a checklist of observable behaviors, such as the willingness to take risks when using the target language or staying on task during the lesson
- Making observations on adhesive notes that can be placed in folders
- Recording anecdotal comments, during or after class, using a cassette recorder.

Knowledge of the criteria you use in your observations gives students a framework for their performance.

HOW ARE PORTFOLIOS EVALUATED?

The portfolio should reflect the process of student learning over a specific period of time. At the beginning of that time period, determine the criteria by which you will assess the final product and convey them to the students. Make this evaluation a collaborative effort by seeking students' input as you formulate these criteria and your instructional goals.

Students need to understand that evaluation based on a predetermined standard is but one phase of the assessment process; demonstrated effort and growth are just as important. As you consider correctness and accuracy in both oral and written work, also consider the organization, creativity, and improvement revealed by the student's portfolio over the time period. The portfolio provides a way to monitor the growth of a student's knowledge, skills, and attitudes, and shows the student's efforts, progress, and achievements.

HOW TO IMPLEMENT PORTFOLIOS

Teacher-teacher collaboration is as important to the implementation of portfolios as teacher-student collaboration. Confer with your colleagues to determine, for example, what kinds of information you want to see in the student portfolio, how the information will be presented, the purpose of the portfolio, the intended purposes (grading, placement, or a combination of the two), and criteria for evaluating the portfolio. Conferring among colleagues helps foster a departmental cohesiveness and consistency that will ultimately benefit the students.

THE PROMISE OF PORTFOLIOS

The high degree of student involvement in developing portfolios and deciding how they will be used generally results in renewed student enthusiasm for learning and improved achievement. As students compare portfolio pieces done early in the year with work produced later, they can take pride in the progress as well as reassess their motivation and work habits.

Portfolios also provide a framework for periodic assessment of teaching strategies, programs, and instruction. They offer schools a tool to help solve the problem of vertical articulation and accurate student placement. The more realistic and accurate assessment of the language learning process that is provided by portfolios is congruent with the strategies that should be used in the proficiency-oriented classroom.

Allez, viens!
supports the use of portfolios in the following ways:

THE PUPIL'S EDITION

- Includes numerous oral and written activities that can be easily adapted for student portfolios, such as **Mon journal, Ecrivons!,** and **Jeu de rôle.**

THE ANNOTATED TEACHER'S EDITION

- Suggests activities in the Portfolio Assessment feature that may serve as portfolio items.

THE ANCILLARY PROGRAM

- Includes criteria in the *Alternative Assessment Guide* for evaluating portfolios.
- Provides Speaking Tests in the Testing Program for each chapter that can be adapted for use as portfolio assessment items.
- Offers several oral and written scenarios on the *Interactive CD-ROM Program* that students can develop and include in their portfolios.

Professional References

This section provides information about several resources that can enrich your French class. Included are addresses of government offices of francophone countries, pen pal organizations, subscription agencies, and many others. Since addresses change frequently, you may want to verify them before you send your requests. You may also want to refer to the HRW web side at **http://www.hrw.com** *for current information.* ◆

CULTURAL AGENCIES

For historic and tourist information about France and francophone countries, contact:

French Cultural Services
972 Fifth Ave.
New York, NY 10021
(212) 439-1400

French Cultural Services
540 Bush St.
San Francisco, CA 94108
(415) 397-4330

TOURIST OFFICES

French Government Tourist Office
444 Madison Ave.
New York, NY 10022
(212) 838-7800

Délégation du Québec
53 State Street
Exchange Place Bldg., 19th floor
Boston, MA 02109
(617) 723-3366

Caribbean Tourism Association
20 E. 46th St., 4th floor
New York, NY 10017
(212) 682-0435

INTERCULTURAL EXCHANGE

American Field Service
198 Madison Ave.
New York, NY 10016
(212) 299-9000

CIEE Student Travel Services
205 East 42nd St.
New York, NY 10017
(212) 661-1414

PEN PAL ORGANIZATIONS

For the names of pen pal groups other than those listed below, contact your local chapter of AATF. There are fees involved, so be sure to write for information.

**Student Letter Exchange
(League of Friendship)**
211 Broadway, Suite 201
Lynbrook, NY 11563
(516) 887-8628

World Pen Pals
1694 Como Avenue
St. Paul, MN 55108
(612) 647-0191

PERIODICALS

Subscriptions to the following cultural materials are available directly from the publishers. See also the section on Subscription Services.

- *Phosphore* is a monthly magazine for high school students.
- *Okapi* is a bimonthly environmentally-oriented magazine for younger teenagers in France.
- *Le Monde* is the major daily newspaper in France.
- *Le Figaro* is an important newspaper in France. Daily or Saturday editions are available by subscription.
- *Elle* is a weekly fashion magazine for women.
- *Paris Match* is a general interest weekly magazine.
- *Le Point* is a current events weekly magazine.
- *L'Express* is a current events weekly magazine.

SUBSCRIPTION SERVICES

French-language magazines can be obtained through subscription agencies in the United States. The following companies are among the many that can provide your school with subscriptions.

EBSCO Subscription Services
5724 Hwy 280 E
Birmingham, AL 35242
(205) 991-6600

Continental Book Company
8000 Cooper Ave., Bldg. 29
Glendale, NY 11385
(718) 326-0560

PROFESSIONAL ORGANIZATIONS

The two major organizations for French teachers at the secondary-school level are:

The American Council on the Teaching of Foreign Languages (ACTFL)
6 Executive Blvd.
Upper Level
Yonkers, NY 10701
(914) 963-8830

The American Association of Teachers of French (AATF)
Mailcode 4510
Southern Illinois University
Carbondale, IL 61820

A Bibliography for the French Teacher

This bibliography is a compilation of several resources available for professional enrichment. ◆

SELECTED AND ANNOTATED LIST OF READINGS

▶ I. METHODS AND APPROACHES

Cohen, Andrew D. *Assessing Language Ability in the Classroom,* (2nd ed.). Boston, MA: Heinle, 1994.
• Assessment processes, oral interviews, role-playing situations, dictation, and portfolio assessment.

Hadley, Alice Omaggio. *Teaching Language in Context,* (2nd ed.). Boston, MA: Heinle, 1993.
• Overview of the proficiency movement and a survey of past language-teaching methods and approaches; application of the five skills in language education; includes sample activities, teaching summaries, and references.

Lafayette, R. (Ed.). *National Standards: A Catalyst for Reform.* Lincolnwood, IL: National Textbook Co., 1996.
• Outline and implications of the National Standards for the modern language classroom; addresses technology, teacher training, materials development, and the changing learning environment.

Lee, James F., and Bill VanPatten. *Making Communicative Language Teaching Happen.* New York: McGraw-Hill, 1995.
• Task-based approach to language education, includes activities and test sections to encourage communicative interaction in the classroom.

▶ II. SECOND LANGUAGE THEORY

Brown, H. Douglas. *Principles of Language Learning and Teaching* (3rd. ed.). Englewood Cliffs, NJ: Prentice Hall Regents, 1994.
• Addresses the cognitive, psychological, and sociocultural factors influencing the language-learning process; also includes theories of learning, styles and strategies, motivation, and culture; as well as assessment, error analysis, communicative competence, and theories of acquisition.

Ellis, Rod. *The Study of Second Language Acquisition.* Oxford: Oxford University Press, 1994.
• Provides an overview of second language acquisition: error analysis, acquisition orders, social factors, affective variables, individual differences, and the advantages and disadvantages of classroom instruction.

Krashen, Stephen. *The Power of Reading.* New York: McGraw, 1994.
• Updates Optimal Input Theory by incorporating the reading of authentic texts.

▶ III. TECHNOLOGY-ENHANCED INSTRUCTION

Bush, Michael D., and Robert M. Terry, (Eds.), in conjunction with ACTFL. *Technology Enhanced Language Learning.* Lincolnwood, IL: National Textbook Co., 1997.
• Articles deal with the application of technology in the modern language classroom, including: computer-mediated communication, electronic discussions, hypermedia, the Internet, multimedia, videos, and the WWW.

Muyskens, Judith Ann (Ed.). *New Ways of Learning and Teaching: Focus on Technology and Foreign Language Education.* Boston: Heinle and Heinle, 1997.
• Compilation of articles on the use of technology in the classroom; techniques for applying technology tools to the four skills and culture; also discusses implementation, teacher training, and language laboratories.

Steen, Douglas R., Mark R. Roddy, Derek Sheffield, and Michael Bryan Stout. *Teaching With the Internet: Putting Teachers before Technology.* Bellevue, WA: Resolution Business Press, Inc., 1995.
• Designed for K–12 teachers and based on educational theory, provides tips and strategies for using the Internet in and out of the classroom, cites specific case studies; topics include the Internet, e-mail, mailing lists, newsgroups, the WWW, creating a Web page, and other research services.

▶ IV. PROFESSIONAL JOURNALS

Calico
(Published by the Computer Assisted Language Instruction Consortium)
• Dedicated to the intersection of modern language learning and high technology. Research articles on videodiscs, using computer-assisted language learning, how-to articles, and courseware reviews.

The Foreign Language Annals
(Published by the American Council on the Teaching of Foreign Languages)
• Consists of research and how-to-teach articles.

The French Review
(Published by the American Association of Teachers of French)
• Articles on French-language literature.

The IALL Journal of Language Learning Technologies
(Published by the International Association for Learning Laboratories)
• Research articles as well as practical discussions pertaining to technology and language instruction.

The Modern Language Journal
• Primarily features research articles.

CHAPITRE PRELIMINAIRE : ALLEZ, VIENS!

Functions
- Introducing yourself
- Spelling
- Counting
- Understanding classroom instructions

Grammar
- French alphabet
- French accent marks

Culture
- The French-speaking world
- Famous French-speaking people
- The importance of learning French
- French gestures for counting

CHAPITRE 1 : FAISONS CONNAISSANCE!

Location: Poitiers

Functions
- Greeting people and saying goodbye
- Asking how people are and telling how you are
- Asking someone's name and age and giving yours
- Expressing likes, dislikes, and preferences about things
- Expressing likes, dislikes, and preferences about activities

Grammar
- ne... pas
- The definite articles le, la, l', and les and the gender of nouns
- The connectors et and mais
- Subject pronouns
- -er verbs

Culture
- Greetings and goodbyes
- Hand gestures
- Leisure-time activities

Re-entry
- Introductions
- Numbers 0–20
- Expressing likes, dislikes, and preferences about things

CHAPITRE 2 : VIVE L'ECOLE!

Location: Poitiers

Functions
- Agreeing and disagreeing
- Asking for and giving information
- Telling when you have class
- Asking for and expressing opinions

Grammar
- Using si instead of oui to contradict a negative statement
- The verb avoir

Culture
- The French educational system/le bac
- L'heure officielle
- Curriculum in French schools
- The French grading system

Re-entry
- Greetings
- The verb aimer
- Numbers for telling time

CHAPITRE 3 : TOUT POUR LA RENTREE

Location: Poitiers

Functions
- Making and responding to requests
- Asking others what they need and telling what you need
- Telling what you'd like and what you'd like to do
- Getting someone's attention
- Asking for information
- Expressing thanks

Grammar
- The indefinite articles un, une, and des
- The demonstrative adjectives ce, cet, cette, and ces
- Adjective agreement and placement

Culture
- Bagging your own purchases
- Buying school supplies in French-speaking countries
- French currency (francs and euros)

Re-entry
- The verb avoir
- Expressing likes and dislikes
- Numbers

CHAPITRE 4 : SPORTS ET PASSE-TEMPS

Location: Quebec

Functions
- Telling how much you like or dislike something
- Exchanging information
- Making, accepting, and turning down suggestions

Grammar
- Expressions with faire and jouer
- Question formation
- de after a negative verb
- The verb faire

- The pronoun on
- Adverbs of frequency

Culture
- Old and new in Quebec City
- Celsius and Fahrenheit
- Sports in francophone countries
- Maison des jeunes et de la culture

Re-entry
- Expressing likes and dislikes
- The verb aimer; regular -er verbs
- Agreeing and disagreeing

CHAPITRE 5 : ON VA AU CAFE?

Location: Paris

Functions
- Making suggestions and excuses
- Making a recommendation
- Getting someone's attention
- Ordering food and beverages
- Inquiring about and expressing likes and dislikes
- Paying the check

Grammar
- The verb prendre
- The imperative

Culture
- Food served in a café
- Waitpersons as professionals
- La litote
- Tipping

Re-entry
- Accepting and turning down a suggestion
- Expressing likes and dislikes
- Numbers 20–100

CHAPITRE 6 : AMUSONS-NOUS!

Location: Paris

Functions
- Making plans
- Extending and responding to invitations
- Arranging to meet someone

Grammar
- Using le with days of the week
- The verb aller and aller + infinitive
- Contractions with à
- The verb vouloir
- Information questions

Culture
- Going out
- Dating in France
- Conversational time

Re-entry
- Expressing likes and dislikes
- Days of the week
- Making, accepting, and turning down suggestions
- Sports and hobbies
- **L'heure officielle**

CHAPITRE 7 : LA FAMILLE
Location: Paris

Functions
- Identifying people
- Introducing people
- Describing and characterizing people
- Asking for, giving, and refusing permission

Grammar
- Possession with **de**
- Possessive adjectives
- Adjective agreement
- The verb **être**

Culture
- Family life
- Pets in France

Re-entry
- Asking for and giving people's names and ages
- Adjective agreement

CHAPITRE 8 : AU MARCHE
Location: Abidjan

Functions
- Expressing need
- Making, accepting, and declining requests
- Telling someone what to do
- Offering, accepting, or refusing food

Grammar
- The partitive articles
- **avoir besoin de**
- The verb **pouvoir**
- **de** with expressions of quantity
- The pronoun **en**

Culture
- The Ivorian market
- Shopping for groceries in francophone countries
- The metric system
- Foods of Côte d'Ivoire
- Mealtimes in francophone countries

Re-entry
- Food vocabulary
- Activities
- The imperative

CHAPITRE 9 : AU TELEPHONE
Location: Arles

Functions
- Asking for and expressing opinions

- Inquiring about and relating past events
- Making and answering a telephone call
- Sharing confidences and consoling others
- Asking for and giving advice

Grammar
- The **passé composé** with **avoir**
- Placement of adverbs with the **passé composé**
- The -**re** verbs: **répondre**
- The object pronouns **le, la, les, lui,** and **leur**

Culture
- History of Arles
- The French telephone system
- Telephone habits of French-speaking teenagers

Re-entry
- Chores
- Asking for, giving, and refusing permission
- **aller** + infinitive

CHAPITRE 10 : DANS UN MAGASIN DE VETEMENTS
Location: Arles

Functions
- Asking for and giving advice
- Expressing need; inquiring
- Asking for an opinion; paying a compliment; criticizing
- Hesitating; making a decision

Grammar
- The verbs **mettre** and **porter**
- Adjectives used as nouns
- The -**ir** verbs: **choisir**
- The direct object pronouns **le, la,** and **les**
- **c'est** versus **il/elle est**

Culture
- Clothing sizes
- Fashion in francophone countries
- Responding to compliments

Re-entry
- The future with **aller**
- Colors
- Likes and dislikes

CHAPITRE 11 : VIVE LES VACANCES!
Location: Arles

Functions
- Inquiring about and sharing future plans
- Expressing indecision; expressing wishes

- Asking for advice; making, accepting, and refusing suggestions
- Reminding; reassuring
- Seeing someone off
- Asking for and expressing opinions
- Inquiring about and relating past events

Grammar
- The prepositions **à** and **en**
- The -**ir** verbs: **partir**

Culture
- **Colonies de vacances**
- Vacations

Re-entry
- **aller** + infinitive
- Asking for advice
- Clothing vocabulary
- The imperative
- Weather expressions
- The **passé composé**
- The verb **vouloir**

CHAPITRE 12 : EN VILLE
Location: Fort-de-France
(Review)

Functions
- Pointing out places and things
- Making and responding to requests
- Asking for advice
- Making suggestions
- Asking for and giving directions

Grammar
- The pronoun **y**
- Contractions with **de**

Culture
- Store hours in France and Martinique
- Making "small talk" in francophone countries
- Getting a driver's license in francophone countries
- **DOMs** and **TOMs**
- Public areas downtown

Re-entry
- Contractions with **à**
- The partitive
- Contractions with **de**
- Family vocabulary
- Possessive adjectives
- The **passé composé**
- Expressing need
- Making excuses
- Inviting

Scope and Sequence: French Level 2

CHAPITRE 1 : BON SEJOUR!
Location: Paris region
(Review)

Functions
- Describing and characterizing yourself and others
- Expressing likes, dislikes, and preferences
- Asking for information
- Asking for and giving advice
- Asking for, making, and responding to suggestions
- Relating a series of events

Grammar
- The verbs **avoir** and **être**
- Adjective agreement
- The interrogative adjective **quel**
- **Choisir** and other -ir verbs
- The imperative
- The future with **aller**

Culture
- Travel documents for foreign countries
- Ethnic restaurants
- Studying abroad

Re-entry
- Adjectives to characterize people
- Pronunciation: **liaison**
- Family vocabulary
- Clothing and colors
- Weather expressions and seasons
- Telling time

CHAPITRE 2 : BIENVENUE A CHARTRES!
Location: Paris region
(Review)

Functions
- Welcoming someone and responding to someone's welcome
- Asking about how someone is feeling and telling how you're feeling
- Pointing out where things are
- Paying and responding to compliments
- Asking for and giving directions

Grammar
- Using **tu** and **vous**
- Question formation
- Adjectives that precede the noun
- Contractions with **à**

Culture
- Paying and receiving compliments

- Polite behavior for a guest
- Teenagers' bedrooms in France
- **Notre-Dame-de-Chartres**
- Houses in francophone countries

Re-entry
- Pronunciation: intonation
- Prepositions of location
- Contractions with **de**
- Making suggestions

CHAPITRE 3 : UN REPAS A LA FRANÇAISE
Location: Paris region

Functions
- Making purchases
- Asking for, offering, accepting, and refusing food
- Paying and responding to compliments
- Asking for and giving advice
- Extending good wishes

Grammar
- The object pronoun **en**
- The partitive articles
- The indirect object pronouns **lui** and **leur**

Culture
- Neighborhood stores
- Typical meals in the francophone world
- Courses of a meal
- The euro
- Special occasions

Re-entry
- Giving prices
- Expressions of quantity
- Food vocabulary
- The verbs **vouloir** and **pouvoir**

CHAPITRE 4 : SOUS LES TROPIQUES
Location: Martinique

Functions
- Asking for information and describing a place
- Asking for and making suggestions
- Emphasizing likes and dislikes
- Relating a series of events

Grammar
- Recognizing reflexive verbs
- The reflexive pronouns **se** and **me**
- The relative pronouns **ce qui** and **ce que**
- The present tense of reflexive verbs
- Adverbs of frequency

Culture
- **La ville de Saint-Pierre**
- Places to visit in different regions
- **Yoles rondes**
- The **créole** language
- **Carnaval**
- Music and dance in Martinique

Re-entry
- **De** with adjectives and plural nouns
- Connectors for sequencing events
- Adverbs of frequency
- Pronunciation: **e muet**
- Sports vocabulary
- Weather expressions

CHAPITRE 5 : QUELLE JOURNEE!
Location: Touraine

Functions
- Expressing concern for someone
- Inquiring; expressing satisfaction and frustration
- Sympathizing with and consoling someone
- Giving reasons and making excuses
- Congratulating and reprimanding someone

Grammar
- The **passé composé** with **avoir**
- Introduction to the **passé composé** with **être**

Culture
- **Carnet de correspondance**
- Meals at school
- French grades and report cards
- School life in francophone countries

Re-entry
- Connector words
- Sports and leisure activities
- Pronunciation: the nasal sound [ɛ̃]
- Question words
- Reflexive verbs

CHAPITRE 6 : A NOUS, LES CHATEAUX!
Location: Touraine

Functions
- Asking for opinions; expressing enthusiasm, indifference, and dissatisfaction
- Expressing disbelief and doubt
- Asking for and giving information

Grammar
- The phrase **c'était**
- The **passé composé** with **être**

- Formal and informal phrasing of questions
- The verb **ouvrir**

Culture
- Types of châteaux in France
- Buses and trains in France
- Studying historical figures in school

Re-entry
- Pronunciation: [y] versus [u]
- The **passé composé** with **avoir**
- Expressing satisfaction and frustration
- Telling time

CHAPITRE 7 : EN PLEINE FORME
Location: Touraine

Functions
- Expressing concern for someone and complaining
- Giving advice; accepting and rejecting advice
- Expressing discouragement and offering encouragement
- Justifying your recommendations; advising against something

Grammar
- Reflexive verbs in the **passé composé**
- The pronoun **en** with activities
- The verbs **devoir** and **se nourrir**

Culture
- Pharmacies in France
- Figures of speech
- Teenagers' exercise habits
- Staying healthy
- Mineral water

Re-entry
- Expressing doubt
- Telling how often you do something
- Pronunciation: the [r] sound
- Sports activities

CHAPITRE 8 : C'ETAIT COMME ÇA
Location: Côte d'Ivoire

Functions
- Telling what or whom you miss; reassuring someone
- Asking and telling what things were like
- Reminiscing
- Making and responding to suggestions

Grammar
- The **imparfait** of **avoir** and **être**
- Formation of the **imparfait**
- **Si on** + the **imparfait**

Culture
- Village life in Côte d'Ivoire

- Ethnic groups in West Africa
- High school in Côte d'Ivoire
- Félix Houphouët-Boigny
- Abidjan
- City versus country living

Re-entry
- Pronunciation: the [ɛ] sound
- Adjectives of physical traits and personality
- Chores
- Places in a city

CHAPITRE 9 : TU CONNAIS LA NOUVELLE?
Location: Provence

Functions
- Wondering what happened; offering possible explanations
- Accepting and rejecting explanations
- Breaking some news; showing interest
- Beginning, continuing, and ending a story

Grammar
- **Avoir l'air** + adjective
- The **passé composé** vs. the **imparfait**
- The **passé composé** and the **imparfait** with interrupted actions
- Using **être en train de** and the **imparfait**

Culture
- The **cours Mirabeau,** Aix-en-Provence
- **Histoires marseillaises**
- Friendship

Re-entry
- School-related mishaps
- The **passé composé** of reflexive verbs
- Accidents and injuries
- The relative pronouns **ce qui** and **ce que**
- Explanations and apologies

CHAPITRE 10 : JE PEUX TE PARLER?
Location: Provence

Functions
- Sharing a confidence
- Asking for and giving advice
- Asking for and granting a favor; making excuses
- Apologizing and accepting an apology; reproaching someone

Grammar
- Object pronouns and their placement
- Direct object pronouns with the **passé composé**
- Object pronouns before an infinitive

Culture
- Paul Cézanne
- Roman ruins in Aix-en-Provence
- Provençale cuisine
- Talking about personal problems

Re-entry
- Accepting and refusing advice
- Personal happenings
- Pronunciation: the nasal sound [ã]
- Making excuses

CHAPITRE 11 : CHACUN SES GOUTS
Location: Provence

Functions
- Identifying people and things
- Asking for and giving information
- Giving opinions
- Summarizing

Grammar
- The verb **connaître**
- **C'est** versus **il/elle est**
- The relative pronouns **qui** and **que**

Culture
- **La Fête de la Musique**
- Musical tastes
- Movie theaters in France
- The **Minitel**

Re-entry
- Emphasizing likes and dislikes
- Making and responding to suggestions

CHAPITRE 12 : A LA BELLE ETOILE
Location: Quebec (Review)

Functions
- Asking for and giving information; giving directions
- Complaining; expressing discouragement and offering encouragement
- Asking for and giving advice
- Relating a series of events; describing people and places

Grammar
- The verb **emporter**
- The **passé composé** and the **imparfait**

Culture
- **Le parc de la Jacques-Cartier**
- Ecology in Canada
- Endangered animals
- French-Canadian expressions

Re-entry
- Sports and activities
- Clothing vocabulary
- Making and responding to suggestions

Scope and Sequence: French Level 3

CHAPITRE 1 : FRANCE, LES REGIONS
Location: France
(Review)

Functions
- Renewing old acquaintances
- Inquiring; expressing enthusiasm and dissatisfaction
- Exchanging information
- Asking and describing what a place was like
- Expressing indecision
- Making recommendations
- Ordering and asking for details

Grammar
- The **passé composé**
- The **imparfait**

Culture
- Traditional regional clothing
- Regional specialties
- Regional foods

Re-entry
- Sports and activities
- Food vocabulary
- Definite, indefinite, and partitive articles
- Question formation

CHAPITRE 2 : BELGIQUE, NOUS VOILA!
Location: Belgium
(Review)

Functions
- Asking for and giving directions
- Expressing impatience
- Reassuring someone
- Expressing enthusiasm and boredom
- Asking and telling where things are

Grammar
- The verb **conduire**
- The imperative
- Pronouns and their placement

Culture
- Languages in Belgium
- Favorite comic book characters
- Overview of Belgium

Re-entry
- The future with **aller**
- Making, accepting, and refusing suggestions

CHAPITRE 3 : SOYONS RESPONSABLES!
Location: Switzerland

Functions
- Asking for, granting, and refusing permission

- Expressing obligation
- Forbidding
- Reproaching
- Justifying your actions and rejecting others' excuses

Grammar
- The subjunctive
- **Ne... pas** + infinitive

Culture
- Swiss work ethic
- Switzerland's neutrality
- Overview of Switzerland
- Environmental issues
- **La minuterie**

Re-entry
- The verb **devoir**
- Complaining
- Chores
- Negative expressions

CHAPITRE 4 : DES GOUTS ET DES COULEURS
Location: France

Functions
- Asking for and giving opinions
- Asking which one(s)
- Pointing out and identifying people and things
- Paying and responding to compliments
- Reassuring someone

Grammar
- The interrogative and demonstrative pronouns
- The causative **faire**

Culture
- French clothing stores
- Fashion and personal style
- French sense of fashion

Re-entry
- Clothing vocabulary
- Adjectives referring to clothing
- Family vocabulary
- Chores

CHAPITRE 5 : C'EST NOTRE AVENIR
Location: Senegal

Functions
- Asking about and expressing intentions
- Expressing conditions and possibilities
- Asking about future plans
- Expressing wishes
- Expressing indecision
- Giving advice

- Requesting information
- Writing a formal letter

Grammar
- The future
- The conditional
- Question formation with inversion

Culture
- Careers and education in Senegal
- Overview of Senegal
- Planning for a career
- Types of job training

Re-entry
- The subjunctive
- Giving advice
- The **passé composé**
- The imperfect
- Making a telephone call
- Expressing likes and preferences

CHAPITRE 6 : MA FAMILLE, MES COPAINS ET MOI
Location: Morocco

Functions
- Making, accepting, and refusing suggestions
- Making arrangements
- Making and accepting apologies
- Showing and responding to hospitality
- Expressing and responding to thanks
- Quarreling

Grammar
- Reciprocal verbs
- The past infinitive

Culture
- Bargaining in North Africa
- Values of francophone teenagers
- Overview of Morocco
- Hospitality in Morocco

Re-entry
- Reflexive verbs
- Expressing thanks

CHAPITRE 7 : UN SAFARI-PHOTO
Location: Central African Republic

Functions
- Making suppositions
- Expressing doubt and certainty
- Asking for and giving advice
- Expressing astonishment
- Cautioning someone
- Expressing fear
- Reassuring someone
- Expressing relief

Grammar
- Structures and their complements
- Using the subjunctive
- Irregular subjunctive forms

Culture
- Overview of the Central African Republic
- Animal conservation in the Central African Republic
- Stereotypical impressions of francophone regions

Re-entry
- The subjunctive
- Travel items
- The conditional

CHAPITRE 8 : LA TUNISIE, PAYS DE CONTRASTES
Location: Tunisia

Functions
- Asking someone to convey good wishes
- Closing a letter
- Expressing hopes or wishes
- Giving advice
- Complaining
- Expressing annoyance
- Making comparisons

Grammar
- **Si** clauses
- The comparative

Culture
- Overview of Tunisia
- Traditional and modern life in Tunisia
- Carthage
- Modernization in francophone countries
- Traditional and modern styles of dress in Tunisia

Re-entry
- The imperfect
- Intonation
- Adjective agreement
- Describing a place

CHAPITRE 9 : C'EST L'FUN!
Location: Canada

Functions
- Agreeing and disagreeing
- Expressing indifference
- Making requests
- Asking for and making judgments
- Asking for and making recommendations
- Asking about and summarizing a story

Grammar
- Negative expressions
- The expression **ne... que**
- The relative pronouns **qui, que,** and **dont**

Culture
- Multilingual broadcasting in Canada
- Overview of Montreal
- Favorite types of movies
- The Canadian film industry

Re-entry
- Expressing opinions
- Quarreling
- Agreeing and disagreeing
- Types of films
- Summarizing a story
- Continuing and ending a story
- Relating a series of events
- Relative pronouns

CHAPITRE 10 : RENCONTRES AU SOLEIL
Location: Guadeloupe

Functions
- Bragging; flattering
- Teasing
- Breaking some news; showing interest
- Expressing disbelief; telling a joke

Grammar
- The superlative
- The past perfect

Culture
- Climate and natural assets of Guadeloupe
- Overview of Guadeloupe
- **La Fête des Cuisinières**
- Daily routines of francophone teenagers
- Greetings in Guadeloupe

Re-entry
- Forms of the comparative
- Reciprocal verbs
- Adjective agreement
- Breaking some news

CHAPITRE 11 : LAISSEZ LES BONS TEMPS ROULER!
Location: Louisiana

Functions
- Asking for confirmation
- Asking for and giving opinions
- Agreeing and disagreeing
- Asking for explanations
- Making observations
- Giving impressions

Culture
- **Mardi Gras** and festivals in Louisiana
- Cajun French
- Cajun music
- History of Louisiana
- Parties and celebrations in francophone countries

Re-entry
- Renewing old acquaintances
- Food vocabulary
- Types of music
- Agreeing and disagreeing
- Asking for and giving opinions
- Emphasizing likes
- Making suggestions
- Expressing opinions
- The relative pronouns **ce qui** and **ce que**

CHAPITRE 12 : ECHANGES SPORTIFS ET CULTURELS
Location: Worldwide (Review)

Functions
- Expressing anticipation
- Making suppositions
- Expressing certainty and doubt
- Inquiring
- Expressing excitement and disappointment

Grammar
- The future after **quand** and **dès que**

Culture
- International sporting events in francophone countries
- Stereotypes of people in francophone countries

Re-entry
- Sports vocabulary
- Making suppositions
- **Si** clauses
- Expressing certainty and doubt
- The future
- Prepositions with countries
- Greeting people
- Introducing people
- Asking someone's name and age and giving yours
- Offering encouragement

Contents

RESOURCES FOR CHAPITRE PRELIMINAIRE

PRINT
- *Lesson Planner,* pp. 1–2
- *Practice and Activity Book,* pp. 1–2
- *Listening Activities,* pp. 2, 101

MEDIA
- *Video Program,* Videocassette 1
  Video Guide, pp. 1–2
- *Videodisc Program,* Videodisc 1, Side A
  Videodisc Guide, pp. 1–3
- *Teaching Transparencies*
  Map Transparency 4: *Le Monde francophone*
- *Audio Compact Discs*
  Textbook Listening Activities, CD 1, Trs. 1–10

Textbook Listening Activities Scripts

For Student Response Forms, see *Listening Activities,* p. 2.

*N*oms de filles/Noms de garçons

For this script, see *Pupil's Edition,* p. 5.

*L'*alphabet

For this script, see *Pupil's Edition,* p. 6.

3 Ecoute! p. 7
1. k–a–n–g–o–u–r–o–u
2. s–e–r–p–e–n–t
3. p–i–n–g–o–u–i–n
4. c–r–a–b–e
5. s–i–n–g–e
6. t–i–g–r–e

Answers to Activity 3
1.f 2.e 3.b 4.a 5.d 6.c

*L*es accents

For this script, see *Pupil's Edition,* p. 8.

5 Ecoute! p. 8
1. p–o–è–m–e
2. h–ô–p–i–t–a–l
3. a–m–é–r–i–c–a–i–n
4. c–a–n–o–ë
5. f–r–a–n–ç–a–i–s
6. s–é–v–è–r–e

*L*es chiffres de 0 à 20

For this script, see *Pupil's Edition,* p. 9.

6 Ecoute! p. 10
1. Moi, mon numéro de téléphone, c'est le zéro trois, vingt, quatorze, zéro huit, douze.
2. Téléphone-moi au zéro trois, vingt, seize, zéro cinq, dix-sept.
3. Mon numéro, c'est le zéro trois, vingt, dix-huit, onze, dix-neuf.
4. Voilà le numéro : zéro trois, vingt, quinze, zéro quatre, treize.

Answers to Activity 6
1. e 2. a 3. b 4. d

A l'école

For this script, see *Pupil's Edition,* p. 11.

9 Ecoute! p. 11
1. Allez au tableau!
2. Fermez la porte!
3. Regardez la carte!
4. Levez la main!
5. Ouvrez le livre!
6. Sortez une feuille de papier!
7. Levez-vous!

Answers to Activity 9
1. Lynn   5. Paul
2. Emilio   6. Dena
3. Brian   7. Evelyne
4. Alison

Projects

Pourquoi apprendre le français?
(Individual Project)

ASSIGNMENT

In this project, students will consider their reasons (motivation) for studying French and set personal objectives and goals. Students will share their ideas with the class through oral presentations, using creative posters that might also be displayed in the classroom to provide motivation later in the term. This project is meant to be done in English.

MATERIALS

✂ **Students may need**
- Posterboard
- Construction paper
- Scissors
- Glue or tape
- Magazines
- Catalogues
- Travel brochures (some in French, if possible)

PLANNING

Students should address the following areas in planning their posters:

Motivation   What are two or three major reasons why you are studying French?

Objectives   What are two or three realistic objectives you would like to achieve in this class this term?

Long-Term Goals   What are your long-range goals in your study of French?

SUGGESTED SEQUENCE

1. Talk with students about the importance of being motivated and setting objectives and goals for language learning. Mention that initial motivation, objectives, and goals are likely to change throughout the learning process. You may want to share your own story with students, explaining the reasons why you began to learn French and describing how your motivation, objectives, and goals may have changed.

2. Describe the project and assign a date for the oral presentations. Write the three planning considerations on the board or on a project assignment sheet. Be sure to set a time limit for the presentations.

3. Go over each of the planning considerations and elicit a few responses from the class to serve as examples. If no one has any ideas at first, you might want to give a few of the examples listed here. Stress that students should be honest with themselves, even if their motivation, objectives, and goals are not what others think they should be.

Motivation
- I need credit to graduate.
- I need foreign language for college or future career.
- I have French-speaking relatives.
- I like French food.
- I want to learn about the culture and people in francophone countries.

Objectives
- I want to be able to carry on a simple conversation in French.
- I want to be able to write a letter to a French-speaking pen pal.
- I want to get a good grade in this class.

Long-Term Goals
- I would like to test out of the foreign language requirement in college.
- I would like to speak fluently enough to order a meal in a French restaurant.
- I would like to travel in francophone countries.
- I would like to study at a French university.

4. Give students some time in class for introspection and organizing their thoughts.

5. Have students create posters based on their personal motivation, objectives, and goals. This might be done in class or as homework. Encourage students to be as creative as possible, using words, photos, and drawings to express themselves.

6. Have students make their presentations to the class, showing their posters and explaining their motivation, objectives, and long-term goals.

GRADING THE PROJECT

The purpose of this project is to encourage students to examine their reasons for learning French and the various outcomes they expect for themselves. Because of the personal nature of the project, it would be counterproductive to assign a grade to the subjective content of the project. Instead, the project might be designated as a component of the students' portfolios. Students might review it later in the term or at the end of the term to assess their progress, or to note any changes in their motivation or goals and examine the reasons for the changes. If, however, you feel a grade is necessary, it might be based on completion of all aspects of the assignment, presentation, and creativity.

Suggested point distribution (total = 100 points):

Completion of assignment . . . . 40 points

Poster and presentation . . . . 40 points

Creativity . . . . 20 points

TEACHER NOTE

Simulations and games can provide effective learning experiences that lower student anxiety and promote language acquisition. Games often improve group dynamics, particularly when they require students to cooperate rather than compete. Here are some points to consider when you think of incorporating games in your lesson plans.

1. Games should be played in French. However, ground rules might be explained in English.

2. Games should be simple so that precious class time is not taken up explaining the rules.

3. Games should have a pedagogical objective. Is the game for language recognition only? For language production? To recycle previously presented material? To practice a particular skill? To develop higher-order thinking skills?

4. There should be a time limit for every game. If you consistently enforce announced time limits, students will help one another to stay on task.

5. When you find that a game is effective and that your students enjoy it, recycle it throughout the year in new contexts with different content.

MINI-LOTO

This game will give students practice in recognizing and saying numbers in French.

Students make a grid with four squares across and four down. They fill in all the squares randomly with numbers 20 and below, using each number once. To begin, call out numbers at random or have a student do it. Students cross off those numbers that appear on their grids. Students win by crossing off four numbers in a row horizontally, vertically, or diagonally, but they must be able to correctly read aloud the winning row of numbers!

Variation This game can also be played using letters of the alphabet or the names or pictures of objects in this chapter.

9	4	1	3
12	8	19	17
5	6	14	20
2	11	13	18

JE PEUX LAISSER UN MESSAGE?

In this game, students will practice letters of the alphabet and numbers in French.

Have students write down fictitious French names and phone numbers on slips of paper. You can refer them to page 10 for some examples of French phone numbers. Collect the papers, and tell students to imagine they're exchange students in France taking phone messages for their host families. As you read and spell the names and read the phone numbers, have students write down the messages — names and numbers. Then, ask individual students to read aloud what they have written. As an extra challenge, students might read their own messages to one another.

GEOGRAPHY CONTEST

This game will test students' knowledge of the location of francophone countries.

Cover any maps visible in the classroom and have students close their books. Form teams of three or four players. Name an area of the world such as Africa, Europe, or the Caribbean. For each area you name, teams must think of a francophone country or department in that area and write their answer correctly on the board or on a transparency. After each item, ask the teams to hold up their answers. Each team with a correct answer wins a point. For more challenge or to break a tie, ask teams to name cities, additional countries, or departments in each area.

PRELIMINAIRE
Allez, viens!

VIDEO PROGRAM
Videocassette 1
01:23–05:39

OR **VIDEODISC PROGRAM,**
Videodisc 1, Side A

Search 1, Play To 7725

The video for the Preliminary Chapter will introduce your students to some of the people they will see in the rest of *Allez, viens!* Some are actors in the **romans-photos** found in the **Mise en train** sections, and others are people interviewed for the **Panorama Culturel.** You may wish to play the video to preview the program and to give your students an introduction to the French language.

Motivating Activity

Before students open their books, ask them to answer the following questions. What comes to mind when you think of the French-speaking countries of the world? Besides France, do you know any other countries where French is spoken? Can you think of any cities in the United States with French names? (Des Moines, Iowa; Beaumont, Texas; Pierre, South Dakota; Baton Rouge, Louisiana; Detroit, Michigan; St. Louis, Missouri; La Crosse, Wisconsin)

Teaching Suggestion

You might want to use *Map Transparency 4* (**Le Monde francophone**) as you introduce students to the countries where French is spoken.

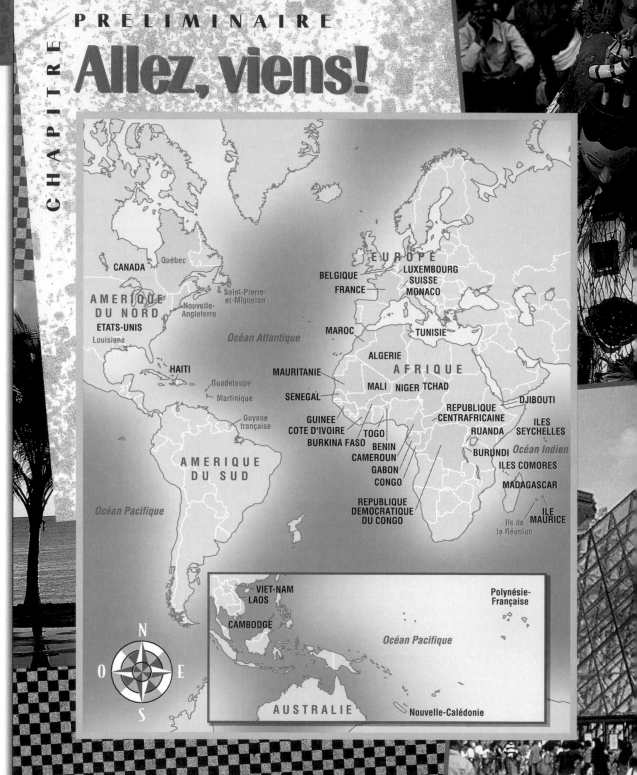

Language Note

The title of this French program, *Allez, viens!*, is a popular idiomatic expression meaning *Come along!, Come on!,* or *Let's go! Allez, viens!* is particularly appropriate as the title of this program because it is an invitation to each student of French to *Come along!* on an exciting trip to a new culture and a new language.

History Link

Ask students if they know anything about the French exploration of the Western Hemisphere. They may have heard of the French explorers Marquette, Joliet, and La Salle. Marquette and Joliet explored the Wisconsin, Mississippi, and Illinois rivers, and La Salle explored the Ohio River, the Great Lakes, and the Mississippi River. Cartier and Champlain were explorers of Canada.

Bienvenue dans le monde francophone!

Welcome to the French-speaking world!

You know, of course, that French is spoken in France, but did you know that French is spoken by many people in North America? About one-third of Canadians speak French, mostly in Quebec province (**le Québec**). In the United States, about 375,000 people in New England (**la Nouvelle-Angleterre**), whose ancestors immigrated from Canada, speak or understand French. French is also an official language in the state of Louisiana (**la Louisiane**).

French is the official language of France's overseas possessions. These include the islands of Martinique (**la Martinique**) and Guadeloupe (**la Guadeloupe**) in the Caribbean Sea, French Guiana (**la Guyane française**) in South America, the island of Réunion (**la Réunion**) in the Indian Ocean, and several islands in the Pacific Ocean. French is also spoken in Haiti (**Haïti**).

Did you know that French is also widely used in Africa? Over twenty African countries have retained French as an official language. Many people in West and Central African countries, such as Senegal (**le Sénégal**), the Republic of Côte d'Ivoire (**la République de Côte d'Ivoire**), Mali (**le Mali**), Niger (**le Niger**), and Chad (**le Tchad**), speak French. In North Africa, French has played an important role in Algeria (**l'Algérie**), Tunisia (**la Tunisie**), and Morocco (**le Maroc**). Although Arabic is the official language of these North African countries, French is used in many schools across North Africa and in parts of the Middle East.

Take a minute to find France on the map. Several of the countries bordering France use French as an official language. It's the first or second language of many people in Belgium (**la Belgique**), Switzerland (**la Suisse**), Luxembourg (**le Luxembourg**), and Andorra (**l'Andorre**), as well as in the principality of Monaco (**Monaco**).

As you look at the map, what other places can you find where French is spoken? Can you imagine how French came to be spoken in these places?

un 1

Background Information

1. **Léopold Senghor** served in the French Parliament from 1946 to 1960, when he was elected president of Senegal. He founded the magazine *L'Etudiant noir* with Aimé Césaire. In the first issue in 1934, they presented the principles of **Négritude**, a literary movement that emphasized the black experience. Senghor is a member of the **Institut de France.** In June of 1983, he was elected to the prestigious **Académie française.** In October 1996, a large celebration was held in Paris in honor of Senghor's ninetieth birthday.

2. **Isabelle Adjani** started a theater troupe with some friends at age 12, and at 15, she began her acting career at the **Comédie-Française,** a historic theater in Paris. While playing Agnès in Molière's *L'Ecole des femmes,* she continued to study for the **baccalauréat.** Her film portrayals have won her three **Césars,** the French equivalent of the Oscars.

3. **Victor Hugo,** noted at an early age for his poetry, won a prize from Louis XVIII at age 19. His first volume of poetry was published in 1822, the same year he was awarded a royal pension. Hugo was a royalist during his youth, but he became more and more liberal and was elected to the National Assembly in 1848. He was exiled in 1851 for speaking out against Napoleon III. Hugo's exile, spent mostly in the Channel Islands, lasted 19 years, during which time he continued to write. Because of his popularity during his lifetime, his 80th birthday was widely celebrated. His principal works include eight novels *(Les Misérables),*

TU LES CONNAIS? *Do you know them?*

In science, politics, technology, and the arts, French-speaking people have made important contributions. How many of these people can you match with their descriptions?

1. **Léopold Senghor** (b. 1906)
   A key advocate of **Négritude,** which asserts the values and the spirit of black African civilization, Senghor is a man of many talents. He was the first black African high school teacher in France. He was President of Senegal from 1960 to 1980. He was also the first black member of the **Académie Française.**

2. **Isabelle Adjani** (b. 1955)
   A talented actress and producer, Isabelle Yasmine Adjani is well known for her award-winning roles in French films. In the 1980s, Adjani publicly acknowledged her Algerian heritage and began a personal campaign to raise consciousness about racism in France.

3. **Victor Hugo** (1802-1885)
   Novelist, poet, and political activist, Hugo led the Romantic Movement in French literature. In his most famous works, *Notre-Dame de Paris (The Hunchback of Notre Dame)* and *Les Misérables,* he sympathizes with the victims of poverty and condemns a corrupt political system.

4. **Marie-José Pérec** (b. 1968)
   At the 1996 Olympic Games®, Pérec became only the second woman in history to win the 200 m. and 400 m. titles in the same Olympics. Her numerous victories have made her one of the premier female track athletes of our time.

2 *deux*

nine plays *(Hernani),* and 22 volumes of poetry *(Les Feuilles d'automne).*

4. **Marie-José Pérec** was born on the island of Guadeloupe, a French DOM. At the age of 16, she moved to Paris. Pérec won her first World Championships title in the 400-meter event in 1991. She left France in 1994 to escape her new fame and to work with her new coach, John Smith, at UCLA.

5. **Jacques-Yves Cousteau** won over 20 film awards and produced numerous TV series and specials. His interest in inventing and ocean exploration manifested itself early, and at age 11, he made a patentable improvement on a marine crane. During World War II, he worked for the resistance movement. His voyages in his vessel *Calypso* began in 1951, and in 1959, he helped invent a mini-submarine that holds two people and photography equipment. He founded the Cousteau Society in 1973 to alert the public about pollution in the oceans.

e.

f.

g.

h.

5. *Jacques Cousteau* (1910-1997)
Jacques-Yves Cousteau first gained worldwide attention for his undersea expeditions as the commander of the *Calypso* and for inventing the aqualung. In order to record his explorations, he invented a process for filming underwater.

6. *Céline Dion* (b. 1968)
A native of Quebec, Dion is an award-winning singer whose work includes hit songs in both English and French. In 1996, her album *Falling Into You* was awarded the Grammy® for Album of the Year and Best Pop Album. Dion also performed in the opening ceremonies of the 1996 Olympic Games in Atlanta, Georgia.

7. *Gérard Depardieu* (b. 1948)
Gérard Depardieu is a popular actor, director, and producer, who has appeared in over 70 films. His performance in the 1990 movie *Green Card,* which won him a Golden Globe award, marked his American film debut.

8. *Marie Curie* (1867-1934)
Along with her husband Pierre, Marie Curie won a Nobel prize in physics for her study of radioactivity. Several years later, she also won an individual Nobel prize for chemistry. Marie Curie was the first woman to teach at the Sorbonne in Paris.

1e 2a 3h 5g 6f 7d 8c 4b

trois **3**

7. **Gérard Depardieu,** one of six children of an illiterate sheet metal worker, had a rough childhood, which included arrests for petty theft and truancy. By his late teens, he was in jail and had become mute. A prison official sent him to a speech therapist who helped him discover acting. When he started his career, he had difficulty reading scripts, but was quickly noticed for his talent in an extremely wide range of roles. His films include *My Father the Hero, Danton* (about the French Revolution), *Jean de Florette, Le Retour de Martin Guerre* (remade in the United States as *Sommersby*), *Cyrano de Bergerac,* and *Tous les Matins du monde,* which also starred his son Guillaume.

8. **Marie Curie,** famous for giving radioactivity its name, was born in Poland and moved to Paris where she attended the Sorbonne. After discovering several radioactive elements, she and her husband finally isolated radium in 1902. She drove an ambulance and provided X-ray service to hospitals during World War I. She is the only person to win two Nobel prizes in science, but she was denied entrance into the French Academy by one vote because of her gender. She died of leukemia.

 For Individual Needs

Challenge Ask students if they know of other famous French-speaking people. You might have students prepare oral reports on them.

6. **Céline Dion** is from Charlemagne, a town 20 kilometers east of Montreal. The youngest of 14 children, Dion began her musical career at the age of 12. Raised in Quebec, a francophone region of Canada, she did not learn English until she was in her late teens. At the 1997 World Music Awards, she was named World's Overall Best-Selling Artist and World's Best-Selling Pop Artist. Some of her hit songs include *Des mots qui sonnent,* "Because You Loved Me" from the movie *Up Close and Personal,* and "My Heart Will Go On" from the movie *Titanic.*

Teaching Suggestion

Have students work in pairs or small groups to identify the careers shown in some of the photos and think of products and brand names from franco-phone countries. Examples include Perrier® and Evian® mineral water, Le Lion (Food Lion®) supermarkets, Air France®, Peugeot® cars, Michelin® tires, Sea-Doo® jet skis, CCM® skates and hockey gear, Rossignol® skis, DeBeers diamonds, Cartier® jewelry, and Yves Saint-Laurent® fashions. You might also ask students to bring in products from home that were made in francophone countries and have French directions. Some examples are food, shampoo, clothes, and perfume.

Career Path

Ask students to discuss why French is necessary in business, travel, and other areas if "everyone speaks English." Ask them why it is different to read something in the language in which it was written rather than in translation. Ask if any of the professions listed on this page interest them and why. In addition, have students find classified ads for employment that either require or prefer knowledge of a foreign language. You might bring in a variety of ads from different newspapers for this activity.

POURQUOI APPRENDRE LE FRANÇAIS? *Why learn French?*

When you study a language, you learn much more than vocabulary and grammar. You learn about the people who speak the language and the influence they've had on our lives. Francophone (French-speaking) cultures continue to make notable contributions to many fields, including art, literature, movies, fashion, cuisine, science, and technology.

Someday you may live, travel, or be an exchange student in one of the more than 30 countries all over the world where French is spoken. You can imagine how much more meaningful your experience will be if you can talk to people in their own language.

Being able to communicate in another language can be an advantage when you're looking for employment in almost any field. As a journalist, sportscaster, hotel receptionist, tour guide, travel agent, buyer for a large company, lawyer, engineer, economist, financial expert, flight attendant, diplomat, translator, teacher, writer, interpreter, publisher, or librarian, you may have the opportunity to use French in your work. Did you know that nearly 4,000 American companies have offices in France?

Perhaps the best reason for studying French is for the fun of it. Studying another language is a challenge to your mind, and you'll get a great feeling of accomplishment the first time you have a conversation in French.

Teacher Note

Some activities suggested in the *Teacher's Edition* ask students to contact various people, businesses, and organizations in the community. Before assigning these activities, it is advisable to request parental permission. In some cases, you may also want to obtain permission from the parties the students will be asked to contact.

QUI SUIS-JE? *Who am I?*

Here's how you introduce yourself to young people who speak French.

To ask someone's name:
Tu t'appelles comment?

To give your name:
Je m'appelle...

NOTE CULTURELLE

French-speaking people use **tu** *(you)* when they talk to a friend, a family member, or a person their own age or younger. In Chapter 1, you'll learn how to address an adult using the more formal **vous.**

Here's a list of some popular French names for girls and boys. Can you find your name, or a name similar to yours?

CD 1 Trs. 1–2

NOMS de FILLES

Delphine
Christelle
Nathalie
Aurélie
Laurence
Karine
Céline
Laetitia
Elodie
Valérie
Sophie
Virginie
Séverine
Sandrine
Sabrina
Claudine
Emilie
Dominique
Audrey
Corinne Stéphanie Julie

NOMS de GARÇONS

Bernard Vincent Pierre
Etienne
Stéphane
Gilles
Eric
Marc
Jean
Laurent
Daniel
David
Philippe
Christian
Frédéric
Mathieu
Cédric
Christophe
Nicolas
Jérôme
Michel Olivier

1 Présente-toi! *Introduce yourself!*

If you like, choose a French name for yourself. Introduce yourself to two or three students in the class, using your own name or your new French name. Ask them their names, too.

Culture Note

For Catholics in francophone countries, each day of the year commemorates a saint. French-speaking Catholics choose a personal saint when they are confirmed as members of the Church. They sometimes celebrate their saint's day **(la fête)** with a cake and cards as they do their own birthdays. People in France sometimes refer to well-known saints' days instead of saying the date; for example, **On se verra avant la Sainte-Catherine.** *(We'll see each other before November 25th.)* Ask students to try to guess which saint is commemorated on February 14. The answer is **Saint-Valentin!** Another example is St. Patrick's Day on March 17.

Teaching Suggestion

Ask students if the English language ever had an informal or intimate way of saying *you.* (The pronouns *thou* and *thee,* to address close friends and family, are still used by groups such as the Quakers.)

Presentation

You might want to have students make name cards for their desks; this will help you learn their names. They might want to choose a French name.

For videodisc application, see *Videodisc Guide.*

Teacher Notes

- Other French boys' names are Antoine, Emmanuel, François, Guillaume, and Julien.
- Additional French girls' names are Anne, Béatrice, Charlotte, Claire, Françoise, Hélène, Jeanne, Nicole, and Véronique.
- Some French African boys' names (from Côte d'Ivoire) are Koffi, Kouassi, Yapo, Séka, Alidou, Moussa, Kouamé, and Daba.
- Some French African girls' names (from Côte d'Ivoire) are Amenan, Aya, Awa, Ami, Fatoumata, Adjoua, Assika, Aminata, Djeneba, and Ahou.

Language-to-Language

Just as in English, some French names have a masculine and feminine form, which sometimes sound the same: Michel/Michèle, René(e), and Frédéric/Frédérique. Still other names are used for both boys and girls: Claude and Dominique.

Motivating Activity

Ask students to suggest situations in which you use the alphabet. These situations might include taking or leaving phone messages, making reservations, understanding acronyms (FBI, FDA), and distinguishing between homonyms, such as *pear* and *pair,* or **mère** *(mother)* and **maire** *(mayor)*. You might use the "Alphabet Song" to help students learn the pronunciation of the letters.

Additional Practice

- Ask students to spell their names or the names of the famous people mentioned on pages 2 and 3. You might also spell other names aloud — Jean-Claude, Eliane, Maryse, Hélène, Blondine — and have students write them on the board and try to pronounce them. You might also ask students to spell classroom objects that you have labeled.
- To practice letters, write a short run-on message, interspersing extra letters throughout. Distribute copies. Then, dictate only the letters of your message. Students circle each letter as they hear it. The circled letters should spell out your message. For example, you would dictate the boldfaced letters in the following series to spell out the message **J'adore le français.**

```
v y j n a w m p c d y l h o
r c u e b x l t e q g f z v y r
a m b n w ç h a g u i p s k
```

For videodisc application, see *Videodisc Guide.*

L'ALPHABET

The French alphabet looks the same as the English alphabet. The difference is in pronunciation. Look at the letters and words below as your teacher pronounces them or as you listen to the audio recording. Which letters sound similar in English and French? Which ones have a different sound?

CD 1 Tr. 3

A artiste

B banane

C cinéma

D dessert

E Europe

F fantôme

G géométrie

H hélicoptère

I igloo

J jardin

K kangourou

L lion

M monstre

N Noël

O orange

P parachute

Q question

R rose

S serpent

T trompette

U uniforme

V voyage

W western

X xylophone

Y yo-yo

Z zèbre

6   *six*   CHAPITRE PRELIMINAIRE   Allez, viens!

Language Note

You might want to tell students that learning to pronounce the alphabet, especially the vowels, can help with their French pronunciation.

Have you noticed that many French words look like English words? Words in different languages that look alike are called *cognates*. Although they're pronounced differently, cognates have the same meaning in French and English. You may not realize it, but you already know hundreds of French words.

Can you figure out what these words mean?

carotte   chocolat   adresse   musique   examen

2 Le dictionnaire

Scan the French-English vocabulary list in the back of your book to see if you can find ten cognates.

CD 1 Tr. 4

3 Ecoute! *Listen!* See scripts on p. T61. **1.** f **2.** e **3.** b **4.** a **5.** d **6.** c

Write down the words as you hear them spelled. Then, match the words you've written with the pictures. Be careful! One of the words isn't a cognate.

a. crabe

b. pingouin

c. tigre

d. singe

e. serpent

f. kangourou

4 Tu t'appelles comment?

Can you spell your name, pronouncing the letters in French?

Language-to-Language

2 Explain one of the sources of cognates. Both French and English have words with Latin roots; for example, *unitas* (Latin), **unité** (French), *unity* (English). You may also want to warn students about false cognates (**faux amis**): words in two languages that look alike but have different meanings. **Librairie** and *library* look alike, but **librairie** is the French word for *bookstore*. The French word for *library* is **bibliothèque**. Other examples of false cognates are the French word **pain**, which means *bread*, not *pain*; **raisin**, which means *grape*, not *raisin*; and **sympathique**, which means *nice*, not *sympathetic*.

Group Work

2 This activity might be done in groups, with one student in each group responsible for compiling the list. Set a time limit within which each group must find and write down ten cognates.

Teaching Suggestion

3 Ask students to repeat the letters or have them try to pronounce the animals' names.

For Individual Needs

4 **Challenge** If students have made name cards, you might collect them and redistribute them to different individuals. Each student should spell the name on the card and point out that particular student. As a variation, the student who hears his or her name spelled might say **C'est moi.**

Presentation

Make an overhead transparency of several French words, some with accents and some without. Ask students if they notice any peculiarities. As they mention the accents, explain each one. Let them know that accents can sometimes change the meaning of a word, like **où** *(where)* and **ou** *(or)* or **sûr** *(sure)* and **sur** *(on)*.

Teaching Suggestion

5 Five of these six words are cognates. Write the six words on the board and have students check their answers to this listening activity. Then, have students give the equivalent English words and practice pronouncing the French words.

LES ACCENTS *Accent marks*

CD 1 Tr. 5

Have you noticed the marks over some of the letters in French words? These marks are called accents. They're very important to the spelling, the pronunciation, and even the meaning of French words.

- The **accent aigu** (´) tells you to pronounce an *e* similar to the *a* in the English word *date:*

  éléphant   **Sénégal**

- The **accent grave** (`) tells you to pronounce an *e* like the *e* in the English word *jet:*

  zèbre   **chèque**

  However, an **accent grave** over an *a* or *u* doesn't change the sound of these letters:

  à   **où**

- The **accent circonflexe** (ˆ) can appear over any vowel, and it doesn't change the sound of the letter:

  pâté   **forêt**   **île**   **hôtel**   **flûte**

- The **cédille** (¸) under a *c* tells you to pronounce the *c* like an *s:*

  français   **ça**

- When two vowels appear next to each other, a **tréma** (¨) over the second one tells you to pronounce each vowel separately:

  Noël   **Haïti**

- You usually will not see accents on capital letters.

  île   **Ile**   **état**   **Etats-Unis**

- When you spell a word aloud, be sure to say the accents, as well as the letters.

5 **Ecoute!** See scripts on p. T61.

Write down the words as you hear them spelled.

CD 1 Tr. 6

1. poème	**3.** américain	**5.** français
2. hôpital	**4.** canoë	**6.** sévére

Language Note

Students will sometimes recognize English words in French words if they imagine an *s* after a circumflex: **forêt** — *forest,* **hôpital** — *hospital.* You may want to explain the rules for a "soft" and "hard" *c* sound to show the need for a cedilla: A *c* followed by an *a, o,* or *u* is a hard *c* pronounced like a *k* (**carte**), unless it is written with a cedilla, in which case, it is a soft *c* pronounced like an *s* (**ça**).

LES CHIFFRES DE 0 A 20

Numbers from 0 to 20

CD 1 Tr. 7

How many times a day do you use numbers? Giving someone a phone number, checking grades, and getting change at the store all involve numbers. Here are the French numbers from 0 to 20.

0	1	2	3
zéro	un	deux	trois
4	5	6	7
quatre	cinq	six	sept
8	9	10	11
huit	neuf	dix	onze
12	13	14	15
douze	treize	quatorze	quinze
16	17	18	19
seize	dix-sept	dix-huit	dix-neuf

20

vingt

> ### NOTE CULTURELLE
>
> When you count on your fingers, which finger do you start with? The French way is to start counting with your thumb as number *one,* your index finger as *two,* and so on. How would you show *four* the French way? And *eight?*
>
>

Motivating Activity
Ask students to suggest why numbers are important. They might list flight numbers, time, temperature, phone numbers, train platform numbers, prices, dates, ages, TV channels, radio stations, and money changing. Point out that the spelling of numbers is also important for writing checks and other banking transactions.

Presentation
You might teach numbers using only numerals before students see the words. Call out the numbers that correspond to the age range of your students and ask them to raise their hands when they hear their age.

For Individual Needs

Slower Pace Students may learn numbers more easily if they group them in short sequences; for example, 1–3, 4–6, 7–9, and then 1–9.

For videodisc application, see *Videodisc Guide.*

Teacher Note

6 You might tell students that phone numbers in France consist of four sets of two-digit numbers preceded by a two-digit number similar to an area code in the United States.

Teaching Suggestion

6 After this listening activity, have students pair off to practice reading the phone numbers aloud. They might also practice saying their own phone numbers in French.

 For Individual Needs

Auditory Learners Read pairs of numbers aloud and tell students to write down the smaller (or larger) number.

Teaching Suggestion

Have students figure out the words below using the following code. Next, have students choose other French words and encode them. Have students work in pairs with one student reading aloud the numbers of an encoded word, and the other student figuring out the word.

0=A	7=D	14=M
1=E	8=F	15=N
2=I	9=G	16=P
3=O	10=H	17=R
4=U	11=J	18=S
5=B	12=K	19=T
6=C	13=L	20=V

L	A	F	R	A	N	C	E
13	0	8	17	0	15	6	1

V	I	N	G	T
20	2	15	9	19

L	'	E	C	O	L	E
13		1	6	3	13	1

6 **Ecoute!** See scripts on p. T61.

CD 1 Tr. 8

Listen as Nicole, Paul, Vincent, and Corinne tell you their phone numbers. Then, match the numbers with their names.

a. 03. 20. 16. 05. 17   d. 03. 20. 15. 04. 13

b. 03. 20. 18. 11. 19   e. 03. 20. 14. 08. 12

c. 03. 20. 17. 07. 18

1. Nicole e
2. Paul a
3. Vincent b
4. Corinne d

7 **Devine!** *Guess!*

Think of a number between one and twenty. Your partner will try to guess your number. Help out by saying **plus** *(higher)* or **moins** *(lower)* as your partner guesses. Take turns.

8 **Plaques d'immatriculation** *License plates*

Look at the license plates pictured below. Take turns with a partner reading aloud the numbers and letters you see.

1.

2.

3.

4.

5.

6.

Math Link

Have students count backwards from 20 or forward by twos and threes. You could also have students identify the prime numbers **(les nombres premiers)** from 0 to 20. **(2, 3, 5, 7, 11, 13, 17, 19)**

A L'ECOLE   *At school*

CD 1 Tr. 9

You should familiarize yourself with these common French instructions. You'll hear your teacher using them in class.

Ecoutez!   *Listen!*
Répétez!   *Repeat!*
Levez-vous!   *Stand up!*
Levez la main!   *Raise your hand!*
Asseyez-vous!   *Sit down!*
Ouvrez vos livres à la page... !
   Open your books to page . . . !

Fermez la porte!   *Close the door!*
Sortez une feuille de papier!
   Take out a sheet of paper!
Allez au tableau!
   Go to the blackboard!
Regardez la carte!   *Look at the map!*

9 Ecoute!   See scripts on p. T61.

CD 1 Tr. 10

Listen to the teacher in this French class tell his students what to do. Then, decide which student is following each instruction.

1. Lynn
2. Emilio
3. Brian
4. Alison
5. Paul
6. Dena
7. Evelyne

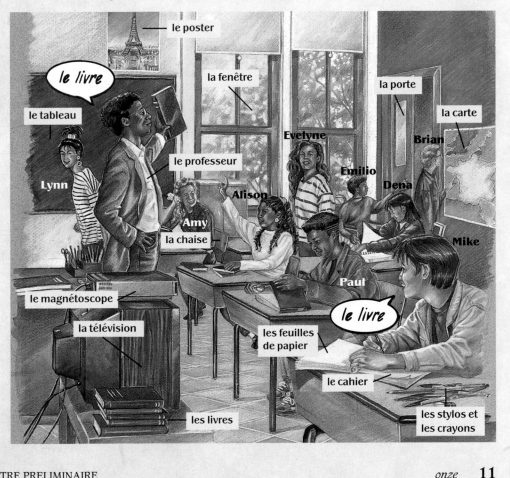

CHAPITRE PRELIMINAIRE   *onze* **11**

Presentation

First, demonstrate the commands without English by using gestures and actions. Point out to students that many of the commands are also useful in settings other than the classroom.

Teacher Note

Here are some additional commands and/or statements you might want to give your students:

Effacez le tableau! *Erase the board.*
Ecrivez au tableau! *Write on the board.*
Est-ce que je peux aller aux toilettes? *May I go to the bathroom?*
Silence, s'il vous plaît. *Quiet, please.*
Comment dit-on... en français? *How do you say . . . in French?*
Regardez le tableau. *Look at the chalkboard.*
Ecrivez votre nom. *Write your name.*

Additional Practice

9 Have students look at the classroom illustration and tell whether the following statements are true or false.
1. Alison lève la main.
2. Emilio ouvre la porte.
3. Evelyne se lève.
4. Amy ferme la porte.
5. Lynn est au tableau.
6. Brian regarde le professeur.
7. Mike répète le vocabulaire.
8. Dena prend une feuille de papier.
9. Paul ouvre un livre.

TPR Have students carry out the commands as you say them aloud. Students might then practice giving and following the commands in pairs or small groups.

Allez, viens à Poitiers! pp. 12–89

VIDEO PROGRAM
Videocassette 1
05:40–07:45

OR *VIDEODISC PROGRAM,*
Videodisc 1, Side A

Search 7725, Play To 11574

Motivating Activity

Have students tell what they know about France: the people, culture, food, cities, tourist attractions, and so on. Then, have them compare their impressions with the photos of Poitiers on pages 12–15.

Teacher Note

La place Aristide Bruant

The beautiful square shown on pages 12 and 13 was named after Aristide Bruant, a popular singer-songwriter (**chansonnier**), who sang his own songs in various cafés near Montmartre in Paris. Aristide Bruant was immortalized in the works of painter Henri de Toulouse-Lautrec. He lived from 1851 to 1925.

Language Note

The earliest inhabitants of the region were the **Pictaves,** or **Pictons,** a Gallic tribe of sailors and tradesmen. Their name is a possible origin of the name of the region, Poitou, and of the city, Poitiers.

 go.hrw.com
WAO POITIERS

Visit the HRW Web site at **http://go.hrw.com** and enter the keyword **WAO POITIERS** for student resources related to this location. For detailed access instructions, see page T45.

CHAPITRES 1, 2, 3

Allez, viens à Poitiers!

Poitiers — ville d'art et d'histoire

Background Information

Poitiers, often called **Ville d'art et d'histoire** and **Ville de tous les âges,** is an ancient city. It is the capital of Poitou-Charentes, one of the 22 regions into which France is now divided. In 56 B.C., the town came under Roman control, which lasted for several centuries. A famous battle occurred near Poitiers in 732 when Charles Martel, grandfather of Charlemagne, defeated the invading Saracens, Muslims who had crossed from North Africa into Spain and settled there. In the twelfth century, Poitiers was the city from which **Aliénor d'Aquitaine,** and later her son Richard I the Lionhearted (**Richard Cœur de Lion**), ruled the provinces of Aquitaine and Poitou.

Poitiers

Map 1

Capital of Poitou-Charentes
Population: more than 120,000
Points of interest: the Futuroscope theme park, the Saint-Pierre Cathedral, the Palais de Justice
Museums: Sainte-Croix, Hypogée des Dunes
Industries: agriculture, fishing, electrical and mechanical manufacturing, forestry, furniture production
Famous people: Saint-Hilaire, Diane de Poitiers, Aliénor d'Aquitaine
Regional specialties: goat cheese, nougat, snails, cream-cheese pastries, chocolates

HRW **go.hrw.com**
WA0 POITIERS

treize **13**

Using the Almanac and Map

Terms in the Almanac

- **Le Palais de Justice** is a courthouse built in the nineteenth century around the remains of the palais des Ducs d'Aquitaine.
- **Le musée Sainte-Croix,** located on the site of the Abbaye Sainte-Croix, houses a fine arts collection and an archeological museum.
- **L'Hypogée des Dunes,** an underground chapel from the seventh century, is built over an ancient Roman cemetery.
- **Saint-Hilaire** was the first bishop of Poitiers.
- **Aliénor d'Aquitaine** (1122–1204) was Duchess of Aquitaine. Among her nine children with Henry II of England were Richard the Lionhearted and John Lackland, the English king who was forced to sign the Magna Carta in 1215.

Teaching Suggestion

Have students research and report on the many fascinating historical figures from this region, such as **Aliénor d'Aquitaine, Henri II,** Richard the Lionhearted, and others. Have them make a timeline of the events of the eleventh and twelfth centuries that occurred in Aquitaine and Poitou.

Language Note

You might give students the French equivalents of the regional specialties listed in the almanac: *goat cheese* (**chabichou**), *nougat* (**nougâtines**), *snails* (**escargots**), *cream-cheese pastries* (**tourteau fromager**), and *chocolates* (**marguerites**).

Using the Map

1. Have students name the bodies of water and the countries surrounding France.
2. Have students locate the island of Corsica (**Corse**) in the Mediterranean Sea. Corsica is part of France and is located about 115 miles east-southeast of the city of Nice.

History/Literature Link

Henry II of England, the husband of **Aliénor d'Aquitaine,** was responsible for the assassination of Sir Thomas Becket, Archbishop of Canterbury. Their story was the basis for T. S. Eliot's play *Murder in the Cathedral* and Jean Anouilh's play *Becket*.

Using the Photo Essay

① Two other impressive attractions of **le Futuroscope** are the "Showscan," which produces a realistic image at 60 frames per second, and the "Dynamic Simulator," which has moving seats that are synchronized with the action on the screen.

② **Le centre-ville** Because Poitiers is an ancient city, the oldest streets are very narrow and unsuitable for automobile traffic. Some have been converted to pedestrian shopping areas where traffic is not allowed.

Thinking Critically

② **Observing** Ask students if there are any particular features they notice about the buildings in this photo.

③ **Le marché aux fleurs** The French are generally very fond of flowers and gardening, and flower markets are a common sight throughout France. French gardens (**les jardins à la française**) are defined by their sculpted shrubs and plants laid out in intricate, symmetrical designs.

Thinking Critically

Observing Call students' attention to the flowers and gardens in the photographs on pages 12–15. Would they find similar decorations around American buildings or towns?

③ **Drawing Inferences** Ask students for the name of the café at the end of the street in this photo. Tell them that **la gargouille** means *gargoyle* and ask why this name was chosen for the café and where they think this area might be located (possibly near a church or cathedral — see Art Link). Finally, ask students what they think a **glacier** is (*ice cream shop*).

Poitiers

CD-ROM
Disc 1

Poitiers is famous for its art and history. It was here in 732 A.D. that Charles Martel defeated the Saracens in the Battle of Poitiers. Home to an important university and attractions such as a futuristic park devoted to cinematic technology, Poitiers is also a very modern city.

① People of all ages enjoy the **Futuroscope**, a popular futuristic theme park filled with cinematic exhibits. Of particular interest are the 360-degree theater and the **Kinémax** with its 600-square-meter screen.

② The heart of French cities and towns is called **le centre-ville**. In Poitiers, it is the bustling center of town where people gather in cafés and frequent the many shops.

③ At least once a week, French towns usually have an outdoor market such as this **marché aux fleurs**.

14   *quatorze*

Culture Note
② Since most train stations in France are located in the **centre-ville**, train travel is very convenient, and people generally do not need their cars for travel outside the metropolitan area or even within the city itself.

Art Link
③ **Les gargouilles**, or *gargoyles*, are decorative sculptures on cathedrals and churches. They serve to drain off rainwater and are often carved in the form of grotesque animals and monsters.

④ The **Pierre Levée** is a dolmen, a prehistoric monument constructed of upright stones supporting a horizontal stone. Found especially in Britain and France, dolmens are believed to be tombs. This one dates from about 3000 B.C.

④ **La Pierre Levée** This monument was a popular gathering place for students in the sixteenth century when the author François Rabelais was a frequent visitor to Poitiers.

Multicultural Link

④ Ask students if they know of other huge stone structures in the world that were built in ancient times (the pyramids in Egypt, Mexico, and South America, and the stone structures on Easter Island and at Stonehenge in England). Ask students to imagine how these structures were built without modern machinery.

⑤ Construction on the **cathédrale Saint-Pierre** was begun towards the end of the twelfth century. It is a cathedral of impressive proportions. Built in the gothic style, its facade has three gabled portals and a rose window.

⑥ In most French cities you will find the **Hôtel de ville**, which houses the government administration offices.

Culture Note

⑤ On most cathedrals, the sculptures over the central door (**le portail**) depict the Last Judgment. God is surrounded by St. Peter, Mary, angels, or other holy figures. Below are the souls condemned to Purgatory, and at the very bottom are those in Hell. The figures in the four arches over the door include apostles, prophets, and saints.

Architecture Link

⑤ The **gothique angevin** style of the **cathédrale Saint-Pierre** marked a transition from Roman to Gothic architecture. Roman architecture was characterized by rounded arches, heavy, solid walls, few windows, and dark interiors. In contrast, the development of **arcs boutants** *(flying buttresses),* which supported the weight of the roof, permitted higher walls and large numbers of **vitraux** *(stained-glass windows).* Gothic architecture was characterized by the pointed **arc brisé** *(Gothic arch).*

Culture Note

④ Dolmens are enormous stone structures, somewhat like tables, with a large stone placed horizontally on other stones standing vertically. About 150 are found in the Poitou region. Menhirs are tall, free-standing stones. Both dolmens and menhirs date from between 5000 and 2000 B.C.

History Link

⑥ The French flag flying over the **Hôtel de ville** is known as **le tricolore** because of its three colors: blue, white, and red (**bleu, blanc et rouge**). The tricolor flag first appeared shortly after the French Revolution in 1789. Ask students if they know the nickname of the flag of the United States (the Star-Spangled Banner).

Chapitre 1 : Faisons connaissance!
Chapter Overview

Mise en train pp. 18–20	Salut, les copains!		

	FUNCTIONS	GRAMMAR	CULTURE	RE-ENTRY
Première étape pp. 21–25	• Greeting people and saying goodbye, p. 22 • Asking how people are and telling how you are, p. 23 • Asking someone's name and giving yours, p. 24 • Asking someone's age and giving yours, p. 25		• **Rencontre Culturelle**, Greetings and goodbyes, p. 21 • **Note Culturelle**, Gestures, p. 23	• Introductions (**Chapitre Préliminaire**) • Numbers 0–20 (**Chapitre Préliminaire**)
Deuxième étape pp. 26–30	• Expressing likes, dislikes, and preferences about things, p. 26	• **ne... pas,** p. 26 • The definite articles **le, la, l', les,** and the gender of nouns, p. 28	• Realia: French movie ad for *Casablanca*, p. 26 • **Panorama Culturel**, Leisure-time activities, p. 30	
Troisième étape pp. 31–35	• Expressing likes, dislikes, and preferences about activities, p. 32	• Subject pronouns and **-er** verbs, p. 33		

Prononciation p. 35	**Intonation** Audio CD 1, Tracks 25–26	**A écrire** (dictation) Audio CD 1, Tracks 27–29
Lisons! pp. 36–37	**Petites annonces**	**Reading Strategy** Using titles, subtitles, illustrations, and captions
Review pp. 38–41	**Mise en pratique,** pp. 38–39	**Que sais-je?** p. 40 **Vocabulaire,** p. 41

Assessment Options	*Testing Program* • Première étape, Quiz 1-1A, Quiz 1-1B, pp. 1–4 • Deuxième étape, Quiz 1-2A, Quiz 1-2B, pp. 5–8 • Troisième étape, Quiz 1-3A, Quiz 1-3B, pp. 9–12 • Chapter Test, pp. 13–18 • Speaking Test, p. 343 *Audio Compact Discs* • Audio CD 1, Tracks 31–36	*Interactive CD-ROM Program* • Mise en pratique (A toi de parler, A toi d'écrire) • *CD-ROM Teacher's Guide*, Assessment Options, p. 4 *Alternative Assessment Guide* • Portfolio Assessment, p. 18 • Performance Assessment, p. 32 • CD-ROM Assessment, p. 46 *Test Generator* • Chapter 1

PRINT	MEDIA

Pupil's Edition, pp. 16–41

 Audio Compact Discs
- Textbook Listening Activities: Audio CD 1, Tracks 11–30

**Interactive CD-ROM Program
Teacher's Guide,** pp. 1–4

 Interactive CD-ROM Program
- Disc 1

Videodisc Guide
- Teaching Suggestions, pp. 9–13
- Activity Masters, pp. 14–16

 Videodisc Program
- Videodisc 1, Side A

Video Guide
- Teaching Suggestions, pp. 6–7
- Activity Masters, pp. 8–10

 Video Program
- Videocassette 1
- Videocassette 5 (captioned version)*

Listening Activities
- Student Response Forms for Textbook Listening Activities, pp. 3–5
- Additional Listening Activities 1-1 to 1-6, pp. 7–9
- Additional Listening Activities (song), p. 10
- Scripts and Answers, pp. 102–106

 Audio Compact Discs
- Textbook Listening Activities: Audio CD 1, Tracks 11–30
- Additional Listening Activities: Audio CD 1, Tracks 37–43

Teaching Transparencies
- Teaching Transparency Masters 1-1 to 1-3 (Situations) and 1-A to 1-D (Vocabulary)
- Teaching Suggestions 1-1 to 1-3 and 1-A to 1-D

 Teaching Transparencies
- Situations 1-1 to 1-3
- Vocabulary 1-A to 1-D

Testing Program
- Grammar and Vocabulary Quizzes, **Etape** Quizzes, and Chapter Test, pp. 1–18
- Score Sheet, Scripts, and Answers, pp. 19–26

 Audio Compact Discs
- Assessment Items: Audio CD 1, Tracks 31–36

 Test Generator
- Chapter 1

Alternative Assessment Guide
- Portfolio Assessment, p. 18
- Performance Assessment, p. 32
- CD-ROM Assessment, p. 46

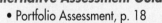 **Grammar and Vocabulary Workbook,** pp. 1–9

 Practice and Activity Book, pp. 3–12

Activities for Communication
- Communicative Activities, pp. 1–6
- Realia and Teaching Suggestions, pp. 75–79
- Situation Cards, pp. 137–138

> ***Videocassette 5**
> contains **Mise en train** and **Suite** with French captions.

Lesson Planner
- Lesson Plan, pp. 3–7

Chapitre 1 : Faisons connaissance!
Technology Applications

MISE EN TRAIN, pp. 18–20

Video
- Show *Salut, les copains!* For Video Synopsis, Teaching Suggestions, Activity Master, and Scripts, see the *Video Guide* or the *Videodisc Guide*.

Audio
- Play the recording of the **Mise en train** with pauses as students read along. Have students practice pronunciation by repeating individual sentences after they hear them.

PREMIERE ETAPE, pp. 21–25

Video
- While students watch *Salut, les copains!*, have them listen for exchanges that model saying hello and introducing oneself. For more suggestions, see p. 10 of the *Videodisc Guide*.

Audio
- Use Textbook Listening Activity 6 to have students practice greeting expressions.
- Textbook Listening Activity 9 practices expressions for asking how people are.
- To have students practice expressions for giving their names and introducing people, play Textbook Listening Activities 12 and 13.
- Textbook Listening Activity 15 and Additional Listening Activities 1-1 and 1-2 practice expressions for introducing oneself.

Transparencies
- Use *Teaching Transparency 1-1* and the Teaching Suggestions to present and practice the expressions for asking and giving someone's name and age.
- Use *Teaching Transparencies 1-A* and *1-B* and the Teaching Suggestions to have students practice telling what they like and dislike.

CD-ROM (Disc 1)
- **Chacun à sa place** and **Méli-mélo** (Activities 1 and 2) practice greetings, telling how you are, and asking how someone else is doing.
- **Le bon choix** (Activity 3) practices the numbers from 1 to 20.
- For suggestions, see p. 2 of the *CD-ROM Teacher's Guide*.

DEUXIEME ETAPE, pp. 26–29

Video
- While students watch *Salut, les copains!*, have them listen for exchanges that model expressing likes and dislikes about things. For more suggestions, see p. 11 of the *Videodisc Guide*.

Audio
- Use Textbook Listening Activity 18 to have students practice **aimer** and **ne pas aimer.**
- Use Textbook Listening Activity 20 to have students practice the words and expressions for telling what they like and dislike.
- Additional Listening Activities 1-3 and 1-4 practice numbers and expressing likes and dislikes.

Transparencies
- Use *Teaching Transparency 1-2* and the Teaching Suggestions to have students practice expressing likes and dislikes.
- Use *Teaching Transparencies 1-C* and *1-D* and the Teaching Suggestions to have students talk about activities they like and dislike.

CD-ROM (Disc 1)
- **Jeu des paires** (Activity 4) practices expressing likes and dislikes. For suggestions, see p. 2 of the *CD-ROM Teacher's Guide*.

PANORAMA CULTUREL, p. 30

Video
- Show the interviews. For Video Synopsis, Teaching Suggestions, Activity Masters, and Scripts, see the *Video Guide* or the *Videodisc Guide*.

Audio
- Play the **Panorama Culturel** as students read along. Remind students that they might not be able to understand everything each person says, but they should try to recognize words and deduce global meaning.

CD-ROM (Disc 1)
- Have students do the **Panorama Culturel** activity for Chapter 1 after showing them the video. For suggestions, see p. 3 of the *CD-ROM Teacher's Guide*.

TROISIEME ETAPE, pp. 31–35

Video
- While students watch *Salut, les copains!*, have them listen for exchanges that model expressing likes and dislikes about activities. For more suggestions, see p. 11 of the *Videodisc Guide*.

Audio
- Use Textbook Activity 24 to have students practice telling what people like and dislike.
- Additional Listening Activities 1-5 and 1-6 practice phrases for expressing likes, dislikes, and preferences.

Transparencies
- Use *Teaching Transparency 1-3* and the Teaching Suggestions to have students practice phrases for expressing likes and dislikes. For another activity using *Transparency 1-3,* see **Chasse au trésor** (Activity 5) in Chapter 1 of the *Interactive CD-ROM Program*.

CD-ROM (Disc 1)
- **Chasse au trésor** (Activity 5) practices the verb **aimer** and the vocabulary on page 31.
- **Les mots qui manquent** (Activity 6) practices definite articles and the verb **aimer**.
- For suggestions, see p. 3 of the *CD-ROM Teacher's Guide*.

MISE EN PRATIQUE, pp. 38–39

Captioned Video
- To review, replay *Salut, les copains!* in its entirety and ask students to identify the exchanges in which the characters greet people and say goodbye, ask people how they are and how old they are, give their names and ask for someone else's name, and express likes, dislikes, and preferences.

CD-ROM (Disc 1)
- Have students do the **En contexte** to practice introducing themselves and talking about their likes and dislikes. See the suggestions on p. 2 of the *CD-ROM Teacher's Guide*.
- Have students practice their writing and speaking skills using the **A toi d'écrire** and **A toi de parler** activities. For a detailed description of these features, see pp. 3–4 of the *CD-ROM Teacher's Guide*.
- For Assessment Options, see p. 4 of the *CD-ROM Teacher's Guide*.

Test Generator
- Use the Test Generator to create review material for students taking the Chapter Test or to prepare an alternate Test.

VIDEOCLIPS

Video
- Show the **Vidéoclips**. For Video Synopsis, Teaching Suggestions, Activity Master, and Scripts, see the *Video Guide* or the *Videodisc Guide*.

Videodisc Program
Videodisc 1, Side A
Videodisc Guide, pp. 7–16

Chapitre 1 : Faisons connaissance!
Barcode Directory

Barcodes A and B access **Mise en train** and **Mise en train (suite)** in their entirety. Subsequent barcodes show specific segments of **Salut, les copains!** The barcode numbers correspond to the scene numbers as they appear on the video.

MISE EN TRAIN

Salut, les copains! **A**

Search 11575, Play To 20690

Thuy–Introduction **3**

Search 13095, Play To 14562

Didier–Introduction **6**

Search 16632, Play To 17532

Claire, Marc, and Jérôme **9**

Search 19873, Play To 20690

Claire–Introduction **1**

Search 11575, Play To 12285

Ahmed–Introduction **4**

Search 14575, Play To 15685

Emilie–Introduction **7**

Search 17549, Play To 18561

Salut, les copains! (suite) **B**

Search 20690, Play To 26765

Djeneba–Introduction **2**

Search 12300, Play To 13078

Stéphane–Introduction **5**

Search 15702, Play To 16618

André–Introduction **8**

Search 18572, Play To 19857

PANORAMA CULTUREL

Qu'est-ce que tu aimes faire après l'école?
These barcodes access the three interviews of the **Panorama Culturel** presented in the *Pupil's Edition* as well as additional interviews.

First three interviews **1**
Search 26765, Play To 28245

Fabienne **4**
Search 27841, Play To 28075

Karina **7**
Search 28456, Play To 28590

Thomas **10**
Search 28925, Play To 29041

Marie-Bertille **13**
Search 29790, Play To 30054

All interviews **2**
Search 26765, Play To 30414

Caroline **5**
Search 28076, Play To 28245

Isabelle **8**
Search 28591, Play To 28800

Catherine **11**
Search 29042, Play To 29519

Lucie **14**
Search 30055, Play To 30188

Gabrielle **3**
Search 27614, Play To 27840

Matthieu **6**
Search 28246, Play To 28455

Léontine **9**
Search 28801, Play To 28924

Charlotte **12**
Search 29520, Play To 29789

Louis **15**
Search 30189, Play To 30414

BARCODE DIRECTORY
CHAPTER 1

ETAPES

To practice the grammar, vocabulary, and functions presented in each **étape**, see the barcodes and accompanying suggestions on pages 11–12 of the *Videodisc Guide*.

MISE EN PRATIQUE

This is additional footage modeling some of the expressions practiced in this chapter. You may want to use it to review the chapter.

Mise en pratique **1**

Search 35550, Play To 37047

Mise en pratique **2**

Search 37047, Play To 38807

VIDEOCLIPS

These are authentic French commercials. You may want to preview them before showing them to students.

Crunch®: chocolate bars **1**

Search 30414, Play To 31811

Tornado®: vacuum cleaners **2**

Search 31811, Play To 32735

Chapitre 1 : Faisons connaissance!
CD-ROM Directory ⊙ DISC 1

The following directory lists the *Interactive CD-ROM Program* activities for Chapter 1. For details and suggestions on how to use them, see pages 1–4 of the *CD-ROM Teacher's Guide*.

	GLOBAL TASK	COMMUNICATIVE GOALS	ACTIVITY TYPE
	On fait connaissance Students meet and respond to teenagers from around the francophone world. Students learn how old these teenagers are and what they like and dislike.	To use chapter functions, vocabulary, and grammar in a lifelike conversation	En contexte *Interactive conversation*

	SUPPORTING ACTIVITIES	PUPIL'S EDITION	COMMUNICATIVE GOALS	ACTIVITY TYPE
Première étape	1. Comment dit-on... ?	pp. 22–23	To identify expressions for saying hello, saying goodbye, and telling how you are	**Chacun à sa place** *Categories*
	2. Comment dit-on... ?	pp. 22–23	To sequence expressions for saying hello, asking how people are, and telling how you are	**Méli-mélo** *Sequencing*
	3. Vocabulaire	pp. 9, 25	To use numbers from 1 to 20	**Le bon choix** *Multiple choice*
Deuxième étape	4. Vocabulaire	p. 27	To express likes and dislikes	**Jeu des paires** *Concentration®*
Troisième étape	5. Vocabulaire	p. 31	To talk about activities and use the verb **aimer**	**Chasse au trésor Explorons!/Vérifions!** *Interactive image*
	6. Grammaire	pp. 28, 33	To use definite articles and the verb **aimer**	**Les mots qui manquent** *Tic Tac Toe*
Panorama Culturel	Panorama Culturel	p. 30	To listen to and understand native speakers talking about what they like to do after school	**Qu'est-ce que tu aimes faire après l'école?** *Presentation* **Le bon choix** *Multiple choice*

	APPLICATION	PUPIL'S EDITION	COMMUNICATIVE GOALS	ACTIVITY TYPE
Mise en pratique	A toi de parler	pp. 38–39	To create and record a conversation with a French teenager	*Guided recording*
	A toi d'écrire	pp. 38–39	To write lists, an e-mail message, or a journal entry	*Guided writing*

🏠 *Homework Suggestions*

CHAPTER SECTION	PRESENTATION	HOMEWORK OPTIONS
Première étape	**Comment dit-on... ?** p. 22	Practice and Activity Book, p. 4, Activity 3
	Comment dit-on... ? p. 23	Practice and Activity Book, p. 4, Activity 4 Grammar and Vocabulary Workbook, p. 1, Activity 1 CD-ROM, Disc 1, Activities 1–2
	Comment dit-on... ? p. 24	Grammar and Vocabulary Workbook, p. 2, Activity 5
	Comment dit-on... ? p. 25	Pupil's Edition, p. 25, Activity 17; p. R26, Activity 1 Grammar and Vocabulary Workbook, p. 2, Activities 4, 6 CD-ROM, Disc 1, Activity 3
Deuxième étape	**Comment dit-on... ?** p. 26	Pupil's Edition, p. 29, Activity 23
	Note de grammaire, p. 26	Pupil's Edition, p. R26, Activity 2 Grammar and Vocabulary Workbook, p. 3, Activities 7–8
	Vocabulaire, p. 27	Practice and Activity Book, p. 8, Activity 12 Grammar and Vocabulary Workbook, p. 4, Activities 9–11 CD-ROM, Disc 1, Activity 4
	Grammaire, p. 28	Pupil's Edition, pp. R26–R27, Activities 3–4 Grammar and Vocabulary Workbook, p. 5, Activities 12–14
Troisième étape	**Vocabulaire,** p. 31	Pupil's Edition, p. 35, Activity 30 Practice and Activity Book, p. 10, Activities 18–19 Grammar and Vocabulary Workbook, pp. 6–7, Activities 15–17 CD-ROM, Disc 1, Activity 5
	Comment dit-on... ? p. 32	Practice and Activity Book, p. 9, Activity 16
	Grammaire, p. 33	Pupil's Edition, pp. R27–R28, Activities 5–8 Practice and Activity Book, p. 10, Activity 17 Grammar and Vocabulary Workbook, pp. 7–9, Activities 18–23 CD-ROM, Disc 1, Activity 6

Chapitre 1 : Faisons connaissance!
Textbook Listening Activities Scripts

For Student Response Forms, see *Listening Activities,* pp. 3–5.

Première étape

6 Ecoute! p. 22

1. — Bonjour, Philippe!
   — Bonjour, Elodie!

2. — Au revoir, Mlle Latour!
   — Au revoir, Paul!

3. — Salut, Julien.
   — Salut. Au revoir.

4. — Tchao, Sophie!
   — A tout à l'heure, Christelle!

5. — Salut, Gilles.
   — Bonjour, M. Dupont.

Answers to Activity 6
1. hello 2. goodbye 3. goodbye 4. goodbye 5. hello

9 Ecoute! p. 23

1. — Alors, Valérie, ça va?
   — Super!

2. — Tiens, salut, Jean-Michel. Comment ça va?
   — Oh, ça va.

3. — Et toi, Anne?
   — Moi, ça va très bien!

4. — Bonjour, Marie. Ça va?
   — Pas terrible!

5. — Et toi, Karim?
   — Pas mal.

Answers to Activity 9
1. good 2. fair 3. good 4. bad 5. fair

12 Ecoute! p. 24

1. Il s'appelle Michel.
2. Elle s'appelle Corinne.
3. Elle, elle s'appelle Danielle.
4. Il s'appelle Mathieu.
5. Lui, il s'appelle Stéphane.
6. Elle s'appelle Laurence.

Answers to Activity 12
1. garçon 2. fille 3. fille 4. garçon 5. garçon 6. fille

13 Ecoute! p. 25

Il s'appelle comment?
Comment s'appelle-t-il?
Il aime les concerts!
Il s'appelle Robert.
Elle s'appelle comment?
Comment s'appelle-t-elle?
Elle est très sympa!
Elle s'appelle Linda.
Comment s'appelle-t-il?
Il s'appelle comment?
Le garçon blond là-bas.
Il s'appelle Thomas!
Comment s'appelle-t-elle?
Elle s'appelle comment?
Elle aime faire du ski.
Elle s'appelle Julie!
Comment t'appelles-tu?
Tu t'appelles comment?
Moi, je m'appelle Jean.
Voilà! J'me présente!

Answers to Activity 13
Robert, Linda, Thomas, Julie, Jean

15 Ecoute! p. 25

1. Salut! Je m'appelle Bruno. J'ai quinze ans.
2. Bonjour! Je m'appelle Véronique. J'ai dix-sept ans.
3. Salut! Ça va? Je m'appelle Laurent. J'ai seize ans.
4. Salut! Je m'appelle Céline. J'ai treize ans.

Answers to Activity 15
Bruno–15   Véronique–17   Laurent–16   Céline–13

Deuxième étape

18 Ecoute! p. 26

PAUL Claude, c'est bien pour un garçon, mais je n'aime pas ça pour une fille. Claudette, Claudine ou...

SOPHIE Oh, je n'aime pas Claudette!

PAUL OK, OK. Pour une fille, j'adore Sandrine.

SOPHIE Oui, Sandrine, c'est adorable. J'aime bien Sandrine aussi, mais j'aime mieux Laetitia. C'est original, non?

PAUL Laetitia Dubois? Hum? Possible, mais j'aime mieux Sandrine.

Answers to Activity 18a
Paul prefers Sandrine.
Sophie prefers Laetitia.

20 Ecoute! p. 28

1. C'est Pierre. Moi, j'adore le ski.
2. Salut. C'est Monique. Moi, j'aime les hamburgers.
3. C'est Robert. Moi, j'aime les concerts.
4. Bonjour! C'est Suzanne. Moi, je n'aime pas la glace.
5. C'est Paul. J'aime la plage.
6. C'est Emilie. Moi, j'aime les amis.

Answers to Activity 20

a. Paul   b. Suzanne   c. Emilie   d. Monique   e. Robert   f. Pierre

Troisième étape

24 Ecoute! p. 32

1. J'aime parler au téléphone.
2. J'aime étudier.
3. J'aime danser.
4. J'aime faire le ménage.
5. J'aime dormir.
6. J'aime regarder la télé.

Answers to Activity 24

1. Nicolas   2. Danielle   3. Solange   4. Hervé   5. Olivier   6. Stéphanie

Prononciation, p. 35

For the script for Part A, see p. 35.

B. A écouter

1. Tu t'appelles Nicole?   question
2. Moi, je m'appelle Marie.   statement
3. Elle aime les maths.   statement
4. Nous aimons les escargots et les frites.   statement
5. Ça va?   question

C. A écrire

(Dictation)

1. — Pierre, tu aimes regarder la télé?
   — Oui, mais j'aime mieux sortir avec les copains.
2. — Salut, Sylvie. Ça va?
   — Très bien. Et toi?
   — Ça va.

Mise en pratique

2 p. 38

Bonjour, c'est Sandrine Dupont à l'appareil de l'O.I.C. J'ai des détails sur votre correspondant. C'est un garçon, Robert Perrault. Il a quinze ans et il est parisien. Il aime faire du sport, écouter de la musique et sortir avec les copains. Par contre, il n'aime pas danser. Voilà, j'espère que ça va. Pour plus de détails, téléphonez au zéro un, dix-sept, treize, quinze, zéro neuf.

Answers to Mise en pratique Activity 2

Name–Robert Perrault
Age–15
Phone number–01.17.13.15.09
Likes–sports, listening to music, and going out with friends
Dislikes–dancing

Chapitre 1 : Faisons connaissance!
Projects

Moi!
(Individual Project)

ASSIGNMENT

Students make a collage, like those in the **Mise en train**, showing their favorite and least favorite activities.

MATERIALS

✂ **Students may need**
- Magazines
- Scissors
- Glue or tape
- Colored pens, pencils, and markers
- Construction paper or posterboard

SUGGESTED SEQUENCE

1. Working individually, students start by making a list of activities they can name in French that they like and don't like to do.
2. Students plan how to present their likes and dislikes visually.
3. Students find pictures in magazines or make their own drawings that illustrate their likes and dislikes and start writing what they want to say in French. Students should mount their illustrations around the text on a large sheet of construction paper or posterboard, using paper clips or small pieces of removable tape to hold the illustrations and text in place until they decide on the final layout.
4. Students write their text on a sheet of paper, double-checking it before they ask you or another student to edit it.

5. Students edit a partner's text, checking for comprehensibility, spelling, and language use.
6. Finally, students write the final version of the text and arrange the final placement of the illustrations.

Students might show their projects to a family member or a friend who is not taking French to see if they have made themselves understood.

GRADING THE PROJECT

As students present their projects to the class, have them cover the French text on their project and tell their classmates in French about their likes and dislikes as they show their pictures.

To evaluate the written content of the projects, you might collect the projects and grade them, or you might display them all around the classroom, giving you time to evaluate and grade each one.

Instead of grading these projects, or after grading them, you might suggest that students place them in their portfolios. If the projects are destined for the portfolio, tell students to include the notes they made in French as well as the initial and final drafts of the French texts.

Suggested Point Distribution: (total = 100 points)

    Content . . . . 20 points
    Oral presentation . . . . 20 points
    Presentation/appearance . . . . 20 points
    Language use . . . . 20 points
    Creativity . . . . 20 points

♖ *Games*

INTRODUCTIONS

In this game, students will practice giving their name and age.

Before you begin the game, you might want to put the following incomplete sentences on the board or on a transparency. Explain that you use **Il/Elle a...** to give another person's age.

> **Je m'appelle...**
> **J'ai... ans.**
> **Il/Elle s'appelle...**
> **Il/Elle a... ans.**

This game can be played by the whole class or by two or three large groups. Student A begins by giving his or her name and age in French. Student B must repeat A's name and age and then give his or her own name and age. Student C must repeat the names and ages of *A* and *B* and then give his or her own name and age, and so on. The game continues until a student makes a mistake. At this point, the game can start over, beginning with the student who made the mistake or with the following student.

EXAMPLE:

ÉLÈVE 1   **Je m'appelle Louise. J'ai quinze ans.**
ÉLÈVE 2   **Elle s'appelle Louise. Elle a quinze ans. Moi, je m'appelle Todd. J'ai quatorze ans.**
ÉLÈVE 3   **Elle s'appelle Louise. Elle a quinze ans. Il s'appelle Todd. Il a quatorze ans. Moi, je m'appelle Keesha. J'ai quatorze ans.**

JACQUES A DIT

In this game, students will practice giving commands.

As you begin the game, tell students that they must carry out the commands that are preceded by **Jacques a dit...** If you don't say **Jacques a dit...** , students who carry out the command are eliminated from the game. Before you start, you may want to demonstrate gestures students might use to carry out the commands: cupping a hand behind the ear in response to **Ecoutez!** or pretending to carry bags or pay for purchases in response to **Faites les magasins!** Students who are eliminated from the game can stay involved by acting as monitors or by writing down the commands that are used.

Here are some commands you might use:

Dansez!	**Faites le ménage!**
Parlez au téléphone!	**Dormez!**
Lisez!	**Regardez la télévision!**
Voyagez!	**Etudiez!**
Ecoutez de la musique!	**Faites du sport!**
Faites les magasins!	**Faites du vélo!**
Nagez!	

In addition to the above-mentioned commands, you might use the following commands from the Preliminary Chapter: **Ecoutez! Répétez! Levez-vous! Asseyez-vous!**

Chapitre 1
Faisons connaissance!
pp. 16–41

𝒰sing the Chapter Opener

Motivating Activity

Ask students the following questions. What do you say to someone you've just met? What differences would there be between meeting someone your own age and introducing yourself to an adult? Why?

Teacher Notes

- You might want to point out to your students that fountain pens, or **stylos plumes**, are still quite common in France and other francophone countries. There is no need for an inkwell, as the ink is contained in disposable cartridges (**cartouches**) that are easily replaced when the ink runs out.
- The passport shown on this page is a European passport, which is available to citizens of most countries in Europe. It allows the bearer to travel more freely among the countries of Europe and avoid long lines at borders.

CHAPITRE

1 Faisons connaissance!

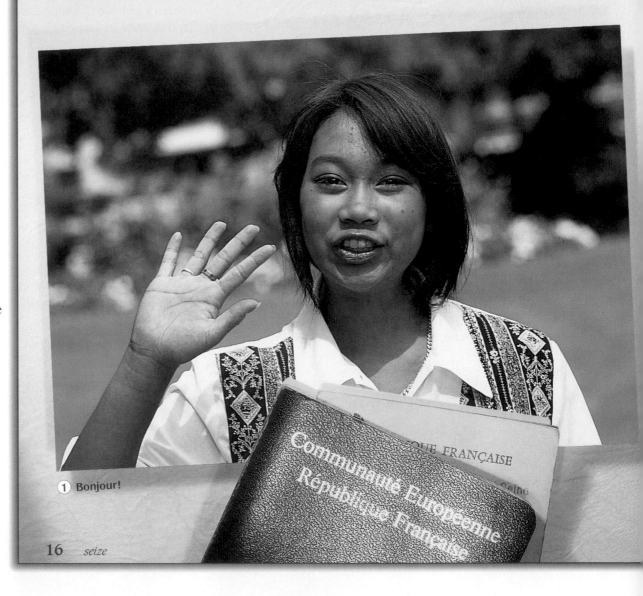

① Bonjour!

16   seize

When you meet new people, it's fun to find out what you have in common with them—and even what you don't!

In this chapter you will learn

- to greet people and say goodbye; to ask how people are and tell how you are; to ask someone's name and age and give yours
- to express likes, dislikes, and preferences about things
- to express likes, dislikes, and preferences about activities

And you will

- listen to French-speaking students tell what they like to do
- read about French-speaking teenagers who are looking for pen pals
- write a letter of introduction to a pen pal
- find out how French-speaking people greet one another

② Ça va?

③ J'aime les desserts!

Focusing on Outcomes

- Have students suggest as many English expressions as possible to say hello and goodbye. When would they use each expression? What gestures (if any) do they use with these greetings (a handshake, a kiss, a hug)?
- Have students brainstorm what they would write about if they were introducing themselves in a letter to a pen pal.
- Ask students to match the photos with the appropriate outcomes.

NOTE: You may want to use the video to support the objectives. The self-check activities in **Que sais-je?** on page 40 help students assess their achievement of the objectives.

Photo Flash!

③ This **pâtisserie** window display shows several popular French pastries. The **baba** on the left is a soft cake pastry; the round **amandine** in the middle is a type of almond tart; the **ganache** on the right is a chocolate tart filled with chocolate cream; the **religieuses** in the back row are made up of two cream puffs filled with pastry cream and topped with chocolate. Pastries may also be in the form of different animals, such as the pink raspberry-filled pigs (**cochons à la framboise**) seen here.

Block Scheduling

For suggestions about how to use *Allez, viens!* with block scheduling, see the *Lesson Planner*, pages 3–7.

VIDEO PROGRAM
Videocassette 1
07:46–12:52
Videocassette 5
(captioned version)
00:46–05:49

OR VIDEODISC PROGRAM,
Videodisc 1, Side A

Search 11575, Play To 20690

Video Synopsis

In this segment of the video, Claire introduces herself and welcomes us to the city of Poitiers. Next, teenagers from around the French-speaking world say hello and introduce themselves. They each talk about the things they like and what they like to do. We then return to Claire, who is joined by some of her friends in Poitiers. They also introduce themselves.

Motivating Activity

To focus students' attention on making introductions, ask the following questions:
- When was the last time you introduced yourself? What information did you give?
- Why is it a good idea to practice introducing yourself and others in French? (Imagine being an exchange student or hosting one.)
- What could happen if you didn't understand someone's introduction? (You might call the person by the wrong name.)

The **roman-photo** is an abridged version of the video episode.

Mise en train

Salut, les copains! p. 3, Acts. 1–2

CD 1
Trs. 11–12

What can you tell about these teenagers just by looking at their photos?

Claire

Bonjour! Ça va? Je m'appelle Claire. J'ai 15 ans. Je suis française, de Poitiers. J'adore le cinéma. Mais j'aime aussi danser, lire, voyager et écouter de la musique.

Djeneba

Salut! Je m'appelle Djeneba. J'ai 16 ans. Je suis ivoirienne. J'aime étudier, mais j'aime mieux faire du sport. C'est super cool!

Ahmed

Salut! Je m'appelle Ahmed. Je suis marocain. J'aime tous les sports, surtout le football. J'aime aussi faire du vélo.

Thuy

Salut! Ça va? Je m'appelle Thuy. J'ai 14 ans. Je suis vietnamienne. J'aime faire les magasins. En général, je n'aime pas la télévision. J'aime mieux aller au cinéma.

RESOURCES FOR **MISE EN TRAIN**	
PRINT	**MEDIA**
• *Practice and Activity Book*, p. 3	• *Video Program*, Videocassette 1,
• *Video Guide*, pp. 5–6, 8	Videocassette 5 (captioned version)
• *Videodisc Guide*, pp. 7–10, 14	• *Videodisc Program*, Videodisc 1, Side A
	• *Audio Compact Discs*, CD 1, Trs. 11–12

Didier

Salut! Je m'appelle Didier. J'ai 13 ans. Je suis belge. J'aime écouter de la musique. J'aime aussi les vacances. J'aime surtout voyager!

Stéphane

Bonjour! Je m'appelle Stéphane. J'ai 15 ans et je suis martiniquais. J'aime la plage, la mer, le soleil, la musique et j'aime aussi nager. J'aime surtout danser.

André

Tiens, bonjour! Comment ça va? Je m'appelle André. J'ai 17 ans et je suis suisse. Je parle français et allemand. J'aime beaucoup la télévision. J'aime aussi parler au téléphone avec mes copains.

Emilie

Bonjour! Je m'appelle Emilie. J'ai 16 ans. Je suis québécoise. J'adore faire du sport, surtout du ski et du patin. J'aime bien aussi faire de l'équitation.

MISE EN TRAIN

dix-neuf 19

Presentation

Have students look at the questions in Activity 1 on page 20 before you play the video, so that they will have an idea of what they will see and hear. Then, show *Map Transparency 4* (Le Monde francophone) on the overhead projector, or use a wall map if you have one. Ask students to locate the places on the map where the teenagers say they live.

Captioned Video

You may also wish to present **Salut, les copains!** using the captioned version on Videocassette 5. As students watch the video, have them identify the activities that the teenagers say they like and dislike.

Teaching Suggestion

Have students identify any statements made by the teenagers that also apply to them.

 Video Integration

- **VIDEO PROGRAM,**
  Videocassette 1, 12:53–16:13
  Videocassette 5, 05:54–09:14
- **VIDEODISC PROGRAM,**
  Videodisc 1, Side A

Search 20690, Play To 26765

You may choose to continue with **Salut, les copains! (suite)** at this time or wait until later in the chapter. At this point in the story, Marc arrives at school on his bicycle and sees M. Balland, the math teacher. They greet each other and ask how things are going. Then, Claire arrives and introduces Ann, an American exchange student. M. Balland leaves, and Jérôme arrives on his moped, which breaks down. Later that day, Claire, Ann, Marc, and Jérôme go to a café. Marc, Jérôme, and Claire pay for Ann's part of the check to welcome her to Poitiers.

For Individual Needs

2 Slower Pace Have students find the cognates in the activity and write them down. Have them find the name of the person in each sentence in **Salut, les copains!** They should then find the name(s) of the activity(-ies) in that person's remarks and decide whether the information in both the true-false statement and the basic text are the same.

2 Challenge Have students work individually or in pairs to write three or four additional true-false statements based on **Salut, les copains!** Students might exchange papers and mark their answers, or you might call on individuals to read one of their statements and have other students respond.

Teaching Suggestion

3 Play the video of **Salut, les copains!** Have students call out when they identify each of these functions. Then, stop the video and have students repeat the French expressions.

For videodisc application, see *Videodisc Guide.*

These activities check for comprehension only. Students should not yet be expected to produce language modeled in **Mise en train.**

1 Tu as compris? *Did you understand?*

Answer the following questions about the teenagers you've just met. Look back at **Salut, les copains!** if you have to. Don't be afraid to guess. See answers below.

1. What are these teenagers talking about?
2. What information do they give you in the first few lines of their introductions?
3. What are some of the things they like?
4. Which of them have interests in common?

2 Vrai ou faux? *True or false?*

According to **Salut, les copains!**, are the following statements true (**vrai**) or false (**faux**)?

1. André aime parler au téléphone.   vrai
2. Ahmed n'aime pas le sport.   faux
3. Stéphane aime écouter de la musique.   vrai
4. Claire aime voyager et danser.   vrai
5. Didier n'aime pas voyager.   faux
6. Emilie aime faire de l'équitation.   vrai
7. Thuy aime la télévision.   faux
8. Djeneba n'aime pas faire du sport.   faux

3 Cherche les expressions *Look for the expressions*

Look back at **Salut, les copains!** How do the teenagers . . .

1. say hello?   Bonjour./Salut.
2. give their name?   Je m'appelle...
3. give their age?   J'ai... ans.
4. say they like something?   J'aime...

J'ai... ans.   J'aime...   Je suis...
Bonjour.   Salut.   Je m'appelle...

4 Qui est-ce? *Who is it?*

Can you identify the teenagers in **Salut, les copains!** from these descriptions?

1. Elle est québécoise.   Emilie
2. Il parle allemand.   André
3. Il a quinze ans.   Stéphane
4. Il aime voyager.   Didier
5. Elle adore le ski.   Emilie
6. Elle n'aime pas la télévision.   Thuy
7. Il adore le football.   Ahmed
8. Elle aime étudier.   Djeneba

5 Et maintenant, à toi *And now, it's your turn*

Which of the students in **Salut, les copains!** would you most like to meet? Why? Jot down your thoughts and share them with a classmate.

Possible answers
1 1. names, ages, interests, and nationalities
2. name, age, nationality, what they like to do
3. music, dancing, sports, movies, reading, traveling, shopping, television
4. Claire and Thuy — movies; Djeneba, Ahmed, and Emilie — sports; Claire, Didier, and Stéphane — music; Claire and Didier — traveling

RENCONTRE CULTURELLE

Look at what the people in these photos are doing.

—Salut, Mireille!
—Salut, Lucien!

—Bonjour, maman!
—Bonjour, mon chou!

—Salut, Lucien!
—Salut, Jean-Philippe!

—Salut, Agnès!
—Tchao, Mireille!

—Bonjour, Monsieur
Balland.
—Bonjour, Marc.

—Au revoir, Monsieur
Legrand.
—Au revoir, Isabelle.

Qu'en penses-tu?   *What do you think?*   See answers below.

1. How do the teenagers greet adults? Other teenagers? What gestures do they use?
2. How do they say goodbye? What gestures do they use?
3. Is this similar to the way you greet people and say goodbye in the United States?

Savais-tu que...?   *Did you know . . . ?*

   In France, girls kiss both girls and boys on the cheek when they meet or say good-bye. The number of kisses varies from two to four depending on the region. Boys shake hands with one another. Teenagers may kiss adults who are family members or friends of the family, but they shake hands when they greet other adults.

   To address adults who aren't family members, teenagers generally use the titles **madame, mademoiselle,** or **monsieur. Mme, Mlle,** and **M.** are the written abbreviations of these titles.

ENTREE POUR UNE PERSONNE

Answers
1. Adults: Bonjour, maman! Bonjour, Monsieur Balland.
   Teenagers: Salut!
   Gestures—adults: kiss (relatives); handshake
   Gestures—teenagers: kiss; handshake
2. Adults: Au revoir, Monsieur Legrand.
   Teenagers: Salut! Tchao!
   Gestures—adults: handshake
   Gestures—teenagers: kiss

Culture Notes
• In France, people say **Bonjour** only the first time they see someone on a given day. If they see that person again during the same day, they might just say **Ça va?**
• In Djoula, the market language of Côte d'Ivoire, greeting one another is truly an art form. There are separate greetings for men, women, a person who is working, a person you haven't seen in a long time, and a person who is going to the market.

Jump Start!

Write several numbers between 0 and 20 at random on the board. Have students write the words for these numbers. Then, have them correct their papers by turning to page 9 in the Preliminary Chapter.

MOTIVATE

Ask students to identify as many situations as they can in which people are required to give their name and age.

TEACH

Presentation

Comment dit-on... ? Say these expressions, using appropriate gestures. Have students repeat after you and imitate your gestures.

Language Note

Explain to students that **A tout à l'heure** is used to say goodbye only when you will see a person later the same day. Although it literally means *See you within the hour,* it translates more generally as *See you later (by the end of the day).* To say *See you later* in a more general way, young people now use the expression **A plus!**, short for **A plus tard.** Tell students that they should pronounce the "s" in **A plus.**

For Individual Needs

Kinesthetic Learners Have students practice saying the expressions while making the corresponding gestures.

Teaching Suggestions

8 Have students draw or cut out pictures of people greeting each other or saying goodbye. Have them add captions or speech bubbles in French.

PREMIERE ETAPE TPR

Storytelling Book pp. 1, 4

Greeting people and saying goodbye; asking how people are and telling how you are; asking someone's name and age and giving yours

COMMENT DIT-ON... ?
Greeting people and saying goodbye

 p. 4, Act. 3
1-1

To anyone:	**Bonjour.** *Hello.*	**Au revoir.** *Goodbye.*
		A tout à l'heure. *See you later.*
		A bientôt. *See you soon.*
		A demain. *See you tomorrow.*
To someone your own age or younger:	**Salut.** *Hi.*	**Salut.** *Bye.*
		Tchao. *Bye.*

6 Ecoute! See scripts and answers on p. 15G.

Imagine you overhear the following short conversations on the street in Poitiers. Listen carefully and decide whether the speakers are saying hello or goodbye.

CD 1 Tr. 13

7 Comment le dire? *How should you say it?*

How would you say hello to these people in French?

| **Mme Leblanc** | **M. Diab** | **Nadia** | **Eric** | **Mme Desrochers** |
| Bonjour! | Bonjour! | Salut! | Salut! | Bonjour! |

8 Comment répondre? *How should you answer?* H

How would you respond to the greeting from each of the following people?

1. Bonjour!

2. Au revoir!/A tout à l'heure!/ A bientôt!/A demain!

3. Au revoir!/A tout à l'heure!/ A bientôt!/Salut!/Tchao!

4. Salut!

22 *vingt-deux*

CHAPITRE 1   Faisons connaissance!

RESOURCES FOR PREMIERE ETAPE

PRINT
- *Lesson Planner,* p. 4
- *Practice and Activity Book,* pp. 4–6
- *Grammar and Vocabulary Workbook,* pp. 1–2
- *Activities for Communication,* pp. 1–2, 75, 78–79, 137–138
- *Listening Activities,* pp. 3–4, 7
- *Testing Program,* pp. 1–4
- *Alternative Assessment Guide,* p. 32

MEDIA
- *Video Program,* Videocassette 1
  Video Guide, pp. 5–10
- *Videodisc Program,* Videodisc 1, Side A
  Videodisc Guide, p. 11
- *Teaching Transparency 1-1*
- *Interactive CD-ROM Program,* Disc 1
  CD-ROM Teacher's Guide, p. 2
- *Audio Compact Discs*
  Textbook Listening Activities, CD 1, Trs. 13–17
  Additional Listening Activities 1-1, 1-2, CD 1, Trs. 37–38
  Quiz 1-1B, CD 1, Tr. 31

COMMENT DIT-ON... ?

Asking how people are and telling how you are

p. 4, Act. 4

p. 1, Act. 1

To ask how your friend is: **Comment ça va?** *or* **Ça va?**

To tell how you are:

CD-ROM
Disc 1

Super! *Great!*
Très bien. *Very well.*

Ça va. *Fine.*
Comme ci, comme ça. *So-so.*
Pas mal. *Not bad.*
Bof! *(expression of indifference)*

Pas terrible. *Not so great.*

To keep a conversation going: **Et toi?** *And you?*

---

^Ala française

To ask an adult how he or she is, you can say:
Comment allez-vous?

To keep a conversation with an adult going, you can say:
Et vous?

You'll learn more about using **vous** later in this chapter.

---

9 Ecoute! See scripts and answers on p. 15G.

CD 1 Tr. 14

You're going to hear a student ask Valérie, Jean-Michel, Anne, Marie, and Karim how they're feeling. Are they feeling good, fair, or bad?

NOTE CULTURELLE

Gestures are an important part of communication. They often speak louder than words. Can you match the gestures with these expressions?

a. Super!
b. Comme ci, comme ça.
c. Pas terrible!

1. c   2. b   3. a

When you say **super**, use a thumbs-up gesture. When you say **comme ci, comme ça**, hold your hand in front of you, palm down, and rock it from side to side. When you say **pas terrible**, shrug your shoulders and frown.

Presentation

Comment dit-on... ? Draw the three faces to represent the expressions in **Comment dit-on... ?** on a transparency and number them. Say the expressions in the box aloud in random order and ask students to call out or write down the number of the face that corresponds to the expression.

For videodisc application, see *Videodisc Guide.*

For Individual Needs

Visual Learners Have students add the functional expressions to their notebooks. You might want to illustrate the intonation pattern by drawing on the board or on a transparency lines that curve upward above **Et toi?** and **Ça va?**

Teaching Suggestion

Have students pair off and practice the expressions, using the appropriate gestures. One student gives an expression, and his or her partner makes the appropriate gesture.

Culture Note

The gesture for **comme ci, comme ça** can also show uncertainty. For example, if someone says that the bus will arrive at eight o'clock while making this gesture, then it means that the bus will arrive around eight, more or less.

Presentation

Comment dit-on... ? Give your name and ask several individuals theirs. Students should recall these expressions using **je** and **tu** from the Preliminary Chapter. Have students practice in pairs asking and giving their names. Then, point to boys and girls in the class, naming them. Occasionally, give a wrong name and encourage students to correct you, saying **Non, il/elle s'appelle...**

For Individual Needs

12 Slower Pace Before doing this listening activity, ask students to say **il** or **elle** as you point to different students. Or you might say **Il/Elle s'appelle...** as you point to individuals, having students complete the sentence with the person's name. Then, hold up pictures of people, asking **C'est un garçon?** or **C'est une fille?** Remind students that some French girls' and boys' names sound the same, such as Dominique, Michel/Michèle, and Claude.

10 Méli-mélo! *Mishmash!*

Work with a classmate to rewrite this conversation in the correct order, using your own names. Then, act it out with your partner. Remember to use the appropriate gestures. See answers below.

> Super! Et toi?
> Très bien.
> Tchao.   Salut,... ! Ça va?
> Bonjour,... !
> Bon. Alors, à tout à l'heure!

11 Et ton voisin (ta voisine)? *And your neighbor?*

Create a conversation with a partner. Be sure to greet your partner, ask how he or she is feeling, respond to any questions your partner asks you, and say goodbye. Don't forget to include the gestures you learned in the **Note Culturelle** on page 23.

1-1

G V
p. 2, Act. 5

COMMENT DIT-ON... ?
Asking someone's name and giving yours

—Tu t'appelles comment?
—Je m'appelle Magali.

To ask someone his or her name:
  Tu t'appelles comment?

To ask someone else's name:
  Il/Elle s'appelle comment? *What is his/her name?*

To give your name:
  Je m'appelle...

To give someone else's name:
  Il/Elle s'appelle... *His/Her name is . . .*

12 Ecoute! See scripts and answers on p. 15G.

Listen as some French teenagers tell you about their friends. Are they talking about a boy **(un garçon)** or a girl **(une fille)**?

CD 1 Tr. 15

Answers
10 Bonjour,... !
   Salut,... ! Ça va?
   Super! Et toi?
   Très bien.
   Bon. Alors, à tout à l'heure!
   Tchao.

13 Ecoute! *See scripts and answers on p. 15G.*

CD 1 Tr. 16

You're going to hear a song called **S'appeler rap.** Which of the following names are mentioned in the song?

Emilie   Jean   Thomas
Laurence   Pierre
Linda   Robert
Laurent   Julie

14 Je te présente... *Let me introduce . . .*

Select a French name for yourself from the list of names on page 5, or ask your teacher to suggest others. Then, say hello to a classmate, introduce yourself, and ask his or her name. Now, introduce your partner to the rest of the class, using **il s'appelle** or **elle s'appelle.**

COMMENT DIT-ON... ?
Asking someone's age and giving yours

To find out someone's age:
Tu as quel âge?

To give your age:
J'ai douze **ans.**
treize
quatorze
quinze
seize
dix-sept
dix-huit

1-1

pp. 1–2,
Acts. 2–4, 6

For additional practice,
see p. R26.

CD-ROM
Disc 1

15 Ecoute! *See scripts and answers on p. 15G.*

CD 1 Tr. 17

Listen as Bruno, Véronique, Laurent, and Céline introduce themselves to you. Write down each student's age.

16 Faisons connaissance! *Let's get to know one another!*

Create a conversation with two other classmates. Introduce yourself, ask your partners' names and ages, and ask how they are.

17 Mon journal *My journal*

A good way to learn French is to use it to express your own thoughts and feelings. From time to time, you'll be asked to write about yourself in French in a journal. As your first journal entry, identify yourself—give your name, your age, and anything else important to you that you've learned how to say in French.

PREMIERE ETAPE
CHAPITRE 1

Building on Previous Skills

14 Review the alphabet in the Preliminary Chapter. Have partners practice spelling their names after introducing each other.

Presentation

Comment dit-on... ?
Review the numbers 1–20. Then, write **âge** on the board and ask the students what they think it means. Now, write **14 ans** and ask what they think **ans** means. Tell the students we get the words *annual* and *anniversary* from the same root. Next, have students pair off and practice the question and response several times.

CLOSE

Group Work

Teams of 3–5 students create short dialogues like the one in Activity 10 on page 24 and write lines on separate strips of paper. Teams mix up their strips of paper and exchange them. Team members work together to arrange the slips of paper in the correct order. Then, teams line up in the order of the dialogue, each member holding a line of dialogue on a slip of paper. Each team reads its dialogue aloud in order, one student at a time.

ASSESS

Quiz 1-1A, Quiz 1-1B, *Testing Program,* pp. 1–4
Audio CD 1, Tr. 31

Performance Assessment

Have students act out their conversations from Activity 16, using the appropriate gestures.

Culture Note

Next to Activity 13 is a photo of the popular French rapper known as MC Solaar. A native of Senegal, Claude M'Barali created his stage name from the English abbreviation for *Master of Ceremonies* and the French word for sun, **le soleil.** In his music, which is a combination of jazz, funk, and soul, Solaar advocates peace and tries to serve as a voice for young people. Solaar has created many tongue twisters to describe his philosophy;

one example is **Ma tactique attaque tous tes tics avec tact.** *(My tactics attack all your tics with tact.)* Among his most popular albums are *Qui sème le vent récolte le tempo* ("He Who Sows the Wind Reaps the Tempo") and *Prose combat.*

Language Note

You might want to tell your students that in everyday speech, they might give a short answer when asked their age: **Quatorze ans.**

Jump Start!

Have students write the answers to the following questions: Ça va? Tu t'appelles comment? Tu as quel âge?

MOTIVATE

Ask students what they ask about, besides name and age, when they meet someone. Tell students that finding out what others like and dislike is a good way to get to know people.

TEACH

Presentation

Comment dit-on... ?
Gather pictures of various things you like and dislike; some may be in **Comment dit-on... ?** Tell the class in French which ones you like, which you really like, which you prefer, and which you dislike, using the expressions in **Comment dit-on... ?** Then, ask students in French if they like or dislike the same things. They might just answer **Oui** or **Non** at first.

For videodisc application, see *Videodisc Guide.*

Teaching Suggestions

• Students might draw smiling, neutral, and unhappy faces and write sentences about what they like and dislike under the appropriate faces.

19 Students might also discuss music groups or sports teams, in addition to movies.

DEUXIEME ETAPE

 Storytelling Book pp. 2, 4

Expressing likes, dislikes, and preferences about things

COMMENT DIT-ON... ?

Expressing likes, dislikes, and preferences about things

To ask if someone likes something:
Tu aimes les hamburgers?
Tu aimes le vélo **ou** le ski? *Do you like . . . , or . . .?*

To say that you like something:
J'adore le chocolat.
J'aime bien le sport.
J'aime les hamburgers.

To say that you dislike something:
Je n'aime pas les hamburgers.

To say that you prefer something:
J'aime les frites, **mais j'aime mieux** le chocolat. *I like . . ., but I prefer . . .*
Je préfère le français.

NOTE DE GRAMMAIRE

Look at the sentences in the illustrations to the left. Can you figure out when to use **ne (n')... pas**? You put **ne (n')... pas** around the verb **aime** to make the sentence negative. Notice the contraction **n'** before the vowel.

J'aime le sport.
Je n'aime pas le sport.

p. 3,
Acts. 7–8

Additional Grammar Practice, p. R26

18 Ecoute!   See scripts and answers on p. 15G.

 CD 1 Tr. 18

a. Listen to Paul and Sophie Dubois discuss names for their baby girl. Which of the names does Paul prefer? And Sophie?

b. Do you agree with Paul and Sophie's choices? With a partner, discuss whether you like or dislike the names Paul and Sophie mention. What's your favorite French girl's name? And your favorite French boy's name? You might refer to the list of names on page 5.

> — Tu aimes... ?
> — Oui, mais je n'aime pas...

Claude   Sandrine   Claudette
Laetitia   Claudine

19 Quel film?   *Which movie?*

With two of your classmates, decide on a movie you all like.

> — J'aime *Twister*®! Et toi?
> — Moi, je n'aime pas *Twister.* Tu aimes *Independence Day*®?
> — Oui, j'aime *Independence Day,* mais j'aime mieux *Casablanca*!

CASABLANCA RE
1942. 1h40. Film d'aventures américain en noir et blanc de Michael Curtiz avec Humphrey Bogart, Ingrid Bergman, Paul Henreid, Conrad Veidt, Claude Rains.
Casablanca à l'heure de Vichy. Un réfugié américain retrouve une femme follement aimée et fuit la persécution nazie. Une distribution étincelante et une mise en scène efficace.
• V.O. Saint Lambert 96

RESOURCES FOR DEUXIEME ETAPE

PRINT

• *Lesson Planner,* p. 5
• *Practice and Activity Book,* pp. 7–8
• *Grammar and Vocabulary Workbook,* pp. 3–5
• *Activities for Communication,* pp. 3–4, 76, 78–79, 137–138
• *Listening Activities,* pp. 4–5, 8
• *Testing Program,* pp. 5–8
• *Alternative Assessment Guide,* p. 32

MEDIA

• *Video Program,* Videocassette 1
  Video Guide, pp. 5–10
• *Videodisc Program,* Videodisc 1, Side A
  Videodisc Guide, p. 11
• *Teaching Transparencies* 1-2, 1-A, 1-B
  Interactive CD-ROM Program, Disc 1
• *CD-ROM Teacher's Guide,* p. 2
• *Audio Compact Discs*
  Textbook Listening Activities, CD 1, Trs. 18–19
  Additional Listening Activities 1-3, 1-4, CD 1, Trs. 39–40
  Quiz 1-2B, CD 1, Tr. 32

VOCABULAIRE

PA p. 8, Act. 12   1-A, 1-B   GV p. 4, Acts. 9–11   CD-ROM Disc 1

les amis (m.)

le cinéma

le ski

le football

le magasin

la plage

le vélo

la glace

l'école (f.)

le français

les frites (f.)

le chocolat

l'anglais (m.)

les examens (f.)

les vacances (f.)

les escargots (m.)

You can probably guess what these words mean:

les concerts (m.)   les hamburgers (m.)   les maths (f.)   la pizza   le sport

DEUXIEME ETAPE   *vingt-sept* **27**

Presentation

Vocabulaire Have students scan the vocabulary for cognates (**cinéma, ski, examens, vacances, chocolat**). Make sure they are also aware of the **faux amis** (**magasins, football, glace**). Have students make flashcards of this vocabulary with the French on one side and drawings or magazine pictures on the other.

For Individual Needs

Visual Learners Bring in magazine illustrations of the vocabulary items. Ask students **Qu'est-ce que c'est?** as you hold up each illustration. Ask individual students whether they like the item, using **Tu aimes... ?** Then, have partners practice asking each other.

Language Note

You might tell students that **examen** rarely translates as *exam* in English. **Examen** usually refers to comprehensive tests such as the **CAP** (**certificat d'aptitude professionnelle**) or the **baccalauréat** (at the end of **lycée**) that French students take at the end of a school cycle. Depending on the type of **examen** a student takes, he or she can obtain a professional certification or be admitted into specialized schools or universities. In French elementary and secondary schools, students are tested through **contrôles** or **interros** (**interrogations écrites** and **interrogations orales**).

Culture Note

As students learn the words **plage** and **vélo,** they may be interested in learning about the beaches of the Riviera (**la Côte d'Azur**), or about the Tour de France, the famous bicycle race that covers more than 4,000 km (2,500 miles).

Language Note

Explain that **le football** means *soccer.* Tell students they must say **le football américain** if they mean *football.* Also, point out that the word for *vacation* is always plural in French: **les vacances.**

For Individual Needs

20 Slower Pace Before they hear the recording, students might look back at the **Vocabulaire** on page 27 to find the words for the things shown in the pictures and practice them orally with a partner. After correcting their answers, students might write the letters of the pictures in the order of their own preference and compare their list with a partner's.

20 Challenge Ask students to check their answers with a partner by telling what each teenager likes or dislikes.

Presentation

Grammaire Tell students that many languages have several ways of saying *the.* Explain that French has four different articles that depend on the type of noun they're used with (masculine, feminine, an initial vowel sound, and plural). Have students repeat the articles and nouns after you. You might hold up vocabulary flashcards and have students identify each item, using the correct article.

20 Ecoute! See scripts and answers on p. 15H.

CD 1 Tr. 19

Listen as several French teenagers call in to a radio talk-show poll of their likes and dislikes. Match their names with the pictures that illustrate the activities they like or dislike.

Paul Pierre Robert
Monique Suzanne Emilie

a. b. c.

d. e. f.

G|V

p. 5,
Acts. 12–14

Additional Grammar
Practice, pp. R26–R27

GRAMMAIRE The definite articles le, la, l', and les

There are four ways to say *the* in French: **le, la, l', and les.** These words are called *definite articles.* Look at the articles and nouns below. Can you tell when to use **les**? When to use **l'**?

| le français | la glace | l'école | les escargots |
| le football | la pizza | l'anglais | les magasins |

- As you may have guessed, you always use **les** before plural nouns.
- Before a singular noun, you use **l'** if the noun begins with a vowel sound, **le** if the noun is masculine, or **la** if the noun is feminine. How do you know which nouns are masculine and which are feminine? While it is usually true that nouns that refer to males are masculine (**le garçon** *the boy*) and those that refer to females are feminine (**la fille** *the girl*), there are no hard-and-fast rules for other nouns. You'll just have to learn the definite article that goes with each one.

28   *vingt-huit*   CHAPITRE 1   Faisons connaissance!

For Individual Needs

Kinesthetic Learners Read aloud some sentences that contain nouns and articles from the **Vocabulaire** on page 27, some singular, some plural. Have students hold up one hand if the noun they hear is singular and both hands if it's plural. For example, if you say **J'aime la pizza,** they would raise one hand; if you say **J'aime les magasins,** they would raise both hands.

21 Et toi, qu'est-ce que tu aimes?

 Lucie and Gilbert are talking about the things they like. With a partner, complete their conversation according to the pictures.

la plage

LUCIE   Moi, j'aime bien . Et toi?

les copains

le cinéma

GILBERT   Moi, j'aime mieux . J'aime bien aussi sortir avec .

J'adore le sport aussi. Et toi, tu aimes le sport?

le vélo   le ski

LUCIE   Oui, j'adore et j'aime bien aussi.

How can you remember if a noun is masculine or feminine? Here are a few hints. Choose the one that works best for you.

De bons conseils

- Practice saying each noun aloud with **le** or **la** in front of it. (NOTE: This won't help with nouns that begin with vowels!)
- Write the feminine nouns in one column and the masculine nouns in another. You might even write the feminine nouns in one color and the masculine nouns in a second color.
- Make flash cards of the nouns, writing the feminine and masculine nouns in different colors.

---

22 Tu aimes...?   *Do you like . . . ?*

 Choose six things from the vocabulary on page 27. Next, write down which of those things you like and which you dislike. Then, with a partner, try to guess each other's likes and dislikes by asking **Tu aimes... ?**

À la française

Two common words you can use to connect your ideas are **et** *(and)* and **mais** *(but)*. Here's how you can use them to combine sentences.

J'aime les hamburgers. J'aime le chocolat.
J'aime les hamburgers **et** le chocolat.

J'aime le français. Je n'aime pas les maths.
J'aime le français, **mais** je n'aime pas les maths.

23 Mon journal

In your journal, write down some of your likes and dislikes. Use **et** and **mais** to connect your sentences. You might want to illustrate your journal entry.

Teacher Note

When giving assignments that entail the disclosure of personal information, keep in mind that some students and their families may consider these matters private. In some cases, you may want to give an alternate assignment in which students may substitute fictitious information.

 Mon journal

23 For an additional journal entry suggestion for Chapter 1, see *Practice and Activity Book,* page 145.

For Individual Needs

Visual/Auditory Learners

To review vocabulary, put pictures or drawings of the vocabulary on the board or on a transparency and number them. Then, say the French words for the pictures in random order. Students should call out the numbers of the corresponding pictures in French. Finally, call out the numbers of the pictures and have students say the corresponding French words.

CLOSE

To close this **étape**, have pairs of students use the **Vocabulaire** on page 27 to describe orally the likes and dislikes of the young people shown in the pictures: **Il aime les frites. Elle aime le football.** Then, referring to the pictures, students should tell what they themselves like and dislike. You might have them do this as a written activity.

ASSESS

Quiz 1-2A, Quiz 1-2B, *Testing Program,* pp. 5–8

Audio CD 1, Tr. 32

Performance Assessment

Have students make a collage of the things they like and dislike. See page 15I for a full description of this project. You might refer students to the Additional Vocabulary, which begins on page R7, for additional likes and dislikes. Have students present their collage to the class, telling whether they like or dislike the objects pictured.

VIDEO PROGRAM
Videocassette 1
16:14–18:16

OR VIDEODISC PROGRAM,
Videodisc 1, Side A

Search 26765, Play To 28245

Teacher Notes

• See the *Video Guide,* the *Videodisc Guide,* and the *CD-ROM Teacher's Guide* for activities related to the **Panorama Culturel.**

• Remind students that cultural material may be included in the Chapter Quizzes and Test.

• The interviewees' language represents informal, unrehearsed speech. Occasionally, edits have been made for clarification.

Motivating Activity

Have students name several activities they enjoy. Ask them if there are certain activities that are particularly popular in their city or region.

Presentation

First, have students view the video. Next, ask simple yes-no questions based on the video or have students tell in English what they have understood about these people. Then, ask them the following **Questions** and have them answer the questions in **Qu'en penses-tu?** This might be done in small groups or as a writing assignment.

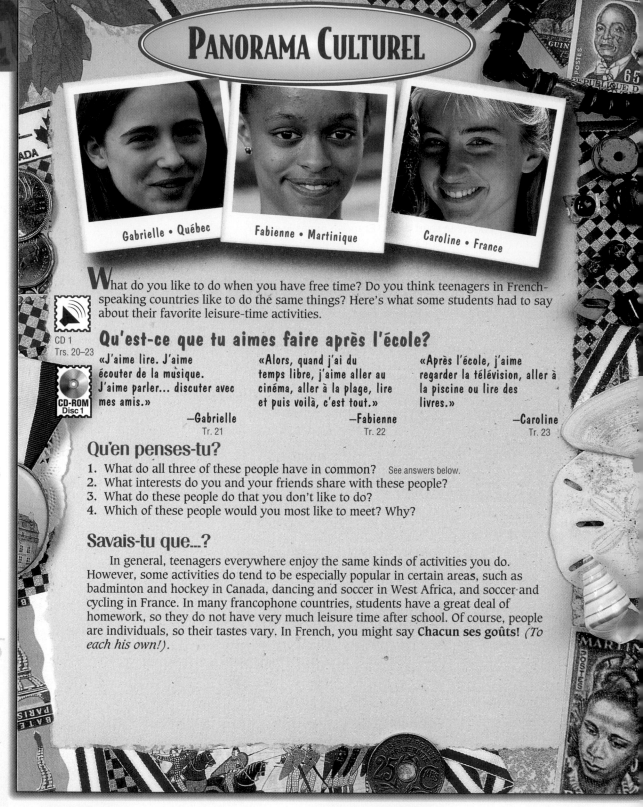

PANORAMA CULTUREL

Gabrielle • Québec

Fabienne • Martinique

Caroline • France

What do you like to do when you have free time? Do you think teenagers in French-speaking countries like to do the same things? Here's what some students had to say about their favorite leisure-time activities.

CD 1
Trs. 20–23

CD-ROM
Disc 1

Qu'est-ce que tu aimes faire après l'école?

«J'aime lire. J'aime écouter de la musique. J'aime parler... discuter avec mes amis.»

—Gabrielle
Tr. 21

«Alors, quand j'ai du temps libre, j'aime aller au cinéma, aller à la plage, lire et puis voilà, c'est tout.»

—Fabienne
Tr. 22

«Après l'école, j'aime regarder la télévision, aller à la piscine ou lire des livres.»

—Caroline
Tr. 23

Qu'en penses-tu?

1. What do all three of these people have in common?   See answers below.
2. What interests do you and your friends share with these people?
3. What do these people do that you don't like to do?
4. Which of these people would you most like to meet? Why?

Savais-tu que...?

In general, teenagers everywhere enjoy the same kinds of activities you do. However, some activities do tend to be especially popular in certain areas, such as badminton and hockey in Canada, dancing and soccer in West Africa, and soccer and cycling in France. In many francophone countries, students have a great deal of homework, so they do not have very much leisure time after school. Of course, people are individuals, so their tastes vary. In French, you might say **Chacun ses goûts!** *(To each his own!).*

Questions

1. Qu'est-ce que Gabrielle aime faire? (Elle aime lire, écouter de la musique, parler et discuter avec des amis.)
2. Est-ce que Fabienne aime la plage? Où est-ce qu'elle aime aussi aller? (Oui. Elle aime aussi aller au cinéma.)
3. Qu'est-ce que Caroline aime faire après l'école? (Elle aime regarder la télévision, aller à la piscine ou lire des livres.)

Language Note

You might want to define the following terms for students: **du temps libre** *(free time),* **la piscine** *(swimming pool).*

Answers
1. They all like to read.

TROISIEME ETAPE Storytelling Book pp. 3, 4

Expressing likes, dislikes, and preferences about activities

 p. 10, Acts. 18–19   1-C, 1-D   pp. 6–7, Acts. 15–17   CD-ROM Disc 1

VOCABULAIRE

Stéphanie adore **regarder la télé.**

Etienne aime **sortir avec les copains.**

Nicolas aime **parler au téléphone.**

Olivier aime **dormir.**

Danielle aime **étudier.**

Sylvie aime bien **faire du sport.**

Michèle aime **faire les magasins.**

Hervé aime **faire le ménage.**

Raymond aime **faire de l'équitation.**

Serge aime **voyager.**

Eric aime **écouter de la musique.**

Laurence aime bien **nager.**

Solange adore **danser.**

Annie aime **lire.**

---

*J*ump Start!

Ask students to write sentences telling two things they like and two things they dislike.

MOTIVATE

Ask students to tell in English what activities they like to do. Make a list of the activities they mention on the board or on a transparency. Have students vote for their favorite activity by a show of hands. If their most popular activities are not represented in the **Vocabulaire,** have them check the Additional Vocabulary on page R7, or write the French equivalents for the students.

TEACH

Presentation

Vocabulaire   To present this vocabulary, you might want to show pictures of the activities or mime the activities yourself, while saying aloud what you like to do. (**J'aime écouter de la musique.**) After students have repeated the expressions, have volunteers tell what they like to do. Then, ask other students in the class to tell what their classmates like to do. (**Jennifer adore danser.**) Finally, have students work in small groups, with each student miming an activity while the others try to guess what it is.

(TPR) Give commands using the activities in the **Vocabulaire: Regarde(z) la télé! Fais/Faites de l'équitation! Nage(z)!** Have students mime the activities to show that they understand.

RESOURCES FOR TROISIEME ETAPE

PRINT
- *Lesson Planner,* p. 6
- *Practice and Activity Book,* pp. 9–10
- *Grammar and Vocabulary Workbook,* pp. 6–9
- *Activities for Communication,* pp. 5–6, 77, 78–79, 137–138
- *Listening Activities,* pp. 5, 9
- *Testing Program,* pp. 9–12
- *Alternative Assessment Guide,* p. 32

MEDIA
- *Video Program,* Videocassette 1 Video Guide, pp. 5–10
- *Videodisc Program,* Videodisc 1, Side A Videodisc Guide, p. 12
- *Teaching Transparencies* 1-3, 1-C, 1-D
- *Interactive CD-ROM Program,* Disc 1 CD-ROM Teacher's Guide, p. 3
- *Audio Compact Discs* Textbook Listening Activities, CD 1, Trs. 24–29 Additional Listening Activities 1-5, 1-6, CD 1, Trs. 41–42 Quiz 1-3B, CD 1, Tr. 33

Presentation

Comment dit-on... ?
Review briefly the expressions of liking and disliking from page 26. Then, tell the students that they can use the same expressions, substituting activities for things, to tell what they like to do. Next, as you act out the activities or refer to the pictures in the **Vocabulaire** on page 31, ask **Qui aime... ?** completing the question with the activity. Have individuals raise their hands and answer **Moi, et j'aime aussi...** if they want to add another activity that they like. Point out that the verbs following the forms of **aimer** are in the infinitive form. You might explain to your students that the *infinitive* is the *to* form of a verb and that **-er**, **-re**, and **-ir** are typical infinitive endings for French verbs.

Group Work

25 Have students number a piece of paper from 1–6 and write down one response for each category. Then, have them ask other students if they like these same items: **Tu aimes... ?** If another student agrees (**Oui, j'aime...**), he or she signs the interviewer's paper next to the appropriate item. Students must get six different signatures to complete the activity.

24 Ecoute! See scripts and answers on p. 15H.

CD 1 Tr. 24

You're going to hear six students tell you what they like to do. For each statement you hear, decide which of the students pictured on page 31 is speaking.

CD-ROM Disc 1

P A
p. 9, Act. 16

1-3

COMMENT DIT-ON... ?
Expressing likes, dislikes, and preferences about activities

To ask if someone likes an activity:
Tu aimes voyager?

To tell what you like to do:
J'aime voyager.
J'adore danser.
J'aime bien dormir.

To tell what you don't like to do:
Je n'aime pas aller aux concerts.

To tell what you prefer to do:
J'aime mieux regarder la télévision.
Je préfère lire.

25 Sondage *Poll*

a. Complete the following poll.

1. J'aime...
a. faire de l'équitation.
b. sortir avec les copains.
c. parler français.
d. dormir.
e. écouter le professeur.
f. faire du sport.

2. Chez moi, j'aime...
a. regarder la télévision.
b. écouter de la musique.
c. dormir.
d. parler au téléphone.

3. Avec mes copains, j'aime mieux...
a. faire du sport.
b. manger au restaurant.
c. faire les magasins.
d. danser.
e. nager.
f. aller au cinéma.

4. J'aime surtout...
a. le chocolat.
b. les hamburgers.
c. la salade.
d. les frites.
e. la pizza.

5. J'aime aussi...
a. le ski.
b. le vélo.
c. le volley.
d. le basket-ball.

6. Je n'aime pas...
a. les escargots.
b. la pollution.
c. l'école.
d. la violence.
e. les dentistes.
f. les examens.

b. Compare your responses to the poll with those of a classmate. Which interests do you have in common?

32 *trente-deux*   CHAPITRE 1   Faisons connaissance!

GRAMMAIRE · Subject pronouns and -er verbs

Additional Grammar Practice, pp. R27–R28

The verb **aimer** has different forms. In French, the verb forms change according to the subjects just as they do in English: *I like, you like,* but *he* or *she like_s_.*

Look at the chart below. Most **-er** verbs, that is, verbs whose infinitive ends in **-er,** follow this pattern.

aimer *(to like)*

J'aime ⎫	Nous aim**ons** ⎫
Tu aim**es** ⎬ les vacances.	Vous aim**ez** ⎬ les vacances.
Il/Elle aime ⎭	Ils/Elles aim**ent** ⎭

PA
pp. 9–10,
Acts. 14, 17

GV
pp. 7–9,
Acts. 18–23

• The forms **aime, aimes,** and **aiment** sound the same.

• The subject pronouns in French are **je/j'** *(I)*, **tu** *(you)*, **il** *(he* or *it)*, **elle** *(she or it)*, **nous** *(we)*, **vous** *(you)*, **ils** *(they)*, and **elles** *(they)*.

• Notice that there are two pronouns for *they.* Use **elles** to refer to a group of females. Use **ils** to refer to a group of males or a group of males and females.

• **Tu** and **vous** both mean *you.* Use **vous** when you talk to more than one person or to an adult who is not a family member. Use **tu** when you talk to a friend, family member, or someone your own age.

• Noun subjects take the same verb forms as their pronouns.

Philippe aime la salade.	**Sophie et Julie aiment** faire du sport.
Il aime la salade.	**Elles aiment** faire du sport.

26 «Tu» ou «vous»?

a. Would you use **tu** or **vous** to greet the following people? How would you ask them if they like a certain thing or activity?

M. et Mme Roland	**Mlle Normand**	**Flore et Loïc**	**Lucie**
Vous aimez... ?	Vous aimez... ?	Vous aimez... ?	Tu aimes... ?

b. Now complete the following phrases to tell what these people like, according to the illustrations above.   Answers may vary.

1. M. et Mme Roland...   aiment l'anglais.
2. Mlle Normand...   aime voyager.
3. Flore et moi, nous...   aimons faire du sport.
4. Moi, je m'appelle Lucie. J'...   aime étudier.

Presentation

Grammaire Introduce this section by reviewing subject pronouns. Ask students to recall any subject pronouns they have learned in French. Supply the ones they don't know, without using English, by pointing to individuals and groups as you say the pronouns in French: **nous, ils, elles...** Then, have students look at the **Grammaire** and repeat the pronouns and verb forms after you. You might want to discuss **liaison** and **élision** at this time. See **Prononciation** on page 59 for information on **liaison** and **élision.**

Teaching Suggestions

Grammaire This would be a good time for students to play a variation of the game "Introductions" on page 15J, using the verb **aimer.** Student A might start by saying **J'aime faire les magasins.** Student B repeats that and then adds his or her own preferred activity. The game continues until a student makes a mistake, at which point the game could start all over again with the student who made the mistake, or with the following student.

26 To extend this activity, have students pair off. Call out two names of people pictured here: Lucie and Mlle Normand. Partners should assume the identity of these people and create a brief dialogue between them, using **tu** or **vous** appropriately.

Additional Practice

26 You might want to hold up pictures of people of various ages, asking **tu ou vous?**

27 Qu'est-ce qu'ils aiment faire?

Your French pen pal wants to know what your friends like to do. Use the following photographs as cues.

Julio
Il aime lire.

Robert
Il aime voyager.

Mark, David et Thomas
Ils aiment nager.

Pam
Elle aime faire les magasins.

Marie
Elle aime faire de l'équitation.

Eric
Il aime parler au téléphone.

Karen
Elle aime écouter de la musique.

Blair
Elle aime dormir.

Emily et Raymond
Ils aiment danser.

28 Les vedettes! *Celebrities!*

a. Make a list of three public figures you admire (movie stars, musicians, athletes, and so on). Write down one or two things you think each person might like to do.

   Shaquille O'Neal aime faire du sport, surtout *(especially)* du basket-ball!

b. Now, get together with a classmate. Tell your partner what one of the celebrities you've chosen likes to do. Use **il** or **elle** instead of the person's name. Your partner will try to identify the celebrity. Take turns.

34 *trente-quatre* CHAPITRE 1 Faisons connaissance!

29 Enquête *Survey*

Get together with three classmates. Ask questions to find out who shares your likes and dislikes. After you've discovered what you have in common, report your findings to the rest of the class.

> Paul et moi, nous aimons le français et l'anglais, mais nous n'aimons pas le sport.

30 Mon journal

Expand your previous journal entry by adding the activities you like and dislike. Tell which activities you and your friends like to do together. Find or draw pictures to illustrate the activities.

P R O N O N C I A T I O N

Intonation
See scripts and answers on p. 15H.

CD 1 Trs. 25–29

As you speak, your voice rises and falls. This is called *intonation*.

A. A prononcer

In French, your voice rises at the end of each group of words within a statement and falls at the end of a statement. Repeat each of the following phrases:

J'aime les frites, les hamburgers et la pizza.

Il aime le football, mais il n'aime pas le vélo.

If you want to change a statement into a question, raise your voice at the end of the sentence. Repeat these questions.

Tu aimes l'anglais?

Tu t'appelles Julie?

B. A écouter

Decide whether each of the following is a statement or a question.

C. A écrire

You're going to hear two short dialogues. Write down what the people say.

Mon journal

30 For an additional journal entry suggestion for Chapter 1, see *Practice and Activity Book,* page 145.

Language Note

Prononciation You might tell students that the rising intonation indicates a yes-no question, rather than a question that seeks information.

Teaching Suggestion

Have students read the **Mise en train** again, silently or aloud in small groups. They might copy some of the text into their notebooks, underlining functional expressions, circling activities or things, and highlighting **ne... pas** or other structures. This will help them to review functions, vocabulary, and grammar.

CLOSE

To close this **étape,** have students tell, either orally or in writing, what activities they like to do, both on their own and with friends. You might have volunteers speak at the beginning or end of class over several days. You might also want to play **Jacques a dit...** on page 15J at this point.

ASSESS

Quiz 1-3A, Quiz 1-3B, *Testing Program,* pp. 9–12

Audio CD 1, Tr. 33

Performance Assessment

When students have finished Activity 28 on page 34, have them pair off and take turns interviewing the celebrities they have chosen to be. The interviewer might use a dummy microphone, and the celebrity might dress in an identifiable costume. If possible, have students videotape their interviews.

Teaching Suggestion

Prononciation After students have finished the activities, you might have them make up their own statements and questions about likes and dislikes and have them practice in pairs or small groups. Pairs or groups could then volunteer to recite their statements and questions in front of the class, using the proper intonation.

READING STRATEGY

Using titles, subtitles, illustrations, and captions

Teacher Note

For an additional reading, see *Practice and Activity Book,* page 11.

PREREADING
Activities A–C

Motivating Activity

Ask students if they have pen pals or friends they write to, why people want pen pals, and when writing is better than phoning. You might pass around postcards from abroad or any ads for pen pals you may have found. Let students know that many students abroad want pen pals and that a number of organizations exist that match up young people who want to correspond. See page T52 for addresses. Point out that exchanging letters often leads to exchanging visits.

READING
Activities D–F

Thinking Critically

Analyzing Ask students to group the pen pals by interest. Then, ask them to choose the pen pal(s) they would most like to correspond with.

Teaching Suggestion

To check for understanding, ask simple questions about the pen pals. **(Il/Elle s'appelle comment? Qui aime la musique?)**

LISONS!

When you look through French magazines, you'll often find a section where people place personal or business ads.

DE BONS CONSEILS
You can often figure out what a reading selection is about simply by looking at the titles, subtitles, illustrations, and captions.

A. Look at the pictures and titles of this article from a French magazine. What do you think the article is about? pen pals

B. Do you remember what you've learned about cognates? Can you find at least five cognates in this article? See answers below.

C. What do you think **Petites annonces** means? Classified ads

D. Which of the pen pals would you choose if you were searching for the following? See answers below.

Quelqu'un qui *(someone who)*…

aime faire les boutiques

aime les animaux

parle français et espagnol

aime la musique et le cinéma

aime le rap et la techno

36 *trente-six*

COPAINS ★ COPINES ★ COPAINS

PETITES

Christiane Saulnier
Marseille

Si vous aimez la télévision, les animaux et les vacances, qu'est-ce que vous attendez pour m'écrire et m'envoyer votre photo! Je voudrais correspondre avec des filles ou des garçons de 13 à 16 ans. J'attends votre réponse avec impatience!

Karim Marzouk
Tunis, Tunisie

J'adorerais recevoir des lettres de personnes habitant le monde entier; j'adore voyager, écouter de la musique, aller au concert et lire sur la plage. J'aime bien les langues et je parle aussi l'arabe et l'espagnol. A bientôt.

Mireille Lacombe
Nantes

J'ai 15 ans et je voudrais bien correspondre avec des filles et des garçons de 13 à 17 ans. J'aime le rap et surtout la techno. Je fais aussi de l'équitation. Ecrivez-moi vite et je promets de vous répondre (photos S.V.P.)!

Didier Kouassi
Abidjan, Côte d'Ivoire

La techno me fait délirer et je suis aussi très sportif. Je cherche des correspondants filles ou garçons entre 15 et 17 ans. N'hésitez pas à m'écrire!

NARFON CASTLE

Answers

B *Possible answers*
correspondre, réponse, lettres, musique, science-fiction, fan, âge, adresse, photo d'identité

D Aime faire les boutiques—Hugues Vallet
Aime les animaux—Christiane Saulnier
Parle français et espagnol—Karim Marzouk
Aime la musique et le cinéma—Amélie Perrin
Aime le rap et la techno—Mireille Lacombe

COPINES ★ COPAINS ★ COPINES

ANNONCES

Laurence Simon
Le Marin, Martinique

J'ai 16 ans, je suis dingue de sport, j'aime les soirs de fête entre copains. Le week-end, j'aime faire les magasins. Alors, si vous me ressemblez, dépêchez-vous de m'écrire. Réponse assurée à 100%!

Etienne Hubert
Poitiers

Je suis blond aux yeux bleus, assez grand, timide mais très sympa. J'aime sortir et j'aime lire la science-fiction. Je cherche des amis entre 14 et 16 ans. Répondez vite!

Hugues Vallet
La Rochelle

Je voudrais correspondre avec des filles et des garçons de 16 à 18 ans. J'aime sortir, délirer et faire les boutiques. Je suis fan de Vanessa Paradis et de Julia Roberts. Alors, j'attends vos lettres!

Amélie Perrin
Périgord

Je voudrais correspondre avec des jeunes de 14 à 17 ans qui aiment faire la fête, écouter de la musique et aller au cinéma. Moi, j'étudie la danse et la photographie. Ecrivez-moi et je me ferai une joie de vous répondre.

Vous voulez correspondre avec des gens sympa? Écrivez votre petite annonce en précisant vos nom, prénom, âge et adresse, et en y joignant une photo d'identité.

E. Several of your friends are looking for pen pals. Based on their wishes, find a good match for each of them in **Petites annonces.**

1. My pen pal should like sports.
   Didier Kouassi
   Laurence Simon

2. I'd like to hear from someone who likes going out.
   Etienne Hubert,
   Hugues Vallet

3. I'm looking for a pen pal who likes to go to the movies.
   Amélie Perrin

4. It would be great to have a pen pal who enjoys shopping.
   Laurence Simon,
   Hugues Vallet

5. I'd like to hear from someone from Africa.
   Karim Marzouk,
   Didier Kouassi

6. I'd like a pen pal who likes to travel.
   Karim Marzouk

F. If you want to place an ad for a pen pal, what should you do?
   See answers below.

G. One of your classmates is looking for a pen pal. Make a short list of questions that will help you identify which pen pal has the most in common with your classmate. Then, interview your classmate, compare his or her answers with the ads included in **Petites annonces,** and decide which pen pal would be the best match. Find out if your classmate agrees with your decision.

H. Jot down a few things you might like to include in your own letter requesting a pen pal. Using your notes, write your own request for a pen pal like the ones you read in **Petites annonces.**

POSTREADING
Activities G-H

Teaching Suggestion

French exchange students in your area or advanced students of French are possible pen pals. You might have classes exchange letters. It might be fun for students to assume a pen name (**nom de plume**) so that they are corresponding with a mystery pen pal. Later in the year, you can arrange a party where the correspondents finally meet.

Thinking Critically

Analyzing Ask students the following: What can be gained from corresponding with someone from another culture? Are you already familiar with other cultures? Is there any culture in particular that interests you? Have you traveled to other regions in the United States? What, if anything, seemed strange or different to you? If your region has several ethnic groups, how do they interact? Are there any students from other cultures at your school? Students might interview them to find out what was difficult for them when they came to this country (being careful, of course, to respect their privacy). You might discuss with students appropriate ways to begin their interviews with foreign students.

Answers
F Send your name, age, photo, and address to the magazine.

The **Mise en pratique** reviews and integrates all four skills and culture in preparation for the Chapter Test.

 For Individual Needs

1 Kinesthetic Learners You might ask groups to prepare and act out two scenes that contrast French and American greetings.

2 Challenge You might have students pretend to call the O.I.C. and leave information about themselves on the organization's answering machine. Students might make an audiocassette, which could be used as an oral portfolio entry.

 Portfolio

3 Oral This activity is appropriate for students' oral portfolios. For portfolio suggestions, see the *Alternative Assessment Guide,* page 18.

MISE EN PRATIQUE

CD-ROM Disc 1

The *CD-ROM Program* offers guided recording and writing activities to practice oral and written skills and to review material from each chapter.

1 Do the following photos represent French culture, American culture, or both?

1. French

2. both

3. French

4. American

5. French

 2 **L'Organisation internationale de correspondants (l'O.I.C.),** a pen pal organization you wrote to, has left a phone message on your answering machine. Listen carefully to the message and write down your pen pal's name, age, phone number, likes, and dislikes.
CD 1 Tr. 30
See scripts and answers on p. 15H.

 3 Tell a classmate in French about your new pen pal.

Nom :

Age :

Numéro :

Aime :

N'aime pas :

Career Path

Have students imagine that they are employed by an organization like the **Organisation internationale de correspondants.** How would their knowledge of French and English help them with their job? With whom would they most likely be working? Have students think of similar jobs that would require knowledge of a foreign language (coordinator of an exchange program, working for a college study abroad office).

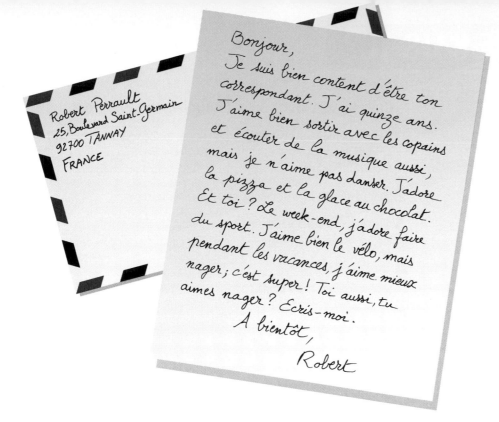

Bonjour,

Je suis bien content d'être ton correspondant. J'ai quinze ans. J'aime bien sortir avec les copains et écouter de la musique aussi, mais je n'aime pas danser. J'adore la pizza et la glace au chocolat. Et toi ? Le week-end, j'adore faire du sport. J'aime bien le vélo, mais pendant les vacances, j'aime mieux nager ; c'est super ! Toi aussi, tu aimes nager ? Écris-moi.

A bientôt,

Robert

Robert Perrault
25, Boulevard Saint-Germain
92700 TANNAY
FRANCE

Teaching Suggestion

5 Remind students to use Robert's letter as a model for their own.

 Portfolio

5 Written You may want to ask students to write their letters on stationery and keep them in their portfolios. Students might also record their letter as if they were going to send an audiocassette to Robert. They might want to include their favorite song or get members of their family to say **Bonjour!** Have students write a script for the recording. For portfolio suggestions, see the *Alternative Assessment Guide,* page 18.

4 You've received your first letter from Robert Perrault. Read it twice— the first time for general understanding, the second time for details. Then, answer the questions below in English.

1. How old is Robert? 15
2. What sports does he like? biking, swimming
3. What foods does he like? pizza, chocolate ice cream
4. What doesn't he like to do? dance

 5 Now, answer Robert's letter. Begin your reply with **Cher Robert.** Be sure to . . .

- introduce yourself.
- ask how he's doing.
- tell about your likes and dislikes.
- ask him about other likes and dislikes he might have.
- answer his questions to you.
- say goodbye.

6

JEU DE ROLE

A French exchange student has just arrived at your school. How would you find out his or her name? Age? Likes and dislikes? Act out the scene with a partner. Take turns playing the role of the French student.

Video Wrap-Up

- **VIDEO PROGRAM,**
  Videocassette 1, 07:46–19:46
- **VIDEODISC PROGRAM,**
  Videodisc 1, Side A

At this time, you might want to use the video resources for additional review and enrichment. See *Video Guide* or *Videodisc Guide* for suggestions regarding the following:
- **Salut, les copains!**
  (Dramatic episode)
- **Panorama Culturel**
  (Interviews)
- **Vidéoclips**
  (Authentic footage)

QUE SAIS-JE?

This page is intended to help students prepare for the Chapter Test. It is a brief checklist of the major points covered in the chapter. The students should be reminded that this is only a checklist and does not necessarily include everything that will appear on the test.

Teaching Suggestions

This section can be used as a written review assignment, as an oral review in class, or as the basis for a review game. One possible game is tic tac toe. Divide the class into two teams, one representing X, the other O. Contestants choose a square, and you ask them a question from **Que sais-je?** If they answer correctly, they win the square they chose. If their answer is incorrect, the other team may choose the same or another square. The team that wins three squares in a row wins the game.

7 To review the **vous** form, have students ask pairs of students if they like what is pictured here.

Can you greet people and say goodbye? p. 22

Can you ask how people are and tell how you are? p. 23

Can you ask someone's name and age and give yours? pp. 24–25

Can you express likes, dislikes, and preferences? pp. 26, 32

Can you use what you've learned in this chapter?

1 How would you say hello and goodbye to the following people? What gestures would you use?   See answers below.

   1. a classmate   2. your French teacher

2 Can you ask how someone is?   Ça va?/Comment ça va?

3 If someone asks you how you are, what do you say if . . .

   1. you feel great?   2. you feel OK?   3. you don't feel well?
      Super!   Pas mal.   Pas terrible.

4 How would you . . .

   1. ask someone's name?   2. tell someone your name?
      Tu t'appelles comment?   Je m'appelle...

5 How would you . . .

   1. find out someone's age?   2. tell someone how old you are?
      Tu as quel âge?   J'ai... ans.

6 Can you tell what you like and dislike, using the verb **aimer**?   See answers below.

   1. horseback riding   4. shopping
   2. soccer   5. the movies
   3. going out with friends

7 Can you ask a friend in French if he or she likes . . .   See answers below.

a.   b.   c.

d.   e.

8 Can you tell in French what these people like, dislike, or prefer?

   1. Robert never studies.   Robert n'aime pas étudier.
   2. Emilie thinks reading is the greatest.   Emilie adore lire.
   3. Hervé prefers pizza.   Hervé préfère la pizza.
   4. Nathalie never goes to the beach.   Nathalie n'aime pas la plage.
   5. Nicole is always biking or playing soccer.   Nicole aime le vélo et le football.

Answers
1 1. Hello—bonjour, salut; Goodbye—au revoir, salut, tchao, à bientôt, à tout à l'heure; boys shake hands with other boys and use the **bise** with girls, and girls use the **bise** with both boys and girls
   2. Hello—bonjour; Goodbye—au revoir, à demain, à bientôt, à tout à l'heure; hand wave/no specific gesture

6 *Possible answers*
   1. J'aime faire de l'équitation.
   2. Je n'aime pas le football.
   3. J'aime mieux sortir avec les copains.
   4. Je n'aime pas faire les magasins.
   5. J'aime le cinéma.
7 a. Tu aimes étudier?
   b. Tu aimes regarder la télévision?
   c. Tu aimes danser?
   d. Tu aimes le ski?
   e. Tu aimes l'école?

PREMIERE ETAPE

Greeting people and saying goodbye

Bonjour! *Hello!*
Salut! *Hi! or Goodbye!*
Au revoir! *Goodbye!*
A tout à l'heure! *See you later!*
A bientôt. *See you soon.*
A demain. *See you tomorrow.*
Tchao! *Bye!*
madame (Mme) *ma'am; Mrs.*
mademoiselle (Mlle) *miss; Miss*
monsieur (M.) *sir; Mr.*

Asking how people are and telling how you are

(Comment) ça va? *How's it going?*

Ça va. *Fine.*
Super! *Great!*
Très bien. *Very well.*
Comme ci, comme ça. *So-so.*
Bof! *(expression of indifference)*
Pas mal. *Not bad.*
Pas terrible. *Not so great.*
Et toi? *And you?*

Asking someone's name and giving yours

Tu t'appelles comment? *What's your name?*
Je m'appelle... *My name is . . .*
Il/Elle s'appelle comment? *What's his/her name?*

Il/Elle s'appelle... *His/Her name is . . .*

Asking someone's age and giving yours

Tu as quel âge? *How old are you?*
J'ai... ans. *I am . . . years old.*
douze *twelve*
treize *thirteen*
quatorze *fourteen*
quinze *fifteen*
seize *sixteen*
dix-sept *seventeen*
dix-huit *eighteen*

Teaching Suggestion
You might want to use the *Teaching Transparencies* for Chapter 1 to review functional expressions and vocabulary.

DEUXIEME ETAPE

Expressing likes, dislikes, and preferences about things

Moi, j'aime (bien)... *I (really) like . . .*
Je n'aime pas... *I don't like . . .*
J'aime mieux... *I prefer . . .*
Je préfère... *I prefer . . .*
J'adore... *I adore . . .*
Tu aimes... ? *Do you like . . . ?*
les amis (m.) *friends*
l'anglais (m.) *English*
le chocolat *chocolate*

le cinéma *the movies*
les concerts (m.) *concerts*
l'école (f.) *school*
les escargots (m.) *snails*
les examens (m.) *tests*
le football *soccer*
le français *French*
les frites (f.) *French fries*
la glace *ice cream*
les hamburgers (m.) *hamburgers*
les magasins (m.) *stores*
les maths (f.) *math*
la pizza *pizza*

la plage *beach*
le ski *skiing*
le sport *sports*
les vacances (f.) *vacation*
le vélo *biking*

Other useful expressions

et *and*
mais *but*
non *no*
oui *yes*
ou *or*

CHAPTER 1 ASSESSMENT

CHAPTER TEST
• *Testing Program*, pp. 13–18
• *Audio Compact Discs*, Audio CD 1, Tracks 34–36

SPEAKING TEST
• *Testing Program*, p. 343

TEST GENERATOR
 • Chapter 1

ALTERNATIVE ASSESSMENT

Performance Assessment
• You might want to use the **Jeu de Rôle** on page 39 as a cumulative performance assessment activity.
• *Alternative Assessment Guide*, p. 32

 Portfolio Assessment
• *Alternative Assessment Guide*
Oral: p. 18
Written: p. 18

CD-ROM ASSESSMENT
• *Interactive CD-ROM Program*, Disc 1
A toi de parler
A toi d'écrire
• *Alternative Assessment Guide*, p. 46

TROISIEME ETAPE

Expressing likes, dislikes, and preferences about activities

aimer *to like*
danser *to dance*
dormir *to sleep*
écouter de la musique *to listen to music*
étudier *to study*

faire de l'équitation *to go horseback riding*
faire les magasins *to go shopping*
faire le ménage *to do housework*
faire du sport *to play sports*
lire *to read*
nager *to swim*
parler au téléphone *to talk on the phone*

regarder la télé *to watch TV*
sortir avec les copains *to go out with friends*
voyager *to travel*

Other useful expressions

aussi *also*
surtout *especially*

For subject pronouns, see page 33.

🏰 Game

DESSINER, C'EST GAGNER Divide the class into two or more teams. A volunteer from the first team goes to the board. Show the student a vocabulary word or expression by pointing it out in the book or by using a flashcard. The student has 30 seconds to illustrate the word for his or her team, who must say the correct French word or expression within the time limit. Teams alternate turns.

Chapitre 2 : Vive l'école!
Chapter Overview

Mise en train pp. 44–46	La rentrée

	FUNCTIONS	GRAMMAR	CULTURE	RE-ENTRY
Première étape pp. 47–50	• Agreeing and disagreeing, p. 50	• Using **si** instead of **oui** to contradict a negative statement, p. 50	• **Note Culturelle,** The French educational system/**Le bac,** p. 49 • Realia: *Baccalauréat 1996,* p. 49	• Greetings (**Chapitre 1**) • The verb **aimer** (**Chapitre 1**) • The definite articles **le, la, l',** and **les** (**Chapitre 1**) • Subject pronouns (**Chapitre 1**)
Deuxième étape pp. 51–56	• Asking for and giving information, p. 51 • Telling when you have class, p. 54	• The verb **avoir,** p. 51	• Realia: French class schedule, p. 52 • **Note Culturelle,** 24-hour time, p. 54 • **Panorama Culturel,** Curriculum in French schools, p. 56	• Numbers for telling time (**Chapitre 1**) • Subject pronouns (**Chapitre 1**)
Troisième étape pp. 57–59	• Asking for and expressing opinions, p. 57		• **Note Culturelle,** The French grading system, p. 57	• The verb **aimer** (**Chapitre 1**) • Expressing likes, dislikes, and preferences about things (**Chapitre 1**)

Prononciation p. 59	**Liaison** Audio CD 2, Tracks 12–14	**À écrire** (dictation) Audio CD 2, Tracks 15–17	
Lisons! pp. 60–61	**Sondage : Les lycéens ont-ils le moral?**	**Reading Strategy** Using visual clues to determine meaning	
Review pp. 62–65	**Mise en pratique,** pp. 62–63	**Que sais-je?** p. 64	**Vocabulaire,** p. 65

Assessment Options

Testing Program
- Première étape, Quiz 2-1A, Quiz 2-1B, pp. 27–30
- Deuxième étape, Quiz 2-2A, Quiz 2-2B, pp. 31–34
- Troisième étape, Quiz 2-3A, Quiz 2-3B, pp. 35–38
- Chapter Test, pp. 39–44
- Speaking Test, p. 343

Audio Compact Discs
- Audio CD 2, Tracks 19–24

Interactive CD-ROM Program
- Mise en pratique (A toi de parler, A toi d'écrire)
- *CD-ROM Teacher's Guide,* Assessment Options, p. 8

Alternative Assessment Guide
- Portfolio Assessment, p. 19
- Performance Assessment, p. 33
- CD-ROM Assessment, p. 47

Test Generator
- Chapter 2

PRINT	MEDIA

Pupil's Edition, pp. 42–65

 Audio Compact Discs
• Textbook Listening Activities: Audio CD 2, Tracks 1–18

Interactive CD-ROM Program Teacher's Guide, pp. 5–8

 Interactive CD-ROM Program
• Disc 1

Videodisc Guide
• Teaching Suggestions, pp. 19–23
• Activity Masters, pp. 24–26

 Videodisc Program
• Videodisc 1, Side B

Video Guide
• Teaching Suggestions, pp. 12–13
• Activity Masters, pp. 14–16

 Video Program
• Videocassette 1
• Videocassette 5 (captioned version)

Listening Activities
• Student Response Forms for Textbook Listening Activities, pp. 11–13
• Additional Listening Activities 2-1 to 2-6, pp. 15–17
• Additional Listening Activities (song), p. 18
• Scripts and Answers, pp. 107–111

 Audio Compact Discs
• Textbook Listening Activities: Audio CD 2, Tracks 1–18
• Additional Listening Activities: Audio CD 2, Tracks 25–31

Teaching Transparencies
• Teaching Transparency Masters 2-1 to 2-3 (Situations) and 2-A to 2-B (Vocabulary)
• Teaching Suggestions 2-1 to 2-3 and 2-A to 2-B

 Teaching Transparencies
• Situations 2-1 to 2-3
• Vocabulary 2-A to 2-B

Testing Program
• Grammar and Vocabulary Quizzes, **Etape** Quizzes, and Chapter Test, pp. 27–44
• Score Sheet, Scripts, and Answers, pp. 45–52

 Audio Compact Discs
• Assessment Items: Audio CD 2, Tracks 19–24

 Test Generator
• Chapter 2

Alternative Assessment Guide
• Portfolio Assessment, p. 19
• Performance Assessment, p. 33
• CD-ROM Assessment, p. 47

 Grammar and Vocabulary Workbook, pp. 10–16

 Practice and Activity Book, pp. 13–24

Activities for Communication
• Communicative Activities, pp. 7–10
• Realia and Teaching Suggestions, pp. 80–84
• Situation Cards, pp. 139–140

Lesson Planner
• Lesson Plan, pp. 8–12

MISE EN TRAIN, pp. 44–46

Video
- Show *La rentrée.* For Video Synopsis, Teaching Suggestions, Activity Master, and Scripts, see the *Video Guide* or the *Videodisc Guide.*

Captioned Video
- Play *La rentrée* on Videocassette 5 and have students identify the classes that the students discuss.

Audio
- Play the recording of the **Mise en train** with pauses as students read along. Have students practice pronunciation by repeating individual sentences after they hear them.

PREMIERE ETAPE, pp. 47–50

Video
- While students watch *La rentrée,* have them listen for exchanges that model talking about school subjects. For more suggestions, see p. 21 of the *Videodisc Guide.*

Audio
- Textbook Listening Activity 7 practices the vocabulary for school subjects.
- To have students practice the expressions for agreeing and disagreeing, play Textbook Listening Activity 11.
- Additional Listening Activities 2-1 and 2-2 practice school subject vocabulary.

Transparencies
- Use *Teaching Transparencies 2-1* and *2-A* and the Teaching Suggestions to present and practice the vocabulary for school subjects.

CD-ROM (Disc 1)
- **Jeu des paires** (Activity 1) practices the vocabulary for school subjects. For suggestions, see p. 6 of the *CD-ROM Teacher's Guide.*

DEUXIEME ETAPE, pp. 51–55

Video
- While students watch *La rentrée,* have them listen for exchanges that model asking for and giving information about school subjects. For more suggestions, see pp. 21–22 of the *Videodisc Guide.*

Audio
- To have students practice the days of the week and the vocabulary for school subjects, use Textbook Listening Activity 18.
- Use Textbook Listening Activity 20 to have students practice official time and the vocabulary for school subjects.
- Additional Listening Activity 2-3 practices the days of the week and official time.
- To have students review expressions for asking for and giving information, use Additional Listening Activity 2-4.

Transparencies
- Use *Teaching Transparency 2-2* and the Teaching Suggestions to have students practice using official time and the vocabulary for school subjects.
- Use *Teaching Transparency 2-B* and the Teaching Suggestions to present and have students practice the days of the week.

CD-ROM (Disc 1)
- **Les mots qui manquent** (Activity 2) practices the verb **avoir.**
- To have students practice school subject vocabulary, official time, and days of the week, use **Le bon choix** (Activity 3).
- **Jeu des paires** (Activity 4) practices official time and numbers from 0 to 59.
- For suggestions, see pp. 6–7 of the *CD-ROM Teacher's Guide.*

PANORAMA CULTUREL, p. 56

Video
- Show the interviews. For Video Synopsis, Teaching Suggestions, Activity Masters, and Scripts, see the *Video Guide* or the *Videodisc Guide.*

Audio
- Play the **Panorama Culturel** as students read along. Remind students that they might not be able to understand everything each person says, but they should try to recognize words and deduce global meaning.

CD-ROM (Disc 1)
- Have students do the **Panorama Culturel** activity for Chapter 2 after showing them the video. For suggestions, see p. 7 of the *CD-ROM Teacher's Guide.*

TROISIEME ETAPE, pp. 57–59

Video
- While students watch *La rentrée,* have them listen for exchanges that model expressing opinions. For more suggestions, see p. 22 of the *Videodisc Guide.*

Audio
- Use Textbook Listening Activity 24 to have students practice expressing opinions.
- Additional Listening Activity 2-5 practices the phrases for expressing opinions.

Transparencies
- Use *Teaching Transparency 2-3* and the Teaching Suggestions to have students practice giving opinions about school subjects.

CD-ROM (Disc 1)
- **Chacun à sa place** (Activity 5) practices expressions for agreeing and disagreeing and for expressing favorable and unfavorable opinions.

- **Méli-mélo** (Activity 6) practices sequencing the days of the week and expressing favorable and unfavorable opinions.
- For suggestions, see p. 7 of the *CD-ROM Teacher's Guide.*

MISE EN PRATIQUE, pp. 62–63

Video
- Replay *La rentrée* in its entirety and ask students to listen for the exchanges in which the characters agree and disagree, ask for and give information, and ask for and express opinions.

CD-ROM (Disc 1)
- Have students do the **En contexte** to practice giving opinions, agreeing and disagreeing, and giving information about school subjects and schedules. You may want to use the suggestions on p. 6 of the *CD-ROM Teacher's Guide.*
- Have students practice their writing and speaking skills using the **A toi d'écrire** and **A toi de parler** activities. For a detailed description of these features, see pp. 7–8 of the *CD-ROM Teacher's Guide.*
- For Assessment Options, see p. 8 of the *CD-ROM Teacher's Guide.*

Test Generator
- Use the Test Generator to create review material for students taking the Chapter Test or to prepare an alternate test.

VIDEOCLIPS

Video
- Show the **Vidéoclip.** For Video Synopsis, Teaching Suggestions, Activity Master, and Scripts, see the *Video Guide* or the *Videodisc Guide.*

Videodisc Program
Videodisc 1, Side B
Videodisc Guide, pp. 17–26

Chapitre 2 : Vive l'école!
Barcode Directory

Barcodes A and B access **Mise en train** and **Mise en train (suite)** in their entirety. Subsequent barcodes show specific segments of *La rentrée.* The barcode numbers correspond to the scene numbers as they appear on the video.

MISE EN TRAIN

La rentrée **A**
Search 1, Play To 6820

Tiens, salut, Claire... **1**
Search 1, Play To 1868

Ecoutez,... **2**
Search 1869, Play To 2381

Salut! **3**
Search 2382, Play To 3368

Qu'est-ce qu'il y a? **4**
Search 3369, Play To 3547

Moi, j'adore... **5**
Search 3548, Play To 3702

Et après,... **6**
Search 3703, Play To 4144

Et toi, Jérôme,... **7**
Search 4145, Play To 4540

Tu aimes l'allemand? **8**
Search 4541, Play To 5230

Dis, tu as sport? **9**
Search 5231, Play To 5813

Tu vas voir... **10**
Search 5814, Play To 6820

La rentrée (suite) **B**
Search 6820, Play To 13490

PANORAMA CULTUREL

Tu as quels cours?

These barcodes access the three interviews of the **Panorama Culturel** presented in the *Pupil's Edition* as well as additional interviews.

First three interviews **1**
Search 13500, Play To 16170

All interviews **2**
Search 13500, Play To 20210

Patrice **3**
Search 14298, Play To 14674

Yannick **4**
Search 14675, Play To 15715

Amadou **5**
Search 15716, Play To 16170

Onélia **6**
Search 16171, Play To 16717

Eva **7**
Search 16718, Play To 17165

Lily-Christine **8**
Search 17166, Play To 17605

Morgan **9**
Search 17606, Play To 17976

Séverine **10**
Search 17977, Play To 18452

Julie **11**
Search 18453, Play To 18721

Isabelle **12**
Search 18722, Play To 19172

Jean-Christophe **13**
Search 19173, Play To 19753

Arnaud **14**
Search 19754, Play To 20210

ETAPES

To practice the grammar, vocabulary, and functions presented in each **étape**, see the barcodes and accompanying suggestions on pages 21–22 of the *Videodisc Guide.*

MISE EN PRATIQUE

This is additional footage modeling some of the expressions practiced in this chapter. You may want to use it to review the chapter.

Mise en pratique **1**

Search 31145, Play To 32103

Mise en pratique **2**

Search 32104, Play To 33663

VIDEOCLIPS

This is an authentic French music video.

Music video: *Tout ce que j'ai, tout ce que j'aime* **1**

Search 20705, Play To 30907

Chapitre 2 : Vive l'école!
CD-ROM Directory ● DISC 1

The following directory lists the *Interactive CD-ROM Program* activities for Chapter 2. For details and suggestions on how to use them, see pages 5–8 of the *CD-ROM Teacher's Guide*.

GLOBAL TASK	COMMUNICATIVE GOALS	ACTIVITY TYPE
Le jour de la rentrée Students talk to their new friend Cédric about schedules. They tell each other when they have certain classes and what they think of them.	To use chapter functions, vocabulary, and grammar in a lifelike conversation	**En contexte** *Interactive conversation*

	SUPPORTING ACTIVITIES	PUPIL'S EDITION	COMMUNICATIVE GOALS	ACTIVITY TYPE
Première étape	1. Vocabulaire	p. 47	To identify school subjects	**Jeu des paires** *Concentration®*
Deuxième étape	2. Grammaire	p. 51	To use the verb **avoir**	**Les mots qui manquent** *Tic Tac Toe*
	3. Vocabulaire	pp. 51–52	To understand school subjects, days of the week, official times, and parts of the school day	**Le bon choix** *Multiple choice*
	4. Comment dit-on... ?	pp. 52–54	To use official times and numbers from 0 to 59	**Jeu des paires** *Concentration®*
Troisième étape	5. Comment dit-on... ?	pp. 50, 57	To classify expressions for agreeing and disagreeing and for expressing favorable and unfavorable opinions	**Chacun à sa place** *Categories*
	6. Comment dit-on... ?	pp. 52, 57	To sequence the days of the week and to express opinions about classes	**Méli-mélo** *Sequencing*
Panorama Culturel	Panorama Culturel	p. 56	To listen to and understand native speakers talking about the classes they have	**Tu as quels cours?** *Presentation* **Le bon choix** *Multiple choice*

	APPLICATION	PUPIL'S EDITION	COMMUNICATIVE GOALS	ACTIVITY TYPE
Mise en pratique	A toi de parler	pp. 62–63	To create and record a conversation with a French teenager about classes	*Guided recording*
	A toi d'écrire	pp. 62–63	To write a journal entry, a schedule, a script, or a survey	*Guided writing*

Homework Suggestions

CHAPTER SECTION	PRESENTATION	HOMEWORK OPTIONS
Première étape	**Vocabulaire,** p. 47	Pupil's Edition, p. 49, Activity 10 Practice and Activity Book, pp. 14–15, Activities 2–5 Grammar and Vocabulary Workbook, pp. 10–11, Activities 1–4 CD-ROM, Disc 1, Activity 1
	Comment dit-on... ? p. 50	Practice and Activity Book, p. 15, Activity 6
	Note de grammaire, p. 50	Pupil's Edition, p. R28, Activities 1–2 Practice and Activity Book, p. 16, Activity 8 Grammar and Vocabulary Workbook, p. 11, Activity 5
Deuxième étape	**Vocabulaire,** p. 51	Grammar and Vocabulary Workbook, p. 12, Activity 6
	Grammaire, p. 51	Pupil's Edition, p. R29, Activities 3–4 Practice and Activity Book, p. 17, Activity 12 Grammar and Vocabulary Workbook, pp. 12–13, Activities 7–9 CD-ROM, Disc 1, Activity 2
	Vocabulaire, p. 52	Practice and Activity Book, pp. 18–19, Activities 14–15 Grammar and Vocabulary Workbook, pp. 13–14, Activities 10–12 CD-ROM, Disc 1, Activity 3
	Vocabulaire, p. 53	Practice and Activity Book, p. 17, Activity 11 Grammar and Vocabulary Workbook, pp. 14–15, Activities 13–14
	Comment dit-on... ? p. 54	Pupil's Edition, p. 55, Activity 23 Practice and Activity Book, p. 18, Activity 13 Grammar and Vocabulary Workbook, p. 15, Activities 15–17 CD-ROM, Disc 1, Activity 4
Troisième étape	**Comment dit-on... ?** p. 57	Pupil's Edition, p. 58, Activity 26; p. R29, Activities 5–6 Practice and Activity Book, pp. 20–21, Activities 17–19 Grammar and Vocabulary Workbook, p. 16, Activities 18–20 CD-ROM, Disc 1, Activities 5–6

Chapitre 2 : Vive l'école!
Textbook Listening Activities Scripts

For Student Response Forms, see *Listening Activities,* pp. 11–13.

Première étape

7 Ecoute! p. 48

CELINE Mais non! C'est de l'espagnol!

AURELIE Zut!

AURELIE Alors, qu'est-ce que c'est?

CELINE C'est un cours d'arts plastiques.
C'est ici, le français?

AURELIE Non. C'est la salle d'informatique.

AURELIE Voilà! Enfin. C'est le français.

CELINE Mais non! C'est de l'histoire!
Oh là là! Ce n'est pas ici non plus.

AURELIE Et là, qu'est-ce que c'est?

CELINE C'est la salle de travaux pratiques de chimie.

Answers to Activity 7
L'espagnol — 022
Les arts plastiques — 023
L'informatique — 323
L'histoire — 223
Les travaux pratiques de chimie — 222

11 Ecoute! p. 50

HELENE Salut, Gérard. Tu as physique maintenant?

GERARD Euh, oui.

HELENE Tu aimes ça?

GERARD Non, pas trop.

HELENE Moi, si! J'aime bien la physique!

GERARD Et toi, tu as quoi maintenant?

HELENE J'ai géométrie. J'adore!

GERARD Moi aussi! C'est super intéressant, mais j'aime mieux l'informatique.

Answers to Activity 11
Agree — la géométrie
Disagree — la physique

Deuxième étape

18 Ecoute! p. 53

1. Salut, Stéphanie. C'est Frédéric. Tu as quoi le lundi matin? Moi, le lundi, j'ai allemand, français, sport et sciences nat.

2. Salut, Stéphanie. C'est Nadine. Tu as quoi le jeudi? Le matin, j'ai maths, sciences nat et allemand. L'après-midi, j'ai français, géographie et musique. Et toi?

3. Salut! Ça va? Ici Georges. Tu as quoi le mercredi? Moi, j'ai maths, anglais, français et histoire/géo.

Answers to Activity 18
Frédéric — same
Nadine — different
Georges — same

20 Ecoute! p. 54

ANNE Salut, Jérôme. Tu as quoi maintenant?

JEROME C'est huit heures? Alors, j'ai anglais!

ANNE Et tu as espagnol à quelle heure?

JEROME Euh... quatorze heures quinze.

ANNE Moi, j'ai histoire à quatorze heures quinze. Et toi, tu as histoire à quelle heure?

JEROME J'ai histoire à neuf heures et après, j'ai maths à dix heures vingt. La récré, c'est à dix heures. J'aime ça!

Answers to Activity 20
Anglais — 8h00
Espagnol — 14h15
Histoire — 9h00
Maths — 10h20

*T*roisième étape

24 Ecoute! p. 57

ERIC   Dis, tu as sciences nat avec moi ce matin?

AURELIE   Oui. Comment tu trouves ça, les sciences nat?

ERIC   C'est génial!

AURELIE   Et on a aussi géographie cet aprèm, n'est-ce pas? Ça te plaît, la géo?

ERIC   Oui. C'est super! Tu n'aimes pas, toi?

AURELIE   Non, pas trop. Mais j'adore l'allemand. C'est cool.

ERIC   L'allemand? Mais c'est nul, l'allemand! J'aime mieux l'anglais. C'est plus intéressant.

AURELIE   Mais c'est plus difficile.

Answers to Activity 24
Eric aime les sciences nat, la géographie et l'anglais.
Eric n'aime pas l'allemand.
Aurélie aime l'allemand.
Aurélie n'aime pas la géographie.

*P*rononciation, p. 59

For the scripts for Parts A and B, see p. 59.

C. A écrire

(Dictation)

1. — Nous aimons l'informatique. C'est cool.
   — Moi, j'aime mieux les arts plastiques.

2. — Ils ont quoi mardi?
   — Ils ont anglais et physique.

*M*ise en pratique

1 p. 62

Le lycée aux Etats-Unis, c'est bizarre! On a chimie tous les matins à neuf heures cinq! Et on a sport, mais à quatorze heures quarante-six! Pourquoi «quarante-six»? On a latin à onze heures trente. Ça, c'est normal. Mais on a informatique l'après-midi à treize heures cinquante-deux! Je ne comprends pas l'emploi du temps américain!

Answers to Mise en pratique Activity 1
André thinks that his schedule is strange because some classes don't start exactly on the hour or half hour.
chimie — 9h05
sport — 14h46 (2:46 P.M.)
latin — 11h30
informatique — 13h52 (1:52 P.M.)

Chapitre 2 : Vive l'école!
Projects

Notre école
(Group Project)

ASSIGNMENT
Have small groups create a school map to help exchange students find their way around. If your school consists of more than one building, assign each group part of the school. Individual group maps may be combined to show the whole school.

MATERIALS
✂ **Students may need**
- Large pieces of paper or posterboard
- Pens and pencils
- Correction fluid
- Glue
- Markers or colored pencils

PREPARATION
Each group should make a list of the subjects taught in their assigned part of the school. They might need to see existing school maps and teacher rosters.

SUGGESTED SEQUENCE
First Sketch Groups should begin sketching their part of the school in pencil on a large piece of paper or posterboard. For the final drawing, students can retrace their work in pen, crayon, or marker. You might assign a different color to each section of the school. Then, referring to the lists they wrote, groups should label each room in French with the teacher's name, room number, and subject(s) taught in that room. You might want to give students the words for *hallway* (**le couloir**), *lockers* (**les casiers**), *ground floor* (**le rez-de-chausée**), *second floor* (**le premier étage**), *lunchroom* (**la cantine**), *teachers' lounge* (**la salle des professeurs**), and so on.

Peer Editing Groups should review one another's work to check for accuracy of content and spelling.

Final Drawing Encourage students to make their maps decorative as well as informative. They might add small drawings or photos to illustrate their maps. The maps can then be joined together to show the entire school. You might display them in the classroom or hallway.

Mon avenir
(Individual Project)

ASSIGNMENT
Students will make posters that show pictures of themselves and illustrate their career goals and the steps toward these goals. See the **Teacher Note** and **Group Work** for Activity 15 on page 52 for French names of professions.

MATERIALS
✂ **Students may need**
- Large pieces of plain or construction paper
- Scissors
- Pens or crayons
- Glue
- Magazines

PREPARATION
Students make a short list in French or English of several careers that interest them. They then add the names of several school subjects that are helpful for each career.

SUGGESTED SEQUENCE
First Draft Students pick their top career choice, which they will represent in a dream bubble above their picture. Next, to illustrate themselves, their goals, and the steps toward their goals, students might draw or cut out pictures from magazines. They might want to sketch a layout before they assemble the final poster.

Final Draft Students paste their illustrations on the poster and then label the pictures of their career choice with the names of the subjects necessary to prepare for that career. The posters might be displayed in the classroom.

GRADING THE PROJECT
You might base students' grades on timely completion of the assignment, presentation, and creativity.

Suggested Point Distribution (total = 100 points)

Completion of assignment . . . . 40 points

Presentation (spelling, neatness, organization) . . . . 40 points

Creativity . . . . 20 points

TEACHER NOTE
The posters might be included in students' portfolios along with the notes they made about career possibilities and the subjects required for each.

LOTO

In this game, students will practice telling time using the 24-hour system.

Have students make a grid, five squares across and five squares down. They should write **libre** in the center square. Have them fill in the squares by drawing clocks that show times on the hour, quarter past the hour, quarter to the hour, or half past the hour. Call out various times, using the 24-hour system. Students should make a small pencil mark in the corner of the appropriate square when their clock shows the time called. A student who marks a complete row of clocks horizontally, vertically, or diagonally wins, provided that he or she is able to say the times in each square correctly. After erasing the pencil marks, students are ready for another game.

Variation   Instead of clocks, students fill in their **Loto** grids with numbers from 20–59. Call out numbers or easy addition or subtraction problems. Students make a small pencil mark in the corner of the appropriate square when their number is called or the solution to the problem is given. Ask students who win to write additional problems while the rest of the class continues to play. They might then call out the problems they've written.

DESSIN ANIME

In this game, students will practice the names of school subjects in French.

Form two or more teams and have one player from one team go to the board. Whisper to the player the name of a subject in French. In 60 seconds or less, the student must make a drawing to represent that subject; letters and symbols are not allowed. The first team to correctly guess the French word for the subject wins a point. The turn then passes to another team. This game might also be played in small groups with individuals competing against one another. In this situation, students can choose subjects from the vocabulary list at the end of the chapter and draw them on paper or on transparencies.

Variation   You might want to have students act out the subjects instead of drawing them.

Chapitre 2
Vive l'école!

pp. 42–65

𝒰sing the Chapter Opener

Motivating Activity

Ask students what subjects they are taking and which ones are required of all students. Ask them if they like their schedules and their classes. Find out how much homework they have.

Teaching Suggestion

Have students look at the photos and identify the subjects depicted. Then, as you say the French name of each subject, ask students to raise their hand if they are currently taking the subject. Ask them if they like that particular subject. Next, ask students to look at the chapter objectives at the top of page 43 and try to match each photo caption with one of these objectives. (Photo 1: agreeing; Photo 2: telling time and giving information; Photo 3: expressing opinions)

Photo Flash!

① These teenagers are playing volleyball at a recreation center. In France, the **MJC (Maison des jeunes et de la culture)** offers numerous recreational activities, such as sports classes, art and drama classes, musical performances, and movies. Physical education **(EPS)** is just one of the courses students will discuss in this chapter.

C H A P I T R E

2
Vive l'école!

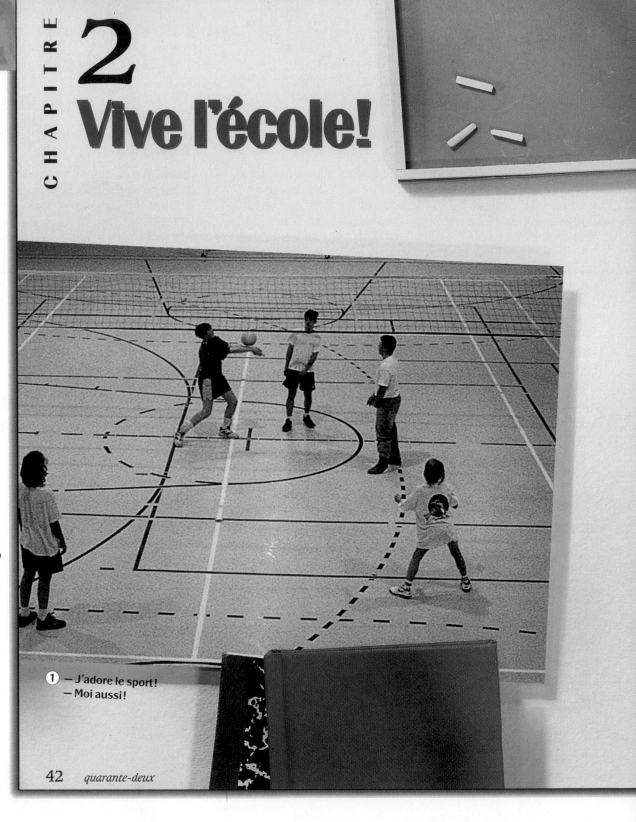

① — J'adore le sport!
— Moi aussi!

42   *quarante-deux*

When school starts, new schedules are the main topic of conversation, at least for a while. What classes do you have? How do you feel about them?

In this chapter you will learn

- to agree and disagree
- to ask for and give information
- to ask for and express opinions

And you will

- listen to French-speaking students talk about their classes
- read a French student's class schedule
- write about your own classes
- compare schools in francophone countries with schools in the United States

② J'ai latin à dix heures quinze.

③ Les arts plastiques, c'est génial!

quarante-trois **43**

Focusing on Outcomes

Call students' attention to the chapter objectives. Ask small groups to brainstorm expressions in English they might use to accomplish the chapter objectives. For example, to express opinions, they might list *boring, fun, OK,* and *interesting.*
NOTE: You may want to use the video to support the objectives. The self-check activities in **Que sais-je?** on page 64 help students assess their achievement of the objectives.

Teacher Note

In this chapter, students will ask about time (**à quelle heure?**), days of the week (**quel(s) jour(s)?**), school subjects (**quel(s) cours?**), and opinions (**comment tu trouves...?**). Other interrogative expressions will be presented later.

Photo Flash!

③ The students in this photo are busy in an art class. **Les arts plastiques** is a class that includes painting and sculpture as well as art history.

Block Scheduling

For suggestions about how to use *Allez, viens!* with block scheduling, see the *Lesson Planner,* pages 8–12.

Language-to-Language

You might tell students that **plastique** is not only a material, but like the English word *plastic,* it also means *capable of being shaped or formed,* and can be used to describe clay.

VIDEO PROGRAM
Videocassette 1
19:47–23:34
Videocassette 5
(captioned version)
09:17–13:03

OR VIDEODISC PROGRAM,
Videodisc 1, Side B

Search 1, Play To 6820

Video Synopsis

In this segment of the video, Claire and Ann meet Delphine on the way to school. They talk about their classes and whether or not they like them. Delphine is worried that she will be late, so she leaves. As Claire and Ann approach the school, they meet Marc and Jérôme. The four of them compare their schedules and express opinions about their classes. They discover they all have gym at the same time. Jérôme realizes he forgot his sneakers.

Motivating Activity

Before presenting the material, ask students to scan the photos and text to find the names of subjects they may be taking. Ask them if they can find any cognates other than school subjects (**super, courage, cool**). You may also wish to play the captioned version on Videocassette 5 without sound and have students watch for words that will give them clues about the teenagers' conversation.

Presentation

Before playing the video, have students answer the questions at the top of this page. After students view the video, ask the questions in Activity 1 on page 46 to check comprehension.

The **roman-photo** is an abridged version of the video episode.

Mise en train

La rentrée p. 13, Act. 1

CD 2
Trs. 1–2

Where do you think these teenagers are?
What do you think they're talking about?
How do you know?

Les jeunes de Poitiers :

Claire   Delphine   Marc

et du
Texas :

Jérôme   Ann

C'est la première semaine de cours…

Tu as quel cours maintenant?

Allemand. J'adore. Et toi, tu as quoi?

Sciences nat.

1

Ecoutez. Je ne veux pas être en retard. Bon courage!

Pourquoi?

2

C'est difficile, les sciences nat.

Mais non, c'est passionnant. Et le prof est sympa.

Alors, les garçons, ça boume?

3

Super.

Bof. Pas terrible.

Qu'est-ce qu'il y a?

Oh rien. J'ai maths.

4

Tu n'aimes pas les maths?

Non, c'est nul.

RESOURCES FOR MISE EN TRAIN

PRINT
• *Practice and Activity Book*, p. 13
• *Video Guide*, pp. 11–12, 14
• *Videodisc Guide*, pp. 17–20, 24

MEDIA
• *Video Program*, Videocassette 1, Videocassette 5 (captioned version)
• *Videodisc Program*, Videodisc 1, Side B
• *Audio Compact Discs*, CD 2, Trs. 1–2

Thinking Critically

Comparing and Contrasting
Ask students to examine the photos for similarities and differences between their school experience and schools in France. Students might consider the subjects offered, how students arrive at school, and how students dress.

Teaching Suggestion
Have students give the meanings for the following abbreviations:

nat = naturelles
maths = mathématiques
baskets = chaussures de basket-ball
aprèm = après-midi
géo = géographie

Ask students to list as many examples as they can of abbreviations of school subjects used in English. Some examples are *PE* or *phys ed* (physical education), *math* (mathematics), *psych* (psychology), *home ec* (home economics), *trig* (trigonometry), *ag* (agriculture), and *bio* (biology).

Culture Note
French students entering the **collège (en sixième)** must take a foreign language. Most **baccalauréat** exams require two foreign languages. Ask students why there might be more emphasis on foreign languages in French schools than in American schools. (Geographical location, greater need to communicate with other countries, and trade among countries in the European Union are some of the reasons students might give.)

MISE EN TRAIN

quarante-cinq 45

Video Integration

- **VIDEO PROGRAM,**
  Videocassette 1, 23:35–27:17
  Videocassette 5, 13:06–16:49
- **VIDEODISC PROGRAM,**
  Videodisc 1, Side B

Search 6820, Play To 13490

You may choose to continue with **La rentrée (suite)** at this time or wait until later in the chapter. The story continues later in the school day. Marc meets Jérôme after the last class of the morning. Marc tells him how he likes his math class. Jérôme is preoccupied about his sneakers and decides to go home during lunch to get them. He rides through the streets of Poitiers, rushing to get back to school in time. He returns, shoes in hand, only to find that gym class has been canceled! The teacher is sick, and they have study hall. Jérôme can't believe he went to all that trouble for nothing.

For Individual Needs

2 Challenge Have students correct the false statements.

 For videodisc application, see Videodisc Guide.

Building on Previous Skills

4 Have students answer each item in French, either orally or in writing, using the expressions they learned in Chapter 1 to express likes and dislikes. **(Il/Elle aime les maths. Il/Elle n'aime pas les sciences nat.)** Then, have them give their own opinions of each subject.

Teaching Suggestion

5 Have students identify the numbers of the frames in the **Mise en train** that support their answers.

Teaching Suggestion

Ask students to find a synonym in the **Mise en train** for the greeting **Ça va? (Ça boume?)** Have them try to guess the meaning of Jérôme's statement **Si, tu as raison.**

These activities check for comprehension only. Students should not yet be expected to produce language modeled in **Mise en train.**

1 Tu as compris?

Answer the following questions about **La rentrée.**

1. What are the students discussing? their schedules
2. What do you think **La rentrée** means? back to school
3. What class do they all have together? gym class
4. Why are they in a hurry at the end of the conversation? They are late for class.
5. What is Jérôme worried about? He forgot his shoes for P.E.

2 Vrai ou faux?

1. Ann est américaine. vrai
2. Jérôme n'aime pas l'espagnol. faux
3. Ann et Marc n'aiment pas les maths. faux
4. Jérôme a allemand. vrai
5. Marc n'a pas sport cet aprèm. faux

3 Cherche les expressions

In **La rentrée**, what do the students say to . . . See answers below.

1. ask what class someone has?
2. tell why they like a class?
3. tell why they don't like a class?
4. tell which class they prefer?
5. ask what time it is?

> C'est difficile. C'est nul. Il est quelle heure?
> C'est super intéressant. J'aime encore mieux...
> Tu as quel cours? C'est plus cool. Tu as quoi?
> Le prof est sympa. J'aime mieux... C'est passionnant.

4 Ils aiment ou pas?

Do these students like or dislike the subjects or teachers they're talking about?

1. «Les sciences nat, c'est passionnant.» like
2. «Les maths, c'est nul.» dislike
3. «C'est super intéressant, les maths.» like
4. «Le prof est sympa.» like

5 Qu'est-ce qui manque? *What's missing?*

Choose the correct words from the box to complete these sentences based on **La rentrée.**

1. Après maths, Marc a _____. géographie
2. Jérôme a _____. allemand   l'espagnol
3. Jérôme aime mieux _____ que l'allemand.
4. On a tous sport à _____ heures. quatorze
5. On est en retard! Il est _____ heures. huit

> géographie   allemand   quatorze
> huit   l'espagnol

6 Et maintenant, à toi

Which students in **La rentrée** share your own likes or dislikes about school subjects?

46 *quarante-six*   CHAPITRE 2   Vive l'école!

---

3 1. Tu as quoi? Tu as quels cours?
   2. C'est passionnant. Le prof est sympa. C'est super intéressant. C'est plus cool.
   3. C'est difficile. C'est nul.
   4. J'aime mieux... ; J'aime encore mieux...
   5. Il est quelle heure?

PREMIERE ETAPE Storytelling Book pp. 5, 8

Agreeing and disagreeing

VOCABULAIRE

 PA pp. 14–16, Acts. 2–5, 7   2-A, 2-1   GV pp. 10–11, Acts. 1–4   CD-ROM Disc 1

l'algèbre (f.)	*algebra*	la chorale	*choir*	la musique	*music*
la biologie	*biology*	le cours de développement		le cours	*course, school subject*
la chimie	*chemistry*	personnel et social (DPS)	*health*	les devoirs (m.)	*homework*
la géométrie	*geometry*	la danse	*dance*	l'élève (m./f.)	*student*
la physique	*physics*	le latin	*Latin*	le professeur	*teacher*

*You can abbreviate **Education Physique et Sportive** as **EPS**. In conversation, students often say **le sport** instead of **EPS**.

PREMIERE ETAPE   *quarante-sept* **47**

RESOURCES FOR PREMIERE ETAPE

PRINT
- *Lesson Planner,* p. 9
- *Practice and Activity Book,* pp. 14–16
- *Grammar and Vocabulary Workbook,* pp. 10–11
- *Activities for Communication,* pp. 7–8, 80, 83–84, 139–140
- *Listening Activities,* pp. 11, 15
- *Testing Program,* pp. 27–30
- *Alternative Assessment Guide,* p. 33

MEDIA
- *Video Program,* Videocassette 1
  Video Guide, pp. 11–16
- *Videodisc Program,* Videodisc 1, Side B
  Videodisc Guide, p. 21
- *Teaching Transparencies* 2-1, 2-A
- *Interactive CD-ROM Program,* Disc 1
  CD-ROM Teacher's Guide, p. 6
- *Audio Compact Discs*
  Textbook Listening Activities, CD 2, Trs. 3–4
  Additional Listening Activities 2-1, 2-2, CD 2, Trs. 25–26
  Quiz 2-1B, CD 2, Tr. 19

PREMIERE ETAPE
CHAPITRE 2

Jump Start!

Have students write sentences telling three things they like to do and three things they don't like to do.

MOTIVATE

Re-enter **l'anglais, les maths,** and **le français** from Chapter 1 by asking students how they feel about each of these classes. (**Tu aimes mieux l'anglais ou les maths?**)

TEACH

Presentation

Vocabulaire   Begin by asking **Qui aime la biologie?** Students who raise their hands might say simply **Moi** or **Moi, j'aime la biologie.** Continue asking about other subjects. Have students categorize the vocabulary. Write the categories on the board or on a transparency. Categories might include **les sciences, les langues, l'éducation civique** *(government),* **les maths, les cours facultatifs** *(electives),* and **les cours obligatoires** *(required courses).* Make sure students understand the meaning of all the categories. Then, give the name of a subject and ask **Quelle catégorie?** Write the subject under the proper category on the board and have students copy the information in their notebooks.

Teacher Note

You might want to tell students that **sciences naturelles** is sometimes referred to as **biologie-géologie** or **sciences de la vie et de la terre (SVT).** This area of study includes both lectures and a lab.

Teaching Suggestions

7 Before students hear the recording, have them locate and give the numbers of each classroom.

8 Students might pair off and ask each other questions based on the pictures: **Qui aime le français?**

For Individual Needs

8 Slower Pace Before doing this activity, ask students to imagine what they think the interests of the two students might be.

8 Challenge You might have students draw their own pictures illustrating their interests. Then, have partners exchange papers and tell what subjects their classmate likes.

Additional Practice

9 Give various items (a compass, a Spanish dictionary) to different students. Have students use facial expressions to indicate whether they like or dislike the subject associated with the item. Have the class tell what each student likes and dislikes. **(Joel aime les maths. Jennifer n'aime pas l'espagnol.)**

---

7 **Ecoute!** See scripts and answers on p. 41G.

CD 2 Tr. 3

On the first day of school, Céline and Aurélie are looking for their French class. As you listen to their conversation, look at the drawing of the school on page 47 and write the numbers of the classrooms they're looking into.

8 **Ils aiment quels cours?** *What subjects do they like?*

Name three subjects Nicole and Gérard probably like, according to their interests.

Nicole
l'algèbre, la chimie, les mathématiques

Gérard
la géographie, l'histoire, le français

9 **C'est qui?** *Who is it?*

Tell your partner what subject one of these students likes, without naming the person. Your partner will try to guess the person's name. Take turns until you've identified all of the students.

— Il aime le français.
— C'est Michel.

Michel

Julien
Il aime le sport.

Nathalie
Elle aime la chorale.

Virginie
Elle aime la danse.

Guillaume
Il aime la géographie.

Franck
Il aime l'anglais.

Karine
Elle aime la chimie.

48 *quarante-huit*

CHAPITRE 2   Vive l'école!

Study at regular intervals. It's best to learn language in small chunks and to review frequently. Cramming will not usually work for French. Study at least a little bit every day, whether you have an assignment or not. The more often you review words and structures, the easier it will be for you to understand and participate in class.

NOTE CULTURELLE

In France and other countries that follow the French educational system, the grade levels are numbered in descending order. When students begin junior high (**le collège**) at about 10 or 11 years of age, the grade they are in is called **sixième**. Then they go into **cinquième**, **quatrième**, and **troisième**. The grade levels at the high school (**le lycée**) are called **seconde**, **première**, and **terminale**.

Le baccalauréat, or le bac, is a national exam taken at the end of study at a **lycée**. Not all students take the **bac**, but those who plan to go on to a university must pass it. It's an extremely difficult oral and written test that covers all major subjects. Students spend the final year of the **lycée, la terminale,** preparing for this exam. There are three major categories of **baccalauréat** exams: **le bac général, le bac technologique,** and **le bac professionnel.** Each category is divided into a more specialized series of exams, depending upon a student's chosen field of study. For example, a student specializing in literature would take the **bac général littéraire,** or simply **le bac L.**

Baccalauréat 1996: Les hauts et les bas

Taux de réussite par série (en %).

Examen et série	Total	En 1995	Changement
Bac Général			
Littéraire (L)	71,9	71,7	+0,2
Economique et social (ES)	71,1	73,2	- 2,1
Sciences (S)	77,8	78,4	- 0,6
Bac Technologique			
Sciences et technologies industrielles (STI)	73,4	67,5	+5,9
Sciences et technologies de laboratoire (STL)	79,7	75,2	+4,5
Sciences médico-sociales (SMS)	81	73,5	+8,5
Sciences et technologies tertiaires (STT)	80,6	80,6	0
Bac Professionnel			
Industriel			
Tertiaire	74,3	70,2	+4,1
	81	74,8	+6,2
Total France métropolitaine	76	75,2	+0,8

10 Mon journal

Make a list of your favorite school subjects in your journal. If you were taking these subjects in France, which **bac** do you think you would take?

Je passerais le bac... (*I would take* **bac** . . .)

Language-to-Language

Tell students that **passer** can be a false cognate. **Passer un examen** means *to take an exam.* To say *I passed the bac,* you would say **J'ai réussi au bac.**

Culture Note

Children may enter **l'école maternelle** as early as two years of age. These schools are subsidized by the government and are strictly monitored. Some families have in-home child care, which is also licensed and monitored by the government.

Teacher Note

There are many types of **baccalauréat** exams. Each one tests students on a number of subjects that are weighted differently according to the student's major. For example, a student who is majoring in literature needs to score higher in literature, philosophy, and languages than in math in order to pass. Students who don't score high enough must try to get a better grade by taking oral exams. If students fail, they must repeat their last year at the **lycée (terminale)** before retaking the **baccalauréat.** Students who don't have their **baccalauréat** need to pass a college entrance exam called **l'ESEU (Examen spécial d'entrée à l'université)** in order to be admitted to college.

Thinking Critically

Comparing and Contrasting
Have students compare passing the **baccalauréat** with graduating from high school in the United States. How does the Scholastic Assessment Test (SAT) or the American College Test (ACT) compare with the **baccalauréat?**

Mon journal

10 You might ask students to write about their most difficult subjects and their favorite ones. Give them these sentence starters: **Pour moi, les cours les plus difficiles sont...** and **Mes cours préférés sont...** For an additional journal entry suggestion for Chapter 2, see *Practice and Activity Book,* page 146.

Additional Practice

10 Have students work in pairs and write sentences in their journals about the subjects their partner likes. (**Les cours préférés de... sont...**)

Presentation

Comment dit-on... ? Read the text of the illustrations to students, using appropriate intonation and facial gestures. Ask them to guess whether each character likes or dislikes the subjects. Have students tell you what subjects they like. Agree with some and disagree with others. Then, tell them what you like and elicit their responses. You might have students form groups of three and role-play the mini-dialogues in the illustrations, changing the names of the subjects to reflect their own feelings.

For videodisc application, see *Videodisc Guide.*

For Individual Needs

11 Slower Pace Distribute a list of school subjects. Have students listen to the dialogue and circle the subjects they hear mentioned. After you give the correct subjects, tell students to listen again to decide whether Hélène and Gérard like or dislike these courses.

13 Challenge Ask the group reporter to differentiate among the students when giving the final report: **Pierre et moi, nous aimons la glace, mais Marie n'aime pas ça. Elle aime mieux la pizza.**

CLOSE

Ask students to draw cartoons with speech bubbles to show their opinions about different subjects. You might have students add them to their portfolios or use them as part of **"Mon avenir,"** one of the chapter projects on page 41I.

COMMENT DIT-ON... ?
Agreeing and disagreeing

PA
p. 15, Act. 6

2-1

To agree:
Oui, beaucoup. *Yes, very much.*
Moi aussi. *Me too.*
Moi non plus. *Neither do I.*

To disagree:
Moi, non. *I don't.*
Non, pas trop. *No, not too much.*
Moi, si. *I do.*
Pas moi. *Not me.*

11 Ecoute!   See scripts and answers on p. 41G.

CD 2 Tr. 4

Listen as Hélène and Gérard talk about the subjects they like and dislike. Which one do they agree on? Which one do they disagree on?

12 Parlons!   *Let's talk!*

Ask your partner's opinion about several subjects and then agree or disagree. Take turns.

— Tu aimes les arts plastiques?
— Non, pas trop.
— Moi, si.

13 Ça te plaît?   *Do you like it?*

Get together with two classmates. Find at least two things or activities that you all like. Then, tell the rest of the class what you agree on.

ELEVE 1 — J'aime les hamburgers. Et toi?
ELEVE 2 — Oui, beaucoup.
ELEVE 3 — Moi aussi.
ELEVE 1 — Nous aimons tous *(all)* les hamburgers.

NOTE DE GRAMMAIRE

PA
p. 16, Act. 8

Use **si** instead of **oui** to contradict a negative statement or question.

— Tu **n'**aimes **pas** la biologie?
— Mais **si!** J'adore la bio!

GV
p. 11, Act. 5   Additional Grammar Practice, p. R28

le cinéma   le foot   les concerts
la pizza   faire du sport
écouter de la musique
la glace   faire les magasins   le ski

50   *cinquante*   CHAPITRE 2   Vive l'école!

ASSESS

Quiz 2-1A, Quiz 2-1B, *Testing Program,* pp. 27–30
Audio CD 2, Tr. 19

Performance Assessment

Have partners prepare and act out a conversation between a student and a school counselor in which they discuss the student's interests and the subjects he or she likes and dislikes.

DEUXIEME ETAPE Storytelling Book pp. 6, 8

Asking for and giving information

? COMMENT DIT-ON... ?
Asking for and giving information

2-2

To ask about someone's classes:
Tu as quels cours aujourd'hui?
What classes do you have . . . ?

Tu as quoi le matin?
What do you have . . . ?

Vous avez espagnol l'après-midi?
Do you have . . . ?

To tell what classes you have:
J'ai arts plastiques et physique.
I have . . .

J'ai algèbre, DPS et sport.

Oui, et **nous avons** aussi géo.
. . . we have . . .

14 On a quoi? *What do we have?*

a. Find out what subjects your partner has in the morning and in the afternoon.

— Tu as quoi le matin
(l'après-midi)?
— Bio, algèbre et chorale.
Et toi?
— Moi, j'ai algèbre, chimie,
chorale et DPS.

b. Now, tell the rest of the class
which subjects you and your
partner have in common.

Marc et moi, nous avons
algèbre et chorale.

VOCABULAIRE
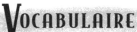

GV
p. 12, Act. 6

le matin	*in the morning*
l'après-midi	*in the afternoon*
aujourd'hui	*today*
demain	*tomorrow*
maintenant	*now*

GRAMMAIRE *The verb* **avoir**

PA
p. 17,
Act. 12

Avoir is an irregular verb. That means it doesn't follow the pattern of the -er
verbs you learned in Chapter 1.

avoir *(to have)*

GV
pp. 12–13,
Acts. 7–9

J' **ai**
Tu **as** } chimie maintenant.
Il/Elle/On **a**

Nous **avons**
Vous **avez** } chimie maintenant.
Ils/Elles **ont**

Additional Grammar
Practice, p. R29

As you saw in Chapter 1, you often use an article (**le, la, l'**, or **les**)before a
noun. When you're telling which school subjects you have, however, you don't
use an article.

DEUXIEME ETAPE

cinquante et un **51**

RESOURCES FOR **DEUXIEME ETAPE**

PRINT
- *Lesson Planner,* p. 10
- *Practice and Activity Book,* pp. 17–19
- *Grammar and Vocabulary Workbook,*
  pp. 12–15
- *Activities for Communication,* pp. 9–10,
  81, 83–84, 139–140
- *Listening Activities,* pp. 12, 16
- *Testing Program,* pp. 31–34
- *Alternative Assessment Guide,* p. 33

MEDIA
- *Video Program,* Videocassette 1
  Video Guide, pp. 11–16
- *Videodisc Program,* Videodisc 1, Side B
  Videodisc Guide, p. 21–22
- *Teaching Transparencies* 2-2, 2-B
- *Interactive CD-ROM Program,* Disc 1
  CD-ROM Teacher's Guide, pp. 6–7
- *Audio Compact Discs*
  Textbook Listening Activities, CD 2, Trs. 5–6
  Additional Listening Activities 2-3, 2-4, CD 2, Trs. 27–28
  Quiz 2-2B, CD 2, Tr. 20

---

*J*ump Start!

Write on the board or on a
transparency: **Tu aimes
l'algèbre? Tu aimes l'histoire?** and **J'aime l'anglais.
Je n'aime pas les sciences
naturelles.** Have students
write answers to the questions
and responses to the statements, agreeing or disagreeing
with each one.

MOTIVATE

Ask students in English
whether they prefer their
morning or afternoon class
schedule and why.

TEACH

Presentation

**Comment dit-on... ?/
Vocabulaire** Teach **le matin,
l'après-midi,** and **aujourd'hui**
by drawing pictures and using
a clock or calendar. Play the
role of a student and tell which
subjects you have today, in the
morning and in the afternoon.
Then, as you ask students the
questions, have them respond.
Next, have students pair off
and practice.

Grammaire Have students
review the forms of **avoir** they
already know by asking them
what classes they have. Then,
model the other forms of the
verb **avoir.** (**David et Paul
ont maths.**) Write the
paradigm of **avoir** on the
board or on a transparency.
Then, erase the forms at
random and have students say
them aloud from memory.
Have students tell what class
they have first period. (**J'ai
maths.**) Then, have them tell
what their classmates have at
that time.

**For videodisc
application, see
*Videodisc Guide.***

Teacher Note

15 Professions will be presented later, but students might want to know the names of the professions pictured here: **le/la pilote, le/la vétérinaire, l'archéologue, la femme (l'homme) d'affaires, le danseur (la danseuse), le chanteur (la chanteuse).**

Group Work

15 Students might do this activity in groups, with each person naming a subject suggested by each illustration. Each student might then name another profession, in English or French, and ask group members to name appropriate subjects. You might want to give students the French names for other professions: **un(e) journaliste, un(e) météorologiste, un acteur (une actrice), un instituteur (une institutrice), un ingénieur, un(e) avocat(e), un médecin (une femme médecin), un homme (une femme) politique.**

Presentation

Vocabulaire Start by presenting the days of the week. Ask students **Quel jour est-ce aujourd'hui?** Next, call out a certain day and time **(le mardi matin, à 10h15)** and have students call out the class that Stéphanie has then. You might also say the name of a subject and have students tell the day(s) that Stéphanie has that subject. Practice the days of the week by naming one and having students name the following day or the preceding day. To elicit quick responses, you might point forward for the following day and backwards for the preceding day.

15 Ils ont quels cours?

Some students are day-dreaming about the future. What classes are they taking to prepare for these careers?

> Ils ont géométrie, physique et géographie.

Possible answers:

1. Elle a chimie et biologie.

2. Il a histoire et géographie.

3. Ils ont informatique et espagnol.

4. Il a danse et musique.

Vocabulaire

PA pp. 18–19, Acts. 14–15   2-B   GV pp. 13–14, Acts. 10–12   CD-ROM Disc 1

Voilà l'emploi du temps de Stéphanie Lambert.

EMPLOI DU TEMPS		**NOM:** Stéphanie Lambert				**CLASSE:** 3ᵉ	
	LUNDI	**MARDI**	**MERCREDI**	**JEUDI**	**VENDREDI**	**SAMEDI**	**DIMANCHE**
8h00	Allemand	Arts plastiques	Mathématiques	Mathématiques	Français		
9h00	Français	Arts plastiques	Anglais	Sciences nat	Français	Anglais	
10h00	**Récréation**	**Récréation**	**Récréation**	**Récréation**	**Récréation**	TP physique	
10h15	EPS	Allemand	Français	EPS	Sciences nat	TP physique	
11h15	Sciences nat	**Etude**	Histoire/Géo	**Etude**	Arts plastiques	**[Sortie]**	
12h15	**Déjeuner**	**Déjeuner**	**[Sortie]**	**Déjeuner**	**Déjeuner**	**APRES-MIDI**	
14h00	Histoire/Géo	Mathématiques	**APRES-MIDI**	Histoire/Géo	Allemand	**LIBRE**	
15h00	Anglais	Physique/Chimie	**LIBRE**	Physique/Chimie	Mathématiques		
16h00	**Récréation**	**[Sortie]**		**Récréation**	**[Sortie]**		
16h15	Mathématiques			Arts plastiques			
17h15	**[Sortie]**			**[Sortie]**			

(Row labels: MATIN for 8h00–11h15; APRES-MIDI for 14h00–17h15. DIMANCHE column reads "LIBRE" vertically.)

Teacher Note

In Chapter 2, students learn the days of the week to tell when they have class. In Chapter 6, students will learn how to use the days of the week with and without a definite article to tell when they do certain activities.

Culture Note

In France and many other countries, the first day of the week is Monday, not Sunday, as it is in the United States.

Thinking Critically

Analyzing Ask students what they think are the advantages and disadvantages of the French schedule.

16 Tu comprends?

1. lundi, mardi, mercredi, jeudi, vendredi, samedi, dimanche
2. lunch and break

Answer the following questions about Stéphanie Lambert's schedule on page 52.

1. Can you find and copy the words in the schedule that refer to days of the week?
2. **Déjeuner** and **Récréation** don't refer to school subjects. What do you think they mean?
3. What do you think **14h00** means? 2:00 P.M.
4. If **étudier** means *to study,* what do you think **Etude** means? study hall
5. You know that **sortir** means *to go out.* What do you think **Sortie** means?
6. Can you list two differences between Stéphanie's schedule and yours?

5. school is out (literally: exit)
6. She goes to school on Saturdays and gets out early on Wednesdays.

17 L'Emploi du temps de Stéphanie

Stéphanie is telling a friend about her schedule. Complete her statements according to her schedule on page 52.

Le __1__ matin, j'ai allemand, français, EPS et sciences nat. Je n'aime pas trop les sciences. J'ai histoire-géo le __2__, le __3__ et le __4__. J'adore l'histoire! Et le mercredi __5__, je n'ai pas cours. Normalement, j'ai __6__ à 10h00, mais le __7__, j'ai travaux pratiques de physique à 10h00. Je n'ai pas cours le __8__.

1. lundi 2. lundi 3. mercredi 4. jeudi 5. après-midi 6. récréation 7. samedi 8. dimanche

18 Ecoute! See scripts and answers on p. 41G.

CD 2 Tr. 5

Look at Stéphanie's schedule as you listen to three of her friends call her on the phone. They're going to tell her what subjects they have on a certain day of the week. Do they have the same subjects as Stéphanie on that day?

 PA p. 17, Act. 11   GV pp. 14–15, Acts. 13–14

VOCABULAIRE

You've already learned the numbers 0–20. Here are the numbers 21–59 in French.

21 vingt et un	**22** vingt-deux	**23** vingt-trois	**24** vingt-quatre	**25** vingt-cinq
26 vingt-six	**27** vingt-sept	**28** vingt-huit	**29** vingt-neuf	**30** trente
31 trente et un	**32** trente-deux	**40** quarante	**41** quarante et un	**42** quarante-deux
50 cinquante	**51** cinquante et un	**52** cinquante-deux	**59** cinquante-neuf	

Math Link

Divide the class into two or more teams. Ask each student to write an addition or subtraction problem on a piece of paper, making sure that neither the numbers used in the problem nor the answers are more than 59. Collect the papers and ask a contestant from each team to go to the board. For the first round, read aloud one of the problems. The first contestant to write the correct answer in numerals wins a point for his or her team. For the second round, contestants must write out the numbers in words in order to win a point. You will need to teach the words **plus/et** *(plus),* **moins** *(minus),* and **font** *(equals).* (**Deux et deux font quatre. Quatre moins deux font deux.**)

Teaching Suggestion

16 Ask how many times a week Stéphanie has various classes, how many different classes she has, and what **TP de physique** means (**travaux pratiques de physique,** *physics lab*).

For Individual Needs

18 Slower Pace Have students form small groups. Play the recording, stopping it after each speaker. Have students in each group write down the subjects each speaker has that day.

Teaching Suggestion

18 After students have done this activity, you might want to give a typed copy of the script for the first, second, or third schedule to small groups of students. Then, have them write sentences using **aussi** and the connectors **et** and **mais** to compare and contrast each schedule with Stéphanie's. (**Le mercredi, Georges a maths, et Stéphanie a maths aussi. Le jeudi, Nadine a musique, mais Stéphanie n'a pas musique.**)

Presentation

Vocabulaire Review the numbers 1–20. Then, before students open their books, start with the number **vingt** and have students count after you from 20–29. Point out that 21 is different from 22 through 29. Teach the word **trente** and ask students to count from 31–39 based on what they have just learned about the 20s. Repeat this process with **quarante** and **cinquante.**

Motivating Activity

Have each student make a clock face with movable hands, using a paper plate and brads or pipe cleaners. Ask students why they might need to know how to tell time in French (to check on movie or flight times and make appointments or dates).

Presentation

Comment dit-on... ? Use a clock to teach official time. Explain that if you add 12 to every hour after noon, you will have the correct 24-hour time. (1 + 12 = 13) Then, say a time and have students indicate that time on their clocks from the Motivating Activity and repeat the time in French. This could be a game played with teams of 3–4. When you call out a time, each team holds up its clock to show the time. A point is awarded for the correct time. Then, write these and other times on the board or on a transparency: 10 P.M., 8:15 P.M., 7:45 P.M., 3 P.M. Ask students to state the times in French, according to the 24-hour system.

Teacher Note

Point out that **heure** is used in both the question and the answer, but that the spelling is plural) after all numbers beyond *one.* The question is always in the singular, however. (**Il est quelle heure?**)

For Individual Needs

Kinesthetic Learners In pairs, one student mimes a daily action, such as brushing one's teeth. The partner tells at what time that action might normally take place and shows the time on his or her clock.

---

19 Quels sont les nombres?

1. Say these numbers in French.
   a. 25   **b.** 37   **c.** 46   **d.** 53

2. Write the numerals for these numbers.
   a. vingt-huit   **b.** trente-quatre   **c.** quarante et un   **d.** cinquante-cinq
   28   34   41   55

1. **a.** vingt-cinq
   b. trente-sept
   c. quarante-six
   d. cinquante-trois

COMMENT DIT-ON... ?
Telling when you have class

p. 18, Act. 13   2-2   p. 15, Acts. 15–17   CD-ROM Disc 1

To find out at what time someone has a certain class:
Tu as maths **à quelle heure**?

To tell at what time you have a certain class:
J'ai maths **à neuf heures.**

| **huit heures** | **dix heures quinze** | **sept heures vingt** | **quinze heures trente** | **seize heures quarante-cinq** |

---

20 Ecoute!   See scripts and answers on p. 41G.

CD 2 Tr. 6

Listen as Jérôme answers Ann's questions about his schedule. At what time does he have these classes: **anglais, espagnol, histoire,** and **maths**?

À la française

In casual conversation, you might try using the abbreviated forms of words just as French teenagers do. For example, **la récréation** can be abbreviated to **la récré.** Do you recall the abbreviated forms of the words listed below? If not, look for them in **La rentrée** or in Stéphanie's schedule.

les sciences naturelles
la géographie
l'éducation physique et sportive
l'après - midi
les mathématiques
le professeur

NOTE CULTURELLE

Although in familiar conversation people may use the 12-hour system to give the time, they use the 24-hour system (**l'heure officielle**) to give schedules for transportation, schools, stores, and movies. For example, the school day generally begins at 8h00 (**huit heures**) and continues until 17h00 (**dix-sept heures**) or 18h00 (**dix-huit heures**) with a break from 12h00 (**douze heures**) to 14h00 (**quatorze heures**). You will learn about the 12-hour system in Chapter 6.

54   *cinquante-quatre*   CHAPITRE 2   Vive l'école!

Additional Practice

Have students write six-digit locker combinations grouped in three double digits (not greater than 59) on small pieces of paper. Then, ask them to work in pairs, with one partner reading aloud the numbers in double digits, and the other writing them down.

21 Une journée chargée

A busy day

Claudine is busy today. What does she have at each of the times listed? See answers below.

A huit heures, elle a géographie.

1. 8h00   2. 9h35

3. 11h50   4. 14h05   5. 16h20

22 Nos emplois du temps *Our schedules*

a. You and your partner prepare schedules showing only the times classes meet at your school. Take turns asking at what time you each have the classes listed here. Fill in each other's schedule, writing the subjects next to the appropriate times.

— Tu as histoire à quelle heure?
— A onze heures trente.

b. Now complete the schedules by asking what subjects you each have at the remaining times.

— Tu as quoi à treize heures?

français   histoire   sport
maths   sciences   anglais

23 Mon journal

In your journal, make a list of your classes. Include the days and times you have them and the names of your teachers.

DEUXIEME ETAPE

cinquante-cinq 55

Answers

21 2. A neuf heures trente-cinq, elle a maths.
    3. A onze heures cinquante, elle a récréation.
    4. A quatorze heures cinq, elle a espagnol.
    5. A seize heures vingt, elle a biologie/sciences naturelles.

Teaching Suggestions

21 You might have students add what they are doing at the times shown in the pictures, according to their own schedules.

Block Scheduling

22 Students on block schedules may want to know the following terms when talking about their schedules: **tous les deux jours** *(every other day)* and **deux/trois fois par semaine** *(two/three times a week)*.

Portfolio

22 Oral Students might want to include this conversation in their oral portfolios. For portfolio suggestions, see the *Alternative Assessment Guide,* page 19.

Mon journal

23 For an additional journal entry suggestion for Chapter 2, see *Practice and Activity Book,* page 146.

CLOSE

To close this **étape,** have pairs of students describe their schedules to each other, including days and times. You might also play the variation of "Loto" as described on page 41J.

ASSESS

Quiz 2-2A, Quiz 2-2B, *Testing Program,* pp. 31–34

Audio CD 2, Tr. 20

Performance Assessment

Have students write their schedules entirely in French, including days, classes, and times according to the 24-hour clock. Then, have students pair off, ask each other what classes they have and when, and tell which subjects they like and dislike.

VIDEO
PROGRAM
Videocassette 1
27:18–31:00

OR VIDEODISC PROGRAM,
Videodisc 1, Side B

Search 13500, Play To 16170

Teacher Notes

• See the *Video Guide,* the *Videodisc Guide,* and the *CD-ROM Teacher's Guide* for activities related to the **Panorama Culturel.**
• Remind students that cultural material may be included in the Chapter Quizzes and Test.
• The interviewees' language represents informal, unrehearsed speech. Occasionally, edits have been made for clarification.

Presentation

Ask students what courses they are required to take and what courses they think French-speaking students might be required to take. Play the video, and then ask if there were any unfamiliar courses mentioned. You might use the **Questions** below to check comprehension.

Thinking Critically

Analyzing Have students compare the subjects they are taking with those the interviewees are taking and make lists of the ones they don't have in common. Have them give advantages and disadvantages of the courses that the interviewees are taking, such as Portuguese or geography, as well as American courses, such as band and home economics.

PANORAMA CULTUREL

Amadou • Burkina Faso Yannick • Martinique Patrice • Québec

What is your school day like? At what time does it start and end? What classes do you have? Here's what some francophone students had to say about their school day.

CD 2
Trs. 7–10

CD-ROM
Disc 1

Tu as quels cours?

«A l'école, j'ai comme cours français, anglais, sciences physiquès, sciences naturelles, éducation civique et morale, géographie, physique.»

—Amadou
Tr. 8

«Comme je suis en première S, j'ai de l'économie. Je fais de l'anglais, du portugais, du français, de l'éducation physique, de l'histoire, de la géographie et des maths.»

Tu peux décrire ton emploi du temps?

«Je commence à huit heures. Je termine à midi. J'ai l'interclasse de midi à deux heures et [j'ai cours] de deux heures à dix-sept heures.»

—Yannick
Tr. 9

«Comme cours, j'ai le français, l'anglais, les maths. J'ai aussi éducation physique. J'ai l'art plastique, l'informatique... beaucoup de matières comme ça.»

—Patrice
Tr. 10

Qu'en penses-tu?

1. What classes do you have in common with these students?
2. What subjects were mentioned that aren't taught at your school?
3. Would you like to trade schedules with any of these students? Why or why not?

Savais-tu que...?

Students in francophone countries commonly have Wednesday afternoons free and attend classes on Saturday mornings. In general, they follow the same core curriculum, which includes French, math, science, history, geography, physical education, and at least one foreign language. Courses like industrial arts and band are not often taught.

Questions

1. Qu'est-ce qu'Amadou a comme cours? (français, anglais, sciences physiques, sciences naturelles, éducation civique et morale, géographie, physique)
2. Qu'est-ce que Yannick étudie comme matières principales? (économie)
3. Quelles langues est-ce que Yannick étudie? (anglais, portugais, français)
4. A quelle heure est-ce que Yannick a l'interclasse? (de midi à deux heures)
5. Les cours de Yannick finissent à quelle heure? (à dix-sept heures)
6. Qu'est-ce que Patrice a comme cours? (français, anglais, maths, éducation physique, art plastique, informatique)

Multicultural Link

Have students research the educational systems in francophone countries, such as Canada and Côte d'Ivoire.

TROISIEME ETAPE

TPR **S**torytelling **B**ook
pp. 7, 8

Asking for and expressing opinions

COMMENT DIT-ON... ?
Asking for and expressing opinions

pp. 20–21,   2-3   p. 16,
Acts. 17–19   Acts. 18–20

For additional practice, see p. R29.

To ask someone's opinion:
 Comment tu trouves ça?
 Comment tu trouves le cours de biologie?

CD-ROM Disc 1

To express a favorable opinion:	To express indifference:	To express an unfavorable opinion:
C'est... *It's . . .*	**C'est pas mal.** *It's not bad.*	**C'est...** *It's . . .*
facile. *easy.*	**Ça va.** *It's OK.*	**difficile.** *hard.*
génial. *great.*		**pas terrible.** *not so great.*
super. *super.*		**pas super.** *not so hot.*
cool. *cool.*		**zéro.** *a waste of time.*
intéressant. *interesting.*		**nul.** *useless.*
passionnant. *fascinating.*		**barbant.** *boring.*

A la française

In informal conversation, French speakers will often leave out the **ne** in a negative sentence.

> **J'aime pas** les hamburgers, moi.
> **C'est pas** super, la géo.

In writing, you should include the **ne** in negative sentences.

For additional practice, see p. R29.

24 Ecoute!   See scripts and answers on p. 41H.

Listen as Aurélie and Eric talk about their subjects. Which ones does Eric like? Which doesn't he like? And Aurélie?

CD 2 Tr. 11

les sciences nat   la géo
l'anglais   l'allemand
      l'espagnol
l'histoire   les maths

NOTE CULTURELLE

The French system of grading is based on a scale of 0–20. A score of less than 8 isn't a passing grade. Students are usually pleased with a score of 10 or higher. They must work very hard to receive a 17 or an 18, and it's very rare to earn a 19 or a 20.

TROISIEME ETAPE

cinquante-sept **57**

RESOURCES FOR **TROISIEME ETAPE**	
PRINT	**MEDIA**
• *Lesson Planner,* p. 11	• *Video Program,* Videocassette 1
• *Practice and Activity Book,* pp. 20–22	*Video Guide,* pp. 11–16
• *Grammar and Vocabulary Workbook,* p. 16	• *Videodisc Program,* Videodisc 1, Side B *Videodisc Guide,* p. 22
• *Activities for Communication,* pp. 11–12, 82, 83–84, 139–140	• Teaching Transparency 2-3
• *Listening Activities,* pp. 13, 17	• *Interactive CD-ROM Program,* Disc 1 *CD-ROM Teacher's Guide,* p. 7
• *Testing Program,* pp. 35–38	• *Audio Compact Discs*
• *Alternative Assessment Guide,* p. 33	Textbook Listening Activities, CD 2, Trs. 11–17
	Additional Listening Activities 2-5, 2-6, CD 2, Trs. 29–30
	Quiz 2-3B, CD 2, Tr. 21

Jump Start!

Ask students to write down their daily class schedules, showing official times and the subjects in French.

MOTIVATE

Have students rate each of their classes on a scale of 1–10. Ask them what makes a class fun or boring.

TEACH

Presentation

Comment dit-on... ? Use appropriate facial expressions and gestures as you present the new vocabulary. Have students repeat the words after you. Then, make the facial expressions and gestures and have students try to recall the appropriate words.

For videodisc application, see *Videodisc Guide.*

Teaching Suggestion

Call out the words **cinéma, télévision, concert,** and **école** and have students react to each word with an appropriate French expression of opinion.

For Individual Needs

24 Slower Pace Distribute a list of the subjects mentioned in the script. Tell students to listen for the subjects the speakers don't like and circle them. Play the recording again. This time, students are to identify the speakers who don't like the subjects they have circled and write the speakers' names next to the subjects.

25 Qu'est-ce qu'on dit? *What are they saying?*

What do you think these students are saying? *Possible answers:*

1. L'histoire, c'est...
   nul.

2. La géométrie, c'est...
   pas terrible.

3. L'algèbre, c'est...
   facile.

4. La biologie, c'est...
   intéressant.

5. L'espagnol, c'est...
   difficile.

6. Les arts plastiques, c'est...
   génial.

26 La vie scolaire *School life* 🏠

Read this letter that your new pen pal Laurent wrote to you after his first day of class. Then, write your reply.

27 Comment tu trouves?

With your partner, discuss how you feel about your classes.

— Tu as maths?
— Oui, à neuf heures.
— Comment tu trouves ça?
— C'est super!

Salut !
Ça va au lycée ? Tu aimes tes cours ? Moi, mes cours sont pas mal. J'adore les maths, c'est facile. Mais la physique, c'est barbant. Et la bio, c'est difficile. Et toi ? Tu aimes les sciences ? Pas moi. J'aime mieux les langues. C'est génial, et c'est plus intéressant. J'ai sport l'après-midi. J'aime bien ; c'est cool. Et toi ? Tu as sport aussi ? Ça te plaît ?
        A bientôt,
        Laurent

58 *cinquante-huit*

CHAPITRE 2   Vive l'école!

28 Un sondage

What is your favorite in each of the following categories? Ask at least three of your classmates how they like your favorites.

— Comment tu trouves *Star Wars*®?
— C'est pas terrible.

les groupes
(musical groups)   les films

les cours   les bandes dessinées
                   (comic strips)

PRONONCIATION

Liaison
See scripts and answers on p. 41H.

CD 2 Trs. 12–17

In French you don't usually pronounce consonants at the end of a word, such as the **s** in **les** and the **t** in **c'est**. But you do pronounce some final consonants if the following word begins with a vowel sound. This linking of the final consonant of one word with the beginning vowel of the next word is called **liaison**.

les examens	C'est intéressant.	vous avez	deux élèves
z	t	z	z

A. A prononcer

Repeat the following phrases and sentences.

les maths / les escargots
nous n'aimons pas / nous aimons
C'est super. / C'est intéressant.
les profs / les élèves

B. A lire

Take turns with a partner reading the following sentences aloud. Make all necessary liaisons.

1. Ils ont maths.
2. Elles ont histoire.
3. Elles aiment l'espagnol.
4. Elle a deux examens lundi.
5. Vous avez cours le samedi?
6. Nous aimons les arts plastiques.

C. A écrire

You're going to hear two short dialogues. Write down what you hear.

Teaching Suggestion

28 Have students write down their classmates' reactions next to each of their favorites. Collect the papers and have volunteers make a list of the top two or three choices in each category.

Presentation

Prononciation Ask students to think of examples of liaison they've already learned (between **ils/elles** and the forms of **aimer, écouter,** and **avoir**). Then, draw the liaison links between each set of words and have students repeat them. Have them deduce the rule for using liaison.

Teaching Suggestion

Prononciation When students have completed the dictation in Part C, have them indicate on their paper where liaison occurs by linking the appropriate words with a pencil mark.

CLOSE

To close this **étape,** have students list the subjects they like and those they dislike. Next to each subject, have them write when the class meets and give their opinion of it.

ASSESS

Quiz 2-3A, Quiz 2-3B, *Testing Program,* pp. 35–38
Audio CD 2, Tr. 21

Language Note

Make sure students make a *z* sound, not an *s* sound, when making liaison with phrases like **les élèves** and **ils ont.**

Performance Assessment

Have students work in pairs to create a conversation between a French student and an American student, comparing and contrasting their school schedules and times. They should express opinions and agreement or disagreement.

READING STRATEGY

Using visual clues to determine meaning

Teacher Note

For an additional reading, see *Practice and Activity Book*, page 23.

PREREADING
Activities A–C

Motivating Activity

Bring in newspapers or textbooks that contain graphs and ask what information they convey. Discuss the advantages of graphs over written explanations.

Teaching Suggestion

A, B You might want to ask students to support the choices they made in these activities.

READING
Activities D–G

Teaching Suggestions

• Have students read the title boxes and pick out the cognates. Next, have them determine what information is displayed in each graph and in what way. They might do this in small groups.
• Have students read the graphs carefully and then do Activities D through G.

LISONS!

How do most American students feel about their classes and their teachers? Do you think French students feel the same way?

DE BONS CONSEILS
You'll find photos, drawings, charts, and other visual clues when you read newspapers, magazines, and even your textbooks! These illustrations will usually give you an idea of what you're going to read before you begin.

A. First, look at the illustrations. Based on what you see, do you think you're going to read . . .
1. price lists?
2. math exercises?
3. results from a survey?
4. ads from a sales catalogue?

B. Now, scan the titles and texts. Based on the titles and the drawings, do you think these articles are about . . .
1. teenagers' favorite pastimes?
2. grades given to students on exams?
3. students' attitudes toward school?
4. prices at several stores?

C. Here are some cognates from the graph entitled **Profs.** What do you think these words mean in English? See answers below.

distants   respectueux
compétents   absents

SONDAGE
Les lycéens ont-ils le moral?

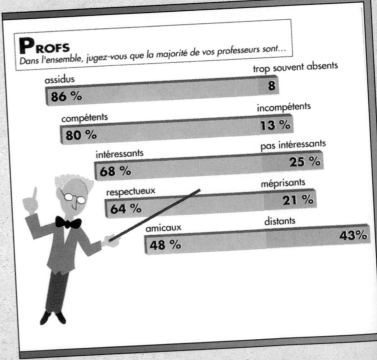

PROFS
Dans l'ensemble, jugez-vous que la majorité de vos professeurs sont...

assidus	trop souvent absents
86 %	8
compétents	incompétents
80 %	13 %
intéressants	pas intéressants
68 %	25 %
respectueux	méprisants
64 %	21 %
amicaux	distants
48 %	43%

Answers
C Distants – *distant, aloof*
Respectueux – *respectful, considerate*
Compétents – *competent*
Absents – *absent*

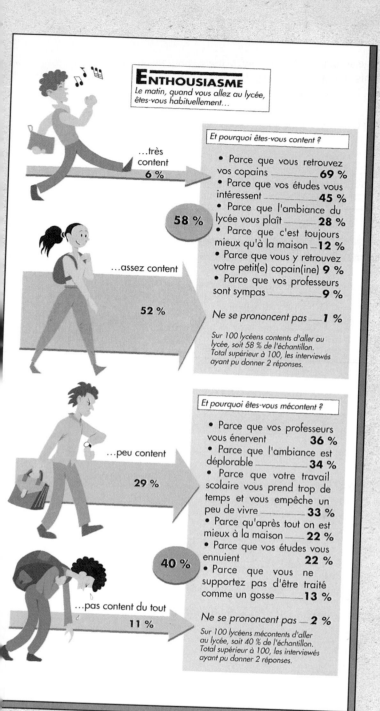

ENTHOUSIASME

Le matin, quand vous allez au lycée, êtes-vous habituellement...

...très content — **6 %**

58 %

...assez content — **52 %**

Et pourquoi êtes-vous content ?

• Parce que vous retrouvez vos copains _____ **69 %**
• Parce que vos études vous intéressent _____ **45 %**
• Parce que l'ambiance du lycée vous plaît _____ **28 %**
• Parce que c'est toujours mieux qu'à la maison **12 %**
• Parce que vous y retrouvez votre petit(e) copain(ine) **9 %**
• Parce que vos professeurs sont sympas _____ **9 %**

Ne se prononcent pas ____ **1 %**

Sur 100 lycéens contents d'aller au lycée, soit 58 % de l'échantillon. Total supérieur à 100, les interviewés ayant pu donner 2 réponses.

...peu content — **29 %**

40 %

...pas content du tout — **11 %**

Et pourquoi êtes-vous mécontent ?

• Parce que vos professeurs vous énervent _____ **36 %**
• Parce que l'ambiance est déplorable _____ **34 %**
• Parce que votre travail scolaire vous prend trop de temps et vous empêche un peu de vivre _____ **33 %**
• Parce qu'après tout on est mieux à la maison ____ **22 %**
• Parce que vos études vous ennuient _____ **22 %**
• Parce que vous ne supportez pas d'être traité comme un gosse _____ **13 %**

Ne se prononcent pas __ **2 %**

Sur 100 lycéens mécontents d'aller au lycée, soit 40 % de l'échantillon. Total supérieur à 100, les interviewés ayant pu donner 2 réponses.

D. Knowing that the words at each end of the bar on the graph are opposites, what do you think the following words mean?

1. **assidus**   regular, constant
2. **incompétents**   incompetent
3. **pas intéressants**   uninteresting
4. **méprisants**   disdainful
5. **amicaux**   friendly

E. According to the graph . . .

1. do French students generally have a positive or negative image of their teachers?
2. how do most of the students feel about their teachers?
3. what do the students criticize the most?   See answers below.

F. Look at the drawings for **Enthousiasme.** What do you think the following categories mean in English? Which category is the best? Which is the worst?   See answers below.

> peu content   très content
>
> pas content du tout
>
> assez content

G. According to the percentages, do most of the students have a positive or a negative attitude when they go to the **lycée?**   positive

H. Conduct the same surveys in your class and compile the results. How do the attitudes of your classmates compare with those of the French **lycéens?**

soixante et un **61**

Teaching Suggestion

Ask students for examples of student and teacher behavior that would illustrate the different categories.

POSTREADING
Activity H

Teaching Suggestion

H. You might have students present the results of their survey in a colorful graph.

Thinking Critically

Analyzing   Discuss the results of the class survey. Ask students for suggestions on improving student and teacher attitudes and behavior. After comparing the results with those in **Lisons!,** have students suggest reasons why the results of the two surveys are similar or different.

Answers

E 1. positive
2. They think they are diligent, competent, interesting, respectful, and friendly.
3. They criticize them for being distant.

F Très content – *very happy (best)*
Assez content – *somewhat happy*
Peu content – *not very happy*
Pas content du tout – *not happy at all (worst)*

The **Mise en pratique** reviews and integrates all four skills and culture in preparation for the Chapter Test.

For Individual Needs

1 Visual Learners

Students might benefit from seeing the typed script after hearing it once. You might have students circle the subjects and times.

Teaching Suggestion

2 Make a list of true/false statements referring to the schedule: **Eliane a EPS à 10h le lundi.** (false) Read the statements to the students and ask them to tell you whether they are true or false.

Group Work

3 Have students work in groups of four. One student in each group might be selected to report the number of votes for and against Eliane's schedule and to explain why the group feels the way it does.

Teaching Suggestion

4 You might extend this activity to include a comparison of the grading system in French and American high schools. Have students refer back to the **Note Culturelle** on page 57 for an explanation of the French grading scale.

MISE EN PRATIQUE

The *CD-ROM Program* offers guided recording and writing activities to practice oral and written skills and to review material from each chapter.

1 Listen as André, a French exchange student, tells you how he feels about his American schedule. What is his reaction to his schedule in general? At what times does he have the following subjects: **chimie, sport, latin, informatique**? See scripts and answers on p. 41H.

CD 2 Tr. 18

2 Answer these questions according to Eliane's schedule. See answers below.

1. Eliane a quoi le lundi matin?
2. Elle a quels cours le jeudi après-midi?
3. Quels jours et à quelle heure est-ce qu'elle a histoire? Anglais? Maths?

EMPLOI DU TEMPS						NOM: Eliane Soulard		CLASSE: 3ᵉ
		LUNDI	**MARDI**	**MERCREDI**	**JEUDI**	**VENDREDI**	**SAMEDI**	**DIMANCHE**
MATIN	8h00	Anglais	Arts plastiques	Histoire/Géo	Mathématiques	Musique		
	9h00	Français	Musique	Anglais	Sciences nat	Arts plastiques	Anglais	
	10h00	Récréation	Récréation	Récréation	Récréation	Récréation	TP physique	L
	10h15	EPS	Mathématiques	Sciences nat	EPS	Sciences nat	TP physique	I
	11h15	Sciences nat	Etude	Arts plastiques	Etude	Français	[Sortie]	
	12h15	**Déjeuner**	**Déjeuner**	**[Sortie]**	**Déjeuner**	**Déjeuner**	**APRES-MIDI**	B
APRES-MIDI	14h00	Arts plastiques	Mathématiques	**APRES-MIDI**	Histoire/Géo	Physique	**LIBRE**	
	15h00	Musique	Physique	**LIBRE**	Physique	Anglais		R
	16h00	Récréation	[Sortie]		Récréation	[Sortie]		
	16h15	Mathématiques			Français			E
	17h15	[Sortie]			[Sortie]			

3 Tell three classmates whether or not you like Eliane's schedule and why. Then, ask them if they like it.

> J'aime l'emploi du temps d'Eliane. Elle a étude et arts plastiques. C'est cool! Et vous?

4 How does an American class schedule compare with Eliane's? With a partner, make a list of similarities and differences.

SIMILARITES

DIFFERENCES

Eliane n'a pas cours le mercredi après-midi.

Answers

2 1. anglais, français, EPS et sciences nat
2. histoire/géographie, physique et français
3. Histoire – mercredi à 8h00, jeudi à 14h00
   Anglais – lundi à 8h00, mercredi à 9h00, vendredi à 15h00, samedi à 9h00
   Maths – lundi à 16h15, mardi à 10h15 et à 14h00, jeudi à 8h00

5 Answer these questions according to Eliane's report card.   See answers below.

1. What are Eliane's best subjects?
2. What would she probably say about French class? Music class? Science class?

BULLETIN TRIMESTRIEL

Année scolaire : 19 98 - 19 99

NOM et Prénom: _Soulard Eliane_   Classe de: 3ᵉ

MATIERES D'ENSEIGNEMENT	Moyenne de l'élève	OBSERVATIONS
Français	5	Montre peu d'enthousiasme
Anglais	8	Assez mauvais travail!
Mathématiques	18	Très bonne élève!
Histoire-Géographie	11	Travail moyen
Sciences naturelles	17	Élève sérieuse
Education physique	12	Un peu paresseuse
Physique-Chimie	18	Très douée pour la physique
Arts plastiques	14	Bon travail.
Musique	15	Fait des efforts.

Ce bulletin doit être conservé précieusement par les parents.
Il n'en sera pas délivré de duplicata.

---

6 Create your ideal schedule showing subjects, days, and times. Write it down in the form of a French **emploi du temps.**

7

JEU DE ROLE

Create a conversation with two classmates. Talk about . . .

a. the subjects you like best and your opinion of them.
b. the subjects you don't like and your opinion of them.
c. whether or not you agree with your classmates' likes and dislikes.

Answers

5 1. mathématiques, physique-chimie, sciences naturelles
2. *Possible answers:* Le français, c'est barbant/c'est difficile/c'est nul/c'est zéro.
La musique, c'est pas mal/c'est pas super/c'est pas terrible.
Les sciences nat, c'est cool/c'est facile/c'est génial/c'est intéressant/c'est passionnant.

Career Path

Many college students pursuing degrees in foreign language spend a year teaching English abroad. Ask students if they can think of other careers that might require people to teach English in a foreign country (Peace Corps). If students were to spend a year teaching English in a French **lycée,** what information from this chapter will help them? What else would they need to learn?

Building On Previous Skills

5 Have students find cognates in the teacher's comments to help them understand the meaning.

Teaching Suggestion

5 Have students make their own French report card. They should give themselves the grades they think they deserve in each subject using the French grading system.

For Individual Needs

6 Auditory Learners
Have partners dictate their ideal schedules to each other and write down the classes and times as they hear them. Then, have them exchange the schedules to check each other's work.

Video Wrap-Up

- *VIDEO PROGRAM,* Videocassette 1, 19:47–37:11
- *VIDEODISC PROGRAM,* Videodisc 1, Side B

At this time, you might want to use the video resources for additional review and enrichment. See *Video Guide* or *Videodisc Guide* for suggestions regarding the following:
- **La rentrée** (Dramatic episode)
- **Panorama Culturel** (Interviews)
- **Vidéoclips** (Authentic footage)

This page is intended to help students prepare for the Chapter Test. It is a brief checklist of the major points covered in the chapter. The students should be reminded that this is only a checklist and does not necessarily include everything that will appear on the test.

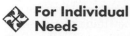 **For Individual Needs**

6 Challenge Encourage students to come up with as many phrases as possible to express each reaction to the geography class.

QUE SAIS-JE?

Can you agree and disagree? p. 50

Can you ask for and give information? pp. 51, 54

Can you tell when you have class? p. 54

Can you ask for and express opinions? p. 57

Can you use what you've learned in this chapter?

1 How would you agree if your friend said the following? How would you disagree with your friend?

1. J'adore l'histoire!   *agree* — Moi aussi! *disagree* — Moi, non.
2. J'aime les sciences nat. Et toi?   *agree* — Oui, beaucoup! *disagree* — Non, pas trop.
3. Je n'aime pas le français.   *agree* — Moi non plus. *disagree* — Moi, si!

2 How would you ask . . .

1. what subjects your friend has in the morning?   Tu as quoi le matin?
2. what subjects your friend has in the afternoon?   Tu as quoi l'après-midi?
3. what subjects your friend has on Tuesdays?   Tu as quoi le mardi?
4. if your friend has music class?   Tu as musique?
5. if your friend has English today?   Tu as anglais aujourd'hui?

3 How would you say in French that the following students have these classes, using the verb **avoir**?   See answers below.

1. you / French and choir
2. Paul / physics
3. we / gym
4. Francine and Séverine / Spanish

4 How would you ask your friend at what time he or she has these classes?   See answers below.

1.   2.   3.

5 How would you tell your friend that you have the following classes at the times given?
See answers below.

1. 9h15   2. 11h45   3. 15h50

6 How would you tell your friend that your geography class is . . .   See answers below.

1. fascinating?   2. not so great?   3. boring?

Answers

3 1. Tu as français et chorale.
2. Paul a physique.
3. Nous avons sport.
4. Francine et Séverine ont espagnol.

4 1. Tu as géométrie à quelle heure?
2. Tu as informatique à quelle heure?
3. Tu as arts plastiques à quelle heure?

5 1. J'ai sport à neuf heures quinze.
2. J'ai allemand à onze heures quarante-cinq.
3. J'ai DPS à quinze heures cinquante.

6 1. C'est passionnant!
2. C'est pas terrible.
3. C'est barbant.

VOCABULAIRE

PREMIERE ETAPE

School subjects

l'algèbre (f.)   *algebra*
l'allemand (m.)   *German*
les arts (m.) plastiques   *art class*
la biologie   *biology*
la chimie   *chemistry*
la chorale   *choir*
le cours de développement
  personnel et social (DPS)
  health
la danse   *dance*
l'éducation (f.) physique et
  sportive (EPS)   *physical
  education*

l'espagnol (m.)   *Spanish*
la géographie   *geography*
la géométrie   *geometry*
l'histoire (f.)   *history*
l'informatique (f.)   *computer
  science*
le latin   *Latin*
la musique   *music*
la physique   *physics*
les sciences (f.) naturelles
  natural science
le sport   *gym*
les travaux (m.) pratiques   *lab*

School-related words

le cours   *course*
les devoirs (m.)   *homework*
l'élève (m./f.)   *student*
le professeur (le prof)   *teacher*

Agreeing and disagreeing

Oui, beaucoup.   *Yes, very much.*
Moi aussi.   *Me too.*
Moi, non.   *I don't.*
Non, pas trop.   *No, not too much.*
Moi non plus.   *Neither do I.*
Moi, si.   *I do.*
Pas moi.   *Not me.*

DEUXIEME ETAPE

Asking for and giving information

Tu as quels cours... ?   *What
  classes do you have . . . ?*
Tu as quoi... ?   *What do you
  have . . . ?*
J'ai...   *I have . . .*
Vous avez... ?   *Do you have . . . ?*
Nous avons...   *We have . . .*
avoir   *to have*

Telling when you have class

Tu as... à quelle heure?   *At what
  time do you have . . . ?*
à... heures   *at . . . o'clock*
à... heures quinze   *at . . . fifteen*

à... heures trente   *at . . . thirty*
à... heures quarante-cinq   *at . . .
  forty-five*
aujourd'hui   *today*
demain   *tomorrow*
maintenant   *now*
le matin   *in the morning*
l'après-midi (m.)   *in the afternoon*
le lundi   *on Mondays*
le mardi   *on Tuesdays*
le mercredi   *on Wednesdays*
le jeudi   *on Thursdays*
le vendredi   *on Fridays*
le samedi   *on Saturdays*
le dimanche   *on Sundays*

Parts of the school day

la récréation   *break*
l'étude (f.)   *study hall*
le déjeuner   *lunch*
la sortie   *dismissal*
l'après-midi libre   *afternoon off*

Numbers

See page 53 for the numbers 21
  through 59.

TROISIEME ETAPE

Asking for and expressing opinions

Comment tu trouves... ?   *What do
  you think of . . . ?*
Comment tu trouves ça?   *What
  do you think of that/it?*
Ça va.   *It's OK.*

C'est...   *It's . . .*
  super.   *super.*
  cool.   *cool.*
  facile.   *easy.*
  génial.   *great.*
  intéressant.   *interesting.*
  passionnant.   *fascinating.*

pas mal.   *not bad.*
barbant.   *boring.*
difficile.   *difficult.*
nul.   *useless.*
pas super.   *not so hot.*
pas terrible.   *not so great.*
zéro.   *a waste of time.*

VOCABULAIRE

soixante-cinq   **65**

Teaching Suggestion

You might want to have students list the feminine nouns together and the masculine nouns together in their notebooks. Ask them also to note any similarities within each group. For example, many of the feminine nouns end in -**ie**.

CHAPTER 2 ASSESSMENT

CHAPTER TEST
- *Testing Program*, pp. 39–44
- *Audio Compact Discs*,
   Audio CD 2,
  Tracks 22–24

SPEAKING TEST
- *Testing Program*, p. 343

TEST GENERATOR
 • Chapter 2

ALTERNATIVE ASSESSMENT
Performance Assessment
- You might want to use the **Jeu de Rôle** on page 63 as a cumulative performance assessment activity.
- *Alternative Assessment Guide*, p. 33

 Portfolio Assessment
- *Alternative Assessment Guide*
  Oral: p. 19
  Written: p. 19

CD-ROM Assessment
- *Interactive CD-ROM Program*, Disc 1
  A toi de parler
  A toi d'écrire
- *Alternative Assessment Guide*, p. 47

Game

TIC TAC TOE   Divide the class into two teams and draw a grid on the board or on a transparency. In each square, write one of the chapter functions or vocabulary categories in English: agreeing, disagreeing, telling time, school subjects, expressing positive and negative opinions, the numbers 20–59, days of the week, and so on. Call out a French expression or sentence. If the contestant chooses the correct functional objective your remark represents, the team symbol goes in the square. If not, a player from the other team may try. You can also reverse the procedure by supplying French expressions in the grid and calling out the functional objectives in English.

Chapitre 3 : Tout pour la rentrée
Chapter Overview

Mise en train pp. 68–70	Pas question!			

	FUNCTIONS	GRAMMAR	CULTURE	RE-ENTRY
Première étape pp. 71–75	• Making and responding to requests, p. 72 • Asking others what they need and telling what you need, p. 74	• The indefinite articles **un, une,** and **des,** p. 73	• **Note Culturelle,** Bagging your own purchases, p. 72 • **Panorama Culturel,** Buying school supplies in French-speaking countries, p. 75	• The verb **avoir** (**Chapitre 2**) • Using **ne... pas** (**Chapitre 1**)
Deuxième étape pp. 76–79	• Telling what you'd like and what you'd like to do, p. 77	• The demonstrative adjectives **ce, cet, cette,** and **ces,** p. 77 • Adjective agreement and placement, p. 79		• Expressing likes and dislikes (**Chapitre 1**) • Activities (**Chapitre 1**) • The verb **avoir** (**Chapitre 2**)
Troisième étape pp. 80–83	• Getting someone's attention, asking for information, and expressing thanks, p. 82		• **Note Culturelle,** French currency, p. 80 • Realia: Radio station logos, p. 80 • Realia: French money, p. 80 • **Note Culturelle,** Expressing prices, p. 82	• Numbers 0–59 (**Chapitres 1–2**)

Prononciation p. 83	The **r** sound Audio CD 3, Tracks 13–15	**A écrire** (dictation) Audio CD 3, Tracks 16–18
Lisons! pp. 84–85	Advertisements for school supplies	**Reading Strategy** Scanning for specific information
Review pp. 86–89	**Mise en pratique**, pp. 86–87 **Ecrivons!** Cluster Diagrams Creating a department store	**Que sais-je?** p. 88 **Vocabulaire,** p. 89

Assessment Options

Testing Program
- Première étape, Quiz 3-1A, Quiz 3-1B, pp. 53–56
- Deuxième étape, Quiz 3-2A, Quiz 3-2B, pp. 57–60
- Troisième étape, Quiz 3-3A, Quiz 3-3B, pp. 61–64
- Chapter Test, pp. 65–70
- Speaking Test, p. 344

Audio Compact Discs
- Audio CD 3, Tracks 20–25

Interactive CD-ROM Program
- Mise en pratique (A toi de parler, A toi d'écrire)
- *CD-ROM Teacher's Guide,* Assessment Options, p. 12

Alternative Assessment Guide
- Portfolio Assessment, p. 20
- Performance Assessment, p. 34
- CD-ROM Assessment, p. 48

Test Generator
- Chapter 3

PRINT

Pupil's Edition, pp. 66–89

**Interactive CD-ROM Program
Teacher's Guide,** pp. 9–12

Videodisc Guide
- Teaching Suggestions, pp. 29–33
- Activity Masters, pp. 34–36

Video Guide
- Teaching Suggestions, pp. 18–19
- Activity Masters, pp. 20–22

Listening Activities
- Student Response Forms for Textbook Listening Activities, pp. 19–21
- Additional Listening Activities 3-1 to 3-6, pp. 23–25
- Additional Listening Activities (song), p. 26
- Scripts and Answers, pp. 112–116

Teaching Transparencies
- Teaching Transparency Masters 3-1 to 3-3 (Situations) and 3-A to 3-D (Vocabulary)
- Teaching Suggestions 3-1 to 3-3 and 3-A to 3-D

Testing Program
- Grammar and Vocabulary Quizzes, **Etape** Quizzes, and Chapter Test, pp. 53–70
- Score Sheet, Scripts, and Answers, pp. 71–78

Alternative Assessment Guide
- Portfolio Assessment, p. 20
- Performance Assessment, p. 34
- CD-ROM Assessment, p. 48

  Grammar and Vocabulary Workbook, pp. 17–24

Practice and Activity Book, pp. 25–36

Activities for Communication
- Communicative Activities, pp. 13–18
- Realia and Teaching Suggestions, pp. 85–89
- Situation Cards, pp. 141–142

Lesson Planner
- Lesson Plan, pp. 13–17

MEDIA

 Audio Compact Discs
- Textbook Listening Activities: Audio CD 3, Tracks 1–19

 Interactive CD-ROM Program
- Disc 1

 Videodisc Program
- Videodisc 2, Side A

 Video Program
- Videocassette 1
- Videocassette 5 (captioned version)

 Audio Compact Discs
- Textbook Listening Activities: Audio CD 3, Tracks 1–19
- Additional Listening Activities: Audio CD 3, Tracks 26–33

 Teaching Transparencies
- Situations 3-1 to 3-3
- Vocabulary 3-A to 3-D

 Audio Compact Discs
- Assessment Items: Audio CD 3, Tracks 20–25

 Test Generator
- Chapter 3

Chapitre 3 : Tout pour la rentrée
Technology Applications

Video

• Show *Pas question!* For Video Synopsis, Teaching Suggestions, Activity Master, and Scripts, see the *Video Guide* or the *Videodisc Guide.*

Captioned Video

• You may wish to play *Pas question!* with captions on Videocassette 5 after playing the non-captioned version of the video. Have students identify the vocabulary for school supplies and expressions for telling what they need.

Audio

• Play the recording of the **Mise en train** with pauses as students read along. You might have them practice pronunciation by repeating individual sentences after hearing them.

Video

• While students watch *Pas question!,* have them listen for exchanges that model asking others what they need and telling what you need. For more suggestions, see p. 31 of the *Videodisc Guide.*

Audio

• Textbook Listening Activity 6 presents and practices the vocabulary for school supplies.

• To have students practice indefinite articles and the vocabulary for school supplies, play Textbook Listening Activity 9.

• Use Additional Listening Activities 3-1 and 3-2 to have students practice vocabulary for school supplies and numbers.

Transparencies

• Use *Teaching Transparencies 3-1* and *3-A* along with the Teaching Suggestions to have students practice the vocabulary for school supplies.

CD-ROM (Disc 1)

• To have students practice vocabulary for school supplies, use **Jeu des paires** (Activity 1).

• **Le bon choix** (Activity 2) targets the use of indefinite articles.

• For suggestions, see p. 10 of the *CD-ROM Teacher's Guide.*

Video

• Show the interviews. For Video Synopsis, Teaching Suggestions, Activity Masters, and Scripts, see the *Video Guide* or the *Videodisc Guide.*

Audio

• Play the **Panorama Culturel** as students read along. Remind students that they might not be able to understand everything each person says, but they should try to recognize words and deduce global meaning.

CD-ROM (Disc 1)

• Have students do the **Panorama Culturel** activity for Chapter 3 after showing them the video. For suggestions, see p. 11 of the *CD-ROM Teacher's Guide.*

Video

• While students watch *Pas question!,* have them listen for exchanges that model **je voudrais** and vocabulary for school and fun. For more suggestions, see p. 32 of the *Videodisc Guide.*

Audio

• Textbook Listening Activity 14 practices additional vocabulary for school and fun.

• To have students practice **Je voudrais** and the vocabulary for things to buy, use Textbook Listening Activity 15.

• Use Additional Listening Activities 3-3 and 3-4 to have students practice the new vocabulary and numbers.

Transparencies

• Use *Teaching Transparency 3-2* and the Teaching Suggestions to have students practice telling what they would like to buy.

• Use *Teaching Transparencies 3-B* and *3-C* and the Teaching Suggestions to present or to have students practice vocabulary for school and things to do for fun.

• Use *Teaching Transparency 3-D* and the Teaching Suggestions to present or have students practice vocabulary for colors.

CD-ROM (Disc 1)

• To have students practice the new vocabulary, use **Chasse au trésor** (Activity 3).

• **Méli-mélo** (Activity 4) targets adjective placement.

• **Les mots qui manquent** (Activity 5) has students practice demonstrative adjectives and adjective agreement.

• For suggestions, see pp. 10–11 of the *CD-ROM Teacher's Guide.*

Video

• While students watch *Pas question!,* have them listen for exchanges that model getting someone's attention, asking for a price, and expressing thanks. For more suggestions, see p. 32 of the *Videodisc Guide.*

Audio

• Use Textbook Activity 23 to have students practice numbers.

• Additional Listening Activities 3-5 and 3-6 practice asking for and telling prices.

Transparencies

• Use *Teaching Transparency 3-3* and the Teaching Suggestions to practice interacting with a salesperson at a store. You might use them after presenting the phrases for getting someone's attention, asking for information, and expressing thanks.

CD-ROM (Disc 1)

• After presenting the vocabulary on p. 80, have students do **Le bon choix** (Activity 6). For suggestions, see p. 11 of the *CD-ROM Teacher's Guide.*

Video

• Replay *Pas question!* in its entirety and ask students to listen for the exchanges in which the characters express needs and respond to requests, tell what they'd like, get someone's attention, ask for information, and express thanks.

CD-ROM (Disc 1)

• Have students do the **En contexte** to practice expressing needs and purchasing items in a store. You may want to use the suggestions on p. 10 of the *CD-ROM Teacher's Guide.*

• Have students practice their writing and speaking skills using the **A toi d'écrire** and **A toi de parler** activities. For a detailed description of these activities, see p. 12 of the *CD-ROM Teacher's Guide.*

• For Assessment Options, see p. 12 of the *CD-ROM Teacher's Guide.*

Test Generator

• Use the Test Generator to create review material for students taking the Chapter Test or to prepare an alternate test.

Video

• Show the **Vidéoclips.** For Video Synopsis, Teaching Suggestions, Activity Master, and Scripts, see the *Video Guide* or the *Videodisc Guide.*

Videodisc Program
Videodisc 2, Side A
Videodisc Guide, pp. 27–36

Chapitre 3 : Tout pour la rentrée!
Barcode Directory

Barcodes A and B access **Mise en train** and **Mise en train (suite)** in their entirety. Subsequent barcodes show specific segments of **Pas question!** The barcode numbers correspond to the scene numbers as they appear on the video.

MISE EN TRAIN

Pas question! **A**

[barcode]
Search 1, Play To 8145

Alors, où sont les fournitures scolaires? **1**

[barcode]
Search 1, Play To 1786

Pardon, mademoiselle... **2**

[barcode]
Search 1787, Play To 2056

Combien de crayons il te faut? **3**

[barcode]
Search 2057, Play To 5524

Oh, regarde, maman... **4**

[barcode]
Search 5225, Play To 5770

C'est combien, s'il vous plaît?... **5**

[barcode]
Search 5771, Play To 5891

590 F!... **6**

[barcode]
Search 5892, Play To 6048

Et cette calculatrice-là?... **7**

[barcode]
Search 6049, Play To 6692

Eh, maman, regarde ce sac vert!... **8**

[barcode]
Search 6693, Play To 7491

Oh, non! Il est horrible!... **9**

[barcode]
Search 7492, Play To 7742

Non. Je voudrais ce sac-ci...**10**

[barcode]
Search 7743, Play To 8144

Pas question! (suite) **B**

[barcode]
Search 8145, Play To 16400

PANORAMA CULTUREL

Qu'est-ce qu'il te faut comme fournitures scolaires?
These barcodes access the three interviews of the **Panorama Culturel** presented in the *Pupil's Edition* as well as additional interviews.

First three interviews **1**

Search 16400, Play To 18510

All interviews **2**

Search 16400, Play To 20209

Séverine **3**

Search 17076, Play To 17649

Onélia **4**

[barcode]
Search 17650, Play To 18213

Marius **5**

[barcode]
Search 18214, Play To 18507

Virginie **6**

[barcode]
Search 18508, Play To 18695

Eva **7**

[barcode]
Search 18696, Play To 18981

Evelyne **8**

[barcode]
Search 18982, Play To 19385

Arnaud **9**

[barcode]
Search 19386, Play To 19558

Matthieu **10**

[barcode]
Search 19559, Play To 19724

Jean-Christophe **11**

[barcode]
Search 19725, Play To 20209

ETAPES

To practice the grammar, vocabulary, and functions presented in each **étape**, see the barcodes and accompanying suggestions on pages 31–32 of the *Videodisc Guide*.

MISE EN PRATIQUE

This is additional footage modeling some of the expressions practiced in this chapter. You may want to use it to review the chapter.

Mise en pratique **1**

Search 24840, Play To 27966

VIDEOCLIPS

These are authentic French commercials. You may want to preview them before showing them to students.

Waterman® : pens **1**

Search 20696, Play To 22401

France Télécom® : French telephone company **2**

Search 22402, Play To 23790

Chapitre 3 : Tout pour la rentrée
CD-ROM Directory DISC 1

The following directory lists the *Interactive CD-ROM Program* activities for Chapter 3. For details and suggestions on how to use them, see pages 9–12 of the *CD-ROM Teacher's Guide*.

GLOBAL TASK		COMMUNICATIVE GOALS	ACTIVITY TYPE
Qu'est ce qu'il te faut pour la rentrée? Students talk to their friend Patrick about what they need, and then purchase these items at the store.		To use chapter functions, vocabulary, and grammar in a lifelike conversation	**En contexte** *Interactive conversation*

	SUPPORTING ACTIVITIES	PUPIL'S EDITION	COMMUNICATIVE GOALS	ACTIVITY TYPE
Première étape	1. Vocabulaire	p. 71	To identify school supplies	**Jeu des paires** *Concentration®*
	2. Grammaire	p. 73	To use indefinite articles	**Le bon choix** *Multiple choice*
Deuxième étape	3. Vocabulaire	p. 76	To identify items you may want to buy for school	**Chasse au trésor Explorons!/Vérifions!** *Interactive image*
	4. Grammaire	p. 79	To place adjectives correctly	**Méli-mélo** *Sequencing*
	5. Grammaire	pp. 77, 79	To use demonstrative adjectives and practice adjective agreement	**Les mots qui manquent** *Tic Tac Toe*
Troisième étape	6. Vocabulaire	p. 80	To identify numbers from 60 to 201	**Le bon choix** *Multiple choice*
Panorama Culturel	Panorama Culturel	p. 75	To listen to and understand native speakers talking about the school supplies they need	**Qu'est-ce qu'il te faut comme fournitures scolaires?** *Presentation* **Le bon choix** *Multiple choice*

	APPLICATION	PUPIL'S EDITION	COMMUNICATIVE GOALS	ACTIVITY TYPE
Mise en pratique	A toi de parler	pp. 86–87	To create and record a conversation between a salesperson and a customer	*Guided recording*
	A toi d'écrire	pp. 86–87	To write lists, a note, or a survey	*Guided writing*

Chapitre 3 : Tout pour la rentrée
🏠 *Homework Suggestions*

CHAPTER SECTION	PRESENTATION	HOMEWORK OPTIONS
Première étape	**Vocabulaire,** p. 71	Practice and Activity Book, p. 26, Activities 2–3 Grammar and Vocabulary Workbook, pp. 17–18, Activities 1–3 CD-ROM, Disc 1, Activity 1
	Comment dit-on... ?, p. 72	Practice and Activity Book, p. 27, Act. 4b
	Grammaire, p. 73	Pupil's Edition, p. R30, Activities 1–2 Grammar and Vocabulary Workbook, pp. 18–19, Activities 4–7 CD-ROM, Disc 1, Activity 2
	Comment dit-on... ? p. 74	Pupil's Edition, p. 74, Activity 12 Practice and Activity Book, p. 28, Activities 5–6
Deuxième étape	**Vocabulaire,** p. 76	Pupil's Edition, p. 77, Activity 17 Grammar and Vocabulary Workbook, p. 20, Activities 8–9 CD-ROM, Disc 1, Activity 3
	Grammaire, p. 77	Pupil's Edition, pp. R30–R31, Activities 3–4 Practice and Activity Book, p. 29, Activities 7–8 Grammar and Vocabulary Workbook, p. 21, Activities 10–11
	Vocabulaire, p. 78	Practice and Activity Book, pp. 29–30, Activity 9–10 Grammar and Vocabulary Workbook, p. 22, Activity 12
	Grammaire, p. 79	Pupil's Edition, p. R31, Activities 5–6 Practice and Activity Book, p. 30, Activities 11–12 Grammar and Vocabulary Workbook, pp. 22–23, Activities 13–15 CD-ROM, Disc 1, Activities 4–5
Troisième étape	**Vocabulaire,** p. 80	Pupil's Edition, p. 81, Activity 25 Practice and Activity Book, p. 32, Activities 15–16 Grammar and Vocabulary Workbook, p. 24, Activities 16–18 CD-ROM, Disc 1, Activity 6
	Comment dit-on... ? p. 82	Pupil's Edition, pp. R31–R32, Activities 7–8 Practice and Activity Book, p. 34, Activities 18–19

Chapitre 3 : Tout pour la rentrée
Textbook Listening Activities Scripts

For Student Response Forms, see *Listening Activities,* pp. 19–21.

Première étape

6 Ecoute! p. 71

1. HAFAIDH   Qu'est-ce qu'il y a dans mon sac? Voilà le cahier de français. J'ai aussi des stylos et des crayons dans ma trousse et une gomme.

2. KARINE   Bon, qu'est-ce qu'il y a dans mon sac? Je ne peux rien trouver! Tiens, voilà le cahier de français. Il y a, bien sûr, des feuilles de papier et ma trousse, avec un crayon et des stylos dedans. Ah, voilà la règle pour les maths.

Answers to Activity 6
a. neither   b. Karine   c. Hafaïdh

9 Ecoute! p. 73

1. — Jacqueline, tu as une feuille de papier?
   — Ben, oui. Voilà.

2. — Ali, tu as un crayon?
   — Non, mais j'ai un stylo.

3. — Paul, tu as un crayon?
   — Oui. Le voilà.

4. — Xavier, tu as une calculatrice?
   — Je regrette. Je n'ai pas de calculatrice.

Answers to Activity 9
1. c   2. a   3. b   4. e

Deuxième étape

14 Ecoute! p. 76

1. Je voudrais un jean.

2. Moi, j'aime faire du sport. Je voudrais des baskets.

3. Je voudrais acheter un portefeuille.

4. J'aime beaucoup la musique. Je voudrais un disque compact.

5. J'adore lire. Je voudrais acheter un roman.

Answers to Activity 14
1. Dorothée   4. Stéphane
2. Odile   5. Denis
3. M. Prévost

15 Ecoute! p. 77

Euh..., je voudrais aller à la plage ce week-end, il me faut un short et un tee-shirt. Alors, pour l'école je voudrais des baskets et un dictionnaire. Je voudrais aussi acheter une montre parce que je suis toujours en retard. Enfin, j'adore écouter de la musique, donc je voudrais une radio.

Answers to Activity 15
un short, un tee-shirt, des baskets, un dictionnaire, une montre et une radio

*T*roisième étape

23 Ecoute! p. 80

1. Vous écoutez quatre-vingt-dix-neuf FM, le rock des Lillois!
2. Génial, phénoménal et amical, c'est canal B sur quatre-vingt-quatorze mégahertz de plaisir.
3. Quatre-vingt-neuf virgule cinq pour swinger dans les chaumières.
4. Qui m'aime? Moi, FM cent deux virgule trois. La station des copains.

Answers to Activity 23
1. a   2. e   3. c   4. b

27 Ecoute! p. 82

1. — Bonjour. C'est combien, ce classeur?
   — Vingt-cinq francs.
   — Merci beaucoup.
2. — C'est cinquante-neuf francs, cette calculatrice?
   — Oui.
   — Merci.
   — A votre service.
3. — Pardon, madame. C'est combien, ce cahier?
   — Quatorze francs.
   — Merci, madame.
4. — Une règle, c'est combien?
   — Onze francs.
   — Merci.
   — A votre service.
5. — Pardon, madame.
   — Oui.
   — Vous avez des trousses?
   — Oui. Ces trousses-là font trente-deux francs.
   — Eh bien, ce n'est pas cher.
6. — C'est combien, ce livre?
   — Quarante-huit francs.
   — Merci, madame.

Answers to Activity 27
1. classeur — 25 F
2. calculatrice — 59 F
3. cahier — 14 F
4. règle — 11 F
5. trousse — 32 F
6. livre — 48 F

*P*rononciation, p. 83

For the scripts for Parts A and B, see p. 83.

C. A écrire, p. 83

(Dictation)
— Pardon, monsieur.
— Oui?
— Je voudrais un crayon rouge et une trousse rose.
— Trente-trois francs, s'il vous plaît.

*M*ise en pratique

1 p. 86

J'aime beaucoup faire du sport. Il me faut des baskets. J'adore écouter de la musique. Je voudrais des cassettes. Je n'ai pas de dictionnaire pour le cours d'espagnol. Je voudrais une calculatrice pour le cours d'algèbre.

Answers to Mise en pratique, Activity 1
des baskets, des cassettes, un dictionnaire et une calculatrice

Projects

La publicité
(Individual or Group Project)

ASSIGNMENT

Students will create advertisements for their own stores, either by creating an illustrated catalogue or by preparing and performing a television or radio commercial. This project can be done individually, in pairs, or in groups.

MATERIALS

✄ **Students may need**
• Paper
• Magazines
• Scissors
• Colored pens and pencils
• Glue or tape

PREPARATION

Have students determine the type of store or the products they want to advertise. They should make a list of their products, looking up any words they might need, and assign a price to each item. (See **Mise en pratique,** Activity 7, page 87.)

SUGGESTED SEQUENCE

First Draft Have students choose the format for their advertisement, either a catalogue or a commercial.

If they choose to make a catalogue, they will need to find or create illustrations for their products and design an attractive layout. They should arrange their text and illustrations before gluing or taping them.

If students choose to create a commercial, they should start writing the script. They can treat their products seriously or make outrageous claims. Students will probably need some guidance; encourage them to find visual aids to get their message across. You may choose to have them memorize their scripts.

Peer Editing Those students who create commercials should now rehearse them to determine if their commercials are convincing and easy to understand. The catalogue producers might serve as an audience.

Those students doing catalogues should ask for feedback from the commercial writers regarding the descriptions and prices of the items as well as the layout.

Final Draft Students doing commercials should correct any mistakes pointed out in peer editing, gather all their visual aids, and present the commercial to the class.

Students making catalogues should revise their projects according to the feedback from their classmates and display them around the classroom.

GRADING THE PROJECT

You might assign grades for this project based on completion of the assignment, language use, presentation, and content.

Suggested Point Distribution (total = 100 points)

Completion of assignment . . . . 20 points
Language use. 20 points
Presentation. . . . . 30 points
Content . . . . 30 points

GO FISH

In this game, students will practice vocabulary for school supplies.

Procedure   This game should be prepared ahead of time. Draw or glue pictures of school supplies onto index cards. You will need four cards of each item for a complete deck and a complete deck for each pair or group playing the game. Deal each player five cards and place the remaining cards face down on the table. Then, players should remove all matching pairs from their hands and set them aside. The dealer begins by asking a player for a card. **(Stan, tu as un stylo?)** If the player has the card, he or she must give it to the person who asks for it, who then sets the pair aside and takes another turn. If the player doesn't have the card, the person requesting the card must draw one from the pile, and the next player takes a turn. The game ends when one player puts down or gives away the last card. All players count their pairs, and the player with the most pairs wins.

JE VOIS QUELQUE CHOSE (*I SPY*)

This game will help students review colors and classroom vocabulary.

Procedure   Have students think of an item in the classroom. It must be visible, and it should be an item that students can name in French. Ask a volunteer to tell only the color of his or her item. **(Je vois quelque chose de bleu, de blanc...)** Other students then try to guess what the item is. **(C'est un stylo?)** You might want to set a one-minute time limit for each item. You might even limit the number of guesses to keep a fast pace. The student who guesses correctly then tells the color of his or her item. If one student guesses correctly more than once, he or she may choose another student to continue the game. If no one guesses correctly, the student should name the item and choose another student to continue.

Chapitre 3
Tout pour la rentrée
pp. 66–89

𝒰sing the Chapter Opener

Motivating Activity

Ask students if they usually go shopping before the beginning of the school year. If so, ask the following questions. Do you go shopping for school supplies or clothes? Are you taking classes now that require extra or special supplies? Have you ever had to buy a book for a class, either for required reading or to replace a lost textbook? How much do school supplies cost? Are certain items considered better or less acceptable than others? Why?

Photo Flash!

① Claire and her mother are trying to decide whether to buy a **calculatrice** *(calculator)* or a **calculatrice**-**traductrice** *(calculator-translator),* which is a calculator and an electronic dictionary in one.

Teaching Suggestion

Ask students to identify the theme in the photos on pages 66 and 67 (shopping) and tell what each person is looking for. Ask students to match a chapter objective with each caption (Photo 1: asking for information; Photo 2: telling what you need; Photo 3: telling what you would like). Ask students what vocabulary they think they will learn in this chapter (school supplies, clothing, more numbers).

CHAPITRE
3
Tout pour la rentrée

① C'est combien, cette calculatrice?

66   *soixante-six*

Literature Link

Antoine de Saint-Exupéry, a well-known French aviator and writer, appears on the 50-franc bill, which is partially visible on these pages. One of his best known works is *Le Petit Prince (The Little Prince),* a story that emphasizes love and friendship rather than wealth and material possessions.

At the start of a new school year, French students have to buy supplies, including their textbooks, at the store. They may also buy things that are less essential for school, like compact discs and clothes.

In this chapter you will learn

- to make and respond to requests; to ask others what they need and tell what you need
- to tell what you'd like and what you'd like to do
- to get someone's attention; to ask for information; to express thanks

And you will

- listen to teenagers talk about what they need for school
- read a page from a French catalogue
- write a list of supplies you need for your classes
- find out about the school supplies French teenagers buy

② Il me faut un sac.

③ Je voudrais ce tee-shirt.

Focusing on Outcomes

Call students' attention to the chapter objectives. Ask small groups to brainstorm expressions in English they might use to accomplish the chapter objectives. For example, to express what they'd like to do, they might suggest *I'd like to . . .*, *I feel like . . .*, *I want to . . .*, and so on.
NOTE: You may want to use the video to support the objectives. The self-check activities in **Que sais-je?** on page 88 help students assess their achievement of the objectives.

Teacher Note

Students will learn **je voudrais** in this chapter; the present tense forms of **vouloir** are presented later.

Photo Flash!

② Claire is shopping for a schoolbag in Poitiers. There are usually no lockers in French schools, so students must have a sturdy bookbag in which to carry their supplies from class to class.

Block Scheduling

For suggestions about how to use *Allez, viens!* with block scheduling, see the *Lesson Planner*, pages 13–17.

VIDEO PROGRAM
Videocassette 1
37:12–41:25
Videocassette 5
(captioned version)
16:52–21:25

OR VIDEODISC PROGRAM,
Videodisc 2, Side A

Search 1, Play To 8145

Video Synopsis

In this segment of the video, Claire and her mother, Mme Millet, are shopping for school supplies. Claire's mother asks her what she needs and asks a saleswoman for help. They pick out pencils, notebooks, a pencil case, and other supplies. Claire sees a schoolbag that she really likes, but her mother tells her it's too expensive. Mme Millet wants to buy a less expensive bag. Claire says she would rather go without a bag than have one she doesn't like.

Motivating Activity

Ask students if they shop with friends, a family member, or alone. Have them think of possible difficulties that might arise while shopping with a parent.

Presentation

Before playing the video, have students read the questions in Activity 1 on page 70. Tell them to look for the answers as they view the episode. You might also ask them to guess the moods of Claire and her mother and what the problem might be.

The **roman-photo** is an abridged version of the video episode.

Mise en train

Pas question!

CD 3
Trs. 1–2

p. 25, Act. 1

Where are Claire and Mme Millet?
What do you think they are shopping for?

Claire   Mme Millet   La vendeuse

1. *Alors, qu'est-ce qu'il te faut?*
   Eh bien, des crayons, des stylos, une gomme, une calculatrice, un pot de colle...

2. *Pardon, mademoiselle, vous avez des trousses, s'il vous plaît?*
   Bien sûr. Là, à côté des cahiers.
   Merci.

3. *C'est combien, ces cahiers-ci?*
   12 F.

4. *Ah, regarde, maman, une calculatrice-traductrice.*
   C'est pour les maths ou pour l'anglais?
   Euh, il me faut une calculatrice pour les maths... Mais une calculatrice-traductrice, c'est pratique pour l'anglais.

RESOURCES FOR MISE EN TRAIN	
PRINT	**MEDIA**
• *Practice and Activity Book*, p. 25	• *Video Program*, Videocassette 1, Videocassette 5 (captioned version)
• *Video Guide*, pp. 17–18, 20	• *Videodisc Program*, Videodisc 2, Side A
• *Videodisc Guide*, pp. 27–29, 34	• *Audio Compact Discs*, CD 3, Trs. 1–2

Teacher Note

The monetary exchange rate has remained fairly steady since the mid-1980s: between five and six francs to the dollar. In the early 80s, the rate went as high as ten francs per dollar.

Language-to-Language

You might point out the connection between the word **colle** *(glue)* and the word **collage**, which is also used in English (illustrations glued together to make a picture).

Cooperative Learning

Have students calculate in dollars the prices of the items in the story. Form groups of four: a recorder, a reader to call out prices in francs, a money-changer to calculate the dollar price, and a checker to review the calculations. Students will need a copy of the latest money exchange rates, which can be found in the newspaper. Students may also want to calculate the prices in euros.

Video Integration

- **VIDEO PROGRAM,**
  Videocassette 1, 41:46–46:19
  Videocassette 5, 21:29–26:02
- **VIDEODISC PROGRAM,**
  Videodisc 2, Side A

Search 8145, Play To 16400

You may choose to continue with **Pas question! (suite)** at this time or wait until later in the chapter. The story continues the next day as Claire and Ann are leaving for school. Claire is carrying her supplies in her arms and drops everything. Her mother shows her a bag in a catalogue. Claire tries to order it through Minitel, but it is out of stock. She goes back to the store she went to with her mother and finds the same 70 F bag in a different color. Claire buys the bag as well as two T-shirts, one for herself and one as a gift for her mother. Mme Millet is surprised to see that Claire bought the inexpensive bag after all.

For videodisc application, see *Videodisc Guide.*

 For Individual Needs

2 Slower Pace Students might work in pairs to find the answers. To check their answers, you might have students repeat each sentence, replacing **elle** with either Claire or Mme Millet.

3 Slower Pace Before students watch the video, have them match the functions and the expressions in the box. Then, play the video and have students raise their hands when they hear these expressions.

Teaching Suggestion

5 You might suggest several possible endings to the story:
a) **Claire va à l'école sans sac.**
b) **Mme Millet achète le sac à 215 F.**
c) **Mme Millet achète le sac à 70 F.**
You might write these on a transparency and have the class vote on an ending for the story.

Additional Practice

Quote at random the characters in the video and have students identify the speakers.

These activities check for comprehension only. Students should not yet be expected to produce language modeled in **Mise en train**.

1 Tu as compris?

Answer the following questions based on **Pas question!**

1. What is the relationship between Claire and Mme Millet? How do you know? *daughter and mother; Claire calls her maman.*
2. Where are they? *at a store*
3. What are they doing there? *buying school supplies*
4. Why does Claire need a calculator? *for math class*
5. What is Mme Millet's main concern? *saving money*
6. What do you think of Claire's decision at the end of **Pas question!**?

2 Claire ou sa mère?

Does **elle** in each of the following sentences refer to Claire or Mme Millet?

1. Elle aime la calculatrice à 590 F. *Claire*
2. Elle voudrait une calculatrice-traductrice. *Claire*
3. Elle aime mieux le sac à 70 F. *Mme Millet*
4. Elle aime mieux le sac vert. *Claire*
5. Elle va aller à l'école sans sac. *Claire*
6. Elle n'achète pas un sac à 215 F. *Mme Millet*

3 Cherche les expressions

Can you find an expression in **Pas question!** to . . . *See answers below.*

1. ask what someone needs?
2. tell what you need?
3. get a salesperson's attention?
4. ask the price of something?
5. say you like or prefer something?
6. say you don't like something?

> Il est horrible!   C'est combien?
> Il me faut... J'aime mieux...
> Il est super! Pardon, mademoiselle...
> Qu'est-ce qu'il te faut?

4 Mets en ordre

Put these sentences about **Pas question!** in chronological order.

1. Mme Millet asks the price of a calculator. *4*
2. Mme Millet asks a salesperson if she has any pencil cases. *2*
3. Claire says she will go to school without a bag. *6*
4. Mme Millet asks Claire what she needs for school. *1*
5. Mme Millet asks the price of the notebooks. *3*
6. Claire points out a bag she likes. *5*

5 Et maintenant, à toi

What do you think will happen next in the story? Discuss your ideas with a partner.

3 1. Qu'est-ce qu'il te faut?
2. Il me faut...
3. Pardon, mademoiselle...
4. C'est combien?
5. Il est super! J'aime mieux...
6. Il est horrible!

PREMIERE ETAPE TPR Storytelling Book pp. 9, 12

Making and responding to requests; asking others what they need and telling what you need

 PA p. 26, Acts. 2–3   3-A **GV** pp. 17–18, Acts. 1–3   CD-ROM Disc 1

VOCABULAIRE

 un cahier

un crayon

une gomme

 un taille-crayon

une calculatrice

un stylo

 une trousse

 un classeur

un livre

 des feuilles (f.) de papier

une règle

 un sac (à dos)

De bons conseils

Make flashcards to learn new words. On one side of a card, write the French word you want to learn. (If the word is a noun, include an article to help you remember the gender.) On the other side, paste or draw a picture to illustrate the meaning of the word. Then, ask a classmate to show you the picture while you try to name the object, or use the cards to test yourself.

---

6 Ecoute! See scripts and answers on p. 65G.

CD 3 Tr. 3

Listen as Hafaïdh and Karine check the contents of their bookbags. Then, look at the pictures and decide which bag belongs to each of them.

a.

b.

c.

PREMIERE ETAPE
CHAPITRE 3

*J*ump Start!

Have students list all the classes they have this semester and tell whether they like them or not.

MOTIVATE

Have students pair off. Give them one minute to write down in English as many school supplies as they can. Call time and check the lists. You might give a prize to the pair who listed the most items.

TEACH

Presentation

Vocabulaire Before students see the French words, gather the objects pictured. Hold them up as you say the French words, having students repeat after you. Then, say the French words for various items and have students try to identify them by pointing to the correct item.

For Individual Needs

Auditory/Kinesthetic Learners After presenting all the words, ask **Qui a un(e)... ?** Have students hold up the object you named and say **Moi. J'ai un(e)...**

6 Slower Pace Before playing the recording, have students identify the items in each bookbag.

6 Auditory Learners Describe the contents of each bookbag and have students give the letter of the corresponding photo.

RESOURCES FOR PREMIERE ETAPE

PRINT
- *Lesson Planner*, p. 14
- *Practice and Activity Book*, pp. 26–28
- *Grammar and Vocabulary Workbook*, pp. 17–19
- *Activities for Communication*, pp. 13–14, 85, 88–89, 141–142
- *Listening Activities*, pp. 19, 23
- *Testing Program*, pp. 53–56
- *Alternative Assessment Guide*, p. 34

MEDIA
- *Video Program*, Videocassette 1
  Video Guide, pp. 17–22
- *Videodisc Program*, Videodisc 2, Side A
  Videodisc Guide, p. 31
- *Teaching Transparencies* 3-1, 3-A
- *Interactive CD-ROM Program*, Disc 1
  CD-ROM Teacher's Guide, p. 10
- *Audio Compact Discs*
  Textbook Listening Activities, CD 3, Trs. 3–4
  Additional Listening Activities 3-1, 3-2, CD 3, Trs. 26–27
  Quiz 3-1B, CD 3, Tr. 20

Thinking Critically

Drawing Inferences
Note Culturelle Have students consider these questions. What are the advantages and disadvantages of having to bag your own purchases? Of having shoppers bring their own bags? Do American stores encourage shoppers to bring their own bags? Why or why not?

Teaching Suggestion

8 Have partners make a list of 3 or 4 items and ask each other if they have these items. Then, have individuals tell which items their partners have and don't have.

Presentation

Comment dit-on... ?
Circulate among the students asking for certain items. (**Tu as une règle?**) Prompt the responses **Voilà** and **Non, je regrette.** Then, have students practice the same exchange in pairs. Next, have students ask you for certain things, saying **Vous avez... ?** Have them ask a partner for two things they need.

Thinking Critically

Drawing Inferences Ask students whether they should use **tu** or **vous** with a classmate and with a salesperson in a store (classmate — **tu**; salesperson — **vous**). Ask students what they think the reaction would be if they used the wrong pronoun (surprised, offended). You might give comparable examples in English (calling someone by their first name when you don't know him or her very well).

7 Objets trouvés
Lost and found

When Paulette gets home from the store, she realizes that she forgot to put some of her school supplies into her bag. Look at the receipt showing what she bought and make a list, in French, of the missing items. See answers below.

Elle n'a pas le...

```
VEN 13-05-99              3004
047CA  BELLIOT Stephanie

GOMME CAOUTCH          3.30
CRAYONS GRAH.          5.15
REGLE GRADUEE          5.20
CAH. BROUILLON         1.90
COPIES DBLES PF GC     4.25
CLASSEUR 17X22        16.15
TROUSSE               28.10
SOUS/TOTAL            64.05

TOTAL                 64.05

REÇU                 100.00
RENDU                 35.95

00617    7 ARTC     16:36TM
```

NOTE CULTURELLE

In large stores in France, customers are expected to place their items on the conveyer belt and then remove and bag them as well. Most stores provide small plastic sacks, but many shoppers bring their own basket (**un panier**) or net bag (**un filet**). Since space is limited in small stores and boutiques, browsing inside stores is not common. Instead, items and their prices are placed in window displays. Most people window-shop until they are ready to make a purchase. A store that reads **Entrée libre** welcomes browsers.

8 Devine!

Write down the name of one of the objects from the **Vocabulaire** on page 71. Don't let the other members of your group know what you've chosen. They will then take turns guessing which object you chose.

—C'est un taille-crayon?
—Oui, c'est ça. *or* Non, ce n'est pas ça.

COMMENT DIT-ON... ?
Making and responding to requests

To ask someone for something:
Tu as un stylo?
Vous avez un crayon?

To respond:
Oui. **Voilà.** *Here.*
Non. **Je regrette. Je n'ai pas de** crayons. *Sorry. I don't have . . .*

—Tu as une calculatrice, Paul?
—J'ai un stylo, un crayon, une règle et des feuilles de papier, mais je n'ai pas de calculatrice!

p. 27, Act. 4b
3-1

Multicultural Link

You might want to have students brainstorm a list of school supplies and other items they need for school. Have them look for two or three of the items at home with labels and/or instructions in different languages.

Answers
7 Elle n'a pas le classeur. Elle n'a pas le cahier. Elle n'a pas la gomme. Elle n'a pas la règle. Elle n'a pas les copies.

CD-ROM
Disc 1

GRAMMAIRE The indefinite articles **un**, **une**, and **des**

The articles **un** and **une** both mean *a* or *an.* Use **un** with masculine nouns and une with feminine nouns. Use **des** *(some)* with plural nouns. Notice that **un**, **une**, and **des** change to **de** after **ne... pas.**

J'ai **un** crayon, mais je n'ai pas **de** papier.

pp. 18–19, Acts. 4–7

Additional Grammar Practice, p. R30

9 Ecoute! See scripts and answers on p. 65G.

CD 3 Tr. 4

Listen as Nadine asks her friends for some school supplies. Match her friends' responses to the appropriate pictures.

a.

b.

c.

d.

e.

10 Tu as ça, toi?

With a partner, take turns pointing out the differences you notice between Christophe's desk and Annick's.

Regarde! Christophe a une gomme, mais Annick n'a pas de gomme.

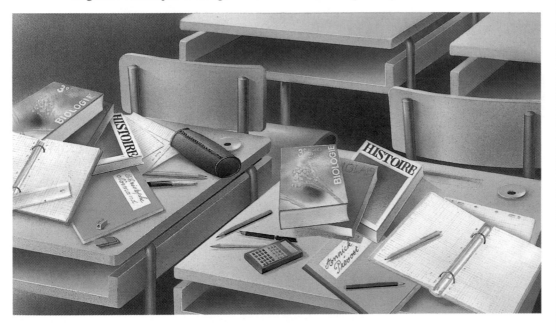

PREMIERE ETAPE

soixante-treize **73**

Presentation

Grammaire Hold up an object that is a masculine noun in French, such as a pencil, and have students tell you what you have. (**Vous avez un crayon.**) Repeat with a feminine noun (**Vous avez une gomme.**) and with several other objects. (**Vous avez des crayons et des gommes.**) Put the items away, show your empty hands, and have students tell you that you don't have these objects. (**Vous n'avez pas de...**) Then, have students make a chart in their notebooks with two columns and four rows. Down the left-hand side of the chart, they should write *masculine, feminine, vowel sound,* and *plural.* They should label the columns *Definite articles* and *Indefinite articles.* Have students fill in the chart with **le, la, l', les, un, une,** and **des,** and keep it for later use.

Teacher Note

Demonstrative adjectives can be added to the chart when they are presented later in this chapter.

Teaching Suggestion

10 As a variation, form small groups or teams for a competition. Set a time limit within which groups must write down all of the items they see on one of the desks in the illustration.

Culture Note

French notebook paper is usually graph paper rather than lined. It is sold either as **copies simples** *(single-page sheets)* or **copies doubles,** which are two-page sheets used for **rédactions** or **interros écrites.**

Presentation

Comment dit-on... ? Have pairs of students role-play the short dialogue in the illustration, substituting other courses and objects. Students might want to know the negative **Il ne me faut pas de...**

For videodisc application, see *Videodisc Guide.*

Thinking Critically

Synthesizing Ask students to imagine situations other than shopping for school supplies when they might use the expressions in **Comment dit-on... ?** (at a pharmacy, library, or post office, and when cooking).

CLOSE

To close this **étape**, display ten school supplies on a tray or table and allow students one minute to look at them. Then, cover the objects and have students write down as many objects as they can remember. You might give a prize or extra credit to the student who remembers the most objects and give credit for completion to the others.

ASSESS

Quiz 3-1A, Quiz 3-1B, *Testing Program,* pp. 53–56

Audio CD 3, Tr. 20

Performance Assessment

Show *Teaching Transparency 3-1.* Have students assume the identity of one of the shoppers and tell what they need for school.

COMMENT DIT-ON... ?
Asking others what they need and telling what you need

To ask what someone needs:
Qu'est-ce qu'il te faut pour la bio?
What do you need for . . . ? (informal)
Qu'est-ce qu'il vous faut pour la géo?
What do you need for . . . ? (formal)

To tell what you need:
Il me faut un stylo et un classeur.

PA
p. 28,
Acts. 5–6

3-1

11 Qu'est-ce qu'il te faut?

Make a list of your school subjects. Exchange lists with a partner. Then take turns asking each other what you need for various classes.

— Qu'est-ce qu'il te faut pour les maths?
— Il me faut une calculatrice et un crayon.

12 Aide-mémoire

Write a note to remind yourself of the school supplies you need to buy for two or three of your classes.

13 Un petit service

You're late for class, and you've forgotten your supplies. Ask a friend if he or she has what you need. Your friend should respond appropriately. Then, change roles.

— Oh là là! J'ai histoire! Il me faut un stylo et un cahier. Tu as un stylo?
— Non, je regrette.
— Zut! *(Darn!)*

Vocabulaire *à la carte*

Here are some additional words you can use to talk about your school supplies.

un compas	*a compass*
des crayons (m.) **de couleur**	*some colored pencils*
un feutre	*a marker*
du liquide correcteur	*some correction fluid*
du ruban adhésif (m.)	*some transparent tape*
une tenue de gymnastique	*a gym suit*

74 *soixante-quatorze*

CHAPITRE 3 Tout pour la rentrée

Language Notes
Vocabulaire à la carte

• Make sure students don't pronounce the **s** at the end of **compas. Feutre** also means *felt,* as in felt-tip pen.

• You might want to give students the names of other items they might like to know in French: **un surligneur** *(highlighter);* **la craie** *(chalk);* and **un cahier de textes** *(memo book or personal calendar for young people).*

PANORAMA CULTUREL

Séverine • Martinique   Onélia • France   Marius • Côte d'Ivoire

We asked some francophone students what supplies they bought for the opening of school, **la rentrée.** Here's what they had to say.

Qu'est-ce qu'il te faut comme fournitures scolaires?

CD 3
Trs. 5–8

CD-ROM
Disc 1

«Alors, donc pour l'école j'ai acheté un nouveau sac à dos, des livres pour étudier, des vêtements, entre autres des jeans, des chaussures, bien sûr et puis bon, des tee-shirts, des jupes, des robes.»

—Séverine
Tr. 6

«Il faut des classeurs, des cahiers, des crayons, des règles, des instruments de géométrie, [une] calculatrice pour les mathématiques, des feuilles... C'est tout.»

—Onélia
Tr. 7

«Pour l'école, il faut des règles, des bics, des stylos, des cahiers, des livres et la tenue.»

—Marius
Tr. 8

Qu'en penses-tu? Answers may vary.

1. What school supplies did you have to purchase for the school year?
2. What did these students buy that is usually provided by schools in the United States?
3. What are the advantages and disadvantages of each system? textbooks
4. What other items do you usually buy at the beginning of a school year?

Savais-tu que...?

In French-speaking countries, students usually buy their own textbooks and even maintain their own grade book, **un livret scolaire.** Some schools require students to purchase school uniforms. A store that specializes in school supplies, textbooks, and paper products is called **une librairie-papeterie.**

PANORAMA CULTUREL
CHAPITRE 3

VIDEO PROGRAM
Videocassette 1
46:20–48:26

OR VIDEODISC PROGRAM,
Videodisc 2, Side A

Search 16400, Play To 18510

Teacher Notes

• See the *Video Guide,* the *Videodisc Guide,* and the *CD-ROM Teacher's Guide* for activities related to the **Panorama Culturel.**
• Remind students that cultural material may be included in the Chapter Quizzes and Test.
• The interviewees' language represents informal, unrehearsed speech. Occasionally, edits have been made for clarification.

Presentation

As students view the video or listen to the recording, have them jot down the items mentioned by the interviewees. Then, in pairs or in small groups, have them take turns reading the interviews aloud. Next, ask students the **Questions** to check comprehension. Finally, have them discuss the questions in **Qu'en penses-tu?** in small groups or as a class.

Culture Note

You might tell students that Ivorian students wear school uniforms. In high school, the boys wear khaki shirts and pants, while the girls wear blue skirts and white blouses.

Questions

1. Qu'est-ce que Séverine a acheté comme vêtements pour l'école? (des jeans, des chaussures, des tee-shirts, des jupes et des robes)
2. Onélia a besoin de quelles fournitures scolaires? (des classeurs, des cahiers, des crayons, des règles, des instruments de géométrie, une calculatrice et des feuilles) Pour quel cours? (les maths, la géométrie)
3. Qu'est-ce que Marius a acheté pour l'école? (des règles, des bics, des stylos, des cahiers, des livres et la tenue)

Language Note

Some new terms are **une tenue** *(a school uniform)* and **des bics** *(ballpoint pens).* See *Video Guide* or *Videodisc Guide* for additional vocabulary.

Jump Start!

Have students make a list of five things they have with them for class and anything they did not bring. They might begin with **Aujourd'hui, j'ai...** and **Je n'ai pas de...**

MOTIVATE

Have students mention one item they would most like to have in each of these categories: clothes, gifts, and reading material. Next, have them tell what they would like to do if they had a free afternoon.

TEACH

Presentation

Vocabulaire Say the cognates at the bottom of the **Vocabulaire** and have students guess their English equivalents. Then, present the other words (**baskets, ordinateur, montre, portefeuille,** and **roman**) by showing the actual items, drawing them on the board, or showing pictures of them.

For Individual Needs

Tactile/Kinesthetic Learners
Name an item in the classroom and have students point to it or pick it up from among items you have displayed on a table.

14 Challenge Have students write down the item each person would like to buy as well as the person's name.

Building on Previous Skills

To review previously learned vocabulary, have students tell why they think the people in the **Vocabulaire** are looking at the objects. (**Hervé aime faire les magasins.**)

DEUXIEME ETAPE TPR

Storytelling Book pp. 10, 12

Telling what you'd like and what you'd like to do

3-B, 3-C   GV   p. 20, Acts. 8–9   CD-ROM Disc 1

VOCABULAIRE

Qu'est-ce qu'on va acheter?

Hervé regarde **un short**.

Odile regarde **des baskets**.

Denis regarde **un roman**.

Stéphane regarde **un disque compact/un CD**.

Dorothée regarde **un jean**.

Mme Roussel regarde **un ordinateur**.

M. Beauvois regarde **une montre**.

M. Prévost regarde **un portefeuille**.

You can probably figure out what these words mean:

un bracelet	un magazine	une radio	une télévision
une cassette	un poster	un sweat-shirt	une vidéocassette
un dictionnaire	un pull-over	un tee-shirt	

14 Ecoute! See scripts and answers on p. 65G.

Several shoppers in the **Vocabulaire** are going to tell you what they would like to buy. As you listen to each speaker, look at the illustrations above and identify the person. Write down his or her name.

CD 3 Tr. 9

76 *soixante-seize*   CHAPITRE 3   Tout pour la rentrée

RESOURCES FOR DEUXIEME ETAPE

PRINT
- *Lesson Planner,* p. 15
- *Practice and Activity Book,* pp. 29–31
- *Grammar and Vocabulary Workbook,* pp. 20–23
- *Activities for Communication,* pp. 15–16, 86, 88–89, 141–142
- *Listening Activities,* pp. 20, 24
- *Testing Program,* pp. 57–60
- *Alternative Assessment Guide,* p. 34

MEDIA
- *Video Program,* Videocassette 1
  Video Guide, pp. 17–22
- *Videodisc Program,* Videodisc 2, Side A
  Videodisc Guide, p. 32
- *Teaching Transparencies* 3-2, 3-B, 3-C
- *Interactive CD-ROM Program,* Disc 1
  CD-ROM Teacher's Guide, pp. 10–11
- *Audio Compact Discs*
  Textbook Listening Activities, CD 3, Trs. 9–10
  Additional Listening Activities 3-3, 3-4, CD 3, Trs. 28–29
  Quiz 3-2B, CD 3, Tr. 21

COMMENT DIT-ON... ?

Telling what you'd like and what you'd like to do

3-2

Je voudrais un sac. *I'd like . . .*
Je voudrais acheter un tee-shirt. *I'd like to buy . . .*

15 **Ecoute!** See scripts and answers on p. 65G.

CD 3 Tr. 10

Georges has just won a gift certificate from his favorite department store. Listen as he tells you what he would like to buy and make a list of his choices.

16 **Vive le week-end!**

What would you like to do this weekend? Find three classmates who want to do the same thing.

—Je voudrais sortir avec des copains. Et toi?
—Moi aussi. *or* Moi, je voudrais faire du sport.

faire les magasins   dormir
danser   écouter de la musique
parler au téléphone   étudier
regarder la télévision
nager   sortir avec des copains
faire le ménage   faire du sport

17 **Un cadeau** *A gift* **H**

Make a list of what you would like to buy for . . .

1. a friend who likes horror movies and books.
2. a friend who loves sports.
3. someone who's always late for class.
4. a friend who loves music.
5. someone who loves French.
6. your best friend.

18 **Mon journal**

You earned 100 dollars this summer. Write down three or four items you'd like to buy for yourself.

GRAMMAIRE The demonstrative adjectives ce, cet, cette, and ces

Ce, cet, and **cette** mean *this* or *that.* **Ces** means *these* or *those.*

PA
p. 29,
Acts. 7–8

	Singular	Plural
Masculine before a consonant sound	**ce** stylo	**ces** stylos
Masculine before a vowel sound	**cet** examen	**ces** examens
Feminine	**cette** école	**ces** écoles

GV
p. 21,
Acts. 10–11

When you want to specify *that* as opposed to *this,* add -**là** *(there)* to the end of the noun.

Additional Grammar
Practice, pp. R30–R31

—J'aime **ce sac.**
—Moi, j'aime mieux **ce sac-là.**

DEUXIEME ETAPE

soixante-dix-sept **77**

DEUXIEME ETAPE
CHAPITRE 3

Presentation

Comment dit-on... ? After modeling the function, hold up various items or illustrations of items or activities and have individual students say what they would like or what they would like to do.

Teaching Suggestion

17 After students complete this activity, name gifts you are buying for imaginary friends (**un poster de Paris pour Pierre**). Ask students to suggest why you are buying that gift for the person. (**Pierre aime voyager.**)

Presentation

Grammaire Show students two of the same item and ask them which one they would choose. For example, hold up two different pens and ask **Tu aimes mieux quel stylo?** Students should answer **Ce stylo-là** as they point to the one they choose. Tell students that forms of *this* and *that* are called demonstrative adjectives because they point out or demonstrate one or more things among many.

For videodisc application, see *Videodisc Guide.*

Teaching Suggestion

Grammaire Review definite and indefinite articles. If you had students make the suggested chart of articles (see **Presentation** on page 73), you might have them add **ce, cet, cette,** and **ces** to it now.

Teacher Note

You might tell students that if they want to specify *this* as opposed to *that,* they can add -**ci** to the end of the first noun. (**Moi, je préfère ce sac-ci, mais je n'aime pas ce sac-là.**) The suffix "-**ci**" is no longer very common in spoken French.

Language Notes

• French teenagers often use the abbreviation **CD** for **disque compact.**
• Tell students that the infinitive, the *to* form of a verb *(to go, to have, to buy),* is used after **Je voudrais.** You might also tell them that this is a polite way to express a desire.

For Individual Needs

19 Slower Pace Have students determine the gender and number of the noun in each sentence before they choose the correct article or adjective.

Presentation

Vocabulaire Say each color as you point out items of that color. Then, name three colors in a row and challenge a volunteer to point to items of those colors in the order in which the colors were mentioned. Ask students if they see any similarities or associations with English. Then, ask students to give the colors of the sky, a Valentine, fall, Halloween, and the French flag.

Additional Practice

You might want to hold up various items and ask about the color: **C'est bleu ou rouge?** Have individuals or the entire class respond. For more of a challenge, ask **C'est de quelle couleur?**

---

19 Le cadeau parfait *The perfect gift*

Claire is shopping for a gift for her mother. The salesperson is making suggestions. Choose the correct articles to complete their conversation.

LE VENDEUR   Vous aimez (**ce**/**cette**) montre, mademoiselle?
CLAIRE   Oui, mais ma mère a déjà (**un**/**une**) montre.
LE VENDEUR   Et (**ces**/**ce**) roman?
CLAIRE   Non, elle n'aime pas lire.
LE VENDEUR   Elle aime (**la** /**l'**) musique?
CLAIRE   Oui. Elle adore le jazz.
LE VENDEUR   (**Cet**/**Cette**) cassette de Wynton Marsalis, peut-être?
CLAIRE   C'est une bonne idée.

20 Qu'est-ce que tu aimes mieux?

Take turns with a partner asking and answering questions about the items below.

— Tu aimes ce sac?
— Non. J'aime mieux ce sac-là!

Moi aussi.   Non, je n'aime pas ça.
   Non.   Oui, j'adore!
Oui, mais j'aime mieux...
J'aime bien.   Moi non plus.

1.   2.   3.   4.

 pp. 29–30, Acts. 9–10   3-D   p. 22, Act. 12

VOCABULAIRE

De quelle couleur est...

le sac?	la trousse?		le sac?	la trousse?
ROUGE	ROUGE		ROSE	ROSE
ORANGE	ORANGE		BLANC	BLANCHE
JAUNE	JAUNE		GRIS	GRISE
VERT	VERTE		NOIR	NOIRE
BLEU	BLEUE		MARRON	MARRON
VIOLET	VIOLETTE			

21 Vrai ou faux?

Tell whether the statements below are true (**vrai**) or false (**faux**) according to the picture.

1. Claire a un sac jaune.   *vrai*
2. Claire et Thierry ont des tee-shirts bleus.   *faux*
3. Claire a un short marron.   *faux*
4. Thierry a des baskets bleues.   *faux*
5. Thierry a un classeur rouge.   *vrai*
6. Claire et Thierry ont des shorts noirs.   *faux*

GRAMMAIRE Adjective agreement and placement

Did you notice in the **Vocabulaire** on page 78 that the spelling of some colors changes according to the nouns they describe?

	Singular	Plural
Masculine	le classeur vert	les classeurs verts
Feminine	la gomme verte	les gommes vertes

- Usually, you add an **e** to make an adjective feminine; however, when an adjective ends in an unaccented **e**, you don't have to add another **e**: **le classeur rouge, la gomme rouge.**
- Some adjectives don't follow this pattern: **blanc, blanche; violet, violette.**
- Usually, you add an **s** to make an adjective plural; however, when an adjective ends in an **s**, you don't have to add another **s**: **les crayons gris.**
- Some adjectives don't change form. Two examples are **orange** and **marron.**
- What do you notice about where the adjectives are placed in relation to the nouns they describe?*

PA p. 30, Acts. 11–12

GV pp. 22–23, Acts. 13–15

Additional Grammar Practice, p. R31

22 Chasse au trésor *Scavenger hunt*

Create a list of six objects. Ask your classmates if they have the items on your list. When you find someone who does, find out what color each item is and write the person's name next to the appropriate item.

un tee-shirt	une montre	un short
des baskets	un stylo	un pull-over
une trousse		un portefeuille

* Colors and many other adjectives are placed **after** the nouns they describe.

DEUXIEME ETAPE

soixante-dix-neuf **79**

DEUXIEME ETAPE
CHAPITRE 3

For Individual Needs

21 Visual Learners First, ask students to identify in French the clothes in the illustration.

Presentation

Grammaire Have students deduce how the feminine forms of colors are formed by studying the **Vocabulaire** on page 78. Then, ask students how they think the spelling of the colors would change if they described several things. Show various combinations of school supplies in certain colors (two red binders, one green pencil, three white rulers) and have volunteers write the French equivalents on the board (**les classeurs rouges, le crayon vert, les règles blanches**).

For Individual Needs

22 Slower Pace Review the colors in French before starting this activity. You might say **Cette personne a des baskets noires** and have students call out the name of the person in class wearing those sneakers.

CLOSE

 Game

Play the game "**Je vois quelque chose**" on page 65J to practice vocabulary and colors. Extend it to refer to people: **Je vois quelqu'un qui a des baskets blanches.** You might also re-enter previously learned vocabulary: **Je vois quelqu'un qui a une calculatrice noire.**

ASSESS

Quiz 3-2A, Quiz 3-2B, *Testing Program,* pp. 57–60
Audio CD 3, Tr. 21

Performance Assessment

Have students form groups, gather ten of their own school supplies, and make a list of the objects. Have one student tell what the group has. (**Nous avons ces stylos verts, cette calculatrice blanche...**)

CHAPITRE 3   DEUXIEME ETAPE   79

Jump Start!

Have students make a list of three things they would like or would like to do.

MOTIVATE

Ask students to count in French from 0–50 by tens and then by fives.

TEACH

Presentation

Vocabulaire After students have done the motivating activity, write the word **soixante** on the board, pointing out the similarity with **six**. Ask students to count aloud from 60–69. Next, write **soixante-dix** on the board and ask students what number it represents. After establishing that it is 70, ask students to guess how to count from 71–79. Next, write **quatre-vingts** on the board and ask students how to continue; do the same with **quatre-vingt-dix**. Finally, write **cent** and ask students to suggest English words that have the same root *(century, cent, centennial)*. Make sure students understand that **quatre-vingts** and **deux cents** end in -**s** only if no other numbers follow. Have students count by hundreds from 200–900. You might want to refer students to the list of numbers on page R55.

Teaching Suggestion

23 After this activity, ask students to say the frequency and call letters of their favorite radio stations. (**Moi, j'écoute KVMJ 95.5 FM.**) You might take a poll to see which three stations are the most popular.

TROISIEME ETAPE TPR

Storytelling Book
pp. 11, 12

Getting someone's attention; asking for information; expressing thanks

PA p. 32, Acts. 15–16   GV p. 24, Acts. 16–18   CD-ROM Disc 1

VOCABULAIRE

60 soixante	70 soixante-dix	71 soixante et onze	72 soixante-douze	80 quatre-vingts	81 quatre-vingt-un
90 quatre-vingt-dix	91 quatre-vingt-onze	100 cent	101 cent un	200 deux cents	201 deux cent un

23 Ecoute! See scripts and answers on p. 65H.

CD 3 Tr. 11

Listen to four French disc jockeys announce the dial frequencies of their radio stations. Then, match the frequency to the station logo.

a. RADIOS ROCK — RCV 99 MHZ (LILLE)

b. NRJ 100.3 MHZ

c. C'ROCK 89.5 MHZ (VIENNE)

d. OUÏ FM 102.3 MHZ (PARIS)

e. CANAL B — 94 MHZ

NOTE CULTURELLE

Prices in French stores will be given in **francs,** the French monetary unit or in **euros,** the European currency. In addition to French francs, there are Swiss francs, Belgian francs, Luxembourg francs, and C.F.A. (**Communauté financière africaine**) francs in many African countries. There are 100 **centimes** in one French franc. Coins are available in denominations of 5, 10, and 20 centimes, 1/2 franc, 1 franc, and 2, 5, 10, and 20 francs. Bills come in denominations of 20, 50, 100, 200, and 500 francs. Beginning in 1999, the euro was introduced in France. The French franc will gradually be replaced by the euro by the year 2002. Euro bills come in denominations of 5, 10, 15, 20, 50, 100, 200, and 500 euro bills. Coins are in denominations of 1, 2, 5, 10, 20, and 50 eurocents.

80 *quatre-vingts*   CHAPITRE 3   Tout pour la rentrée

RESOURCES FOR **TROISIEME ETAPE**	
PRINT	**MEDIA**
• *Lesson Planner,* p. 16	• *Video Program,* Videocassette 1
• *Practice and Activity Book,* pp. 32–34	*Video Guide,* pp. 17–22
• *Grammar and Vocabulary Workbook,* p. 24	• *Videodisc Program,* Videodisc 2, Side A
• *Activities for Communication,* pp. 17–18, 87, 88–89, 141–142	*Videodisc Guide,* p. 32
• *Listening Activities,* pp. 21, 25	• *Teaching Transparencies* 3-3, 3-D
• *Testing Program,* pp. 61–64	• *Interactive CD-ROM Program,* Disc 1
• *Alternative Assessment Guide,* p. 34	*CD-ROM Teacher's Guide,* pp. 10–11
	• *Audio Compact Discs*
	Textbook Listening Activities, CD 3, Trs. 11–12
	Additional Listening Activities 3-5, 3-6, CD 3, Trs. 30–31
	Quiz 3-3B, CD 3, Tr. 22

24 Ça fait combien? *How much is it?*

How much money is shown in each illustration? Give the totals in French.

1. quatre-vingt-sept francs
2. soixante-trois francs

25 C'est combien?

Look at the drawing of the store display below. How much money does each of these customers spend in **Papier Plume**?

1. Alain achète deux stylos et une trousse.   20F70
2. Geneviève achète un classeur, un dictionnaire et un cahier.   266F15
3. Paul achète six crayons et un taille-crayon.   5F95
4. Marcel achète une règle, une gomme et un stylo.   8F10
5. Sarah achète deux cahiers et un dictionnaire.   250F20
6. Cécile achète une règle et une calculatrice.   123F20

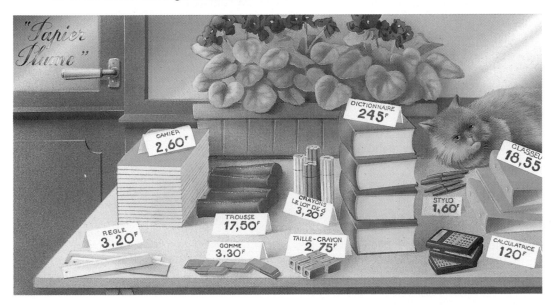

TROISIEME ETAPE

quatre-vingt-un **81**

Math Link

Using either the present exchange rate or an estimate of five and a half francs per dollar, have students calculate the cost in dollars of some of the school supplies in the ad in Activity 25. Ask students whether supplies seem to cost more, less, or about the same in France as in the US. (Generally, school supplies are a little more expensive in France.) Then, have students calculate the amounts in euros.

Culture Note

Euro bills, like French franc bills, increase in size according to the value of the bill. Euro bills are illustrated with architectural elements and bridges. As for euro coins, one side features a common European theme, and the other side contains a national symbol surrounded by the European Union's twelve stars. By 2002, all current national currencies will be replaced by the euro.

Teaching Suggestion

25 For listening comprehension, make some true–false statements as students look at the illustration. (**La trousse coûte 20 F. (faux) Les règles coûtent 3F20. (vrai)**)

Reteaching

25 School supplies, numbers Write on the board the prices of several items in francs:

> **un crayon = 2F30**
> **un cahier = 14F80**
> **une trousse = 39F50**
> **six stylos = 75 F**

Say the names of the items and their prices and have students repeat them. Then, write several more items on the board and have individual students suggest prices for them. Next, have students work in pairs, with one student naming items and prices at random, and the other student calculating the total cost and the change due from a **100 F** bill.

Language Notes

- Ask students to suggest slang terms we use in English to refer to money (dough, bucks). You might give them some other terms in French for money. Money in slang is **le fric. Les sous** is used for **francs** in slang expressions like **Je n'ai pas un sou** or **Il est sans le sou.**
- Some idiomatic expressions with numbers include **couper les cheveux en quatre** *(to split hairs),* **voir trente**-six **chandelles** *(to see stars),* **faire les cent pas** *(to pace up and down).*
- Francophone Swiss and Belgians say **septante** and **nonante** for 70 and 90. For 80, the Belgians say **quatre-vingts,** while the Swiss say **octante.**

Mon journal

26 For an additional journal entry suggestion for Chapter 3, see *Practice and Activity Book,* page 147. You might also refer students to additional school supplies listed in the Additional Vocabulary on page R10.

Motivating Activity

Ask students what else they need to know besides numbers in order to buy something at a store. Ask them how they get the clerk's attention and how they ask for help.

Presentation

Comment dit-on... ? Ask students to look first at the illustrations. Then, have them read the two dialogues and infer which functions the girl is expressing in each (1st: asking how much something costs; 2nd: expressing thanks). After introducing the expressions, have students role-play the dialogues, changing the item and price.

Language Note

Explain to students that although **A votre service** means *you're welcome/at your service,* it is used only in certain situations. The expression will be used by people who work in service-oriented businesses, such as restaurants and shops, but not in casual conversation.

Teaching Suggestion

28 You might want to have students use their own school supplies as props for their dialogues.

---

26 Mon journal

Do you budget your money? Make a list of the items you've bought in the last month and the approximate price of each in francs. To convert American prices to francs, look up the current exchange rate in the newspaper.

COMMENT DIT-ON... ?
Getting someone's attention; asking for information; expressing thanks

p. 34,
Acts. 18–19 3-3

For additional practice, see pp. R31–R32.

To get someone's attention:
Pardon, monsieur/madame/
mademoiselle.
Excusez-moi, monsieur/madame/
mademoiselle.

To ask how much something costs:
C'est combien?

To express thanks:
Merci.

27 Ecoute!   See scripts and answers on p. 65H.

In a department store in France, you overhear shoppers asking salespeople for the prices of various items. As you listen to the conversations, write down the items mentioned and their prices.

CD 3 Tr. 12

28 Jeu de rôle

You're buying school supplies in a French **librairie-papeterie.** For each item you want, get the salesperson's attention and ask how much the item costs. The salesperson will give you the price. Act out this scene with a partner. Then, change roles.

NOTE CULTURELLE

Prices in French stores will be expressed in francs or in euros. Prices expressed in francs can be said and written in two ways, either **quarante-cinq francs cinquante** (45F50) or **quarante-cinq cinquante** (45,50). Notice that a comma is used instead of a decimal point.

82 *quatre-vingt-deux*   CHAPITRE 3   Tout pour la rentrée

Career Path

26 Have students work in pairs to think of careers that would involve foreign currencies, such as the **euro** and the **franc.** Ask them how a knowledge of French could benefit them in these careers. You may want to have students do research on the Internet for ideas.

29 Les magazines

 You've decided to subscribe to a French magazine. Take turns with a partner playing the roles of a customer and a salesperson. Use the advertisement to discuss the prices of several magazines.

Abonnez-vous à :

FEMME A LA MODE	(12 numéros) France 210 FF
DECOUVERTE SCIENTIFIQUE	(22 numéros) France 499 FF
L'AFRIQUE DE NOS JOURS	(12 numéros) France 250 FF, Europe 250 FF, Dom-Tom 250 FF, Afrique 265 FF
TELE-TUBE	(52 numéros) France et Dom-Tom 580 FF, USA $140, Canada $180, Autres pays 855 FF
LA VOIX DU MONDE	(52 numéros) France 728 FF
LES GRANDS MOUVEMENTS DE L'ECONOMIE	(12 numéros) France 170 FF
LA VIE SPORTIVE	(12 numéros) France 215 FF

PRONONCIATION

The r sound

See scripts and answers on p. 65H.

CD 3 Trs. 13–18

The French **r** is quite different from the American *r*. To pronounce the French **r**, keep the tip of your tongue pressed against your lower front teeth. Arch the back of your tongue upward, almost totally blocking the passage of air in the back of your throat.

A. A prononcer

Repeat the following words.

1. Raoul	rouge	roman	règle
2. crayon	trente	calculatrice	barbe
3. terrible	intéressant	Europe	quarante
4. poster	rare	vert	montre

B. A lire

Take turns with a partner reading the following sentences aloud.

1. Fermez la porte.
2. Regardez le livre de français.
3. Prenez un crayon.
4. Ouvrez la fenêtre.
5. Je voudrais une montre.
6. Je regrette. Je n'ai pas de règle.

C. A écrire

You're going to hear a short dialogue. Write down what you hear.

TROISIEME ETAPE

quatre-vingt-trois **83**

Teacher Note

For descriptions of French-language periodicals and subscription information, see page T54.

For Individual Needs

29 Slower Pace Ask individuals to name the different magazines and the prices shown here. Ask them what kinds of magazines they think these are.

Teaching Suggestion

Prononciation To make the French **r** sound, have students practice the correct position of the tongue by pronouncing the French word **garage**. At first, they may simply say **gara**, since the two consonants are produced in the back of the throat. Then, have them say the whole word **garage**.

CLOSE

Read aloud some addition and subtraction problems for students to solve. You might have students work individually, in pairs, or in small groups. You will need to teach the words **et/plus** *(plus)* and **moins** *(minus)*. Sample problems: 83 + 156; 92 – 16; 64 + 71; 48 + 27; 212 – 13 (Answers: 239, 76, 135, 75, 199). Ask volunteers to write the problems and answers on the board and read them aloud.

ASSESS

Quiz 3-3A, Quiz 3-3B, *Testing Program,* pp. 61–64

Audio CD 3, Tr. 22

Performance Assessment

Have partners make lists of what they have and what they need for their courses. Then, have them act out a scene in a store where they purchase the items they need.

READING STRATEGY

Scanning for specific information

Teacher Note

For an additional reading, see *Practice and Activity Book*, page 35.

PREREADING
Activities A–B

Motivating Activity

Ask students where they go shopping for school supplies and why they go there. Next, ask students to imagine they are going to school in another country. Ask them how they would find the supplies and clothes they want.

Teaching Suggestion

Have students identify the type of reading they are faced with so that they will know what type of information to look for. Ask them for examples of words or phrases that give clues as to what the ad is about.

Teacher Note

There are several large discount store chains in France, including **Monoprix**, **Prisunic**, **Nouvelles Galeries**, and **Tati**.

READING
Activities C–J

 For Individual Needs

Visual/Auditory Learners

You might want to read the selection aloud or have students read it to each other in pairs.

$\mathcal{L}$ook at the information presented on this page. Where would you expect to find a text like this? Would you normally use information like this for a specific purpose? What would it be?

DE BONS CONSEILS

When you read material like this, you are generally looking for specific information—prices, colors, or sizes, for example. When that is your purpose, you don't have to read or understand every word. You can simply scan the material until you find what you are looking for.

A. At what time of year would you expect to see an advertisement like this?   fall

B. When you buy school supplies, what is most important to you? Color? Price? Brand name?

C. Working with a partner, scan the ad for information about price, size, and quantity. Make a list of the words you find in the text that fit each of these categories.

D. What do you think **les 3** means?

E. The word **écolier** is used to describe the notebook. Do you recognize a word you've learned before in this word? What do you think **écolier** means?

F. What is the most expensive item? The least expensive?
See answers below.

C. See answers below.
D. See answer below.
E. See answers below.

UNIVERS
TOUT POUR LA RENTREE

VENEZ VOIR NOS PRIX REMARQUABLES!

ENSEMBLE D'ARDOISE: ardoise naturelle, éponge, crayon.

10F20

27F95

STYLO PLUME

2F75

SURLIGNEUR LUMINEUX
divers coloris

5F60

REGLE
Graduation millimétrique, 30cm.

5F80

COMPAS POINTE FIXE

5F95

BOITE DE GOUACHE
12 pastilles de 30 mm et un pinceau.

Answers
C *Price:* 10F20, 27F95, 2F75, 5F60, 5F80, 5F95, 13F61, 14F, 4F20, 1F75, 8F45, 16F97, 1F70
   Size: 30 cm., 30 mm., 19 mm. × 33 m., 24 × 32 cm., 0,50 × 2 m.
   Quantity: 12 pastilles, 8 chiffres, 4 opérations
D for three
E école; *for school use*
F *Most expensive*—stylo plume
   Least expensive—rouleau protège-livres

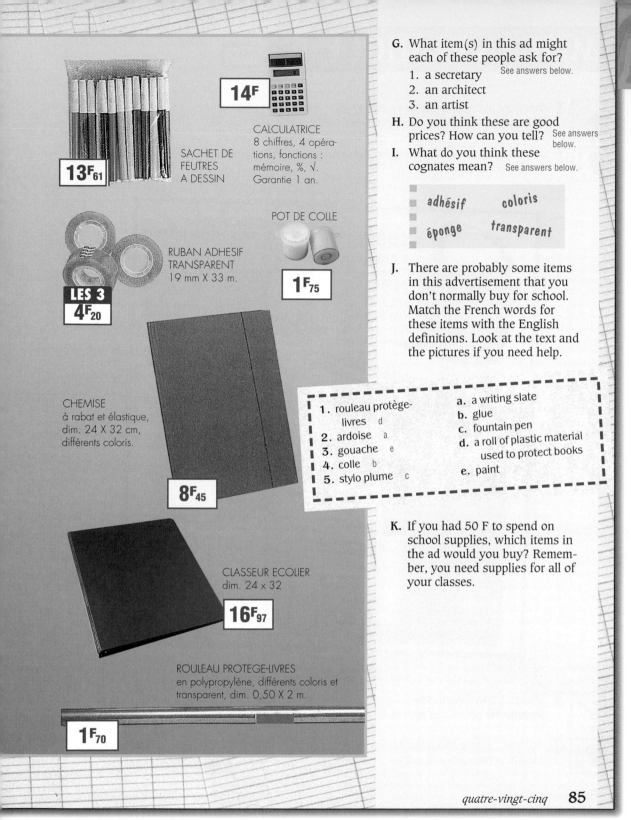

Left column (advertisement)

14F

CALCULATRICE
8 chiffres, 4 opéra-
tions, fonctions :
mémoire, %, √.
Garantie 1 an.

SACHET DE
FEUTRES
A DESSIN

13F61

POT DE COLLE

RUBAN ADHESIF
TRANSPARENT
19 mm X 33 m.

1F75

LES 3
4F20

CHEMISE
à rabat et élastique,
dim. 24 X 32 cm,
différents coloris.

8F45

CLASSEUR ECOLIER
dim. 24 x 32

16F97

ROULEAU PROTEGE-LIVRES
en polypropylène, différents coloris et
transparent, dim. 0,50 X 2 m.

1F70

G. What item(s) in this ad might each of these people ask for?

1. a secretary   See answers below.
2. an architect
3. an artist

H. Do you think these are good prices? How can you tell?   See answers below.

I. What do you think these cognates mean?   See answers below.

> adhésif   coloris
>
> éponge   transparent

J. There are probably some items in this advertisement that you don't normally buy for school. Match the French words for these items with the English definitions. Look at the text and the pictures if you need help.

1. rouleau protège-livres   d
2. ardoise   a
3. gouache   e
4. colle   b
5. stylo plume   c

   a. a writing slate
   b. glue
   c. fountain pen
   d. a roll of plastic material used to protect books
   e. paint

K. If you had 50 F to spend on school supplies, which items in the ad would you buy? Remember, you need supplies for all of your classes.

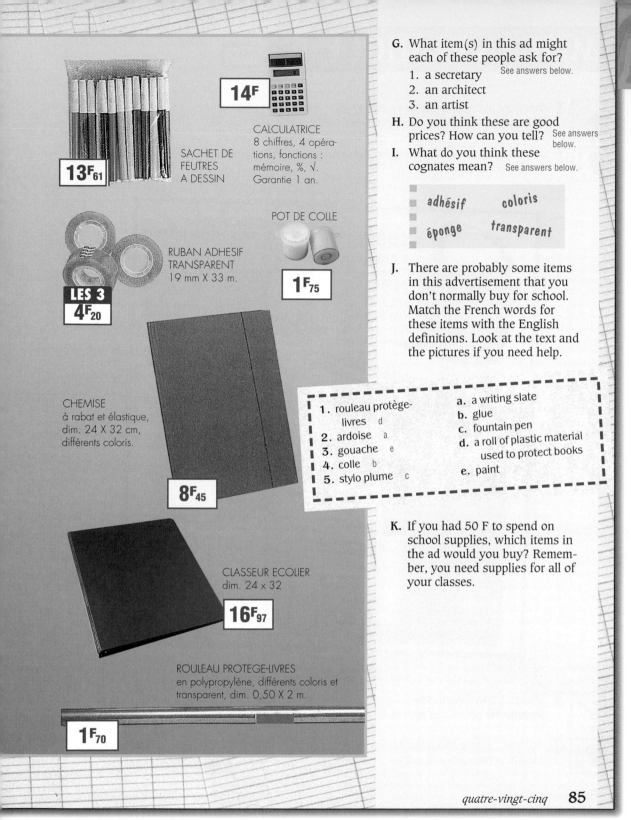

quatre-vingt-cinq **85**

Language Note

In addition to the school supplies presented in Activity J, students might be interested in the following items:

- **chemise:** folder with flaps that fold in to hold papers and elastic bands to keep the folder shut
- **stylo plume:** fountain or ink pen that can be refilled
- **ardoise:** small chalkboard (slate) used instead of scratch paper

POSTREADING
Activity K

Thinking Critically

Analyzing   Have students examine the ad and determine why they think it is effective or ineffective.

Comparing and Contrasting
Have students compare the items in the selection to the one(s) they usually see. Do the items shown seem similar to those used by American students? How do they differ in price or appearance? Which supplies would high school students use?

Answers

G *Possible answers*
1. *Secretary:* stylo plume, surligneur
2. *Architect:* feutres à dessin, compas, règle
3. *Artist:* gouache, feutres à dessin

H Our prices are impressive/competitive.

I adhésif: *adhesive*
éponge: *sponge*
coloris: *colors*
transparent: *transparent*

The **Mise en pratique** reviews and integrates all four skills and culture in preparation for the Chapter Test.

 For Individual Needs

1 Challenge Have students listen to the recording again. This time they should note the reasons why the speaker would like each gift.

Teaching Suggestions

2 Encourage students to use the expressions of agreement and disagreement they learned in Chapter 2: **Moi aussi, Moi non plus, Moi si,** and so forth.

Additional Practice

2 Have students use the advertisement to do a "chain" activity to practice telling what they would like and the vocabulary for colors and objects. One student could begin by saying **Je voudrais un classeur vert.** The next student might say **Marc voudrait un classeur vert et moi, je voudrais un stylo bleu.** and so on.

 Portfolio

3 Written This activity is appropriate for students' written portfolios. For portfolio suggestions, see page 20 of the *Alternative Assessment Guide.*

4 Oral This activity might be included in students' oral portfolios and/or performed for the class. For portfolio suggestions, see page 20 of the *Alternative Assessment Guide.*

MISE EN PRATIQUE

The *CD-ROM Program* offers guided recording and writing activities to practice oral and written skills and to review material from each chapter.

1 You want to buy your friend a birthday gift. Listen as she gives you some ideas and then make a list of the things she would like. See scripts and answers on p. 65H.

2 You and a friend are browsing through a magazine. Point out several items you like and several you dislike.

3 Make a list in French of two or three of the items pictured above that you'd like to buy. Include the colors and prices of the items you choose.

4 Tell your partner about the items you've chosen in Activity 3. Give as much detail as you can, including the color and price.

5 Your friend has been passing notes to you during study hall. Write a response to each one.

Il me faut un stylo!

Qu'est-ce qu'il faut pour l'algèbre?

Qu'est-ce qu'il faut pour la chimie?

6 If you were in France, what differences would you notice in these areas?

1. money

2. school supplies

3. stores

See answers below.

7 *Ecrivons!*

You're creating your own department store. First, make a list of possible names for your store. Then, create a list of items you would like to sell in your store, and begin thinking about how these items might be grouped together. Before you start, organize your ideas in a cluster diagram.

STRATEGIE
Cluster diagrams are a helpful way to organize the ideas you develop in your brainstorming. Start by drawing a circle and label it with the name you chose for your store. Then draw two or three other circles, each connected to the first circle. In each of the new circles you draw, write the name of an item you plan to sell. Add more circles as you need them. Connect your circles with lines to group similar items together as they might be organized in a department store.

les trousses
les classeurs
Le Grand Magasin

8

J E U   D E   R O L E

Visit the "store" your partner created and decide on something you'd like to buy. Your partner will play the role of the salesperson. Get the salesperson's attention, tell what you want, ask the price(s), pay for your purchase(s), thank the salesperson, and say goodbye. Your partner should respond appropriately. Then, change roles, using the store you created. Remember to use **madame, monsieur,** or **mademoiselle,** and **vous.**

MISE EN PRATIQUE

quatre-vingt-sept **87**

Possible answers
6 1. French money has more coins.
  2. Notebook paper looks like graph paper.
  3. One is expected to bag one's own purchases.

Teaching Suggestion
5 Extend this activity by asking students to write notes of their own to one another, exchange them, and write replies.

Process Writing
7 Beginning with this chapter, students will have the opportunity to develop their writing skills with the **Ecrivons!** feature. This feature will be presented in each chapter in the **Mise en pratique** review section, before the **Jeu de rôle.** The Ecrivons! feature gives students a writing strategy to apply to their assignment. In subsequent chapters, students will learn to use all the steps of the writing process. For rubrics and evaluation guidelines for written assignments, see pages 6–9 of the *Alternative Assessment Guide.*

Video Wrap-Up

• *VIDEO PROGRAM,*
  Videocassette 1, 37:12–50:26
• *VIDEODISC PROGRAM,*
  Videodisc 2, Side A

At this time, you might want to use the video resources for additional review and enrichment. See *Video Guide* or *Videodisc Guide* for suggestions regarding the following:
• **Pas question!**
  (Dramatic episode)
• **Panorama Culturel**
  (Interviews)
• **Vidéoclips**
  (Authentic footage)

QUE SAIS-JE?

This page is intended to help students prepare for the Chapter Test. It is a brief checklist of the major points covered in the chapter. Students should be reminded that this is only a checklist and does not necessarily include everything that will appear on the test.

Teaching Suggestion

In pairs, have students ask and respond to each of the questions in Activities 1–5.

Can you use what you've learned in this chapter?

Can you make and respond to requests? p. 72

1 How would you ask for the following items using the verb **avoir**? How would you respond to someone's request for one of these items?
See answers below.

1. 2. 3.

Can you ask others what they need? p. 74

2 How would you ask your friend what he or she needs for each of these school subjects? See answers below.

1. 2. 3.

Can you tell what you need? p. 74

3 How would you tell a friend that you need . . . See answers below.

1 a calculator and an eraser for math?
2. a binder and some sheets of paper for Spanish class?
3. some pens and a notebook for English?
4. a pencil and a ruler for geometry?
5. a backpack and a book for history?

Can you tell what you'd like and what you'd like to do? p. 77

4 How would you tell your friend that you'd like . . . See answers below.

1. those white sneakers?
2. this blue bag?
3. that purple and black pencil case?
4. to listen to music and talk on the phone?
5. to go shopping?

Can you get someone's attention, ask for information, and express thanks? p. 82

5 What would you say in a store to . . .

1. get a salesperson's attention? Pardon, madame/mademoiselle/monsieur...
2. politely ask the price of something? C'est combien, s'il vous plaît?
3. thank a clerk for helping you? Merci.

Answers

1 *Questions*
1. Vous avez/Tu as un stylo, s'il vous/te plaît?
2. Vous avez/Tu as une calculatrice?
3. Vous avez/Tu as des feuilles de papier?
Possible responses
Non, je regrette; Non, je n'ai pas de... ; Oui, voilà.

2 1. Qu'est-ce qu'il te faut pour le sport?
2. Qu'est-ce qu'il te faut pour l'allemand?

3. Qu'est-ce qu'il te faut pour les arts plastiques?

3 1. Il me faut une calculatrice et une gomme pour les maths.
2. Il me faut un classeur et des feuilles pour l'espagnol.
3. Il me faut des stylos et un cahier pour l'anglais.
4. Il me faut un crayon et une règle pour la géométrie.

5. Il me faut un sac et un livre pour l'histoire.

4 1. Je voudrais ces baskets blanches.
2. Je voudrais ce sac bleu.
3. Je voudrais cette trousse violette et noire.
4. Je voudrais écouter de la musique et parler au téléphone.
5. Je voudrais faire les magasins.

PREMIERE ETAPE

Making and responding to requests

Tu as... ?   *Do you have . . . ?*
Vous avez... ?   *Do you have . . . ?*
Voilà.   *Here.*
Je regrette.   *Sorry.*
Je n'ai pas de...   *I don't have . . .*

Asking others what they need and telling what you need

Qu'est-ce qu'il vous faut pour... ?
   What do you need for . . . ?
   (formal)

Qu'est-ce qu'il te faut pour... ?
   What do you need for . . . ?
   (informal)
Il me faut...   *I need . . .*
un   *a; an*
une   *a; an*
des   *some*

School supplies

un cahier   *notebook*
une calculatrice   *calculator*
un classeur   *loose-leaf binder*
un crayon   *pencil*

des feuilles (f.) de papier   *sheets of paper*
une gomme   *eraser*
un livre   *book*
une règle   *ruler*
un sac (à dos)   *bag; backpack*
un stylo   *pen*
un taille-crayon   *pencil sharpener*
une trousse   *pencil case*

Other useful expressions

Zut!   *Darn!*

Teaching Suggestions

• Encourage students to try to remember words by association. For example, **un porte-feuille** carries (**porte**) little pieces of paper (**feuilles**), such as franc or euro notes.
• Have students group the vocabulary by categories, such as *things you write with, things you wear, things you listen to,* and *things you use to organize.*

DEUXIEME ETAPE

Telling what you'd like and what you'd like to do

Je voudrais...   *I'd like . . .*
Je voudrais acheter...   *I'd like to buy . . .*

For school and fun

des baskets (f.)   *sneakers*
un bracelet   *bracelet*
une cassette   *cassette tape*
un dictionnaire   *dictionary*
un disque compact/un CD   *compact disc/CD*
un jean   *(a pair of) jeans*
un magazine   *magazine*

une montre   *watch*
un ordinateur   *computer*
un portefeuille   *wallet*
un poster   *poster*
un pull-over   *pullover*
une radio   *radio*
un roman   *novel*
un short   *(a pair of) shorts*
un sweat-shirt   *sweatshirt*
un tee-shirt   *T-shirt*
une télévision   *television*
une vidéocassette   *videotape*
ce, cet, cette   *this; that*
ces   *these; those*
-là   *there (noun suffix)*

Colors

De quelle couleur est... ?   *What color is . . . ?*
blanc(he)   *white*
bleu(e)   *blue*
gris(e)   *grey*
jaune   *yellow*
marron   *brown*
noir(e)   *black*
orange   *orange*
rose   *pink*
rouge   *red*
vert(e)   *green*
violet(te)   *purple*

CHAPTER 3 ASSESSMENT

CHAPTER TEST
• *Testing Program,* pp. 65–70
• *Audio Compact Discs,*
   Audio CD 3,
   Tracks 23–25

SPEAKING TEST
• *Testing Program,* p. 344

TEST GENERATOR
 • Chapter 3

ALTERNATIVE ASSESSMENT
Performance Assessment
• You might want to use the **Jeu de Rôle** on page 87 as a cumulative performance assessment activity.
• *Alternative Assessment Guide,* p. 34

📁 **Portfolio Assessment**
• *Alternative Assessment Guide*
Oral: p. 20
Written: p. 20
CD-ROM Assessment
• *Interactive CD-ROM Program,* Disc 1
A toi de parler
A toi d'écrire
• *Alternative Assessment Guide,* p. 48

TROISIEME ETAPE

Getting someone's attention; asking for information; expressing thanks

Pardon.   *Pardon me.*
Excusez-moi.   *Excuse me.*
C'est combien?   *How much is it?*
Merci.   *Thank you.*

A votre service.   *At your service; You're welcome.*
s'il vous/te plaît   *please*
franc   *(the French monetary unit)*
soixante   *sixty*
soixante-dix   *seventy*
quatre-vingts   *eighty*

quatre-vingt-dix   *ninety*
cent   *one hundred*
deux cents   *two hundred*

Other useful expressions

Bien sûr.   *Of course.*

VOCABULAIRE

quatre-vingt-neuf **89**

Science Link

Have students arrange the colors according to the spectrum they learned about in science or art class.

Allez, viens à Québec! pp. 90–119

VIDEO PROGRAM
Videocassette 2
01:22–03:33

OR **VIDEODISC PROGRAM**,
Videodisc 2, Side B

Search 1, Play To 3945

Motivating Activity

Have students recall what they already know about Canada and Quebec concerning history, climate, food, culture, relationship with the United States, historical sites, tourist attractions, and other aspects. Then, have them look at the photos on pages 90–93. Ask them to find features that seem European and others that seem North American.

Geography Link

Given its northern location, it is not surprising that the region around Quebec City receives approximately 130 inches of snow each winter and has average temperatures of -16 to -7 degrees Celsius (3 to 19 degrees Fahrenheit) in January, and 13 to 25 degrees Celsius (55 to 77 degrees Fahrenheit) in July. As they say in Quebec, there are two seasons: winter and July.

go.hrw.com
WAO QUEBEC

Visit the HRW Web site at **http://go.hrw.com** and enter the keyword **WAO QUEBEC CITY** for student resources related to this location. For detailed access instructions, see page T45.

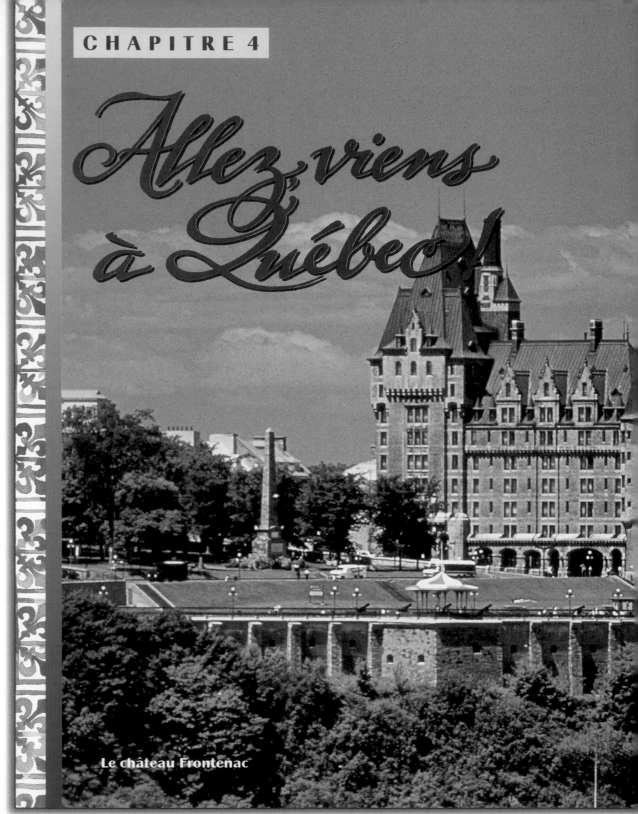

CHAPITRE 4

Allez, viens à Québec!

Le château Frontenac

Background Information

La Nouvelle-France, claimed for the French by the explorer Jacques Cartier in 1534, was ceded to the British by the Treaty of Paris in 1763 at the end of the Seven Years' War (known in North America as the French and Indian War). Quebec City, one of the oldest cities in North America, was founded in 1608 by Samuel de Champlain. It is known for its old-world charm, narrow streets, beautiful parks, and numerous cafés. The name **Québec** comes from the Algonquian word **Kébec,** meaning *narrowing of the river* (referring to its strategic location where the St. Lawrence River narrows). With a current population of more than half a million, Quebec City has been the capital of the province of Quebec since 1791.

Québec

Map 3

Capitale de la province du Québec

Population : plus de 600.000

Points d'intérêt : le château Frontenac, l'université Laval, la terrasse Dufferin, le musée du Québec, les fortifications de Québec, les chutes Montmorency, le mont Sainte-Anne, Québec Expérience

Québécois célèbres : Samuel de Champlain, François de Montmorency-Laval, le marquis de Montcalm

Ressources et industries : dérivés du bois, du cuir et de l'érable; tourisme

Spécialités : ragoût de boulettes, tourtière, cretons, soupe aux pois, tarte au sucre, tarte à la ferlouche

HRW   go.hrw.com
WAO QUEBEC CITY

quatre-vingt-onze 91

Using the Almanac and Map

Terms in the Almanac

- **Le château Frontenac,** named for the comte de Frontenac, governor of la Nouvelle-France in the late seventeenth century, was built on a site that once served as a residence for colonial governors. The building is now a luxury hotel.
- **L'université Laval,** formerly the Quebec Seminary, founded in 1852, is the oldest French-language university in North America.
- **Les chutes Montmorency** This impressive waterfall is 1.5 times the height of Niagara Falls.
- **Le mont Sainte-Anne,** located 40 kilometers east of Quebec City, is famous for its ski slopes.
- **Québec Expérience** is a multimedia 3-D sound and light presentation spotlighting the Amerindian, French, and English influences in Quebec City's history.
- **Le marquis de Montcalm** commanded the French troops during the French and Indian War.
- **dérivés de l'érable:** Canada is known for its maple products. A favorite treat of children, **tire,** is formed by pouring maple syrup on snow where it congeals to form a sort of caramel.
- **ragoût de boulettes:** pork stew with meatballs, eaten on special occasions
- **tourtière:** a meat pie usually eaten at Christmastime
- **cretons:** similar to **pâté,** made from ground pork
- **tarte au sucre:** a sugar pie made with brown sugar or sometimes maple syrup
- **tarte à la ferlouche:** a pie made with molasses or maple syrup and raisins

Language Notes

- Because the owners of the logging companies in Quebec were generally English speakers, much of the lumberjack's language contained anglicisms. For example, the men who floated the lumber downriver were called **draveurs** *(drivers),* they used a **bécosses** *(backhouse* or *outhouse),* and they ate in the **cookerie.**
- After the passage of **la Loi 101** in 1976, which required all advertising and documen-

tation to be in French, the **Office de la langue française** was created to help develop appropriate French terminology. La Loi 101 was declared unconstitutional in 1988.

Using the Map

You might tell students that the vast majority of place names in Quebec are derived from geographic features, Amerindian words, or saints' names.

Using the Photo Essay

① **Typical houses in Vieux-Québec** The narrow streets and stone structures of the older parts of Quebec City are reminiscent of European cities, but many buildings also represent the long, low, one-story construction typical of French-Canadian houses.

② **Les chutes Montmorency** Overlooking these impressive falls is the Manoir Montmorency, built in 1780 for Edward, Duke of Kent, then governor-general of the colony and future father of Queen Victoria. Today it is a restaurant and conference center.

③ **Street performers** For years, **Québécois** families and friends have gathered for **veillées** where people sing, dance, and tell stories. This tradition lives on in the street performers often seen in Quebec City or Montreal. Each July, the **Festival d'été international** brings francophone musicians and performers from all over the world to play their music in Quebec City.

④ **Le quartier Petit-Champlain** The cobblestone pedestrian street in this photo dates from 1680. It is linked with the upper part of the city by a cable car **(le funiculaire).** Recent restoration efforts have transformed the district into an animated gathering place with cafés, restaurants, and shops.

Thinking Critically

④ **Observing** Ask students to identify the most striking feature of the buildings here. The proliferation of plants and flowers is typically **québécois,** but at the same time, very reminiscent of the French love of flowers and gardens.

Québec

CD-ROM
Disc 1

*Quebec City, one of the oldest cities in North America, is the capital of **La Nouvelle-France**, as the French-speaking province of Quebec used to be called. The **Québécois** people are fiercely proud of their heritage and traditions, and they work hard to maintain their language and culture. The narrow streets and quaint cafés of **Vieux-Québec** have an old-world feeling, but Quebec is also a dynamic, modern city — as exciting as any you'll find in North America!*

① Typical houses in **Vieux-Québec.**

② The spectacular **chutes Montmorency** are just outside of the city.

③ Musicians, jugglers, and other entertainers perform frequently in the streets of **Vieux-Québec.**

④ Le quartier Petit-Champlain is a picturesque shopping district filled with boutiques and cafés.

92   *quatre-vingt-douze*

Culture Note

① Following several disastrous fires in Quebec City, new regulations require structures to be made of stone with slate roofs and to have high fire walls between buildings.

History Link

The early European inhabitants of Quebec included settlers **(colons),** fur trappers, and **voyageurs** who traveled by canoe to the interior to trade with the Indians.

Geography Link

② The Canadian Shield **(le bouclier canadien),** a range of mountains and peaks, reaches down toward the Great Lakes. Many of the rivers that empty into the St. Lawrence River "fall off" the edge of this shield in impressive waterfalls.

⑤ **La rue du Trésor** is where local artists sell their work. This street in the heart of the old section of town is very popular among tourists.

⑥ **Les plaines d'Abraham,** now a 250-acre park, was the site of the battle in which the English defeated the French on September 13, 1759.

⑦ **La Grande Allée,** a boulevard lined with businesses and cafés, is the longest road in Quebec.

⑧ **La terrasse Dufferin** is a bustling six-kilometer boardwalk that overlooks the St. Lawrence River.

History Links
⑥ During the famous battle in 1759, the British forces under General Wolfe scaled the cliff to attack and defeat the outnumbered French forces under General Montcalm.

⑤ **La rue du Trésor** is a tiny pedestrian street (**rue piétonne**) where local artists sell their paintings, watercolors, drawings, and engravings.

Teacher Note
Although many Americans, French, and English-speaking Canadians visit Quebec, a large percentage of tourists are **Québécois** from other regions of Quebec who come to visit the capital.

⑥ **Les Plaines d'Abraham,** located in **le parc des Champs de Bataille,** are named after Abraham Martin, a seventeenth-century settler.

Thinking Critically
⑥ **Drawing inferences**
Ask students to suggest other activities that people might do in the park. (Cycling, jogging, and walking are common pastimes. In the winter, one might find sledders or cross-country skiers.)

⑦ **La Grande Allée** This boulevard holds the same place in **Québécois** hearts as the Champs-Elysées does in the hearts of Parisians. It was originally an Indian trail used to transport furs to sell to the French. In the seventeenth century, it was only a country lane separating two properties, and in later centuries, the address of several luxurious residences. Today, it is a busy street lined with many restaurants, cafés, shops, and offices.

⑧ **La terrasse Dufferin**
This 671-meter walkway overlooks the lower town and the river. The part facing the château Frontenac was built over the remains of the château Saint-Louis (the governor-general's residence), which burned down in 1834.

Chapitre 4 : Sports et passe-temps
Chapter Overview

Mise en train pp. 96–98	Nouvelles de Québec

	FUNCTIONS	GRAMMAR	CULTURE	RE-ENTRY
Première étape pp. 99–103	• Telling how much you like or dislike something, p. 102	• Expressions with **faire** and **jouer,** p. 101 • Question formation with **est-ce que,** p. 103	• **Rencontre Culturelle,** Old and new in Quebec City, p. 99	• Expressing likes and dislikes (**Chapitre 1**) • The verb **aimer** (**Chapitre 2**) • Agreeing and disagreeing (**Chapitre 2**)
Deuxième étape pp. 104–109	• Exchanging information, p. 104	• **De** after a negative verb, p. 104 • The verb **faire,** p. 104 • The pronoun **on,** p. 105	• **Note Culturelle,** Celsius and Fahrenheit, p. 107 • **Panorama Culturel,** Sports in francophone countries, p. 109	• The verb **jouer,** regular **-er** verbs (**Chapitre 1**) • Agreeing and disagreeing (**Chapitre 2**) • Using **ne... pas** (**Chapitre 1**) • Expressing likes and dislikes (**Chapitre 1**) • Activities (**Chapitre 1**)
Troisième étape pp. 110–113	• Making, accepting, and turning down suggestions, p. 110	• Adverbs of frequency, p. 110		• Expressing opinions (**Chapitre 2**) • Expressing likes and dislikes (**Chapitre 1**)

Prononciation p. 113	The sounds **[u]** and **[y]** Audio CD 4, Tracks 12–14	**A écrire** (dictation) Audio CD 4, Tracks 15–17
Lisons! pp. 114–115	**Allez, c'est à vous de choisir!**	**Reading Strategy** Predicting what you're going to read
Review pp. 116–119	**Mise en pratique**, pp. 116–117 **Ecrivons!** Arranging ideas logically Writing a letter	**Que sais-je?** p. 118 **Vocabulaire**, p. 119

Assessment Options	*Testing Program* • Première étape, Quiz 4-1A, Quiz 4-1B, pp. 79–82 • Deuxième étape, Quiz 4-2A, Quiz 4-2B, pp. 83–86 • Troisième étape, Quiz 4-3A, Quiz 4-3B, pp. 87–90 • Chapter Test, pp. 91–96 • Speaking Test, p. 344 *Audio Compact Discs* • Audio CD 4, Tracks 19–24	*Interactive CD-ROM Program* • Mise en pratique (A toi de parler, A toi d'écrire) • CD-ROM Teacher's Guide, Assessment Options, p. 17 *Alternative Assessment Guide* • Portfolio Assessment, p. 21 • Performance Assessment, p. 35 • CD-ROM Assessment, p. 49 *Test Generator* • Chapter 4

PRINT	MEDIA

Pupil's Edition, pp. 94–119

 Audio Compact Discs
- Textbook Listening Activities: Audio CD 4, Tracks 1–18

**Interactive CD-ROM Program
Teacher's Guide,** pp. 14–17

 Interactive CD-ROM Program
- Disc 1

Videodisc Guide
- Teaching Suggestions, pp. 42–46
- Activity Masters, pp. 47–49

 Videodisc Program
- Videodisc 2, Side B

Video Guide
- Teaching Suggestions, pp. 26–27
- Activity Masters, pp. 28–30

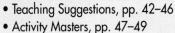 **Video Program**
- Videocassette 2
- Videocassette 5 (captioned version)

Listening Activities
- Student Response Forms for Textbook Listening Activities, pp. 27–29
- Additional Listening Activities 4-1 to 4-6, pp. 31–33
- Additional Listening Activities (song), p. 34
- Scripts and Answers, pp. 117–121

 Audio Compact Discs
- Textbook Listening Activities: Audio CD 4, Tracks 1–18
- Additional Listening Activities: Audio CD 4, Tracks 25–31

Teaching Transparencies
- Teaching Transparency Masters 4-1 to 4-3 (Situations) and 4-A to 4-D (Vocabulary)
- Teaching Suggestions 4-1 to 4-3 and 4-A to 4-D

 Teaching Transparencies
- Situations 4-1 to 4-3
- Vocabulary 4-A to 4-D

Testing Program
- Grammar and Vocabulary Quizzes, **Etape** Quizzes, and Chapter Test, pp. 79–96
- Score Sheet, Scripts, and Answers, pp. 97–104

 Audio Compact Discs
- Assessment Items: Audio CD 2, Tracks 19–24

 Test Generator
- Chapter 4

Alternative Assessment Guide
- Portfolio Assessment, p. 21
- Performance Assessment, p. 35
- CD-ROM Assessment, p. 49

 Grammar and Vocabulary Workbook, pp. 25–34

 Practice and Activity Book, pp. 37–48

Activities for Communication
- Communicative Activities, pp. 19–24
- Realia and Teaching Suggestions, pp. 90–94
- Situation Cards, pp. 143–144

Lesson Planner
- Lesson Plan, pp. 18–22

Chapitre 4 : Sports et passe-temps
Technology Applications

MISE EN TRAIN, pp. 96–98

Video
- Show *Nouvelles de Québec.* For Video Synopsis, Teaching Suggestions, Activity Master, and Scripts, see the *Video Guide* or the *Videodisc Guide.*

Audio
- Play the recording of the **Mise en train** with pauses as students read along. You might have them practice pronunciation by repeating individual sentences after hearing them.

PREMIERE ETAPE, pp. 100–103

Video
- While students watch *Nouvelles de Québec,* have them listen for **faire + de** and **jouer + à** with vocabulary for sports and activities. For more suggestions, see p. 44 of the *Videodisc Guide.*

Audio
- Textbook Listening Activities 6 and 9 practice expressions with **faire** and **jouer.**
- To give students more work with the vocabulary for sports and activities, use Additional Listening Activities 4-1 and 4-2.

Transparencies
- Use *Teaching Transparency 4-1* and the Teaching Suggestions to have students practice telling what sports people like.
- Use *Teaching Transparencies 4-A* and *4-B* and the Teaching Suggestions to present and have students practice vocabulary for sports and hobbies.

CD-ROM (Disc 1)
- Have students review the vocabulary for sports and activities by using **Jeu des paires** (Activity 1).

- **Les mots qui manquent** (Activity 2) practices expressions with **faire** and **jouer.**
- For suggestions, see p. 15 of the *CD-ROM Teacher's Guide.*

DEUXIEME ETAPE, pp. 104–108

Video
- While students watch *Nouvelles de Québec,* have them listen for exchanges that model asking and telling what sports and activities people do. See pp. 44–45 of the *Videodisc Guide* for more suggestions.

Audio
- Textbook Listening Activity 21 practices the vocabulary for seasons, sports, and activities.
- To review expressing likes and dislikes with sports and activities, use Additional Listening Activities 4-3 and 4-4.

Transparencies
- Use *Teaching Transparency 4-2* and the Teaching Suggestions to have students practice telling about the weather.
- Use *Teaching Transparency 4-C* and the Teaching Suggestions to present and have students practice talking about weather.
- Use *Teaching Transparency 4-D* and the Teaching Suggestions to present and have students practice vocabulary for seasons, months, and times.

CD-ROM (Disc 1)
- To have students practice forms of the verb **faire,** use **Les mots qui manquent** (Activity 3).
- **Chasse au trésor** (Activity 4) targets the vocabulary for weather and the seasons.
- For suggestions, see pp. 15–16 of the *CD-ROM Teacher's Guide.*

PANORAMA CULTUREL, p. 109

Video
- Show the interviews. For Video Synopsis, Teaching Suggestions, Activity Master, and Scripts, see the *Video Guide* or the *Videodisc Guide.*

Audio
- Play the **Panorama Culturel** as students read along. Remind them they might not understand everything, but they should try to recognize words and deduce global meaning.

CD-ROM (Disc 1)
- Have students do the **Panorama Culturel** activity for Chapter 4 after showing them the video. For suggestions, see p. 16 of the *CD-ROM Teacher's Guide.*

TROISIEME ETAPE, pp. 110–113

Video
- As students watch *Nouvelles de Québec,* have them listen for characters accepting and turning down suggestions and telling how often they do activities. See pp. 45–46 of the *Videodisc Guide* for more suggestions.

Audio
- Use Textbook Listening Activity 26 to have students practice accepting and turning down suggestions.
- Use Textbook Listening Activity 28 to have students tell how often they practice sports.
- Additional Listening Activity 4-5 practices making and accepting suggestions.
- Additional Listening Activity 4-6 targets telling how often people do activities.

Transparencies
- Use *Teaching Transparency 4-3* and the Teaching Suggestions to have students practice making, accepting, and turning down suggestions.

CD-ROM (Disc 1)
- After presenting the phrases for making, accepting, and turning down suggestions, have students do **Chacun à sa place** (Activity 5).
- To practice the verb **faire** and the adverbs of frequency, have students do **Le bon choix** (Activity 6).
- For suggestions, see p. 16 of the *CD-ROM Teacher's Guide.*

MISE EN PRATIQUE, pp. 116–117

Captioned Video
- Replay *Nouvelles de Québec* on Videocassette 5 and ask students to listen for the exchanges for expressing likes and dislikes, exchanging information, and making, accepting, and turning down suggestions.

CD-ROM (Disc 1)
- Have students do the **En contexte** to practice discussing sports and activities they enjoy. For suggestions, see p. 15 of the *CD-ROM Teacher's Guide.*
- Have students practice their writing and speaking skills using the **A toi d'écrire** and **A toi de parler** activities. For a detailed description of these activities, see p. 17 of the *CD-ROM Teacher's Guide.*
- For Assessment Options, see p. 17 of the *CD-ROM Teacher's Guide.*

Test Generator
- Use the Test Generator to create review material for students taking the Chapter Test or to prepare an alternate test.

VIDEOCLIPS

Video
- Show the **Vidéoclips.** For Video Synopsis, Teaching Suggestions, Activity Master, and Scripts, see the *Video Guide* or the *Videodisc Guide.*

Chapitre 4: Sports et passe-temps
Barcode Directory

MISE EN TRAIN

Barcodes A and B access **Mise en train** and **Mise en train (suite)** in their entirety. Subsequent barcodes show specific segments of **Nouvelles de Québec.** The barcode numbers correspond to the scene numbers as they appear on the video.

ETAPES

To practice the grammar, vocabulary, and functions presented in each **étape**, see the barcodes and accompanying suggestions on pages 44–46 of the *Videodisc Guide.*

Nouvelles de Québec **A**
Search 3945, Play To 13170

Salut, Leticia! **1**
Search 3945, Play To 6395

Bonjour, Leticia! **2**
Search 6396, Play To 7132

Salut, Leticia! **3**
Search 7133, Play To 7815

Au printemps,... **4**
Search 7816, Play To 8905

Ça, c'est le Centre... **5**
Search 8906, Play To 9438

Ici, on joue au basket... **6**
Search 9439, Play To 10765

Souvent, nous aimons... **7**
Search 10766, Play To 11408

Salut, Michel! **8**
Search 11432, Play To 13170

Nouvelles de Québec (suite) **B**
Search 13171, Play To 31080

MISE EN PRATIQUE

This is additional footage modeling some of the expressions practiced in this chapter. You may want to use it to review the chapter.

Mise en pratique **1**
Search 38191, Play To 40070

PANORAMA CULTUREL

Qu'est-ce que tu fais comme sport?
These barcodes access the three interviews of the **Panorama Culturel** presented in the *Pupil's Edition* as well as additional interviews.

VIDEOCLIPS

These are authentic French commercials. You may want to preview them before showing them to students.

First three interviews **1**
Search 31080, Play To 33370

All interviews **2**
Search 31080, Play To 35120

Marius **3**
Search 32028, Play To 32374

Noky®: paper products **1**
Search 35605, Play To 36116

Aljosa **4**
Search 34919, Play To 35006

Mélanie **5**
Search 35006, Play To 35120

Matthieu **6**
Search 33364, Play To 33518

Casino®: grocery store **2**
Search 36117, Play To 37570

Patricia **7**
Search 33519, Play To 33754

Stéphanie **8**
Search 33755, Play To 33895

Eva **9**
Search 33896, Play To 34010

Lily-Christine **10**
Search 34011, Play To 34193

Cinthia **11**
Search 34194, Play To 34313

Antoine **12**
Search 34314, Play To 34393

Olivier **13**
Search 34394, Play To 34918

Claire **14**
Search 34919, Play To 35006

Richard et Yannick **15**
Search 35006, Play To 35120

Chapitre 4: Sports et passe-temps
CD-ROM Directory 💿 DISC 1

The following directory lists the *Interactive CD-ROM Program* activities for Chapter 4. For details and suggestions on how to use them, see pages 14–18 of the *CD-ROM Teacher's Guide*.

GLOBAL TASK	COMMUNICATIVE GOALS	ACTIVITY TYPE
Salut de Québec Students watch a video with their friend Juliette and discuss the sports and activities they enjoy.	To use chapter functions, vocabulary, and grammar in a lifelike conversation	**En contexte** *Interactive conversation*

	SUPPORTING ACTIVITIES	PUPIL'S EDITION	COMMUNICATIVE GOALS	ACTIVITY TYPE
Première étape	1. Vocabulaire	p. 100	To identify activities and sports	**Jeu des paires** *Concentration®*
	2. Grammaire	p. 101	To use contractions with **à** and **de** with **jouer** and **faire**	**Les mots qui manquent** *Tic Tac Toe*
Deuxième étape	3. Grammaire	p. 104	To produce the forms of the verb **faire**	**Les mots qui manquent** *Tic Tac Toe*
	4. Vocabulaire	pp. 106, 108	To identify and use weather expressions and seasons	**Chasse au trésor Explorons!/Vérifions!** *Interactive image*
Troisième étape	5. Comment dit-on... ?	p. 110	To classify expressions for accepting and turning down suggestions	**Chacun à sa place** *Categories*
	6. Grammaire	pp. 100, 104, 110	To identify vocabulary for sports and activities and to use the verb **faire** and adverbs of frequency	**Le bon choix** *Multiple choice*
Panorama Culturel	Panorama Culturel	p. 109	To listen to and understand native speakers talking about the sports they play	**Qu'est-ce que tu fais comme sport?** *Presentation* **Le bon choix** *Multiple choice*

	APPLICATION	PUPIL'S EDITION	COMMUNICATIVE GOALS	ACTIVITY TYPE
Mise en pratique	A toi de parler	pp. 116–117	To create and record a conversation about activities students like to do	*Guided recording*
	A toi d'écrire	pp. 116–117	To create a note, a survey, a list, or a script	*Guided writing*

CHAPTER SECTION	PRESENTATION	HOMEWORK OPTIONS
Première étape	**Vocabulaire,** p. 100	Practice and Activity Book, p. 38, Activity 4 Grammar and Vocabulary Workbook, p. 25, Activities 1–2 CD-ROM, Disc 1, Activity 1
	Grammaire, p. 101	Pupil's Edition, p. 101, Activity 7; p. R32, Activities 1–2 Practice and Activity Book, p. 38, Activity 3 Grammar and Vocabulary Workbook, p. 26, Activities 3–4 CD-ROM, Disc 1, Activity 2
	Comment dit-on... ?, p. 102	Practice and Activity Book, p. 39, Activity 5
	Grammaire, p. 103	Pupil's Edition, p. R33, Activity 3 Practice and Activity Book, p. 40, Activity 8 Grammar and Vocabulary Workbook, p. 27, Activities 5–6
Deuxième étape	**Note de grammaire,** p. 104	Pupil's Edition, p. R33, Activity 4 Practice and Activity Book, p. 41, Activity 10 Grammar and Vocabulary Workbook, p. 28, Activities 7–8
	Grammaire, p. 104	Pupil's Edition, pp. R33–R34, Activities 5–6 Practice and Activity Book, p. 41, Activity 11 Grammar and Vocabulary Workbook, p. 29, Activities 9–10 CD-ROM, Disc 1, Activity 3
	Grammaire, p. 105	Pupil's Edition, p. R34, Activity 7 Practice and Activity Book, p. 41, Activity 9 Grammar and Vocabulary Workbook, p. 30, Activity 11
	Vocabulaire, p. 106	Pupil's Edition, p. 107, Activity 22 Grammar and Vocabulary Workbook, p. 30, Activity 12
	Vocabulaire, p. 107	Practice and Activity Book, p. 44, Activity 17 Grammar and Vocabulary Workbook, p. 31, Activities 13–14
	Vocabulaire, p. 108	Practice and Activity Book, p. 42, Activities 12–14 Grammar and Vocabulary Workbook, p. 32, Activity 16 CD-ROM, Disc 1, Activity 4
Troisième étape	**Comment dit-on... ?,** p. 110	Practice and Activity Book, p. 45, Activity 19 CD-ROM, Disc 1, Activity 5
	Grammaire, p. 110	Pupil's Edition, p. 112, Activity 33; p. R35, Activities 9–10 Practice and Activity Book, pp. 45–46, Activities 20–22 Grammar and Vocabulary Workbook, p. 34, Activities 18–20 CD-ROM, Disc 1, Activity 6

For Student Response Forms, see *Listening Activities,* pp. 27–29.

Première étape

6 Ecoute! p. 100

PHILIPPE   Eh, salut, Pascal! Tu vas en vacances à la montagne! Quelle chance! Tu vas faire des photos?

PASCAL   Des photos? Non, je ne fais jamais de photos.

PHILIPPE   Tu vas faire du ski?

PASCAL   Non, pas moi. Je n'aime pas le ski.

PHILIPPE   Qu'est-ce que tu aimes faire, alors?

PASCAL   Mais des tas de choses. J'aime faire de la natation. Et puis, le champion du patin à glace, c'est moi. J'adore ça. J'aime aussi beaucoup faire de la vidéo. A la rentrée, on va regarder une vidéo formidable de mes vacances.

Answers to Activity 6

Likes: swimming, ice-skating, making videos
Dislikes: taking pictures, skiing

9 Ecoute! p. 102

— Tu aimes faire du sport?

— Le sport, j'adore ça, surtout le roller en ligne et le hockey. Par contre, je n'aime pas beaucoup le volley. Et toi, tu aimes faire du sport?

— Le volley, pas du tout. Le roller en ligne, pas tellement. Je n'aime pas les sports d'équipe. J'aime bien faire du ski, et je fais du jogging tous les matins à sept heures.

Answers to Activity 9

Canadian student likes: in-line skating, hockey
Canadian student dislikes: volleyball
Your classmate likes: skiing, jogging
Your classmate dislikes: volleyball, in-line skating, team sports

Deuxième étape

21 Ecoute! p. 107

JOURNALISTE   Bonjour, Paul. Qu'est-ce que tu aimes faire en hiver?

PAUL   J'écoute de la musique, et je regarde la télévision.

JOURNALISTE   Tu ne fais pas de sport?

PAUL   Si. Je fais du ski, et je joue au hockey.

JOURNALISTE   Est-ce que tu fais du sport, Anne?

ANNE   De temps en temps, mais j'aime mieux aller au cinéma. Je regarde souvent la télé aussi.

JOURNALISTE   Et toi, Julie, tu regardes la télévision?

JULIE   Jamais. Je fais du sport. J'adore faire du ski et du patin.

JOURNALISTE   Tu es sportive! Est-ce que tu écoutes de la musique aussi?

JULIE   Oui, très souvent.

JOURNALISTE   Et toi, Anne, tu aimes la musique?

ANNE   Oui, beaucoup. Et j'aime aussi danser.

Answers to Activity 21

1. Julie
2. Paul, Julie, Anne
3. Paul
4. Anne
5. Anne

*T*roisième étape

26 Ecoute! p. 110

1. — Allô?
   — Allô, Lise? C'est Germain. Tiens, vendredi après-midi, on joue au volley-ball?
   — Vendredi après-midi? D'accord. Bonne idée.

2. — Allô, oui?
   — Salut, Renaud! Dis, tu fais quoi vendredi après-midi?
   — Eh ben, rien. Pourquoi?
   — On joue au volley-ball?
   — Le volley... euh, ça ne me dit rien, le volley. C'est barbant.

3. — Allô?
   — Salut, Philippe. C'est Germain. Qu'est-ce que tu fais ce week-end?
   — Je ne sais pas. Et toi?
   — J'ai une idée. On joue au volley-ball?
   — Bonne idée! Le volley, c'est le fun!

4. — Allô?
   — Allô, Monique? C'est Germain. On joue au volley?
   — Je n'aime pas tellement le volley.

Answers to Activity 26
1. Lise: accepts
2. Renaud: turns down
3. Philippe: accepts
4. Monique: turns down

28 Ecoute! p. 111

1. EMILE Thierry, tu fais souvent du sport?
   THIERRY Oui, je fais du jogging une fois par semaine.

2. EMILE Salut, Odile. Dis-moi, tu fais du sport?
   ODILE Non, jamais. Je déteste le sport.

3. EMILE Et toi, Martine?
   MARTINE Oh, de temps en temps. J'aime bien jouer au basket-ball.

4. EMILE Dis, François, tu fais souvent du sport?
   FRANÇOIS Euh, pas vraiment. Quelquefois, je joue au tennis ou au base-ball.

5. EMILE Et toi, Vincent?
   VINCENT Oui, je fais de l'aérobic deux fois par semaine.

Answers to Activity 28
1. Thierry: once a week
2. Odile: never
3. Martine: from time to time
4. François: sometimes
5. Vincent: twice a week

*P*rononciation, p. 113

For the scripts for Parts A and B, see p. 113.

C. A écrire

(Dictation)
— Salut! On joue au foot?
— Non. J'ai musique.
— Tu aimes la musique?
— Oui, bien sûr. C'est super.

*M*ise en pratique

1 p. 116

Vous aimez le ski, le patin, le hockey? Venez au Village des Sports. C'est le fun en hiver! Au printemps aussi, c'est le fun. Faites de l'athlétisme et du roller en ligne. Vous venez en été? Eh bien, c'est aussi le fun quand il fait chaud. Jouez au base-ball et faites du ski nautique. Et l'automne au Village des Sports, c'est super! Avec du volley et du football, Le Village des Sports, c'est le fun des quatre saisons!

Answers to Mise en pratique, Activity 1
Winter: skiing, skating, hockey
Spring: track and field, in-line skating
Summer: baseball, water-skiing
Fall: volleyball, soccer

Projects

Mon calendrier
(Individual Project)

ASSIGNMENT
Students will make a calendar for one month showing the activities they participate in each day.

MATERIALS
✂ **Students may need**
- Large sheets of paper
- Magazines
- Scissors
- Colored pens and pencils
- Glue or tape

SUGGESTED SEQUENCE
Prewriting After students choose a month, have them make a list of the activities they participate in (or would like to participate in) during that month.

Students might want to add illustrations to their calendars, so they should begin to look for photos or make drawings of the activities they want to depict.

First Draft Have students draw a calendar of the month they chose and write their activities in the appropriate squares. Then, on a separate sheet of paper, have them write at least four sentences describing their activities, telling how much they like them and how often they participate in each one.

Peer Editing Have students exchange their lists of activities and sentences with at least one other student. Students should check each other's work for comprehensibility and accuracy (spelling, verb forms, and word order).

Final Draft Have students rewrite their lists and sentences, making any necessary corrections. Then, have them write their information around the calendar and glue or tape their photos or illustrations to the appropriate calendar days. Finally, have students display and describe their calendars to the class.

Le sport
(Individual Project)

ASSIGNMENT
Students will make a poster or collage presenting their favorite sport or team.

MATERIALS
✂ **Students may need**
- Large sheets of paper or posterboard
- Magazines
- Scissors
- Colored pens and pencils
- Glue or tape

SUGGESTED SEQUENCE
Prewriting Have students do research on their favorite sport or team. They might want to look through the **Vocabulaire** sections of Chapters 1–4 to find useful vocabulary. You might also refer them to the Additional Vocabulary on page R10.

First Draft Have students write at least four sentences describing their poster topic and choose photos or drawings to illustrate their posters. They should also begin to organize the information for their poster and plan where they will write the information and position their photos and drawings.

Peer Editing Have students exchange their sentences with at least one other student. Have them check each other's work for comprehensibility and accuracy (spelling, verb forms, and word order). They should also comment on the poster layout and choice of illustrations.

Final Draft Have students rewrite their sentences, making any necessary corrections. Then, have them copy their information onto the poster and glue or tape their photos or illustrations in place. Have students display their posters in the classroom and describe them to the class.

GRADING THE PROJECTS
You might assign grades for both projects based on the completeness of the assignment, presentation, language use, and content.

Suggested Point Distribution (total = 100 points)

Completeness of assignment . . . . 20 points

Presentation . . . . 30 points

Language use . . . . 20 points

Content . . . . 30 points

Chapitre 4: Sports et passe-temps
Games

GAMES — CHAPTER 4

CHARADES

In this game, students will review the verbs they've learned so far.

Have teams of three or four students recall the verbs they've learned in Chapters 1-4. Distribute index cards and have each group write a different verb on each one. Collect the cards, decide which team will start, and give the first player from that team one of the cards. The player has thirty seconds to mime the action and have his or her team call out the correct French verb. If the player succeeds, the team wins a point. In order to give all team members a chance to guess, no team member may make consecutive guesses. If the first team is unable to guess correctly, allow the other teams to try. Repeat the process with the other teams. After you have gone through all the verbs, use any that weren't guessed as tie-breakers.

MEMOIRE

This game provides an entertaining way for students to practice and review vocabulary.

Have students make two cards for each vocabulary word from this chapter. On one card, they should write the French word; on the other, they should illustrate the word or write the English equivalent. Mix the cards and number them on the blank side. You will need to write the number so that the vocabulary or illustration is right-side up when the card is flipped up. Tape the cards to the board so that the numbers show. Each player calls out two of the numbers in French. Turn up the two cards bearing those numbers to reveal the vocabulary word or illustration on the reverse side. The object is to find the two cards that match. Each player or team wins a point for each correct match. If the two cards do not match, be sure to turn the cards back to the number side so that they will remain in play.

Chapitre 4
Sports et passe-temps

pp. 94–119

*U*sing the Chapter Opener

Motivating Activity

Ask students what activities are represented by the pictures and objects on pages 94 and 95. Have them tell what activities they would like to learn to say in French. Write their suggestions on a transparency. You might want to show this transparency at the end of the chapter and have students give the French equivalents for the activities listed.

Teaching Suggestion

Have students look at the photos and try to guess the meanings of the captions.

Photo Flash!

① These photos were taken in Quebec City and the surrounding area.

① The young people in this photo are rehearsing a play during a drama class at a recreation center.

CHAPITRE

4
Sports et passe-temps

① On aime faire du théâtre !

94 *quatre-vingt-quatorze*

① **Culture Note**

Centres d'animation and **Maisons des jeunes** are French organizations that offer teenagers a place to meet with other young people who share the same interests. These are also places where teenagers can find information on summer jobs, student travel opportunities, and many other topics. They also give classes on a variety of subjects such as: dancing, music, art, acting, and various sports. **Centres Communautaires** offer the same type of activities, but they are open to people of all ages. Some of them may focus on issues of interest to specific demographic groups. For more information on the **Maisons des jeunes,** see page 106.

Teenagers in French-speaking countries find plenty of time for hobbies. They play sports, watch television, listen to music, take photos, and go out with friends. Many of their spare-time activities are similar to yours.

In this chapter you will learn

- to tell how much you like or dislike something
- to exchange information
- to make, accept, and turn down suggestions

And you will

- listen to French-speaking students talk about what they do for fun
- read about a sports resort in Canada
- write about your hobbies and what you do to have fun
- find out about sports and hobbies in francophone countries

② On fait du patin à glace de temps en temps.

③ En automne, on fait du vélo.

Focusing on Outcomes

Have students read the three functional objectives listed on this page. Ask them which objectives correspond to the photos and captions on pages 94 and 95. You might also ask students if they like the activities pictured.

NOTE: You may want to use the video to support the objectives. The self-check activities in **Que sais-je?** on page 118 help students assess their achievement of the objectives.

Photo Flash!

② Ice-skating has long been a popular activity in Quebec City. In 1856, the city acquired the first covered skating rink in North America in order to accommodate **les Nordiques,** a former hockey team of Quebec. When a second skating arena **(Le Colisée)** was built in 1949, it was the most modern of all covered rinks. Skating is not exclusively an indoor sport for the **Québécois,** however. When the Saint Charles River freezes in the winter, people go there to skate **en plein air.**

③ This cyclist is riding a mountain bike in the **parc du mont Sainte-Anne** near Quebec City. In the fall and spring, mountain biking and hiking are popular activities in the thirty-square-mile park. In the winter, the park is even more popular as the largest ski resort in Quebec. With the latest in timing technology, the park has hosted famous ski races such as the World Cup.

Teacher Note

Some activities suggested in the *Teacher's Edition* ask students to contact various people, businesses, and organizations in the community. Before assigning these activities, it is advisable to request parental permission. In some cases, you may also want to obtain permission from the parties the students will be asked to contact.

Community Link

Have students research one of the sports in this chapter and any famous events or athletes associated with that sport in francophone countries. Have them share what they have learned with their classmates.

Block Scheduling

For suggestions about how to use *Allez, viens!* with block scheduling, see the *Lesson Planner,* pages 18–22.

VIDEO PROGRAM
Videocassette 2
03:34–08:41
Videocassette 5
(captioned version)
26:05–31:12

OR VIDEODISC PROGRAM,
Videodisc 2, Side B

Search 3945, Play To 13170

Video Synopsis

In this segment of the video, Emilie is making a video for Leticia, her pen pal in San Diego, to tell her about Quebec City and the sports and hobbies she likes. Emilie introduces her friends Michel, François, and Marie. Emilie and her friends talk about the sports and hobbies they like, the weather, and the different things you can do in each season in Quebec. We see scenes of Emilie, her friends, and other people participating in these activities.

Motivating Activity

Ask students what they would include in a videotape to a French pen pal. Would they show their city, their friends, or what they like to do?

Presentation

Since the letter is not read on the video, you might first read the letter aloud to students and have them listen with their books closed. Ask them what they understood, or have them answer the questions in Activity 1 on page 98. Then, tell students they're going to see the video Emilie made for Leticia. Play the video and then have students open their books and read the letter and photo captions.

This is an abridged version of the video episode.

Mise en train 📖 PA

p. 37, Act. 1

Nouvelles de Québec

CD 4
Trs. 1–2

Emilie is eager to get to know her American pen pal Leticia. What kind of information do you think Emilie might include in a letter to her new pen pal?

*Emilie Tremblay
185, rue des Grisons
Québec, Québec
G1R 4M9
Canada*

*Leticia Garza
10286 Balboa Ave.
San Diego, CA 9212[
... S.A.*

Salut, Leticia!

Comment ça va? Juste une petite lettre pour accompagner ces photos, une brochure sur le mont Sainte-Anne, une montagne près de Québec et aussi une cassette vidéo sur Québec... et sur moi! Comme ça, tu as une idée des activités ici... C'est l'automne à Québec et il fait déjà froid! Heureusement, il y a du soleil, mais il y a du vent. Quel temps est-ce qu'il fait à San Diego? Est-ce qu'il fait froid aussi? J'aime beaucoup Québec. C'est très sympa. Il y a beaucoup de choses à faire. En automne, je fais du patin et de la natation. J'adore le sport. En été, je fais du deltaplane et de la voile. Au printemps, je fais de l'équitation et je joue au tennis. Et en hiver, bien sûr, je fais du ski. C'est super ici pour le ski. Il neige de novembre à avril! Tu imagines? Est-ce qu'il neige à San Diego? Qu'est-ce qu'on fait comme sport? Du ski? Du base-ball? Quand il fait trop froid, je regarde la télévision et j'écoute de la musique. J'adore le rock et la musique québécoise. Et toi? Qu'est-ce que tu écoutes comme musique? Qu'est-ce qu'on fait à San Diego les fins de semaine? J'ai aussi une autre passion : de temps en temps, je fais des films avec un caméscope. C'est le fun! Tu sais, c'est super, Québec. Et la Californie, c'est comment ? C'est le fun ou pas?

A très bientôt

Emilie

96   *quatre-vingt-seize*   CHAPITRE 4   Sports et passe-temps

---

RESOURCES FOR MISE EN TRAIN

PRINT	MEDIA
• *Practice and Activity Book,* p. 37 • *Video Guide,* pp. 25–26, 28 • *Videodisc Guide,* pp. 40–43, 47	• *Video Program,* Videocassette 2, Videocassette 5 (captioned version) • *Videodisc Program,* Videodisc 2, Side B • *Audio Compact Discs,* CD 4, Trs. 1–2

Language Note

You might explain that the expression **C'est le fun** is Canadian slang; it is often contracted as **l'fun.**

① *Ça, c'est notre café préféré.*

② *La musique, c'est super!*
Tu fais de la musique, toi?

③ *Au printemps, on joue*
au tennis. J'adore!

④ *C'est mon copain Michel.*
En été, on fait du vélo.

⑤ *En automne, on fait*
de l'équitation.

⑥ *C'est moi! En hiver,*
on fait du patin.

Thinking Critically

Drawing Inferences Have students try to guess the seasons, climate, and activities shown on page 97. Ask if they can think of an English word that looks like **hiver** and has to do with winter? (Some animals *hibernate* in winter, living off their stored energy sources.)

Teaching Suggestion

Have students find examples of the chapter objectives and activities in the letter and in the photo captions. (Examples include talking about how much someone likes an activity, asking someone about his or her pastimes, talking about hobbies and sports, and sharing information about Canada.)

For Individual Needs

Kinesthetic Learners Have students or pairs of students come to the front of the class and mime the action in one of the photos. The first person to call out the number of the corresponding photo takes the next turn. As a challenge, you might also have students find the sentence in Emilie's letter where she talks about the activity being mimed.

Video Integration

- VIDEO PROGRAM,
  Videocassette 2, 08:42–18:38
  Videocassette 5, 31:15–41:05
- VIDEODISC PROGRAM,
  Videodisc 2, Side B

Search 13171, Play To 31080

You may choose to continue with **Nouvelles de Québec (suite)** at this time or wait until later in the chapter. The story continues with Michel filming Emilie as she talks about Quebec City. We see scenes of different parts of the city as Emilie goes window-shopping, and Michel goes to a hockey match. Next, Emilie and some friends go to **mont Sainte-Anne,** where they hike and ride mountain bikes. Finally, Emilie and Michel go to a skating rink. They interview a man who talks about sports. Emilie and Michel say goodbye to Leticia and suggest that she make a video for them about San Diego.

MISE EN TRAIN
CHAPITRE 4

Teaching Suggestion

2 This activity can be used as a listening comprehension exercise. Read the sentences aloud and have students write **Oui** or **Non** on their papers.

For videodisc application, see *Videodisc Guide.*

Captioned Video

3 You may want to play **Nouvelles de Québec** on Videocassette 5 to help students find the targeted expressions.

 For Individual Needs

4 Slower Pace Go over the list of sports with students to make sure they understand them before completing the activity. You might mime the sports to avoid using English.

Language Note

4 Tell students that a good way to remember whether to use **en** or **au** with the seasons is that **en** is used with the seasons that begin with a vowel sound (**été**, **automne**, and **hiver**), and **au** is used with **printemps**, which doesn't begin with a vowel sound.

These activities check for comprehension only. Students should not yet be expected to produce language modeled in **Mise en train**.

1 Tu as compris?

Answer the following questions about Emilie's letter to Leticia. Don't be afraid to guess. *See answers below.*

1. What is Emilie sending to Leticia along with her letter?
2. What are some of Emilie's hobbies and pastimes?
3. What would she like to know about Leticia and San Diego?
4. What does Emilie tell Leticia about the city of Quebec?
5. What else have you learned about Emilie from her letter?

2 C'est Emilie?

Tell whether Emilie would be likely or unlikely to say each of the statements below.

1. «J'adore faire du sport.» *likely*
2. «Le ski? Ici on n'aime pas beaucoup ça.» *unlikely*
3. «Pour moi, Québec, c'est barbant en hiver.» *unlikely*
4. «Faire des films avec un caméscope, pour moi, c'est passionnant.» *likely*
5. «Je regarde la télé en hiver quand il fait trop froid.» *likely*
6. «La musique? Bof! Je n'aime pas beaucoup ça.» *unlikely*

3 Cherche les expressions

In **Nouvelles de Québec**, what does Emilie say to . . . *See answers below.*

1. greet Leticia?
2. ask how Leticia is?
3. ask about the weather?
4. tell what she likes?
5. express her opinion about something?
6. inquire about California?
7. say goodbye?

C'est super. Comment ça va? J'adore...
A très bientôt. J'aime... C'est très sympa.
Quel temps est-ce qu'il fait?
C'est le fun. Salut!
Et la Californie, c'est comment?

4 Les saisons et les sports

D'après la lettre d'Emilie, quels sports est-ce qu'elle fait? En quelle saison? Choisis des sports pour compléter ces phrases.

1. Au printemps, Emilie fait... *de l'équitation.*
2. En hiver, elle fait... *du ski.*
3. En automne, elle fait... *du patin et de la natation.*
4. En été, elle fait... *du deltaplane et de la voile.*

de l'équitation   du ski
du deltaplane   de la voile
du patin   de la natation

5 Et maintenant, à toi

Emilie fait beaucoup de choses! Tu fais les mêmes choses? Pour chaque activité, réponds **Moi aussi** ou **Moi, non.**

1. Emilie fait du ski.
2. Elle écoute de la musique.
3. Emilie fait des films avec un caméscope.
4. Elle fait de l'équitation.
5. Quand il fait trop froid pour sortir, Emilie regarde la télé.
6. Emilie joue au tennis.

98 *quatre-vingt-dix-huit*   CHAPITRE 4   Sports et passe-temps

---

Answers

1 1. photographs, a brochure, and a videocassette
2. ice-skating, swimming, hang gliding, sailing, horseback riding, tennis, skiing, watching TV, listening to music, and making video films
3. her favorite hobbies and pastimes, what the weather is like, what music she listens to, what California is like
4. It's already cold in autumn. It's sunny, but windy. There are a lot of things to do there. It snows from November to April.

5. *Possible answers:* She's athletic, active, friendly, and extroverted.

3 1. Salut!
2. Comment ça va?
3. Quel temps est-ce qu'il fait?
4. J'aime...; J'adore...
5. C'est super. C'est le fun. C'est très sympa.
6. Et la Californie, c'est comment?
7. A très bientôt.

RENCONTRE CULTURELLE

What do you know about Quebec? What impressions do you get of Quebec when you look at these photos?

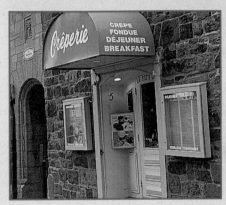

Qu'en penses-tu? See answers below.

1. What things do you see that are typically American?
2. What do you see in these photos that you might not see in the United States?

Savais-tu que... ?

One of the first things you'll notice about Quebec City is its fascinating blend of styles—old and new, European and North American. Old Quebec (**le Vieux-Québec**) is filled with quaint neighborhood cafés and shops that maintain the old-world flavor of Europe. And yet, it is surrounded by a vibrant, modern city with high-rise hotels, office buildings, and a complex network of freeways. All of these elements together give the city its unique character.

Geography Link

Have students find Quebec on a map of Canada. You might have them calculate the distance between their city and Quebec. Have them look at a globe or world map to find out what other cities are on the same latitude as Quebec.

History Link

Have students look up information about the founding of Quebec, the exploration of the region, and the important people involved. You might also have them refer to the Location Opener on pages 90–93.

Motivating Activity

Ask students what they already know about Quebec. Based on the Location Opener and Emilie's letter, what are their impressions?

Presentation

Have students describe the photos orally, and then answer the questions in **Qu'en penses-tu?** Ask them if they would like to visit or study in Quebec and have them explain why or why not.

Thinking Critically

Comparing and Contrasting
In English, have students compare their city with Quebec, writing or naming several similarities and differences. You might have them consult an encyclopedia to obtain more information about Quebec.

Teaching Suggestion

Have students choose one of the pictures of Quebec and write a short note as if they were sending it as a postcard.

Multicultural Link

Have students research cities in the United States where there is evidence of more than one major culture. They might choose New Orleans (French), Miami (Hispanic), or any city with a large Asian population (San Francisco). Have students research how these cultures have enriched the city and what contributions citizens of these cultures have made to their city and state.

Possible answers
1. freeways, freeway signs, skyscrapers, and other modern buildings
2. cobblestone streets, European-style cafés and shops, French signs

Jump Start!

Have students write sentences telling two things they like to do after school and two things they don't like to do.

MOTIVATE

Ask students what activities they participate in, both in and out of school, and which ones they really enjoy or dislike. Ask them if their friends like the same activities.

TEACH

Presentation

Vocabulaire Write the activities on a transparency and cover it with a sheet of paper. Then, mime the activities one at a time. After you mime each one, say the French equivalent and have students repeat it as you uncover that expression. Then, hold up magazine pictures of people playing various sports and make true-false statements. (**Il joue au tennis.**)

Teaching Suggestions

• Have students categorize the activities by season and keep their notes to use in later activities.
• Show *Teaching Transparencies 4-A* and *4-B* and ask students which sport each person likes.

(TPR) Tell students to do some of these activities (**Joue au tennis!**) and have them mime the activity in response to your instruction.

Language-to-Language

In Canada, *soccer* is called **le soccer** instead of **le foot(ball)** because Canadian football, which is similar to American football, also exists.

PREMIERE ETAPE Storytelling Book pp. 13, 16

Telling how much you like or dislike something

 P A p. 38, Act. 4   4-A, 4-B   G V p. 25, Acts. 1–2   CD-ROM Disc 1

VOCABULAIRE

Qu'est-ce que tu aimes faire après l'école?

jouer au foot(ball)

jouer au football américain

faire de la vidéo

faire du roller en ligne

faire du patin à glace

faire du théâtre

faire de l'athlétisme

faire du vélo

faire de la natation *

You can probably guess what these activities are:

faire de l'aérobic	faire du ski (nautique)	jouer au basket(-ball)	jouer à des jeux vidéo
faire du jogging	jouer aux cartes	jouer au golf	jouer au tennis
faire de la/des photo(s)	jouer au base-ball	jouer au hockey	jouer au volley(-ball)

6 Ecoute!   See scripts and answers on p. 93G.

 Listen to this conversation between Philippe and Pascal. List at least two activities Pascal likes and two he doesn't like.

CD 4 Tr. 3   * Remember that **nager** also means *to swim.*

100   *cent*   CHAPITRE 4   Sports et passe-temps

RESOURCES FOR PREMIERE ETAPE

PRINT

• *Lesson Planner,* p. 19
• *Practice and Activity Book,* pp. 38–40
• *Grammar and Vocabulary Workbook,* pp. 25–27
• *Activities for Communication,* pp. 19–20, 90, 93–94, 143–144
• *Listening Activities,* pp. 27, 31
• *Testing Program,* pp. 79–82
• *Alternative Assessment Guide,* p. 35

MEDIA

• *Video Program,* Videocassette 2
  Video Guide, pp. 25–30
• *Videodisc Program,* Videodisc 2, Side B
  Videodisc Guide, p. 44
• *Teaching Transparencies* 4-1, 4-A, 4-B
• *Interactive CD-ROM Program,* Disc 1
  CD-ROM Teacher's Guide, p. 15
• *Audio Compact Discs*
  Textbook Listening Activities, CD 4, Trs. 1–4
  Additional Listening Activities 4-1, 4-2, CD 4, Trs. 25–26
  Quiz 4-1B, CD 4, Tr. 19

CD-ROM
Disc 1

GRAMMAIRE Expressions with faire and jouer

You use **faire** *(to make, to do)* followed by the preposition **de** with activities, including sports.

- When the sport is a masculine noun, **de** becomes **du.**
  faire **du** ski   faire **du** patin

- If the activity is plural, **de** becomes **des.**
  faire **des** photos

- The preposition **de** doesn't change before **la** or **l'.**
  faire **de la** natation   faire **de l'**aérobic

PA
p. 38, Act. 3

GV
p. 26,
Acts. 3–4

Additional Grammar
Practice, p. R32

You use **jouer** *(to play)* with games or sports that you <u>play</u>. It is followed by the preposition **à.**

- When the game or sport is a masculine noun, **à** becomes **au.**
  jouer **au** football

- When the game or sport is plural, **à** becomes **aux.**
  jouer **aux** cartes

- The preposition **à** doesn't change before **la, l'** or **des.**

7 Qu'est-ce que tu aimes faire? ⓗ

Ariane and Serge are telling each other about the activities they like to do after school. Complete their conversation by substituting the activities suggested by the pictures.

ARIANE   Qu'est-ce que tu aimes faire après l'école?

SERGE   Moi, j'aime avec mes copains. Et toi?
         jouer au football

ARIANE   Moi, j'aime et j'adore .
         faire du roller en ligne   *faire des photos*

SERGE   Tu aimes ? On va jouer à la plage demain. Tu viens?
         jouer au volley-ball

ARIANE   Non, merci. J'aime mieux avec des copains.
         faire du ski nautique

8 Après l'école

You and a Canadian student are discussing what you like to do after school on different days of the week. Create the conversation with one of your classmates.

— Qu'est-ce que tu aimes faire le lundi après l'école?
— J'aime jouer au basket le lundi. Et toi?
— Moi, j'aime faire du vélo.

Teacher Note

Students will learn more about contractions with **à** in Chapter 6 and contractions with **de** in Chapter 12. You may want to refer to these presentations on pages 157 and 320.

Presentation

Grammaire Play "Jeter et attraper" (see page 123J) with activities. First, have students look back at the **Vocabulaire** on page 100, noticing which activities use **faire** and which ones use **jouer** and explain why. Then, have them close their books. Call out an activity (**ski**) and toss a ball to a student, who catches it and calls out the full expression (**faire du ski**). For an extra challenge, students who drop the ball should be given two activities.

For videodisc application, see *Videodisc Guide.*

Teacher Note

You may want to explain to students that **faire de la photo** means *to do photography,* while **faire des photos** means *to take pictures.*

Language Note

Some other activities using **faire** that students might like to know are: **faire du vélo tout terrain** *(to mountain bike),* **faire de la gymnastique** *(to do gymnastics, to exercise in general),* **faire de la boxe** *(to box),* and **faire de l'alpinisme** *(to climb mountains).*

Teacher Note

7 Remind students that they will need to fill in the verb as well as the name of the activity.

◆ **For Individual Needs**

7 Challenge After students have completed the activity, have them pair off and rewrite the dialogue to express their own preferences.

Motivating Activity

Ask students if they always answer questions in complete sentences. Have them suggest short answers they might give in English if someone asked whether they liked or disliked something. Have them compare their short answers to those in **Comment dit-on... ?**

Presentation

Comment dit-on... ? Have a volunteer ask you if you like soccer. Then, give all of the short answers listed here, delivering each with exaggerated facial expressions and gestures to get the meaning across. Tell students how much you like certain activities. (**J'aime beaucoup nager.**) Have them indicate what they understood by using the thumbs-up gesture, the **comme-ci, comme ça** gesture, or the thumbs-down gesture.

Additional Practice

Give each student a card with a smiling face, a face with a straight line for a mouth, or a frowning face drawn on it. Then, have partners ask each other about certain activities and respond according to the card they have.

For Individual Needs

9 Slower Pace Play the recording twice. The first time, tell students to listen only for those activities the speakers say they like. The second time, have students listen for those activities the speakers dislike.

COMMENT DIT-ON... ?
Telling how much you like or dislike something

p. 39, Act. 5

4-1

To tell how much you like something:
J'aime **beaucoup** le sport. *I like . . . a lot!*
J'aime **surtout** faire du ski. *I especially like . . .*

To tell how much you dislike something:
Je n'aime **pas tellement** le football. *I don't like . . . too much.*
Je n'aime **pas beaucoup** le volley-ball. *I don't like . . . very much.*
Je n'aime **pas du tout** la natation. *I don't like . . . at all.*

You can use the expressions in bold type alone as short answers:
— Tu aimes faire du sport?
— Oui, **beaucoup!** *or*
  Non, **pas tellement.**

9 Ecoute! See scripts and answers on p. 93G.

CD 4 Tr. 4

On a school trip to Quebec, you listen to your classmate talk to a Canadian student. Write down at least one sport or game each speaker likes and one each speaker dislikes.

10 Pas d'accord!

You and a Canadian exchange student want to watch sports on TV, but you can't agree on what to watch. Each time one of you finds something you like, the other doesn't like it and changes the channel. Act this out with a partner.

— Oh! J'aime bien le football. Et toi, tu aimes?
— Pas beaucoup. Regarde, un match de tennis. Tu aimes le tennis?

le patin à glace   le hockey   le football américain

oui, beaucoup   le basket-ball   pas tellement

pas du tout   pas beaucoup

le ski   moi, si   la natation

Teaching Suggestion

10 Remind students of the expression **Moi, si** and practice it briefly in contradictory responses.
—Tu aimes le hockey?
—Non, pas beaucoup.
—Moi, si!

11 Qu'est-ce qu'ils aiment faire?

The Canadian exchange student is visiting your school. He'd like to get to know your friends better, so he asks you about their interests. Tell him how much each of your friends likes or dislikes the activity pictured, using the cue provided.

—Est-ce que Marc aime... ? —Non, il n'aime pas trop...

(–) (+) (+) (–) (+)

Marc   Isabelle   Antoine   Jean-Paul   Anne-Marie

Answers may vary.

1. Est-ce que Marc aime... ?   1. Non, il n'aime pas trop jouer au tennis.
2. Est-ce qu'Isabelle aime... ?   2. Oui, elle aime beaucoup jouer aux cartes.
3. Et Antoine, est-ce qu'il aime... ?   3. Oui, il aime surtout faire du ski nautique.
4. Et Jean-Paul, est-ce qu'il aime... ?   4. Non, il n'aime pas tellement faire des photos.
5. Est-ce qu'Anne-Marie aime... ?   5. Oui, elle aime beaucoup faire du patin à glace.

GRAMMAIRE Question formation

PA p. 40, Act. 8   GV p. 27, Acts. 5–6

You've already learned to make a yes-or-no question by raising the pitch of your voice at the end of a sentence. Another way to ask a yes-or-no question is to say **est-ce que** before a statement and raise your voice at the very end.

Additional Grammar Practice, p. R33

Est-ce que tu aimes faire du vélo?

12 Et toi?

With a partner, discuss the sports and hobbies you both like to do. Take turns asking and answering questions. Be sure to vary the kinds of questions you ask.

— Est-ce que tu aimes jouer au football américain?
— Non! J'aime mieux faire de l'aérobic, du théâtre et du roller en ligne.

Vocabulaire à la carte

faire un pique-nique	to have a picnic
faire de la randonnée	to go hiking
faire des haltères	to lift weights
faire de la gymnastique	to do gymnastics
faire du surf	to surf
faire de la voile	to go sailing

13 Enquête

Poll five of your classmates about the sports and hobbies they like to do. Which activity is the most popular? Which is the least popular?

Presentation

Grammaire Before students look at the explanation, write the sentence *You like to go bike riding* on the board or on a transparency. Ask students to turn it into a question in as many different ways as they can. (They might just use a rising intonation, place *Do* at the beginning of the sentence, or put *don't you?* at the end.) Next, have them look at the expression in the box and repeat it after you. Write the following sentences on the board or on a transparency and have students use **est-ce que** to turn them into questions:
1. **Tu aimes faire du roller en ligne.**
2. **Tu aimes faire de la natation.**
3. **Tu aimes étudier.**
4. **Tu aimes faire le ménage.**
Then, write the questions they form on the transparency and have pairs of students ask and answer them.

Teacher Note

Grammaire You might tell students that a third, more formal way to form questions in French is by using *inversion,* reversing the order of the subject pronoun and the verb (**Aimez-vous. . .? Aimes-tu. . .?**) You might also tell students that a **-t-** is inserted after a third person singular verb that ends with a vowel. (**Aime-t-il faire du vélo?**) As an example of inversion, point out the expression **Comment dit-on. . .?** and the question **Quel temps fait-il?** on page 106.

Performance Assessment

Have pairs of students interview each other to find out their most and least favorite activities. You might have them act out their interviews for the class.

CLOSE

Have students give all appropriate responses to the following questions and statements:
1. **Tu aimes le sport? (Oui, beaucoup! Non, pas trop. Oui, un peu. Pas tellement. Pas du tout.)**
2. **Moi, j'aime le volley-ball. (Moi aussi! Moi, non.)**
3. **Je n'aime pas le ski. (Moi, si! Moi non plus.)**

ASSESS

Quiz 4-1A, Quiz 4-1B, *Testing Program,* pp. 79–82

Audio CD 4, Tr. 19

Jump Start!

Have students draw pictures of three activities from the previous **étape**. Then, have them exchange drawings and write captions identifying the activities in French.

MOTIVATE

Ask students what they would like to find out about someone they've just met.

TEACH

Presentation

Comment dit-on... ? Write **est-ce que** on the board and ask students how it is used. Next, add **qu'** to the beginning of the expression to make **qu'est-ce que.** Explain that it means *what* and is used to begin an information question. Next, have students find examples of **qu'est-ce que** in Emilie's letter on page 96 or play the captioned video for **Nouvelles de Québec** on Videocassette 5. Then, hold a toy microphone out to "interview" various students, asking **Qu'est-ce que tu fais comme sport?** You might call students' attention to the **Note de grammaire,** which explains the use of **de** in a negative sentence.

Grammaire Write the forms of **faire** on a transparency and have students repeat them after you. Then, form four teams. Have each team make a set of flashcards showing the forms of **faire.** Call out a subject pronoun and have teams hold up the card that shows the appropriate verb form.

 For videodisc application, see *Videodisc Guide.*

DEUXIEME ETAPE   Storytelling Book pp. 14, 16

Exchanging information

 COMMENT DIT-ON... ?
Exchanging information
To find out a friend's interests:
   Qu'est-ce que tu fais comme sport? *What sports do you play?*
   Qu'est-ce que tu fais pour t'amuser? *What do you do to have fun?*

To tell about your interests:
4-2
   Je fais de l'athlétisme. *I do . . .*
   Je joue au volley-ball. *I play . . .*
   Je ne fais pas de ski. *I don't . . .*
   Je ne joue pas au foot. *I don't play . . .*

NOTE DE GRAMMAIRE
Du, de la, and **de l'** usually become **de** (or **d'**) in a negative sentence.

Je ne fais pas **de** jogging.
Je ne fais pas **d'**athlétisme.

14 **Qu'est-ce que tu fais pour t'amuser?**
With a partner, take turns asking each other about your sports and hobbies.

PA p. 41, Act. 10   GV p. 28, Acts. 7–8   Additional Grammar Practice, p. R33

— Qu'est-ce que tu fais pour t'amuser?
— Je fais du jogging et du ski. Et toi?
— Moi, je...

GRAMMAIRE   The verb **faire**
The irregular verb **faire** is used in many different expressions.

faire *(to do, to play, or to make)*

Je **fais**		Nous **faisons**	
Tu **fais**	du sport.	Vous **faites**	du sport.
Il/Elle/On **fait**		Ils/Elles **font**	

 PA p. 41, Act. 11

 GV p. 29, Acts. 9–10

Additional Grammar Practice, pp. R33–R34

15 **Quels sports?**
Complete the following conversation with the correct forms of the verb **faire.**

— Tu __1__ quels sports?   fais
— Moi, je __2__ surtout du ski et du patin.   fais
— Et tes copains, qu'est-ce qu'ils __3__ comme sport?   font
— Michel __4__ de la natation et Hélène __5__ du roller en ligne.   fait, fait
— Hélène et toi, est-ce que vous __6__ du sport ensemble?   faites
— Oui, nous __7__ souvent du vélo.   faisons

RESOURCES FOR DEUXIEME ETAPE

PRINT
- *Lesson Planner,* p. 20
- *Practice and Activity Book,* pp. 41–44
- *Grammar and Vocabulary Workbook,* pp. 28–32
- *Activities for Communication,* pp. 21–22, 91, 93–94, 143–144
- *Listening Activities,* pp. 28, 32
- *Testing Program,* pp. 83–86
- *Alternative Assessment Guide,* p. 35

MEDIA
- *Video Program,* Videocassette 2
    Video Guide, pp. 25–30
- *Videodisc Program,* Videodisc 2, Side B
    Videodisc Guide, pp. 44–45
- *Teaching Transparencies* 4-2, 4-C
- *Interactive CD-ROM Program,* Disc 1
    CD-ROM Teacher's Guide, pp. 15–16
- *Audio Compact Discs*
    Textbook Listening Activity, CD 4, Tr. 5
    Additional Listening Activities 4-3, 4-4, CD 4, Trs. 27–28
    Quiz 4-2B, CD 4, Tr. 20

16 Jean et Luc

Jean and Luc are identical twins. They even enjoy the same activities. Tell what activities they do, based on what you see in their room.   See answers below.

GRAMMAIRE   The pronoun on

PA

p. 41,
Act. 9

GV

p. 30,
Act. 11

Additional Grammar
Practice, p. R34

- The subject pronoun **on** is used with the **il/elle** form of the verb. In conversational French, **on** usually means *we.*
  Le samedi, **on** fait du sport.   *On Saturdays, we play sports.*
- **On** can mean *they* or *you* when it refers to people in general.
  En France, **on** parle français.
- You will have to use context, the surrounding words and phrases, to tell how a speaker is using **on.**

17 Au Cercle français   *At the French Club*

Based on the activities shown in the photos, talk about some of the activities you do or don't do with your friends.

Mes copains et moi, on fait...

1.   2.   3.   4.   5.

16 Have pairs of students ask and answer questions about what Jean and Luc like to do, based on the illustration. Remind them to use **Est-ce que.** (**Est-ce qu'ils aiment faire du ski? Est-ce qu'ils aiment jouer au hockey?**)

Presentation

Grammaire   Hold up several pictures of various sports and activities and give students some generalizations about the sport or activity pictured. (**On joue au foot au Texas. On fait du ski en France.**) Have students guess the meaning of **on** based on what you say and the pictures they see. Tell students that **on** can mean *we, they,* or *you* when referring to people in general. You might want to mention that **on** corresponds to *one* in English. (In order to be healthy, *one* needs to get enough sleep.) Then, have students complete the statement **Après l'école, on...**

Teaching Suggestions

17 Students might work in pairs to do this activity, asking their partner **Et toi?** after each activity they identify.

Possible answers
16 Ils font du ski, du patin à glace, des photos, du théâtre. Ils jouent au football, au hockey.

4-C,
4-2
GV p. 30,
Act. 12

Presentation

Vocabulaire Present the weather expressions by talking about the weather conditions that prevail on the day of your presentation. Present other weather conditions by miming, drawing on the board, or showing pictures or props, such as an umbrella, mittens, and suntan lotion. Then, have students repeat the expressions after you as they read along in their books. Make several statements about weather conditions and have students point to the appropriate prop.

Teaching Suggestion

18 Have students change the pleasant weather conditions to make them unpleasant and vice-versa.

 For Individual Needs

18 Visual/Auditory Learners You might hold up a magazine picture or drawing of each type of weather (a rainy day) and say an activity (**jouer au football américain**). Have students respond with a thumbs-up gesture if they find it pleasant (**agréable**) and a thumbs-down gesture if they think it's unpleasant (**désagréable**).

 Portfolio

19 Written This activity is appropriate for students' written portfolios. For portfolio information, see the *Alternative Assessment Guide,* pages iv–17.

VOCABULAIRE

Quel temps fait-il?

Il fait beau.

Il fait chaud.

Il fait froid.

Il fait frais.

Il pleut.

Il neige.

18 C'est agréable ou désagréable?

Is each of these activities pleasant (**agréable**) or unpleasant (**désagréable**)?

1. faire du vélo quand *(when)* il fait froid   désagréable
2. faire de la natation quand il fait chaud   agréable
3. regarder la télé quand il neige   agréable
4. faire du jogging quand il fait frais   agréable
5. jouer au football américain quand il pleut   désagréable

19 Et toi?

Qu'est-ce que tu aimes faire quand...

1. il fait froid?
2. il pleut?
3. il fait beau?
4. il neige?

Additional Practice

Have the class keep a local weather chart for a week, with one student responsible for recording the weather conditions each day. After the data has been recorded each day, ask students about the weather.

Language-to-Language

If you have native speakers of Spanish in your classroom, you may want to point out the similarity between the verbs **hacer** *(to make* or *to do)* and **faire** when talking about the weather. (**Hace calor. = Il fait froid.**) Have students tell how using **faire** and **hacer** is different from the way weather is described in English.

VOCABULAIRE

Les mois de l'année

PA p. 44, Act. 17 GV p. 31, Acts. 13–14

janvier	juillet
février	août
mars	septembre
avril	octobre
mai	novembre
juin	décembre

NOTE CULTURELLE

Francophone countries, like most other countries of the world, use the metric system, so temperature is measured in degrees centigrade or Celsius rather than Fahrenheit. This means that the freezing point of water is 0°C, and its boiling point is 100°C. A comfortable temperature would be 25°C (77°F). If the temperature were more than 35°C, it would be very hot. If the temperature were 18°C (64.4°F), you would probably need a jacket. If the temperature were 15°C, what month might it be?

20 Il fait quel temps?

In these months, what is the weather usually like where you live?

1. en mai
2. en février
3. en juillet
4. en octobre
5. en avril
6. en décembre

> Il fait froid. Il pleut.
> Il neige. Il fait frais.
> Il fait beau. Il fait chaud.

Tu te rappelles ?

GV p. 31, Act. 15

Do you remember the endings that you learned to use with the verb **aimer** in Chapter 1? Those endings are exactly the same for all regular **-er** verbs, which include many French verbs. Here's how the verb **jouer** fits the pattern.

jouer *(to play)*

Je **joue** ⎫	Nous **jouons** ⎫
Tu **joues** ⎬ au tennis.	Vous **jouez** ⎬ au tennis.
Il/Elle/On **joue** ⎭	Ils/Elles **jouent** ⎭

For additional practice, see p. R34.

21 Écoute! See scripts and answers on p. 93G.

CD 4 Tr. 5

Listen as a newspaper reporter asks three Canadian teenagers, Paul, Anne, and Julie, about their hobbies and pastimes. Then, answer the questions below.

1. Which teenagers don't watch TV?
2. Which ones like to listen to music?
3. Which ones play hockey?
4. Which ones like to dance?
5. Which teenagers like to go to the movies?

22 Prisonnier des neiges

Imagine that you've been snowed in during a winter storm. Write a note to a friend telling him or her about the weather, what you're doing to pass the time, and how you feel about the situation.

Math Link

Note Culturelle To convert Fahrenheit to Celsius, subtract 32 and then multiply by 5/9. To convert Celsius to Fahrenheit, multiply by 9/5 and then add 32. Ask students if they know the freezing and boiling temperatures for water in degrees Celcius and Fahrenheit (Answer: 32° and 212°). Students might want to practice converting some of the temperatures shown on the chart.

Game

 VERB BEE Play this game to review -er verbs. Divide the class into two teams and have one player from each team go to the board. Call out an infinitive (**jouer**) and a subject (**vous**). Award a point to the team of the first player to write the correct verb form.

Presentation

Vocabulaire Divide a transparency into four sections. Label each section with a simple drawing to represent a season (a flower for spring, a sun for summer, and so on). Write the names of the months in French under the appropriate season. Present the months a season at a time, having students repeat each one after you. Then, call out months at random and have students raise their hand if their birthday is in that month. You might also hold up an illustration or an object associated with a holiday and have students name the month in which that holiday falls.

For Individual Needs

20 Challenge Have students answer in complete sentences, either orally or in writing. Then, have them give at least one activity they do in each weather condition and/or in each month. (**En juillet, j'aime nager. En mai, je fais du vélo. Quand il neige, je fais du ski.**)

Building on Previous Skills

22 You might orally review some activities students learned in Chapter 1 (**regarder la télévision, écouter de la musique, étudier, parler au téléphone, danser**).

Teaching Suggestion

22 Students might prefer to write about a heat wave (**une vague de chaleur**) instead.

Portfolio

22 Written This activity could be a portfolio entry or a writing assessment activity. For portfolio information, see the *Alternative Assessment Guide,* pages iv–17.

Presentation

Vocabulaire Show or draw pictures of the four seasons. Write the French words for the seasons on the board next to the pictures. Say aloud a sentence describing an activity. **(On fait du patin à glace.)** Have students identify the appropriate season. Re-enter some activities from previous chapters: **faire de l'équitation, nager,** and **voyager.** Present **en vacances** and **le week-end** using these activities. Present **le matin, l'après-midi,** and **le soir** by drawing the route of the sun from sunrise to sunset on the board. Give various times in the 24-hour system (**13h30, 8h50, 23h15**) and have students tell whether it's **le matin, l'après-midi,** or **le soir.** Teach the phrase **en vacances** by referring to the calendar as you talk about school vacations.

Teaching Suggestion

23 Have students give their own preferred activity if they choose **fais autre chose.**

For Individual Needs

25 **Slower Pace** Before students write their letters, have them think of activities a Canadian pen pal might enjoy.

CLOSE

To close this **étape,** show *Teaching Transparencies 4-A* and *4-2.* Have students describe the activities and weather conditions shown. You might prompt students with **Quand il... , ils...**

VOCABULAIRE

Qu'est-ce que tu fais...

p. 42,
Acts. 12–14

4-D

p. 32,
Act. 16

en vacances?

le soir?

le week-end?

en automne?

en hiver?

au printemps?

en été?

23 Un questionnaire

To help pair up campers for activities, a camp counselor has sent out the survey you see on the right. Give one answer in each category.

24 Et toi?

Tell other students in your class what activities you do in each season and ask what they do. Try to find someone who does at least two of the same things that you do.

— En hiver, je fais du patin à glace. Et toi?
— Moi, non! Quand il fait froid, j'écoute de la musique.

25 Une lettre

In preparation for a visit to Canada, you've decided to write to your French-Canadian pen pal. Write a brief paragraph, asking about your pen pal's sports and hobbies and telling which ones you do and don't do.

1. En automne, je...
a. fais du patin à glace.
b. joue au hockey.
c. écoute de la musique.
d. fais du ski.
e. fais autre chose.

2. En hiver, je...
a. joue au football américain.
b. joue au foot.
c. fais du théâtre.
d. joue au volley.
e. fais autre chose.

3. Au printemps, je...
a. joue au base-ball.
b. fais de l'athlétisme.
c. fais du vélo.
d. fais de la vidéo.
e. fais autre chose.

4. En été, je...
a. fais de la natation.
b. fais du roller en ligne.
c. regarde la télé.
d. fais du ski nautique.
e. fais autre chose.

ASSESS

Quiz 4-2A, Quiz 4-2B, *Testing Program,* pp. 83–86
Audio CD 4, Tr. 20

Performance Assessment

Have pairs of students create a conversation in which they talk about and compare what they like to do in each season of the year. Be sure that both students tell what they like to do and react to their partner's comments.

PANORAMA CULTUREL

Marius • Côte d'Ivoire

Aljosa • France

Mélanie • Québec

VIDEO PROGRAM
Videocassette 2
18:38–20:52

OR VIDEODISC PROGRAM,
Videodisc 2, Side B

Search 31080, Play To 33370

What sports do you play? Where do you go to practice them? We asked some young people about their favorite sports. Here's what they had to say.

Qu'est-ce que tu fais comme sport?

CD 4
Trs. 6–9

CD-ROM
Disc 1

«Je fais beaucoup de sport, mais surtout le football. Je fais le football et le skate, le patin à roulettes et puis j'aime aussi le tennis.»

—Marius
Tr. 7

«Comme sport, j'aime bien faire le tennis. J'aime bien aller à la piscine, voilà. J'aime bien [le] bowling.»

—Aljosa
Tr. 8

«Avec mes amies, moi je fais beaucoup de sport. Je fais partie de l'équipe interscolaire de volley-ball et de badminton de l'école. Je fais de la natation. Je fais du patinage. Je fais de la course. Je fais du tennis aussi souvent l'été. L'hiver, je patine.»

—Mélanie
Tr. 9

Qu'en penses-tu?

1. Which of these students enjoy the same sports that you do?
2. Which sports that they mention are not played in your area?
3. Can you guess which sports are associated with the following events and places?*

   a. La Coupe du monde
   b. Le Grand Prix de Monaco
   c. Le Tour de France
   d. Le stade Roland-Garros

Savais-tu que... ?

While schools in francophone countries do offer extracurricular sports, serious athletes often participate through clubs outside of school. Activities such as swimming, tennis, or volleyball are often organized by parent volunteers or communities. In France, recreation centers (**Maisons des jeunes et de la culture** or **MJC**) sponsor all kinds of social, cultural, and educational activities for young people.

*a. soccer b. auto racing c. cycling d. tennis (the French Open)

Culture Note

Savais-tu que... ? **Maisons des jeunes et de la culture** provide a variety of sports, movies, and other activities such as music, dance, computer science, photography, and arts and crafts. Annual dues are charged based on the number of activities in which a person participates.

Questions

1. **Qu'est-ce que Marius fait comme sport?** (du football, du skate, du patin à roulettes, du tennis)
2. **Est-ce qu'Aljosa aime le bowling?** (Oui)
3. **Est-ce que Mélanie fait du sport à l'école?** (Oui)
4. **Qu'est-ce qu'elle fait en été?** (du tennis) **En hiver?** (Elle patine.)

Teacher Notes

- See the *Video Guide,* the *Videodisc Guide,* and the *CD-ROM Teacher's Guide* for activities related to the **Panorama Culturel.**
- Remind students that cultural material may be included in the Chapter Quizzes and Test.
- The interviewees' language represents informal, unrehearsed speech. Occasionally, edits have been made for clarification.

Presentation

Tell students to listen for the sports that each interviewee mentions. Play the video, and then hold up pictures of various activities, asking **Qui fait ça?** Students call out the name of the interviewee who mentioned that activity.

Thinking Critically

Analyzing Have students give advantages and disadvantages of having school-sponsored sports teams (football, cheerleaders, drill team).

Teaching Suggestion

Have students prepare short reports in English on francophone sporting events. They might look up in *The World Almanac* the most recent winners of the events listed in question 3 of **Qu'en penses-tu?**

TROISIEME ETAPE (TPR)
Storytelling Book
pp. 15, 16

Making, accepting, and turning down suggestions

Jump Start!

Have students write six sentences using a different form of **faire** and a different activity in each.

MOTIVATE

Make suggestions to students in English (Let's go eat lunch! How about a pop quiz?) and write their English responses on the board.

TEACH

Presentation

Comment dit-on... ? Make several suggestions using **On... ?** (On fait du jogging?) Ask students to guess what you are doing (making suggestions). Have students open their books to page 110 or write the new expressions on the board. Then, name a sport or hold up a picture of it and ask a student to suggest doing that sport using the new expression. Respond by accepting or turning down the suggestion. (**D'accord./Ça ne me dit rien.**) Next, suggest various activities and have students accept or reject your suggestions with the appropriate expressions.

Grammaire Ask students how often they participate in various sports and activities. Then, draw a timeline on the board with **souvent** and **d'habitude** at one end, **quelquefois** and **de temps en temps** in the middle, and **rarement** and **jamais** at the other end. Name several pastimes (**le vélo**) and have individual students indicate on the timeline how often they do each activity. Then, say the complete sentence and have students repeat. (**Je ne fais jamais de vélo.**)

 For videodisc application, see *Videodisc Guide.*

COMMENT DIT-ON... ?
Making, accepting, and turning down suggestions

 PA p. 45, Act. 19   4-3

To make a suggestion:
On fait du patin?
How about . . . ?
On joue au foot?
How about . . . ?

To accept a suggestion:
D'accord. *OK.*
Bonne idée. *Good idea.*
Oui, c'est génial!
Allons-y! *Let's go!*

To turn down a suggestion:
Désolé(e), mais je ne peux pas.
Sorry, but I can't.
Ça ne me dit rien.
That doesn't interest me.
Non, c'est barbant!

CD-ROM Disc 1

26 Ecoute! See scripts and answers on p. 93H.

Listen as Germain calls his friends Lise, Renaud, Philippe, and Monique to suggest activities for the weekend. Do his friends accept or turn down his suggestions?

CD 4 Tr. 10

27 Qu'est-ce qu'on fait?

Write down one or two things that you'd like to do this weekend. Then, find three classmates who'd like to join you.

— On fait du jogging ce week-end?
— Le jogging, c'est barbant! *or* D'accord. C'est génial, le jogging.

 CD-ROM Disc 1

PA pp. 45–46, Acts. 20–22

GV pp. 33–34, Acts. 18–20

Additional Grammar Practice, p. R35

GRAMMAIRE   Adverbs of frequency

- To tell how often you do something, use **quelquefois** (*sometimes*), **de temps en temps** (*from time to time*), une **fois par semaine** (*. . . time(s) a week*), **souvent** (*often*), **d'habitude** (*usually*), **rarement** (*rarely*), and **ne... jamais** (*never*).
- Short adverbs usually come after the verb. Longer adverbs can be placed at the beginning or the end of a sentence. Put **d'habitude** at the beginning of a sentence and **une fois par semaine** at the end. Put **ne... jamais** around the verb, as you do with **ne... pas.**

Je fais **souvent** du ski.   Je fais du ski **une fois par semaine.**
D'habitude, je fais du ski au printemps.   Je **ne** fais **jamais** de ski.

110   *cent dix*   CHAPITRE 4   Sports et passe-temps

RESOURCES FOR **TROISIEME ETAPE**

28 Ecoute! See scripts and answers on p. 93H.

Listen as Emile, a reporter for the school newspaper in Quebec City, interviews his classmates about sports. How often does each person practice sports?

CD 4 Tr. 11

29 L'agenda de Pauline *Pauline's planner*

Pauline is an active, French-Canadian teenager. Based on her calendar, take turns with a partner asking about her activities and how often she does them.

— Est-ce qu'elle fait de l'aérobic?
— Oui, de temps en temps.

N O V E M B R E						
DIMANCHE	**LUNDI**	**MARDI**	**MERCREDI**	**JEUDI**	**VENDREDI**	**SAMEDI**
		1 *jogging*	2 *photo*	3 *jogging*	4 *théâtre*	5 *patin à glace*
6 *aérobic*	7 *jogging*	8 *photo*	9	10 *jogging*	11	12 *jogging*
13 *photo*	14 *jogging*	15	16 *aérobic*	17 *jogging*	18 *théâtre*	19
20 *patin à glace*	21 *jogging*	22 *jogging*	23 *photo*	24 *ski*	25	26 *aérobic*
27 *jogging*	28	29 *jogging*	30 *photo*			

30 Moi, je fais souvent....

With a partner, discuss your favorite pastimes and how often you do them. Ask questions to keep the conversation going.

— Qu'est-ce que tu fais pour t'amuser?
— En été, je fais souvent du ski nautique. Et toi?
— Je fais du vélo. Et toi? Tu fais du vélo... ?

le week-end?   en vacances?
quand il fait froid?   en été?
quand il fait beau?

TROISIEME ETAPE

cent onze **111**

TROISIEME ETAPE
CHAPITRE 4

Teaching Suggestion
28 Stop the recording after each interview and have students write the adverb of frequency. You may prefer to have individuals volunteer the answer orally.

For Individual Needs

28 Challenge Have students give the sport that each person practices as well as tell how often he or she does the activity.

29 Slower Pace You might want to go over Pauline's schedule orally before students pair off to discuss it. You might also call out the activity and have students give the days and times when Pauline does that activity, and vice-versa.

29 Challenge Have students make two calendars of their own, one blank and one with their activities filled in like Pauline's. Have them give the blank calendar to a partner, who asks questions about the other's activities and fills in the blank calendar appropriately. They should compare the calendar to the original, and then reverse roles.

30 Kinesthetic Learners You might have students create interview skits based on this activity.

Culture Note
Tell students that calendars in France begin on Monday, but those in Canada begin on Sunday, as in the United States.

Language Note
You might point out that students can replace the number in **une fois par semaine** to fit their situation (**deux fois...**, **trois fois...**).

Teaching Suggestion

31 You might give students examples of questions for this activity (**Tu aimes... ? Comment tu trouves... ? Est-ce que tu fais/joues... ?**). You might also have students recall ways to express their opinion of activities. (**C'est super, génial, nul, barbant.**)

 Portfolio

31 Written This activity is suitable for students' written portfolios. Students may also want to record the conversation they have with their classmates. For portfolio suggestions, see page 21 of the *Alternative Assessment Guide.*

 For Individual Needs

32 Auditory Learners Students might read the letter aloud in small groups, or you might read it aloud to the class.

Teaching Suggestion

33 Type copies of Lucien's letter, deleting all the activities and the opinion words. Have students fill in the blanks with their own activities and opinions.

 Portfolio

33 Written This activity might be added to students' portfolios or used at the end of this **étape** as an assessment activity. For portfolio information, see the *Alternative Assessment Guide,* pages iv–17.

---

31 Sondage

a. Make a chart like the one shown here. In the left-hand column, list the activities you enjoy. In the middle column, tell when you do them, and in the right-hand column, tell how often.

ACTIVITE	SAISON	FREQUENCE
Je fais du ski. Je fais...	en hiver	de temps en temps

b. Now, share this information with three other classmates. Ask questions to find out what you have in common and what you don't.

— Je fais du ski de temps en temps.
— Pas moi! Je ne fais jamais de ski.

32 Le sportif

Your French pen pal Lucien is coming to visit soon. Read his letter and tell whether he would answer **D'accord** or **Ça ne me dit rien** if you were to suggest the following activities.

1. On fait de la vidéo ce week-end? D'accord.
2. On fait du ski nautique? Ça ne me dit rien.
3. On joue au foot? D'accord.
4. On fait de la natation ce soir? D'accord.
5. On joue au football américain ce week-end? Ça ne me dit rien.

Salut!

J'espère que ça va. Moi, ça va bien. Je fais beaucoup de sport maintenant. Et toi, tu aimes faire du sport? Moi, j'aime jouer au foot, mais je n'aime pas trop le football américain; c'est barbant. D'habitude, le week-end, je joue au tennis ou je fais de la natation. La natation, c'est génial. Mais je n'aime pas faire du ski nautique; c'est nul. Quand il fait froid, je fais de l'aérobic. A part le sport, quelquefois, je fais de la vidéo. Et toi? Qu'est-ce que tu fais le week-end? Ecris-moi vite!

A bientôt,

Lucien

33 Cher Lucien, ...

Now, answer Lucien's letter. Be sure to . . .

- tell him what activities you like and why you like them.
- tell him when and how often you do each activity.

- tell him what you don't like to do and why not.
- suggest one or two things you might do together and when.

34 Une interview

a. You are a guest at a French-Canadian school and you'll soon be interviewed on local television. You've received a list of questions you'll be asked. Write down your answers.

1. Tu fais souvent du sport?
2. Qu'est-ce que tu fais comme sport en hiver?
3. Tu regardes souvent la télé?
4. Qu'est-ce que tu fais le week-end?
5. Qu'est-ce que tu fais en vacances?
6. Tu fais quoi le soir?
7. Tu écoutes souvent de la musique? (Du rock? Du jazz? De la musique classique?)
8. Qu'est-ce que tu fais quand il fait froid?

b. With a partner, take turns asking and answering the questions.

35 Mon journal

Using the information in the chart you made for Activity 31, tell about your favorite weekend and after-school activities and how often you do them. Give your opinions of the activities, too.

PRONONCIATION

 The sounds [u] and [y]   See scripts and answers on p. 93H.

CD 4 Trs. 12–17

The sound [u] occurs in such English words as *Sue, shoe,* and *too.* The French [u] is shorter, tenser, and more rounded than the vowel sound in English. Listen to these French words: **tout, nous, vous.** The sound [u] is usually represented by the letter combination **ou.**

The sound [y] is represented in the words **salut, super,** and **musique.** This sound does not exist in English. To pronounce [y], start by saying [i], as in the English word *me.* Then, round your lips as if you were going to say the English word *moon,* keeping your tongue pressed behind your lower front teeth.

A. A prononcer

Now, practice first the sound [u] and then [y]. Repeat these words.

1. vous
2. nous
3. douze
4. rouge
5. cours
6. joue
7. tu
8. musique
9. nul
10. étude
11. une
12. du

B. A lire

Take turns with a partner reading the following sentences aloud.

1. Salut! Tu t'appelles Louis?
2. J'ai cours aujourd'hui.
3. Tu aimes la trousse rouge?
4. Elle n'aime pas du tout faire du ski.
5. Nous aimons écouter de la musique.
6. Vous jouez souvent au foot?

C. A écrire

You're going to hear a short dialogue. Write down what you hear.

Teaching Suggestion

Prononciation Tell students that when they see the letter *u* by itself, it always represents the sound [y]. Have them make their own lists of words containing the sounds [u] and [y]. Read aloud words from the students' lists and ask them to raise their left hand to signal [u] and their right hand to signal [y]. You might also read the list of words from Part A.

For Individual Needs

Slower Pace Have students copy the sentences from **Prononciation** Part B into their notebooks as you write them on the board or on a transparency. Have students circle all the [u] sounds. As they read the words aloud that contain this sound, circle the correct words in your sentences so students can correct their papers. Then, have students pair off to practice reading the sentences aloud. Do the same for the sound [y].

CLOSE

TPR To close this **étape**, tell students in French to do a certain activity and have them respond by miming the activity.

ASSESS

Quiz 4-3A, Quiz 4-3B, *Testing Program,* pp. 87–90
Audio CD 4, Tr. 21

Performance Assessment

Meet with students individually and have them respond orally to some of the questions in Activity 34.

Mon journal

35 For an additional journal entry suggestion for Chapter 4, see *Practice and Activity Book,* page 148.

READING STRATEGY

Predicting what you're going to read

Teacher Note

For an additional reading, see *Practice and Activity Book,* page 47.

PREREADING
Activities A–C

Motivating Activity

Ask students what sports and activities they would like to participate in. Have them tell what they would need to do to get started and identify the equipment they would need.

Teaching Suggestion

A–C Ask students to read the introduction silently or read it to them as they read along. Ask them what they think it means. Then, have students try to guess what type of information will be provided in the selection. List their responses on the board. Ask them for what age group this article is intended. Then, have students scan the article. Have them see how many of the items they listed on the board are in the article.

READING
Activities D–N

Language-to-Language

Ask students to think about the word origin of **le karting.** How did they recognize what the word means? Can they think of any other words used in the French language that end in —*ing*? Students might want to know **le bowling, le parking, le jogging,** and **le camping.**

LISONS!

*W*hat are your favorite free-time activities? In this article, you will get some additional information about the activities enjoyed by francophone students.

DE BONS CONSEILS

When you first glance at a reading selection, you might try to predict what information the article will give you. This will give you a better idea of what you're going to read. Remember to use headings, subheadings, and the organization of the text to help you understand what you're reading.

A. The title of this selection is **Allez, c'est à vous de choisir!** What do you think this title means? What do you think the article will be about? See answers below.

B. Look at the organization of the article and the two major headings. What type of information do you think will be included under **Pour les artistes?** What about **Pour les sportifs?** What do you know about the activities in each category? See answers below.

C. What type of information do you find in each section? Do all the sections have the same type of information? If not, how do they differ? See answers below.

Pour les artistes

D. Scan the sections titled **La musique, Le théâtre,** and **La danse.** Make a list of the cognates you find. You should find at least ten. See answers below.

Allez, c'est à vous de choisir!

Cette année, c'est décidé, vous vous lancez dans une activité! Nous vous en proposons ici quelques exemples, à vous de choisir...

POUR LES ARTISTES

LA MUSIQUE

- Il n'y a pas d'âge pour commencer. L'important, c'est d'être motivé. Et de bien choisir son instrument.
- Vous devez avoir votre instrument. Au début, il est possible de le louer.
- Rythme : en général 1 heure de solfège par semaine et 1/2 h de cours d'instrument. Pour progresser, il faut prévoir 1/4 h de travail chaque jour.

LE THEATRE

- C'est souvent à l'adolescence qu'on commence. On découvre à la fois les joies (et les doutes) de l'improvisation et les grands auteurs.
- Rythme : entre 2 et 3 heures par semaine, plus des textes à apprendre.
- Renseignez-vous auprès de votre mairie ou à l'École de Musique, 4, rue Beaubourg, 75004 Paris. Tel : 01 42 71 25 07.

LA DANSE

- Peu de garçons s'inscrivent au cours de danse et c'est bien dommage car la danse apprend à aimer et maîtriser son corps... et à s'éclater aussi!
- Débutant à tout âge!
- Pour commencer un caleçon chaud (pour les muscles) et un tee-shirt près du corps (pour que le prof voie vos mouvements) peuvent suffire. Et des chaussures ballerines ou rythmiques.
- Rythme : 1 heure et demie par semaine.
- Fédération française de danse : 12, rue Saint-Germain-d'Auxerrois, 75013 Paris. Tel : 01 42 36 12 61.

A. *Come on, it's your choice!;* choosing different activities to do in your spare time

B. *Pour les artistes:* information about artistic activities
Pour les sportifs: Information about sports/athletic activities
Answers will vary.

C. required equipment; best ages to begin the activity; how often the activity should be done; addresses and telephone numbers for more information; No, some sections tell how much equipment might cost. Also, there is no address or telephone number under the section entitled **La musique.**

D. *Possible answers:* musique, âge, commencer, important, motivé, instrument, début, possible, rythme, général, progresser, théâtre, adolescence, improvisation, textes, danse, muscles, tee-shirt, mouvements, rythmiques, fédération

POUR LES SPORTIFS

LE TENNIS

- Des matchs sont organisés par les clubs. Ils permettent de se préparer à la compétition.

- Le coût varie selon les clubs et votre niveau. Choisissez un forfait qui comprend les cours et l'accès aux courts.

- Comptez au moins 250 francs pour une raquette de bonne qualité et choisissez des chaussures adaptées, pas les tennis mode que vous portez tous les jours!

- Rythme : 1 heure par semaine, plus les tournois. Si vous jouez beaucoup, faites un autre sport en complément, pour éviter les problèmes de dos.

- Fédération française de tennis : Stade Roland Garros, 2 avenue Gordon Bennett, 75016 Paris. Tel : 01 47 43 48 00.

LE FOOTBALL

- Avec quelques copains et un ballon, on peut s'amuser presque partout. Mais pour jouer dans les règles de l'art, mieux vaut s'inscrire dans un club.

- Souvent, le short et le maillot sont fournis par le club, mais les chaussures à crampons vissés coûtent entre 150 et 900 francs.

- Rythme : en général 2 heures par semaine. Rencontres entre clubs le samedi ou le dimanche.

- Fédération française de football : 60 bis, avenue d'Iéna, 75763 Paris cédex 16. Tel : 01 44 31 73 00.

LE KARTING

- Il existe une formule de location de kart avec cours adaptés dès 12 ans.

- Coût : environ 3.000 francs par an, comprenant les cours et le matériel.

- Rythme : 1 heure par semaine, plus quelques courses (souvent le samedi ou le dimanche).

- Groupement national de karting : 203, rue Lafayette, 75010 Paris. Tel : 01 42 05 09 44.

beginning; debutante, debut

E. What do you think the word **débutant** means? Can you think of any words in English that are related to this word?

F. At what age do people usually...
   1. learn how to play an instrument   any age
   2. begin drama?   as a teenager/adolescent
   3. learn how to dance?   any age

G. According to the article, how often do you need to practice playing an instrument to improve quickly?   1/4 hour per day

Pour les sportifs

H. What do you think **Rythme** means? How do you know?
   pace; Answers will vary.

I. What do you think Le Karting means? Is this an activity that is popular in your area?   go–carting; Answers will vary.

J. According to the article, how much does a tennis racket cost?   about 250 F

K. Which of these activities...
   1. require(s) special shoes?   tennis and soccer
   2. require(s) two or more hours a week?   soccer

L. For which activities is it recommended that you join a club?   tennis and soccer

M. Which activity costs the most to participate in? Why?

N. Conduct a survey among your classmates to see which of these activities are the most and least popular and why. You might also find out in how many of these activities your classmates have participated, which ones are the most interesting, and why. Make a list of questions you need to include in your survey.

M. go-carting; Participants must pay for classes and materials.

Teaching Suggestion

Have pairs of students create a conversation in which they discuss which activity from this article they would prefer to do and why. Have them support their opinions with details from the reading.

Terms in Lisons!

Students might want to know the following words: **rythme** *(rate, pace);* **solfège** *(music theory);* **s'inscrire** *(to join, to enroll);* and **corps** *(body).*

Teaching Suggestion

Divide students into six groups and assign each group one section of the reading. Have them find at what age they should start the activity, how often they should participate, the cost and/or items needed to begin, and where to find more information. Have each group report its findings to the class.

POSTREADING
Activity O

Thinking Critically

Comparing and Contrasting
O. After students have answered the questions and surveyed one another to determine which of these activities are and are not popular among Americans, ask them whether young people in France seem to have interests similar to young people in the Unites States. What activities listed here are not common in the United States? What popular activities aren't suggested here?

Analyzing

What activities seem to take the most amount of dedication and practice, which activities are most mentally or physically beneficial?

Teaching Suggestion

Have students find out more information about an activity they would like to pursue that is not included in this article. You might have them research what equipment or supplies they might need, a good age to start, and how often they would probably do the activity. Have them share their findings by creating a poster with the information in French.

The **Mise en pratique** reviews and integrates all four skills and culture in preparation for the Chapter Test.

For Individual Needs

1 Slower Pace Before students listen to the recording, have them recall the names of the seasons. Write them on the board. Then, ask students to imagine what activities might be appropriate in each season. Write a couple of examples for each season.

1 Challenge Have students list more than one activity mentioned for each season. You might give a small prize to the student who lists the most activities mentioned on the recording.

Teaching Suggestion

2 Have students choose one activity that they like from the choices listed under each season in the ad and tell why they like that particular activity. Ask them if there are any other activities that they participate in during each of the four seasons.

Additional Practice

2 Have students describe each of the photos in the ad. They should identify the season, give the weather conditions, and tell where the people are and what they are doing.

MISE EN PRATIQUE

CD-ROM Disc 1

The *CD-ROM Program* offers guided recording and writing activities to practice oral and written skills and to review material from each chapter.

1 Listen to this radio commercial for the **Village des Sports,** a resort in Quebec. List at least one activity offered in each season.   See scripts and answers on p. 65H.

CD 4 Tr. 18

2 You've decided to spend part of your vacation at the **Village des Sports.** Read the information you've received about the resort. Then, answer the questions that follow.

Village des Sports

c'est l'fun fun fun!

en hiver comme en été

Le plus grand centre du sport au Canada offre du plaisir pour toute la famille. Services d'accueil, de restauration et de location sur place.

EN ETE
- le tennis
- le volley
- l'athlétisme
- le base-ball
- le roller en ligne
- le ski nautique
- la natation
- l'équitation
- la voile

EN AUTOMNE
- le football
- l'équitation
- la randonnée
- le volley

EN HIVER
- le hockey
- le ski
- le patin à glace
- la luge

AU PRINTEMPS
- le base-ball
- la randonnée
- le roller en ligne
- le tennis

Village des Sports
1860, boul. Vlaicartier
(418) 844-3725
à 24 km du centre-ville de Québec via la route 371 Nord

116   *cent seize*   CHAPITRE 4   Sports et passe-temps

Culture Note

You might point out to students that Canadian phone numbers follow the American rather than the French pattern, with a three-digit area code and numbers of three and four digits separated by a dash. To call long-distance, Canadians dial 1 before the area code and number, just as in the United States.

1. Would the **Village des Sports** be good for a family vacation? Why or why not?
2. According to the brochure, in what season(s) can you go . . .
   a. in-line skating? c. hiking?
   b. water skiing? d. horseback riding?
3. You have a friend who doesn't like cold weather. What three activities could your friend do at the **Village des Sports**?

 3 a. You've arrived at the **Village des Sports.** You meet your three roommates, get to know them, and ask them about the activities they enjoy.
   b. You and your roommates decide to participate in an activity together. Each of you suggests an activity until you all agree on one.

4 What differences are there between the way students in your area and students in Quebec spend their free time?

 5 *Ecrivons!*

You're going to write a letter to your French class back home describing your activities at the **Village des Sports.** Organizing your ideas using the strategy below will help you create your letter.

STRATEGIE
Arranging ideas logically is a helpful way to organize your ideas before you begin writing.
1. Divide a sheet of paper into three separate columns.
2. Label the first column on your paper **J'aime…** , the next column **Je n'aime pas…** , and the third column **Le temps.**
3. In the first column, list the activities that you like to participate in at the **Village des Sports.** In the next column, list the activities you dislike, and in the third column, tell what the weather is like there.
4. Now you are ready to write your letter.

J'aime	Je n'aime pas	Le temps
faire du ski		Il fait froid.

6 **J E U   D E   R O L E**

You're a famous Canadian athlete. Your partner, a reporter for the local television station, will interview you about your busy training routine. Tell the interviewer what you do at different times of the year, in various weather conditions, and how often. Then, take the role of the reporter and interview your partner, who will assume the identity of a different Canadian athlete.

MISE EN PRATIQUE   *cent dix-sept* **117**

2 1. Yes; the resort offers activities for all the family.
2. a. in-line skating: summer; b. water skiing: summer; c. hiking: fall; d. horseback riding: summer and fall
3. *Answers may vary. Possible answers:* swimming, water skiing, volleyball

Career Path
6 Have students think about why knowing French would be valuable for a career in journalism. Have them tell how their skills in French would help them with research, interviewing, writing, and reporting. You might also have students use the Internet to find sites of French news magazines.

Teaching Suggestion
3 Either of these activities could be used in addition to or in place of one of the chapter projects. Have students write and practice these skits and then perform them in front of the class. Students might record them as an oral portfolio entry.

Process Writing
5 If students want to write about activities other than sports, have them describe their stay at a summer camp (**une colonie de vacances**).

 For Individual Needs
5 Challenge Have students add another column to their charts to record how often they do each activity (**Quand?**). Have them include this information in their letters as well.

 Portfolio
6 Oral This activity is appropriate as an oral portfolio entry. For portfolio suggestions, see the *Alternative Assessment Guide,* page 21.

 Video Wrap-Up
• *VIDEO PROGRAM,* Videocassette 2, 03:34–22:38
• *VIDEODISC PROGRAM,* Videodisc 2, Side B

At this time, you might want to use the video resources for additional review and enrichment. See *Video Guide* or *Videodisc Guide* for suggestions regarding the following:
• **Nouvelles de Québec** (Dramatic episode)
• **Panorama Culturel** (Interviews)
• **Vidéoclips** (Authentic footage)

This page is intended to help students prepare for the Chapter Test. It is a brief checklist of the major points covered in the chapter. Students should be reminded that this is only a checklist and does not necessarily include everything that will appear on the test.

Teaching Suggestions

1, 4 To review the months and seasons of the year, have students tell in which month(s) and/or season(s) the people in the illustrations are doing the activities.

5 You might have students tell how frequently they do each activity, using appropriate adverbs.

6, 7 For further practice, students might use the illustrations on this page to make, accept, and turn down suggestions.

QUE SAIS-JE?

Can you tell how much you like or dislike something? p. 102

Can you exchange information? p. 104

Can you make, accept, and turn down suggestions? p. 110

Can you use what you've learned in this chapter?

1 Can you tell someone how much you like or dislike these activities? See answers below.

1.　　2.　　3.　　4.　　5.

2 Can you tell someone which sports and activities you enjoy a lot? Which ones you don't enjoy at all?　See answers below.

3 How would you tell someone about a few of your sports and hobbies, using the verbs **jouer** and **faire**?　See answers below.

4 How would you find out if someone plays these games?　See answers below.

1.　　　　2.　　　　3.

5 How would you tell someone in French . . .　See answers below.

1. what you do in a certain season?
2. what you like to do in a certain month?
3. what you do in certain weather?
4. what you like to do at a certain time of day?

6 How would you suggest that . . .

1. you and a friend go waterskiing?　On fait du ski nautique?
2. you and your friends play baseball?　On joue au base-ball?

7 If a friend asked you to go jogging, how would you accept the suggestion? How would you turn it down?　See answers below.

Answers

1 *Like:* J'aime beaucoup... ; J'aime surtout...
Dislike: Je n'aime pas tellement... ; Je n'aime pas beaucoup... ; Je n'aime pas du tout...
1. jouer au golf.
2. faire de la natation.
3. jouer au tennis.
4. faire des photos.
5. faire du roller en ligne.

2 *Enjoy:* J'aime beaucoup... ; J'aime surtout...
Don't enjoy: Je n'aime pas tellement... ; Je n'aime pas beaucoup... ; Je n'aime pas du tout...

3 Je joue... ; Je fais...

4 1. Tu joues au football?/Est-ce que tu joues au football?
2. Tu joues au hockey?/Est-ce que tu joues au hockey?
3. Tu joues au volley-ball?/Est-ce que tu joues au volley-ball?

5 1. Au printemps/En été/En automne/En hiver, je...
2. En janvier/février/mars/avril/mai/juin/juillet/août/septembre/octobre/novembre/décembre, j'aime...
3. Quand il fait froid/il fait frais/il fait beau/il fait chaud/il pleut/il neige, je...
4. Le matin/L'après-midi/Le soir, j'aime...

7 *Accept:* D'accord. Bonne idée. Oui, c'est génial. Oui, c'est super! Allons-y!
Turn down: Désolé(e), mais je ne peux pas. Ça ne me dit rien. Non, c'est barbant. Non, c'est nul!

PREMIERE ETAPE

Telling how much you like or dislike something

Beaucoup. *A lot.*
surtout *especially*
Pas tellement. *Not too much.*
Pas beaucoup. *Not very much.*
Pas du tout. *Not at all.*

Sports and hobbies

faire de l'aérobic *to do aerobics*
  de l'athlétisme *to do track and field*
  du jogging *to jog*
  de la natation *to swim*

du patin à glace *to ice-skate*
de la photo *to do photography*
des photos *to take pictures*
du roller en ligne *to in-line skate*
du ski *to ski*
du ski nautique *to water-ski*
du théâtre *to do drama*
du vélo *to bike*
de la vidéo *to make videos*
jouer au base-ball *to play baseball*
  au basket(-ball) *to play basketball*
  au foot(ball) *to play soccer*

au football américain *to play football*
au golf *to play golf*
au hockey *to play hockey*
à des jeux vidéo *to play video games*
au tennis *to play tennis*
au volley(-ball) *to play volleyball*
aux cartes *to play cards*

Other useful expressions

Est-ce que *(introduces a yes-or-no question)*

DEUXIEME ETAPE

Exchanging information

Qu'est-ce que tu fais comme sport? *What sports do you play?*
Qu'est-ce que tu fais pour t'amuser? *What do you do to have fun?*
Je fais... *I play/do . . .*
Je joue... *I play . . .*
Je ne fais pas de... *I don't play/do . . .*
Je ne joue pas... *I don't play . . .*
faire *to do, to play, to make*
jouer *to play*

Weather

Quel temps fait-il? *What's the weather like?*

Il fait beau. *It's nice weather.*
Il fait chaud. *It's hot.*
Il fait frais. *It's cool.*
Il fait froid. *It's cold.*
Il pleut. *It's raining.*
Il neige. *It's snowing.*

Seasons, months, and times

Qu'est-ce que tu fais... *What do you do . . .*
  le week-end? *on weekends?*
  le soir? *in the evening?*
  en vacances? *on vacation?*
  au printemps? *in the spring?*
  en été? *in the summer?*
  en automne? *in the fall?*

en hiver? *in the winter?*
en janvier?
en février?
en mars?
en avril?
en mai?
en juin?
en juillet?
en août?
en septembre?
en octobre?
en novembre?
en décembre?

Other useful expressions

on *we, they, you*

TROISIEME ETAPE

Making, accepting, and turning down suggestions

On... ? *How about . . . ?*
D'accord. *OK.*
Bonne idée. *Good idea.*
Allons-y! *Let's go!*
Oui, c'est... *Yes, it's . . .*

Désolé(e), mais je ne peux pas. *Sorry, but I can't.*
Ça ne me dit rien. *That doesn't interest me.*
Non, c'est... *No, it's (that's) . . .*

Expressions of frequency

quelquefois *sometimes*

...fois par semaine *. . . time(s) a week*
de temps en temps *from time to time*
souvent *often*
rarement *rarely*
ne... jamais *never*
d'habitude *usually*

VOCABULAIRE

cent dix-neuf **119**

Teaching Suggestions

• To review vocabulary, you might have students list all of the cognates they can find on this page.
• You might play the game "Mémoire" described on page 93J.

CHAPTER 4 ASSESSMENT

CHAPTER TEST

• *Testing Program,* pp. 91–96
• *Audio Compact Discs,* Audio CD 4, Tracks 22–24

SPEAKING TEST

• *Testing Program,* p. 344

TEST GENERATOR

 • Chapter 4

ALTERNATIVE ASSESSMENT

Performance Assessment

• You might want to use the **Jeu de rôle** on page 117 as a cumulative performance assessment activity.
• *Alternative Assessment Guide,* p. 35

Portfolio Assessment

• *Alternative Assessment Guide*
Oral: p. 21
Written: p. 21

CD-ROM Assessment

• *Interactive CD-ROM Program,* Disc 1
A toi de parler
A toi d'écrire
• *Alternative Assessment Guide,* p. 49

VIDEO PROGRAM
Videocassette 2
22:39–25:14

OR *VIDEODISC PROGRAM,*
Videodisc 3, Side A

Search 1, Play To 4660

Motivating Activity

Ask students if they can name any well-known monuments or places in Paris. Then, have them look at the photos on pages 120–123 and make inferences about Paris.

Background Information

The earliest known inhabitants of Paris were the **Parisii,** who settled on the Ile de la Cité in the third century B.C. Paris has often played a central role in the political and cultural evolution of France. The major political events of the French Revolution occurred in Paris in 1789. Today, Paris is an important university center. The **quartier Latin** has been home to many students since the Middle Ages. In the mid-nineteenth century, Baron Haussmann, working under Emperor Napoléon III, razed many areas of the city and created **les grands boulevards.**

go.hrw.com
WAO PARIS

Visit the HRW Web site at **http://go.hrw.com** and enter the keyword **WAO PARIS** for student resources related to this location. For detailed access instructions, see page T45.

CHAPITRES 5, 6, 7

Allez, viens à Paris !

L'avenue des Champs-Elysées et l'Arc de triomphe

Architecture Link

L'avenue des Champs-Elysées extends from the place de la Concorde to the place Charles-de-Gaulle. In the courtyard of the Louvre museum is the Arc de triomphe du Carrousel; in the center of the place de la Concorde is the obélisque de Louxor, a stone pillar brought back from Egypt in 1831; at the end of the avenue is the famous Arc de triomphe. These monuments are all perfectly aligned.

History Link

L'Arc de triomphe, situated in the middle of the place Charles-de-Gaulle (the former place de l'Etoile) where twelve avenues intersect, was constructed on the orders of Napoléon I. Underneath the Arc is the tomb of the French Unknown Soldier, placed there after World War I.

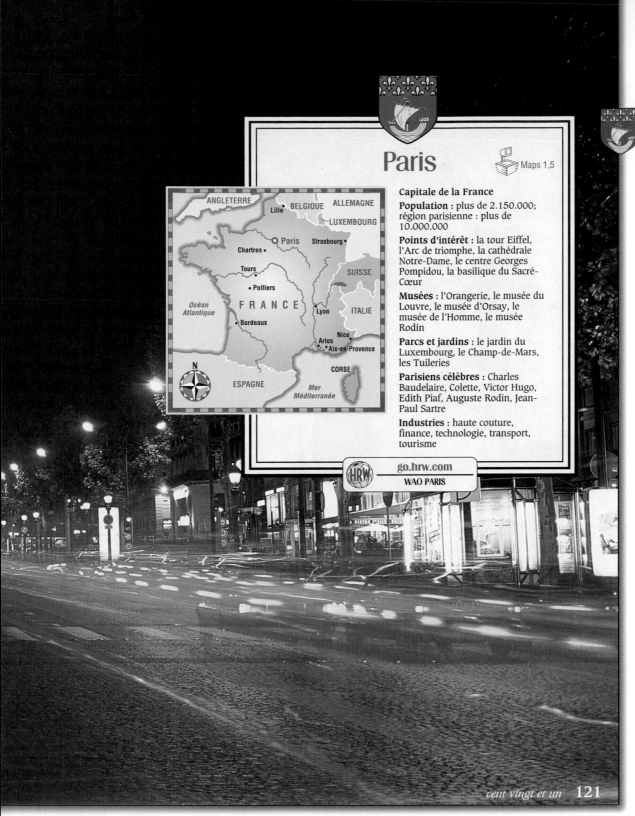

Paris

Maps 1,5

Capitale de la France

Population : plus de 2.150.000; région parisienne : plus de 10.000.000

Points d'intérêt : la tour Eiffel, l'Arc de triomphe, la cathédrale Notre-Dame, le centre Georges Pompidou, la basilique du Sacré-Cœur

Musées : l'Orangerie, le musée du Louvre, le musée d'Orsay, le musée de l'Homme, le musée Rodin

Parcs et jardins : le jardin du Luxembourg, le Champ-de-Mars, les Tuileries

Parisiens célèbres : Charles Baudelaire, Colette, Victor Hugo, Edith Piaf, Auguste Rodin, Jean-Paul Sartre

Industries : haute couture, finance, technologie, transport, tourisme

HRW go.hrw.com
WAO PARIS

cent vingt et un **121**

Using the Almanac and Map

Terms in the Almanac

- **La tour Eiffel,** built by Gustave Eiffel for the **Exposition universelle** of 1889, was the tallest structure in the world at the time.
- **La cathédrale Notre-Dame** dates from 1163.
- **Le centre Georges Pompidou,** finished in 1977, is also known as **Beaubourg.** It contains the Museum of Modern Art of Paris.
- **La basilique du Sacré-Cœur,** built between 1876 and 1914, is located on Montmartre, the highest point in Paris.
- **Le musée du Louvre,** the largest museum in the world, houses such works as the *Mona Lisa* (**La Joconde**) and the *Venus de Milo.*
- **Le musée d'Orsay,** formerly a train station, was turned into a museum in 1986, and is devoted to sculpture, painting, and architecture of the nineteenth century.
- **Le musée Rodin** houses many of Rodin's most famous sculptures, including *Le Penseur* and *Les Bourgeois de Calais.*
- **Le jardin du Luxembourg** is a famous Parisian park.
- **Les Tuileries** is a park à l'italienne with fountains and sculptures.
- **Charles Baudelaire** (1821–1867), was a poet in the romantic tradition. His most famous work is *Les Fleurs du mal.*
- **Colette** (1873–1954) was a famous novelist.
- **Victor Hugo** (1802–1885) See page 2 in the Preliminary Chapter.
- **Edith Piaf** (1915–1963) was a singer famous for her heartrending songs.
- **Jean-Paul Sartre** (1905–1980), philosopher, novelist, and playwright, was a proponent of existentialism.

Art Link

Have students research various French artists (David, Monet, Manet, Degas, Rodin, Matisse, Renoir, Chagall) or artists who worked in France (Van Gogh and Picasso).

Using the Map

Have students look at the map and try to determine why Paris was an important crossroads throughout history.

History Link

Even though **Notre-Dame** is one of the most famous cathedrals, it was not the scene of royal coronations or funerals. Kings of France were crowned in the cathedral in Reims where Clovis, the first Christian king of France, was baptized. Many of the French kings are buried in the basilica of Saint-Denis, just north of Paris.

Using the Photo Essay

① **Le centre Georges Pompidou,** a museum named after the second president of the Fifth Republic, offers a splendid view of Paris. The upper floors are reached via escalators encased in glass tubes that allow visitors to look out over Paris as they ascend. The public square in front of the museum is always bustling with all kinds of entertainment, from magicians, to fire-eaters, to mimes.

② **Montmartre** is the highest point in Paris. Many of its steep, narrow streets end in staircases. Both Sacré-Cœur and Saint-Pierre-de-Montmartre, one of the earliest Roman-Gothic churches, are located in Montmartre. There is some disagreement about how the name **Montmartre** originated. Some speculate that it came from the *mount of Mars,* a Roman temple that stood on top of the hill. Others say it means *mount of martyrs,* referring to the site of the execution of Saint Denis, the first bishop of Paris.

③ Each **bouquiniste** has a green metal box affixed to the stone wall along the Seine. When the **bouquinistes** are not there, their wares are locked inside the box.

Career Path

Have students discuss why knowing several languages would be useful in a city like Paris. Have groups of students make lists of jobs in Paris that might require the knowledge of more than one language (tour guide, travel agent, bank teller). Ask students to think of cities in the United States that, like Paris, receive tourists from around the world. How would knowing a foreign language be beneficial in these places? Which languages would be most helpful?

Paris CD-ROM Disc 2

Paris is a city that has no equal. It is the intellectual and cultural capital of the French-speaking world and also the largest city in Europe, if you include the greater Parisian area. Whether you like to visit museums, go to the theater, sit in cafés, or stroll along tree-lined boulevards, there's something for everyone here. Paris is one of the world's most beautiful and exciting cities!

① **Le centre Georges Pompidou** houses a major library and the National Museum of Modern Art. Outside, you can see jugglers, magicians, and all kinds of entertainers. It is one of Paris's most popular tourist attractions.

② Many of the streets in the **Montmartre** district are lined with artists who sell their work and will even paint your portrait.

③ In the shadow of **la cathédrale Notre-Dame,** booksellers, called **bouquinistes,** sell rare books and posters along the banks of the river Seine.

Architecture Link

① The structure of the **centre Georges Pompidou,** because of its skeletal design of pipes and tubes, has often been the subject of both amusement and controversy for Parisians, who refer to it as **la raffinerie,** *the refinery.* In reality, the pipes and tubes are quite functional, as they serve as casing for the heating, air-conditioning, electrical, and telephone conduits.

Culture Note

③ Efforts were made in the past to limit or reduce the number of **bouquinistes** along the Seine. However, the public outcry was so great that the project was abandoned, and these traditional fixtures remain along the banks of the Seine.

⑤ **La tour Eiffel** was erected as a temporary exhibit for the Centennial Exposition in 1889 and has been the object of controversy ever since. It is 320.75 meters tall, including the television antenna added in 1957. To reach the top platform, ride one of the hydraulic elevators or climb the 1,792 stairs!

④ In Paris, the terrace of a café is a wonderful place to sit and watch the world go by.

⑥ The Paris subway, **le métro,** is one of the world's most efficient mass-transit systems.

⑦ **Le stade Roland-Garros** is the site of the French Open, one of the Grand-Slam tennis tournaments.

Culture Notes
⑥ French transportation systems are among the best in the world. A network of **autoroutes** crisscrosses the country. The **TGV** (**Train à grande vitesse**) and other trains run by the **SNCF** (**Société nationale de chemins de fer**) reach every corner of France. In addition, the Paris **métro** is the envy of the world. French firms also have designed and built subways in Cairo and Mexico City.

⑦ **Roland Garros** was a famous French aviator who, in 1913, was the first to fly successfully across the Mediterranean.

④ Paris is full of sidewalk cafés, some of which date from the eighteenth century. The most famous include **Les Deux Magots** (see photo page 124), the nearby **Café de Flore,** and the **Café Procope,** frequented by Voltaire in the eighteenth century.

⑤ Among the many illuminated monuments in Paris is **la tour Eiffel.** Until 1986, it was illuminated by giant projectors located on the ground. In 1986, lights were installed on the tower itself. These lights give the tower greater depth, making it look like a jewel.

⑥ The Paris **métro** began service with the Vincennes-Maillot line in 1900, several years after both the London and Boston subways. Today, there are 16 lines with over 350 stations. Each day the **métro,** run by the **RATP** (**Régie autonome des transports parisiens**), carries over 5 million passengers. The system extends to the suburbs with four **RER** (**Réseau express régional**) lines. **RER** trains are slightly larger than **métro** trains, and outside the city limits, they travel above ground.

Teaching Suggestion
⑥ Have students look at a map of the Paris **métro** to determine which stations are named after people, which after events, and which after places in Paris. Ask students if they can figure out why the names of so many lines include the word **porte,** such as **Porte de Clignancourt** and **Porte d'Orléans.** (In the Middle Ages, Paris was a walled city whose gates were closed at dusk. Gates (**portes**) were located around the city and named. As the city grew, the wall was extended several times.)

Chapitre 5 : On va au café?
Chapter Overview

Mise en train pp. 126–128	Qu'est-ce qu'on prend?			

	FUNCTIONS	GRAMMAR	CULTURE	RE-ENTRY
Première étape pp. 129–134	• Making suggestions, p. 129 • Making excuses, p. 129 • Making a recommendation, p. 132	• The verb **prendre**, p. 133	• **Panorama Culturel,** Food served in a café, p. 134	• Accepting and turning down a suggestion **(Chapitre 4)** • Likes and dislikes **(Chapitre 1)** • Activities **(Chapitre 1)**
Deuxième étape pp. 135–137	• Getting someone's attention, p. 135 • Ordering food and beverages, p. 135	• The imperative, p. 136	• Realia: Café menu, p. 136 • **Note Culturelle,** Waitpersons as professionals, p. 137 • Realia: Menu from **La Crêperie Normande,** p. 137	• Expressing likes, dislikes, and preferences **(Chapitre 1)**
Troisième étape pp. 138–141	• Inquiring about and expressing likes and dislikes, p. 138 • Paying the check, p. 139		• **Note Culturelle, La litote,** p. 138 • **Note Culturelle,** Tipping, p. 140 • Realia: Café bill, p. 140 • Realia: Menu from **Café Sport,** p. 140	• Expressing likes and dislikes **(Chapitre 1)** • Numbers 20–100 **(Chapitres 2, 3)**

Prononciation p. 141	The nasal sound [ɑ̃] Audio CD 5, Tracks 12–14	**A écrire** (dictation) Audio CD 5, Tracks 15–17
Lisons! pp. 142–143	French menus	**Reading Strategy** Using what you already know
Review pp. 144–147	**Mise en pratique,** pp. 144–145 **Que sais-je?** p. 146 **Vocabulaire,** p. 147 **Ecrivons!** Arranging ideas spatially Creating a poster	

Assessment Options

Testing Program
• Première étape, Quiz 5-1A, Quiz 5-1B, pp. 105–108
• Deuxième étape, Quiz 5-2A, Quiz 5-2B, pp. 109–112
• Troisième étape, Quiz 5-3A, Quiz 5-3B, pp. 113–116
• Chapter Test, pp. 117–122
• Speaking Test, p. 345

Audio Compact Discs
• Audio CD 5, Tracks 19–24

Interactive CD-ROM Program
• Mise en pratique (A toi de parler, A toi d'écrire)
• *CD-ROM Teacher's Guide,* Assessment Options, p. 22

Alternative Assessment Guide
• Portfolio Assessment, p. 22
• Performance Assessment, p. 36
• CD-ROM Assessment, p. 50

Test Generator
• Chapter 5

PRINT	MEDIA
Pupil's Edition, pp. 124–147	**Audio Compact Discs** • Textbook Listening Activities: Audio CD 5, Tracks 1–18
Interactive CD-ROM Program Teacher's Guide, pp. 19–22	**Interactive CD-ROM Program** • Disc 2
Videodisc Guide • Teaching Suggestions, pp. 55–59 • Activity Masters, pp. 60–62	**Videodisc Program** • Videodisc 3, Side A
Video Guide • Teaching Suggestions, pp. 34–35 • Activity Masters, pp. 36–38	**Video Program** • Videocassette 2 • Videocassette 5 (captioned version)
Listening Activities • Student Response Forms for Textbook Listening Activities, pp. 35–37 • Additional Listening Activities 5-1 to 5-6, pp. 39–41 • Additional Listening Activities (song), p. 42 • Scripts and Answers, pp. 122–126	**Audio Compact Discs** • Textbook Listening Activities: Audio CD 5, Tracks 1–18 • Additional Listening Activities: Audio CD 5, Tracks 25–31
Teaching Transparencies • Teaching Transparency Masters 5-1 to 5-3 (Situations) and 5-A to 5-B (Vocabulary) • Teaching Suggestions 5-1 to 5-3 and 5-A to 5-B	**Teaching Transparencies** • Situations 5-1 to 5-3 • Vocabulary 5-A to 5-B
Testing Program • Grammar and Vocabulary Quizzes, **Etape** Quizzes, and Chapter Test, pp. 105–122 • Score Sheet, Scripts, and Answers, pp. 123–130	**Audio Compact Discs** • Assessment Items: Audio CD 5, Tracks 19–24 **Test Generator** • Chapter 5
Alternative Assessment Guide • Portfolio Assessment, p. 22 • Performance Assessment, p. 36 • CD-ROM Assessment, p. 50	
Grammar and Vocabulary Workbook, pp. 35–40	
Practice and Activity Book, pp. 49–60	
Activities for Communication • Communicative Activities, pp. 25–30 • Realia and Teaching Suggestions, pp. 95–99 • Situation Cards, pp. 145–146	
Lesson Planner • Lesson Plan, pp. 23–27	

Chapitre 5 : On va au café?

Technology Applications

MISE EN TRAIN, pp. 126–128

Video
- Show *Qu'est-ce qu'on prend?* For Video Synopsis, Teaching Suggestions, Activity Master, and Scripts, see the *Video Guide* or the *Videodisc Guide*.

Captioned Video
- If students have trouble understanding *Qu'est-ce qu'on prend?*, you may want to show the captioned version on Videocassette 5.

Audio
- Play the recording of the **Mise en train** with pauses as students read along. You might have them practice pronunciation by repeating individual sentences after hearing them.

PREMIERE ETAPE, pp. 129–133

Video
- While students watch *Qu'est-ce qu'on prend?*, have them listen for exchanges that model making suggestions, excuses, and recommendations. For more suggestions, see p. 57 of the *Videodisc Guide*.

Audio
- Textbook Listening Activity 6 practices the expressions for accepting and turning down suggestions.
- To have students practice the vocabulary for food and drinks served in a café, play Textbook Listening Activity 9.
- Additional Listening Activities 5-1 and 5-2 target the expressions for making suggestions and excuses and recommending food and drink items. Use these activities as a challenge for students.

Transparencies
- Use *Teaching Transparencies 5-1, 5-A,* and *5-B* along with the Teaching Suggestions to

present and have students practice vocabulary for food and drink items.

CD-ROM (Disc 2)
- **Jeu des paires** and **Chasse au trésor** (Activities 1 and 2) practice vocabulary for food and drinks to order in a café.
- **Les mots qui manquent** (Activity 3) practices the present tense of the verb **prendre**.
- For suggestions, see p. 20 of the *CD-ROM Teacher's Guide*.

PANORAMA CULTUREL, p. 134

Video
- Show the interviews. For Video Synopsis, Teaching Suggestions, Activity Masters, and Scripts, see the *Video Guide* or the *Videodisc Guide*.

Audio
- Play the **Panorama Culturel** as students read along. Remind students that they might not be able to understand everything each person says, but they should try to recognize words and deduce global meaning.

CD-ROM (Disc 2)
- Have students do the **Panorama Culturel** activity for Chapter 5 after showing them the video. For suggestions, see p. 21 of the *CD-ROM Teacher's Guide*.

DEUXIEME ETAPE, pp. 135–137

Video
- While students watch *Qu'est-ce qu'on prend?*, have them listen for exchanges that model getting someone's attention and ordering food and beverages. For more suggestions, see p. 57 of the *Videodisc Guide*.

Audio
- Use Textbook Listening Activity 14 to have students classify phrases that a customer or a server might say.

- Additional Listening Activities 5-3 and 5-4 target vocabulary and expressions for ordering food and beverages.

Transparencies
- Use *Teaching Transparency 5-2* and the Teaching Suggestions to have students practice the expressions for ordering food and beverages in a café.

CD-ROM (Disc 2)
- **Les mots qui manquent** (Activity 4) practices the imperative. For suggestions, see p. 21 of the *CD-ROM Teacher's Guide*.

TROISIEME ETAPE, pp. 138–141

Video
- While students watch *Qu'est-ce qu'on prend?*, have them listen for exchanges that model asking for the check and how the server answers. For more suggestions, see p. 58 of the *Videodisc Guide*.

Audio
- Use Textbook Listening Activity 25 to have students practice ordering and getting ready to pay the check.
- Additional Listening Activities 5-5 and 5-6 target phrases for expressing likes and dislikes. Use these activities as a challenge for students.

Transparencies
- Use *Teaching Transparency 5-3* and the Teaching Suggestions to have students practice phrases for expressing likes and dislikes and for paying the check.

CD-ROM (Disc 2)
- **Chacun à sa place** (Activity 5) practices expressions that a customer and a server might use.
- **Le bon choix** (Activity 6) practices expressions used in a café or restaurant.
- For suggestions, see p. 21 of the *CD-ROM Teacher's Guide*.

MISE EN PRATIQUE, pp. 144–145

Video
- Replay *Qu'est-ce qu'on prend?* in its entirety and ask students to listen for the exchanges in which the characters make a recommendation, make an excuse, get the server's attention, order food and drinks, inquire about and express likes and dislikes, and pay the check.

CD-ROM (Disc 2)
- Have students do the **En contexte** to practice ordering food and drinks, talking about their likes and dislikes, making recommendations, and asking for the check. You may want to use the suggestions on p. 20 of the *CD-ROM Teacher's Guide*.
- Have students practice their writing and speaking skills by doing the **A toi d'écrire** and **A toi de parler** activities. For a detailed description of these features, see p. 22 of the *CD-ROM Teacher's Guide*.
- For Assessment Options, see p. 22 of the *CD-ROM Teacher's Guide*.

Test Generator
- Use the Test Generator to create review material for students taking the Chapter Test or to prepare an alternate test.

VIDEOCLIPS

Video
- Show the **Vidéoclips**. For Video Synopsis, Teaching Suggestions, Activity Master, and Scripts, see the *Video Guide* or the *Videodisc Guide*.

Videodisc Program
Videodisc 3, Side A
Videodisc Guide, pp. 53 – 62

Chapitre 5 : On va au café?
Barcode Directory

Barcodes A and B access **Mise en train** and **Mise en train (suite)** in their entirety. Subsequent barcodes show specific segments of ***Qu'est-ce qu'on prend?*** The barcode numbers correspond to the scene numbers as they appear on the video.

MISE EN TRAIN

Qu'est-ce qu'on prend? **A**

Search 4660, Play To 10515

Qu'est-ce que vous faites? **1**

Search 4660, Play To 5734

Qu'est-ce que vous prenez?**2**

Search 5748, Play To 6368

C'est combien... ? **3**

Search 6368, Play To 6705

Vous avez choisi? **4**

Search 6705, Play To 7235

Vous avez des pizzas? **5**

Search 7235, Play To 7603

Bien, un croque-monsieur... **6**

Search 7604, Play To 7952

Parfait... **7**

Search 7953, Play To 9765

Monsieur, l'addition... **8**

Search 9797, Play To 9948

Eh, je ne trouve pas... **9**

Search 9949, Play To 10515

Qu'est-ce qu'on prend? (suite)**B**
Search 10531, Play To 17750

ETAPES

To practice the grammar, vocabulary, and functions presented in each **étape**, see the barcodes and accompanying suggestions on pages 57–58 of the *Videodisc Guide*.

MISE EN PRATIQUE

This is additional footage modeling some of the expressions practiced in this chapter. You may want to use it to review the chapter.

Mise en pratique **1**

Search 25443, Play To 27552

VIDEOCLIPS

These are authentic French commercials. You may want to preview them before showing them to students.

Vidéoclip 1: Badoit® mineral water **1**

Search 22060, Play To 23489

Vidéoclip 2 : Orangina® orange drink **2**

Search 23489, Play To 24377

PANORAMA CULTUREL

Où retrouves-tu tes amis?
These barcodes access the three interviews of the **Panorama Culturel** presented in the *Pupil's Edition* as well as additional interviews.

First three interviews **1**

Search 17750, Play To 19965

All interviews **2**

Search 17750, Play To 22056

Déjan **3**

Search 18562, Play To 19010

Clémentine **4**

Search 19011, Play To 19592

Armande **5**

Search 19593, Play To 19955

Elisa **6**

Search 19987, Play To 20309

Séverine **7**

Search 20310, Play To 21023

Sébastien **8**

Search 21024, Play To 21295

Caroline **9**

Search 21296, Play To 21426

Céline **10**
Search 21427, Play To 21649

Pauline **11**
Search 21650, Play To 21771

Yvette **12**
Search 21772, Play To 22045

Chapitre 5 : On va au café?
CD-ROM Directory DISC 2

The following directory lists the *Interactive CD-ROM Program* activities for Chapter 5. For details and suggestions on how to use them, see pages 19–22 of the *CD-ROM Teacher's Guide*.

GLOBAL TASK	COMMUNICATIVE GOALS	ACTIVITY TYPE
Au café Students order lunch in a café with their friend François.	To use chapter functions, vocabulary, and grammar in a lifelike conversation	**En contexte** *Interactive conversation*

	SUPPORTING ACTIVITIES	PUPIL'S EDITION	COMMUNICATIVE GOALS	ACTIVITY TYPE
Première étape	1. Vocabulaire	p. 131	To identify food and drinks served in a café	**Jeu des paires** *Concentration®*
	2. Vocabulaire	p. 131	To listen to and understand vocabulary for food and drinks	**Chasse au trésor Explorons!/Vérifions!** *Interactive image*
	3. Grammaire	p. 133	To produce the forms of the verb **prendre**	**Les mots qui manquent** *Tic Tac Toe*
Deuxième étape	4. Grammaire	p. 136	To create commands with the imperative	**Les mots qui manquent** *Tic Tac Toe*
Troisième étape	5. Comment dit-on... ?	pp. 135, 139	To classify phrases that a customer or server might say	**Chacun à sa place** *Categories*
	6. Comment dit-on... ?	pp. 129, 132, 135, 138, 139	To use functional expressions and vocabulary to complete conversations	**Le bon choix** *Multiple choice*
Panorama Culturel	Panorama Culturel	p. 134	To listen to and understand native speakers talking about where they go with their friends	**Où retrouves-tu tes amis?** *Presentation* **Le bon choix** *Multiple choice*

	APPLICATION	PUPIL'S EDITION	COMMUNICATIVE GOALS	ACTIVITY TYPE
Mise en pratique	A toi de parler	pp. 144–145	To create and record a conversation between a server and a customer in a restaurant	*Guided recording*
	A toi d'écrire	pp. 144–145	To write a note, a menu, an advertisement, or a script	*Guided writing*

Chapitre 5 : On va au café?
Homework Suggestions

CHAPTER SECTION	PRESENTATION	HOMEWORK OPTIONS
Première étape	**Comment dit-on... ?** p. 129	Practice and Activity Book, pp. 51–52, Activities 7–8
	Vocabulaire, p. 131	Pupil's Edition, p. 132, Activity 11 Practice and Activity Book, p. 50, Activity 3 Grammar and Vocabulary Workbook, pp. 35–36, Activities 1–4 CD-ROM, Disc 2, Activities 1–2
	Comment dit-on... ? p. 132	Grammar and Vocabulary Workbook, p. 36, Activity 5
	Grammaire, p. 133	Pupil's Edition, pp. R35–R36; Activities 1–2 Practice and Activity Book, p. 51, Activity 5 Grammar and Vocabulary Workbook, p. 37, Activities 6–7 CD-ROM, Disc 2, Activity 3
Deuxième étape	**Comment dit-on... ?** p. 135	Pupil's Edition, p. 137, Activity 20 Practice and Activity Book, p. 53, Activities 10–12
	Grammaire, p. 136	Pupil's Edition, pp. R36–R37, Activities 3–5 Practice and Activity Book, p. 54, Activities 13, 15 Grammar and Vocabulary Workbook, p. 38, Activities 8–10 CD-ROM, Disc 2, Activity 4
Troisième étape	**Comment dit-on... ?** p. 138	Pupil's Edition, p. 139, Activity 24 Practice and Activity Book, pp. 56–57, Activities 19–21 Grammar and Vocabulary Workbook, p. 39, Activities 11–12
	Comment dit-on... ? p. 139	Pupil's Edition, p. R37, Activities 6–7 Practice and Activity Book, pp. 57–58, Activities 23–24 CD-ROM, Disc 2, Activities 5–6

Chapitre 5 : On va au café?
Textbook Listening Activities Scripts

For Student Response Forms, see *Listening Activities,* pp. 35–37.

Première étape

6 Ecoute! p. 129

1. — On va au café?
   — Oui, allons-y!
2. — On fait du jogging?
   — Ça ne me dit rien.
3. — On écoute de la musique?
   — Oui, d'accord. C'est une bonne idée.
4. — On joue au basket?
   — Je ne peux pas. J'ai des devoirs à faire.
5. — On fait des photos?
   — Désolé, mais j'ai des courses à faire.

Answers to Activity 6
1. accepts
2. turns down
3. accepts
4. turns down
5. turns down

9 Ecoute! p. 132

1. Moi, je voudrais une pizza et un coca, s'il vous plaît.
2. Un croque-monsieur, s'il vous plaît.
3. Je voudrais un jus de fruit.
4. Et moi, je vais prendre un steak-frites, s'il vous plaît.
5. Un sandwich au fromage pour moi.

Answers to Activity 9
1. Paul
2. Minh
3. Didier
4. Mamadou
5. Nabil

Deuxième étape

14 Ecoute! p. 135

1. Je vais prendre un steak-frites, s'il vous plaît.
2. Vous avez choisi?
3. Donnez-moi un croque-monsieur, s'il vous plaît.
4. Qu'est-ce que vous avez comme sandwiches?
5. Vous prenez?
6. Apportez-moi un jus de pomme, s'il vous plaît.

Answers to Activity 14
1. customer
2. server
3. customer
4. customer
5. server
6. customer

Troisième étape

21 Ecoute! p. 138
1. Cette pizza, elle n'est pas très bonne.
2. La glace au chocolat, c'est délicieux!
3. Il n'est pas terrible, ce hot-dog.
4. Ne mange pas ça! C'est dégoûtant!
5. Il est bon, ce croque-monsieur.

Answers to Activity 21
1. dislikes
2. likes
3. dislikes
4. dislikes
5. likes

25 Ecoute! p. 139
1. Apportez-moi un coca, s'il vous plaît.
2. L'addition, s'il vous plaît.
3. Je vais prendre un jus de pomme, s'il vous plaît.
4. Ça fait combien, s'il vous plaît?
5. Donnez-moi une limonade, s'il vous plaît.

Answers to Activity 25
1. ordering
2. getting ready to pay the check
3. ordering
4. getting ready to pay the check
5. ordering

Prononciation, p. 141

For the scripts for Parts A and B, see p. 141.

C. A écrire
(Dictation)
— Ça fait combien, un jus d'orange et un sandwich?
— Soixante francs.

Mise en pratique

1 p. 144
1. — Michel, on prend un sandwich?
   — D'accord. Je voudrais un sandwich au jambon et de l'eau minérale.
2. — Je vais prendre une pizza.
   — Moi aussi.
3. — Vous avez choisi?
   — Apportez-moi un steak-frites et un coca, s'il vous plaît.
4. — Je voudrais une coupe melba.
   — Bonne idée.

Answers to Mise en pratique Activity 1
1. Café de la gare
2. Café Américain
3. Café Américain
4. Café de Paris

Chapitre 5 : On va au café?
Projects ✂

Notre café
(Cooperative Learning Project)

ASSIGNMENT

Have groups of three or four students design a menu for a café they will open.

MATERIALS

✂ **Students may need**
- Construction paper
- Markers or colored pencils
- Magazines
- Tape or glue
- Scissors

SUGGESTED SEQUENCE

Prewriting Students should come up with ideas for their café, including the theme or style of the café and the price range. One student should write down the different ideas; the group should then decide which ideas to follow.

First Draft Different tasks should be assigned to individual group members: writing down menu items, designing the menu, editing, and choosing appropriate prices in francs for each item.

Peer Editing Have students check one another's work. Are there enough items for the menu? Do the items have reasonable and consistent prices? Is the spelling correct, and are the items in the correct section of the menu? Is the menu design attractive, and does it reflect the restaurant's style?

Final Draft Students should add their assigned parts to the menu and complete it with illustrations or graphics according to the design. They should also check for any mistakes before handing it in.

GRADING THE PROJECT

You might base students' grades on the following: content, attractive menu design, accurate spelling and placement of items on the menu, and participation.

Suggested Point Distribution (total = 100 points)

Content	25 points
Menu design	25 points
Spelling/placement of items	25 points
Participation	25 points

TEACHING SUGGESTION

These menus might be displayed in the classroom and/or used in skits or for reading comprehension.

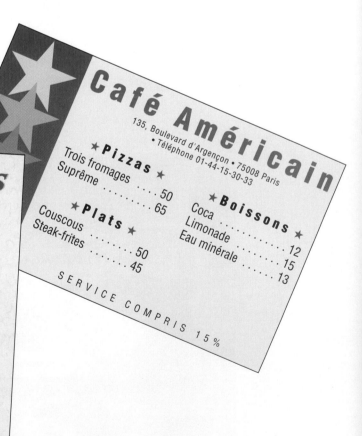

Café Américain
135, Boulevard d'Argençon • 75008 Paris
• Téléphone 01-44-15-30-33

★ **Pizzas** ★
Trois fromages 50
Suprême 65

★ **Plats** ★
Couscous
Steak-frites 50
.........45

★ **Boissons** ★
Coca 12
Limonade 15
Eau minérale 13

SERVICE COMPRIS 15 %

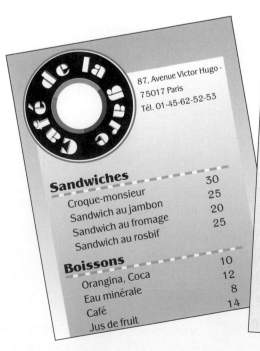

Café de la gare
87, Avenue Victor Hugo -
75017 Paris
Tél. 01-45-62-52-53

Sandwiches
Croque-monsieur 30
Sandwich au jambon ..25
Sandwich au fromage ..20
Sandwich au rosbif ...25

Boissons
Orangina, Coca 10
Eau minérale 12
Café 8
Jus de fruit 14

Café de Paris
15, Place du Palais - 75004 Paris
Téléphone 01-43-54-20-21

Nos **glaces**
Coupe Melba 50
Coupe Nougat 46
Banana Split 42

Nos **boissons**
Eau minérale 14
Jus de fruit 16
Café 10
Thé 8

SERVICE COMPRIS 15%

JETER ET ATTRAPER

This game will help students review vocabulary from this chapter and from previous chapters. It is recommended at the end of the first étape.

Procedure List various categories (food, drink, activities, the infinitive of a particular verb, and so on) on the board or on a transparency. Call out a category and toss a ball or other soft object to a student. The student must catch the ball and name an appropriate item in that category within three seconds. Then, that student will call out a category and toss the ball to another student. The game continues in this manner. You can vary the game by having students conjugate verbs as you call out the subject pronoun and the infinitive, count by threes, and so on. Keep the game moving as quickly as possible. You might choose to start the game with all students standing, having any students who do not respond correctly or quickly enough sit down and monitor the others. To motivate students who are hesitant to catch the ball, have them answer two items if they drop it.

JEU DE CONCOURS

This game will help students review words and expressions in a variety of categories.

Procedure Draw a game grid on a transparency, or on a large sheet of paper hanging on the wall. The grid should have six columns, each of which has a header that represents a category. Below each category are five boxes that contain numbers ranging from 100–500 and words and/or expressions that students should figure out. The game grid below can be used as a model. The object of the game is to give the French words for the words or expressions in the boxes. Players who do so are awarded the points in the box they selected. Divide the class into two teams and decide the order of play. The first player selects a category and a box, and then attempts to say in French the word or expression given in the box. For example, if a student selects the category "Ordering" and the box "200, ask for menu," then that student should say "**La carte, s'il vous plaît.**" If the player answers correctly, the box is crossed out, and the team receives the given number of points. If the player answers incorrectly, the other team will have the opportunity to give the words or expressions. You may want to have one student keep score and mark off boxes and another student act as an impartial judge in cases where an answer is different from the expected one but perhaps also correct, or where the answer is not pronounced very clearly.

Example:

Suggestions/ Excuses	Menu	Prendre	Ordering	Commands	Potpourri
100 play basketball	100 coffee	100 je	100 get attention	100 watch a film	100 homework
200 go jogging	200 steak & fries	200 elle	200 ask for menu	200 play soccer	200 yummy
300 I have homework	300 hot chocolate	300 nous	300 ask for check	300 do sports	300 how much
400 I have errands to do	400 apple juice	400 vous	400 ask for hot dog	400 have a sandwich	400 gross
500 I have things to do	500 grilled ham & cheese	500 ils	500 ask for types of drinks	500 bring me…	500 to be hungry and thirsty

Chapitre 5
On va au café?

pp. 124–147

Using the Chapter Opener

Motivating Activity

Ask students if they ever eat out with friends, where they go, and what they consider when choosing a place to go. Ask students if they have any preconceptions about French cafés and if they can imagine going there and enjoying themselves.

Photo Flash!

① As was the practice in 1950's Paris, young writers such as Ernest Hemingway and F. Scott Fitzgerald frequented **Les Deux Magots** to discuss their ideas with other writers and even to do some of their writing. Other cafés, such as the **Café de Flore,** were also frequented by such intellectuals as Simone de Beauvoir and Jean-Paul Sartre, who discussed philosophy and current events.

Teaching Suggestion

Ask students if there are any restaurants where they live that have both indoor and outdoor seating. Do many people choose to eat outside? Ask students what factors they consider when deciding whether to eat inside or outside. Ask if they have a preference and why.

CHAPITRE

5
On va au café?

① On va au café?

124   *cent vingt-quatre*

Where are your favorite places to meet and relax with your friends? In France, people of all ages meet at cafés to talk, have a snack, or just watch the people go by!

In this chapter you will learn

- to make suggestions; to make excuses; to make a recommendation
- to get someone's attention; to order food and beverages
- to inquire about and express likes and dislikes; to pay the check

And you will

- listen to people ordering in a café
- read a café menu
- write about your food and drink preferences
- find out about French cafés

② Miam, miam! Je vais prendre un croque-monsieur.

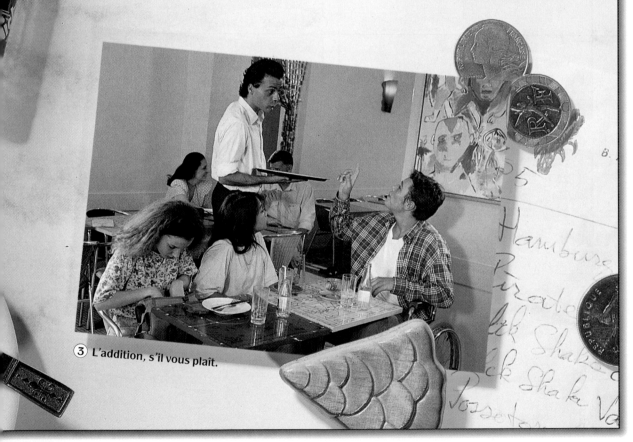

③ L'addition, s'il vous plaît.

Focusing on Outcomes

After reading the list of outcomes with students, have them look at the photo captions. Then, have students point out which outcomes are illustrated in the photos and photo captions. Can students imagine how the functions could be used in a café setting?
NOTE: You may want to use the video to support the objectives. The self-check activities in **Que sais-je?** on page 146 help students assess their achievement of the objectives.

Photo Flash!

② A waiter is about to serve a **croque-monsieur**, a grilled cheese and ham sandwich that is often served open-faced. There is also a **croque-madame**, which is a **croque-monsieur** topped with a fried egg. Point out that **Miam, miam!** is an expression that means *Yum-yum.*

③ Call student's attention to the gesture the boy uses to signal the waiter. Ask them if they would make the same gesture or a different one.

Block Scheduling

For suggestions about how to use *Allez, viens!* with block scheduling, see the *Lesson Planner,* pages 23–27.

Video Synopsis

In this segment of the video, Simon suggests to Isabelle, Thuy, and Mathieu that they go to a café. Mathieu is busy and makes an excuse. At the café, they ask for a menu and discuss what they will have. When the waiter arrives, Simon and Thuy order right away. Isabelle has trouble deciding, but finally orders a **croque-monsieur**. When they've finished their snack, Simon asks for the check. Isabelle discovers that she can't find her wallet. When the waiter brings the check, they don't know what to do.

Motivating Activity

Ask students where the teenagers are and why. You might also ask students where they go for a snack or to people-watch.

Teaching Suggestion

You might have students read the questions in Activity 1 on page 128 to prepare them for viewing the video or reading the story.

The **roman-photo** is an abridged version of the video episode.

Mise en train

Simon   Thuy

Isabelle   Mathieu

Qu'est-ce qu'on prend? PA

p. 49, Act. 1

CD 5
Trs. 1–2

Where does this story take place? What are the people doing? Why do you think they look upset at the end?

1

On va au café?

Oui, d'accord.

Si tu veux. Tu viens, Mathieu?

Désolé. J'ai des devoirs à faire. A demain!

2

Qu'est-ce que vous prenez?

Je vais prendre une menthe à l'eau.

Euh... je ne sais pas.

3

22 F.

C'est combien, un croque-monsieur?

LA CARTE

CAFE	8 F
CHOCOLAT	10 F
JUS DE FRUIT	13 F
COCA	14 F
LIMONADE	11 F
SANDWICH	16 F
HOT-DOG	17 F
GLACE	12 F

SERVICE ◆ COMPRIS

126 *cent vingt-six*

CHAPITRE 5   On va au café?

RESOURCES FOR MISE EN TRAIN

PRINT	MEDIA
• *Practice and Activity Book*, p. 49	• *Video Program*, Videocassette 2,
• *Video Guide*, pp. 33–34, 36	Videocassette 5 (captioned version)
• *Videodisc Guide*, pp. 53–56, 60	• *Videodisc Program*, Videodisc 3, Side A
	• *Audio Compact Discs*, CD 5, Trs. 1–2

④ Vous avez choisi?

Apportez-moi une menthe à l'eau, s'il vous plaît.

Euh, je ne sais toujours pas.

Moi, je vais prendre une coupe melba et une bouteille d'eau minérale, s'il vous plaît. Et toi, Isabelle?

⑤ Vous avez des pizzas?

Non, je regrette. Nous n'avons pas de pizzas.

Tu aimes les sandwiches? Eh bien, prends un croque-monsieur.

D'accord. Un croque-monsieur pour moi.

Et comme boisson, qu'est-ce que vous prenez?

Qu'est-ce que vous avez comme jus de fruit?

⑥ Nous avons du jus d'orange, du jus de pomme...

Un jus d'orange, s'il vous plaît.

Parfait. C'est tout?

⑦ Non... Une coupe melba aussi pour moi, s'il vous plaît.

⑧

Plus tard...

⑨ Monsieur! L'addition, s'il vous plaît.

Tout de suite.

Eh, je ne trouve pas mon porte-monnaie! Je n'ai pas d'argent!

⑩ Ce n'est pas vrai!

Voilà, ça fait 129 F.

Presentation

Read (or have students read) the items on the menu. Ask students to give the price of each item as it is read. Have them guess which items are food and which are beverages. You might have them figure out some of the prices in dollars or euros, using the current exchange rates. Then, have students view the video and read the episode in groups.

Teaching Suggestions

• Read aloud a line from **Qu'est-ce qu'on prend?**, such as **Parfait. C'est tout?** and have students locate the line that follows it. (**Non... une coupe melba aussi pour moi, s'il vous plaît.**) You might have the first person to answer choose the next line to read aloud.

• You might also type and distribute copies of the dialogue with some of the words deleted. Have students work in pairs to complete the dialogue. You might give a small prize to the pair that finishes first.

Video Integration

• **VIDEO PROGRAM,**
  Videocassette 2, 28:31–32:31
  Videocassette 5, 44:14–48:14
• **VIDEODISC PROGRAM,**
  Videodisc 3, Side A

Search 10515, Play To 17750

You may choose to continue with **Qu'est-ce qu'on prend? (suite)** or wait until later in the chapter. When the story continues, Simon, Thuy, and Isabelle find that they need six francs more to pay the bill. Then, they learn that they have been given the bill for another table. They need even more money for their own! As they try to figure out what to do, some tourists start a conversation with them. When the tourists learn of the situation, they insist on paying the difference. As Simon, Thuy, and Isabelle are leaving, Isabelle finds her wallet on the ground.

For Individual Needs

2 Slower Pace Before they begin, have students look for cognates in the title and the sentences in this activity (en ordre, commande, propose).

Teaching Suggestions

2 As a variation, make the actual remarks that are paraphrased here (**Apportez-moi une menthe à l'eau, s'il vous plaît.**) and have students choose the correct paraphrase. (**Thuy commande une menthe à l'eau.**)

3 You might choose to have students work in pairs, taking turns asking a question and finding an appropriate response.

 For videodisc application, see Videodisc Guide.

5 Have each pair of students brainstorm several solutions to this situation. Then, have them explain the solution they prefer to the class. Once all the solutions have been presented, ask the class to vote on the best one.

These activities check for comprehension only. Students should not yet be expected to produce language modeled in **Mise en train.**

1 Tu as compris? See answers below.

Answer the following questions about **Qu'est-ce qu'on prend?**

1. What is the relationship between the teenagers in **Qu'est-ce qu'on prend?**
2. Where are they at the beginning of the story?
3. Where do they decide to go?
4. What does each person order?
5. Who has trouble deciding what to order?
6. What is the problem at the end of the story?

2 Mets en ordre

Mets les phrases suivantes en ordre d'après **Qu'est-ce qu'on prend?**

1. Thuy commande une menthe à l'eau. 2
2. Simon demande l'addition. 4
3. Simon propose à Isabelle, Thuy et Mathieu d'aller au café. 1
4. Isabelle ne retrouve pas son argent. 5
5. Le serveur apporte l'addition. 6
6. Isabelle commande un jus d'orange. 3

3 Les deux font la paire

Choisis la bonne réponse d'après **Qu'est-ce qu'on prend?**

1. On va au café? c
2. Qu'est-ce que vous prenez? b
3. C'est combien, un croque-monsieur? d
4. Vous avez des pizzas? e
5. Qu'est-ce que vous avez comme jus de fruit? a

a. Nous avons du jus d'orange, du jus de pomme...
b. Je vais prendre une menthe à l'eau.
c. Désolé. J'ai des devoirs à faire.
d. Vingt-deux francs.
e. Non, je regrette.

4 Cherche les expressions

Look back at **Qu'est-ce qu'on prend?** What do the students say to . . . See answers below.

1. suggest that everyone go to the café?
2. give an excuse?
3. ask what someone's going to order?
4. order food?
5. ask what kind of fruit juice the restaurant serves?
6. ask how much something costs?
7. ask for the check?

> On va au café?   Qu'est-ce que vous prenez?
>
> Apportez-moi...   L'addition, s'il vous plaît.
>
> Désolé. J'ai des devoirs à faire.
>
> Je vais prendre...
>
> C'est combien,... ?   Qu'est-ce que vous avez comme jus de fruit?

5 Et maintenant, à toi

 Isabelle is in an embarrassing situation. What do you think she is going to do? Take turns with a partner suggesting ways Isabelle and her friends might resolve their problem.

128 *cent vingt-huit*   CHAPITRE 5   On va au café?

Answers

1 1. friends, classmates
2. in front of the school
3. to a café
4. Thuy: une menthe à l'eau, une coupe melba
Simon: une coupe melba, une bouteille d'eau minérale
Isabelle: un croque-monsieur, un jus d'orange
5. Isabelle
6. Isabelle can't find her wallet. She has no money.

4 1. On va au café?
2. Désolé. J'ai des devoirs à faire.
3. Qu'est-ce que vous prenez?
4. Je vais prendre... ; Apportez-moi...
5. Qu'est-ce que vous avez comme jus de fruit?
6. C'est combien,... ?
7. L'addition, s'il vous plaît.

PREMIERE ETAPE Storytelling Book pp. 17, 20

Making suggestions; making excuses; making a recommendation

COMMENT DIT-ON... ?
Making suggestions; making excuses

PA
pp. 51–52,
Acts. 7–8

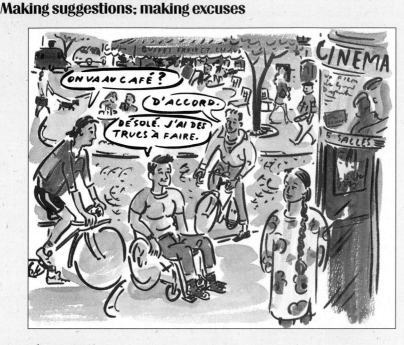

To make suggestions:
> **On** va au café? *How about going to the café?*
> **On** fait du ski?
> **On** joue au base-ball?

To make excuses:
> **Désolé(e). J'ai** des devoirs à faire. *Sorry. I have homework to do.*
> **J'ai** des courses à faire. *I have errands to do.*
> **J'ai** des trucs à faire. *I have some things to do.*
> **J'ai** des tas de choses à faire. *I have lots of things to do.*
> **Je** ne peux pas parce que... *I can't because . . .*

6 Ecoute! See scripts and answers on p. 123G.

Listen to the following dialogues. Do the speakers accept or turn down the suggestions?

CD 5 Tr. 3

---

*J*ump Start!

Have students write whether they like or dislike the following foods: **le chocolat, la glace, les escargots, les hamburgers, les frites, la pizza.**

MOTIVATE

Ask students which French foods they have heard of or eaten. Ask them to suggest French words we use to talk about food (**purée, à la mode, sautée, entrée**).

TEACH

Presentation

Comment dit-on... ? Read aloud the conversation in the cartoon as students read along silently. Ask them which student is going to the café and which one isn't and why. Ask them how they know. Then, suggest activities to students (**On joue au basket?**), prompting various excuses. Write activities on the board or on a transparency, or display pictures of them, and have pairs of students use them to make suggestions and respond with excuses.

For videodisc application, see *Videodisc Guide.*

For Individual Needs

6 Slower Pace Before students listen to the recording, have them practice distinguishing acceptance from refusal. Say aloud several expressions (**D'accord./Bonne idée./Ça ne me dit rien.**) and tell students to gesture thumbs up if they hear an acceptance and thumbs down if they hear a refusal.

Building on Previous Skills

7 Have students recall or look up expressions for accepting and refusing from previous chapters. (Examples include **C'est le fun! Allons-y! Oui, c'est génial/super. Non, c'est barbant/zéro/nul.**)

Teaching Suggestion

8 Have students exchange papers and edit each other's work. They should not make any corrections, but simply underline whatever is incorrect and return the papers. Students should then make their own corrections and rewrite their notes.

📁 Portfolio

8 Written This item is appropriate for students' written portfolios. For portfolio information, see the *Alternative Assessment Guide,* pages iv–17.

Tu te rappelles ❓

Do you remember the following ways to accept a suggestion?

D'accord.
Bonne idée.

Do you remember the following ways to turn down a suggestion?

Ça ne me dit rien. J'aime mieux…
Désolé(e), mais je ne peux pas.

7 Qu'est-ce qu'on fait?

Suggest to your friends that you all do these activities after class. They will either accept your suggestions or turn them down and make excuses. Take turns making suggestions.

—On… ?
—D'accord,… or Désolé(e),…

1. On va au café?

2. On joue au football?

3. On regarde la télévision?

4. On écoute de la musique?

5. On va au concert?

8 Un petit mot

You and your friend have agreed to go to the café on Saturday. You can't make it. Write your friend a note saying that you can't go, make an excuse, and suggest another activity at another time.

Mon ami(e),
Je suis désolé(e), mais…

Language Notes

The term **trucs** (used in **Comment dit-on… ?** on page 129) is informal and very commonly used. Students can use **truc(s)** when they don't know the word for something: **J'aime bien ces trucs.** *(I like these things.)*; **Tu as vu ce truc-là?** *(Did you see that thingamajïg over there?).* Ask students if they know other words in English that can be used in this situation.

8 Ask students why they think **désolé** is sometimes spelled with an extra **-e.** Tell them that because it is an adjective, the spelling depends on the gender of the speaker. Point out that the pronunciation doesn't change, however.

Vocabulaire

Au café...

Language Notes

- Another way to say *lemonade,* is **une citronnade.**
- Slang terms for *to eat* and *food* are **bouffer** and **la bouffe.** The slang term for *water* is **la flotte.**
- Make sure students don't pronounce the final **-m** of **faim.** Ask if they can think of an English word related to **faim** *(famished).*

Culture Notes

- In France, milk is generally not drunk at meals. Coffee is generally taken black after meals. At breakfast, people might have **café au lait** in a bowl (**un bol de café**).
- You might want to let students know that most café sandwiches are made on pieces of **baguettes.**

Presentation

Vocabulaire Collect containers of the beverages shown in the illustration. Or, draw or paste pictures of the containers on large file cards. Present the terms for the drinks first. Say **J'ai soif** aloud with appropriate gestures to get the meaning across. Then say **Je voudrais...** , showing a container and naming the beverage. Repeat this with the food items, using pictures, drawings, or toys.

Language Note

In France, flavored syrups are used in several popular drinks. Syrups are served with either non-carbonated water (**Vittel® menthe** *(mint),* **Vittel® grenadine**) or lemon soda (**diabolo menthe, diabolo grenadine**). Other flavors of syrups include **fraise** *(strawberry),* **framboise** *(raspberry),* **groseille** *(red currant),* and **orgeat** *(barley water).* When ordering a syrup drink in a café, it is a good idea to specify that you want non-alcoholic syrup (**sirop sans alcool**).

Language-to-Language

Remind students that one way languages influence one another is through "loan words," words one language adopts from another. One category of loan words is food. Ask students to give examples of French food items (from this lesson or from previous chapters) that have been borrowed from English. Then, have students brainstorm food words that English has borrowed from other languages *(hors d'oeuvres, sauerkraut, tortilla).* Discuss why words for food might be so readily shared among languages.

Language Note

Point out to students that **croque-monsieur** doesn't change form in the plural: **les croque-monsieur.**

 For Individual Needs

9 Slower Pace Have students identify in French the food shown in the thought bubbles. Stop the recording after each person orders and have students write or say the name of the boy ordering.

Teaching Suggestion

9 Have students write or say **Il a faim** or **Il a soif,** as appropriate for each of the boys.

 For Individual Needs

11 Challenge Students may want to use dictionaries or books on food to help them create a longer list. You might also refer students to the Additional Vocabulary on page R8 for more food-related vocabulary. Students might consult with friends in German, Spanish, and other language classes to learn the names of other cultural dishes to make the fair truly international. They might also learn simple greetings in these languages, and the classes might all participate in a real international fair at school.

Presentation

Comment dit-on... ? Place various food and drink items or pictures of them on a table and recommend them to students. Students should pick up the item or picture you recommend. Then, hold up pictures of various food and drink items and prompt students to recommend them to you.

---

9 **Ecoute!** See scripts and answers on p. 123G.

CD 5 Tr. 4

Look at the picture. As the boys tell the waiter what they would like, decide which boy is ordering.

Didier   Minh   Paul   Mamadou   Nabil

10 **Vous désirez?**

Now, take the role of the server in Activity 9. Write down each boy's order. See answers below.

11 **La fête internationale**

Your French class is going to participate in an international food fair at school. You've been assigned to poll your classmates about the types of food and drink they would like to have at the party. Make a list of five questions you might ask.

COMMENT DIT-ON... ?

Making a recommendation

To recommend something to eat or drink:

Prends une limonade. (informal) *Have . . .*
Prenez un sandwich. (formal) *Have . . .*

p. 36,
Act. 5

5-1

 Multicultural Link

11 You might also expand this activity into a project, with student groups reporting on and even making dishes from different francophone regions. They might present their report to the class in the form of a poster or collage.

Answers

10 Paul: une pizza et un coca
Minh: un croque-monsieur
Didier: un jus de fruit
Mamadou: un steak-frites
Nabil: un sandwich au fromage

CD-ROM
Disc 2

GRAMMAIRE The verb prendre

Prendre is an irregular verb.

PA p. 51, Act. 5
GV p. 37, Acts. 6–7

prendre *(to take; to have food or drink)*	
Je **prends** ⎱	Nous **prenons** ⎱
Tu **prends** ⎬ des frites.	Vous **prenez** ⎬ un croque-monsieur.
Il/Elle/On **prend** ⎰	Ils/Elles **prennent** ⎰

Additional Grammar Practice, pp. R35–R36

12 Qu'est-ce que je vais prendre?

You and your friends are deciding what to have in a café. Complete the conversation with the appropriate forms of the verb **prendre**.   1. prenez 2. prends 3. prends 4. prenons 5. prend 6. prennent

—Alors, qu'est-ce que vous __1__ ?
—Moi, j'ai très faim, je __2__ un steak-frites.
—Et toi, Anne, qu'est-ce que tu __3__ ?
—Michel et moi, nous __4__ une pizza.
—Et Isabelle, qu'est-ce qu'elle __5__ ?
—Isabelle et Sylvie n'ont pas faim mais elles ont très soif, alors elles __6__ un coca.

De bons conseils

Resist the temptation to match English with French word-for-word. In many cases, it doesn't work. For example, in English you say *I am hungry,* while in French you say **J'ai faim** (literally, *I have hunger*).

13 Qu'est-ce qu'ils prennent?

Michel prend un steak-frites.
Paul et Julie prennent un sandwich.
Sandrine et Eric prennent un hot-dog.
Fabienne prend une eau minérale.

Paul et Julie
Sandrine
Eric
Michel
Fabienne

PREMIERE ETAPE

cent trente-trois **133**

Teaching Suggestion

You might want to introduce the **Prononciation** section on page 141 at this time and practice the nasal sound [ã].

Language-to-Language

You might want to tell students who are native speakers of Spanish that the verb **prendre** is similar in meaning and usage to the verb *tomar* in Spanish.

Language Note

Have students compare the plural forms of **prendre** to the infinitive. Point out that the **d** of the infinitive does not appear in the plural forms. Point out also that the singular forms are pronounced with the nasal vowel [ã], while the plurals have an [n] sound.

Presentation

Grammaire Introduce the singular forms of **prendre** first, asking students what they notice about the pronunciation (they all sound the same). Then, present the plural forms, making sure students pronounce the [n] sound. Next, say the forms in random order, having students tell whether the form is singular or plural. Finally, give pictures of food (**des frites**) to various students and have the class tell what the students are having (**Ils prennent des frites.**)

Thinking Critically

Synthesizing — De bons conseils Ask students to think of expressions they've learned that can't be matched word for word with an English equivalent. (**Tu t'appelles comment? Tu as quel âge?**)

CLOSE

Have students pair off and take turns recommending five things to eat and telling why.

ASSESS

Quiz 5-1A, Quiz 5-1B, *Testing Program,* pp. 105–108
Audio CD 5, Tr. 19

Performance Assessment

On a table, display food or beverage items or pictures of these items. Have two students come up to the table. One asks for an item without pointing to it, saying **Je voudrais...** The other student picks up the correct item and hands it to his or her classmate, saying **Voilà.** Have students take turns asking for items.

VIDEO PROGRAM
Videocassette 2
32:32–34:54

OR VIDEODISC PROGRAM,
Videodisc 3, Side A

Search 17750, Play To 19965

Teacher Notes

- See the *Video Guide,* the *Videodisc Guide,* and the *CD-ROM Teacher's Guide* for activities related to the **Panorama Culturel.**
- Remind students that cultural material may be included in the Chapter Quizzes and Test.
- The interviewees' language represents informal, unrehearsed speech. Occasionally, edits have been made for clarification.

Presentation

Have students view the video. To check comprehension, ask the **Questions** below. Then, replay the video, pausing after each interview to ask questions 1 and 2 of **Qu'en penses-tu?**

Thinking Critically

Comparing and Contrasting
Have students discuss or list similarities and differences between a fast-food restaurant in the United States and a French café. You might pick a specific local establishment to use in the comparison.

Teacher Note

Students may want to know the following words: **baby** (-**foot**) *(Foosball®, table soccer);* **flipper** *(pinball);* **piscine** *(swimming pool).*

PANORAMA CULTUREL

Déjan • France

Clémentine • France

Armande • Côte d'Ivoire

Where do you go to meet with your friends? Here's what some francophone students had to say about where they go and what they do.

CD 5
Trs. 5–8

CD-ROM
Disc 2

Où retrouves-tu tes amis?

«J'aime bien aller au café après l'école. On va jouer un peu au baby, au flipper et après, je rentre chez moi faire les devoirs. On a un parc à côté de chez nous et on rencontre tous nos amis.»
—Déjan
Tr. 6

«Nous allons dans des cafés ou chez d'autres amis. Quand il fait beau, [on va] à la piscine. Ça dépend du temps qu'il fait.»
—Clémentine
Tr. 7

«Je vais à la maison, soit chez moi, ou bien chez eux [mes amis]. Puis on va à l'Alocodrome, enfin pour prendre un peu d'aloco, puis on revient à la maison.»
—Armande
Tr. 8

Qu'en penses-tu?

1. Where do these students go to meet their friends? See answers below.
2. Do you and your friends like to go to the same places and do the same things as these teenagers? Where do you go? What do you do?

Savais-tu que... ?

Many cultures have a particular kind of place where people gather. In many francophone countries, a café is more than just a place to eat; it's a social institution! Cafés primarily serve beverages. They may also serve bread (**pain**) or flaky crescent rolls (**croissants**) in the morning, and some cafés serve lunch. If you order something, you may stay in most cafés as long as you like. In some African countries, people like to go to open-air restaurants called **maquis.** They usually open only in the evening and serve traditional snack foods such as fried plantains (**aloco**), as well as full meals.

Questions

1. Où est-ce que Déjan va après l'école? (au café) Qu'est-ce qu'il fait là-bas? (Il joue au baby et au flipper.)
2. Quand est-ce que Clémentine va à la piscine? (quand il fait beau)
3. Qu'est-ce qu'Armande fait à l'Alocodrome? (Elle prend de l'aloco.)

Answers

1. café, park, friends' houses, Alocodrome

DEUXIEME ETAPE (TPR)

Storytelling Book
pp. 18, 20

Getting someone's attention; ordering food and beverages

COMMENT DIT-ON... ?

Getting someone's attention; ordering food and beverages

PA
p. 53,
Acts. 10–12

5-2

To get the server's attention:

Excusez-moi.

Monsieur! Madame! Mademoiselle!

La carte, s'il vous plaît. *The menu, please.*

The server may ask:

Vous avez choisi? *Have you decided/chosen?*

Vous prenez? *What are you having?*

You might want to ask:

Vous avez des jus de fruit?

Qu'est-ce que vous avez comme boissons? *What kind of drinks do you have?*

Qu'est-ce qu'il y a à boire? *What is there to drink?*

To order:

Je voudrais un hamburger.

Je vais prendre un coca, **s'il vous plaît.** *I'll have . . . , please.*

Un sandwich, **s'il vous plaît.** *. . . , please.*

Donnez-moi un hot-dog, **s'il vous plaît.** *Please give me . . .*

Apportez-moi une limonade, **s'il vous plaît.** *Please bring me . . .*

14 Ecoute!   See scripts and answers on p. 123G.

CD 5 Tr. 9

Listen to these remarks and decide whether the server (**le serveur/la serveuse**) or the customer (**le client/la cliente**) is speaking.

15 Méli-mélo!

Unscramble the following conversation between a server and a customer. Then, act it out with a partner.

—Qu'est-ce qu'il y a comme
  sandwiches?   2

—Bien sûr.   5

—Eh bien, donnez-moi un sandwich
  au fromage, s'il vous plaît.   4

—Vous avez choisi?   1

—Il y a des sandwiches au
  jambon, au saucisson, au fromage...   3

À la française

If you need time to think during a conversation, you can say **Eh bien**... and pause for a moment before you continue speaking.

—Vous prenez, mademoiselle?
—Eh bien... un steak-frites, s'il vous plaît.

At first you'll have to make a conscious effort to do this. The more you practice, the more natural it will become.

DEUXIEME ETAPE

cent trente-cinq   **135**

Presentation

Grammaire Before you begin, review the classroom commands from page 11. Then, contrast a command and a declarative statement that have the same verb. (**Va au tableau! Elle va au tableau.**) Ask students what the structural difference is between the command and the statement (no subject in the command). Finally, say or write some declarative sentences and have students restate or rewrite them as commands.

Grammaire Give students or pairs of students the following commands and have them perform the actions. **Apporte(z)-moi un stylo! Parle(z) français! Donne(z)-moi une feuille de papier! Danse(z)! Nage(z)! Apporte(z)-moi un crayon jaune! Prends/Prenez ce livre!** After some practice, have students give the commands to one another. You might want to play **Jacques a dit,** described on page 15J.

Language-to-Language

If you have students who speak Spanish, you might have them tell how informal commands in Spanish are similar to informal commands for -**er** verbs in French. (They both drop the final -**s.**) You might also stress that verbs in French that do not end in -**er** keep the final -**s** in informal commands, but in Spanish, the -**s** is dropped from all regular verbs.

---

16 On prend un sandwich?

You've stopped at a café for lunch. Get the server's attention, look at the menu, and order. Take turns playing the role of the server.

LA MAISON DU SANDWICH

NOS SANDWICHES

au jambon de Paris	19 F	au gruyère	19 F
au jambon de pays	25 F	au camembert	19 F
au saucisson	19 F	au saumon	34 F
au pâté	21 F	au crabe	32 F
mixte (jambon et gruyère)	26 F	végétarien	28 F

CD-ROM
Disc 2

PA
p. 54,
Acts. 13, 15

GV
p. 38,
Acts. 8–10

Additional Grammar
Practice, pp. R36–R37

GRAMMAIRE The imperative

Did you notice the subject **vous** isn't used in **Donnez-moi...** and **Apportez-moi...** ? When you give a command in French, you leave off the subject pronoun **tu** or **vous,** just as we leave off the subject pronoun *you* in English commands.

- When you write the **tu** form of an -**er** verb as a command, drop the final **s** of the usual verb ending.

Tu écoutes...	⟶	**Ecoute!**
Tu regardes...	⟶	**Regarde!**

- If the verb isn't a regular -**er** verb, the spelling of the command form doesn't change.

Tu fais...	⟶	**Fais** les devoirs!
Tu prends...	⟶	**Prends** un hot-dog, Paul!

- Remember to use the **tu** form when you talk with family members and people your own age or younger. Use the **vous** form when you talk with people older than you or with more than one person.

  Prenez un coca, Marc et Eve.

17 Que faire?

Your friends can't decide how they want to spend their Saturday afternoon. You're the one they always turn to for advice. Respond to each of their statements below by telling them what they should do. See answers below.

—Nous avons faim.
—Prenez un sandwich.

1. Nous avons soif.
2. J'aime beaucoup la musique.
3. Il fait beau aujourd'hui.
4. Nous avons un examen demain.
5. Il fait frais.
6. Je voudrais faire du sport.

---

18 Que prendre?

You don't know what to order at the café. The server makes some suggestions for you, but you don't like the suggestions. Take turns playing the server.

> —Prenez un sandwich au fromage.
> —Non, je n'aime pas le fromage.
> —Alors, prenez un sandwich au jambon.
> —Non, apportez-moi un hot-dog, s'il vous plaît.

19 A la crêperie

You and some friends get together at a **crêperie**. Look at the menu and order. Take turns playing the server.

NOTE CULTURELLE

In France, waiters and waitresses are considered professionals. In better restaurants, waiters and waitresses must not only be good servers but they must also be knowledgeable about food and wine. Even in simple restaurants or cafés, servers take great pride in their work. Contrary to what you may have seen in American movies, it is impolite to address a waiter as **Garçon**. It is more polite to say **Monsieur** to a waiter, and **Madame** or **Mademoiselle** to a waitress. It is expected that diners will take time to enjoy their food, so service in French restaurants may seem slow to Americans. It is not uncommon for a meal to last several hours.

La Crêperie Normande

Crêpes salées :

Jambon - fromage	35
Epinards - crème fraîche	35
Champignons	38

Crêpes sucrées :

Sucre	28
Banane - Chantilly	35
Chocolat	32
Glace vanille - sauce noisette	38

20 Mon journal

Make a list of the foods and drinks you like to have when you go out with your friends. Then, mention several items you'd try if you were at a café in France.

Culture Notes

19 Students may be interested to know that **crêpes** are a specialty of Brittany (**Bretagne**). Traditionally, they are served during **la fête de la chandeleur,** a Christian religious holiday in February celebrating the presentation of Jesus in the temple. **Crêperies** usually serve both dessert and dinner **crêpes** as well as sparkling apple cider.

Note Culturelle Although the number of cafés is dwindling, the café remains a viable, important institution in French life. In some cafés, you will find pinball machines (**les flippers**), table soccer (**le baby-foot**), and video games (**les jeux vidéo**). Video games may be located in a separate room at the back of the café. Decks of cards and checker games are also available in many cafés.

 For Individual Needs

20 Challenge Have students give their reactions to some of the items (J'aime beaucoup... , Nous n'aimons pas... , Je voudrais...).

 Mon journal

20 For an additional journal entry suggestion for Chapter 5, see *Practice and Activity Book,* page 149.

 Cooperative Learning

After students practice the vocabulary orally, have groups of four or five role-play a restaurant scene. One student is the server, one is the chef, and the others are the customers. The customers give their orders to the server who writes them down. The server then goes to the chef and reads aloud the orders. The chef writes down the items, while repeating the orders aloud. Finally, the server "serves" the customers, restating each person's order. At this point, limit students to the use of **Je voudrais** when they order.

CLOSE

To close this **étape,** show *Teaching Transparency 5-2* and have students imagine what the people are saying.

ASSESS

Quiz 5-2-A, Quiz 5-2B, *Testing Program,* pp. 109–112
Audio CD 5, Tr. 20

Performance Assessment

Have students form groups of three: two customers and one server. They should enact a scene in a café in which the customers call the server, ask for the menu, ask the server some questions about the food, and order. The server responds accordingly.

Jump Start!

Have students write commands using the **tu** forms of **écouter, faire, regarder, prendre,** and **jouer.** (Ecoute le prof! Joue au foot!)

MOTIVATE

Ask students what else they need to know about eating in a café now that they know how to get a waiter's attention and order.

TEACH

Presentation

Comment dit-on... ? Begin by asking students their opinions of certain classes. (**Comment tu trouves le cours de... ?**) List on the board the responses they recall (**super, cool, barbant, difficile, passionnant**). Model some of the expressions dealing with food and have students repeat them. Using magazine pictures or drawings of food, point to an item and ask a student **Comment tu trouves ça?** Students should use the new expressions to express their opinion of the given food item.

◆ For Individual Needs

21 Slower Pace Before playing the recording, write on the board the expressions of opinion students will hear. Then, ask them if each one expresses a like or a dislike.

Language Note

Note Culturelle Other examples of **la litote** are **Ça casse pas des briques** (It's not earth-shattering) and **Ce n'est pas mal** (It's very good).

TROISIEME ETAPE
 TPR
Storytelling Book pp. 19, 20

Inquiring about and expressing likes and dislikes; paying the check

COMMENT DIT-ON... ?
Inquiring about and expressing likes and dislikes

PA

pp. 56–57, Acts. 19–21

To ask how someone likes the food or drink:
   Comment tu trouves ça? *How do you like it?*

To say you like your food/drink:
   C'est... *It's . . .*
      bon! *good!*
      excellent! *excellent!*
      délicieux! *delicious!*
      pas mauvais. *pretty good.*

To say you don't like your food/drink:
   C'est... *It's . . .*
      pas bon. *not good.*
      pas terrible. *not so great.*
      dégoûtant. *gross.*
      mauvais. *bad.*

5-3

GV

p. 39, Acts. 11–12

21 Ecoute!

See scripts and answers on p. 123H.

Listen to the following remarks. Do the speakers like or dislike the food they've been served?

CD 5
Tr. 10

> ### NOTE CULTURELLE
>
> French speakers have a tendency to use understatement (**la litote**). For instance, if the food were bad, they might say **C'est pas terrible.** Similarly, rather than saying something is good, they would say **C'est pas mauvais.**

22 A mon avis...

The school cafeteria is thinking of adding some items to the menu. A poll is being taken among the students. Discuss each of the items below with a partner.

1.

2.

3.

4.

RESOURCES FOR TROISIEME ETAPE

PRINT
- *Lesson Planner,* p. 26
- *Practice and Activity Book,* pp. 56–58
- *Grammar and Vocabulary Workbook,* pp. 39–40
- *Activities for Communication,* pp. 29–30, 97, 98–99, 145–146
- *Listening Activities,* pp. 37, 41
- *Testing Program,* pp. 113–116
- *Alternative Assessment Guide,* p. 36

MEDIA
- *Video Program,* Videocassette 2
  Video Guide, pp. 33–38
- *Videodisc Program,* Videodisc 3, Side A
  Videodisc Guide, p. 58
- *Teaching Transparency* 5-3
- *Interactive CD-ROM Program,* Disc 2
  CD-ROM Teacher's Guide, p. 21
- *Audio Compact Discs*
  Textbook Listening Activities, CD 5, Trs. 10–11
  Additional Listening Activities 5-5, 5-6, CD 5, Trs. 29–30
  Quiz 5-3B, CD 5, Tr. 21

23 Ça, c'est bon.

You and your partner are in a café. Ask if your partner has decided what to order and tell what you think of his or her choice.

— Tu as choisi? Qu'est-ce que tu vas prendre?
— Euh... je vais prendre un hot-dog.
— Un hot-dog? C'est dégoûtant! *or* Bonne idée. C'est délicieux.

24 Chère correspondante

Your French pen pal Cécile asked you what teenagers in America eat or drink when they get together. Write a brief note in French telling her what you and your friends have when you go out and what you think of each item.

COMMENT DIT-ON... ?
Paying the check

pp. 57–58,
Acts. 23–24

5-3

CD-ROM
Disc 2

L'addition, s'il vous plaît.

Tout de suite, madame.

To ask for the check:
L'addition, s'il vous plaît. *The check, please.*

To ask how much something is:
C'est combien, un sandwich?
Ça fait combien, s'il vous plaît?
How much is it, . . . ? (total)

The server might answer:
Oui, tout de suite. *Yes, right away.*
Un moment, s'il vous plaît.

C'est huit **francs.**
Ça fait cinquante **francs.** *It's . . . francs. (total)*

---

25 Ecoute!

See scripts and answers on p. 123H.

Listen to the following remarks. Are the speakers ordering or getting ready to pay the check?

CD 5 Tr. 11

pp. 39–40,
Acts. 13–14

For additional practice, see p. R37.

Tu te rappelles ?

Do you remember the numbers from 20–100?

20 **vingt**	50 **cinquante**	80 **quatre-vingts**
30 **trente**	60 **soixante**	90 **quatre-vingt-dix**
40 **quarante**	70 **soixante-dix**	100 **cent**

TROISIEME ETAPE

cent trente-neuf **139**

Teaching Suggestion
23 Students will need to practice **Tu as choisi?** before doing this activity. You might have students look at the food items on page 131 or the menus in the **Lisons!** section as they do this activity.

Language Note
24 Remind students that in negative sentences, **de** replaces the indefinite article. (**Nous prenons un sandwich au jambon, mais nous ne prenons jamais de hot-dog.**)

For Individual Needs
24 Slower Pace Before starting this activity, review the food items orally. You might also want to make a list of adverbs of frequency on the board: **souvent, une fois par semaine, quelquefois, ne... jamais.**

Presentation
Comment dit-on... ? Ask students to look back at the **Mise en train** or view the video to identify these functions. Then, act out both asking for and paying the check in front of the class. Act out the dialogue a second time, having students repeat after you. You might have students refer to the menu on page 140 as you ask the prices of various items. (**C'est combien, un croque-monsieur?**) Finally, have students practice both roles in pairs.

For videodisc application, see *Videodisc Guide.*

Culture Note
Most people in France pay for purchases at a café in cash or with personal checks, which are accepted throughout the country. Cafés rarely accept credit cards, but restaurants often take them. It is a good idea to ask before ordering a meal.

Portfolio
24 Written This activity is appropriate for students' written portfolios. You might have students edit one another's note before they write a final draft. For portfolio suggestions, see the *Alternative Assessment Guide,* page 22.

Additional Practice

26 Partners might also use the menu in the **Mise en train** to practice asking and telling each other the price of different items.

Language Note

26 Have students look at the receipt next to Activity 26. Point out that capital letters in French are sometimes printed without accents (**MINERALE, AGREABLE**).

Group Work

27 While students are writing their captions, draw four large columns on the board and number them 1–4. Ask for volunteers to come to the board and write one of their captions in the appropriate column. Then, have students tell as many logical stories as they can by combining the captions.

 Portfolio

28 Oral This activity is appropriate for students' oral portfolios. For portfolio information, see the *Alternative Assessment Guide,* pages iv–17.

```
        LA GIRAFE
      Port de Cavalaire
   Tél : 04 94 64 40 31

   28-09-99

CROQUE-MONSIEUR 23,00
STEAK-FRITES    29,00
EAU MINERALE     9,00
COCA            14,00

TOTAL          75,00 F

La Direction souhaite
que cet instant de
détente vous ait été
AGREABLE
```

NOTE CULTURELLE

In cafés and restaurants, a 15% tip is included in the check if the words **service compris** are posted or written on the menu. If you're not sure, it's acceptable to ask **Le service est compris?** It's customary, however, to leave a little extra if the service is particularly good.

26 **Ça fait combien?**

You and your friend have just finished eating at a café. Look at the check, tell what you had (**Moi, j'ai pris...**), and figure out how much each of you owes.

—Moi, j'ai pris...
—Ça fait... francs.

27 **Qu'est-ce qu'on dit?**

Write what you think the people in this scene are saying. Then, with a partner, compare what you both have written.

CAFE SPORT

Sandwiches		BOISSONS	
Fromage	15 F	Jus de fruit	13 F
Jambon	19 F	orange, pomme,	
Saucisson	18 F	pamplemousse	
Hamburger	22 F	Limonade	11 F
Hot-dog	17 F	Café	8 F
Steak-frites	33 F	Cola	14 F
Croque-monsieur	22 F	Eau minérale	10 F
Pizza	20 F	Chocolat	10 F
Frites	10 F		
Glace	12 F		

28 **Jeu de rôle**

Act out a scene in a café. One student is the server and the others are customers. The customers should get the server's attention, order, comment on the food, and then pay the check.

140 *cent quarante*   CHAPITRE 5   On va au café?

Culture Note

28 Now might be a good time to discuss French table manners with students: keep both hands above the table (people sometimes rest their wrists on the table edge); keep your fork in your left hand to eat; and avoid eating with your hands (even fries and pizza).

The nasal sound [ã]

CD 5 Trs. 12–17

See scripts and answers on p. 123H.

Listen carefully to the vowel sounds in the following words: **ans, en.** These words contain the nasal sound [ã]. It's called a nasal sound because part of the air goes through the back of your mouth and nose when you make the sound. Listen to the English word *sandwich,* and the French **sandwich.** Is the first syllable pronounced the same in the two words? The sound in French is a pure nasal sound, with no trace of the *n* sound in it. In English you say *envy,* but in French you say **envie.** The nasal sound [ã] has four possible spellings: **an, am, en,** and **em.**

These letter combinations don't always represent a nasal sound. If another vowel follows the **n** or the **m,** or if the **n** or **m** is doubled, there may not be a nasal sound. You'll have to learn the pronunciation when you learn the word.

Listen to the following pairs of words and compare the sounds.

Fr*an*ce/*ani*mal   pr*en*d/pr*en*ez   j*am*bon/*ami*   *en*vie/*enn*emi

A. A prononcer

Repeat the following words.

en France	attendez	comment	soixante
anglais	dimanche	jambon	temps
orange	tellement	vent	souvent

B. A lire

Take turns with a partner reading the following sentences aloud.

1. Il a cent francs.
2. J'ai un excellent roman allemand.
3. Elle a danse et sciences nat vendredi.
4. Moi, je vais prendre un sandwich au jambon.

C. A écrire

You're going to hear a short dialogue. Write down what you hear.

Teaching Suggestion

Prononciation   Write the sentences in Part B on the board or on a transparency. Have students tell you which words contain the nasal sound and circle or underline them. Practice these words first, making sure students pronounce them correctly. Then, have students practice reading the sentences.

CLOSE

To close this **étape,** show *Teaching Transparency 5-3.* Have students suggest a dialogue for the first scene, and then have them tell what each person in the second scene might be saying about his or her food.

ASSESS

Quiz 5-3A, Quiz 5-3B, *Testing Program,* pp. 113–116

Audio CD 5, Tr. 21

Performance Assessment

Have students form groups of three and act out a restaurant scene in which the customers give opinions about the food and pay the check. The server should take and verify their orders and bring their check.

Language Note

Prononciation   Have students read the second paragraph above. In French, syllables usually begin with a consonant. When a consonant has a vowel on each side, the consonant will attach itself to the following vowel, preventing the nasal sound. This can be illustrated by dividing words into syllables: **a-ni-mal, pre-nez.**

LISONS!

$\mathcal{D}$o you like to go out to eat with your friends? Where do you like to go?

DE BONS CONSEILS
When you're faced with something new to read, look for anything that is familiar, anything that will help you identify the type of reading selection that you're dealing with. For example, a quick glance at these reading selections tells you that they're menus. Since you're familiar with menus, you should have a general idea of the kind of information these will contain, even if you don't know what all the words mean.

A. When you look at menus, what information are you usually looking for? Can you find this type of information on these menus?   See answers below.

B. French cuisine is enjoyed the world over. However, you can often find dishes from other cultures at French cafés and restaurants.   See answers below.
   1. Which items on the menus are typical American dishes?
   2. What French words might you find on American menus?
   3. What other French words do you know that are related to food and restaurants?

C. In the Café des Lauriers, what ingredients do the **salade niçoise,** the **salade mexicaine,** and the **salade sicilienne** have in common?   green lettuce and tomatoes

READING STRATEGY
Using what you already know

Teacher Note
For an additional reading, see *Practice and Activity Book,* page 59.

PREREADING
Activity A

Motivating Activity
You might use the first question of Activity A as an opener to get students thinking about menus and what they reveal about a restaurant. Have students look at the illustrations on the menus. What do they notice?

READING
Activities B–H

Teaching Suggestion
Working in pairs or small groups, have students skim the menus quickly and answer the questions in Activities B, C, and D.

SNACK • BAR
Café
DES LAURIERS

SALADE VERTE	20
SALADE NIÇOISE	38
(salade verte, tomates, œufs, haricots verts, thon, olives)	
SALADE MEXICAINE	40
(salade verte, tomates, maïs, poivrons, thon, olives)	
SALADE SICILIENNE	40
(salade verte, tomates, basilic, mozzarella, huile d'olive)	
ASSIETTE ANGLAISE	45
(jambon blanc, saucisson, rôti de porc, beurre)	
SANDWICHES	
jambon blanc	28
saucisson	28
pâté	30
fromage	26
CROQUE–MONSIEUR	27
PORTION FROMAGE	18
PIZZA	30
QUICHE	30
HAMBURGER	30

Math Link
Have students calculate how much the most expensive item at each café is in dollars. You may need to review with students how to convert francs to dollars. You might also have students convert francs to euros.

Answers
A food choices, prices; Yes
B 1. hamburger, hot-dog, pizza, banana split, cola
   2. Answers will vary.
   3. *Possible answers:* Bon appétit!, bistro, à la mode, soupe du jour, entrée, à la carte, hors d'œuvres, chef, sauté, parfait

FONTAINE ELYSÉE

SANDWICHES
Jambon cru	30
Jambon de Paris	24
Pâté	24
Mixte	36
Roquefort aux noix	28

OMELETTES
Jambon	35
Fromage	35
Mixte	41

PLATS DIVERS
Croque-monsieur	30
Escargots (les 6)	52
Hot-Dog 1 Saucisse	32
Hot-Dog 2 Saucisses	57

BOISSONS CHAUDES
Café express	15
Décaféiné	15
Café ou chocolat viennois	32
Café crème	27
Cappuccino	33

BOISSONS FRAICHES
Eau minérale, limonade	26
Cola	28
Jus de fruit	28
raisin, poire, abricot, pamplemousse, ananas	

SPECIALITES
COUPE CHAMPS-ELYSEES :	
Chocolat - Pistache - Caramel - Sauce Chocolat - Mandarine Impériale - Chantilly	53
BANANA SPLIT :	
Glace -Vanille - Chocolat - Banane Fruit - Sauce Chocolat - Chantilly	44
COUPE MELBA :	
Vanille - Pêche Fruit - Chantilly - Sauce Fraise	44

For Activities D–G, see answers below.

D. Which café lists the beverages served? Do you recognize any of them? What is the difference between **BOISSONS FRAICHES** and **BOISSONS CHAUDES**?

E. How many different cognates can you find on the menus? (You should be able to find at least ten!)

F. Read the following statements about your friends' likes and dislikes. Which café would you recommend to each one?

1. Chantal a soif, mais elle n'a pas faim. Elle aime les jus de fruit.
2. Michel adore la glace.
3. Jean-Paul est végétarien.
4. Mai voudrait une omelette.
5. Alain aime les quiches.

G. Judging from the menus, what are the differences between the two cafés? What are the specialties of each one?

H. If your parents invited you to go out, which café would you choose? Why? Which would you choose if you had to pay?

I. If you had 100 F to spend, what would you order?

J. Now, make your own menu. Plan what you want to serve and how you want the menu to look. Will you have any illustrations? Don't forget to include prices.

cent quarante-trois **143**

Teaching Suggestions

F. Have students pair off to create a conversation in French in which one person asks the other how he or she likes each café:
— **Comment tu trouves le café Fontaine Elysée?**
— **C'est très cher, mais les sandwiches sont très bons.**

H. You might have students work in groups of three to create a conversation in French that might take place in this situation.

POSTREADING
Activity I

Teacher Note

J. This activity could be expanded as the Chapter Project. See page 123I for the project description.

Answers

D Fontaine Elysée; boissons fraîches *(cold drinks)*, boissons chaudes *(hot drinks)*

E *Possible answers:* salade, tomates, olives, porc, omelette, vanille, sauce, banane, abricot, caramel, spécialités, sandwiches, mexicaine

F 1. Fontaine Elysée
2. Fontaine Elysée
3. Café des Lauriers
4. Fontaine Elysée
5. Café des Lauriers

G Fontaine Elysée has more choices; Café des Lauriers has no specialty. Fontaine Elysée's specialty is ice cream.

MISE EN PRATIQUE

The *CD-ROM Program* offers guided recording and writing activities to practice oral and written skills and to review material from each chapter.

The **Mise en pratique** reviews and integrates all four skills and culture in preparation for the Chapter Test.

For Individual Needs

1 Slower Pace Before doing this activity, go over the menus with students. Ask them to identify as many differences as they can among the cafés, particularly concerning the type of food offered.

1 Challenge Have students write down the items that are ordered in each dialogue.

Math Link

1 Replay the recording. Pause the recording after each dialogue and ask students to calculate the amount of the check.

Portfolio

2 Oral You might want to have students add this to their oral portfolios or use it as an oral assessment tool. For portfolio suggestions, see the *Alternative Assessment Guide*, page 22.

1 In which café would you most likely hear these conversations? See scripts and answers on p. 123H.

CD 5 Tr. 18

Café de Paris

15, Place du Palais - 75004 Paris
Téléphone 01-43-54-20-21

Nos glaces

Coupe Melba	50
Coupe Nougat	46
Banana Split	42

Nos boissons

Eau minérale	14
Jus de fruit	16
Café	10
Thé	8

SERVICE COMPRIS 15%

Café de la gare

87, Avenue Victor Hugo -
75017 Paris
Tél. 01-45-62-52-53

Sandwiches

Croque-monsieur	30
Sandwich au jambon	25
Sandwich au fromage	20
Sandwich au rosbif	25

Boissons

Orangina, Coca	10
Eau minérale	12
Café	8
Jus de fruit	14

Café Américain

135, Boulevard d'Argençon • 75008 Paris
• Téléphone 01-44-15-30-33

★ Pizzas ★

Trois fromages	50
Suprême	65

★ Plats ★

Couscous	50
Steak-frites	45

★ Boissons ★

Coca	12
Limonade	15
Eau minérale	13

SERVICE COMPRIS 15 %

2 You and your partner are hungry. Suggest that you go to a café, decide what you both want to eat, and choose one of the cafés above.

144 *cent quarante-quatre*

CHAPITRE 5 On va au café?

3 From what you know about French cafés, are these statements true or false?

1. If you don't see **service compris** on the menu, you should leave a tip.   true
2. To call the waiter, you should say **Garçon!**   false
3. It is usually acceptable to stay in a French café for a long time, as long as you've ordered something to eat or drink.   true
4. If a French person says **C'est pas mauvais,** he or she doesn't like the food.   false

4 *Ecrivons!*

The French Club at your school is going to have a picnic to raise money. Plan the picnic with two classmates and then create your own poster announcing it.

STRATEGIE
Arranging ideas spatially is a useful way to organize information before you write. It's a way of creating a type of blueprint to show how your finished product will look.

First, create a name and catchy slogan to attract attention to your event. Determine the time and place of the picnic, the food, and the activities. Include a brief description of the purpose of the event. You should also decide how much each item will cost. Jot down all of your decisions.

Now, you're ready to create your blueprint. On a sheet of paper, draw a box for each item that will be included on your poster (title, slogan, date, time, place, food, and so on) indicating where you want the information to appear. Label each box with the type of information that will go in that space.

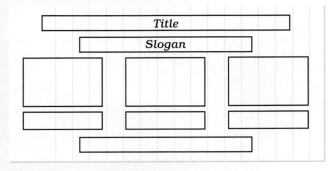

Next, using the blueprint you've developed, create your poster promoting the French Club picnic. Use the material you've learned in this chapter, such as commands. You might add drawings or magazine cutouts to illustrate your poster.

5

JEU DE ROLE

The day of the French Club picnic has arrived. One person in your group will act as host, the others will be the guests. The host will ask people what they want. Guests will tell what they want and talk about how they like the food and drink. After eating, suggest activities and decide which one you'll participate in.

MISE EN PRATIQUE   *cent quarante-cinq*   **145**

Process Writing
4 Have students create a radio announcement for the picnic they're planning. They might record their announcements for their class and play them for other French classes.

Teaching Suggestion
4,5 Both of these activities could be used as class projects.

 Video Wrap-Up

• *VIDEO PROGRAM,*
  Videocassette 2, 25:15–36:17
• *VIDEODISC PROGRAM,*
  Videodisc 3, Side A

At this time, you might want to use the video resources for additional review and enrichment. See *Video Guide* or *Videodisc Guide* for suggestions regarding the following:
• **Qu'est-ce qu'on prend?**
  (Dramatic episode)
• **Panorama Culturel**
  (Interviews)
• **Vidéoclips**
  (Authentic footage)

This page is intended to help students prepare for the Chapter Test. It is a brief checklist of the major points covered in the chapter. The students should be reminded that this is only a checklist and does not necessarily include everything that will appear on the test.

Teaching Suggestion

2 Encourage students to give several different responses.

♜ Game

LE BASE-BALL Draw a baseball diamond on the board. Divide the class into two teams. The player up first may try to answer a single question for one base, two questions for a double, and so on. You might want to use the more difficult questions for players trying for extra-base hits.

QUE SAIS-JE?

Can you make suggestions, excuses, and recommendations? pp. 129, 132

Can you get someone's attention and order food and beverages? p. 135

Can you inquire about and express likes and dislikes? p. 138

Can you pay the check? p. 139

Can you use what you've learned in this chapter?

1 How would you suggest to a friend that you . . .
1. go to the café?
On va au café?
2. play tennis?
On joue au tennis?

2 How would you turn down a suggestion and make an excuse?
See answers below.

3 How would you recommend to a friend something . . . Possible answers:
1. to eat?
Prends un sandwich au jambon.
2. to drink?
Prends un coca.

4 In a café, how would you . . . See answers below.
1. get the server's attention?
2. ask what kinds of sandwiches they serve?
3. ask what there is to drink?

5 How would you say that you're . . .
1. hungry? J'ai faim.
2. thirsty? J'ai soif.

6 How would you order . . . See answers below.
1. something to eat?
2. something to drink?

7 How would you tell what people are having, using the verb **prendre**?
See answers below.

1. il
2. tu
3. nous
4. ils

8 How would you ask a friend how he or she likes a certain food?
Comment tu trouves ça?

9 How would you tell someone what you think of these items?
See answers below.

1.
2.
3.
4.

10 How would you ask how much each item in number 9 costs?
See answers below.

11 How would you ask for the check? L'addition, s'il vous plaît.

12 How would you ask what the total is? Ça fait combien, s'il vous plaît?

Answers

2 *Possible answers:* Désolé(e), j'ai des devoirs à faire. J'ai des courses à faire. J'ai des trucs à faire. J'ai des tas de choses à faire.

4 1. Excusez-moi. Monsieur! Madame! Mademoiselle! La carte, s'il vous plaît.
2. Qu'est-ce que vous avez comme sandwiches?
3. Qu'est-ce qu'il a à boire?

6 *Possible answers:*
1. Je voudrais... ; Je vais prendre... ; Donnez-moi... ; Apportez-moi un steak-frites, s'il vous plaît.
2. Je voudrais... ; Je vais prendre... ; Donnez-moi... ; Apportez-moi une limonade, s'il vous plaît.

7 1. Il prend un sandwich au jambon.
2. Tu prends un steak-frites.
3. Nous prenons un jus d'orange.
4. Ils prennent une limonade.

9 *Possible answers:* C'est bon! C'est excellent! C'est délicieux! C'est pas bon. C'est pas terrible. C'est dégoûtant.

10 1. C'est combien, un hot-dog?
2. C'est combien, une pizza?
3. C'est combien, une glace?
4. C'est combien, une salade?

PREMIERE ETAPE

**Making suggestions;
making excuses**

On va au café? *How about going
to the café?*
On... ? *How about . . . ?*
Désolé(e). J'ai des devoirs à
faire. *Sorry. I have homework
to do.*
J'ai des courses à faire. *I have
errands to do.*
J'ai des trucs à faire. *I have some
things to do.*
J'ai des tas de choses à faire. *I
have lots of things to do.*
Je ne peux pas parce que... *I
can't because . . .*

Foods and beverages

un sandwich au jambon *ham
sandwich*
  au saucisson *salami sandwich*
  au fromage *cheese sandwich*
un hot-dog *hot dog*
un croque-monsieur *toasted
cheese and ham sandwich*
un steak-frites *steak and French
fries*
une quiche *quiche*
une omelette *omelet*
une crêpe *very thin pancake*
une eau minérale *mineral water*
une limonade *lemon soda*
un citron pressé *lemonade*

un sirop de fraise (à l'eau)
  water with strawberry syrup
un coca *cola*
un jus d'orange *orange juice*
un jus de pomme *apple juice*
un café *coffee*
un chocolat *hot chocolate*

Making a recommendation

Prends/Prenez... *Have . . .*
prendre *to take; to have food or
drink*

Other useful expressions

avoir soif *to be thirsty*
avoir faim *to be hungry*

Teaching Suggestions

• As a comprehensive review
of vocabulary, have students
write a conversation among
two customers and a server
in a café using vocabulary
from all three **étapes**. Students might do this in pairs.
• Have students write down all
the cognates they can find on
this page.

DEUXIEME ETAPE

**Getting someone's
attention**

Excusez-moi. *Excuse me.*
Monsieur! *Waiter!*
Madame! *Waitress!*
Mademoiselle! *Waitress!*
La carte, s'il vous plaît. *The
menu, please.*

**Ordering food and
beverages**

Vous avez choisi? *Have you
decided/chosen?*

Vous prenez? *What are you
having?*
Vous avez... ? *Do you have . . . ?*
Qu'est-ce que vous avez comme
boissons? *What do you have
to drink?*
Qu'est-ce qu'il y a à boire?
What is there to drink?
Je voudrais... *I'd like . . .*
Je vais prendre... , s'il vous plaît.
I'll have . . . , please.

... , s'il vous plaît. *. . . , please.*
Donnez-moi... , s'il vous plaît.
Please give me . . .
Apportez-moi... , s'il vous plaît.
Please bring me . . .

CHAPTER 5 ASSESSMENT

CHAPTER TEST

• *Testing Program*, pp. 117–122

  • *Audio Compact Discs,*
  Audio CD 5,
  Tracks 22–24

SPEAKING TEST

• *Testing Program*, p. 345

TEST GENERATOR
  • Chapter 5

ALTERNATIVE ASSESSMENT

Performance Assessment

• You might want to use the **Jeu
de Rôle** on page 145 as a
cumulative performance
assessment activity.
• *Alternative Assessment Guide,*
p. 36

TROISIEME ETAPE

**Inquiring about and
expressing likes and
dislikes**

Comment tu trouves ça? *How do
you like it?*
C'est... *It's . . .*
  bon! *good!*
  excellent! *excellent!*
  délicieux! *delicious!*

pas mauvais! *pretty good!*
pas bon. *not good.*
pas terrible. *not so great.*
dégoûtant. *gross.*
mauvais. *bad.*

Paying the check

L'addition, s'il vous plaît. *The
check, please.*

Oui, tout de suite. *Yes, right
away.*
Un moment, s'il vous plaît. *One
moment, please.*
C'est combien,... ? *How much
is . . . ?*
Ça fait combien, s'il vous plaît?
How much is it, please?
C'est... francs. *It's . . . francs.*
Ça fait... francs. *It's . . . francs.*

Portfolio Assessment

• *Alternative Assessment Guide*
Oral: p. 22
Written: p. 22

CD-ROM ASSESSMENT

• *Interactive CD-ROM Program,*
Disc 2

A toi de parler

A toi d'écrire

• *Alternative Assessment Guide*
p. 50

Chapitre 6 : Amusons-nous!
Chapter Overview

Mise en train pp. 150–152	**Projets de week-end**			

	FUNCTIONS	**GRAMMAR**	**CULTURE**	**RE-ENTRY**
Première étape pp. 153–158	• Making plans, p. 153	• Using **le** with days of the week, p. 153 • The verb **aller** and **aller** + infinitive, p. 154 • Contractions with **à**, p. 157	• **Panorama Culturel,** Going out with friends, p. 158	• Expressing likes and dislikes (**Chapitre 1**) • Days of the week (**Chapitre 2**)
Deuxième étape pp. 159–162	• Extending and responding to invitations, p. 159	• The verb **vouloir,** p. 160	• Realia: Leisure activities, p. 159 • **Rencontre Culturelle,** Dating in France, p. 162	• Making, accepting, and turning down suggestions (**Chapitre 4**) • Sports and hobbies (**Chapitre 4**)
Troisième étape pp. 163–167	• Arranging to meet someone, p. 163	• Information questions, p. 165	• **Note Culturelle,** Conversational time, p. 164 • Realia: Movie schedule, p. 166	• Official time (**Chapitre 2**) • **Est-ce que** (**Chapitre 4**) • Days of the week (**Chapitre 2**) • Time expressions (**Chapitre 2**)

Prononciation p. 167	The vowel sounds **[ø]** and **[œ]** Audio CD 6, Tracks 12–14	**A écrire** (dictation) Audio CD 6, Tracks 15–17
Lisons! pp. 168–169	Theme-park ads	**Reading Strategy** Using context to determine meaning
Review pp. 170–173	**Mise en pratique**, pp. 170–171 **Ecrivons!** Arranging ideas chronologically Planning a day in Paris	**Que sais-je?** p. 172 **Vocabulaire,** p. 173

Assessment Options

Testing Program
• Première étape, Quiz 6-1A, Quiz 6-1B, pp. 131–134
• Deuxième étape, Quiz 6-2A, Quiz 6-2B, pp. 135–138
• Troisième étape, Quiz 6-3A, Quiz 6-3B, pp. 139–142
• Chapter Test, pp. 143–148
• Speaking Test, p. 345

Audio Compact Discs
• Audio CD 6, Tracks 19–24

Interactive CD-ROM Program
• Mise en pratique (A toi de parler, A toi d'écrire)
• *CD-ROM Teacher's Guide,* Assessment Options, p. 26

Alternative Assessment Guide
• Portfolio Assessment, p. 23
• Performance Assessment, p. 37
• CD-ROM Assessment, p. 51

Test Generator
• Chapter 6

MIDTERM EXAM

Testing Program
• Midterm Exam, pp. 157–164
• Score Sheet, pp. 165–167
• Listening Scripts, pp. 168–169
• Answers, p. 170

Audio Compact Discs
• Audio CD 6, Tracks 25–30

PRINT	MEDIA

Pupil's Edition, pp. 148–173

 Audio Compact Discs
• Textbook Listening Activities: Audio CD 6, Tracks 1–18

**Interactive CD-ROM Program
Teacher's Guide,** pp. 23–26

 Interactive CD-ROM Program
• Disc 2

Videodisc Guide
• Teaching Suggestions, pp. 65–69
• Activity Masters, pp. 70–72

 Videodisc Program
• Videodisc 3, Side B

Video Guide
• Teaching Suggestions, pp. 40–41
• Activity Masters, pp. 42–44

 Video Program
• Videocassette 2
• Videocassette 5 (captioned version)

Listening Activities
• Student Response Forms for Textbook Listening Activities, pp. 43–45
• Additional Listening Activities 6-1 to 6-6, pp. 47–49
• Additional Listening Activities (song), p. 50
• Scripts and Answers, pp. 127–131

 Audio Compact Discs
• Textbook Listening Activities: Audio CD 6, Tracks 1–18
• Additional Listening Activities: Audio CD 6, Tracks 31–37

Teaching Transparencies
• Teaching Transparency Masters 6-1 to 6-3 (Situations) and 6-A to 6-B (Vocabulary)
• Teaching Suggestions 6-1 to 6-3 and 6-A to 6-B

 Teaching Transparencies
• Situations 6-1 to 6-3
• Vocabulary 6-A to 6-B

Testing Program
• Grammar and Vocabulary Quizzes, **Etape** Quizzes, Chapter Test, and Midterm, pp. 131–148, 157–164
• Score Sheet, Scripts, and Answers, pp. 149–156, 165–170

 Audio Compact Discs
• Assessment Items: Audio CD 6, Tracks 19–30

 Test Generator
• Chapter 6

Alternative Assessment
• Portfolio Assessment, p. 23
• Performance Assessment, p. 37
• CD-ROM Assessment, p. 51

 Grammar and Vocabulary Workbook, pp. 41–50

 Practice and Activity Book, pp. 61–72

Activities for Communication
• Communicative Activities, pp. 31–36
• Realia and Teaching Suggestions, pp. 100–104
• Situation Cards, pp. 147–148

Lesson Planner
• Lesson Plan, pp. 28–32

Chapitre 6 : Amusons-nous!
Technology Applications

MISE EN TRAIN, pp. 150–152

Video
• Show *Projets de week-end.* For Video Synopsis, Teaching Suggestions, Activity Master, and Scripts, see the *Video Guide* or the *Videodisc Guide.*

Captioned Video
• Play the captioned video for *Projets de week-end* on Videocassette 5 and have students raise their hands when they see expressions for extending and responding to invitations and for arranging to meet someone.

Audio
• Play the recording of the **Mise en train** with pauses as students read along. You might have them practice pronunciation by repeating individual sentences after hearing them.

PREMIERE ETAPE, pp. 153–157

Video
• While students watch *Projets de week-end,* have them listen for exchanges that model making plans. For more suggestions, see p. 67 of the *Videodisc Guide.*

Audio
• Textbook Listening Activity 7 practices expressions for making plans.
• To have students practice using **aller** with an infinitive to express the near future, play Textbook Listening Activity 9.
• Additional Listening Activities 6-1 and 6-2 target the vocabulary for places around town.

Transparencies
• Use *Teaching Transparencies 6-1, 6-A,* and *6-B* along with the Teaching Suggestions to present and have students practice the vocabulary for leisure activities and places around town.

CD-ROM (Disc 2)
• **Les mots qui manquent** (Activity 1) practices the forms of the verb **aller.**
• **Chasse au trésor** and **Jeu des paires** (Activities 2 and 3) use the vocabulary for places and activities in town.
• For suggestions, see p. 24 of the *CD-ROM Teacher's Guide.*

PANORAMA CULTUREL, p. 158

Video
• Show the interviews. For Video Synopsis, Teaching Suggestions, Activity Master, and Scripts, see the *Video Guide* or the *Videodisc Guide.*

Audio
• Play the **Panorama Culturel** as students read along. Remind students they might not be able to understand everything each person says, but they should try to recognize words and deduce global meaning.

CD-ROM (Disc 2)
• Have students do the **Panorama Culturel** activity for Chapter 6 after showing them the video. For suggestions, see p. 25 of the *CD-ROM Teacher's Guide.*

DEUXIEME ETAPE, pp. 159–161

Video
• While students watch *Projets de week-end,* have them listen for exchanges that model extending and responding to invitations. For more suggestions, see p. 68 of the *Videodisc Guide.*

Audio
• Use Textbook Listening Activity 17 to have students classify phrases that accept or refuse an invitation.

Transparencies
• Use *Teaching Transparency 6-2* and the Teaching Suggestions to have students practice the

expressions for extending and responding to invitations.

CD-ROM (Disc 2)
• **Chacun à sa place** (Activity 4) practices the expressions for extending, accepting, and refusing invitations.
• **Les mots qui manquent** (Activity 5) practices the forms of the verb **vouloir.**
• For suggestions, see pp. 24–25 of the *CD-ROM Teacher's Guide.*

TROISIEME ETAPE, pp. 163–167

Video
• While students watch *Projets de week-end,* have them listen for exchanges that model arranging to meet someone. For more suggestions, see p. 68 of the *Videodisc Guide.*

Audio
• Use Textbook Listening Activities 24 and 26 to have students arrange to meet someone.
• Additional Listening Activities 6-5 and 6-6 practice phrases for arranging to meet someone. Use these activities as a challenge for students.

Transparencies
• Use *Teaching Transparency 6-3* and the Teaching Suggestions to have students practice phrases for arranging to meet someone.

CD-ROM (Disc 2)
• **Le bon choix** (Activity 6) targets expressions for arranging to meet someone. For suggestions, see p. 25 of the *CD-ROM Teacher's Guide.*

MISE EN PRATIQUE, pp. 170–171

Video
• Replay *Projets de week-end* in its entirety and ask students to listen for the exchanges in which the characters make

plans, extend and respond to invitations, and arrange to meet someone.

CD-ROM (Disc 2)
• Have students do the **En contexte** to practice making suggestions, deciding on an activity to do, and arranging a time and place to meet someone. You might want to use the suggestions on p. 24 of the *CD-ROM Teacher's Guide.*
• Have students practice their writing and speaking skills by doing the **A toi d'écrire** and **A toi de parler** activities. For a detailed description of these activities, see pp. 25–26 of the *CD-ROM Teacher's Guide.*
• For Assessment Options, see p. 26 of the *CD-ROM Teacher's Guide.*

Test Generator
• Use the Test Generator to create review material for students taking the Chapter Test or to prepare an alternate test.

VIDEOCLIPS

Video
• Show the **Vidéoclips.** For Video Synopsis, Teaching Suggestions, Activity Master, and Scripts, see the *Video Guide* or the *Videodisc Guide.*

Chapitre 6 : Amusons-nous!
Barcode Directory

Barcodes A and B access **Mise en train** and **Mise en train (suite)** in their entirety. Subsequent barcodes show specific segments of **Projets de week-end.** The barcode numbers correspond to the scene numbers as they appear on the video.

MISE EN TRAIN

Projets de week-end **A**

Search 1, Play To 5705

Salut, Isabelle. **1**

Search 1, Play To 1942

Il y a un concert... **2**

Search 1943, Play To 2325

Et dimanche après-midi... **3**

Search 2326, Play To 3029

Alors, allons au Louvre! **4**

Search 3030, Play To 3297

Mais non,... **5**

Search 3298, Play To 3458

Je ne sais pas. **6**

Search 3459, Play To 4271

On va au Sacré-Cœur? **7**

Search 4272, Play To 4394

Bon, eh bien,... **8**

Search 4395, Play To 5223

Oh non,... **9**

Search 5224, Play To 5705

Projets de week-end (suite) **B**

Search 5705, Play To 13810

PANORAMA CULTUREL

Qu'est-ce que tu fais quand tu sors?
These barcodes access the three interviews of the **Panorama Culturel** presented in the *Pupil's Edition* as well as additional interviews.

First three interviews **1**

Search 13810, Play To 16011

All interviews **2**

Search 13810, Play To 19308

Julie **3**

Search 14613, Play To 15024

Arnaud **4**

Search 15025, Play To 15370

Céline **5**

Search 15371, Play To 16011

Emmanuel **6**

Search 16012, Play To 16539

Léna **7**

Search 16540, Play To 16716

Elodie **8**

Search 16717, Play To 16941

Frédéric **9**

Search 16942, Play To 17265

Aminata **10**

Search 17266, Play To 17616

Marieke **11**

Search 17617, Play To 18135

Matthieu **12**

Search 18136, Play To 18400

Evelyne **13**

Search 18401, Play To 18654

Onélia **14**

Search 18655, Play To 18953

Louise **15**

Search 18954, Play To 19323

ETAPES

To practice the grammar, vocabulary, and functions presented in each **étape**, see the barcodes and accompanying suggestions on pages 67–68 of the *Videodisc Guide*.

MISE EN PRATIQUE

This is additional footage modeling some of the expressions practiced in this chapter. You may want to use it to review the chapter.

Mise en pratique 1 **1**

Search 21511, Play To 23983

Mise en pratique 2 **2**

Search 23984, Play To 25146

VIDEOCLIPS

These are authentic French commercials. You may want to preview them before showing them to students.

Panach'® : beverage **1**

Search 19323, Play To 20604

Folies® chocolat liégeois : dairy dessert **2**

Search 20605, Play To 21236

Chapitre 6 : Amusons-nous!
CD-ROM Directory 💿 DISC 2

The following directory lists the *Interactive CD-ROM Program* activities for Chapter 6. For details and suggestions on how to use them, see pages 23–26 of the *CD-ROM Teacher's Guide*.

GLOBAL TASK	COMMUNICATIVE GOALS	ACTIVITY TYPE
Vivement le week-end! Students make plans for the weekend with their friend Cédric.	To use chapter functions, vocabulary, and grammar in a lifelike conversation	**En contexte** *Interactive conversation*

	SUPPORTING ACTIVITIES	PUPIL'S EDITION	COMMUNICATIVE GOALS	ACTIVITY TYPE
Première étape	1. Grammaire	p. 154	To produce the forms of the verb **aller**	**Les mots qui manquent** *Tic Tac Toe*
	2. Vocabulaire	pp. 153, 156	To identify vocabulary for places and activities in town	**Chasse au trésor Explorons!/Vérifions!** *Interactive image*
	3. Vocabulaire	pp. 153, 156	To identify vocabulary for places and activities in town	**Jeu des paires** *Concentration®*
Deuxième étape	4. Comment dit-on... ?	p. 159	To classify expressions for extending, accepting, and refusing invitations	**Chacun à sa place** *Categories*
	5. Grammaire	p. 160	To use the forms of the verb **vouloir**	**Les mots qui manquent** *Tic Tac Toe*
Troisième étape	6. Comment dit-on... ?	p. 163	To use expressions for arranging to meet someone	**Le bon choix** *Multiple choice*
Panorama Culturel	Panorama Culturel	p. 158	To listen to and understand native speakers talking about what they do when they go out	**Qu'est-ce que tu fais quand tu sors?** *Presentation* **Le bon choix** *Multiple choice*

	APPLICATION	PUPIL'S EDITION	COMMUNICATIVE GOALS	ACTIVITY TYPE
Mise en pratique	A toi de parler	pp. 170–171	To create and record a conversation about weekend plans	*Guided recording*
	A toi d'écrire	pp. 170–171	To write an e-mail message, a brochure, a survey, or a note	*Guided writing*

🏠 *Homework Suggestions*

CHAPTER SECTION	PRESENTATION	HOMEWORK OPTIONS
Première étape	**Note de grammaire,** p. 153	Pupil's Edition, p. R38, Activity 1 Grammar and Vocabulary Workbook, p. 42, Activities 3–4
	Vocabulaire, p. 153	Grammar and Vocabulary Workbook, p. 41, Activities 1–2
	Grammaire, p. 154	Pupil's Edition, p. R38, Activities 2–3 Practice and Activity Book, p. 63, Activity 7 Grammar and Vocabulary Workbook, p. 43, Activities 5–6 CD-ROM, Disc 2, Activity 1
	Vocabulaire, p. 156	Pupil's Edition, p. 156, Activity 13 Practice and Activity Book, pp. 63–64, Activities 6, 8 Grammar and Vocabulary Workbook, pp. 44–45 Activities 7–9 CD-ROM, Disc 2, Activities 2–3
	Grammaire, p. 157	Pupil's Edition, p. R38, Activity 4 Grammar and Vocabulary Workbook, p. 45, Activities 10–11
Deuxième étape	**Comment dit-on... ?** p. 159	Practice and Activity Book, pp. 65–66, Activities 11–14 CD-ROM, Disc 2, Activity 4
	Grammaire, p. 160	Pupil's Edition, p. 161, Activity 20; p. R39, Activities 5–6 Practice and Activity Book, pp. 66–67, Activities 15–16 Grammar and Vocabulary Workbook, p. 46, Activities 12–13 CD-ROM, Disc 2, Activity 5
Troisième étape	**Comment dit-on... ?** p. 163	Pupil's Edition, p. 167, Activity 32 Practice and Activity Book, pp. 68–69, Activities 19–20 Grammar and Vocabulary Workbook, pp. 47–48, Activities 14–17 CD-ROM, Disc 2, Activity 6
	Grammaire, p. 165	Pupil's Edition, pp. R39–R40, Activities 7–8 Practice and Activity Book, p. 69, Activities 21–22 Grammar and Vocabulary Workbook, pp. 49–50, Activities 18–21

Chapitre 6 : Amusons-nous!
Textbook Listening Activities Scripts

For Student Response Forms, see *Listening Activities,* pp. 43–45.

Première étape

7 Ecoute! p. 153

SOPHIE   Alors, qu'est-ce que tu vas faire ce week-end?

THERESE   Ce week-end? Oh là là! Plein de choses! Samedi matin, je vais faire une vidéo à la Maison des jeunes. Samedi après-midi, je vais faire les magasins et le soir, je vais au cinéma avec des copains.

SOPHIE   C'est tout?

THERESE   Non, attends, ce n'est pas fini! Dimanche matin, je vais au café et l'après-midi, je vais aller au Parc Astérix.

SOPHIE   Eh bien, bon week-end!

Possible answers to Activity 7
make a video, go shopping, go to the movies, go to the café, go to Parc Astérix

9 Ecoute! p. 154

1. Samedi après-midi, je vais jouer au football.
2. Michel et moi, nous regardons la télévision.
3. Je prends un sandwich et un coca.
4. Tu vas faire un pique-nique?
5. Nous allons faire une promenade.

Answers to Activity 9

1. going to do	3. doing	5. going to do
2. doing	4. going to do	

Deuxième étape

17 Ecoute! p. 159

1. — Dis, Marc, tu veux aller nager?
   — Désolé, je ne peux pas.

2. — Tu veux bien faire les magasins avec nous, Nathalie?
   — A quelle heure?
   — Vers cinq heures.
   — Pourquoi pas?

3. — On va jouer au foot ce week-end. Tu viens, Malika?
   — Oui, je veux bien.

4. — Stéphane, on va faire un pique-nique. Tu viens?
   — Un pique-nique? Désolé, je suis occupé. J'ai un match de tennis.

5. — Salut, Ferdinand. On va écouter de la musique?
   — Je ne peux pas. J'ai des trucs à faire.
   — Dommage.

6. — Tu veux venir manger un sandwich avec nous, Serge?
   — Oui, je veux bien. A quelle heure?
   — Maintenant.
   — D'accord. J'arrive.

Answers to Activity 17

1. refuse	3. accepte	5. refuse
2. accepte	4. refuse	6. accepte

Troisième étape

24 Ecoute! p. 164

Salut, Paul. C'est moi, Sylvie! Ça va?... Demain, je vais au musée d'Orsay. Tu veux venir avec moi?... Oui, demain... A quelle heure? Bon, vers midi. Tu viens?... Super! Alors, on se retrouve devant le musée... C'est ça. Midi, devant le musée, demain. A demain, Paul...

Answers to Activity 24
1. c   2. a   3. c   4. c

26 Ecoute! p. 164

1. Salut. C'est Laurent. On va au zoo ce week-end avec Nathalie. Est-ce que tu veux venir avec nous? Voilà. On y va samedi après-midi, vers trois heures. On se retrouve devant le zoo à trois heures moins le quart. D'accord? Alors, à demain peut-être.

2. Allô! C'est moi, Patricia. Comment ça va? Je vais au stade dimanche avec Pascal. Tu veux venir avec nous? On va voir un match de foot. On se retrouve à huit heures au métro Saint-Michel. A dimanche. Tchao!

3. Bonjour. Ici Eric. Je vais à la piscine demain matin à dix heures. Est-ce que tu peux venir? Rendez-vous devant la piscine. Au revoir.

Answers to Activity 26
1. Laurent; to the zoo; Saturday afternoon at 2:45; in front of the zoo
2. Patricia; to the stadium; Sunday at 8:00; at the Saint-Michel metro stop
3. Eric; to the swimming pool; tomorrow morning at 10:00; in front of the swimming pool

Prononciation, p. 167

For the scripts for Parts A and B, see p. 167.

C. A écrire

(Dictation)
— Tu veux aller à la Maison des jeunes jeudi?
— A quelle heure?
— Vers neuf heures.
— Désolé, je ne peux pas.

Mise en pratique

2 p. 170

— Tu viens avec moi visiter la Tour Montparnasse? J'ai un bon de réduction. On a une vue magnifique de la terrasse.
— Bof. Je vais avoir le vertige là-haut.
— Tu veux aller au cinéma ou au musée?
— Non, je voudrais aller écouter les grandes orgues de Notre-Dame. C'est tellement beau.
— D'accord. Tu veux y aller quand?
— Dimanche, si tu veux.
— Pourquoi pas? On se retrouve à quelle heure?
— Le concert est à six heures moins le quart. On peut se donner rendez-vous vers cinq heures et demie.
— Où ça?
— Devant la cathédrale.
— OK. Notre-Dame, dimanche, à cinq heures et demie. Bonne idée. Ça coûte cher?
— Mais non, c'est gratuit.
— Génial! C'est vraiment une excellente idée.

Answers to Mise en pratique Activity 2
Notre-Dame; Sunday at 5:30, in front of the cathedral

Chapitre 6 : Amusons-nous!
Projects

Les vacances parfaites
(Individual or Group Project)

ASSIGNMENT

Students will create a poster or brochure of a vacation spot in the francophone world. This can be done in English or French.

SUGGESTED VACATION SPOTS

Any francophone location is appropriate. You might suggest Chamonix (ski resort near the highest peak in the French Alps), Fort-de-France, Tahiti, Paris, Monte-Carlo, Dakar, Abidjan, Quebec, Casablanca, or Brussels.

MATERIALS

✄ **Students may need**

- Atlases
- Magazines
- Catalogues
- Travel information from newspapers, travel guides, or travel agencies
- Encyclopedias
- Other reference books
- Scissors
- Glue or tape
- Colored pens and pencils
- Construction paper or posterboard

You might want to have photos of some of the places suggested above, or suitcases and tourist gear.

PREPARATION

Have students choose a vacation spot that interests them. Then, have them gather information about the place, using atlases, magazines, catalogues, newspaper articles, and travel brochures.

SUGGESTED SEQUENCE

1. Have students make a list of information tourists might need for their particular destination, including attractions, average weather conditions, local customs, currency, and so on. Have them also draw or photocopy illustrations of the chosen destination.

2. Have students organize their materials and notes and begin planning their posters. If the posters are to be in French, students might also look up unfamiliar words they will need.

3. Next, students either show you their organized materials, or have classmates look over their work to check spelling and provide feedback on the appropriateness of the content and arrangement of the layout.

4. Students then finish putting their posters together, adding illustrations, captions, and other written information.

GRADING THE PROJECT

You might want to base students' grades on the appropriateness of the content they provide for their destination, presentation and appearance, correct use of language, and creativity.

Suggested Point Distribution: (total = 100 points)

Content . . . . 30 points
Presentation/appearance . . . . 30 points
Language use (if in French) . . . . 20 points
Creativity . . . . 20 points

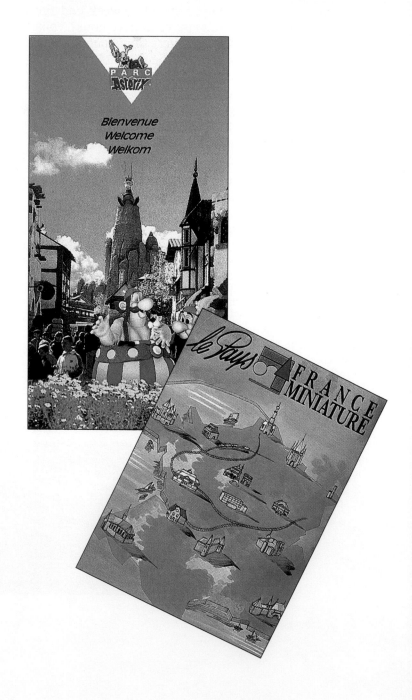

LE MOT JUSTE *(CIRCUMLOCUTION GAME)*

This game will help your students develop the skill of circumlocution, the linguistic art of communicating when a person doesn't know the precise word he or she needs. Explain to students that they will learn to paraphrase, use synonyms, describe essential elements, and apply key phrases to communicate when they find themselves at a loss for the exact word.

Materials   To play this game, you will need index cards.

Preparation   Create a list of words related to the vocabulary presented in the chapter or **étape.** On each card, write one word from the list. Arrange four desks at the front of the room so that the two partners from each team can face each other. Place the cards face down where they can easily be reached by the players from any of the desks. On the board or a transparency, write the following key phrases:

C'est un(e)...
C'est un(e) truc, personne, animal que/qui...
Il/Elle est grand(e)/âgé(e). C'est... rouge/grand.
Ça ressemble à...
C'est le contraire de...
C'est un endroit où...
Il/Elle a...
... est fait(e)(s) en plastique/bois/verre/coton.
On l'utilise pour...

Procedure   Divide the class into two teams and select a scorekeeper and a timekeeper. Have two players from each team sit at the desks. A player from Team A selects a card and shows it to one of the players from Team B. Using circumlocution, the Team A player makes a statement about the vocabulary word without saying the word itself. (For an elephant, one could say **C'est un animal gris.**) If the player's partner guesses the word, Team A receives five points. (Allow 30 seconds per guess.) If not, the Team B player in turn gives a clue to his or her partner. If the partner guesses correctly, Team B receives four points. Play alternates between the two teams, with point value dropping by one after each incorrect guess. If no team scores a point after five clues, any student on Team A may guess to earn one point. If Team A can't guess correctly, a student from Team B is given the same opportunity. Announce the answer if no one guesses correctly. After four words, select four new players for the next round.

AROUND THE WORLD

This is a fast vocabulary review game that is easy to set up and fun to play.

Materials   To play this game, you will need flashcards with pictures of vocabulary items.

Teacher Note   Before the game begins, tell students that after the game, they will have to write down as many vocabulary words as they can remember. You may want to have students clear their desks so they won't be tempted to write down the vocabulary as the game proceeds.

Procedure   Arrange students in rows. The first two students in the first row stand next to each other. These are the two players. Hold up a flashcard so that all students can see it. The first player to identify the picture wins and moves to stand beside the next person in the row. The player who loses sits down. The round continues in this manner until each student has had a chance to play. The winner is the student who has eliminated the most players in the course of the round. Play as many rounds as you like. When the game ends, have students write down as many of the vocabulary words used in the game as they can remember. You might give a prize to the student who recalls the most vocabulary.

Chapitre 6
Amusons-nous!
pp. 148–173

𝒰sing the Chapter Opener

Motivating Activity

After they read the introduction at the top of page 149, ask students to recall what they learned about Paris from the Location Opener on pages 120–123. This would also be a good time to show a travel video or slides of Paris.

Photo Flash!

① The fountain shown in this photo is called *Hommage à Stravinsky* by Niki de Saint-Phalle. It is located near the modern Georges Pompidou Center in Beaubourg. The **centre Pompidou**, officially the **Centre national d'art et de culture Georges Pompidou**, was named after the second president of the Fifth Republic. For more information on the Pompidou Center, see pages 121–122.

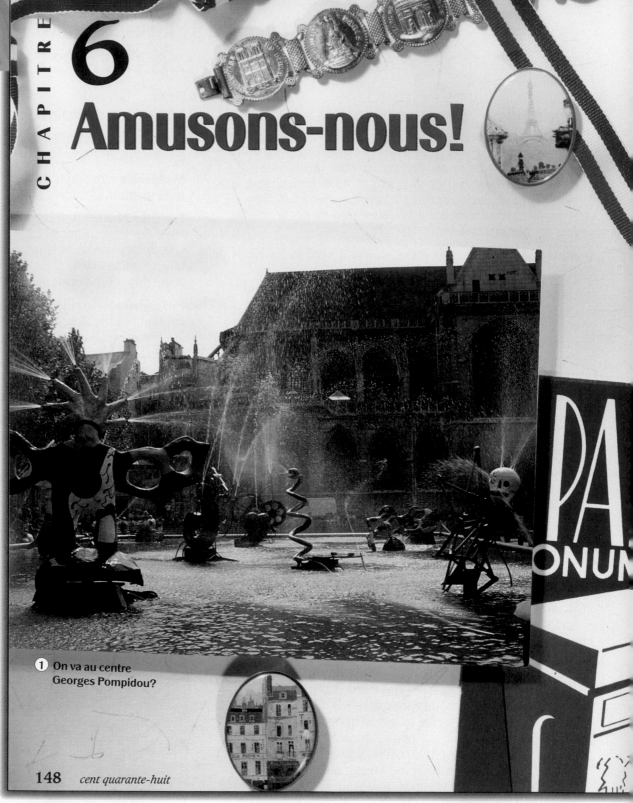

CHAPITRE **6**
Amusons-nous!

① On va au centre Georges Pompidou?

148 *cent quarante-huit*

Culture Note

You might ask students if they can identify the monument pictured in the medallion at the top of this page **(la tour Eiffel)**. Ask them to recall what they learned about it in the Location Opener on pages 121 and 123. When it was built, **la tour Eiffel** was first declared to be a "monstrosity" although later it was considered to be one of the identifying symbols of Paris. The tower was built on the hundred-year anniversary of the storming of the Bastille and was also the centerpiece of the 1889 International Exhibition of Paris. In addition to being a popular tourist attraction, the tower has been used as a radio and meteorological post since World War I, and in 1985, equipment for France's fifth television channel was installed there.

Teenagers everywhere love to go out with their friends. In Paris there are so many events and activities that it is almost impossible to choose. If you were in Paris, what would you want to do?

In this chapter you will learn

- to make plans
- to extend and respond to invitations
- to arrange to meet someone

And you will

- listen to French teenagers talk about where they go to have fun
- read brochures and advertisements
- write about your plans for the weekend
- find out what French-speaking young people do and where they go to have fun

② On se retrouve au métro Palais-Royal?

③ Je voudrais bien aller au cinéma.

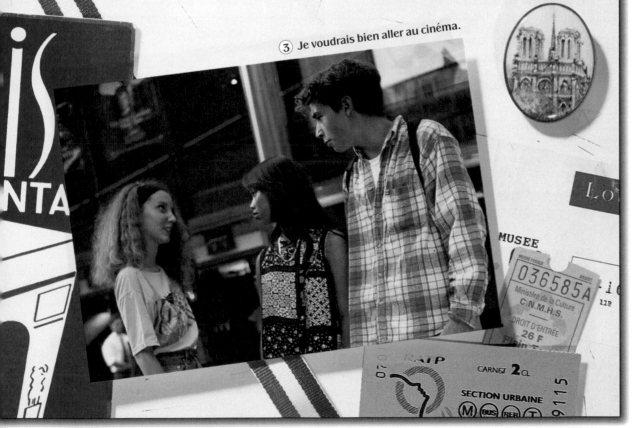

Focusing on Outcomes

Have students look at the chapter outcomes and match them with the three photos. Have them determine which photos show making plans, inviting and responding to invitations, and arranging to meet someone.
NOTE: You may want to use the video to support the objectives. The self-check activities in **Que sais-je?** on page 172 help students assess their achievement of the objectives.

Photo Flash!

② The **Palais-Royal** was built as a royal residence for Cardinal Richelieu by Lemercier in the seventeenth century. Although most of the building was destroyed in 1871, it was rebuilt in the latter part of the nineteenth century and now houses the **Conseil d'Etat,** the supreme administrative court. The **métro** station in the photo is in the Art Nouveau style of the late nineteenth and the early twentieth century, which is characterized by curvilinear designs and organic forms.

Block Scheduling

For suggestions about how to use *Allez, viens!* with block scheduling, see the *Lesson Planner,* pages 28–32.

Culture Notes

• You might call students' attention to the metro ticket at the bottom of this page. Remind students that **RATP** stands for **Régie autonome des transports parisiens.**
• You might ask students to identify the cathedral (**Notre-Dame**) pictured in the medallion to the right of the third photo.

Ask them to recall what they learned about **Notre-Dame** from the Location Opener on page 122. You might also tell them that during the French Revolution, the cathedral was converted from a Catholic place of worship into a **Temple de la raison,** the name given to all churches under the new state religion.

VIDEO PROGRAM
Videocassette 2
36:27–39:37
Videocassette 5
(captioned version)
48:20–51:29

OR VIDEODISC PROGRAM,
Videodisc 3, Side B

Search 1, Play To 5705

Video Synopsis

In this segment of the video, Mathieu asks Isabelle what she is going to do tomorrow. She tells him about her plans for the day and says she is free in the evening. Mathieu asks her if she would like to go to a concert, but she is not interested. Mathieu suggests they go to the zoo, but Isabelle doesn't like zoos. They each make several more suggestions but cannot agree on any of them. During their conversation, we see scenes of their suggested activities. They finally agree to go to the movies, but then can't agree on what film to see!

Motivating Activity

Show *Map Transparency 5* (**Paris**). Call on students to point out the places mentioned in the **Mise en train.** Point out other major places of interest. Ask students which of the places they would like to visit and have them explain why.

Culture Note

The Louvre was first used as a defensive structure in 1204 by Philippe II Auguste. Over the years, it has served as a royal residence to several kings, notably Francis I. Now one of the largest museums in the world, the Louvre welcomes visitors through its newly renovated main entrance under the huge glass pyramid designed by I. M. Pei.

The **roman-photo** is an abridged version of the video episode.

Mise en train

Projets de week-end   p. 61, Acts. 1–2

CD 6
Trs. 1–2

What do you think Mathieu and Isabelle are talking about? Why do you think so?

Vendredi après-midi...

1 Salut, Isabelle. Dis, qu'est-ce que tu vas faire demain?

Oh, pas grand-chose. Le matin, je vais aller à mon cours de danse. L'après-midi, je vais faire les magasins. Mais le soir, je suis libre.

2 Il y a un concert super à Bercy : Patrick Bruel. J'aimerais bien y aller. Tu veux venir avec moi?

Oh non, je n'ai pas envie d'aller à un concert.

Ah, dommage...

3 Et dimanche après-midi, tu es libre?

Dimanche? Oui, je n'ai rien de prévu.

Tu veux aller au zoo?

Ah, non, je déteste les zoos.

4 Alors, allons au Louvre!

Non, je n'aime pas trop les musées.

150   *cent cinquante*   CHAPITRE 6   Amusons-nous!

RESOURCES FOR MISE EN TRAIN

PRINT
- *Practice and Activity Book*, p. 61
- *Video Guide*, pp. 39–40, 42
- *Videodisc Guide*, pp. 63–66, 70

MEDIA
- *Video Program*, Videocassette 2, Videocassette 5 (captioned version)
- *Videodisc Program*, Videodisc 3, Side B
- *Audio Compact Discs*, CD 6, Trs. 1–2

5 Qu'est-ce que tu veux faire, alors?

6 S'il fait beau, on peut faire une promenade au palais de Chaillot. On peut même monter au sommet de la tour Eiffel.

Bof.

7 J'ai une idée! Tu ne veux pas aller faire un tour dans un bateau-mouche?

Ça, non. C'est pas terrible.

8 On va au Sacré-Cœur?

Non, j'ai pas envie.

On peut tout simplement aller au cinéma. Tu veux?

9 D'accord. Je veux bien. Qu'est-ce que tu veux voir comme film?

Moi, je propose *Dracula*. Ça passe à 16h40 et à 18h55.

10 Oh non, je n'aime pas les films d'horreur. Je préfère aller voir un film comique.

Oh non! Encore un film comique?! Tu sais, c'est bizarre. On n'est jamais d'accord!

MISE EN TRAIN   *cent cinquante et un* **151**

Presentation

Before viewing the video, have students look at the title and pictures and guess what Mathieu and Isabelle are talking about. Play the video and ask students to listen for what the two friends will do on Saturday, what Mathieu suggests for Sunday, and what, if anything, the two friends finally decide to do.

Culture Notes

• To verify movie listings, Mathieu and Isabelle consult *Pariscope,* a weekly entertainment guide that lists movies, shows, and exhibits in Paris. Other major cities have similar publications available.

• The **palais de Chaillot** was built in 1937 on the site of the old **palais du Trocadéro.** Its two curving wings house five different museums: the **musée de la Marine,** the **musée de l'Homme,** the **musée des Monuments français,** the **Cinémathèque française,** and the **musée du Cinéma.** Its beautifully terraced gardens and fountains lead down to the Seine River.

• The huge Romanesque-Byzantine church **Sacré-Cœur** offers a breathtaking view of Paris. It was built after France was defeated in the Franco-Prussian War of 1870-1871. Its belltower houses the **Savoyarde,** a bell weighing over 18,000 kilos.

 Video Integration

• *VIDEO PROGRAM,*
Videocassette 2, 39:38–44:08
Videocassette 5, 51:30–55:59

• *VIDEODISC PROGRAM,*
Videodisc 3, Side B

Search 5705, Play To 13810

You may choose to continue with **Projets de week-end (suite)** at this time or wait until later in the chapter. When the story continues, Mathieu and Isabelle agree on a film. Mathieu and Isabelle invite Simon to join them, but he is too busy with schoolwork. Mathieu and Isabelle then meet Thuy, who is interested in going to the movies but wants to see a different film. Mathieu checks the times in his *Pariscope.* They all meet in front of the theater, but the movie is not playing. Mathieu discovers that he has last week's *Pariscope!*

For Individual Needs

1 **Slower Pace** If students have difficulty with this activity, you might indicate the photos where the answers can be found. (1. Photo 1; 2. Photo 1; 3. Photos 2, 3, 4, and 9; 4. Photos 6, 7, 8, and 10; 5. Photos 9 and 10).

Teaching Suggestion

2 If the sentence is true, have students find the text that verifies it.

For Individual Needs

3 **Slower Pace** Play the video of the **Mise en train**. Ask students to watch and listen carefully for any mention of places to go or things to do. Compile a list on the board and then have pairs or small groups do the activity.

For videodisc application, see *Videodisc Guide.*

Teaching Suggestions

5 You might want to review expressions for making excuses in Chapter 5. (See page 129.)

6 Students might refer to the activities in Activity 4, or they might reread the story.

These activities check for comprehension only. Students should not yet be expected to produce language modeled in **Mise en train**.

1 Tu as compris?

Answer the following questions according to **Projets de week-end.** Don't be afraid to guess. See answers below.

1. What are Isabelle's plans for tomorrow?
2. What day and time of day is it?
3. Can you name three places where Mathieu suggests they go?
4. Can you name three things that Isabelle prefers to do?
5. What do they finally agree to do? What problem remains?

2 Vrai ou faux?

1. Isabelle aime aller au zoo. faux
2. Isabelle a un cours de danse. vrai
3. Mathieu aime la musique de Patrick Bruel. vrai
4. Isabelle aime bien les musées. faux
5. Isabelle veut voir un film d'horreur dimanche après-midi. faux

3 Mets en ordre

Mets les phrases en ordre d'après **Projets de week-end.**

1. Isabelle propose d'aller au palais de Chaillot. 3
2. Mathieu propose d'aller au zoo. 2
3. Isabelle propose d'aller au Sacré-Cœur. 5
4. Mathieu ne veut pas faire de promenade. 4
5. Isabelle refuse d'aller au concert. 1
6. Isabelle accepte d'aller au cinéma. 6

4 Où est-ce qu'on veut aller?

Choisis les activités qu'Isabelle veut faire et les activités que Mathieu préfère. See answers below.

> aller voir un film comique
> aller à un concert aller voir un film d'horreur faire une promenade au palais de Chaillot
> aller au musée
> aller au zoo faire un tour en bateau aller au Sacré-Cœur

5 Invitations et refus

Match Mathieu's suggestions for weekend activities with Isabelle's refusals.

Tu veux...

1. aller au concert de Patrick Bruel? d
2. aller au Louvre? c
3. aller au zoo? a
4. aller voir *Dracula*? b

Désolée, mais...

a. je déteste les zoos.
b. je préfère aller voir un film comique.
c. je n'aime pas trop les musées.
d. je n'ai pas envie.

6 Et maintenant, à toi

How would you react to Mathieu and Isabelle's suggestions for the weekend? Which would you choose to do? Why? Compare your answers with a partner's.

152 *cent cinquante-deux*　　　　　CHAPITRE 6　　Amusons-nous!

Answers

1 1. A.M. dance class, P.M. shopping, free evening
2. Friday afternoon
3. concert, zoo, museum, movies
4. take a walk at the palais de Chaillot, go to the top of the Eiffel Tower, take a boat ride, go to Sacré-Cœur
5. Isabelle and Mathieu decide to go to a movie, but they cannot agree on which one to see.

4 *Isabelle:* aller voir un film comique, faire une promenade au palais de Chaillot, faire un tour en bateau, aller au Sacré-Cœur
Mathieu: aller à un concert, aller au zoo, aller voir un film d'horreur, aller au musée

PREMIERE ETAPE TPR
Storytelling **B**ook
pp. 21, 24

Making plans

COMMENT DIT-ON... ?
Making plans

6-1

To ask what a friend's planning to do:
Qu'est-ce que tu vas faire demain? *What are you going to do . . . ?*
Tu vas faire quoi ce week-end? *What are you going to do . . . ?*

To tell what you're going to do:
Vendredi, **je vais** faire du vélo.
Samedi après-midi, **je vais** aller au café. ⎫ *I'm going to . . .*
Dimanche, **je vais** regarder la télé. ⎭
Pas grand-chose. *Not much.*
Rien de spécial. *Nothing special.*

 7 **Ecoute!** See scripts and answers on p. 147G.

 Listen as Sophie asks Thérèse about her plans for the weekend. Write down at least three things Thérèse plans to do.

CD 6 Tr. 3

8 **Qu'est-ce que tu vas faire?**

GV

a. Write down three activities you have planned for the weekend.

p. 42, Acts. 3–4   Additional Grammar Practice, p. R38

 b. Now, tell your partner what you plan to do and ask about his or her plans.

Je vais voir un film. Et toi, qu'est-ce que tu vas faire?

NOTE DE GRAMMAIRE

If you want to say that you do an activity regularly on a certain day of the week, use the article **le** before the day of the week.

Je fais du patin à glace **le mercredi** *(on Wednesdays)*.

To say that you are doing something only on one particular day, use the day of the week without an article before it.

Je vais faire du patin à glace **mercredi** *(on Wednesday)*.

VOCABULAIRE

6-A   GV

p. 41, Acts. 1–2

regarder un match	*to watch a game (on TV)*
manger quelque chose	*to eat something*
voir un film	*to see a movie*
aller voir un match	*to go see a game*
voir une pièce	*to see a play*
faire une promenade	*to go for a walk*
faire les vitrines	*to window-shop*
faire un pique-nique	*to have a picnic*
aller à une boum	*to go to a party*

PREMIERE ETAPE   *cent cinquante-trois* **153**

RESOURCES FOR **PREMIERE ETAPE**	
PRINT	**MEDIA**
• *Lesson Planner,* p. 29	• *Video Program,* Videocassette 2
• *Practice and Activity Book,* pp. 62–64	*Video Guide,* pp. 39–44
• *Grammar and Vocabulary Workbook,* pp. 41–45	• *Videodisc Program,* Videodisc 3, Side B
	Videodisc Guide, p. 67
• *Activities for Communication,* pp. 31–32, 100, 103–104, 147–148	• *Teaching Transparencies* 6-1, 6-A, 6-B
	• *Interactive CD-ROM Program,* Disc 2
• *Listening Activities,* pp. 43, 47	*CD-ROM Teacher's Guide,* p. 24
• *Testing Program,* pp. 131–134	• *Audio Compact Discs*
• *Alternative Assessment Guide,* p. 37	Textbook Listening Activities, CD 6, Trs. 3–4
	Additional Listening Activities 6-1, 6-2, CD 6, Trs. 31–32
	Quiz 6-1B, CD 6, Tr. 19

---

*J*ump Start!

Have students suggest the following activities in writing: **faire une vidéo, nager, jouer au basket.**

MOTIVATE

Ask students to write down two or three things they are going to do this weekend.

TEACH

Presentation

Comment dit-on... ? Tell students what you're going to do next weekend, using expressions from the **Vocabulaire** in Chapters 1 and 4. (**Dimanche, je vais faire du ski.**) Then, ask students about their weekends, real or imaginary. (**Qu'est-ce que tu vas faire samedi?**) Have partners practice asking and telling each other about their plans.

Note de grammaire Ask individual students questions, such as **Tu fais tes devoirs le samedi? Qu'est-ce que tu fais le mardi à 10h?**

Vocabulaire Hold up pictures of the various activities as you say the French expressions and have students repeat after you. Then, say what you're going to do this weekend (**Je vais voir une pièce.**) and ask volunteers to tape the appropriate picture to the board.

 For videodisc application, see *Videodisc Guide.*

Language Note

Vocabulaire You might remind students that **faire** is used with a variety of idiomatic expressions and does not always mean *to make* or *to do*.

Presentation

Grammaire After introducing **aller**, explain that it is also used with an infinitive to express the immediate future. Mention a certain day or time of day (**mercredi à 6h**), and tell students what you're going to do then. (**Je vais voir un film.**) Then, give a certain day and time and have students tell what they are going to do. To practice the third-person forms, ask students to tell about their classmates' plans. (**Qu'est-ce que José va faire mercredi à 6h?**)

Teaching Suggestion

Grammaire On the board or on a transparency, draw three columns. Write the six subject pronouns in the first column, the infinitive **aller** at the top of the second, and activities students suggest in the third. Ask students to write as many sentences as possible in five minutes, using the items in these three columns. You might also have them make a few of the sentences negative. For example, for **ils/aller/regarder un match,** students would write **Ils ne vont pas regarder un match.** Have them exchange and correct papers.

For Individual Needs

9 Slower Pace Before they do this activity, ask students for examples of sentences in the present (**Ils jouent au foot.**) and the immediate future. (**Ils vont jouer au foot.**)

---

p. 63, Act. 7

p. 43, Acts. 5–6

Additional Grammar Practice, p. R38

GRAMMAIRE The verb **aller**

Aller is an irregular verb.

aller *(to go)*

Je **vais**	Nous **allons**
Tu **vas** ⎬ au café.	Vous **allez** ⎬ au café.
Il/Elle/On **va**	Ils/Elles **vont**

- You can use a form of the verb **aller** with the infinitive of another verb to say that you're *going to do something* in the future.

  Je vais jouer au base-ball demain.

- To say that you're *not going to do something* in the near future, put **ne... pas** around the conjugated form of the verb **aller**.

  Je *ne* vais *pas* jouer au base-ball demain.

---

9 Ecoute!   See scripts and answers on p. 147G.

CD 6 Tr. 4

Listen to the following sentences and decide whether the people are talking about what they're doing or what they're going to do.

10 Qu'est-ce que tu vas faire?

You have a busy weekend planned! Tell what you're going to do and on what day you plan to do it.   Answers may vary. Possible answers:

1.   Je vais voir un match dimanche.

2.   Je vais voir un film vendredi.

3.   Je vais faire un pique-nique dimanche.

4.   Je vais aller à une boum vendredi.

5.   Je vais faire les vitrines vendredi.

6.   Je vais manger quelque chose samedi.

154   *cent cinquante-quatre*   CHAPITRE 6   Amusons-nous!

Game

TROP A FAIRE Begin the game by telling what you're going to do tomorrow. (**Je vais jouer au volley-ball.**) Then, have a student repeat what you're going to do and add what he or she is planning to do. (**Julie va jouer au volley-ball, et je vais étudier.**) Each student continues by repeating all the previous activities and adding another. If someone makes a mistake, the next student starts a new sequence with an activity he or she is going to do.

Language Note

You might remind students that the *infinitive* is the *to* form of a verb.

11 Qu'est-ce qu'ils vont faire?

What are these people going to do?

1. Elles Elles vont faire les vitrines.

2. Ils Ils vont manger/aller au café.

3. Je Je vais jouer au football.

4. Nous Nous allons faire un pique-nique.

5. Vous Vous allez voir un film.

6. Elle Elle va faire une promenade.

À la française

The French often use the present tense of a verb to say that something will happen in the near future, just as we do in English.

Samedi matin, je vais jouer au tennis. *Saturday morning, I'm going to play tennis.*

Samedi matin, je joue au tennis. *Saturday morning, I'm playing tennis.*

12 Enquête

Ask the members of your group what they're going to do this weekend and tell them what you're planning. Then, tell the class what you're all planning to do.

—Qu'est-ce que tu fais ce week-end, Nicole?
—Samedi après-midi, je fais du ski nautique. Et toi?
—Moi, je vais à une boum.
  (to the class)
—Je vais à une boum et Nicole fait du ski nautique samedi après-midi.

For Individual Needs

11 Slower Pace As you tell in French what the people in the photos are going to do, have students write down the numbers of the photos you describe. Then, have students pair off and take turns telling each other what the people in the photos are going to do.

Kinesthetic Learners Have small groups of students play "Charades." One member of the group acts out an activity he or she plans to do, and the other students try to guess the activity the person is miming. The first student to say what the person is going to do (**Tu vas faire du jogging.**) chooses who will take the next turn.

12 Challenge Have two groups compare their activities and summarize the results. (**Maria, Pam et Damon font du ski nautique samedi, mais Tori joue au tennis.**)

Teacher Note

You might make the following suggestions to students.

• Encourage students to visualize new vocabulary as they study it. To learn the word **la bibliothèque**, for example, they might visualize their local library as they say the French word aloud.

• You might suggest that students create memory devices to learn new material. For example, students might use the first letters (BCCMMPP) of a list of new words (**bibliothèque, centre commercial, cinéma, Maison des jeunes, musée, parc, piscine**) to make a sentence. (Bruno Couldn't Cook Mom's Meat Pizza Precisely.)

PA pp. 63–64, Acts. 6, 8   6-B   **GV** pp. 44–45, Acts. 7–9

CD-ROM
Disc 2

Presentation

Vocabulaire After introducing the **Vocabulaire**, hold up illustrations (a zebra, a movie star) or props (sunglasses, a shopping bag) to suggest the places, asking **On va où?** Ask students to name local examples of these places. Then, name these local places, and have students call out the French term for the place (for example, *Huntington Beach* —**une plage**; *the Galleria*—**un centre commercial**). Another place students might want to go is *downtown*—**au centre-ville.**

(TPR) Tell students to go to a place (**Va à la plage!**) and have them mime what they would do there. As a variation, you might whisper the place to a student and have the class try to guess where that student is going as he or she mimes a related activity.

Teaching Suggestion

13 Ask students to suggest other possible completions for these sentences. You might also ask them to prepare similar sentence starters for other locations to be used as a quiz for their classmates.

Vocabulaire

Where do you and your friends like to go in your spare time?

au restaurant

au cinéma

au parc

au stade

au zoo

au centre commercial

à la plage

à la piscine

au musée

à la Maison des jeunes

au théâtre

à la bibliothèque

13 Où vas-tu?

Où est-ce que tu vas pour faire ces activités?

1. Je vais faire de la natation... d
2. Je vais faire les vitrines... c
3. Je vais voir un film... a
4. Je vais manger quelque chose... e
5. Je vais voir un match... f
6. Je vais voir une pièce... b

    a. au cinéma.
    b. au théâtre.
    c. au centre commercial.
    d. à la piscine.
    e. au café.
    f. au stade.

156 *cent cinquante-six*   CHAPITRE 6   Amusons-nous!

Game

CONCENTRATION® For each vocabulary word or expression, make two cards. On one card, write the phrase in French (**au théâtre**). On the other, draw a picture or tape a magazine picture of the item. Number the back of each card and tape them to the board with the numbers visible. Divide the class into two teams. Have the first player from the first team call out two numbers. Turn over the corresponding cards. If the cards match, the player keeps them and takes another turn. If not, the turn passes to the other team.

GRAMMAIRE Contractions with à

GV

p. 45,
Acts. 10–11

Additional Grammar
Practice, p. R38

The preposition **à** usually means *to* or *at*.
When you use **à** before **le** or **les**, make the following contractions:

à + le = au	Je vais **au** stade.
à + les = aux	Martine va aller **aux** Tuileries.

The preposition **à** doesn't contract with **l'** or **la**:

Cet après-midi, on ne va pas **à la** Maison des jeunes. On va **à l'**école.

14 Projets de week-end

Christine and Alain are talking about where they like to go on weekends. Complete their conversation according to the pictures.

CHRISTINE Moi, j'adore aller avec mes copains. Après, on va

souvent . Et toi?
au café

au cinéma

ALAIN Moi, j'aime mieux aller . J'adore le sport. J'aime bien
au stade

aller aussi. On y joue souvent au foot.
au parc

CHRISTINE Qu'est-ce que tu vas faire ce week-end? On va _____ ? à la piscine/à
la plage

ALAIN Ah, non, je n'aime pas trop nager. Tu veux aller _____ ? au zoo

15 Qu'est-ce qu'on fait?

You're trying to decide what to do after school. With a partner, take turns suggesting places to go. Then, accept or reject each other's suggestions.

> le café   le musée   la piscine   le parc
>
> la piscine   la Maison des jeunes   le zoo
>
> la bibliothèque   le centre commercial

16 Mon journal

Tu as des projets pour le week-end? Qu'est-ce que tu vas faire? Où vas-tu? Quand?

Vendredi après-midi, je vais faire mes devoirs. Samedi, je...

Performance Assessment

Have students write a letter to a French pen pal who is coming for a visit. Have them suggest what to do during the pen pal's stay, using **on**.

📁 Portfolio

16 Written This activity is appropriate for students' written portfolios. Students might draw and label a calendar of their plans to accompany the entry. For portfolio information, see the *Alternative Assessment Guide*, pages iv–17.

Presentation

Grammaire Draw two columns on the board. One should be labeled *masculine* and the other *feminine*. Have students look at the **Vocabulaire** on page 156 and ask volunteers to come to the board and write each word, including its definite article, in the appropriate column according to the gender of the word. Then, have other volunteers come to the board and write whether they would use **au** or **à la** with each of the words listed. Ask students to try to deduce when to use **au** and **à la**. Then, read the **Grammaire** and point out that while **à** never combines with **l'**, it always contracts with **les** to form **aux**, regardless of the gender of the word.

◆ For Individual Needs

14 Challenge Have partners rewrite the conversation to reflect their own interests. They could then include this in their written portfolios. Students could also rewrite their conversations on posterboard, inserting pictures of the places they like to go.

CLOSE

To close this **étape**, use *Teaching Transparencies 6-A and 6-B* to practice vocabulary. You might say that you're going to do various activities (**Je vais lire un livre.**) and have students tell where in town you're going. (**Vous allez à la bibliothèque municipale.**)

ASSESS

Quiz 6-1 A, Quiz 6-1 B, *Testing Program,* pp. 131–134
Audio CD 6, Tr. 19

VIDEO PROGRAM
Videocassette 2
44:09–47:10

OR VIDEODISC PROGRAM,
Videodisc 3, Side B

Search 13810, Play To 16015

Teacher Notes

• See the *Video Guide,* the *Videodisc Guide,* and the *CD-ROM Teacher's Guide* for activities related to the **Panorama Culturel.**

• Remind students that cultural material may be included in the Chapter Quizzes and Test.

• The interviewees' language represents informal, unrehearsed speech. Occasionally, edits have been made for clarification.

Motivating Activity

Ask students what they do when they go out with friends.

Presentation

Have students view the video and write down the activities that the interviewees mention. To check comprehension, you might ask yes-no questions, such as **Arnaud achète des disques?** as well as the **Questions** below.

Teaching Suggestion

Hold up magazine illustrations of the activities and ask **Qui fait ça?**

PANORAMA CULTUREL

Julie • Côte d'Ivoire

Arnaud • France

Céline • Viêt-nam

CD 6
Trs. 5–8

CD-ROM
Disc 2

When you go out with your friends, where do you go? What do you do? We asked some French-speaking students what they like to do on weekends with their friends. Here's what they said.

Qu'est-ce que tu fais quand tu sors?

«Quand je sors, je me balade. Je vais manger un peu. Souvent, on va jouer de la musique. On joue au tennis... souvent, au basket aussi.»

—Julie
Tr. 6

«Je vais au cinéma. Je vais dans une discothèque. J'achète des disques.»

—Arnaud
Tr. 7

«Je vais à la patinoire, ou [je vais] faire les boutiques, ou [je vais] au restaurant, enfin dans les fast-foods, ou alors je vais faire du sport, du tennis. Je vais nager.»

—Céline
Tr. 8

Qu'en penses-tu?

1. Do you and your friends like to do any of the things these teenagers mentioned?
2. Do they mention anything that you wouldn't do? Why wouldn't you do these things?
3. What do you and your friends like to do that these teenagers haven't mentioned?

Savais-tu que...?

Teenagers around the world generally like to do the same things. They usually have favorite places where they go to meet with their friends, just as you do. In most towns, students can find films, plays, concerts, and **discothèques** to go to in their free time. Dance parties (**boums**) are very popular. Most cities in France also have a **Maison des jeunes et de la culture (la MJC)** where a variety of activities, such as photography, music, dance, drama, arts and crafts, and computer science, is available to young people.

Culture Notes

• Many French movie theaters and museums have student rates (**tarif réduit**) that are usually available to young tourists with student ID cards or proof of age.

• In Paris, most **métro** trains begin their final runs between midnight and 1:00 A.M. Thus, parties or evenings out usually end in time for everyone to get to the closest subway station in time for the last train.

Questions

1. **Julie fait quels sports? (Elle joue au tennis, au basket.)**
2. **Arnaud va où quand il sort? (au cinéma, dans une discothèque)**
3. **Où est-ce que Céline va quand elle sort? (à la patinoire, dans les restaurants, dans les fast-foods)**
4. **Qu'est-ce qu'elle fait comme sport? (Elle fait du tennis; elle nage.)**

DEUXIEME ETAPE TPR

Storytelling Book pp. 22, 24

Extending and responding to invitations

COMMENT DIT-ON... ?
Extending and responding to invitations

pp. 65–66, Acts. 11–14

6-2

To extend an invitation:
Allons au parc! *Let's go . . . !*
Tu veux aller au café **avec moi?** *Do you want to . . . with me?*
Je voudrais aller faire du vélo. **Tu viens?** *Will you come?*
On peut faire du ski. *We can . . .*

To accept an invitation:
D'accord.
Bonne idée.
Je veux bien. *I'd really like to.*
Pourquoi pas? *Why not?*

To refuse an invitation:
Ça ne me dit rien.
J'ai des trucs à faire.
Désolé(e), je ne peux pas.
Désolé(e), je suis occupé(e).
Sorry, I'm busy.

17 Ecoute!
See scripts and answers on p. 147G.

Ecoute ces dialogues. Est-ce qu'on accepte ou refuse l'invitation?

CD 6 Tr. 9

Les loisirs préférés	15-25 ans
Cinéma	90
Discothèque	69
Fête foraine	58
Concert de rock	42
Parc d'attractions	37
Match (payant)	36
Monument historique	31
Bal public	30
Musée	27
Théâtre	17
Concert de jazz	11
Cirque	10
Concert classique	6
Spectacle de danse	5
Opéra	3

DEUXIEME ETAPE

cent cinquante-neuf **159**

Jump Start!
Have students write their plans for next weekend.

MOTIVATE
Ask students what they say in English to invite their friends to do things. Ask them if they've ever made polite excuses to decline an invitation. What did they say?

TEACH

Presentation
Comment dit-on... ? Have students tell which animal in the cartoon is extending an invitation, which one is refusing, and which one is accepting. Ask students for expressions they've already learned for inviting someone and for accepting and refusing an invitation (see Chapter 5). Then, present the new expressions with gestures and have students tell whether you are extending, accepting, or refusing an invitation.

Additional Practice
Have two students stand up. Call out an expression from **Comment dit-on... ?** The first student to identify it correctly as an invitation, an acceptance, or a refusal remains standing, while the other sits down, and the next student stands up. Continue until all students have had a chance to respond.

For videodisc application, see *Videodisc Guide.*

For Individual Needs

17 Challenge Have students write down the suggested activity as well as the type of response.

Additional Practice

18 Ask students to suggest different ways to make the same invitations. This could be done orally or as a written assignment.

For Individual Needs

19 Slower Pace First, have students identify the activities shown. Then, ask them to suggest other places or activities that could be used in refusing the invitations.

Presentation

Grammaire Ask students **Qu'est-ce que tu veux faire après l'école?** Then, as students give different answers (**écouter de la musique, faire les magasins, jouer au tennis**), write them on the board or on a transparency. Next, have partners ask each other whether they want to do those activities. (**Tu veux... ?**) Finally, ask students when they might use **Je voudrais** (when asking for something in a store or restaurant, when asking permission to do something).

For Individual Needs

Kinesthetic Learners Toss a ball to a student as you call out a subject pronoun (**il, singulier**). The student catches the ball, calls out the corresponding verb form of **vouloir** (**veut**), and tosses the ball to a classmate, calling out a different subject pronoun. This game, **"Jeter et Attraper,"** is described in more detail on page 123J.

---

18 Et toi? Tu veux?

Choisis la bonne réponse.

1. J'ai faim. d
2. Je voudrais faire un pique-nique. a
3. Tu ne viens pas? b
4. Je voudrais voir un match de foot. e
5. Tu veux voir une pièce? c

a. Allons au parc!
b. J'ai des trucs à faire.
c. Pourquoi pas? Allons au théâtre!
d. Tu veux aller au café?
e. Allons au stade!

19 Tu acceptes?

Your partner will invite you to participate in some of the following activities. Accept or refuse, telling where you're going or what you're going to do instead. Exchange roles.
Possible answers:

1. On peut regarder la télévision.

2. Tu veux faire les vitrines?

3. Allons danser!

4. Tu veux jouer au tennis?

5. Je vais voir un film. Tu viens?

6. Tu veux aller à la piscine?

GRAMMAIRE   The verb **vouloir**

Vouloir is an irregular verb.

vouloir *(to want)*

Je **veux**	Nous **voulons**
Tu **veux** } aller au café.	Vous **voulez** } aller au café.
Il/Elle/On **veut**	Ils/Elles **veulent**

Je voudrais *(I would like)* is a more polite form of **je veux**.

PA
pp. 66–67,
Acts. 15–16

GV
p. 46,
Acts. 12–13

Additional Grammar Practice, p. R39

Language Note

Grammaire You might point out that all of the singular forms of **vouloir** are pronounced the same, and that the "boot" forms (**je, tu, il/elle,** and **ils/elles**) all contain **eu**.

20 Qu'est-ce qu'on veut faire ce soir? See answers below.

1. Pierre et Marc

2. Alain

3. Moi, je...

4. Elodie et Guy

5. Mes copains et moi, nous...

6. David et Monique

21 Invitations pour le week-end

You're making plans for the upcoming weekend. Take turns with a partner suggesting activities and accepting or politely refusing the suggestions.

23 A la boum!

The French Club is having a party. Invite three students. Before they accept or refuse your invitation, they want to know what you're planning to do. Tell them about the activities you're planning. Your friends will either accept or refuse.

- écouter de la musique québécoise
- danser
- voir un film français
- parler français avec des copains
- manger des escargots

22 Vous voulez faire quoi?

You and your friends can't decide what to do this weekend. Each of you makes a suggestion, and the others react to it. See if you can find three things you'd all like to do.

—Vous voulez faire du vélo?
—Oui, je veux bien.
—Moi, je ne veux pas. Je n'aime pas faire du vélo.

L'ambiance sera extra!

Le Cercle Français
t'invite
à une fête
le 10 mai
de 7h à 10h

Si tu viens, ce sera plus sympa!

DEUXIEME ETAPE

cent soixante et un **161**

DEUXIEME ETAPE
CHAPITRE 6

Teaching Suggestions

21 Students might use the activities in the **Vocabulaire** on page 153.

23 • Have students also decide upon a time and place for the party, and then create a colorful invitation to pass out to guests. They might include illustrations or a list of the activities offered to encourage people to come.
• Show *Teaching Transparency 6-2* and assign each person in the illustration to a student or group of students. Provide them with a strip of transparency and a pen and have them create a speech bubble for that person.

Teacher Note

23 Remind students to use **nous** or **on** as the subject of **aller** in their suggestions.

CLOSE

To close this **étape,** have students pair off. Provide one student in each pair with a vocabulary card picturing a place in town (**le musée**) or a sports activity (**jouer au tennis**). Give the other student a card with *accept* or *refuse* written on it. Have students act out a dialogue according to their cards.

ASSESS

Quiz 6-2A, Quiz 6-2B, *Testing Program,* pp. 135–138
Audio CD 6, Tr. 20

Performance Assessment

Have students act out their dialogues from Activity 21.

Answers
20 1. Ils veulent aller au zoo.
2. Il veut aller à la Maison des jeunes.
3. Moi, je veux aller au restaurant.
4. Ils veulent faire du vélo.
5. Nous voulons aller au théâtre.
6. Ils veulent aller au musée.

Motivating Activity

Ask students how they would describe a typical American date to someone from France or another francophone country. They might include who goes out, where they might go, and who pays.

Presentation

Give each photo a number. Then, have students, individually or in pairs, write at least three phrases or sentences in English describing each photo. They might want to tell what the people are doing or wearing, where they are, and any other details they notice. Collect students' papers and read aloud one or two sentences from each. Ask students to identify the photo you are describing by saying **un, deux,** or **trois.**

Teaching Suggestions

• You might have students form small groups to discuss the questions in **Qu'en penses-tu?** Have the group choose a reporter to tell the class their answers.

• Tell students that their French pen pal has asked some questions about going out in the United States. Ask them what they would take pictures of (a movie theater, the mall, their favorite restaurant) to make an informative photo-collage about going out in their town, similar to the one on this page.

Teacher Note

You may want to refer to the list of professional resources on page T54 for a list of publications that students may want to read to learn more about the habits of francophone teenagers. Visit the HRW Web site at **http://www.hrw.com** for online resources and additional information.

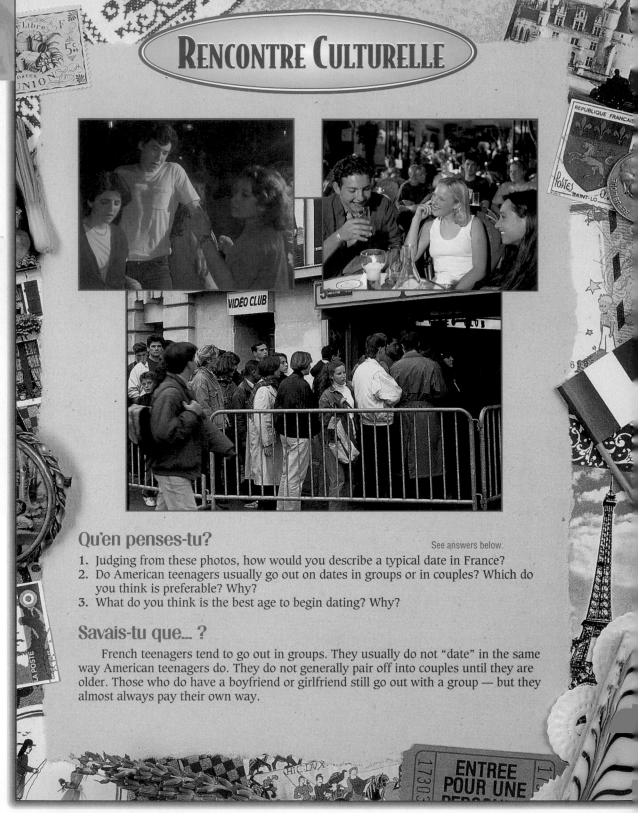

RENCONTRE CULTURELLE

Qu'en penses-tu?

See answers below.

1. Judging from these photos, how would you describe a typical date in France?
2. Do American teenagers usually go out on dates in groups or in couples? Which do you think is preferable? Why?
3. What do you think is the best age to begin dating? Why?

Savais-tu que... ?

French teenagers tend to go out in groups. They usually do not "date" in the same way American teenagers do. They do not generally pair off into couples until they are older. Those who do have a boyfriend or girlfriend still go out with a group — but they almost always pay their own way.

Multicultural Link

Have students research dating habits and customs in other countries. They might interview exchange students or community members with different cultural backgrounds to find out the normal age to begin dating, popular places to go on dates, and who pays.

Answers

1. French teenagers go out in groups rather than in couples.

COMMENT DIT-ON... ?
Arranging to meet someone

 pp. 68–69, Acts. 19–20   6-3   pp. 47–48, Acts. 14–17

To ask when:	To tell when:
Quand?	**Lundi./Demain matin./Ce week-end.**
Quand ça?	**Tout de suite.** *Right away.*

To ask where:	To tell where:
Où?	**Au café.** *At the . . .*
	Devant le cinéma. *In front of . . .*
Où ça?	**Dans** le café. *In . . .*
	Au métro Saint-Michel. *At the . . . subway stop.*
	Chez moi. *At . . . house.*

To ask with whom:	To tell with whom:
Avec qui?	**Avec** Ahmed et Nathalie.

To ask at what time:	To tell at what time:
A quelle heure?	**A dix heures du matin.** *At ten in the morning.*
	A cinq heures de l'après-midi. *At five in the afternoon.*
	A cinq heures et quart. *At quarter past five.*
	A cinq heures et demie. *At half past five.*
	Vers six heures. *About six o'clock.*

To ask the time:	To give the time:
Quelle heure est-il?	**Il est six heures.** *It's six o'clock.*
What time is it?	**Il est six heures moins le quart.** *It's a quarter to six.*
	Il est six heures dix. *It's ten after six.*
	Il est midi. *It's noon.*/**Il est minuit.** *It's midnight.*

To confirm:
Bon, on se retrouve à trois heures. *OK, we'll meet . . .*
Rendez-vous mardi au café. *We'll meet . . .*
Entendu. *OK.*

TROISIEME ETAPE · *cent soixante-trois* · **163**

*J*ump Start!

Write three invitations on the board or on a transparency and have students write a different response to each one.

MOTIVATE

Ask students what information they need to set up a date or a meeting (when, where, with whom, what time).

TEACH

Presentation

Comment dit-on... ? Act out both sides of a phone conversation in which you arrange to meet someone. Check comprehension by asking **Où ça? Quand ça?** and so on. Then, pretend to arrange a meeting with the class by asking individual students when, where, and at what time to meet. Have pairs of students practice arranging to meet after school. Introduce conversational time expressions by drawing a clock on the board with the minute hand at 15, 30, and 45 minutes past; label them **et quart, et demie,** and **moins le quart.** Show students various times on a clock and have them repeat the time expressions after you. Then, call out various times and have students display them on the clock.

 For videodisc application, see *Videodisc Guide.*

Teaching Suggestion

To practice question words, give possible answers (**Au stade.**) and have students say the appropriate question word. (**Où?**)

RESOURCES FOR **TROISIEME ETAPE**

PRINT
- *Lesson Planner,* p. 31
- *Practice and Activity Book,* pp. 68–70
- *Grammar and Vocabulary Workbook,* pp. 47–50
- *Activities for Communication,* pp. 35–36, 102, 103–104, 147–148
- *Listening Activities,* pp. 44–45, 49
- *Testing Program,* pp. 139–142
- *Alternative Assessment Guide,* p. 37

MEDIA
- *Video Program,* Videocassette 2
  Video Guide, pp. 39–44
- *Videodisc Program,* Videodisc 3, Side B
  Videodisc Guide, p. 68
- *Teaching Transparency 6-3*
- *Interactive CD-ROM Program,* Disc 2
  CD-ROM Teacher's Guide, p. 25
- *Audio Compact Discs*
  Textbook Listening Activities, CD 6, Trs. 10–11
  Additional Listening Activities 6-5, 6-6, CD 6, Trs. 35–36
  Quiz 6-3B, CD 6, Tr. 21

Building on Previous Skills

Note Culturelle To re-enter official time from Chapter 2, call out times in French according to the 24-hour system (**quinze heures quarante-cinq**). Have students tell you the time in the 12-hour system, adding **du matin, de l'après-midi,** or **du soir** (**quatre heures moins le quart de l'après-midi**).

Cooperative Learning

25 Have students form groups of three. For each illustration, one person gives the time (**neuf heures**), a second gives the activity or place (**faire du jogging**), and the third puts these elements into a sentence. (**A neuf heures, ils vont faire du jogging.**) Roles change for each illustration.

For Individual Needs

26 Challenge After they do this activity, have students write a similar message that they might leave on a friend's answering machine. Then, in small groups, each student reads aloud his or her message while the others write down the important information. You might have students record their messages and add them to their oral portfolios.

Language Note

Explain to students that the masculine form **demi** is used after **minuit** and **midi.** The feminine form **demie** is used after **heure(s),** as in **Il est trois heures et demie.**

---

24 Ecoute!   See scripts on p. 147H.

While you're waiting to use a public phone in Paris, you overhear a young woman inviting a friend to go out. Listen to the conversation and then choose the correct answers to these questions.

CD 6 Tr. 10

1. Sylvie parle **avec qui?**
   a. Marc   b. Anna   c. <u>Paul</u>

2. Elle va **où?**
   a. <u>au musée</u>   b. au parc   c. au stade

3. A **quelle heure?**
   a. 1h30   b. 10h15   c. <u>12h00</u>

4. Où est-ce qu'ils se retrouvent?
   a. au métro Solférino   b. dans un café   c. <u>devant le musée</u>

NOTE CULTURELLE

You've already learned that train, airline, school, and other official schedules use a 24-hour system called **l'heure officielle.** When you look in an entertainment guide such as *Pariscope,* you may see that a movie starts at 20h00, which is 8:00 P.M. In everyday conversation, however, people use a 12-hour system. For example, for 1:30 P.M., you may hear, **une heure et demie de l'après-midi,** rather than **treize heures trente.** Expressions such as **et demie, et quart,** and **moins le quart** are used only in conversational time, never in official time.

---

25 A quelle heure?

Où est-ce que Christian et Noëlle vont aujourd'hui? Qu'est-ce qu'ils vont faire? A quelle heure?   See answers below.

1. 9h00   2. 12h00   3. 5h45   4. 8h30

26 Ecoute!   See scripts and answers on p. 147H.

Listen to these three messages on your answering machine and write down who they're from and where you're being invited to go. Listen a second time and write down the meeting time and place.

CD 6 Tr. 11

164   *cent soixante-quatre*   CHAPITRE 6   Amusons-nous!

Language-to-Language

If you have students who speak Spanish, you may want to point out the similarities in telling time in Spanish and French. **Moins** in French and *menos* in Spanish function the same way. (**Il est dix heures moins dix.** *Son las diez menos diez.*) The expressions **et quart** and **et demie** are equivalent to *y cuarto* and *y media.* Have your Spanish-speaking students identify some differences in telling time in the two languages. (For minutes past the hour, Spanish uses *y* while French does not. French uses the word **heure** while Spanish does not. **Il est deux heures cinq.** *Son las dos y cinco.*)

Answers

25 1. Ils vont faire du jogging à neuf heures.
    2. Ils vont à la bibliothèque à midi.
    3. Ils vont au zoo à six heures moins le quart.
    4. Ils vont au musée à huit heures et demie.

27 Qu'est-ce que tu vas faire ce soir?

a. Make a list of at least three things that you're going to do tonight. Be sure to include the time and place.

b. Now, ask what your partner is going to do tonight. Then, continue to ask questions about his or her plans.

GRAMMAIRE Information questions

PA p. 69, Acts. 21–22
GV pp. 49–50, Acts. 18–21

There are several ways to ask information questions in French.

- People often ask information questions using only a question word or phrase. They will sometimes add **ça** after the question word to make it sound less abrupt.

  Où ça?

  Quand ça?

Additional Grammar Practice, pp. R39–R40

- Another way to ask an information question is to attach the question word or phrase at the end of a statement.

  Tu vas **où?**

  Tu veux faire **quoi?**

  Tu vas au cinéma **à quelle heure?**

  Tu vas au parc **avec qui?**

- Still another way is to begin an information question with the question word or phrase, followed by **est-ce que (qu')**.

  Où est-ce que tu vas?

  Qu'est-ce que tu veux faire ce soir?

  Avec qui est-ce que tu vas au cinéma?

  A quelle heure est-ce qu'on se retrouve?

---

28 On va où?

Some friends are inviting you to join them. Ask questions to get more information about their plans. Complete the conversation with the appropriate words or phrases.

— Tu veux aller au cinéma?

— Quand ça?

— Demain soir.

— A quelle heure?

— Vers six heures.

— Où ça?

— Au cinéma Gaumont.

— Avec qui?

— Avec Catherine et Michel.

— D'accord!

— Bon, on se retrouve...

📁 Portfolio

27 Oral Part **b** of this activity might be recorded and included in students' oral portfolios. For portfolio information, see the *Alternative Assessment Guide,* page 23.

Presentation

Grammaire Ask students to recall all the question words they can (**comment, à quelle heure, combien, qu'est-ce que, quoi, quand, où,** and **avec qui**). Using these words, ask students simple questions and have them give short answers. (**Tu vas où après l'école?**) Next, write on the board these three questions: **Où? Tu vas où? Où est-ce que tu vas?** Then, have students follow this model to write more questions, substituting **quand, avec qui,** and **à quelle heure** for **où.**

Additional Practice

Ask a question using the informal pattern with the question word(s) at the end. (**Tu étudies à quelle heure?**) Ask students to restate the question using the formal pattern with **est-ce que**. (**A quelle heure est-ce que tu étudies?**) Then, reverse the procedure.

🔷 For Individual Needs

28 Challenge Have partners supply their own information for the invitation (what, when, where, with whom, what time). You might have several students present their conversations to the class. As the other students listen, have them write down the information they hear. You might videotape these conversations and include them in students' oral portfolios.

🏰 Game

AROUND THE WORLD Play the game "Around the World" described on page 147J, using questions instead of vocabulary items. Give the first two students an answer to a question, such as **A l'école.** The first student to call out an appropriate question (**Où est-ce que tu vas?**) continues the game.

29 **Qu'est-ce qu'on fait chez toi?**

You'd like to find out more about what teenagers in France normally do. Write down at least six questions to ask your pen pal about his or her classes, activities, and hobbies.

30 **Allons au cinéma!**

Look at the movie schedule below. Choose a movie you want to see and invite your partner to go with you. When you've agreed on a movie to see, decide at which time you want to go and arrange a time and place to meet.

> ## Le Beaumont 15, Bd des Italiens • 75002 PARIS
>
> ○ **Astérix chez les Bretons,** *v.f. Séances : 12h, 14h15, 16h30, 18h45, 21h00*
> ○ **Les Randonneurs,** *v.f. Séances : 11h55, 13h55, 15h55*
> ○ **Roméo et Juliette,** *v.f. Séances : 13h40, 16h15, 18h55, 21h30*
> ○ **La Guerre des étoiles,** *v.o. Séances : 11h30, 14h, 16h30, 19h, 21h30*
> ○ **Le Cinquième Elément,** *v.f. Séances : 13h30, 15h, 16h30*
> ○ **Les 101 Dalmatiens,** *v.o. Séances : 11h05, 13h45, 16h20, 19h, 21h35*
> ○ **Hercules,** *v.f. Séances : 21h*
> ○ **Les Visiteurs,** *v.f. Séances : 13h30, 16h30*
> ○ **Volcan,** *v.f. Séances : 12h30, 14h, 16h*
> ○ **Casablanca,** *v.o. Séances : 16h30, 19h*

31 **Ça te dit?**

A friend has written you this note suggesting some things to do this weekend. Write an answer, accepting the invitations or making suggestions of your own.

> *Salut! Ça va? Tu veux faire quoi ce week-end? Moi, je voudrais faire les magasins vendredi soir et jouer au tennis samedi après-midi. On va au ciné samedi soir vers huit heures et demie. Tu viens? Et dimanche matin, tu veux aller au café? Qu'est-ce que tu en penses? Fabienne*

32 Mon journal

What are you and your friends going to do during the next school vacation? Write about your plans. Tell what you're going to do, with whom, when, where, and so on.

P R O N O N C I A T I O N

The vowel sounds [ø] and [œ]   See scripts and answers on p. 147H.
CD 6 Trs. 12–17

The vowel sound [ø] in **veux** is represented by the letter combination **eu.** It is pronounced with the lips rounded and the tongue pressed against the back of the lower front teeth. To produce this sound, first make the sound **è**, as in **algèbre**, and hold it. Then round the lips slightly to the position for closed **o**, as in **photo**. Repeat these words.

| jeudi | veux | peu | deux |

The vowel sound [œ] in the word **heure** is similar to the sound in **veux** and is also represented by the letters **eu.** This sound is more open, however, and occurs when these letters are followed by a consonant sound in the same syllable. To produce this sound, first make the sound **è**, as in **algèbre**, and hold it. Then round the lips slightly to the position for open **o**, as in **short**. Repeat these words.

| classeur | feuille | heure |

A. A prononcer
Repeat the following words.

1. jeudi   déjeuner   peux
2. deux   veut   mieux
3. ordinateur   jeunes   heure
4. feuille   classeur   veulent

B. A lire
Take turns with a partner reading each of the following sentences aloud.

1. Tu as deux ordinateurs? On peut étudier chez toi jeudi?
2. Tu veux manger des escargots? C'est délicieux!
3. On va à la Maison des jeunes? A quelle heure?
4. Tu as une feuille de papier? Je n'ai pas mon classeur.

C. A écrire
You're going to hear a short dialogue. Write down what you hear.

Mon journal
32 For an additional journal entry suggestion for Chapter 6, see *Practice and Activity Book,* page 150.

Portfolio
32 This activity is appropriate for students' written portfolios. For portfolio information, see the *Alternative Assessment Guide,* page 23.

CLOSE

To close this **étape,** have students think about what they're planning to do this weekend: where, when, and with whom. Then, have them write a sentence about their plans, omitting the activity: **Samedi après-midi, à trois heures, je vais ____ à la piscine avec des copains.** Have students read their sentences to a partner, who will try to fill in the blanks.

ASSESS

Quiz 6-3A, Quiz 6-3B, *Testing Program,* pp. 139–142

Audio CD 6, Tr. 21

Performance Assessment

Tell students that you'd like to join them for the activities they wrote about for Activity 31 on page 166. Have them tell you what they are doing and when and where to meet. Alternatively, you might have students ask you about your weekend plans.

Teaching Suggestion

Prononciation   Have students use the end-of-chapter **Vocabulaire** to find all the words that contain the **eu** combination. Then, have them write sentences like the ones in Part B, using as many of these words as possible. Remind them that the sentences must be logical! You might give groups of students a transparency on which to write their sentences, and then, as they read their sentences aloud for the class, project their transparency.

LISONS!

READING STRATEGY

Using context to determine meaning

Teacher Note

For an additional reading, see *Practice and Activity Book*, page 71.

Motivating Activity

Bring in brochures or advertisements from amusement parks or tourist attractions. Pass them around and ask students if they have gone to any of these places or would like to visit them. You might offer students a "free vacation" and ask where they would spend it. Ask them what they consider to be an enjoyable vacation.

Language Arts Link

Read aloud (or have students read) **De bons conseils**. Choose a passage from a Language Arts reading selection and delete every seventh word. Have students use the context to suggest words that could complete the passage.

PREREADING
Activity A

Teaching Suggestion

Begin by having students scan the brochures to answer the question in this activity. You might also ask what types of brochures there are and what information students would expect to find in them.

READING
Activities B–D

Teaching Suggestion

B. Have students correct the inaccurate statements.

$\mathcal{W}$here do you like to go on the weekend? Look at these brochures to see where Parisians go for fun.

Le Pays FRANCE MINIATURE, c'est la France comme vous ne l'avez jamais vue! Sur une immense carte en relief, sont regroupées les plus belles richesses de notre patrimoine : 166 monuments historiques, 15 villages typiques de nos régions, les paysages et les scènes de la vie quotidienne à l'échelle 1/30ème... au cœur d'un environnement naturel extraordinaire.

CALENDRIER :
Ouverture : 15 mars au 15 novembre.
Tous les jours de 10h à 19h.

TARIFS :
Individuels : Adultes : 75 F.
Enfants : 50 F (de 11 à 16 ans).

RESTAURATION
Deux restaurants de 300 places chacun et 2 kiosques proposent des menus de différentes régions de France (un restaurant ouvert le samedi soir). Aire de pique-nique aménagée.

 DE BONS CONSEILS

When you run across a word you don't know, use context to guess the meaning of the word. You automatically use this strategy in your own language. For example, you may not know the English word *dingo*, but when you see it in a sentence, you can make an intelligent guess about what it means. Read this sentence: *He thought that the kangaroos and the koala bears were cute, but that the dingos were mean-looking.* You can guess that a *dingo* is a possibly vicious animal found in Australia. It is, in fact, a wild dog.

A. What kinds of places do these brochures describe? theme parks and zoo

B. One of your friends visited **France Miniature** and told you about it. Check the brochure to see if what he said was accurate or not.
  1. "I saw more than 150 monuments!" accurate
  2. "There were twenty villages represented." inaccurate
  3. "The size of everything was on a scale of 1/25." inaccurate
  4. "It was more expensive than **Parc Astérix**." inaccurate
  5. "We stayed until midnight." inaccurate
  6. "We went on my birthday, June 15th." accurate

168 *cent soixante-huit*

Culture Note

The photo of model castles on the **France Miniature** brochure shows several châteaux of the Loire Valley, including Chenonceau (foreground) and Chambord (background).

Math Link

France Miniature Make sure students understand the concept of building on a scale of 1/30. How tall would a 60-meter building be on this reduced scale? (2 meters)

PARC ZOOLOGIQUE DE PARIS

Porte de St Mandé

vautours
caprins loutres

M St-Mandé-Tourelle (1.5 km)
Bus 46-325-86

cerfs

entrée du
Grand Rocher

wapiti

tigre lion éléphants

oryx algazelle

macaque

tétracère hippo nain

babouin

tamarin addax rhino

lémur gibbon

okapi ours

zèbre

oryx lémuriens girafe élan

zèbre panda hippo flamants

damalis andou guépard otarie phoque loup

anaco autruche antilopes renne

springbok

chameau

kangourou

Porte de Service

accueil-point rencontre
restaurant
aire de pique-nique
toilettes
expositions et
projections temporaires
crêperie-friandises
téléphone
poste de secours
week-end ap.midi
verrier
souvenirs
friandises
aire de jeux

Porte de Charenton

Bus 325

OUVERT TOUS LES JOURS
de 9 h à 18 h ou 18h30 l'été*
de 9 h à 17 h ou 17h30 l'hiver*
Entrée : 40 F* Tarif réduit : 30 F*
Groupes scolaires : 10 F* par enfant
Accès au Grand Rocher : 20 F*

REPAS
Panda - 9h15 - 16h
Pélicans - 14h15
Manchots - 14h30
Phoques et Otaries - 16h30
Les chiens ne sont pas admis.

ouverte dimanche et
jours fériés après-midi

53, avenue de Saint-Maurice 75012 PARIS
Tél.: 01 44 75 20 10 Fax : 01 43 43 54 73

PARC ASTERIX

Bienvenue
Welcome
Welkom

PARC ASTERIX

Bienvenue en Gaule pour une journée mémorable !

Pour passer une journée partagée entre l'émotion et l'aventure. Pour retrouver cette bonne humeur légendaire et communicative. Pour faire un voyage mémorable en Gaule, au pays du bien-vivre et de l'histoire…

Venez au Parc Astérix! Astérix et tous ses amis vous y attendent…

Départ de Paris les mercredi et samedi à 9h, du 10 avril au 2 octobre. Retour du site à 18 h et arrivée à Paris vers 19h30.

Prix par personne: **340 F**
Enfants de 3 à 11 ans inclus: **260 F**
Le prix inclut l'hébergement.

C. Look at the brochure for **Parc Astérix** and answer the following questions. See answers below.

1. During which months would you not be able to go on this trip?
2. On which days of the week can you take this trip to **Parc Astérix?**
3. If you took the trip in the advertisement, at what time would you leave Paris?
4. At what time would you leave the park for the trip back?
5. If you go with three friends and one of you brings your ten-year-old sister, how much will it cost?

D. Imagine you and a friend want to go to the **Parc zoologique de Paris.** See answers below.

1. Is the park open on Sundays? Is there a restaurant?
2. How much is it going to cost? Will it make a difference if you're students?
3. How late can you stay in the summer? In the winter?
4. What are some of the animals you'll get to see?
5. At what time do the pelicans eat? The pandas?
6. How many picnic areas are there? What is near the first-aid station? Where can you buy a gift?

E. Which of these places would you like to go to most? Why?

cent soixante-neuf **169**

Teaching Suggestions

C. As part of this activity, you might want to show students an **Astérix** book. These books are published in numerous languages and might be available at local bookstores.

D. Students might enjoy planning their visit to the zoo and listing the animals they would like to see. You might refer them to the names of animals in the Preliminary Chapter or the Additional Vocabulary on page R9.

Terms in Lisons!

• An important expression from **France Miniature** is **aire de pique-nique aménagée**—*equipped picnic area*.
• Terms that might interest students from the **Parc Astérix** brochure include: **retrouver**—*to find again* **bien-vivre**—*good living, the good life*
• Students might want to know some of the other expressions from the zoo brochure: **friandises**—*sweets, desserts* **manchots**—*penguins* **fauves**—*wildcats* **otaries**—*sea lions*

POSTREADING
Activity E

Teaching Suggestion

Use Activity E as a closing discussion question. You might also ask students to name the brochures that give them the most and the least information. Students might enjoy creating a brochure in French to advertise a nearby attraction in their own community to French tourists.

Answers
C 1. November through March
2. Wednesdays and Saturdays
3. 9:00 A.M.
4. 6:00 P.M.
5. 1.620 francs; Exchange rate will vary.
D 1. Yes; Yes
2. 40 F or 30 F; student groups: 10 F

3. Summer: 6:00 or 6:30 P.M.; Winter: 5:00 or 5:30 P.M.
4. *Possible answers:* elephants, tigers, kangaroos
5. Pelicans: 2:15 P.M.; Pandas: 9:15 A.M. and 4:00 P.M.
6. three picnic areas; lions and tigers; souvenirs, friandises *(souvenir shop)*

MISE EN PRATIQUE

The *CD-ROM Program* offers guided recording and writing activities to practice oral and written skills and to review material from each chapter.

The **Mise en pratique** reviews and integrates all four skills and culture in preparation for the Chapter Test.

Teaching Suggestions

1 You might use this activity as a game. Have students form small groups and give them a time limit to answer as many questions as possible. You might give a prize to the group that correctly answers the most questions.

1 Ask students which place they would prefer to visit and why.

Career Path

Have students list the types of services provided by a travel agency for someone planning to visit Paris (provide information about various attractions, make hotel reservations, and so on). Ask students how they might use French if they were a travel agent. Then, have them identify the services on the list that would require knowing French. You might have students visit travel agency sites on the Internet for more ideas.

La tour Eiffel est le monument parisien le plus connu au monde. Elle a été construite pour l'Exposition universelle de 1889. Jusqu'à la construction de l'Empire State Building de New York en 1931, la tour Eiffel était la plus haute tour du monde avec ses 320 mètres, antenne comprise. La Tour a trois étages. Il y a un restaurant au premier et au deuxième étages. Le troisième étage offre un superbe point de vue sur la ville. Horaires : 9h30 à 23 h. Tarifs : 20 F à 56 F.

Le musée d'Orsay a été installé dans l'ancienne gare d'Orsay, construite par Victor Laloux et inaugurée en 1900 au moment de l'Exposition universelle. C'est en 1977 qu'un Conseil des ministres a décidé de transformer la gare et son hôtel en un musée consacré à la création artistique du XIXe siècle (1848-1914). Collections : Arts Décoratifs, Histoire, Littérature, Mobilier, Peinture, Photographie, Sculpture. L'intérieur a été réalisé par l'architecte italienne Gae Aulenti. 1, rue de Bellechasse, 7e. Tél. : 01 40 49 48 14. Métro : Solférino. Horaires : tous les jours sauf le lundi de 10h-18h, le jeudi jusqu'à 21h45. Tarifs : 35 F.

Notre-Dame de Paris est un chef-d'œuvre de l'art gothique français, construite entre 1163 et 1330. La façade principale est composée de trois gigantesques portails. Visite guidée et gratuite de la cathédrale tous les jours : à 12 h du lundi au vendredi, à 14h30 le samedi, à 14 h le dimanche. Visite payante des tours tous les jours de 10 h à 17h30. Concerts gratuits tous les dimanches à 17h45. Visites et ascension fermées les jours fériés. Tél : 01 42 34 56 10. Tarifs : Visite des tours : 31 F.

1 Look over the advertisements and answer the questions below. See answers below.

1. Which place(s) offer(s) a view of Paris?
2. Where can you go to a free concert? On what day?
3. Are any of these places open in the evening? If so, which ones?
4. Where can you see nineteenth-century French art?
5. Which attraction is closed on holidays?
6. Which places list their prices?
7. Which attraction is closed on Mondays?
8. Which attraction costs the most to visit?
9. At which place can you buy something to eat?

CD 6 Tr. 18

2 Your French friends are discussing which Paris attraction to visit. Listen to their conversation and write down the attraction they decide on. Listen again and tell when and where they agree to meet. See scripts and answers on p. 147H.

Answers

1 1. la tour Eiffel, Notre-Dame de Paris
2. Notre-Dame de Paris; Sunday
3. Yes; la tour Eiffel, le musée d'Orsay
4. le musée d'Orsay

5. Notre-Dame de Paris
6. All of them
7. le musée d'Orsay
8. la tour Eiffel
9. la tour Eiffel

3 Using what you've learned about French culture, answer the following questions. See answers below.

1. Where do French teenagers like to go to have fun?
2. Would a French teenager be surprised at American dating customs? Why?

4 *Ecrivons!*

You have one day in Paris to do whatever you like. Write a note to your French class back home telling everyone what you plan to do during your day in Paris.

STRATEGIE

Arranging your ideas chronologically is helpful when planning activities for the day. To do this, take a sheet of paper, turn it sideways, and divide it into five columns. Label the first column **de 8h à 10h**, the second column **de 10h à midi**, and so on, in two-hour increments up to 6:00 in the evening. Next, decide what you would like to do at these times and write the information in the appropriate columns.

de 8h à 10h	de 10h à midi	de midi à 2h
visiter la tour Eiffel	aller au zoo	

Now, using the information from the chart you've prepared, write the note to your French class. Tell everyone what you plan to see and do throughout the day. Here are some connecting words that may help your writing flow more smoothly: **d'abord** *(first)*, **ensuite** *(next)*, and **après ça** *(after that)*.

5

JEU DE ROLE

Get together with some classmates. Choose one place in Paris you'd all like to visit and decide on a meeting time and place. Make sure that the Paris attraction you choose to visit will be open when you plan to go. Act this out with your group.

Possible answers

3 1. films, plays, concerts, discothèques, dance parties, **Maisons des jeunes**
   2. Yes, because French teenagers tend to go out in groups rather than couples.

📁 **Portfolio**

4 Written You might have students include this assignment in their written portfolios. For portfolio information, see the *Alternative Assessment Guide,* pages iv–17.

5 Oral Students might include this conversation in their oral portfolios.

Process Writing

4 If students have problems getting started or would like more options, refer them to the Location Opener on pages 120–123 for sites and activities in Paris.

Teaching Suggestion

5 Extend this activity by having students find several classmates who have planned an activity similar to theirs. Then, ask the groups to research three of the sites or attractions they want to see. Students might use the information on pages 120–123, or locate additional information on the Internet or in encyclopedias. Have each group do a short oral presentation about the attractions they research.

 Video Wrap-Up

• *VIDEO PROGRAM,*
  Videocassette 2, 36:27–48:15
• *VIDEODISC PROGRAM,*
  Videodisc 3, Side B

At this time, you might want to use the video resources for additional review and enrichment. See *Video Guide* or *Videodisc Guide* for suggestions regarding the following:

• **Projets de week-end**
  (Dramatic episode)
• **Panorama Culturel**
  (Interviews)
• **Vidéoclips**
  (Authentic footage)

This page is intended to help students prepare for the Chapter Test. It is a brief checklist of the major points covered in the chapter. Students should be reminded that this is only a checklist and does not necessarily include everything that will appear on the test.

Building on Previous Skills

1 Have students add a day and time to their answers. You might have them practice with the **tu, vous, il,** and **elle** forms as well.

Teaching Suggestion

3, 4 Encourage students to vary the ways they express each function.

Additional Practice

5 Suggest other places these or other people might want to visit.

Teaching Suggestion

7 After students have given possible answers, read the following message left on a telephone answering machine and have them answer the questions in this activity based on the message. (**Salut, c'est Monique! Ecoute, tu veux aller au musée? On y va samedi avec Daniel vers deux heures—il veut y voir une exposition de photos. Alors, tu peux? Rendez-vous devant le musée—à bientôt!**)

QUE SAIS-JE?

Can you use what you've learned in this chapter?

Can you make plans?
p. 153

1 How would you say that these people are going to these places?

1. **Je** vais au match.
2. **Nous** allons au centre commercial.
3. **Anne et Etienne** vont au cinéma.

2 How would you tell what you're planning to do this weekend?
Je vais... ce week-end.

3 How would you invite a friend to . . .   See answers below.
1. go window shopping?
2. go for a walk?
3. go see a basketball game?
4. go to the café?

Can you extend and respond to invitations?
p. 159

4 How would you accept the following invitations? How would you refuse them?   See answers below.
1. Je voudrais aller faire du ski. Tu viens?
2. Allons à la Maison des jeunes!
3. On va au restaurant. Tu viens?
4. Tu veux aller au cinéma?

5 How would you say that the following people want to go to these places?   See answers below.

1. **Ahmed**
2. **Isabelle et Ferdinand**
3. **Mon amie et moi**

Can you arrange to meet someone?
p. 163

6 If someone invited you to go to the movies, what are three questions you might ask to find out more information?
Possible answers: Où ça? Quand ça? A quelle heure? Avec qui?

7 What are some possible answers to the following questions?   See answers below.
1. Où ça?
2. Avec qui?
3. A quelle heure?
4. Quand ça?

Possible answers
3 1. Tu veux faire les vitrines avec moi?
2. Je voudrais faire une promenade. Tu viens?
3. On peut aller voir un match de basket.
4. Allons au café!
4 *Accepting:* D'accord. Bonne idée. Je veux bien. Pourquoi pas?
Refusing: Ça ne me dit rien. J'ai des trucs à faire. Désolé(e), je ne peux pas. Je suis occupé(e).

5 1. Ahmed veut aller à la bibliothèque.
2. Isabelle et Ferdinand veulent aller au théâtre.
3. Mon amie et moi, nous voulons aller au musée.
7 1. au cinéma, devant le stade, au café
2. avec Anne, avec mes amis, avec moi
3. vers trois heures, à huit heures et demie, à midi
4. demain, ce soir, lundi après-midi

PREMIERE ETAPE

Making plans

Qu'est-ce que tu vas faire... ?
What are you going to do . . . ?
Tu vas faire quoi...? *What are you going to do . . . ?*
Je vais... *I'm going . . .*
Pas grand-chose. *Not much.*
Rien de spécial. *Nothing special.*

Things to do

aller à une boum *to go to a party*
faire une promenade *to go for a walk*
faire un pique-nique *to have a picnic*

faire les vitrines *to window-shop*
manger quelque chose *to eat something*
regarder un match *to watch a game (on TV)*
voir un film *to see a movie*
aller voir un match *to go see a game*
voir une pièce *to see a play*

Places to go

la bibliothèque *the library*
le centre commercial *the mall*
le cinéma *the movie theater*

la Maison des jeunes et de la culture (MJC) *the recreation center*
le musée *the museum*
le parc *the park*
la piscine *the swimming pool*
la plage *the beach*
le restaurant *the restaurant*
le stade *the stadium*
le théâtre *the theater*
le zoo *the zoo*

Other useful expressions

aller *to go*
au/à la/à l'/aux *to, at*

DEUXIEME ETAPE

Extending invitations

Allons... ! *Let's go . . . !*
Tu veux... avec moi? *Do you want . . . with me?*
Tu viens? *Will you come?*
On peut... *We can . . .*

Accepting invitations

D'accord. *OK.*
Bonne idée. *Good idea.*

Je veux bien. *I'd really like to.*
Pourquoi pas? *Why not?*

Refusing invitations

Ça ne me dit rien. *I don't feel like it.*
J'ai des trucs à faire. *I've got things to do.*
Désolé(e), je ne peux pas. *Sorry, I can't.*

Désolé(e), je suis occupé(e). *Sorry, I'm busy.*

Other useful expressions

je voudrais... *I'd like . . .*
vouloir *to want*

TROISIEME ETAPE

Arranging to meet someone

Quand (ça)? *When?*
tout de suite *right away*
Où (ça)? *Where?*
dans *in*
devant *in front of*
au (métro)... *at the . . . (metro stop)*
chez... *at . . . ('s) house*
Avec qui? *With whom?*
avec... *with . . .*
A quelle heure? *At what time?*

A cinq heures. *At five o'clock.*
et demie *half past*
et quart *quarter past*
moins le quart *quarter to*
moins cinq *five to*
Quelle heure est-il? *What time is it?*
Il est midi. *It's noon.*
Il est minuit. *It's midnight.*
Il est midi (minuit) et demi. *It's half past noon (midnight).*
vers *about*

Bon, on se retrouve... *OK, we'll meet . . .*
Rendez-vous... *We'll meet . . .*
Entendu. *OK.*

Other useful expressions

ce week-end *this weekend*
demain *tomorrow*
est-ce que *(introduces a yes-no question)*

Game

MOTS CROISÉS Have groups of students choose five or six vocabulary words and design a crossword puzzle with pictures or fill-in-the-blank sentences as clues. Have groups exchange and fill out the puzzles.

CHAPTER 6 ASSESSMENT

CHAPTER TEST
• *Testing Program,* pp. 143–148
• *Audio Compact Discs,* Audio CD 6, Tracks 22–24

SPEAKING TEST
• *Testing Program,* p. 345

TEST GENERATOR
• Chapter 6

MIDTERM EXAM
• *Testing Program,* pp. 157–164
• *Audio Compact Discs,* Audio CD 6, Tracks 25–30

ALTERNATIVE ASSESSMENT
Performance Assessment
• You might want to use the **Jeu de Rôle** on page 171 as a cumulative performance assessment activity.
• *Alternative Assessment Guide,* p. 37

Portfolio Assessment
• *Alternative Assessment Guide*
Oral: p. 23
Written: p. 23

CD-ROM Assessment
• *Interactive CD-ROM Program,* Disc 2
A toi de parler
A toi d'écrire
• *Alternative Assessment Guide,* p. 51

Circumlocution

Have students act out a conversation in which a tourist in a French city wants to visit certain places, but hasn't yet learned the French words for them. One partner will play the role of the tourist, and the other partner will guess the name of the place based on what the tourist says. (**–Où est-ce qu'on peut faire les vitrines? –Au centre commercial.**) Students can use vocabulary for activities and places from previous chapters as well. You may want to give students the list of circumlocution expressions on page 147J.

Chapitre 7 : La famille
Chapter Overview

Mise en train pp. 176–178	Sympa, la famille!

	FUNCTIONS	GRAMMAR	CULTURE	RE-ENTRY
Première étape pp. 179–183	• Identifying people, p. 179 • Introducing people, p. 183	• Possession with **de**, p. 180 • Possessive adjectives, p. 181	• **Note Culturelle,** Family life, p. 182	• Asking for and giving people's names and ages **(Chapitre 1)** • Sports and hobbies **(Chapitre 4)** • Adverbs of frequency **(Chapitre 4)**
Deuxième étape pp. 184–188	• Describing and characterizing people, p. 185	• Adjective agreement, p. 186 • The verb **être**, p. 187	• **Panorama Culturel,** Pets in France, p. 188	• Adjective agreement and placement **(Chapitre 3)** • **Et** and **mais** **(Chapitre 1)**
Troisième étape pp. 189–191	• Asking for, giving, and refusing permission, p. 189			• Sports and activities **(Chapitres 1, 4)** • The verb **vouloir** **(Chapitre 6)**

Prononciation p. 191	The nasal sounds [5], [ɛ̃], and [œ̃] Audio CD 7, Tracks 14–16	**A écrire** (dictation) Audio CD 7, Tracks 17–19
Lisons! pp. 192–193	**En direct des refuges**	**Reading Strategy** Finding the main idea
Review pp. 194–197	**Mise en pratique**, pp. 194–195 **Ecrivons!** Using details to describe people Describing a family photo	**Que sais-je?** p. 196 **Vocabulaire,** p. 197

Assessment Options	**Testing Program** • Première étape, Quiz 7-1A, Quiz 7-1B, pp. 171–174 • Deuxième étape, Quiz 7-2A, Quiz 7-2B, pp. 175–178 • Troisième étape, Quiz 7-3A, Quiz 7-3B, pp. 179–182 • Chapter Test, pp. 183–188 • Speaking Test, p. 346 **Audio Compact Discs** • Audio CD 7, Tracks 21–26	**Interactive CD-ROM Program** • Mise en pratique (A toi de parler, A toi d'écrire) • CD-ROM Teacher's Guide, Assessment Options, p. 30 **Alternative Assessment Guide** • Portfolio Assessment, p. 24 • Performance Assessment, p. 38 • CD-ROM Assessment, p. 52 **Test Generator** • Chapter 7

PRINT	MEDIA

Pupil's Edition, pp. 174–197

 Audio Compact Discs
- Textbook Listening Activities: Audio CD 7, Tracks 1–20

Interactive CD-ROM Program
Teacher's Guide, pp. 27–30

 Interactive CD-ROM Program
- Disc 2

Videodisc Guide
- Teaching Suggestions, pp. 75–79
- Activity Masters, pp. 80–82

 Videodisc Program
- Videodisc 4, Side A

Video Guide
- Teaching Suggestions, pp. 46–47
- Activity Masters, pp. 48–50

 Video Program
- Videocassette 3
- Videocassette 5 (captioned version)

Listening Activities
- Student Response Forms for Textbook Listening Activities, pp. 51–53
- Additional Listening Activities 7-1 to 7-6, pp. 55–57
- Additional Listening Activities (song), p. 58
- Scripts and Answers, pp. 132–136

 Audio Compact Discs
- Textbook Listening Activities: Audio CD 7, Tracks 1–20
- Additional Listening Activities: Audio CD 7, Tracks 27–33

Teaching Transparencies
- Teaching Transparency Masters 7-1 to 7-3 (Situations) and 7-A to 7-D (Vocabulary)
- Teaching Suggestions 7-1 to 7-3 and 7-A to 7-D

 Teaching Transparencies
- Situations 7-1 to 7-3
- Vocabulary 7-A to 7-D

Testing Program
- Grammar and Vocabulary Quizzes, **Etape** Quizzes, and Chapter Test, pp. 171–188
- Score Sheet, Scripts, and Answers, pp. 189–196

 Audio Compact Discs
- Assessment Items: Audio CD 7, Tracks 21–26

 Test Generator
- Chapter 7

Alternative Assessment Guide
- Portfolio Assessment, p. 24
- Performance Assessment, p. 38
- CD-ROM Assessment, p. 52

 Grammar and Vocabulary Workbook, pp. 51–60

 Practice and Activity Book, pp. 73–84

Activities for Communication
- Communicative Activities, pp. 37–42
- Realia and Teaching Suggestions, pp. 105–109
- Situation Cards, pp. 149–150

Lesson Planner
- Lesson Plan, pp. 33–37

Chapitre 7 : La famille
Technology Applications

MISE EN TRAIN, pp. 176–178

Video
- Show *Sympa, la famille!* For Video Synopsis, Teaching Suggestions, Activity Masters, and Scripts, see the *Video Guide* or the *Videodisc Guide.*

Audio
- Play the recording of the **Mise en train** with pauses as students read along. You might have them practice pronunciation by repeating individual sentences after hearing them.

PREMIERE ETAPE, pp. 179–183

Video
- While students watch *Sympa, la famille!,* have them listen for exchanges that model identifying and introducing people. For more suggestions, see pp. 76–77 of the *Videodisc Guide.*

Audio
- Textbook Listening Activity 8 practices the vocabulary for family members.
- To have students practice possessive adjectives and the vocabulary for pets, play Textbook Listening Activity 9.
- Textbook Listening Activity 12 practices expressions for identifying and introducing someone.
- Use Additional Listening Activities 7–1 and 7–2 to have students practice the vocabulary for family members.

Transparencies
- Use *Teaching Transparencies 7–1* and *7–A* along with the Teaching Suggestions to have students practice the vocabulary for family members and the expressions for identifying and introducing people.

CD-ROM (Disc 2)
- To have students practice using vocabulary for family members, use **Chasse au trésor** (Activity 1).

DEUXIEME ETAPE, pp. 184–187

Video
- While students watch *Sympa, la famille!,* have them listen for exchanges that model describing and characterizing people. For more suggestions, see p. 77 of the *Videodisc Guide.*

Audio
- Textbook Listening Activities 15 and 16 practice vocabulary and expressions for describing people.
- Use Additional Listening Activities 7–3 and 7–4 to have students practice the vocabulary and the expressions for describing and characterizing someone.

Transparencies
- Use *Teaching Transparencies 7–2, 7–B,* and *7–C* along with the Teaching Suggestions to have students practice describing someone.

CD-ROM (Disc 2)
- **Les mots qui manquent** (Activity 2) targets adjective agreement.
- To have students practice the vocabulary for describing people, use **Chasse au trésor** (Activity 3).
- **Les mots qui manquent** (Activity 4) has students produce forms of the verb **être.**
- For suggestions, see pp. 28–29 of the *CD-ROM Teacher's Guide.*

PANORAMA CULTUREL, p. 188

Video
- Show the interviews. For Video Synopsis, Teaching Suggestions, Activity Master, and Scripts, see the *Video Guide* or the *Videodisc Guide.*

Audio
- Play the **Panorama Culturel** as students read along. Remind students they might not be able to understand everything each person says, but they should try to recognize words and deduce global meaning.

CD-ROM (Disc 2)
- Have students do the **Panorama Culturel** activity for Chapter 7 after showing them the video. For suggestions, see p. 29 of the *CD-ROM Teacher's Guide.*

TROISIEME ETAPE, pp. 189–191

Video
- While students watch *Sympa, la famille!,* have them listen for exchanges that model asking for, giving, and refusing permission. For more suggestions, see p. 78 of the *Videodisc Guide.*

Audio
- Use Textbook Activity 23 to have students practice expressions for giving and refusing permission.
- Textbook Listening Activity 24 practices the vocabulary for chores.
- Additional Listening Activities 7–5 and 7–6 target the vocabulary for chores and the expressions for asking for, giving, and refusing permission.

Transparencies
- Use *Teaching Transparencies 7–3* and *7–D* along with the Teaching Suggestions to practice the vocabulary for chores and the expressions for asking for, giving, and refusing permission.

CD-ROM (Disc 2)
- **Chacun à sa place** (Activity 5) has students classify expressions for asking for, giving, and refusing permission.
- After presenting the vocabulary on p. 189, have students do **Jeu des paires** (Activity 6).
- For suggestions, see p. 29 of the *CD-ROM Teacher's Guide.*

MISE EN PRATIQUE, pp. 194–195

Video
- Replay *Sympa, la famille!* in its entirety and ask students to listen for the exchanges in which the characters identify and introduce people, describe and characterize people, and ask for, give, and refuse permission.

CD-ROM (Disc 2)
- Have students do the **En contexte** to practice describing family members and pets, and discussing chores. You may want to use the suggestions on p. 28 of the *CD-ROM Teacher's Guide.*
- Have students practice their writing and speaking skills by doing the **A toi d'écrire** and **A toi de parler** activities. For a detailed description of these activities, see p. 30 of the *CD-ROM Teacher's Guide.*
- For Assessment Options, see p. 30 of the *CD-ROM Teacher's Guide.*

Test Generator
- Use the Test Generator to create review material for students taking the Chapter Test or to prepare an alternate test.

VIDEOCLIPS

Video
- Show the **Vidéoclips.** For Video Synopsis, Teaching Suggestions, Activity Masters, and Scripts, see the *Video Guide* or the *Videodisc Guide.*

Videodisc Program
Videodisc 4, Side A
Videodisc Guide, pp. 73–82

Chapitre 7 : La famille
 Barcode Directory

BARCODE DIRECTORY
CHAPTER 7

Barcodes A and B access **Mise en train** and **Mise en train (suite)** in their entirety. Subsequent barcodes show specific segments of *Sympa, la famille!* The barcode numbers correspond to the scene numbers as they appear on the video.

MISE EN TRAIN

Sympa, la famille! **A**

Search 1, Play To 7100

Qui est-ce? **3**

Search 2451, Play To 2852

Tiens, là, c'est moi. **6**

Search 4631, Play To 5363

Et toi, tu n'as pas... ? **9**

Search 6532, Play To 7100

Salut, Thuy! **1**

Search 1, Play To 1831

Et là, ce sont... ? **4**

Search 2853, Play To 4285

Et là, qui est... ? **7**

Search 5364, Play To 5909

Sympa, la famille! (suite) **B**

Search 7100, Play To 14605

Et voilà ma chambre. **2**

Search 1832, Play To 2450

Comment s'appelle-t-elle? **5**

Search 4286, Play To 4630

Et là, c'est qui... ? **8**

Search 5910, Play To 6531

PANORAMA CULTUREL

Tu as un animal domestique? Il est comment?
These barcodes access the three interviews of the **Panorama Culturel** presented in the *Pupil's Edition* as well as additional interviews.

First three interviews **1**

Search 14605, Play To 17084

Onélia **4**

Search 16025, Play To 16634

Céline **7**

Search 17277, Play To 17442

Yvette **10**

Search 17890, Play To 17999

Matthieu **13**

Search 18678, Play To 18832

All interviews **2**

Search 14605, Play To 19374

Marie-Emmanuelle **5**

Search 16635, Play To 17084

Antoine **8**

Search 17443, Play To 17676

Isabelle **11**

Search 18000, Play To 18245

Marie-Laure **14**

Search 18833, Play To 19053

Olivier **3**

Search 15533, Play To 16024

Bosco **6**

Search 17085, Play To 17276

Emmanuel **9**

Search 17677, Play To 17889

Céline **12**

Search 18246, Play To 18677

Virginie **15**

Search 19054, Play To 19374

ETAPES

To practice the grammar, vocabulary, and functions presented in each **étape**, see the barcodes and accompanying suggestions on pages 76–78 of the *Videodisc Guide*.

MISE EN PRATIQUE

This is additional footage modeling some of the expressions practiced in this chapter. You may want to use it to review the chapter.

Mise en pratique 1 **1**

Search 22231, Play To 24066

Mise en pratique 2 **2**

Search 24067, Play To 25382

VIDEOCLIPS

These are authentic French commercials. You may want to preview them before showing them to students.

César®: dog food **1**

Search 19375, Play To 20480

Jockey®: yogurt **2**

Search 20481, Play To 21414

Chapitre 7 : La famille
CD-ROM Directory 💿 DISC 2

The following directory lists the *Interactive CD-ROM Program* activities for Chapter 7. For details and suggestions on how to use them, see pages 27–30 of the *CD-ROM Teacher's Guide*.

GLOBAL TASK	COMMUNICATIVE GOALS		ACTIVITY TYPE
La famille de Dominique Students talk with their French teacher on the phone about their friend Dominique and her family.	To use chapter functions, vocabulary, and grammar in a lifelike conversation		**En contexte** *Interactive conversation*

	SUPPORTING ACTIVITIES	PUPIL'S EDITION	COMMUNICATIVE GOALS	ACTIVITY TYPE
Première étape	1. Vocabulaire	p. 180	To identify family members	**Chasse au trésor Explorons!/Vérifions!** *Interactive image*
Deuxième étape	2. Grammaire	p. 186	To make adjectives agree	**Les mots qui manquent** *Tic Tac Toe*
	3. Vocabulaire	pp. 184, 186	To describe and characterize people	**Chasse au trésor Explorons!/Vérifions!** *Interactive image*
	4. Grammaire	p. 187	To produce forms of the verb **être**	**Les mots qui manquent** *Tic Tac Toe*
Troisième étape	5. Comment dit-on... ?	p. 189	To classify expressions for asking for, giving, and refusing permission	**Chacun à sa place** *Categories*
	6. Vocabulaire	p. 189	To identify chores	**Jeu des paires** *Concentration®*
Panorama Culturel	Panorama Culturel	p. 188	To listen to and understand native speakers talking about their pets	**Tu as un animal domestique? Il est comment?** *Presentation* **Le bon choix** *Multiple choice*

	APPLICATION	PUPIL'S EDITION	COMMUNICATIVE GOALS	ACTIVITY TYPE
Mise en pratique	A toi de parler	pp. 194–195	To create and record a conversation between a parent and a teenager asking for permission to do something	*Guided recording*
	A toi d'écrire	pp. 194–195	To create a lost-and-found ad, a cast of characters, an interview, or a list	*Guided writing*

CHAPTER SECTION	PRESENTATION	HOMEWORK OPTIONS
Première étape	**Vocabulaire,** p. 180	Practice and Activity Book, p. 75, Activity 4 Grammar and Vocabulary Workbook, p. 51, Activities 1–2 CD-ROM, Disc 2, Activity 1
	Note de Grammaire, p. 180	Pupil's Edition, p. R40, Activity 1 Practice and Activity Book, pp. 74, 76, Acts. 2b, 7b Grammar and Vocabulary Workbook, p. 52, Activities 3–4
	Grammaire, p. 181	Pupil's Edition, p. 183, Activity 14; pp. R40–R41, Activities 2–4 Practice and Activity Book, p. 75, Activity 6 Grammar and Vocabulary Workbook, p. 53, Activities 5–7
	Comment dit-on... ? p. 183	Practice and Activity Book, p. 76, Activity 8
Deuxième étape	**Vocabulaire,** p. 184	Practice and Activity Book, p. 77, Activities 9–10 Grammar and Vocabulary Workbook, p. 54, Activities 8–9
	Comment dit-on... ? p. 185	Practice and Activity Book, p. 78, Activity 13
	Grammaire, p. 186	Pupil's Edition, p. R41, Activity 5 Practice and Activity Book, pp. 77–78, Activities 11–12 Grammar and Vocabulary Workbook, pp. 55–57, Activities 10–14 CD-ROM, Disc 2, Activities 2–3
	Grammaire, p. 187	Pupil's Edition, p. 187, Activity 22; p. R41, Activity 6 Practice and Activity Book, pp. 78–79, Activities 14–15 Grammar and Vocabulary Workbook, pp. 57–58, Activities 15–17 CD-ROM, Disc 2, Activity 4
Troisième étape	**Comment dit-on... ?** p. 189	Pupil's Edition, p. 191, Activity 27; pp. R41–R42, Activities 7–8 Practice and Activity Book, p. 81, Activity 21 CD-ROM, Disc 2, Activity 5

	Vocabulaire, p. 189	Pupil's Edition, p. 190, Activity 26
		Practice and Activity Book, pp. 80–82, Activities 17–18,
		   20, 22–23
		Grammar and Vocabulary Workbook, pp. 59–60,
		   Activities 18–21
		CD-ROM, Disc 2, Activity 6

Chapitre 7 : La famille
Textbook Listening Activities Scripts

For Student Response Forms, see *Listening Activities*, pp. 51–53.

*P*remière étape

8 Ecoute! p. 181

1. Voilà mon grand-père. Il n'est pas jeune, mais il est toujours actif. Regarde. Là, il fait du vélo.

2. Et voici ma mère et mon père. Là, ils sont en vacances à la Martinique. Qu'est-ce qu'il fait beau, hein?

3. Et ça, c'est ma sœur. Elle adore jouer au volley!

4. Ce sont mes deux frères. Ils jouent souvent au football.

5. Et ça, c'est moi avec mon chien. Il est mignon, n'est-ce pas?

Answers to Activity 8
1. d   2. b   3. a   4. e   5. c

9 Ecoute! p. 181

1. Notre chien s'appelle Chouchou.

2. Nos poissons aiment beaucoup manger.

3. Leurs chats aiment sortir le matin.

4. Son canari est jaune.

5. Votre chien, il a quel âge?

6. Et vos chats, est-ce qu'ils aiment beaucoup dormir?

7. Ses poissons sont noirs ou rouges?

Answers to Activity 9
1. their own; dog
2. their own; fish
3. someone else's; cats
4. someone else's; canary
5. someone else's; dog
6. someone else's; cats
7. someone else's; fish

12 Ecoute! p. 183

1. Salut, Michèle! Je te présente mon amie Anne-Marie.

2. Regarde. Voilà Mademoiselle Simonet.

3. Maman, je te présente Annick.

4. Voilà Isabelle. C'est une amie.

5. Madame Martin, je vous présente Monsieur Poulain.

Answers to Activity 12
1. introducing
2. identifying
3. introducing
4. identifying
5. introducing

*D*euxième étape

15 Ecoute! p. 185

1. Elle est grande et blonde.

2. Il est petit, roux et très fort.

3. Il est grand et brun.

4. Elle est petite, mince et brune.

5. Elle est petite et rousse.

Answers to Activity 15
1. Julie
2. Martin
3. Roger
4. Carmen
5. Denise

16 Ecoute! p. 185

1. Dominique est grande, brune et très intelligente.

2. Ça, c'est Andrée. Andrée est mince et blonde. Euh, un peu pénible.

3. Tu vois, là, c'est Joëlle. Joëlle aime bien faire du sport. Petite mais assez forte. Elle est amusante.

4. Ici, c'est Gabriel. Gabriel est mignon et tellement gentil!

5. Et Danielle. Danielle est brune. Toujours embêtante. Pas facile du tout!

Answers to Activity 16
1. Dominique — favorable
2. Andrée — unfavorable
3. Joëlle — favorable
4. Gabriel — favorable
5. Danielle — unfavorable

*T*roisième étape

23 Ecoute! p. 189

1. — Je voudrais sortir. Tu es d'accord?
   — Non. C'est impossible.

2. — Je peux aller à la plage?
   — Pas question.

3. — Je voudrais aller au restaurant avec mes amis. Tu es d'accord?
   — Oui, si tu fais d'abord tes devoirs.

4. — On va jouer au football. Je peux y aller?
   — Oui, bien sûr.

5. — Est-ce que je peux aller au cinéma?
   — Oui, si tu veux.

Answers to Activity 23
1. refused   3. given   5. given
2. refused   4. given

24 Ecoute! p. 190

1. — Maman, Stéphanie et Emilie vont au cinéma ce soir. Je peux y aller?
   — Non, tu dois garder ta sœur.

2. — Je voudrais sortir avec Jean-Luc. Je peux?
   — Si tu promènes le chien, c'est d'accord.

3. — Maman, je peux sortir avec Marc ce soir?
   — Si tu passes d'abord l'aspirateur.

4. — On va au parc cet après-midi pour faire un pique-nique. Je voudrais y aller.
   — Mais non. Tu sais bien, tu dois ranger ta chambre!

5. — Je voudrais aller à la piscine avec Elise et Cécile. D'accord?
   — D'accord, si tu fais d'abord tes devoirs.

6. — Je peux aller au centre commercial ce soir avec Arnaud?
   — Oui, si tu fais d'abord la vaisselle.

Answers to Activity 24
1. c   2. e   3. d   4. a   5. f   6. b

*P*rononciation, p. 191

For the scripts for Parts A and B, see p. 191.

C. A écrire

(Dictation)
— Voilà mon cousin américain.
— Son chien est très mignon.

*M*ise en pratique

1 p. 194

Je m'appelle Nathalie. Ma famille habite à Paris. J'ai un frère qui s'appelle Jean-Paul. Il a douze ans. Il est très gentil avec moi. J'ai aussi un chat. Il s'appelle Câlin. Il n'est pas vieux, il a deux ans seulement. Et moi, quel âge j'ai? Eh bien, j'ai quinze ans.

Answers to Mise en pratique Activity 1
1. Jean-Paul
2. douze ans
3. un chat
4. Il n'est pas vieux, il a deux ans.

Chapitre 7 : La famille
Projects

Ma famille
(Individual Project)

ASSIGNMENT

Students will draw their family trees, labeling at least three generations with the names of family members and their relationships to the student. Students who don't want to give their own family background can draw the family tree of a royal family, a famous family, or an imaginary family.

MATERIALS

✂ **Students may need**
- Construction paper or posterboard
- Colored pens, pencils, or markers
- Photos of family members or magazine photos
- Tape or glue

SUGGESTED SEQUENCE

1. Have students list all of their family members for at least three generations. They should begin with one pair of grandparents and add all their children. Then, have them add any descendants from the second generation, and so on. They should do the same for the other pair of grandparents.

2. Have students sketch the tree in pencil on a large piece of paper or posterboard. Then, have them write in the names and relationships in pencil, using their lists. Remind them to leave space for photos or drawings. Have them exchange sketches with a classmate to edit.

3. Have students position their photos or drawings on their trees and make any necessary adjustments.

4. Have students give an oral presentation in which they identify each family member in French. You might want to display students' sketches around the classroom.

GRADING THE PROJECT

You might base each student's grade on completeness, presentation and appearance, correct use and spelling of vocabulary, and oral presentation.

Suggested Point Distribution (total = 100 points)

Completeness	30 points
Presentation/appearance	30 points
Use/spelling of vocabulary	20 points
Oral presentation	20 points

FAMILY LINK

Encourage students to take their projects home to share with their families.

Mon album de famille
(Individual Project)

ASSIGNMENT

Students will make a family photo album with descriptions of each family member similar to the one on pages 176–177. This project provides more challenge and requires more language use than **Ma famille**. Students might describe a cartoon, television, or royal family instead of their own.

MATERIALS

✂ **Students may need**
- Construction paper
- Stapler and staples
- Colored markers or pens
- Family photos or magazine pictures
- Tape or glue

SUGGESTED SEQUENCE

1. Have students choose at least five family members to present in their photo albums. They should make a list of words and phrases to describe each member. For each person, have students list his or her age, at least three adjectives, and two things that he or she likes or dislikes.

2. Have students choose photos or draw sketches of the family members they are featuring in their album.

3. Have students write rough drafts of their descriptions. They might give their descriptions to a classmate to edit.

4. Give students some construction paper and have them tape or glue one photo or drawing on each page and copy their final description of that family member below it.

5. Have students design and draw a cover for their album and staple it to the other pages.

GRADING THE PROJECT

You might base students' grades on the completion of the assignment, use of vocabulary, presentation and creativity, and accurate language use.

Suggested Point Distribution (total = 100 points)

Completion of assignment	25 points
Vocabulary use	25 points
Presentation/creativity	25 points
Language use	25 points

QUI SUIS-JE?

In this game, students will interact and practice question formation.

Procedure   The day before the game, have each student write the name of a well-known person on an index card. Collect the cards and make sure there are no duplicates. You might want to include the principal or other staff members. On the day of the game, tape a card to each student's back, without letting him or her see the card. Have students try to determine their new identity by asking members of their group yes-no questions. **(Je suis grand(e)?)** Circulate to monitor and help out as needed. You might set a time limit for this game and give prizes to the first few students who guess the name affixed to their back.

Variation   An alternate way to play this game is to have students write their own names and a brief but detailed description of themselves on an index card. Have them include their likes and dislikes, their hobbies, and so on. Collect and redistribute the cards, taping one to each student's back. Continue with the game as described above.

TREE FILL-IN

In this game, students will practice family vocabulary.

Procedure   In this game, students will try to fill in a family tree as they listen to an oral description of the family relationships. To prepare the game, draw different family trees on pieces of paper and write in only first names. Have students pair off or form small groups. Distribute a family tree to one student in each pair or group. The person in each pair or group who receives the tree will describe it to the other(s). **(Pierre est le père de Marie.)** The other student(s) must draw the family tree according to the description. Those listening may ask for clarification, as long as they do so in French. After students have drawn their trees, they should compare them to the original and make corrections.

POSSESSIFS

In this game, students will practice using possessive adjectives.

Procedure   Prepare in advance two sets of flashcards, one set with subject pronouns and the other set with nouns from the first seven chapters. Divide the class into two or three teams and appoint a timekeeper. One player from each team will play at a time. Hold up two flashcards, one showing a subject pronoun and the other a noun. The player must say the possessive adjective appropriate to the subject together with the noun within a set amount of time (five seconds should be long enough). For example, if **ils** and **amis** are shown on the two cards, the player should say **leurs amis.** Give points for all correct answers. Make sure all players have a turn and play as many rounds as you choose. By mixing the pronouns and nouns, you can use the same cards over and over.

Variation   This game can also be played by forming smaller teams so all of the students can play at once. In this case, each team would write their answer on a piece of paper within a specific time limit (perhaps 5–10 seconds). This way, all students and all teams will play each round.

Chapitre 7
La famille
pp. 174–197

𝒰sing the Chapter Opener

Teaching Suggestions
• Ask several students to come to the front of the room. Introduce them to the class, using the caption of the first photo and changing **tu** to **vous.** Show two photos of your family members and introduce and describe them as in the caption of Photo 2.
• Call attention to the document at the bottom of the page. Ask students what they think it is.

Culture Notes
  • The candies shown on this page are called **dragées,** sugar-coated almonds that are traditionally given out at weddings and baptisms. They might be offered in small net bags or small boxes. Wedding **dragées** are usually white and may be mixed with silver candies. The pink candies shown here are probably for a girl's baptism; they might be blue if a boy were being baptized.
• French weddings are similar to traditional American weddings. However, some customs that students might be familiar with aren't practiced in France. For example, no showers are held before the wedding, and there are no bridesmaids or groomsmen in the wedding party. Instead, **demoiselles d'honneur** and **garçons d'honneur,** who are usually young children from the bride's and groom's families, accompany

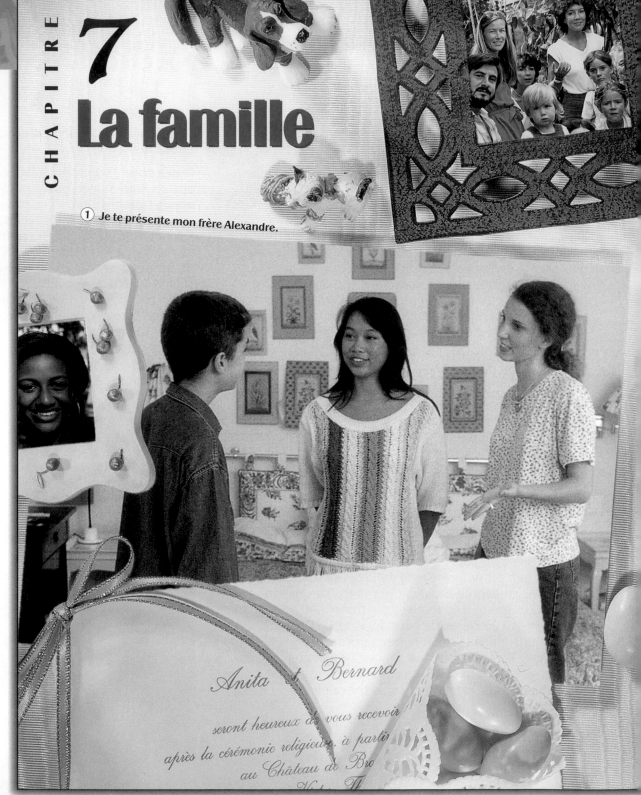

CHAPITRE

7
La famille

① Je te présente mon frère Alexandre.

the bride down the aisle. In addition to a civil ceremony, which is required to make the marriage legally binding, some French couples also choose to have a religious service.
• The traditional French wedding cake **(la pièce montée)** is very distinctive. It is often made up of layers of stacked cream puffs covered with caramel sauce.

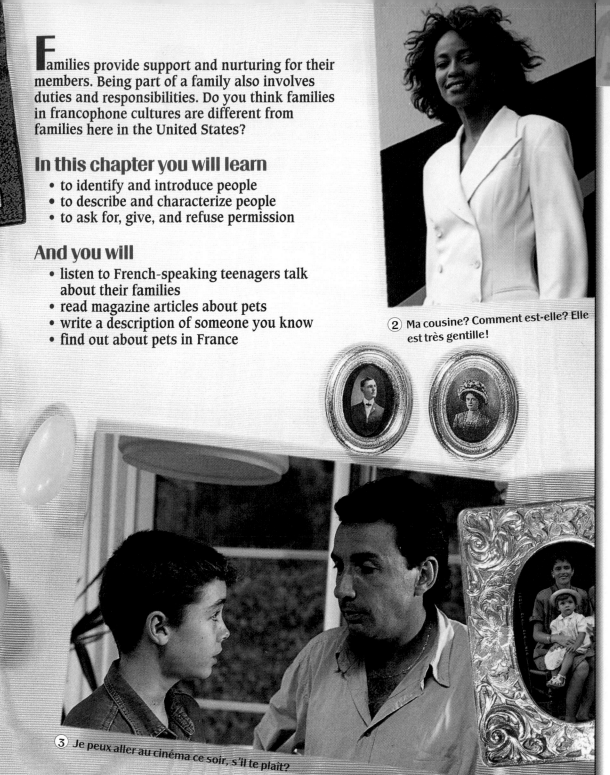

F amilies provide support and nurturing for their members. Being part of a family also involves duties and responsibilities. Do you think families in francophone cultures are different from families here in the United States?

In this chapter you will learn

- to identify and introduce people
- to describe and characterize people
- to ask for, give, and refuse permission

And you will

- listen to French-speaking teenagers talk about their families
- read magazine articles about pets
- write a description of someone you know
- find out about pets in France

② Ma cousine? Comment est-elle? Elle est très gentille!

③ Je peux aller au cinéma ce soir, s'il te plaît?

cent soixante-quinze 175

Focusing on Outcomes

Have students read the chapter outcomes and match them to the photos. Ask them to think of some situations in which these functions would be used, such as introducing people at parties or telling stories. NOTE: You may want to use the video to support the objectives. The self-check activities in **Que sais-je?** on page 196 help students assess their achievement of the objectives.

Teacher Notes

- Also included in this chapter are possessive adjectives and vocabulary describing family relationships, as well as household chores.
- Some suggestions in this chapter ask students to cut pictures from magazines. Consider keeping old issues in the classroom for this purpose. You might also want to begin a subscription for a French magazine. See page T54 for a list of periodicals and subscription services.

Block Scheduling

For suggestions about how to use *Allez, viens!* with block scheduling, see the *Lesson Planner,* pages 33–37.

🌐 Culture Note

In Africa, members of the extended family often live under the same roof as the nuclear family. It is normal for all family members to be intimately involved in every aspect of one another's lives, including business matters, health care, education, child care, and employment. Even as more Africans move to the cities, they still manage to keep in close touch with family members in town as well as with those still living in the village. It might be noted that marriage is considered a means of acquiring more family, both by gaining in-laws and by having children.

VIDEO PROGRAM
Videocassette 3
01:22–05:18
Videocassette 5
(captioned version)
56:00–59:55

OR **VIDEODISC PROGRAM,**
Videodisc 4, Side A

Search 1, Play To 7100

Video Synopsis

In this segment of the video, Thuy arrives at Isabelle's house for a visit. Isabelle introduces Thuy to her father. Thuy notices Isabelle's family photo album and asks if she can look at it. As they look at the photos, Isabelle explains who all the family members are and describes them. Thuy says that she is an only child and asks about Isabelle's brother Alexandre. Isabelle tells her that he can be difficult.

Motivating Activity

You might ask students if they take pictures, of whom or of what, and if they keep photo albums.

Teaching Suggestion

Have students look at the pictures on pages 176–177 and guess how the people are related to Isabelle.

Presentation

Show the video, stopping after each photo Isabelle describes to ask students to name the relative and describe him or her in English. You might draw Isabelle's family tree without the names and have students fill them in as they view the video.

This is an abridged version of the video episode.

Mise en train

Sympa, la famille! p. 73, Act. 1

CD 7
Trs. 1–2

Look at the people pictured in the photo album. Can you guess how they're related to Isabelle?

Tiens, j'adore regarder les photos. Je peux les voir?

Bien sûr!

Ce sont mes grands-parents. Ils sont heureux sur cette photo. Ils fêtent leur quarantième anniversaire de mariage.

C'est une photo de papa et maman.

Là, c'est mon oncle et ma tante, le frère de ma mère et sa femme. Et au milieu, ce sont leurs enfants, mes cousins. Ils habitent tous en Bretagne. Ça, c'est Loïc. Il a 18 ans.

Loïc

Ma tante

Julie

Patricia

Mon oncle

C'est Julie. Elle a 8 ans. Elle est adorable.

Et elle, c'est ma cousine Patricia. Elle est très intelligente. En maths, elle a toujours 18 sur 20!

176 *cent soixante-seize*

CHAPITRE 7   La famille

RESOURCES FOR MISE EN TRAIN

PRINT
- *Practice and Activity Book,* p. 73
- *Video Guide,* pp. 45–46, 48
- *Videodisc Guide,* pp. 73–76, 80

MEDIA
- *Video Program,* Videocassette 3
  Videocassette 5 (captioned version)
- *Videodisc Program,* Videodisc 4, Side A
- *Audio Compact Discs,* CD 7, Trs. 1–2

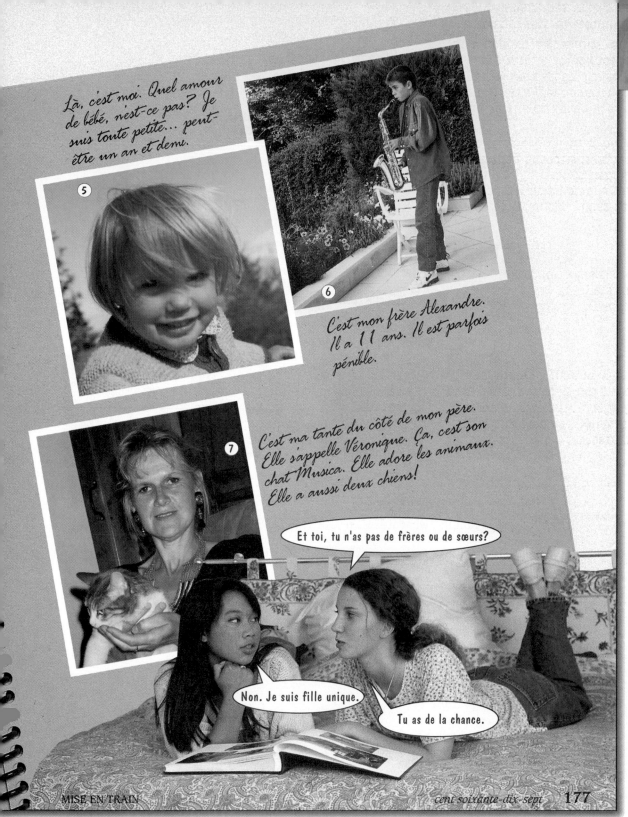

Là, c'est moi. Quel amour de bébé, n'est-ce pas? Je suis toute petite... peut-être un an et demi.

C'est mon frère Alexandre. Il a 11 ans. Il est parfois pénible.

C'est ma tante du côté de mon père. Elle s'appelle Véronique. Ça, c'est son chat Musica. Elle adore les animaux. Elle a aussi deux chiens!

Et toi, tu n'as pas de frères ou de sœurs?

Non. Je suis fille unique.

Tu as de la chance.

MISE EN TRAIN · *cent soixante-dix-sept* **177**

For Individual Needs

Challenge You might have partners read the text together. As they read, have students draw a family tree to illustrate the relationships that are mentioned. They can check their drawings by looking at Isabelle's family tree in the **Vocabulaire** on page 180.

Visual Learners Have students watch the video without the sound to encourage them to use visual clues to figure out who the people are and what they're like.

Building on Previous Skills

Have students use their reading strategies to match the following French cognates with their English equivalents.

1. **grands-parents**   a. *mom*
2. **papa**   b. *uncle*
3. **maman**   c. *baby*
4. **oncle**   d. *dad*
5. **cousins**   e. *grandparents*
6. **bébé**   f. *cousins*

 Video Integration

- **VIDEO PROGRAM,**
  Videocassette 3, 05:19–09:28
  Videocassette 5, 59:56–1:04:05
- **VIDEODISC PROGRAM,**
  Videodisc 4, Side A

Search 7100, Play To 14605

You may choose to continue with **Sympa, la famille! (suite)** at this time or wait until later in the chapter. When the story continues, Alexandre enters Isabelle's room without knocking or saying hello and asks where his CD is. Isabelle is annoyed at Alexandre but introduces him to Thuy. Next, the doorbell rings. It is Aunt Véronique, who has brought a kitten as a surprise for Isabelle and Alexandre. Isabelle introduces Thuy. Isabelle's father is not enthusiastic about the kitten, but the others convince him to let them keep it.

Teaching Suggestion

2 Have students find a quote from the story to confirm the true statements.

 For videodisc application, see *Videodisc Guide.*

For Individual Needs

4 Auditory Learners You might have students view the video or listen to the recording of **Sympa, la famille!** to find these expressions.

Captioned Video

4 To help students identify the expressions in Activity 4, play the captioned version of **Sympa, la famille!** on Videocassette 5.

Teaching Suggestions

5 Students might want to talk about their own families, or they might invent an imaginary family, select a TV or comic book family, or refer to the photo of the family on page 179 to compare to Isabelle's.

5 Students might also sketch a family tree in their journals and write a comparison in English.

These activities check for comprehension only. Students should not yet be expected to produce language modeled in **Mise en train**.

1 Tu as compris?

Answer these questions about **Sympa, la famille!**

1. What are Isabelle and Thuy talking about? Isabelle's family photos
2. Does Isabelle have brothers or sisters? If so, what are their names? Yes, a brother; Alexandre
3. How many cousins does she have? three
4. Who are some of the other family members she mentions? grandparents, parents, an uncle, two aunts
5. How does Isabelle feel about her family? How can you tell? She likes her family; She speaks favorably of them.

2 Vrai ou faux?

1. Julie a huit ans. vrai
2. Julie est blonde. faux
3. Les cousins d'Isabelle habitent à Paris. faux
4. Tante Véronique n'a pas d'animaux. faux
5. Thuy a un frère. faux

3 Quelle photo?

De quelle photo est-ce qu'Isabelle parle?

1. Il a onze ans. b
2. En maths, elle a toujours 18 sur 20. a
3. J'ai un an et demi, je crois... c
4. Elle a huit ans. d

a.　　　　　　　b.　　　　　　　c.　　　　　　　d.

4 Cherche les expressions

In **Sympa, la famille!**, what does Isabelle or Thuy say to . . . See answers below.

1. ask permission?
2. identify family members?
3. describe someone?
4. pay a compliment?
5. tell someone's age?
6. complain about someone?

> Je peux... ?　　C'est...　　Elle est très intelligente.
>
> Elle est adorable.　　Ce sont...　　Il/Elle a... ans.
>
> Il est parfois pénible.　　Ils sont heureux.

5 Et maintenant, à toi

How does Isabelle's family resemble or differ from families you know?

Answers
4 1. Je peux... ?
 2. C'est... ; Ce sont...
 3. *Possible answers:* Ils sont heureux. Elle est adorable. Elle est très intelligente.
 4. *Possible answers:* Elle est adorable. Elle est très intelligente.
 5. Il/Elle a... ans.
 6. Il est parfois pénible.

PREMIERE ETAPE (TPR) Storytelling Book pp. 25, 28

Identifying and introducing people

COMMENT DIT-ON... ?
Identifying people

7-1

To identify people:

C'est ma tante Véronique.
Ce sont mes cousins Loïc et Julie. *These/Those are . . .*
Voici mon frère Alexandre. *Here's . . .*
Voilà Patricia. *There's . . .*

6 C'est qui?

With a partner, take turns creating identities for the people in this picture.

𝒥ump Start!

Have students write answers to the following questions: **Tu t'appelles comment? Tu as quel âge? Ça va?**

MOTIVATE

Have students describe different types of families. Ask them to evaluate today's TV families. Are they realistic?

TEACH

Presentation

Comment dit-on... ? Before students open their books, use the expressions in the box to identify several students in the classroom and some pictures you've brought in of faculty members or of family members. After several examples, point to one or more people and ask **C'est qui?** Then, identify students who are close by or far away, using **voici** and **voilà**.

Teaching Suggestion

6 If students need help with French names, refer them to page 5 of the Preliminary Chapter.

Additional Practice

If you made a family tree transparency for the **Mise en train** (see Presentation, page 176), show it again and call on volunteers to identify the various family members. If not, have students turn to pages 176 and 177 and take turns identifying the people in Isabelle's family.

RESOURCES FOR PREMIERE ETAPE

PRINT
• *Lesson Planner,* p. 34
• *Practice and Activity Book,* pp. 74–76
• *Grammar and Vocabulary Workbook,* pp. 51–53
• *Activities for Communication,* pp. 37–38, 105, 108–109, 149–150
• *Listening Activities,* pp. 51, 55
• *Testing Program,* pp. 171–174
• *Alternative Assessment Guide,* p. 38

MEDIA
• *Video Program,* Videocassette 3
  Video Guide, pp. 45–50
• *Videodisc Program,* Videodisc 4, Side A
  Videodisc Guide, pp. 76–77
• *Teaching Transparencies* 7-1, 7-A
• *Interactive CD-ROM Program,* Disc 2
  CD-ROM Teacher's Guide, p. 28
• *Audio Compact Discs*
  Textbook Listening Activities, CD 7, Trs. 3–5
  Additional Listening Activities 7-1, 7-2, CD 7, Trs. 27–28
  Quiz 7-1B, CD 7, Tr. 21

PA pp. 74–75, Acts. 2a, 4

7-A, 7-1

GV p. 51, Acts. 1–2

CD-ROM Disc 2

Presentation

Vocabulaire Draw a transparency of the family tree with no labels. Uncover one generation at a time and identify each family member, writing in the person's relationship to Isabelle (**ma tante Véronique**). Then, create fill-in-the-blank sentences, such as **Véronique est la _____ d'Alexandre. (tante)**, and have students complete them.

For Individual Needs

Note de grammaire— Slower Pace Demonstrate this structure by pointing out students' school supplies and telling to whom they belong. For example, pick up a notebook and say **C'est le cahier de Steven.** Then, pick up an object and have a student tell whose it is.

Additional Practice

7 Say the names of two of the people on the family tree (**Julie et Loïc**). Have students tell or write the relationship between them. (**Julie est la sœur de Loïc.**) You might also have students write sentences identifying the relationship between two celebrities or cartoon characters. (**Bart Simpson est le frère de Lisa Simpson.**)

Language-to-Language

Have Spanish-speaking students tell how **de** is also used to show possession in Spanish. Explain how **de** contracts to **d'** before a vowel in French, where it doesn't in Spanish. (**Es el libro de Ana.**) Ask students if they know of other languages in which **de** is used in this way.

VOCABULAIRE

Les membres de la famille d'Isabelle

Ma grand-mère et mon grand-père, Eugénie et Jean-Marie Ménard

Other family relationships:
la femme *wife*
le mari *husband*
la fille *daughter*
le fils *son*
l'enfant *child*
le parent *parent, relative*

Ma tante Véronique, la sœur de mon père

Mon père et ma mère, Raymond et Josette Guérin

Mon oncle et ma tante, Guillaume et Micheline Ménard

Mon frère Alexandre

C'est moi!

Mes cousines Patricia et Julie, et mon cousin Loïc

Mon chien   Mon chat

Mon canari   Mon poisson

7 Qui est-ce? See answers below.

Which member of Isabelle's family does each of these statements refer to?

Le frère de Véronique, c'est Raymond.

1. C'est le père d'Alexandre.
2. C'est la femme de Guillaume.
3. C'est le grand-père de Julie.
4. C'est la mère de Patricia.
5. Ce sont les sœurs de Loïc.
6. C'est le cousin de Patricia.

NOTE DE GRAMMAIRE

Use **de (d')** to indicate relationship or ownership.

C'est la mère **de** Paul.
That's Paul's mother.

PA pp. 74, 76, Acts. 2b, 7b

Voici le chien **d'**Agnès.
Here's Agnès' dog.

C'est le copain **du** prof.
That's the teacher's friend.

GV p. 52, Acts. 3–4

Additional Grammar Practice, p. R40

180   *cent quatre-vingts*   CHAPITRE 7   La famille

Language Note

Students might want to know the following common expressions: **les gosses, les mômes,** or **les gamins** *(kids, brats);* **tonton** *(uncle,* also used sometimes to refer to former President François Mitterrand); **tata, tatie,** or **tantine** *(aunt);* **mémé** *(grandma);* **pépé** *(grandpa).*

Answers

7 1. Le père d'Alexandre, c'est Raymond.
  2. La femme de Guillaume, c'est Micheline.
  3. Le grand-père de Julie, c'est Jean-Marie.
  4. La mère de Patricia, c'est Micheline.
  5. Les sœurs de Loïc, ce sont Patricia et Julie.
  6. Le cousin de Patricia, c'est Alexandre.

8 Ecoute!

See scripts on p. 173G. 1. d 2. b 3. a 4. e 5. c

CD 7 Tr. 3

Alain montre des photos de sa famille à Jay. De quelle photo est-ce qu'il parle?

a.

b.

c.

d.

e.

GRAMMAIRE Possessive adjectives

	Before a masculine singular noun	Before a feminine singular noun	Before a plural noun
my	mon	ma	mes
your	ton	ta	tes
his/her/its	son	sa	ses
our	notre	notre	nos
your	votre	votre	vos
their	leur	leur	leurs

(mon/ton/son/notre/votre/leur } frère; ma/ta/sa/notre/votre/leur } sœur; mes/tes/ses/nos/vos/leurs } frères)

- **Son, sa,** and **ses** may mean either *her* or *his*.

C'est **son** père.	That's *her* father. *or* That's *his* father.
C'est **sa** mère.	That's *her* mother. *or* That's *his* mother.
Ce sont **ses** parents.	Those are *her* parents. *or* Those are *his* parents.

  PA pp. 75–76, Acts. 6–7a

- **Mon, ton,** and **son** are used before all singular nouns that begin with a vowel sound, whether the noun is masculine or feminine.

  C'est **ton** amie Marianne?
  C'est **mon** oncle Xavier.

  GV p. 53, Acts. 5–7

  Additional Grammar Practice, pp. R40–R41

- Liaison is always made with **mon, ton,** and **son,** and with all the plural forms.

  mon école   nos amis

- Can you figure out when to use **ton, ta, tes,** and when to use **votre** and **vos?***

9 Ecoute!

See scripts and answers on p. 173G.

Listen to Roland and Odile. Are they talking about their own pets or someone else's? Then, listen again to find out what kind of pets they're talking about.

CD 7 Tr. 4

*Use **ton, ta,** and **tes** with people you would normally address with **tu**. Use **votre** and **vos** with people you would normally address with **vous**.

PREMIERE ETAPE

cent quatre-vingt-un **181**

Teacher Note

Grammaire You might work only with the singular forms during one class period and leave **notre, votre, leur, nos, vos,** and **leurs** for the following day.

Language-to-Language

Point out to students that they should choose **son, sa,** or **ses** based on the gender and number of the object, <u>not</u> of the owner, as they would in English. Tell them that **son stylo** means either *his pen* or *her pen* and that **sa gomme** means *his eraser* or *her eraser*.

Teaching Suggestion

8 You might have students describe the pictures before you play the recording. Tell them to listen for key words to get the general meaning and not to try to translate every word.

Presentation

Grammaire Before students see these structures, ask them for the different ways to say *the* (**le, la, l', les**). Ask them how they choose the correct article (gender, number). Then, pick up classroom objects and say they belong to you. (**C'est mon livre.**) You might also ask about ownership by asking **C'est ton livre?** Next, pick up a boy's pencil and say **C'est son crayon.** Do the same with a girl's pencil. Ask students what they notice about **son** (it means both *his* and *her*). Finally, pick up items belonging to various students and ask the class **C'est mon stylo?**, prompting the response **Non, c'est son stylo!** You might also pick up an item from your desk to prompt the response **Oui, c'est votre...** or choose a book that two students are sharing to prompt **Non, c'est leur livre!**

For Individual Needs

9 Slower Pace Before starting this activity, you might ask students to determine which of the possessive adjectives they would use to speak about their own pets (**mon, ma, mes, notre, nos**) and which they would use to speak about someone else's (**son, sa, ses, leur, leurs, ton, ta, tes, votre, vos**).

Reteaching

10 Adverbs of frequency
Review adverbs of frequency such as **souvent, jamais,** and **une fois par semaine** by giving students a subject and a verb phrase (**ils/jouer au golf**), and asking them to form a sentence. (**Ils jouent souvent au golf.**)

 For Individual Needs

10 Slower Pace Have students tell how they think the people in the illustration are related. Then, have them identify the activities the people like to do. You might write these on the board or on a transparency as students suggest them. Finally, have partners use this information in their questions and answers.

Teaching Suggestion

10 In order to practice **ton, ta,** and **tes,** have partners ask each other to verify the relationships by asking questions such as **C'est ta sœur?**

Additional Practice

11 This activity could be extended by asking students to find a picture in a magazine that illustrates a familial relationship. Have students write on a separate piece of paper what they think the relationship between the people in the picture might be. Then, tell them to exchange pictures with a partner and write down the relationship they imagine in their partner's picture. Finally, have partners compare their impressions.

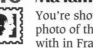 **NOTE CULTURELLE**

Family life plays an important role in French society. Although modern times have brought changes to the family's daily life (more working mothers, less time for family activities, more divorces, and so on), France is working hard to maintain the family unit. To do this, the French government provides subsidies (**allocations familiales**) to all families with two or more children. Other social benefits also encourage larger families in a country with an ever-decreasing birth rate. These benefits include a paid maternity leave of at least 14 weeks, a renewable maternity or paternity leave of one year, free day-care, and a birth allowance (**allocation de naissance**) for every child after the second. Families also receive subsidies for each child attending school or college.

10 **Ma famille française**

You're showing a classmate a photo of the family you stayed with in France. Take turns with a partner identifying the people and asking questions about them.

—C'est qui, ça?
—C'est ma sœur.
—Elle joue souvent au tennis?
—Oui. Une fois par semaine.

11 Devine! *Guess!*

Identify the teenagers in the photos below and tell how you think the other people in the photos are related to them. Take turns with a partner.

C'est Nadine et son grand-père.

Nadine

Hassan

Thierry

Liliane

Monique et Annie

 For Individual Needs

Tactile Learners Have students cut out three magazine pictures of men, four of women, two of boys, and three of girls. Give each student an unlabeled drawing of a family tree, then have students pair off. One student will call out a family member (**C'est le père de la famille.**), and the other will glue a picture in the appropriate place on the family tree. Partners should take turns calling out the names of family members.

COMMENT DIT-ON...❓

Introducing people

To introduce someone to a friend:
   C'est Jean-Michel.
   Je te présente mon ami Jean-Michel.
      I'd like you to meet . . .

p. 76,
Act. 8

To introduce someone to an adult:
   Je vous présente Jean-Michel.

7-1

To respond to an introduction:
   Salut, Jean-Michel. **Ça va?**
   Bonjour.
   Très heureux (heureuse). *Pleased to meet you.* (FORMAL)

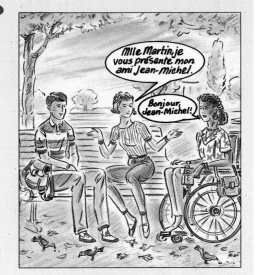

12 Ecoute!   See scripts and answers on p. 173G.

CD 7 Tr. 5

Are the people in these conversations identifying someone or introducing someone?

13 Je te présente...

A new student from France has just arrived at your school and asks you the names and ages of some students in your class. Introduce him or her to those classmates. Act this out in your group, changing roles.

14 Mon journal

Write about your family, giving the names and ages of each person. Tell what each of them likes to do. You may choose to create an imaginary family or you may want to write about a famous family in real life or on TV.

Tu te rappelles❓

Do you remember how to ask for and give people's names and ages?
—Elle s'appelle comment?
—Magali.
—Elle a quel âge?
—Seize ans.

 à la carte

Here are some other words you might need to talk about your family.

des petits-enfants	*grandchildren*
un demi-frère	*stepbrother; half brother*
une demi-sœur	*stepsister; half sister*
un(e) enfant unique	*an only child*
une belle-mère	*stepmother/mother-in-law*
un beau-père	*stepfather/father-in-law*
un petit-fils	*grandson*
une petite-fille	*granddaughter*
une nièce	*niece*
un neveu	*nephew*

Presentation

Comment dit-on... ?
Demonstrate the expressions by introducing students to stuffed animals you bring in, and then by introducing one student to another. Then, use **Je vous présente...** to introduce one student to the entire class.

 For videodisc application, see *Videodisc Guide.*

📁 Portfolio

13 Oral   This activity can be used for oral assessment or can be added to students' oral portfolios. For portfolio information, see the *Alternative Assessment Guide,* pages iv–17.

📖 Mon journal

14   For additional family vocabulary, refer students to the Additional Vocabulary on pages R7–R11. Students might want to include a family tree or photos in their journal entry. For an additional journal entry suggestion for Chapter 7, see *Practice and Activity Book,* page 151.

CLOSE

To close this **étape,** have students bring in family photos or magazine pictures to represent an imaginary family. Have partners identify the people. Encourage them to ask questions to find out more about the people in the pictures.

ASSESS

Quiz 7-1A, Quiz 7-1B, *Testing Program,* pp. 171–174
Audio CD 7, Tr. 21

Performance Assessment

Have students form groups of three. In each group, one person will introduce another to the third member. This person asks questions to get to know the newcomer, who can take on any identity. Have students present these introductions to the class.

DEUXIEME ETAPE
 Storytelling Book pp. 26, 28

Describing and characterizing people

PA p. 77, Acts. 9–10   7-B, 7-C   GV p. 54, Acts. 8–9

VOCABULAIRE

Ils sont comment?

PETITE   GRAND   BRUNE   BLOND   ROUX

JEUNE   AGEE   MINCE   GROS

You can also use these descriptive words:

> **mignon(mignonne)(s)** *cute*   **ne... ni grand(e)(s) ni petit(e)(s)** *. . . neither tall nor short*

You can use these words to characterize people:

amusant(e)(s)	*funny*	**sympathique(s)/sympa**	*nice*	**embêtant(e)(s)**	*annoying*
timide(s)	*shy*	**intelligent(e)(s)**	*smart*	**pénible(s)**	*a pain in the neck*
gentil(le)(s)	*nice*	**content(e)(s)**	*happy*	**mechant(e)(s)**	*mean*
		fort(e)(s)	*strong*		

De bons conseils

Organizing vocabulary in various ways can help you remember words. Group words by categories, like foods, sports, numbers, colors, and so forth. Try to associate words with a certain context, such as school (school subjects, classroom objects) or a store (items for sale, salesperson). Try to use associations like opposites, such as **petit— grand** or **gros—mince.**

Jump Start!

Write **stylos, mère, livre, amie, feuilles de papier,** and **sport préféré** on the board. Have students write sentences claiming ownership. (**Ce sont mes stylos.**)

MOTIVATE

Ask students to describe their favorite celebrity or a celebrity you suggest.

TEACH

Presentation

Vocabulaire Present the vocabulary using magazine pictures. Then, ask students to name celebrities whom these adjectives describe. (**Qui est amusant?**) You might also ask about the hair color of class members. (**Qui est blond(e)? brun(e)? roux(rousse)?**)

Teaching Suggestion

De bons conseils Suggest that students make flash cards pairing adjectives that are opposites (**gentil/méchant**), associating a person with each one (**fort — Superman®**), or drawing a facial expression to represent each one.

Additional Practice

Create true-false statements about celebrities and have the class respond to them. (**Michael Jordan est grand.**)

RESOURCES FOR **DEUXIEME ETAPE**

PRINT
- *Lesson Planner,* p. 35
- *Practice and Activity Book,* pp. 77–79
- *Grammar and Vocabulary Workbook,* pp. 54–58
- *Activities for Communication,* pp. 39–40, 106, 108–109, 149–150
- *Listening Activities,* pp. 52, 56
- *Testing Program,* pp. 175–178
- *Alternative Assessment Guide,* p. 38

MEDIA
- *Video Program,* Videocassette 3
  Video Guide, pp. 45–50
- *Videodisc Program,* Videodisc 4, Side A
  Videodisc Guide, p. 77
- *Teaching Transparencies* 7-2, 7-B, 7-C
- *Interactive CD-ROM Program,* Disc 2
  CD-ROM Teacher's Guide, pp. 28–29
- *Audio Compact Discs*
  Textbook Listening Activity, CD 7, Trs. 6–7
  Additional Listening Activities 7-3, 7-4, CD 7, Trs. 29–30
  Quiz 7-2B, CD 7, Tr. 22

15 Ecoute! <small>See scripts and answers on p. 173G.</small>

<small>CD 7 Tr. 6</small>

Match the descriptions you hear with the students' names.

Roger   Denise   Julie   Martin   Carmen

COMMENT DIT-ON... ?
Describing and characterizing people

p. 78, Act. 13   7-2

To ask what someone is like:
Il est comment? *What is he like?*
Elle est comment? *What is she like?*
Ils/Elles sont comment? *What are they like?*

To describe someone:
Il n'est ni grand **ni** petit.
Elle est brune.
Ils/Elles sont âgé(e)s.

To characterize someone:
Il est pénible.
Elle est timide.
Ils/Elles sont amusant(e)s.

16 Ecoute! <small>See scripts and answers on p. 173G.</small>

<small>CD 7 Tr. 7</small>

Ariane is telling a friend about her cousins. Does she have a favorable or unfavorable opinion of them?

17 Des familles bizarres

Comment sont les membres de ces familles?
<small>See answers below.</small>

Answers
17 *Possible answers for first photo:* L'oncle est gros, et la mère est mince. Les enfants sont pénibles. *Possible answers for second photo:* Bart est petit, pénible et jaune. Maggie est mignonne. Lisa est intelligente et gentille. Homer est gros et amusant.

Language Note
17 Tell students that they should not add an **-s** to family names in French: **Ce sont les Simpson. Voilà les Ménard.**

For Individual Needs
15 Slower Pace Before playing the recording, ask students to suggest adjectives they might use to describe each person in the picture. Write their suggestions on a transparency for them to refer to as they listen to the recording.

Presentation
Comment dit-on... ? Begin by asking **Je suis comment? Grand(e)? Petit(e)? Jeune? Agé(e)? Amusant(e)?** Then, hold up pictures of people and ask what they are like. (**Il/Elle est comment? Ils/Elles sont comment?**) Next, name or show a photo of a celebrity and ask the class various questions about the person, such as **Il est petit? Il est fort? Il est brun? Il est comment?** You might also play the **Mise en train** video episode, pausing after each person is described to ask **Il/Elle est comment?**

For videodisc application, see *Videodisc Guide.*

Teaching Suggestion
16 Before students hear the recording, have them suggest what Ariane might say that would be favorable or unfavorable. Remind students that these categories are matters of opinion.

Portfolio
17 Written This activity could be included in students' written portfolios. For portfolio information, see the *Alternative Assessment Guide,* pages iv–17.

Presentation

Grammaire Draw stick figures of a boy, a girl, two boys, and two girls on the board. Have students suggest descriptions for each one, using adjectives they can recall. (**Il est...** , **Elle est...** , **Ils/Elles sont...**) Write the adjectives in the correct form under each figure. Have students suggest rules for adjective formation illustrated by the adjectives you have written. Then, point to the appropriate stick figure as you say the sentences in the grammar box. Have students suggest reasons for the differences. Repeat this with adjectives that don't change and ask students what they notice about these adjectives.

Teaching Suggestions

18 This activity could be written or done orally in pairs, with students taking turns identifying similarities and differences.

18 Have students compare themselves to either Frédéric or Denise.

19 Students may prefer to describe fictitious friends.

19 This activity could be written and included in students' portfolios or used as a journal entry.

Additional Practice

Ask students questions about celebrities or mythical figures, such as **Santa Claus est gros ou grosse? Tom Cruise est brun ou brune?** You might also ask students to describe them. (**Comment est Santa Claus? Et Michael Jordan?**)

GRAMMAIRE Adjective agreement

As you may remember from Chapter 3, you often change the pronunciation and spelling of adjectives according to the nouns they describe.

- If the adjective describes a feminine noun, you usually add an **e** to the masculine form of the adjective.
- If the adjective describes a plural noun, you usually add an **s** to the singular form, masculine or feminine.
- If an adjective describes both males and females, you always use the masculine plural form.
- Some adjectives have special (irregular) feminine or plural forms. Here are some irregular adjectives that you've seen in this chapter.

P A
pp. 77–78,
Acts. 11–12

G V
pp. 55–57,
Acts. 10–14

Additional Grammar
Practice, p. R41

Il est **roux**.	Elle est **rousse**.
Ils sont **roux**.	Elles sont **rousses**.
Il est **mignon**.	Elle est **mignonne**.
Ils sont **mignons**.	Elles sont **mignonnes**.
Il est **gentil**.	Elle est **gentille**.
Ils sont **gentils**.	Elles sont **gentilles**.
Il est **gros**.	Elle est **grosse**.
Ils sont **gros**.	Elles sont **grosses**.

- In the masculine forms, the final consonant sound is silent. In the feminine forms, the final consonant sound is pronounced.
- A few adjectives don't ever change. Here are some that you've already seen.

marron   orange   cool   super   sympa

18 On est différents!

Frédéric and Denise are brother and sister. Look at the picture and tell how they're alike and how they're different. See answers below.

Frédéric est grand, mais Denise est petite.

19 Les meilleurs amis

Take turns with a partner describing your best friends. Tell about your friends' appearance, personality, and interests.

Language Note

Tell students that some adjectives, such as **cool** and **super,** are invariable because they come from another language. Others, such as **marron** and **orange,** are invariable because their adjective forms were derived from nouns (*chestnut* and *orange*).

Possible answers

18 Frédéric est blond, grand et gentil, mais Denise est brune, petite, mince et embêtante. Ils sont contents.

CD-ROM
Disc 2

GRAMMAIRE The verb être

Être is an irregular verb.

pp. 78–79
Acts. 14–15

pp. 57–58,
Acts. 15–17

être *(to be)*

Je **suis** intelligent(e).	Nous **sommes** intelligent(e)s.
Tu **es** intelligent(e).	Vous **êtes** intelligent(e)(s).
Il/Elle/On **est** intelligent(e).	Ils/Elles **sont** intelligent(e)s.

Additional Grammar
Practice, p. R41

20 On est très différents

Albain is describing everyone, including himself. Complete his descriptions with the appropriate forms of **être**. 1. suis 2. sont 3. êtes 4. es 5. est 6. est 7. sont 8. sommes

Je __1__ blond, mais Rénato et Jacob, ils __2__ bruns. Francette et Babette, vous __3__ rousses. Et toi, Francette, tu __4__ grande aussi. Rénato aussi __5__ grand, et pénible. Babette __6__ très gentille et mignonne. Mais les différences ne __7__ pas importantes. Nous __8__ tous intelligents.

21 Devine!

Describe a member of the Louvain family to your partner, without naming the family member. He or she will try to figure out who it is. Take turns.

22 Mon journal

Write a paragraph describing a family member whom you admire. Tell what he or she likes to do and where he or she likes to go. If you prefer, choose a member of your favorite TV family and describe and characterize that person.

DEUXIEME ETAPE

cent quatre-vingt-sept **187**

ASSESS

Quiz 7-2A, Quiz 7-2B, *Testing Program,*
pp. 175–178
Audio CD 7, Tr. 22

Performance Assessment

Have students bring in a photo of someone and describe that person to the class, giving a physical description and telling what the person is like. The photo might be of a family member, a relative, a friend, or a famous person. Students might also choose to bring in a picture from a magazine.

Presentation

Grammaire Make two sets of flashcards, one with the forms of **être** and the other with the subject pronouns. Tape the flashcards in random order on the board and have students match the subjects and verbs. Then, remove the verb cards from the board and ask for volunteers to write the verb forms next to the subject cards. Finally, divide the class into two teams. Have the first player from each team come to the board. Give a subject pronoun and an adjective (**elle/brun**). The first player to combine them in a correct sentence on the board wins a point. (**Elle est brune.**) Continue until all players have had a turn.

Additional Practice

21 Extend this activity by having partners also tell how the person described might be related to Gabrielle.

Mon journal

22 As a prewriting activity, name a member of a popular TV family and ask students to describe him or her. For an additional journal entry suggestion for Chapter 7, see *Practice and Activity Book*, page 151.

CLOSE

To close this **étape,** have students mime adjectives before the whole class or a small group who will try to guess the adjectives. (**Tu es âgé(e)!**) The mimers might select adjectives from a stack of flashcards or mime an adjective of their choice.

VIDEO PROGRAM
Videocassette 3
09:29–12:06

OR **VIDEODISC PROGRAM,**
Videodisc 4, Side A

Search 14605, Play To 17090

Teacher Notes

• See the *Video Guide,* the *Videodisc Guide,* and the *CD-ROM Teacher's Guide* for activities related to the **Panorama Culturel.**

• Remind students that cultural material may be included in the Chapter Quizzes and Test.

• The interviewees' language represents informal, unrehearsed speech. Occasionally, edits have been made for clarification.

Motivating Activity

Before students view the interviews, ask them if they have a pet, and if so, what it is.

Presentation

Ask students for common pet names for dogs, cats, and other pets in the United States. Then, play the video and have them listen for the kind of pet each person has and its name.

Thinking Critically

Analyzing Have students consider the advantages of tatooing pets versus using identification tags. Which system is more effective?

Language Note

Students might want to know these words: **se promener** *(to go for a walk)*; **au garrot** *(at the withers)*; **faire des balades** *(to go for walks).*

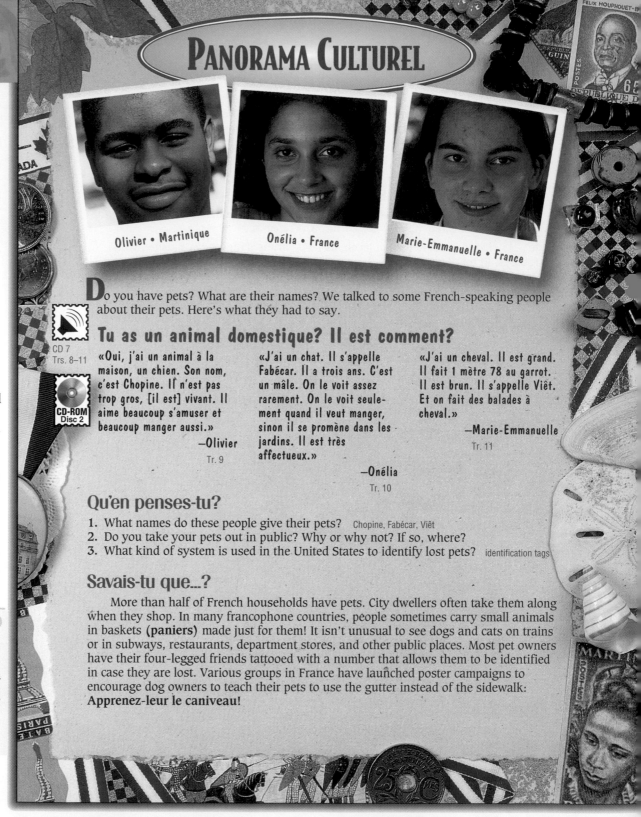

PANORAMA CULTUREL

Olivier • Martinique

Onélia • France

Marie-Emmanuelle • France

Do you have pets? What are their names? We talked to some French-speaking people about their pets. Here's what they had to say.

CD 7
Trs. 8–11

CD-ROM
Disc 2

Tu as un animal domestique? Il est comment?

«Oui, j'ai un animal à la maison, un chien. Son nom, c'est Chopine. Il n'est pas trop gros, [il est] vivant. Il aime beaucoup s'amuser et beaucoup manger aussi.»
—Olivier
Tr. 9

«J'ai un chat. Il s'appelle Fabécar. Il a trois ans. C'est un mâle. On le voit assez rarement. On le voit seulement quand il veut manger, sinon il se promène dans les jardins. Il est très affectueux.»
—Onélia
Tr. 10

«J'ai un cheval. Il est grand. Il fait 1 mètre 78 au garrot. Il est brun. Il s'appelle Viêt. Et on fait des balades à cheval.»
—Marie-Emmanuelle
Tr. 11

Qu'en penses-tu?

1. What names do these people give their pets?   Chopine, Fabécar, Viêt
2. Do you take your pets out in public? Why or why not? If so, where?
3. What kind of system is used in the United States to identify lost pets?   identification tags

Savais-tu que...?

More than half of French households have pets. City dwellers often take them along when they shop. In many francophone countries, people sometimes carry small animals in baskets (**paniers**) made just for them! It isn't unusual to see dogs and cats on trains or in subways, restaurants, department stores, and other public places. Most pet owners have their four-legged friends tattooed with a number that allows them to be identified in case they are lost. Various groups in France have launched poster campaigns to encourage dog owners to teach their pets to use the gutter instead of the sidewalk: **Apprenez-leur le caniveau!**

Questions

1. Qui est Chopine? Et Fabécar? Et Viêt? (le chien d'Olivier; le chat d'Onélia; le cheval de Marie-Emmanuelle)
2. Comment sont-ils? (Chopine—pas trop gros, vivant; Fabécar—très affectueux; Viêt—brun et grand)
3. Qu'est-ce que Chopine aime faire? (s'amuser, manger)

Language Note

Students might want to know these animal-related expressions: **minou** *(kitty,* used to call a cat, or as a generic name for a cat); **ouah-ouah** *(bow-wow);* **aboyer** *(to bark);* **miaou** *(meow);* **miauler/faire miaou** *(to mew, whine).*

TROISIEME ETAPE

(TPR) Storytelling Book pp. 27, 28

Asking for, giving, and refusing permission

COMMENT DIT-ON... ?

Asking for, giving, and refusing permission

To ask for permission:

Je voudrais aller au cinéma. **Tu es d'accord?**
Is that OK with you?

(Est-ce que) je peux sortir? *May I . . .*

To give permission:

Oui, si tu veux. *Yes, if you want to.*
Pourquoi pas?
Oui, bien sûr.
D'accord, si tu fais d'abord la vaisselle.
OK, if you . . . first.

To refuse permission:

Pas question! *Out of the question!*
Non, c'est impossible. *No, that's impossible.*
Non, tu dois faire tes devoirs.
No, you've got to . . .
Pas ce soir. *Not . . .*

CD-ROM Disc 2

PA p. 81, Act. 21

7-3

For additional practice, see pp. R41–R42.

23 Ecoute! See scripts and answers on p. 173H.

Listen to these people ask for permission.
Are they given or refused permission?

CD 7 Tr. 12

VOCABULAIRE

PA pp. 80–82, Acts. 17–18, 20, 22–23

7-D

GV pp. 59–60, Acts. 18–21

débarrasser la table	to clear the table
faire les courses	to do the shopping
faire le ménage	to clean house
faire la vaisselle	to do the dishes
garder ta petite sœur	to look after . . .
laver la voiture	to wash the car
passer l'aspirateur	to vacuum
promener le chien	to walk the dog
ranger ta chambre	to pick up your room
sortir la poubelle	to take out the trash
tondre le gazon	to mow the lawn

CD-ROM Disc 2

TROISIEME ETAPE

cent quatre-vingt-neuf **189**

Jump Start!

Ask students to write the opposites of **gros, grand, méchant,** and **âgé.**

MOTIVATE

Ask students to suggest activities that require permission.

TEACH

Presentation

Comment dit-on... ? Write the headings *asking for permission, giving permission,* and *refusing permission* on a transparency. Model the new expressions, using gestures. Write the new expressions on strips of transparency. Have students select an expression and place the strip under the appropriate heading.

For videodisc application, see *Videodisc Guide.*

◆ For Individual Needs

23 Slower Pace To give an example, have a student ask you for permission. Give a positive or negative response and then ask the class if you granted or refused permission.

Presentation

Vocabulaire Use props (a leash, trash bag, dishes) to mime the activities, telling students in French what you're doing. Ask either-or questions (**Je fais la vaisselle ou les courses?**) to verify comprehension.

(TPR) Tell students to do various chores and have them respond by miming the appropriate activity.

RESOURCES FOR TROISIEME ETAPE

PRINT
- *Lesson Planner,* p. 36
- *Practice and Activity Book,* pp. 80–82
- *Grammar and Vocabulary Workbook* pp. 59–60
- *Activities for Communication,* pp. 41–42, 107, 108–109, 149–150
- *Listening Activities,* pp. 52–53, 57
- *Testing Program,* pp. 179–182
- *Alternative Assessment Guide,* p. 38

MEDIA
- *Video Program,* Videocassette 3
  Video Guide, pp. 45–50
- *Videodisc Program,* Videodisc 4, Side A
  Videodisc Guide, p. 78
- *Teaching Transparencies* 7-3, 7-D
- *Interactive CD-ROM Program,* Disc 2
  CD-ROM Teacher's Guide, p. 29
- *Audio Compact Discs*
  Textbook Listening Activities, CD 7, Trs. 12–13
  Additional Listening Activities 7-5, 7-6, CD 7, Trs. 31–32
  Quiz 7-3B, CD 7, Tr. 23

Teaching Suggestion

24 You might have students tell or write what is happening in the pictures.

 Portfolio

25 Written This activity could be a written exercise, with students writing a paragraph about who does what chores in their homes. Have them list the chores to be done at home with a person's name next to each. Students might exchange rough drafts to read and edit. The first and final drafts might be included in students' written portfolios. For portfolio information, see the *Alternative Assessment Guide,* pages iv–17.

Group Work

26 After students have written their captions, make four columns on the board, each representing one of the illustrations. Have students write one of their captions in the appropriate column. Then, have small groups make up a story, using one caption from each column.

For Individual Needs

26 Auditory Learners For additional listening practice, call out two expressions for each illustration and have students choose the correct one. For example, for the second illustration, you might say **Oui, si tu veux** or **Pas question.**

Teaching Suggestions

- Have partners role-play asking a parent for permission to attend a party at a friend's house on a week night.
- Show *Teaching Transparency 7-3* and have groups of four students role-play the situation shown.

---

24 **Ecoute!** See scripts on p. 173H. 1. c 2. e 3. d 4. a 5. f 6. b

Listen to some French teenagers ask permission to go out with their friends. Which picture represents the outcome of each dialogue?

CD 7 Tr. 13

a.

b.

c.

d.

e.

f.

25 **Qui doit le faire?**

Ask your partner who does various chores at his or her house. Then, change roles.

—Qui promène le chien?
—Mon frère. Et moi aussi quelquefois.

26 **Qu'est-ce qu'ils disent?** *What are they saying?*

1.

2.

3.

4.

190 *cent quatre-vingt-dix*

CHAPITRE 7   La famille

Language Note

Point out that **aujourd'hui, ce week-end, ce matin,** and **cet après-midi** can be substituted for **ce soir** in the expression **Pas ce soir.**

Career Path

Have students imagine that they work for a French family as an **au pair** or a nanny. How would the vocabulary they have learned in this chapter help them with their daily tasks? (family vocabulary, vocabulary for chores around the house) Have them discuss their ideas, and then have them think about other types of vocabulary that would help them in that situation.

27 Et toi?

Give or refuse permission in these situations.

1. Your little sister or brother asks to listen to your cassette.
2. Your friend wants to read your novel.
3. Your little sister or brother wants to go to the movies with you and your friend.

28 Jeu de rôle

Pretend you're a parent. Your partner asks permission to do several activities this weekend. Refuse permission for some, give permission for others, and give reasons. Change roles.

P R O N O N C I A T I O N

The nasal sounds [ɔ̃], [ɛ̃], and [œ̃]

See scripts and answers on p. 173H.

CD 7 Trs. 14–19

In Chapter 5 you learned about the nasal sound [ɑ̃]. Now listen to the other French nasal sounds [ɔ̃], [ɛ̃], and [œ̃]. As you repeat the following words, try not to put a trace of the consonant **n** in your nasal sounds.

on hein un

How are these nasal sounds represented in writing? The nasal sound [ɔ̃] is represented by a combination of **on** or **om**. Several letter combinations can represent the sound [ɛ̃], for example, **in, im, ain, aim, (i)en**. The nasal sound [œ̃] is spelled **un** or **um**. A vowel after these groups of letters or, in some cases, a doubling of the consonants **n** or **m** will result in a non-nasal sound, as in **limonade** and **ennemi**.

A. A prononcer

Repeat the following words.

1. ton	blond	pardon	nombre
2. cousin	impossible	copain	faim
3. un	lundi	brun	humble

B. A lire

Take turns with a partner reading the following sentences aloud.

1. Ils ont très faim. Ils vont prendre des sandwiches au jambon. C'est bon!
2. Allons faire du patin ou bien, allons au concert!
3. Ce garçon est blond et ce garçon-là est brun. Ils sont minces et mignons!
4. Pardon. C'est combien, cette montre? Cent soixante-quinze francs?

C. A écrire

You're going to hear a short dialogue. Write down what you hear.

Language Note

Point out that even though the nasal sound [ɛ̃] can be spelled in a variety of ways, the letter **i** is always part of the syllable. Make sure that students pronounce the nasal [ɔ̃] with their mouths small and rounded, with most of the sound passing through the nose (**pardon**). For the nasal [ɛ̃], the mouth is wider but still not very open (**jardin**). For the nasal [œ̃] (**lundi**), the jaw should be dropped more than for the [ɛ̃] sound.

Game

CHASSE AU TRÉSOR Provide each student with a list of ten instructions, such as **Trouve quelqu'un qui...** (1) **a deux tantes.** (2) **a un poisson.** (3) **ne fait jamais les courses.** Students circulate, asking questions in French. When they find someone who can answer a question affirmatively, they should have that student sign his or her name next to the item. The first student to complete the list wins.

📁 Portfolio

28 Oral This activity is appropriate for students' oral portfolios. You might have volunteers perform their dialogues for the class. For portfolio information, see the *Alternative Assessment Guide,* pages iv–17.

Music Link

Prononciation To have students listen to the nasal sound in words like **ton** and **blond,** play the song *Il était une bergère,* available on Audio CD 10. Before you play the song, you might want to give students a copy of the script. (See *Listening Activities,* page 82.)

CLOSE

To close this **étape,** have students choose one family member (real or fictitious), present and describe this person to the class, and tell what chore(s) the person does or does not do around the house. This might be an oral or written activity.

ASSESS

Quiz 7-3A, Quiz 7-3B, *Testing Program,* pp. 179–182
Audio CD 7, Tr. 23

Performance Assessment

Have students write three things they would like to do and three chores they must do. Then, tell them to pair off and create a skit in which a student asks a parent for permission to do something and the parent grants or refuses permission. Alternatively, students might create an oral or written monologue in which they complain about all the chores they have to do.

READING STRATEGY

Finding the main idea

Teacher Note

For an additional reading, see *Practice and Activity Book*, page 83.

PREREADING
Activities A–B

Motivating Activity

Ask students if they've ever adopted a pet and how they went about finding and choosing one (newspaper, animal shelter, pet shop).

READING
Activities C–G

Teaching Suggestion

You might form small groups and assign each group one of the animals. Students should look for a physical description, personality characteristics, where the pet is located, and how it got to be in the shelter. Have groups share their information with the class. You might also have groups read their information aloud and have the class guess which pet they are describing.

Terms in Lisons!

Write the following terms on the board or on a transparency to help students in their reading:
recueilli *(picked up)*
maître(sse) *(pet owner)*
course *(race)*
courir *(to run)*
s'entendre bien avec *(to get along well with)*

LISONS!

Have you ever read an article about animals in an American magazine or newspaper? Here are some articles that appeared in the French magazine *Femme Actuelle*.

DE BONS CONSEILS

When you read something, it's important to separate the main idea from the supporting details. Sometimes the main idea is clearly stated at the beginning, other times it's just implied.

A. Which completion best expresses the main idea of these articles?
These articles are about . . .
1. animals that are missing.
2. animals that have performed heroic rescues.
3. animals that are up for adoption.
4. animals that have won prizes at cat and dog shows.

B. Now that you've decided what the main idea of the reading is, make a list of the kinds of details you expect to find in each of the articles. See answers below.

C. How is Mayo different from the other animals? What is the main idea of the article about him? See answers below. What other details are given?

D. Each of the articles includes a description of the animal. Look at the articles again and answer these questions.
1. Which animal is the oldest? The youngest? Camel; Jupiter
2. Which animals get along well with children? Camel, Jupiter, Flora

192 *cent quatre-vingt-douze*

EN DIRECT DES REFUGES

miaou

IL VOUS ATTEND, ADOPTEZ-LE
CAMEL, 5 ANS

Ce sympathique bobtail blanc et gris est arrivé au refuge à la suite du décès accidentel de son maître. Il est vif, joyeux, a bon caractère et s'entend très bien avec les enfants. En échange de son dévouement et de sa fidélité, ce sportif robuste demande un grand espace afin de pouvoir courir et s'ébattre à son aise.

Continuez à nous écrire, et envoyez-nous votre photo avec votre protégé, une surprise vous attend!

Cet animal vous attend au refuge de la Société normande de protection aux animaux, 7 bis, avenue Jacques-Chastellain, Ile Lacroix 76000 Rouen. Tél.: (02) 35.70.20.36. Si Camel a été adopté, pensez à ses voisins de cage.

ELLE VOUS ATTEND, ADOPTEZ-LA
DADY, 2 ANS

Toute blanche, à l'exception de quelques petites taches et des oreilles noires bien dressées, Dady a un petit air de spitz, opulente fourrure en moins. Gentille, enjouée, très attachante, elle a été abandonnée après la séparation de ses maîtres et attend une famille qui accepterait de s'occuper d'elle un peu, beaucoup, passionnément.

Cet animal vous attend au refuge de l'Eden, Rod A'char, 29430 Lanhouarneau. Tél.: (02) 98.61.64.55. Colette Di Faostino tient seule, sans aucune subvention, ce havre exemplaire mais pauvre. Si Dady avait été adoptée, pensez à ses compagnons de malchance !

Mayo a trouvé une famille

Mayo a été adopté à la SPA de Valenciennes par Françoise Robeaux qui rêvait d'un chat gris ! Il a ainsi rejoint l'autre «fils» de la famille, un superbe siamois âgé de 13 ans.

Teacher Note

Remind students that they don't need to know the meaning of every word to understand the reading selections.

Answers

B *Possible answers:* what kinds of animals are available, how to adopt the animals, each animal's age, appearance, and personality

C Mayo is no longer up for adoption; Mayo has found a family; where Mayo was adopted, the name of Mayo's new owner, Mayo's color, the fact that the owner already has a thirteen-year-old Siamese cat

ELLE VOUS ATTEND, ADOPTEZ-LA

POUPETTE, 3 ANS

Cette jolie chatte stérilisée au regard tendre et étonné a été recueillie à l'âge de quelques semaines par une vieille dame, dont elle a été la dernière compagne. Sa maîtresse est malheureusement décédée après un long séjour à l'hôpital. Poupette, l'orpheline, ne comprend pas ce qui lui arrive et commence à trouver le temps long ! Elle a hâte de retrouver un foyer «sympa», des bras caressants et une paire de genoux pour ronronner.

Cet animal vous attend avec espoir au refuge Grammont de la SPA 30, av. du Général-de-Gaulle 92230 Gennevilliers. Tél.: (01) 47.98.57.40. Rens. sur Minitel: 36.15 SPA. Si Poupette est déjà partie, pensez aux autres!

IL VOUS ATTEND, ADOPTEZ-LE

JUPITER, 7 MOIS

Cet adorable chaton tigré et blanc vient tout juste d'être castré et est dûment tatoué. Très joueur et affectueux, il a été recueilli au refuge parce que, malheureusement, sa maîtresse a dû être hospitalisée pour un séjour de longue durée. Sociable, il s'entend très bien avec les jeunes enfants et accepterait volontiers un chien pour compagnon.

Cet animal vous attend au refuge de la fondation Assistance aux animaux, 8, rue des Plantes 77410 Villevaudé. Tél.: (01) 60.26.20.48 (l'après-midi seulement).

-ouaf

miaou

ELLE VOUS ATTEND, ADOPTEZ-LA

FLORA, 3 ANS

C'est une pure braque Saint Germain roux et blanc. Elle ne pense qu'à jouer, s'entend bien avec les enfants et témoigne d'une gentillesse infatigable. Flora a été abandonnée car elle ne s'intéressait pas à la chasse. Son sport passion : la course derrière la «baballe».

Elle vous attend au refuge de l'Eden, Rod A'char, 29430 Lanhouarneau. Tél.: (02) 98.61.64.55. Colette Di Faostino tient seule, sans aucune subvention, ce havre exemplaire mais pauvre ! Si Flora est adoptée, pensez à ses compagnons !

Vous avez recueilli un animal par notre intermédiaire ? Envoyez-nous votre photo avec votre protégé, une surprise vous attend!

---

3. Which animal needs a lot of space? Camel

4. Which animals love to play? Jupiter, Flora

E. Make a list of all the adjectives of physical description that you can find in the articles. Now, list the adjectives that describe the animals' characteristics. See answers below.

F. Each article also explains why these animals were sent to the animal shelter. See answers below.

1. Which animal wasn't interested in hunting?

2. Whose owner was involved in an accident?

3. Whose owner had to go to the hospital for a long time?

4. Whose family got separated?

G. A third kind of detail tells where you can go to adopt these animals. Can you find the French word for *animal shelter*? le refuge

H. Now, write your own classified ad to try to find a home for a lost pet. Remember to give the animal's name and age, tell what the animal looks like, and describe his or her character.

or

Write a letter to the animal shelter telling them what kind of pet you would like to adopt.

1. First, make a list of all of the characteristics you're looking for in a pet. Will you choose to adopt a cat or a dog? What will he or she look like? Act like? Like to do?

2. Write a short letter, including all the important information about your desired pet.

3. Don't forget to give your address and telephone number!

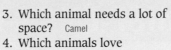

POSTREADING
Activity H

Teaching Suggestions

• Have students write three or four true-false statements about the selections. They should then exchange papers, mark the items either **vrai** or **faux,** and return them to be corrected. You might also have students work in groups to create three or four true-false statements and then include one statement from each group on a short quiz.

• Have students convert their ads into posters or into a class newspaper with the information neatly displayed and a drawing or photo of the pet, if possible. Display the posters around the room and have each student choose a pet to "adopt." They might write a short paragraph explaining why they chose that particular pet.

📁 Portfolio

H. Written Activity H is appropriate as an entry in students' written portfolios. For portfolio information, see the *Alternative Assessment Guide,* pages iv–17.

Teaching Suggestion

Ask students to explain which of the animals pictured they might like to adopt and why.

Answers

E *Physical:* blanc et gris, robuste, toute blanche, noires, opulente, gris, jolie, adorable, tigré et blanc, tatoué, pure, roux et blanc

Character: sympathique, vif, joyeux, gentille, enjouée, attachante, tendre, étonné, joueur, affectueux, sociable, infatigable

F 1. Flora
2. Camel's
3. Jupiter's, Poupette's
4. Dady's

MISE EN PRATIQUE

The *CD-ROM Program* offers guided recording and writing activities to practice oral and written skills and to review material from each chapter.

The **Mise en pratique** reviews and integrates all four skills and culture in preparation for the Chapter Test.

Teaching Suggestion

1 Have students read the questions to themselves before you play the recording. Tell them they only need to jot down one word or a number to answer each question as they listen.

Group Work

2 Have students form small groups. Assign one of the announcements to each group. Have the groups read the announcement and answer the related questions. Reporters from each group can give the group's answers to the class. Ask groups to share any other details they gleaned from the announcement.

For Individual Needs

2 Tactile Learners Have students make their own birth announcements. Supply stationery or construction paper and markers. You might also have students bring in a baby picture to attach to the announcement. If students don't want to make their own birth announcements, have them create one for a TV or cartoon character.

Language Note

You might tell students that the announcements shown here, as well as other official announcements, are called **les faire-part.** The birth announcement would be **un faire-part de naissance,** and the wedding announcement would be **un faire-part de mariage**.

1 Ecoute Nathalie qui va te parler de sa famille. Puis, réponds aux questions. See scripts and answers on p. 173H.

CD 7 Tr. 20

1. Comment s'appelle le frère de Nathalie?
2. Il a quel âge?
3. Est-ce qu'elle a un chien ou un chat?
4. Comment est son animal?

2 Skim these documents. Then, read them more thoroughly and answer the questions below. *See answers below.*

1. What kind of document is this? How do you know?
2. Who is Michel Louis Raymond?
3. Who are Denise Morel-Tissot and Raymond Tissot?
4. What happened on May 20, 1999?

Nous avons la joie de vous annoncer la naissance de notre fils

Michel Louis Raymond
20 mai 1999

Denise Morel-Tissot
Raymond Tissot

Christelle et Nicolas

ont le plaisir de vous faire part de leur mariage

qui aura lieu le treize février 1999 à 15 heures, en la Mairie de Saint-Cyr-sur-Loire

M. et Mme Lionel Desombre
305 Rue des Marronniers
37540 Saint-Cyr-sur-Loire

5. What kind of document is this? How do you know?
6. Who are Christelle and Nicolas?
7. What happened on February 13, 1999, at three o'clock?
8. Who do you think M. and Mme Lionel Desombre are?

Answers

2 1. birth announcement; *Possible answers:* It is similar to an American birth announcement. The names at the bottom have the same last name.
2. the son of Denise Morel-Tissot and Raymond Tissot
3. the parents
4. Michel Louis Raymond was born.
5. wedding announcement; *Possible answers:* The word **mariage** looks like *marriage.* Christelle and Nicolas are a couple.
6. a couple announcing their wedding plans
7. Christelle and Nicolas got married.
8. Christelle's or Nicolas's parents

3 Are the following sentences representative of French culture, American culture, or both?

1. Dogs are not allowed in restaurants or department stores.   American culture
2. The government gives money to all families with two or more children.   French culture
3. Pets are tattooed with an identification number.   French culture
4. Women have a paid maternity leave of 14 weeks.   French culture

4 ## Ecrivons!

Write a paragraph describing the family in the picture. Give French names to all the family members, tell their ages, give brief physical descriptions, say something about their personalities, and mention one or two things they each like to do.

A cluster diagram, like the one you created in Chapter 3, will help you organize your thoughts. Make a large circle for each family member, then attach smaller circles for age, physical description, and so on.

STRATEGIE
Using details to describe people will enable you to help your reader develop a clearer mental picture of what you're writing about. The more detailed the writing, the sharper the mental image the reader gets of the subject.

Using the information you organized in your cluster diagram, write a paragraph describing the family in the picture. Imagine that your readers have never seen this picture before. After reading your paragraph, they should feel as if they know the members of the family personally. Be sure to use descriptive words you learned in this chapter, but remember those you've learned in previous chapters as well!

5

J E U   D E   R O L E

Your friends arrive at your door and suggest that you go out with them. Your parent tells them that you can go out if you finish your chores, so your friends offer to help. As you work around the house, you discuss where to go and what to do. Create a conversation with your classmates. Be prepared to act out the scene, using props.

Process Writing
4 To extend this activity, have students bring pictures or magazine cutouts of other families (real or fictional). Have them write a short paragraph describing the family they chose. Tell students to use their work for Activity 4 as a model. Collect the papers and tape the pictures students brought to the board. Divide the class into several teams. Then, read aloud one of the descriptions to the class. The first student to correctly identify the family being described wins a point for his or her team.

Teaching Suggestion
4 Give each person in the illustration a name (**Adèle, Jean-Paul, Sophie, Laurent, Céline, Danielle, Emile**) and write the names across the board. Have students read their description of one of the people and have the class tell which person is being described.

 Video Wrap-Up
* ***VIDEO PROGRAM,*** *Videocassette 3, 01:22–13:45*
* ***VIDEODISC PROGRAM,*** *Videodisc 4, Side A*

At this time, you might want to use the video resources for additional review and enrichment. See *Video Guide* or *Videodisc Guide* for suggestions regarding the following:
* **Sympa, la famille!** (Dramatic episode)
* **Panorama Culturel** (Interviews)
* **Vidéoclips** (Authentic footage)

This page is intended to help students prepare for the Chapter Test. It is a brief checklist of the major points covered in the chapter. The students should be reminded that this is only a checklist and does not necessarily include everything that will appear on the test.

Teaching Suggestions

3 Have students write descriptions of the people in the illustrations. Collect the papers, read some of the descriptions at random, and have students write the number of the illustration that fits each description you read.

4 You might expand this activity by having students describe their best friend.

7 Have pairs of students use the answers they gave in Activity 7 to create and act out a conversation between a child and a parent. The child should ask for permission to go somewhere. The parent should grant permission on the condition that the child do the three things the students mentioned in Activity 7. Then, have students reverse roles.

QUE SAIS-JE?

Can you use what you've learned in this chapter?

Can you identify people? p. 179

1 How would you point out and identify Isabelle's relatives? How would you give their names and approximate ages? See page 180.
1. her grandparents   Ce sont les grand-parents d'Isabelle. Ils s'appellent Jean-Marie et Eugénie Ménard. Ils ont soixante ans.
2. her uncle   C'est l'oncle d'Isabelle. Il s'appelle Guillaume Ménard. Il a quarante ans.
3. her cousin Loïc   C'est le cousin d'Isabelle. Il s'appelle Loïc. Il a dix-huit ans.
4. her brother   C'est le frère d'Isabelle. Il s'appelle Alexandre. Il a onze ans.

Can you introduce people? p. 183

2 How would you introduce your friend to . . .
1. an adult relative?   Je vous présente...
2. a classmate?   C'est... ; Je te présente...

Can you describe and characterize people? p. 185

3 How would you describe these people?   See answers below.

1.

2.

4 How would you . . .
1. tell a friend that he or she is nice?   Tu es gentil(gentille).
2. tell several friends that they're annoying?   Vous êtes embêtant(e)s/pénibles.
3. say that you and your friend are intelligent?   Nous sommes intelligent(e)s.

Can you ask for, give, and refuse permission? p. 189

5 How would you ask permission to . . .   See answers below.
1. go to the movies?
2. go out with your friends?
3. go shopping?
4. go ice-skating?

6 How would you give someone permission to do something? How would you refuse?   See answers below.

7 What are three things your parents might ask you to do before allowing you to go out with your friends?   See answers below.

196   *cent quatre-vingt-seize*   CHAPITRE 7   La famille

Answers

3 *Possible answers*
1. La femme est brune, l'homme est blond et le garçon est roux.
2. Ils sont forts.

5 1. Je peux aller au cinéma? Est-ce que je peux aller au cinéma?
2. Je peux sortir avec des copains? Est-ce que je peux sortir avec des copains?
3. Je peux faire les magasins? Est-ce que je peux faire les magasins?
4. Je peux faire du patin à glace? Est-ce que je peux faire du patin à glace?

6 *Possible answers*
Giving permission: Oui, si tu veux. Pourquoi pas? Oui, bien sûr. D'accord, si tu... d'abord...
Refusing: Pas question! Non, c'est impossible. Non, tu dois... Pas ce soir.

7 *Possible answers:* faire la vaisselle, faire le ménage, ranger ma chambre, promener le chien, garder ma petite sœur, sortir la poubelle, débarrasser la table, laver la voiture, tondre le gazon, passer l'aspirateur

VOCABULAIRE

PREMIERE ETAPE

Identifying people

C'est...   *This/That is . . .*
Ce sont...   *These/those are . . .*
Voici...   *Here's . . .*
Voilà...   *There's . . .*

Family members

la famille   *family*
le grand-père   *grandfather*
la grand-mère   *grandmother*
la mère   *mother*
le père   *father*
le parent   *parent, relative*
la femme   *wife*
le mari   *husband*
la sœur   *sister*

le frère   *brother*
la fille   *daughter*
le fils   *son*
l'enfant (m./f.)   *child*
l'oncle (m.)   *uncle*
la tante   *aunt*
la cousine   *girl cousin*
le cousin   *boy cousin*
le chat   *cat*
le chien   *dog*
le canari   *canary*
le poisson   *fish*

Possessive adjectives

mon/ma/mes   *my*
ton/ta/tes   *your*

son/sa/ses   *his, her*
notre/nos   *our*
votre/vos   *your*
leur/leurs   *their*

Introducing people

C'est...   *This is . . .*
Je te/vous présente...   *I'd like you to meet . . .*
Très heureux (heureuse).   *Pleased to meet you.* (FORMAL)

Other useful expressions

de   *of (indicates relationship or ownership)*

DEUXIEME ETAPE

Describing and characterizing people

Il est comment?   *What is he like?*
Elle est comment?   *What is she like?*
Ils/Elles sont comment?   *What are they like?*
Il est...   *He is . . .*
Elle est...   *She is . . .*
Ils/Elles sont...   *They're . . .*
amusant(e)   *funny*

content(e)   *happy*
embêtant(e)   *annoying*
fort(e)   *strong*
gentil (gentille)   *nice*
intelligent(e)   *smart*
méchant(e)   *mean*
pénible   *annoying; a pain in the neck*
sympa(thique)   *nice*
timide   *shy*
âgé(e)   *older*
blond(e)   *blond*

brun(e)   *brunette*
grand(e)   *tall*
gros (grosse)   *fat*
jeune   *young*
mince   *slender*
mignon (mignonne)   *cute*
ne... ni grand(e) ni petit(e)   *neither tall nor short*
petit(e)   *short*
roux (rousse)   *redheaded*
être   *to be*

TROISIEME ETAPE

Asking for, giving, and refusing permission

Tu es d'accord?   *Is that OK with you?*
(Est-ce que) je peux... ?   *May I . . . ?*
Oui, si tu veux.   *Yes, if you want to.*
Pourquoi pas?   *Why not?*
Oui, bien sûr.   *Yes, of course.*
D'accord, si tu... d'abord...   *OK, if you . . . first.*
Pas question!   *Out of the question!*

Non, c'est impossible.   *No, that's impossible.*
Non, tu dois...   *No, you've got to . . .*
Pas ce soir.   *Not tonight.*

Chores

débarrasser la table   *to clear the table*
faire la vaisselle   *to do the dishes*
faire le ménage   *to do housework*
faire les courses   *to do the shopping*

garder...   *to look after . . .*
laver la voiture   *to wash the car*
passer l'aspirateur   *to vacuum*
promener le chien   *to walk the dog*
ranger ta chambre   *to pick up your room*
sortir la poubelle   *to take out the trash*
tondre le gazon   *to mow the lawn*

VOCABULAIRE

cent quatre-vingt-dix-sept **197**

 Circumlocution

Have students use the vocabulary from this chapter to come up with riddles for their partner to figure out. (—**C'est la femme du père.** —**La mère.**) You may want to award a prize to the student who can think of the most riddles, or to the pair who can answer the riddles with the fewest guesses.

CHAPTER 7 ASSESSMENT

CHAPTER TEST

• *Testing Program,* pp. 183–188
• *Audio Compact Discs,* Audio CD 7, Tracks 24–26

SPEAKING TEST

• *Testing Program,* p. 346

TEST GENERATOR,

• Chapter 7

ALTERNATIVE ASSESSMENT

Performance Assessment

You might want to use the **Jeu de Rôle** on page 195 as a cumulative performance assessment activity.

• *Alternative Assessment Guide,* p. 38

Portfolio Assessment

• *Alternative Assessment Guide*
Oral: p. 24
Written: p. 24

CD-ROM Assessment

• *Interactive CD-ROM Program,* Disc 2
A toi de parler
A toi d'écrire
• *Alternative Assessment Guide,* p. 52

Game

JEU D'ASSOCIATION   Have students form small groups and arrange their desks in circles. You will need a small ball for each group. Start the game by calling out a word or expression from the **Vocabulaire (le chien)** and tossing the ball to a member of the group, who calls out a related word or expression (**le chat**). Then, that student calls out another word and tosses the ball to another student who must catch the ball and say a related word, and so on. If a student drops the ball or can't think of a word, he or she is out. You might assign an arbiter to monitor each group. The last remaining player wins. As an alternative, you might play for points instead of eliminating players.

Allez, viens à Abidjan! pp. 198–227

VIDEO
PROGRAM
Videocassette 3
13:50–16:05

OR VIDEODISC PROGRAM,
Videodisc 4B

Search 1, Play To 4085

Motivating Activity

Ask students to share what they know about French-speaking Africa, or Africa in general. Then, have them compare what they know with what they see in the photos of Abidjan on pages 198–201.

Background Information

Abidjan, the largest city of Côte d'Ivoire, is considered to be the economic capital of the country. Abidjan is located on a series of islands and drained lowlands and lies along the Ebrié Lagoon. In 1950, the construction of the Vridi Canal provided an effective passageway between the lagoon and the Gulf of Guinea, part of the Atlantic Ocean. This construction, along with Côte d'Ivoire's independence from France in 1960, has allowed the city to expand into one of the busiest seaports and financial centers of francophone West Africa.

go.hrw.com
WAO ABIDJAN

Visit the HRW Web site at **http://go.hrw.com** and enter the keyword **WAO ABIDJAN** for student resources related to this location. For detailed access instructions, see page T45.

CHAPITRE 8

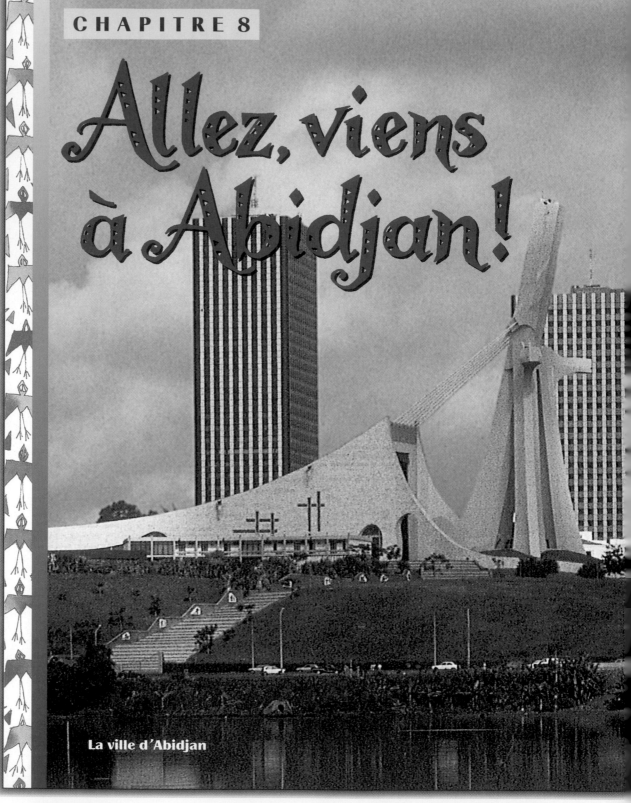

Allez, viens à Abidjan!

La ville d'Abidjan

Photo Flash

Call students' attention to the skyline of Abidjan on this page and point out the **Cathédrale Saint-Paul.** This eye-catching modern cathedral was consecrated by the Pope in 1985.

Teacher Note

Even though Abidjan is still the economic capital of Côte d'Ivoire, Yamoussoukro, the home town of former President Houphouët-Boigny, has been the official capital of the country since 1983.

Abidjan
Map 2

Ville principale de la République de Côte d'Ivoire

Population : plus de 2.100.000

Points d'intérêt : l'Assemblée nationale, le palais du Président, le parc national du Banco, le Musée national

Abidjanais célèbres : Bernard Dadié, Goffi Jadeau, Amon d'Aby, Abdoulaye Traoré

Ressources et industries : café, cacao, bananes, textiles, bois

Spécialités : foutou, aloco, kedjenou, attiéké, sauce arachide, sauce graine, sauce claire

MALI

BURKINA FASO

GUINEE

Korhogo

CÔTE D'IVOIRE

Bouaké

Yamoussoukro

GHANA

LIBERIA

Abidjan

Océan Atlantique

HRW go.hrw.com
WAO ABIDJAN

cent quatre-vingt-dix-neuf 199

Using the Map

As students look at the map, ask them to name the five countries that share a border with Côte d'Ivoire (Liberia, Guinée *(Guinea)*, Mali, Burkina Faso, and Ghana). Ask students if they know that the former name of Burkina Faso was Upper Volta. Have students identify the capital city of Côte d'Ivoire (Yamoussoukro).

Culture Notes

• Côte d'Ivoire has consistently been one of the world's leading producers of both coffee and cocoa. In recent years, production has diversified, adding cotton and rubber to the country's list of profitable exports.

• Two other sauces served with various Ivorian dishes are **sauce djoumbre,** made with okra, and **sauce feuille,** made with various leafy green vegetables, such as spinach.

Using the Almanac and Map

Terms in the Almanac

• **L'Assemblée nationale,** the legislative body whose chamber is located in the Plateau, has 124 representatives, most of whom belong to the ruling political party, the **Parti Démocratique de Côte d'Ivoire (PDCI).**

• **Le palais du Président** is the residence of the Ivorian president. Overlooking the Ebrié Lagoon, the palace has several magnificent gardens.

• **Le parc national du Banco,** a 7,500-acre park outside of Abidjan, is the site of a thriving laundry business. Every morning in the park, hundreds of laundrymen come to the Banco River, pound the clothes on stones to get them clean, and spread them out to dry.

• **Le Musée national** gives ample evidence of Côte d'Ivoire's rich cultural heritage. The collection of over 20,000 art objects includes wooden statues and masks, jewelry, pottery, musical instruments, and furniture.

• **foutou:** a dish made from boiled plantains, manioc, or yams, which is served with any one of several sauces

• **aloco:** a dish of fried plantain bananas

• **kedjenou:** a traditional main dish made with chicken or meat, vegetables (usually tomatoes and onions), and seasonings

• **attiéké:** grated manioc, a starchy root, which is served with braised chicken or fish and covered with tomatoes and onions

• **sauce arachide:** a sauce made from ground peanuts

• **sauce palme:** a sauce made from palm oil nuts

• **sauce claire:** a sauce made with eggplant, tomatoes, and other vegetables

Using the Photo Essay

① The **Treichville market** in Abidjan is the city's best source of a variety of fabrics, such as wax prints, kente cloth, indigo fabric, and woven cloth. Kente cloth is a brightly colored fabric with intricate patterns made by the Ashanti in Ghana.

② Parts of **le parc Banco** serve as coffee and cocoa plantations, managed by villagers who live in the area. There is also a small zoo in the center of the park near the lake.

Teaching Suggestion

② Ask students if they have ever visited a national park. Have them brainstorm activities in French that they might do there (**faire du vélo, faire des photos**). Have them come up with a list of any animals that they might see in a national park.

③ **Le Plateau** is sometimes known as "little Manhattan" because of its imposing, tall buildings and its dominant position overlooking the water of the lagoon.

Architecture Link

③ **La Pyramide,** the building shown in this photo, is located in the heart of the **Plateau** on avenue Franchet-d'Esperey. Because of its triangular, asymmetrical structure, **la Pyramide** is one of the city's most impressive examples of modern architecture.

Abidjan

CD-ROM
Disc 2

*Abidjan is a modern city that lies on the **baie de Cocody** in Côte d'Ivoire. It is a bustling metropolitan area sometimes called the "melting pot of Africa." The office buildings and hotels of **Le Plateau** contrast sharply with the lively and colorful district of **Treichville**, the cultural heart of Abidjan.*

① Côte d'Ivoire is famous for its brightly colored fabrics and weavings.

② **Le parc Banco**, a national park since 1953, is a beautiful rain forest reserve.

③ **Le Plateau** is Abidjan's center of commerce and government.

Geography Link

② **Le parc Banco** was established in 1926 outside of Abidjan as a forest reserve and was declared a national park in 1953. The southern part of Côte d'Ivoire, including **le parc Banco,** is dominated by tropical rain forests, which include many varieties of trees, such as palms, fruit trees, ebony, and mahogany. As you move north in the direction of the desert, the land becomes savanna, which is grassland covered with plants that withstand drought and fire. Côte d'Ivoire is fairly flat, except for the hills of Man and Odienné in the western and northwestern parts of the country.

④ The port of **Adjamé** is one of the busiest in West Africa.

⑤ Many different kinds of traditional masks are displayed in the National Museum in Abidjan.

⑥ **Treichville** is the main shopping district of Abidjan. The combination of colors, sounds, and aromas of this lively quarter of town will awaken all the senses.

④ Many of the workers who built the city of Abidjan originally settled in the **Adjamé** area (a neighborhood north of the **Plateau**) before moving on to Treichville. In the Ebrié language, Adjamé means *place of meeting.* The busy port allows Côte d'Ivoire to maintain its trade in cocoa, coffee, and other products, although economic problems have slowed this trade in recent years.

⑤ Several ethnic groups in Côte d'Ivoire are known for their traditional masks. For example, the **Poro** system of life, on which the **Sénoufo** culture is based, follows a complex social code and philosophy. These people use wooden masks to communicate the teachings of their society. Many of these masks are made in artisan villages surrounding Korhogo in northern Côte d'Ivoire. The ceremonial masks of the **Dan** people, who belong to the larger **Malinké** region surrounding the city of Man in western Côte d'Ivoire, represent the powerful traditions of their group and can be found in museums all over the world.

⑥ **Treichville** is the African hub of Abidjan and is a very lively section of town, day and night. The Treichville market is the largest market in the city and is located across the street from the headquarters of the PDCI, the major political party of the country. This neighborhood is also known for its African restaurants and nightclubs, many of which are situated around the **avenue de la Reine-Pokou,** named for the ancient queen who gave the **Baoulé** people their name (see History Link on this page).

History Link

In the eighteenth century, Queen Abla Pokou, the niece of King Osei Toutou, was leading several families out of Ghana after the king's death when they came upon the Comoë River and could not continue. The high priest asked that a child be given up in exchange for safe passage across the river. Legend has it that Pokou threw her only child into the waters, crying **"Baoulé"** *("The child is dead"),* and a group of hippos formed a "bridge" on which the families crossed the river. Through this experience, Queen Pokou gave a name to the people who had followed her into what is now central Côte d'Ivoire.

Chapitre 8 : Au marché
Chapter Overview

Mise en train pp. 204–206	Une invitée pour le déjeuner			

	FUNCTIONS	GRAMMAR	CULTURE	RE-ENTRY
Première étape pp. 207–211	• Expressing need, p. 210	• The partitive and indefinite articles **du, de la, de l'**, and **des**, p. 208 • **Avoir besoin de**, p. 210	• **Note Culturelle,** The Ivorian market, p. 209 • **Panorama Culturel,** Shopping for groceries in francophone countries, p. 211	• Food vocabulary **(Chapitre 5)** • The verb **avoir (Chapitre 2)** • Asking others what they need and telling what you need **(Chapitre 3)**
Deuxième étape pp. 212–216	• Making, accepting, and declining requests, p. 212 • Telling someone what to do, p. 212	• The verb **pouvoir**, p. 213 • **De** with expressions of quantity, p. 214	• **Note Culturelle,** The metric system, p. 214 • **Rencontre Culturelle,** Foods of Côte d'Ivoire, p. 216	• Activities **(Chapitre 1)** • The imperative **(Chapitre 5)**
Troisième étape pp. 217–221	• Offering, accepting, or refusing food, p. 219	• The pronoun **en,** p. 220	• **Note Culturelle,** Mealtimes in francophone countries, p. 218	• The verb **vouloir (Chapitre 6)**

Prononciation p. 221	The sounds **[o]** and **[ɔ]** Audio CD 8, Tracks 13–15	**A écrire** (dictation) Audio CD 8, Tracks 16–18		
Lisons! pp. 222–223	**La cuisine africaine**	**Reading Strategy** Recognizing false cognates		
Review pp. 224–227	**Mise en pratique**, pp. 224–225 **Ecrivons!** Arranging ideas spatially Writing a food ad	**Que sais-je?** p. 226	**Vocabulaire,** p. 227	

Assessment Options

Testing Program
- Première étape, Quiz 8-1A, Quiz 8-1B, pp. 197–200
- Deuxième étape, Quiz 8-2A, Quiz 8-2B, pp. 201–204
- Troisième étape, Quiz 8-3A, Quiz 8-3B, pp. 205–208
- Chapter Test, pp. 209–214
- Speaking Test, p. 346

Audio Compact Discs
- Audio CD 8, Tracks 20–25

Interactive CD-ROM Program
- Mise en pratique (A toi de parler, A toi d'écrire)
- CD-ROM Teacher's Guide, Assessment Options, p. 35

Alternative Assessment Guide
- Portfolio Assessment, p. 25
- Performance Assessment, p. 39
- CD-ROM Assessment, p. 53

Test Generator
- Chapter 8

PRINT	**MEDIA**

Pupil's Edition, pp. 202–227

 Audio Compact Discs
• Textbook Listening Activities: Audio CD 8, Tracks 1–19

Interactive CD-ROM Program Teacher's Guide, pp. 31–35

 Interactive CD-ROM Program
• Disc 2

Videodisc Guide
• Teaching Suggestions, pp. 88–92
• Activity Masters, pp. 93–95

Videodisc Program
• Videodisc 4, Side B

Video Guide
• Teaching Suggestions, pp. 54–55
• Activity Masters, pp. 56–58

Video Program
• Videocassette 3
• Videocassette 5 (captioned version)

Listening Activities
• Student Response Forms for Textbook Listening Activities, pp. 59–61
• Additional Listening Activities 8-1 to 8-6, pp. 63–65
• Additional Listening Activities (song), p. 66
• Scripts and Answers, pp. 137–141

Audio Compact Discs
• Textbook Listening Activities: Audio CD 8, Tracks 1–19
• Additional Listening Activities: Audio CD 8, Tracks 26–32

Teaching Transparencies
• Teaching Transparency Masters 8-1 to 8-3 (Situations) and 8-A to 8-D (Vocabulary)
• Teaching Suggestions 8-1 to 8-3 and 8-A to 8-D

 Teaching Transparencies
• Situations 8-1 to 8-3
• Vocabulary 8-A to 8-D

Testing Program
• Grammar and Vocabulary Quizzes, **Etape** Quizzes, and Chapter Test, pp. 197–214
• Score Sheet, Scripts, and Answers, pp. 215–222

 Audio Compact Discs
• Assessment Items: Audio CD 8, Tracks 20–25

 Test Generator
• Chapter 8

Alternative Assessment
• Portfolio Assessment, p. 25
• Performance Assessment, p. 39
• CD-ROM Assessment, p. 53

 Grammar and Vocabulary Workbook, pp. 61–70

 Practice and Activity Book, pp. 85–96

Activities for Communication
• Communicative Activities, pp. 43–48
• Realia and Teaching Suggestions, pp. 110–114
• Situation Cards, pp. 151–152

Lesson Planner
• Lesson Plan, pp. 38–42

Chapitre 8 : Au marché
Technology Applications

MISE EN TRAIN, pp. 204–206

Video
• Show *Une invitée pour le déjeuner.* For Video Synopsis, Teaching Suggestions, Activity Masters, and Scripts, see the *Video Guide* or the *Videodisc Guide.*

Captioned Video
• If students have trouble understanding *Une invitée pour le déjeuner,* you might play the captioned version on Videocassette 5.

Audio
• Play the recording of the **Mise en train** with pauses as students read along. You might have them practice pronunciation by repeating individual sentences after hearing them.

PREMIERE ETAPE, pp. 207–210

Video
• While students watch *Une invitée pour le déjeuner,* have them listen for exchanges that model expressing need. For more suggestions, see pp. 89-90 of the *Videodisc Guide.*

Audio
• Textbook Listening Activity 7 has students classify food items according to food groups.
• Use Additional Listening Activities 8-1 and 8-2 to have students practice the vocabulary for food items.

Transparencies
• Use *Teaching Transparencies 8-A* and *8-B* along with the Teaching Suggestions to have students practice the vocabulary for food items.

CD-ROM (Disc 2)
• After presenting the vocabulary on p. 207, have students do **Chasse au trésor** (Activity 1).
• To have students practice classifying food items according to

food groups, use **Chacun à sa place** (Activity 2).
• **Le bon choix** (Activity 3) targets partitive articles.
• For suggestions, see p. 33 of the *CD-ROM Teacher's Guide.*

PANORAMA CULTUREL, p. 211

Video
• Show the interviews. For Video Synopsis, Teaching Suggestions, Activity Masters, and Scripts, see the *Video Guide* or the *Videodisc Guide.*

Audio
• Play the **Panorama Culturel** as students read along. Remind students they might not be able to understand everything each person says, but they should try to recognize words and deduce global meaning.

CD-ROM (Disc 2)
• Have students do the **Panorama Culturel** activity for Chapter 8 after showing them the video. For suggestions, see p. 34 of the *CD-ROM Teacher's Guide.*

DEUXIEME ETAPE, pp. 212–215

Video
• While students watch *Une invitée pour le déjeuner,* have them listen for exchanges that model making, accepting, and declining requests, and telling someone what to do. For more suggestions, see pp. 90-91 of the *Videodisc Guide.*

Audio
• Textbook Listening Activity 14 practices the expressions for making, accepting, and declining requests, and telling someone what to do.
• Textbook Listening Activity 17 targets the vocabulary for food items and quantities.
• Use Additional Listening Activities 8-3 and 8-4 to have students work with food vocab-

ulary and the expressions of quantity.

Transparencies
• Use *Teaching Transparencies 8-2* and *8-C* along with the Teaching Suggestions to have students practice the vocabulary for food items and quantities, and the expressions for making, accepting, and declining requests, and telling someone what to do.

CD-ROM (Disc 2)
• **Les mots qui manquent** (Activity 4) has students produce the forms of the verb **pouvoir.**
• To have students practice expressions of quantity, use **Jeu des paires** (Activity 5).
• For suggestions, see p. 34 of the *CD-ROM Teacher's Guide.*

TROISIEME ETAPE, pp. 217–221

Video
• While students watch *Une invitée pour le déjeuner,* have them listen for exchanges that model offering, accepting, and refusing food. For more suggestions, see p. 91 of the *Videodisc Guide.*

Audio
• Use Textbook Listening Activity 21 to have students practice the vocabulary for breakfast foods.
• Textbook Listening Activity 25 practices expressions for offering, accepting, and refusing food.
• Additional Listening Activities 8-5 and 8-6 practice meal vocabulary and the expressions for offering, accepting, and refusing food.

Transparencies
• Use *Teaching Transparencies 8-3* and *8-D* along with the Teaching Suggestions to practice the vocabulary for food items and meals and the

expressions for offering, accepting, and refusing food.

CD-ROM (Disc 2)
• **Chacun à sa place** (Activity 6) has students classify expressions for telling someone what to do, and for offering, refusing, and accepting food.

MISE EN PRATIQUE, pp. 224–225

Video
• Replay *Une invitée pour le déjeuner* in its entirety and ask students to listen for the exchanges in which the characters express need, make, accept, and decline requests, tell someone what to do, and offer, accept, and refuse food.

CD-ROM (Disc 2)
• Have students do the **En contexte** to practice using the vocabulary for food items, meals, and quantities, and the expressions for making, accepting, and declining requests. You might use the suggestions on p. 33 of the *CD-ROM Teacher's Guide.*
• Have students practice their writing and speaking skills by doing the **A toi d'écrire** and **A toi de parler** activities. For a detailed description of these activities, see p. 35 of the *CD-ROM Teacher's Guide.*
• For Assessment Options, see p. 35 of the *CD-ROM Teacher's Guide.*

Test Generator
• Use the Test Generator to create review material for students taking the Chapter Test or to prepare an alternate test.

VIDEOCLIPS

Video
• Show the **Vidéoclips.** For Video Synopsis, Teaching Suggestions, Activity Masters, and Scripts, see the *Video Guide* or the *Videodisc Guide.*

Videodisc Program
Videodisc 4, Side B
Videodisc Guide, pp. 86–95

Chapitre 8 : Au marché
Barcode Directory

BARCODE DIRECTORY
CHAPTER 8

MISE EN TRAIN

Barcodes A and B access **Mise en train** and **Mise en train (suite)** in their entirety. Subsequent barcodes show specific segments of *Une invitée pour le déjeuner.* The barcode numbers correspond to the scene numbers as they appear on the video.

ETAPES

To practice the grammar, vocabulary, and functions presented in each **étape**, see the barcodes and accompanying suggestions on pages 89–91 of the *Videodisc Guide.*

Une invitée pour le déjeuner **A**

Search 4085, Play To 12035

Encore du pain... ? **1**

Search 4085, Play To 6302

Tiens, te voilà... **2**

Search 6302, Play To 6659

Il me faut... **3**

Search 6659, Play To 7388

Au marché **4**

Search 7403, Play To 9051

Maman, je suis de retour. **5**

Search 9067, Play To 10971

Viens, Djeneba. **6**

Search 10986, Play To 12035

Une invitée pour le déjeuner (suite) **B**

Search 12035, Play To 19035

MISE EN PRATIQUE

This is additional footage modeling some of the expressions practiced in this chapter. You may want to use it to review the chapter.

Mise en pratique 1 **1**

Search 26431, Play To 27786

Mise en pratique 2 **2**

Search 27786, Play To 29301

PANORAMA CULTUREL

Où est-ce que tu aimes faire des provisions?
These barcodes access the three interviews of the **Panorama Culturel** presented in the *Pupil's Edition* as well as additional interviews.

First three interviews **1**

Search 19035, Play To 21125

All interviews **2**

Search 10935, Play To 23764

Louise **3**

Search 20011, Play To 20340

Angèle **4**

Search 20341, Play To 20592

Micheline **5**

Search 20593, Play To 21099

Jocelyne **6**

Search 21140, Play To 21522

Armande **7**

Search 21523, Play To 21882

Joël **8**

Search 21883, Play To 22093

Lucie **9**

Search 22094, Play To 22643

Elodie **10**

Search 22644, Play To 22834

Danielle **11**

Search 22835, Play To 23177

Sylviane **12**

Search 23178, Play To 23764

VIDEOCLIPS

These are authentic French commercials. You may want to preview them before showing them to students.

Andros®: fruit compote **1**

Search 23764, Play To 25210

Garbit®: paëlla (Spanish dish made with rice and seafood) **2**

Search 25210, Play To 25824

Chapitre 8 : Au marché
CD-ROM Directory — Disc 2

The following directory lists the *Interactive CD-ROM Program* activities for Chapter 8. For details and suggestions on how to use them, see pages 32–35 of the *CD-ROM Teacher's Guide*.

GLOBAL TASK	COMMUNICATIVE GOALS	ACTIVITY TYPE
Tu peux aller au marché? Students talk with Madame Mabo about shopping for groceries.	To use chapter functions, vocabulary, and grammar in a lifelike conversation	**En contexte** *Interactive conversation*

	SUPPORTING ACTIVITIES	PUPIL'S EDITION	COMMUNICATIVE GOALS	ACTIVITY TYPE
Première étape	1. Vocabulaire	p. 207	To identify food items	**Chasse au trésor** Explorons!/Vérifions! *Interactive image*
	2. Vocabulaire	p. 207	To classify food items according to food groups	**Chacun à sa place** *Categories*
	3. Grammaire	p. 208	To use partitive articles	**Le bon choix** *Multiple choice*
Deuxième étape	4. Grammaire	p. 213	To produce forms of the verb **pouvoir**	**Les mots qui manquent** *Tic Tac Toe*
	5. Vocabulaire	p. 214	To identify expressions of quantity	**Jeu des paires** *Concentration®*
Troisième étape	6. Comment dit-on... ?	pp. 212, 219	To classify expressions for telling someone what to do, and for offering, refusing, and accepting food	**Chacun à sa place** *Categories*
Panorama Culturel	Panorama Culturel	p. 211	To listen to and understand native speakers talking about where they like to shop for groceries	**Où est-ce que tu aimes faire des provisions?** *Presentation* **Le bon choix** *Multiple choice*

	APPLICATION	PUPIL'S EDITION	COMMUNICATIVE GOALS	ACTIVITY TYPE
Mise en pratique	A toi de parler	pp. 224–225	To create and record a conversation between a host or hostess and a guest who are finishing a meal together	*Guided recording*
	A toi d'écrire	pp. 224–225	To create a list, a conversation, a newspaper article, or a menu	*Guided writing*

Homework Suggestions

CHAPTER SECTION	PRESENTATION	HOMEWORK OPTIONS
Première étape	**Vocabulaire,** p. 207	Practice and Activity Book, pp. 86–87, Activities 3–5 Grammar and Vocabulary Workbook, pp. 61–62, Activities 1–4 CD-ROM, Disc 2, Activities 1–2
	Grammaire, p. 208	Pupil's Edition, p. R42, Activities 1–2 Practice and Activity Book, p. 87, Activity 6 Grammar and Vocabulary Workbook, pp. 63–65, Activities 5–9 CD-ROM, Disc 2, Activity 3
	Comment dit-on... ? p. 210	Pupil's Edition, p. 210, Activity 11 Practice and Activity Book, p. 88, Activity 8
	Note de grammaire, p. 210	Pupil's Edition, p. R42, Activity 3 Practice and Activity Book, p. 88, Activity 9 Grammar and Vocabulary Workbook, p. 65, Activity 10
Deuxième étape	**Comment dit-on... ?** p. 212	Practice and Activity Book, p. 89, Activities 10–12
	Grammaire, p. 213	Pupil's Edition, p. 213, Activity 15; p. R43, Activities 4–5 Practice and Activity Book, p. 90, Activities 13–14 Grammar and Vocabulary Workbook, p. 66, Activities 11–12 CD-ROM, Disc 2, Activity 4
	Vocabulaire, p. 214	Practice and Activity Book, pp. 90–91, Activities 15–17 Grammar and Vocabulary Workbook, p. 67, Activity 13 CD-ROM, Disc 2, Activity 5
	Note de grammaire, p. 214	Pupil's Edition, p. R43, Activity 6 Grammar and Vocabulary Workbook, pp. 67–68, Activities 14–16
Troisième étape	**Vocabulaire,** p. 217	Practice and Activity Book, p. 92, Activities 19–20 Grammar and Vocabulary Workbook, p. 69, Activities 17–18
	Comment dit-on... ? p. 219	Pupil's Edition, p. 221, Activity 29 Practice and Activity Book, pp. 92–93, Activities 21–22 CD-ROM, Disc 2, Activity 6
	Grammaire, p. 220	Pupil's Edition, p. 220, Activity 27; pp. R43–R44, Activities 7–8 Practice and Activity Book, p. 93, Activity 23 Grammar and Vocabulary Workbook, p. 70, Activities 19–20

For Student Response Forms, see *Listening Activities,* pp. 59–61.

Première étape

7 Ecoute! p. 208

1. — Comment sont ces fraises?
   — Bof, elles ne sont pas très mûres.

2. — Tu aimes ce poisson?
   — Ça va. Rien de spécial.

3. — Elle est comment, cette mangue?
   — Elle est délicieuse. Mais moi, j'adore les mangues!

4. — Comment est ce poulet?
   — Pas mauvais.

5. — Alors? Ces haricots? Ils sont bons?
   — Pas terribles.

Answers to Activity 7
1. fruit   4. poultry
2. fish   5. vegetables
3. fruit

Deuxième étape

14 Ecoute! p. 213

1. — Eh bien, Jean-Luc, tu peux aller faire les courses aujourd'hui?
   — Euh, je regrette, mais je n'ai pas le temps.

2. — Sylvie, tu me rapportes du lait cet après-midi?
   — Bon, d'accord.

3. — Robert! Rapporte-moi du beurre! N'oublie pas!
   — Mais, maman, je ne peux pas maintenant!

4. — Annie, tu peux acheter des fraises pour le dîner?
   — Tout de suite.

5. — Euh, Chantal, achète-moi un paquet de riz cet après-midi!
   — Je veux bien.

Answers to Activity 14
a. 1. making a request
     2. making a request
     3. telling someone what to do
     4. making a request
     5. telling someone what to do
b. 1. declines
     2. accepts
     3. declines
     4. accepts
     5. accepts

17 Ecoute! p. 215

1. — Bonjour, monsieur. Je voudrais douze tranches de jambon, s'il vous plaît.
   — Voilà.
   — C'est combien?
   — Cinquante-trois francs.

2. — Bonjour, madame. Est-ce que vous avez des fraises, s'il vous plaît?
   — Oui, regardez, elles sont mûres!
   — Alors, je vais prendre un kilo de fraises.
   — Voilà. Ça fait vingt-six francs.
   — Tenez.
   — Merci bien. Au revoir.

3. — Bonjour, madame. C'est combien, l'eau minérale, s'il vous plaît?
   — Trois francs soixante-quinze la bouteille.
   — Bien, je vais prendre trois bouteilles.
   — Tenez.
   — Merci. Ça fait combien?
   — Onze francs vingt-cinq.
   — Tenez.
   — Merci.

4. — Je voudrais un morceau de fromage, s'il vous plaît, monsieur.
   — Voilà.
   — Je vais aussi prendre une douzaine d'œufs.
   — C'est tout?
   — Oui.
   — Alors, ça vous fait... vingt-neuf francs.
   — Voilà.
   — Merci.

Answers to Activity 17
1. twelve slices of ham
2. a kilo of strawberries
3. three bottles of mineral water
4. a piece of cheese, a dozen eggs

Troisième étape

21 Ecoute! p. 218

1. — Dis, Anne, qu'est-ce que tu prends d'habitude au petit déjeuner?
   — Oh, d'habitude, je prends un chocolat, du pain, du beurre et de la confiture.

2. — Pardon, monsieur. Qu'est-ce que vous prenez en général au petit déjeuner?
   — Je prends un café, un jus d'orange et des fruits.

3. — Bonjour, madame. Qu'est-ce que vous prenez d'habitude au petit déjeuner?
   — J'aime bien prendre du lait avec des céréales, du pain avec du beurre et un jus d'orange.

Answers to Activity 21

1. c   2. a   3. b

25 Ecoute! p. 219

1. Vous prenez de la salade?
2. Merci. Je n'ai plus faim.
3. Oui, avec plaisir.
4. Encore du poisson?
5. Non, merci.

Answers to Activity 25

1. offering   4. offering
2. refusing   5. refusing
3. accepting

Prononciation, p. 221

For the scripts for Parts A and B, see p. 221.

C. A écrire

(Dictation)
— Tu peux aller faire les courses aujourd'hui?
— D'accord. Qu'est-ce qu'il te faut?
— Il me faut deux kilos de pommes de terre, du fromage et un gâteau.

Mise en pratique

1 p. 224

Mesdames, messieurs, aujourd'hui, profitez de nos prix exceptionnels sur l'alimentation! Le kilo de carottes à huit francs, le kilo de pommes de terre à quatre francs et les deux kilos d'oranges, onze francs. Et ce n'est pas fini! Trente-deux francs, le poulet. Quarante-quatre francs, le kilo de jambon. Des prix aussi sur les produits laitiers! Trois francs, le litre de lait, quatre francs vingt, la douzaine d'œufs! Alors, vous hésitez encore? Dépêchez-vous. Remplissez vos placards! Faites de bonnes affaires!

Possible answers to Mise en pratique Activity 1

1 kilo of carrots, 8 francs; 1 kilo of potatoes, 4 francs; 2 kilos of oranges, 11 francs; 1 chicken, 32 francs; 1 kilo of ham, 44 francs; 1 liter of milk, 3 francs; 1 dozen eggs, 4F20

Jour de marché
(Group Project)

ASSIGNMENT

Students will role-play a marketplace scene, acting as vendors and customers.

TEACHER NOTE

You might have students do this project after they complete the **Première étape,** where they will learn about a variety of food items from Côte d'Ivoire.

MATERIALS

✄ **Students may need**

- A variety of foods
- Plates, platters, or bowls
- A small knife for cutting food
- Cardboard or posterboard
- Tape or glue
- Colored markers
- Paper
- Pen or pencil

SUGGESTED SEQUENCE

1. Before "market day," ask students to find out if there are any tropical fruits available locally. Have them refer to the **Vocabulaire** on page 207. Then, bring in or have students bring in some of these foods.

2. Ask for five or six volunteers to be the vendors; the others will be the customers. Have the vendors make signs for their stands and set up the marketplace. Several students might work together on one stand. The customers should make CFA francs out of paper and cardboard. (Refer students to page 203 for sample CFA bills.)

3. On "market day," have the vendors set up their stands and clean and cut the foods into portions so that everyone can "buy" some. All the shopping, bargaining, and purchasing should then be conducted in French.

4. After everyone has shopped and tried some of the foods, have students clean up. Then, have them write about the experience in French, giving their opinions of the foods they tried.

GRADING THE PROJECT

This is an ungraded project, but you might choose to give participation grades or a grade for the writing assignment.

TEACHER NOTE

In the Postreading section of **Lisons!** on page 223, you will find another suggested project that can be graded.

DESSIN ANIME

In this game, students will practice food vocabulary from this chapter.

Procedure Divide the class into two or more teams. A player from one team goes to the board. Tell him or her the name of a food in French so that the other students cannot hear. The student must draw a picture of that food on the board. Set a time limit of 30 to 60 seconds. The player's team wins a point if they guess the correct French word for the picture. The other team then takes a turn. This game may also be played in small groups. In this case, students choose words from the vocabulary list at the end of the chapter and draw their illustrations on paper.

QUELS INGREDIENTS?

In this game, students will practice expressing need as well as food vocabulary.

Procedure The game begins with one student naming a particular dish or meal: **un sandwich, une salade, une salade de fruits, une omelette, le déjeuner.** The next student names one ingredient needed for that particular dish or meal. Subsequent students repeat all the previously mentioned ingredients and add another. For example, the first student might say **un sandwich.** The next student would say **Il faut du pain.** The third student would say **Il faut du pain et du jambon.** When a student is unable to repeat the order correctly, start a new round with a different food item. This game can be played either by going in order around the class, or by randomly calling on students, which is more difficult. You might want to have one or two students act as judges, who write down the ingredients mentioned to verify the correct order.

QU'EST-CE QU'ON FAIT?

This game will test students' recognition of the ingredients for various recipes.

Procedure This game can be played by individuals, partners, or small groups. Read aloud a list of ingredients for a particular dish that students are familiar with. Students will try to guess what dish it is within a given time. You might want to consult a cookbook for recipes, or use the recipes that students create for the **Lisons!** activity on page 223. Students may guess in English if they have not learned the French name of a particular dish.

Examples:
1. **du pain, du fromage, du jambon, du beurre (un croque-monsieur)**
2. **du chocolat, du sucre, du beurre, des œufs, de la farine (un gâteau au chocolat)**
3. **des œufs, des champignons, du fromage, du lait (une omelette)**
4. **de la salade, des tomates, des carottes, des oignons (une salade)**
5. **des bananes, des oranges, des pommes (une salade de fruits)**

Chapitre 8
Au marché
pp. 202–227

𝒰sing the Chapter Opener

Motivating Activity

Have students find the name of a country (Côte d'Ivoire) on these pages. Have them locate it on the map of Africa on page xxiv or on *Map Transparency 2.* Ask students to share their knowledge, experiences, and/or impressions of Africa. Then, direct students' attention to the photos. Ask them to identify features that are uniquely African.

Thinking Critically

Comparing and Contrasting
Have students compare the Ivorian market they see to outdoor markets they've seen in the United States or photos they've seen of French markets. How are they similar? Different?

Photo Flash!

① The photos on pages 202 and 203 show typical outdoor markets in Côte d'Ivoire. Although there are no set rules as to who sells what, generally women sell fruits, vegetables, and fish, while men sell bread and meat. Both men and women sell fabric.

Block Scheduling

For suggestions about how to use *Allez, viens!* with block scheduling, see the *Lesson Planner,* pages 38–42.

CHAPITRE

8
Au marché

① Le marché en Côte d'Ivoire, c'est un plaisir pour les yeux.

202   *deux cent deux*

🌐 Culture Note

Call students' attention to the jewelry shown on pages 202 and 203. There is an abundance of handcrafted jewelry made in Côte d'Ivoire, and the beautiful bracelets, necklaces, rings, and earrings are made out of a variety of raw materials. Jewelry made of bone may be intricately carved like the necklace at the top of this page. Gold, silver, and brass are popular metals used for jewelry. Malachite is a popular, dark green stone used for earrings and rings. Leather is used extensively as are cowry shells (see the mask on page 201). Ebony and other kinds of wood may also be used. Beads come in all colors and shapes, and a particularly wide selection can be found in Abidjan's Treichville market.

Imagine shopping for food in the Republic of Côte d'Ivoire—the tropical fruits, lively marketplace, and Ivorian merchants would make it an adventure. You'd also gain experience with the metric system and the currency of francophone Africa, *le franc de la Communauté financière africaine (CFA)*.

In this chapter you will learn

- to express need
- to make, accept, and decline requests; to tell someone what to do
- to offer, accept, or refuse food

And you will

- listen to French-speaking people talk about the foods they like
- read recipes for African dishes
- write about your favorite and least favorite foods
- find out about the metric system of weights and measures

② Tu me rapportes des fruits?

③ Tiens, Djeneba, tu peux m'aider?

Culture Note

You might point out the CFA (**Communauté financière africaine**) bills at the bottom of this page. The CFA, used throughout francophone Africa, comes in bills of 100, 500, 1,000, 2,500, 5,000, and 10,000 CFA. Coins are available in 5, 10, 25, and 100 CFA. There are actually *two* CFAs in Africa, which are more or less equal in value. The West African CFA is used in Côte d'Ivoire, Senegal, Mali, Burkina Faso, Niger, Togo, and Benin. The Central African CFA is used in Cameroon, Central African Republic, Chad, Congo, Equatorial Guinea, and Gabon.

Focusing on Outcomes

Have students think of different situations where the functions listed in the outcomes might be used. You might write their ideas on the board or on a transparency. Ask students to match the outcomes to the photo captions. NOTE: You may want to use the video to support the objectives. The self-check activities in **Que sais-je?** on page 226 help students assess their achievement of the objectives.

Photo Flash!

② In Côte d'Ivoire, it is common to see women carrying food, firewood, a bucket of water, or various other loads on their heads. If the object is heavy, two women might lift it onto a third woman's head. High school girls will sometimes carry their books on their heads as they walk to and from school. In the market, it is not uncommon to see a woman carrying a bowl of food items on her head, a baby riding on her back, and a bag in one hand. With this arrangement, the woman still has the other hand free to carry on her business, and the baby has a cozy place to sleep!

Career Path

Have students look at the photos on pages 202–203. Ask them what types of items are sold in the markets. Have students imagine themselves as owners of a stall or buyers for a market. What would be their job responsibilities? What if they worked for a market that imported goods from other countries? How would knowing French or other languages help them in this career?

VIDEO PROGRAM

Videocassette 3
16:03–20:26
Videocassette 5
(captioned version)
1:04:12–1:08:35

OR VIDEODISC PROGRAM,
Videodisc 4, Side B

Search 4085, Play To 12035

Video Synopsis

In this segment of the video, Djeneba's mother (Mme Diomandé) and aunt (Aminata) are discussing what to prepare for lunch. Djeneba's mother asks her to go shopping at the market. She tells her what she needs to make lunch, specifying different quantities of the items. At the market, Djeneba buys fish, tomatoes, rice, and the other things her mother asked for. When she returns home, she and her mother prepare lunch. When they are almost done, someone knocks at the door, and Djeneba realizes that she forgot to tell her mother that she invited a guest for lunch!

Motivating Activities

• Have students imagine what the climate, crops, and culture are like in Côte d'Ivoire. Ask them to find evidence in the photos to support their ideas. Ask them if they can name parts of the United States that are similar to Côte d'Ivoire with respect to climate and crops (southern Texas, California).

• Ask students what they normally eat for lunch. What would they make if a guest were coming for lunch?

Teacher Note

Foutou and **sauce arachide** are described on page 216.

The **roman-photo** is an abridged version of the video episode.

Mise en train

p. 85, Acts. 1–2

Djeneba   Mme Diomandé   Aminata

CD 8
Trs. 1–2

Une invitée pour le déjeuner

Where does Djeneba go to do the grocery shopping?
Do you recognize any of the food items she buys?

Le matin chez les Diomandé, à Abidjan. C'est l'heure du petit déjeuner.

1 kilo de riz
250 grammes de pâte d'arachide
1 poisson
7 oignons
1 douzaine de tomates
3 citrons
un paquet de beurre
du pain

Encore du pain, Aminata?

Non, merci. Je n'ai plus faim.

Je pense faire du foutou avec de la sauce arachide pour le déjeuner.

①

Plus tard...

Tiens, te voilà, Djeneba. Tu me fais le marché?

Volontiers! Qu'est-ce qu'il te faut?

②

Il me faut des légumes, du riz, du poisson... Tu me rapportes aussi du pain... Et prends de la pâte de tomates.

Bon, d'accord.

③

204   *deux cent quatre*   CHAPITRE 8   Au marché

RESOURCES FOR MISE EN TRAIN	
PRINT	**MEDIA**
• *Practice and Activity Book*, p. 85 • *Video Guide*, pp. 53–54, 56 • *Videodisc Guide*, pp. 86–88, 93	• *Video Program*, Videocassette 3 Videocassette 5 (captioned version) • *Videodisc Program*, Videodisc 4, Side B • *Audio Compact Discs*, CD 8, Trs. 1–2

Djeneba va au marché...

...puis, elle rentre chez elle.

Voilà le poisson, les 250 grammes de pâte d'arachide, les oignons, les tomates et les citrons. J'ai aussi acheté un paquet de beurre, de la pâte de tomates, du pain et du riz.

Merci, chérie.

Mme Diomandé fait la cuisine.

Viens. Goûte voir. C'est bon?

Oui, très bon.

Toc toc toc!

Ah, j'ai oublié... Devine qui j'ai vu au marché.

Aucune idée... Va voir qui est à la porte.

MISE EN TRAIN

deux cent cinq **205**

Presentation

Before students view the video, introduce the characters in the story. Write their names on the board and ask students to guess what their relationships are. Then, have students watch the episode to get the gist of the story. When they have finished viewing the episode for the first time, ask them to tell what they think is happening in the story. You might have students look over the questions in Activity 1 on page 206 and keep them in mind as they watch the episode again. Ask students to name the items that Djeneba buys at the market.

Teaching Suggestion

Ask students if they are familiar with the units of measurement used in the shopping list. The metric system is presented on page 214.

Photo Flash!

⑦ ⑨ In these photos, Djeneba is holding a pestle that she is using to make **foutou**. This dish is usually made by pounding boiled yams, **manioc** *(cassava)*, or plantains in a mortar until they are the consistency of paste. They are then shaped into round balls for serving (see page 216).

Multicultural Link

Ask students if they have tried food specialties from other countries and how they liked them. You might also have them choose a country and research its food specialties. Have students list specialties of their own town or area.

 Video Integration

- **VIDEO PROGRAM,**
  Videocassette 3, 20:27–24:19
  Videocassette 5, 1:08:36–1:12:28
- **VIDEODISC PROGRAM,**
  Videodisc 4, Side B

Search 12035, Play To 19035

You may choose to continue with **Une invitée pour le déjeuner (suite)** at this time or wait until later in the chapter. When the story continues, we discover that Miss Riggs, Djeneba's English teacher, is at the door. The next scene is a flashback to the market where Miss Riggs is asking Djeneba how to make **sauce arachide.** Djeneba tells her that her mother is making it for lunch and invites Miss Riggs. Back home, Djeneba's mother tells Miss Riggs about **sauce arachide.** At the table, Djeneba's mother offers everyone **foutou** and **sauce arachide.**

Teaching Suggestions

1 You might have students work in pairs to answer these questions.

2 Have students identify the photo that proves or disproves each statement.

2–4 Have students do these activities individually or in pairs. You might check answers orally.

3 Bring in these food items or pictures of them and hold them up. Have students call out the numbers of the corresponding names.

Additional Practice

4 Have students tell who said each of the following:
1. **Qu'est-ce qu'il te faut?** (Djeneba)
2. **Encore du pain... ?** (Mme Diomandé)
3. **Et prends de la pâte de tomates.** (Mme Diomandé)
4. **Oui, très bon.** (Djeneba)

For videodisc application, see *Videodisc Guide.*

These activities check for comprehension only. Students should not yet be expected to produce language modeled in **Mise en train.**

1 Tu as compris? See answers below.
1. What time of day is it?
2. What does Mme Diomandé want Djeneba to do? Why?
3. What are some of the things Djeneba buys?
4. What happens at the end of the story?
5. Judging from the story title, what do you think Djeneba forgot to tell Mme Diomandé?

2 Vrai ou faux?
1. Aminata va au marché.   faux
2. Mme Diomandé va faire du foutou avec de la sauce arachide.   vrai
3. Djeneba ne veut pas aller au marché.   faux
4. Djeneba achète des bananes au marché.   faux
5. Djeneba oublie *(forgets)* le pain.   faux

3 Choisis la photo
Match the foods that Djeneba bought with their pictures.

1. du poisson b   2. des tomates d   3. des oignons e   4. des citrons a   5. du pain c

a.   b.   c.   d.   e.

4 C'est qui?
1. «Non, merci. Je n'ai plus faim.»   Aminata
2. «Tu me fais le marché?»   Mme Diomandé
3. «J'ai aussi acheté un paquet de beurre, de la pâte de tomates, du pain et du riz.»   Djeneba
4. «Ah, j'ai oublié... »   Djeneba
5. «Va voir qui est à la porte.»   Mme Diomandé

5 Cherche les expressions See answers below.
In **Une invitée pour le déjeuner,** how does . . .
1. Mme Diomandé offer more food to Aminata?
2. Aminata refuse the offer?
3. Mme Diomandé ask Djeneba to do the shopping?
4. Mme Diomandé tell Djeneba what she needs?
5. Djeneba agree to do what Mme Diomandé asks?

> Volontiers! Tu me fais le marché?
> Non, merci. Je n'ai plus faim.
> Bon, d'accord.
> Encore du pain?   Il me faut...

6 Et maintenant, à toi
Who does the grocery shopping in your family? Where do they do the shopping?

Answers

1 1. morning
2. She wants her to go to the market. Mme Diomandé needs some ingredients for a dish she is planning to make.
3. fish, peanut butter, onions, tomatoes, lemons, rice, butter, bread, and tomato paste
4. Someone knocks at the door.
5. Djeneba forgot to tell her that she had invited a guest for lunch.

5 1. Encore du pain?
2. Non, merci. Je n'ai plus faim.
3. Tu me fais le marché?
4. Il me faut...
5. Volontiers! Bon, d'accord.

PREMIERE ETAPE Storytelling Book pp. 29, 32

Expressing need

VOCABULAIRE

 pp. 86–87, Acts. 3–5   8-A, 8-B   pp. 61–62, Acts. 1–4   CD-ROM Disc 2

Qu'est-ce qu'on trouve **au marché? Au supermarché?**

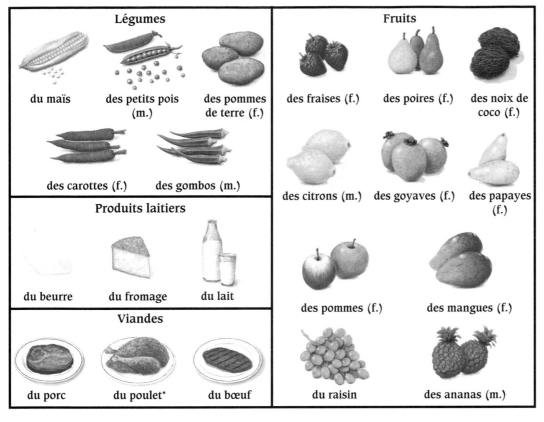

Légumes

du maïs · des petits pois (m.) · des pommes de terre (f.)

des carottes (f.) · des gombos (m.)

Produits laitiers

du beurre · du fromage · du lait

Viandes

du porc · du poulet* · du bœuf

Fruits

des fraises (f.) · des poires (f.) · des noix de coco (f.)

des citrons (m.) · des goyaves (f.) · des papayes (f.)

des pommes (f.) · des mangues (f.)

du raisin · des ananas (m.)

du pain	bread	**de la farine**	flour	**des tomates** (f.)	tomatoes
de la confiture	jam	**du sucre**	sugar	**des avocats** (m.)	avocados
des yaourts (m.)	yogurt	**des gâteaux** (m.)	cakes	**une/de la salade**	a/some salad
des œufs (m.)	eggs	**de la tarte**	pie	**des salades** (f.)	heads of lettuce
du riz	rice	**des oranges** (f.)	oranges	**des oignons** (m.)	onions
du poisson	fish	**des bananes** (f.)	bananas	**des haricots verts** (m.)	green beans
		des pêches (f.)	peaches	**des champignons** (m.)	mushrooms

* **Poule** usually refers to live chickens, while **poulet** usually refers to chicken as a food item.

RESOURCES FOR PREMIERE ETAPE

PRINT
- *Lesson Planner*, p. 39
- *Practice and Activity Book*, pp. 86–88
- *Grammar and Vocabulary Workbook*, pp. 61–65
- *Activities for Communication*, pp. 43–44, 110, 113–114, 151–152
- *Listening Activities*, pp. 59, 63
- *Testing Program*, pp. 197–200
- *Alternative Assessment Guide*, p. 39

MEDIA
- *Video Program*, Videocassette 3
  Video Guide, pp. 53–58
- *Videodisc Program*, Videodisc 4, Side B
  Videodisc Guide, pp. 89–90
- *Teaching Transparencies* 8-1, 8-A, 8-B
- *Interactive CD-ROM Program*, Disc 2
  CD-ROM Teacher's Guide, p. 33
- *Audio Compact Discs*
  Textbook Listening Activities, CD 8, Tr. 3
  Additional Listening Activities 8-1, 8-2, CD 8, Trs. 26–27
  Quiz 8-1B, CD 8, Tr. 20

---

*J*ump Start!

Have students list three things they might order in a café.

MOTIVATE

Ask students if they ever go grocery shopping, what their favorite foods are, and if they like to cook.

TEACH

Presentation

Vocabulaire Bring in real or toy food items or magazine pictures to present this vocabulary. Present the new words by food groups, holding up the object or illustration as you say the word for each one. Then, hold up the items or pictures again, asking **Qu'est-ce que c'est?** Encourage students to make charts for each food group. Have them create a set of picture flashcards.

Language Notes

- Make sure students pronounce **poisson** with an *s* sound, not with a *z* sound as in **poison**.
- The final -**f** is pronounced in **œuf**, but not in the plural **œufs**. Teach students the phrase *One egg is* **un œuf** *("enough")* to help them remember to pronounce the -**f** only in the singular form.

Game

ATTRAPE-LE! Place three food items on a table (**une mangue, une tomate, un citron**). Call two students to the front. Say what you'd like to have. (**Je voudrais un citron.**) The first student to grab the item and hand it to you wins. The winner stays at the table and another player comes to the front. You might add more items to make the game more challenging.

For Individual Needs

7 Challenge Before playing the recording, you might have students practice categorizing the vocabulary. Distribute the flashcards (see the **Vocabulaire** presentation on page 207) randomly to students. Write **Fruits, Légumes, Viandes, Volailles** *(poultry)*, **Poissons,** and **Produits laitiers** on the board at the top of five columns, and ask students to tape their flashcards under the correct category. If cards are not available, number the categories 1 to 5 and have students give the number of the appropriate category as you say different vocabulary words.

Presentation

Grammaire To present the partitive article, first draw a whole pizza and a whole cake on the board. Identify them orally, using the indefinite article: **une pizza, un gâteau.** Then, divide each into pieces and shade one of the pieces. Identify the portions, using the partitive article: **de la pizza, du gâteau.** Next, bring in a whole food item (**une tarte, un pain, une orange**) and have students ask for some or all of it. (**Je voudrais de la tarte/du pain/une orange, s'il vous plaît.**) Remind students that they learned how to use **de** after **ne... pas** in Chapter 3.

Additional Practice

Grammaire Hold up real or toy food items or the picture side of vocabulary flashcards and ask students if they want some of them. (**Tu veux du gâteau?**)

7 Écoute! See scripts and answers on p. 201G.

Listen to the dialogues and decide if the people are talking about fruit, vegetables, fish, or poultry.

CD 8 Tr. 3

GRAMMAIRE The partitive and indefinite articles

You already know how to use **un** and **une** with singular nouns and **des** with plural nouns. Use **du, de la, de l',** or **des** to indicate *some of* or *part of* something.

> Je voudrais **du** gâteau.
> Tu veux **de la** salade?
> Elle va prendre **de l'**eau minérale.
> Il me faut **des** oranges.

P/A p. 87, Act. 6

G/V pp. 63–65, Acts. 5–9

Additional Grammar Practice, p. R42

• If you want to talk about a whole item, use the indefinite articles **un** and **une.**

Il achète **une** tarte.

Il prend **de la** tarte.

• In a negative sentence, **du, de la, de l',** and **des** change to **de/d'** *(none or any)*.
> —Tu as **du** pain?   —Tu prends **de la** viande?
> —Désolée, je n'ai pas **de** pain.   —Merci, je ne prends jamais **de** viande.

• You can't leave out the article in French as you do in English.
> Elle mange **du** fromage. *She's eating cheese.*

8 Qu'est-ce qu'on mange?

Complète ce dialogue avec du, de la, de l', de, d', ou des.

ASSIKA Dis, maman, qu'est-ce qu'on mange à midi? J'ai très faim!
MAMAN __1__ poisson, __2__ riz et __3__ haricots verts.   Du, du, des
ASSIKA Est-ce qu'on a encore __4__ pain?   du
MAMAN Non. Et on n'a pas __5__ bananes non plus. Est-ce que tu peux aller en acheter? de
ASSIKA Bon, d'accord. C'est tout?
MAMAN Non. Prends aussi __6__ yaourts, __7__ farine et __8__ sucre. Je vais faire un gâteau pour ce soir.   des, de la, du
ASSIKA Super!
MAMAN Merci, ma chérie.

Teaching Suggestion

8 Have students rewrite the dialogue, substituting their favorite foods for the items mentioned and leaving the numbered blanks empty. Have them exchange papers with a partner, who fills in the blanks and then returns the paper for correction.

9 Qu'est-ce qu'elles achètent?

What are Prisca, Clémentine, and Adjoua buying at the market? See answers below.

1.   2.   3.

NOTE CULTURELLE

Shopping at a market in Côte d'Ivoire can be an exciting and colorful experience. Every city, town, and village has an open-air market where people come to buy and sell food, cloth, housewares, medicine, and herbal remedies. Although French is the official language in Côte d'Ivoire, more than 60 different African languages are spoken there. To make shopping easier for everyone, there is a common market language called **Djoula**. Here are a few phrases in **Djoula**.

í ní sɔgɔma   (ee nee sogoma)   *Good morning.*
í ní wúla   (ee *nee* woulah)   *Good afternoon./Hello.*
í ká kɛnɛ wá?   (ee kah keh*neh* wah)   *How are you?/How's it going?*
n ká kɛnɛ kósobɛ   (nnkah keh*neh* kuh*sohb*eh)   *I'm fine.*

ETIENNE NANDEC

10 Qu'est-ce qu'il y a dans le chariot?

Your partner has mixed his or her shopping cart with five others whose contents are listed below. Ask about the contents until you have enough information to guess which cart belongs to your partner. Then, change roles.

— Tu as acheté des tomates?   — Non.
— Tu as acheté du poisson?   — Oui.
— Ton chariot, c'est le numéro... ?   — Oui.

1. du poisson
   des tomates
   des bananes
   du fromage
   du lait

2. du pain
   des œufs
   des oignons
   du poisson
   des haricots verts

3. du sucre
   des ananas
   du lait
   du maïs
   des tomates

4. des tomates
   des haricots verts
   des œufs
   du sucre
   du maïs

5. des ananas
   des bananes
   du fromage
   des oignons
   des haricots verts

6. des bananes
   des œufs
   du poisson
   du pain
   des tomates

PREMIERE ETAPE   *deux cent neuf*   209

Teacher Note

You might invite someone from West Africa or someone who has traveled there to speak to your class. Try contacting the international student office at a local college or university. Returned Peace Corps volunteers might also be classroom visitors. Write to Peace Corps, Office of World Wise Schools, 1990 K Street, Washington, D.C. 20526, or call the Peace Corps Africa desk at 1-800-424-8580, extension 2262.

Teaching Suggestion

Note Culturelle Have partners practice greeting each other in Djoula. They might also choose to use these greetings in activities and skits later in the chapter.

For videodisc application, see *Videodisc Guide.*

Culture Notes

• Prices in West African markets are not fixed and customers are expected to bargain. With the buyer's first inquiry, the vendor often extols the virtues of the item and quotes a high price, sometimes triple the price usually paid. The customer should never pay this price, but make a counteroffer of approximately half the usual price. The vendor and customer will usually bargain to a happy compromise.

• In many African countries, it is believed that a vendor who allows the first customer of the day to leave without purchasing something will have bad luck for the rest of the day.

Language Note

For *seller* or *merchant,* the words **vendeur**(**-euse**) and **commerçant**(**e**) are generally interchangeable.

For Individual Needs

10 Slower Pace/Visual Learners Hold up pictures of the foods mentioned in this activity and have students give the number of the cart that contains each one. For example, if you hold up a picture of pineapples, the class would respond **trois et cinq.**

Presentation

Comment dit-on... ?
Distribute vocabulary cards to students. Then, ask various students **De quoi est-ce que tu as besoin?** or **Qu'est-ce qu'il te faut?** and have them respond by naming the item on their cards (**ananas**). Then, have groups of five or six play the game "**Quels ingrédients?**" To play, each student repeats all the previously mentioned ingredients and adds another. This game is explained in more detail on page 201J.

Language-to-Language

A la française Have students think of additional expressions in English that involve food. (*It's food for thought. Don't cry over spilled milk.*) You might want to share the following French expressions with your students and have them guess what they mean: **C'est du beurre!** *It's a cinch.* **Il mange son pain blanc le premier.** *He eats his cake first.* **Ce n'est pas mes oignons.** *It's none of my business.* Ask students who speak Spanish to share similiar expressions involving food. **Es una papa sin sal.** *He or she is a dull person (literally, a potato without salt).* **Ese huevo quiere sal.** *He or she wants to take advantage of you (literally, that egg wants salt).*

CLOSE

To close this **étape**, show *Teaching Transparencies 8-A* and *8-B* and have students identify the food items shown.

ASSESS

Quiz 8-1A, Quiz 8-1B, *Testing Program,* pp. 197–200
Audio CD 8, Tr. 20

COMMENT DIT-ON... ?

Expressing need

p. 88, Act. 8   8-1

— Qu'est-ce qu'il te faut?
— **Il me faut** des bananes, du riz et de l'eau minérale.

— De quoi est-ce que tu as besoin? *What do you need?*
— **J'ai besoin de** riz pour faire du foutou. *I need . . .*

NOTE DE GRAMMAIRE

PA
p. 88, Act. 9

The expression **avoir besoin de** can be followed by a noun or a verb. The partitive article is not used with this expression.

GV
p. 65, Act. 10

Tu **as besoin de** tomates?
Nous **avons besoin d'œufs** pour l'omelette.
J'**ai besoin d'**aller au marché.

Additional Grammar Practice, p. R42

A la française

Many French expressions involve foods: **On est dans la purée** (*We're in trouble*); **C'est pas de la tarte** (*It's not easy*). Can you guess what **C'est du gâteau** means? *

Vocabulaire à la carte

Here are some additional words you may want to know:

du concombre	*cucumber*
des cornichons (m.)	*pickles*
de la mayonnaise	*mayonnaise*
de la moutarde	*mustard*
des noix (f.)	*nuts*
du poivre	*pepper*
du sel	*salt*

11 **Que faut-il?** See answers below.

Tu as besoin de quoi pour faire...

1. un bon sandwich?
2. une quiche?
3. une salade?
4. une salade de fruits?
5. un banana split?

12 **Un repas entre amis**

Sandrine is having a party, but she's keeping the menu a secret. Based on what she needs, try to guess what she's preparing.

1. J'ai besoin de salade, de tomates, de carottes, d'oignons...   une salade
2. J'ai besoin de fromage, de pain, de jambon...   un sandwich
3. J'ai besoin d'œufs, de champignons, de fromage, de lait...   une omelette
4. J'ai besoin de bananes, de pommes, d'oranges...   une salade de fruits

une tarte aux pommes
un banana split   une salade de fruits
une salade   un sandwich   une omelette

13 **De quoi est-ce que tu as besoin?**

You're going to cook a special meal for your host family. Decide what you want to make. Then, go to the market and buy what you need. Take turns with a partner playing the role of the merchant.

* It means *It's easy; it's a piece of cake.*

Performance Assessment

Have students make a shopping list of at least five items, using the partitive articles. Then, have them pair off and take turns asking what their partner needs.

Possible answers

11 1. du pain, du fromage, de la viande, des cornichons, de la moutarde
2. des œufs, du fromage, du lait, des champignons, des oignons
3. de la salade, des tomates, des carottes, des champignons, du concombre
4. des oranges, des fraises, des bananes, un ananas
5. des bananes, de la glace, des noix

PANORAMA CULTUREL

Louise • France

Angèle • Côte d'Ivoire

Micheline • Belgique

VIDEO PROGRAM
Videocassette 3
24:20–26:57

OR VIDEODISC PROGRAM,
Videodisc 4, Side B

Search 19035, Play To 21125

Where does your family go to shop for groceries? People in francophone countries have several options. We asked these people where they shop. Here's what they had to say.

CD 8
Trs. 4–7

CD-ROM
Disc 2

Où est-ce que tu aimes faire des provisions?

«Je vais le plus souvent au supermarché, mais je préfère le marché, parce que le marché, c'est dehors et puis, l'ambiance est meilleure.»
—Louise
Tr. 5

«Je préfère aller au supermarché pour aller faire des achats parce que là-bas, c'est plus sûr et bien conservé.»
—Angèle
Tr. 6

«Je préfère aller au marché, chez les petits commerçants, parce qu'il y a le contact personnel, il y a le choix, il y a les odeurs, les couleurs, le plaisir de la promenade aussi dans le marché.»
—Micheline
Tr. 7

Qu'en penses-tu? See answers below.

1. Where do these people shop for groceries?
2. What are the advantages and disadvantages of shopping in these different places?
3. Are there outdoor farmers' markets in your community? What can you buy there?
4. Does your family sometimes shop in small specialty stores? If so, what do they buy there?

Savais-tu que... ?

Many people in francophone countries grocery shop in supermarkets (**supermarchés**) or hypermarkets (**hypermarchés**) because it's convenient. Others prefer to shop in small grocery stores (**épiceries**) or outdoor markets (**marchés en plein air**). **Supermarchés** are similar to their American counterparts. **Hypermarchés** are very large stores that carry just about anything you can imagine—all under one roof! Americans may be surprised to learn, however, that stores are not open 24 hours a day or even late in the evening. **Epiceries** are usually closed between 12:30 P.M. and 4 P.M. and all day on either Sunday or Monday.

Teacher Notes

• See the *Video Guide,* the *Videodisc Guide,* and the *CD-ROM Teacher's Guide* for activities related to the **Panorama Culturel.**
• Remind students that cultural material may be included in the Chapter Quizzes and Test.
• The interviewees' language represents informal, unrehearsed speech. Occasionally, edits have been made for clarification.

Presentation

After students view the video and read the interviews, ask them the **Questions** below. Have them tell where they would prefer to shop and why. This could be done orally or in writing. Ask students if they choose different places to shop for different things.

Language Note

Students might want to know the following words from the interviews: **dehors** *(outside)*; **ambiance** *(atmosphere, mood)*; **bien conservé** *(well-preserved)*; **commerçants** *(shopkeepers)*; **meilleure** *(better).*

Answers
1. in the supermarket and market
2. *Possible answers*
In a supermarket, everything is conveniently under one roof and well-refrigerated, but the atmosphere can be impersonal. At the market, the atmosphere is lively, and the food is fresh, but you may have to visit several vendors to complete all of your shopping, and shopping carts aren't available.

Questions

1. **Pourquoi est-ce que Louise préfère aller au marché? (C'est dehors; l'ambiance est meilleure.)**
2. **Pourquoi est-ce qu'Angèle préfère aller au supermarché pour faire ses achats? (C'est plus sûr et bien conservé.)**
3. **Pourquoi est-ce que Micheline préfère aller au marché? (Il y a le contact personnel, le choix, les odeurs, les couleurs, le plaisir de la promenade.)**

DEUXIEME ETAPE Storytelling Book pp. 30, 32

Making, accepting, and declining requests; telling someone what to do

COMMENT DIT-ON... ?
Making, accepting, and declining requests; telling someone what to do

p. 89, Acts. 10–12   8-2

To make requests:
Tu peux aller faire les courses?
  Can you . . . ?
Tu me rapportes des œufs?
  Will you bring me . . . ?

To tell someone what to do:
Rapporte(-moi) du beurre.
  Bring (me) back . . .
Prends du lait. *Get . . .*
Achète(-moi) du riz. *Buy (me) . . .*
N'oublie pas d'acheter le lait.
  Don't forget to . . .

To accept:
Pourquoi pas?
Bon, d'accord.
Je veux bien. *Gladly.*
J'y vais tout de suite.
  I'll go right away.

To decline:
Je ne peux pas maintenant.
Je regrette, mais je n'ai pas le temps. *I'm sorry, but I don't have time.*
J'ai des trucs à faire.
J'ai des tas de choses à faire.

14 Ecoute!   See scripts and answers on p. 201G.

a. Listen to these dialogues. Is the first speaker making a request or telling someone what to do?

b. Now, listen again. Does the second speaker accept or decline the request or command?

CD 8
Trs. 8–9

À la française

You already know that the verb **faire** means *to do.* What do you think the verb **refaire** might mean? The prefix **re-** in front of a verb means *to redo* something; to do something again. Use **r-** in front of a verb that begins with a vowel.

Tu dois **re**lire ce livre. *You need to reread this book.*
On va **r**acheter du lait. *We'll buy milk again.*
Rapporte-moi du beurre! *Bring me back some butter!*

Does this same rule apply in English?

GRAMMAIRE   The verb **pouvoir**

 p. 90, Acts. 13–14   p. 66, Acts. 11–12

Pouvoir is an irregular verb. Notice how similar it is to the verb **vouloir,** which you learned in Chapter 6.

Additional Grammar Practice, p. R43

pouvoir   *(to be able to, can, may)*

Je **peux**	Nous **pouvons**
Tu **peux** } faire les courses?	Vous **pouvez** } promener le chien?
Il/Elle/On **peut**	Ils/Elles **peuvent**

15 Qui va faire les courses? 🏠

Complete this conversation with the appropriate forms of **pouvoir.**

M. BONFILS   Sim, tu __1__ aller au marché pour moi?   peux

SIM   Non, je ne __2__ pas. J'ai des trucs à faire!   peux

ARMANDE   Papa, Julie et moi, nous __3__ y aller si tu veux.   pouvons

M. BONFILS   Merci, les filles. Vous __4__ me prendre un ananas et des mangues?   pouvez
Ah, et du pain aussi.

JULIE   On __5__ acheter les fruits, mais Sim et Marius ne font jamais rien. Ils __6__ bien acheter le pain pour une fois!   peut, peuvent

16 On peut?

Find out if your classmates can do these things with or for you.

—Vous pouvez écouter de la musique après l'école?
—Non, nous ne pouvons pas.

regarder la télé après l'école

aller nager

faire des courses avec moi

me rapporter un sandwich

jouer au foot demain

sortir ce soir

Teaching Suggestion

14 Ask students to listen to the speakers' intonation for clues, as well as to what they say.

Presentation

Grammaire   First, ask students to recall the forms of the verb **vouloir.** Have individuals write one form they remember on the board until the paradigm is complete. Write the forms of **pouvoir** next to those of **vouloir.** Next, say a subject pronoun and toss a ball to a student, who must say the correct verb form as he or she catches the ball. Then, that student continues by tossing the ball to another student while calling out a subject pronoun.

For Individual Needs

16 Challenge   Encourage students to offer excuses for declining their classmates' requests. Have students find at least two classmates who accept to do each activity with them.

Language-to-Language

Review with students the difference between the use of *can* and *may* in English. Point out that the verb **pouvoir** means both *can* and *may.*

Language Notes

• **A la française** Ask students to try to guess the meanings of the following verbs that are formed with the prefix **re-: reprendre, redonner, recommencer** *(to take back, to give back, to begin again).*

• A famous French proverb is **Vouloir, c'est pouvoir.** Have students try to guess the English equivalent. *(Where there's a will, there's a way.)*

Presentation

Vocabulaire/Note de grammaire Say the expressions of quantity as you hold up the corresponding amount or container of each item. Have partners or small groups list other items that are packaged or sold in these quantities (**un litre de coca**). Collect their lists, call out the foods or beverages, and have students give a possible quantity for each one.

For videodisc application, see *Videodisc Guide.*

Teacher Note

Note de grammaire Make sure students understand that only **de** or **d'** is used after expressions of quantity, regardless of the gender and number of the noun that follows.

Language Notes

• Other common expressions of quantity are **une brique de lait, un pot de yaourt,** and **une plaquette de beurre** (two quarter-pound sticks).

• Explain that **une livre** is an old unit of measure equivalent to half a kilo (1 kilo equals 2.2 pounds), so it equals approximately one pound.

Thinking Critically

Analyzing Ask students to give advantages of the American system of weights and measures. Have them discuss the advantages and disadvantages of changing to the metric system.

PA pp. 90–91, Acts. 15–17   8-C   GV p. 67, Act. 13

CD-ROM Disc 2

VOCABULAIRE

Vous en voulez combien?

un kilo(gramme) de pommes de terre et **une livre d'**oignons

une bouteille d'eau minérale

une douzaine d'œufs

une boîte de tomates   **un paquet de** sucre

une tranche de jambon

un morceau de fromage   **un litre de** lait

NOTE DE GRAMMAIRE

Notice that you always use **de** or **d'** after expressions of quantity.

Une tranche **de** jambon, s'il vous plaît.

Je voudrais un kilo **d'**oranges.

GV pp. 67–68, Acts. 14–16

Additional Grammar Practice, p. R43

NOTE CULTURELLE

The metric system was created shortly after the French Revolution and has since been adopted by nearly all countries in the world. Although the United States is officially trying to convert to the metric system, many people aren't yet used to it. In the metric system, lengths are measured in centimeters and meters, rather than inches and yards. Distances are measured in kilometers. Grams and kilograms are the standard measures of weight. **Une livre** is half a kilogram. Liquids, including gasoline, are measured in liters. To convert metric measurements, use the following table:

1 centimeter = .39 inches	1 gram = .035 ounces
1 meter = 39.37 inches	1 kilogram = 2.2 pounds
1 kilometer = .62 miles	1 liter = 1.06 quarts

Math Link

Note Culturelle Have students figure out their height in meters and centimeters or their weight in kilos. They could also calculate speed limits in kilometers per hour (55 mph = 89 kph; 65 mph = 105 kph). Students may be sensitive about discussing their own measurements, so you might discuss the height and weight of different celebrities instead.

Culture Note

In Côte d'Ivoire, meat, potatoes, flour, sugar, popcorn, rice, and milk are sold by weight (kilos or grams). Vegetables and fruits are priced according to size, freshness, and availability. Items such as hot pepper (**piment**) and okra are sold in bunches. Small items are often placed in large banana leaves that are folded to make containers.

17 Ecoute!
See scripts and answers on p. 201G.

Listen to Sophie as she does her shopping. Write down the items and the quantities she asks for.

CD 8 Tr. 10

18 Qu'est-ce que tu veux?

Your mother and grandmother are planning a dinner party. They have asked you to go to the market for them. Complete the conversation below with an appropriate quantity from the expressions given. See answers below.

une boîte de/d'   une douzaine de/d'   un morceau de/d'

un litre de/d'   une livre de/d'   une bouteille de/d'

un paquet de/d'   un kilo de/d'

—Alors, Maman, qu'est-ce qu'il te faut?
—Il me faut __1__ bœuf, __2__ fromage et __3__ eau minérale.
—Et pour le dessert?
—Achète-moi __4__ farine, __5__ pêches et __6__ œufs.
—Et toi, Mémé, de quoi est-ce que tu as besoin?
—Rapporte-moi __7__ oignons et __8__ lait, s'il te plaît.
—D'accord. A tout à l'heure.

19 Allons au marché!

You're shopping for groceries. Make sure that you place your orders in appropriate quantities. Your partner will be the merchant. Then, change roles.

Vous avez choisi?

Et avec ça?   Voilà.

Vous désirez?   C'est tout?

Je voudrais...   Il me faut...

Je prends...

avocats
tomates
vinaigre
oignons
œufs
pain
huile d'olive
fromage
riz
haricots verts
raisin
sucre

20 Jeu de rôle

You're working as a volunteer to pick up groceries for senior citizens. Make a list of what you need to get and the quantity of each item. Take turns with your partner playing the role of the senior citizen.

DEUXIEME ETAPE

deux cent quinze **215**

Teaching Suggestions

17 You might have partners listen to the recording together, with one writing the item as the other writes the quantity.

19 Have students list the quantities they intend to buy before working with a partner.

20 Before they begin the activity, have students make a list of what they need to get. Then, after the partners have read their lists to each other, they might exchange them to check for accuracy.

Additional Practice

Show *Teaching Transparency 8-2* and have partners act out the situation.

CLOSE

To close this **étape**, hold up various food items and have students ask for a specific quantity of each one.

ASSESS

Quiz 8-2A, Quiz 8-2B, *Testing Program,* pp. 201–204
Audio CD 8, Tr. 21

Performance Assessment

In groups of four, students will plan a typical American dinner for a guest from Côte d'Ivoire. Have them make a grocery list (**Nous avons besoin de...**). Then, one student asks the others to go get the various items at the supermarket. The others respond appropriately.

Possible answers
18 1. une livre de
2. un morceau de
3. une bouteille d'
4. un paquet de
5. une boîte de
6. une douzaine d'
7. un kilo d'
8. un litre de

Motivating Activity

Ask students if they've ever tried food from another country. Have them describe what the food looked like and how it tasted. Ask them if they used any special utensils or if certain customs were connected with eating the food.

Presentation

Have students look at the pictures and guess what each dish is made of. Then, have three volunteers read the descriptions. Have small groups of students answer the questions in **Qu'en penses-tu?** and report back to the class.

Culture Notes

• In Ivorian villages, **foutou** is eaten without silverware and only with the right hand. It is considered rude to eat with the left hand, which is reserved for personal hygiene. To eat **foutou**, individuals break off a piece, form a small ball, and then dip it in the sauce accompanying the meal.

• Tell students that when they are guests for dinner in Africa, they should at least taste everything that they are served. When they are offered a second helping, it is polite to accept at least some, even though they may not want more.

• Since most meals are not made with prepared foods, a typical meal might take from six to seven hours, including a visit to the market and cleaning up afterwards. For this reason, the sauce that is eaten for lunch is often eaten for dinner on the same day.

RENCONTRE CULTURELLE

◀ **Le foutou,** the national dish of Côte d'Ivoire, is a paste made from boiled plantains, manioc, or yams. It is eaten with various sauces, such as peanut sauce or palm oil nut sauce.

▼ **La sauce arachide** is one of the many sauces eaten in Côte d'Ivoire. It is made from peanut butter with beef, chicken, or fish, hot peppers, peanut oil, garlic, onions, tomato paste, tomatoes, and a variety of other vegetables. It is usually served over rice.

▶ **L'aloco,** a popular snack food in Côte d'Ivoire, is a dish of fried plantain bananas. It is usually eaten with a spicy sauce (**sauce pimentée**).

Qu'en penses-tu? See answers below.

1. Do these dishes resemble any that are eaten in the United States?
2. Which ingredients in these dishes can you find in your neighborhood grocery store? Which ingredients are unfamiliar?
3. What dishes are typical of your part of the country? Why are they more common than others?

Savais-tu que... ?

Yams (**ignames**) and plantains are abundant in the Republic of Côte d'Ivoire, which explains why **foutou** is a popular dish. A typical lunch consists of one main course — often **foutou**, rice, or **attiéké** (ground manioc root) with a sauce; and a dessert — usually tropical fruits such as guavas, pineapples, or papayas. Lunch is traditionally followed by an hour-long siesta. To accommodate this custom, stores are closed from noon until 3:00 P.M., even in large cities such as Abidjan. Unlike lunch, dinner tends to be a much lighter meal. Heavy foods are rarely eaten in the evening.

Community Link

Call the local parks and recreation association, community education program, or community college and try to find someone who teaches African cooking. Invite this person to come and speak to your students about popular recipes and their ingredients or even prepare a dish.

Possible answers

1. **Le foutou** is a unique dish that has no American equivalent. **La sauce arachide** resembles a dark sauce, stew, or soup. **L'aloco** resembles banana fritters.

TROISIEME ETAPE Storytelling Book pp. 31, 32

Offering, accepting, or refusing food

 p. 92, Acts. 19–20   8-D   p. 69, Acts. 17–18

VOCABULAIRE

Qu'est-ce qu'on mange au...

petit déjeuner?

déjeuner?

goûter?

dîner?

TROISIEME ETAPE

deux cent dix-sept **217**

RESOURCES FOR TROISIEME ETAPE

PRINT
- *Lesson Planner,* p. 41
- *Practice and Activity Book,* pp. 92–94
- *Grammar and Vocabulary Workbook,* pp. 69–70
- *Activities for Communication,* pp. 47–48, 112, 113–114, 151–152
- *Listening Activities,* pp. 60–61, 65
- *Testing Program,* pp. 205–208
- *Alternative Assessment Guide,* p. 39

MEDIA
- *Video Program,* Videocassette 3
  Video Guide, pp. 53–58
- *Videodisc Program,* Videodisc 4, Side B
  Videodisc Guide, p. 91
- *Teaching Transparencies* 8-3, 8-D
- *Interactive CD-ROM Program,* Disc 2
  CD-ROM Teacher's Guide, p. 34
- *Audio Compact Discs*
  Textbook Listening Activities, CD 8, Trs. 11–12
  Additional Listening Activities 8-5, 8-6, CD 8, Trs. 30–31
  Quiz 8-3B, CD 8, Tr. 22

Jump Start!

Have students write two sentences for each of these food items: **eau minérale** and **fraises.** In the first sentence, students say they need the item, and in the second sentence, they ask or tell someone to get a specified quantity of the item.

MOTIVATE

Ask students if they have ever been served food they didn't like and what they did in that situation. Discuss how to avoid being rude in such a situation. Have students consider the consequences of being an inconsiderate guest. Ask students how they would feel if a guest refused to taste something they had prepared.

TEACH

Presentation

Vocabulaire Ask students to name the different foods shown on each table. Ask them **A quelle heure est-ce que tu manges ça?** Then, tell what you have for breakfast, lunch, a snack, and dinner. Hold up pictures of various foods and beverages and have students name the meal at which they would have them.

Culture Notes
- Point out that in France, **le déjeuner** is usually the main meal of the day, whereas **le dîner** is typically a light, simple meal.
- In Côte d'Ivoire, people might have popcorn (**du pop-corn**), peanuts (**des arachides**), roasted yams, or **aloco** with hot sauce (**sauce pimentée**) for an afternoon snack.

For Individual Needs

21 Slower Pace Before playing the recording, have pairs of students name the foods shown in each illustration, or you might name the items in each breakfast and have students identify the letter of the illustration you're describing.

Culture Note

Nutella® is a spread made from hazelnuts and chocolate. It is very popular in Europe and is sometimes eaten at breakfast or for a snack (**le goûter**).

Thinking Critically

Comparing and Contrasting
Ask students to compare a French breakfast with what Americans normally eat for breakfast. Ask students if they generally have a light breakfast or a heavy one.

Culture Note

In Africa, as in France, people almost never drink milk with meals. Ask students which French or African eating habits might be difficult to adopt.

21 Ecoute! See scripts on p. 201H. 1. c 2. a 3. b

CD 8 Tr. 11

Listen to these people tell what they have for breakfast. Match each speaker with his or her breakfast.

a. b. c.

NOTE CULTURELLE

In the morning, most people in francophone countries have a very light breakfast. Coffee with hot milk (**café au lait**) and hot chocolate are the drinks of choice. They are usually served with bread or croissants, butter, and jam. Children may eat cereal for breakfast as well, sometimes with warm milk. The largest meal of the day, **le déjeuner**, has traditionally been between noon and 1:00 P.M. Dinner (**le dîner**) is eaten after 7:00 P.M.

22 Un repas typique

Look at each illustration below and tell at which meal(s) you might eat the items. Then, decide whether each set of items would typically be served in the United States, in a francophone country, or in both.   See answers below.

1. 2. 3.

4. 5. 6.

218 *deux cent dix-huit* CHAPITRE 8 Au marché

Possible answers:
22 1. au dîner; both
   2. au goûter; United States
   3. au déjeuner; francophone country
   4. au petit déjeuner; United States
   5. au dîner; francophone country
   6. au petit déjeuner; francophone country

Language Note

Students might be interested to know that **jeûner** means *to fast,* so **déjeuner** is *to break a fast.* **Goûter** means *to taste* or *to have a snack,* and **dîner** is *to dine.*

23 Quel repas?

 Describe one of these meals to your partner. He or she will try to guess which meal you're talking about. Take turns. See answers below.

Il y a du poulet,...

1.   2.   3.

24 Devine!

 Write down what you think you'll have for your meals tomorrow, using the **Vocabulaire** on page 207. Your partner will do the same. Take turns guessing what each of you will have.

—Au petit déjeuner, tu vas manger... ?
—Oui, c'est ça. *or* Non, pas de...

COMMENT DIT-ON... ?
Offering, accepting, or refusing food

CD-ROM
Disc 2

To offer food to someone:
Tu veux du riz?
Vous voulez de l'eau minérale?
Vous prenez du fromage?
Tu prends du fromage?
Encore du pain? *More . . . ?*

To accept:
Oui, s'il vous/te plaît.
Oui, j'en veux bien. *Yes, I'd like some.*
Oui, avec plaisir. *Yes, with pleasure.*

To refuse:
Non, merci.
Je n'en veux plus. *I don't want any more.*
Non, merci. Je n'ai plus faim. *No thanks. I'm not hungry anymore.*

pp. 92–93,
Acts. 21–22
 8-3

---

25 Ecoute! See scripts and answers on p. 201H.

 Is the speaker offering, accepting, or refusing food?

CD 8 Tr. 12

TROISIEME ETAPE   *deux cent dix-neuf*   **219**

Answers
23 1. Il y a du poulet, du riz, du maïs, du pain, du fromage, une salade avec des tomates, des fraises et de l'eau minérale.
  2. Il y a du poulet, du riz, des haricots, du pain, du beurre, une salade avec des tomates, des pêches et de l'eau minérale.
  3. Il y a du bifteck, du riz, du maïs, du pain, du fromage, une salade avec des œufs, des fraises et du lait.

Language Note
Tell students that responding to an offer of food by saying **Merci** alone might be taken as a refusal. Another expression of acceptance is **Oui, je veux bien.**

For Individual Needs
23 Slower Pace Before having students do the activity, you might have them point out the differences among the three meals, using **Il n'y a pas de...**

Teaching Suggestion
23 This activity could also be done by having students write a description of one of the meals. Then, have them exchange papers with a partner, who will guess which meal is described.

Presentation

Comment dit-on... ? Bring in real food items or pictures of them. Offer different items to individuals, varying your expressions. (**Tu veux du poulet? Tu prends de l'eau?**) Next, have students offer you the food items, using the **vous** form. Alternately accept and refuse the various food items, having students repeat after you.

 For videodisc application, see *Videodisc Guide*.

For Individual Needs

Tactile Learners Bring in mineral water, sliced bread, or food that can be broken into pieces. Offer some to the first person in each row. After that student responds, give him or her the food. He or she then offers some to the next student, and so on.

26 Slower Pace You might have the class orally identify the food items shown before beginning the activity.

Teaching Suggestion

26 Have students change roles after offering several items.

Portfolio

26 Oral This activity is appropriate for students' oral portfolios. For portfolio information, see the *Alternative Assessment Guide,* pages iv–17.

Presentation

Grammaire On five separate index cards, write each word and the question mark of the question **Tu veux des mangues?** Write **en** on a sixth card. Give one card, with the exception of **en,** to each of five students and have them stand side by side and hold up their cards to form the question **Tu veux des mangues?** Then, remove the two students holding the cards for **des** and **mangues** and substitute another student holding the card for **en** in the proper position to form **Tu en veux?** Have students repeat both questions and explain what has happened. Repeat this procedure for the other examples.

Additional Practice

27 Have students tell or write about three things that Aïssata doesn't have in her basket. For example, **Du chocolat? Elle n'en a pas.**

---

26 Encore du pain?

An Ivorian exchange student is having dinner at your house. Encourage him or her to try some of the foods on the table. Your friend will accept or politely refuse.

De bons conseils Look for opportunities to practice your French wherever you go. Try to meet French-speaking people and talk with them. Ask your teacher to help you find a pen pal in a French-speaking country. Rent videocassettes of French films. See how many French products you can find at the grocery store and the cosmetic counter, and how many French dishes you can find on restaurant menus.

GRAMMAIRE The pronoun en

En takes the place of a phrase beginning with **du, de la, de l', des,** or **de** to avoid repetition. **En** usually means *some (of it/them)* or simply *it/them.*

— Tu veux **des mangues**?
— Oui, j'**en** veux bien.
— Tu manges **des légumes**?
— Oui, j'**en** mange souvent.

In a negative sentence, **en** means *any* or *none.*

— Tu veux **du beurre**?
— Merci, je n'**en** veux pas.

p. 93, Act. 23

p. 70, Acts. 19–20

Additional Grammar Practice, pp. R43–R44

27 Elle en a combien?

What quantity of each of these items does Aïssata have in her basket?

Des haricots? Elle en a un kilo.

1. Du lait? Elle en a un litre.
2. Du beurre? Elle en a un paquet.
3. Des tomates? Elle en a trois.
4. Du riz? Elle en a un kilo.
5. Des œufs? Elle en a six.
6. De l'eau minérale? Elle en a une bouteille.
7. Des ananas? Elle n'en a pas.

220 *deux cent vingt*

CHAPITRE 8 Au marché

Teacher Note

De bons conseils For information on international pen pal organizations, see page T54.

Music Link

Grammaire To have students listen to the pronoun **en** modeled in a song, play *Il n'y en a pas comme nous* available on Audio CD 8.

28 Tu en veux?

Take turns with a partner asking each other if you eat the foods shown in Activity 26. Use the pronoun **en** in your answers.

— Tu manges du poulet?
— Oui, j'en mange souvent.

29 Bienvenue chez nous!

Write a conversation between an Ivorian family and an American family who are having dinner together. During the meal, the hosts offer various foods to their guests, who respond politely and comment favorably on what they're eating.

P R O N O N C I A T I O N

 The sounds [o] and [ɔ]   See scripts and answers on p. 201H.

CD 8 Trs. 13–18

The sound [o] is similar to the vowel sound in the English word *boat.* To make the sound [o], hold your mouth in a whistling position. Keep the lips and tongue steady to avoid the glide heard in *boat.* Repeat each of these words: **trop, kilo, mot.** The spellings **au, eau, ô,** and sometimes **o** represent the sound [o]. Now, repeat these words: **jaune, chaud, beau, rôle.**

The sound [ɔ] is between the vowel sounds in the English words *boat* and *bought.* Usually, this sound is followed by a consonant sound in the same syllable. The sound [ɔ] is more open, so hold your mouth in a semi-whistling position to produce it. This sound is usually spelled with the letter **o.** Now repeat these words: **bof, donne, fort, carotte.**

A. A prononcer

Repeat the following words and phrases.

1. au revoir   un stylo jaune   au restaurant
2. un gâteau   moi aussi   des haricots verts
3. des pommes   d'abord   une promenade
4. encore   dormir   l'école

B. A lire

Take turns with a partner reading each of the following sentences aloud.

1. Elle a une gomme violette et un stylo jaune.
2. Tu aimes les carottes? Moi, j'adore. J'aime bien aussi les escargots et le porc.
3. Elle est occupée aujourd'hui. Elle a informatique et biologie.
4. Il me faut un short parce qu'il fait trop chaud.
5. Tu peux sortir si tu promènes d'abord le chien.

C. A écrire

You're going to hear a short dialogue. Write down what you hear.

 For Individual Needs

29 Challenge Students might do this activity in pairs, practicing the conversation aloud before writing it down. They could act the conversations out as skits (with props), if time permits. Students might also imagine they are having dinner with a French family or a family from Quebec.

Teaching Suggestion

Prononciation After correcting the dictation in Part C, have students underline the letters that represent the [o] sound and circle the letters that represent [ɔ].

CLOSE

To close this **étape,** write a list of food items on a transparency and have students tell whether they would be eaten **au petit déjeuner, au déjeuner, au goûter,** or **au dîner** in a francophone country.

ASSESS

Quiz 8-3A, Quiz 8-3B, *Testing Program,* pp. 205–208
Audio CD 8, Tr. 22

Performance Assessment

On separate index cards, write the names of the meals in French. Have students pair off and have one partner in each pair draw a card. Partners must then offer and accept or refuse four items that would normally be served at that meal. Encourage students to bring in the food items, paper plates, and plastic eating utensils to make their skits more realistic.

Teacher Note

Prononciation Notice that in Part A, rows 1 and 2 contain examples of the [o] sound, and rows 3 and 4, examples of the [ɔ] sound.

READING STRATEGY
Recognizing false cognates

Teacher Note
For an additional reading, see *Practice and Activity Book,* page 95.

PREREADING
Activities A–D

Motivating Activity
Have students look at the photos and describe the foods.

Teaching Suggestions
A–C Have students do these activities on their own and check them orally.
• Have students create a list of common cooking instructions in English, such as *bake, slice, stir, mix,* and so on. Tell students to place them in the order in which they are usually performed. For example, *stir* would come before *bake.* Tell students that they will be able to guess the meanings of some unfamiliar French instructions by their order in the recipe.

Teaching Suggestion
Students might also enjoy compiling a list of French cooking terms used in English, such as **sauté, julienne,** and **purée.**

READING
Activities E–H

Terms in Lisons!
Students may want to know the following expressions: **pâte** *(dough);* **étaler** *(to roll out);* **cuire** *(to cook);* **four** *(oven);* **ail** *(garlic);* **éplucher** *(to peel);* **évider** *(to empty out).*

LISONS!

Skim the titles and photographs. What will you be reading?

DE BONS CONSEILS
Remember to look for cognates to help you figure out what you're reading. Occasionally, you will encounter false cognates, words that look alike in two languages but have different meanings.
Context clues can sometimes help you recognize false cognates. An example of a false cognate is the French phrase **fruits de mer.** **Fruits de mer** may make you think of the English word *fruit,* but it means *seafood.*

A. You already know a few false cognates. Try to figure out the meaning of the false cognates in the sentences below.

1. Je vais à San Francisco à 11h00. Maintenant, il est 10h40, et **j'attends** le train.
   a. I'm attending
   b. I'm late for
   c. I'm waiting for

2. J'adore les sciences. Ce soir, je vais **assister** à une conférence sur l'ozone.
   a. to attend
   b. to assist
   c. to teach

222 *deux cent vingt-deux*

la cuisine autour du monde

LA CUISINE AFRICAINE

SAEP

Les desserts

Croissants au coco et au sésame
(Afrique occidentale)

✕ ⚭

Prép. : 30 mn. - Cuiss. : 10 mn.
Repos : 1 h. - 8 pers.

2 œufs
140 g de sucre
190 g de noix de coco râpée

170 g de farine
Vanille en poudre
Graines de sésame

Mélanger la noix de coco râpée, le sucre, la vanille et les œufs entiers. Incorporer la farine. Travailler la pâte. Former une boule. Laisser reposer 1 heure au frais.
Etaler la pâte sur 1/2 cm. Découper en croissants. Les rouler dans le sésame. Cuire au four à 200 °C, (th. 6-7), 10 minutes.

Math Link
Have students figure out the American measurements of the ingredients in the cookie recipe. They might refer to the conversion chart in the **Note Culturelle** on page 214.

Language Note
Students might notice that the recipe directions are given in the infinitive form. This is common in written instructions to a general audience.

Signification des symboles accompagnant les recettes

Recettes

✗ élémentaire

✗✗ facile

✗✗✗ difficile

Recettes

○ peu coûteuse

○○ raisonnable

○○○ chère

Les entrées

Mousseline africaine de petits légumes

(Afrique occidentale - Bénin - Togo)

✗ ○○

Prép. : 40 mn. - Cuiss. : 15 mn.

4 pers.

2 petits concombres
Ail
1 lime
1 radis noir
1/2 papaye

1 avocat
1 épi de maïs
Graines de carvi
4 petites brioches
Sel.

Eplucher les concombres. Les détailler en dés. Faire la même chose avec l'avocat.
Débarrasser l'épis de maïs des feuilles et des barbes. Le faire cuire durant 15 minutes à l'eau bouillante. Saler en fin de cuisson.
Egréner le maïs. Débarrasser la papaye de ses graines. La découper en petits dés. Emincer le radis noir. Parfumer de graines de carvi et d'ail haché. Arroser la salade de jus de lime.
Retirer le chapeau des brioches. Les évider. Les garnir de la salade parfumée.

Les brioches ne doivent pas être sucrées. Si on les fabrique, il convient d'ôter le sucre. Ne pas saler l'épi de maïs au début de la cuisson mais à la fin afin d'éviter qu'il durcisse.

B. With a partner, scan the reading and write down all of the cognates you can find in these selections.   See answers below.

C. Did you find any false cognates? Were you able to figure out what they mean? If so, how? See answers below.

D. Where would you expect to find these reading selections? Where are these dishes from? cookbook; Africa

E. Which of the dishes would make a good dessert?   croissants

F. Are these dishes easy or difficult to make? How do you know? Are they expensive or inexpensive to make? How do you know?   See answers below.

G. To make **croissants**, how long do you need to chill the dough? At what temperature do you bake them? What temperature is that on the Fahrenheit scale? (To convert from Celsius to Fahrenheit, multiply by $\frac{9}{5}$ and add 32.)   See answers below.

H. To make **mousseline**, how long do you have to cook the corn? Do you think this dish would taste sweet or salty? How many people does this dish serve?
See answers below.

I. Now, with a partner, write the instructions for an easy recipe that you know how to make. Include the ingredients, the steps required to prepare the dish, and the cooking and preparation time required.

The background design on the two **Lisons!** pages is from a piece of cloth purchased in Côte d'Ivoire.

deux cent vingt-trois **223**

Thinking Critically

Comparing and Contrasting
After students have read the recipes carefully, ask them if the ingredients listed would be difficult to find in local stores. Ask students if the recipes sound appetizing and if they are similar to dishes that they have eaten.

(TPR) Say various cooking instructions, having students mime the actions. You might provide props such as a bowl, a spoon, and a baking pan.

POSTREADING
Activity I

Teaching Suggestion

I. Ask students to use metric measurements in their recipes. You might have students demonstrate how to prepare their dishes in front of the class, using props if they choose. Have one partner read aloud the recipe while the other acts out the instructions. You might also have students make their dishes at home and bring them in for the class to sample.

For Individual Needs

Challenge   As an additional chapter project, students might compile all the recipes into a class cookbook. They might design and draw a cover and illustrate each recipe. You might have them make copies to distribute to the entire class.

Answers

B *Possible answers:* africaine, coco, sésame, vanille, symboles, raisonnable, desserts, avocat

C *Possible answers:* parfumer *(to flavor),* former *(to mold),* détailler *(to cut separately),* fabriquer *(to make)*

F Symbols show that both recipes are very easy (**élémentaire**) and moderately priced (**raisonnable**).

G one hour; 200°C; 392°F

H 15 minutes; salty; four people

Math Link

I. If students use the oven for their recipes, have them give the oven temperature in Celsius. The formula for converting Fahrenheit to Celsius is F – 32 × 5/9.

The **Mise en pratique** reviews and integrates all four skills and culture in preparation for the Chapter Test.

Teaching Suggestion

1 Before you play the recording, tell students that they should not expect to hear the prices given immediately after the food item. You might pause the recording after one or two items are mentioned to give students time to write.

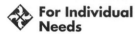 **For Individual Needs**

1 Challenge As a follow-up activity, students might prepare and record similar advertisements.

Health Link

Have students bring in the latest charts of recommended foods and of foods to avoid. If possible, have them describe the foods in French.

MISE EN PRATIQUE

 The *CD-ROM Program* offers guided recording and writing activities to practice oral and written skills and to review material from each chapter.

CD 8
Tr. 19

1 Listen to this supermarket advertisement. List four of the foods that are on sale. Then, listen again for the prices of the four items you listed. See scripts and answers on p. 201H.

2

LES GROUPES D'ALIMENTS

Les aliments sont regroupés en 6 catégories selon leurs caractéristiques nutritionnelles :

- **Le lait et les produits laitiers** sont nos principaux fournisseurs de calcium.
- **Viandes, poissons et œufs** sont nos sources essentielles de protéines de bonne qualité.
- **Le groupe du pain, des féculents et des légumes secs** apporte les «glucides lents» libérant progressivement l'énergie nécessaire à notre organisme.
- **Légumes et fruits** sont nos sources de fibres, vitamines et minéraux.
- **Les matières grasses** sont les sources énergétiques les plus importantes pour notre corps.
- **Le sucre et ses dérivés** apportent les «glucides rapides» nécessaires au bon fonctionnement cérébral et musculaire.

Groupe	Lait Produits Laitiers	Viandes Poissons Œufs	Pains Féculents	Fruits Légumes	Matières Grasses	Sucre Dérivés
Intérêt Principal	Calcium	Protéines	Glucides	Fibres Vitamines A et B	Lipides	Glucides
Intérêt Secondaire	Protéines Vitamines A, B, D	Fer Vitamine B	Fibres	Glucides	Vitamines (A, E, selon mat. grasses)	

L'ensemble de ces catégories permet, au sein d'une alimentation diversifiée, de couvrir tous nos besoins.

See answers below.

1. What kind of chart is this?
2. What do the six categories listed mean?
3. According to the chart, what are some of the nutrients found in . . .
   a. produits laitiers?
   b. viandes?
   c. pain?
   d. fruits et légumes?
   e. matières grasses?
   f. sucre et ses dérivés?
4. Give some examples of foods you know in French that fall into each category.
5. Name three foods that are high in protein and three that are high in calcium.

224 *deux cent vingt-quatre*
CHAPITRE 8   Au marché

Answers
2 1. food groups
2. milk and milk products; meats, fish, and eggs; breads (starches); fruits and vegetables; fats; sugar
3. a. calcium, protein, vitamins A, B, and D
   b. protein, iron, vitamin B
   c. carbohydrates, fiber
   d. fiber, vitamins A and B, carbohydrates
   e. lipids, vitamins A and E
   f. carbohydrates
4. *Possible answers*
   Lait : lait, fromage, yaourt
   Viandes : poulet, bifteck, porc
   Pain/féculents : pain, pommes de terre, riz
   Fruits/légumes : oranges, petits pois, carottes
   Matières grasses : beurre
   Sucre : gâteau, glace, confiture
5. *Answers will vary.*

3 What are some differences between meals in Africa, France, and the United States?

See answers below.

4 *Ecrivons!*

Imagine that you're the producer of a certain food item that you're trying to market. Write an ad that encourages people to buy the item, telling when they might eat it and why it's good. Consider who would be likely to buy your product. Include logos and pictures in your ad as well.

STRATEGIE

Arranging your ideas spatially is a good way to organize ideas for your advertisement. First, brainstorm some catchy phrases and convincing arguments you might write in your ad to persuade people to buy your product. Also, decide what types of illustrations you might use (photos, logos, and so on) and where to place them in your ad. Then, create a sketch of how you want your ad to look.

Persuasive writing encourages people to do a certain thing or to think a certain way. Advertisements are a type of persuasive writing because advertisers try to convince people that their products are better than any others.

Using the sketch you prepared, create the ad for your product. Structure is very important in persuasive writing. You should choose what you feel is the greatest benefit or most appealing characteristic of the product and draw attention to it. You can do this by writing it in larger print or in an eye-catching color. Less attention should be drawn to what you feel are your product's weaker points. However, try to avoid relying too heavily on illustrations and layout; your ad should be informative as well as eye-catching. Be sure to use descriptive terms that illustrate the qualities of your product.

5

JEU DE ROLE

a. Make a list in French of what you've eaten for the last two days. Use the food vocabulary that you've learned in this chapter.

b. Now, you go to a nutrition counselor. The counselor will evaluate your diet, telling you what you need to eat more of and what you shouldn't eat anymore. Act out this scene with a partner. Then, change roles.

3 *Possible answers:* In Africa and France, lunch is often the largest meal of the day, while in the United States, dinner is the largest meal. Dinner is eaten later in Africa and France than in the United States. In Africa, lunch is followed by an hour-long siesta and stores are generally closed from noon to 3:00 P.M.

Process Writing

4 Before students begin their ad, have them look at magazines and newspapers for ideas. When students have completed their ads, you may want to compile them into a food catalog that can be displayed in the classroom, or award a prize for the most creative advertisement.

 Portfolio

5 Oral This activity might be included in students' oral portfolios and/or performed as a skit for the class. For portfolio information, see the *Alternative Assessment Guide*, pages iv–17.

 Video Wrap-Up

- *VIDEO PROGRAM,* Videocassette 3, 16:03–28:23
- *VIDEODISC PROGRAM,* Videodisc 4, Side B

At this time, you might want to use the video resources for additional review and enrichment. See *Video Guide* or *Videodisc Guide* for suggestions regarding the following:

- **Une invitée pour le déjeuner** (Dramatic episode)
- **Panorama Culturel** (Interviews)
- **Vidéoclips** (Authentic footage)

QUE SAIS-JE?

This page is intended to help students prepare for the Chapter Test. It is a brief checklist of the major points covered in the chapter. The students should be reminded that this is only a checklist and does not necessarily include everything that will appear on the test.

Additional Practice

1 Have students write a grocery list specifying quantities of these items.

Teaching Suggestion

7 Have students tell what they would have for these meals in France or Côte d'Ivoire.

? Circumlocution

Have students imagine that they're shopping in a food market in Côte d'Ivoire, but they don't know the vocabulary for food items very well. Have them work with a partner, who will play the role of a merchant. Have students think of five items that they need to purchase, without naming them. Students will circumlocute the item they need to the merchant, who will try to help them with their purchase. (—**C'est un fruit jaune.**—**C'est une banane?**—**Oui, c'est ça.**) You might provide students with the list of circumlocution expressions on page 147J.

Can you use what you've learned in this chapter?

Can you express need? p. 210

1 How would you tell someone that you need these things? *See answers below.*

1.   2.   3.

4.   5.

Can you make, accept, and decline requests or tell someone what to do? p. 212

2 How would you . . .
1. ask someone to go grocery shopping for you? *Tu peux aller faire les courses?*
2. tell someone to bring back some groceries for you? *Tu me rapportes... ?*

3 How would you accept the requests in Activity 2? How would you refuse? *Accept: Bon, d'accord. Je veux bien. J'y vais tout de suite.*
Refuse: Je ne peux pas maintenant. Je regrette, mais je n'ai pas le temps.

4 How would you ask for a specific quantity of these foods? *See answers below.*
1. œufs	4. beurre
2. lait	5. jambon
3. oranges	6. eau minérale

Can you offer, accept, or refuse food? p. 219

5 How would you offer someone these foods? *See answers below.*
1. some rice
2. some oranges
3. some milk

6 How would you accept the foods listed in number 5 if they were offered? How would you refuse them? *Accept: Oui, s'il vous/te plaît. Oui, avec plaisir.*
Refuse: Non, merci. Je n'en veux plus. Je n'ai plus faim.

7 How would you tell someone what you have for . . . *See answers below.*
1. breakfast?	3. an afternoon snack?
2. lunch?	4. dinner?

Answers

1 1. Il me faut du poisson. J'ai besoin de poisson.
   2. Il me faut des pommes de terre. J'ai besoin de pommes de terre.
   3. Il me faut du riz. J'ai besoin de riz.
   4. Il me faut du gâteau. J'ai besoin de gâteau.
   5. Il me faut un ananas. J'ai besoin d'ananas.

4 *Possible answers*
Je voudrais... ; Je prends... ; Il me faut...
1. une douzaine d'œufs.
2. un litre de lait.
3. un kilo d'oranges.
4. un paquet de beurre.
5. une tranche de jambon.
6. une bouteille d'eau minérale.

5 *Possible answers:* Tu veux... ; Vous voulez... ;
Tu prends... ; Vous prenez... ; Encore...
1. du riz?
2. des oranges?
3. du lait?

7 *Possible answers*
1. Pour le petit déjeuner, je prends...
2. Pour le déjeuner, je prends...
3. Pour le goûter, je prends...
4. Pour le dîner, je prends...

PREMIERE ETAPE

Expressing need

Qu'est-ce qu'il te faut? *What do you need?*
Il me faut... *I need ...*
De quoi est-ce que tu as besoin? *What do you need?*
J'ai besoin de... *I need ...*
du, de la, de l' *some*

Foods; Shopping

des ananas (m.) *pineapples*
des avocats (m.) *avocados*
des bananes (f.) *bananas*
du beurre *butter*
du bœuf *beef*
des carottes (f.) *carrots*
des champignons (m.) *mushrooms*
des citrons (m.) *lemons*
de la confiture *jam*
de la farine *flour*

des fraises (f.) *strawberries*
du fromage *cheese*
des fruits (m.) *fruit*
des gâteaux (m.) *cakes*
des gombos (m.) *okra*
des goyaves (f.) *guavas*
des haricots verts (m.) *green beans*
du lait *milk*
des légumes (m.) *vegetables*
du maïs *corn*
des mangues (f.) *mangoes*
des noix de coco (f.) *coconuts*
des œufs (m.) *eggs*
des oignons (m.) *onions*
des oranges (f.) *oranges*
du pain *bread*
des papayes (f.) *papayas*
des pêches (f.) *peaches*
des petits pois (m.) *peas*

des poires (f.) *pears*
du poisson *fish*
des pommes (f.) *apples*
des pommes de terre (f.) *potatoes*
du porc *pork*
des poules (f.) *live chickens*
du poulet *chicken*
des produits (m.) laitiers *dairy products*
du raisin *grapes*
du riz *rice*
une/de la salade *a/some salad*
des salades *heads of lettuce*
du sucre *sugar*
de la tarte (f.) *pie*
des tomates (f.) *tomatoes*
de la viande *meat*
des yaourts (m.) *yogurt*
le marché *market*
le supermarché *supermarket*

DEUXIEME ETAPE

Making, accepting, and declining requests

Tu peux... ? *Can you ... ?*
Tu me rapportes... ? *Will you bring me ... ?*
Bon, d'accord. *Well, OK.*
Je veux bien. *Gladly.*
J'y vais tout de suite. *I'll go right away.*
Je regrette, mais je n'ai pas le temps. *I'm sorry, but I don't have time.*

Je ne peux pas maintenant. *I can't right now.*

Telling someone what to do

Rapporte(-moi)... *Bring (me) back ...*
Prends... *Get ...*
Achète(-moi)... *Buy (me) ...*
N'oublie pas de... *Don't forget ...*
pouvoir *to be able to, can, may*

Quantities

une boîte de *a can of*
une bouteille de *a bottle of*
une douzaine de *a dozen*
un kilo(gramme) de *a kilogram of*
un litre de *a liter of*
une livre de *a pound of*
un morceau de *a piece of*
un paquet de *a package/box of*
une tranche de *a slice of*

TROISIEME ETAPE

Offering, accepting, or refusing food

Tu veux... ? *Do you want ... ?*
Vous voulez... ? *Do you want ... ?*
Vous prenez... ? *Will you have ... ?*
Tu prends... ? *Will you have ... ?*

Encore de... ? *More ... ?*
Oui, s'il vous/te plaît. *Yes, please.*
Oui, j'en veux bien. *Yes, I'd like some.*
Oui, avec plaisir. *Yes, with pleasure.*
Non, merci. *No, thank you.*
Je n'en veux plus. *I don't want any more.*

Non, merci. Je n'ai plus faim. *No thanks. I'm not hungry anymore.*
en *some, of it, of them, any*

Meals

le petit déjeuner *breakfast*
le déjeuner *lunch*
le goûter *afternoon snack*
le dîner *dinner*

VOCABULAIRE

deux cent vingt-sept 227

Teaching Suggestion

To review vocabulary, you might play the game "**Quels ingrédients?**" described on page 201J.

Language Note

Point out to students that in French, unlike in English, **carotte** is spelled with one **r** and two **t**'s.

CHAPTER 8 ASSESSMENT

CHAPTER TEST

- *Testing Program,* pp. 209–214
- *Audio Compact Discs,* Audio CD 8, Tracks 23–25

SPEAKING TEST

- *Testing Program,* p. 346

TEST GENERATOR,
- Chapter 8

ALTERNATIVE ASSESSMENT
Performance Assessment

You might want to use the **Jeu de Rôle** on page 225 as a cumulative performance assessment activity.

- *Alternative Assessment Guide,* p. 39

Portfolio Assessment
- *Alternative Assessment Guide*
  Oral: p. 25
  Written: p. 25

CD-ROM Assessment
- *Interactive CD-ROM,* Disc 2
  A toi de parler
  A toi d'écrire
- *Alternative Assessment Guide,* p. 53

Game

CONCOURS DE VOCABULAIRE Have students bring in pictures of the food listed on this page. Form two teams and have one player from each team go to the board. Show them one of the pictures. Writing on the board, the players must identify the item (**du lait**), give an appropriate quantity of it (**un litre de lait**), say that they need the item (**J'ai besoin de lait**), ask someone to buy it (**Tu peux acheter du lait?**), and offer it to someone (**Encore du lait?**). Give a point to the player who first writes all the information correctly.

Allez, viens en Arles! pp. 228–305

> **VIDEO PROGRAM**
> **Videocassette 3**
> **28:33–31:21**

OR VIDEODISC PROGRAM,
Videodisc 5, Side A

Search 1, Play To 5059

Motivating Activity

Ask students if they can name any cities in southern France (Nice, Cannes, Marseille, Avignon). You might have students turn to the detailed map of France on page xxiii, or show them *Map Transparency 1.*

Background information

In 46 B.C., Julius Caesar established a Roman colony in Arles, and in 306 A.D., Constantine the Great made the city a capital in his empire. It became known as "the little Rome of the Gauls." In 1239, Arles became part of Provence, which, in 1481, became part of France. Vincent Van Gogh painted 300 pictures in Arles, which is typical of southern French towns with its pale-colored buildings with tiled roofs.

Language Note

The preposition **en** is used instead of **à** with the town of Arles.

go.hrw.com
WAO ARLES

Visit the HRW Web site at **http://go.hrw.com** and enter the keyword **WAO ARLES** for student resources related to this location. For detailed access instructions, see page T45.

La ville d'Arles

Thinking Critically

Observing Have students compare the photo of the city of Arles on pages 228 and 229 with the photos of Poitiers on pages 12–15. Ask students if they notice any differences (the tiled roofs) or similarities (the window shutters and number of stories in a building). What mixture of ancient and modern times can they find? (The ancient church on this page is surrounded by television antennas and even a satellite dish.)

Geography Link

The smallest administrative division of France is a **commune,** which consists of a town and some of the surrounding area. Arles is the largest **commune** in France because of its location near the **Camargue** (see page 231). The entire area covers approximately 190,000 acres.

Using the Almanac and Map

Terms in the Almanac

- **Les thermes de Constantin** once served as public baths for the Romans.
- **Les Baux-de-Provence,** the ruins of a medieval city, sits on a rock promontory in the **Alpilles** *(little Alps).* The mineral bauxite, discovered in the area in 1821, was named after **Les Baux.**
- **Les Antiques à St-Rémy-de-Provence** is home to two ancient monuments: the best preserved mausoleum in the world and a small **arc de triomphe.**
- **Le moulin d'Alphonse Daudet,** located in Fontvieille, is where Daudet supposedly wrote *Les Lettres de mon moulin.*
- **Alphonse Daudet** (1840–1897), the author of several short stories and novels that celebrate Provence, wrote the novel *Les Aventures prodigieuses de Tartarin de Tarascon* (1872) and a collection of short stories entitled *Les Lettres de mon moulin* (1866).
- **Frédéric Mistral** (1830–1914) wrote a narrative poem, *Mirèio* (1859) in Provençal, a language spoken in Provence.
- **Le musée Réattu** contains Italian, French, Dutch, and Provençal paintings from the sixteenth through eighteenth centuries.
- **Le musée de l'Arles Antique** is home to statues and artifacts uncovered in archeological excavations.
- **Le Museon Arlaten** is a folklore museum of Provençal life founded in 1896 by Frédéric Mistral.

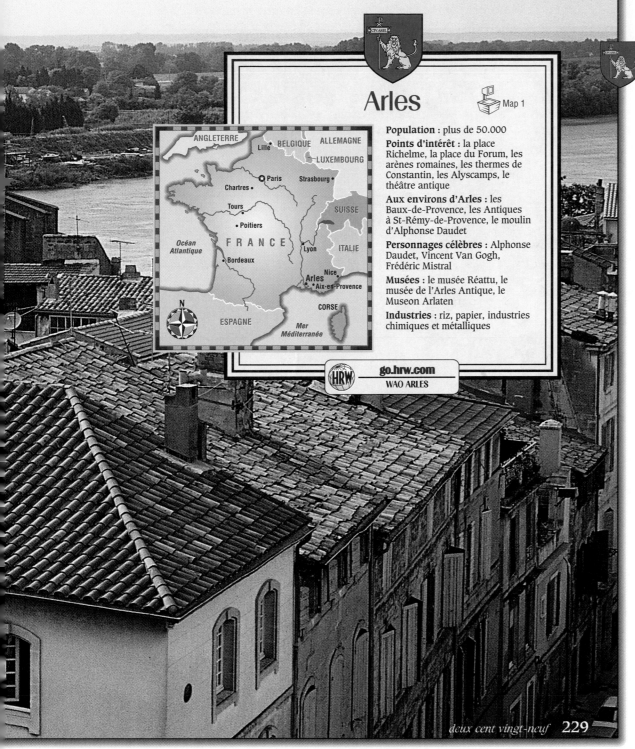

Arles
Map 1

Population : plus de 50.000

Points d'intérêt : la place Richelme, la place du Forum, les arènes romaines, les thermes de Constantin, les Alyscamps, le théâtre antique

Aux environs d'Arles : les Baux-de-Provence, les Antiques à St-Rémy-de-Provence, le moulin d'Alphonse Daudet

Personnages célèbres : Alphonse Daudet, Vincent Van Gogh, Frédéric Mistral

Musées : le musée Réattu, le musée de l'Arles Antique, le Museon Arlaten

Industries : riz, papier, industries chimiques et métalliques

go.hrw.com
WAO ARLES

deux cent vingt-neuf 229

Using the Map

Have students look at the map above or at the map of the francophone world on page xxvi, and suggest reasons why the Greeks and Romans were the first to colonize what is now southern France.

Geography Link

Ask students if they can name the mountain ranges in France (**les Pyrénées, les Alpes, le Jura, le Massif Central,** and **les Vosges**).

History Link

Ask students if they can name any other areas of the world where the Romans established settlements (southern Europe, the Middle East, North Africa, Germany, Belgium, and Great Britain).

Culture Note

In addition to founding the city of Arles, the Greeks introduced grape cultivation to France.

Using the Photo Essay

① **Les arènes romaines,** when originally built in the first century, could seat approximately 25,000 spectators. After the fall of the Roman Empire, 200 houses and even a church were constructed inside the arena. Restoration began in 1825. The structure had been severely damaged throughout the centuries as stones were removed for other construction. In fact, the third level of galleries is completely gone. The view from the upper level, overlooking the Rhône River and the surrounding countryside, is magnificent.

② **Les Alyscamps** is a famous cemetery that was established from Roman times through the Middle Ages. Tombs of more than 80 generations of people who were buried there were discovered in three layers. Unfortunately, in later centuries, stones and sarcophagi were taken for building projects and souvenirs. Today, a shaded pathway lined with ancient tombs offers the visitor an eerie glimpse of history.

② **Vincent Van Gogh** (1853–1890) was a postimpressionistic Dutch painter who spent most of his life in France. From 1888–1890, he lived in Arles, where he produced 300 paintings, including *Starry Night, The Bridge at Arles,* and *L'Arlésienne.* His use of bright colors and harsh brush strokes was revolutionary. In fact, one of his paintings, *Sunflowers,* sold at that time for the highest price ever paid for a painting. Van Gogh suffered from mental problems and spent time in an asylum. He cut off one of his ears after an argument with painter Paul Gauguin and eventually committed suicide. Many of his works are now on display in Paris at the **musée d'Orsay.**

Arles CD-ROM Disc 3

Founded by the Greeks in the fifth century B.C., Arles later prospered for hundreds of years under Roman rule. It was the largest city in Provence and the capital of ancient Gaul. In the Middle Ages, Arles was an important religious center. It did not become a part of France until 1481. In 1888, Vincent Van Gogh moved to Arles and painted some of his most famous works. Today, Arles still attracts artists, as well as historians and archeologists. Festivals, the many museums, and the beautiful countryside draw thousands of other visitors every year to this very special place known to some as "the soul of Provence."

① **Les arènes romaines** is one of the most ancient Roman amphitheaters in the world. Measuring 136 meters long and 107 meters wide, it is also one of the largest arenas, holding 12,000 spectators.

② **Les Alyscamps** is well-known as an ancient Christian burial site. Both Vincent Van Gogh and Paul Gauguin immortalized it in their paintings.

230 *deux cent trente*

Geography Link

Located on the Rhône River, the city of Arles is officially known as Arles-sur-Rhône to distinguish it from Arles-sur-Tech, which is located in the eastern Pyrenees Mountains.

Art Link

Van Gogh generally painted three types of subjects: still life, landscape, and figure, most of which portrayed the daily lives of the peasants, the hardships they endured, and the countryside they cultivated. During the time Van Gogh spent in Arles, he painted blossoming fruit trees, views of the town, self-portraits, portraits of Roulin the postman, his own family and friends, interiors and exteriors of houses, a series of sunflowers, and a sky full of stars.

③ The marshland known as **la Camargue** is a stunningly beautiful nature reserve. It is particularly known for its pink flamingos and wild horses.

④ Arles is home to several festivals that feature dancers from all over Provence dressed in their traditional costumes.

⑤ **Le théâtre antique**, constructed in the first century B.C., is still in use. It is here that the Festival d'Arles, the Rencontres internationales de la photographie, and numerous shows are staged.

③ **La Camargue,** established as a nature preserve in 1927, is the delta of the Rhône River. The river splits into two arms: **le Grand Rhône,** which makes up nine-tenths of the volume, and **le Petit Rhône,** just upstream from Arles. In certain areas, the delta area advances from 10 to 50 meters a year because of silt deposits, but it has receded in other areas. **La Camargue** is famous for its pink flamingos, bulls, and the white horses shown in the photo. Scattered throughout the delta are **mas,** or *farms,* where the **gardians** work herding the bulls.

④ Many festivals are held in Arles every year. **Le festival d'Arles** lasts the entire month of July and consists of concerts, theatrical and dance performances, and exhibitions. **La fête des gardians,** a version of a rodeo, takes place on May 1. **Le Salon international des santonniers,** held every December, is famous for its Nativity scenes (**crèches**) and ornamental figures (**santons**).

⑤ **Le théâtre antique,** a Roman theater located a short distance from the **arènes,** is the site for many drama and dance performances, as well as the **festival d'Arles,** held every July. When the **théâtre antique** was built, it was able to hold approximately 7,000 spectators. After the fifth century A.D., it was used as a quarry, and all that remains today are some of the seats and two marble Corinthian columns from the original wall behind the acting area.

Culture Notes

③ The village of Saintes-Maries-de-la-Mer, the unofficial capital of the **Camargue,** is the destination of an annual pilgrimage on May 24 and 25 by European gypsies.

③ The famous bulls raised in the **Camargue** are often reluctant participants in bullfights held in southern France. Bullfights in France are different from those in Spain; the bull lives after the fight. For a lively description of a Provençal bullfight, read *Caravan to Vaccares,* a novel by Alistair Maclean. Bullfights and other events are held in the **arènes** in Arles and Nîmes, a city northwest of Arles considered to be the gateway to the Rhône Valley and Provence.

Chapitre 9 : Au téléphone
Chapter Overview

Mise en train pp. 234–236	Un week-end spécial

	FUNCTIONS	GRAMMAR	CULTURE	RE-ENTRY
Première étape pp. 237–242	• Asking for and expressing opinions, p. 237 • Inquiring about and relating past events, p. 238	• The **passé composé** with **avoir,** p. 239 • Placement of adverbs with the **passé composé,** p. 240	• **Note Culturelle,** History of Arles, p. 240	• Chores **(Chaptire 7)** • Asking for, giving, and refusing permission **(Chaptire 7)** • The verb **avoir (Chaptire 2)** • Activities **(Chaptire 1)**
Deuxième étape pp. 243–246	• Making and answering a telephone call, p. 244	• The **-re** verbs: **répondre,** p. 245	• Realia: Ad for phone services, p. 243 • **Note Culturelle,** The French telephone system, p. 244 • Realia: **Télécartes** from **France Télécom,** p. 244 • **Panorama Culturel,** Telephone habits of French-speaking teenagers, p. 246	• **aller** + infinitive **(Chaptire 6)** • The verb **pouvoir (Chaptire 6)**
Troisième étape pp. 247–249	• Sharing confidences and consoling others, p. 247 • Asking for and giving advice, p. 247	• The object pronouns **le, la, les, lui,** and **leur,** p. 247		• The imperative **(Chaptire 5)** • The verb **pouvoir (Chaptire 8)**

Prononciation p. 249	The vowel sounds **[e]** and **[ɛ]** Audio CD 9, Tracks 13–15	**A écrire** (dictation) Audio CD 9, Tracks 16–18
Lisons! pp. 250–251	**Je passe ma vie au téléphone!**	**Reading Strategy** Combining different reading strategies
Review pp. 252–255	**Mise en pratique,** pp. 252–253 **Ecrivons!** Answering the five "w" questions Writing a letter asking advice	**Que sais-je?** p. 254 **Vocabulaire,** p. 255

Assessment Options

Testing Program
- Première étape, Quiz 9-1A, Quiz 9-1B, pp. 223–226
- Deuxième étape, Quiz 9-2A, Quiz 9-2B, pp. 227–230
- Troisième étape, Quiz 9-3A, Quiz 9-3B, pp. 231–234
- Chapter Test, pp. 235–240
- Speaking Test, p. 347

Audio Compact Discs
- Audio CD 9, Tracks 20–25

Interactive CD-ROM Program
- Mise en pratique (A toi de parler, A toi d'écrire)
- CD-ROM Teacher's Guide, Assessment Options, p. 40

Alternative Assessment Guide
- Portfolio Assessment, p. 26
- Performance Assessment, p. 40
- CD-ROM Assessment, p. 54

Test Generator
- Chapter 9

PRINT	MEDIA

Pupil's Edition, pp. 232–255

 Audio Compact Discs
• Textbook Listening Activities: Audio CD 9, Tracks 1–19

Interactive CD-ROM Program Teacher's Guide, pp. 36–40

 Interactive CD-ROM Program
• Disc 3

Videodisc Guide
• Teaching Suggestions, pp. 101–105
• Activity Masters, pp. 106–108

 Videodisc Program
• Videodisc 5, Side A

Video Guide
• Teaching Suggestions, pp. 62–63
• Activity Masters, pp. 64–66

 Video Program
• Videocassette 3
• Videocassette 5 (captioned version)

Listening Activities
• Student Response Forms for Textbook Listening Activities, pp. 67–69
• Additional Listening Activities 9-1 to 9-6, pp. 71–73
• Additional Listening Activities (song), p. 74
• Scripts and Answers, pp. 142–146

 Audio Compact Discs
• Textbook Listening Activities: Audio CD 9, Tracks 1–19
• Additional Listening Activities: Audio CD 9, Tracks 26–32

Teaching Transparencies
• Teaching Transparency Masters 9-1 to 9-3 (Situations) and 9-A to 9-B (Vocabulary)
• Teaching Suggestions 9-1 to 9-3 and 9-A to 9-B

 Teaching Transparencies
• Situations 9-1 to 9-3
• Vocabulary 9-A to 9-B

Testing Program
• Grammar and Vocabulary Quizzes, **Etape** Quizzes, and Chapter Test, pp. 223–240
• Score Sheet, Scripts, and Answers, pp. 241–248

 Audio Compact Discs
• Assessment Items: Audio CD 9, Tracks 20–25

 Test Generator
• Chapter 9

Alternative Assessment Guide
• Portfolio Assessment, p. 26
• Performance Assessment, p. 40
• CD-ROM Assessment, p. 54

 Grammar and Vocabulary Workbook, pp. 71–78

 Practice and Activity Book, pp. 97–108

Activities for Communication
• Communicative Activities, pp. 49–54
• Realia and Teaching Suggestions, pp. 115–119
• Situation Cards, pp. 153–154

Lesson Planner
• Lesson Plan, pp. 43–47

Chapitre 9 : Au téléphone
Technology Applications

MISE EN TRAIN, pp. 234–236

Video
- Show *Un week-end spécial.* For Video Synopsis, Teaching Suggestions, Activity Master, and Scripts, see the *Video Guide* or the *Videodisc Guide.*

Audio
- Play the recording of the **Mise en train** with pauses as students read along. You might have them practice pronunciation by repeating individual sentences after hearing them.

PREMIERE ETAPE, pp. 237–242

Video
- While students watch *Un week-end spécial,* have them listen for exchanges that model inquiring about and relating past events and asking for and expressing opinions. For more suggestions, see pp. 102–103 of the *Videodisc Guide.*

Audio
- Textbook Listening Activity 7 practices the expressions for asking for and expressing opinions.
- Textbook Listening Activity 10 has students recognize the **passé composé.**
- To have students use the vocabulary for relating past events, have them complete Additional Listening Activity 9-1.
- To review the **passé composé** with **avoir,** use Additional Listening Activity 9-2.

Transparencies
- Use *Teaching Transparency 9-1* and the Teaching Suggestions to present and have students practice talking about past events.
- Use *Teaching Transparencies 9-A* and *9-B* and the Teaching Suggestions to present and have students practice vocabulary for daily activities and events.

CD-ROM (Disc 3)
- **Les mots qui manquent** (Activity 1) practices the **passé composé** with **avoir.**
- Have students practice the vocabulary for daily activities by using **Jeu des paires** (Activity 2).
- **Chasse au trésor** (Activity 3) targets the **passé composé** with **avoir** and the vocabulary for daily activities.
- For suggestions, see p. 38 of the *CD-ROM Teacher's Guide.*

DEUXIEME ETAPE, pp. 243–245

Video
- While students watch *Un week-end spécial,* have them listen for exchanges that model making and answering a telephone call. For more suggestions, see p. 103 of the *Videodisc Guide.*

Audio
- Textbook Listening Activities 19 and 21 practice the expressions for making and answering a phone call.
- To review the expressions for making and answering a phone call, use Additional Listening Activities 9-3 and 9-4.

Transparencies
- Use *Teaching Transparency 9-2* and the Teaching Suggestions to have students practice the expressions for making and answering a phone call.

CD-ROM (Disc 3)
- To have students practice making and answering a phone call, use **Méli-mélo** (Activity 4).
- **Chacun à sa place** (Activity 5) practices the expressions for making and answering a phone call and expressing opinions.
- For suggestions, see p. 39 of the *CD-ROM Teacher's Guide.*

PANORAMA CULTUREL, p. 246

Video
- Show the interviews. For Video Synopsis, Teaching Suggestions, Activity Master, and Scripts, see the *Video Guide* or the *Videodisc Guide.*

Audio
- Play the **Panorama Culturel** as students read along. Remind students they might not be able to understand everything each person says, but they should try to recognize words and deduce global meaning.

CD-ROM (Disc 3)
- Have students do the **Panorama Culturel** activity for Chapter 9 after showing them the video. For suggestions, see p. 39 of the *CD-ROM Teacher's Guide.*

TROISIEME ETAPE, pp. 247–249

Video
- While students watch *Un week-end spécial,* have them listen for exchanges that model sharing confidences, consoling others, and asking for and giving advice. For more suggestions, see p. 104 of the *Videodisc Guide.*

Audio
- Use Textbook Listening Activity 24 to have students practice giving and asking for advice.
- Use Textbook Listening Activity 25 to have students practice sharing confidences and asking for and giving advice.
- Additional Listening Activities 9-5 and 9-6 practice the expressions for sharing confidences, consoling others, and asking for and giving advice.

Transparencies
- Use *Teaching Transparency* 9-3 and the Teaching Suggestions to have students practice shar-ing confidences, consoling oth-ers, and asking for and giving advice.

CD-ROM (Disc 3)
- After presenting the expressions for asking for and giving advice, have students do **Le bon choix** (Activity 6).
- For suggestions, see p. 39 of the *CD-ROM Teacher's Guide.*

MISE EN PRATIQUE, pp. 252–253

Captioned Video
- Replay *Un week-end spécial* in its entirety on Videocassette 5 and ask students to identify the functional expressions presented in the chapter.

CD-ROM (Disc 3)
- Have students do the **En contexte** to practice making a phone call, asking for and expressing opinions, inquiring about and relating past events, and asking for and giving advice. You might use the suggestions on p. 38 of the *CD-ROM Teacher's Guide.*
- Have students practice their writing and speaking skills by doing the **A toi d'écrire** and **A toi de parler** activities. For a detailed description of these activities, see p. 40 of the *CD-ROM Teacher's Guide.*
- For Assessment Options, see p. 40 of the *CD-ROM Teacher's Guide.*

Test Generator
- Use the Test Generator to create review material for students taking the Chapter Test or to prepare an alternate test.

VIDEOCLIPS

Video
- Show the **Vidéoclips.** For Video Synopsis, Teaching Suggestions, Activity Masters, and Scripts, see the *Video Guide* or the *Videodisc Guide.*

Chapitre 9 : Au téléphone
🔘 *Barcode Directory*

Barcodes A and B access **Mise en train** and **Mise en train (suite)** in their entirety. Subsequent barcodes show specific segments of **Un week-end spécial.** The barcode numbers correspond to the scene numbers as they appear on the video.

MISE EN TRAIN

Un week-end spécial **A**

Search 5060, Play To 11745

Et toi? Tu as passé... ? **3**

Search 7006, Play To 7355

Et après... **6**

Search 10074, Play To 10504

Un week-end spécial (suite) **B**

Search 11745, Play To 18905

Allô? **1**

Search 5060, Play To 6715

Il m'a présenté... **4**

Search 7355, Play To 8686

Et Ahmed? Tu as revu... ? **7**

Search 10505, Play To 10871

Samedi, j'ai fait... **2**

Search 6715, Play To 7006

Alors, qu'est-ce que vous avez fait... ? **5**

Search 8687, Play To 10073

Qu'est-ce que vous avez fait... ? **8**

Search 10871, Play To 11745

PANORAMA CULTUREL

Tu aimes téléphoner?

These barcodes access the three interviews of the **Panorama Culturel** presented in the *Pupil's Edition* as well as additional interviews.

First three interviews **1**

Search 18905, Play To 21180

Virgile **4**

Search 20440, Play To 20761

Karina **7**

Search 21411, Play To 21566

Elodie **10**

Search 22301, Play To 22405

Onélia **13**

Search 22869, Play To 23459

All interviews **2**

Search 18905, Play To 24058

Marie **5**

Search 20762, Play To 21158

Marieke **8**

Search 21567, Play To 22048

Armande **11**

Search 22406, Play To 22726

Karina **14**

Search 23460, Play To 23737

Nicole **3**

Search 19689, Play To 20439

Marie-Emmanuelle **6**

Search 21190, Play To 21410

Léna **9**

Search 22049, Play To 22300

Arnaud **12**

Search 22727, Play To 22868

Céline **15**

Search 23738, Play To 24058

ETAPES

To practice the functions, grammar, and vocabulary presented in each **étape,** see the barcodes and accompanying suggestions on pages 102–104 of the *Videodisc Guide.*

MISE EN PRATIQUE

This is additional footage modeling some of the expressions presented in this chapter. You may want to use it to review the chapter.

Mise en pratique **1**

Search 26430, Play To 27900

Mise en pratique **2**

Search 27900, Play To 28955

Mise en pratique **3**

Search 28955, Play To 30099

VIDEOCLIPS

These are authentic French commercials. You may want to preview them before showing them to students.

Groupe Azur®: insurance **1**

Search 24058, Play To 25430

Petits Cœurs®: cookies **2**

Search 25430, Play To 26115

Chapitre 9 : Au téléphone
CD-ROM Directory 💿 Disc 3

The following directory lists the *Interactive CD-ROM Program* activities for Chapter 9. For details and suggestions on how to use them, see pages 37–40 of the *CD-ROM Teacher's Guide*.

	GLOBAL TASK		COMMUNICATIVE GOALS	ACTIVITY TYPE
	Tu as passé un bon week-end? Students find out what Magali did over the weekend.		To use chapter functions, vocabulary, and grammar in a lifelike conversation	**En contexte** *Interactive conversation*

	SUPPORTING ACTIVITIES	PUPIL'S EDITION	COMMUNICATIVE GOALS	ACTIVITY TYPE
Première étape	1. Grammaire	p. 239	To use the **passé composé** with **avoir**	**Les mots qui manquent** *Tic Tac Toe*
	2. Vocabulaire	p. 241	To identify daily activities	**Jeu des paires** *Concentration®*
	3. Vocabulaire	pp. 239, 241	To name daily activities and use the **passé composé** with **avoir**	**Chasse au trésor Explorons!/Vérifions** *Interactive image*
Deuxième étape	4. Comment dit-on... ?	p. 244	To make and answer a telephone call	**Méli-mélo** *Sequencing*
	5. Comment dit-on... ?	pp. 237, 244	To express opinions and make and answer a telephone call	**Chacun à sa place** *Categories*
Troisième étape	6. Comment dit-on... ?	p. 247	To ask for and give advice	**Le bon choix** *Multiple choice*
Panorama Culturel	Panorama Culturel	p. 246	To listen to and understand native speakers talking about their telephone habits	**Tu aimes téléphoner?** *Presentation* **Le bon choix** *Multiple choice*

	APPLICATION	PUPIL'S EDITION	COMMUNICATIVE GOALS	ACTIVITY TYPE
Mise en pratique	A toi de parler	pp. 252–253	To create and record a phone conversation	*Guided recording*
	A toi d'écrire	pp. 252–253	To create a journal entry, a note, e-mail messages, or a letter	*Guided writing*

CHAPTER SECTION	PRESENTATION	HOMEWORK OPTIONS
Première étape	**Comment dit-on... ?** p. 237	Practice and Activity Book, p. 98, Activity 2
	Comment dit-on... ? p. 238	Practice and Activity Book, p. 98, Activity 3
	Grammaire, p. 239	Pupil's Edition, pp. R44–R45, Activities 1–3 Practice and Activity Book, pp. 98–99, Activities 4, 6–7 Grammar and Vocabulary Workbook, pp. 71–74, Activities 1–7 CD-ROM, Disc 3, Activity 1
	Note de grammaire, p. 240	Pupil's Edition, p. R45, Activity 4 Grammar and Vocabulary Workbook, p. 74, Activity 8
	Vocabulaire, p. 241	Pupil's Edition, p. 242, Activity 17 Grammar and Vocabulary Workbook, p. 75, Activities 9–10 CD-ROM, Disc 3, Activities 2–3
Deuxième étape	**Comment dit-on... ?** p. 244	Pupil's Edition, p. 245, Activity 20 Practice and Activity Book, p. 102, Activities 13–14 Grammar and Vocabulary Workbook, p. 76, Activities 11–12 CD-ROM, Disc 3, Activities 4–5
	Grammaire, p. 245	Pupil's Edition, pp. R45–R46, Activities 5–6 Practice and Activity Book, p. 103, Activities 15–16 Grammar and Vocabulary Workbook, p. 77, Activities 13–14
Troisième étape	**Comment dit-on... ?** p. 247	Pupil's Edition, p. 248, Activity 26 Practice and Activity Book, pp. 104–105, Activities 18–22 CD-ROM, Disc 3, Activity 6
	Note de grammaire, p. 247	Pupil's Edition, p. R46, Activities 7–8 Grammar and Vocabulary Workbook, p. 78, Activities 15–16

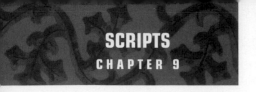
Chapitre 9 : Au téléphone
Textbook Listening Activities Scripts

For Student Response Forms, see *Listening Activities,* pp. 67–69.

Première étape

7 Ecoute! p. 237

1. — Salut. Alors, tu as passé un bon week-end?
   — Oh, c'était épouvantable!

2. — Dis, tu as passé un bon week-end?
   — Ça a été.

3. — Tu as passé un bon week-end?
   — Oui, très bon.

4. — Tiens, tu as passé un bon week-end?
   — Oui, très chouette.

5. — Tu as passé un bon week-end?
   — Oh, pas mauvais.

Answers to Activity 7
1. no fun at all
2. mildly good
3. really good
4. really good
5. mildly good

10 Ecoute! p. 239

1. — Bonjour, Serge. Ça va? Tu as passé un bon week-end?
   — Ça a été. Je suis allé au cinéma avec Sandrine.

2. — Tiens, Eric! Qu'est-ce que tu vas faire ce week-end?
   — Oh, je ne sais pas. Je vais peut-être regarder un match à la télé.

3. — Dominique, ça va?
   — Oui, ça va bien. Et toi?
   — Ça va. Ecoute. On va danser samedi soir. Tu viens?
   — Bonne idée!

4. — Salut, Christine!
   — Salut!
   — Tu as passé un bon week-end?
   — Oui, très bon.
   — Qu'est-ce que tu as fait?
   — Je suis allée à la plage, et j'ai rencontré des copains.

5. — Tiens, Sylvie, tu es allée où ce week-end?
   — Je suis allée au café avec Patrick.
   — Tu as passé un bon week-end?
   — Oui, très chouette.

Answers to Activity 10
1. last weekend
2. next weekend
3. next weekend
4. last weekend
5. last weekend

Deuxième étape

19 Ecoute! p. 244

1. — Allô?
   — Bonjour. Je suis bien chez Michel Perrault?
   — Oui. Qui est à l'appareil?
   — C'est Françoise.
   — Salut, Françoise! C'est moi, Paul.
   — Ah salut, Paul. Michel est là?
   — Une seconde, s'il te plaît.
   — D'accord.

2. — Allô?
   — Salut, Suzanne! C'est Jeanne à l'appareil. Ça va?
   — Oui, ça va bien.
   — Je peux parler à Thierry?
   — Thierry n'est pas là. Tu peux rappeler plus tard?
   — D'accord.

3. — Allô?
   — Bonjour, Anne?
   — Non, c'est Brigitte.
   — Ah, Anne est là?
   — Euh, je ne sais pas. Une seconde, s'il vous plaît. Vous pouvez rappeler? Elle est occupée.
   — Je peux lui laisser un message?
   — Bien sûr.
   — Vous pouvez lui dire que Daniel a téléphoné?
   — D'accord. C'est noté.

Answers to Activity 19
1. Françoise; Michel   2. Jeanne; Thierry   3. Daniel; Anne

21 Ecoute! p. 245

1. — Allô?
   — Bonjour. Est-ce que Madame Tissot est là?
   — Non, elle n'est pas là.
   — Je peux laisser un message?
   — Bien sûr.
   — Vous pouvez lui dire que Madame Morel a téléphoné?
   — Madame Moran?
   — Non, Morel. M-O-R-E-L.
   — Ah, Morel. D'accord.
   — Merci. Au revoir.
   — Au revoir.

2. — Allô?
   — Bonjour. Je peux parler à Monsieur Tissot? C'est son frère, Roger.
   — Désolé, mais il n'est pas là.
   — Vous pouvez lui dire que je ne peux pas aller au restaurant samedi soir?
   — D'accord.
   — Merci. Allez, au revoir.
   — Au revoir.

3. — Allô?
   — Bonjour! C'est Claire Laroche à l'appareil. Anne est là, s'il vous plaît?
   — Non, elle n'est pas là. Vous pouvez rappeler plus tard?
   — Oui. Mais, est-ce que je peux laisser un message?
   — Bien sûr.
   — Vous pouvez lui dire qu'on va au cinéma à neuf heures moins le quart?
   — Euh, à quelle heure? Vous pouvez répéter?
   — A neuf heures moins le quart.
   — D'accord.
   — Bon, merci. Au revoir.
   — Au revoir.

4. — Allô?
   — Bonjour. Je suis bien chez Philippe?
   — Oui. Qui est à l'appareil?
   — C'est Marc. Je peux lui parler?
   — Désolé, mais il n'est pas là.
   — Alors, je peux laisser un message?
   — Bien sûr.
   — Vous pouvez lui dire qu'on va jouer au foot samedi après-midi?
   — D'accord.
   — Merci bien. Au revoir.
   — Au revoir.

Answers to Activity 21
Possible answers
1. Mme Tissot — Mme Morel a téléphoné.
2. M. Tissot — Votre frère Roger ne peut pas aller au restaurant samedi soir.
3. Anne — Claire Laroche a téléphoné. Vous allez au cinéma à neuf heures moins le quart.
4. Philippe — Marc a téléphoné. Vous allez jouer au foot samedi après-midi.

Troisième étape

24 Ecoute! p. 247

1. — Je veux sortir avec Jean-Luc. Tu crois que je peux l'inviter?

2. — Eh bien, si tu ne veux pas rater ton examen, tu devrais étudier.

3. — Bruno? Moi, je trouve qu'il n'est pas très gentil. Oublie-le!

4. — Moi, je voudrais bien aller au concert de Vanessa Paradis, mais ça coûte très cher! Qu'est-ce que je fais?

5. — Alors, si tu veux acheter une voiture, pourquoi tu ne travailles pas cet été?

6. — Je ne mange pas beaucoup, mais je trouve que je suis un peu gros quand-même. Qu'est-ce que tu me conseilles?

7. — Si elle n'a pas encore téléphoné, téléphone-lui!

Answers to Activity 24

1. asking	4. asking	7. giving
2. giving	5. giving	
3. giving	6. asking	

25 Ecoute! p. 247

— Allô?
— Salut, Mireille. C'est Simone. Ça va?
— Oui, ça va. Et toi?
— Pas terrible. Je peux te parler? Tu as une minute?
— Oui.
— J'ai un petit problème.
— Je t'écoute.
— Ben, j'ai raté mon examen de maths. Je ne sais pas quoi faire.
— Ne t'en fais pas, Simone!
— Mais, j'ai beaucoup étudié. J'ai bien préparé mes réponses, et j'ai quand même raté.
— Qu'est-ce que je peux faire?
— Je peux étudier avec toi, Mireille?
— Bien sûr! Ne t'en fais pas. Ça va aller mieux!

Answer to Activity 25
Elle a raté son examen de maths.

Prononciation, p. 249

For the scripts for Parts A and B, see p. 249.

C. A écrire

(Dictation)
— Allô?
— Salut, Hélène. Tu peux parler? J'ai un problème.
— Je t'écoute.

Mise en pratique

1 p. 252

Salut, c'est Martin. Comment vas-tu? Tu as passé un bon week-end? Moi, j'ai passé un week-end génial. Je suis allé à la plage. Il a fait un temps superbe. Samedi, j'ai fait du ski nautique et après, j'ai joué au volley-ball. Ensuite, dimanche, j'ai fait du jogging. Et toi, qu'est-ce que tu as fait? Appelle-moi quand tu rentres. Salut!

Answers to Mise en pratique Activity 1

1. false	3. true	5. true
2. true	4. false	6. false

La Provence
(Individual Project)

ASSIGNMENT

Have students work individually to research topics associated with the region of Provence. Projects should include a written report and an oral and visual presentation, all in English.

MATERIALS

✂ **Students may need**
- Reference books
- Posterboard
- Colored markers

PREPARATION

Ask each student to select a topic. Possible topics include:
- tourist attractions or history of Avignon, Arles, Aix-en-Provence, the Camargue, Marseilles, Cannes, or Nice
- natural resources or geography of the region
- regional dishes or products
- the Roman occupation or architecture
- the artist Vincent Van Gogh in Arles
- the poet Frédéric Mistral
- the **santons**

SUGGESTED SEQUENCE

1. Students choose a topic and begin looking for reference materials. They may use encyclopedias, almanacs, travel guides, history books, and so on.

2. Students gather information and begin organizing their reports. They should also gather or make illustrations and plan how their visuals will look.

3. Once students have a rough draft of their report, they should ask you or other students to go over it for suggestions and feedback on language use. For their oral presentations, students should submit an outline of their presentation either to you or to other students to check for clarity and organization.

4. After making any necessary changes in their rough drafts, students should edit them again for accuracy. They should also prepare and organize their visual aids.

5. Have students give their oral presentations. You might display their posters around the classroom.

GRADING THE PROJECT

You might base students' grades on content, language use, presentation, creativity, and appearance of visuals.

Suggested Point Distribution (total = 100 points)

Correct content	20 points
Language use	20 points
Oral presentation	20 points
Creativity	20 points
Appearance of visuals	20 points

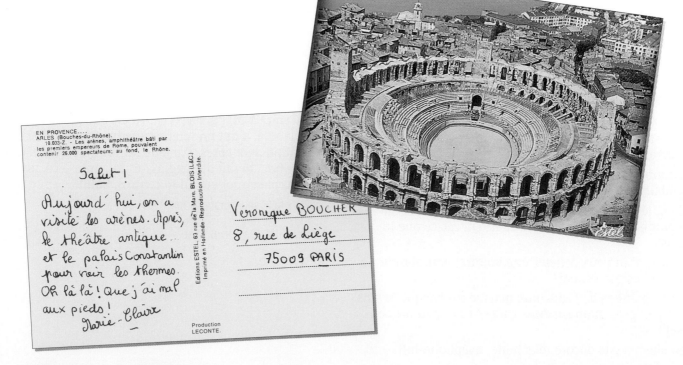

MESSAGE TELEPHONIQUE

In this game, students will practice using telephone vocabulary.

Procedure Whisper one of the short messages below only once to one student. Then, have that student whisper what you said to the next student, and so on. Once the message reaches the last student, ask that person to say the message aloud to compare it with the original. Follow the same procedure with the other messages. If the class is very large, this game might be played by two or three groups simultaneously. You might whisper the message to the first person in each group, wait for all groups to finish, and have the final student in each group say the message aloud. Try to begin each time with different students so that the same students aren't always first and last. The suggested messages here can be shortened or extended, depending on the class' success with the first few messages.

Ne quittez pas.
C'était épouvantable.
Qui est à l'appareil?
J'ai un petit problème.
Vous pouvez rappeler plus tard?
Qu'est-ce que tu me conseilles?
Qu'est-ce que tu as fait vendredi soir?

VERB TENSE RACE

In this game, students will practice various verb conjugations.

Procedure This game can be played by two to five teams. Begin by saying a regular -er verb, a subject pronoun, and a tense (past, present, or future). Students should write the subject and the correct verb form. For example, if you say **apporter, nous, passé composé,** the students should write **nous avons apporté.** Vary the subjects and tenses. You might point out the accent changes for **acheter** and **répéter.** To play with two teams, have one student from each team race to the board to write the correct verb form when you give a verb, a subject, and a tense. To play with three or more teams, provide each team with an overhead transparency and marker or pieces of scrap paper. Have students work together to figure out and write down the answer. The first team to hold up a correctly written answer wins. If you need a tiebreaker, give two points for correct irregular past participles. For a list of -er verbs and irregular past participles that students know, see the chapter vocabulary list on page 255 under **Première étape.**

Chapitre 9
Au téléphone

pp. 232–255

*U*sing the Chapter Opener

Motivating Activity

Have students look at the objects and photos on pages 232 and 233 and guess what the teenagers might be talking about (sports, concerts, chores, friends, a picnic).

Teaching Suggestion

Ask students to describe the three photos. Then, read the captions aloud. Have students read the outcomes and relate them to what is happening in each photo. Ask students why understanding a phone conversation might be difficult in a foreign language. (There are no hints from body language or facial expressions.)

Photo Flash!

① Hélène is talking on the phone to a friend. In France, local calls are charged by the minute, just like long-distance calls in the United States. **France Télécom** is the national public phone company responsible for all local and long-distance service.

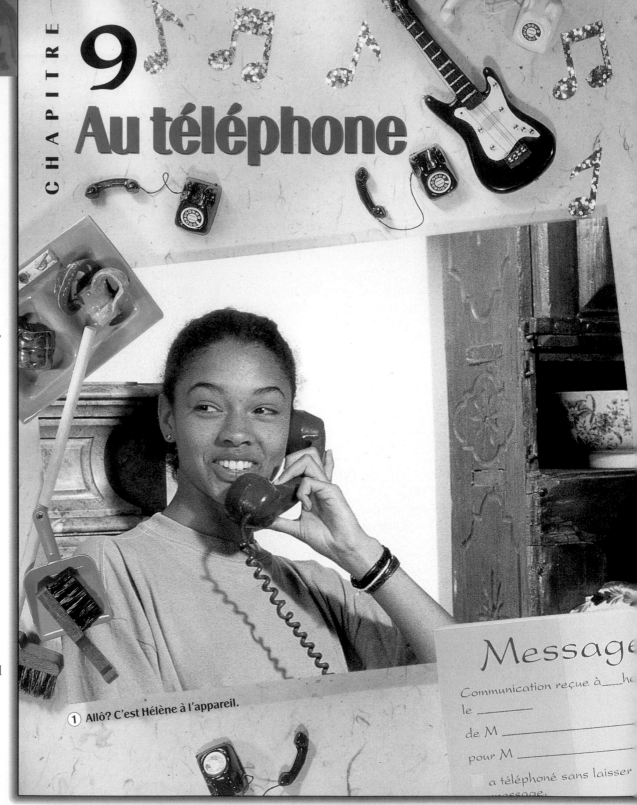

CHAPITRE

9
Au téléphone

① Allô? C'est Hélène à l'appareil.

Message

Communication reçue à ___ he___

le _____

de M _____

pour M _____

a téléphoné sans laisser
message.

🌐 Culture Note

In West Africa, telephone service is limited. Smaller towns and villages may not have service at all. Even in large cities, every household may not have a telephone. Public phones are scarce as well, but calls can be made from the post office. International calls can be made through hotel operators or long-distance operators in local post offices and are usually expensive. Since telephones are not always available, visits to friends and relatives often replace phone calls. In fact, it is not uncommon for visitors to drop by unannounced to catch up on the latest news of friends and family.

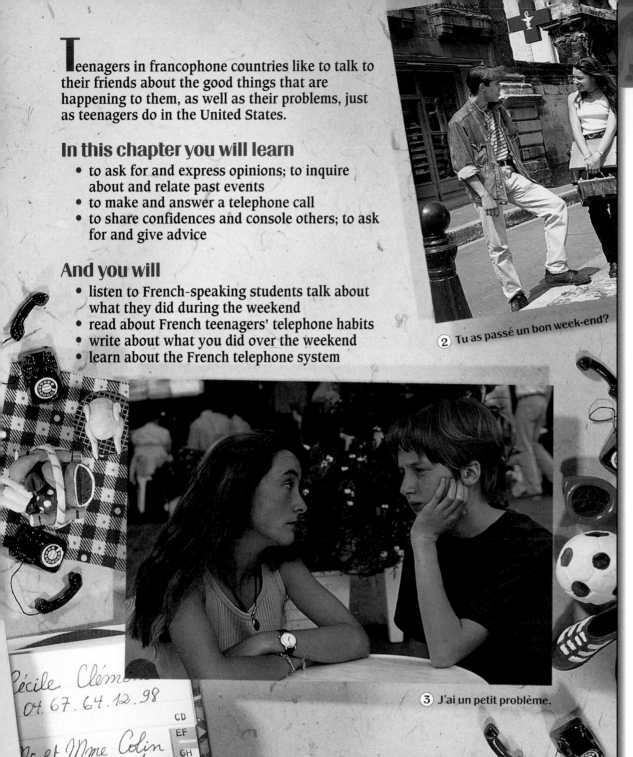

Teenagers in francophone countries like to talk to their friends about the good things that are happening to them, as well as their problems, just as teenagers do in the United States.

In this chapter you will learn

- to ask for and express opinions; to inquire about and relate past events
- to make and answer a telephone call
- to share confidences and console others; to ask for and give advice

And you will

- listen to French-speaking students talk about what they did during the weekend
- read about French teenagers' telephone habits
- write about what you did over the weekend
- learn about the French telephone system

② Tu as passé un bon week-end?

③ J'ai un petit problème.

Cécile Clém[...]
04.67.64.12.98

Mr. et Mme Colin
rue Victor Hugo
[...]000 Montpellier

deux cent trente-trois 233

Focusing on Outcomes

Have students describe the situations when they last performed the functions in the list of outcomes. Ask them how often they do these things. Then, ask what expressions they might expect to learn in this chapter.
NOTE: You may want to use the video to support the objectives. The self-check activities in **Que sais-je?** on page 254 help students assess their achievement of the objectives.

Thinking Critically

Drawing Inferences Have students look at the third photo and guess whether the girl had a good or a bad weekend. What might have happened to make it good or bad?

Teacher Note

You might remind students that French phone numbers consist of five sets of two digits, separated by periods (03.24.13.93.12).

Block Scheduling

For suggestions about how to use *Allez, viens!* with block scheduling, see the *Lesson Planner,* pages 43–47.

VIDEO PROGRAM
Videocassette 3
31:22–35:04
Videocassette 5
(captioned version)
1:12:34–1:16:16

OR VIDEODISC PROGRAM,
Videodisc 5, Side A

Search 5060, Play To 11745

Video Synopsis

In this segment of the video, Magali calls her friend Hélène, and they tell each other what they did over the weekend. We see a flashback of Magali with her friends at **les arènes**, where Florent introduced her to Ahmed. Magali tells Hélène about Ahmed and how she and her friends went to **les Baux-de-Provence** on Sunday. Hélène is anxious to hear the rest, but Magali's father needs to use the telephone, so she tells Hélène she will call back.

Motivating Activity

Ask students why they call their friends on the phone. Do they discuss homework, school, parents, or friends? When is a good time to call? Do they have their friends' numbers memorized?

Presentation

Have students look at the photos for **Un week-end spécial** and answer the general questions at the top of this page. Show the video, and then have students read the dialogue and use the photos to understand the general meaning. Ask them to answer the questions in Activity 1 on page 236 as they read.

The **roman-photo** is an abridged version of the video episode.

Mise en train [PA]

p. 97, Act. 1

Un week-end spécial

CD 9
Trs. 1–2

What is the subject of Hélène and Magali's telephone conversation? How do you know?

Hélène

Magali

Florent

Ahmed

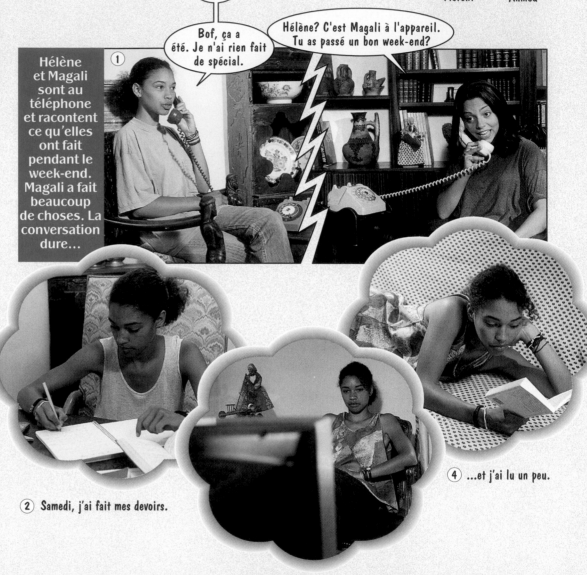

Allô?

Bof, ça a été. Je n'ai rien fait de spécial.

Hélène? C'est Magali à l'appareil. Tu as passé un bon week-end?

① Hélène et Magali sont au téléphone et racontent ce qu'elles ont fait pendant le week-end. Magali a fait beaucoup de choses. La conversation dure...

② Samedi, j'ai fait mes devoirs.

③ Dimanche, j'ai regardé la télévision...

④ ...et j'ai lu un peu.

234   *deux cent trente-quatre*   CHAPITRE 9   Au téléphone

RESOURCES FOR **MISE EN TRAIN**

PRINT
- *Practice and Activity Book,* p. 97
- *Video Guide,* pp. 61–62, 64
- *Videodisc Guide,* pp. 99–101, 106

MEDIA
- *Video Program,* Videocassette 3 Videocassette 5 (captioned version)
- *Videodisc Program,* Videodisc 5, Side A
- *Audio Compact Discs,* CD 9, Trs. 1–2

(5) Et toi? Tu as passé un bon week-end?

Excellent! J'ai passé un week-end super!

Ah oui? Qu'est-ce que tu as fait?

Je suis allée au théâtre antique avec Florent.

(6) Il m'a présenté un garçon très sympa. Il s'appelle Ahmed. Il est super gentil.

(7) Nous avons beaucoup parlé. Tu sais, il adore le sport. Il aime le tennis, comme moi.

(8) Dimanche, nous sommes tous allés aux Baux-de-Provence.

Qu'est-ce que vous avez fait là-bas?

Je vais te raconter une histoire incroyable!

(10) Mais, qu'est-ce qui s'est passé aux Baux-de-Provence?

Je t'écoute.

(9) Attends une seconde... Ecoute, Hélène, mon père veut téléphoner. Je te rappelle plus tard.

MISE EN TRAIN · deux cent trente-cinq · **235**

Thinking Critically
Comparing and Contrasting
Ask students to discuss the girls' weekends in small groups or as a class. Have them compare their recent weekends with Magali's and Hélène's. Ask if they discuss their weekends on the phone with friends and if they ever have to get off the phone for another family member. Ask them what they would consider an entertaining weekend spent locally.

For Individual Needs
Visual/Tactile Learners
On a transparency, draw pictures to illustrate the activities the girls did over the weekend. For example, you might draw a book to illustrate Hélène's statement **J'ai lu un peu.** Then, write the girls' dialogue in speech bubbles on strips of transparency. Call on students to match the speech bubbles to the illustrations.

Culture Notes
• The **théâtre antique** in downtown Arles dates back to the time of the Emperor Augustus.
• **Les Baux-de-Provence** is a lively village of winding streets and small shops which is perched on a rocky promontory. A medieval castle dating from the thirteenth century offers a beautiful view of the surrounding countryside.
• **Santons** are ceramic figures that depict characters from Nativity scenes as well as people of different occupations, such as shepherds or weavers, dressed in traditional **provençal** attire.

 Video Integration

• **VIDEO PROGRAM,**
  Videocassette 3, 35:05–39:04
  Videocassette 5, 1:16:18–1:20:18
• **VIDEODISC PROGRAM,**
  Videodisc 5, Side A

Search 11745, Play To 18905

You may choose to continue with **Un week-end spécial (suite)** at this time or wait until later in the chapter. When the story continues, Magali calls Hélène back and tells her about her trip to **les Baux-de-Provence** as we see flashbacks of Magali and her friends there. Magali tells Hélène about the sites they visited. At the end of the episode, we see a flashback of Magali opening a package. It is a gift from Ahmed, a **santon** that Magali admired at the souvenir boutique at **les Baux-de-Provence.** Magali asks Hélène for advice about getting to know Ahmed.

Teaching Suggestion

Teaching Suggestion

1, 2 Have students do these activities first without looking back at the text. Then, have them look back to check their answers.

For videodisc application, see *Videodisc Guide.*

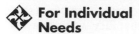

For Individual Needs

3 Tactile Learners You might write the statements on strips of paper and tape them in random order on the board. Then, write the numbers 1–4 to the side. Have a student move one sentence to its correct position. Repeat the process until all sentences are in order. If there is a mistake, a student can use his or her turn to correct it.

Captioned Video

5 To help students locate the expressions in this activity, play the captioned version of **Un week-end spécial** on Videocassette 5.

Group Work

6 Form small groups. Have each group imagine a sequel to the story and share it with the class. Have the class choose the most imaginative, the most realistic, the most probable, and so on.

These activities check for comprehension only. Students should not yet be expected to produce language modeled in **Mise en train**.

1 Tu as compris?

1. How was Hélène's weekend? OK.
2. Did Magali have a good weekend? Yes. Why? Why not? She met a nice boy.
3. Do you think Magali likes Ahmed? Yes. How can you tell? She says he is very nice.
4. Why does Magali have to hang up? Her father needs to make a phone call.

2 Magali ou Hélène?

Qui a fait ça, Magali ou Hélène?

1. aller aux Baux Magali
2. faire ses devoirs Hélène
3. lire Hélène
4. aller au théâtre antique Magali
5. regarder la télévision Hélène
6. ne rien faire de spécial Hélène

3 Mets en ordre

Put Magali's activities in order according to **Un week-end spécial.** 1, 4, 2, 3

1. Elle est allée au théâtre antique.
2. Elle est allée aux Baux-de-Provence.
3. Elle a parlé avec Hélène au téléphone.
4. Elle a rencontré un garçon sympa.

4 C'est qui?

Match the photos of these people with the sentences that refer to them.

Magali

Hélène

Ahmed

le père de Magali

1. Cette personne veut téléphoner. le père de Magali
2. Cette personne a passé un bon week-end. Magali
3. Cette personne est super gentille. Ahmed
4. Pendant le week-end, cette personne n'a rien fait de spécial. Hélène
5. Cette personne va téléphoner plus tard. Magali

5 Cherche les expressions

According to **Un week-end spécial,** what do you say in French . . . See answers below.

1. to answer the phone?
2. to identify yourself on the phone?
3. to ask if someone had a good weekend?
4. to ask what someone did?
5. to tell someone to hold?
6. to ask what happened?

> C'est... à l'appareil.   Qu'est-ce qui s'est passé?
> Attends une seconde.
> Allô?   Qu'est-ce que tu as fait?
> Tu as passé un bon week-end?

6 Et maintenant, à toi

What do you think happened to Magali at les Baux?

Answers
5 1. Allô?
2. C'est... à l'appareil.
3. Tu as passé un bon week-end?
4. Qu'est-ce que tu as fait?
5. Attends une seconde.
6. Qu'est-ce qui s'est passé?

PREMIERE ETAPE Storytelling Book pp. 33, 36

Asking for and expressing opinions; inquiring about and relating past events

COMMENT DIT-ON... ?
Asking for and expressing opinions

 p. 98, Act. 2   9-1

To ask for someone's opinion:
Tu as passé un bon week-end?
Did you have a good weekend?

To express indifference:
Oui, ça a été. *Yes, it was OK.*
Oh, pas mauvais.

To express satisfaction:
Oui, très chouette. *Yes, super.*
Oui, excellent.
Oui, très bon.

To express dissatisfaction:
Très mauvais.
C'était épouvantable.
It was horrible.

7 **Ecoute!** See scripts and answers on page 231G.

Listen to these people talk about their weekend. Tell if they had a really good time, a mildly good time, or no fun at all.

CD 9 Tr. 3

8 **Tu as passé un bon week-end?**

Find out if some of your classmates had a good or bad weekend. Then, tell them how your weekend was.

PREMIERE ETAPE   *deux cent trente-sept* **237**

Jump Start!

Have students write opinions of three of their favorite classes or activities and three of their least favorite. (**Le français, c'est génial. La biologie, c'est nul.**)

MOTIVATE

Ask students what they talk about when they see friends at school on Monday morning.

TEACH

Presentation

Comment dit-on... ? Draw three faces showing satisfaction, indifference, and dissatisfaction on the board. Read each response, making appropriate facial expressions, and have students tell which face expresses it. List the expressions on the board. Then, name a weekend activity, such as **un concert de rock.** Tell students to imagine they did that activity over the weekend. Have them point to the expression listed on the board that would express their opinion of the activity you named.

For Individual Needs

7 **Visual Learners** Show magazine pictures of people who are happy, indifferent, or unhappy and ask **Il/Elle a passé un bon week-end?**

7 **Kinesthetic Learners** Have students respond by making the thumbs-up gesture, the **comme ci, comme ça** gesture, or the thumbs-down gesture.

Presentation

Comment dit-on... ? Tell students that you're going to talk about your weekend. Have them listen for what you did and in what order. Then, tell about your weekend activities again, writing **d'abord, ensuite, après, après ça,** and **finalement** on the board as you proceed. Next, write five of the activities you mentioned on five flashcards, and give the flashcards to five students. Have them recall in what order you recounted your activities and hold the flashcards under the appropriate sequencing expressions on the board. Have students repeat the sequencing expressions and activities. **(D'abord, j'ai fait les courses.)**

For videodisc application, see *Videodisc Guide.*

  For Individual Needs

9 Slower Pace Copy these sentences randomly on a sheet of paper and give copies to pairs of students. Have students begin by finding the sentence that might start the conversation. Then, have partners underline or circle the sequencing expressions and number the sentences to show the correct order.

COMMENT DIT-ON... ?
Inquiring about and relating past events

 p. 98, Act. 3   9-1

To inquire about past events:

Qu'est-ce qui s'est passé (hier)?
What happened (yesterday)?

Qu'est-ce que tu as fait vendredi?
What did you do . . . ?

Et après? *And then?*
Tu es allé(e) où? *Where did you go?*

To relate past events:

Nous avons parlé. *We talked.*

D'abord, j'ai fait mes devoirs.
First, . . .

Ensuite, j'ai téléphoné à un copain.
Then, . . .

Après, je suis sorti(e).
Afterwards, I went out.

Et après ça, j'ai téléphoné à Luc.
And after that, . . .

Finalement/Enfin, je suis allé(e) chez Paul.
Finally, I went . . .

9 Méli-mélo! 🏠

Remets la conversation entre Albert et Marcel dans le bon ordre.

1
—Salut, Marcel! Ça va?

3
—Pas mal. Dis, qu'est-ce que tu as fait ce week-end?

9
—Et après ça?

4
—Vendredi et samedi, rien de spécial.

10
—Après, nous sommes allés au café et avons parlé jusqu'à minuit.

6
—Dimanche, j'ai téléphoné à Gisèle et nous avons décidé de sortir.

7
—Vous êtes allés où?

5
—Et dimanche?

8
—D'abord, nous avons fait un pique-nique. Ensuite, nous sommes allés au cinéma.

2
—Oui, ça va bien. Et toi?

238 *deux cent trente-huit*   CHAPITRE 9   Au téléphone

CD-ROM
Disc 3

GRAMMAIRE The passé composé with avoir

To tell what happened in the past, use the **passé composé** of the verb. The **passé composé** is composed of two parts: *(a)* a present-tense form of the helping verb **avoir** or **être**—which you've already learned—and *(b)* the past participle of the verb you want to use. You use **avoir** as the helping verb with most verbs. Only with a small number of French verbs, like **aller,** do you use **être** as the helping verb. You'll learn more about these verbs later.

Helping Verb +	*Past Participle*
J' **ai**	
Tu **as**	
Il/Elle/On **a**	**parlé** au téléphone.
Nous **avons**	
Vous **avez**	
Ils/Elles **ont**	

PA
pp. 98–99,
Acts. 4, 6–7

GV
pp. 71–74,
Acts. 1–7

Additional Grammar
Practice, pp. R44–R45

- To form the past participle of a verb that ends in **-er,** drop the **-er** and add **-é.**
- To make a verb in the **passé composé** negative, put **ne (n')... pas** around the helping verb.

Je **n'**ai **pas** étudié.

- Some French verbs have irregular past participles, that is, they don't follow a regular pattern. You'll have to memorize them when you learn the verb. Here are the past participles of some irregular verbs that you've already seen.

faire	fait	J'ai **fait** mes devoirs.
prendre	pris	Ils ont **pris** un taxi.
voir	vu	Il a **vu** sa grand-mère.
lire	lu	Elle a **lu** un roman français.

10 Ecoute! See scripts and answers on page 231G.

CD 9 Tr. 4

Listen to these conversations and decide whether the speakers are talking about what they did last weekend or what they're going to do next weekend.

11 Une journée à la plage

Qu'est-ce que Claire et ses amis ont fait à la plage?

1. Ils ont joué au volley. **2.** Ils ont fait un pique-nique. **3.** Claire a écouté de la musique.

Language-to-Language

Some students may be confused by the **passé composé** in French (**j'ai parlé**), since they are used to using one verb for the past in English *(I spoke)*. Have them think about compound tenses that exist in English *(I had spoken, I will have spoken,* and so on) and point out the similarities. If you have native speakers of Spanish in your classroom, explain to them that the **passé composé** is very similar in usage (although not in form) to the preterite in Spanish. Have these students give examples.

Presentation

Grammaire Write the sentence **Nous avons parlé** on the board and ask students to tell what they can deduce about the past tense. Then, review the forms of **avoir** by handing students items such as a book or some pencils and asking **Qui a mon livre/mes crayons? (Tim a votre livre. Alicia et John ont vos crayons.)** Explain that the **passé composé** is formed with the present tense of **avoir** plus a past participle. Then, hold up pictures that illustrate activities such as **voir un film, manger du gâteau,** and **faire du jogging.** Call on students to give the correct past participle.

Teaching Suggestions

10 Before starting this activity, review the use of **aller** + infinitive to express future time. Write an activity on the board (**faire les devoirs**) and have one volunteer create a sentence, using that verb in the **passé composé.** Then, have a second volunteer create a second sentence with the same verb, using **aller.** You might also ask students **Qu'est-ce que tu vas faire demain?**

11 As a variation, make up several sentences about the pictures. (**Ils ont joué au volley-ball. Ils ont fait un pique-nique. Elle a écouté la radio.**) Say them at random and have students write the number of the picture each one refers to.

For Individual Needs

12 Slower Pace Have students look at the expressions in the word box and form the **passé composé** of the infinitives given in each expression.

Game

Loto! Have each student draw a 4 × 4 grid and fill the squares with different past tense forms (**j'ai pris, il a lu**). Write the infinitives of these verbs on slips of paper (**prendre, lire**) and put them in a box. Then, begin the "bingo" game. Select a slip of paper, call out the infinitive in French, and have students mark the square on the grid if it contains a past-tense form of the verb you called. When a student has marked four squares in a row, horizontally, vertically, or diagonally, he or she calls out **Loto!** and reads the items in French.

Teaching Suggestion

Note de grammaire Have one student suggest an activity (**voyager**). Then, have a second student give the **passé composé**. (**J'ai voyagé.**) Have a third student repeat the sentence, adding an adverb that relates to his or her own experience. (**J'ai beaucoup voyagé.**)

Additional Practice

Distribute the verb slips from the **Loto!** game and have students write a sentence, using the verb in the **passé composé** and adding an appropriate adverb.

---

12 Qu'est-ce qu'on a fait?

Take turns with a partner asking and telling what you did and didn't do over the weekend. Then, tell another classmate about your partner's weekend activities.

faire mes devoirs   laver la voiture
acheter une montre   sortir la poubelle
faire le ménage   ranger ma chambre
promener le chien
prendre un café avec mes amis
faire un pique-nique   lire un roman
voir un film français

NOTE DE GRAMMAIRE

G V

p. 74,
Act. 8

Additional
Grammar
Practice, p. R45

When you use the **passé composé** with adverbs such as **trop, beaucoup, pas encore** *(not yet)*, **bien** *(well)*, **mal** *(badly)*, and **déjà** *(already)*, place the adverb before the past participle of the verb.

J'ai **déjà** mangé.

Nadine n'a **pas encore** vu ce film.

13 Mais pourquoi? See answers below.

Using the words in the box, give a logical explanation for each of the statements below. Be sure to put the verbs in the **passé composé**.

Céline a gagné le match de tennis.
Elle a bien joué.

1. Marie-Louise a eu 18 à son interro de maths!
2. Jérôme n'a pas d'énergie.
3. Sabine veut aller voir *Les Misérables*.
4. Luc n'a plus faim.
5. Etienne ne veut pas lire *Le Petit Prince*.

bien   étudier   travailler
déjà   voir   pas encore
manger   lire   beaucoup
trop

NOTE CULTURELLE

In the first centuries A.D., its location on the Rhône river made Arles the most important port and trading center in the Roman province of Southern Gaul, called Provincia. The Roman influence can still be seen today in Arles. You can visit the Roman amphitheater, which is still in use, an ancient theater, and the largest existing thermal baths in Provence.

History Link/Language Link

The French word **Provence** comes from the latin word **Provincia,** the name the Romans gave to their province in Gaul. You might have students find out more about the Roman occupation and different Roman ruins in the area. Students might want to research how the aqueducts and baths functioned and were used. This might be done as a chapter project. (See page 231I.)

Possible answers
13 1. Elle a bien étudié.
2. Il a beaucoup travaillé.
3. Elle n'a pas encore vu *Les Misérables.*
4. Il a trop mangé.
5. Il a déjà lu *Le Petit Prince.*

VOCABULAIRE

J'ai raté le bus.

J'ai trouvé cinquante francs.

J'ai oublié mes devoirs.

J'ai déjeuné à la cantine.

J'ai rencontré une fille (un garçon) sympa.

J'ai chanté dans la chorale.

J'ai acheté un CD.

J'ai travaillé au fast-food.

Here are some other verbs and expressions you may want to use to talk about what you've done during your day.

apporter	to bring	gagner	to win, to earn	répéter	to rehearse, to practice music
chercher	to look for	montrer	to show		
commencer	to begin, to start	passer un examen	to take an exam	retrouver	to meet with
dîner	to have dinner	rater une interro	to fail a quiz	visiter	to visit (a place)

Additional Practice

Write each sequencing expression on a strip of transparency and distribute them to five students. Have students write an activity they did over the weekend on their strips. Then, display the strips on the overhead and have the class use them to create a story. You might use this activity as a writing assignment.

Language Notes

• Point out that **commencer** is followed by **à** when used with an infinitive: **J'ai commencé à comprendre.**

• Remind students that **chercher** means *to look for* and isn't followed by a preposition. (**J'ai cherché mes devoirs.**)

Presentation

Vocabulaire Gather props to help present the sentences (a 50-franc bill, a fork, a CD). Act out each sentence and have students repeat it, imitating your gestures. Next, call on eight students to mime one sentence each and have the class tell what happened to them. Then, make statements using the verbs at the bottom of the page and have students respond by miming the actions.

Teaching Suggestion

Ask students if they have ever done these things. (**Qui a (déjà) raté le bus?**)

For Individual Needs

Kinesthetic Learners Write several sentences with words from the **Vocabulaire** on strips of transparency. (**Après l'école, j'ai cherché mon chat. Ensuite, Emile et Laurent ont retrouvé des amis.**) Cut the sentences into sequencing words, subjects, auxiliary verbs, past participles, and objects or complements and shuffle them. Have two students come up to the overhead and arrange the pieces to make sentences.

Teaching Suggestion

Have students write down three activities from the **Vocabulaire** that they did last week. Then, have them try to find one other student who also did these activities by saying **J'ai déjeuné à la cantine. Et toi?** Have them report back to the class.

For Individual Needs

14 Visual Learners Have students bring in magazine pictures of people engaged in different activities. As they hold up each picture, have the class tell what the people did last weekend.

Language-to-Language

DE BONS CONSEILS To show students how words that look alike are often related in meaning in other languages as well as French and English, give them the following examples in Spanish. Ask students to guess what a **pintor**, a **patinador**, and a **cantante** are if **pintar** means *to paint*, **patinar** means *to skate*, and **cantar** means *to sing* (*painter*, *skater*, and *singer*). If you have native speakers of Spanish in your classroom, have them give other examples.

Teaching Suggestion

16 Set either a time limit or a goal of five names.

 Mon journal

17 For an additional journal entry suggestion for Chapter 9, see *Practice and Activity Book,* page 153.

CLOSE

To close this **étape,** have partners ask each other what they did yesterday.

ASSESS

Quiz 9-1A, Quiz 9-1B, *Testing Program,* pp. 223–226
Audio CD 9, Tr. 20

Performance Assessment

Have students imagine they are spending a weekend in Provence. Have them write a postcard home, telling what they did or didn't do.

---

14 Qu'est-ce qu'ils ont fait le week-end dernier? Answers may vary.

1.
Elle a étudié.

2.
Elle a rencontré un garçon sympa.

3.
Il a raté une interro.

4.
Il a dîné avec sa grand-mère.

5.
Il a écouté de la musique.

6.
Elles ont acheté des livres.

15 Pierre a fait quoi?

Pierre spent a week at a sports camp. Which of the activities below do you think he did and which do you think he didn't do? See answers below.

chanter avec des copains

rater le bus

gagner un match

faire du ski nautique

rater un examen   nager

acheter un CD

manger des escargots

De bons conseils

French words that look similar are often related in meaning, so you can use words you already know to guess the meanings of new words. If you already know what **chanter** means, you can probably guess the meaning of **une chanteuse.** You know what **commencer** means, so what do you think **le commencement** means? Likewise, you should be able to figure out **le visiteur** from the verb **visiter.**

16 Tu as déjà fait ça?

Make a list of ten activities that you or a classmate might have done last week. Then, try to find a classmate who did each activity. When you find someone who did one of the activities, write his or her name on your list next to the activity. Try to find a different person for each activity.

Activités	Nom
1. J'ai gagné cent dollars.	Jeff
2. J'ai chanté dans la chorale.	Lisa

17 Mon journal Ⓗ

Write down five things you did last weekend. Be sure to tell when you did each activity, with whom, and add as many other details as you can think of.

Language Note

Remind students that **du, de la, de l', des, un,** and **une** all become **de** after a negative expression, but the definite articles **le, la,** and **les** do not change.

Answers

15 Pierre a : gagné un match, fait du ski nautique, nagé, chanté avec des copains.
Pierre n'a pas : raté d'examen, mangé d'escargots, raté le bus, acheté de CD.

DEUXIEME ETAPE TPR Storytelling Book pp. 34, 36

Making and answering a telephone call

—Allô, Anita?
—Oui. C'est moi.
—Salut. C'est François.

—Allô? C'est Michel. Véronique est là, s'il vous plaît?
—Une seconde.
—Merci.

—Allô? Est-ce que Xuan est là, s'il vous plaît?
—Non, il est chez Robert.
—Est-ce que je peux laisser un message?
—Bien sûr.
—Vous pouvez lui dire qu'Emmanuel a téléphoné?
—D'accord.
—Merci.

18 Au téléphone

Answer these questions about the conversations.

1. What do the people say to begin the conversation? Allô?
2. Who has to wait a few seconds to speak to his or her friend? Michel
3. Who gets to talk right away to the person he or she is calling? François
4. Who isn't home? Xuan

Allô, allô?
Les spécialistes du téléphone

Microcommutateurs • Téléphones sans fil • Téléphones de voiture • Répondeurs • Télécopieurs personnels • Interphones • Alarmes

18, rue Lafayette — **13200 ARLES**   **04-90-96-45-75**
26, rue de la Liberté — **13200 ARLES**   04-90-49-54-16

DEUXIEME ETAPE

deux cent quarante-trois **243**

Presentation

Comment dit-on... ? Act as both the caller and the person called in a simple conversation, using the expressions from **Comment dit-on... ?** Then, dial a number, make telephone ringing sounds, turn to the class, and say **Ça ne répond pas.** Dial again, making busy signal sounds, and tell the class **C'est occupé.** Then, pretend to answer the phone, pause, and say **Ne quittez pas.** Turn to the class and hand the phone to a student, saying **C'est pour toi.** Have students repeat the new expressions.

For videodisc application, see *Videodisc Guide.*

Language Notes

• Other useful telephone expressions are: **composer le numéro** *(to dial the number);* **l'annuaire** *(phone book);* **décrocher** *(to pick up the receiver);* **raccrocher** *(to hang up).*

• Have students practice difficult sounds, as in **l'appareil** and **seconde** (the c is pronounced like a **g**). Point out that **lui** can mean either *(to) him* or *(to) her.*

Additional Practice

19 After doing this activity, hand out typed copies of the script and have partners read the conversations aloud. You might also delete parts of the conversations and have students supply their own substitutions.

COMMENT DIT-ON... ?
Making and answering a telephone call

To make a phone call:	To answer a phone call:
Bonjour.	**Allô?**
Je suis bien chez Véronique?	**Qui est à l'appareil?**
Is this . . . 's house?	*Who's calling?*
C'est Michel.	
(Est-ce que) Véronique **est là, s'il vous plaît?**	**Vous pouvez rappeler plus tard?**
	Can you call back later?
Je peux parler à Véronique?	**Une seconde, s'il vous plaît.**
Je peux laisser un message?	**D'accord.**
May I leave a message?	
Vous pouvez lui dire que j'ai téléphoné?	**Bien sûr.**
Can you tell her/him that I called?	

CD-ROM Disc 3

P A
p. 102,
Acts. 13–14

9-2

G V
p. 76,
Acts. 11–12

Here are some additional phrases you may need:

Ne quittez pas. *Hold on.*

Ça ne répond pas. *There's no answer.*

C'est occupé. *It's busy.*

19 Ecoute! See scripts and answers on page 231G.

CD 9 Tr. 5

Ecoute ces conversations téléphoniques. Qui téléphone? A qui voudrait-il/-elle parler?

NOTE CULTURELLE

The French telephone system is run by the **France Télécom** office. You can make telephone calls at the post office, where you will always find a telephone booth. Coin-operated telephones **(téléphones à pièces)** are gradually being replaced by card-operated ones **(publiphones à cartes)**, which has greatly reduced vandalism. These modern phones accept "smart cards" **(télécartes)**, which can be purchased at the post office and at newsstands. Each card contains credits for a specific number of units. Units are deducted according to the distance and the duration of a call. To make a call, you simply insert the card in the phone. A readout will tell you how many units you have remaining on your card.

244   *deux cent quarante-quatre*   CHAPITRE 9   Au téléphone

Culture Note

Students might be interested to know that even local calls from public phones in France have a time limit, approximately six minutes. After this, a signal warns that more money must be deposited, or the call will be cut off. One advantage of using **télécartes** to make long-distance calls is that they operate silently; otherwise, the caller's coins drop during the conversation, often causing noise on the line.

Multicultural Link

Have students compare the French public phone system to the one they're used to. You might want to assign countries to students and have them find out how public phones work there. They might ask someone who has traveled to their assigned country, or call or write to the nearest tourist office. Then, have them report their findings to the class.

20 Méli-mélo!

Mets cette conversation dans le bon ordre.

9 **D'accord.**

1 **Allô?**

4 **C'est Aurélie.**

8 **Tu peux lui dire que j'ai téléphoné?**

5 **Salut, Aurélie. Désolée, elle n'est pas là.**

2 **Allô, bonjour. Je peux parler à Nicole?**

3 **Qui est à l'appareil?**

7 **Bien sûr.**

6 **Est-ce que je peux laisser un message?**

21 Ecoute! See scripts and answers on pages 231G–231H.

CD 9 Tr. 6

During your exchange visit to France, you stay with a French family, **les Tissot.** You're the only one at home today. Several of their friends call and leave messages. Write down the messages and compare your notes with a classmate's.

22 Jeu de rôle

The friend you're phoning isn't home, so you leave a message. Take turns playing the role of the friend's parent.

GRAMMAIRE -re verbs

Like **-er** verbs, most verbs that end in **-re** follow a regular pattern. Drop the **-re** from the infinitive and add the endings below. Notice that you don't add an ending to the **il/elle/on** form of the verb.

répondre *(to answer)*

je répon**ds**	nous répond**ons**
tu répon**ds**	vous répond**ez**
il/elle/on répon**d**	ils/elles répond**ent**

p. 103, Acts. 15–16

p. 77, Acts. 13–14

- **Répondre** is followed by a form of the preposition **à**.
  Nathalie répond **à** Lucas. Je réponds **au** professeur.

- Some other **-re** verbs you might want to use are **vendre** *(to sell)*, **attendre** *(to wait for)*, and **perdre** *(to lose)*.

Additional Grammar Practice, pp. R45–R46

- To form the past participle of an **-re** verb, drop the **-re** and add **-u**.
  Il a **répondu** à sa lettre.   Nous avons **perdu** nos cahiers.

23 A l'école

Sébastien overhears the following comments before class. Complete the comments with the appropriate forms of the verbs **répondre, vendre, attendre,** and **perdre.**

1. «Nous ____ le professeur. Il est en retard.» attendons
2. «Attention, Luc! Tu ____ ton argent. Tu dois fermer *(to close)* ton sac à dos.» perds
3. «Ils ____ toujours bien aux questions du professeur!» répondent
4. «Est-ce qu'on ____ des calculatrices à la Papeterie Simonet? Il me faut une calculatrice.» vend
5. «Je ____ à la lettre de Marianne. Elle est à Nice avec sa famille.» réponds
6. «On va ____ des tee-shirts pour gagner de l'argent pour le Cercle français.» vendre

---

Additional Practice

20 Have students give an appropriate response to each of the following questions: **Allô? Qui est à l'appareil? Je peux parler à Nicole? Tu peux rappeler plus tard?**

For Individual Needs

21 Slower Pace Stop the recording after each phone call to allow students time to jot down a few words to help them recall the message.

Presentation

Grammaire Bring in props to help you illustrate the four **-re** verbs presented. For example, you might hold up a sign that says "For Sale" and tell the students **Je vends ma maison.** You might look in your desk drawer and say **Où est mon stylo... ? J'ai perdu mon stylo.** To present the other forms, you might hold up pictures of people doing various activities. For example, you might hold up a picture of some people at a bus stop and tell the students **Ils attendent le bus.** Write the forms on the board as you present them, and then have students identify the endings. As the class becomes familiar with the forms, ask them questions such as **Qu'est-ce que je fais?** as you act out the different verbs.

CLOSE

Say some of the telephone expressions and have students tell whether you are the caller or the person receiving the call.

ASSESS

Quiz 9-2A, Quiz 9-2B, *Testing Program,* pp. 227–230
Audio CD 9, Tr. 21

Teacher Note

Students might want to know these terms: *cellular phone* (**un téléphone mobile**); *cordless phone* (**un téléphone sans fil**).

Performance Assessment

Have students act out a phone conversation between two friends who are asking about each other's weekends.

Language Note

You might point out that **un coup de téléphone** or **un coup de fil** is an informal way of saying *a phone call.* One might give someone a call (**donner un coup de téléphone/un coup de fil à quelqu'un**) or get a call from someone (**recevoir un coup de téléphone/un coup de fil de quelqu'un**).

VIDEO PROGRAM
Videocassette 3
39:05–41:53

OR VIDEODISC PROGRAM,
Videodisc 5, Side A

Search 18905, Play To 21180

Teacher Notes

• See the *Video Guide,* the *Videodisc Guide,* and the *CD-ROM Teacher's Guide* for activities related to the **Panorama Culturel.**

• Remind students that cultural material may be included in the Chapter Quizzes and Test.

• The interviewees' language represents informal, unrehearsed speech. Occasionally, edits have been made for clarification.

Motivating Activity

Before students view the video, you might have them answer questions 2 and 3 in **Qu'en penses-tu?**

Presentation

Play the video. Pause after each interview to ask **Il/Elle aime téléphoner?** Ask what else students understand from the first viewing. Then, write the **Questions** below on the board or on a transparency and have students answer them as they read the interviews in pairs.

Thinking Critically

Synthesizing Ask students how they would keep in touch with friends and family in a French home where phone calls are very expensive.

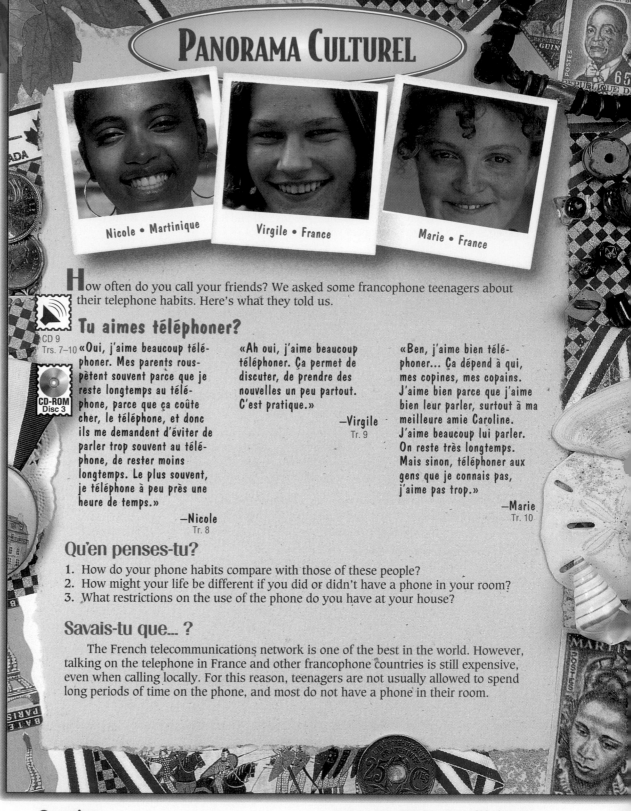

PANORAMA CULTUREL

Nicole • Martinique

Virgile • France

Marie • France

How often do you call your friends? We asked some francophone teenagers about their telephone habits. Here's what they told us.

Tu aimes téléphoner?

CD 9
Trs. 7–10

«Oui, j'aime beaucoup téléphoner. Mes parents rouspètent souvent parce que je reste longtemps au téléphone, parce que ça coûte cher, le téléphone, et donc ils me demandent d'éviter de parler trop souvent au téléphone, de rester moins longtemps. Le plus souvent, je téléphone à peu près une heure de temps.»

—Nicole
Tr. 8

«Ah oui, j'aime beaucoup téléphoner. Ça permet de discuter, de prendre des nouvelles un peu partout. C'est pratique.»

—Virgile
Tr. 9

«Ben, j'aime bien téléphoner... Ça dépend à qui, mes copines, mes copains. J'aime bien parce que j'aime bien leur parler, surtout à ma meilleure amie Caroline. J'aime beaucoup lui parler. On reste très longtemps. Mais sinon, téléphoner aux gens que je connais pas, j'aime pas trop.»

—Marie
Tr. 10

Qu'en penses-tu?

1. How do your phone habits compare with those of these people?
2. How might your life be different if you did or didn't have a phone in your room?
3. What restrictions on the use of the phone do you have at your house?

Savais-tu que... ?

The French telecommunications network is one of the best in the world. However, talking on the telephone in France and other francophone countries is still expensive, even when calling locally. For this reason, teenagers are not usually allowed to spend long periods of time on the phone, and most do not have a phone in their room.

Questions

1. Pourquoi est-ce que les parents de Nicole rouspètent? (parce qu'elle reste longtemps au téléphone)
2. Pourquoi est-ce que Virgile aime téléphoner? (Ça permet de discuter, de prendre des nouvelles. C'est pratique.)
3. A qui est-ce que Marie aime téléphoner? (à ses copines et à ses copains, à Caroline)
4. Est-ce que Marie aime téléphoner aux gens qu'elle ne connaît pas? (Non)

Thinking Critically

Drawing Inferences Have students guess what **rouspètent** means from the context of Nicole's interview *(moan, grumble, grouse).* Have students ever seen adults do this? Under what circumstances?

TROISIEME ETAPE

 TPR Storytelling Book pp. 35, 36

Sharing confidences and consoling others; asking for and giving advice

COMMENT DIT-ON... ?

Sharing confidences and consoling others; asking for and giving advice

 pp. 104–105, Acts. 18–22

To share a confidence:

J'ai un petit problème.
I've got a little problem.

Je peux te parler?
Can I talk to you?

Tu as une minute?
Do you have a minute?

To ask for advice:

A ton avis, qu'est-ce que je fais?
In your opinion, what do I do?

Qu'est-ce que tu me conseilles?
What do you advise me to do?

To console someone:

Je t'écoute. *I'm listening.*

Qu'est-ce que je peux faire? 9-3
What can I do?

Ne t'en fais pas! *Don't worry!*

Ça va aller mieux!
It's going to get better!

To give advice:

Oublie-le/-la/-les!
Forget him/her/it/them!

Téléphone-lui/-leur!
Call him/her/them!

Tu devrais lui/leur parler.
You should talk to him/her/them.

Pourquoi tu ne téléphones **pas?**
Why don't you . . . ?

NOTE DE GRAMMAIRE

In the expressions above, **le, la,** and **les** *(him, her, it, them)* are object pronouns that refer to people or things. The pronouns **lui** and **leur** *(to him, to her, to them)* refer only to people. You will learn more about these pronouns later. **GV**

Additional Grammar Practice, p. R46

p. 78, Acts. 15–16

 Study at regular intervals. It's best to learn language in small chunks and to review frequently. Cramming will not usually work for French. Study at least a little bit every day, whether you have an assignment or not. The more often you review words and structures, the easier it will be for you to understand and speak in class. And don't forget to talk to yourself or to a classmate in French!

24 Ecoute! See scripts and answers on page 231H.

Are these people giving advice or asking for advice?

CD 9 Tr. 11

25 Ecoute! See scripts and answers on page 231H.

Ecoute cette conversation entre Mireille et Simone. Simone a un problème. Quel est son problème?

CD 9 Tr. 12

TROISIEME ETAPE

deux cent quarante-sept **247**

Jump Start!

Have students write responses to the following: **Bonjour! Je peux laisser un message? Qui est à l'appareil? Vous pouvez lui dire que j'ai téléphoné?**

MOTIVATE

Have students list the qualities they look for in a friend. Ask students when they might ask for a friend's help or in what circumstances they might need to help a friend.

TEACH

Presentation

Comment dit-on... ? Act out the following scenes with a toy telephone, having students guess which functions you're demonstrating:
1. Call a friend to get help with a problem.
2. Answer a call from a friend who has a problem.

Continue your conversation until all the new expressions have been identified.

 For videodisc application, see *Videodisc Guide.*

Language-to-Language

Point out that the verb **conseiller** is related to *counselor.* Ask students if they have seen a French word related to *counsel* (**conseils**).

Teaching Suggestion

De bons conseils Have individuals or pairs design a weekly study schedule. Offer small prizes a week later to students who followed it.

Group Work

26 Have groups of students make up additional problems with a solution for each, using this activity as a model. Have them number the problems and letter the solutions. They should provide an answer key on a separate sheet of paper. Then, have groups exchange papers with another group and match their problems to the suggested solutions.

Teaching Suggestion

27 This activity might be done in pairs. One student is Hervé who explains his problem. The other consoles him. Have students reverse roles.

 For Individual Needs

28 Slower Pace Review the suggested problems by having students match them to props you hold up: want ads (**ne peut pas trouver de travail pour l'été**), a party hat (**veut faire une boum...**), a toy phone, and tennis shoes. Have students change the verbs and possessive adjectives to the **je** and **tu** forms in preparation for the activity.

 Cooperative Learning

28 Have students do this activity in small groups. One student poses a problem and each of the others offers advice. Then, they all collaborate to decide on the best advice. You might want to re-enter expressions for agreeing and disagreeing, such as **Tu es d'accord?** and **Je ne suis pas d'accord.**

Teaching Suggestion

28 This activity might be done as a skit with toy phones or as a written activity in the form of a letter to an advice column.

---

26 J'ai un petit problème

Match each of the following problems with a logical solution.

1. Mon frère ne me parle plus depuis *(for)* cinq jours.   d
2. Je veux acheter un vélo, mais je n'ai pas d'argent.   b
3. J'ai oublié mes devoirs.   c
4. Je vais rater l'interro d'anglais.   a

a. Tu devrais étudier plus souvent.
b. Pourquoi tu ne travailles pas?
c. Refais-les!
d. Parle-lui!

27 Pauvre Hervé!

Console Hervé.

Possible answers:

1.   Ça va aller mieux!

2.   Oublie-la!

3.   Ne t'en fais pas!

28 Et à ton avis?

 Your friend phones and asks to speak to you. He or she has some problems and wants to ask your advice about them. Console your friend and offer some advice. Then, change roles.

Il/Elle...

veut rencontrer de nouveaux copains.

n'a pas acheté de cadeau pour l'anniversaire de sa sœur.

veut faire une boum, mais ses parents ne sont pas d'accord.

n'a pas d'argent pour acheter des baskets.

a raté un examen.

ne peut pas trouver de travail pour l'été.

n'aime pas le prof de biologie.

n'a pas parlé avec son petit ami (sa petite amie) depuis *(for)* 3 jours.

n'a pas gagné son match de tennis.

a oublié ses devoirs.

29 Ne t'en fais pas!

 Your friend asks you to listen to his or her account of a very bad day. Console your friend. Act this out with a partner. Then, change roles.

📁 **Portfolio**

29 Oral   This activity is suitable for students' oral portfolios. For portfolio information, see the *Alternative Assessment Guide*, page 26.

PRONONCIATION

The vowel sounds [e] and [ɛ]

CD 9 Trs. 13–18

See scripts and answers on page 231H.

Listen to the vowels in the word **préfère.** How are they different? The first one is pronounced [e], and the second one [ɛ]. To make the vowel sound [e], hold your mouth in a closed smiling position. Keep your lips and tongue steady to avoid the glide as in the English word *day.* Repeat these words.

été   désolé   occupé   répondre

Now, take a smiling position once again, but this time open your mouth wider. This will produce the vowel sound [ɛ]. Repeat these words.

règle   algèbre   achète   frère

In the examples, you can see that **é** represents the sound [e], while **è** represents the sound [ɛ] in writing. You've probably noticed that **e** with no accent and some other letter combinations can represent these sounds as well. Repeat these words.

apportez   trouver

You see that the spellings **ez** and **er** normally represent the sound [e]. This is true of all infinitives ending in -**er**. Now repeat these words.

fait   français   neige   bête

elle   cassette   examen   cherche

Some spellings of the vowel sound [ɛ] are **ait, ais, ei,** and **ê.** An unaccented **e** is pronounced as open [ɛ] when it is followed by a double consonant, such as **ll** or **tt,** when followed by **x,** and, in most cases, when followed by **r,** or by any pronounced consonant.

A. A prononcer

Repeat the following words.

1. délicieux   méchant   théâtre   vélo
2. après-midi   père   mère   très
3. février   chanter   chez   prenez
4. cette   française   treize   pêches

B. A lire

Take turns with a partner reading each of the following sentences aloud.

1. Ne quittez pas! Je vais chercher mon frère.
2. Marcel a visité Arles en mai. Il est allé au musée, à la cathédrale et aux arènes.
3. Elle n'aime pas trop l'algèbre et la géométrie, mais elle aime bien l'espagnol.
4. Tu ne peux pas aller au cinéma. Tu n'as pas fait la vaisselle.

C. A écrire

You're going to hear a short dialogue. Write down what you hear.

Teaching Suggestions

Pononciation   Make sure students look over their work for accents before the dictation in Part C is corrected. Look over their sentences for common errors, and review accent and sound correlations, if necessary.

Additional Practice

Show *Teaching Transparency 9-3* and ask students to give the problem for each situation illustrated. Then, have volunteers role-play asking a friend or family member for advice about one of the problems.

CLOSE

To close this **étape,** copy onto a transparency some of the problems and solutions that students wrote for Group Work (Activity 26) on page 248. Have the class match the problems with the solutions.

ASSESS

Quiz 9-3A, Quiz 9-3B, *Testing Program,* pp. 231–234

Audio CD 9, Tr. 22

Performance Assessment

Have students work in pairs to write a phone conversation in which one person brings up a problem and the other offers consolation and advice. Have students act it out in front of the class. If last year's class videotaped their skits, you might show them to get students started on their own conversations.

Language Note

Pononciation   Make sure students don't make a diphthong out of the [e] sound, commonly pronounced by Americans as *ay-ee.*

READING STRATEGY

Combining different reading strategies

Teacher Note

For an additional reading, see *Practice and Activity Book,* page 107.

PREREADING
Activities A–B

Motivating Activity

Ask students how many hours they spend per week on average talking on the telephone and if they have ever had discussions with their parents about the amount of time they spend talking on the telephone or about expensive long-distance bills? How did they resolve this issue? Have the students think of ways in which they might be able to reduce their long-distance bill.

READING
Activities C–J

Teaching Suggestion

Complete Activities C, D, and E as a class and then have students complete Activities F–J in pairs. Encourage them to use the strategies they have learned to guess the meaning of unfamiliar words.

Terms in Lisons!

Students might want to know the following words: **chaleureux** *(warm)*, **gâterie** *(little treat)*, **maîtrise** *(mastery)*, **combiné magique** *(magic receiver)*, **quotidiennement** *(daily)*, **fil** *(cord)*.

Thinking Critically

Analyzing Ask students how their lives would be different if local calls in the United States were charged by the minute.

LISONS!

$\mathcal{D}$o you talk on the telephone much? Whom do you call? What do you talk about? What advantages are there to talking on the phone? Are there disadvantages? Based on the title of this article, what do you think it will be about?

DE BONS CONSEILS

As you read, you use many different reading strategies at the same time. You may start by looking at illustrations, then move on to the titles and subtitles. You may need to skim the passage to get the general idea, then scan for specific details, and finally read the passage for more complete comprehension.

A. Skim the article. What kind of information do you expect to find? See answers below.

B. What is the purpose of each section? How does the second section differ from the others? See answers below.

Emmanuelle

C. How old was Emmanuelle when she started using the telephone? How did her parents feel about her using the telephone? See answers below.

D. Read Emmanuelle's statement and list all the cognates you find. Then, match these terms with their English equivalents.

1. carte téléphonique b
2. cervelle c
3. remboursement d
4. cabine téléphonique e
5. papier à lettres a

a. stationery
b. phone card
c. brain
d. reimbursement
e. telephone booth

Possible answers:
A. telephone habits of teenagers
B. The first and second sections are statements from teenagers about how they like the telephone. The third section is general information.
C. around the age of 10 or 11; her parents punished her for using the phone too much

---

Et moi, et moi... et eux !

Je passe ma vie au téléphone

$\mathbf{I}$L y en a qui chantent : «Qui a eu cette idée folle, un jour, d'inventer l'école?» Moi, si j'en avais le talent, je chanterais : «Qui a eu cette idée folle, un jour, d'inventer le phone?»

Je ne pouvais plus me passer du téléphone. Et pourtant, j'ai tout essayé : punitions des parents, remboursement des communications, cures de quinze jours et plus en colonie... J'en ai découvert l'usage à dix ou onze ans, l'utilisation quasi quotidienne à treize ans. Et cela pour n'importe quel motif : discuter du travail scolaire, appeler les copains de colo qui habitent parfois à plus de 100 km de chez moi...

C'est à ce moment-là que mes parents sont intervenus. Au début, mes coups de fil ne se voyaient pas sur la note car mes parents restent assez longtemps, eux aussi, au téléphone. Mais du coup, j'ai pris l'habitude des longues conversations et des cris se sont fait entendre. Jusqu'au jour où, las de me réprimander, ils ont

décidé de m'acheter une carte téléphonique et des timbres. J'ai vite eu la flemme d'aller à la cabine téléphonique et j'ai donc jeté mon dévolu sur le papier à lettres. En écrivant, j'utilise ma petite cervelle et quel plaisir de recevoir

Emmanuelle : «Qui a eu l'idée, un jour, d'inventer le phone ?»

en retour une lettre que je peux lire et relire où et quand je veux! Il ne se passe pas une journée sans que je reçoive ma lecture préférée, celle qui vient du fond du cœur, celle des copains. D'accord, le téléphone est rapide et chaleureux, mais la lettre l'est peut-être encore plus. Bref, le téléphone est une gâterie à consommer avec modération.

Emmanuelle, 15 ans

Language-to-Language

Ask students if they know how people answer the phone in other countries. You might tell them that in Germany, people often answer the phone by giving their last name. In Italy, they're likely to hear **Pronto.** In Spanish-speaking countries, they might hear various exspressions, such as **Bueno, Diga,** and **Aló.**

LE bon usage du téléphone passe par une certaine maîtrise de l'appareil. Il faut savoir se présenter, être clair, précis, articuler... Après quelques années de pratique s'installe une véritable relation avec le combiné magique, merveilleux messager des peines et des espoirs. On attend une soirée entière une hypothétique sonnerie, on sursaute à chaque «Dring!», redoutant que Sylvain annule le rendez-vous pour lequel il a fallu passer trois heures dans la salle de bains. Combien de fois ai-je tourné, hésitante, autour de cet objet mystérieux au clavier soudain terrifiant? Combien de fois a-t-il, avec patience et sans jamais rien dire, recueilli mes rires et mes larmes? C'est pourquoi, aujourd'hui, je tiens à confesser publiquement et solennellement que j'aime mon téléphone!

Géraldine, 17 ans

Géraldine : «Je le confesse : mon téléphone, je l'aime!»

Pour dire bonjour, pour un rien...

Un quart d'heure, une demi-heure, une heure pendus au bout du fil... L'opération se répète quotidiennement. «Mes enfants téléphonent à leurs amis pour un rien, pour se dire bonjour et parfois pour faire leurs devoirs. Ça commence dès qu'ils rentrent du lycée et ça peut durer très longtemps... C'est à croire qu'ils sont nés avec un téléphone à l'oreille!», confie Véronique. Comme le dit Aurélie : «De retour chez soi, la seule façon de conserver un lien avec ceux qu'on vient de quitter, c'est le téléphone.»

Au sens propre comme au sens figuré, l'appareil est un fil qui vous relie au monde, qui vous rassure sur l'amitié des copains. C'est-à-dire sur ce qui est le plus important. Parce que dans l'amitié, on trouve la confiance, le respect, la tolérance et la sécurité dont on a tant besoin, à tout moment. Faute de lien, le risque est de se retrouver seul face à ses angoisses.

D'ailleurs, peu importe parfois qui vous appelez; quand l'interlocuteur décroche, vous finissez toujours par trouver quelque chose à raconter ou une confidence à partager.

Le téléphone, c'est un fil qui vous relie au monde, qui rassure sur l'amitié des copains. Et c'est ce qui est le plus important.

E. How did Emmanuelle break her telephone addiction? How does she communicate with her friends now? Why does she prefer this means of communication? See answers below.

Pour dire bonjour, pour un rien...

F. In this section, Véronique and Aurélie each make a statement. Which person is a parent? How do you know? See answers below.

G. Read the selection again and find three reasons why people enjoy talking on the phone. Which reason do you think is most important? See answers below.

Géraldine

H. What advice does Géraldine give at the beginning of her statement? How does she describe her relationship with the telephone? See answers below.

I. Who might have made each of the following statements?

"My telephone is my best friend." Géraldine

"Finally, Arlette answered the letter I wrote her last week!" Emmanuelle

"You may not make any more long-distance calls!" Emmanuelle's parents

J. Which people give the following reasons for talking on the phone? See answers below.

1. to say hello to friends
2. to do homework

K. In English, write a statement similar to Emmanuelle's and Geraldine's in which you tell how you feel about the telephone. Give examples to show why you feel the way you do.

deux cent cinquante et un 251

LISONS!
CHAPITRE 9

Teaching Suggestion

You might ask students to discuss the following questions about **Je passe ma vie au téléphone:** Which of the reasons given for talking on the phone are valid? Which are not? What are some other justifiable reasons for staying on the phone?

POSTREADING
Activity K

Thinking Critically

Analyzing In Emmanuelle's letter, she writes **«Qui a eu cette idée folle d'inventer le phone?»**. Ask students to think of other forms of communication that have been invented in the last decade. Have them discuss the positive and negative ways in which these new inventions and the speed and accessibility of communicating have changed people's lives. Have any of the new inventions changed the way students communicate?

Possible answers:

E. She started writing letters. Now, she writes letters all the time. She can read and reread the letters whenever she likes.

F. Véronique: she says "mes enfants..."

G. Students sometimes talk on the phone about assignments; the phone keeps you connected to the world and to your friends; there is always something to share. Answers will vary.

H. She says you need to know how to present yourself and how to be precise and clear on the telephone. She loves her telephone.

J. 1. les enfants de Véronique
2. les enfants de Veronique, Emmanuelle

The **Mise en pratique** reviews and integrates all four skills and culture in preparation for the Chapter Test.

Teaching Suggestion

1 Have students read the statements before they listen to the recording.

For Individual Needs

1 Challenge Have students correct the false statements to make them true. You might also have them tell whether or not they did the activities the speaker mentioned last weekend.

Teacher Note

3 If students have problems with any of these questions, tell them to reread the **Note Culturelle** on page 244.

MISE EN PRATIQUE

The *CD-ROM Program* offers guided recording and writing activities to practice oral and written skills and to review material from each chapter.

1 A friend has left a message on your answering machine telling you what he did over the weekend. Listen, then decide if these sentences are true or false. *See scripts and answers on page 231H.*

CD 9 Tr. 19

1. Martin a passé un mauvais week-end.
2. Il est allé à la plage.
3. Il a fait beau pendant le week-end.
4. Il a joué au football samedi.
5. Il n'a pas joué au tennis.
6. Dimanche, il a fait de l'aérobic.

2 Scan these letters first and then read them more carefully. What are they about? Who is Agnès? Then, answer the questions that follow. *See answers below.*

Chère Agnès	Il me dit qu'il veut sortir avec moi. Est-ce vrai?	Toute ma famille me déteste.
Agnès vous comprend. Vous pouvez lui confier tous vos problèmes. Elle trouve toujours une solution!	**Chère Agnès,** J'aime beaucoup un garçon, Pierre, qui me dit, dans une lettre très tendre, qu'il veut sortir avec moi. Mais il ne m'appelle jamais. Se moque-t-il de moi? Aide-moi car je suis dingue de lui! --Monique... Ne te décourage pas! Tu aimes ce garçon et il t'aime également. Tu t'imagines qu'il se moque de toi, mais lui aussi doit se demander s'il a ses chances. A toi d'aller vers lui. Bonne chance!	**Chère Agnès,** J'ai 14 ans et j'ai un problème : tout le monde dans ma famille me déteste, sauf ma mémé. Mes parents et ma sœur se moquent toujours de moi et me disent que je suis laide. Je suis très déprimée. Au secours! --S Ah S...! N'écoute pas ce que ta famille te dit. Et puis, il y a toujours ta mémé qui t'aime. Tu as 14 ans et tes parents ont sûrement peur de perdre leur petite fille. Parle-leur de tes sentiments et tu verras, tout ira mieux.

1. What is Monique's problem?
2. How does Agnès respond?
3. Who is S having difficulties with?
4. What does Agnès advise her to do?

3 Based on what you know about the French telephone system, tell whether the statements below are true or false.

1. The only way to make a call from a public phone in France is to use coins. *false*
2. You can generally find a public phone at the post office. *true*
3. You can't buy phone cards at the post office. *false*
4. Card-operated phones are being replaced by coin-operated ones. *false*
5. If you make a call using a phone card, you will be charged based on the distance and duration of the call. *true*

252 *deux cent cinquante-deux*   CHAPITRE 9   Au téléphone

Answers

2 1. A boy asked her out, and she doesn't know if he's serious.
2. She tells Monique not to be discouraged and to approach the boy.
3. her family
4. She tells S not to pay attention to the negative comments and to tell her family she's unhappy.

4 *Ecrivons!*

Think of a problem that many teenagers face. Describe the problem in a letter to Agnès and ask her to give you some advice. Then, exchange letters with a classmate and write a response offering advice about his or her problem.

STRATEGIE
Answering the five "W" questions (Who? What? Where? When? and Why?) can help you clarify your ideas. It can also help you make sure you don't leave out important information for your audience.

Prewriting
On a sheet of paper, brainstorm ways to explain the problem by asking yourself the "W" questions. Who is involved in the problem? What exactly is the problem? Where do you see the problem? At home? At school? When is the problem most evident? Why do you think this problem occurs?

Writing
Using the answers to your "W" questions, write a letter to Agnès describing the problem. Be as specific as you can in your description. However, don't try to use vocabulary and expressions you don't know or aren't familiar with. Use what you know as effectively as you can; other words and expressions will come later.

Now, exchange letters with a classmate. Each of you should write a response to the other's letter, offering advice on the problem. In writing your response, try to use some of the expressions you've learned for giving advice. After your classmate has read your response, have him or her return it to you, along with the letter you wrote. You're now ready for the final step of the writing process.

Revising
Evaluating your work is another important part of writing. This process involves several steps:

1. Self-evaluation: Reread both your letter and the response you wrote. Are they both arranged well? Are they easy to understand? Are they too wordy or are they lacking information?

2. Proofreading: Now, go over your writing again. This time, look just for misspelled words, punctuation errors, and grammatical mistakes.

3. Revising: Make any changes you feel are necessary.

After these steps are completed, you can submit, or publish, the final copy of your work.

5

JEU DE ROLE

You haven't seen your friend in a while. You want to find out what he or she has been doing. Phone and ask to speak to your friend. Talk about what you both did last weekend. Find out also what your friend is planning to do next summer. Act this out with a partner.

MISE EN PRATIQUE · *deux cent cinquante-trois* · **253**

Process Writing
4 You may want to have the class brainstorm some imaginary problems. Make a list on the board and allow students to either choose problems from this list or think of one on their own.

Portfolio
4 Written This activity is appropriate for students' written portfolios. For portfolio information, see the *Alternative Assessment Guide*, pages iv–17.

Teacher Note
To help students edit one another's work for the **Ecrivons!** writing assignments, you might give them the Peer Editing Rubric on page 9 of the *Alternative Assessment Guide.* Students complete the rubric by checking content and proofreading their classmate's work.

Video Wrap-Up
• *VIDEO PROGRAM,*
  Videocassette 3, 31:22–43:03
• *VIDEODISC PROGRAM,*
  Videodisc 5, Side A

At this time, you might want to use the video resources for additional review and enrichment. See *Video Guide* or *Videodisc Guide* for suggestions regarding the following:
• **Un week-end spécial**
  (Dramatic episode)
• **Panorama Culturel**
  (Interviews)
• **Vidéoclips**
  (Authentic footage)

This page is intended to help students prepare for the Chapter Test. It is a brief checklist of the major points covered in the chapter. The students should be reminded that this is only a checklist and does not necessarily include everything that will appear on the test.

Additional Practice

2 To extend this activity and review the **passé composé**, have students tell what they did during their weekend after they have told how it was.

Teacher Note

4 You might have students review other forms of the **passé composé** in addition to the **je** form as suggested in the activity.

Teaching Suggestions

• You might play the "Verb Tense Race" described on page 231J to review the verbs used in the chapter.
• You might also have students review regular -**re** verbs, such as **répondre** and **attendre**.

QUE SAIS-JE?

Can you use what you've learned in this chapter?

Can you ask for and express opinions? p. 237

1 How would you ask a friend how his or her weekend went?
Tu as passé un bon week-end?

2 How would you tell someone that your weekend was . . .
1. great? C'était très chouette.
2. OK? Ça a été. Pas mauvais.
3. horrible? C'était épouvantable. Très mauvais.

Can you inquire about and relate past events using the passé composé? p. 238

3 If you were inquiring about your friend's weekend, how would you ask . . .
1. what your friend did? Qu'est-ce que tu as fait?
2. where your friend went? Tu es allé(e) où?
3. what happened? Qu'est-ce qui s'est passé?

4 How would you tell someone that you did these things?

1. J'ai chanté.
2. J'ai gagné le match de tennis.
3. J'ai raté le bus.

Can you make and answer a telephone call? p. 244

5 If you were making a telephone call, how would you . . . See answers below.
1. tell who you are?
2. ask if it's the right house?
3. ask to speak to someone?
4. ask to leave a message?
5. ask someone to say you called?
6. tell someone the line's busy?

6 If you were answering a telephone call, how would you . . .
1. ask who's calling? Qui est à l'appareil?
2. ask someone to hold? Une seconde, s'il vous plaît.
3. ask someone to call back later? Vous pouvez rappeler plus tard?

Can you share confidences, console others, and ask for and give advice? p. 247

7 How would you approach a friend about a problem you have?
J'ai un petit problème. Je peux te parler? Tu as une minute?

8 What would you say to console a friend?
Ne t'en fais pas! Ça va aller mieux!

9 How would you ask a friend for advice?
A ton avis, qu'est-ce que je fais? Qu'est-ce que tu me conseilles?

10 How would you tell a friend what you think he or she should do?
Tu devrais... ; Pourquoi tu ne... pas?

254   *deux cent cinquante-quatre*   CHAPITRE 9   Au téléphone

Answers
5 1. C'est...
 2. Je suis bien chez... ?
 3. (Est-ce que)... est là, s'il vous plaît? (Est-ce que) je peux parler à... ?
 4. Je peux laisser un message?
 5. Vous pouvez lui dire que j'ai téléphoné?
 6. C'est occupé.

PREMIERE ETAPE

Asking for and expressing opinions

Tu as passé un bon week-end?
Did you have a good weekend?
Oui, très chouette. *Yes, super.*
Oui, excellent. *Yes, excellent.*
Oui, très bon. *Yes, very good.*
Oui, ça a été. *Yes, it was OK.*
Oh, pas mauvais. *Oh, not bad.*
Très mauvais. *Very bad.*
C'était épouvantable. *It was horrible.*

Inquiring about and relating past events

Qu'est-ce qui s'est passé (hier)?
What happened (yesterday)?
Nous avons parlé. *We talked.*
Qu'est-ce que tu as fait... ? *What did you do . . . ?*

D'abord,... *First, . . .*
Ensuite,... *Then, . . .*
Après, je suis sorti(e).
Afterwards, I went out.
Et après (ça)... *And after (that) . . .*
Finalement/Enfin,... *Finally, . . .*
Tu es allé(e) où? *Where did you go?*
Je suis allé(e)... *I went . . .*
j'ai fait *I did, I made*
j'ai pris *I took*
j'ai vu *I saw*
j'ai lu *I read*
déjà *already*
bien *well*
mal *badly*
ne... pas encore *not yet*
acheter *to buy*
apporter *to bring*
chanter *to sing*
chercher *to look for*
commencer *to begin, to start*

déjeuner à la cantine *to have lunch at the cafeteria*
dîner *to have dinner*
gagner *to win, to earn*
montrer *to show*
oublier *to forget*
passer un examen *to take an exam*
rater le bus *to miss the bus*
rater une interro *to fail a quiz*
rencontrer *to meet for the first time*
répéter *to rehearse, to practice music*
retrouver *to meet with*
travailler au fast-food *to work at a fast-food restaurant*
trouver *to find*
visiter *to visit (a place)*
une fille *girl*
un garçon *boy*

 Game

CE WEEK-END Have students form groups of five or six. The first person in each group begins by telling one thing he or she did last weekend. (**Ce week-end, j'ai dîné avec mes parents.**) The next person repeats the first activity and adds another. (**Ce week-end, j'ai dîné avec mes parents, et j'ai étudié.**) Groups compete to see which one can go on the longest without making a mistake.

DEUXIEME ETAPE

Making and answering a telephone call

Allô? *Hello?*
Je suis bien chez... ? *Is this . . . 's house?*
Qui est à l'appareil? *Who's calling?*
(Est-ce que)... est là, s'il vous plaît? *Is . . . there, please?*

Une seconde, s'il vous plaît. *One second, please.*
(Est-ce que) je peux parler à... ?
May I speak to . . . ?
Bien sûr. *Certainly.*
Vous pouvez rappeler plus tard?
Can you call back later?
Je peux laisser un message?
May I leave a message?

Vous pouvez lui dire que j'ai téléphoné? *Can you tell her/him that I called?*
Ne quittez pas. *Hold on.*
Ça ne répond pas. *There's no answer.*
C'est occupé. *It's busy.*
attendre *to wait for*
perdre *to lose*
répondre (à) *to answer*
vendre *to sell*

TROISIEME ETAPE

Sharing confidences and consoling others

J'ai un petit problème. *I've got a little problem.*
Je peux te parler? *Can we talk?*
Tu as une minute? *Do you have a minute?*
Je t'écoute. *I'm listening.*
Qu'est-ce que je peux faire? *What can I do?*
Ne t'en fais pas! *Don't worry!*

Ça va aller mieux! *It's going to get better!*

Asking for and giving advice

A ton avis, qu'est-ce que je fais?
In your opinion, what do I do?
Qu'est-ce que tu me conseilles?
What do you advise me to do?
Oublie-le/-la/-les! *Forget him/her/it/them!*

Téléphone-lui/-leur! *Call him/her/them!*
Tu devrais lui/leur parler. *You should talk to him/her/them.*
Pourquoi tu ne... pas? *Why don't you . . . ?*
le *him, it*
la *her, it*
les *them*
lui *to him, to her*
leur *to them*

VOCABULAIRE

deux cent cinquante-cinq **255**

 Game

REPONDS! For each student, write a question from one of the **Comment dit-on... ?** boxes on an index card. (**Tu as passé un bon week-end? Je peux parler à... ? Qu'est-ce que tu me conseilles?**) Have students stand in two lines facing each other. Each student reads the question on his or her card, and the student facing him or her has ten seconds to respond. At your signal, the students in one line move down one, and the person at the end moves to the front. The other row of students remains stationary. Repeat the process until students are back in their original positions.

CHAPTER 9 ASSESSMENT

CHAPTER TEST
• *Testing Program,* pp. 235–240
• *Audio Compact Discs,* Audio CD 9, Tracks 23–25

SPEAKING TEST
• *Testing Program,* p. 347

TEST GENERATOR
• Chapter 9

ALTERNATIVE ASSESSMENT
Performance Assessment
• You might want to use the **Jeu de rôle** on page 253 as a cumulative performance assessment activity.
• *Alternative Assessment Guide,* p. 40

Portfolio Assessment
• *Alternative Assessment Guide*
Oral: p. 26
Written: p. 26

CD-ROM Assessment
• *Interactive CD-ROM,* Disc 3
A toi de parler
A toi d'écrire
• *Alternative Assessment Guide,* p. 54

Chapitre 10 : Dans un magasin de vêtements
Chapter Overview

Mise en train pp. 258–260	Chacun ses goûts			

	FUNCTIONS	GRAMMAR	CULTURE	RE-ENTRY
Première étape pp. 261–264	• Asking for and giving advice, p. 264	• The verbs **mettre** and **porter**, p. 263		• The future with **aller** (**Chapitre 6**) • Sequencing adverbs (**Chapitre 9**) • Colors (**Chapitre 3**) • Family members (**Chapitre 7**)
Deuxième étape pp. 265–269	• Expressing need; inquiring, p. 265	• Adjectives used as nouns, p. 265 • The **-ir** verbs: **choisir**, p. 267	• Realia: Clothing ad, p. 266 • Realia: French size chart, p. 267 • **Note Culturelle,** Clothing sizes, p. 267 • **Panorama Culturel,** Fashion in francophone countries, p. 269	• Likes and dislikes (**Chapitre 1**) • The **passé composé** with **avoir** (**Chapitre 9**) • Expressing need (**Chapitre 8**)
Troisième étape pp. 270–275	• Asking for an opinion; paying a compliment; criticizing, p. 270 • Hesitating; making a decision, p. 274	• The direct object pronouns **le, la,** and **les,** p. 273 • **C'est** versus **il/elle est,** p. 274	• **Rencontre Culturelle,** Responding to compliments, p. 272	• Demonstrative adjectives (**Chapitre 3**) • The imperative (**Chapitre 5**)

Prononciation p. 275	The glides **[j], [w],** and **[ɥ]** Audio CD 10, Tracks 13–15	**A écrire** (dictation) Audio CD 10, Tracks 16–18

Lisons! pp. 276–277	**La mode au lycée**	**Reading Strategy** Distinguishing fact from opinion

Review pp. 278–281	**Mise en pratique,** pp. 278–279 **Ecrivons!** Paraphrasing Writing an article on fashion trends	**Que sais-je?** p. 280	**Vocabulaire,** p. 281

Assessment Options

Testing Program
• Première étape, Quiz 10-1A, Quiz 10-1B, pp. 249–252
• Deuxième étape, Quiz 10-2A, Quiz 10-2B, pp. 253–256
• Troisième étape, Quiz 10-3A, Quiz 10-3B, pp. 257–260
• Chapter Test, pp. 261–266
• Speaking Test, p. 347

Audio Compact Discs
• Audio CD 10, Tracks 20–25

Interactive CD-ROM Program
• Mise en pratique (A toi de parler, A toi d'écrire)
• CD-ROM Teacher's Guide, Assessment Options, p. 44

Alternative Assessment Guide
• Portfolio Assessment, p. 27
• Performance Assessment, p. 41
• CD-ROM Assessment, p. 55

Test Generator
• Chapter 10

PRINT	MEDIA

Pupil's Edition, pp. 256–281

Audio Compact Discs
• Textbook Listening Activities: Audio CD 10, Tracks 1–19

Interactive CD-ROM Program
Teacher's Guide, pp. 41–44

Interactive CD-ROM Program
• Disc 3

Videodisc Guide
• Teaching Suggestions, pp. 111–115
• Activity Masters, pp. 116–118

Videodisc Program
• Videodisc 5, Side B

Video Guide
• Teaching Suggestions, pp. 68–69
• Activity Masters, pp. 70–72

Video Program
• Videocassette 4
• Videocassette 5 (captioned version)

Listening Activities
• Student Response Forms for Textbook Listening Activities, pp. 75–77
• Additional Listening Activities 10-1 to 10-6, pp. 79–81
• Additional Listening Activities (song), p. 82
• Scripts and Answers, pp. 147–151

Audio Compact Discs
• Textbook Listening Activities: Audio CD 10, Tracks 1–19
• Additional Listening Activities: Audio CD 10, Tracks 26–32

Teaching Transparencies
• Teaching Transparency Masters 10-1 to 10-3 (Situations) and 10-A (Vocabulary)
• Teaching Suggestions 10-1 to 10-3 and 10-A

Teaching Transparencies
• Situations 10-1 to 10-3
• Vocabulary 10-A

Testing Program
• Grammar and Vocabulary Quizzes, **Etape** Quizzes, and Chapter Test, pp. 249–266
• Score Sheet, Scripts, and Answers, pp. 267–274

Audio Compact Discs
• Assessment Items: Audio CD 10, Tracks 20–25

Test Generator
• Chapter 10

Alternative Assessment Guide
• Portfolio Assessment, p. 27
• Performance Assessment, p. 41
• CD-ROM Assessment, p. 55

Grammar and Vocabulary Workbook, pp. 79–87

Practice and Activity Book, pp. 109–120

Activities for Communication
• Communicative Activities, pp. 55–60
• Realia and Teaching Suggestions, pp. 120–124
• Situation Cards, pp. 155–156

Lesson Planner
• Lesson Plan, pp. 48–52

Chapitre 10 : Dans un magasin de vêtements
Technology Applications

MISE EN TRAIN, pp. 258–260

Video

• Show *Chacun ses goûts.* For Video Synopsis, Teaching Suggestions, Activity Master, and Scripts, see the *Video Guide* or the *Videodisc Guide.*

Audio

• Play the recording of the **Mise en train** with pauses as students read along. You might have them practice pronunciation by repeating individual sentences after hearing them.

PREMIERE ETAPE, pp. 261–264

Video

• While students watch *Chacun ses goûts,* have them listen for exchanges that model asking for and giving advice. For more suggestions, see pp. 112–113 of the *Videodisc Guide.*

Audio

• Textbook Listening Activity 7 practices the vocabulary for clothes and accessories.

• Textbook Listening Activity 13 has students distinguish between asking for and giving advice.

• To review vocabulary for clothes and accessories, have students do Additional Listening Activities 10-1 and 10-2.

Transparencies

• Use *Teaching Transparency 10-A* and the Teaching Suggestions to present and have students practice the vocabulary for clothing items.

• Use *Teaching Transparency 10-1* and the Teaching Suggestions to present and have students practice asking for and giving advice about clothing items.

CD-ROM (Disc 3)

• **Jeu des paires** (Activity 1) and **Chasse au trésor** (Activity 2)

target the vocabulary for clothing items.

• For suggestions, see p. 42 of the *CD-ROM Teacher's Guide.*

DEUXIEME ETAPE, pp. 265–268

Video

• While students watch *Chacun ses goûts,* have them listen for exchanges that model expressing need and inquiring. For more suggestions, see p. 113 of the *Videodisc Guide.*

Audio

• Textbook Listening Activity 17 targets the expressions for expressing need and inquiring.

• Textbook Listening Activity 18 practices talking about colors, prices, and sizes of clothing items.

• To review expressing need, inquiring, and the vocabulary for clothing items, use Additional Listening Activities 10-3 and 10-4.

Transparencies

• Use *Teaching Transparency 10-2* and the Teaching Suggestions to have students practice expressing need and inquiring.

CD-ROM (Disc 3)

• To have students practice the forms of the verb **mettre** and -ir verbs, use **Les mots qui manquent** (Activity 3).

• For suggestions, see p. 42 of the *CD-ROM Teacher's Guide.*

PANORAMA CULTUREL, p. 269

Video

• Show the interviews. For Video Synopsis, Teaching Suggestions, Activity Master, and Scripts, see the *Video Guide* or the *Videodisc Guide.*

Audio

• Play the **Panorama Culturel** as students read along. Remind students they might not be able

to understand everything each person says, but they should try to deduce global meaning.

CD-ROM (Disc 3)

• Have students do the **Panorama Culturel** activity after showing them the video. For suggestions, see p. 43 of the *CD-ROM Teacher's Guide.*

TROISIEME ETAPE, pp. 270–275

Video

• While students watch *Chacun ses goûts,* have them listen for exchanges that model asking for an opinion, paying a compliment, criticizing, hesitating, and making a decision. For more suggestions, see p. 114 of the *Videodisc Guide.*

Audio

• Use Textbook Listening Activity 26 to have students practice complimenting and criticizing clothing.

• Use Textbook Listening Activity 31 to have students practice the expressions for hesitating and making a decision.

• Additional Listening Activities 10-5 and 10-6 review the expressions for asking for an opinion, paying a compliment, criticizing, hesitating, and making a decision.

Transparencies

• Use *Teaching Transparency 10-3* and the Teaching Suggestions to have students practice asking for an opinion, paying a compliment, criticizing, hesitating, and making a decision.

CD-ROM (Disc 3)

• **Méli-mélo** (Activity 4) has students practice the placement of the direct object pronouns.

• After presenting the expressions for expressing need and inquiring, have students do **Chacun à sa place** (Activity 5).

• **Le bon choix** (Activity 6) targets the pronouns **le, la,** and **les,** and using **c'est** versus **il/elle est.**

• For suggestions, see p. 43 of the *CD-ROM Teacher's Guide.*

MISE EN PRATIQUE, pp. 278–279

Video

• Replay *Chacun ses goûts* in its entirety and ask students to listen for the exchanges in which the characters use expressions for asking for and giving advice, expressing need, inquiring, asking for an opinion, paying a compliment, criticizing, hesitating, and making a decision.

CD-ROM (Disc 3)

• Have students do the **En contexte** to practice identifying clothing items, inquiring about sizes, colors, and prices, criticizing, complimenting, hesitating, and making a decision. For suggestions, see p. 42 of the *CD-ROM Teacher's Guide.*

• Have students practice their writing and speaking skills by doing the **A toi d'écrire** and **A toi de parler** activities. For a detailed description of these activities, see p. 44 of the *CD-ROM Teacher's Guide.*

• For Assessment Options, see p. 44 of the *CD-ROM Teacher's Guide.*

Test Generator

• Use the Test Generator to create review material for students taking the Chapter Test or to prepare an alternate Test.

VIDEOCLIPS

Video

• Show the **Vidéoclips**. For Video Synopsis, Teaching Suggestions, Activity Masters, and Scripts, see the *Video Guide* or the *Videodisc Guide.*

Chapitre 10 : Dans un magasin de vêtements
Barcode Directory

MISE EN TRAIN

Barcodes A and B access **Mise en train** and **Mise en train (suite)** in their entirety. Subsequent barcodes show specific segments of **Chacun ses goûts.** The barcode numbers correspond to the scene numbers as they appear on the video.

ÉTAPES

To practice the grammar, vocabulary, and functions presented in each **étape**, see the barcodes and accompanying suggestions on pages 112–114 of the *Videodisc Guide*.

Chacun ses goûts! **A**

Search 1, Play To 9405

Oh là là! **1**

Search 1, Play To 1482

Bonjour. Je peux... ? **2**

Search 1483, Play To 2773

Si vous voulez,... **3**

Search 2773, Play To 3868

Nous avons... **4**

Search 3868, Play To 4870

J'aime bien... **5**

Search 4874, Play To 6228

Très joli... **6**

Search 6228, Play To 7427

Ah, très chic! **7**

Search 7437, Play To 7786

Nous avons ces chemisiers...**8**

Search 7786, Play To 9405

MISE EN PRATIQUE

This is additional footage modeling some of the expressions practiced in this chapter. You may want to use it to review the chapter.

Mise en pratique **1**

Search 24960, Play To 26039

Mise en pratique **2**

Search 26412, Play To 28421

Chacun ses goûts (suite) **B**

Search 9405, Play To 16950

PANORAMA CULTUREL

Qu'est-ce que tu aimes comme vêtements?
These barcodes access the three interviews of the **Panorama Culturel** presented in the *Pupil's Edition* as well as additional interviews.

First three interviews **1**

Search 16950, Play To 18765

All interviews **2**

Search 16950, Play To 22269

Marie-Emmanuelle **3**

Search 17613, Play To 18122

VIDEOCLIPS

These are authentic French commercials. You may want to preview them before showing them to students.

Kelton®: watches **1**

Search 22269, Play To 23717

Alain Afflelou®: eyeglasses **2**

Search 23717, Play To 24664

Thomas **4**

Search 18123, Play To 18475

Aminata **5**

Search 18476, Play To 18752

Jean-Christophe **6**

Search 18787, Play To 19292

Epie **7**

Search 19293, Play To 19352

Marieke **8**

Search 19353, Play To 19693

Narcisse **9**

Search 19694, Play To 19802

Clémentine **10**

Search 19803, Play To 20482

Emmanuel **11**

Search 20483, Play To 20877

Marie-Laure **12**

Search 20878, Play To 21127

Carole **13**

Search 21128, Play To 21375

Pascal **14**

Search 21376, Play To 21887

Nicole **15**

Search 21888, Play To 22269

Chapitre 10 : Dans un magasin de vêtements
CD-ROM Directory 💿 Disc 3

The following directory lists the *Interactive CD-ROM Program* activities for Chapter 10. For details and suggestions on how to use them, see pages 41–44 of the *CD-ROM Teacher's Guide*.

GLOBAL TASK	COMMUNICATIVE GOALS	ACTIVITY TYPE
Au magasin Students talk with Pascale's friend Juliette about an upcoming birthday party for Etienne. Then, students go shopping for a gift and also buy clothing for the party.	To use chapter functions, vocabulary, and grammar in a lifelike conversation	**En contexte** *Interactive conversation*

	SUPPORTING ACTIVITIES	PUPIL'S EDITION	COMMUNICATIVE GOALS	ACTIVITY TYPE
Première étape	1. Vocabulaire	p. 261	To identify clothing items	**Jeu des paires** *Concentration®*
	2. Vocabulaire	p. 261	To use vocabulary for clothing items	**Chasse au trésor Explorons!/Vérifions!** *Interactive image*
Deuxième étape	3. Grammaire	pp. 263, 267	To use the verb **mettre** and **-ir** verbs	**Les mots qui manquent** *Tic Tac Toe*
Troisième étape	4. Grammaire	p. 273	To correctly place the pronouns **le, la,** and **les** in a sentence	**Méli-mélo** *Sequencing*
	5. Comment dit-on...?	pp. 265, 270	To classify expressions that a customer or salesperson might use	**Chacun à sa place** *Categories*
	6. Grammaire	pp. 273–274	To use the pronouns **le, la,** and **les** and to demonstrate when to use **c'est** versus **il/elle est**	**Le bon choix** *Multiple choice*
Panorama Culturel	Panorama Culturel	p. 269	To listen to and understand native speakers talking about the kinds of clothing they like	**Qu'est-ce que tu aimes comme vêtements?** *Presentation* **Le bon choix** *Multiple choice*

	APPLICATION	PUPIL'S EDITION	COMMUNICATIVE GOALS	ACTIVITY TYPE
Mise en pratique	A toi de parler	pp. 278–279	To create and record a conversation between a customer and a salesperson in a clothing store	*Guided recording*
	A toi d'écrire	pp. 278–279	To create a survey, a note, a conversation, or an advertisement	*Guided writing*

🏠 *Homework Suggestions*

CHAPTER SECTION	PRESENTATION	HOMEWORK OPTIONS
Première étape	**Vocabulaire,** p. 261	Pupil's Edition, p. 262, Activity 9 Practice and Activity Book, p. 110, Activities 2–4 Grammar and Vocabulary Workbook, pp. 79–80, Activities 1–3 CD-ROM, Disc 3, Activities 1–2
	Grammaire, p. 263	Pupil's Edition, p. R47, Activities 1–2 Practice and Activity Book, p. 111, Activities 6–7 Grammar and Vocabulary Workbook, pp. 80–81, Activities 4–6
	Comment dit-on... ? p. 264	Practice and Activity Book, p. 112, Activities 8–9
Deuxième étape	**Comment dit-on... ?** p. 265	Practice and Activity Book, p. 113, Activities 10–11 Grammar and Vocabulary Workbook, p. 82, Activity 7
	Note de grammaire, p. 265	Pupil's Edition, p. R47, Activity 3 Practice and Activity Book, p. 114, Activity 12 Grammar and Vocabulary Workbook, p. 82, Activity 8
	Grammaire, p. 267	Pupil's Edition, p. 268, Activity 24; p. R48, Activities 4–6 Practice and Activity Book, p. 115, Activities 14–16 Grammar and Vocabulary Workbook, pp. 83–84, Activities 9–12 CD-ROM, Disc 3, Activity 3
Troisième étape	**Comment dit-on... ?** p. 270	Practice and Activity Book, pp. 116–117, Activities 17–19 Grammar and Vocabulary Workbook, pp. 85–86, Activities 13–15 CD-ROM, Disc 3, Activity 5

	Grammaire, p. 273	Pupil's Edition, p. 273, Activity 30; pp. R48–R49,
		    Activities 7–8
		Practice and Activity Book, p. 117, Activity 21
		Grammar and Vocabulary Workbook, pp. 86–87,
		    Activities 16–17
		CD-ROM, Disc 3, Activity 4

	Comment dit-on... ? p. 274	Practice and Activity Book, p. 128, Activity 22
	Note de grammaire, p. 274	Pupil's Edition, p. R49, Activity 9 Practice and Activity Book, p. 118, Activity 23 Grammar and Vocabulary Workbook, p. 87, Activity 18 CD-ROM, Disc 3, Activity 6

For Student Response Forms, see *Listening Activities,* pp. 75–77.

Première étape

7 Ecoute! p. 262

ARMELLE J'ai acheté des tas de vêtements pour la rentrée. J'ai trouvé une jupe orange en coton avec la ceinture qui va avec. Elle est super, tu vas voir. Je vais la mettre demain. J'ai aussi acheté un chemisier noir avec le cardigan assorti. Très chic.

AMIE Tu n'as pas acheté de chaussures cette fois-ci? C'est ton habitude.

ARMELLE Non, il me faut des chaussures, mais c'était trop cher. Mais j'ai acheté des chaussettes en solde et aussi une paire de boucles d'oreilles pour l'anniversaire de ma sœur.

Answer to Activity 7
c

13 Ecoute! p. 264

1. — Je vais au cinéma avec Chantal ce soir. Dis, Pierre, qu'est-ce que je mets?

2. — Si tu veux être chic, Dianne, pourquoi tu ne mets pas ta nouvelle robe?

3. — Mais non! Il ne faut pas mettre ton jean! Pourquoi est-ce que tu ne mets pas un pantalon?

4. — Je ne sais pas quoi mettre pour aller à la boum. J'aimerais quelque chose de joli.

5. — Tu vas avoir trop chaud, Luc. Mets un short et des sandales!

Answers to Activity 13
1. asking   4. asking
2. giving   5. giving
3. giving

Deuxième étape

17 Ecoute! p. 265

1. — Je cherche un maillot de bain.

2. — Vous avez ça en quarante?

3. — Je peux vous aider?

4. — J'aimerais des chaussures pour aller avec ma robe.

5. — Non, mais nous l'avons en bleu.

6. — Je peux l'essayer?

7. — Vous avez choisi?

Answers to Activity 17
1. customer   5. salesperson
2. customer   6. customer
3. salesperson   7. salesperson
4. customer

18 Ecoute! p. 266

1. — Vous avez ça en quarante-quatre?

2. — Il me faut des chaussettes noires.

3. — Ça coûte cent vingt francs.

4. — Je peux essayer la jupe blanche?

5. — Le blouson en cuir, c'est huit cent quatre-vingt-quinze francs.

6. — Vous l'avez en trente-huit?

Answers to Activity 18
1. size   3. price   5. price
2. color   4. color   6. size

Troisième étape

26 Ecoute! p. 271

1. — Dis, comment tu trouves ma jupe?
   — Euh, je la trouve un peu démodée.

2. — Elle est super chic, ta robe!
   — Tu trouves?

3. — Dis, Nicole, tu sais, ces chaussures, elles ne vont pas du tout avec ta jupe!
   — Ah oui? C'est vrai?

4. — Il n'est pas trop serré, ce chemisier?
   — Euh, si, je le trouve un peu serré.

5. — Il est sensas, ton pantalon!
   — Tu crois?
   — Oui, il te va très bien!

6. — Elle me va, cette robe?
   — C'est tout à fait ton style!

Answers to Activity 26
1. criticizing   4. criticizing
2. complimenting   5. complimenting
3. criticizing   6. complimenting

31 Ecoute! p. 274

1. VENDEUR Ce manteau vous va très bien, monsieur. Vous le prenez?
   CLIENT Il me plaît, mais il est beaucoup trop cher.

2. VENDEUR Alors, vous avez décidé de prendre cette casquette, monsieur?
   CLIENT Elle est super. Je la prends.

3. VENDEUR Et ces baskets? Vous les prenez?
   CLIENT Euh, j'hésite. Elles sont sensas, mais pas vraiment mon genre.

4. VENDEUR Très bien, monsieur. Et vous avez décidé pour ces bottes?
   CLIENT Pourquoi pas? Je les prends aussi.

5. VENDEUR Et cette chemise, vous la prenez, monsieur?
   CLIENT Je ne sais pas. J'aime la couleur, mais elle est chère.

6. VENDEUR C'est tout à fait votre style, ce blouson. Vous le prenez?
   CLIENT Euh, je ne sais pas. Il est un peu trop court.

Answers to Activity 31
1. doesn't take   4. takes
2. takes   5. can't decide
3. can't decide   6. can't decide

Prononciation, p. 275

For the scripts for Parts A and B, see p. 275.

C. A écrire

(Dictation)
— Je cherche un maillot de bain.
— Voilà.
— Je peux l'essayer?
— Oui, bien sûr.

Mise en pratique

1 p. 278

VENDEUSE Bonjour. Je peux vous aider?
PHILIPPE Oui, euh... je voudrais une chemise.
VENDEUSE Quel genre de chemise cherchez-vous?
PHILIPPE Bof, je ne sais pas. Quelque chose de cool, de branché. Une chemise bleue ou kaki, à carreaux peut-être.
VENDEUSE Et bien, nous avons des chemises américaines, style western. Ça vous intéresse?
PHILIPPE Ouais, ...
VENDEUSE Les voilà. Comment les trouvez-vous?
PHILIPPE Pas mal. Ouais, j'aime bien celle-ci.
VENDEUSE Vous faites quelle taille?
PHILIPPE Euh... je ne sais pas... Vous l'avez en trente-sept/trente-huit?
VENDEUSE Voici.
PHILIPPE Je peux l'essayer?
VENDEUSE Bien sûr.

plus tard

VENDEUSE Elle vous va très bien. C'est tout à fait votre style! Et c'est tellement à la mode!
PHILIPPE Mais moi, je la trouve un peu serrée. Vous avez ça en trente-neuf/quarante?
VENDEUSE Oui, en trente-neuf/quarante, mais en rouge.
PHILIPPE Euh... j'hésite. J'aime pas trop la rouge. J'aime mieux la bleue. Bon, alors. Ça va. C'est combien?
VENDEUSE Deux cent quarante-neuf francs.
PHILIPPE Ah? Deux cent quarante-neuf francs! Je regrette, c'est trop cher. Je ne la prends pas.

Answers to Mise en pratique Activity 1
1. a shirt
2. blue and khaki
3. The shirt suits him. It's his style, and it's in fashion.
4. It's a little tight.
5. No.

Chapitre 10 : Dans un magasin de vêtements
Projects

Un défilé de mode
(Group Project)

ASSIGNMENT

This project may be oral or written. Students will organize a fashion show. They may actually model clothes on a runway, accompanied by an oral commentary, or draw their designs and provide a written description on a poster.

MATERIALS

✂ **Students may need**
- Clothing or fabric
- Posterboard
- Colored pencils or markers
- Fashion magazines
- French-English dictionaries

SUGGESTED SEQUENCE

1. Have students form groups of three or four. Have each group decide on the general style of their fashion line: grunge, evening wear, retro, modern, and so on. They should also choose the colors and patterns they would like to feature.

2. Have students look through fashion magazines for ideas. If they plan to do a runway show, they might also list their favorite clothing items from their own closets.

3. Have students sketch or collect the items for their show. Have them write out complete descriptions of each item. They might consult a dictionary for French words to describe the fashions. Remind students that their goal is to sell the clothes, so their commentaries should include when and where they can be worn as well as a description of the overall look.

4. Have students organize their projects and decide in what order to present the items or plan the layout of their poster. Have them exchange their written descriptions with peers for editing.

5. Have students recopy or type their descriptions and finalize their visuals if they are doing a written project.

If they are making a poster, they might attach samples of fabric or jewelry to add texture to their illustrations. If they are doing a runway presentation, have them present the fashions to the class as a narrator from the group reads the description of each item. Have them change narrators after every few items.

GRADING THE PROJECT

You might want to base students' grades on completion of the assignment, creativity, accuracy of language use, and presentation.

Suggested Point Distribution (total = 100 points)

Completion of assignment	20 points
Creativity	30 points
Language use	20 points
Presentation	30 points

Games

DESSINEZ-MOI!

In this game, students will review clothing vocabulary.

Describe an outfit to students (see examples below) and have them draw the outfit on a piece of paper as they listen to you. Say each item of clothing only once. After the outfit is complete, have students hold up their drawings and award a point for each correct one, or you might have volunteers draw their version of the outfit on the board. The outfits might be serious, humorous, or even bizarre.

Examples of outfits:

1. **un maillot de bain, un chapeau, un manteau large, une ceinture trop serrée, des bottes moches, des lunettes de soleil**

2. **un sweat-shirt court, des baskets trop grandes, une écharpe, un jean, des boucles d'oreilles longues, un cardigan large**

3. **un pantalon court, une chemise, une petite cravate, une casquette, de grandes chaussettes**

Variation Give students pieces of paper and crayons or transparencies and colored markers and have them draw color illustrations as you describe them.

MEMOIRE

This game will test students' recognition of clothing vocabulary.

This game is played like Concentration®. First, assign sections of the **Vocabulaire** on page 281 to groups of students. Have them create two cards for each item: one with the French word or expression on it, and the other with an illustration of the item. Collect the cards, mix them thoroughly, and number them consecutively on the back. Tape them to the board or wall in numerical order so that only the numbers show. Then, have players ask to see two cards by saying the numbers in French **(trois, douze)**. Turn over the two cards. If they match, the player wins a point, keeps the cards, and the next player takes a turn. Continue until all students have had a chance to guess or until all cards have been matched. You might want to give out small prizes to the students who get the most points.

**Chapitre 10
Dans un magasin
de vêtements**
pp. 256–281

𝒰sing the Chapter Opener

Motivating Activity

Ask students how they would rate the importance of clothing in their lives on a scale of 1 to 10, with 10 being the most important. Have them explain their ratings. Ask what they consider more important than clothing.

Teaching Suggestion

Have students read the caption for each photo and ask them to pick out words or phrases they already know. Have them use context and the photos to guess the meaning of the other words. After having students match the outcomes with the photos, ask them to explain how the outcomes are reflected in the photos.

Photo Flash!

① This photo shows a girl shopping for an outfit to wear to a party. Point out that **faire les boutiques** or **faire les magasins** refers to *shopping,* while **faire les vitrines** or **faire du lèche-vitrines** refers to *window shopping,* or shopping without the intent to buy.

CHAPITRE

10
Dans un magasin de vêtements

① Je ne sais pas quoi mettre pour aller à la boum.

It's not easy to decide what to wear on a special occasion. It's often a welcome excuse to buy something new. But what? It depends on the statement you want to make. Chic? Casual? How do you create just the right look?

In this chapter you will learn

- to ask for and give advice
- to express need; to inquire
- to ask for an opinion; to pay a compliment; to criticize; to hesitate; to make a decision

And you will

- listen to French-speaking students talk about what they like to wear on different occasions
- read about the clothing styles French-speaking teenagers like
- write about what you wear on different occasions
- find out how francophone teenagers feel about fashion

② J'aimerais un foulard pour aller avec cette jupe.

③ C'est tout à fait ton style!

deux cent cinquante-sept 257

Focusing on Outcomes

Ask students to tell how the outcomes could be used to discuss clothing. Then, have them suggest other situations in which these outcomes could be used and how (when buying school supplies or gifts, when discussing new hairstyles). NOTE: You may want to use the video to support the objectives. The self-check activities in **Que sais-je?** on page 280 help students assess their achievement of the objectives.

Teaching Suggestion

Have students read the introductory paragraph on this page. Ask if they agree that clothing makes a statement. Find out what clothing styles students like.

Building on Previous Skills

② Ask students which colors Hélène prefers, judging from the skirt she's considering buying. Have them describe the colors in their favorite outfit.

Block Scheduling

For suggestions about how to use *Allez, viens!* with block scheduling, see the *Lesson Planner,* pages 48–52.

Family Link

Ask students to interview their family members about what they like to wear and why. Have students report their results to the class and give possible explanations for the different preferences. Students can provide results for a famous or imaginary family if they prefer.

VIDEO PROGRAM
Videocassette 4
01:22–06:35
Videocassette 5
(captioned version)
1:20:21–1:25:35

OR *VIDEODISC PROGRAM,*
Videodisc 5, Side B

Search 1, Play To 9405

Video Synopsis

In this segment of the video, Magali and Hélène discuss what they are going to wear to Sophie's birthday party. Later, we see Sophie leaving a clothing boutique. Magali enters the same boutique. Inside, she is helped by a saleswoman and tries on several items. When Magali finally finds something she likes, she discovers that it costs 670 F! She is reluctant to spend that much money and doesn't know what to do.

Motivating Activity

Ask students to suggest expressions that salespeople in a clothing store might say to customers. Ask students what their favorite stores are and what they wear to parties or to go out with friends.

Presentation

After viewing the video, play the recording and have students follow along in their books. Stop the recording to ask the questions in Activity 1 on page 260 to check students' comprehension: after the first scene, question 1; after the second, question 2; after the third, question 3; after the ninth, question 4; after the tenth, question 5.

Language Note

The expression **Chacun ses goûts** is the French equivalent of *To each his own.*

The **roman-photo** is an abridged version of the video episode.

Mise en train ▣ PA

p. 109, Act. 1

CD 10
Trs. 1–2

Chacun ses goûts

What event are Hélène and Magali discussing at the beginning of the story? Where does Magali go? Why do you think Hélène doesn't go with her?

> Oh là là! Je ne sais pas quoi mettre demain. C'est l'anniversaire de Sophie. J'ai envie d'acheter quelque chose de joli. Et toi, qu'est-ce que tu vas mettre?

> Oh, je ne sais pas. Sans doute un jean et un tee-shirt.

> Pourquoi est-ce que tu ne trouves pas quelque chose d'original? De mignon?

> Ecoute, Magali. Moi, j'aime bien être en jean et en tee-shirt. C'est simple et agréable à porter. Chacun ses goûts.

Au magasin...

> Bonjour. Je peux vous aider?

> Je cherche quelque chose pour aller à une fête. J'aimerais quelque chose d'original et pas trop cher.

> Qu'est-ce que vous faites comme taille?

> Je fais du 38.

258   *deux cent cinquante-huit*   CHAPITRE 10   Dans un magasin de vêtements

---

RESOURCES FOR MISE EN TRAIN

PRINT
- *Practice and Activity Book,* p. 109
- *Video Guide,* pp. 67–68, 70
- *Videodisc Guide,* pp. 109–112, 116

MEDIA
- *Video Program,* Videocassette 4 Videocassette 5 (captioned version)
- *Videodisc Program,* Videodisc 5, Side B
- *Audio Compact Discs,* CD 10, Trs. 1–2

Thinking Critically

Analyzing Have students discuss the questions that Magali asks at the clothing store. Ask students if they ask the same questions and if there are other things to consider when buying clothes. Ask them whether they agree with the saleswoman that it's worth any price to look original.

For Individual Needs

Auditory Learners Describe each photo aloud in random order. For example, for Photo 5, you might say **Magali trouve une jupe, mais ce n'est pas son style.** Have students call out the number of the photo you're describing.

Culture Note

The outfit that Magali tries on is made of **provençal** fabric. These prints are characterized by one or more distinctive **provençal** motifs, which are recognizable by their floral designs, medallions, or paisleys.

MISE EN TRAIN   *deux cent cinquante-neuf* **259**

Video Integration

- **VIDEO PROGRAM,**
  Videocassette 3, 06:36–10:47
  Videocassette 5, 1:25:37–1:29:49
- **VIDEODISC PROGRAM,**
  Videodisc 5, Side B

Search 9405, Play To 16950

You may choose to continue with **Chacun ses goûts (suite)** at this time or wait until later in the chapter. When the story continues, Hélène enters the clothing boutique and sees Magali. Magali asks her about the outfit she has on, and Hélène compliments her on it. Magali is unsure and still can't figure out what to do. Later, at Sophie's, everything is ready for the party. Malika arrives, and then Ahmed, Charles, and Florent. When Magali arrives, she and Sophie discover they've bought the same shirt! Magali is upset at first, but then smiles. Florent takes a photo of Magali and Sophie.

For Individual Needs

2 Slower Pace/Visual Learners If students have difficulty with this activity, show the video, stop it when you come to each of these quotes, and have students identify the speaker.

For videodisc application, see *Videodisc Guide.*

Auditory Learners

4 Read the sentences aloud in random order and have students tell whether the salesperson or customer is speaking.

Teaching Suggestion

6 This activity might be done orally as a class or in pairs. You might also have students write down their answers.

Additional Practice

Write down some sentences from the conversation between Magali and the salesperson on strips of transparency and place the strips on the overhead in random order. Have students identify the person who said each sentence. Then, have students put the sentences in order to recreate the conversation.

These activities check for comprehension only. Students should not yet be expected to produce language modeled in **Mise en train**.

1 Tu as compris?

1. Why does Magali want to buy something new?   She is going to a birthday party.
2. What is Hélène going to wear? Why?   jeans and a T-shirt; They are simple and comfortable.
3. What type of clothing is Magali looking for?   something original and not too expensive
4. What outfit does Magali like?   a green skirt and a shirt
5. What does she think of the price?   She thinks it is expensive.

2 C'est qui?

Qui parle? C'est Magali, Hélène ou la vendeuse?

1. «J'aimerais quelque chose d'original et pas trop cher.»   Magali
2. «Je peux vous aider?»   la vendeuse
3. «Moi, j'aime bien être en jean et en tee-shirt. C'est simple et agréable à porter.»   Hélène
4. «Qu'est-ce que vous faites comme taille?»   la vendeuse
5. «Chacun ses goûts.»   Hélène
6. «Est-ce que vous l'avez en vert?»   Magali
7. «C'est tout à fait votre style.»   la vendeuse
8. «Ce n'est pas tellement mon style.»   Magali

3 Chacun ses goûts

What does Magali say about these things?

1. le jean et le tee-shirt d'Hélène   Pourquoi est-ce que tu ne trouves pas quelque chose d'original? De mignon?
2. la jupe verte en 38   C'est pas mal, mais elle est un peu large.
3. le prix de l'ensemble   C'est cher.

4 Qu'est-ce qu'elle répond?

Qu'est-ce que Magali répond à la vendeuse?

1. Qu'est-ce que vous faites comme taille?   b
2. Comment la trouvez-vous?   d
3. Je peux vous aider?   c
4. Ça vous fait 670 francs.   a

a. C'est cher!
b. Je fais du 38.
c. Je cherche quelque chose pour aller à une fête.
d. Bof. Ce n'est pas tellement mon style.

5 Cherche les expressions   See answers below.

According to **Chacun ses goûts,** how would you . . .

1. express indecision?
2. express satisfaction with your clothes?
3. tell a salesperson what you want?
4. tell what size you wear?
5. express dissatisfaction with clothes?
6. ask for a certain color or size?
7. ask what all of your purchases cost?

> Je fais du...   Ça fait combien, ...?
>
> C'est simple et agréable à porter.   J'aimerais quelque chose de...
>
> Je ne sais pas quoi mettre.   Est-ce que vous l'avez en... ?
>
> C'est pas tellement mon style.

6 Et maintenant, à toi

Do you prefer Magali's style or Hélène's? What sort of clothes do you like to wear?

---

260   *deux cent soixante*   CHAPITRE 10   Dans un magasin de vêtements

Answers

5 1. Je ne sais pas quoi mettre.
  2. C'est simple et agréable à porter.
  3. J'aimerais quelque chose de...
  4. Je fais du...
  5. C'est pas tellement mon style.
  6. Est-ce que vous l'avez en... ?
  7. Ça fait combien, ... ?

PREMIERE ETAPE Storytelling Book pp. 37, 40

Asking for and giving advice

 p. 110, Acts. 2–4   10-A   pp. 79–80, Acts. 1–3   CD-ROM Disc 3

VOCABULAIRE

VETEMENTS

maillot de bain bleu et rouge 119F

blouson bleu ou noir 925F

chaussures marron 309F

chemise blanche ou bleue 129F

veste bleue 720F

chemisier blanc 149F

jupe grise 199F

robe verte à fleurs 439F

blouson marron ou noir 1160F

bottes noires 499F

Accessoires

noires blanches bleues

chaussettes 10,20F la paire

pêche

lunettes de soleil 61,50F

cravate bleue à rayures 83F

montre noire 449F

écharpe rose ou blanche 101,50F

ceinture noire ou marron 99,90F

chapeau gris 255F

boucles d'oreilles 249F

casquette rouge 161F

Here are some other words you may want to use to talk about what you're wearing.

un bracelet	un manteau	des sandales (f.)
un cardigan	un pantalon	un short
un jean	un pull (-over)	un sweat-shirt

PREMIERE ETAPE   *deux cent soixante et un*   **261**

RESOURCES FOR PREMIERE ETAPE

PRINT
- *Lesson Planner,* p. 49
- *Practice and Activity Book,* pp. 110–112
- *Grammar and Vocabulary Workbook,* pp. 79–81
- *Activities for Communication,* pp. 55–56, 120, 123–124, 155–156
- *Listening Activities,* pp. 75, 79
- *Testing Program,* pp. 249–252
- *Alternative Assessment Guide,* p. 41

MEDIA
- *Video Program,* Videocassette 4
  Video Guide, pp. 67–72
- *Videodisc Program,* Videodisc 5, Side B
  Videodisc Guide, pp. 112–113
- *Teaching Transparencies* 10-1, 10-A
- *Interactive CD-ROM Program,* Disc 3
  CD-ROM Teacher's Guide, p. 42
- *Audio Compact Discs*
  Textbook Listening Activities, CD 10, Trs. 3–4
  Additional Listening Activities 10-1, 10-2, CD 10, Trs. 26–27
  Quiz 10-1B, CD 10, Tr. 20

Jump Start!

Have students list three colors they're wearing today.

MOTIVATE

Ask students if they shop alone or with family or friends, whether they pay for or make their own clothes, if they hunt for bargains or for a certain brand, and whether they ask for advice from friends when buying clothes.

TEACH

Presentation

Vocabulaire Present the vocabulary with real clothing items or magazine pictures. Then, ask individuals how much various items in the ads cost. (**Combien coûte la montre noire?**) Next, point to various items of clothing that students are wearing, asking **Qu'est-ce que c'est?** You might also hold up an item or illustration and ask students what other item(s) of clothing they would suggest to go with it.

For Individual Needs

Visual/Kinesthetic Learners
With a permanent marker, draw stick figures on a transparency. Write the names of the items in the **Vocabulaire** on cards and distribute them to students. Then, call on students to draw the item written on the card on one of the figures on the transparency.

For Individual Needs

7 Slower Pace Before playing the recording, have students identify the items in the illustrations. Have them point out the similarities and differences among the three groups. You might want to play the recording twice.

Building on Previous Skills

8 Before students begin, you might review family vocabulary from Chapter 7 by showing *Teaching Transparency 7-A.* Ask questions about the family members. **(Raymond est le père ou la mère d'Isabelle?)** Have students recall the use of **son, sa,** and **ses** as well. This activity might also be written.

9 Have students include colors for the clothing on their lists. They might want to use the phrase **en or** *(gold).*

Reteaching

Adjective agreement Ask students to recall how they form the feminine and the plural of most adjectives. Then, remind them that the last consonant may be doubled before the **-e** is added: **violet(te),** or that the feminine form may be irregular: **blanc(blanche).** Show various clothing articles and have students describe them, including colors. You might also have students write the descriptions on the board to check adjective agreement.

Teaching Suggestion

10 Have students write out this activity. They might use this list as a point of departure for Activity 33 on page 274.

---

7 Ecoute!   See scripts on page 255G.

CD 10 Tr. 3

Listen as Armelle tells her friend about her big shopping trip. Then, choose the illustration that represents her purchases.   c

a.   b.   c.

8 Des cadeaux

Look at the picture and tell what Lise bought for her family.   See answers below.

Elle a acheté... pour...

9 Pas de chance!

On your way to France, the airline lost your luggage. Fortunately, the airline is paying you $500 for new clothes. Make a list of the clothes you'll buy.

D'abord, je vais acheter...

10 La fête

Imagine that you've been invited to a party. Of the clothes you listed in Activity 9, which would you choose to wear? What clothes would you need that aren't on your list?

Language Note

Another term for **un cardigan** is **un gilet.** A sweatsuit is called **un jogging.**

Culture Note

Teenagers and adults in France and Canada don't often wear shorts. In Martinique's warm climate, however, shorts are popular.

Answers

8 Lise a acheté une cravate pour son père, des boucles d'oreilles pour sa mère, une casquette pour son frère, des chaussettes pour sa sœur, un bracelet pour sa grand-mère et une écharpe pour son grand-père.

GRAMMAIRE The verbs **mettre** and **porter**

 p. 111,
Acts. 6–7

 pp. 80–81,
Acts. 4–6

Additional Grammar
Practice, p. R47

mettre *(to put, to put on, to wear)*

Je **mets**	Nous **mettons**
Tu **mets** } un pull.	Vous **mettez** } un pull.
Il/Elle/On **met**	Ils/Elles **mettent**

- **Mets** and **met** are pronounced alike. You don't pronounce the final consonant(s) **ts** and **t**.
- The past participle of **mettre** is **mis**: Elle **a mis** une jupe.
- You can also use the regular **-er** verb **porter** to tell what someone is wearing: Elle **porte** une robe.

11 Qu'est-ce qu'on met pour sortir?

1. met une jupe, une ceinture et un pull. 2. mettent des robes et des chaussures. 3. mets un blouson. 4. mettons des baskets.

1. Pour aller à l'école, Sophie…

2. Pour aller à une boum, elles…

3. Pour aller au café, toi, tu…

4. Pour aller au stade, nous…

12 Qu'est-ce que tu as mis hier?

Ask your partner what he or she wore yesterday and tell what you wore.

De bons conseils Although it's common to feel a little uncomfortable when speaking a new language, the best way to overcome it is to talk and talk and talk. Whenever you answer a question or have a conversation with a partner, try to keep the conversation going as long as possible. Don't worry about making a mistake. The more you think about making mistakes, the less likely you will be to talk.

Language Note

Porter also means *to wear,* but most people prefer to use **mettre** *(to put on, to wear)* in everyday conversation. Caution your students, however, that **mettre** cannot be used to tell what someone is wearing now. **Elle met une jupe** means either *She is putting on a dress,* or *She is going to wear a dress (tonight)*. To say that someone is wearing a dress now, **porter** must be used. (**Elle porte une robe aujourd'hui.**)

Teacher Note

De bons conseils Encourage students to speak French by telling them that native French speakers, just like English speakers, often make errors when they speak. Also, point out that when students speak to their friends in English, they probably concentrate on the message rather than on saying every word correctly.

Grammaire Write the forms of **mettre** on large flashcards and shuffle them. Write the subject pronouns on the board. As you show each card, have students tell you what they think the subject pronouns might be. Have them repeat the subject and verb as you tape the card next to the subject pronoun on the board. Then, bring in magazine photos of boys and girls and ask students **Qu'est-ce qu'il/elle met pour la boum ce soir?** You might also tell students there's a party tonight and ask them what they're going to wear. (**Qu'est-ce que tu mets pour la boum ce soir?**)

Additional Practice

Grammaire Describe what a student is wearing, asking the class **Qui a mis des baskets, un jean et un tee-shirt rouge?** The first person to call out the correct student's name asks the next question. You might also show *Teaching Transparency 10-1* and ask students **Qu'est-ce qu'elles mettent?**

For Individual Needs

11 Auditory Learners Tell students what the people in the pictures are putting on. (**Elle met une jupe.**) Have students write the number of the appropriate illustration.

12 Kinesthetic/Visual Learners As one partner describes a classmate's outfit, the other one draws it, writing in the colors. The first student then checks the drawing for accuracy.

Teaching Suggestion

12 You might suggest that students imagine an original outfit to describe.

Presentation

Comment dit-on... ? Ask individuals for advice on what to wear to a party (à une boum), to school (à l'école), and to a restaurant (au restaurant). Write prompts for their responses on the board. Then, have them ask you for advice.

For videodisc application, see Videodisc Guide.

Language Note

Remind students that the **tu** form of **mettre** retains the final **-s** in the command form since it is not an **-er** verb.

◆ For Individual Needs

14 Visual Learners
Assign a clothing item to each student. Have them draw and color a picture of their assigned item on one side of an index card and write the French word for it on the other side. Distribute the cards to partners and have them ask for and give advice about what to wear with the item.

Mon journal

16 For an additional journal entry suggestion for Chapter 10, see *Practice and Activity Book,* page 154.

CLOSE

To close this **étape**, list various places on the board (à l'école, à un mariage). Have one student ask a second student **Qu'est-ce que je mets pour... ?** The second student gives advice, and then asks a third student what to wear for another occasion. Continue until all students have asked a question.

COMMENT DIT-ON... ?

Asking for and giving advice

To ask for advice:

Je ne sais pas quoi mettre pour aller à la boum. *I don't know what to wear for (to) . . .*

Qu'est-ce que je mets? *What shall I wear?*

P A
p. 112, Acts. 8–9

To give advice:

Pourquoi est-ce que tu ne mets pas ta robe? *Why don't you wear . . . ?*

10-1

Mets ton jean. *Wear . . .*

---

13 Ecoute! See scripts and answers on page 255G.

Are these people asking for or giving advice?

CD 10 Tr. 4

14 Harmonie de couleurs

Ask your partner's advice on what you should wear with the following items. Take turns.

—Qu'est-ce que je mets avec ma jupe noire?
—Pourquoi tu ne mets pas ton pull gris?

1. Avec mon pantalon bleu?
2. Avec ma chemise rouge?
3. Avec mes baskets violettes?
4. Avec mon pull gris?
5. Avec mon short orange?
6. Avec ma veste verte?

15 Qu'est-ce que je mets?

Tell your partner where you'll go and what you'll do during your stay as an exchange student in France. Ask for advice about what you should wear. Then, change roles.

—Pour aller au café, qu'est-ce que je mets?
—Mets un jean et un sweat-shirt.

pour aller à une boum

pour aller au café

pour aller à la plage

pour dîner dans un restaurant élégant

pour jouer au football

pour aller au parc

pour aller au théâtre

pour faire du patin à glace

pour aller au musée

pour faire du ski

16 Mon journal

Write about what you normally wear to school, to parties, to go out with friends, or what you wear to dress up for a special occasion.

ASSESS

Quiz 10-1A, Quiz 10-1B, *Testing Program,* pp. 249–252

Audio CD 10, Tr. 20

Performance Assessment

Have partners write and act out a short conversation between friends who are deciding what to wear to a school party that will include a picnic and dancing.

DEUXIEME ETAPE

 Storytelling Book
pp. 38, 40

Expressing need; inquiring

COMMENT DIT-ON... ?

Expressing need; inquiring

 p. 113, Acts. 10–11

 10-2

 p. 82, Act. 7

The salesperson might ask you:

Vous désirez?

(Est-ce que) je peux vous aider?

May I help you?

To express need, you might answer:

Oui, il me faut un chemisier vert.

Oui, vous avez des chapeaux?

Je cherche quelque chose pour
aller à une boum.
I'm looking for something to . . .

J'aimerais un chemisier **pour aller**
avec ma jupe.
I'd like . . . to go with . . .

Non, merci, je regarde.
No, thanks, I'm just looking.

Je peux l'/les essayer?
Can I try it/them on?

Je peux essayer le/la/l'/les
bleu(e)(s)?
Can I try on the . . . ?

To inquire about prices:

C'est combien,... ?

Ça fait combien?

To ask about sizes, colors, and fabrics:

Vous avez ça en (taille) 36?
Do you have that in (size) . . . ?
en bleu?
en coton? *cotton?*
en jean? *denim?*
en cuir? *leather?*

BONJOUR, J'AIMERAIS UN PANTALON POUR ALLER AVEC MON TEE-SHIRT!

VOUS AVEZ CES CHAUSSURES EN 43?

17 Ecoute! See scripts and answers on page 255G.

Listen and decide whether a customer or salesperson is speaking.

CD 10 Tr. 5

 p. 114, Act. 12

 p. 82, Act. 8

Additional Grammar
Practice, p. R47

NOTE DE GRAMMAIRE

You can use colors and other adjectives as nouns by putting **le, la,** or **les** before them. Change their spelling according to the things they refer to: **le bleu, la bleue** = *the blue one;* **les verts, les vertes** = *the green ones.*

DEUXIEME ETAPE

deux cent soixante-cinq **265**

RESOURCES FOR DEUXIEME ETAPE

PRINT
- *Lesson Planner,* p. 50
- *Practice and Activity Book,* pp. 113–115
- *Grammar and Vocabulary Workbook,* pp. 82–84
- *Activities for Communication,* pp. 57–58, 121, 123–124, 155–156
- *Listening Activities,* pp. 75–76, 80
- *Testing Program,* pp. 253–256
- *Alternative Assessment Guide,* p. 41

MEDIA
- *Video Program,* Videocassette 4
  Video Guide, pp. 67–72
- *Videodisc Program,* Videodisc 5, Side B
  Videodisc Guide, p. 113
- *Teaching Transparency 10-2*
- *Interactive CD-ROM Program,* Disc 3
  CD-ROM Teacher's Guide, p. 42
- *Audio Compact Discs*
  Textbook Listening Activities, CD 10, Trs. 5–6
  Additional Listening Activities 10-3, 10-4, CD 10, Trs. 28–29
  Quiz 10-2B, CD 10, Tr. 21

Jump Start!

Display a picture of an outfit and have students write a description of it.

MOTIVATE

Ask students what they would need to say when shopping for clothes in France. Then, ask them to list appropriate expressions they already know in French. You might also ask students if they have ever worked in a clothing store and, if so, how they addressed their customers.

TEACH

Presentation

Comment dit-on... ? Begin by playing the video for **Chacun ses goûts (Mise en train),** pausing it for students to repeat each of the expressions in **Comment dit-on... ?** as they are used in the video. Then, act as a salesperson and ask students **Je peux vous aider?** Bring in real clothing items or pretend to show them. Criticize the fit and color to encourage students to ask for different sizes and colors. Next, practice clothing and colors by having students describe different items that you point to. (**C'est un sac en cuir. C'est une jupe en jean.**)

For videodisc application, see *Videodisc Guide.*

Teaching Suggestion

Note de grammaire Practice this structure by holding up two items, such as notebooks, which are the same except for the color. Ask individual students to choose the one they prefer. (**Tu aimes mieux le blanc ou le jaune?**)

Teaching Suggestion
18 You might have students write their answers, using C for color, S for size, and P for price.

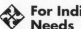 **For Individual Needs**
18 **Challenge** Have students tell the color, price, or size of each item.

19 **Challenge/Visual Learners** Show *Teaching Transparency 10-2*. Have partners write another conversation based on what they see, cut it into strips line by line, and exchange it with another pair. Students should then reassemble the conversation and hand it back to the pair who wrote it to be checked. You might also have them act out the conversation.

21 **Challenge** Have students make their own clothing catalogue. Have them draw items or cut out pictures from magazines. They should label the items and give a price for each in francs or euros. Be sure they give their store a name. You might choose to use this as a chapter project.

18 **Ecoute!**   See scripts and answers on page 255G.

Listen and decide whether these people are talking about the color, price, or size of the items they're looking at.

CD 10 Tr. 6

19 **Méli-mélo!**

Mets cette conversation dans le bon ordre.

6 —C'est combien?

5 —Oui. Nous les avons en bleu, en rouge et en orange.

3 —Voilà, ces maillots de bain sont très chic.

8 —Oh là là! C'est trop cher, ça!

1 —Je peux vous aider?

7 —C'est 450 F.

2 —Oui, je cherche un maillot de bain.

4 —Euh, je n'aime pas trop la couleur. Vous les avez en bleu?

20 **Quelle couleur?**

Blondine and Claire are getting ready for a party. Complete their conversation with **le, la, l',** or **les** and a color.   Answers may vary.

—Et avec ma jupe bleue, est-ce que je mets mon chemisier orange ou mon chemisier blanc?
—Pas l'orange! Mets plutôt __1__.   le blanc
—Et pour les chaussures? __2__ vont mieux avec ma jupe, non?   Les blanches
—Mais non. Mets __3__.   les bleues
—Et mon sac rose ou le noir? Le rose, non?
—Mmm... je n'aime pas __4__. Tu as une ceinture noire?   le rose
—Oui, mais j'ai aussi une ceinture jaune.
—Ah non! Pas la jaune! Mets __5__.   la noire

21 **Préférences**

You and a partner are looking at some clothes in a catalogue. Tell each other which items you like and in which colors.

—J'aime bien ce polo en bleu. Et toi?
—Moi, j'aime mieux le noir.

COLLECTION D'ETE

LES POLOS à 155F

LES JEANS à 245F

blanc

rouge
jaune
bleu

noir

orange

noir

blanc

bleu

266   *deux cent soixante-six*   CHAPITRE 10   Dans un magasin de vêtements

Math Link
21 You might extend this activity by having students add up the cost of their favorite items. You might also have them convert the amounts to dollars or euros.

NOTE CULTURELLE

The French don't use the same clothing sizes as Americans. Look at this size conversion chart to find the size you'd ask for if you were shopping in France.

TABLE DE COMPARAISON DE TAILLES

Robes, chemisiers et pantalons femmes.

France	34	36	38	40	42	44
USA	3	5	7	9	11	13

Chaussures femmes.

France	36	37	38	38½	39	40
USA	5-5½	6-6½	7-7½	8	8½	9

Tricots, pull-overs, pantalons hommes.

France	36	38	40	42	44	46
USA	26	28	30	32	34	36

Chemises hommes.

France	36	37	38	39	40	41
USA	14	14½	15	15½	16	16½

Chaussures hommes.

France	39	40	41	42	43	44
USA	6½-7	7½	8	8½	9-9½	10-10½

22 Jeu de rôle

You need something to go with some of the items below. Tell the salesperson what you need and ask about prices and sizes. Act out this scene with a partner. Then, change roles.

un jean
un blouson en jean
une veste en cuir noir
un pull jaune
un short noir
une chemise en coton

Vocabulaire à la carte

à rayures	striped	en laine	wool
à carreaux	checked	en rayonne	rayon
à pois	polka dot	en lin	linen
à fleurs	flowered	en soie	silk
bleu clair	light blue	bleu foncé	dark blue

GRAMMAIRE -ir verbs

p. 115, Acts. 14–16 | pp. 83–84, Acts. 9–12 | Additional Grammar Practice, p. R48

You've already learned the forms of regular **-er** and **-re** verbs. There is one more regular verb pattern for you to learn. Here are the forms of regular **-ir** verbs.

choisir *(to choose, to pick)*

Je **choisis**
Tu **choisis** } un manteau noir.
Il/Elle/On **choisit**

Nous **choisissons**
Vous **choisissez** } ce jean-là.
Ils/Elles **choisissent**

- The past participle of regular **-ir** verbs ends in **-i**: Elle a choisi une belle robe.
- Other regular **-ir** verbs you might want to use when talking about clothes are: **grandir** *(to grow)*, **maigrir** *(to lose weight)*, and **grossir** *(to gain weight)*.

Math Link

Have students figure out the pattern of conversion from American to French sizes.

Language Notes

Vocabulaire à la carte Point out that **bleu clair** and **bleu foncé** are invariable.

Grammaire Point out that a single **s** between vowels sounds like a *z*, while double **s** sounds like an *s*. Have students practice saying **choisissons**, pronouncing the first **s** like a *z* and the double **s** like an *s*.

Building on Previous Skills

Note Culturelle Re-enter numbers by naming a type of clothing, the gender of the wearer, and an American size. (**chemise, homme, quinze et demi.**) Have students give the corresponding French size. Then, reverse the procedure. You might also have students determine the French equivalents of their own sizes for shirts, shoes, dresses, and pants.

📁 Portfolio

22 Oral This activity is appropriate for students' oral portfolios. For portfolio information, see the *Alternative Assessment Guide,* pages iv–17.

Presentation

Grammaire Write the stem **chois-** on a piece of paper. Then, write each subject pronoun and each of the verb endings on separate pieces of paper. Pass out all of the papers to students in the class. The student who receives the paper with **chois-** on it should come to the front of the class and remain there throughout the activity. As you call out a subject pronoun and the corresponding verb ending, the student holding the subject pronoun and the student holding the appropriate verb ending should come to the front of the class, displaying their papers on either side of the student with the stem **chois-** to form the correct subject and verb. Then, hold up pictures of two different hats. Ask a student **Quel chapeau est-ce que tu choisis?** When the student responds, ask the class **Quel chapeau est-ce que Pierre a choisi?** Continue with pictures of different clothing items.

Additional Practice

23 Have partners ask and tell each other what they would choose. For example, one student says **Elle choisit les chaussures rouges** and asks **Et toi?** The other answers **Moi, je choisis...** and tells which shoes he or she would wear with the outfit. Students might suggest an item not shown in the illustration. They might also use the past tense or the future with **aller**.

Additional Practice

Show pictures of a baby, Santa Claus, and a stick figure. Ask students **Qu'est-ce qu'ils doivent** (should) **faire?** (grandir, maigrir, grossir) You might write **grandir, grossir,** and **maigrir** on the board and ask students to come up and write the different verb forms.

CLOSE

🏰 **Game**

C'EST QUI? Have one student name an item of clothing, including the color, that someone in the room is wearing. Then, the others try to guess the student's identity. If they have difficulty, the student may name a second item the person is wearing. The student who guesses correctly names a clothing item worn by a different student, and so on.

ASSESS

Quiz 10-2A, Quiz 10-2B, *Testing Program,* pp. 253–256
Audio CD 10, Tr. 21

Performance Assessment

Have students perform their skits from Activity 25 with props. The skits may also be done by groups of three.

23 Qu'est-ce qu'ils choisissent?

Qu'est-ce qu'ils choisissent pour aller avec leurs vêtements? See answers below.

1. Elle...   2. Nous...   3. Il...   4. Vous...

24 Ça ne me va plus! 🏠

1. Il a maigri.   2. Ils ont grandi.   3. Il a grossi.   4. Elle a grandi.

Why don't these clothes fit anymore? Remember to use the **passé composé** in your answer.

1.   2.

3.   4.

25 Dans un grand magasin

With a partner, act out a scene in a department store between a customer and salesperson. The customer, who's going on a winter vacation, should tell what he or she is looking for, ask about size, colors, styles, fabrics, and prices, and ask to try things on. The salesperson should respond appropriately. Change roles.

268 *deux cent soixante-huit*   CHAPITRE 10   Dans un magasin de vêtements

Language Note

Point out to students that **un grand magasin** is a large department store, and a smaller shop is called **une boutique** or **un magasin.** You might ask students **Tu préfères les boutiques ou les grands magasins?**

Possible answers

23 1. Elle choisit les chaussures rouges.
   2. Nous choisissons le blouson noir.
   3. Il choisit la cravate rouge.
   4. Vous choisissez le chemisier bleu.

PANORAMA CULTUREL

Marie-Emmanuelle • France

Thomas • France

Aminata • Côte d'Ivoire

VIDEO PROGRAM
Videocassette 4
10:48–13:44

OR **VIDEODISC PROGRAM,**
Videodisc 5, Side B

Search 16950, Play To 18765

We asked some francophone people what they like to wear. Here's what they said.

Qu'est-ce que tu aimes comme vêtements?

CD 10
Trs. 7–10

CD-ROM
Disc 3

«J'aime bien mettre des jeans, des tee-shirts, des affaires simples, mais de temps en temps, j'aime bien être originale et porter des jupes longues, ou euh... quelque chose de plus classique ou plus moderne.»

—Marie-Emmanuelle
Tr. 8

«J'aime les jeans, les chemises, les grosses chaussures et les casquettes aussi.»

—Thomas
Tr. 9

«J'adore beaucoup les jupes droites, les robes, les pagnes. J'aime beaucoup me mettre aussi en tissu.»

—Aminata
Tr. 10

Qu'en penses-tu?

1. How do you and your friends like to dress? How is this different from the way these people like to dress?
2. Which of these people share your tastes in clothing?

Savais-tu que...?

In France and other francophone countries, it is common to see people dressed quite well on the streets, on trains, at work, and in restaurants, even fast-food restaurants. In Africa, women commonly drape themselves in brightly-colored fabrics called **pagnes**. Martinique is famous for its **madras** patterns, and southern France is known for its pretty **provençal** prints. Although Paris has the reputation of being a fashion capital, ordinary Parisians don't wear fashions created by well-known designers. Most young people like to wear jeans, just like American teenagers.

Teacher Notes

- See the *Video Guide*, the *Videodisc Guide*, and the *CD-ROM Teacher's Guide* for activities related to the **Panorama Culturel**.
- Remind students that cultural material may be included in the Chapter Quizzes and Test.
- The interviewees' language represents informal, unrehearsed speech. Occasionally, edits have been made for clarification.

Motivating Activity

Ask students to describe their favorite outfit. Ask what is important when choosing clothes (color, comfort, style, fabric, cost).

Presentation

Have students write the interviewees' names at the top of three columns on a sheet of paper. Tell them to listen for and write down two things that each person likes to wear. Then, play the video. You might compile a complete list on a transparency and have students check their answers.

For Individual Needs

Visual Learners Draw or hold up the items of clothing mentioned in the interviews and have students tell which of the teenagers mentioned each article of clothing.

Questions

1. Qu'est-ce que Marie-Emmanuelle aime mettre comme vêtements? (des jeans, des tee-shirts, des jupes longues)
2. Comment sont les vêtements qu'elle préfère? (simples, classiques, modernes)
3. Thomas aime quelles sortes de vêtements? (les jeans, les chemises, les grosses chaussures et les casquettes)
4. Aminata adore quelles sortes de vêtements? (les jupes droites, les robes, les pagnes) En quoi est-ce qu'elle aime se mettre? (en tissu)

Culture Note

Tell students that **madras** is a brightly colored plaid fabric commonly worn in Martinique. See Photo 4 on page 309. A **pagne** is a length of cloth that African women wrap around their waist to make a skirt.

TROISIEME ETAPE

Storytelling Book
pp. 39, 40

Asking for an opinion; paying a compliment; criticizing; hesitating; making a decision

COMMENT DIT-ON... ?

pp. 116–117, Acts. 17–19 · 10-3 · pp. 85–86, Acts. 13–15

Asking for an opinion, paying a compliment, and criticizing

To ask for an opinion:
Comment tu trouves... ?
Elle me va, cette robe?
  Does . . . suit me?
Il te/vous plaît, ce jean?
  Do you like . . . ?
Tu aimes mieux le bleu **ou** le noir?

To pay a compliment:
C'est parfait. *It's perfect.*
C'est tout à fait ton/ votre style. *It looks great on you!*
Elle te/vous va très bien, cette jupe.
  . . . suits you really well.
Il/Elle va très bien avec ta chemise. *It goes very well with . . .*
Je le/la/les trouve... *I think it's/they're . . .*
    très à la mode. *in style.*
    chic.
    mignon(mignonne)(s). *cute.*
    sensationnel(le)/sensas. *fantastic.*
    rétro.

To criticize:
Il/Elle ne te/vous va pas du tout. *That doesn't look good on you at all.*
Il/Elle est (Ils/Elles sont) trop serré(e)(s). *It's/They're too tight.*
    large(s). *baggy.*
    petit(e)(s). *small.*
    grand(e)(s). *big.*
    court(e)(s). *short.*
    long(longue)(s). *long.*
Il/Elle ne va pas du tout avec tes chaussures. *That doesn't go at all with . . .*
Je le/la/les trouve moche(s). *I think it's/they're tacky.*
    démodé(e)(s). *out of style.*
    horrible(s). *terrible.*

26 Ecoute! See scripts and answers on page 255H.

Listen to the following conversations and decide if the speakers are complimenting or criticizing each other's clothing.

CD 10 Tr. 11

27 Un après-midi au grand magasin

You and a friend are spending the afternoon shopping at **Le Printemps.** If these people asked you for advice, what would you say? See answers below.

28 Sondage

Complete this survey from a French fashion magazine. How many points did you get? Which category do you fall into? Compare your answers with your partner's.

ENQUETE: LA MODE

Es-tu à la mode?

Fais notre petit test pour savoir si tu es vraiment à la dernière mode.

En général, quelle sorte de vêtements est-ce que tu portes?
a. Des vêtements super chic. (3 points)
b. Ça dépend de l'occasion. (2 points)
c. Des jeans, des tee-shirts et des baskets. (1 point)

Tu achètes de nouveaux vêtements...
a. très souvent. (3 points)
b. quelquefois. (2 points)
c. presque jamais. (1 point)

Quand tu achètes des vêtements, en général, tu...
a. achètes ce qui est à la dernière mode. (3 points)
b. achètes quelque chose que tu aimes. (2 points)
c. achètes ce qui est en solde. (1 point)

Dans un magazine de mode, tu vois que les chemises en plastique fluorescentes sont très populaires. Tu...
a. achètes 4 chemises de 4 couleurs différentes. (3 points)
b. attends patiemment pour voir si les autres en portent. (2 points)
c. refuses d'en acheter! Tu ne veux pas être ridicule! (1 point)

Réponses :
10 -12 points : Tu es vraiment à la mode! Attention! Tu risques de perdre ton originalité.
5 - 9 points : Parfaitement raisonnable! Tu es à la mode tout en gardant ton propre style.
0 - 4 points : Tu ne t'intéresses pas à la mode! Tu sais, il y a quelquefois des styles uniques. Essaie de les trouver.

NE PRENDS PAS CE TEST TROP AU SERIEUX!

Possible answers
27 Ce pantalon bleu est trop court. Cette chemise bleue est trop serrée. Ce pantalon noir est trop long. Ce pantalon rouge est trop large et trop long.

Teacher Note
27 Le Printemps is a major French department store.

Teaching Suggestion
26 Have students write a plus sign to indicate a compliment and a minus sign to indicate criticism. You might also ask them to write the key words that support their answers: **démodé(e), super chic, trop serré(e),** and so on.

Group Work
27 Have groups of three students act out the scene. One is trying on the clothes, the friend offers criticism, and the salesperson offers compliments and help finding different colors and sizes.

Teaching Suggestions
28 Before students complete the survey, have them guess what the following words mean from context: **la dernière mode** *(the latest fashion),* and **en solde** *(on sale).* You might also have them read the descriptions under **Réponses** in the right-hand column and try to guess which description fits them.

28 Have students hand in their results anonymously and have a few volunteers compile them to find out which styles are most common in the class.

For Individual Needs
28 Challenge Have groups create their own three- or four-question fashion survey and administer it to the class.

Motivating Activity

Ask students when they might compliment someone and what they would say. Ask how they respond to compliments. You might have two students role-play a scene in English in which one compliments an item of clothing and the other responds.

Presentation

Have two students read each dialogue for the class. Then, ask students the first question in **Qu'en penses-tu?** Next, have partners act out one of the dialogues. You might have volunteers perform their dialogue for the class.

Additional Practice

Have partners pay each other compliments and respond in French.

For Individual Needs

Visual Learners   Have students draw their own scenes, illustrating a situation in which one person is paying a compliment and the other person is responding. Have them write the French dialogue in speech bubbles. This item would be appropriate for students' written portfolios.

Thinking Critically

Analyzing   Have students read **Savais-tu que... ?** and give possible reasons why the French don't pay compliments freely. Ask them how they think the French might view people from other cultures who pay compliments frequently and why.

RENCONTRE CULTURELLE

Read the following dialogues to find out how French people compliment one another.

—J'aime bien ta chemise.
—Ah oui?
—Oui, elle est pas mal.
—Tu trouves? Tu sais, c'est une vieille chemise.

—Il est super, ce chapeau!
—Tu crois?
—Oui, il te va très bien.
—C'est gentil.

—Tu es ravissante aujourd'hui!
—Vraiment? Je n'ai rien fait de spécial.

Qu'en penses-tu?

1. How do these people react to a compliment?   *They downplay the compliment.*
2. How do you usually react to a compliment? How is that different from the French reactions you've just read?   *Answers will vary; Americans often say thank you, while the French tend to downplay compliments.*

Savais-tu que...?

The French do not compliment freely and generally do so only in exceptional cases. It is common to respond to compliments with **Merci.** However, French people will often respond with a modest expression of disbelief, such as **Vraiment? Tu crois? Tu trouves? Ah oui?** or a comment downplaying the importance of the item complimented, such as **Oh, c'est vieux.**

Multicultural Link

You might have students interview people from different cultures or people who have studied other cultures to find out acceptable ways to pay and accept compliments in those cultures. Discuss their findings in class.

Culture Note

In West Africa, it is wise to use caution when paying compliments. Normally, when someone compliments you on what you are wearing or on something you own, you are expected to offer it to that person. Likewise, when you compliment someone on something, he or she will often offer it to you, even if it is the last shirt a man owns or a woman's favorite earrings.

29 Fais des compliments!

Compliment two things that your partner is wearing. He or she should respond in the French way.

> —Elles sont sensas, tes baskets!
> —Vraiment?
> —Oui, elles sont très à la mode!

GRAMMAIRE The direct object pronouns le, la, and les

The pronouns **le,** *him* or *it*, **la,** *her* or *it*, and **les,** *them*, refer to people or things. In the sentences below, what do the pronouns **le, la,** and **les** refer to?*

> — Ce pull, il te plaît?   — Oui, je **le** trouve assez chic.
> — Comment tu trouves cette   — Je **la** trouve démodée.
>   robe?
> — Vous aimez ces chaussures?   — Oui, je vais **les** prendre.

 p. 117, Act. 21

- You normally place the direct object pronouns before the conjugated verb.
  Je **le** prends.   Je **l'**ai pris.
  Je ne **la** prends pas.   Ne **les** prends pas!

pp. 86–87, Acts. 16–17

- There are two exceptions to this rule. You place the direct object pronoun after the conjugated verb in a positive command and before an infinitive. Additional Grammar Practice, pp. R48–R49
  Prends-**le!**
  Je vais **la** prendre.

- When **le** or **la** comes before a verb that starts with a vowel sound, it changes to **l'**.
  Je vais essayer **le pull.** Je vais **l'**essayer.

30 Qu'en penses-tu?

Elise and Karim are shopping for clothes. Complete their conversation, using **le, la, l',** and **les.**

ELISE	Dis, Karim, tu aimes ce pantalon, toi?
KARIM	Bof... Je __1__ trouve un peu démodé, mais enfin... le
ELISE	Et cette chemise-là?
KARIM	Oui, je __2__ aime bien. Eh! Tu as vu ces chaussures? Elles sont l' super, non?
ELISE	Oui! Tu vas __3__ prendre? les
KARIM	Oh, je sais pas...
ELISE	Si, allez! Prends- __4__ ! les
KARIM	Bon. Je vais __5__ essayer. Et toi, essaie la chemise. Je __6__ les, la trouve vraiment chouette.
ELISE	D'accord. Mmm... et ce pull violet, il est beau, non?
KARIM	Oui, mais je __7__ préfère en bleu. le

* the pullover, the dress, the shoes

Portfolio

29 Oral This item is appropriate for students' oral portfolios. For portfolio information, see the *Alternative Assessment Guide,* pages iv–17.

For Individual Needs

29 Kinesthetic Learners
Have students bring in clothing items and arrange them around the classroom, simulating departments of a clothing store. Have students pair off and walk around the room to shop and compliment each other on the items they select.

Presentation

Grammaire Bring to class the following items or pictures of them: a sweater, a dress, and a pair of shoes. Show each item, ask **Qu'est-ce que c'est?** and write the responses on the board. Then, ask the question **Ce pull (cette robe, ces chaussures), comment tu le/la/les trouves?** as you hold up each item. Model the answers **Je le/la/les trouve...** Then, ask individual students how they like each item. Continue with additional items or illustrations. Read the grammar explanation. Then, pretend to be a salesperson and ask individuals **Tu prends ce pull (cette robe, ces chaussures)?** Have students answer **Oui, je le/la/les prends** or **Non,...**

Motivating Activity

Ask students if they ever have difficulty deciding whether or not to buy something and why.

Presentation

Comment dit-on... ? Write the expressions for *hesitating* and *making a decision* on a transparency. Then, hold up various clothing items or pictures of them. Give a price for each and ask students **Vous le/la/les prenez?** Make some prices outrageously high (6.000 F for a pair of socks) and some unbelievably low (2 F for a dress).

For Individual Needs

Visual Learners Write **Je le/la/les prends** or **C'est trop cher** on cards for each student. Then, give a card and a picture of an item of clothing to pairs of students. Have them act out the dialogues suggested by their cards.

Additional Practice

Note de grammaire Write the following sentences on the board or on a transparency and have students complete them: ____ est trop serrée, cette robe. On n'a pas école demain. ____ est génial! Tu aimes ce pantalon? ____ est chic, n'est-ce pas? J'aime parler au téléphone parce que ____ est agréable.

31 Type the listening script with some of the words deleted. Make copies and have partners fill in the blanks.

COMMENT DIT-ON... ?

Hesitating; making a decision

When the salesperson asks you:
Vous avez choisi?
Vous avez décidé de prendre ce pantalon? *Have you decided to take . . . ?*
Vous le/la/les prenez? *Are you going to take it/them?*

p. 128, Act. 22

To hesitate, say:
Je ne sais pas.
Euh... J'hésite.
Oh, I'm not sure.
Il/Elle me plaît, mais il/elle est cher/chère.
I like it, but it's expensive.

10-3

To make a decision, say:
Je le/la/les prends.
I'll take it/them.
C'est trop cher.
It's too expensive.

NOTE DE GRAMMAIRE

- Use **il/elle/ils/elles** when you are referring to a specific item. Comment tu trouves cette robe? **Elle** est chouette, non?

- Use **c'est** when you are speaking in general about an action or something that happened. J'aime porter des pantalons parce que **c'est** pratique. J'ai réussi à mon examen de maths! **C'est** super!

p. 118, Act. 23

p. 87, Act. 18

In the sentences above, **c'est** refers to the general ideas of wearing pants and passing a test.

Additional Grammar Practice, p. R49

---

31 **Ecoute!** See scripts and answers on page 255H.

CD 10 Tr. 12

Listen to these exchanges between a customer and a salesperson. Tell whether the customer takes the item, doesn't take it, or can't decide.

---

32 **Qu'est-ce qu'ils disent?**

Write down what you think these people are saying. Then, get together with a partner and compare what you both have written.

1.   2.   3.   4.

---

33 **J'hésite**

You're shopping for something new to wear to a party. The salesperson helps you find something. You're unsure, but your friend offers you advice. Take turns.

For Individual Needs

32 **Kinesthetic Learners** Have partners act out their conversation. The first person to guess which illustration they're dramatizing acts out his or her conversation with a partner.

32 **Auditory Learners** Collect the conversations students wrote and read one scene aloud. Have students write the number of the corresponding illustration.

Portfolio

33 **Oral** This activity is appropriate for students' oral portfolios. For portfolio information, see the *Alternative Assessment Guide*, pages iv–17.

The glides [j], [w], and [ɥ]   See scripts and answers on page 255H.

CD 10 Trs. 13–18

As you listen to people speak French, you may notice a sound that reminds you of the first sound in the English word *yes*. This sound is called a *glide*, because one sound glides into another. Now, try making the sound [j] in these common French words: **mieux, chemisier, bien.** Did you notice that this gliding sound often occurs when the letter **i** is followed by **e**? The sound is also represented by the letters **ill** in words such as **maillot** and **gentille.**

There are two more glides in French. [w] sounds similar to the *w* sound you hear in *west wind.* Listen to these French words: **moi, Louis, jouer.**

The last glide sound is the one you hear in the French word **lui.** It sounds like the French vowel sounds [y] and [i] together. This sound is often written as **ui.** Listen to the glide [ɥ] in these words: **cuir, huit, juillet.**

A. A prononcer

Repeat the following words.

1. travailler	monsieur	combien	conseiller
2. pouvoir	soif	poires	moins
3. suis	minuit	suite	juillet

B. A lire

Take turns with a partner reading each of the following sentences aloud.

1. J'aime bien tes boucles d'oreilles. Elles sont géniales!
2. Il me faut des feuilles de papier, un taille-crayon et un cahier.
3. Elle a choisi un blouson en cuir et une écharpe en soie. C'est chouette!
4. Tu as quoi aujourd'hui? Moi, j'ai histoire et ensuite, je vais faire mes devoirs.
5. —Tu veux promener le chien avec moi?
   —Pourquoi pas?

C. A écrire

You're going to hear a short dialogue. Write down what you hear.

Slower Pace   Have students begin by breaking the sentences in Part B into three- or four-word phrases, and work up to saying entire sentences.

Teaching Suggestion

Show *Teaching Transparency 10-3* and have students suggest what the customers and salespeople might be saying. You might have partners write a brief dialogue between a customer and a salesperson.

CLOSE

To close this **étape,** have partners ask and respond to the following questions:

1. **Comment tu trouves les jeans courts?**
2. **Qu'est-ce que tu as mis hier?**
3. **Qu'est-ce que tu mets pour aller à une fête?**

ASSESS

Quiz 10-3A, Quiz 10-3B, *Testing Program,* pp. 257–260

Audio CD 10, Tr. 22

Performance Assessment

Have students bring in a picture of an outfit from a magazine. Have them work in groups of three, with one person acting as the salesperson and the other two as friends. The friends ask for and give their opinions of each other's outfits and compliment or criticize the outfits. The salesperson offers help and compliments. Have students take turns playing the role of the salesperson.

Language Note

Prononciation   Make sure students don't split the glides into two separate syllables.

Teacher Note

For an additional reading, see *Practice and Activity Book*, page 119.

Motivating Activity

Ask students why they think fashion is important to some people and not to others. Have them look at the photos and tell what they can guess about the personalities of these people based on their clothing.

PREREADING
Activities A–C

Teaching Suggestion

A., B. Have students answer the questions in these activities in small groups.

◆ For Individual Needs

B. Kinesthetic/Visual Learners Provide large sheets of paper and have students draw the styles pictured and write their opinions of them.

Thinking Critically

Comparing and Contrasting
Have students compare present styles with those of the past and discuss the differences.

READING
Activities D–H

Teaching Suggestion

D. Have students suggest words or phrases in French that teenagers might say if they consider fashion important and if they consider it unimportant. (**C'est cool; C'est nul.**)

LISONS!

How important is fashion to you? Do you generally favor one style or do you like to vary the look of what you wear?

DE BONS CONSEILS

When you read, be careful to separate facts from opinions. A fact is something that can be proven by observation or specific information. **Le jean est rouge** is a fact that you could prove by looking at the jeans to see if they're red or not. An opinion is someone's personal view of something. **La mode, c'est important** is an opinion. While some people may believe that to be true, it cannot be proven.

A. Think for a moment about the role fashion plays in your life.

1. Do you follow trends you see in magazines or at school?
2. How much influence do your parents have on your wardrobe?
3. Do you think clothing is a reflection of a person's personality or lifestyle?

B. How would you categorize styles that are popular at your school or in your town? What words would you use to describe them?

C. What can you tell about the people who wrote these essays?
Answers will vary.

D. Which of the students consider fashion important? Which consider it unimportant? Answers will vary.

LA MODE AU LYCÉE

Mélanie

• 15 ans. En seconde au lycée Théodore Aubanel, Avignon.

Ce que je trouve dommage aujourd'hui, c'est que les filles ressemblent de plus en plus à des garçons. Au lycée, presque toutes mes copines portent des jeans ou des pantalons avec des sweat-shirts. Moi aussi, j'aime bien les jeans, mais de temps en temps, je préfère m'habiller «en fille» avec des robes ou des jupes. Je porte aussi beaucoup de bijoux, surtout des boucles d'oreilles; j'adore ça. Et puis en même temps, ça fait plaisir à mes parents quand je suis habillée comme ça; ils préfèrent ça au look garçon manqué.

Christophe

• 17 ans. En terminale au lycée Henri IV, Paris.

Moi, ce qui m'énerve avec la mode, c'est que si tu ne la suis pas, tout le monde te regarde d'un air bizarre au lycée. Moi, par exemple, le retour de la mode des années 70, les pattes d'eph et le look grunge, c'est vraiment pas mon truc. Je trouve ça horrible. Alors, je ne vois pas pourquoi je devrais m'habiller comme ça, simplement parce que c'est la mode. Je préfère porter des pantalons à pinces, des blazers et des chemises avec des cravates. Mes copains trouvent que ça fait trop sérieux, trop fils-à-papa, mais ça m'est égal. Je suis sûr que dans quelques années, quand ils travailleront, ils seront tous habillés comme moi et quand ils regarderont des photos de terminale, ils rigoleront bien en voyant les habits qu'ils portaient à 18 ans!

Terms in Lisons!

Some useful expressions that you might write on the board or on a transparency are **ce qui m'énerve** *(what annoys me)*; **fabriquer** *(to make)*; **un foulard** *(a decorative scarf)*.

Serge

- 16 ans. En première au lycée Ampère de Lyon.

Pour moi, ce qui est vraiment important, c'est d'avoir des vêtements confortables. Je suis très sportif et j'aime pouvoir bouger dans mes habits. Mais, je veux aussi des trucs cool. Pas question de porter des vêtements très serrés ou très chers, par exemple. Je ne vois pas l'intérêt d'avoir un blouson qui coûte 4 000 F. Je préfère un blouson bon marché dans lequel je peux jouer au foot avec les copains. Comme ça, si je tombe ou si je l'abîme, c'est pas tragique. En général, je mets des jeans parce que c'est pratique et sympa. En été, je porte des tee-shirts très simples et en hiver, des sweat-shirts. Et comme chaussures, je préfère les baskets.

Emmanuelle

- 17 ans et demi. Lycée Mas de Tesse, Montpellier.

Pour moi, la façon dont quelqu'un s'habille est un reflet de sa personnalité. Au lycée, j'étudie les arts plastiques, et comme on le dit souvent, les artistes sont des gens originaux et créatifs. Je n'aime pas dépenser beaucoup pour mes vêtements. Je n'achète jamais de choses très chères, mais j'utilise mon imagination pour les rendre plus originales. Par exemple, j'ajoute toujours des accessoires sympa : bijoux fantaisie que je fabrique souvent moi-même, foulards, ceintures, sacs... Parfois, je fais même certains de mes vêtements, surtout les jupes car c'est facile. Et comme ça, je suis sûre que personne ne portera la même chose que moi!

E. Although many people consider France a fashion capital, the U.S. also influences fashion. What English words can you find in the essays? See answers below.

F. Look for the words in the box below in the essays. Then, try to match them with their English equivalents.

1. bijoux d		a. fashion
2. la mode a		b. things
3. pattes d'eph f		c. ruin
4. bouger e		d. jewelry
5. abîme c		e. to move
6. les trucs b		f. bell-bottoms

G. Which student . . .

1. likes clothes that are practical and comfortable? Serge
2. makes some of his or her clothing and jewelry? Emmanuelle
3. doesn't buy expensive clothes? Serge, Emmanuelle
4. thinks girls should wear feminine clothes sometimes? Mélanie

H. Which of the following sentences are facts and which are opinions?

1. En été, je porte des tee-shirts. fact
2. Les artistes sont des gens originaux et créatifs. opinion
3. Les filles ressemblent de plus en plus à des garçons. opinion
4. Je n'achète jamais de choses très chères. fact
5. La façon dont on s'habille est un reflet de sa personnalité. opinion

I. Write a short paragraph in French telling what you like to wear. Mention colors and any other details you feel are important.

deux cent soixante-dix-sept 277

Teaching Suggestions

H. Have students give their reactions to each of these statements. If they disagree, have them tell why.

H. Have students write two sentences, one fact and one opinion. You might have them form groups to compile their statements and determine whether they are labeled accurately. Then, have the groups turn in their statements.

Thinking Critically

Analyzing Have students discuss their reactions to the reading. Would these teenagers fit in at their school? Why or why not? Do students agree or disagree with the attitudes expressed in the interviews?

POSTREADING
Activity I

📁 Portfolio

I. Written Students may want to add a drawing of themselves to illustrate their paragraphs. Have them use pictures from magazines to make a collage that illustrates their sense of fashion. This activity is appropriate for students' written portfolios. For portfolio information, see the *Alternative Assessment Guide,* pages iv–17.

♜ Game

C'EST QUI? In small groups, one student names an item worn by one of the teenagers or quotes from one of the essays. The other students try to identify the person. The student who guesses correctly takes the next turn.

The **Mise en pratique** reviews and integrates all four skills and culture in preparation for the Chapter Test.

Teaching Suggestions

1 Tell students to read the questions before they listen to the recording. Encourage them to listen to the entire conversation before they write their answers. Then, play the recording again so students can check their work or complete the activity.

Additional Practice

2 Have students give the price and color of each clothing item in the ad. You might assign each item to a group of students. Have them note the sizes and colors it is available in, the price, and the fabric. Since most of the colors in the ad are cognates, encourage students to guess what the colors might be.

For Individual Needs

2 Challenge Have students create an ad for an article of clothing they're wearing or for a favorite article of clothing, using this ad as a model.

MISE EN PRATIQUE

CD-ROM
Disc 3

The *CD-ROM Program* offers guided recording and writing activities to practice oral and written skills and to review material from each chapter.

1 Listen to this conversation between Philippe and a saleswoman at a French department store. Then, answer these questions. See scripts and answers on page 255H.

CD 10 Tr. 19

1. What does Philippe want to buy?
2. What colors does he prefer?
3. What does the salesperson say about the first item Philippe tries on?
4. How does Philippe feel about the way the item fits?
5. Does he end up buying it?

2 Look over the advertisement below. Then, answer the questions that follow.

NOUVELLE COLLECTION ARIELLE DE LA BRETTINIERE

FEMME : Pantalon à pinces uni, 100 % soie. Du 36 au 44, **399 F**. Existe en vert, bleu, rouge, blanc et noir. **Cardigan** en coton, taille unique, **299 F**. Existe en noir et blanc cassé. **Tee-shirt** cache-cœur noir, manches courtes, **129 F**. **Boucles d'oreilles** et **bracelet** fantaisie, **45 F** et **65 F**. **ENFANT : Robe** bleu clair à fleurs multicolores, 100 % coton. Du 2 au 8 ans, **79 F**. **Tee-shirt** uni rose, 100 % coton, **29 F**. Du 2 au 8 ans. Existe en 17 coloris. **Sandales** en cuir blanc, **119 F**. Du 24 au 34. **HOMME : Pantalon** à pinces, 100 % lin. Du 38 au 52, **439 F**. Existe en noir, bleu marine, beige et marron. **Chemise** en jean, manches longues. Du 2 au 6, **259 F**. **Pull** rouge, 100 % coton. Du 2 au 6, **299 F**.

VENDUE DANS LES GRANDS MAGASINS

1. Who does **Arielle de la Brettinière** make clothes for? men, women, and children
2. How many colors does the child's T-shirt come in? 17
3. The women's pants are available in what sizes? 36 to 44
4. What material is the men's shirt made of? denim
5. What's the most expensive men's item on the page? The most expensive women's item? *Most expensive:* men's pants, 439 F; women's pants, 399 F

3 From what you know about French culture, are these statements true or false?

1. The French are famous for giving lots of compliments. false
2. The French tend to downplay the compliments they receive. true
3. **Merci** is the only appropriate way to respond to a compliment. false
4. A common French way to respond to a compliment on something you're wearing is to say **Tu trouves?** true

278 *deux cent soixante-dix-huit* CHAPITRE 10 Dans un magasin de vêtements

Career Path

The fashion industry is international. Photo shoots and fashion shows take place in many locations around the world. Ask students to name some international designers and some cities that they associate with the fashion industry. To help students think of fashion designers, you might clip out pages from men's and women's fashion magazines showing names and clothing of international designers. Ask students which languages would be useful if they were to work in the fashion industry.

4 *Écrivons!*

You've been hired by a French magazine to write about fashion trends among American teenagers today. Interview two or three classmates about their tastes in clothing. Then, write a short article in French based on your interviews.

STRATEGIE

Paraphrasing is a useful tool for organizing and simplifying information for your readers. To paraphrase a quote or other piece of information you collect, you state the main points in your own words. At the same time, be sure you don't change the meaning of what was said.

Prewriting

First, brainstorm a list of interview questions that you might ask your classmates about their fashion preferences. You might ask what they like to wear, what they wear to parties (**les boums**), what colors they like, and what their favorite article of clothing is. Arrange your questions in a logical order. You may want to arrange them so that you begin with more general questions and progress to more specific ones.

Next, conduct your interview with two or three classmates. Be sure to take notes on their responses to each of your questions.

Before you begin your article, rearrange the information you've collected into a logical order. For example, you might group different answers to each question together.

Writing

Expository writing is a process of converting information you've collected into a readable or easily understandable form. Newspaper and magazine articles are good examples of expository writing. Reporters collect information on newsworthy events, fashion trends, etc., and then take that information and turn it into articles that readers can easily understand.

Now, referring to the information you've collected and organized, write a short article that reveals what you found out. It's not necessary to include every detail of the information you collect. For example, if a quote from your interview is too long, you may paraphrase the main points of the quote in your own words.

Revising

Peer evaluation is another helpful step in the evaluation process. Give your article to a classmate and have him or her give you suggestions on how to improve it. After your classmate evaluates your article, make any revisions you feel are necessary, including those you find in proofreading. Now you're ready to submit your finished article.

5

JEU DE ROLE

Choose one of the items from the advertisement on page 278 and ask the salesperson about it. Do they have it in your size? Can you try it on? The salesperson should compliment the way it looks, and you should decide whether to buy it or not. Take turns playing the role of the salesperson.

Process Writing

4 • Give students the following quotes and have the class practice paraphrasing them aloud.

a. "I like to wear skirts and shorts to parties, well, sometimes dresses too. It just depends on the party. Also, I like to wear shorts in the winter sometimes and always in the summer, and on the weekends, I really love to wear them. I love to wear shorts at school too. I like black and red ones the best."

b. "I really don't care what I wear most of the time. I just wear warm clothes in winter and cool clothes in summer, and in the other seasons, it just depends on weather. I just go day by day, you know. And I don't like to shop at the mall, either. I let my mom do it for me."

• You may also want to have students paraphrase the three interviews from the **Panorama Culturel** on page 269.

 Video Wrap-Up

• *VIDEO PROGRAM,*
  Videocassette 4, 01:22–15:18
• *VIDEODISC PROGRAM,*
  Videodisc 5, Side B

At this time, you might want to use the video resources for additional review and enrichment. See *Video Guide* or *Videodisc Guide* for suggestions regarding the following:
• **Chacun ses goûts**
  (Dramatic episode)
• **Panorama Culturel**
  (Interviews)
• **Vidéoclips**
  (Authentic footage)

Captioned Video

As a chapter review, write the conversation from a section of the **Mise en train** and leave out targeted expressions presented in this chapter. Play the video of **Chacun ses goûts** on Videocassette 4 and have students fill in the missing expressions. Then, play the captioned version for **Chacun ses goûts** on Videocassette 5 and have students check their work.

QUE SAIS-JE?

This page is intended to help students prepare for the Chapter Test. It is a brief checklist of the major points covered in the chapter. The students should be reminded that this is only a checklist and does not necessarily include everything that will appear on the test.

Teaching Suggestions

2 To practice the **passé composé**, have students say that their friend wore these clothes to a party yesterday.

6 Ask students what else they might ask a friend when they try on clothing.

9 Remind students to give examples of both positive and negative responses.

Teacher Note

You might want to have students review other forms of **mettre** and **choisir** as well by playing the "Verb Tense Race" described on page 231J.

Can you use what you've learned in this chapter?

Can you ask for and give advice? p. 264

1 How would you ask a friend what you should wear to a party?
Qu'est-ce que je mets pour aller à la boum?

2 How would you advise a friend to wear these clothes, using the verb **mettre?**   See answers below.

1.   2.

Can you express need and inquire? p. 265

3 How would you tell a salesperson . . .

1. that you're just looking?
   Je regarde.
2. what you would like?
   J'aimerais... ; Je cherche...

4 How would you ask a salesperson . . .

1. if you can try something on?
2. if they have what you want in a different size?
   Vous avez ça en... (36)?
3. if they have what you want in a particular color? Vous avez ça en... (rouge)?
4. how much something costs?
   C'est combien? Ça fait combien?

1. Je peux l'/les essayer?
   Je peux essayer le/la/les... ?

5 How would you tell what these people are choosing?   See answers below.

| Charles | Jean-Marc et Farid | Astrid | Delphine et Camille |

Can you ask for an opinion, pay a compliment, and criticize? p. 270

6 If you were shopping with a friend, how would you ask . . .

1. if your friend likes what you have on?   Comment tu trouves... ? Ça te plaît?
2. if something fits?   Ça me va?
3. if it's too short?   Il/Elle est trop court(e)?

7 How would you compliment a friend's clothing? How would you criticize it?   See answers below.

Can you hesitate and make a decision? p. 274

8 How can you express your hesitation?
J'hésite. Je ne sais pas. Ça me plaît, mais c'est cher.

9 How would you tell a salesperson what you've decided to do?
Je le/la/les prends. C'est trop cher.

280   *deux cent quatre-vingts*   CHAPITRE 10   Dans un magasin de vêtements

Answers

2 1. Pourquoi est-ce que tu ne mets pas ton pantalon bleu? Mets ton pantalon bleu.
2. Pourquoi est-ce que tu ne mets pas ton pull? Mets ton pull.

5 1. Charles choisit une veste bleue et verte.
2. Jean-Marc et Farid choisissent un manteau en cuir bleu.
3. Astrid choisit des chaussures en cuir.
4. Delphine et Camille choisissent des chaussettes blanches.

7 *Possible answers*

Complimenting: C'est tout à fait ton style. Il/Elle te va très bien. Il/Elle va très bien avec... ; Je le/la/les trouve chic/à la mode/mignon(ne)(s)/sensas. C'est parfait.

Criticizing: Il/Elle ne te va pas du tout. Il/Elle ne va pas du tout avec... ; Il/Elle est (Ils/Elles sont) trop serré(e)(s)/large(s)/petit(e)(s)/grand(e)(s)/court(e)(s). Je le/la/les trouve moche(s)/démodé(e)(s)/horrible(s).

PREMIERE ETAPE

Clothes

un blouson	*jacket*
des bottes (f.)	*boots*
des boucles d'oreilles (f.)	*earrings*
un bracelet	*bracelet*
un cardigan	*cardigan*
une casquette	*cap*
une ceinture	*belt*
un chapeau	*hat*
des chaussettes (f.)	*socks*
des chaussures (f.)	*shoes*
une chemise	*shirt (men's)*

un chemisier	*shirt (women's)*
une cravate	*tie*
une écharpe	*scarf*
une jupe	*skirt*
des lunettes de soleil (f.)	*sunglasses*
un maillot de bain	*bathing suit*
un manteau	*coat*
un pantalon	*(a pair of) pants*
une robe	*dress*
des sandales (f.)	*sandals*
une veste	*suit jacket, blazer*
des vêtements	*clothes*

Asking for and giving advice

Je ne sais pas quoi mettre pour... *I don't know what to wear for (to) . . .*
Qu'est-ce que je mets? *What shall I wear?*
Pourquoi est-ce que tu ne mets pas... ? *Why don't you wear . . . ?*
Mets... *Wear . . .*
mettre *to put, to put on, to wear*
porter *to wear*

DEUXIEME ETAPE

Expressing need; inquiring

Vous désirez? *What would you like?*
(Est-ce que) je peux vous aider? *May I help you?*
Je cherche quelque chose pour... *I'm looking for something to . . .*
J'aimerais... pour aller avec... *I'd like . . . to go with . . .*

Non, merci, je regarde. *No, thanks, I'm just looking.*
Je peux l'/les essayer? *Can I try it/them on?*
Je peux essayer le/la/les... ? *Can I try on the . . . ?*
Vous avez ça... ? *Do you have that . . . ? (size, fabric, color)*
en taille... ? *in size . . . ?*
en bleu *in blue*

en coton	*cotton*
en jean	*denim*
en cuir	*leather*

Other useful expressions

choisir	*to choose, to pick*
grandir	*to grow*
maigrir	*to lose weight*
grossir	*to gain weight*

TROISIEME ETAPE

Asking for an opinion; paying a compliment; criticizing

Comment tu trouves... ? *How do you like . . . ?*
Il/Elle me va? *Does . . . suit me?*
Il/Elle te/vous plaît? *Do you like it?*
C'est parfait. *It's perfect.*
C'est tout à fait ton style. *It looks great on you!*
Il/Elle te/vous va très bien. *It suits you really well.*
Il/Elle va très bien avec... *It goes very well with . . .*
Il/Elle est (Ils/Elles sont) trop... *It's/They're too . . .*
Je le/la/les trouve... *I think it's/ they're . . .*

très à la mode	*in style*
chic	*chic*
mignon (mignonne) (s)	*cute*
sensationnel (le) (s)/sensas	*fantastic*
rétro	*retro*
serré(e) (s)	*tight*
large (s)	*baggy*
petit(e) (s)	*small*
grand(e) (s)	*big*
court(e) (s)	*short*
long(longue) (s)	*long*
moche(s)	*tacky*
démodé(e) (s)	*out of style*
horrible(s)	*terrible*

Il/Elle ne te/vous va pas du tout. *It doesn't look good on you at all.*

Il/Elle ne va pas du tout avec... *It doesn't go at all with . . .*

Hesitating; making a decision

Vous avez choisi? *Have you decided?*
Vous avez décidé de prendre... ? *Have you decided to take . . . ?*
Vous le/la/les prenez? *Are you taking it/them?*
Je ne sais pas. *I don't know.*
Euh... J'hésite. *Well, I'm not sure.*
Il/Elle me plaît, mais il/elle est cher/chère. *I like it, but it's expensive.*
Je le/la/les prends. *I'll take it/ them.*
C'est trop cher. *It's too expensive.*

VOCABULAIRE *deux cent quatre-vingt-un* **281**

Circumlocution

Have students imagine that they are staying with a French family and that they're looking for a certain item of their clothing they have misplaced. They are having difficulty remembering the French word for the item and are trying to communicate to the host family member what they need. **(On le porte pour nager.)** Have students work with a partner, one playing the role of the exchange student and the other playing the role of the host family member. Then have students change roles.

CHAPTER 10 ASSESSMENT

CHAPTER TEST
• *Testing Program,* pp. 261–266
• *Audio Compact Discs,* Audio CD 10, Tracks 23–25

SPEAKING TEST
• *Testing Program,* p. 347

TEST GENERATOR
 • Chapter 10

ALTERNATIVE ASSESSMENT
Performance Assessment
• You might want to use the **Jeu de Rôle** on page 279 as a cumulative performance assessment activity.
• *Alternative Assessment Guide,* p. 41

Portfolio Assessment
• *Alternative Assessment Guide* Oral: p. 27 Written: p. 27

CD-ROM Assessment
• *Interactive CD-ROM,* Disc 3 A toi de parler A toi d'écrire
• *Alternative Assessment Guide,* p. 55

Game

CONCOURS DE FAMILLE This game is played like Family Feud®. First, group the chapter vocabulary into categories: what you wear every day, what you wear for special occasions, what a salesperson might say, what you might say if something doesn't fit, and so on. Then, divide the class into two or more teams and have a player from each team go to the board. Call out a category. The team whose player first gives an appropriate expression has one minute to list on the board all the words or expressions that fit into that category. Award points for correctly spelled answers. You may play up to a certain number of points or until you have exhausted all the categories.

Chapitre 11 : Vive les vacances!
Chapter Overview

Mise en train pp. 284–286	Bientôt les vacances!

	FUNCTIONS	GRAMMAR	CULTURE	RE-ENTRY
Première étape pp. 287–292	• Inquiring about and sharing future plans, p. 289 • Expressing indecision; expressing wishes, p. 289	• The prepositions **à** and **en**, p. 290	• **Note Culturelle, Colonies de vacances**, p. 288 • **Panorama Culturel**, Annual vacations in France, p. 292	• The verb **aller** + infinitive **(Chapitre 6)** • Asking for advice **(Chapitre 9)** • Making, accepting, and refusing suggestions **(Chapitres 4, 5)** • Telling what you like and what you'd like to do **(Chapitre 3)**
Deuxième étape pp. 293–296	• Reminding; reassuring, p. 293 • Seeing someone off, p. 296	• The **-ir** verbs: **partir, sortir**, and **dormir**, p. 294	• Realia: Itinerary for **Provence**, p. 295	• Clothing **(Chapitre 10)** • The imperative **(Chapitre 5)** • Weather expressions **(Chapitre 4)** • **L'heure officielle (Chapitre 2)**
Troisième étape pp. 297–299	• Asking for and expressing opinions, p. 297 *Review* • Inquiring about and relating past events, p. 297			• The **passé composé (Chapitre 9)** • The verb **vouloir (Chapitre 6)** • Asking for and expressing opinions **(Chapitre 9)**

Prononciation p. 299	Aspirated **h; th, ch**, and **gn** Audio CD 11, Tracks 13–15	**A écrire** (dictation) Audio CD 11, Tracks 16–18
Lisons! pp. 300–301	Tourist information for Provence	**Reading Strategy** Reading for a purpose
Review pp. 302–305	**Mise en pratique**, pp. 302–303 **Ecrivons!** Using connecting words Writing a letter to an exchange student	**Que sais-je?** p. 304 **Vocabulaire**, p. 305

Assessment Options	

Testing Program
• Première étape, Quiz 11-1A, Quiz 11-1B, pp. 275–278
• Deuxième étape, Quiz 11-2A, Quiz 11-2B, pp. 279–282
• Troisième étape, Quiz 11-3A, Quiz 11-3B, pp. 283–286
• Chapter Test, pp. 287–292
• Speaking Test, p. 348

Audio Compact Discs
• Audio CD 11, Tracks 20–25

Interactive CD-ROM Program
• Mise en pratique (A toi de parler, A toi d'écrire)
• *CD-ROM Teacher's Guide*, Assessment Options, p. 48

Alternative Assessment Guide
• Portfolio Assessment, p. 28
• Performance Assessment, p. 42
• CD-ROM Assessment, p. 56

Test Generator
• Chapter 11

PRINT	MEDIA

Pupil's Edition, pp. 282–305

 Audio Compact Discs
- Textbook Listening Activities: Audio CD 11, Tracks 1–19

**Interactive CD-ROM Program
Teacher's Guide,** pp. 45–48

 Interactive CD-ROM Program
- Disc 3

Videodisc Guide
- Teaching Suggestions, pp. 121–125
- Activity Masters, pp. 126–128

 Videodisc Program
- Videodisc 6, Side A

Video Guide
- Teaching Suggestions, pp. 74–75
- Activity Masters, pp. 76–78

 Video Program
- Videocassette 4
- Videocassette 5 (captioned version)

Listening Activities
- Student Response Forms for Textbook Listening Activities, pp. 83–85
- Additional Listening Activities, 11-1 to 11-6, pp. 87–89
- Additional Listening Activities (song), p. 90
- Scripts and Answers, pp. 152–156

 Audio Compact Discs
- Textbook Listening Activities: Audio CD 11, Tracks 1–19
- Additional Listening Activities: Audio CD 11, Tracks 26–32

Teaching Transparencies
- Teaching Transparency Masters 11-1 to 11-3 (Situations) and 11-A to 11-C (Vocabulary)
- Teaching Suggestions 11-1 to 11-3 and 11-A to 11-C

 Teaching Transparencies
- Situations 11-1 to 11-3
- Vocabulary 11-A to 11-C

Testing Program
- Grammar and Vocabulary Quizzes, **Etape** Quizzes, and Chapter Test, pp. 275–292
- Score Sheet, Scripts, and Answers, pp. 293–300

 Audio Compact Discs
- Assessment Items: Audio CD 11, Tracks 20–25

 Test Generator
- Chapter 11

Alternative Assessment Guide
- Portfolio Assessment, p. 28
- Performance Assessment, p. 42
- CD-ROM Assessment, p. 56

 Grammar and Vocabulary Workbook, pp. 88–97

 Practice and Activity Book, pp. 121–132

Activities for Communication
- Communicative Activities, pp. 61–66
- Realia and Teaching Suggestions, pp. 125–129
- Situation Cards, pp. 157–158

Lesson Planner
- Lesson Plan, pp. 53–57

Chapitre 11 : Vive les vacances!
Technology Applications

MISE EN TRAIN, pp. 284–286

Video
• Show *Bientôt les vacances!* For Video Synopsis, Teaching Suggestions, Activity Master, and Scripts, see the *Video Guide* or the *Videodisc Guide.*

Audio
• Play the recording of the **Mise en train** with pauses as students read along. You might have them practice pronunciation by repeating individual sentences after hearing them.

PREMIERE ETAPE, pp. 287–291

Video
• While students watch *Bientôt les vacances!*, have them listen for exchanges that model inquiring about and sharing future plans, expressing indecision and wishes, asking for advice, and making, accepting, and refusing suggestions. See p. 123 of the *Videodisc Guide.*

Audio
• Textbook Listening Activity 6 practices the vocabulary for vacation places and activities.
• Textbook Listening Activities 8 and 13 feature expressions for inquiring about and sharing future plans and expressing wishes and indecision.
• To have students review expressions for inquiring about and sharing future plans, expressing wishes and indecision, and the vocabulary for vacation places and activities, use Additional Listening Activities 11-1 and 11-2.

Transparencies
• Use *Teaching Transparency 11-1* and the Teaching Suggestions to present and practice expressions for inquiring about and sharing vacation plans and expressing indecision and wishes.

• Use *Teaching Transparencies 11-A* and *11-B* and the Teaching Suggestions to present and have students practice the vocabulary for places to go and things to do on vacation.

CD-ROM (Disc 3)
• **Le bon choix** (Activity 1) practices the vocabulary for vacation places and activities.
• For suggestions, see p. 46 of the *CD-ROM Teacher's Guide.*

PANORAMA CULTUREL, p. 292

Video
• Show the interviews. For Video Synopsis, Teaching Suggestions, Activity Master, and Scripts, see the *Video Guide* or the *Videodisc Guide.*

Audio
• Play the **Panorama Culturel** as students read along. Remind students they might not be able to understand everything each person says, but they should deduce global meaning.

Audio
• Have students do the **Panorama Culturel** activity after showing them the video. For suggestions, see p. 47 of the *CD-ROM Teacher's Guide.*

DEUXIEME ETAPE, pp. 293–296

Video
• While students watch *Bientôt les vacances!*, have them listen for exchanges that model reminding, reassuring, and seeing someone off. See p. 124 of the *Videodisc Guide.*

Audio
• Textbook Listening Activity 18 practices the expressions for reminding and reassuring someone.
• Textbook Listening Activity 25 has students recognize expressions for seeing someone off.
• To review the vocabulary for items to take on a trip, and the

expressions for reminding, reassuring and seeing someone off, use Additional Listening Activities 11-3 and 11-4.

Transparencies
• Use *Teaching Transparency 11-C* and the Teaching Suggestions to present and practice the vocabulary for items to take on a trip.
• Use *Teaching Transparency 11-2* and the Teaching Suggestions to have students practice the expressions for reminding, reassuring, and seeing someone off.

CD-ROM (Disc 3)
• To have students practice the vocabulary for items to take on a trip, use **Jeu des paires** (Activity 2).
• **Les mots qui manquent** (Activity 3) targets the verbs **partir**, **sortir**, and **dormir**.
• For suggestions, see p. 46 of the *CD-ROM Teacher's Guide.*

TROISIEME ETAPE, pp. 297–299

Video
• While students watch *Bientôt les vacances!*, have them listen for exchanges that model asking for and expressing opinions and inquiring about and relating past events. See p. 124 of the *Videodisc Guide.*

Audio
• Use Textbook Listening Activity 29 to practice asking for and expressing opinions.
• Additional Listening Activities 11-5 and 11-6 review the expressions for asking for and expressing opinions and inquiring about and relating past events.

Transparencies
• Use *Teaching Transparency 11-3* and the Teaching Suggestions to practice relating past events and asking for and expressing opinions.

CD-ROM (Disc 3)
• In **Le bon choix** (Activity 4), students will respond to statements and questions about vacations.
• **Méli-mélo** (Activity 5) has students unscramble sentences using the **passé composé**.
• **Les mots qui manquent** (Activity 6) has students produce the **passé composé**.
• For suggestions, see p. 47 of the *CD-ROM Teacher's Guide.*

MISE EN PRATIQUE, pp. 302–303

Video
• Replay *Bientôt les vacances!* in its entirety and ask students to listen for the functional expressions presented in the chapter.

CD-ROM (Disc 3)
• In the **En contexte** activity, students talk to a friend about their vacations. Students inquire about future plans, express indecision, ask for and express opinions, and see someone off. See p. 46 of the *CD-ROM Teacher's Guide.*
• Have students practice their writing and speaking skills by doing the **A toi d'écrire** and **A toi de parler** activities. See p. 48 of the *CD-ROM Teacher's Guide.*
• For Assessment Options, see p. 48 of the *CD-ROM Teacher's Guide.*

Test Generator
• Use the Test Generator to create review material for students taking the Chapter Test or to prepare an alternate test.

VIDEOCLIPS

Video
• Show the **Vidéoclips**. For Video Synopsis, Teaching Suggestions, Activity Masters, and Scripts, see the *Video Guide* or the *Videodisc Guide.*

Videodisc Program
Videodisc 6, Side A
Videodisc Guide, pp.119–128

Chapitre 11 : Vive les vacances!
Barcode Directory

MISE EN TRAIN

Barcodes A and B access **Mise en train** and **Mise en train (suite)** in their entirety. Subsequent barcodes show specific segments of *Bientôt les vacances!* The barcode numbers correspond to the scene numbers as they appear on the video.

ETAPES

To practice the grammar, vocabulary, and functions presented in each **étape**, see the barcodes and accompanying suggestions on pages 123–124 of the *Videodisc Guide*.

Bientôt les vacances! **A**
Search 1, Play To 4400

Alors, les copains... **1**
Search 1, Play To 1771

Et en août... **2**
Search 1771, Play To 2137

Et toi, Ahmed,... ? **3**
Search 2137, Play To 2367

Et en août? **4**
Search 2375, Play To 2807

Et toi, Florent? **5**
Search 2807, Play To 3563

Tu peux aller... **6**
Search 3563, Play To 3705

Bon, je dois... **7**
Search 3705, Play To 4400

Bientôt les vacances! (suite) **B**
Search 4400, Play To 17600

MISE EN PRATIQUE

This is additional footage modeling some of the expressions practiced in this chapter. You may want to use it to review the chapter.

Mise en pratique **1**

Search 27180, Play To 31082

Mise en pratique **2**

Search 31082, Play To 32645

PANORAMA CULTUREL

Qu'est-ce que tu fais pendant les vacances?
These barcodes access the three interviews of the **Panorama Culturel** presented in the *Pupil's Edition* as well as additional interviews.

First three interviews **1**
Search 17600, Play To 20340

All interviews **2**
Search 17600, Play To 23566

Sim **3**
Search 18386, Play To 19049

Nicole **4**
Search 19050, Play To 19418

Céline **5**
Search 19419, Play To 20320

Karina **6**
Search 20352, Play To 20900

Sylviane **7**
Search 20901, Play To 21341

Emmanuel **8**
Search 21342, Play To 21868

Viviane **9**
Search 21869, Play To 22205

Thomas **10**
Search 22206, Play To 22434

Céline **11**
Search 22435, Play To 22620

Caroline **12**
Search 22621, Play To 22786

Eva **13**
Search 22787, Play To 22905

Aristide **14**
Search 22906, Play To 23146

Marieke **15**
Search 23147, Play To 23566

VIDEOCLIPS

These are authentic French commercials. You may want to preview them before showing them to students.

TGV Atlantique®:
train service **1**

Search 23566, Play To 25468

SNCF Carte Kiwi®: discount
train travel **2**

Search 25468, Play To 26412

Chapitre 11 : Vive les vacances!
CD-ROM Directory 💿 DISC 3

The following directory lists the *Interactive CD-ROM Program* activities for Chapter 11. For details and suggestions on how to use them, see pages 45–48 of the *CD-ROM Teacher's Guide*.

	GLOBAL TASK		COMMUNICATIVE GOALS	ACTIVITY TYPE
	Vivement les vacances! Students talk to their friend Nathalie about their summer vacation plans.		To use chapter functions, vocabulary, and grammar in a lifelike conversation	**En contexte** *Interactive conversation*

	SUPPORTING ACTIVITIES	PUPIL'S EDITION	COMMUNICATIVE GOALS	ACTIVITY TYPE
Première étape	1. Vocabulaire	p. 287	To identify things to do and places to go on vacation	**Le bon choix** *Multiple choice*
Deuxième étape	2. Vocabulaire	p. 293	To identify items you might need on vacation	**Jeu des paires** *Concentration®*
	3. Grammaire	p. 294	To use the verbs **partir, sortir,** and **dormir**	**Les mots qui manquent** *Tic Tac Toe*
Troisième étape	4. Comment dit-on... ?	pp. 289, 293, 296–297	To identify expressions for reminding and reassuring, inquiring about and sharing future plans, expressing indecision, expressing wishes, seeing someone off, and asking for and expressing opinions	**Le bon choix** *Multiple choice*
	5. Grammaire	p. 298	To sequence sentences containing the **passé composé**	**Méli-mélo** *Sequencing*
	6. Grammaire	p. 298	To produce the **passé composé**	**Les mots qui manquent** *Tic Tac Toe*
Panorama Culturel	Panorama Culturel	p. 292	To listen to and understand native speakers talking about what they do on vacation	**Qu'est-ce que tu fais pendant les vacances?** *Presentation* **Le bon choix** *Multiple choice*

	APPLICATION	PUPIL'S EDITION	COMMUNICATIVE GOALS	ACTIVITY TYPE
Mise en pratique	A toi de parler	pp. 302–303	To create and record a conversation with Madame Dulac about what students did on vacation	*Guided recording*
	A toi d'écrire	pp. 302–303	To create a letter, a note, a conversation, or an advertisement	*Guided writing*

Homework Suggestions

CHAPTER SECTION	PRESENTATION	HOMEWORK OPTIONS
Première étape	**Vocabulaire,** p. 287	Practice and Activity Book, p. 122, Activity 2 Grammar and Vocabulary Workbook, pp. 88–89, 　　Activities 1–4 CD-ROM, Disc 3, Activity 1
	Comment dit-on... ? p. 289	Pupil's Edition, p. 291, Activity 16 Practice and Activity Book, p. 123, Activity 6
	Note de grammaire, p. 290	Pupil's Edition, p. R50, Activities 2–3 Grammar and Vocabulary Workbook, p. 91, Activity 7
Deuxième étape	**Vocabulaire,** p. 293	Practice and Activity Book, p. 125, Activities 10–11 Grammar and Vocabulary Workbook, p. 92, 　　Activities 8–9 CD-ROM, Disc 3, Activity 2
	Comment dit-on... ? p. 293	Practice and Activity Book, p. 126, Activity 13
	Grammaire, p. 294	Pupil's Edition, p. 295, Activity 24; pp. R50–R51, 　　Activities 4–5 Practice and Activity Book, p. 125, Activity 12 Grammar and Vocabulary Workbook, pp. 93–94, 　　Activities 11–12 CD-ROM, Disc 3, Activity 3
	Comment dit-on... ? p. 296	Pupil's Edition, p. 296, Activity 28 Practice and Activity Book, p. 127, Activities 14–16
Troisième étape	**Comment dit-on... ?** p. 297	Practice and Activity Book, pp. 128–129, Activities 17–19 CD-ROM, Disc 3, Activity 4
	Tu te rappelles? p. 298	Pupil's Edition, p. 298, Activity 31; p. R51, Activity 7 Practice and Activity Book, p. 130, Activity 21 Grammar and Vocabulary Workbook, pp. 96–97, 　　Activities 16–18 CD-ROM, Disc 3, Activities 5–6

For Student Response Forms, see *Listening Activities,* pp. 83–85.

Première étape

6 Ecoute! p. 287

1. — Bonjour, Nathalie. Qu'est-ce que tu vas faire pendant tes vacances?
   — Je ne sais pas encore, mais je voudrais aller au bord de la mer et faire du bateau.
   — Eh bien, bonnes vacances.
   — Merci beaucoup.

2. — Alors, Bruno. Qu'est-ce que tu vas faire cet été?
   — Je vais aller à Paris avec mes parents.
   — Ah, c'est génial. Tu aimes Paris, toi?
   — Je n'y suis jamais allé.
   — Tu vas voir, c'est très joli. J'espère qu'il va faire beau.
   — Moi aussi!

3. — Bonjour, Pauline. Où est-ce que tu vas aller en vacances?
   — Au mois de juillet, je vais aller chez mes cousins à La Rochelle.
   — C'est chouette, La Rochelle.
   — Je sais, mais, moi, j'aimerais mieux aller en colonie de vacances avec des copains.
   — Amuse-toi bien quand même.
   — Merci.

4. — Alors, Emile, tu as décidé? Où est-ce que tu vas aller en vacances?
   — Euh, je pense aller à la montagne.
   — Pour faire de la randonnée?
   — Oui, mais c'est cher.
   — Dommage. Tu n'y vas pas alors?
   — Si. J'y vais quand même.
   — Et bien, bonnes vacances.
   — Merci beaucoup.

Answers to Activity 6
1. Nathalie is going boating on the coast.
2. Bruno is going to Paris with his parents.
3. Pauline is going to visit her cousins in La Rochelle.
4. Emile is going hiking in the mountains.

8 Ecoute! p. 289

1. — Qu'est-ce que tu vas faire pendant les vacances, Sabine?
   — Euh, je n'ai rien de prévu. Je voudrais bien aller chez mes grands-parents, mais j'ai envie de travailler aussi.

2. — Dis, Gilbert, où est-ce que tu vas aller pendant les vacances?

— Oh, ça va être super! En juillet, je vais voir mon oncle au Canada, et en août, je vais voyager en Afrique.

3. — Qu'est-ce que tu vas faire cet été, Ariane?
   — Euh, j'hésite. Je voudrais bien aller à la plage, mais je ne sais pas.

4. — Tu vas travailler cet été?
   — Euh, je me demande. Je voudrais bien si je peux trouver du travail. Est-ce qu'il y a du travail à la station-service?

5. — Qu'est-ce que tu vas faire pendant les vacances?
   — Je vais dans un camp de tennis. C'est chouette, hein? On va jouer au tennis trois heures par jour.

Answers to Activity 8
1. undecided   3. undecided   5. definite plans
2. definite plans   4. undecided

13 Ecoute! p. 291

ALAIN Je ne sais pas où aller pendant les vacances. Tu as une idée?

VALÉRIE Tu devrais aller à la Martinique.

ALAIN Ah oui?

VALÉRIE Oui, j'y suis allée plusieurs fois.

ALAIN C'est comment?

VALÉRIE C'est chouette. Il fait toujours beau. Les gens sont très sympa.

ALAIN Qu'est-ce qu'on peut y faire?

VALÉRIE Oh, plein de choses. Il y a des plages superbes. Tu peux y faire de la planche à voile, du bateau, de la plongée. Tu peux aussi visiter Fort-de-France. C'est une ville très intéressante.

ALAIN Qu'est-ce qu'on peut voir à Fort-de-France?

VALÉRIE Le marché aux poissons, le marché aux fruits et aux légumes ou la place de la Savane, qui est très belle.

ALAIN Eh bien, c'est une bonne idée. J'ai envie d'y aller!

Answers to Activity 13
1. vrai   2. faux   3. vrai   4. faux

Deuxième étape

18 Ecoute! p. 294

1. — Tu as les cadeaux, Frédéric? N'oublie surtout pas les cadeaux!

2. — J'ai mon manteau, mon écharpe, ma cravate. J'ai pensé à tout!

3. — Tu as pensé à ton dictionnaire? Il ne faut pas que tu l'oublies. Il te faut absolument un dictionnaire.

4. — Eh bien, j'ai regardé ma liste deux fois. Je suis sûr, je n'ai rien oublié.

5. — Tu n'as pas oublié tes sandales? Tu sais, il va faire très chaud.

6. — Oui, j'ai mon appareil-photo. Ne t'en fais pas.

7. — Tu ne prends pas ton maillot de bain? Pourquoi? Tu vas en avoir besoin.

Anwers to Activity 18

1. reminding	3. reminding	5. reminding	7. reminding
2. reassuring	4. reassuring	6. reassuring	

25 Ecoute! p. 296

1. — Salut, Michel! Ça va? Ça fait longtemps! Qu'est-ce que tu fais?

2. — A bientôt, Nathalie! Amuse-toi bien!

3. — Eh bien, bon voyage, Luc! N'oublie pas de m'écrire! Je vais penser à toi!

4. — Salut, Amira! Tu vas mieux? On va au cinéma ce soir. Tu viens?

5. — Salut, Paul! Tu as de la chance, toi, d'aller en Italie! Passe de bonnes vacances!

6. — Salut, Albert! Ça s'est bien passé, le week-end? Qu'est-ce que tu as fait?

Answers to Activity 25

1. arrive	2. part	3. part	4. arrive	5. part	6. arrive

*T*roisième étape

29 Ecoute! p. 297

1. — Tu as passé un bon été?
   — Oh, pas mauvais. J'ai beaucoup travaillé, mais j'ai gagné de l'argent.

2. — Ça s'est bien passé, tes vacances en Italie?
   — C'était un véritable cauchemar! Il a fait tellement chaud, et c'était trop cher!

3. — Tu t'es bien amusée en vacances, Fabienne?
   — Ah oui, c'était formidable! Il a fait très beau! On est allés à la plage tous les jours!

4. — Dis, Etienne, tu as passé un bon week-end?
   — Euh, pas vraiment. Je suis allé chez mes cousins à la montagne. C'est barbant chez eux!

5. — Tu t'es bien amusé en colonie de vacances?
   — Oh, ça a été. On a beaucoup joué au football, mais moi, j'aime mieux le tennis.

6. — Ça s'est bien passé, tes vacances à la montagne?
   — C'était épouvantable! J'y suis allé pour faire du ski, et il n'y avait pas de neige!

7. — Tu t'es bien amusé à Paris?
   — C'était formidable! On est allés au Louvre, à Notre-Dame, à la tour Eiffel et au Sacré-Cœur.

Answers to Activity 29

1. fair	3. good	5. fair	7. good
2. bad	4. bad	6. bad	

*P*rononciation, p. 299

For the scripts for Parts A and B, see p. 299.

C. A écrire

(Dictation)

— Salut, Michel! Qu'est-ce que tu fais cet été?
— Je vais chez mon oncle à la campagne. Il a trois chats mignons et quatre chiens méchants.

*M*ise en pratique

1 p. 302

Vous voulez découvrir de nouveaux horizons? Vous avez l'esprit d'aventure? Pierre et Vacances peut vous aider à partir au bout du monde! Grands voyages pour petits budgets!

Envie de soleil, de plages tranquilles, de musique exotique? Sortez votre maillot de bain et votre crème solaire. Venez passer une semaine au Maroc y faire de la planche à voile et de la plongée sous-marine.

Envie de neige et de descentes olympiques? Les montagnes de Grenoble vous attendent. Hôtel, location de skis et chaussures, forfait téléski, voyage en train compris, au départ de Paris, deux mille cinq cents francs.

Envie de sensation forte et de paysages spectaculaires? La randonnée de votre vie vous attend! Descente du Grand Canyon avec un guide. Campez au bord des eaux vertes du Colorado. Pour les amoureux du risque, rafting possible.

Pour profiter des prix hors saison, voyagez avant le quinze juin. Nous avons des prix étudiant et des prix de groupes. Si les voyages vous intéressent, venez nous voir ou téléphonez Pierre et Vacances, zéro deux, quarante-sept, vingt-trois, trente-deux, vingt-deux.

Answers to Mise en pratique Activity 1

1. travel agency
2. *Possible answers:* Morocco, Grenoble, the Grand Canyon, Colorado
3. windsurfing, scuba diving, skiing, hiking, camping, rafting
4. students and groups

Chapitre 11 : Vive les vacances!
Projects

Le monde du voyageur
(Individual or Group Project)

ASSIGNMENT

Students will create posters of travel scenes.

MATERIALS

✄ **Students may need**
- French-English dictionary
- Posterboard or construction paper
- Markers or colored pencils
- Magazines and catalogues

SUGGESTED SEQUENCE

1. Students might work alone or in small groups. Tell them that they will depict an airport, train station, or vacation scene, with labels on important items and speech bubbles for the people in the scene. Individuals might create a scene on construction paper and groups might use a piece of posterboard. You might show *Teaching Transparency 11-2* as an example of a travel scene. As preparation for their own projects, have students suggest labels for objects and speech bubbles for the people in the scene. You might write their suggestions on a transparency overlay.

2. Students choose the location for their scenes and begin gathering or drawing pictures to illustrate it. They may wish to present a story or simply show people doing different things.

3. Before they create the final draft, have students plan the layout of their pictures and look up words they don't know in the dictionary. They might cut out pictures from magazines as well. Have them label as many items as possible, such as clothes, travel items, objects in the scene, activities, and so on. Remind them to check their spelling.

4. Next, have students write speech bubbles for the people shown. They might choose to demonstrate greeting or seeing people off, giving advice, or other appropriate functions.

5. Have students edit one another's work; they should make any corrections in labels or language use. They should then add any final touches to their posters to make them complete and attractive.

GRADING THE PROJECT

You might want to base students' grades on completion of the assignment, creativity, language use, and appearance.

Suggested Point Distribution (total = 100 points)

Completion of assignment	30 points
Creativity	30 points
Language use	20 points
Appearance	20 points

DESSIN ANIME

In this game, students will review vocabulary related to vacation activities.

Procedure   First, divide the class into two or more teams and have a player from the first team go to the board. Give the player the name of a vacation place or activity in French and have him or her draw a representation of that activity or place. If the player's team correctly guesses the activity or place within 15 seconds, that team wins a point. The turn then goes to the second team.

Variation   This game can also be played in small groups. In this case, students choose an activity from the vocabulary list at the end of the chapter and draw their illustrations on paper or on a transparency.

JE L'AI TROUVE!

The object of this game is to have students recognize the names of francophone countries and identify their location on a map.

Procedure   Before playing this game, give students a few minutes to look over the map of the francophone world on page xxvi in their books. You might also show *Map Transparency 4.* Then, display two world maps and divide the class into two teams. Have a player from each team stand by a map. Call out the name of a country in French. The first player to point out the country on the map and say **Je l'ai trouvé!** wins a point. Give each team a point in case of a tie.

REPONDS VITE!

In this game, students will practice verb forms.

Procedure   Divide the class into two teams and place a bell or squeaky toy on top of a desk. Then, have one player from each team come forward. Name a subject, a verb, and a tense (**je, partir, présent**). Give the first student to ring the bell a chance to respond with the correct verb form. If that student is wrong, the other player has a chance to respond. A correct answer wins a point for the team. Then, both players return to their seats, and two other players come forward. In case of confusion due to mispronunci–ation, have the player write the verb form on the board. In addition to verb forms, you can also ask students to give functional expressions, such as *see someone off* or *suggest that someone go to the beach.*

Chapitre 11
Vive les vacances!
pp. 282–305

*U*sing the Chapter Opener

Motivating Activity

Ask students where they would go on vacation if they had unlimited time and money. You might also have them recall popular vacation spots mentioned in previous chapters.

Teaching Suggestions

• Have partners ask and answer the questions about vacations in the introduction at the top of page 283.
• Ask students if they can name any of the countries whose flags appear at the top of this page.

Photo Flash!

① The beach is a popular vacation destination for the French. Many flock to the beaches of the **Côte d'Azur** in southern France or the trendy resort town of Biarritz on the Atlantic coast. The beaches of Grand-Bassam and Assinie in Côte d'Ivoire attract both African and European tourists. The teenager in this photo is relaxing on **La plage des Salines** in Martinique, a popular overseas vacation destination. Since Martinique is a **département** and officially a part of France, French citizens do not need a passport to travel there.

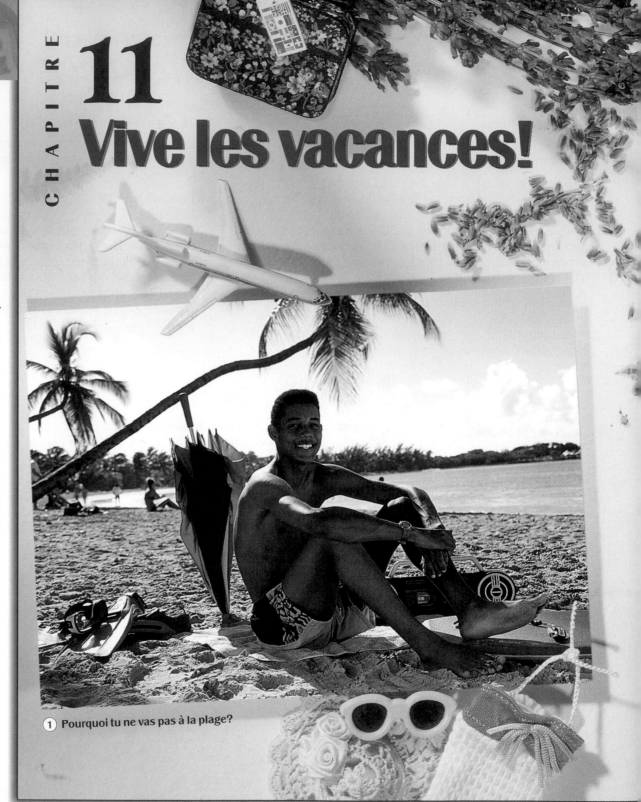

CHAPITRE

11
Vive les vacances!

① Pourquoi tu ne vas pas à la plage?

Multicultural Link

Ask students which holidays they have off from school. Have them suggest both national holidays, such as Martin Luther King Day or Columbus Day, and religious holidays, such as Yom Kippur, Christmas, or Ramadan. Then, have them research national and religious holidays in other countries and how they're celebrated.

Language Note

Have students guess what **Vive** in the expression **Vive les vacances!** means. You might write **Vive le roi!** or **Vive la France!** on the board as additional examples.

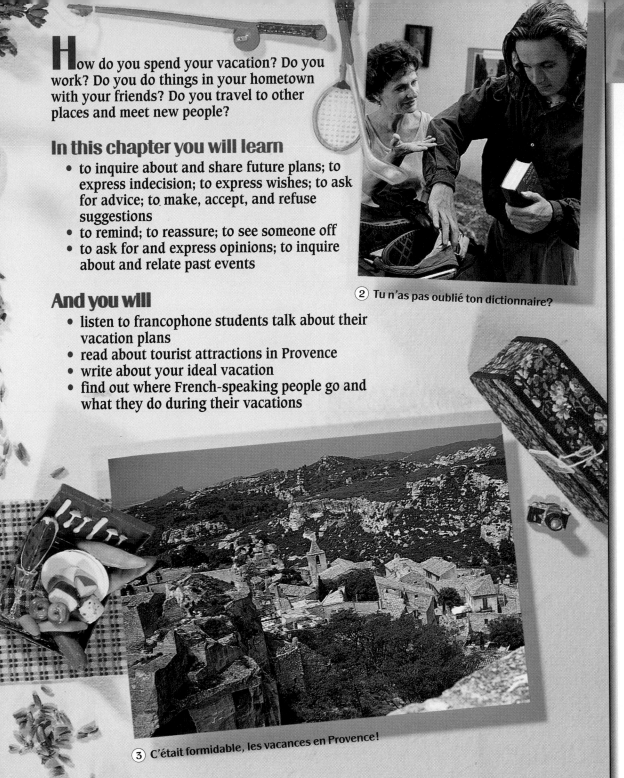

How do you spend your vacation? Do you work? Do you do things in your hometown with your friends? Do you travel to other places and meet new people?

In this chapter you will learn

- to inquire about and share future plans; to express indecision; to express wishes; to ask for advice; to make, accept, and refuse suggestions
- to remind; to reassure; to see someone off
- to ask for and express opinions; to inquire about and relate past events

And you will

- listen to francophone students talk about their vacation plans
- read about tourist attractions in Provence
- write about your ideal vacation
- find out where French-speaking people go and what they do during their vacations

② Tu n'as pas oublié ton dictionnaire?

③ C'était formidable, les vacances en Provence!

deux cent quatre-vingt-trois **283**

CHAPTER OPENER
CHAPTER 11

Focusing on Outcomes

Ask students to describe a vacation they have taken or an imaginary vacation and tell why they enjoyed it. Then, have partners suggest how they would express the chapter outcomes, using vocabulary and expressions they already know. Ask them to list English expressions related to the outcomes.
NOTE: You may want to use the video to support the objectives. The self-check activities in **Que sais-je?** on page 304 help students assess their achievement of the objectives.

Building on Previous Skills

Ask students to recall and name in French particular sports and activities they might do on vacation.

Photo Flash!

③ The region of Provence, known as **Provincia** by the Romans, is famous for its mild climate, which is characterized by long, warm summers and mild winters.

Teaching Suggestions

- Ask students if they like to take pictures when they visit a different city or country and what they might take pictures of.
- Ask students if they would have guessed that Photo 3 was taken in the south of France, and if so, why.

Block Scheduling

For suggestions about how to use *Allez, viens!* with block scheduling, see the *Lesson Planner,* pages 53–57.

CHAPTER 11   CHAPTER OPENER   283

VIDEO PROGRAM
Videocassette 4
15:19–17:45
Videocassette 5
(captioned version)
1:29:50–1:32:17

OR VIDEODISC PROGRAM,
Videodisc 6, Side A

Search 1, Play To 4400

Video Synopsis

In this segment of the video, Ahmed and Florent are playing soccer when Magali comes up to greet them. They talk about their plans for the summer. Magali is going to a summer camp, and Ahmed plans to go camping and then work at a gas station in Arles. Florent doesn't have any vacation plans yet. Magali and Ahmed each make suggestions. Florent wants to do something interesting, but he doesn't know what!

Motivating Activity

Ask students what they did during summer vacation last year and what they would like to do this year. Ask what types of jobs are available during the summer. If students would like to work, what would they save for?

Presentation

As a prereading activity, have students answer the questions at the top of page 284. Play the video and then have students answer the questions in Activity 1 on page 286. Ask them to suggest advantages and disadvantages of each teenager's vacation plans.

Geography Link

Ask students to look in an atlas and locate **Sisteron** and **les Gorges du Verdon.** Have them find information on the attractions at these places and what the weather is like.

The **roman-photo** is an abridged version of the video episode.

Mise en train

 CD 11 Trs. 1–2

Bientôt les vacances! p. 121, Act. 1

What are these teenagers discussing? What clues do you have? What is Florent's dilemma?

1 Alors, les copains, qu'est-ce que vous allez faire pendant les vacances?

C'est sympa!

Moi, je pars en colonie de vacances.

2 Et en août, je vais voir mes cousins à la montagne. Ils habitent à Sisteron, dans les Alpes de Haute-Provence. C'est super joli là-bas.

3 Non. En juillet, je vais faire du camping dans les Gorges du Verdon.

Et toi, Ahmed, tu vas à l'étranger?

En août, je travaille dans une station-service. J'aimerais bien acheter une mobylette.

4 C'est génial!

284 *deux cent quatre-vingt-quatre* CHAPITRE 11 Vive les vacances!

RESOURCES FOR MISE EN TRAIN

PRINT	MEDIA
• *Practice and Activity Book,* p. 121 • *Video Guide,* pp. 73–74, 76 • *Videodisc Guide,* pp. 119–122, 126	• *Video Program,* Videocassette 4 Videocassette 5 (captioned version) • *Videodisc Program,* Videodisc 6, Side A • *Audio Compact Discs,* CD 11, Trs. 1–2

Teaching Suggestion

Stop the recording or video periodically to ask students where the teenagers are going on vacation. (**Il/Elle va où en vacances?**)

Thinking Critically

Comparing and Contrasting

Ask students to compare what these French teenagers are planning to do for the summer with what they themselves usually do. Do they find any of the activities mentioned by the French students unusual? Why? What might an American teenager do that these French teenagers didn't mention?

 Video Integration

- *VIDEO PROGRAM,*
  Videocassette 4, 17:46–25:05
  Videocassette 5, 1:32:18–1:39:40
- *VIDEODISC PROGRAM,*
  Videodisc 6, Side A

Search 4400, Play To 17600

You may choose to continue with **Bientôt les vacances! (suite)** at this time or wait until later in the chapter. When the story continues, Florent's father sees an ad for a **séjour linguistique** in England and thinks Florent should participate. Florent tells Ahmed of his plans. Ahmed says that it won't be fun and that it rains all the time in England. Florent is reluctant to go to England, but his parents finally persuade him to go. At the end of the story, Florent's parents receive a package from him. He has sent back his rain gear and is having a great time after all!

For videodisc application, see *Videodisc Guide.*

For Individual Needs

3 Challenge Have students create one or two additional true-false statements based on **Bientôt les vacances!** They might read their statements aloud to the class, or they might exchange papers with a partner.

Captioned Video

4 You might show the captioned version of **Bientôt les vacances**, available on Videocassette 5, and have students point out the indicated words and phrases.

Thinking Critically

4 Synthesizing Ask students to name other situations in which these expressions might be used.

Teaching Suggestion

5 This activity could be a class discussion or a writing assignment for individuals or groups.

These activities check for comprehension only. Students should not yet be expected to produce language modeled in **Mise en train**.

1 Tu as compris? See answers below.

1. What time of year is it? How do you know?
2. Who is planning to travel during the vacation? Where?
3. Who is going to work during the vacation? Why?
4. What is Florent going to do?

2 C'est qui?

D'après **Bientôt les vacances!** qui a l'intention de (d')...

Florent

Ahmed

Magali

Magali — aller dans les Alpes?

Ahmed — travailler en Arles?

Florent — rester en Arles?

Magali — partir en colonie de vacances?

aller voir ses cousins?
Magali

aller à la montagne?
Magali

faire du camping?
Ahmed

3 Vrai ou faux?

1. Tous les jeunes restent en France pendant les vacances.   vrai
2. Les cousins de Magali habitent à la montagne.   vrai
3. Ahmed va faire du camping dans les Alpes.   faux
4. Ahmed va travailler dans un café.   faux
5. Ahmed veut aller au Festival de la photographie.   faux
6. Florent part en colonie de vacances.   faux

4 Cherche les expressions

According to **Bientôt les vacances!**, what can you say in French. . .   See answers below.

1. to ask what someone is going to do?
2. to tell what a place looks like?
3. to express an opinion?
4. to express indecision?
5. to make a suggestion?
6. to express a preference?

> C'est génial! C'est super joli...
>   Je préfère...
> Pourquoi est-ce que tu ne... pas?
> Qu'est-ce que vous allez faire... ?
>   Je n'ai pas encore décidé.

5 Et maintenant, à toi

Whose vacation plans are the most interesting to you? Why?

286   *deux cent quatre-vingt-six*   CHAPITRE 11   Vive les vacances!

Answers

1 1. almost summer; July and August are mentioned.
2. Magali: colonie de vacances and Sisteron, dans les Alpes de Haute-Provence; Ahmed: les Gorges du Verdon
3. Ahmed; He needs money to buy a moped.
4. He doesn't know.

4 1. Qu'est-ce que vous allez faire... ?
2. C'est super joli...
3. C'est génial!
4. Je n'ai pas encore décidé.
5. Pourquoi est-ce que tu ne... pas... ?
6. Je préfère...

PREMIERE ETAPE TPR

Storytelling Book
pp. 41, 44

Inquiring about and sharing future plans; expressing indecision; expressing wishes; asking for advice; making, accepting, and refusing suggestions

 p. 122, Act. 2   11-A, 11-B   pp. 88–89, Acts. 1–4   CD-ROM Disc 3

VOCABULAIRE

Où est-ce que tu vas aller pendant tes vacances?

à la montagne

à la campagne

au bord de la mer

en forêt

en colonie de vacances

chez mes grands-parents

Qu'est-ce qu'on peut y faire? On peut y...

faire du camping.

faire de la randonnée.

faire du bateau.

faire de la plongée.

faire de la planche à voile.

faire de la voile.

6   Ecoute! See scripts and answers on p. 281G.

Listen as Nathalie, Bruno, Pauline, and Emile tell about their vacation plans. What is each teenager going to do?

CD 11 Tr. 3

RESOURCES FOR PREMIERE ETAPE

PRINT
- *Lesson Planner*, p. 54
- *Practice and Activity Book*, pp. 122–124
- *Grammar and Vocabulary Workbook*, pp. 88–91
- *Activities for Communication*, pp. 61–62, 125, 128–129, 157–158
- *Listening Activities*, pp. 83–84, 87
- *Testing Program*, pp. 275–278
- *Alternative Assessment Guide*, p. 42

MEDIA
- *Video Program*, Videocassette 4
  Video Guide, pp. 73–78
- *Videodisc Program*, Videodisc 6, Side A
  Videodisc Guide, p. 123
- *Teaching Transparencies* 11-1, 11-A, 11-B
- *Interactive CD-ROM Program*, Disc 3
  CD-ROM Teacher's Guide, p. 46
- *Audio Compact Discs*
  Textbook Listening Activities, CD 11, Trs. 3–5
  Additional Listening Activities 11-1, 11-2, CD 11, Trs. 26–27
  Quiz 11-1B, CD 11, Tr. 20

Jump Start!

Have students write sentences telling whether or not they do the following: **faire de l'aérobic, faire de la natation, faire du vélo, jouer au football, jouer au tennis, faire du ski nautique.**

MOTIVATE

Tell students to imagine they are starting a summer camp for their friends and classmates. Ask them where they would have the camp and what activities they would offer.

Teach

Presentation

Vocabulaire   Use magazine illustrations to present the new vocabulary. Then, ask **On est où?** as you show pictures of the places, and **Qu'est-ce qu'on fait?** as you show pictures of activities. Next, ask if students have been to these places. (**Tu es déjà allé(e) à la montagne?**) Finally, have pairs of students do a clustering activity. Tell them to write down one of the locations and circle it; this is the center of a diagram. Then, have them write related words, expressions, and activities in French in the circles of the diagram.

Teaching Suggestion

6   Stop the recording after each person speaks to elicit answers.

For Individual Needs

Visual/Kinesthetic Learners
To practice the vacation vocabulary, have students play the game "Dessin animé," described on page 281J.

Teaching Suggestions

De bons conseils Have students look back at the vocabulary pages in previous chapters to find examples of words with these endings. Examples include **éducation, sortie, vaisselle, piscine, heure, plage, ménage, devoir, classeur,** and **manteau.** You might have groups compete to find the most words.

Tu te rappelles? You might review the forms of **aller** with students before they do Activity 7.

Additional Practice

7 Ask students to tell or write whether they are going to do the same activities, using **je** or **nous.**

Game

VRAI OU FAUX? Have students write three true-false statements about what Vincent and Roland are going to do on vacation. Then, form two teams. Have the first player from one team read a statement. The player from the other team tells whether the statement is true or false. If the player is correct, he or she reads a statement to the first team. If not, the second player of the first team reads another statement. Award points for correct answers.

Teaching Suggestion

Note Culturelle You might want to take a poll of how many students have ever attended a summer camp. Ask them if they enjoyed it, how long they stayed there, and what activities were offered. You might have students compare the activities they've enjoyed at summer camps or seen in movies about summer camps with the types of activities offered in the **colonies de vacances.**

Although there are few hard-and-fast rules to help you remember if a noun is masculine or feminine, you can often predict the gender of a word by its ending. Some of the endings that usually indicate a feminine word are **-tion, -sion, -ie, -ette, -elle, -ine, -ude,** and **-ure.** Endings that often signal a masculine word are **-ment, -age, -oir, -ier, -et,** and **-eau.** But be careful! There are exceptions.

p. 122, Act. 4   p. 90, Acts. 5–6   **Tu te rappelles?**
Do you remember how to tell what is going to happen? Use a form of the verb **aller** *(to go)* plus the infinitive of another verb.
Demain, je **vais faire** du bateau.

Si tu as oublié the verb aller va à la page 154.

7 Dans une colonie de vacances

Qu'est-ce que Vincent et Roland vont faire en colonie de vacances?

Ils vont... **1.** faire de la planche à voile.　**2.** faire de la plongée.　**3.** faire du ski nautique.

4. jouer au football.　**5.** faire de l'équitation.　**6.** faire de la voile.

NOTE CULTURELLE

In francophone countries, many children and teenagers attend summer camps **(colonies de vacances),** where they learn folklore, folk dances, arts and crafts, foreign languages, and many other subjects. Of course, they also participate in sports. The camps are usually run by young adults called **animateurs.** In France alone there are hundreds of **colonies de vacances.**

288 *deux cent quatre-vingt-huit*　CHAPITRE 11　Vive les vacances!

Language Notes

• The word **animateur (animatrice)** is also used to describe hosts of TV shows or anyone who plans and leads group activities.
• You might point out that **au bord de la mer** *(to/on the coast)* is not exactly synonymous with **à la plage,** which refers specifically to the beach.

Language-to-Language

De bons conseils You might tell students that many languages in addition to French assign genders to nouns. Nouns in Spanish are masculine or feminine, and nouns in German are masculine, feminine, or neuter. Ask students to think of English words that are thought of as feminine. (A *ship* is often referred to as *she.)*

COMMENT DIT-ON... ?

Inquiring about and sharing future plans; expressing indecision; expressing wishes

  p. 123, Act. 6   11-1

QU'EST-CE QUE TU VAS FAIRE PENDANT TES VACANCES ?

JE NE SAIS PAS. J'HÉSITE. JE VOUDRAIS BIEN ALLER À LA MONTAGNE... MAIS J'AI AUSSI ENVIE DE RESTER ICI POUR VOIR MES GRANDS-PARENTS !

To inquire about someone's plans:
Qu'est-ce que tu vas faire cet été?
Où est-ce que tu vas aller pendant les vacances?

To express indecision:
J'hésite.
Je ne sais pas.
Je n'en sais rien. *I have no idea.*
Je n'ai rien de prévu. *I don't have any plans.*

To share your plans:
En juillet, **je vais** travailler.
En août, **j'ai l'intention d'**aller en Italie. *. . . I intend to . . .*

To express wishes:
Je voudrais bien aller chez mes cousins.
J'ai envie de travailler. *I feel like . . .*

8 Ecoute! <small>See scripts and answers on p. 281G.</small>

Listen to these speakers talk about their vacations. Do they have definite plans or are they undecided?

CD 11 Tr. 4

9 Les vacances en France

Imagine you're going to France on vacation next summer. Your partner will ask about your vacation plans. Tell what you feel like doing or plan to do there. Then, change roles.

visiter le Louvre   faire des photos   faire du ski   rencontrer de jeunes Français

voir la tour Eiffel   parler français   aller à un concert de rock français   aller au café

Presentation

Comment dit-on... ? To introduce the new expressions, prompt three students to ask you the questions. In response to one student, express indecision. In response to another student, share your plans, and in response to a third, express your wishes. Then, ask students what they would like to do tonight and what they're going to do tonight.

 For videodisc application, see *Videodisc Guide.*

Teaching Suggestions

8 You might have students write down the destination(s) or activities mentioned by the speakers.

9 Have students suggest other things they'd like to do. Write their suggestions on a transparency for reference during the activity. Remind students to reverse roles.

For Individual Needs

9 Visual Learners Show *Teaching Transparency 11-1.* Have students look at the posters displayed in the travel agency for additional vacation destinations and activities.

♖ Game

LES VACANCES Write different answers to the question **Qu'est-ce que tu vas faire cet été?** on index cards. Write each answer on two separate cards. Include plans that your students would be likely to have, such as **Je vais travailler comme maître nageur** *(lifeguard)* **à la piscine.** Distribute one card to each student. Students circulate and ask about one another's plans until they find the person whose card matches theirs.

Presentation

Note de grammaire After explaining the use of **à** with cities and **en** and **au** with countries, have students practice by asking one another where they would like to go for their next vacation. You might also have small groups make suggestions and decide together on a vacation destination. Write **Pourquoi pas aller... ?** and **On peut aller... ?** on the board as prompts.

🏰 Game

OÙ SE TROUVE... ? Hold a geography contest. Students on one team name a well-known city; their opponents tell in which country or state it is located. Refer students to the Additional Vocabulary on pages R10–R11 for additional country names.

◆ For Individual Needs

10 Challenge Have students write one or two sentences describing what they would like to see or do on vacation, read them aloud, and have the class guess where each student would like to go. Encourage them to use the locations previously presented in the book (Poitiers, Quebec, Paris, Abidjan, Arles).

Teaching Suggestion

12 Before students do this activity, re-enter the expressions in **Tu te rappelles?** by asking students for advice on where to go for vacation.

📁 Portfolio

12 Oral This activity is appropriate for students' oral portfolios. For portfolio information, see the *Alternative Assessment Guide,* pages iv–17.

NOTE DE GRAMMAIRE

p. 91, Act. 7

Additional Grammar Practice, p. R50

- To say *to* or *in* before the names of most cities, use **à**.

  Tu vas **à** Paris pendant les vacances?

- Names of countries are either masculine or feminine. Feminine countries end in **-e,** but there are exceptions, such as **le Mexique.** Use **au** *(to, in)* before masculine names and **en** *(to, in)* before feminine names and before names of countries that begin with a vowel. Before plural names, use **aux.**

  Vous allez **au** Canada?

  Hélène va **en** Allemagne.

  Nous allons **aux** Etats-Unis.

- States and provinces follow slightly different rules.

10 Où vont-ils?

Dans quel pays *(country)* vont-ils passer leurs vacances?

1. Murielle va prendre des photos de la tour Eiffel.   *en France*
2. Monique va visiter le château Frontenac.   *au Canada*
3. Joseph va visiter la tour de Londres.   *en Angleterre*
4. Mathieu va voir les pyramides.   *en Egypte*
5. Than et Laure vont visiter le Texas.   *aux Etats-Unis*
6. Dominique va voir le Kremlin.   *en Russie*
7. Paul et Gilles vont aller à Casablanca.   *au Maroc*

11 On y fait quoi?

Select two of the countries from Activity 10 and decide with your group on at least three activities you would all like to do on vacation in each country.

12 Un voyage gratuit

You've won a trip to go anywhere you want. Where will you go? Why? What will you do there? Discuss this with a partner. Take turns.

290 *deux cent quatre-vingt-dix*

Vocabulaire à la carte

en Angleterre	en France
en Allemagne	en Floride
en Australie	en Italie
en Belgique	au Maroc
au Brésil	au Mexique
en Californie	en Russie
en Chine	au Sénégal
en Egypte	en Suisse
en Espagne	au Texas
aux Etats-Unis	au Viêt-Nam

au Canada   au Maroc

aux Etats-Unis

en Russie   en Angleterre

en Egypte   en France

Tu te rappelles?

Do you remember how to ask for advice?
Make, accept, and refuse suggestions?

To ask for advice:
Je ne sais pas quoi faire (où aller).
Tu as une idée?
Qu'est-ce que tu me conseilles?

To make suggestions:
Je te conseille de…
Tu devrais…

To accept suggestions:
C'est une bonne idée!
Pourquoi pas?
D'accord!
Allons-y!

To refuse suggestions:
Non, ce n'est pas possible.
Non, je ne peux pas.
Ça ne me dit rien.
C'est trop cher.

Geography Link

To practice the country names, you might play the game **"Je l'ai trouvé,"** which is described on page 281J. To prepare your students for the game, divide the class into small groups and give each group a list of ten or twelve countries to locate on a world map.

Language Note

The preposition **en** is used instead of **à** with the town of Arles.

13 Ecoute! See scripts and answers on p. 281G.

Ecoute Alain et Valérie qui parlent de leurs vacances. Est-ce que ces phrases sont vraies ou fausses?

CD 11 Tr. 5

1. Alain ne sait pas quoi faire.
2. Valérie n'a pas d'idées.
3. Valérie est déjà allée à la Martinique.
4. Alain ne veut pas aller à la Martinique.

A la française

Use the words **alors** *(so, then, well, in that case)* and **donc** *(so, then, therefore)* to connect your sentences.

  J'adore faire de la plongée, **donc** je vais en Australie.
  Tu aimes faire du bateau? **Alors**, tu devrais aller à Marseille.

14 Des conseils

Ces élèves rêvent *(are dreaming)* de ce qu'ils aiment. Ils ne savent pas où aller pendant les vacances. Tu as une idée? *Possible answers:* Tu devrais aller… ; Je te conseille d'aller…

Malika   au musée.

Marion   en forêt.

Hai   en Egypte.

Christian   au bord de la mer.

Adrienne   en Afrique.

Ali   en colonie de vacances.

15 Où aller?

Tell your partner what you like to do on vacation. Your partner will then make some suggestions about where you might want to go. Accept your partner's suggestions, or refuse them and give an excuse. Then, change roles.

16 Mon journal

Décris un voyage que tu vas faire ou que tu voudrais faire. Où veux-tu aller? Quand? Avec qui? Qu'est-ce que tu vas y faire?

PREMIERE ETAPE   *deux cent quatre-vingt-onze* **291**

For Individual Needs

13 Slower Pace   Before playing the recording, read the statements aloud. Ask students what they think the conversations will be about, based on these statements.

Teaching Suggestion

A la française   Write the following sentences on a transparency. Have students match and then combine them, using **donc** or **alors**.

1. J'aime faire du camping.
2. Je vais chez ma tante.
3. J'aime faire de la voile.
4. Je vais au bord de la mer.

a. Je vais au Québec.
b. Je vais au bord de la mer.
c. J'apporte un cadeau.
d. J'ai besoin de mon maillot de bain.

Mon journal

16 For an additional journal entry suggestion for Chapter 11, see *Practice and Activity Book,* page 155.

CLOSE

To close this **étape,** have students choose cards with vacation destinations written on them (**au Québec, à la montagne, en Côte d'Ivoire**) and list at least two things they plan to do there.

ASSESS

Quiz 11-1A, Quiz 11-B, *Testing Program,* pp. 275–278
Audio CD 11, Tr. 20

Performance Assessment

Have students create radio commercials to promote their favorite vacation destination. They should describe the activities available there as well as the weather.

Career Path

Tourism is an industry in which speaking a foreign language is almost a necessity. Tour guides generally speak three or more languages fluently. Some of the job responsibilities include meeting the tour group upon their arrival, assisting with hotel accommodations, and accompanying the tourists on tours during their vacation. Tour guides with a historical or specialized knowledge of a region might conduct specific tours and work with many tour groups during any given day. Have students discuss which languages would be most useful for someone who works as a tour guide and why.

VIDEO PROGRAM
Videocassette 4
25:06–28:24

OR VIDEODISC PROGRAM,
Videodisc 6, Side A

Search 17600, Play To 20340

Teacher Notes

• See the *Video Guide,* the *Videodisc Guide,* and the *CD-ROM Teacher's Guide* for activities related to the **Panorama Culturel.**

• Remind students that cultural material may be included in the Chapter Quizzes and Test.

• The interviewees' language represents informal, unrehearsed speech. Occasionally, edits have been made for clarification.

Presentation

Before playing the video, ask students to listen for what the people do on vacation. Remind them that they don't need to understand every word, just the general idea. After playing the video, have students read the interviews in groups and write answers to the questions in **Qu'en penses-tu?** Then, have groups share their answers.

Thinking Critically

Drawing Inferences After reading **Savais-tu que... ?,** have groups discuss the following questions: Why do you think people in the United States aren't guaranteed five weeks of vacation a year? Why do you think it is different in France?

PANORAMA CULTUREL

Sim • Côte d'Ivoire

Nicole • Martinique

Céline • France

We asked some francophone people where they go and what they do on vacation. Here are their responses.

CD 11
Trs. 6–9

CD-ROM
Disc 3

Qu'est-ce que tu fais pendant les vacances?

«Pendant les vacances, d'habitude je vais au village chez les parents qui sont restés au village. Et après une année scolaire, il faut aller les voir parce que ça... il y a longtemps qu'on se voit pas. Donc, ça fait plaisir aux parents de revoir les enfants quand ils vont au village. Voilà. Ça fait changer de climat. On va se reposer un peu.»

—Sim
Tr. 7

«Pendant les vacances, alors, je vais généralement à la plage, au cinéma. Le soir, je sors, enfin je vais dans des fêtes, chez des amis. On danse. On s'amuse. On rigole. On joue aux cartes. Les vacances se passent comme ça.»

Quand est-ce que tu as des vacances?

«J'ai des vacances en juillet, à partir de juillet. Les vacances durent deux mois et nous reprenons l'école en septembre.»

—Nicole
Tr. 8

«Ben, pendant les vacances, bon, des fois je pars. L'année dernière, je suis partie en Espagne, cette année je pars en Corse. Je pars souvent avec des copains ou... sinon, je reste à Aix.»

—Céline
Tr. 9

Qu'en penses-tu? See answers below.

1. Where do these people like to go and what do they like to do during their vacations?
2. Where do you go and what do you do on vacation? How does this differ from what these people do?

Savais-tu que...?

Salaried employees in France are guaranteed five weeks of vacation time per year. Most people take a month off in July or August and take the fifth week at some other time of the year, often in winter.

Questions

1. Pourquoi est-ce que Sim va au village? (pour voir les parents, parce que ça fait changer de climat)
2. Qu'est-ce que Nicole fait aux fêtes de ses amis? (Elle danse, s'amuse, rigole, joue aux cartes.)
3. Nicole a combien de mois de vacances? (deux)
4. Avec qui est-ce que Céline part en vacances? (avec des amis)

Multicultural Link

Have students choose a country and find out how much vacation time the people usually have and when they usually take their vacations.

Answers

1. parents' village, the beach, the movies, parties, friends' homes, Spain, Corsica; dance, have fun, laugh, play cards

DEUXIEME ETAPE Storytelling Book pp. 42, 44

Reminding; reassuring; seeing someone off

Vocabulaire

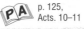 p. 125, Acts. 10–11   11-C   p. 92, Acts. 8–9   CD-ROM Disc 3

un appareil-photo
une valise
un parapluie
un cadeau
de l'argent
un billet d'avion
un passeport
un billet de train

17 Qu'est-ce qu'il te faut?

1. Qu'est-ce qu'il faut quand il pleut?   un parapluie
2. Qu'est-ce qu'il faut pour prendre le train? L'avion?   un billet de train, un billet d'avion
3. Qu'est-ce qu'il faut pour acheter des souvenirs?   de l'argent
4. Qu'est-ce qu'il faut pour prendre des photos?   un appareil-photo

COMMENT DIT-ON... ?
Reminding; reassuring

 p. 126, Act. 13   11-2

To remind someone of something:
N'oublie pas ton passeport!
Tu n'as pas oublié ton billet d'avion? *You didn't forget . . . ?*
Tu ne peux pas partir sans ton écharpe! *You can't leave without . . . !*
Tu prends ton manteau? *Are you taking . . . ?*

To reassure someone:
Ne t'en fais pas.
J'ai pensé à tout. *I've thought of everything.*
Je n'ai rien oublié. *I didn't forget anything.*

DEUXIEME ETAPE   *deux cent quatre-vingt-treize*   **293**

RESOURCES FOR DEUXIEME ETAPE

PRINT
- *Lesson Planner*, p. 55
- *Practice and Activity Book*, pp. 125–127
- *Grammar and Vocabulary Workbook*, pp. 92–95
- *Activities for Communication*, pp. 63–64, 126, 128–129, 157–158
- *Listening Activities*, pp. 84, 88
- *Testing Program*, pp. 279–282
- *Alternative Assessment Guide*, p. 42

MEDIA
- *Video Program*, Videocassette 4
  Video Guide, pp. 73–78
- *Videodisc Program*, Videodisc 6, Side A
  Videodisc Guide, p. 124
- *Teaching Transparencies* 11-2, 11-C
- *Interactive CD-ROM Program*, Disc 3
  CD-ROM Teacher's Guide, p. 46
- *Audio Compact Discs*
  Textbook Listening Activities, CD 11, Trs. 10–11
  Additional Listening Activities 11-3, 11-4, CD 11, Trs. 28–29
  Quiz 11-2B, CD 11, Tr. 21

Jump Start!
Have students write where the following people could be going on vacation: **Nous voulons voir les pyramides. Anne-Marie et Yvette aiment faire du ski. Marco veut pratiquer son espagnol.**

MOTIVATE
Have students tell in English what they would pack for a vacation in Martinique, France, Canada, or Côte d'Ivoire.

TEACH

Presentation

Vocabulaire/Comment dit-on... ? Introduce the vocabulary, using real items or pictures from magazines. Bring in a suitcase or large travel bag with items from the **Vocabulaire**. Then, introduce the expressions from **Comment dit-on... ?** and have students help you pack your suitcase. Say an expression for reminding with the new vocabulary. (**N'oublie pas ton passeport!**) Then, let students pack the item in your suitcase. Use expressions for reassuring as you go along, for example: **Oui, j'ai pensé à tout.** Every time you reassure them, you realize you've forgotten something else, so you have to ask them to pack another item. Continue until all items are packed.

 For videodisc application, see *Videodisc Guide.*

Culture Note
Ask students who the gift in the **Vocabulaire** is for (the host family). In many francophone regions, it is considered polite for a guest to bring a small gift for his or her host. Have students suggest small gifts they might bring.

For Individual Needs

18 Slower Pace Before playing the recording, read aloud in random order expressions from **Comment dit-on... ?** on page 293 and ask students to indicate whether you are reminding or reassuring someone.

19 Slower Pace Before students list what Jean-Paul has forgotten, have them copy his list and check off what he remembered to pack.

19 Challenge You might also have students make a list of things Jean-Paul may have packed that are not on his list.

Teaching Suggestion

20 Before they do this activity, have students make a short list of items they might need.

Presentation

Grammaire Walk out the door, saying **Salut! Je pars!** Then, have various students walk towards the door as you describe their actions, using the forms of **partir**. Have students repeat the forms after you, and then have them deduce the forms of **sortir** and **dormir**. Write their guesses on a transparency, correcting any mistakes. Next, have students mime sleeping or leaving and ask the class **Qu'est-ce qu'il/elle fait?**

Game

TIC TAC TOE Draw a tic tac toe grid on the board. Write a subject pronoun and the infinitive **sortir**, **dormir**, or **partir** in each square and have students copy the grid. In order to mark an *X* or an *O* in a square, players must write the correct verb form in that square. Have students play the game with a partner.

---

18 Ecoute! See scripts and answers on p. 281G.

Listen to these speakers. Are they reminding or reassuring someone?

CD 11 Tr. 10

19 Qu'est-ce qu'il a oublié?

GV p. 93, Act. 10

Read the list of things Jean-Paul needs for his trip. Make a list of what he's forgotten to pack. Next, play the role of Jean-Paul's parent and remind him what to take. Then, change roles.

Si tu as oublié clothing va à la page 261.

appareil-photo — casquette
billet d'avion — baskets
billet de train — shorts
passeport — chaussures
dictionnaire — chaussettes
magazines — cadeaux

20 Jeu de rôle

You're going on a trip to France this summer with the French Club. Ask your friend, who went last year, what you should take. He or she will remind you of some things you'll need. Act this out with a partner and then change roles.

CD-ROM Disc 3

GRAMMAIRE The verb partir

PA p. 125, Act. 12

A small group of verbs whose infinitives end in **-ir** follow a pattern different than the one you learned in Chapter 10.

partir *(to leave)*

Je **pars**		Nous **partons**		
Tu **pars**	à dix heures.	Vous **partez**	à dix heures.	
Il/Elle/On **part**		Ils/Elles **partent**		

GV pp. 93–94, Acts. 11–12

Additional Grammar Practice, pp. R50–R51

• Don't pronounce the **s** or **t** in **pars** or **part**.
• **Sortir** *(to go out)* and **dormir** *(to sleep)* also follow this pattern.

À la française

French speakers often use the present tense to talk about the future.

Je **pars** à neuf heures. *I'm leaving/I'm going to leave/I will leave . . .*
Je **sors** avec Aline ce soir. *I'm going out/I'm going to go out/I will go out . . .*

294 *deux cent quatre-vingt-quatorze*   CHAPITRE 11   Vive les vacances!

Teacher Note

Students might want to know this additional travel-related vocabulary: **la gare** *(train station);* **l'aéroport** *(airport);* **des chèques de voyage** *(traveler's checks);* **une pellicule/un film** *(roll of film).*

Language Notes

• You might explain to your students that **partir** means *to leave* and is used to stress the action of going away. **Sortir**, however, implies that one is *going out* for a short period of time and will be returning soon.
• Remind students that **partir**, **sortir**, and **dormir** follow a different pattern than **-ir** verbs like **choisir** and **finir**.

21 D'habitude, qu'est-ce que tu fais?

You're exchanging information with your host family about your daily routines. Complete each sentence with the correct form of **partir**, **sortir**, or **dormir**.

1. Je _____ pour l'école à huit heures du matin.   pars
2. Ma sœur et moi, nous _____ jusqu'à dix heures le samedi matin.   dormons
3. Mon père et ma mère _____ toujours avant moi le matin.   partent
4. Quand est-ce que vous _____ en vacances?   partez
5. Est-ce que tu _____ beaucoup le week-end?   sors
6. Mon frère Emile _____ le vendredi soir avec son amie Agnès.   sort

22 Vacances en Provence   See answers below.

Regarde l'itinéraire de Marianne. Ensuite, réponds aux questions.

1. D'où part Marianne samedi?
2. Où est-ce qu'elle va?
3. Son voyage va durer *(last)* combien de temps?
4. Qu'est-ce qu'elle a l'intention de faire?

23 Jeu de rôle

You're going to take the same trip as Marianne. Your partner will ask you questions about the trip and remind you what to take.

24 Bonjour de Provence!

Pendant ton voyage en Provence, écris une carte postale à ton ami(e), à tes camarades de classe ou à ton professeur.

Bienvenue en Provence!

SAMEDI :
départ d'Arles, bus de 9h35;
arrivée aux Baux-de-Provence à 10h10;
* visite de la Cathédrale d'Images;
  dîner : Auberge de la Benvengudo

DIMANCHE :
départ pour Saint-Rémy-de-Provence, bus de 9h15;
arrivée à 9h45;
* visite du musée Van Gogh; déjeuner : pique-nique à Fontvieille;

* visite du moulin de Daudet;
  retour aux Baux-de-Provence;
  départ pour Avignon, bus de 18h16;
  arrivée à 19h10 Hôtel le Midi;
  dîner

LUNDI :
* visite de la Cité des Papes, le Pont St-Bénezet, promenade du Rocher des Doms, le musée du Petit-Palais;
* spectacle folklorique;
  départ pour Grasse 20h15;
  arrivée à 22h10 Hôtel les Arômes

MARDI :
* visite de la Parfumerie Fragonard;
* Musée d'Art et d'Histoire de Provence; retour en Arles 17h42;
  arrivée à 19h20

Additional Practice

21 To practice the other forms of these verbs, you might use large flashcards with different subject pronouns written on them and a clock with moveable hands. Set the clock to a certain time and hold up a subject flashcard, asking **On part à quelle heure?**

For Individual Needs

22 Challenge Have students write a short paragraph describing what Marianne is going to do during one day of her vacation. This might also be done orally. This activity is appropriate for students' written or oral portfolios.

Portfolio

24 Written This activity might be included in students' written portfolios. For portfolio information, see the *Alternative Assessment Guide*, pages iv–17.

Teaching Suggestion

24 Students might write this activity on one side of an index card and illustrate it on the reverse side. Refer them to the Location Opener on pages 228–231 for illustration ideas.

Teacher Note

The postcard below Activity 24 features fields of lavender (**la lavande**), a flower native to the Provence region.

Answers
22 1. d'Arles
2. aux Baux-de-Provence, à Saint-Rémy-de-Provence, à Avignon et à Grasse
3. quatre jours
4. *Possible answers:* visiter une cathédrale, des musées et une parfumerie, assister à un spectacle folklorique

History Link

23 Before they do this activity, you might have groups of students research the historical significance of each of the places Marianne is visiting: **la Cathédrale d'Images, le musée Van Gogh, le moulin de Daudet, la Cité des Papes, le Pont Saint-Bénezet, le Rocher des Doms, le musée du Petit Palais, la Parfumerie Fragonard,** and **le Musée d'Art et d'Histoire de Provence.**

Presentation

Comment dit-on... ? Ask students what they say in English to see someone off at the airport or at the train or bus station. Have several students read the text in the speech bubbles. Then, introduce the expressions while waving goodbye and have students practice them with a partner.

Additional Practice

Ask students what they would say to a friend who was leaving on a long car trip; who was leaving on June 1; who was going to Disneyland™; who was leaving for a band competition.

Teaching Suggestion

26 Encourage students to expand their goodbyes by telling the person what to do during the flight or after he or she gets home. They might use **N'oublie pas de...** or **Pense à...**

Geography Link

27 Encourage students to use atlases or other reference materials to find out more about the climate and topography of their chosen vacation spot.

CLOSE

🏰 Game

N'OUBLIE PAS! Name a vacation destination and have a student remind you of one thing to take. The next student should repeat the first item and remind you of another. Continue until everyone has had a chance to add an item or until a mistake is made, in which case, you might give another destination and restart the game.

COMMENT DIT-ON... ?
Seeing someone off

p. 127, Acts. 14–16   11-2

To wish someone a good trip:
Bon voyage! *Have a good trip!*
Bonnes vacances! *Have a good vacation!*
Amuse-toi bien! *Have fun!*
Bonne chance! *Good luck!*

25 Ecoute! See scripts and answers on p. 281H.

Ecoute ces conversations.
On arrive ou on part?
CD 11 Tr. 11

26 Au revoir!
It's time for your French exchange student to return home. See him or her off at the airport. Act this out with your partner.

27 Un grand voyage

You and a friend have decided to take a trip together to a foreign country. Decide where you will go and what you will do there. Talk about the weather conditions and when you will go. Discuss what clothes and other items you each plan to pack and what you will wear on the plane.

Tu te rappelles ❓
Do you remember how to give commands? Use the **tu** or **vous** form of the verb without a subject.
Attends! Allez!
When you use an **-er** verb, remember to drop the final **s** of the **tu** form. p. 94, Act. 13
Ecoute! For additional practice, see p. R51.
When you use an object pronoun with a positive command, place it after the verb, separated by a hyphen in writing.
Donnez-moi votre billet, s'il vous plaît.

Si tu as oublié weather *va à la page 106.* GV
p. 95, Acts. 14–15

28 Un petit mot 🏠

Your friend is leaving on a trip tomorrow. Write a note wishing him or her well and suggesting things he or she might like to see and do while on vacation.

296 *deux cent quatre-vingt-seize*   CHAPITRE 11   Vive les vacances!

ASSESS

Quiz 11-2A, Quiz 11-2B, *Testing Program,* pp. 279–282
Audio CD 11, Tr. 21

Performance Assessment

Have students write a note to a friend who is going on vacation. They should make up a destination, make suggestions about what to take and do, and say goodbye.

TROISIEME ETAPE TPR

Storytelling Book pp. 43, 44

Asking for and expressing opinions; inquiring about and relating past events

COMMENT DIT-ON...?
Asking for and expressing opinions

pp. 128–129, Acts. 17–19   11-3

To ask someone's opinion:
Tu as passé un bon été?

Ça s'est bien passé?
Did it go well?

Tu t'es bien amusé(e)?
Did you have fun?

To express an opinion:
Oui, très chouette.
Oui, c'était formidable!
  Yes, it was great!
Oui, ça a été.
Oh, pas mauvais.
C'était épouvantable.
Non, pas vraiment. *No, not really.*
C'était un véritable cauchemar!
  It was a real nightmare!
C'était ennuyeux. *It was boring.*
C'était barbant.

29 **Ecoute!** See scripts and answers on p. 281H.

Listen to these conversations and then tell whether these people had a good, fair, or bad vacation.

CD 11 Tr. 12

Tu te rappelles?

Do you remember how to inquire about and relate events that happened in the past?

Tu es allé(e) où?
Qu'est-ce que tu as fait?
D'abord,... Ensuite,... Après,... Finalement,...

30 **Méli-mélo!**

Remets la conversation entre Thierry et Hervé dans le bon ordre.

—Où est-ce que vous êtes allés? 5
—Qu'est-ce que tu as fait? 3
—Et ensuite? 7
—Salut, Hervé! Ça s'est bien passé, l'été? 1

—On est allés chez mon oncle à la campagne. C'est barbant chez lui. 6
—Ah non, alors! C'était ennuyeux! 2
—Après ça, on est rentrés à la maison. 8
—Je suis parti en vacances avec mes parents. 4

RESOURCES FOR TROISIEME ETAPE

PRINT
- *Lesson Planner*, p. 56
- *Practice and Activity Book*, pp. 128–130
- *Grammar and Vocabulary Workbook*, pp. 96–97
- *Activities for Communication*, pp. 65–66, 127–129, 157–158
- *Listening Activities*, pp. 85, 89
- *Testing Program*, pp. 283–286
- *Alternative Assessment Guide*, p. 42

MEDIA
- *Video Program*, Videocassette 4
  Video Guide, pp. 73–78
- *Videodisc Program*, Videodisc 6, Side A
  Videodisc Guide, p. 124
- *Teaching Transparency* 11-3
- *Interactive CD-ROM Program*, Disc 3
  CD-ROM Teacher's Guide, p. 47
- *Audio Compact Discs*
  Textbook Listening Activity, CD 11, Tr. 12
  Additional Listening Activities 11-5, 11-6, CD 11, Trs. 30–31
  Quiz 11-3B, CD 11, Tr. 22

---

*J*ump Start!

Have students write a note to a French friend who is coming to visit, reminding him or her of three things to pack for the trip.

MOTIVATE

Ask students in English how their weekends were. Then, have them list French expressions they've already learned for giving opinions, such as **super, barbant,** and **chouette.**

TEACH

Presentation

Comment dit-on...? Draw three columns on the board and draw a question mark, a happy face, and an unhappy face as column headers. Teach these expressions, using appropriate gestures or facial expressions. As you teach each one, write the expression under the appropriate heading on the board. Then, give students various vacation activities (**garder ma petite sœur, aller à la plage**) and have them identify the expression on the board that they would give if they had done the activity while on vacation.

For Individual Needs

29 Challenge Have students imagine they spent their vacation in a certain place and write a sentence telling how it was. Then, have them read the sentence to a partner, who will indicate whether the student had a good, fair, or bad time.

Reteaching

Passé composé Ask students what they remember about the **passé composé.** Then, review the forms of **avoir** on a transparency. Ask students if they remember how to form the past participles of regular -**er**, -**re**, and -**ir** verbs and if they can recall the irregular past participles of verbs like **faire, lire,** and **voir.** To practice verb forms, you might also want to play the verb game **"Réponds vite!"** described on page 281J.

Additional Practice

Tu te rappelles? You might conduct a short oral practice of the **passé composé** by asking simple questions such as **Qu'est-ce que tu as mis hier? Qu'est-ce que tu as fait pendant le week-end? Qu'est-ce que tu as mangé ce matin?** Then, have partners ask each other what they did yesterday and tell three things they did.

Teaching Suggestion

31 Have students give the itinerary twice, first as if they were Marianne, using **je,** and again as if they went with Marianne, using **nous** or **on.**

Portfolio

32 Written This activity could also be written and would be appropriate for students' written portfolios. For portfolio information, see the *Alternative Assessment Guide,* pages iv–17.

 For videodisc application, see *Videodisc Guide.*

 CD-ROM Disc 3

Tu te rappelles?

Do you remember how to form the **passé composé?** Use a form of **avoir** as a helping verb with the past participle of the main verb. The past participles of regular -**er**, -**re**, and -**ir** verbs end in **é, u,** and **i.**

Nous **avons** beaucoup **mangé.** J'**ai répondu** à leur lettre. Ils **ont fini.**

You have to memorize the past participles of irregular verbs.

J'**ai fait** du camping. Ils **ont vu** un film.

To make a verb in the **passé composé** negative, you place **ne... pas** around the helping verb.

Il **n'a pas** fait ses devoirs.

With **aller, partir,** and **sortir,** you use **être** as the helping verb instead of **avoir.**

 PA
p. 130, Act. 21

 GV
pp. 96–97, Acts. 16–18

For additional practice, see p. R51.

31 Qu'est-ce qu'elle a fait?

Mets ces activités dans le bon ordre d'après l'itinéraire de Marianne à la page 295. See answers below.

D'abord, elle...

visiter le musée Van Gogh

voir un spectacle folklorique

visiter la parfumerie Fragonard

visiter la Cité des Papes

voir le moulin de Daudet

faire la promenade du Rocher des Doms

faire un pique-nique

32 On fait la même chose?

You and your partner took these photographs on a trip to France last year. Take turns telling where you went, what you did, and what you thought of each place or activity.

Un café sur le Cours Mirabeau

Le palais des Papes, c'est formidable.

La mer Méditerranée

Les arènes en Arles

La Côte d'Azur

Answers

31 D'abord, elle a visité le musée Van Gogh. Ensuite, elle a fait un pique-nique, et elle a vu le moulin de Daudet. Après ça, elle a visité la Cité des Papes, et elle a fait la promenade du Rocher des Doms. Ensuite, elle a vu un spectacle folklorique. Enfin, elle a visité la Parfumerie Fragonard.

33 On est de retour

Tu reviens d'un voyage. Ton ami(e) te demande où tu es allé(e), avec qui, ce que tu as fait et comment ça s'est passé.

PRONONCIATION

Aspirated h, th, ch, and gn   See scripts and answers on p. 281H.
CD 11 Trs. 13–18

You've learned that you don't pronounce the letter **h** in French. Some words begin with an aspirated **h** (**h aspiré**). This means that you don't make elision and liaison with the word that comes before. Repeat these phrases: **le haut-parleur; le houx; les halls; les haricots.**

Haut and **houx** begin with an aspirated **h**, so you can't drop the **e** from the article **le**. **Halls** and **haricots** also begin with an aspirated **h**, so you don't pronounce the **s** in the article **les**. How will you know which words begin with an aspirated **h**? If you look the words up in the dictionary, you may find an asterisk (*) before an aspirated **h**.

How do you pronounce the combination **th**? Just ignore the letter **h** and pronounce the **t**. Repeat these words: **mathématiques, théâtre, athlète.**

What about the combination **ch**? In French, **ch** is pronounced like the English *sh,* as in the word *show.* Compare these English and French words: *change/***change,** *chocolate/***chocolat,** *chance/***chance.** In some words, **ch** is pronounced like *k.* Listen to these words and repeat them: **chorale, Christine, archéologie.**

Finally, how do you pronounce the combination **gn**? The English sound /ny/, as in the word *onion* is similar. Pronounce these words: **oignon, montagne, magnifique.**

A. A prononcer

Repeat the following words.

1. le héros	la harpe	le hippie	le hockey
2. thème	maths	mythe	bibliothèque
3. Chine	choisir	tranche	pêches
4. espagnol	champignon	montagne	magnifique

B. A lire

Take turns with a partner reading each of the following sentences aloud.

1. J'aime la Hollande, mais je veux aller à la montagne en Allemagne.
2. Je cherche une chemise, des chaussures et un chapeau.
3. Il n'a pas fait ses devoirs de maths et de chimie à la bibliothèque dimanche.
4. Charles a gagné trois hamsters. Ils sont dans ma chambre! Quel cauchemar!

C. A écrire

You're going to hear a short dialogue. Write down what you hear.

📁 **Portfolio**

33 Oral   This might be included in students' oral portfolios. For portfolio suggestions, see the *Alternative Assessment Guide,* page 28.

Teaching Suggestion

Prononciation   You might have students prepare any two of the sentences in Part B to read aloud for oral assessment.

CLOSE

To close this **étape**, show *Teaching Transparency 11-3.* Ask students what the teenagers did on vacation and how they felt about it. You might have students form groups of four and role-play the teenagers' discussion.

ASSESS

Quiz 11-3A, Quiz 11-3B, *Testing Program,* pp. 283–286
Audio CD 11, Tr. 22

Performance Assessment

Have students act out a phone conversation between two friends who are comparing their weekends. Students should tell how their weekends were and what they did.

Language-to-Language

- The word **le houx** means *holly.*
- Many words with the **h aspiré** are of Germanic rather than Latin origin, or were borrowed from modern German or English. You might point out that words of these origins generally do not have **l'** preceding them, with the exception of **l'héroïne.**

READING STRATEGY

Reading for a purpose

Teacher Note

For an additional reading, see *Practice and Activity Book*, page 131.

PREREADING
Activities A–B

Motivating Activity

Point out Provence on a map. Have students share information they have already learned about Provence through the Location Opener for Chapters 9–11, the **Notes Culturelles**, and their projects for Chapter 9. Ask students what they would do if they were to go on a vacation to Provence. You might show a short video or some slides of Provence, or read a short passage from a book about Provence. See Peter Mayle's books: *A Year in Provence; Provence; Toujours Provence;* and *Hôtel Pastis.*

Teaching Suggestion

Before they begin the activities, have students look at travel guides for New York City, Chicago, Dallas, and so on. You might also ask them to bring in travel guides. Have groups of students go through the guides that are available and identify the general categories of information found in them. Then, do Activities A-B as a class.

$\mathcal{W}$hat would you like to do if you were visiting Provence?

DE BONS CONSEILS

When you read for a purpose, it's a good idea to decide beforehand what kind of information you want. If you're looking for an overview, a quick, general reading may be all that is required. If you're looking for specific details, you'll have to read more carefully.

A. The information at the top of both pages is from a book entitled *Le Guide du Routard.* Do you think this is

1. a history book?
2. a travel guide?
3. a geography book?

B. You usually read a book like this to gather general information about what is going on, or to find details about a certain place or event. What general categories of information can you find? Under what titles?   See answers below.

C. Where should you stay if . . .

1. you plan to visit Provence in November?
2. you want a balcony?
3. you want the least expensive room you can get?
4. you have a tent and a sleeping bag?   See answers below.

D. Do you think the descriptions of the hotels were written by the hotel management? How do you know?   No; Some remarks are unfavorable.

ARLES (13200)

Où dormir?

Très bon marché

Auberge de jeunesse : 20, av. Foch. 04-90-96-18-25. Fax : 04-90-96-31-26. Fermée pendant les vacances de Noël. 100 lits. 75 F la première nuit, 65 F les suivantes, draps et petit déjeuner compris. Fait aussi restaurant. Repas à 47 F.

Prix modérés

Hôtel Gauguin : 5, place Voltaire. 04-90-96-14-35. Fax : 04-90-18-98-87. Fermé du 10 janvier au 15 février et du 15 novembre au 20 décembre. De 170 F à 210 F la double. Sur trois étages. Chambres simples, bien aménagées. Celles qui donnent sur la place ont un balcon. Peu de charme cependant dans ce quartier de l'après-guerre. Le petit plus : tous les matins la météo locale est affichée à la réception!

Plus chic

Hôtel du Musée : 11, rue du Grand-Prieuré. 04-90-93-88-88. Fax : 04-90-49-98-15. Fermé en janvier. Dans une belle demeure du XVIIe siècle, face au musée Réattu et à deux pas du Rhône, une excellente adresse. De 270 F à 300 F la chambre double. Joli patio pour le petit déjeuner. Très bien situé et très bon accueil.

Camping

Camping City : 67, route de Crau. 04-90-93-08-86. Fax : 04-90-93-91-07. Fermé du 30 octobre au 1er mars. En allant vers Raphèle-lès-Arles. Assez ombragé, mais plutôt bruyant. Attention aux moustiques, car situé près d'un marécage. Piscine, épicerie, plats à emporter, restaurant-pizzeria, animations en été.

BATEAU «MIREIO»

BATEAU «MIREIO»
Bateau restaurant de 250 places, chauffé, climatisé. Croisières déjeuner sans escale vers Châteauneuf-du-Pape ou avec escale en Arles – visite de la capitale de la Camargue –, à Roquemaure avec dégustation des vins de Côtes du Rhône, à Villeneuve avec visite du village et de ses monuments. Croisières dîner et soirées spectacle devant Avignon et Villeneuve. Animation dansante et commentaires sur toutes les croisières.

84000 AVIGNON -
Tél. : 04 90 85 62 25
Fax : 04 90 85 61 14

CATHEDRALE D'IMAGES
Aux Baux-de-Provence, dans les anciennes carrières du Val-d'Enfer, CATHEDRALE D'IMAGES propose un spectacle permanent en IMAGE TOTALE. 4.000m² d'écrans naturels, 40 sources de projection, 2 500 diapos créent une féerie visuelle et sonore où déambule le spectateur.
–Couvrez-vous car les carrières sont fraîches!–

13520 LES BAUX-DE-PROVENCE -
Tél. : 04 90 54 38 65
Fax : 04 90 54 42 65

CATHEDRALE D'IMAGES

Science Link

You might have your students do research to find out how caves such as the **Grottes de Thouzon** are formed.

Answers

B what to see (various titles), where to eat *(Où manger?)*, where to sleep *(Où dormir?)*

C 1. Auberge de jeunesse en Arles, Hôtel du Musée
2. Hôtel Gauguin
3. Auberge de jeunesse en Arles
4. Camping City

ARLES (13200)

Où manger?

Bon marché

🍴 **Vitamine** : 04-90-93-77-36. ☎ 16, rue du Docteur-Fanton derrière la place du Forum. Fermé le samedi soir et le dimanche sauf pendant l'été. Une carte de 50 salades différentes, de 20 à 48 F, et 15 spécialités de pâtes de 32 à 80 F, le tout dans une salle agréablement décorée (expos photos) et avec un accueil décontracté.

🍴 **Le Grillon** : rond-point des Arènes. ☎ 04-90-96-70-97. Fermé le mercredi. Ce restaurant-brasserie-crêperie-glacier ne paie pas de mine, mais il y a une agréable terrasse avec une très belle vue sur les arènes. On y découvre de bons petits plats sympathiques. Menu à 81 F (très honnête) le midi, le soir et le week-end, avec soupe de poisson, fricassée de canard à la graine de moutarde, fromage ou dessert. A la carte, compter 70 F pour un plat. Salades copieuses à 49 F.

🍴 **Le Poisson Banane** : 6, rue du Forum. ☎ 04-90-96-02-58. Ouvert uniquement le soir. Fermé le dimanche seulement hors saison. Avec sa grande terrasse et sa tonnelle, ce petit resto caché derrière la place du Forum passe facilement inaperçu et c'est dommage. Il est agréable d'aller y goûter une cuisine sucrée-salée inventive avec un menu à 125 F, et une spécialité antillaise : le «poisson-banane», bien sûr. Autre menu à 79 F servi tous les jours jusqu'à 21h.

CHATEAU MUSEE DE L'EMPERI

CHATEAU MUSEE DE L'EMPERI

Le CHATEAU DE L'EMPERI, la plus importante forteresse médiévale en Provence, abrite une des plus somptueuses collections d'art et d'histoire militaire qui soit en Europe. Cette collection unique illustre l'évolution des uniformes et de l'art militaire de Louis XIV à 1918. La période napoléonienne est la plus présente. Le Château de l'Empéri est situé en plein cœur de la ville ancienne.

13300 SALON DE PROVENCE -
Tél : 04 90 56 22 36

GROTTES DE THOUZON

Les décors de stalactites qui parent « le ciel » de ce réseau naturel forment des paysages souterrains merveilleux. (Photo : M. CROTET) Grotte réputée pour la finesse de ses stalactites (fistuleuses). Parcours aisé pour les personnes âgées et les enfants. Seule grotte naturelle aménagée pour le tourisme en Provence. Ouvert du 1/04 au 31/10. Groupe toute l'année sur rendez-vous.

84250 LE THOR
Tél : 04 90 33 93 65
Fax : 04 90 33 74 90

GROTTES DE THOUZON

E. Which restaurant should you try if . . . *See answers below.*

1. you want the most expensive meal available?
2. you love salad?
3. you want to go out on Saturday night?

F. At the bottom of both pages, you will find descriptions of several tourist attractions in Provence. After you've read them, match attractions listed below with the sites where you would find them.

1. a dinner cruise   b
2. stalactites   c
3. thousands of projection screens   a
4. a collection of military art and uniforms   d

a. Cathédrale d'Images
b. Bateau «Mireio»
c. Grottes de Thouzon
d. Château Musée de l'Empéri

G. If you were working at a tourist information office, what would you recommend to someone who . . . *See answers below.*

1. wants a comfortable cruise package?
2. would like to visit a medieval castle?
3. likes to explore caves?
4. is interested in military art?

H. Are there similar tourist attractions in your area? What are they?

I. You and your friend have three days to spend in Arles. You're on a very tight budget, but you still want to enjoy your trip. Where will you stay? Where will you eat your lunches and dinners? How much will you spend for these three days?

trois cent un **301**

READING
Activities C–H

Thinking Critically

Drawing Inferences Ask students to suggest reasons why the places listed under **Où dormir?** are closed during various times of the year.

Building on Previous Skills

You might assign small groups various categories, such as meals, food, months of the year, days of the week, and so on, and ask them to scan the travel information and list words they recognize that fit their category.

POSTREADING
Activity I

Teaching Suggestion

I. Using Marianne's itinerary on page 295 as an example, students might write out their final itinerary and hand it in.

✦ For Individual Needs

Challenge Have students research lodgings and restaurants in a city they'd like to visit or in their own city. Have them create a brochure for French tourists that rates the hotels and restaurants. Price categories might include **très bon marché, bon marché, prix modérés,** and **plus chic.** They might also find out hotel rates and average menu prices and list them in francs or euros. Current exchange rates can be obtained from the newspaper or from larger banks and the Internet.

Answers

E 1. Le Poisson Banane
2. Vitamine
3. Le Grillon, Le Poisson Banane

G 1. Bateau «Miréio»
2. Château Musée de l'Empéri
3. Grottes de Thouzon
4. Château Musée de l'Empéri

MISE EN PRATIQUE

CD-ROM
Disc 3

The *CD-ROM Program* offers guided recording and writing activities to practice oral and written skills and to review material from each chapter.

The **Mise en pratique** reviews and integrates all four skills and culture in preparation for the Chapter Test.

Teaching Suggestion

1 You might first have students listen to the recording, read the questions, and then listen again for the answers.

 For Individual Needs

1 Slower Pace Have students write a list of the vacation words and expressions they expect to hear in this advertisement; they can look at this list while they listen to the recording. In this ad, three questions about three different types of vacations are posed and then answered. You might pause the recording after each type of vacation to assess comprehension.

2 Challenge After students have answered the questions, have them discuss or write about their reaction to the ad. You might have them design a similar ad aimed at Americans who might like to experience the culture of France or of other francophone countries.

1 Listen to this radio advertisement and then answer these questions. See scripts and answers on p. 281H.

CD 11 Tr. 19

1. What is being advertised?
2. Can you name two places that are mentioned in the advertisement?
3. What activities are mentioned in the advertisement?
4. For whom do they offer discounts?

2 Read the brochure and then answer the questions that follow.

Le rêve américain devient réalité, en séjour Immersion avec EF

Vivre à l'américaine

Qui n'a rêvé un jour de vivre une autre vie ? Ce rêve devient réalité, grâce à la formule EF Immersion : pendant quelques semaines, vous devenez totalement américain. Parce que les familles d'accueil sont soigneusement sélectionnées par EF, votre intégration est immédiate, et vos progrès linguistiques sont aussi spectaculaires que durables. C'est, sans nul doute, la formule qui vous assure la connaissance la plus directe et la plus profonde du mode de vie américain.

Vacances de Printemps

N° de séjour	Date de départ	Date de retour	Durée du séjour	Région	Frais de séjour*
550	11 avril	25 avril	2 sem.	Côte Est	7.730
551	18 avril	2 mai	2 sem.	Côte Est	7.730
552	18 avril	2 mai	2 sem.	Sud-Est	8.170

*Voyage inclus (départ Paris)

1. Where do students go if they sign up for this trip? the United States
2. Where do they stay? with a family
3. What do they learn? English language, American lifestyle
4. In what months can students make this trip? April, May
5. How long does it last? 2 weeks
6. To what regions of the country can students go? the East Coast, the Southeast
7. How much does this trip cost? 7.730 F for the East Coast, 8.170 F for the Southeast

3 Decide whether the statements below are true or false.

1. Only a few French children attend summer camp. false
2. French children can study foreign languages at summer camp. true
3. Most French people take a one-week summer vacation. false

302 *trois cent deux*   CHAPITRE 11   Vive les vacances!

4 *Ecrivons!*

Write a letter to a French-speaking exchange student who is coming to your school. Tell him or her what there is to see and do where you live, what the weather is like there, and what to bring.

STRATEGIE
Using connecting words such as **donc** and **alors** to link your ideas can help your writing flow more naturally.

Prewriting
Before you begin your letter, arrange your ideas logically to make your letter flow more smoothly. You might want to divide a sheet of paper into columns and label each column with a subject you'll address in your letter (**le temps, il te faut…** , and so on). Write each of your ideas in the appropriate column.

Writing
Using the ideas you organized, write a letter to describe the place where you live. Include a lot of detail in your description to help form an image of the places to visit. Try to use connecting words to tie sentences together in the letter. Remember to use expressions you've learned for making suggestions and reminding someone to do something.

Revising
Proofreading is one of the most important steps in the evaluation process. It gives you a chance to correct any mistakes you might have made while you were writing. While writing your first draft, concentrate on being creative. You can make corrections to the grammar, punctuation, and spelling when you proofread.

It's a good idea to proofread in several passes. First, read through your letter to check only for grammar and punctuation mistakes. On your second pass, check for spelling errors. This way, there will be fewer errors in your final draft.

5

JEU DE ROLE

a. You want to take a trip for your vacation, but you're not sure where. Tell your travel agent what you like to do and what you'd like to see. The travel agent will make some suggestions about where you might go and what there is to do there. He or she will also describe the weather conditions and tell you what clothes to take, where you can stay, and when and from where you can leave. The travel agent will also remind you of things you shouldn't forget to take. Act this out with your partner. Then, change roles.

b. You've returned from your trip and your friend wants to know how it went. Tell your friend about your trip and answer any questions he or she has about what you did. Act this out with your partner and then change roles.

Process Writing
4 To expand the Prewriting section, have students list the sights that they think the French exchange student visiting their town would most like to see and the activities he or she would most like to do. Beside each activity, have students write the best time of year or season to visit the sight or to do the activity. Then, next to the time of year, have students list any specific items the French exchange student might need to bring for visiting the sight or doing the activity. For example, **la plage** --> **en été** --> **un maillot de bain.**

Teaching Suggestion
4 For this activity, students may use information they learned about Canada and Côte d'Ivoire from previous chapters, the research they did for projects, or the activities they did in this chapter.

 Video Wrap-Up

- *VIDEO PROGRAM,*
  Videocassette 4, 15:19–30:28
- *VIDEODISC PROGRAM,*
  Videodisc 6, Side A

At this time, you might want to use the video resources for additional review and enrichment. See *Video Guide* or *Videodisc Guide* for suggestions regarding the following:
- **Bientôt les vacances!**
  (Dramatic episode)
- **Panorama Culturel**
  (Interviews)
- **Vidéoclips**
  (Authentic footage)

This page is intended to help students prepare for the Chapter Test. It is a brief checklist of the major points covered in the chapter. The students should be reminded that this is only a checklist and does not necessarily include everything that will appear on the test.

Teaching Suggestions

4 You might encourage students to add other activities, such as hiking or sailing, and other destinations, such as Mexico, England, or Vietnam.

5 Encourage students to offer several different ways to accept and reject the suggestions.

8 You might suggest other subjects and times for more practice with **partir.**

QUE SAIS-JE?

Can you use what you've learned in this chapter?

Can you inquire about and share future plans? Express indecision and wishes? p. 289

1 How would you ask where a friend is going on vacation and what he or she is going to do? How would you answer these questions? See answers below.

2 How would you tell someone . . .   See answers below.

1. you're not sure what to do?   2. where you'd really like to go?

Can you ask for advice? Make, accept, and refuse suggestions? p. 290

3 How would you ask a friend for advice about your vacation?
Je ne sais pas quoi faire (où aller); Tu as une idée? Qu'est-ce que tu me conseilles?

4 How would you suggest to a friend that he or she . . .   See answers below.

1. go to the country?   3. work?
2. go camping?   4. go to Canada?

5 How would you accept and refuse the suggestions in number 4? See answers below.

Can you remind and reassure someone? p. 293

6 How would you remind a friend to take these things on a trip?
See answers below.

1.   2.   3.

7 How would you reassure someone you haven't forgotten these things?

Je n'ai pas oublié...

1.   mon passeport.   2.   mon billet d'avion.   3.   mon billet de train.

Can you see someone off? p. 296

8 How would you tell when these people are leaving, using the verb **partir?** See answers below.

1. Didier / 14h28   3. Nous / 11h15
2. Désirée et Annie / 20h46   4. Tu / 23h59

9 How would you wish someone a good trip?
Bon voyage! Bonnes vacances! Amuse-toi bien!

Can you ask for and express opinions? p. 297

10 How would you ask a friend how his or her vacation went?
Tu as passé un bon été? Ça s'est bien passé? Tu t'es bien amusé(e)?

11 How would you tell how your vacation went?   C'était formidable/très chouette.
Ça a été. Pas mauvais. C'était épouvantable. C'était un véritable cauchemar! C'était ennuyeux.

Can you inquire about and relate past events? p. 297

12 How would you find out what a friend did on vacation?
Qu'est-ce que tu as fait? Tu es allé(e) où?

13 How would you tell what you did on vacation?

304   *trois cent quatre*   CHAPITRE 11   Vive les vacances!

Possible answers

1 Où est-ce que tu vas aller pendant les vacances? Qu'est-ce que tu vas faire?;
Je vais... J'ai l'intention de...

2 1. J'hésite. Je ne sais pas. Je n'en sais rien. Je n'ai rien de prévu.
2. Je voudrais bien aller... J'ai envie d'aller...

4 Je te conseille de (d')... Tu devrais...
1. aller à la campagne.
2. faire du camping.
3. travailler.

4. aller au Canada.

5 *Accept:* Tiens! C'est une bonne idée! Pourquoi pas? D'accord! Allons-y!
Refuse: Non, ce n'est pas possible. Non, je ne peux pas. Ça ne me dit rien. C'est trop cher.

6 N'oublie pas...
Tu n'as pas oublié... ?
Tu ne peux pas partir sans...
1. ton appareil-photo.
2. les cadeaux.
3. ton manteau.

8 1. Didier part à quatorze heures vingt-huit.
2. Désirée et Annie partent à vingt heures quarante-six.
3. Nous partons à onze heures quinze.
4. Tu pars à vingt-trois heures cinquante-neuf.

PREMIERE ETAPE

Inquiring about and sharing future plans

Qu'est-ce que tu vas faire...? *What are you going to do . . . ?*
Où est-ce que tu vas aller... ? *Where are you going to go . . . ?*
Je vais... *I'm going to . . .*
J'ai l'intention de... *I intend to . . .*

Expressing indecision

J'hésite. *I'm not sure.*
Je ne sais pas. *I don't know.*
Je n'en sais rien. *I have no idea.*
Je n'ai rien de prévu. *I don't have any plans.*

Expressing wishes

Je voudrais bien... *I'd really like to . . .*

J'ai envie de... *I feel like . . .*

Vacation places and activities

à la montagne *to/in the mountains*
en forêt *to/in the forest*
à la campagne *to/in the countryside*
en colonie de vacances *to/at a summer camp*
au bord de la mer *to/on the coast*
chez... *to/at . . . 's house*
faire du camping *to go camping*
faire de la randonnée *to go hiking*
faire du bateau *to go boating*

faire de la plongée *to go scuba diving*
faire de la planche à voile *to go windsurfing*
faire de la voile *to go sailing*
à *to, in (a city or place)*
en *to, in (before a feminine noun)*
au *to, in (before a masculine noun)*
aux *to, in (before a plural noun)*

Asking for advice; making, accepting, and refusing suggestions

See **Tu te rappelles?** on page 290.

DEUXIEME ETAPE

Travel items

un passeport *passport*
un billet de train *train ticket*
un billet d'avion *plane ticket*
une valise *suitcase*
de l'argent *money*
un appareil-photo *camera*
un cadeau *gift*
un parapluie *umbrella*

Reminding, reassuring

N'oublie pas... *Don't forget . . .*

Tu n'as pas oublié... ? *You didn't forget . . . ?*
Tu ne peux pas partir sans... *You can't leave without . . .*
Tu prends... ? *Are you taking . . . ?*
Ne t'en fais pas. *Don't worry.*
Je n'ai rien oublié. *I didn't forget anything.*
J'ai pensé à tout. *I've thought of everything.*
partir *to leave*

Seeing someone off

Bon voyage! *Have a good trip!*
Bonnes vacances! *Have a good vacation!*
Amuse-toi bien! *Have fun!*
Bonne chance! *Good luck!*

TROISIEME ETAPE

Asking for and expressing opinions

Tu as passé un bon... ? *Did you have a good . . . ?*
Ça s'est bien passé? *Did it go well?*
Tu t'es bien amusé(e)? *Did you have fun?*

Oui, très chouette. *Yes, very cool.*
C'était formidable! *It was great!*
Oui, ça a été. *Yes, it was OK.*
Oh, pas mauvais. *Oh, not bad.*
C'était épouvantable. *It was horrible.*
Non, pas vraiment. *No, not really.*

C'était un véritable cauchemar! *It was a real nightmare!*
C'était ennuyeux. *It was boring.*
C'était barbant. *It was boring.*

Inquiring about and relating past events

See **Tu te rappelles?** on page 297.

VOCABULAIRE

trois cent cinq **305**

CHAPTER 11 ASSESSMENT

CHAPTER TEST
• *Testing Program*, pp. 287–292
• *Audio Compact Discs*, Audio CD 11, Tracks 23–25

SPEAKING TEST
• *Testing Program*, p. 348

TEST GENERATOR
• Chapter 11

ALTERNATIVE ASSESSMENT
Performance Assessment
• You might want to use the **Jeu de Rôle** on page 303 as a cumulative performance assessment activity.
• *Alternative Assessment Guide*, p. 42

 Portfolio Assessment
• *Alternative Assessment Guide*, Oral: p. 28 Written: p. 28

CD-ROM Assessment
• *Interactive CD-ROM Program*, Disc 3
  A toi de parler
  A toi d'écrire
• *Alternative Assessment Guide*, p. 56

 Circumlocution

Tell students to imagine that they are traveling in a francophone country and they have lost several necessary travel items. Then, tell them that they don't know the words for these travel items, but they need to make a list of the missing items. Have them describe the items they lost to a partner without naming them. The partner will guess the items that are missing. You might give them the expression **On l'utilise pour...** Then, have partners switch roles and describe different items.

VIDEO PROGRAM
Videocassette 4
30:29–32:49

OR VIDEODISC PROGRAM,
Videodisc 6, Side B

Search 1, Play To 4171

Motivating Activity

Have students share whatever they know about the Caribbean, specifically about the French-speaking islands. Ask them if they know where French is spoken in the Caribbean (Guadeloupe, Haiti, and Martinique), and if they're familiar with the climate, history, or customs of this area. Then, have them open their books and compare their impressions with the photos on pages 306–309.

go.hrw.com
WAO FORT-DE-FRANCE

Visit the HRW Web site at http://go.hrw.com and enter the keyword **WAO FORT-DE-FRANCE** for student resources related to this location. For detailed access instructions, see page T45.

CHAPITRE 12

Allez, viens à Fort-de-France!

La ville de Fort-de-France

Background Information

Located on the beautiful Baie des Flamands, Fort-de-France is the largest city and busiest commercial center in the French West Indies. As the region's chief port, its exports include sugarcane, cocoa, and various fruits. Formerly known as Fort-Royal, Fort-de-France is now the **chef**-**lieu** *(administrative seat or capital)* of Martinique, which is a **département d'outre-mer** *(overseas department)* of France. Fort-de-France became the administrative capital of Martinique in 1902, when Saint-Pierre, formerly the largest city of the island, was destroyed by an eruption of Mount Pelée that killed approximately 30,000 people.

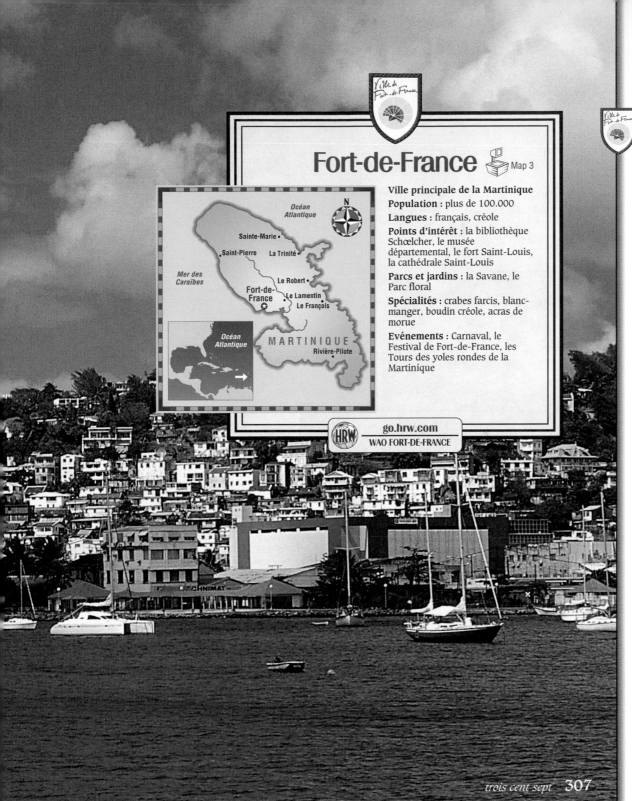

Fort-de-France   Map 3

Ville principale de la Martinique

Population : plus de 100.000

Langues : français, créole

Points d'intérêt : la bibliothèque Schœlcher, le musée départemental, le fort Saint-Louis, la cathédrale Saint-Louis

Parcs et jardins : la Savane, le Parc floral

Spécialités : crabes farcis, blanc-manger, boudin créole, acras de morue

Evénements : Carnaval, le Festival de Fort-de-France, les Tours des yoles rondes de la Martinique

HRW go.hrw.com
WAO FORT-DE-FRANCE

trois cent sept 307

Using the Almanac and Map

Terms in the Almanac

- **Créole,** one of two languages spoken in Martinique, is a blend of French, Spanish, English, and African languages. Words in Creole are usually written the way they sound.
- **Le musée départemental,** a museum devoted to the history of the island, includes artifacts of the Pre-Columbian Arawak and Carib civilizations, exhibits on Napoléon I and Joséphine, and information on **la montagne Pelée** and the history of slavery on the island.
- **La cathédrale Saint-Louis,** a Romanesque cathedral built in 1671, has beautiful stained-glass windows. Many of the island's governors are interred beneath it.
- **Le Parc floral et culturel** introduces visitors to the flowers and plants of the island and also contains an aquarium with native fish.
- **crabes farcis:** deviled land crabs
- **blanc-manger:** coconut pudding
- **boudin créole:** spicy creole sausage
- **acras de morue:** cod fritters

Teacher Note

Carnaval, which is mentioned in the **Culture Note** below, and the **Tour des yoles rondes** are described in detail in Chapter 4 of Level 2.

Using the Map

Ask students if they know on which body of water Fort-de-France is located (the Caribbean Sea). Ask if they can identify other countries that are located near Martinique (Cuba, Haiti and the Dominican Republic, Colombia, Panama, Venezuela).

Culture Note

Several holidays and festivals take place every year in Fort-de-France and throughout Martinique. **Carnaval,** a festival of music, parades, and costumes, is celebrated for four days preceding Ash Wednesday **(le mercredi des Cendres)**. **Le Festival de Fort-de-France** in July offers exhibits, concerts, and theatrical productions.

Using the Photo Essay

① **La bibliothèque Schœlcher** is a public library named after Victor Schœlcher, who fought to abolish slavery in the nineteenth century. Slavery was officially abolished in Martinique in 1848.

② **La Savane** Located here are statues of Pierre Belain d'Esnambuc, who led 80 settlers to Fort Saint-Pierre in 1635, and of Joséphine, the first wife of French Emperor Napoléon I. Joséphine, the daughter of a Martinique planter, was born on the island in 1763.

History Link

France began to colonize Martinique with d'Esnambuc's arrival in 1635, and the island became a domain of the French crown in 1674. The British had possession of the island three times in the eighteenth and early nineteenth centuries (1762, 1794–1802, 1809–1814). In 1815, the island was ceded by treaty to France, and in 1946, it became an overseas department. Martinique sends four deputies to the French National Assembly and is governed by a prefect appointed by the French Minister of the Interior and a general council elected by the people of the island.

③ **Le fort Saint-Louis** was built in the seventeenth century to defend the island of Martinique. Today, special permission is needed to visit the fort.

Teacher Note

③ Call students' attention to the French flag flying atop **fort Saint-Louis.** Explain that since Martinique is a French **département,** its people are French citizens.

Fort-de-France CD-ROM Disc 3

*Clinging to the mountains overlooking the Caribbean coast of Martinique, the city of Fort-de-France lies on the **baie des Flamands**. Nearly one-third of the population of Martinique lives in or near the city. Here you will see a blending of cultures. Although Martinique is 4,261 miles from Paris, it is a **département** of France. While its character is decidedly French, the pastel-colored buildings and wrought-iron balconies may remind you of New Orleans, and the sounds of the **créole** language and **zouk** music are purely West Indian.*

① **La bibliothèque Schœlcher** is a very elaborate building constructed in a blend of byzantine, Egyptian, and romanesque styles. Like the Eiffel Tower, it was built in 1889 for the Paris Exposition. It was later dismantled and rebuilt among the palm trees in Fort-de-France.

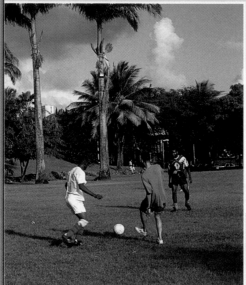

② **La Savane** is a 12½-acre landscaped park filled with tropical trees, fountains, benches, and gardens. This is the place to go to meet with friends, take a walk, or play a casual game of soccer.

③ Built on a rocky peninsula, **le fort Saint-Louis** overlooks the port of Fort-de-France.

History Link

The original inhabitants of Martinique were Indians from South America who gradually migrated through the islands of the Caribbean, most likely reaching Martinique and Guadeloupe in the second century A.D. Gradually, the Arawaks, another Indian people, settled there. Subsequently, a cannibalistic warrior race called the Caribs (who gave their name to the Caribbean Sea) conquered the Arawaks. In the early sixteenth century, when Columbus arrived in Martinique for the first time, he encountered the descendants of the Caribs, whose excellent fighting skills prevented the Europeans from immediately gaining possession of the island.

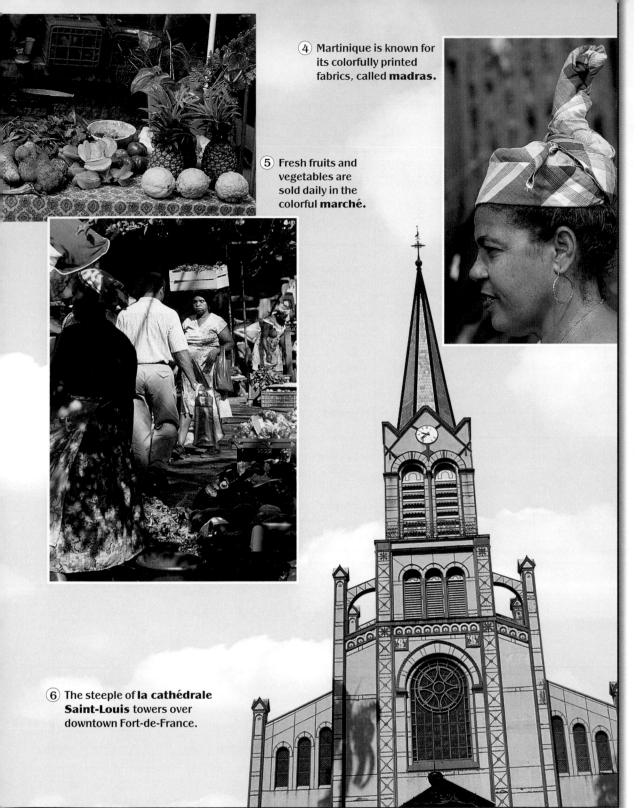

④ Martinique is known for its colorfully printed fabrics, called **madras.**

⑤ Fresh fruits and vegetables are sold daily in the colorful **marché.**

⑥ The steeple of **la cathédrale Saint-Louis** towers over downtown Fort-de-France.

Thinking Critically

④ **Drawing Inferences**
Have students suggest reasons why head coverings are important. (In Martinique, the intense heat and sun of the tropical climate create the need for some sort of head covering. Scarf-like head coverings serve to hold one's hair in place, are decorative and stylish, and often match the outfit being worn.)

⑤ **Observing** Have students try to identify the different fruits and vegetables in the photos. They might recognize the tomatoes and pineapples, but you might have to identify the other food items. Moving from left to right, you can see *yams* (**des ignames**), which students will recall from Chapter 8; *star fruit* (**des caramboles**); breadfruit (**fruit de l'arbre à pain**), sitting in front of the pineapples; and hot peppers (**piments**), in the bowl behind the star fruit and tomatoes. The flowers behind the pineapples are called *anthuriums,* known as the official flower of Martinique.

⑤ **Comparing and Contrasting** Have students recall from Chapter 8 the differences between shopping in an open-air market and in a store. How might the produce be different? What quantities might one buy? Are prices fixed? How does the shopper carry his or her purchases? In Martinique, most produce sold in open-air markets is fresh, and women will often carry their purchases on their heads, as students will notice in Photo 5. Shoppers generally bring their own shopping bags and pay in cash. They might bargain with the seller on the price of a particular item. Tasting is also common before one buys something.

Teaching Suggestion

⑤ Ask students what the advantages and disadvantages are of carrying heavy loads on one's head. If students can't think of any advantages, have them try to carry a book on their head. Although it requires some practice and balance, carrying things on one's head leaves the hands free and is probably easier on the back. It also ensures good posture.

Chapitre 12 : En ville
Chapter Overview

Mise en train pp. 312–314	Un petit service			

	FUNCTIONS	GRAMMAR	CULTURE	RE-ENTRY
Première étape pp. 315–319	• Pointing out places and things, p. 317	*Review* • Contractions with **à**, p. 316	• **Note Culturelle,** Store hours in France and Martinique, p. 316 • **Rencontre Culturelle,** Making "small talk" in francophone countries, p. 319	• School supplies **(Chapitre 3)** • Food items **(Chapitre 8)** • The **passé composé (Chapitre 9)**
Deuxième étape pp. 320–324	• Making and responding to requests, p. 320 • Asking for advice and making suggestions, p. 322	*Review* • The partitive, p. 320 • The pronoun **y,** p. 323	• Realia: A French stamp, p. 321 • **Panorama Culturel,** Getting a driver's license in francophone countries, p. 324	• Expressing need **(Chapitre 8)** • Making an excuse **(Chapitre 5)** • Inviting **(Chapitre 6)**
Troisième étape pp. 325–329	• Asking for and giving directions, p. 327	• Contractions with **de,** p. 325	• **Note Culturelle, DOMs** and **TOMs,** p. 326 • **Note Culturelle,** Public areas downtown, p. 327	• Family vocabulary **(Chapitre 7)** • Possessive adjectives **(Chapitre 7)**

Prononciation p. 329	Review Audio CD 12, Tracks 12–14	**À écrire** (dictation) Audio CD 12, Tracks 15–17	
Lisons! pp. 330–331	**Cheval de bois**	**Reading Strategy** Combining different reading strategies	
Review pp. 332–335	**Mise en pratique**, pp. 332–333 **Écrivons!** Making a writing plan Writing a conversation	**Que sais-je?** p. 334	**Vocabulaire,** p. 335

Assessment Options

Testing Program
- Première étape, Quiz 12-1A, Quiz 12-1B, pp. 301–304
- Deuxième étape, Quiz 12-2A, Quiz 12-2B, pp. 305–308
- Troisième étape, Quiz 12-3A, Quiz 12-3B, pp. 309–312
- Chapter Test, pp. 313–318
- Speaking Test, p. 348

Audio Compact Discs
- Audio CD 12, Tracks 19–24

Interactive CD-ROM Program
- Mise en pratique (A toi de parler, A toi d'écrire)
- CD-ROM Teacher's Guide, Assessment Options, p. 53

Alternative Assessment Guide
- Portfolio Assessment, p. 29
- Performance Assessment, p. 43
- CD-ROM Assessment, p. 57

Test Generator
- Chapter 12

FINAL EXAM

Testing Program
- Final Exam, pp. 327–334
- Score Sheet, pp. 335–337
- Listening Scripts, pp. 338–339
- Answers, p. 340

Audio Compact Discs
- Audio CD 12, Tracks 25–30

PRINT	MEDIA

Pupil's Edition, pp. 310–335

 Audio Compact Discs
• Textbook Listening Activities: Audio CD 12, Tracks 1–18

**Interactive CD-ROM Program
Teacher's Guide,** pp. 50–53

 Interactive CD-ROM Program
• Disc 3

Videodisc Guide
• Teaching Suggestions, pp. 134–138
• Activity Masters, pp. 139–141

 Videodisc Program
• Videodisc 6, Side B

Video Guide
• Teaching Suggestions, pp. 82–83
• Activity Masters, pp. 84–86

 Video Program
• Videocassette 4
• Videocassette 5 (captioned version)

Listening Activities
• Student Response Forms for Textbook Listening Activities, pp. 91–93
• Additional Listening Activities, 12-1 to 12-6, pp. 95–97
• Additional Listening Activities (song), p. 98
• Scripts and Answers, pp. 157–161

 Audio Compact Discs
• Textbook Listening Activities: Audio CD 12, Tracks 1–18
• Additional Listening Activities: Audio CD 12, Tracks 31–37

Teaching Transparencies
• Teaching Transparency Masters 12-1 to 12-3 (Situations) and 12-A to 12-C (Vocabulary)
• Teaching Suggestions 12-1 to 12-3 and 12-A to 12-C

 Teaching Transparencies
• Situations 12-1 to 12-3
• Vocabulary 12-A to 12-C

Testing Program
• Grammar and Vocabulary Quizzes, **Etape** Quizzes, Chapter Test, and Final Exam, pp. 301–318, 327–334
• Score Sheet, Scripts, and Answers, pp. 319–326, 335–340

 Audio Compact Discs
• Assessment Items: Audio CD 12, Tracks 19–30

 Test Generator
• Chapter 12

Alternative Assessment Guide
• Portfolio Assessment, p. 29
• Performance Assessment, p. 43
• CD-ROM Assessment, p. 57

 Grammar and Vocabulary Workbook, pp. 98–107

 Practice and Activity Book, pp. 133–144

Activities for Communication
• Communicative Activities, pp. 67–72
• Realia and Teaching Suggestions, pp. 130–134
• Situation Cards, pp. 159–160

Lesson Planner
• Lesson Plan, pp. 58–62

Chapitre 12 : En ville
Technology Applications

MISE EN TRAIN, pp. 312–314

Video
• Show *Un petit service.* For Video Synopsis, Teaching Suggestions, Activity Master, and Scripts, see the *Video Guide* or the *Videodisc Guide.*

Audio
• Play the recording of the **Mise en train** with pauses as students read along. You might have them practice pronunciation by repeating individual sentences after hearing them.

PREMIERE ETAPE, pp. 315–319

Video
• While students watch *Un petit service,* have them listen for exchanges that model pointing out places and things. See p. 135 of the *Videodisc Guide.*

Audio
• Textbook Listening Activity 7 practices the vocabulary for places and things in town.

• To have students recognize the vocabulary for places in town and errands to do at each place, use Additional Listening Activities 12-1 and 12-2.

Transparencies
• Use *Teaching Transparencies 12-1* and *12-A* and the Teaching Suggestions to present and practice the vocabulary for stores and errands and the expressions for pointing out places in town.

CD-ROM (Disc 3)
• **Chasse au trésor** (Activity 1) practices places in town and errands to do at each place.
• In **Le bon choix** (Activity 2), students respond to statements and questions about places in town and errands to do at each place.
• For suggestions, see p. 51 of the *CD-ROM Teacher's Guide.*

DEUXIEME ETAPE, pp. 320–323

Video
• While students watch *Un petit service,* have them listen for exchanges that model making and responding to requests, asking for advice, and making suggestions. See pp. 135–136 of the *Videodisc Guide.*

Audio
• Textbook Listening Activity 15 has students distinguish between accepting and declining requests.
• Textbook Listening Activity 19 has students practice the vocabulary for means of transportation.
• To review the vocabulary for errands, places in town, and means of transportation, and the expressions for making and responding to requests, and for asking for and responding to suggestions, use Additional Listening Activity 12-3.
• Additional Listening Activity 12-4 reviews the vocabulary for means of transportation.

Transparencies
• Use *Teaching Transparency 12-2* and the Teaching Suggestions to have students practice the expressions for making and responding to requests and for asking for and making suggestions.
• Use *Teaching Transparency 12-B* to present and practice the vocabulary for means of transportation.

CD-ROM (Disc 3)
• To have students review partitive and indefinite articles, use **Les mots qui manquent** (Activity 3).
• **Jeu des paires** (Activity 4) has students identify means of transportation.
• **Méli-mélo** (Activity 5) has students practice the pronoun **y.**
• For suggestions, see pp. 51–52

of the *CD-ROM Teacher's Guide.*

PANORAMA CULTUREL, p. 324

Video
• Show the interviews. For Video Synopsis, Teaching Suggestions, Activity Master, and Scripts, see the *Video Guide* or the *Videodisc Guide.*

Audio
• Play the **Panorama Culturel** as students read along. Remind students they might not be able to understand everything each person says, but they should deduce global meaning.

CD-ROM (Disc 3)
• Have students do the **Panorama Culturel** activity after showing them the video. For suggestions, see p. 52 of the *CD-ROM Teacher's Guide.*

TROISIEME ETAPE, pp. 325–329

Video
• While students watch *Un petit service,* have them listen for exchanges that model asking for and giving directions. See p. 136 of the *Videodisc Guide.*

Audio
• Use Textbook Listening Activity 23 to have students identify the location of places in town.

• Use Textbook Listening Activity 27 to have students follow directions in town.

• Additional Listening Activities 12-5 and 12-6 review the expressions for asking for and giving directions and the vocabulary for places in town.

Transparencies
• Use *Teaching Transparency 12-C* and the Teaching Suggestions to have students talk about the location of places and things in town.
• Use *Teaching Transparency 12-3* and the Teaching

Suggestions to have students practice asking for and giving directions to various places in town.

CD-ROM (Disc 3)
• After presenting the expressions for asking for and giving directions, have students do **Chasse au trésor** (Activity 6).
• For suggestions, see p. 52 of the *CD-ROM Teacher's Guide.*

MISE EN PRATIQUE, pp. 332–333

Video
• Replay *Un petit service* in its entirety and ask students to identify the exchanges in which the characters point out places and things, make and respond to requests, ask for advice, make suggestions, and ask for and give directions.

CD-ROM (Disc 3)
• Have students do the **En contexte** to practice the vocabulary and functional expressions presented in the chapter. See the suggestions on p. 51 of the *CD-ROM Teacher's Guide.*

• Have students practice their writing and speaking skills by doing the **A toi d'écrire** and **A toi de parler** activities. See pp. 52–53 of the *CD-ROM Teacher's Guide.*

• For Assessment Options, see p. 53 of the *CD-ROM Teacher's Guide.*

Test Generator
• Use the Test Generator to create review material for students taking the Chapter Test or to prepare an alternate test.

VIDEOCLIPS

Video
• Show the **Vidéoclips.** For Video Synopsis, Teaching Suggestions, Activity Masters, and Scripts, see the *Video Guide* or the *Videodisc Guide.*

Videodisc Program
Videodisc 6, Side B
Videodisc Guide, pp. 132–141

Chapitre 12 : En ville
Barcode Directory

BARCODE DIRECTORY
CHAPTER 1

MISE EN TRAIN

Barcodes A and B access **Mise en train** and **Mise en train (suite)** in their entirety. Subsequent barcodes show specific segments of **Un petit service.** The barcode numbers correspond to the scene numbers as they appear on the video.

ETAPES

To practice the grammar, vocabulary, and functions presented in each **étape,** see the barcodes and accompanying suggestions on pages 135–136 of the *Videodisc Guide.*

Un petit service **A**

Search 4200, Play To 10245

Où vas-tu... ? **1**

Search 4200, Play To 5829

Avant de rentrer... **2**

Search 5829, Play To 6424

Tu n´as besoin... ? **3**

Search 6424, Play To 7211

Est-ce que... ? **4**

Search 7211, Play To 7954

Dis, Lucien... **5**

Search 7954, Play To 8554

Au retour... **6**
Search 8554, Play To 9892

Bonjour!... **7**
Search 9892, Play To 10245

Un petit service (suite) **B**
Search 10245, Play To 28545

MISE EN PRATIQUE

This is additional footage modeling some of the expressions practiced in this chapter. You may want to use it to review the chapter.

Mise en pratique **1**

Search 42240, Play To 45144

Mise en pratique **2**

Search 45145, Play To 46291

Mise en pratique **3**

Search 46972, Play To 47789

PANORAMA CULTUREL

Qu'est-ce qu´il faut faire pour avoir un permis de conduire? These barcodes access the three interviews of the **Panorama Culturel** presented in the *Pupil's Edition* as well as additional interviews.

First three interviews **1**
Search 28545, Play To 31590

All interviews **2**
Search 28545, Play To 33624

Lily-Christine **3**
Search 29438, Play To 30038

Emmanuel **4**
Search 30039, Play To 31030

Charlotte **5**
Search 31031, Play To 31567

Virgile **6**
Search 31594, Play To 31719

Jean-Christophe **7**
Search 31720, Play To 32126

Olivier **8**
Search 32127, Play To 32381

Matthieu **9**
Search 32382, Play To 32730

Céline **10**
Search 32731, Play To 32915

Léna **11**
Search 32916, Play To 33063

Viviane **12**
Search 33064, Play To 33355

Amadou **13**

Search 33356, Play To 33624

VIDEOCLIPS

These are authentic French commercials. You may want to preview them before showing them to students.

RATP®: Parisian transport system **1**

Search 33624, Play To 35988

Banette®: bread **2**
Search 35988, Play To 36459

Banette®: bread **3**

Search 36459, Play To 36966

Chapitre 12 : En ville
CD-ROM Directory ● DISC 3

The following directory lists the *Interactive CD-ROM Program* activities for Chapter 12. For details and suggestions on how to use them, see pages 50–53 of the *CD-ROM Teacher's Guide*.

GLOBAL TASK		COMMUNICATIVE GOALS	ACTIVITY TYPE
Faisons des courses! Students help their friend Etienne run errands in town.		To use chapter functions, vocabulary, and grammar in a lifelike conversation	**En contexte** *Interactive conversation*

	SUPPORTING ACTIVITIES	PUPIL'S EDITION	COMMUNICATIVE GOALS	ACTIVITY TYPE
Première étape	1. Vocabulaire	p. 315	To identify places in town and errands to run at each place	**Chasse au trésor Explorons!/Vérifions!** *Interactive image*
	2. Vocabulaire	p. 315	To match places in town with errands to run at each place	**Le bon choix** *Multiple choice*
Deuxième étape	3. Grammaire	p. 320	To review partitive and indefinite articles	**Les mots qui manquent** *Tic Tac Toe*
	4. Vocabulaire	p. 322	To identify means of transportation	**Jeu des paires** *Concentration®*
	5. Grammaire	p. 323	To correctly sequence sentences containing the the pronoun **y**	**Méli-mélo** *Sequencing*
Troisième étape	6. Comment dit-on... ?	pp. 325, 327	To give directions to places in town	**Chasse au trésor Explorons!/Vérifions!** *Interactive image*
Panorama Culturel	Panorama Culturel	p. 324	To listen to and understand native speakers talking about what they need to do to get a driver's license where they live	**Qu'est-ce qu'il faut faire pour avoir un permis de conduire?** *Presentation* **Le bon choix** *Multiple choice*

	APPLICATION	PUPIL'S EDITION	COMMUNICATIVE GOALS	ACTIVITY TYPE
Mise en pratique	A toi de parler	pp. 332–333	To create and record a conversation in which students ask their friend Adjoua for help with some errands and give her directions	*Guided recording*
	A toi d'écrire	pp. 332–333	To write a note, a dialogue, a list, or a letter	*Guided writing*

🏠 *Homework Suggestions*

CHAPTER SECTION	PRESENTATION	HOMEWORK OPTIONS
Première étape	**Vocabulaire,** p. 315	Pupil's Edition, p. 318, Activity 13 Practice and Activity Book, pp. 134–135, Activities 2–5 Grammar and Vocabulary Workbook, pp. 98–99, Activities 1–4 CD-ROM, Disc 3, Activities 1–2
	Comment dit-on... ? p. 317	Practice and Activity Book, p. 136, Activity 8
Deuxième étape	**Comment dit-on... ?** p. 320	Practice and Activity Book, p. 137, Activities 9–11
	Vocabulaire, p. 322	Practice and Activity Book, p. 138, Activities 12–14 Grammar and Vocabulary Workbook, pp. 103–104, Activities 11–15 CD-ROM, Disc 3, Activity 4
	Grammaire, p. 323	Pupil's Edition, p. 323, Activity 21; p. R53, Activities 4–5 Practice and Activity Book, p. 139, Activities 15–16 Grammar and Vocabulary Workbook, p. 105, Activities 16–17 CD-ROM, Disc 3, Activity 5
Troisième étape	**Vocabulaire,** p. 325	Pupil's Edition, p. 329, Activity 30 Practice and Activity Book, p. 140, Activities 18–20 Grammar and Vocabulary Workbook, pp. 106–107, Activities 19–21
	Note de grammaire, p. 325	Pupil's Edition, p. R53, Activity 6 Practice and Activity Book, p. 141, Activity 21 Grammar and Vocabulary Workbook, p. 106, Activity 18
	Comment dit-on... ? p. 327	Practice and Activity Book, pp. 141–142, Activities 22–24 CD-ROM, Disc 3, Activity 6

For Student Response Forms, see *Listening Activities,* pp. 91–93.

Première étape

7 Ecoute! p. 316

1. — De l'aspirine, s'il vous plaît.
   — Voilà. C'est tout?
2. — Vous avez des disques compacts en espagnol?
   — Oui, bien sûr.
3. — Je voudrais déposer deux cents francs.
   — Le numéro de votre compte, s'il vous plaît?
4. — Je voudrais des timbres.
   — Vous en voulez combien?
5. — Il me faut du papier, des stylos et des enveloppes.
   — Ça fait trente-neuf francs.
6. — Mmm... il a l'air très bon, ce gâteau-là. Je vais le prendre.
   — N'oublie pas, tu es au régime!

Answers to Activity 7
1. at the drugstore
2. at the record store
3. at the bank
4. at the post office
5. at the book/stationery store
6. at the pastry shop/bakery

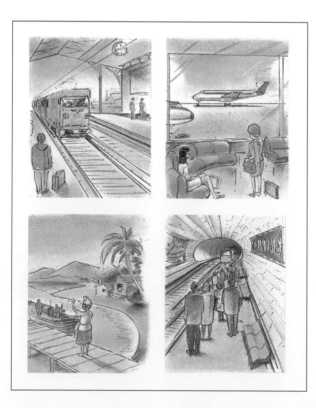

Deuxième étape

15 Ecoute! p. 320

1. — Marie, tu peux aller à la poste acheter des timbres?
   — Désolée, mais je n'ai pas le temps!
2. — Est-ce que tu peux aller à la pharmacie? J'ai mal à la tête, mais je n'ai plus d'aspirine.
   — Oui, d'accord. J'y vais tout de suite.
3. — Tu peux me rendre un petit service? J'ai besoin d'argent. Est-ce que tu peux aller à la banque ce matin?
   — Oui, si tu veux.
4. — Au retour, tu peux passer à la boulangerie? Prends deux baguettes, s'il te plaît.
   — Oui, maman. C'est tout?
5. — Tu pourrais passer par la bibliothèque aujourd'hui? Je veux rendre ces livres.
   — Désolé, je ne peux pas. J'ai des tas de choses à faire.
6. — Zut alors! J'ai oublié les tomates! Tu peux passer au marché pour moi?
   — Oui, je veux bien. Je pars tout de suite.

Answers to Activity 15
1. refuses
2. agrees
3. agrees
4. agrees
5. refuses
6. agrees

19 Ecoute! p. 323

1. — Comment est-ce qu'on va en ville?
   — On peut y aller à vélo, si tu veux.
2. — J'aimerais bien aller au cinéma.
   — Bonne idée. Comment veux-tu y aller?
   — On peut prendre le bus.
3. — Je vais à Paris cet été.
   — Ah oui? Comment est-ce que tu y vas?
   — J'y vais en avion.
4. — Tu veux aller à la plage ce week-end?
   — Oui, on peut y aller à pied.
5. — Comment est-ce que tu vas à Fort-de-France demain?
   — J'y vais en voiture avec mes parents.
6. — Tu ne veux pas aller au musée samedi?
   — Si. On peut prendre un taxi collectif.

Answers to Activity 19
1. to town, by bike
2. to the movies, by bus
3. to Paris, by plane
4. to the beach, on foot
5. to Fort-de-France, by car
6. to the museum, by taxi

Troisième étape

23 Ecoute! p. 325

1. La boulangerie est à côté du cinéma.
2. La banque est au coin de la rue.
3. La pharmacie est loin de la papeterie.
4. Le café est entre la poste et le cinéma.
5. Le cinéma est en face du lycée.
6. La poste est près du café.

Answers to Activity 23

1. false   3. false   5. true
2. true   4. true   6. true

27 Ecoute! p. 327

En sortant de la gare routière, prenez à gauche. Vous serez sur le boulevard du Général de Gaulle. Ensuite, prenez la première rue à gauche, c'est la rue Schœlcher. Continuez jusqu'à la rue Victor Sévère et tournez à gauche. Vous allez passer devant la bibliothèque. Juste après la bibliothèque, prenez à droite, rue de la Liberté. Allez tout droit jusqu'à la rue Antoine Siger. Là, tournez à droite et ce sera le premier bâtiment sur votre gauche.

Answer to Activity 27

to the post office

Prononciation, p. 329

For the scripts for Parts A and B, see p. 329.

C. A écrire

(Dictation)
— Tu pourrais faire des courses pour moi?
— Volontiers!
— Passe à la poste. Prends des timbres. Et n'oublie pas les enveloppes à la papeterie.
— Bon, d'accord.

Mise en pratique

2 p. 332

1. — La bibliothèque Schœlcher est très grande, et elle est aussi très belle, n'est-ce pas?

2. — Les plages de sable blanc de la Martinique sont magnifiques. On peut à la fois s'y baigner et y faire du bateau.

3. — Ça, c'est le marché. C'est un vrai paradis pour les yeux : on y trouve des légumes de toutes les couleurs.

4. — Là, c'est le disquaire où j'ai acheté le dernier CD de Kassav', un groupe de musique zouk, qui est très populaire ici.

Answers to Mise en pratique Activity 2

c, d, a, b

Ma ville
(Individual or Group Project)

ASSIGNMENT

Students will create a brochure for visitors with maps of their town or neighborhood and written directions to important places.

MATERIALS

✂ **Students may need**
- Construction paper
- Scissors
- Local maps
- Glue
- Markers or colored pens
- Telephone directories
- Brochures of local attractions

SUGGESTED SEQUENCE

1. Have students make a list of interesting and important places in their area that visitors might want or need to visit. These might include hospitals, subway or bus stops, bus depots, airports, pharmacies, restaurants, the main post office, the Chamber of Commerce, and so on.

2. Have students find out exactly where each place is located. They might call for directions. Then, have them sketch a rough map of the city with each place correctly indicated. They should also begin to gather or draw pictures to illustrate their maps.

3. Have students write directions to the points of interest from main streets or designated locations. They might use the following vocabulary: **l'autoroute** *(highway)*; **Prenez la 35 jusqu'à...** *(Take highway 35 to . . .)*; **la sortie** Main Street *(the . . . exit)*; **un pont** *(bridge)*; **faire demi-tour** *(to make a U-turn)*; **un carrefour** *(intersection)*; **une rue en sens unique** *(one-way street)*.

4. Have students exchange their written directions for peer editing. Students should check the clarity and accuracy of the directions by trying to follow them on a city map. They should also check for completeness and for accuracy of language use.

5. Have students select their final illustrations and plan the final layout of their maps.

6. Have students finalize their maps. They should copy the final version of the written directions at the bottom or on the reverse side of the map.

These brochures might be displayed at school, added to portfolios, or sent to local tourist offices or Chambers of Commerce.

GRADING THE PROJECT

Suggested Point Distribution (total = 100 points)

Completion of assignment . . . . 20 points

Content/creativity . . . . 30 points

Language use. . . . . 25 points

Presentation. . . . . 25 points

CHASSE L'INTRUS

In this game, students will practice new and previously learned vocabulary.

Procedure Give students index cards. Ask them to write a group of four words on their card: three should have something in common, and the fourth should be unrelated. For example, students might write **banque, pharmacie, avion,** and **boulangerie.** Words can be related according to their meanings or their parts of speech. Collect and shuffle the cards. Divide the class into two teams. Give a card to the first player on the first team. The player says **Chasse l'intrus!** to his or her opponent and reads aloud the four words on the card. If the opposing player correctly identifies the word that doesn't belong within a specified amount of time, his or her team wins a point. Teams alternate, asking questions until all the cards have been read. The team with the most points wins. NOTE: If pronunciation is a problem, have students show their card to the opposing player.

LES MOTS EN FAMILLE

In this game, students will review vocabulary from all twelve chapters.

Procedure Skim the French-English vocabulary list at the back of the book and make a list under several general categories, such as **les vêtements, l'école, à manger,** and **les sports.** Have students pair off or form small groups. Give each pair or group a transparency and a marker. Then, announce a category and give partners or groups 2 or 3 minutes to write down as many related words as they can think of, without consulting their books or dictionaries. Then, project the transparencies and have the class verify the spelling and appropriateness of each item. Give one point for each appropriate word that is spelled correctly. The team with the most points wins. This game might be played with functional expressions as well as with vocabulary words.

Chapitre 12
En ville

pp. 310–335

*U*sing the Chapter Opener

Motivating Activity

Ask students if they have ever been lost and how they reacted. Ask them to imagine getting lost in another country. What strategies would they use to find their way around the United States?

Photo Flash!

① Fort-de-France is the departmental seat of Martinique as well as the island's business center. This view from the **baie des Flamands** also shows the historic, romanesque bell tower of the **cathédrale Saint-Louis.**

Teaching Suggestion

Have students tell where in town they go to run errands.

Teacher Note

Information on Fort-de-France is easily accessible on the Internet. Topics such as maps, weather, restaurants, hotels, transportation, money, arts and culture, tours, festivals, and entertainment are easy to find. Have students create itineraries for a short visit to Fort-de-France, using information that they find.

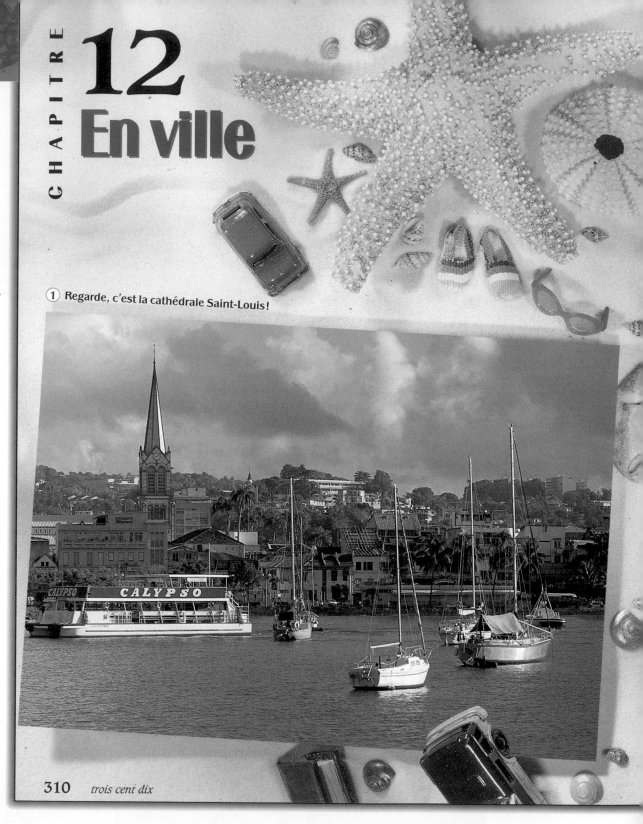

CHAPITRE **12**
En ville

① Regarde, c'est la cathédrale Saint-Louis!

310 *trois cent dix*

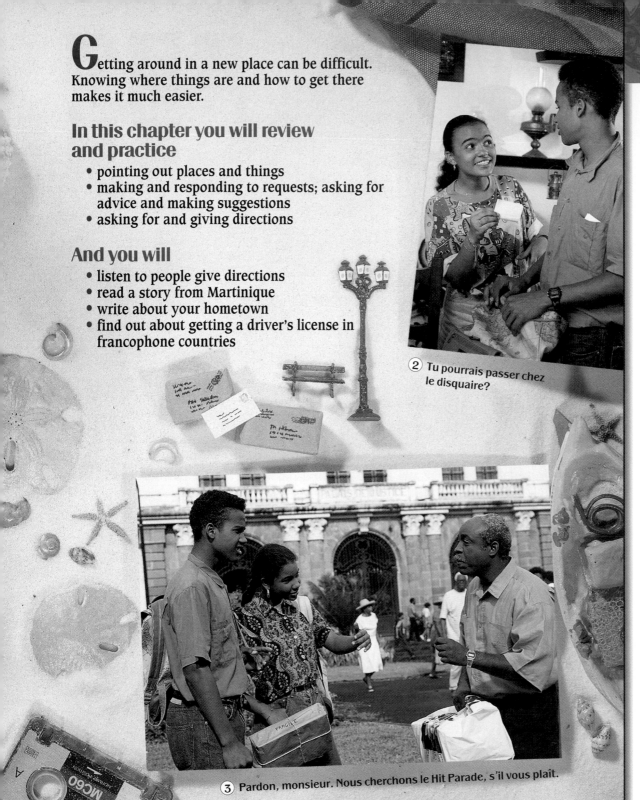

Getting around in a new place can be difficult. Knowing where things are and how to get there makes it much easier.

In this chapter you will review and practice

- pointing out places and things
- making and responding to requests; asking for advice and making suggestions
- asking for and giving directions

And you will

- listen to people give directions
- read a story from Martinique
- write about your hometown
- find out about getting a driver's license in francophone countries

② Tu pourrais passer chez le disquaire?

③ Pardon, monsieur. Nous cherchons le Hit Parade, s'il vous plaît.

Focusing on Outcomes

Begin by having students match the photo captions to the outcomes. Since some of these functions were presented in earlier chapters, you might review them by asking students to recall familiar expressions for each function. NOTE: You may want to use the video to support the objectives. The self-check activities in **Que sais-je?** on page 334 help students assess their achievement of the objectives.

Photo Flash!

③ Lucien and Mireille are asking a man for directions in front of the **Palais de Justice** in Fort-de-France.

Teaching Suggestion

Have students suggest other functions involved in running errands and finding their way around town. Examples include making purchases, making excuses, and hesitating.

Building on Previous Skills

Have students describe the photos in French. You might prompt them by asking **Comment est Lucien? Qu'est-ce qu'il porte? Comment est Fort-de-France? Qu'est-ce qu'il y a à faire là-bas?**

Block Scheduling

For suggestions about how to use *Allez, viens!* with block scheduling, see the *Lesson Planner,* pages 58–62.

VIDEO PROGRAM
Videocassette 4
32:50–36:11
Videocassette 5
(captioned version)
1:39:45–1:43:46

OR *VIDEODISC PROGRAM,*
Videodisc 6, Side B

Search 4200, Play To 10245

Video Synopsis

In this episode, Lucien plans to meet his friend Mireille in town and visit Fort Saint-Louis. As he is getting ready to leave, his mother, father, and sister all ask favors of him. Although they ask him to do a lot of errands, Lucien reluctantly agrees to everyone's requests. When a neighbor enters and asks if anyone is going to town, however, Lucien has had enough.

Motivating Activity

Have students answer the questions in the introduction at the top of this page. Ask them if they would mind doing the errands Lucien is being asked to do. Have students recall the vocabulary for household chores that they learned in Chapter 7 (**sortir la poubelle, faire la vaisselle, débarrasser la table**).

History Link

The Schœlcher Library is at the site of the old **Hôtel du Petit Gouvernement,** where Empress Joséphine of France used to live. The library did not take the name Schœlcher to commemorate Victor Schœlcher's campaign to abolish slavery, but rather to acknowledge his gift of about 10,000 volumes to further the education of the people of Martinique.

The **roman-photo** is an abridged version of the video episode.

Mise en train
p. 133, Act. 1

Un petit service

CD 12
Trs. 1–2

Do you ever run errands for your family? What kinds of things do you have to do? Look at the pictures below and see if you can figure out what Lucien's mother, father, and sister are asking him to do.

Lucien   Lisette   La mère

Le père   Une voisine

1. Maman, je vais en ville. J'ai rendez-vous avec Mireille. On va passer la journée à Fort-de-France. Je vais lui faire visiter le fort Saint-Louis.

2. Avant de rentrer, passe au marché et prends de l'ananas, des oranges et des caramboles.

3. Ah, tu peux rendre ces livres à la bibliothèque aussi, s'il te plaît? Et en échange, tu me prends trois autres livres. Voilà ma carte.

4. Est-ce que tu peux aller à la poste et envoyer ce paquet?

Je ne sais pas si je vais avoir le temps.

RESOURCES FOR MISE EN TRAIN

PRINT	MEDIA
• *Practice and Activity Book,* p. 133 • *Video Guide,* pp. 81–82, 84 • *Videodisc Guide,* pp. 132–134, 139	• *Video Program,* Videocassette 4 Videocassette 5 (captioned version) • *Videodisc Program,* Videodisc 6, Side B • *Audio Compact Discs,* CD 12, Trs. 1–2

MISE EN TRAIN

trois cent treize **313**

Presentation

Before students view the video episode, have them make a chart like this:

WHO?   WHERE?   WHY?
Mother
Lisette
Father
Lisette
Mother
Father

As students view the video, they should briefly note in English where Lucien's family members ask him to go and what they ask him to do there. Play the episode again to allow students to revise their notes. Then, as students tell you their answers, record them on a transparency so they can correct their own charts.

Captioned Video

An alternate way to complete the presentation would be to play the captioned version of **Un petit service** on Videocassette 5.

Teaching Suggestion

Play the recording of **Un petit service**. Have students read along in their books and repeat the text in the pauses provided on the recording. Then, have them form groups of five and read the story aloud.

For Individual Needs

Visual Learners Copy the speech bubbles from Photos 2, 3, 4, 6, 7, and 8 onto a transparency and label them with the letters **a** through **f**. Then, hold up objects to represent each of the errands (a **baguette,** an orange, a library book, a postage stamp, and so on). Have students match the family's requests to the items requested.

Video Integration

- *VIDEO PROGRAM,*
  Videocassette 4, 36:12–46:21
  Videocassette 5, 1:43:47–1:53:25
- *VIDEODISC PROGRAM,*
  Videodisc 6, Side B

Search 10245, Play To 28545

You may choose to continue with **Un petit service (suite)** at this time or wait until later in the chapter. When the story continues, Mireille accompanies Lucien on his errands. They get lost trying to find a record store and ask a man for directions. Then, they take a ferry to deliver a package, and Lucien points out landmarks in Fort-de-France. When Lucien returns home, everyone thanks him for doing his or her errands. His mother asks him about the fort, and he realizes he completely forgot about visiting it!

For videodisc application, see *Videodisc Guide.*

Teaching Suggestion

3 Have students match these errands with the people pictured in Activity 2 who requested them. Have students tell what else they could do in each place.

For Individual Needs

4 Challenge Copy the sentences onto the board or a transparency, omitting several words. (**Lucien va acheter des ____, des pêches et des ____.**) Have students complete these sentences to make them true.

Thinking Critically

6 Comparing and Contrasting Have students list where they go to do each of their errands and compare their list with Lucien's errands.

These activities check for comprehension only. Students should not yet be expected to produce language modeled in **Mise en train.**

1 Tu as compris?

1. What are Lucien's plans for the day?   to visit fort Saint-Louis in Fort-de-France with Mireille
2. What are Lucien and his family talking about?   running errands in town
3. Is Lucien happy with the situation? Why or why not?   No; He's afraid he won't have time for everything.
4. What happens at the end?   Lucien calls for help when a neighbor starts to ask a favor.

2 Qui dit quoi?

Lucien   Lisette   M. Lapiquonne   Mme Lapiquonne

1. «Tu peux aller à la boulangerie?»
2. «Tu peux rendre ces livres à la bibliothèque aussi, s'il te plaît?»
3. «Est-ce que tu peux aller à la poste et envoyer ce paquet?»

4. «Tu peux passer chez le disquaire?»
5. «Passe au marché et prends de l'ananas, des oranges et des caramboles.»
6. «Prends-moi aussi le journal.»

1. Mme Lapiquonne
2. Lisette
3. M. Lapiquonne

4. Lisette
5. Mme Lapiquonne
6. M. Lapiquonne

3 Où va-t-il?

Où est-ce que Lucien va aller pour...

1. acheter des caramboles?
2. envoyer le paquet?
3. rendre les livres?
   1. au marché
   2. à la poste
4. acheter le disque compact?
5. acheter des baguettes?
   3. à la bibliothèque
   4. chez le disquaire
   5. à la boulangerie

à la boulangerie
à la poste
chez le disquaire
au marché
à la bibliothèque

4 Vrai ou faux?

1. Lucien va acheter des caramboles, des pêches et des pommes.   faux
2. Il va rendre des livres à la bibliothèque.   vrai
3. Lucien va à la boulangerie.   vrai

4. Lisette lui donne de l'argent pour acheter un livre.   faux
5. Lucien va chez le disquaire pour son père.
6. Il va acheter le journal pour la voisine.
   5. faux   6. faux

5 Cherche les expressions

According to **Un petit service,** how do you . . .   See answers below.

1. say you're meeting someone?
2. say you don't know if you'll have time?
3. ask someone to do something for you?
4. express your annoyance?
5. call for help?

Est-ce que tu peux... ?   Au secours!
Ça suffit!   J'ai rendez-vous avec...
Je ne sais pas si je vais avoir le temps.

6 Et maintenant, à toi

What errands do you do for your family and friends? Do you go to the same places as Lucien?

314   *trois cent quatorze*   CHAPITRE 12   En ville

Answers
5 1. J'ai rendez-vous avec...
   2. Je ne sais pas si je vais avoir le temps.
   3. Est-ce que tu peux... ?
   4. Ça suffit!
   5. Au secours!

PREMIERE ETAPE

 TPR Storytelling Book
pp. 45, 48

Pointing out places and things

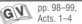 pp. 134–135, Act. 2–5   12-A, 12-1   pp. 98–99, Acts. 1–4

VOCABULAIRE

Où est-ce qu'on va pour faire les courses? On peut aller à ces **endroits :**

à la **boulangerie** pour acheter **des baguettes**

à la **pâtisserie** pour acheter **des pâtisseries**

à l'**épicerie** pour acheter de la confiture

à **la poste** pour acheter **des timbres** et **envoyer des lettres**

à **la banque** pour **retirer** ou **déposer** de l'argent

à la **librairie-papeterie** pour acheter **des livres** ou **des enveloppes**

à la **pharmacie** pour acheter **des médicaments**

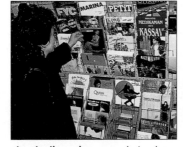

chez le disquaire pour acheter des disques compacts ou des cassettes

à la **bibliothèque** pour **emprunter** ou **rendre** des livres

PREMIERE ETAPE   *trois cent quinze*   **315**

Jump Start!

Have students make a shopping list in French of at least five things they need to buy. They might include groceries, school supplies, or clothing. Have them begin the list with **Il me faut...**

MOTIVATE

Ask students to name three or four places tourists might want to go in their town during a vacation and tell why.

TEACH

Presentation

Vocabulaire Hold up pictures of the items that can be purchased at each store, having students repeat after you. Write the store names and the items available at each one on strips of transparency. Scatter the strips across the overhead. Then, have two students come to the projector and match the stores with the items available at each one. Have students name in French other items they might find at these places. You might want to have students give local equivalents of the places mentioned.

Additional Practice

For listening practice, create and read aloud several true-false statements based on the **Vocabulaire,** such as **On va à la bibliothèque pour acheter du pain.** Call on individual students to correct the false statements.

RESOURCES FOR PREMIERE ETAPE

PRINT
- *Lesson Planner,* p. 59
- *Practice and Activity Book,* pp. 134–136
- *Grammar and Vocabulary Workbook,* pp. 98–101
- *Activities for Communication,* pp. 67–68, 130, 133–134, 159–160
- *Listening Activities,* pp. 91, 95
- *Testing Program,* pp. 301–304
- *Alternative Assessment Guide,* p. 43

MEDIA
- *Video Program,* Videocassette 4
  Video Guide, pp. 81–86
- *Videodisc Program,* Videodisc 6, Side B
  Videodisc Guide, p. 135
- *Teaching Transparencies* 12-1, 12-A
- *Interactive CD-ROM Program,* Disc 3
  CD-ROM Teacher's Guide, p. 51
- *Audio Compact Discs*
  Textbook Listening Activity, CD 12, Tr. 3
  Additional Listening Activities 12-1, 12-2, CD 12, Trs. 31–32
  Quiz 12-1B, CD 12, Tr. 19

Additional Practice

Tu te rappelles? You might have students recall the French names of other places where they might go after school (**au café, au ciné**) and write them on the board. Then, have partners ask and tell where they're going after school today or this weekend.

 For Individual Needs

8 Challenge Have students write a response to Frédéric's letter, describing a similar day that they have had recently.

For Individual Needs

9 Visual Learners In pairs, one student draws a picture of a building that Yvette visited (**la pharmacie, la poste**). When his or her partner correctly identifies the place and calls out what Yvette said there, he or she then draws a different building.

9 Challenge Ask students to write additional statements and have classmates guess where they might hear them.
—Je voudrais acheter le nouveau CD de Vanessa Paradis.
—Chez le disquaire.

Thinking Critically

Analyzing — Note Culturelle Have students consider how late stores usually stay open in the United States. Have them compare these hours to the hours that French stores usually keep. What are the advantages and disadvantages of French hours? Of American hours?

---

7 Ecoute! See scripts and answers on p. 309G.

 CD 12 Tr. 3

Listen to these conversations and tell where the people are.

8 Un petit mot

Read this note that Frédéric wrote to his friend. Then, list three places he went to and tell what he did there. See answers below.

GV pp. 100–101, Acts. 5–8 **Tu te rappelles?**

Remember, **au, à la, à l'**, and **aux** mean *to the* or *at the*. Use **au** before a masculine singular noun, **à la** before a feminine singular noun, **à l'** before any singular noun beginning with a vowel sound, and **aux** before any plural noun.

Je vais { **au** musée. **à la** boulangerie. **à l'** épicerie. }

Je vais { **à l'** hôtel. **aux** Etats-Unis. }

For additional practice, see p. R52.

Cher Pierre,

Ici, rien de bien nouveau. Hier, mes parents sont allés passer la journée chez leurs amis, alors j'étais tout seul. J'en ai profité pour faire des courses. D'abord, je suis allé à la boulangerie acheter du pain. Ensuite, je suis allé à la poste parce que je n'avais plus de timbres, et j'en ai profité pour envoyer une lettre à Jules, mon correspondant québécois. Puis, je suis allé à la bibliothèque emprunter quelques livres parce que j'ai fini de lire toute ma collection. Je n'ai pas trouvé le dernier livre de Stephen King à la bibliothèque (il paraît qu'il est super!), alors je suis allé à la librairie pour l'acheter. Finalement, je suis passé à l'épicerie acheter des légumes et du fromage pour mon déjeuner. Voilà, c'est tout. Ecris-moi vite pour me dire comment tu trouves ton nouveau lycée. Salut.

Frédéric

9 Des courses en ville

Yvette fait des courses en ville. Où est-elle?

1. «Je voudrais ce gâteau au chocolat, s'il vous plaît.»
2. «Je voudrais emprunter ces trois livres, s'il vous plaît.»
3. «Eh bien, je voudrais des médicaments pour ma mère.»
4. «C'est combien pour envoyer cette lettre aux Etats-Unis?»
5. «Zut, alors! Elle est fermée. Je ne peux pas déposer de l'argent!»

9 1. à la pâtisserie   4. à la poste
2. à la bibliothèque   5. à la banque
3. à la pharmacie

NOTE CULTURELLE

Stores in France and Martinique don't stay open 24 hours a day. Between 12:30 P.M. and 3:30 P.M., very few small businesses are open; however, they usually remain open until 7:00 P.M. By law, businesses must close one day a week, usually Sunday. Only grocery stores, restaurants, and certain places related to culture and entertainment, such as museums and movie theaters, may stay open on Sunday.

316 *trois cent seize* CHAPITRE 12 En ville

Culture Note

Stores in Côte d'Ivoire usually follow the French system of closing for a few hours in the early afternoon. To escape the heat, people usually take a short nap (**la sieste**) at this time.

Possible answers

8 to the bakery to buy bread, to the post office to buy stamps and send a letter, to the library to borrow some books, to the bookstore to buy a book, to the grocery store to buy vegetables and cheese.

10 Il va où? See answers below.

a. Regarde la liste d'Armand. Où va-t-il?
b. Qu'est-ce qu'il peut acheter d'autre là où il va?

You've already learned that an ending can often help you guess the gender of a word. An ending can also help you guess the meaning of a word. For example, the ending **-erie** often indicates a place where something is sold or made. Look at these words: **poissonnerie, fromagerie, chocolaterie, croissanterie.** What do you think they mean? Another common ending that carries a particular meaning is **-eur (-euse).** It indicates a person who performs a certain activity. In French, **chasser** means *to hunt.* A person who hunts is a **chasseur.** Since **chanter** means *to sing,* how do you think you would say *singer* in French? If **danser** means *to dance,* how would you say *dancer?* *

For additional practice, see p. R52.

Si tu as oublié *le passé composé* va à la page 239.

11 Devine!

Think of something that you bought. Then, tell your partner where you went to buy it. Your partner will try to guess what you bought there. Take turns.

— Je suis allé(e) à la boulangerie.
— Tu as acheté des croissants?
— Non.

COMMENT DIT-ON... ?
Pointing out places and things

Voici tes timbres.
Regarde, voilà ma maison.
  Look, here/there is/are . . .

p. 136,
Act. 8

Ça, c'est la banque.
  This/That is . . .
Là, c'est mon disquaire préféré.
  There, that is . . .

12-1

Là, tu vois, c'est la maison de mes grands-parents.
  There, you see, this/that is . . .

VOILÀ LA MAISON DE MES GRANDS-PARENTS.

*chanteur, danseur

Answers
10 a. à la librairie-papeterie (classeurs, gomme, enveloppes, livre), chez le disquaire (CD), à la pharmacie (aspirine), à la poste (timbres), à l'épicerie (œufs), à la pâtisserie (tarte), à la boulangerie (baguettes)
  b. Answers will vary.

Language-to Language

De bons conseils The official French term for a *Walkman*® is **un baladeur,** which translates literally as *one who walks around.* A **conteur** is *someone who narrates stories.* **Rapporter** means *to tell on* or *to tattle,* so a **rapporteur** is not a very popular person!

Teaching Suggestions
10 You might have students work in pairs to answer these questions. Have them do **10a** first and then write their answers on the board. Students can then use these place names as the basis for answering **10b.**

Language-to-Language
De bons conseils You might have students think of common suffixes in English, such as *-ly, -er,* and *-ment,* and suggest words that have these endings *(happily, buyer, punishment).*

For Individual Needs

Challenge — De bons conseils Have students guess what the ending **-ant** means from looking at the following words they're already familiar with: **barbant, intéressant, embêtant, dégoûtant.** You might have them go through the French vocabulary at the end of the book to find other endings that signal adjectives (**-é, -eux, -euse,** and so on).

Teaching Suggestion
11 You might ask students to think of two or three additional things that they bought at different stores.

Presentation
Comment dit-on... ? Begin by identifying students or pictures of celebrities that you have brought to class. Then, use the expressions to identify different items in the classroom and pictures of buildings. Finally, hold up pictures of different places or things or point to various objects in the classroom and have students identify them.

For videodisc application, see *Videodisc Guide*.

Teaching Suggestions

12 You might also have students bring in photos they've taken on vacation or pictures they've cut from magazines and identify them to a partner or to the class.

 Circumlocution

After reading **A la française** with students, have them practice using circumlocution to identify the photos in Activity 12. You might also give students some photos of additional places to describe to a partner in French. To help students, provide them with a list of circumlocution expressions from page 147J.

Teacher Note

For more information on the **bibliothèque Schœlcher**, see page 308 of the Location Opener and the History Link on page 312.

📁 Portfolio

13 **Written** This activity might be expanded into the chapter project described on page 309I. This item is appropriate for students' written portfolios. For portfolio information, see the *Alternative Assessment Guide*, pages iv–17.

CLOSE

To close this **étape**, name a local store *(Cathy's Cakes)*. Have one student tell what type of store it is **(une pâtisserie)** and another student name something they could buy there **(des gâteaux)**.

---

12 **A la Martinique**

During your trip to Martinique you took the photos below. Take turns with your partner pointing out and identifying the places and objects in the photos. Possible answers:

> le disquaire   la statue de Joséphine de Beauharnais
> la pharmacie   la boulangerie
> la bibliothèque Schœlcher   le marché

1. Voici la statue de Joséphine de Beauharnais.

2. Regarde, voilà la pharmacie.

3. Ça, c'est le disquaire.

4. Là, c'est le marché.

5. Là, tu vois, c'est la bibliothèque Schœlcher.

6. Voici la boulangerie.

À la française

When you try to communicate in a foreign language, there will always be times when you can't remember or don't know the exact word you need. One way to get around this problem is to use *circumlocution*. Circumlocution means substituting words and expressions you do know to explain what you mean. For example, if you can't think of the French word for *pharmacy*, you might say **l'endroit où on peut acheter des médicaments** *(the place where you can buy medicine)*. Other expressions you can use are **la personne qui/que** *(the person who/whom)*, and **le truc qui/que** *(the thing that)*.

 p. 135, Act. 6

13 **Mon quartier**

An exchange student is coming to stay with your family for a semester. Draw a map of your neighborhood and label the school, post office, grocery store, and so on.

14 **Jeu de rôle**

As your exchange student asks where various places are, point them out on the map you made for Activity 13. Tell what you buy or do there. Take turns playing the role of the exchange student.

ASSESS

Quiz 12-1A, Quiz 12-1B, *Testing Program*, pp. 301–304

Audio CD 12, Tr. 19

Performance Assessment

Have students write a note to a friend, telling all the things they plan to do over the weekend. They should include at least three separate chores, errands, or activities.

RENCONTRE CULTURELLE

Look at the illustrations below. Where are these people? What are they talking about?

— Bonjour, Madame Perrot. Vous avez passé de bonnes vacances?
— Très bonnes. On est allés à la Guadeloupe. Vous savez, ma sœur habite là-bas, et...

— Et votre père, il va bien?
— Oui, merci. Il va beaucoup mieux depuis...

— Qu'est-ce que vous allez faire avec ça?
— Ma voisine m'a donné une très bonne recette. C'est très simple. Tout ce qu'il faut faire, c'est...

Qu'en penses-tu?

1. What are the topics of these conversations? What does this tell you about the culture of Martinique?
2. What kind of relationships do you or your family have with the people who work in your town? Do you know them? Do you often make "small talk" with them?

Savais-tu que... ?

In Martinique, as in many parts of France, people like to take the time to say hello, ask how others are doing, and find out what's going on in one another's lives. Of course, the smaller the town, the more likely this is to occur. While it may be frustrating to Americans in a hurry, especially when they are conducting business, in West Indian culture it is considered rude not to take a few minutes to engage in some polite conversation before talking business.

Culture Notes
• Even in large cities like Paris, owners of small shops often greet customers as they come into the store and say goodbye as they leave. Customers often respond with a polite **Bonjour, madame/monsieur** or **Merci, au revoir!**

• Small talk is also very common in Côte d'Ivoire and can be quite involved. When people run into a friend or acquaintance during the day, they often inquire at length about that person's health, job, and family situation. Friends will also inquire about the health, job, and general situation of that person's entire family and circle of friends.

Motivating Activity
Ask students for examples of "small talk" in English. Ask them in what situations and with whom they might make small talk.

Presentation
Have two students read each conversation aloud. After each one, ask the class where the people are, what they are talking about, and what the other people are doing. (**On est où? De quoi est-ce qu'on parle? Que font les autres?**) Then, have students answer the questions in **Qu'en penses-tu?** as a class or with a partner.

Teaching Suggestion
You might ask students if there are places or situations in the United States in which small talk is expected or discouraged.

Thinking Critically
Comparing and Contrasting
Ask students how Americans behave when they have to stand in line and if their behavior is different from that shown here. Ask students if they consider themselves to be very patient.

Synthesizing Form small groups. Have each group adapt one of these conversations to a similar situation in their town. Have them expand the conversations by involving the other customers who are waiting in line. Groups should act out their conversations.

Jump Start!

Have students list the places they'd go to get the following items: **du pain, des timbres, un livre, une gomme,** and **un CD.**

MOTIVATE

Have students recall French expressions they already know that they would use to tell someone to do something, such as cleaning one's room. **(Range ta chambre! Tu dois ranger ta chambre.)** Write their suggestions on the board. You might also ask students to recall possible responses to the commands.

TEACH

Presentation

Comment dit-on... ? Begin by reviewing the previously learned expressions suggested above for the activity under Motivate. Then, use the expressions in **Comment dit-on... ?** to ask individual students for various favors.

 For videodisc application, see *Videodisc Guide.*

Language Note

You might want to compare **pourrais** with **voudrais,** explaining that the -**ais** ending signals the polite form for **je** and **tu.**

 For Individual Needs

15 Challenge Have students also write down the errand that is requested. Have partners use these notes to make and respond to requests.

DEUXIEME ETAPE

Storytelling Book
pp. 46, 48

Making and responding to requests; asking for advice and making suggestions

COMMENT DIT-ON... ?
Making and responding to requests

p. 137,
Acts. 9–11
12-2

To make a request:

(Est-ce que) tu peux aller au marché?
Tu me rapportes des timbres?
Tu pourrais passer à la poste acheter des timbres?
   Could you go by . . . ?

To accept requests:

D'accord.
Je veux bien.
J'y vais tout de suite.
Si tu veux. *If you want.*

To decline requests:

Je ne peux pas maintenant.
Je suis désolé(e), mais je n'ai pas le temps.

---

15 Ecoute! See scripts and answers on p. 309G.

Listen to the following conversations and decide if the person agrees to or refuses the request.

CD 12 Tr. 4

GV

For additional practice, see p. R52.

p. 102, Acts. 9–10 **Tu te rappelles ?**

Use the partitive articles **du, de la,** and **de l'** when you mean *some* of an item. If you mean a whole item instead of a part of it, use the indefinite articles **un, une,** and **des. Du, de la, de l', des, un,** and **une** usually become **de/d'** in negative sentences.

 CD-ROM Disc 3

RESOURCES FOR DEUXIEME ETAPE

PRINT

- *Lesson Planner,* p. 60
- *Practice and Activity Book,* pp. 137–139
- *Grammar and Vocabulary Workbook,* pp. 102–105
- *Activities for Communication,* pp. 69–70, 131, 133–134, 159–160
- *Listening Activities,* pp. 91–92, 96
- *Testing Program,* pp. 305–308
- *Alternative Assessment Guide,* p. 43

MEDIA

- *Video Program,* Videocassette 4
  Video Guide, pp. 81–86
- *Videodisc Program,* Videodisc 6, Side B
  Videodisc Guide, pp. 135–136
- *Teaching Transparencies* 12-2, 12-B
- *Interactive CD-ROM Program,* Disc 3
  CD-ROM Teacher's Guide, pp. 51–52
- *Audio Compact Discs*
  Textbook Listening Activities, CD 12, Trs. 4–5
  Additional Listening Activities 12-3, 12-4, CD 12, Trs. 33–34
  Quiz 12-2B, CD 12, Tr. 20

16 Un petit service

What would these people say to ask you a favor? See answers below.

1.

2.

3.

4.

17 Il me faut....

Decide which of these items you need and ask your partner to go to the appropriate store. Your partner will accept or decline your request. Take turns.

Si tu as oublié expressing need va à la page 210.

1.

2.

3.

4.

5.

6.

18 Tu pourrais me rendre un service?

Ask your classmates to do these favors for you. They will either accept or decline and make an excuse.

aller chercher un livre à la bibliothèque

acheter un dictionnaire de français à la librairie

acheter un CD chez le disquaire

acheter un sandwich au fast-food

acheter une règle à la papeterie

acheter des timbres à la poste

Si tu as oublié making an excuse va à la page 129.

DEUXIEME ETAPE

trois cent vingt et un **321**

Possible answers

16 1. (Est-ce que) tu peux aller à la poste envoyer des lettres?
2. (Est-ce que) tu pourrais passer à la bibliothèque rendre des livres?
3. Tu me rapportes un CD?
4. (Est-ce que) tu pourrais passer à la pharmacie acheter des médicaments?

Culture Note

The second photo of Activity 17 shows a common French stamp. The stamp bears the allegorical image of **la République française**, known as **Marianne.** This image also appears on French coins.

For Individual Needs

16 Auditory Learners Read aloud appropriate requests and have students match them with the illustrations.

16 Challenge Encourage students to say or write other requests each person might make. Have them expand their requests by telling why the errand needs to be done.

17 Slower Pace Before students do the activity, have them tell which store they would go to for each item.

Additional Practice

17 You might also show the items you used for the **Vocabulaire** presentation on page 315 (a jar of jam, money, medicine, a croissant, and a library book) and have partners make appropriate requests.

Reteaching

17 The partitive Review the use of the partitive, using **Tu te rappelles?** on page 320. You might bring in a loaf of bread to demonstrate **un pain,** and then break off a piece and offer it to students to illustrate the partitive **du pain.** Have students name each item in the photos with the correct partitive article.

Teaching Suggestion

18 Have students vary the way they request and respond to favors.

Additional Practice

Show *Teaching Transparency 12-2.* Assign each of the people shown to one of four groups. Have them write a speech bubble on a strip of transparency for the person they were assigned. Project their transparencies on top of the original transparency and have the class match the speech bubbles to the people.

Presentation

Comment dit-on... ?/ Vocabulaire Ask students if they ever have problems getting where they want to go. Have them name in French several places they might want to visit in a new town. Have students look at the photos and tell which of these means of transportation are available in their town or area. Name local places and ask **Comment est-ce qu'on peut y aller? En voiture? En bus?** Then, display a map of the United States or a world map and make true/false statements about how to get to and from certain locations. Have students say whether the statement is true or false. For example, **San Francisco à New York, on peut y aller à vélo. (faux)** or **Miami à Martinique, on peut y aller en bateau. (vrai)**

Teaching Suggestions

- Ask students what forms of transportation they use. (**Comment est-ce que tu vas à l'école? Au cinéma? Au centre commercial?**)
- Have pairs of students ask each other **Comment est-ce que tu vas à l'école?** and report their findings to the class.

COMMENT DIT-ON... ?
Asking for advice and making suggestions

To ask for advice on how to get somewhere:
Comment est-ce qu'on y va? *How can we get there?*

To suggest how to get somewhere:
On peut y aller en train. *We can go . . .*
On peut prendre le bus. *We can take . . .*

P.A. p. 138, Acts. 12–14   12-B   G.V. pp. 103–104, Acts. 11–15   CD-ROM Disc 3

VOCABULAIRE

Comment est-ce qu'on y va?

en bus (m.)

à pied (m.)

à vélo (m.)

en voiture (f.)

en taxi (m.)

en bateau (m.)

en avion (m.)

en train (m.)

en métro (m.)

Language Notes
- Explain that **à** is used instead of **en** with **pied** and **vélo** because they aren't vehicles you get inside.
- Point out that either the definite article or indefinite article can be used with transportation after **prendre** (**prendre le train, prendre un taxi**).

Multicultural Link
Have students choose a foreign city or country and imagine what form of transportation is the most popular and efficient there. They may want to find out about typical bus, train, metro, and plane fares there.

19 Ecoute! See scripts and answers on p. 309G.

Listen to these conversations. Where are these people going and how are they going to get there?

CD 12 Tr. 5

20 Comment vont-ils voyager?

1. en bateau 2. en métro 3. en train 4. en avion

GRAMMAIRE The pronoun y

You've already seen the pronoun **y** *(there)* several times. Can you figure out how to use it?

—Je vais **à la bibliothèque.** Tu **y** vas aussi?
—Non, je n'**y** vais pas.

—Je vais **chez le disquaire.** Tu veux **y** aller?
—Non, j'**y** suis allé hier.

It can replace an entire phrase meaning *to, at,* or *in* any place that has already been mentioned. Place it before the conjugated verb, or, if there is an infinitive, place **y** before the infinitive: Je vais **y** aller demain.

PA p. 139, Acts. 15–16

GV p. 105, Acts. 16–17

Additional Grammar Practice, p. R53

---

21 On va en ville

How do you and your friends get to these places?

Au cinéma? Nous y allons en bus.

> au cinéma   au supermarché   à la poste   à la bibliothèque
> à la piscine   au centre commercial   au stade
> au parc   à la librairie   au lycée   au concert

Si tu as oublié inviting, va à la page 159.

22 Qu'est-ce qu'on fait vendredi soir?

You call your friend and invite him or her to do something Friday night. When you've decided where you want to go, talk about how to get there.

DEUXIEME ETAPE

trois cent vingt-trois 323

CLOSE

To close this **étape,** have small groups review the forms of transportation by playing charades.

ASSESS

Quiz 12-2A, Quiz 12-2B, *Testing Program,* pp. 305–308

Audio CD 12, Tr. 20

Performance Assessment

Write on index cards the names of the items available at the places on page 315 (**du pain, de l'argent**). Have students draw a card and ask a classmate to go to the appropriate place for it. (**Tu pourrais passer à la boulangerie?**) The partner responds accordingly. (**Je veux bien.**)

For Individual Needs

19 Slower Pace Before they do this activity, have students list expressions they might expect to hear.

20 Challenge You might also have students write brief descriptions of what the people are going to do and why.

Presentation

Grammaire Write **Il, va, à la bibliothèque,** and **y** on separate strips of transparency. Arrange the first three strips to form the sentence **Il va à la bibliothèque** and have students repeat it. Then, replace **à la bibliothèque** with **y** to form the sentence **Il y va.** Write the subjects, verbs, and prepositional phrases of several similar sentences and the pronoun **y** on strips, scramble them, and call on students to arrange them into sentences, first without **y,** and then forming a new sentence using **y.**

Music Link

After teaching the pronoun **y,** you might play the song *Sur le pont d'Avignon* available on Audio CD 9. Have students raise their hand whenever they hear the pronoun **y.**

Additional Practice

Write destinations like **chez le disquaire** and **à la bibliothèque** on cards and distribute them. Then, have students pair off and ask questions until they find out where their partner is going.
—**Tu vas à la bibliothèque?**
—**Non, je n'y vais pas.**
—**Tu vas chez le disquaire?**
—**Oui, je vais y aller aujourd'hui.**

VIDEO PROGRAM
Videocassette 4
46:22–49:09

OR VIDEODISC PROGRAM,
Videodisc 6, Side B

Search 28545, Play To 31590

Teacher Notes

- See the *Video Guide,* the *Videodisc Guide,* and the *CD-ROM Teacher's Guide* for activities related to the **Panorama Culturel.**
- Remind students that cultural material may be included in the Chapter Quizzes and Test.
- The interviewees' language represents informal, unrehearsed speech. Occasionally, edits have been made for clarification.

Motivating Activity

Ask students question 1 of **Qu'en penses-tu?** Ask whether they have or would like to have a driver's license and why or why not.

Presentation

After students view the video, have them scan the interviews for cognates and skim for a general idea of what each person is saying. Then, ask the **Questions** below.

Thinking Critically

Comparing and Contrasting

Have students compare the French, Canadian, and American requirements for a driver's license. Which requirements are most strict? What do students think the requirements for a license should be?

PANORAMA CULTUREL

Lily-Christine • Québec

Emmanuel • France

Charlotte • France

Here's what some francophone people told us about obtaining a driver's license where they live.

CD 12
Trs. 6–9

CD-ROM
Disc 3

Qu'est-ce qu'il faut faire pour avoir un permis de conduire?

«J'ai mon permis probatoire, temporaire. Je n'ai pas encore mon permis de conduire. Premièrement, pour avoir ton permis, tu suis les cours théoriques. Après ça, tu passes ton examen. Si tu passes l'examen, tu as ton permis temporaire. Après, tu suis des cours pratiques. Tu passes un examen sur route. Et puis, si tu as l'examen sur route, eh bien, tu as ton permis.»

—Lily-Christine
Tr. 7

«Non, je n'ai pas encore de permis de conduire parce que je n'ai pas encore 16 ans. Je l'aurai peut-être, [mon] permis accompagné, à 16 ans. Autrement, [pour avoir] un permis de conduire normal, il faut attendre 18 ans en France. Pour avoir un permis de conduire, il faut passer le code. C'est un examen, quoi, c'est le code de la route. Et [il] faut passer la conduite. On est avec un moniteur. On doit faire un trajet qu'il nous indique et puis, suivant si on le fait bien ou pas, on a notre permis.»

—Emmanuel
Tr. 8

«Il faut sans doute bien savoir ses signes, son code de la route. [Il ne faut] pas avoir la tête ailleurs souvent, enfin... [Il] faut être bien dans sa tête. Voilà.»

—Charlotte
Tr. 9

Qu'en penses-tu?

1. Are the requirements for a driver's license that these people mention the same as those in your state?
2. What means of public transportation are available in your area? Do you use them? Why or why not?
3. How does transportation influence your lifestyle? How would your lifestyle change if you lived where these people do?

Language Note

You might define the following terms:
sur route *(on the road);* **conduite** *(driving);* **trajet** *(route);* **ailleurs** *(elsewhere).*

Questions

1. Est-ce que Lily-Christine a son permis de conduire? (Non, elle a son permis probatoire.)

2. D'après Lily-Christine, combien d'examens est-ce qu'on passe pour avoir le permis de conduire? (deux)

3. Est-ce qu'Emmanuel a son permis de conduire? Pourquoi ou pourquoi pas? (Non; Il faut avoir 18 ans.)

4. D'après Charlotte, qu'est-ce qu'il faut bien savoir? (les signes, le code de la route)

TROISIEME ETAPE

 Storytelling Book pp. 47, 48

Asking for and giving directions

PA p. 140, Acts. 18–20   12-C   **GV** pp. 106–107, Acts. 19–21

VOCABULAIRE

le lycée la bibliothèque la banque

Avenue Lamartine

le cinéma le café la poste

Chez Ana le restaurant

la papeterie la pharmacie

Victor Hugo le marché

la boulangerie

La bibliothèque est **entre** le lycée et la banque.
La poste est **à droite du** café.
Le cinéma est **à gauche du** café.

La boulangerie est **au coin de** la rue.
Le café est **en face de** la bibliothèque.

Here are some other prepositions you may want to use to give directions:

à côté de	*next to*	**loin de**	*far from*
devant	*in front of*	**près de**	*near*
derrière	*behind*		

23 Ecoute!   See scripts and answers on p. 309H.

CD 12 Tr. 10

Listen to the following statements and tell whether they are true or false, according to the **Vocabulaire**.

24 Qui est-ce?

Tell where a classmate is seated in your classroom. The others in your group will try to guess who it is.

> Cette personne est derrière David et à côté d'Isabelle.

NOTE DE GRAMMAIRE

The preposition **de** usually means *of* or *from*.

PA p. 141, Act. 21

GV p. 106, Act. 18

Additional Grammar Practice, p. R53

• When you use **de** before **le** or **les**, make the following contractions:

de + le = du	C'est près **du** musée.
de + les = des	Le café est près **des** Alpes.

• **De** doesn't change before **l'** or **la**: C'est au coin **de** la rue.

RESOURCES FOR TROISIEME ETAPE

PRINT

- *Lesson Planner*, p. 61
- *Practice and Activity Book*, pp. 140–142
- *Grammar and Vocabulary Workbook*, pp. 106–107
- *Activities for Communication*, pp. 71–72, 132–134, 159–160
- *Listening Activities*, pp. 92–93, 97
- *Testing Program*, pp. 309–312
- *Alternative Assessment Guide*, p. 43

MEDIA

- *Video Program*, Videocassette 4
  Video Guide, pp. 81–86
- *Videodisc Program*, Videodisc 6, Side B
  Videodisc Guide, p. 136
- *Teaching Transparencies* 12-3, 12-C
- *Interactive CD-ROM Program*, Disc 3
  CD-ROM Teacher's Guide, p. 52
- *Audio Compact Discs*
  Textbook Listening Activities, CD 12, Trs. 10–11
  Additional Listening Activities 12-5, 12-6, CD 12, Trs. 35–36
  Quiz 12-3B, CD 12, Tr. 21

Jump Start!

Have students write down the forms of transportation they take to the following places: **le cinéma, le fast-food, l'école.**

MOTIVATE

Have students brainstorm English expressions they might need to ask for directions if they were lost in a city. Have them list French expressions they already know.

TEACH

Presentation

Vocabulaire Review the places in town by showing pictures or by asking students questions. (**Où est-ce qu'on peut manger? Où est-ce qu'on peut acheter du pain?**) Then, have volunteers hold up signs with the names of different places written on them. Position the students at different locations in the classroom and tell the class where each "building" is located in relation to the others nearby. You might also position yourself near a particular "building" and ask questions about your location. (**Je suis près de la boulangerie?**)

For Individual Needs

Slower Pace You might write incomplete sentences on a transparency (**La boulangerie est près de...**) and have students complete them.

Game

24 Have students form teams and award a point for a correct answer. They might give locations of objects as well as people.

For Individual Needs

25 Challenge Have partners write one or two additional questions Hervé might ask about places in their own town. They might ask their partner these questions, or you might collect them to ask the class.

26 Challenge You might also have students draw their own family pictures like Arianne's (or pictures of a famous or imaginary family) and exchange them with a partner. The partner will ask about the people and places in the drawings and help write appropriate captions. Students might include this "photo album" in their written portfolios.

Additional Practice

26 Ask additional questions about the photos. For example, for the fifth photo, you might ask **Où est l'épicerie? (Elle est à côté de la maison.)**

Reteaching

Family vocabulary Draw the family tree of a TV family or of a royal family and ask students to describe the relationships between the family members. You might expand this activity by having students tell where the families live and what they like to do. You might also ask questions about familial relationships, such as **Le frère de ton père, c'est ton oncle ou ta mère?**

25 Il est perdu!

Your friend, Hervé, has a poor sense of direction. Everything is in just the <u>opposite</u> direction or location from what he thinks. Help him out by answering his questions.

> —La poste est loin de la bibliothèque?
> —Mais non, elle est près de la bibliothèque.

1. Est-ce que la papeterie est près de la pharmacie?
2. Le cinéma est devant le centre commercial?
3. La bibliothèque est à droite?
4. Est-ce que le café est derrière le stade?

1. Mais non, elle est loin de la pharmacie.
2. Mais non, il est derrière le centre commercial.
3. Mais non, elle est à gauche.
4. Mais non, il est devant le stade.

> **NOTE CULTURELLE**
>
> Martinique is an overseas possession of France known as a **département d'outre-mer,** or **DOM.** It has the same administrative status as a department in France, and the people of Martinique, who are citizens of France, have the same rights and responsibilities as other French citizens. Other DOMs include Guadeloupe, French Guiana, and Reunion Island. France also has overseas territories, like New Caledonia and French Polynesia. These territories are called **territoires d'outre-mer,** or **TOMs.**

26 La visite d'Arianne

Arianne a pris des photos pendant sa visite chez son oncle et sa tante. Complète les descriptions des photos avec des prépositions.

1. C'est mon oncle et ma tante dans le jardin _____ leur maison. devant

2. Là, _____ ma tante, c'est mon cousin Daniel. à côté de

3. Et voilà ma cousine Adeline, _____ mon oncle. derrière

4. Il y a une boulangerie _____ leur maison. Les croissants sont délicieux le matin! en face de/près de

5. Leur maison est _____ une autre maison et une épicerie. entre

6. Il y a un parc au coin de la rue, _____ leur maison. près de

326 *trois cent vingt-six* CHAPITRE 12 En ville

 Culture Note
Since Martinique is a **département** of France, people in Martinique refer to continental France as **la métropole.**

COMMENT DIT-ON... ?
Asking for and giving directions

CD-ROM
Disc 3

PA

pp. 141–142,
Act. 22–24

12-3

To ask for directions:

Pardon, madame. La poste, **s'il vous plaît?**

Pardon, mademoiselle. Où est la banque, **s'il vous plaît?**

Pardon, monsieur. Je cherche le musée, **s'il vous plaît.** *Excuse me, sir. I'm looking for . . . please.*

To give directions:

Vous continuez jusqu'au prochain feu rouge. *You keep going until the next light.*

Vous allez tout droit jusqu'au lycée. *You go straight ahead until you get to . . .*

Vous tournez à droite. *You turn . . .*

Prenez la rue Lamartine, **puis traversez la rue** Isambert. *Take . . . Street, then cross . . . Street.*

Vous passez devant la boulangerie. *You'll pass . . .*

C'est tout de suite à gauche. *It's right there on the . . . .*

27 Ecoute!   See scripts on p. 309H.

Guy is at the bus station (**la gare routière**) in Fort-de-France. Follow M. Robinet's directions, using the map on page 328. Where does Guy want to go?   to the post office

CD 12
Tr. 11

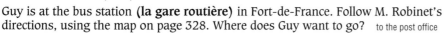

NOTE CULTURELLE

In many French towns, intersections have a traffic circle (**un rond-point**) at the center, which is often decorated with flowers, fountains, or statues. Vehicles enter and continue around the center island, turning off at the various streets that open into the circle. Most towns have at least one public square, often located in front of a public building or a church. Numerous cities have closed off some of the tiny streets in the **centre-ville** and made pedestrian areas where people can stroll freely, without having to worry about traffic.

28 Où est-ce?

Give directions from school to your favorite restaurant or record store. Your partner will try to guess the name of the place. Take turns.

TROISIEME ETAPE

trois cent vingt-sept **327**

Community Link

You might have students look up the history of a public square, town hall, local landmark, or historical building in their town. They might go to the Chamber of Commerce or the local library to find out when the building was built, whether it's been renovated, and what happened there of historical importance.

Teaching Suggestion

28 This activity could also be done using maps of Paris or other francophone cities, or by giving directions to places in the classroom or school.

For Individual Needs

29 **Slower Pace** Before students do this activity, have them locate the two sites in the photos on the map. Then, have them locate the major landmarks and streets mentioned in the letter.

29 **Challenge** Have students write directions to a different location on the map and read them to a partner, who follows the directions and tells where they lead.

Additional Practice

29 Give directions to various locations on the map. (**De la préfecture, vous tournez à droite dans la rue Félix Eboué. Vous passez devant la bibliothèque. Enfin, vous tournez à droite rue Antoine Siger. C'est tout de suite à gauche.**) Have students tell where your directions lead (**la poste**).

29 Quel monument est-ce? la cathédrale Saint-Louis

Your pen pal from Martinique wrote directions to a site that he thinks you should visit. Follow his directions on the map of Fort-de-France to find out which of these sites it is.

la bibliothèque Schœlcher

la cathédrale Saint-Louis

> Quand tu sors de la gare routière, va à droite sur le boulevard du Général de Gaulle. Prends la première à droite — c'est la rue Félix Eboué — et continue tout droit. Tu vas passer devant la préfecture. Traverse l'avenue des Caraïbes et va tout droit dans la rue de la Liberté jusqu'à la poste. Ensuite, tourne à droite rue Blénac et continue tout droit. Ça sera à droite, tout de suite après la rue Schœlcher.

History Link

29 You might have students find out about the people for whom the streets on the map were named and their major accomplishments (General Charles de Gaulle, Victor Schœlcher, Alphonse de Lamartine, or Antoine Siger). They might do the same for streets in their own town.

Community Link

29 Have students create a map and brochure of their own town with directions to help French-speaking tourists get around town. They might include local points of interest, good restaurants, hotels, post offices, and so on. See the project on page 309I for an expanded version of this activity.

30 Mon journal

Write a description of your city or neighborhood. What does it look like? Where are things located? Draw a small map to accompany your description.

PRONONCIATION

 Prononciation   See scripts and answers on p. 309H.

CD 12 Trs. 12–17

Do you remember what you've learned about French pronunciation? Here is a quick pronunciation review. If you've forgotten how to produce any of these sounds, check the Pronunciation Index at the back of the book and go back to the chapters where they were introduced. Repeat these words.

[y]	du	étude	[u]	rouge	voudrais
[o]	escargots	gâteau	[ɔ]	pomme	carottes
[ø]	veut	heureux	[œ]	sœur	beurre
[e]	cinéma	trouver	[ɛ]	frère	anglaise
[ɑ̃]	anglais	il prend	[ɔ̃]	allons	poisson
[ɛ̃]	quinze	pain	[œ̃]	lundi	emprunter
[j]	papier	viande	[w]	moi	pouvoir
[ɥ]	lui	ensuite	[t]	maths	théâtre
[r]	très	roux	[ʃ]	chat	chercher
[']	le héros	le hockey	[ɲ]	montagne	Allemagne

A. A prononcer

Repeat the following words.

1. nourriture	boutique	bateau	poste
2. feu	déposer	près	derrière
3. devant	avion	timbre	emprunter
4. pied	voiture	envoyer	tout de suite
5. rue	gauche	prochain	bibliothèque

B. A lire

Take turns with a partner reading each of the following sentences aloud.

1. Quand le chat n'est pas là, les souris dansent.
2. Il est mieux de travailler que de s'amuser.
3. Beaucoup de bruit pour rien.
4. Un poisson n'est jamais trop petit pour être frit.
5. On n'attrape pas les mouches avec du vinaigre.

C. A écrire

You're going to hear a short dialogue. Write down what you hear.

Portfolio

30 Written   This activity is appropriate for students' written portfolios. For portfolio suggestions, see the *Alternative Assessment Guide,* page 29.

Mon journal

30 If students don't want to write about their towns or neighborhoods, have them describe an ideal city or neighborhood. For an additional journal entry suggestion for Chapter 12, see *Practice and Activity Book,* page 156.

Teaching Suggestion

You might have students match the words in Part A with the corresponding sounds in the list above.

Portfolio

Oral   To assess students' pronunciation, have them record the list at the beginning of **Prononciation** for their oral portfolios. For portfolio information, see the *Alternative Assessment Guide,* pages iv–17.

CLOSE

 To close this **étape,** play **"Jacques a dit,"** using the new expressions from this **étape** as well as vocabulary students have already learned. (**Allez à gauche. Mettez le livre devant/derrière vous. Allez loin de la fenêtre.**)

ASSESS

Quiz 12-3A, Quiz 12-3B, *Testing Program,* pp. 309–312

Audio CD 12, Tr. 21

Performance Assessment

Distribute maps or a section of a map of your city. Have students tell a partner how to get from the school to their house or another place in the city. The partner should follow along on the map and tell where the directions lead. Have students reverse roles. As an alternative, show *Teaching Transparency 12-3* and have students give directions to a place in Fort-de-France.

Language Note

The sentences in Part B are well-known proverbs. You might have students quote similar English proverbs. Students might need to know **souris** *(mice),* **bruit** *(noise, rumor),* **frit** *(fried),* and **mouches** *(flies).*

READING STRATEGY

Combining different reading strategies

Teacher Note

For an additional reading, see *Practice and Activity Book,* page 143.

PREREADING
Activity A

Motivating Activity

Have students answer the introductory questions about stories they like to read. Then, ask them what fairy tales or folk tales they remember from their childhood. Did they have a favorite? Have them describe characters or themes that are usually found in fairy tales. You might also have them discuss the purpose or moral of their favorite fairy tales.

Teaching Suggestion

A. You might want to do this activity with the entire class. Remind students just to look at the titles and pictures. Then, ask them how they arrived at their answers.

READING
Activities B–F

Teaching Suggestion

B. Remind students just to scan for the information and to skip over the other details.

For Individual Needs

C. Slower Pace First, have students use the pictures and key words to find the page of the story on which each event takes place. Then, have them look more closely at each page to finalize the order.

LISONS!

$\mathcal{W}$hat kinds of stories do you like to read? Stories about the past? About the future? About exotic places?

 DE BONS CONSEILS
When you read stories, newspaper and maga-zine articles, or novels that were written for native French speakers, you're bound to come across many unfamiliar words. Just remember to use all the reading tips that you know to try to understand what you're reading.

A. a wooden horse; in Saint-Pierre, Martinique

A. Look at the title and illustrations that accompany the text. What is this story going to be about? Where does the story take place?

B. Scan the story to see if you can find the answers to these questions. See answers below.
1. Who are the main characters in the story?
2. What is going on when the story starts?
3. Why does Congo come to help the horse?
4. How does Congo help the horse?

C. Read the story carefully and then see if you can put these events in the correct order.
1. Congo burns the blue horse. 5
2. A child is frightened by the blue horse. 2
3. Congo first comes to see the blue horse. 4
4. M. Quinquina and his sons play music. 1
5. The blue bird is freed. 6
6. The mayor goes to see Congo. 3

Cheval de bois

$\mathcal{C}$ette année, la ville de Saint-Pierre accueille le manège de la famille Quinquina pour sa fête patronale. Le manège s'est installé sur la place du marché, face à la mer. Madame Quinquina tient une buvette où elle sert des limonades multicolores.

Monsieur Quinquina et ses deux fils jouent de la flûte de bambou et du "ti-bwa". Au rythme de cette musique, le manège de chevaux de bois, poussé par de robustes jeunes gens, tourne, tourne, tourne.

Cheval bleu, bleu comme l'océan.
Cheval noir, noir comme la nuit.
Cheval blanc, blanc comme les nuages.
Cheval vert, vert comme les bambous.
Cheval rouge, rouge comme le flamboyant.
Cheval jaune, jaune comme l'allamanda.

$\mathcal{L}$es chevaux de bois tournent, tournent et, sur leur dos, tous les enfants sont heureux.

Mais quand la nuit parfumée caresse l'île, les chevaux de bois rêvent. Le cheval bleu, bleu comme l'océan, rêve de partir, partir loin, visiter les îles, visiter le monde. Il a entendu dire que la terre est ronde. Vrai ou faux? Il aimerait bien savoir ! Cela fait si longtemps qu'il porte ce rêve dans sa carcasse de bois que cette nuit-là, son rêve devient oiseau. L'oiseau bat des ailes dans le corps du cheval bleu, bleu comme l'océan.

Au matin, un enfant monte sur le cheval bleu.
Tout à coup, il commence à hurler :
— Maman, maman, il y a une bête dans le cheval. J'ai peur ! Je veux descendre.

Language Note

Le flamboyant (used to describe the red horse) is a tree that is between 20 and 40 feet tall with feathery leaves and scarlet or orange flowers. You might ask students what the English word *flamboyant* means and point out the cognate *flame*. **L'allamanda** (used to describe the yellow horse) is a shrub with large, funnel-shaped, golden flowers.

Answers

B 1. The blue horse and Congo
2. There is a fair in town.
3. The mayor asked him to help.
4. He frees him and lets his dream come true.

On arrête la musique, on arrête le manège. C'est un tollé général : les mères rassemblent leurs enfants. En quelques secondes, la place est vide. Le maire et ses conseillers décident d'aller chercher le sage Congo.

...Congo s'approche du manège et caresse les flancs du cheval bleu, bleu comme l'océan :
— Je vais te délivrer ! cheval bleu, bleu comme l'océan, car ton rêve est vivant, il s'est métamorphosé en oiseau.

Congo s'assied près du cheval bleu, bleu comme l'océan. Quand le maire voit Congo tranquillement assis, il sort de la mairie en courant et hurle :

— Que faites-vous?
— J'attends, dit doucement Congo.
— Vous attendez quoi? demande le maire.
— J'attends que la nuit mette son manteau étoilé et ouvre son œil d'or. Je ferai alors un grand feu.

Quand la nuit met son manteau étoilé et ouvre son œil d'or, Congo prend tendrement dans ses bras le cheval bleu, bleu comme l'océan, et le dépose dans les flammes. Le feu crépite, chante, et l'or des flammes devient bleu, bleu comme l'océan. Les habitants de Saint-Pierre voient un immense oiseau bleu, bleu comme l'océan, s'élever dans la nuit étoilée et s'envoler vers l'horizon. Congo, heureux, murmure :
-Bon vent, oiseau-rêve !

RAPPEL As you read the story, you probably came across some unfamiliar words. Remember, you don't have to understand every word to get a sense of what you're reading. If you decide that the meaning of a particular word is necessary to help you understand the story, there are two techniques you've learned that can help: using the context to figure out the meaning of the word, and trying to see a cognate in the word.

D. Below are some cognates that appear in *Cheval de bois*. See if you can match them with their English equivalents.

1. habitants	f	a. counselors
2. fête	d	b. to descend; to get down
3. flammes	e	c. island
4. conseillers	a	d. festival
5. île	c	e. flames
6. descendre	b	f. inhabitants, people who live in a certain area

For Activities E and F, see answers below.

E. Make a list of all of the other cognates you can find in *Cheval de bois*. You should be able to find at least six more. Watch out for false cognates!

F. How can you tell this story was written for a young audience?

G. What stories, fairy tales, or myths have you read or heard that are similar to this story? In what ways are they similar? In what ways are they different?

H. Do you think there really was a bird inside the horse? What do you think the bird represents?

I. Compose a fairy tale of your own. Write it out or record it in French. Keep it simple so that your teacher can use it in the future with students who are beginning to learn French! Illustrate your story to make it easier to understand.

Answers

E *Possible answers:* flûte *(flute),* bambou *(bamboo),* rythme *(rhythm),* musique *(music),* robuste *(robust, strong),* océan *(ocean),* parfumée *(perfumed),* caresse *(caress),* ronde *(round),* carcasse *(carcass),* commence *(commence),* secondes *(seconds),* sage *(sage),* flanc *(flank),* tranquillement *(quietly, tranquilly),* tendrement *(tenderly),* immense *(immense),* horizon *(horizon)*

F It is short, relatively simple, and magical. The illustrations are colorful and simple.

Literature Link

Famous Caribbean authors are Maryse Condé, Jacques Roumain, Léon-Gontran Damas, and Simone Schwartz-Bart. Damas joined Léopold Senghor of Senegal and Aimé Césaire of Martinique in founding the **Négritude** movement, which stressed African cultural, economic, social, and political values.

Terms in Lisons!

Students might want to know these words: **cheval** *(horse);* **bois** *(wood);* **manège** *(merry-go-round);* **rêve** *(dream);* **oiseau** *(bird);* **feu** *(fire);* **devient** *(becomes).*

POSTREADING
Activities G-I

Thinking Critically

Comparing and Contrasting Have students compare the characters in this fairy tale to ones they're familiar with. How are they similar or different? Have them compare the ending of the story to the ending of *Cinderella* or *Beauty and the Beast.* Is there a moral to the story?

Teaching Suggestion

I. You might have students write their stories in a book they make out of construction paper and illustrate them with drawings or magazine pictures. This would also be appropriate for students' written portfolios or as a chapter project.

Cooperative Learning

Have the class act out the story. In small groups, they should choose a director and a narrator, as well as actors to play the characters. You might videotape the performance to show to other classes.

Language Arts Link

Ask students how the use of repetition affects the story. Have them also find examples of symbolic or metaphoric language (**la nuit met son manteau étoilé, les chevaux de bois rêvent, le rêve devient oiseau**).

MISE EN PRATIQUE

The *CD-ROM Program* offers guided recording and writing activities to practice oral and written skills and to review material from each chapter.

The **Mise en pratique** reviews and integrates all four skills and culture in preparation for the Chapter Test.

Additional Practice

1 You might review the means of transportation by showing picture flashcards. After students identify the means of transportation, they might tell where they have gone using that form of transportation.

Teacher Note

For more information on the sites in Martinique, see the Location Opener on pages 306–309 or contact the Caribbean Tourism Association, whose address and phone number are given on page T54.

For Individual Needs

2 Slower Pace Have students list words or phrases they associate with each picture before they listen to the recording.

Teaching Suggestion

2 After doing this activity, have partners identify what is in the photos.

---

1 You're planning a trip to Martinique and you'll need some transportation. Look at these ads. What kinds of transportation are available?   See answers below.

> ### LOCATION TROIS-ILETS
> #### Anse à l'Ane - 97229 Trois-Ilets
>
> **68.40.37**
> Lundi à Vendredi
> 8 H - 13 H
> et 15 H - 18 H
> Week-end :
> à la demande
>
> Avec Location TROIS-ILETS, la moto que vous avez louée par téléphone, 48 heures plus tôt, vient à vous. Chez vous. Si vous vous trouvez dans la commune des Trois-Ilets. Location possible pour une semaine au moins.

> ### TAXI
> ### FORT-DE-FRANCE
> 102 Rue de la République -
> 97200 Fort-de-France
>
> **70.44.08** Tous les jours : 5 H - 20 H
>
> Nos taxis répondent sans délais quand vous téléphonez à Taxi Fort-de-France. Déplacement dans toute l'île.

> # LOCA CENTER
> 3 Km Route de Schœlcher n. 63 -
> 97233 Schœlcher
>
> Livraison de voiture (Opel Corsa, Peugeot 106) à domicile (Nord Caraïbe, Schœlcher, Fort-de-France) pour une durée minimum de trois jours. Pas de frais de déplacement. Pendant la haute saison, pour une location de 10 jours au moins, réserver un mois à l'avance. Pour une location d'une durée de 3 à 7 jours, réserver 48 heures à l'avance. Pendant la basse saison, réserver la veille ou le jour même.
>
> **61.05.95**
> **61.40.12**
> Lundi à
> Vendredi
> 7 H 30 -
> 16 H 30
> Week-end :
> à la
> demande

1. Where can you call if you want a taxi? When is the latest you can call?
2. Where can you call if you want to rent a Renault? What about a motorcycle?
3. What's the minimum length of time you can rent these vehicles?
4. How long in advance do you need to make a reservation?
5. Are these places open on weekends?

2 Listen to Didier tell his family about his trip to Martinique. Put the pictures in order according to Didier's description.   See scripts on p. 309H.   c, d, a, b

CD 12
Tr. 18

a.

b.

c.

d.

Answers
1 motorcycle, taxi, rental car
  1. Taxi Fort-de-France; 8:00 P.M.
  2. Loca Center; Location Trois-Ilets
  3. Renault: three days; motorcycle: one week
  4. Location Trois-Ilets: 48 hours; Taxi Fort-de-France; advance reservation not necessary;

Loca Center: high season, one month (if renting for at least 10 days) or 48 hours (if renting for 3–7 days); low season, the night before or the same day
  5. Location Trois-Ilets and Loca Center: open on request; Taxi Fort-de-France: yes

3 *Ecrivons!*

Write a logical conversation to accompany the picture below.

STRATEGIE

Making a writing plan before you begin is important. Study the illustration carefully. Do you know all the vocabulary you'll need? Will you need to use certain verbs or structures frequently? You might want to use your textbook as a reference.

Prewriting

To help form your writing plan, look at the illustration and jot down ideas that immediately come to mind. You might imagine the situation, names for the people, and things they might be saying. Think about the types of vocabulary and structures you will need.

Writing

Now, using the notes you created in your writing plan, create the conversation that goes with the picture. Keep in mind expressions you've learned, such as asking for and giving directions, and vocabulary for telling where something is located.

Revising

When you've completed your writing, set it aside for a while before you do your self-evaluation. This will give you a fresh perspective on how to make it better. Also, when you evaluate what you've written, focus on only one area at a time. For example, don't look for spelling and punctuation mistakes while you're checking to see how well your writing flows. Focus on finding such mistakes when you proofread.

After you've revised your work, let a classmate give you feedback. Then, you can concentrate on making any other necessary revisions.

4 JEU DE ROLE

While visiting Fort-de-France, you stop and mail some postcards at the post office. You ask the employee for directions to two places in town: the library and the cathedral. Using the map on page 328, the employee gives you directions from the post office to each of these places. Be sure to ask questions if something is not clear. Then, ask the employee what means of transportation you should use to get to these places.

MISE EN PRATIQUE   *trois cent trente-trois* 333

Process Writing

3 You might have students work in groups of three to write the conversation. Once each group has completed its conversation, have students act it out in front of the class.

Teaching Suggestion

3 You might substitute different illustrations for students to write about from the one shown here, or use Photo 3 on page 311. You might also have students find or draw their own illustration.

Video Wrap-Up

- *VIDEO PROGRAM,*
  Videocassette 4, 32:50–51:01
- *VIDEODISC PROGRAM,*
  Videodisc 6, Side B

At this time, you might want to use the video resources for additional review and enrichment. See *Video Guide* or *Videodisc Guide* for suggestions regarding the following:
- **Un petit service**
  (Dramatic episode)
- **Panorama Culturel**
  (Interviews)
- **Vidéoclips**
  (Authentic footage)

This page is intended to help students prepare for the Chapter Test. It is a brief checklist of the major points covered in the chapter. The students should be reminded that this is only a checklist and does not necessarily include everything that will appear on the test.

Teaching Suggestions

1 You might review different types of buildings in town by giving a local example of a place *(Prescriptions To Go)* and asking students to identify it. (**C'est une pharmacie.**)

2, 3 Encourage students to vary the ways they request and respond to favors.

5 You might review other means of transportation in addition to the ones shown.

8 Have students illustrate expressions for giving directions on the board or mime them for their classmates to guess.

QUE SAIS-JE?

Can you point out places and things?
p. 317

Can you make and respond to requests?
p. 320

Can you ask for advice and make suggestions?
p. 322

Can you ask for and give directions?
p. 327

Can you use what you've learned in this chapter?

1 How would you point out and identify . . .   *Possible answers:*
1. a certain building?   *Voici...*
2. a certain store?   *Regarde, voilà...*
3. a certain person?   *Ça, c'est...*

2 How would you ask someone to . . .   *Possible answers:*
1. buy some stamps?   *Tu peux me rapporter des timbres?*
2. go to the bookstore?   *Tu pourrais passer à la librairie?*
3. deposit some money?   *(Est-ce que) tu peux déposer de l'argent?*

3 How would you agree to do the favors you asked in number 2? How would you refuse?   *See answers below.*

4 How would you ask a friend which means of transportation you should use to get to a certain store?   *Comment est-ce qu'on y va?*

5 How would you suggest these means of transportation?   *On peut y aller... On peut prendre...*

1.
en voiture.
la voiture.

3.
en taxi.
un taxi.

2.
en bateau.
un bateau.

4.
en bus.
le bus.

6 How would you tell someone that you're looking for a certain place?
Pardon, monsieur/madame/mademoiselle. Je cherche... , s'il vous plaît.

7 How would you ask someone where a certain place in town is?
Pardon, monsieur/madame/mademoiselle. Où est... , s'il vous plaît?

8 How would you give someone directions to your house from . . .
1. your school?
2. your favorite restaurant?

🏰 Game

Où EST... ?   To practice giving directions, create a city in the classroom by labeling the aisles as streets and areas or objects in the room (your desk, the blackboard, the door) as buildings. Form two teams. A player from one team names a place, and a player from the opposing team must direct the first player there in French.

Answers

3 *Agree:* D'accord. Je veux bien. J'y vais tout de suite. Si tu veux.

Refuse: Je ne peux pas maintenant. Je suis désolé(e), mais je n'ai pas le temps.

PREMIERE ETAPE

Pointing out places and things

Voici...   *Here is/are . . .*
Regarde, voilà...   *Look, here/there is/are . . .*
Ça, c'est...   *This/That is . . .*
Là, c'est...   *There, that is . . .*
Là, tu vois, c'est...   *There, you see, this/that is . . .*
un endroit   *place*
chez   *at (at the place of) . . .*

Buildings

la banque   *bank*

la boulangerie   *bakery*
le disquaire   *record store*
l'épicerie (f.)   *small grocery store*
la librairie   *bookstore*
la papeterie   *stationery store*
la pâtisserie   *pastry shop*
la pharmacie   *drugstore*
la poste   *post office*

Things to do or buy in town

envoyer des lettres   *to send letters*

une baguette   *long, thin loaf of bread*
un timbre   *stamp*
retirer de l'argent (m.)   *to withdraw money*
déposer de l'argent   *to deposit money*
rendre   *to return something*
emprunter   *to borrow*
des médicaments (m.)   *medicine*
une enveloppe   *envelope*
une pâtisserie   *pastry*

Teaching Suggestions
• To review pronunciation and vocabulary, have students find words in the **Vocabulaire** that contain the sounds listed in the **Prononciation** on page 329.
• To review vocabulary from all twelve chapters, play the game **"Les mots en famille"** described on page 309J.

DEUXIEME ETAPE

Making and responding to requests

Tu peux... ?   *Can you . . . ?*
Tu me rapportes... ?   *Will you bring me . . . ?*
Tu pourrais passer à... ?   *Could you go by . . . ?*
D'accord.   *OK.*
Je veux bien.   *Gladly.*
J'y vais tout de suite.   *I'll go right away.*
Si tu veux.   *If you want.*
Je ne peux pas maintenant.   *I can't right now.*

Je suis désolé(e), mais je n'ai pas le temps.   *I'm sorry, but I don't have time.*

Asking for advice and making suggestions

Comment est-ce qu'on y va?   *How can we get there?*
On peut y aller...   *We can go . . .*
On peut prendre...   *We can take . . .*
y   *there*

Means of transportation

en bus (m.)   *by bus*
à pied (m.)   *on foot*
à vélo (m.)   *by bike*
en voiture (f.)   *by car*
en taxi (m.)   *by taxi*
en bateau (m.)   *by boat*
en avion (m.)   *by plane*
en train (m.)   *by train*
en métro (m.)   *by subway*

CHAPTER 12 ASSESSMENT

CHAPTER TEST
• *Testing Program,* pp. 313–318
• *Audio Compact Discs*

Audio CD 12, Tracks 22-24

SPEAKING TEST
• *Testing Program,* p. 348

TEST GENERATOR

• Chapter 12

ALTERNATIVE ASSESSMENT
Performance Assessment
• You might want to use the **Jeu de Rôle** on page 333 as a cumulative performance assessment activity.
• *Alternative Assessment Guide,* p. 43

📁 **Portfolio Assessment**
• *Alternative Assessment Guide*
Oral: p. 29
Written: p. 29

CD-ROM ASSESSMENT
• *Interactive CD-ROM Program,* Disc 3
A toi de parler
A toi d'écrire
• *Alternative Assessment Guide,* p. 57

TROISIEME ETAPE

Asking for and giving directions

Pardon, ..., s'il vous plaît?   *Excuse me, . . . please?*
Pardon, ... Où est..., s'il vous plaît?   *Excuse me, . . . Where is . . . , please?*
Pardon, ... Je cherche..., s'il vous plaît.   *Excuse me, . . . I'm looking for . . . , please.*
Vous continuez jusqu'au prochain feu rouge.   *You keep going until the next light.*

Vous allez tout droit jusqu'à...   *You go straight ahead until you get to . . .*
Vous tournez...   *You turn . . .*
Prenez la rue..., puis traversez la rue...   *Take . . . Street, then cross . . . Street.*
Vous passez...   *You'll pass . . .*
C'est tout de suite à...   *It's right there on the . . .*

Locations

à côté de   *next to*
loin de   *far from*
près de   *close to*
au coin de   *on the corner of*
en face de   *across from*
derrière   *behind*
devant   *in front of*
entre   *between*
à droite (de)   *to the right*
à gauche (de)   *to the left*

VOCABULAIRE   *trois cent trente-cinq* **335**

Career Path

A career in banking provides many interesting opportunities for people who speak a foreign language, as a translator in the United States for customers who do not speak English, or working abroad with an international bank. Ask students to name cities or countries that have many international banks. What languages might be important in these locations?

REFERENCE SECTION

R1

SUMMARY OF FUNCTIONS

Function is another word for the way in which you use language for a specific purpose. When you find yourself in specific situations, such as in a restaurant, in a grocery store, or at school, you'll want to communicate with those around you. In order to communicate in French, you have to "function" in the language.

Each chapter in this book focuses on language functions. You can easily find them in boxes labeled **Comment dit-on... ?** The other features in the chapter—grammar, vocabulary, culture notes—support the functions you're learning.

Here is a list of functions and the French expressions presented in this book. You'll need them in order to communicate in a wide range of situations. Following each function entry, you will find the chapter and page number where each function is presented.

SOCIALIZING

Greeting people   Ch. 1, p. 22

Bonjour.
Salut.

Saying goodbye   Ch. 1, p. 22

Salut.	A bientôt.
Au revoir.	A demain.
A tout à l'heure.	Tchao.

Asking how people are and telling how you are
Ch. 1, p. 23

(Comment) ça va?	Bof.
Ça va.	Pas mal.
Super!	Pas terrible.
Très bien.	Et toi?
Comme ci, comme ça.	

Expressing and responding to thanks   Ch. 3, p. 82

Merci.
A votre service.

Extending invitations   Ch. 6, p. 159

Allons... !
Tu veux... avec moi?
Tu viens?
On peut...

Accepting invitations   Ch. 6, p. 159

Je veux bien.	D'accord.
Pourquoi pas?	Bonne idée.

Refusing invitations   Ch. 6, p. 159

Désolé(e), je suis occupé(e).
Ça ne me dit rien.
J'ai des trucs à faire.
Désolé(e), je ne peux pas.

Identifying people   Ch. 7, p. 179

C'est...
Ce sont...
Voici...
Voilà...

Introducing people   Ch. 7, p. 183

C'est...
Je te/vous présente...
Très heureux (heureuse).   (FORMAL)

Inquiring about past events   Ch. 9, p. 238

Qu'est-ce que tu as fait... ?
Tu es allé(e) où?
Et après?
Qu'est-ce qui s'est passé?

Relating past events   Ch. 9, p. 238

D'abord,...
Ensuite,...
Après,...
Je suis allé(e)...
Et après ça,...
Finalement,/Enfin,...

Inquiring about future plans   Ch. 11, p. 289

Qu'est-ce que tu vas faire... ?
Où est-ce que tu vas aller... ?

Sharing future plans   Ch. 11, p. 289

J'ai l'intention de...
Je vais...

Seeing someone off   Ch. 11, p. 296

Bon voyage!
Bonnes vacances!
Amuse-toi bien!
Bonne chance!

EXCHANGING INFORMATION

Asking someone's name and giving yours
Ch. 1, p. 24

Tu t'appelles comment?
Je m'appelle...

Asking and giving someone else's name
Ch. 1, p. 24

Il/Elle s'appelle comment?
Il/Elle s'appelle...

Asking someone's age and giving yours
Ch. 1, p. 25

Tu as quel âge?
J'ai... ans.

Asking for information Ch. 2, p. 51

Tu as quels cours... ?
Tu as quoi... ?
Vous avez... ?
Tu as... à quelle heure?

Giving information Ch. 2, p. 51

Nous avons...
J'ai...

Telling when you have class Ch. 2, p. 54

à... heure(s)
à... heure(s) quinze
à... heure(s) trente
à... heure(s) quarante-cinq

Making requests Ch. 3, p. 72

Tu as... ?
Vous avez... ?

Responding to requests Ch. 3, p. 72

Voilà.
Je regrette.
Je n'ai pas de...

Asking others what they need and telling what you need Ch. 3, p. 74

Qu'est-ce qu'il te faut pour... ?
Qu'est-ce qu'il vous faut pour... ?
Il me faut...

Expressing need Ch. 8, p. 210; Ch. 10, p. 265

Qu'est-ce qu'il te faut?
Il me faut...
De quoi est-ce que tu as besoin?
J'ai besoin de...
Oui, il me faut...
Oui, vous avez... ?
Je cherche quelque chose pour...
J'aimerais... pour aller avec...
Non, merci, je regarde.

Asking for information Ch. 3, p. 82

C'est combien?

Getting someone's attention
Ch. 3, p. 82; Ch. 5, p. 135

Pardon...
Excusez-moi.
... , s'il vous plaît.
Monsieur!
Madame!
Mademoiselle!

Exchanging information Ch. 4, p. 104

Qu'est-ce que tu fais comme sport?
Qu'est-ce que tu fais pour t'amuser?
Je fais...
Je ne fais pas de...
Je (ne) joue (pas)...

Ordering food and beverages Ch. 5, p. 135

Vous avez choisi?
Vous prenez?
Je voudrais...
Je vais prendre... , s'il vous plaît.
... , s'il vous plaît.
Donnez-moi... , s'il vous plaît.
Apportez-moi... , s'il vous plaît.
Vous avez... ?
Qu'est-ce que vous avez comme boissons?
Qu'est-ce qu'il y a à boire?

Paying the check Ch. 5, p. 139

L'addition, s'il vous plaît.
Oui, tout de suite.
Un moment, s'il vous plaît.
Ça fait combien, s'il vous plaît?
Ça fait... francs.
C'est combien, ... ?
C'est... francs.

Making plans Ch. 6, p. 153

Qu'est-ce que tu vas faire... ?
Tu vas faire quoi... ?
Je vais...
Pas grand-chose.
Rien de spécial.

Arranging to meet someone Ch. 6, p. 163

Quand (ça)?   et quart
tout de suite   moins le quart
Où (ça)?   moins cinq
devant   midi (et demi)
au métro...   minuit (et demi)
chez...   vers
dans...   Quelle heure est-il?
Avec qui?   Il est...
A quelle heure?   On se retrouve...
A cinq heures...   Rendez-vous...
et demie   Entendu.

Describing and characterizing people
Ch. 7, p. 185

Il est comment?
Elle est comment?
Ils/Elles sont comment?
Il est...
Elle est...
Ils/Elles sont...

Making a telephone call Ch. 9, p. 244

Bonjour.
Je suis bien chez... ?
C'est...
(Est-ce que)... est là, s'il vous plaît?

(Est-ce que) je peux parler à... ?
Je peux laisser un message?
Vous pouvez lui dire que j'ai téléphoné?
Ça ne répond pas.
C'est occupé.

Answering a telephone call   Ch. 9, p. 244

Allô?
Qui est à l'appareil?
Une seconde, s'il vous plaît.
D'accord.
Bien sûr.
Vous pouvez rappeler plus tard?
Ne quittez pas.

Inquiring   Ch. 10, p. 265

(Est-ce que) je peux vous aider?
Vous désirez?
Je peux l'(les) essayer?
Je peux essayer... ?
C'est combien, ... ?
Ça fait combien?
Vous avez ça en... ?

Pointing out places and things   Ch. 12, p. 317

Là, tu vois, c'est...
Ça, c'est...
Regarde, voilà...
Là, c'est...
Voici...

Asking for advice   Ch. 12, p. 322

Comment est-ce qu'on y va?

Making suggestions   Ch. 12, p. 322

On peut y aller...
On peut prendre...

Asking for directions   Ch. 12, p. 327

Pardon, ..., s'il vous plaît?
Pardon, ... Où est..., s'il vous plaît?
Pardon, ... Je cherche..., s'il vous plaît.

Giving directions   Ch. 12, p. 327

Vous continuez jusqu'au prochain feu rouge.
Vous tournez...
Vous allez tout droit jusqu'à...
Prenez la rue... puis traversez la rue...
Vous passez...
C'est tout de suite à...

EXPRESSING FEELINGS AND EMOTIONS

Expressing likes, dislikes, and preferences   Ch. 1, pp. 26, 32

J'aime (bien)...   J'aime mieux...
Je n'aime pas...   J'adore...
Je préfère...

Ch. 5, p. 138
C'est...
  bon!
  excellent!
  délicieux!
  pas mauvais!
  pas bon!
  pas terrible!
  dégoûtant!
  mauvais!

Telling what you'd like and what you'd like to do
Ch. 3, p. 77

Je voudrais...
Je voudrais acheter...

Telling how much you like or dislike something
Ch. 4, p. 102

Beaucoup.   Pas du tout.
Pas beaucoup.   surtout
Pas tellement.

Inquiring about likes and dislikes   Ch. 1, p. 26

Tu aimes... ?

Ch. 5, p. 138
Comment tu trouves ça?

Sharing confidences   Ch. 9, p. 247

J'ai un petit problème.
Je peux te parler?
Tu as une minute?

Consoling others   Ch. 9, p. 247

Je t'écoute.
Ne t'en fais pas!
Ça va aller mieux!
Qu'est-ce que je peux faire?

Making a decision   Ch. 10, p. 274

Vous avez décidé de prendre... ?
Vous avez choisi?
Vous le/la/les prenez?
Je le/la/les prends.
Non, c'est trop cher.

Hesitating   Ch. 10, p. 274

Euh... J'hésite.
Je ne sais pas.
Il/Elle me plaît, mais il/elle est...

Expressing indecision   Ch. 11, p. 289

J'hésite.
Je ne sais pas.
Je n'en sais rien.
Je n'ai rien de prévu.

Expressing wishes   Ch. 11, p. 289

J'ai envie de...
Je voudrais bien...

R4

EXPRESSING ATTITUDES AND OPINIONS

Agreeing Ch. 2, p. 50

Oui, beaucoup.
Moi aussi.
Moi non plus.

Disagreeing Ch. 2, p. 50

Moi, non.
Non, pas trop.
Moi, si.
Pas moi.

Asking for opinions Ch. 2, p. 57

Comment tu trouves... ?
Comment tu trouves ça?

Ch. 9, p. 237
Tu as passé un bon week-end?

Ch. 10, p. 270
Il/Elle me va?
Il/Elle te/vous plaît?
Tu aimes mieux... ou... ?

Ch. 11, p. 297
Tu as passé un bon... ?
Tu t'es bien amusé(e)?
Ça s'est bien passé?

Expressing opinions Ch. 2, p. 57

C'est...
   facile.   pas terrible.
   génial.   pas super.
   super.   zéro.
   cool.   barbant.
   intéressant.   nul.
   passionnant.   pas mal.
   difficile.
Ça va.

Ch. 9, p. 237
Oui, très chouette.
Oui, excellent.
Oui, très bon.
Oui, ça a été.
Oh, pas mauvais.
C'était épouvantable.
Très mauvais.

Ch. 11, p. 297
C'était formidable!
Non, pas vraiment.
C'était ennuyeux.
C'était un véritable cauchemar!

Paying a compliment Ch. 10, p. 270

C'est tout à fait ton style.
Il/Elle te/vous va très bien.
Il/Elle va très bien avec...
Je le/la/les trouve...
C'est parfait.

Criticizing Ch. 10, p. 270

Il/Elle ne te/vous va pas du tout.
Il/Elle ne va pas du tout avec...
Il/Elle est (Ils/Elles sont) trop...
Je le/la/les trouve...

PERSUADING

Making suggestions Ch. 4, p. 110

On... ?
On fait... ?
On joue... ?

Ch. 5, p. 129
On va... ?

Accepting suggestions Ch. 4, p. 110

D'accord.
Bonne idée.
Oui, c'est...
Allons-y!

Turning down suggestions; making excuses
Ch. 4, p. 110

Non, c'est...
Ça ne me dit rien.
Désolé(e), mais je ne peux pas.

Ch. 5, p. 129
Désolé(e). J'ai des devoirs à faire.
J'ai des courses à faire.
J'ai des trucs à faire.
J'ai des tas de choses à faire.
Je ne peux pas parce que...

Making a recommendation Ch. 5, p. 132

Prends...
Prenez...

Asking for permission Ch. 7, p. 189

Tu es d'accord?
(Est-ce que) je peux... ?

Giving permission Ch. 7, p. 189

Oui, si tu veux.
Pourquoi pas?
D'accord, si tu... d'abord...
Oui, bien sûr.

Refusing permission Ch. 7, p. 189

Pas question!
Non, c'est impossible.
Non, tu dois...
Pas ce soir.

Making requests   Ch. 8, p. 212

Tu peux (aller faire les courses)?
Tu me rapportes... ?

Ch. 12, p. 320
Est-ce que tu peux... ?
Tu pourrais passer à... ?

Accepting requests   Ch. 8, p. 212

Pourquoi pas?
Bon, d'accord.
Je veux bien.
J'y vais tout de suite.

Ch. 12, p. 320
D'accord.
Si tu veux.

Declining requests   Ch. 8, p. 212

Je ne peux pas maintenant.
Je regrette, mais je n'ai pas le temps.
J'ai des tas de choses (trucs) à faire.

Ch. 12, p. 320
Je suis désolé(e), mais je n'ai pas le temps.

Telling someone what to do   Ch. 8, p. 212

Rapporte(-moi)...
Prends...
Achète(-moi)...
N'oublie pas de...

Offering food   Ch. 8, p. 219

Tu veux... ?
Vous voulez... ?
Vous prenez... ?
Tu prends... ?
Encore... ?

Accepting food   Ch. 8, p. 219

Oui, s'il vous/te plaît.
Oui, avec plaisir.
Oui, j'en veux bien.

Refusing food   Ch. 8, p. 219

Non, merci.
Non, merci. Je n'ai plus faim.
Je n'en veux plus.

Asking for advice   Ch. 9, p. 247

A ton avis, qu'est-ce que je fais?
Qu'est-ce que tu me conseilles?

Ch. 10, p. 264
Je ne sais pas quoi mettre pour...
Qu'est-ce que je mets?

Giving advice   Ch. 9, p. 247

Oublie-le/-la/-les!
Téléphone-lui/-leur!
Tu devrais...
Pourquoi tu ne... pas?

Ch. 10, p. 264
Pourquoi est-ce que tu ne mets pas... ?
Mets...

Reminding   Ch. 11, p. 293

N'oublie pas...
Tu n'as pas oublié... ?
Tu ne peux pas partir sans...
Tu prends... ?

Reassuring   Ch. 11, p. 293

Ne t'en fais pas.
J'ai pensé à tout.
Je n'ai rien oublié.

ADDITIONAL VOCABULARY

This list presents additional vocabulary you may want to use when you're working on the activities in the textbook and workbook. It also includes the optional vocabulary labeled **Vocabulaire à la carte** that appears in several chapters. If you can't find the words you need here, try the French-English and English-French vocabulary lists beginning on page R56.

ADJECTIVES

absurd *absurde*
awesome (impressive) *impressionnant(e)*
boring *ennuyeux/ennuyeuse*
chilly *froid(e), frais* (m.)*/fraîche* (f.)
colorful (thing) *vif/vive*
despicable *ignoble*
eccentric *excentrique*
incredible *incroyable*
tasteless (flavor) *insipide;* (remark, object) *de mauvais goût*
tasteful (remark, object) *de bon goût*
terrifying *terrifiant(e)*
threatening *menaçant(e)*
tremendous (excellent) *formidable*
unforgettable *inoubliable*
unique *unique*

CLOTHING

blazer *un blazer*
button *un bouton*
coat *un manteau*
collar *un col*
eyeglasses *des lunettes* (f.)
gloves *des gants* (m.)
handkerchief *un mouchoir*
high-heeled shoes *des chaussures* (f.) *à talons*
lace *de la dentelle*
linen *du lin*
necklace *un collier*
nylon *du nylon*
pajamas *un pyjama*
polyester *du polyester*
raincoat *un imperméable*
rayon *de la rayonne*
ring *une bague*
sale (discount) *des soldes* (m.)
silk *de la soie*
sleeve *une manche*
slippers *des pantoufles* (f.)
suit (man's) *un costume;* (woman's) *un tailleur*
suspenders *des bretelles* (f.)
velvet *du velours*
vest *un gilet*
wool *de la laine*
zipper *une fermeture éclair®*

COLORS AND PATTERNS

beige *beige*
checked *à carreaux*
colorful *coloré(e), vif/vive*
dark blue *bleu foncé*
dark-colored *foncé(e)*
flowered *à fleurs*
gold (adj.) *d'or, doré(e)*
light blue *bleu clair(e)*
light-colored *clair(e)*
patterned *à motifs*
polka-dotted *à pois*
striped *à rayures*
turquoise *turquoise*

COMPUTERS

l'ordinateur le lecteur de CD-ROM le CD-ROM
le clavier la souris

CD-ROM *le CD-ROM, le disque optique compact*
CD-ROM drive *le lecteur de CD-ROM, l'unité* (f.) *de CD-ROM*
to click *cliquer*
computer *l'ordinateur* (m.)
delete key *la touche d'effacement*
disk drive *le lecteur de disquette, l'unité de disquettes* (f.)
diskette, floppy disk *la disquette, la disquette souple*
to drag *glisser, déplacer*
e-mail *le courrier électronique, la messagerie électronique*

file *le dossier*
file (folder) *le fichier*
hard drive *le disque dur*
homepage *la page d'accueil*
Internet *Internet* (m.)
keyboard *le clavier*
keyword *le mot clé*
log on *l'ouverture* (f.) *de session*
modem *le modem*
monitor *le moniteur, le logimètre*
mouse *la souris*
password *le mot de passe*
to print *imprimer*
printer *l'imprimante* (f.)
to quit *quitter*
to record *enregistrer*
return key *la touche de retour*
to save *sauvegarder, enregistrer*
screen *l'écran* (m.)
to search *chercher, rechercher*
search engine *le moteur de recherche, l'outil* (m.)
  de recherche
to send *envoyer*
software *le logiciel*
Web site *le site du Web, le site W3*
World Wide Web *le World Wide Web, le Web,*
  le W3

ENTERTAINMENT

blues *le blues*
CD player *le lecteur de CD*
camera flash *le flash*
folk music *la musique folklorique*
headphones *les écouteurs*
hit (song) *le tube*
lens *l'objectif* (m.)
microphone *le micro(phone)*
opera *l'opéra* (m.)
pop music *la musique pop*
reggae *le reggae*
roll of film *la pellicule (photo)*
screen *l'écran* (m.)
speakers *les enceintes* (f.), *les baffles* (m.)
to turn off *éteindre*
to turn on *allumer*
turntable *la platine*
walkman *le balladeur*

FAMILY

adopted *adopté(e), adoptif/adoptive*
brother-in-law *le beau-frère*
child *un(e) enfant*
couple *un couple*
daughter-in-law *la belle-fille*
divorced *divorcé(e)*
engaged *fiancé(e)*
goddaughter *la filleule*
godfather *le parrain*

godmother *la marraine*
godson *le filleul*
grandchildren *les petits-enfants*
granddaughter *la petite-fille*
grandson *le petit-fils*
great-granddaughter *l'arrière-petite-fille* (f.)
great-grandfather *l'arrière-grand-père* (m.)
great-grandmother *l'arrière-grand-mère* (f.)
great-grandson *l'arrière-petit-fils* (m.)
half-brother *le demi-frère*
half-sister *la demi-sœur*
mother-in-law *la belle-mère*
only child *un/une enfant unique*
single *célibataire*
sister-in-law *la belle-sœur*
son-in-law *le gendre; le beau-fils*
stepbrother *le demi-frère*
stepdaughter *la belle-fille*
stepfather *le beau-père*
stepmother *la belle-mère*
stepsister *la demi-sœur*
stepson *le beau-fils*
widow *la veuve*
widower *le veuf*

FOODS AND BEVERAGES

appetizer *une entrée*
apricot *un abricot*
asparagus *des asperges* (f.)
bacon *du bacon*
bowl *un bol*
Brussels sprouts *des choux* (m.) *de Bruxelles*
cabbage *du chou*
cauliflower *du chou-fleur*
cereal *des céréales* (f.)
chestnut *un marron*
cookie *un biscuit*
cucumber *un concombre*
cutlet *une escalope*
fried egg *un œuf au plat;* **hard-boiled egg** *un*
  œuf dur; **scrambled eggs** *des œufs brouillés;*
  soft-boiled egg *un œuf à la coque*
eggplant *une aubergine*
French bread *une baguette*
garlic *de l'ail* (m.)
grapefruit *un pamplemousse*
honey *du miel*
liver *du foie*
margarine *de la margarine*
marshmallow *une guimauve*
mayonnaise *de la mayonnaise*
melon *un melon*
mustard *de la moutarde*
nuts *des noix* (f.)
peanut butter *du beurre de cacahouètes*
popcorn *du pop-corn*
potato chips *des chips* (f.)
raspberry *une framboise*
salmon *du saumon*
salt *du sel*

pepper (spice) *du poivre;* (vegetable) *un poivron*
shellfish *des fruits* (m.) *de mer*
soup *de la soupe*
spinach *des épinards* (m.)
spoon *une cuillère*
syrup *du sirop*
veal *du veau*
watermelon *une pastèque*
zucchini *une courgette*
bland *doux (douce)*
hot (spicy) *épicé(e)*
juicy (fruit) *juteux/juteuse;* (meat) *tendre*
rare (cooked) *saignant(e)*
medium (cooked) *à point*
spicy *épicé(e)*
well-done (cooked) *bien cuit(e)*
tasty *savoureux/savoureuse*

HOUSEWORK

to clean *nettoyer*
to dry *faire sécher*
to dust *faire la poussière*
to fold *plier*
to hang *pendre*
to iron *repasser*
to put away *ranger*
to rake *ratisser*
to shovel *enlever à la pelle*
to sweep *balayer*

PETS

bird *un oiseau*
cow *une vache*
frog *une grenouille*
goldfish *un poisson rouge*
guinea-pig *un cochon d'Inde*
hamster *un hamster*
horse *un cheval*
kitten *un chaton*
lizard *un lézard*
mouse *une souris*
parrot *un perroquet*
pig *un cochon*
puppy *un chiot*
rabbit *un lapin*
turtle *une tortue*

PLACES AROUND TOWN

airport *l'aéroport* (m.)
beauty shop *le salon de coiffure*
bridge *le pont*
church *l'église* (f.)
consulate *le consulat*
hospital *l'hôpital* (m.)
mosque *la mosquée*

police station *le commissariat de police*
synagogue *la synagogue*
tourist office *l'office du tourisme* (m.)
town hall *l'hôtel* (m.) *de ville*

PROFESSIONS

Note: If only one form is given, that form is used for both men and women. Note that you can also say **une femme banquier, une femme médecin,** and so forth.

archaeologist *un(e) archéologue*
architect *un(e) architecte*
athlete *un(e) athlète*
banker *un banquier*
businessman/businesswoman *un homme d'affaires (une femme d'affaires)*
dancer *un danseur (une danseuse)*
dentist *un(e) dentiste*
doctor *un médecin*
editor *un rédacteur (une rédactrice)*
engineer *un ingénieur*
fashion designer *un(e) styliste de mode*
fashion model *un mannequin*
hairdresser *un coiffeur (une coiffeuse)*
homemaker *un homme au foyer (une femme au foyer)*
lawyer *un(e) avocat(e)*
manager (company) *un directeur (une directrice);* (store, restaurant) *un gérant (une gérante)*
mechanic *un mécanicien (une mécanicienne)*
painter (art) *un peintre;* (buildings) *un peintre en bâtiment*
pilot *un pilote*
plumber *un plombier*
scientist *un(e) scientifique*
secretary *un(e) secrétaire*
social worker *un assistant social (une assistante sociale)*
taxi driver *un chauffeur de taxi*
technician *un technicien (une technicienne)*
truck driver *un routier*
veterinarian *un(e) vétérinaire*
worker *un ouvrier (une ouvrière)*
writer *un écrivain*

SCHOOL SUBJECTS

accounting *la comptabilité*
business *le commerce*
home economics *les arts* (m.) *ménagers*
foreign languages *les langues* (f.) *étrangères*
marching band *la fanfare*
orchestra *l'orchestre* (m.)
social studies *les sciences* (f.) *sociales*
typing *la dactylographie*
woodworking *la menuiserie*
world history *l'histoire* (f.) *mondiale*

SCHOOL SUPPLIES

calendar   *un calendrier*
colored pencils   *des crayons* (m.) *de couleur*
compass   *un compas*
correction fluid   *du liquide correcteur*
glue   *de la colle*
gym suit   *une tenue de gymnastique*
marker   *un feutre*
rubber band   *un élastique*
scissors   *des ciseaux* (m.)
staple   *une agrafe*
stapler   *une agrafeuse*
transparent tape   *du ruban adhésif*

SPORTS AND INTERESTS

badminton   *le badminton*
boxing   *la boxe*
fishing rod   *la canne à pêche*
foot race   *la course à pied*

to go for a ride (by bike, car, motorcycle, moped)
   faire une promenade, faire un tour (à bicyclette,
   en voiture, à moto, à vélomoteur)
to do gymnastics   *faire de la gymnastique*
hunting   *la chasse*
to lift weights   *faire des haltères*
mountain climbing   *l'alpinisme* (m.)
to play checkers   *jouer aux dames*
to play chess   *jouer aux échecs*
to ride a skateboard   *faire de la*
   planche à roulettes
to sew   *coudre; faire de la couture*
speed skating   *le patinage de vitesse*
to surf   *faire du surf*

WEATHER

barometer   *le baromètre*
blizzard   *la tempête de neige*
cloudy   *nuageux*
drizzle   *la bruine*
fog   *le brouillard*
frost   *la gelée*
hail   *la grêle*
to hail   *grêler*
heat wave   *la canicule*
hurricane   *l'ouragan* (m.)
ice (on the road)   *le verglas*
It's pouring.   *Il pleut à verse.*
It's sleeting.   *Il tombe de la neige fondue.*
It's sunny.   *Il fait du soleil.*
lightning bolt   *l'éclair* (m.)
mist   *la brume*
shower (rain)   *l'averse* (f.)
storm   *la tempête*
thermometer   *le thermomètre*
thunder   *le tonnerre*
thunderstorm   *l'orage* (m.)
tornado   *la tornade*

CITIES

Algiers   *Alger*
Brussels   *Bruxelles*
Cairo   *Le Caire*
Geneva   *Genève*
Lisbon   *Lisbonne*
London   *Londres*
Montreal   *Montréal*
Moscow   *Moscou*
New Orleans   *La Nouvelle-Orléans*
Quebec City   *Québec*
Tangier   *Tanger*
Venice   *Venise*
Vienna   *Vienne*

THE CONTINENTS

Africa   *l'Afrique* (f.)
Antarctica   *l'Antarctique* (f.)
Asia   *l'Asie* (f.)
Australia   *l'Océanie* (f.)
Europe   *l'Europe* (f.)
North America   *l'Amérique* (f.) *du Nord*
South America   *l'Amérique* (f.) *du Sud*

COUNTRIES

Algeria   *l'Algérie* (f.)
Argentina   *l'Argentine* (f.)
Australia   *l'Australie* (f.)
Austria   *l'Autriche* (f.)
Belgium   *la Belgique*
Brazil   *le Brésil*
Canada   *le Canada*
China   *la Chine*
Egypt   *l'Egypte* (f.)
England   *l'Angleterre* (f.)
France   *la France*
Germany   *l'Allemagne* (f.)
Greece   *la Grèce*
Holland   *la Hollande*
India   *l'Inde* (f.)
Ireland   *l'Irlande* (f.)
Israel   *Israël* (m.)
Italy   *l'Italie* (f.)
Ivory Coast   *la République de Côte d'Ivoire*
Jamaica   *la Jamaïque*
Japan   *le Japon*
Jordan   *la Jordanie*
Lebanon   *le Liban*
Libya   *la Libye*
Luxembourg   *le Luxembourg*
Mexico   *le Mexique*
Monaco   *Monaco* (f.)
Morocco   *le Maroc*
Netherlands   *les Pays-Bas* (m.)
North Korea   *la Corée du Nord*
Peru   *le Pérou*

Philippines   *les Philippines* (f.)
Poland   *la Pologne*
Portugal   *le Portugal*
Russia   *la Russie*
Senegal   *le Sénégal*
South Korea   *la Corée du Sud*
Spain   *l'Espagne* (f.)
Switzerland   *la Suisse*
Syria   *la Syrie*
Tunisia   *la Tunisie*
Turkey   *la Turquie*
United States   *les Etats-Unis* (m.)
Vietnam   *le Viêt-nam*

STATES

California   *la Californie*
Florida   *la Floride*
Georgia   *la Géorgie*
Louisiana   *la Louisiane*
New Mexico   *le Nouveau Mexique*
North Carolina   *la Caroline du Nord*
Pennsylvania   *la Pennsylvanie*
South Carolina   *la Caroline du Sud*
Virginia   *la Virginie*

OCEANS AND SEAS

Atlantic Ocean   *l'Atlantique* (m.), *l'océan* (m.)
  Atlantique
Caribbean Sea   *la mer des Caraïbes*
English Channel   *la Manche*

Indian Ocean   *l'océan* (m.) *Indien*
Mediterranean Sea   *la mer Méditerranée*
Pacific Ocean   *le Pacifique, l'océan* (m.) *Pacifique*

OTHER GEOGRAPHICAL TERMS

Alps   *les Alpes* (f.)
border   *la frontière*
capital   *la capitale*
continent   *le continent*
country   *le pays*
hill   *la colline*
lake   *le lac*
latitude   *la latitude*
longitude   *la longitude*
North Africa   *l'Afrique* (f.) *du Nord*
ocean   *l'océan* (m.)
plain   *la plaine*
Pyrenees   *les Pyrénées* (f.)
river   *la rivière, le fleuve*
sea   *la mer*
state   *l'état* (m.)
the North Pole   *le pôle Nord*
the South Pole   *le pôle Sud*
valley   *la vallée*

GRAMMAR SUMMARY

ADJECTIVES

REGULAR ADJECTIVES

In French, adjectives agree in gender and number with the nouns that they modify. A regular adjective has four forms: masculine singular, feminine singular, masculine plural, and feminine plural. To make an adjective agree with a feminine noun, add an **-e** to the masculine singular form of the adjective. To make an adjective agree with a plural noun, add an **-s** to the masculine singular form. To make an adjective agree with a feminine plural noun, add **-es** to the masculine singular form. Adjectives ending in **-é**, like **désolé**, also follow these rules.

	SINGULAR	PLURAL
MASCULINE	un jean **vert**	des jeans **verts**
FEMININE	une ceinture **verte**	des ceintures **vertes**

ADJECTIVES THAT END IN AN UNACCENTED -E

When an adjective ends in an unaccented **-e,** the masculine singular and the feminine singular forms are the same. To form the plural of these adjectives, add an **-s** to the singular forms.

	SINGULAR	PLURAL
MASCULINE	un cahier **rouge**	des cahiers **rouges**
FEMININE	une trousse **rouge**	des trousses **rouges**

ADJECTIVES THAT END IN -S

When the masculine singular form of an adjective ends in an **-s,** the masculine plural form does not change. The feminine forms follow the regular adjective rules.

	SINGULAR	PLURAL
MASCULINE	un sac **gris**	des sacs **gris**
FEMININE	une robe **grise**	des robes **grises**

ADJECTIVES THAT END IN -EUX

Adjectives that end in **-eux** do not change in the masculine plural. The feminine singular form of these adjectives is made by replacing the **-x** with **-se.** To form the feminine plural, replace the **-x** with **-ses.**

	SINGULAR	PLURAL
MASCULINE	un garçon **heureux**	des garçons **heureux**
FEMININE	une fille **heureuse**	des filles **heureuses**

ADJECTIVES THAT END IN -IF

To make the feminine singular form of adjectives that end in -**if,** replace **-if** with **-ive**. To make the plural forms of these adjectives, add an **-s** to the singular forms.

	SINGULAR	PLURAL
MASCULINE	un garçon **sportif**	des garçons **sportifs**
FEMININE	une fille **sportive**	des filles **sportives**

ADJECTIVES THAT END IN -IEN

To make the feminine singular and feminine plural forms of masculine singular adjectives that end in -**ien**, add -**ne** and **-nes.** Add an **-s** to form the masculine plural.

	SINGULAR	PLURAL
MASCULINE	un garçon **canadien**	des garçons **canadiens**
FEMININE	une fille **canadienne**	des filles **canadiennes**

ADJECTIVES THAT DOUBLE THE LAST CONSONANT

To make the adjectives **bon, gentil, gros, mignon, nul,** and **violet** agree with a feminine noun, double the last consonant and add an **-e.** To make the plural forms, add an **-s** to the singular forms. Note that with **gros,** the masculine singular and masculine plural forms are the same.

SINGULAR						
MASCULINE	bon	gentil	gros	mignon	nul	violet
FEMININE	bonne	gentille	grosse	mignonne	nulle	violette

PLURAL						
MASCULINE	bons	gentils	gros	mignons	nuls	violets
FEMININE	bonnes	gentilles	grosses	mignonnes	nulles	violettes

INVARIABLE ADJECTIVES

Some adjectives are invariable. They never change form. **Cool, marron, orange, super,** and **sympa** are examples of invariable adjectives. **Sympa,** the shortened form of **sympathique,** is invariable, whereas **sympathique** follows the rules for adjectives that end in an unaccented -**e**, like **rouge.**

Il me faut une montre **marron** et des baskets **orange.**

IRREGULAR ADJECTIVES

The forms of some adjectives must simply be memorized. This is the case for **blanc** and **roux.**

	SINGULAR	PLURAL
MASCULINE	blanc	blancs
FEMININE	blanche	blanches

	SINGULAR	PLURAL
MASCULINE	roux	roux
FEMININE	rousse	rousses

POSITION OF ADJECTIVES

In French, adjectives are usually placed after the noun that they modify.

C'est une femme **intelligente.**

Certain adjectives precede the noun. Some of these are **bon, jeune, joli, grand,** and **petit.**

C'est un **petit** village.

DEMONSTRATIVE ADJECTIVES

This, that, these, and *those* are demonstrative adjectives. There are two masculine singular forms of these adjectives in French: **ce** and **cet. Cet** is used with masculine singular nouns that begin with a vowel sound. Some examples are **cet ordinateur** and **cet homme.** Demonstrative adjectives always precede the noun that they modify.

	SINGULAR WITH A CONSONANT	SINGULAR WITH A VOWEL SOUND	PLURAL
MASCULINE	ce livre	cet ordinateur	ces posters
FEMININE	cette montre	cette école	ces gommes

POSSESSIVE ADJECTIVES

Possessive adjectives come before the noun that they modify and agree in gender and number with the item that they modify. Nouns that begin with a vowel sound use the masculine singular form, for example **mon ami(e), ton ami(e), son ami(e)**.

	MASCULINE SINGULAR	FEMININE SINGULAR	MASC./FEM. SINGULAR WITH A VOWEL SOUND	MASC./FEM. PLURAL
my	**mon** père	**ma** mère	**mon** oncle	**mes** cousines
your	**ton** livre	**ta** montre	**ton** écharpe	**tes** cahiers
his, her, its	**son** chien	**sa** sœur	**son** école	**ses** cours

The possessive adjectives for *our, your*, and *their* have only two forms, singular and plural.

	MASC./FEM. SINGULAR	MASC./FEM. PLURAL
our	**notre** frère	**nos** tantes
your	**votre** classeur	**vos** amis
their	**leur** copain	**leurs** trousses

ADJECTIVES AS NOUNS

To use an adjective as a noun, add a definite article before the adjective. The article that you use agrees in gender and number with the noun that the adjective is replacing.

—Tu aimes les chemises rouges ou **les blanches?**
Do you like the red shirts or the white ones?
—J'aime **les blanches.**
I like the white ones.

ADVERBS

POSITION OF ADVERBS

Most adverbs follow the conjugated verb. In the **passé composé,** they usually precede the past participle.

Nathalie fait **souvent** des photos.   Je n'ai pas **bien** mangé ce matin.

Adverbs that are made up of more than one word can be placed at the beginning or at the end of a sentence. When you use **ne (n')... jamais,** place it around the conjugated verb.

D'habitude, je fais du tennis le soir.
J'aime faire de l'aérobic **deux fois par semaine.**
Je **n'ai jamais** fait de ski.

ARTICLES

DEFINITE ARTICLES

French has four definite articles: **le, la, l'**, and **les.** The form that you use depends on the gender and number of the noun it modifies. Use **le** with masculine singular nouns, **le livre; la** with feminine singular nouns, **la chemise;** and **les** with both masculine and feminine nouns that are plural, **les crayons.** The form **l'** is used with both masculine and feminine nouns that begin with a vowel sound: **l'ami, l'amie, l'homme.** In French, you sometimes use a definite article when no article is required in English.

J'aime **le** chocolat et toi, tu préfères **le** café.

	SINGULAR WITH A CONSONANT	SINGULAR WITH A VOWEL SOUND	PLURAL
MASCULINE	**le** professeur	**l'**ami	**les** livres
FEMININE	**la** pharmacie	**l'**école	**les** pommes

INDEFINITE ARTICLES

In English, there are three indefinite articles: *a, an*, and *some.* In French there are also three: **un, une,** and **des.** The indefinite articles agree in number and gender with the nouns they modify.

	SINGULAR	PLURAL
MASCULINE	**un** poisson	**des** chats
FEMININE	**une** orange	**des** lunettes

PARTITIVE ARTICLES

To say that you want *part* or *some* of an item, use the partitive articles. Use **du** with a masculine noun and **de la** with a feminine noun. Use **de l'** with singular nouns that begin with a vowel sound whether they are masculine or feminine.

Je veux **de la** tarte aux pommes. *I want some apple pie.*

To indicate the whole as opposed to a part of the item, use the indefinite articles **un, une,** and **des.**

Pour la fête, il me faut **des** tartes. *I need (some) pies for the party.*

NEGATION AND THE ARTICLES

When the main verb of a sentence is negated, the indefinite and the partitive articles change to **de/d'.** Definite articles remain the same after a negative verb.

J'ai **le** livre de maths.   —> Je n'ai pas **le** livre de maths.
J'ai **des** stylos.   —> Je n'ai pas **de** stylos.
J'ai mangé **de la** pizza.   —> Je n'ai pas mangé **de** pizza.

INTERROGATIVES

QUESTION FORMATION

There are several ways to ask yes-no questions. One of these is to raise the pitch of your voice at the end of a statement. The other is to place **est-ce que** in front of a statement.

Tu aimes le chocolat. —> **Tu aimes le chocolat?** (intonation) *or*
Est-ce que tu aimes le chocolat?

NEGATIVE QUESTIONS

The answer to a yes-no question depends on the way the question was stated. If the verb in a question is positive, then the answer is **oui** if you agree, and **non** if you don't. If the verb in a question is negative, then **non** is used to agree with the question and **si** to disagree.

QUESTION	AGREEING WITH THE QUESTION	DISAGREEING WITH THE QUESTION
Tu aimes lire?	**Oui,** j'aime lire.	**Non,** je n'aime pas lire.
Tu n'aimes pas lire?	**Non,** je n'aime pas lire.	**Si,** j'aime lire.

INFORMATION QUESTIONS

To ask for specific kinds of information, use the following question words:

A quelle heure? *At what time?* **Où?** *Where?*
Avec qui? *With whom?* **Quand?** *When?*

These words can be used by themselves, at the beginning of a question, at the beginning of the question followed by **est-ce que**, or at the end of a question.

Avec qui? **Avec qui** est-ce qu'on va au cinéma?
Avec qui on va au cinéma? On va au cinéma **avec qui?**

NOUNS

PLURAL FORMS OF NOUNS

In French, you make most nouns plural by adding an **-s** to the end of the word, unless they already end in **-s** or **-x**. Nouns that end in **-eau** are made plural by adding an **-x,** and nouns that end in **-al** are made plural by replacing the **-al** with **-aux.**

	REGULAR NOUNS	-s or -x	-eau	-al
SINGULAR	table	bus	manteau	hôpital
PLURAL	tables	bus	manteaux	hôpitaux

PREPOSITIONS

THE PREPOSITIONS A AND DE

The preposition **à** means *to, at,* or *in,* and **de** means *from* or *of.* When **à** and **de** are used in front of the definite articles **le** and **les**, they form contractions. If they precede any other definite article, there is no contraction.

Il va **à l'**école et **au** musée. *He's going to school and to the museum.*
Nous sommes loin **du** musée. *We are far from the museum.*

	MASCULINE ARTICLE	FEMININE ARTICLE	VOWEL SOUND	PLURAL
à	à + le = **au**	à + la = **à la**	à + l' = **à l'**	à + les = **aux**
de	de + le = **du**	de + la = **de la**	de + l' = **de l'**	de + les = **des**

De can also indicate possession or ownership.

C'est le livre **de** Laurent. *It's Laurent's book.*
C'est le stylo **du** prof. *It's the professor's pen.*

PREPOSITIONS AND PLACES

To say that you are at or going to a place, you need to use a preposition. With cities, use the preposition **à**: **à Paris**. One notable exception is **en Arles**. When speaking about masculine countries, use **au**: **au Maroc**. With plural names of countries, use **aux**: **aux Etats-Unis**. Most countries ending in **-e** are feminine; in these cases, use **en**: **en France**. **Le Mexique** is an exception. If a country begins with a vowel, like **Israël**, use **en**: **en Israël**.

CITIES	MASCULINE COUNTRIES	FEMININE COUNTRIES OR MASCULINE COUNTRIES THAT BEGIN WITH A VOWEL	PLURAL COUNTRIES
à Nantes **à** Paris **en** Arles	**au** Canada **au** Maroc **au** Mexique	**en** Italie **en** Espagne **en** Israël	**aux** Etats-Unis **aux** Philippines **aux** Pays-Bas

PRONOUNS

In French, as in English, a pronoun can refer to a person, place, or thing. Pronouns are used to avoid repetition. In French, pronouns agree in gender and number with the noun that they replace.

SUBJECT PRONOUNS

Subject pronouns replace the subject in a sentence.

je (j')	*I*	nous	*we*
tu	*you* (familiar)	vous	*you* (plural or formal)
il	*he / it*	ils	*they*
elle	*she / it*	elles	*they*
on	*we / one / they*		

THE IMPERSONAL PRONOUN IL

Many statements in French begin with the personal pronoun **il.** In these statements, **il** does not refer to any particular person or thing. For this reason, these statements are called impersonal statements.

Il fait beau.   *It's nice out.*
Il est huit heures.   *It's eight o'clock.*

Il me/te faut... *I/You need . . .*
Il y a... *There is/are . . .*

DIRECT OBJECT PRONOUNS: LE, LA, LES

A direct object is a noun that receives the action of the verb. It answers the questions *What?* or *Whom?* To say *him, her, it,* or *them,* use the pronouns **le, la,** and **les.** In French, you place the direct object pronoun in front of the conjugated verb.

Il regarde **la télé.** —> Il **la** regarde.

If there is an infinitive in the sentence, the direct object pronoun comes before the infinitive.

Je vais attendre **Pierre.** —> Je vais **l'**attendre.

In an affirmative command, the direct object pronoun follows the verb and is connected to it with a hyphen.

Regarde **la télévision.** —> Regarde-**la**!

	SINGULAR	PLURAL
MASCULINE	le / l'	les
FEMININE	la / l'	les

INDIRECT OBJECT PRONOUNS: LUI, LEUR

The indirect object answers the question *To whom?* and refers only to people. In French an indirect object follows the preposition **à: Il parle à Marie.** The indirect object pronoun replaces the prepositional phrase **à + a person,** and precedes the conjugated verb.

Nous téléphonons **à Mireille.** —> Nous **lui** téléphonons.

If there is an infinitive in the sentence, the indirect object pronoun comes before the infinitive.

Il n'aime pas parler **à ses parents.** —> Il n'aime pas **leur** parler.

In an affirmative command, the indirect object pronoun follows the verb and is connected to it with a hyphen.

Téléphone **à ta sœur.** —> Téléphone-**lui**!

THE PRONOUN Y

To replace a phrase meaning *to, on, at,* or *in* any place that has already been mentioned, you can use the pronoun **y.** It can replace phrases beginning with prepositions of location such as **à, sur, chez, dans,** and **en + a place or thing.** Place **y** before the conjugated verb.

Elle va **à la pharmacie.** —> Elle **y** va.

If there is an infinitive, place **y** before the infinitive.

Elle va aller **à la poste** demain. —> Elle va **y** aller demain.

THE PRONOUN EN

The pronoun **en** replaces a phrase beginning with **de, du, de la, de l',** or **des.** It usually means *about it, some (of it/of them),* or simply *it/them,* and is placed before the conjugated verb.

Tu achètes **des haricots verts?** —> Oui, j'**en** achète pour le dîner.

En in a negative sentence means *not any* or *none.*

Tu ne bois pas **de café.** —> Tu n'**en** bois pas.

En is placed before the conjugated verb.

Je parle **de mes vacances.** —> J'**en** parle.

If there is an infinitive, place **en** before the infinitive.

Vous aimez manger **des fruits.** —> Vous aimez **en** manger.

Notice that with the **passé composé, en** precedes the helping verb.

Il a mangé **du pain.** —> Il **en** a mangé.

VERBS

THE PRESENT TENSE OF REGULAR VERBS

To conjugate a verb in French, use the following formulas. Which formula you choose depends on the ending of the infinitive. There are three major verb categories: -**er**, -**ir**, and -**re**. Each one has a different conjugation. Within these categories, there are regular and irregular verbs. To conjugate regular verbs, you drop the infinitive endings and add these endings.

SUBJECT	aim**er** (to love, to like) STEM	ENDING	chois**ir** (to choose) STEM	ENDING	vend**re** (to sell) STEM	ENDING
je/j' tu il/elle/on	aim	-e -es -e	chois	-is -is -it	vend	-s -s —
nous vous ils/elles		-ons -ez -ent		-issons -issez -issent		-ons -ez -ent

VERBS WITH STEM AND SPELLING CHANGES

Verbs listed in this section are not irregular, but they do have some stem and spelling changes.

With **acheter** and **promener**, add an **accent grave** over the second to last **e** for all forms except **nous** and **vous**. Notice that the accent on the second **e** in **préférer** changes from **é** to **è**.

	acheter (to buy)	préférer (to prefer)	promener (to walk (an animal))
je/j' tu il/elle/on	achète achètes achète	préfère préfères préfère	promène promènes promène
nous vous ils/elles	achetons achetez achètent	préférons préférez préfèrent	promenons promenez promènent
PAST PARTICIPLE	acheté	préféré	promené

The following verbs have different stems for **nous** and **vous**.

	appeler *(to call)*	essayer *(to try)*
je/j'	appelle	essaie
tu	appelles	essaies
il/elle/on	appelle	essaie
nous	appelons	essayons
vous	appelez	essayez
ils/elles	appellent	essaient
PAST PARTICIPLE	appelé	essayé

The following verbs show a difference only in the **nous** form.

	commencer *(to start)*	manger *(to eat)*
je/j'	commence	mange
tu	commences	manges
il/elle/on	commence	mange
nous	commençons	mangeons
vous	commencez	mangez
ils/elles	commencent	mangent
PAST PARTICIPLE	commencé	mangé

	nager *(to swim)*	voyager *(to travel)*
je/j'	nage	voyage
tu	nages	voyages
il/elle/on	nage	voyage
nous	nageons	voyageons
vous	nagez	voyagez
ils/elles	nagent	voyagent
PAST PARTICIPLE	nagé	voyagé

VERBS LIKE DORMIR

These verbs follow a different pattern from the one you learned for regular -**ir** verbs. These verbs have two stems: one for the singular subjects, and one for the plural ones.

	dormir *(to sleep)*	partir *(to leave)*	sortir *(to go out, to take out)*
je/j' tu il/elle/on	dors dors dort	pars pars part	sors sors sort
nous vous ils/elles	dorm**ons** dorm**ez** dorm**ent**	part**ons** part**ez** part**ent**	sort**ons** sort**ez** sort**ent**

VERBS WITH IRREGULAR FORMS

Verbs listed in this section do not follow the pattern of verbs like **aimer**, **choisir**, or **vendre**. Therefore, they are called *irregular verbs.* The following four irregular verbs are used frequently.

	aller *(to go)*	avoir *(to have)*
je/j' tu il/elle/on	vais vas va	ai as a
nous vous ils/elles	allons allez vont	avons avez ont

	être *(to be)*	faire *(to do, to make, to play)*
je/j' tu il/elle/on	suis es est	fais fais fait
nous vous ils/elles	sommes êtes sont	faisons faites font

Devoir, pouvoir, and **vouloir** are also irregular. They are usually followed by an infinitive.

Je peux chanter. *I can sing.*

	devoir *(must, to have to)*	pouvoir *(to be able to, can)*	vouloir *(to want)*
je/j'	dois	peux	veux
tu	dois	peux	veux
il/elle/on	doit	peut	veut
nous	devons	pouvons	voulons
vous	devez	pouvez	voulez
ils/elles	doivent	peuvent	veulent

These verbs also have irregular forms.

	dire *(to say)*	écrire *(to write)*	lire *(to read)*
je/j'	dis	écris	lis
tu	dis	écris	lis
il/elle/on	dit	écrit	lit
nous	disons	écrivons	lisons
vous	dites	écrivez	lisez
ils/elles	disent	écrivent	lisent
PAST PARTICIPLE	dit	écrit	lu

	mettre *(to put, to put on, to wear)*	prendre *(to take, to have food or drink)*	voir *(to see)*
je/j'	mets	prends	vois
tu	mets	prends	vois
il/elle/on	met	prend	voit
nous	mettons	prenons	voyons
vous	mettez	prenez	voyez
ils/elles	mettent	prennent	voient
PAST PARTICIPLE	mis	pris	vu

THE NEAR FUTURE (FUTUR PROCHE)

Like the past tense, the near future is made of two parts. The future tense of a verb consists of the present tense of **aller** plus the infinitive:

Vous **allez sortir** avec vos copains demain. *You're going to go out with your friends tomorrow.*

R24

THE PAST TENSE (PASSE COMPOSE)

The past tense of most verbs is formed with two parts: the present tense form of the helping verb **avoir** and the past participle of the main verb. To form the past participle, use the formulas below. To make a sentence negative in the past, place the **ne... pas** around the helping verb **avoir**.

INFINITIVE	aimer *(to love, to like)*		choisir *(to choose)*		vendre *(to sell)*	
	STEM	ENDING	STEM	ENDING	STEM	ENDING
PAST PARTICIPLE	aim aimé	-é	chois choisi	-i	vend vendu	-u
PASSE COMPOSE	j'ai aimé		j'ai choisi		j'ai vendu	

J'**ai mangé** de la pizza.   Nous **avons choisi** le livre.
Elle n'**a** pas **vendu** sa voiture.   Nous n'**avons** pas **mangé** de pizza.

Some verbs have irregular past participles.

faire —> **fait**   **prendre** —> **pris**
lire —> **lu**   **voir** —> **vu**

With some verbs, you use the helping verb **être** instead of **avoir**, for example the verb **aller.** The past participle of these verbs agrees in gender and number with the subject of the sentence.

Je **suis allé(e)** à l'école.   Ils **sont allés** à la poste.   Elle **est allée** au café.

THE IMPERATIVE (COMMANDS)

To make a request or a command of most verbs, use the **tu, nous,** or **vous** form of the present tense of the verb without the subject. Remember to drop the final -**s** in the **tu** form of an -**er** verb.

Mange!
Ecoute le professeur!
Faites vos devoirs!
Prenons un sandwich!

aimer *(to love, to like)*		choisir *(to choose)*		vendre *(to sell)*	
STEM	ENDING	STEM	ENDING	STEM	ENDING
aim	-e -ons -ez	chois	-is -issons -issez	vend	-s -ons -ez

ADDITIONAL GRAMMAR PRACTICE

CHAPITRE 1 - FAISONS CONNAISSANCE!

Page numbers in parentheses send students to the *Pupil's Edition* page(s) where the targeted grammar is presented.

PREMIERE ETAPE

Greeting people and saying goodbye; asking how people are and telling how you are; asking someone's name and age and giving yours

1 Can you find the pattern in these phone numbers? Figure out which number completes each pattern. Then write out the number in French. (See pp. 9, 25.)

EXAMPLE   02. _____ . 20. 29. 38; _____
          02. <u>11</u>. 20. 29. 38; <u>onze</u>

1. 05. 12. <u>19</u> . 26. 33; dix-neuf
2. 03. 10. <u>17</u> . 24. 31; dix-sept
3. 01. <u>13</u> . 25. 37. 49; treize
4. 05. <u>20</u> . 35. 50. 65; vingt
5. 04. 10. <u>16</u> . 22. 28; seize
6. 02. <u>12</u> . 22. 32. 42; douze

DEUXIEME ETAPE

Expressing likes, dislikes, and preferences about things

2 Complete the following sentences, using the correct form of **aimer** and **ne (n')... pas** when appropriate. (See p. 26.)

EXAMPLE   — Tu adores la plage, mais tu <u>n'aimes pas</u> la piscine.

1. Moi, j'aime bien la musique classique, mais je/j' _____ le rock.   n'aime pas
2. Tu n'aimes pas le sport, mais tu _____ le vélo.   aimes
3. J'adore la glace, mais je/j' _____ le chocolat.   n'aime pas
4. J'aime bien l'école, mais je/j' _____ les examens.   n'aime pas
5. Tu aimes les concerts, mais tu _____ le cinéma.   n'aimes pas
6. Tu n'aimes pas les hamburgers, mais tu _____ les frites.   aimes
7. J'aime la télé, mais je/j' _____ le cinéma.   n'aime pas
8. Tu n'aimes pas l'anglais, mais tu _____ le français.   aimes

3 Complete Gabrielle's journal entry with the appropriate definite articles **le, la, l'**, or **les.** (See p. 28.)   1. l' 2. l' 3. le 4. les 5. le 6. la 7. le 8. le

J'aime __1__ école. J'aime bien __2__ anglais et __3__ français, mais je n'aime pas __4__ examens. J'adore __5__ sport et __6__ plage. J'aime __7__ football et __8__ vélo aussi.

4 Use the following fragments to create four questions and four answers. Remember to add the appropriate definite articles: **le, la, l',** or **les.** (See p. 28.)

EXAMPLE salade/Eric/tu/aimes? aime/j'/hamburgers/aussi (*also*)
<u>Eric, tu aimes la salade?</u> <u>Oui, et j'aime aussi les hamburgers.</u>

1. tu/aimes/frites/Marianne?
   –Marianne, tu aimes les frites?
   aime/j'/pizza/aussi
   —Oui, et...   j'aime aussi la pizza.

2. tu/ne/pas/maths/aimes/Isabelle?
   –Isabelle, tu n'aimes pas les maths?
   français/aussi/aime/j'
   —Si *(yes)*, et...   j'aime aussi le français.

3. aimes/escargots/Nathalie/tu?
   –Nathalie, tu aimes les escargots?
   j'/aussi/aime/chocolat
   —Oui, et...   j'aime aussi le chocolat.

4. tu/aimes/ne/pas/magasins?
   –Tu n'aimes pas les magasins?
   plage/j'/aussi/aime
   —Si, et...   j'aime aussi la plage.

TROISIEME ETAPE

Expressing likes, dislikes, and preferences about activities

5 Séverine is looking for a pen pal. Complete her ad with the appropriate forms of the verbs in parentheses. (See p. 33.) 1. adore 2. aime 3. aimons 4. préférons 5. écoutons 6. adorons 7. danse 8. aimons
9. aimez

J'ai 16 ans. Je/J' __1__ (adorer) faire du sport. Je/J' __2__ (aimer) aussi sortir avec les copains. Nous __3__ (aimer) bien aller au cinéma, mais nous __4__ (préférer) aller danser. Parfois, nous __5__ (écouter) de la musique. Nous __6__ (adorer) le rap, surtout MC Solaar; il __7__ (danser) très bien. Nous __8__ (aimer) aussi les fast-food. Si vous __9__ (aimer) le sport, écrivez-moi! A bientôt!

6 Etienne and Solange don't have much in common. Complete their conversation with the appropriate forms of the verbs in parentheses. (See p. 33.)

ETIENNE   Dis, Solange, tu __1__ (aimer) faire du vélo?   1. aimes
SOLANGE   Non, je n' __2__ (aimer) pas le sport, mais j' __3__ (adorer) danser.   2. aime 3. adore
ETIENNE   Moi, je ne __4__ (danser) pas, mais j' __5__ (écouter) souvent la radio.   4. danse
SOLANGE   Ah oui? Tu __6__ (écouter) quel type de musique?   6. écoutes   5. écoute
ETIENNE   Moi, j' __7__ (adorer) le rap. Mes copains __8__ (aimer) aller à des concerts de rap, mais moi, j' __9__ (aimer) mieux regarder des vidéoclips à la télé. Et toi, tu __10__ (regarder) la télé?   7. adore 8. aiment 9. aime 10. regardes
SOLANGE   Moi, non. J' __11__ (aimer) mieux aller au cinéma.   11. aime

7 There are many things these students like to do, but what do they prefer to do? Complete these conversations with the appropriate subject pronouns. (See p. 33.)

EXAMPLE   —Pierre aime les frites. —Oui, mais <u>il</u> aime mieux les escargots.

1. —Lucie et Marie aiment regarder la télé.
   —Oui, mais <u>elles</u> préfèrent aller au cinéma.

2. —Hugo et toi, vous aimez parler au téléphone?
   —Oui, mais <u>nous</u> préférons sortir avec les copains.

3. —Olivier et Lise aiment faire les magasins.
   —Oui, mais <u>ils</u> aiment mieux faire du sport.

4. —Aurélie aime lire.
   —Oui, mais <u>elle</u> aime mieux dormir.

5. —Christelle et moi, nous aimons le volley.
   —Oui, mais <u>vous</u> préférez le basket-ball, non?

8 Given their likes and dislikes, what do the following students probably do on weekends? Complete each sentence, using a personal pronoun and the correct form of the appropriate verb. (See p. 33.)

EXAMPLE   Hervé et moi, nous aimons danser.
Le week-end, <u>nous dansons.</u>

1. Mary aime bien parler français avec sa copine.
Le week-end, ...   elle parle français avec sa copine.

2. Jules et Loïc aiment regarder des matchs de football.
Le week-end, ...   ils regardent des matchs de football.

3. Moi, j'adore écouter de la musique.
Le week-end, ...   j'écoute de la musique.

4. Sylvie et Marianne aiment bien nager.
Le week-end, ...   elles nagent.

5. Stéphane et toi, vous aimez parler au téléphone.
Le week-end, ...   vous parlez au téléphone.

6. Toi, tu adores danser.
Le week-end, ...   tu danses.

CHAPITRE 2 - VIVE L'ECOLE!

PREMIERE ETAPE

Agreeing and disagreeing

1 Would you answer **si** or **oui** to each of the following questions? (See p. 50.)

1. Hervé n'aime pas faire le ménage?   Si.
2. Vous aimez le cours de physique?   Oui.
3. Tu aimes écouter de la musique?   Oui.
4. Annick et Ahmed n'aiment pas le prof de français?   Si.
5. Jean-Paul aime la chorale?   Oui.
6. Olivia n'aime pas faire du sport?   Si.

2 Complete the following conversations, using **si, oui,** or **non,** as appropriate. (See p. 50.)

1. —Tu aimes les sciences naturelles?
   — <u>Oui</u>, j'adore!
2. —Marc n'aime pas parler au téléphone?
   — <u>Si</u>, il aime bien parler avec ses copains.
3. —Ils aiment la physique?
   — <u>Non</u>, ils n'aiment pas les cours de science.
4. —Tu n'aimes pas le ski?
   — <u>Si</u>, j'aime bien le sport en général.
5. —Tu aimes faire de l'équitation?
   — <u>Oui</u>, mais je préfère lire et regarder la télévision.
6. —Nicole aime les concerts?
   — <u>Oui</u>, elle adore la musique.

DEUXIEME ETAPE

Asking for and giving information

3 Complete the conversation below with the correct forms of the verb **avoir**. (See p. 51.)

—Céline, tu __1__ quels cours aujourd'hui?   1. as
—Le matin, j' __2__ sciences nat et français. L'après-midi, j' __3__ histoire et géométrie.   2. ai 3. ai
—Et Vincent, il __4__ quels cours?   4. a
—Il __5__ chimie et espagnol le matin, et l'après-midi, il __6__ informatique.   5. a 6. a
—Le mardi et le jeudi matin, nous __7__ travaux pratiques de chimie.   7. avons

4 Matthieu and some of his friends are discussing their school schedules. Complete each of the following sentences with the correct form of the verb **avoir**. Then, write out the time given in parentheses. (See pp. 51, 54.)

EXAMPLE Sylvie _____ latin à (9h30). Sylvie a latin à neuf heures trente.

1. J' _____ sciences nat à (8h45).   ai, huit heures quarante-cinq
2. Anne et moi, nous _____ EPS à (13h50).   avons, treize heures cinquante
3. Matthieu et Jeanne, vous _____ latin à (11h20), non?   avez, onze heures vingt
4. Séverine, tu _____ quoi à (15h30)?   as, quinze heures trente
5. Chad et Mireille _____ maths à (16h15).   ont, seize heures quinze

TROISIEME ETAPE

Asking for and expressing opinions

5 Rewrite these informal remarks and questions in formal French. (See pp. 26, 57.)

1. «C'est pas super, l'algèbre.»   Ce n'est pas super, l'algèbre.
2. «Elle aime pas la chimie?»   Elle n'aime pas la chimie?
3. «Ils aiment pas les devoirs.»   Ils n'aiment pas les devoirs.
4. «Mais non! L'anglais, c'est pas difficile!»   Mais non! L'anglais, ce n'est pas difficile.
5. «Tu aimes pas la géographie?»   Tu n'aimes pas la géographie?

6 David and Olivia are discussing their schedules and their classes. Complete their conversation with either the correct form of the verb in parentheses or the word or phrase that expresses their opinion. (See pp. 33, 51, 57.)

—Olivia, tu __1__ (avoir) quels cours le lundi matin?   1. as
—J' __2__ (avoir) histoire, maths et français. Et toi, tu __3__ (avoir) quels cours?   2. ai 3. as
—Florent et moi, nous __4__ (avoir) chimie, allemand et anglais.   4. avons
—Vous __5__ (aimer) la chimie?   5. aimez
—Florent n' __6__ (aimer) pas ça. Mais moi, j' __7__ (adorer) la chimie. C'est __8__ (passionnant/pas super)!   6. aime 7. adore 8. passionnant
—Ah bon! Florent __9__ (avoir) biologie le mardi. Il __10__ (adorer) ça. Et toi, tu __11__ (aimer) ça, la biologie?   9. a 10. adore 11. aimes
—Moi, non. C'est __12__ (pas mal/nul).   12. nul

CHAPITRE 3 - TOUT POUR LA RENTREE

PREMIERE ETAPE

Making and responding to requests; asking others what they need and telling what you need

1 Fill in the missing letters in the following words to find out what Amadou has on his desk. Then write the correct indefinite article for each word. (See p. 73.)

EXAMPLE   C _ _ I _ R -> un cahier

1. L _ _ R _ S   des livres
2. T _ O _ _ S _   une trousse
3. S T _ _ O _   des stylos

4. C _ A _ _ N   un crayon
5. C _ _ C _ L _ T _ _ C _   une calculatrice
6. F _ _ I L _ _ S   des feuilles

2 Rewrite the following conversations, adding **un, une, des,** or **de (d')**. Remember to use the correct form of **avoir**. (See p. 73.)

EXAMPLE   Anne/montre/avoir/tu?—<u>Anne, tu as une montre?</u>
Non/pas/montre/ne/avoir/je—<u>Non, je n'ai pas de montre.</u>

1. —Séverine/tu/sac à dos/avoir?   Séverine, tu as un sac à dos?
   —Non/ne/avoir/je/pas/sac à dos   Non, je n'ai pas de sac à dos.

2. —Raphaël et Philippe/feuilles de papier/avoir/vous?   Raphaël et Philippe, vous avez des feuilles de papier?
   —Non/pas/nous/avoir/ne/feuilles de papier   Non, nous n'avons pas de feuilles de papier.

3. —tu/avoir/Karine/taille-crayon?   Karine, tu as un taille-crayon?
   —je/ne/non/pas/avoir/taille-crayon   Non, je n'ai pas de taille-crayon.

4. —Valérie et Mireille/vous/calculatrices/avoir?   Valérie et Mireille, vous avez des calculatrices?
   —nous/avoir/ne/pas/calculatrices/non   Non, nous n'avons pas de calculatrices.

DEUXIEME ETAPE

Telling what you'd like and what you'd like to do

3 You overheard these conversations at a store having a back-to-school sale. Complete the following conversations using **ce, cet, cette,** or **ces**. (See p. 77.)

1. —Tu aimes ____ montre?   cette
   —Oui, mais je préfère ____ bracelet.   ce

2. —Vous aimez ____ jean?   ce
   —Oui, mais il me faut ____ tee-shirt pour l'EPS.   ce

3. —Je voudrais acheter ____ ordinateur.   cet
   —Moi aussi, mais il te faut ____ calculatrice pour la géométrie.   cette

4. —Comment tu trouves ____ baskets?   ces
   —Super! J'aime ____ short aussi.   ce

5. —Je voudrais acheter ____ cassette.   cette
   —Moi, je préfère acheter ____ disque compact.   ce

6. —Il me faut ____ feuilles de papier.   ces
   —Moi aussi. Il me faut ____ règle aussi.   cette

R30

4 Match a verb from column A with a noun from column B, using each word only once. Then, write six logical sentences telling what you would like to do, using **je voudrais,** and **ce, cet, cette,** or **ces.** (See p. 77.)

EXAMPLE   étudier roman   <u>Je voudrais étudier ce roman.</u>

A	B
1. sortir avec	**a.** magazines
2. regarder	**b.** amis
3. lire	**c.** cours (m. pl.)
4. avoir	**d.** calculatrice
5. acheter	**e.** disque compact
6. écouter	**f.** vidéocassette

Answers may vary. Possible answers:
1. b; Je voudrais sortir avec ces amis.
2. f; Je voudrais regarder cette vidéocassette.
3. a; Je voudrais lire ces magazines.
4. c; Je voudrais avoir ces cours.
5. d; Je voudrais acheter cette calculatrice.
6. e; Je voudrais écouter ce disque compact.

5 Unscramble the colors. Then, use them to describe the items you would like to have. Remember to add the appropriate endings to the colors. (See pp. 73, 79.)

EXAMPLE   LEBU/des tee-shirts   <u>Je voudrais des tee-shirts bleus.</u>

1. RARONM/des trousses   Je voudrais des trousses marron.

2. NLCAB/des calculatrices   Je voudrais des calculatrices blanches.

3. ORUEG/des stylos   Je voudrais des stylos rouges.

4. ETVR/une règle   Je voudrais une règle verte.

5. RNIO/un sac   Je voudrais un sac noir.

6. RIGS/des cahiers   Je voudrais des cahiers gris.

7. OLEVIT/une gomme   Je voudrais une gomme violette.

6 You're telling the store clerk what school supplies you need to buy. Rewrite each sentence to include the given adjective and place it correctly. (See p. 79.)

1. Il me faut une calculatrice. (gris)   Il me faut une calculatrice grise.

2. Il me faut des baskets. (noir)   Il me faut des baskets noires.

3. Il me faut des feuilles de papier. (blanc)   Il me faut des feuilles de papier blanches.

4. Il me faut deux règles. (jaune)   Il me faut deux règles jaunes.

5. Il me faut une trousse. (marron)   Il me faut une trousse marron.

TROISIEME ETAPE

Getting someone's attention; asking for information; expressing thanks

7 Ask how much the following items cost, using **ce, cet, cette,** or **ces,** and the appropriate form of the adjectives. (See pp. 77, 79, 81.)

EXAMPLE   trousse/bleu   <u>C'est combien, cette trousse bleue?</u>

1. crayons/noir   C'est combien, ces crayons noirs?

2. montre/violet   C'est combien, cette montre violette?

3. télévision/gris   C'est combien, cette télévision grise?

4. classeurs/orange   C'est combien, ces classeurs orange?

5. bracelet/rose   C'est combien, ce bracelet rose?

8 Complete this conversation with the appropriate form of the words in parentheses. (See pp. 73, 77, 79.) **1.** cet **2.** marron **3.** cette **4.** grise **5.** cette **6.** blanche **7.** des **8.** violettes **9.** de

JULIE   Excusez-moi, madame, c'est combien, __1__ (ce/cet/cette) ordinateur __2__ (marron)?

VENDEUSE   Neuf cents francs!

JULIE   C'est pas cher! Et __3__ (ce/cet/cette) montre __4__ (gris)?

VENDEUSE   Quatre-vingts francs, mademoiselle. Elle vous plaît?

JULIE   Oui, beaucoup. J'aime aussi __5__ (ce/cet/cette) télévision __6__ (blanc). Et vous avez __7__ (des/de/d') calculatrices __8__ (violet)?

VENDEUSE   Non. Je regrette, mademoiselle. Je n'ai pas __9__ (des/de/d') calculatrices.

CHAPITRE 4 - SPORTS ET PASSE-TEMPS

PREMIERE ETAPE

Telling how much you like or dislike something

1 Complete the following conversations with **faire** or **jouer** as appropriate. (See p. 101.)

1. —Corinne, est-ce-que tu aimes _jouer_ au golf?
   —Non. Je préfère _faire_ du ski.

2. —Frédéric et Arthur, est-ce que vous aimez _faire_ de la vidéo?
   —Pas tellement. Nous aimons mieux _faire_ du théâtre.

3. —Et Malika, est-ce qu'elle aime _jouer_ aux cartes?
   —Pas du tout. Mais elle aime _faire_ de la natation.

4. —Georges, est-ce que tu aimes _faire_ du jogging?
   —Oui. Mais je préfère _jouer_ au hockey.

2 What do you and your friends do in your spare time? Write six sentences telling what you do, using the verbs **faire** and **jouer** and an expression from the box in each sentence. Use each expression only once. (See p. 104.)

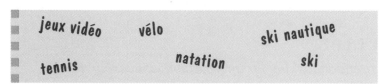

jeux vidéo   vélo   ski nautique

tennis   natation   ski

EXAMPLE   Ariane aime la piscine (*swimming pool*).
            <u>Elle aime faire de la natation.</u>

1. Claude aime tellement la plage.   Il aime faire du ski nautique.

2. Suzanne aime les bicyclettes (*bicycles*).   Elle aime faire du vélo.

3. Olivier et Victor aiment les ordinateurs.   Ils aiment jouer à des jeux vidéo.

4. Moi, j'aime la neige (*snow*).   Moi, j'aime faire du ski.

5. Tu aimes le sport.   Tu aimes faire de l'athlétisme.

3 You have made a list of the activities your classmates like to do. Double-check your list by transforming your notes into questions, using **est-ce que**, and **tu** or **vous** as appropriate. (See p. 103.)

EXAMPLE   Paul et Aurélie aiment faire du ski.
                <u>Est-ce que vous aimez faire du ski?</u>

1. Anne-Marie et Louise aiment jouer au foot.   Est-ce que vous aimez jouer au foot?
2. Marc aime jouer à des jeux vidéo.   Est-ce que tu aimes jouer à des jeux vidéo?
3. Elodie aime faire de la photo.   Est-ce que tu aimes faire de la photo?
4. Jacques et Jules aiment jouer au tennis.   Est-ce que vous aimez jouer au tennis?
5. Alexandrine aime faire du ski nautique.   Est-ce que tu aimes faire du ski nautique?
6. Véronique et Céline aiment faire de l'athlétisme.   Est-ce que vous aimez faire de l'athlétisme?
7. Miriam aime faire du vélo.   Est-ce que tu aimes faire du vélo?
8. Jean et Françoise aiment jouer aux cartes.   Est-ce que vous aimez jouer aux cartes?

DEUXIEME ETAPE

Exchanging information

4 You're having a friend over who doesn't like to do anything. Answer the following questions as your friend would, based on the example. (See p. 104.)

EXAMPLE   Tu joues au volley?   <u>Non, je ne joue pas au volley.</u>
                Tu fais du ski?   <u>Non, je ne fais pas de ski.</u>

1. Tu fais de la natation?   Non, je ne fais pas de natation.
2. Tu joues à des jeux vidéo?   Non, je ne joue pas à des jeux vidéo.
3. Tu fais de l'athlétisme?   Non, je ne fais pas d'athlétisme.
4. Tu fais du jogging?   Non, je ne fais pas de jogging.
5. Tu joues aux cartes?   Non, je ne joue pas aux cartes.
6. Tu fais des photos?   Non, je ne fais pas de photos.
7. Tu fais du patin à glace?   Non, je ne fais pas de patin à glace.
8. Tu fais du roller en ligne?   Non, je ne fais pas de roller en ligne.

5 Pauline and Louise are making plans for the evening. Complete their conversation with the correct forms of **faire**. (See p. 104.)   1. fait 2. fais 3. faire 4. fais 5. faisons 6. font 7. fais

LOUISE   Dis, Pauline, on __1__ de la natation ce soir?
PAULINE   Non. Quand il fait froid, moi, je ne __2__ pas de natation! J'aime mieux
           __3__ du patin à glace! Tu __4__ du patin à glace, toi?
LOUISE   Non, ça ne me dit rien. En hiver, quand il neige, mes copines et moi,
           nous __5__ du ski. C'est génial, le ski!
PAULINE   En été, Gilles et Félix __6__ du ski nautique. J'adore le ski nautique! Mais
           ce soir, moi, je __7__ du patin à glace. C'est décidé!
LOUISE   D'accord. Allons-y!

6 Odile is asking her friends if they play certain sports. Based on their answers, what are her questions? Remember to use the correct forms of **faire**. (See p. 104.)

| EXAMPLE | ODILE | <u>Vous faites du vélo?</u> |
| | JEREMY ET VALENTINE | Oui, on adore faire du vélo. |

1. ODILE _____ Tu fais du jogging?

   SYLVIE Oui, j'aime beaucoup faire du jogging.

2. ODILE _____ Sophie et Marie font de l'aérobic?

   PIERRE Oui, Sophie et Marie adorent faire de l'aérobic.

3. ODILE _____ Arthur fait de la natation?

   DAVID Oui, Arthur aime faire de la natation.

4. ODILE _____ Vous faites du ski?

   MARION ET Oui, nous aimons bien faire du ski.
   FRANCINE

5. ODILE _____ Elodie et Jérôme font du roller en ligne?

   VANESSA Oui, Elodie et Jerôme aiment beaucoup faire du roller en ligne.

6. ODILE _____ Thérèse aime faire de la randonnée?

   CHRISTINE Oui, Thérèse aime faire de la randonnée.

7 Rewrite the following sentences, replacing the subject with the pronoun **on**. Be sure to make any necessary changes. (See p. 105.)

1. Nous allons à la pharmacie aujourd'hui.   On va à la pharmacie aujourd'hui.

2. Marcel et moi aimons faire de la natation après l'école.   On fait de la natation après l'école.

3. Est-ce que vous faites du ski nautique au Texas?   Est-ce qu'on fait du ski nautique au Texas?

4. Vous jouez aux cartes?   On joue aux cartes?

5. Nous faisons de l'aérobic.   On fait de l'aérobic.

6. Est-ce que nous allons faire du roller en ligne ce week-end?   Est-ce qu'on va faire du roller en ligne ce week-end?

7. Est-ce que vous faites du théâtre dans votre école?   Est-ce qu'on fait du théâtre dans votre école?

8 Complete the following sentences with the activity most appropriate for the weather condition or time of year stated. (See p. 107.)   Answers may vary.

> jouer au football américain   regarder la télé
> jouer au tennis
> jouer au hockey   nager   jouer à des jeux vidéo

1. En automne, mon frère _____.   joue au football américain

2. Quand il fait chaud, les enfants _____.   nagent

3. Quand il neige, Jacqueline _____.   joue au hockey

4. Quand il pleut, je _____.   regarde la télé

5. Quand il fait frais, mon frère et moi _____.   jouons au tennis

TROISIEME ETAPE

Making, accepting, and turning down suggestions

9 François is asking Janine how often she plays certain sports. Rewrite their conversation, using the fragments below. Remember to use the correct form of the verbs and to put the adverb in the correct position. (See p. 110.)

FRANÇOIS tu/est-ce que/souvent/faire/de la natation Est-ce que tu fais souvent de la natation?

JANINE faire/de la natation/je/souvent/au printemps/oui Oui, je fais souvent de la natation au printemps.

FRANÇOIS faire/du ski/de temps en temps/tu/est-ce que Est-ce que tu fais du ski de temps en temps?

JANINE faire/du ski/oui/je/quand il neige Oui, je fais du ski quand il neige.

FRANÇOIS quelquefois/tu/est-ce que/jouer/au foot Est-ce que tu joues quelquefois au foot?

JANINE ne...jamais/jouer/non/au foot/je Non, je ne joue jamais au foot.

10 Vanessa has taken a survey to find out how often teenagers play certain sports. Rewrite her notes, using the adverbs from the box. The meaning of the sentences should remain the same. Use each adverb only once. (See p. 110.) Answers may vary. Possible answers:

> ne ... jamais   d'habitude   quelquefois
>
> souvent   une fois par semaine

EXAMPLE Camille fait du vélo trois fois par semaine.
<u>Camille fait souvent du vélo.</u>

1. Koffi joue au tennis de temps en temps.   Quelquefois, Koffi joue au tennis.
2. Estelle et Olivia font du patin à glace le samedi matin. Estelle et Olivia font du patin à glace une fois par semaine.
3. Quand il pleut, Fatima ne fait pas de jogging.   Quand il pleut, Fatima ne fait jamais de jogging.
4. Sébastien joue au golf tous les jours au printemps.   D'habitude, Sébastien joue au golf au printemps.

CHAPITRE 5 - ON VA AU CAFE?

PREMIERE ETAPE

Making suggestions; making excuses; making a recommendation

1 Choose the appropriate completion for each sentence. (See p. 133.)

1. Guillaume et Ludovic... f
2. Paul... g
3. Anne et Lucie... d
4. Marie-Lise et toi... c
5. André et moi... b
6. Alice... a
7. Moi, je... e

a. prend un jus de pomme; elle a soif.
b. prenons des hot-dogs.
c. prenez un chocolat.
d. prennent du jus d'orange; elles ont très soif.
e. prends un croque-monsieur.
f. prennent un sandwich.
g. prend un steak-frites; il a faim.

2 You and your friends are deciding what to order in a café. Complete the sentences that follow with the correct forms of **prendre**. (See p. 133.)

1. Tu _____ un jus de pomme?   prends
2. Eric _____ un hot-dog.   prend
3. Vous _____ un café?   prenez
4. Moi, je _____ une limonade.   prends
5. Elles _____ des sandwichs.   prennent
6. Nous _____ des cocas.   prenons
7. Jean et Alphonse _____ un steak-frites.   prennent
8. Le professeur _____ un croque-monsieur.   prend

DEUXIEME ETAPE

Getting someone's attention; ordering food and beverages

3 You and your friends are browsing through a basket full of items on sale. Tell your friends what to get (**prendre**) based on what they tell you about their favorite colors. (See p. 136.)

> un jean noir   des baskets bleues   un short blanc   un bracelet rose
>
> des sweat-shirts orange   un tee-shirt rouge   des pull-overs verts

EXAMPLE   Céline : J'aime le rouge. <u>Prends le tee-shirt rouge!</u>

1. Valentine et Sophie : On adore l'orange.   Prenez les sweat-shirts orange!
2. Jérôme : Moi, j'aime bien le noir.   Prends le jean noir!
3. Clément : Moi, j'aime le blanc.   Prends le short blanc!
4. Anne et Lydie : On aime bien le bleu.   Prenez les baskets bleues!
5. Aurélie : Moi, j'aime le rose.   Prends le bracelet rose!
6. Marcel et Pascal : On adore le vert.   Prenez les pull-overs verts!

4 A physical education teacher is encouraging her students to exercise. Based on their answers, write what she told them to do. (See p. 136.)

EXAMPLE   —<u>Faites du sport!</u>
          —Mais on n'aime pas faire du sport!

1. —Mais je n'aime pas faire de la natation!   Fais de la natation!
2. —Mais on n'aime pas faire du jogging!   Faites du jogging!
3. —Mais on n'aime pas jouer au basket!   Jouez au basket!
4. —Mais je n'aime pas jouer au tennis!   Joue au tennis!
5. —Mais nous n'aimons pas jouer au football!   Jouez au football!
6. —Mais je n'aime pas faire du roller en ligne!   Fais du roller en ligne!

5 Rewrite the following requests, using the imperative of the verbs in parentheses followed by **-moi**. (See p. 136.)

   EXAMPLE   —Monsieur, je voudrais un café, s'il vous plaît! (apporter)
              —<u>Apportez-moi un café, s'il vous plaît!</u>

   1. —Maman, je voudrais une limonade, s'il te plaît! (apporter)
      —____, s'il te plaît!   Apporte-moi une limonade

   2. —Jérémy, je voudrais un sandwich au fromage, s'il te plaît! (donner)
      —____, s'il te plaît!   Donne-moi un sandwich au fromage

   3. —Monsieur, je voudrais une eau minérale, s'il vous plaît! (donner)
      —____, s'il vous plaît!   Donnez-moi une eau minérale

   4. —Mademoiselle, je voudrais un coca, s'il vous plaît! (apporter)
      —____, s'il vous plaît!   Apportez-moi un coca

   5. —Bérénice, je voudrais un chocolat, s'il te plaît! (apporter)
      —____, s'il te plaît!   Apporte-moi un chocolat

   6. —Papa, je voudrais de l'argent, s'il te plaît! (donner)
      —____, s'il te plaît!   Donne-moi de l'argent

TROISIEME ETAPE

Inquiring about and expressing likes and dislikes; paying the check

6 Maud would like to know how much the following items cost. Write the waiter's answers to her questions. The prices are given in parentheses. Write out the amounts in French. (See p. 139.)

   EXAMPLE   C'est combien, la pizza suprême? (65F) <u>Soixante-cinq francs.</u>

   1. C'est combien, le steak-frites? (45F)   Quarante-cinq francs.
   2. C'est combien, l'omelette au jambon? (36F)   Trente-six francs.
   3. C'est combien, la salade niçoise? (28F)   Vingt-huit francs.
   4. C'est combien, trois sandwiches au rosbif? (75F)   Soixante-quinze francs.
   5. C'est combien, le couscous? (53F)   Cinquante-trois francs.
   6. C'est combien, le croque-monsieur et le café? (61F)   Soixante et un francs.

7 Write out in French the number that would come next in each of the series below. (See p. 139.)

   1. vingt-deux, quarante-quatre, soixante-six...   quatre-vingt-huit
   2. seize, trente-deux, quarante-huit...   soixante-quatre
   3. onze, trente et un, cinquante et un...   soixante et onze
   4. quatre-vingt-quinze, quatre-vingt-dix, quatre-vingt-cinq...   quatre-vingts
   5. soixante-dix, quatre-vingts, quatre-vingt-dix...   cent
   6. vingt-cinq, trente-cinq, quarante-cinq...   cinquante-cinq

CHAPITRE 6 - AMUSONS-NOUS!

PREMIERE ETAPE

Making plans

1 Malika is leaving a message on Axel's answering machine. Complete her message with **le** when appropriate. Be careful! In some cases, you won't need to add anything. (See p. 153.) 1. X 2. le 3. X 4. le 5. X 6. le

Salut, Axel! C'est moi, Malika! Ça va? Ecoute! On va au Café Américain __1__ lundi soir. Tu viens? On va souvent à la crêperie __2__ lundi, mais cette semaine, on va aller au café. Bonne idée, non? __3__ mercredi après-midi, on va aller voir une pièce. On va quelquefois au théâtre __4__ mercredi. C'est super, le théâtre! Est-ce que tu peux venir? Ah, oui, __5__ samedi, on va à la boum de Nadine. Qu'est-ce que tu fais d'habitude __6__ samedi soir? Tu veux venir avec nous? Eh bien, à bientôt peut-être. Tchao!

2 Fernand and Michèle are discussing what to do this coming Saturday. Complete their conversation with the correct forms of **aller**. (See p. 154.) 1. vas 2. va 3. vont 4. va 5. vont 6. allons 7. vais

FERNAND	Dis, Michèle, tu __1__ faire quoi demain?
MICHELE	Bof. Rien de spécial. D'habitude, le samedi, je fais les vitrines.
FERNAND	Eric et moi, on __2__ faire un pique-nique. Tu viens avec nous?
MICHELE	Désolée, mais ça ne me dit rien, les pique-niques.
FERNAND	Mais écoute, Michèle! Les pique-niques, c'est génial! Tous les copains __3__ venir! On __4__ jouer au foot! Julien et Juliette __5__ apporter des hot-dogs! Nous __6__ nous amuser!
MICHELE	D'accord. Pourquoi pas? On se retrouve où?
FERNAND	Devant la MJC. Vers trois heures.
MICHELE	Entendu. Je __7__ passer chez toi vers deux heures et demie.

3 Combine these fragments into sentences. Remember to use the correct form of **aller**. (See p. 154.)

EXAMPLE   Marc et Li/faire les vitrines   <u>Marc et Li vont faire les vitrines</u>.

1. Toi, tu/aller au café   Toi, tu vas aller au café.

2. Moi, je/aller au théâtre   Moi, je vais aller au théâtre.

3. Marc/voir un film   Marc va voir un film.

4. Simone et moi, nous/voir un match   Simone et moi, nous allons voir un match.

5. Pascal et Maurice, vous/faire une promenade   Pascal et Maurice, vous allez faire une promenade.

4 Imagine that you and your friends are going on a trip to Paris this summer. Complete your plans using **à, à la, au,** and **aux**. (See p. 157.)

1. Christine va aller ___ Cathédrale (f.) Notre-Dame.   à la

2. Nous allons aller ___ Louvre et _____ cafés.   au, aux

3. Marc va aller ___ concerts de rock.   aux

4. Moi, je vais ___ Maison des jeunes.   à la

5. Les garçons ne vont pas aller ___ centre commercial.   au

DEUXIEME ETAPE

Extending and responding to invitations

5 Complete the sentences that follow with the correct form of the verb **vouloir**. (See p. 160.)

1. Mes copines _____ aller au restaurant. veulent
2. Mais moi, je _____ aller au café. veux
3. Et vous, vous _____ manger quelque chose? voulez
4. Non. Nous _____ voir un film. voulons
5. Et toi, Eric, tu _____ faire quoi? veux
6. Patricia et moi, on _____ faire les vitrines. veut

6 Based on their preferences, write what the following students want to do. Be sure to use the appropriate subject pronoun, the correct form of **vouloir**, and an expression from the box. Use each expression only once. (See p. 160.)

> voir un film   regarder un match de foot à la télé   voir une pièce   manger quelque chose
>
> aller à une boum   aller à la bibliothèque   aller à la piscine

EXAMPLE   Marianne a faim. <u>Elle veut manger quelque chose.</u>

1. Suzanne et Monique adorent nager. Elles veulent aller à la piscine.
2. J'aime lire. Je veux aller à la bibliothèque.
3. Vous adorez le théâtre. Vous voulez voir une pièce.
4. Gilles aime bien le cinéma. Il veut voir un film.
5. Anne et moi, nous aimons danser. Nous voulons aller à une boum.
6. Tu aimes le football. Tu veux regarder un match de foot à la télé.

TROISIEME ETAPE

Arranging to meet someone

7 Complete this conversation with the correct answer to each question. (See p. 165.)

> Avec Lise.   A sept heures et demie.
>
> Chez moi.   Ce soir.

DIANE	Tu viens manger avec nous, Isabelle?
ISABELLE	Oui. Je veux bien. Quand ça?
DIANE	__1__ Ce soir.
ISABELLE	Où est-ce qu'on se retrouve?
DIANE	__2__ Chez moi.
ISABELLE	Avec qui on va manger?
DIANE	__3__ Avec Lise.
ISABELLE	On se retrouve à quelle heure?
DIANE	__4__ A sept heures et demie.

8 Match the response from column A with the question asked from column B.
(See p. 165.)

A	B
1. Mireille et Matthieu. c	a. Où est-ce qu'on se retrouve?
2. On va voir "Les Randonneurs." b	b. Qu'est-ce tu vas voir?
3. Demain, à deux heures et demie de l'après-midi. d	c. Tu vas avec qui?
4. Je vais voir un film. e	d. Quand ça?
5. Au cinéma Beaubourg. a	e. Qu'est-ce que tu vas faire ce week-end?

CHAPITRE 7 – LA FAMILLE

PREMIERE ETAPE

Identifying and introducing people

1 Ahmed is new to your neighborhood. He needs you to help him identify some people. Answer his questions, using **c'est** or **ce sont** and the words in parentheses in the order in which they are listed. (See p. 180.)

EXAMPLE   C'est qui, Karim et Mohamed? (les oncles/Samira)
<u>Ce sont les oncles de Samira.</u>

1. C'est qui, Claudette? (la grand-mère/Guy)   C'est la grand-mère de Guy.

2. C'est qui, Arnaud et Martin? (les frères/Marie)   Ce sont les frères de Marie.

3. C'est qui, Mourad? (le fils/Fatima)   C'est le fils de Fatima.

4. C'est qui, Jacqueline et Jeanne? (les tantes/Paul)   Ce sont les tantes de Paul.

5. C'est qui, Ismaïl? (le grand-père/Saïdou)   C'est le grand-père de Saïdou.

2 Sabine and Claire are asking their younger brother Luc to bring them some items they forgot in their room. Complete their statements with the appropriate possessive adjectives. (See p. 181.)

EXAMPLE   Luc, apporte-nous nos calculatrices, s'il te plaît!

1. Apporte-nous <u>nos</u> stylos, s'il te plaît!

2. Apporte-moi <u>ma</u> trousse, s'il te plaît!

3. Apporte-moi <u>mes</u> cahiers, s'il te plaît!

4. Apporte-nous <u>notre</u> dictionnaire, s'il te plaît!

3 Luc cannot find the items his sisters want, so he asks them where they are. Complete his questions by adding the appropriate possessive adjectives. (See p. 181.)

1. Ils sont où, <u>vos</u> stylos?

2. Elle est où, <u>ta</u> trousse, Claire?

3. Ils sont où, <u>tes</u> cahiers, Sabrine?

4. Il est où, <u>votre</u> dictionnaire?

4 Mazarine and Jean-Luc are talking about their pets. Complete their conversation with the appropriate possessive adjectives. (See p. 181.)

MAZARINE   Il a quel âge, __1__ chien, Jean-Luc?   ton
JEAN-LUC   __2__ chien? Je n'ai pas de chien. Par contre, j'ai des poissons rouges!   Mon
MAZARINE   Ah, c'est cool, ça! Ils s'appellent comment, __3__ poissons?   tes
JEAN-LUC   Elvis et Presley. Tu aimes les poissons rouges, toi?
MAZARINE   Oui, beaucoup, mais j'aime mieux les chats et les canaris.
                __4__ sœur a deux chats et trois canaris.   Ma
JEAN-LUC   Ils sont comment, les chats de __5__ sœur?   ta
MAZARINE   Très mignons!
JEAN-LUC   Et __6__ canaris?   ses
MAZARINE   Eh bien, ils sont jaunes.
JEAN-LUC   Ah! Très drôle! Est-ce que __7__ parents aiment bien les animaux?   tes
MAZARINE   Oui. Chez moi, tout le monde *(everybody)* adore les animaux.

DEUXIEME ETAPE

Describing and characterizing people

5 Unscramble the adjectives. Then, write the correct form of each adjective. Remember to make the adjective agree with the subject it describes. (See p. 186.)

1. Daniel est UNBR.   brun
2. Ses amis sont LNBOD.   blonds
3. Ses tantes sont NILTEG.   gentilles
4. Ses frères sont TNSUAMA.   amusants
5. Ses sœurs sont OFRT.   fortes

6. Son chien est BNTAMEET.   embêtant
7. Sa grand-mère est ETPIT.   petite
8. Ses chats sont ROGS.   gros
9. Sa mère est XRUO.   rousse
10. Son cousin est ENBLEPI.   pénible

6 Complete the following sentences by choosing the appropriate endings. (See p. 187.)

1. Je...   b
2. Elles...   h
3. Tu...   e
4. Julien et moi, on...   g
5. Jeanne...   a
6. Alice et moi, nous...   d
7. Mes frères...   c
8. Marie et toi, vous...   f

a. est très gentille.
b. suis grand et fort.
c. sont embêtants.
d. sommes très minces.
e. es méchant!
f. êtes un peu pénibles!
g. est roux.
h. sont intelligentes.

TROISIEME ETAPE

Asking for, giving, and refusing permission

7 There are many things Onélia would like to do, but first she has to ask her parents for permission. Complete her questions with the correct forms of **être**. (See pp. 187, 189.)

1. Je voudrais sortir avec mes copains. Tu _____ d'accord, maman?   es
2. Je voudrais aller au cinéma. Vous _____ d'accord?   êtes
3. Je voudrais aller à la MJC. Tu _____ d'accord, papa?   es
4. Je _____ invitée à la boum de Pierre. Vous _____ d'accord?   suis; êtes

ADDITIONAL GRAMMAR PRACTICE   **R41**

8 Mme Ménard is asking her children to do some work around the house. Complete their answers with the correct form of **être.** (See pp. 187, 189.)

1. MME MENARD   Fabienne, tu fais les courses, s'il te plaît?
    FABIENNE   Désolée, je _____ occupée. J'ai des devoirs à faire.   suis
2. MME MENARD   Anne et Eva, vous faites la vaisselle, s'il vous plaît?
    ANNE ET EVA   Désolées, nous _____ occupées.   sommes
3. MME MENARD   Paul et Eric, vous pouvez débarrasser la table?
    PAUL ET ERIC   Désolés, on _____ occupés. On a des trucs à faire.   est
4. MME MENARD   Lise, tu peux promener le chien?
    LISE   Oui, bien sûr!
    MME MENARD   Merci. Tu _____ très gentille!   es

CHAPITRE 8 - AU MARCHE

PREMIERE ETAPE

Expressing need

1 Eric is planning a party and has made a list of what he needs to do to get ready. Complete his list with **du, de la, de l'**, and **des** as needed. (See p. 208.)

Pour ma boum, je vais faire des sandwiches, alors je vais acheter __du__ pain, __du__ fromage et __du__ jambon. Mes amis aiment manger __de la__ salade. Dans la salade, je vais mettre __des__ tomates, __du__ maïs et __des__ champignons. Pour le dessert, je vais préparer une salade de fruits avec __des__ oranges, __des__ bananes et __des__ pommes.

2 Read the recipes below. Then write a note reminding yourself what you need to buy at the market, using the articles **du, de la, de l'**, and **des**. (See p. 208.)

1.

Les crêpes bretonnes
500 g de farine
3 œufs
20 g de beurre
3 g de sel (m.; *salt*)
5 g de levure (f.;*yeast*)
1 cl de jus de pomme
1/4 litre de lait

2.

La sauce arachide
4 oignons
2 tomates
5 cl d'huile d'arachide
100 g de pâte (f.) d'arachide
100 g de pâte (f.) de tomates
10 g de sel
1/4 botte *(bunch)* de piments rouges

Il me faut...   de la farine,
1. de la farine; des œufs; du beurre; du sel; de la levure; du jus de pomme; du lait.

Il me faut...
2. des oignons; des tomates; de l'huile d'arachide; de la pâte d'arachide; de la pâte de tomates; du sel; des piments rouges.

3 Rewrite the following sentences, using the expressions **avoir besoin de** or **il me/te faut** and the partitive article. (See pp. 208, 210.)

EXAMPLE   Il me faut des bananes. <u>J'ai besoin de bananes.</u>
Tu as besoin de lait? <u>Il te faut du lait?</u>

1. Il me faut des noix de coco.
2. Il te faut des papayes?
3. Tu as besoin de confiture?
4. Il me faut du raisin.
5. J'ai besoin d'eau minérale.
6. Il te faut des ananas?

1. J'ai besoin de noix de coco.
2. Tu as besoin de papayes?
3. Il te faut de la confiture?
4. J'ai besoin de raisin.
5. Il me faut de l'eau minérale.
6. Tu as besoin d'ananas?

DEUXIEME ETAPE

Making, accepting, and declining requests; telling someone what to do

4 You and your friends are planning a party and you're writing down what people are volunteering to bring. Fill in the correct forms of the verb **pouvoir**. (See p. 213.)

1. Isabelle _____ acheter des avocats et des tomates.   peut
2. Moi, je _____ acheter des tartes.   peux
3. Henri, tu _____ acheter des fraises et des citrons?   peux
4. Carol et Sylvain, vous _____ acheter de la salade et du pain.   pouvez
5. Barbara, Serge et Françoise _____ acheter une bouteille d'eau.   peuvent

5 Choose the appropriate completion for each sentence. (See p. 213.)

A	B
1. Est-ce que tu... c	**a.** ne peuvent pas aller au cinéma ce soir. Ils sont occupés.
2. Elle... e	**b.** ne peux pas sortir la poubelle. Je n'ai pas le temps.
3. Nous... d	**c.** peux débarrasser la table, s'il te plaît?
4. Angèle et toi, vous... f	**d.** ne pouvons pas faire la vaisselle. Nous avons des trucs à faire.
5. Moi, je... b	**e.** ne peut pas sortir avec ses copines. Elle a des devoirs à faire.
6. Mes copains... a	**f.** pouvez promener le chien?

6 Unscramble the names of the food items. Then combine the fragments to create sentences telling Djeneba what to get you from the market. (See p. 214.)

EXAMPLE   RUERBE / un paquet/s'il te plaît/prends
   Prends un paquet de beurre, s'il te plaît!

1. ITESPT OSPI / une boîte/rapporte-moi/s'il te plaît   Rapporte-moi une boîte de petits pois, s'il te plaît!
2. NDVAIE / s'il te plaît/un morceau/achète-moi   Achète-moi un morceau de viande, s'il te plaît!
3. SECHEP / prends/une douzaine   Prends une douzaine de pêches!
4. SJU ASANAN D' / une bouteille/acheter/n'oublie pas de   N'oublie pas d'acheter une bouteille de jus d'ananas!
5. AMCHNONPIGS / tu peux/s'il te plaît/une livre/acheter   Tu peux acheter une livre de champignons, s'il te plaît?
6. IRNAFE / un kilo/s'il te plaît/rapporte-moi   Rapporte-moi un kilo de farine, s'il te plaît!

TROISIEME ETAPE

Offering, accepting, or refusing food

7 You're asking Didier about his family's eating habits. Write down his answers to your questions, using the pronoun **en** and the correct form of **prendre**. (See pp. 133, 220.)

EXAMPLE   Tu prends du café au lait au petit déjeuner? Oui, j'en prends.

1. Tu prends du lait au dîner? Non, ...   je n'en prends pas.
2. Tes parents prennent du pain avec leur fromage? Oui, ...   ils en prennent.
3. Ta sœur prend des légumes au déjeuner? Oui, ...   elle en prend.
4. Ton petit frère prend des gâteaux au goûter? Non, ...   il n'en prend pas.
5. Ta cousine et toi, vous prenez de la viande au déjeuner? Non, on ...   on n'en prend pas.
6. Tu prends de la sauce arachide avec ton riz? Oui, ...   j'en prends.

8 Read the four sentences in the box below and tell what Armelle's friends like and dislike and how they're feeling. With this information in mind, write down their answers to Armelle's offers of various foods and drinks. Use the correct form of **vouloir** and the pronoun **en** in each answer. (See pp. 160, 220.)

> Marius n'a plus faim, mais il a très soif.
> Irène aime les fruits, mais elle n'aime pas tellement le fromage.
> Isabelle n'aime pas la viande, mais elle adore le poisson.
> Léopold a très faim, mais il n'a plus soif.

EXAMPLE Irène, encore du fromage? <u>Non, merci. Je n'en veux plus.</u>

1. Marius, tu veux de l'eau? Oui, j'en veux bien.
2. Irène, tu veux des pêches? Oui, j'en veux bien.
3. Isabelle, encore du rosbif? Non, merci. Je n'en veux plus.
4. Léopold, tu veux du gâteau? Oui, j'en veux bien.
5. Isabelle, tu veux du poisson? Oui, j'en veux bien.
6. Marius, encore du riz? Non, merci. Je n'en veux plus.

CHAPITRE 9 – AU TELEPHONE

PREMIERE ETAPE

Asking for and expressing opinions; inquiring about and relating past events

1 Françoise and Julie are talking about what they did over the weekend. Complete their conversation with the **passé composé** of the verbs in parentheses. (See p. 239.)

FRANÇOIS Salut Julie. Tu __1__ (passer) un bon week-end? **1.** as passé
JULIE Oh, ça __2__ (être). J' __3__ (visiter) **2.** a été **3.** ai visité
ma grand-mère et j' __4__ (lire) mon roman. **4.** ai lu
Et toi? Qu'est-ce que tu __5__ (faire)? **5.** as fait
FRANÇOIS J' __6__ (prendre) la voiture de ma mère, et mon sœur et moi, nous
__7__ (voir) un film. **6.** ai pris **7.** avons vu

2 Complete Pierre's journal entry about his busy weekend by putting each verb into the **passé composé** (See p. 239.) ai retrouvé, avons déjeuné, avons parlé, a lu, a étudié, ont acheté, n'ont pas gagné, ai vu, ai fait

Hier, j' _____ (retrouver) mes amis Jean et Françoise au café. Nous _____ (déjeuner) ensemble puis nous _____ (parler) de notre week-end. Samedi, Françoise _____ (lire) un livre et Jean _____ (étudier). Le soir, ils _____ (acheter) un billet de loto mais ils _____ (ne pas gagner). Dimanche, j' _____ (voir) un bon film et ensuite j' _____ (faire) mes devoirs.

3 Edouard always wants to do what Milo just did. Read what Edouard says he'll be doing. Then write six sentences saying that Milo did the same thing yesterday. Remember to put the verbs in the **passé composé**, and to make all necessary changes. (See p. 239.)

EXAMPLE Demain, je vais acheter des baskets. <u>Hier, Milo a acheté des baskets.</u>

1. Je vais laver la voiture de mon père demain. Hier,... Milo a lavé la voiture de son père.
2. Je vais déjeuner à la cantine demain. Hier,... Milo a déjeuné à la cantine.
3. Demain, je vais retrouver mes copains. Hier,... Milo a retrouvé ses copains.
4. Demain, je vais répéter avec la chorale. Hier,... Milo a répété avec la chorale.
5. Je vais dîner avec ma grand-mère demain. Hier,... Milo a dîné avec sa grand-mère.
6. Demain, je vais ranger ma chambre. Hier,... Milo a rangé sa chambre.

4 Elissa's mother is asking her if she and her brothers and sisters have done their chores. Write Elissa's answers, using **déjà** or **ne (n')... pas encore**. Remember to make all the necessary changes. (See p. 240.)

EXAMPLE MAMAN   Tu as passé l'aspirateur?
 ELISSA   <u>Non, je n'ai pas encore passé l'aspirateur.</u>

1. MAMAN Claire et toi, vous avez rangé vos chambres?
 ELISSA Non, nous n'avons pas encore rangé nos chambres.
2. MAMAN Tu as débarrassé la table?
 ELISSA Oui, j'ai déjà débarrassé la table.
3. MAMAN Et Guillaume, est-ce qu'il a fait les courses?
 ELISSA Oui, il a déjà fait les courses.
4. MAMAN Est-ce que tu as promené le chien?
 ELISSA Non, je n'ai pas encore promené le chien.
5. MAMAN Est-ce que Claire et Sophie ont fait le ménage?
 ELISSA Non, elles n'ont pas encore fait le ménage.

DEUXIEME ETAPE

Making and answering a telephone call

5 Pierre, David, and Yves are discussing what their friends are doing today. Complete their conversation with the correct forms of **répondre** and **attendre**. (See p. 245.)

1. attendez 2. attendons 3. attend 4. répond 5. attends

PIERRE Tiens, salut! Vous __1__ le bus?
 YVES Non, nous __2__ Paul. Il va au stade avec nous.
PIERRE Où est Lise?
 DAVID Elle est chez elle. Elle __3__ sa mère pour aller au musée.
PIERRE Ah oui! C'est vrai. Et Bruno, qu'est-ce qu'il fait ce matin?
 YVES Il __4__ à la lettre de son correspondant américain. Et toi, qu'est-ce que tu fais, alors?
PIERRE Rien de spécial.
 DAVID Tu __5__ Paul avec nous?
PIERRE Oui, pourquoi pas?

6 Write complete sentences using the fragments below. Watch for clues that tell you when to use the **passé composé.** (See p. 245.)

1. hier/Paul/perdre/son portefeuille/au centre commercial Hier, Paul a perdu son portefeuille au centre commercial.

2. nous/répondre/au téléphone/quand/notre père/travailler Nous répondons au téléphone quand notre père travaille.

3. ne/pas/perdre/votre argent Ne perdez pas votre argent!

4. mes parents/vendre/leur voiture/bleu/la semaine dernière Mes parents ont vendu leur voiture bleue la semaine dernière.

5. Michel/vendre/des bonbons/pour/gagner de l'argent Michel vend des bonbons pour gagner de l'argent.

TROISIEME ETAPE

Sharing confidences and consoling others; asking for and giving advice

7 Léon is asking Diane for advice. Complete their conversation with **le, la, l', or lui.** (See p. 247.)

LEON Dis, Diane, tu as une minute?
DIANE Oui. Bien sûr. Je t'écoute.
LEON Ben, hier, au café, j'ai rencontré une fille. On a parlé pendant *(for)* deux heures. Ce matin, elle m'a téléphoné pour me dire qu'elle veut sortir avec moi. A ton avis, qu'est-ce que je fais?
DIANE Elle est comment cette fille? Tu __1__ (l', les) aimes bien? l'
LEON Oui. Je __2__ (l', la) aime beaucoup. Elle est super sympa. l'
DIANE Qu'est-ce que tu __3__ (lui, leur) as répondu alors? lui
LEON Je ne __4__ (la, lui) ai pas répondu. A ton avis, qu'est-ce que je fais? lui
DIANE Téléphone- __5__ (lui, leur) tout de suite! lui
LEON Mais je ne trouve plus son numéro de téléphone!
DIANE Cherche- __6__ (le, leur)! le
LEON Non, c'est pas possible. Je ne peux pas __7__ (le, lui) téléphoner. Je suis trop timide! lui
DIANE Ah, bon! Alors, oublie- __8__ (la, les)! la

8 You and your friend Max are giving advice to Odile. Repeat Max's advice using an object pronoun **(le, la, les, lui, or leur).** (See p. 247.)

EXAMPLE MAX Achète les pommes rouges!
TOI Oui. Achète-les!

1. Téléphone à tes copains! Oui. Téléphone-leur!
2. Prends la trousse violette! Oui. Prends-la!
3. Apporte tes disques compacts! Oui. Apporte-les!
4. Oublie ce garçon! Oui. Oublie-le!
5. Attends les vacances! Oui. Attends-les!
6. Ecris à Caroline! Oui. Ecris-lui!
7. Parle à tes parents! Oui. Parle-leur!
8. Achète ces stylos! Oui. Achète-les!

CHAPITRE 10 – DANS UN MAGASIN DE VETEMENTS

PREMIERE ETAPE

Asking for and giving advice

1 Fill in the blanks to create the correct present tense form of **mettre** for each of the sentences below. (See p. 263.)

1. Qu'est-ce que je M E T S pour la boum de Charles?

2. Pourquoi tu ne M E T S pas ta robe blanche?

3. Odile et Béatrice M E T T E N T souvent des robes à fleurs.

4. Boris et moi, nous M E T T O N S des lunettes de soleil pour aller à des boums.

5. Vous M E T T E Z des lunettes de soleil quand il pleut comme ça?

6. Oui, on M E T toujours des lunettes de soleil et des baskets.

2 Marie-France is asking Patricia for advice on what to wear to a party. Complete their conversation with the appropriate forms of **mettre** and **porter**. Remember to use the past tense when indicated. (See p. 263.)

MARIE-FRANCE   Je ne sais pas quoi __1__ (mettre) pour aller au théâtre.   **1.** mettre

PATRICIA   __2__ (mettre) ta jupe noire avec ton chemisier blanc.   **2.** Mets

MARIE-FRANCE   Non, ce n'est pas très chic. Et j' __3__ (déjà mettre) mon chemisier blanc avec ma veste cette semaine.   **3.** ai déjà mis

PATRICIA   Pourquoi tu ne __4__ (mettre) pas ton chemisier bleu avec une écharpe alors?   **4.** mets

MARIE-FRANCE   Non, j' __5__ (déjà porter) mon écharpe à la boum de Jean-Marc.   **5.** ai déjà porté

PATRICIA   __6__ (mettre) ta robe noire.   **6.** Mets

MARIE-FRANCE   Bonne idée. Et je vais __7__ aussi mes chaussures noires. Enfin, c'est décidé.   **7.** mettre

DEUXIEME ETAPE

Expressing need; inquiring

3 Nadia is asking Clara what to wear for Raphaël's party. Write Clara's advice, using **mets** and the correct forms of the adjectives in parentheses. (See pp. 263, 265.)

EXAMPLE   NADIA   Je mets ma robe violette? (gris)
CLARA   Je la trouve trop serrée. <u>Mets la grise!</u>

1. NADIA   Je mets mes sandales jaunes? (blanc)
CLARA   Je les trouve un peu démodées. _____   Mets les blanches!

2. NADIA   Je mets mon cardigan orange? (noir)
CLARA   C'est pas ton style. _____   Mets le noir!

3. NADIA   Je mets mon écharpe rouge? (rose)
CLARA   Elle ne te va pas. _____   Mets la rose!

4. NADIA   Je mets ma ceinture verte? (bleu)
CLARA   Elle ne va pas avec ta robe. _____   Mets la bleue!

5. NADIA   Je mets mes boucles d'oreilles marron? (vert)
CLARA   Je les trouve trop grosses. _____   Mets les vertes!

4 Given their likes and dislikes, write what these students choose to wear to Mélanie's party, using the correct form of **choisir**. Remember to make all the necessary changes. (See p. 267.)

EXAMPLE Suzanne aime les jupes courtes. <u>Elle choisit une jupe courte.</u>

1. Pierre et Philippe aiment bien les cravates à pois.   Ils choisissent des cravates à pois.
2. Armelle adore les robes rétro.   Elle choisit une robe rétro.
3. Moi, j'aime les boucles d'oreilles noires.   Je choisis des boucles d'oreilles noires.
4. Tu préfères les chemisiers à fleurs.   Tu choisis un chemisier à fleurs.
5. Elsa et toi, vous aimez bien les chaussures en cuir.   Vous choisissez des chaussures en cuir.
6. Toi et moi, nous adorons les blousons en jean.   Nous choisissons des blousons en jean.

5 Write complete sentences using the words below. Remember to put the verbs in the present tense and to make all necessary changes. (See p. 267.)

1. vous/ne/pas/grossir/parce que/vous/faire du sport   Vous ne grossissez pas parce que vous faites du sport.
2. on/grandir/si/on/manger/assez   On grandit si on mange assez.
3. tu/maigrir/parce que/tu/jouer au foot/tous les jours   Tu maigris parce que tu joues au foot tous les jours.
4. nous/grossir/facilement/si/nous/ne/pas/faire du jogging   Nous grossissons facilement si nous ne faisons pas de jogging.
5. je/grossir/parce que/je/manger/beaucoup de gâteaux   Je grossis parce que je mange beaucoup de gâteaux.
6. mes petites sœurs/grandir/tous les jours   Mes petites sœurs grandissent tous les jours.
7. il/maigrir/si/il/ne/pas/manger/trois fois par jour   Il maigrit s'il ne mange pas trois fois par jour.
8. vous/grandir/quand/vous/manger vos légumes   Vous grandissez quand vous mangez vos légumes.
9. ma sœur/maigrir/facilement/quand/elle/faire de l'aérobic   Ma sœur maigrit facilement quand elle fait de l'aérobic.
10. tu/manger/beaucoup/mais/tu/ne/jamais/grossir   Tu manges beaucoup mais tu ne grossis jamais.

6 Why can't these students wear their clothes anymore? Give the explanation, using the **passé composé** of the verbs in parentheses and the cues provided. (See p. 267.)

EXAMPLE Armelle, ce cardigan ne te va plus. (grandir)   <u>J'ai grandi.</u>

1. Sophie, ce pantalon ne te va plus. (maigrir)   J'ai maigri.
2. Pierre et Jean, ces chemises ne vous vont plus. (grandir)   Nous avons grandi.
3. Valentine, cette robe ne te va plus. (grossir)   J'ai grossi.
4. Ce pantalon ne me va plus. (grandir)   J'ai grandi.
5. Ahmed et Karim, ces vestes ne vous vont plus. (maigrir)   Nous avons maigri.
6. Dis donc, ce blouson ne me va plus. (grossir)   J'ai grossi.

TROISIEME ETAPE

Asking for an opinion; paying a compliment; criticizing; hesitating; making a decision

7 You're shopping with a friend. She is having trouble deciding what to buy and asks for your advice. Respond to each of these statements, replacing the object with **le**, **la**, or **les**. Remember to use commands when necessary. (See p. 273.) Answers may vary.

1. Est-ce que tu aimes cette robe?   Oui, je l'aime bien.
2. Comment tu trouves ce pantalon?   Je le trouve démodé.
3. Je veux acheter cette veste, mais j'hésite.   Prends-la.
4. J'aime bien cette veste mais elle est chère et un peu grande.   Ne la prends pas.
5. Est-ce que tu vas acheter ces chaussures aussi?   Oui, je vais les acheter.

8 Anne is shopping for clothes. Complete her conversations with the salesperson according to the pattern shown in the example. Remember to use the direct object pronouns **le, la, l'**, and **les** in your answers. (See p. 273.)

EXAMPLE	ANNE	Ces bottes vont très bien avec mon manteau. <u>Je peux les essayer?</u>
	VENDEUR	Elles vous vont très bien, mademoiselle! <u>Vous les prenez?</u>
	ANNE	Oui. <u>Je les prends.</u>

1.   ANNE   Ce blouson va très bien avec mon pantalon noir.

                  _____?   Je peux l'essayer?

    VENDEUR   Il vous va très bien, mademoiselle.

                  _____?   Vous le prenez?

        ANNE   Oui. _____.   Je le prends.

2.   ANNE   Ces sandales vont très bien avec ma jupe en jean.

                  _____?   Je peux les essayer?

    VENDEUR   Elles vous vont très bien, mademoiselle.

                  _____?   Vous les prenez?

        ANNE   Euh... J'hésite... Non. _____. Elles sont trop chères.   Je ne les prends pas.

3.   ANNE   Cette robe va très bien avec mes chaussures.

                  _____?   Je peux l'essayer?

    VENDEUR   Elle vous va très bien, mademoiselle.

                  _____?   Vous la prenez?

        ANNE   Elle me plaît beaucoup. Oui. _____.   Je la prends.

4.   ANNE   Ces lunettes de soleil vont très bien avec mon maillot de bain. _____?

    VENDEUR   Elles vous vont très bien, mademoiselle.   Je peux les essayer?

                  _____?   Vous les prenez?

        ANNE   Elles sont super cool. Oui. _____.   Je les prends.

9 Complete Flavien's statements with **il est, elle est,** or **c'est**. (See p. 274.)

1. Comment tu trouves ce chapeau? _____ sensas, non?   Il est

2. Moi, j'aime beaucoup porter un chapeau parce que _____ sympa.   c'est

3. Cédric porte souvent une casquette. _____ en cuir, sa casquette. Très chic!   Elle est

4. Tu aimes les choses en cuir, toi? Moi, non. Je préfère le jean. _____ plus pratique!   C'est

5. Tu dis? Ah, oui. J'adore le look rétro. _____ chouette, le rétro!   C'est

CHAPITRE 11 - VIVE LES VACANCES!

PREMIERE ETAPE

Inquiring about and sharing future plans; expressing indecision; expressing wishes; asking for advice; making, accepting, and refusing suggestions

1 The following sentences state what these people generally do during the summer. Rewrite the sentences in the future using the verb **aller**. (See pp. 154, 288.)

1. Antoine fait du bateau.   Antoine va faire du bateau.

2. Sophie et sa sœur font de la voile.   Sophie et sa sœur vont faire de la voile.

3. Ma famille et moi, nous allons au bord de la mer.   Nous allons aller au bord de la mer.

4. Anne et toi, vous faites de la randonnée.   Vous allez faire de la randonnée.

2 The names of these exchange students begin with the same letter as their countries of origin. Match each of the students with a country listed in the box. Then tell where he or she will be going this summer. (See p. 290.)

> EXAMPLE   Bélinda/le Brésil -> Elle va aller au Brésil.

> 1. Anne/ _____ - _____   l'Australie; Elle va aller en Australie.
> 2. Erin/_____ - _____   les Etats-Unis; Elle va aller aux Etats-Unis.
> 3. Maria/_____ - _____   le Mexique; Elle va aller au Mexique.
> 4. Isabella/_____ - _____   l'Italie; Elle va aller en Italie.
> 5. Céline/ _____ - _____   le Canada; Elle va aller au Canada.

> le Canada   les Etats-Unis
> le Mexique   l'Italie
> le Brésil   l'Australie

3 Jeanne and her friends are asking you for advice. Based on their likes and wishes, write four suggestions, using a location from the box. (See p. 290.)

> la Californie   le Mexique   la Suisse   la France   l'Egypte

> EXAMPLE   J'aime faire de la randonnée! Pourquoi tu ne vas pas en Suisse?

> 1. J'adore les quiches et les croque-monsieur!
> _____   Pourquoi tu ne vas pas en France?
> 2. Nous aimons la plage.
> _____   Pourquoi vous n'allez pas en Californie?
> 3. Je voudrais visiter les pyramides.
> _____   Pourquoi tu ne vas pas en Egypte?
> 4. Nous adorons parler espagnol.
> _____   Pourquoi vous n'allez pas au Mexique?

DEUXIEME ETAPE

Reminding; reassuring; seeing someone off

4 Write six sentences telling when you and your friends usually leave home to go to school, using the verb **partir.** (See p. 294.)

> EXAMPLE   Marianne (8h30) Elle part à huit heures et demie.

> 1. Antoine et moi (6h15)   Nous partons à six heures et quart.
> 2. Et toi, Maryse (7h00)   Tu pars à sept heures.
> 3. Lise et Marie (7h30)   Elles partent à sept heures trente.
> 4. Philippe et toi (8h00)   Vous partez à huit heures.
> 5. Stéphane (8h45)   Il part à neuf heures moins le quart.

ADDITIONAL GRAMMAR PRACTICE

5 Omar and Larissa are getting ready to leave for their grandmother's house. Complete their conversation with the correct forms of the verbs in parentheses. (See p. 294.)

OMAR   Dis, Larissa, tu __1__ (dormir) toujours? dors

LARISSA   Oui. Je __2__ (dormir)! dors

OMAR   Mais c'est pas possible! On __3__ (partir) dans une heure! part

LARISSA   On __4__ (aller) où? va

OMAR   Tu ne te rappelles pas? Nous __5__ (partir) en vacances aujourd'hui! Au bord de la mer! Chez mémé! partons

LARISSA   Ah, mais c'est vrai! J'avais oublié! C'est super! Qu'est-ce que je __6__ (prendre)? Mon maillot de bain? prends

OMAR   Oui. __7__ (prendre) - le! Il __8__ (aller) faire chaud! Et n' __9__ (oublier) pas une robe! On va __10__ (sortir) avec les copains tous les soirs. prends; va ; oublie; sortir

LARISSA   Je __11__ (pouvoir) prendre la valise de maman? peux

OMAR   Oui. Si tu __12__ (vouloir). veux

LARISSA   Dis, Omar, tu, n' __13__ (avoir) pas oublié le cadeau pour mémé? as

OMAR   Mais non. Je n' __14__ (avoir) rien oublié. J' __15__ (avoir) pensé à tout. ai, ai

6 There are some things you and your friends cannot leave without, so your parents are telling you to bring them on vacation. Write what they tell you, using the appropriate object pronoun (**le, la,** or **les**). (See pp. 247, 296.)

EXAMPLE   Je ne peux pas partir sans mon blouson en jean.
<u>Eh bien, prends-le!</u>

1. Je ne peux pas partir sans ma valise! Eh bien, prends-la!
2. Je ne peux pas partir sans mon passeport! Eh bien, prends-le!
3. Nous ne pouvons pas partir sans nos chaussures en cuir! Eh bien, prenez-les!
4. Je ne peux pas partir sans mon appareil-photo! Eh bien, prends-le!
5. Nous ne pouvons pas partir sans nos lunettes de soleil! Eh bien, prenez-les!
6. Je ne peux pas partir sans ma cravate à fleurs. Eh bien, prends-la!

TROISIEME ETAPE

Asking for and expressing opinions; inquiring about and relating past events

7 Combine these fragments into eight complete sentences telling what you and your friends did during your vacation. Remember to put the verb in the **passé composé**. (See pp. 239, 298.)

1. Karim et moi/pièce/voir/une/super/nous   Karim et moi, nous avons vu une pièce super.
2. Tu/de/au bord de/la/faire/mer/voile/la/non?   Tu as fait de la voile au bord de la mer, non?
3. Christelle/jusqu'à midi/dormir   Christelle a dormi jusqu'à midi.
4. Jacques et Simon/la télé/regarder/pendant des heures   Jacques et Simon ont regardé la télé pendant des heures.
5. Jonathan et toi/de/randonnée?/vous/la/faire   Jonathan et toi, vous avez fait de la randonnée?
6. Larissa et moi/des/sensas/lire/romans/nous   Larissa et moi, nous avons lu des romans sensas.
7. Véra et Julie/visiter/le Louvre   Véra et Julie ont visité le Louvre.
8. Moi/à/des/répondre/lettres/je   Moi, j'ai répondu à des lettres.

CHAPITRE 12 - EN VILLE

PREMIERE ETAPE

Pointing out places and things

1 Write five sentences telling where these people are going to go, based on what they need. Use the present tense of **aller** and one word from the box in each sentence. (see pp. 154, 157, 316.)

> la boulangerie   la banque   la papeterie
>
> la poste   l'épicerie   le marché   la pharmacie

EXAMPLE   J'ai besoin de pain. <u>Je vais à la boulangerie.</u>

1. Il me faut des feuilles de papier et des gommes.   Je vais à la papeterie.
2. Tu as besoin de retirer de l'argent.   Tu vas à la banque.
3. Il vous faut des timbres.   Vous allez à la poste.
4. Mme Bonjean a besoin de farine et de beurre.   Elle va à l'épicerie.
5. Pierre et moi, nous avons besoin de médicaments.   Nous allons à la pharmacie.

2 You're asking your friends what they did during the weekend. Write their answers, using the activities in parentheses. Remember to put the verbs in the **passé composé**. (See pp. 239, 317.)

EXAMPLE   Malika, tu as passé un bon week-end? (visiter le fort Saint-Louis)
<u>Oui. J'ai visité le fort Saint-Louis.</u>

1. Lisette, qu'est-ce que tu as fait pendant le week-end? (lire des magazines)
J'...   ai lu des magazines.
2. Cécile et Julien, vous avez passé un bon week-end? (faire de la plongée)
Oui, nous...   avons fait de la plongée.
3. Tu as passé un bon week-end, Martin? (voir un film génial)
Oui, j'...   ai vu un film génial.
4. Romain, tu as passé un bon week-end? (prendre des photos de mes chiens)
Oui, j'...   ai pris des photos de mes chiens.

DEUXIEME ETAPE

Making and responding to requests; asking for advice and making suggestions

3 Rewrite the following sentences, replacing the words indicating a specific amount with the appropriate partitive or indefinite article (**du, de la, de l'**, or **des**). (See pp. 208, 320.)

EXAMPLE   Tu pourrais me rapporter une bouteille de lait?
<u>Tu pourrais me rapporter du lait?</u>

1. Tu me rapportes un kilo de farine, s'il te plaît?   Tu me rapportes de la farine, s'il te plaît?
2. Tu me prends un paquet de beurre, s'il te plaît?   Tu me prends du beurre, s'il te plaît?
3. Tu m'achètes une livre de carottes?   Tu m'achètes des carottes?
4. Rapporte-moi trois tranches de jambon, s'il te plaît!   Rapporte-moi du jambon, s'il te plaît!
5. Tu me rapportes deux bouteilles d'eau minérale?   Tu me rapportes de l'eau minérale?

4 You're asking your friends how they're going to get to their vacation destinations. Write their answers, using the pronoun **y**. (See p. 323.)

EXAMPLE Philippe, comment est-ce que tu vas aux Etats-Unis? (en avion)
J'y vais en avion.

1. Mohamed et Yasmina, comment est-ce que vous allez au bord de la mer? (en train)
Nous... y allons en train.

2. Azzedine, comment tu vas à la campagne? (à vélo)   J'y vais à vélo.

3. Comment est-ce que Fatima va en Angleterre? (en bateau)   Elle y va en bateau.

4. Hannah et Raphaël, comment vous allez à la montagne? (en bus)   On y va en bus.

5. Aziz, comment est-ce que tu vas à Paris? (en voiture)   J'y vais en voiture.

5 Complete the following conversations with **y** and the correct form and tense of the verbs in parentheses. Be careful! Some of the verbs will be in the present tense and some will be in the **passé composé.** (See p. 323.) 1. y vais 2. veux 3. y va 4. as trouvé
5. y ai trouvé 6. as 7. peux 8. ai 9. peux 10. y vais 11. y vas 12. pars

—Salut, Michèle, tu vas à la bibliothèque?

—Oui, je/j' __1__ (y/aller) cet aprèm. J'ai des livres à rendre. Tu __2__ (vouloir) venir?

—Oui, je veux bien. On __3__ (y/aller) à quelle heure?

—Dis, Florence, c'est vrai que tu __4__ (trouver) un billet de cent francs devant la banque?

—Pas tout à fait. Je/j' __5__ (y trouver) une pièce de dix francs.

—Tu __6__ (avoir) de la chance, quand même!

—Tu __7__ (pouvoir) me rendre un service, ma chérie!

—Oui, maman.

—Je/j' __8__ (avoir) besoin de bananes et de citrons. Tu __9__ (pouvoir) aller au marché, s'il te plaît?

—Au marché? C'est loin! Comment est-ce que je/j' __10__ (y/aller)? A pied?

—Mais non. Pourquoi tu ne/n' __11__ (y/aller) pas à vélo?

—Bonne idée. Je __12__ (partir) tout de suite.

TROISIEME ETAPE

Asking for and giving directions

6 Unscramble the following location words. Then combine the fragments to create five sentences telling where the places are located. Use the places in the order in which they are given. (See p. 325.)

EXAMPLE EN CEFA ED/l'école/le café   L'école est en face du café.

1. REDEIRER/la poste/le stade   La poste est derrière le stade.

2. ED TOIRDE A/la pharmacie/la boulangerie   La pharmacie est à droite de la boulangerie.

3. SERP ED/l'épicerie/le cinéma   L'épicerie est près du cinéma.

4. CHUGEA ED A/la pâtisserie/la bibliothèque   La pâtisserie est à gauche de la bibliothèque.

5. ED NOIL/la banque/la papeterie   La banque est loin de la papeterie.

PRONUNCIATION INDEX

CHAPTER	LETTER COMBINATION	IPA SYMBOL	EXAMPLE
Ch. 1, p. 35 Intonation			
Ch. 2, p. 59 Liaison			vous_avez des_amis
Ch. 3, p. 83 The r sound	the letter r	/ʀ/	rouge vert
Ch. 4, p. 113 The sounds [y] and [u]	the letter u the letter combination ou	/y/ /u/	une nous
Ch. 5, p. 141 The nasal sound [ɑ̃]	the letter combination an the letter combination am the letter combination en the letter combination em	/ɑ̃/	anglais jambon comment temps
Ch. 6, p. 167 The vowel sounds [ø] and [œ]	the letter combination eu the letter combination eu	/ø/ /œ/	deux heure
Ch. 7, p. 191 The nasal sounds [ɔ̃], [ɛ̃], and [œ̃]	the letter combination on the letter combination om the letter combination in the letter combination im the letter combination ain the letter combination aim the letter combination (i)en the letter combination un the letter combination um	/ɔ̃/ /ɛ̃/ /œ̃/	pardon nombre cousin impossible copain faim bien lundi humble
Ch. 8, p. 221 The sounds [o] and [ɔ]	the letter combination au the letter combination eau the letter ô the letter o	/o/ /ɔ/	jaune beau rôle carotte
Ch. 9, p. 249 The vowel sounds [e] and [ɛ]	the letter combination ez the letter combination er the letter combination ait the letter combination ais the letter combination ei the letter ê	/e/ /ɛ/	apportez trouver fait français neige bête
Ch. 10, p. 275 The glides [j], [w], and [ɥ]	the letter i the letter combination ill the letter combination oi the letter combination oui the letter combination ui	/j/ /w/ /ɥ/	mieux maillot moi Louis huit
Ch. 11, p. 299 h aspiré, th, ch, and gn	the letter h the letter combination th the letter combination ch the letter combination gn	/'/ /t/ /ʃ/ /ɲ/	les halls théâtre chocolat oignon
Ch. 12, p. 329 Review			

NUMBERS

LES NOMBRES CARDINAUX

0	zéro	20	vingt	80	quatre-vingts
1	un(e)	21	vingt et un(e)	81	quatre-vingt-un(e)
2	deux	22	vingt-deux	82	quatre-vingt-deux
3	trois	23	vingt-trois	90	quatre-vingt-dix
4	quatre	24	vingt-quatre	91	quatre-vingt-onze
5	cinq	25	vingt-cinq	92	quatre-vingt-douze
6	six	26	vingt-six	100	cent
7	sept	27	vingt-sept	101	cent un
8	huit	28	vingt-huit	200	deux cents
9	neuf	29	vingt-neuf	300	trois cents
10	dix	30	trente	800	huit cents
11	onze	31	trente et un(e)	900	neuf cents
12	douze	32	trente-deux	1.000	mille
13	treize	40	quarante	2.000	deux mille
14	quatorze	50	cinquante	3.000	trois mille
15	quinze	60	soixante	10.000	dix mille
16	seize	70	soixante-dix	19.000	dix-neuf mille
17	dix-sept	71	soixante et onze	40.000	quarante mille
18	dix-huit	72	soixante-douze	500.000	cinq cent mille
19	dix-neuf	73	soixante-treize	1.000.000	un million

- The word **et** is used only in 21, 31, 41, 51, 61, and 71.
- **Vingt (trente, quarante,** and so on) **et une** is used when the number refers to a feminine noun: **trente et une cassettes.**
- The **s** is dropped from **quatre-vingts** and is not added to multiples of **cent** when these numbers are followed by another number: **quatre-vingt-cinq; deux cents,** *but* **deux cent six.** The number **mille** never takes an **s: deux mille insectes.**
- **Un million** is followed by **de** + a noun: **un million de francs.**
- In writing numbers, a period is used in French where a comma is used in English.

LES NOMBRES ORDINAUX

1er, 1ère	premier, première	9e	neuvième	17e	dix-septième
2e	deuxième	10e	dixième	18e	dix-huitième
3e	troisième	11e	onzième	19e	dix-neuvième
4e	quatrième	12e	douzième	20e	vingtième
5e	cinquième	13e	treizième	21e	vingt et unième
6e	sixième	14e	quatorzième	22e	vingt-deuxième
7e	septième	15e	quinzième	30e	trentième
8e	huitième	16e	seizième	40e	quarantième

FRENCH-ENGLISH VOCABULARY

This list includes both active and passive vocabulary in this textbook. Active words and phrases are those listed in the **Vocabulaire** section at the end of each chapter. You are expected to know and be able to use active vocabulary. All entries in heavy black type in this list are active. All other words are passive. Passive vocabulary is for recognition only.

The number after each entry refers to the chapter where the word or phrase is introduced. Nouns are always given with an article. If it is not clear whether the noun is masculine or feminine, *m.* (masculine) or *f.* (feminine) follows the noun. Some nouns that are generally seen only in the plural, as well as irregular plurals, are also given with gender indications and the abbreviation *pl.* (plural) following them. An asterisk (*) before a word beginning with *h* indicates an aspirate *h*. Phrases are alphabetized by the key word(s) in the phrase.

The following abbreviations are also used in this vocabulary: *pp.* (past participle), *inv.* (invariable), and *adj.* (adjective).

A

à *to, in (a city or place)*, 11; **à côté de** *next to*, 12; **à la** *to, at*, 6; **A bientôt.** *See you soon.* 1; à carreaux *checked*, 10; **A demain.** *See you tomorrow.* 1; à fleurs *flowered*, 10; à la carte *pick and choose*, 3; à la française *French-style*, 1; **à la mode** *in style*, 10; à part ça *aside from that*, 11; à pois *polka dot*, 10; **A quelle heure?** *At what time?* 6; à rayures *striped*, 10; **A tout à l'heure!** *See you later!* 1; **A votre service.** *At your service; You're welcome.* 3; Et maintenant, à toi. *And now, it's your turn*, 1

l' abbaye (f.) *abbey*, 6
abîmer *to ruin*, 10
s' abonner *to subscribe*; abonnez-vous à... *subscribe to . . .* , 3
l' abricot (m.) *apricot*, 5
abriter *to house*, 11
absent(e) *absent*, 2
accompagner *to accompany*, 4
l' accueil (m.) *reception, welcome*, 4
accueille (accueillir) *to welcome*
acheter *to buy*, 9; **Achète (-moi)...** *Buy (me) . . .* , 8; Je n'achète pas... *I don't buy / I'm not buying . . .* , 3
l' acra de morue (m.) *cod fritter*
l' activité (f.) *activity*, 4
l' addition (f.) *check, bill*, 5; **L'addition, s'il vous plaît.** *The check, please.* 5

adorer *to adore*, 1; **J'adore...** *I adore . . .* 1; J'adorerais... *I would adore . . .* , 1
l' **aérobic** (f.) *aerobics*, 4; **faire de l'aérobic** *to do aerobics*, 4
affectueux (-euse) *affectionate*, 7
afin de *in order to*, 7
l' **âge** (m.) *age*, 1; **Tu as quel âge?** *How old are you?* 1
âgé(e) *older*, 7
l' agenda (m.) *planner*, 4
agit : il s'agit de *it's concerned with; it's about*, 6
agréable *pleasant*, 4
ai : J'ai... *I have . . .* , 2; **J'ai... ans.** *I am . . . years old.* 1; **J'ai besoin de...** *I need . . .* , 8; **J'ai faim.** *I'm hungry.* 5; **J'ai l'intention de...** *I intend to . . .* , 11; **J'ai soif.** *I'm thirsty.* 5; Je n'ai pas de... *I don't have . . .* , 3
aider *to help*, 10; (Est-ce que) je peux vous aider? *May I help you?* 10
l' ail (m.) *garlic*, 8
les ailes (f.) *wings*, 12
aimé(e) (pp. of aimer) *loved*, 1
aimer *to like*, 1; **J'aime mieux...** *I prefer . . .* , 1; **J'aimerais... pour aller avec...** *I'd like . . . to go with . . .* , 10; **Je n'aime pas...** *I don't like . . .* , 1; **Moi, j'aime (bien)...** *I (really) like . . .* 1; **Tu aimes... ?** *Do you like . . . ?* 1
l' aire de pique-nique aménagée (f.) *equipped picnic area*, 6
l' aise (f.) *ease*, 7
ajouter *to add*, 10

l' algèbre (f.) *algebra*, 2
l' Algérie (f.) *Algeria*, 0
l' alimentation (f.) *food*, 12
les aliments (m.) *nutrients*, 8
allé(e) (pp. of aller) *went*, 9; **Je suis allé(e)...** *I went . . .* , 9; **Tu es allé(e) où?** *Where did you go?* 9
l' **allemand** (m.) *German (language)*, 2
aller *to go*, 6; Ça va aller mieux! *It's going to get better!* 9; **On peut y aller...** *We can go there . . .* , 12
allez : Allez au tableau! *Go to the blackboard!* 0; Allez, viens! *Come along!* 0
Allô? *Hello?* 9
l' allocation de naissance (f.) *money provided as a birth allowance by the French government*, 7; l'allocation familiale (f.) *money provided by the French government to large families*, 7
allons : Allons-y! *Let's go!* 4; **Allons...** *Let's go . . .* , 6
l' aloco (m.) *dish from West Africa made from fried plantain bananas and usually eaten as a snack*, 5
alors *well, then*, 3
l' alphabet (m.) *alphabet*, 0
l' ambiance (f.) *atmosphere*, 2
aménagé(e) *equipped*, 6
américain(e) *American* (adj.), 0
l' **ami(e)** *friend*, 1
amical(e) (pl. amicaux) *friendly*, 2
amicalement *sincerely (to close a letter)*, 1
l' amitié (f.) *friendship*, 1

l' amour (m.) *love*, 1
amusant(e) *funny*, 7
s' amuser *to have fun*, 11; Amuse-
toi bien! *Have fun!* 11;
Qu'est-ce que tu fais pour t'a-
muser? *What do you do to
have fun?* 4; Tu t'es bien
amusé(e)? *Did you have fun?*
11
l' an (m.) *year*, 1; J'ai... ans. *I
am . . . years old.* 1
l' ananas (m.) *pineapple*, 8
ancien(ne) *old; former*, 6; l'ancienne gare *the former train
station*, 6
l' Andorre (article not commonly
used) *Andorra*, 0
l' anglais (m.) *English (language)*, 1
l' animal (m.) *animal*, 1
l' animateur (m.) *camp counselor*,
11
les animations (f.) *activities*, 11
l' année (f.) *year*, 4
l' année scolaire (f.) *school year*, 2
l' anniversaire (m.) *anniversary;
birthday*, 7
les annonces (f.) *ads*, 1; les petites
annonces *personal or business
ads*, 1
anthracite *charcoal grey*, 10
antique *ancient*, 9
les antiquités (f.) *antiquities,
antiques*, 6
août *August*, 4; en août *in
August*, 4
l' appareil (m.) *phone*, 9; Qui est
à l'appareil? *Who's calling?* 9
l' appareil-photo (m.) *camera*, 11
appartient (appartenir) à *to
belong to*, 9
s' appeler *to call oneself, to be
called*, 1; Il/Elle s'appelle comment? *What's his/her name?*
1; Il/Elle s'appelle... *His/Her
name is . . .* , 1; Je m'appelle...
My name is . . . , 1; Tu t'appelles comment? *What's
your name?* 1
apporter *to bring*, 9;
Apportez-moi... , s'il vous
plaît. *Please bring me . . .* , 5
apprendre *to learn*, 0
l' aprèm (m.) *afternoon*, 2; cet
aprèm *this afternoon*, 2
après-guerre *post-war*, 11
l' après-midi (m.) *afternoon; in
the afternoon*, 2; l'après-midi
libre *afternoon off*, 2
après *after, afterward*, 9; Et
après? *And afterwards?* 9
l' arabe (m.) *Arabic (language)*,
1

l' ardoise (f.) *writing slate*, 3
l' arène (f.) *amphitheater*, 9
l' argent (m.) *money*, 11
l' arrivée (f.) *arrival*, 6
arroser *to sprinkle*, 8
l' artiste (m./f.) *artist*, 0
les arts plastiques (m. pl.) *art
class*, 2
as : Tu as... ? *Do you have . . . ?*
3; Tu as quel âge? *How old
are you?* 1; De quoi est-ce que
tu as besoin? *What do you
need?* 8
l' ascenseur (m.) *elevator*, 6
l' ascension (f.) *ascent, climb*, 6;
ascension en haut de la tour
*ascent/climb to the top of the
tower*, 6
l' aspirateur (m.) *vacuum cleaner*,
7; passer l'aspirateur *to vacuum*, 7
l' aspirine (f.) *aspirin*, 12
Asseyez : Asseyez-vous! *Sit
down!* 0
assez *enough, fairly*, 2
assidu(e) *regular (punctual)*, 2
l' assiette (f.) *plate*, 5
assuré(e) (pp. of assurer)
assured, 1
l' athlétisme (m.) *track and field*,
4; faire de l'athlétisme *to do
track and field*, 4
attachant(e) *loving*, 7
attendre *to wait for*, 9
l' attiéké (m.) *ground manioc
root*, 8
au *to, at*, 6; *to, in (before a
masculine noun)*, 11; au
métro... *at the metro stop*, 6;
au milieu *in the middle*, 7; au
revoir *goodbye*, 1; au secours
help, 9
l' auberge de jeunesse (f.) *youth
hostel*, 11
aucun(e) *none*, 7
aujourd'hui *today*, 2
aussi *also*, 1; Moi aussi. *Me
too.* 2
l' automne (m.) *autumn, fall*, 4;
en automne *in the fall*, 4
autour de *around*, 8
autre *other*, 4
aux *to, in (before a plural
noun)*, 6
Av. (abbrev. of avenue) *avenue*, 6
avant *before*, 1
avec *with*, 1; avec moi *with
me*, 6; Avec qui? *With
whom?* 6
avez : Qu'est-ce que vous avez
comme ... ? *What kind of . . .
do you have?* 5; Vous avez... ?
Do you have . . . ? 2

l' avion (m.) *plane*, 12; en avion
by plane, 12, un billet d'avion
plane ticket, 11
l' avis (m.) *opinion*, 9; A ton
avis, qu'est-ce que je fais?
In your opinion, what do I do?
9
l' avocat (m.) *avocado*, 8
avoir *to have*, 2; avoir faim *to
be hungry*, 5; avoir hâte de *to
be in a hurry (to do something)*,
7; avoir la flemme *to be lazy*,
9; avoir lieu *to take place*, 7;
avoir raison *to be right*, 2;
avoir soif *to be thirsty*, 5
avons : Nous avons... *We have
. . .* , 2
avril *April*, 4; en avril *in
April*, 4
ayant : ayant pu donner *having been able to give*, 2

B

le baby (foot) *table soccer game*, 5
le bac(calauréat) *secondary school
exam for entering a university*,
2
le bachelier *someone who has
passed the bac*, 2
la baguette *long, thin loaf of
bread*, 12
la baie *bay*
se balader *to stroll*, 6
la balade à cheval *horseback ride*,
7
le ballon *ball*, 4
le bambou *bamboo*, 12
la banane *banana*, 8
les bandes dessinées (f.) *comic
strips*, 2
la banque *bank*, 12
barbant(e) *boring*, 2
le base-ball *baseball*, 4; jouer au
base-ball *to play baseball*, 4
le basilic *basil*, 5
le basket(-ball) *basketball*, 4;
jouer au basket(-ball) *to
play basketball*, 4
les baskets (f.) *sneakers*, 3
le bateau *boat*, 11; en bateau *by
boat*, 12; faire du bateau *to
go boating*, 11
le bâteau-mouche *river boat*, 6
Bd (abbrev. of boulevard) (m.)
boulevard, 6
le beau-père *stepfather; father-in-
law*, 7
beau *nice, pretty*, 4; Il fait
beau. *It's nice weather.* 4
Beaucoup. *A lot.* 4; Oui, beaucoup. *Yes, very much.* 2; Pas
beaucoup. *Not very much.* 4

belge *Belgian* (adj.), 1
la Belgique *Belgium*, 0
la belle-mère *stepmother; mother-in-law*, 7
le besoin *need*, 8; **De quoi est-ce que tu as besoin?** *What do you need?* 8; **J'ai besoin de...** *I need . . . ,* 8
la bête *animal*, 12
le beurre *butter*, 8
la bibliothèque *library*, 6
le bic *ballpoint pen*, 3
bien *well*, 1; **Je veux bien.** *Gladly.* 8; **Je veux bien.** *I'd really like to.* 6; **J'en veux bien.** *I'd like some.* 8; **Moi, j'aime (bien)...** *I (really) like . . . ,* 1; **Très bien.** *Very well.* 1
Bien sûr. *Of course.* 3; *certainly,* 9; **Oui, bien sûr.** *Yes, of course.* 7
bientôt *soon*, 1; **À bientôt.** *See you soon.* 1
le bien-vivre *good living, the good life,* 6
Bienvenue! *Welcome!* 0
le bifteck *steak*, 8
les bijoux (m.) *jewelry*, 10
le billet *ticket*, 11; **un billet d'avion** *plane ticket*, 11; **un billet de train** *train ticket*, 11
la biologie *biology*, 2
bizarre *strange*, 7
blanc(he) *white*, 3
le blanc-manger *coconut pudding*
bleu(e) *blue*, 3; le bleu clair *light blue*, 10; le bleu foncé *dark blue*, 10
blond(e) *blond*, 7
le blouson *jacket*, 10
le bœuf *beef*, 8
Bof! *(expression of indifference),* 1
boire *to drink*, 5; **Qu'est-ce qu'il y a à boire?** *What is there to drink?* 5
la boisson *drink, beverage*, 5; **Qu'est-ce que vous avez comme boissons?** *What do you have to drink?* 5
la boîte *box, can*, 8; **une boîte de** *a can of,* 8
le bon *coupon*, 6
bon *good*, 5; **Bon courage!** *Good luck!* 2; **Bon voyage!** *Have a good trip!* 11; **Bon, d'accord.** *Well, OK.* 8; de bons conseils *good advice*, 1; **Oui, très bon.** *Yes, very good.* 9; **pas bon** *not good*, 5
Bonjour *Hello*, 1
bonne (f. of **bon**) *good,* 5;

Bonne chance! *Good luck!* 11; **Bonne idée.** *Good idea.* 4; **Bonnes vacances!** *Have a good vacation!* 11
le bord *side, edge;* **au bord de la mer** *to/on the coast,* 11
les **bottes** (f.) *boots*, 10
les **boucles d'oreilles** (f.) *earrings,* 10
le boudin créole *spicy creole sausage,* 12
bouger *to move,* 10
bouillant(e) *boiling,* 8
la boulangerie *bakery,* 12
la boule *ball,* 8
la boum *party,* 6; **aller à une boum** *to go to a party,* 6
la bouteille *bottle,* 8; **une bouteille de** *a bottle of,* 8
la boutique *store, shop,* 3; une boutique de souvenirs *souvenir shop,* 3
le bracelet *bracelet,* 3
la brioche *brioche, light slightly sweet bread made with a rich yeast dough,* 8
la brochure *brochure,* 4
la broderie *embroidery,* 10
brun(e) *brunette,* 7
le bulletin trimestriel *report card,* 2
le bus *bus,* 12; **en bus** *by bus,* 12, **rater le bus** *to miss the bus,* 9
la buvette *refreshment stand,* 12

C'est... *It's . . . ,* 2; **C'est... *This is . . . ,* 7; **C'est qui?** *Who is it?* 2; **C'est combien?** *How much is it?* 3; C'est du gâteau. *It's a piece of cake.* 8; **C'est... francs.** *It's . . . francs.* 5; C'est pas de la tarte. *It's not easy.* 8; C'est tout. *That's all.* 1; **Ça, c'est...** *This/That is . . . ,* 12; **Non, c'est impossible.** *No, that's impossible.* 7
C'était barbant! *It was boring!* 11
ça *that; it;* Ça boume? *How's it going?* 2; Ça va. *Fine.* 1; Ça va? *How are things going?* 1; Ça, c'est... *This/That is . . . ,* 12; Ça m'est égal *It doesn't matter; I don't care.* 10; Ça ne me dit rien. *That doesn't interest me.* 4; *I don't feel like it.* 6; ça suffit *that's enough,* 12; Et après ça... *And after that,. . . ,* 9; Oui, ça a été. *Yes, it was fine.* 9

ça fait : Ça fait combien, s'il vous plaît? *How much is it, please?* 5; Ça fait... francs. *It's . . . francs.* 5
le cabinet de toilette *small room with a sink and counter,* 11
caché(e) (pp. of cacher) *hidden,* 11
le cadeau *gift,* 11
le café *coffee, café,* 5; le café au lait *coffee with hot milk,* 8; le café crème *coffee with cream,* 5
le cahier *notebook,* 0
la calculatrice *calculator,* 3; une calculatrice-traductrice *translating calculator,* 3
le caleçon *leggings,* 4
la Californie *California,* 4
le caméscope *camcorder,* 4
la campagne *countryside,* 11; **à la campagne** *to/in the countryside,* 11
le camping *camping,* 11; **faire du camping** *to go camping,* 11
le canal *channel,* 3
le canari *canary,* 7
le caniveau *sidewalk gutter,* 7
la cantine *cafeteria,* 9; **à la cantine** *at the school cafeteria,* 9
car *because,* 4
la carcasse *body,* 12
le cardigan *sweater,* 10
la carrière *quarry,* 11
la carotte *carrot,* 8
la carte *map,* 0; à la carte *pick and choose,* 3; **La carte, s'il vous plaît.** *The menu, please.* 5
les **cartes** (f.) *cards,* 4; **jouer aux cartes** *to play cards,* 4
la cartouche *cartridge,* 3; cartouche d'encre *ink cartridge,* 3
le carvi *cumin* (Afrique), 8; graines de carvi *cumin seeds,* 8
la casquette *cap,* 10
la cassette *cassette tape,* 3
la cassette vidéo *videocassette,* 4
la cathédrale *cathedral,* 1
le cauchemar *nightmare,* 11; **C'était un véritable cauchemar!** *It was a real nightmare!* 11
ce *this; that,* 3; **Ce sont...** *These/Those are . . . ,* 7
la ceinture *belt,* 10
cent *one hundred,* 3; **deux cents** *two hundred,* 3
le centre commercial *mall,* 6
le centre-ville *city center,* 12
cependant *however,* 11
le cercle *circle, group,* 6; au cercle

français *at French Club,* 4
ces *these, those,* 3
cet *this, that,* 3
cette *this; that,* 3
chacun *each (person),* 5;
  Chacun ses goûts! *To each his
  own!* 1
la **chaise** *chair,* 0
  chaleureux (-euse) *warm,* 9
la **chambre** *room,* 7; **ranger ta
  chambre** *to pick up your
  room,* 7
le **champignon** *mushroom,* 8
la **chance** *luck,* 11; **Bonne
  chance!** *Good luck!* 11
  chanter *to sing,* 9
le **chanteur** *singer (male),* 9
la **chanteuse** *singer (female),* 9
  Chantilly : la crème Chantilly
  sweetened whipped cream, 5
le **chapeau** *hat,* 10
  chaque *each,* 4
  chargé(e) *busy,* 2
le **chariot** *shopping cart,* 8
la **chasse** *hunting,* 7; une chasse
  au trésor *treasure hunt,* 3
le **chat** *cat,* 7
le **chaton** *kitten,* 7
  chaud *hot,* 4; **Il fait chaud.**
  It's hot. 4
  chauffé(e) *heated,* 11
les **chaussettes** (f.) *socks,* 10
les **chaussures** (f.) *shoes,* 10; les
  chaussures à crampons
  spikes, 4
le **chef-d'œuvre** *masterpiece,* 6
la **chemise** *shirt (man's),* 10
la chemise *folder,* 3
le **chemisier** *shirt (woman's),* 10
le **chèque** *check,* 0
  cher (chère) *dear,* 1; *expensive,* 3; **C'est trop cher.** *It's
  too expensive.* 10
  chercher *to look for,* 9; **Je
  cherche quelque chose pour...**
  *I'm looking for something
  for . . . ,* 10
le **cheval** *horse,* 12; le cheval de
  bois *wooden horse, carousel
  horse,* 12
  chez... *to/at . . . 's house,* 6;
  chez le disquaire *at the
  record store,* 12; **Je suis bien
  chez...** ? *Is this . . . 's house?*
  9
  chic *chic,* 10
le **chien** *dog,* 7; **promener le
  chien** *to walk the dog,* 7
le **chiffre** *number,* 0
la **chimie** *chemistry,* 2
  chimique *chemical,* 9
le **chocolat** *chocolate,* 1; **un
  chocolat** *hot chocolate,* 5

la chocolaterie *chocolate shop,* 12
  choisi (pp. of choisir) *decided,
  chosen;* **Vous avez choisi?**
  Have you decided/chosen? 5
  choisir *to choose, to pick,* 10
le **choix** *choice,* 8
la **chorale** *choir,* 2
la **chose** *thing,* 5; **J'ai des tas de
  choses (trucs) à faire.** *I have
  lots of things to do.* 5
le **chou** *cabbage,* 1; mon chou *my
  darling, dear,* 1
  chouette *cool,* 9; **Très chouette.**
  Very cool. 9
  chrétien(ne) *Christian,* 9
le **cinéma** *movie theater,* 6;
  movies, 1
le **citron** *lemon,* 8
le **citron pressé** *lemonade,* 5
  clair(e) *light (color),* 10
le **classeur** *loose-leaf binder,* 3
  classique *classical,* 4
le climat *climate,* 11
  climatisé(e) *air-conditioned,* 11
le **coca** *cola,* 5
le **coco** *coconut,* 8
le **code de la route** *rules of
  the road; rules of the road
  test,* 12
le **coin** *corner,* 12; **au coin de** *on
  the corner of,* 12
le **col** *collar,* 10; au col montant
  with turtleneck, 10
le **collant** *hose,* 10
la **colle** *glue,* 3; un pot de colle
  container of glue, 3
le **collège** *junior high school,* 2
la **colonie de vacances** *summer
  camp,* 11
le **coloris** *color, shade,* 3
  combien *how much, how many,*
  3; **C'est combien,... ?** *How
  much is . . . ?* 5; **C'est combien?** *How much is it?* 3; **Ça
  fait combien, s'il vous plaît?**
  How much is it, please? 5
le **combiné** *(telephone) receiver,* 9
  comme *like, as,* 4; **Comme ci,
  comme ça.** *So-so.* 1; Qu'est-ce
  qu'ils aiment comme cours?
  What subjects do they like? 2;
  **Qu'est-ce que tu fais comme
  sport?** *What sports do you
  play?* 4; **Qu'est-ce que vous
  avez comme... ?** *What kind of
  . . . do you have?* 5
le commencement *beginning,* 9
  commencer *to begin, to start,* 9
  comment *what,* 0; *how,* 1;
  (Comment) ça va? *How's it
  going?* 1; Comment dit-on?
  How do you say it? 1;
  Comment le dire? *How should*

you say it? 1; **Comment tu
trouves... ?** *What do you
think of . . . ?* 2; **Comment tu
trouves ça?** *What do you
think of that/it?* 2; **Il/Elle est
comment?** *What is he/she
like?* 7; **Ils/Elles sont comment?** *What are they like?* 7;
Tu t'appelles comment?
What is your name? 0
le **commerçant** *store owner,* 8
le **compagnon** *companion,* 7
le **compas** *compass,* 3
  compétent(e) *competent,* 2
  compléter *to complete,* 4
  compris *included,* 5
  compris (pp. of comprendre): Tu
  as compris? *Did you understand?* 1
le **concert** *concert,* 1
le **concombre** *cucumber,* 8
  conçu(e) (pp. of concevoir) *con-
  ceived,* 9
  confier *to confide,* 9
la **confiture** *jam,* 8
  connais : Tu les connais? *Do you
  know them?* 0
la **connaissance** *acquaintance;*
  Faisons connaissance! *Let's
  get acquainted.* 1
  connu(e) (pp. of connaître)
  knew; known; le plus connu
  the best-known (adj.), 6
le **conseil** *advice,* 1; de bons
  conseils *good advice,* 1
  conseiller *to advise, to counsel;*
  **Qu'est-ce que tu me con-
  seilles?** *What do you advise
  me to do?* 9
le **conseiller** *adviser,* 12
la **conseillère** *adviser,* 12
  conservé(e) (pp. of conserver)
  kept, 2; ce bulletin doit être
  conservé *this report card must
  be kept,* 2
  content(e) *happy, pleased,* 7
  continuer *to continue,* 12; **Vous
  continuez jusqu'au prochain
  feu rouge.** *You keep going
  until the next light.* 12
  contre *against,* 2
  cool *cool,* 2
le **copain** (la copine) *friend,* 1
le **cordon** *cord, string;* le cordon de
  serrage *drawstring,* 10
le **cornichon** *pickle,* 8
le **corps** *body,* 8
le **correspondant** (la correspon-
  dante) *pen pal,* 1
  correspondre *to write; to correspond,* 1
le **côté** *side;* **à côté de** *next to,*
  12; du côté de mon père *on*

FRENCH-ENGLISH VOCABULARY

my father's side (of the family), 7
le coton *cotton*, 10; **en coton** *(made of) cotton*, 10
la couleur *color*, 3; **De quelle couleur est... ?** *What color is . . . ?* 3
le coup *hit, blow;* **le coup de fil** *phone call*, 9
la coupe *dish(ful)*, 5
la coupe melba *vanilla ice cream, peaches, whipped cream, and fruit sauce*, 5
courir *to run*, 7
le cours *course*, 2; **le cours de développement personnel et social (DPS)** *health*, 2; **Tu as quels cours... ?** *What classes do you have . . . ?* 2
les courses (f.) *shopping, errands*, 7; **faire les courses** *to do the shopping*, 7; **J'ai des courses à faire.** *I have errands to do.* 5
court(e) *short (length)*, 10
le cousin *male cousin*, 7
la cousine *female cousin*, 7
coûteux (-euse) *expensive*, 8
les crabes farcis (m.) *deviled land crabs*
la cravate *tie*, 10
le crayon *pencil*, 3; **des crayons de couleur** *colored pencils*, 3
créer *to create*, 11
la crêpe *very thin pancake*, 5
la crêperie *café or restaurant which specializes in crêpes*, 5
crépiter *to crackle*, 12
croire *to believe;* **Tu crois?** *Do you think so?* 10
la croisière *cruise*, 11
la croissanterie *croissant shop*, 12
le croque-monsieur *toasted cheese and ham sandwich*, 5
cru(e) *uncooked*, 5
le cuir *leather*, 10; **en cuir** *(made of) leather*, 10
cuire *to cook, to bake*, 8
culturel(le) *cultural*, 0

D

D'abord, ... *First, . . . ,* 9
D'accord. *OK.* 4; **Bon, d'accord.** *Well, OK.* 8; **D'accord, si tu... d'abord...** *OK, if you. . . , first.* 7; **Tu es d'accord?** *Is that OK with you?* 7
d'habitude *usually*, 4
dans *in*, 6
danser *to dance*, 1
la danse *dance*, 2
de *from*, 0; *of*, 0; **de l'** *some*, 8; **de la** *some*, 8; **Je n'ai pas**

de... *I don't have . . . ,* 3; **Je ne fais pas de...** *I don't play/do . . . ,* 4
déambuler *to stroll*, 11
débarrasser la table *to clear the table*, 7
décaféiné(e) *decaffeinated*, 5
décédé(e) *deceased*, 7
décembre *December*, 4; **en décembre** *in December*, 4
le décès *death*, 7
décider *to decide*, 5; **Vous avez décidé de prendre... ?** *Have you decided to take . . . ?* 10
décontracté(e) *relaxed*, 11
la découverte *discovery*, 3
décrocher *to take down; to unhook;* **quand l'interlocuteur décroche** *when the speaker picks up (the phone)*, 9
dedans *inside*, 3
dégoûtant(e) *gross*, 5
dehors *outside*, 8
déjà *already*, 9
déjeuner *to have lunch*, 9; **le déjeuner** *lunch*, 2
délicieux (-euse) *delicious*, 5
délirer *to be delirious;* **La techno me fait délirer.** *I'm wild about technology.* 1
délivré(e) (pp. of delivrer) : **il n'en sera pas délivré de duplicata** *duplicates will not be issued*, 2
le deltaplane *hang-glider;* **faire du deltaplane** *to go hang-gliding*, 4
demain *tomorrow*, 2; **A demain.** *See you tomorrow.* 1
le demi-frère *stepbrother*, 7; *half-brother*, 7
la demi-sœur *stepsister*, 7; *half-sister*, 7
demi(e) *half;* **et demi** *half past (after **midi** and **minuit**)*, 6; **et demie** *half past*, 6
démodé(e) *out of style*, 10
le dentiste (la dentiste) *dentist*, 1
le départ *departure*, 6
le département d'outre-mer *overseas department*, 12
dépêchez : Dépêchez-vous de... *hurry up and . . . ,* 1
déplorable *deplorable*, 2
déposer *to deposit*, 12
deprimé(e) *depressed*, 9
depuis *for (a certain amount of time)*, 9; *since*, 12
le dérivé *derivative, by-product;* **le sucre et ses dérivés** *sugar and its by-products*, 8
derrière *behind*, 12
des *some*, 3
les dés (m.) *dice;* **découper en dés**

to dice, 8
dès que *as soon as*, 9
désagréable *unpleasant*, 4
désirer *to desire, to want;* **Vous désirez?** *What would you like?* 10
désolé(e) : Désolé(e), je suis occupé(e). *Sorry, I'm busy.* 6; **Désolé(e), mais je ne peux pas.** *Sorry, but I can't.* 4
le dessert *dessert*, 0
le dessin *drawing*, 3
détailler *to slice*, 8
devant *in front of*, 6
deviennent : Que deviennent... ? *What happened to . . . ?* 7
Devine! *Guess!* 0
les devoirs (m.) *homework*, 2; **J'ai des devoirs à faire.** *I've got homework to do.* 5
le dévouement *devotion*, 7
devrais : Tu devrais... *You should . . . ,* 9
la diapo (sitive) *photographic slide*, 11
la dictée *dictation*, 0
le dictionnaire *dictionary*, 3
difficile *difficult*, 2
dimanche *Sunday*, 2; **le dimanche** *on Sundays*, 2
dîner *to have dinner*, 9; **le dîner** *dinner*, 8
dingue *crazy*, 1; **Je suis dingue de...** *I'm crazy about . . . ,* 1
dire *to say;* 1; *to tell*, 9; **Comment le dire?** *How should you say it?* 1; **Dis,...** *Say, . . . ,* 2; **Ça ne me dit rien.** *That doesn't interest me.* 4; **Comment dit-on... ?** *How do you say . . . ?* 1; **Jacques a dit...** *Simon says . . . ,* 0; **Qu'est-ce qu'on se dit?** *What are they saying to themselves?* 2; **Vous pouvez lui dire que j'ai téléphoné?** *Can you tell her/him that I called?* 9
direct(e) *direct;* **en direct** *live*, 7
la discothèque *dance club*, 6
discuter *to discuss*, 7; **Ne discute pas!** *Don't argue!* 3
disponible *available*, 8
le disquaire *record store*, 12; **chez le disquaire** *at the record store*, 12
le disque compact/CD *compact disc/CD*, 3
distant(e) *distant*, 2
la distribution *cast (of a movie, play, etc.)*, 1; **une distribution étincelante** *a brilliant cast*, 1
divers *various*, 3
dois : Non, tu dois... *No, you've*

got to . . . , 7

le **domicile** *place of residence*, 4
dommage *too bad*, 10
donc *so, therefore*, 11
donner *to give*, 5; **Donnez-moi... , s'il vous plaît.** *Please give me . . .* , 5
donner sur *to overlook*, 11
dont *of which*, 7
dormir *to sleep*, 1
le **dos** *back*, 12; **un sac à dos** *backpack*, 3
doucement *gently*, 12
la **douche** *shower*, 11; **avec douche ou bains** *with shower or bath*, 11
doué(e) *gifted, talented*, 2
la **douzaine** *dozen*, 8; **une douzaine de** *a dozen*, 8
les **draps** (m.) *linens, sheets*, 11
dressé(e) *pointed*, 7
droit(e) *straight*, 10
la **droite** *right (direction)*; **à droite (de)** *to the right*, 12
du *some*, 8
le **duplicata** (inv.) *duplicate*; il n'en sera pas délivré de duplicata *duplicates will not be issued*, 2
durable *long-lasting*, 11
durcir *to harden*, 8
la **durée** *duration*, 7
durer *to last*, 11

E

l' **eau** (f.) *water*, 5; **l'eau minérale** *mineral water*, 5; **le sirop de fraise (à l'eau)** *water with strawberry syrup*, 5
s' **ébattre** *to frolic*, 7
l' **échange** (m.) *exchange*, 7; **en échange de** *in exchange for*, 7
l' **échantillon** (m.) *sample*, 2
l' **écharpe** (f.) *scarf*, 10
l' **échelle** (f.) *scale*, 6
s' **éclater** *to have fun, to have a ball*, 4
l' **école** (f.) *school*, 1; **A l'école** *At school*, 0
l' **économie** (f.) *economics*, 2
écouter *to listen*, 1; Ecoute! *Listen!* 0; **écouter de la musique** *to listen to music*, 1; **Ecoutez!** *Listen!* 0; **Je t'écoute.** *I'm listening.* 9
l' **écran** (m.) *screen*, 11
l' **écrin** (m.) *case*, 6
écrire *to write*, 2; Ecris-moi. *Write me.* 1
l' **édifice** (m.) *edifice, building*, 6
l' **éducation physique et sportive (EPS)** (f.) *physical education*, 2; **l'éducation civique et morale**

(f.) *civics class*, 2
efficace *efficient*, 9
égrener *to shell*, 8
égyptien(ne) *Egyptian* (adj.), 6
Eh bien... *Umm . . . (expression of hesitation)*, 5
élastique *elastic* (adj.), 3
élémentaire *elementary; basic*, 8
l' **éléphant** (m.) *elephant*, 0
l' **élève** (m./f.) *student*, 2
l' **emballage** (m.) *packaging*, 9
embêtant(e) *annoying*, 7
émincer *to slice thinly*, 8
l' **émission** (f.) *TV program*, 4
empêche (empêcher) *to prevent, to keep from doing*, 2
l' **emploi** *use; job*; un emploi du temps *schedule*, 2
emprunter *to borrow*, 12
en *in*, 1; **en** *some, of it, of them, any, none*, 8; **en** *to, in (before a feminine country)*, 11; **en coton** *(made of) cotton*, 10; **en cuir** *(made of) leather*, 10; en français *in French*, 1; **en jean** *(made of) denim*, 10; en retard *late*, 2; en solde *on sale*, 10; **en vacances** *on vacation*, 4; Je n'en veux plus. *I don't want anymore*, 8; **Oui, j'en veux bien.** *Yes, I'd like some.* 8; Qu'en penses-tu? *What do you think (about it)?* 1; **Vous avez ça en... ?** *Do you have that in . . . ? (size, fabric, color)*, 10
encore *again, more*; **Encore de... ?** *More. . . ?* 8
l' **endroit** (m.) *place*, 12
énerver *to annoy*, 2
l' **enfant** (m./f.) *child*, 7; l'enfant unique *only child*, 7
enfin *finally*, 9
enjoué(e) *playful*, 7
ennuyer *to bore*, 2
ennuyeux (-euse) *boring*, 11; **C'était ennuyeux.** *It was boring*, 11
l' **enquête** (f.) *survey*, 1
l' **enseignement** (m.) *teaching*, 2
ensemble *together*, 4
l' **ensemble** (m.) *collection, ensemble*, 3
ensuite : Ensuite, ... *Next,/Then, . . . ,* 9
entendre *to hear*; s'entendre avec *to get along with*, 7
entendu dire que : Il a entendu dire que... *He heard that . . . ,* 12
Entendu. *Agreed.* 6
l' **enthousiasme** (m.) *enthusiasm*, 2

entier (-ière) *whole, entire*; le monde entier *all over the world*, 1
entrant *entering*, 2
entre *between*, 12
l' **entrée** (f.) *entry, entrance*; Entrée libre *"Browsers welcomed,"* 3
l' **enveloppe** (f.) *envelope*, 12
l' **envie** (f.) *desire; need*; **J'ai envie de...** *I feel like . . . ,* 11
les **environs** (m. pl.) *surroundings*, 9
s' **envoler** *to fly away*, 12
envoyer *to send*, 12; **envoyer des lettres** *to send letters*, 12
l' **épi** (m.) *ear (of a plant)*, 8; l'épi de maïs *ear of corn*, 8
l' **épicerie** (f.) *grocery store*, 12
éplucher *to clean, to peel*, 8
l' **éponge** (f.) *sponge*, 3
épouvantable *terrible, horrible*, 9; **C'était épouvantable.** *It was horrible.* 9
l' **équipe interscolaire** (f.) *school team*, 4
l' **équitation** (f.) *horseback riding*, 1; **faire de l'équitation** *to go horseback riding*, 1
es : Tu es d'accord? *Is that OK with you?* 7
l' **escale** (f.) *docking (of a boat)*, 11
l' **escalier** (m.) *staircase*, 6
les **escargots** (m.) *snails*, 1
l' **espace** (m.) *space, area*, 7
l' **espagnol** (m.) *Spanish (language)*, 2
espère : J'espère que oui. *I hope so.* 1
l' **espoir** (m.) *hope*, 7
essayer *to try; to try on*, 10; **Je peux essayer... ?** *Can I try on . . . ?* 10; **Je peux l'/les essayer?** *Can I try it/them on?* 10
est : Il/Elle est... *He/She is . . . ,* 7; **Quelle heure est-il?** *What time is it?* 6; **Qui est à l'appareil?** *Who's calling?* 9
Est-ce que *(Introduces a yes-or-no question)*, 4; **(Est-ce que) je peux... ?** *May I . . . ?* 7
et *and*, 1; **Et après ça...** *And after that, . . . ,* 9; **Et toi?** *And you?* 1
l' **étage** (m.) *floor, story (of a building)*, 6
était : C'était épouvantable. *It was horrible.* 9
étaler *to spread*, 8
l' **étape** (f.) *part*, 1; première étape *first part*, 1; deuxième étape

second part, 1; troisième étape *third part,* 1

l' **état** (m.) *state,* 0

les **Etats-Unis** (m. pl.) United States, 0

l' **été** (m.) *summer,* 4; **en été** *in the summer,* 4

été (pp. of être) *was,* 9

étincelant(e) *brilliant,* 1

étoilé(e) *starry,* 12

étonné(e) (pp. of étonner) *surprised,* 7

étranger (-ère) *foreign,* 11

l' **étranger** (m.) *foreign countries;* à l'étranger *abroad,* 11

être *to be,* 7; **C'est...** *This is . . . ,* 7; **Ce sont...** *These (those) are . . . ,* 7; **Elle est...** *She is . . . ,* 7; **Il est...** *He is . . . ,* 7; **Il est...** *It is . . . (time),* 6; **Ils/Elles sont...** *They're . . . ,* 7; **Oui, ça a été.** *Yes, it was fine.* 9

l' **étude** (f.) *study hall,* 2

étudier *to study,* 1

l' **euro** *European Community monetary unit,* 3

l' **Europe** (f.) *Europe,* 0

évider *to scoop out,* 8

éviter *to avoid,* 9

l' **examen** (m.) *exam,* 1; **passer un examen** *to take a test,* 9

excellent(e) *excellent,* 5; **Oui, excellent.** *Yes, excellent.* 9

excusez : Excusez-moi. *Excuse me.* 3

exemplaire *exemplary,* 7

la **face** *face, side;* **en face de** *across from,* 12

facile *easy,* 2

la **façon** *way, manner,* 10

la **faim** *hunger;* **avoir faim** *to be hungry,* 5; **Non, merci. Je n'ai plus faim.** *No thanks. I'm not hungry anymore.* 8

faire *to do, to make, to play,* 4; **Désolé(e), j'ai des devoirs à faire.** *Sorry, I have homework to do.* 5; **J'ai des courses à faire.** *I have errands to do.* 5; **Qu'est-ce que tu vas faire... ?** *What are you going to do . . . ?* 6; **Tu vas faire quoi... ?** *What are you going to do . . . ?* 6; **faire de l'équitation** *to go horseback riding,* 1; faire de la course *to race (running),* 4; faire de la gymnastique *to do gymnastics,* 4; faire des haltères *to lift weights,* 4;

faire du bateau *to go sailing,* **faire du sport** *to play sports,* 1; faire du surf *to surf,* 4; faire la cuisine *to cook, do the cooking,* 8; **faire la vaisselle** *to do the dishes,* 7; **faire le ménage** *to do housework,* 1; faire les boutiques *to go shopping,* 1; **faire les courses** *to do the shopping,* 7; **faire les magasins** *to go shopping,* 1; **faire les vitrines** *to window-shop,* 6; **faire un pique-nique** *to have a picnic,* 6; **faire une promenade** *to go for a walk,* 6

fais : A ton avis, qu'est-ce que je fais? *In your opinion, what do I do?* 9; **Fais-moi...** *Make me . . . ,* 3; **Je fais...** *I play/do . . . ,* 4; **Ne t'en fais pas!** *Don't worry!* 9; **Qu'est-ce que tu fais comme sport?** *What sports do you play?* 4; **Qu'est-ce que tu fais pour t'amuser?** *What do you do to have fun?* 4; **Qu'est-ce que tu fais... ?** *What do you do . . . ?* 4

faisons : Faisons connaissance! *Let's get acquainted.* 1

fait : Quel temps fait-il? *What's the weather like?* 4; **Il fait beau.** *It's nice weather.* 4; **Il fait chaud.** *It's hot.* 4; **Il fait frais.** *It's cool.* 4; **Il fait froid.** *It's cold.* 4

fait (pp. of faire) *done, made,* 9; **J'ai fait...** *I did/made . . . ,* 9; **Qu'est-ce que tu as fait?** *What did you do?* 9

la **famille** *family,* 7

la **fantaisie** *fancy,* 10

le **fantôme** *ghost,* 0

la **farine** *flour,* 8

le **fast-food** *fast-food restaurant,* 6

faut : Il me faut... *I need . . . ,* 3; **Qu'est-ce qu'il te faut pour... ?** *What do you need for . . . ? (informal),* 3; **Qu'est-ce qu'il te faut?** *What do you need?* 8; **Qu'est-ce qu'il vous faut pour... ?** *What do you need for . . . ? (formal),* 3

le **fauve** *wildcat,* 6

faux (fausse) *false,* 2

les **féculents** (m.) *starches,* 8

la **féerie** *extravaganza,* 11

la **femme** *wife,* 7

la **fenêtre** *window,* 0

ferai : je me ferai une joie de... *I'll gladly . . . ,* 1

fermez : Fermez la porte. *Close the door.* 0

la **fête** *party,* 1; faire la fête *to*

live it up, 1

le **feu** *fire,* 12

le **feu rouge** *traffic light,* 12; **Vous continuez jusqu'au prochain feu rouge.** *You keep going until the next light.* 12

la **feuille** *sheet; leaf;* **une feuille de papier** *sheet of paper,* 0

le **feutre** *marker,* 3

février *February,* 4; **en février** *in February,* 4

la **fidélité** *loyalty,* 7

le **filet** *a type of net or mesh bag,* 3

la **fille** *girl,* 0; **la fille** *daughter,* 7

le **film** *movie,* 6; **voir un film** *to see a movie,* 6; un film d'aventures *adventure film,* 1

le **fil** *cord, thread;* sans fil *cordless,* 9

le **fils** *son,* 7

fils-à-papa *daddy's boy,* 10

la **fin** *end,* 4

finalement *finally,* 9

fistuleux (-euse) *hollow,* 11

la **flamme** *flame,* 12

le **flanc** *side; flank,* 12

le **flipper** *pinball,* 5

la **flûte** *flute,* 0

la **fois** *time;* **une fois par semaine** *once a week,* 4

follement *madly,* 1

foncé(e) *dark (color),* 10

le **foot** *soccer,* 4

le **football** *soccer,* 1; **le football américain** *football,* 4; **jouer au foot(ball)** *to play soccer,* 4; **jouer au football américain** *to play football,* 4

la **forêt** *forest,* 0; **en forêt** *to/in the forest,* 11

formidable : C'était formidable! *It was great!* 11

fort(e) *strong,* 7

fou (folle) *crazy,* 9

le **foulard** *scarf,* 10

le **four** *oven,* 8

le **fournisseur** *supplier,* 8

les **fournitures** (f. pl.) scolaires *school supplies,* 3

la **fourrure** *fur,* 7

le **foutou** *a paste made from boiled plantains, manioc, or yams; It is common in Côte d'Ivoire.* 8

le **foyer** *home,* 7

fraîche *cool, cold,* 5

le **frais** *cool place,* 8; au frais *in a cool place,* 8

les **frais** (m. pl.) *cost, expenses,* 11

frais *cool (temperature),* 4; **Il fait frais.** *It's cool.* 4

la **fraise** *strawberry,* 8; **un sirop de fraises (à l'eau)** *water with strawberry syrup,* 5 le franc *(the French monetary unit)*, 3; **C'est... francs.** *It's . . .francs.* 5

le franc de la Communauté financière africaine (CFA) *the currency of francophone Africa*, 8

le français *French (language)*, 1; français(e) *French (adj.)*, 0; *A la française* *French-style*, 2

francophone *French-speaking*, 0

le frère *brother*, 7

les friandises (f.) *sweets*, 6

les frites (f. pl.) *French fries*, 1

froid *cold*, 4; **Il fait froid.** *It's cold.* 4

le fromage *cheese*, 5

la fromagerie *cheese shop*, 12

les fruits (m.) *fruit*, 8

fui (pp. of fuir) *fled*, 1

le fun *fun*, 4; C'est le fun! (in Canada) *It's fun!* 4

G

gagner *to win, to earn*, 9

le garçon *boy*, 9

garder *to look after*, 7

la gare *train station*, 6

le garrot *withers, shoulder height of an animal, such as a horse*, 7

le gâteau *cake*, 8

la gâterie *little treat*, 9

la gauche *left (direction)*; à gauche *to the left*, 12

le gazon *lawn*, 7; tondre le gazon *to mow the lawn*, 7

généralement *in general, usually*, 11

génial(e) *great*, 2

le génie *genius*, 6

les genoux (m.) *knees*, 7; une paire de genoux *pair of knees, lap*, 7

les gens (m. pl.) *people*, 9

gentil(le) *nice*, 7

la géographie *geography*, 2

la géométrie *geometry*, 2

la glace *ice cream*, 1

la glace *ice*; faire du patin à glace *to ice-skate*, 4

le golf *golf*, 4; jouer au golf *to play golf*, 4

les gombos (m.) *okra*, 8

la gomme *eraser*, 3

la gosse *kid*, 2; être traité comme une gosse *to be treated like a kid*, 2

le gouache *paint*, 3

le goûter *afternoon snack*, 8

goûter *to taste*, 8

le goût (m.) *taste*, 4

la goyave *guava*, 8

grâce à *thanks to*, 11

gradué(e) *graduated*, 3; une règle graduée *graduated ruler*, 3

la graine *seed*, 8

grammaire *grammar*, 1

grand(e) *tall*, 7; *big*, 10

grand-chose : Pas grand-chose. *Not much.* 6

la grand-mère *grandmother*, 7

le grand-père *grandfather*, 7

grandir *to grow*, 10

gratuit(e) *free*, 6

grec *Greek (adj.)*, 6

gris(e) *grey*, 3

gros(se) *fat*, 7

grossir *to gain weight*, 10

la grotte *cave*, 11

le groupe *musical group*, 2

la Guadeloupe *Guadeloupe*, 0

le guichet *ticket window*, 6

la Guyane Française *French Guiana*, 0

H

habitant : habitant le monde entier *living all over the world*, 1

habite : J'habite à... *I live in . . .*, 1

l' habitude (f.) *habit*, 4; d'habitude *usually*, 4

habituellement *usually*, 2

* haché(e) (pp of hacher) *minced*, 8

Haïti (no article) *Haiti*, 0

*le hamburger *hamburger*, 1

*les haricots (m.) *beans*, 8; les haricots verts (m. pl.) *green beans*, 8

*la harpe *harp*, 11

*la hâte *hurry, haste*; Elle a hâte de... *She can't wait to . . .*, 7

* haut(e) *tall, high*, 6

*le haut-parleur *loudspeaker*, 11

*le havre *haven*, 7

l' hébergement (m.) *lodging*, 6

l' hélicoptère (m.) *helicopter*, 0

*le héros *hero*, 11

hésite : Euh... J'hésite. *Well, I'm not sure.* 10

l' heure (f.) *hour; time*, 1; à l'heure de *at the time of*, 1; A quelle heure? *At what time?* 6; A tout à l'heure! *See you later!* 1; l'heure officielle *official time (24-hour system)*, 2; Quelle heure est-il? *What time is it?* 6; Tu as... à quelle heure? *At what time do you have . . . ?* 2

heures *o'clock*, 2; à... heures *at . . . o'clock*, 2; à... heures quarante-cinq *at . . . forty-five*, 2; à... heures quinze *at . . . fifteen*, 2; à... heures trente *at . . . thirty*, 2

heureusement *luckily, fortunately*, 4

heureux (-euse) *happy*; Très heureux-(-euse). *Pleased to meet you.* 7

hier *yesterday*, 9

l' histoire (f.) *history*, 2

l' hiver (m.) *winter*, 4; en hiver *in the winter*, 4

*le hockey *hockey*, 4; jouer au hockey *to play hockey*, 4

l' hôpital (pl. -aux) *hospital*, 0

horrible *terrible*, 10

*le hot-dog *hot dog*, 5

l' hôtel (m.) *hotel*, 0

*le houx *holly*, 11

l' huile d'olive (f.) *olive oil*, 5

* hurler *to shriek, to cry out*, 12

I

l' idée (f.) *idea*, 4; Bonne idée. *Good idea.* 4

l' identité (f.) *identity*; une photo d'identité *photo ID*, 1

l' igloo (m.) *igloo*, 0

l' igname (f.) *yam*, 8

il y a *there is, there are*, 5; il y a du soleil/du vent *it's sunny/windy*, 4; Qu'est-ce qu'il y a à boire? *What is there to drink?* 5

l' île (f.) *island*, 0

imagines : Tu imagines? *Can you imagine?* 4

imprimé(e) *printed*, 10

inaperçu(e) *unnoticed*, 11

inclus(e) *included*, 6

incompétent(e) *incompetent*, 2

incroyable *unbelievable*, 9

l' informatique (f.) *computer science*, 2

intelligent(e) *smart*, 7

l' intention (f.) *intention*; J'ai l'intention de... *I intend to . . .*, 11

l' interclasse (m.) *break (between classes)*, 2

intéressant(e) *interesting*, 2

international(e) *international*, 5

l' interphone (m.) *intercom*, 9

l' interro(gation) (f.) *quiz*, 9; rater une interro *to fail a quiz*, 9

intervenu(e) (pp. of intervenir) *intervened*, 9

l' interviewé(e) (m./f.) *interviewee*, 2
intime *personal*, 1
l' invité(e) (m./f.) *guest*, 8
ivoirien(ne) *from the Republic of Côte d'Ivoire*, 1

J

jamais : ne... jamais *never*, 4
le jambon *ham*, 5
janvier *January*, 4; en janvier *in January*, 4
le jardin *garden*, 0
jaune *yellow*, 3
le jazz *jazz*, 4
je *I*, 0
le jean *(pair of) jeans*, 3; en jean *made of denim*, 10
le jeu *game*; un jeu de rôle *role-playing exercise*, 1; jouer à des jeux vidéo *to play video games*, 4
jeudi *Thursday*, 2; le jeudi *on Thursdays*, 2
jeune *young*, 7; les jeunes *youths*, 4
le jogging *jogging*, 4; faire du jogging *to jog*, 4
la joie *joy*, 1
joignant (joindre) *attached*, 1
joli(e) *pretty*, 4
jouer *to play*, 4; Je joue... *I play . . .*, 4; Je ne joue pas... *I don't play . . .*, 4; jouer à... *to play (a game) . . .*, 4
joueur (-euse) *playful*, 7
le jour *day*, 2; le jour férié (m.) *holiday*, 6
le journal *journal*, 1; *newspaper*, 12
la journée *day*, 2
juillet *July*, 4; en juillet *in July*, 4
juin *June*, 4; en juin *in June*, 4
la jupe *skirt*, 10
le jus d'orange *orange juice*, 5
le jus de fruit *fruit juice*, 5
le jus de pomme *apple juice*, 5
jusqu'à *up to, until*, 12; Vous allez tout droit jusqu'à... *You go straight ahead until you get to . . .*, 12
juste *just*, 4

K

le kangourou *kangaroo*, 0
le kilo(gramme) *kilogram*, 8; un kilo de *a kilogram of*, 8

L

la *the*, 1; *her, it* (f.), 9
là *there*, 12; -là *there (noun suffix)*, 3; (Est-ce que)... est là, s'il vous plaît? *Is . . . , there, please?* 9; là-bas *there; over there*, 8
laid(e) *ugly*, 9
la laine *wool*, 10
laisser *to leave*, 9; Je peux laisser un message? *Can I leave a message?* 9
le lait *milk*, 8
laitier (-ière) *dairy*, 8; les produits laitiers (m.) *dairy products*, 8
la langue *language*, 1
large *baggy*, 10
le latin *Latin, (language)*, 2
laver *to wash*, 7; laver la voiture *to wash the car*, 7
le *the*, 1; *him, it*, 9
la légèreté *lightness*, 6
les légumes (m.) *vegetables*, 8
la lettre *letter*, 12; envoyer des lettres *to send letters*, 12
les *the*, 1; *them*, 9
leur *to them*, 9
leur/leurs *their*, 7
levez : Levez la main! *Raise your hand!* 0; Levez-vous! *Stand up!* 0
la librairie *bookstore*, 12
la librairie-papeterie *bookstore and stationary store*, 3
libre *free*, 2
liégeois : café ou chocolat liégeois *coffee or chocolate ice cream with whipped cream*, 5
le lieu *place*; avoir lieu *to take place*, 7; ... aura lieu... *. . . will take place . . .*, 7
la limonade *lemon soda*, 5
le lin *linen*, 10
le lion *lion*, 0
le liquide correcteur *correction fluid*, 3
lire *to read*, 1
lisons : Lisons! *Let's read!* 1
la litote *understatement*, 5
le litre *liter*, 8; un litre de *a liter of*, 8
la livraison *delivery*, 12
la livre *pound*, 8; une livre de *a pound of*, 8
le livre *book*, 0
le livret scolaire *a student's personal gradebook*, 3
la location *rental*, 4
loin *far*, 12; loin de *far from*, 12
long(ue) *long*, 10
la longueur *length*, 10

louer *to rent*, 12
la Louisiane *Louisiana*, 0
lu (pp. of lire) *read*, 9
lui *to him, to her*, 9
lundi *Monday*, 2; le lundi *on Mondays*, 2
les lunettes de soleil (f. pl.) *sunglasses*, 10
le Luxembourg *Luxembourg*, 0
le lycée *high school*, 2
le lycéen *high school student*, 2

M

ma *my*, 7
madame (Mme) *ma'am; Mrs.*, 1; Madame! *Waitress!* 5
mademoiselle (Mlle) *miss; Miss*, 1; Mademoiselle! *Waitress!* 5
le magasin *store*, 1; faire les magasins *to go shopping*, 1
le magazine *magazine*, 3
le magnétoscope *videocassette recorder, VCR*, 0
mai *May*, 4; en mai *in May*, 4
maigrir *to lose weight*, 10
le maillot de bain *bathing suit*, 10
la main *hand*, 0
maintenant *now*, 2; Je ne peux pas maintenant. *I can't right now.* 8
le maire *mayor*, 12
la mairie *city hall*, 4
mais *but*, 1
le maïs *corn*, 8
la Maison des jeunes et de la culture (MJC) *recreation center*, 6
le maître *master, owner*, 7
maîtriser *to master*, 4
la majorité *majority*, 2
mal *bad*, 1; Pas mal. *Not bad.* 1
la malchance *misfortune*, 7
le mâle *male (refers to animals)*, 7
malheureusement *unfortunately*, 7
le Mali *Mali*, 0
la manche *sleeve*, 10
le manchot *penguin*, 6
le manège *carousel*, 12
manger *to eat*, 6
la mangue *mango*, 8
manqué(e) (pp. of manquer) *missed*; garçon manqué *tomboy*, 10
manque : Qu'est-ce qui manque? *What's missing?* 2
le manteau *coat*, 10
le marché *market*, 8
mardi *Tuesday* 2; le mardi *on Tuesdays*, 2
le mari *husband*, 7

le mariage *marriage*, 7
le Maroc *Morocco*, 0
   marocain(e) *Moroccan* (adj.), 1
   marron (inv.) *brown*, 3
   mars *March*, 4; **en mars** *in March*, 4
   martiniquais(e) *from Martinique*, 1
la Martinique *Martinique*, 0
le match *game*, 6; **regarder un match** *to watch a game (on TV)*, 6; **aller voir un match** *to go see a game (in person)*, 6
les maths (les mathématiques) (f. pl.) *math*, 1
la matière *school subject*, 2
les matières grasses (f.) *fat*, 8
le matin *morning; in the morning*, 2
   mauvais(e) *bad*, 5; **C'est pas mauvais!** *It's pretty good!* 5; **Oh, pas mauvais.** *Oh, not bad.* 9; **Très mauvais.** *Very bad.* 9
   méchant(e) *mean*, 7
   mécontent(e) *unhappy*, 2
les médicaments (m.) *medicine*, 12
   meilleur(e) *best*, 7; les meilleurs amis *best friends*, 7
   mélanger *to mix*, 8
   méli-mélo *mishmash*, 1
la mémé *granny, grandma*, 9
le ménage *housework*, 1; **faire le ménage** *to do housework*, 1
le mensuel *monthly publication*, 9
méprisant(e) *contemptuous*, 2
la mer *sea;* **au bord de la mer** *to/on the coast*, 11
   Merci. *Thank you*, 3; **Non, merci.** *No, thank you.* 8
   mercredi *Wednesday*, 2; **le mercredi** *on Wednesdays*, 2
la mère *mother*, 7
   mes *my*, 7
le message *message*, 9; **Je peux laisser un message?** *May I leave a message?*, 9
le métro *subway*, 12; **au métro...** *at the . . . metro stop*, 6; **en métro** *by subway*, 12
métropolitain(e) *metropolitan*, 2
mets : mets en ordre *put into order*, 6
mettre *to put, to put on, to wear*, 10; **Je ne sais pas quoi mettre pour...** *I don't know what to wear for (to) . . .* , 10; **Mets...** *Wear . . .* , 10; **Qu'est-ce que je mets?** *What shall I wear?* 10
meublé(e) *furnished*, 11
miam, miam *yum-yum*, 5
midi *noon*, 6; **Il est midi.** *It's noon.* 6; **Il est midi et demi.** *It's half past noon.* 6

mieux *better*, 9; **Ça va aller mieux!** *It's going to get better!* 9; **J'aime mieux...** *I prefer . . .* , 1
mignon(ne) *cute*, 7
mince *slender*, 7
minuit *midnight*, 6; **Il est minuit.** *It's midnight.* 6; **Il est minuit et demi.** *It's half past midnight.* 6
la minute *minute*, 9; **Tu as une minute?** *Do you have a minute?* 9
la mise en scène *production*, 1
la mise *putting, setting;* mise en pratique *putting into practice*, 1; mise en train *getting started*, 1
mixte *mixed*, 5
le mobilier *furniture*, 6
la mobylette *motor scooter*, 11
   moche *tacky*, 10
le mode d'emploi *instructions*, 9
la mode *style*, 10; **à la mode** *in style*, 10; à la dernière mode *in the latest fashion*, 10
modéré(e) *moderate*, 11
moi *me*, 2; **Moi aussi.** *Me too.* 2; **Moi, non.** *I don't.* 2; **Moi non plus.** *Neither do I.* 2; **Moi, si.** *I do.* 2; **Pas moi.** *Not me.*
le mois *month*, 4
   moins *(with numbers) minus, lower*, 0; **moins cinq** *five to*, 6; **moins le quart** *quarter to*, 6
le moment *moment*, 5; **Un moment, s'il vous plaît.** *One moment, please.* 5
mon *my*, 7
Monaco *Monaco*, 0
le monde *world*, 0
le moniteur *monitor*, 12
   monsieur (M.) *sir (Mr.)* 1; **Monsieur!** *Waiter!* 5
le monstre *monster*, 0
la montagne *mountain*, 4; **à la montagne** *to/in the mountains*, 11
la montée *ascent*, 6
la montre *watch*, 3
   montrer *to show*, 9
le monument *monument*, 6
se moquer de *to make fun of*, 9
le moral *morale*, 2
le morceau *piece*, 8; **un morceau de** *a piece of*, 8
le motif *reason*, 9
la moto(cyclette) *motorcycle*, 12
le moulin *windmill*, 9
la mousseline *chiffon*, 8
la moutarde *mustard*, 8
moyen(ne) *average*, 2; travail moyen *average work*, 2

la moyenne *average*, 2
le musée *museum*, 6
la musique *music*, 2; **écouter de la musique** *to listen to music*, 1; la musique classique *classical music*, 4
le mystère *mystery*, 5

nager *to swim*, 1
le nain *dwarf*, 6
la naissance *birth*, 7
la natation *swimming*, 4; **faire de la natation** *to swim*, 4
   nautique *nautical;* **faire du ski nautique** *to water ski*, 4
   ne : ne... pas *not*, 1; **ne... pas encore** *not yet*, 9; **ne... jamais** *never*, 4; **ne... ni grand(e) ni petit(e)** *neither tall nor short*, 7
né(e) (pp. of naître) *born*, 9
la Négritude *movement which asserts the values and spirit of black African civilizations*, 0
   neige : Il neige. *It's snowing.* 4
le neveu *nephew*, 7
la nièce *niece*, 7
le Niger *Niger*, 0
le niveau *level*, 6
le nocturne *late-night opening*, 6
le Noël *Christmas*, 0
   noir(e) *black*, 3
la noisette *hazelnut*, 5
la noix *nut*, 5
la noix de coco *coconut*, 8
le nom *name*, 1; nom de famille *last name*
le nombre *number*, 2
   non *no*, 1; **Moi non plus.** *Neither do I.* 2; **Moi, non.** *I don't.* 2; **Non, c'est...** *No, it's . . .* , 4; **Non, merci.** *No, thank you.* 8; **Non, pas trop.** *No, not too much.* 2
   nos *our*, 7
   notre *our*, 7
la Nouvelle-Angleterre *New England*, 0
les nouvelles (f.) *news*, 9
   novembre *November*, 4; **en novembre** *in November*, 4
le nuage *cloud*, 12
   nul(le) *useless*, 2
le numéro *number*, 0; un numéro de téléphone *telephone number*, 3; les numéros *issues (for magazines, etc.)*, 3

l' objet (m.) *object*, 6; objets trouvés *lost and found*, 3

occupé(e) : C'est occupé. *It's busy.* 9; **Désolé(e), je suis occupé(e).** *Sorry, I'm busy.* 6; **s'occuper de** *to take care of,* 7
octobre *October,* 4; **en octobre** *in October,* 4
l' **odeur** (f.) *aroma; smell,* 8
l' **œil** (m.) *eye,* 12
l' **œuf** (m.) *egg,* 8
l' **oignon** (m.) *onion,* 8
l' **oiseau** (m.) *bird,* 12
ombragé(e) (pp. of ombrager) *shaded,* 11
l' **omelette** (f.) *omelette,* 5
on *one, we, you, they,* 1; **Comment dit-on... ?** *How do you say . . . ?* 1; **On est dans la purée.** *We're in trouble.* 8; **On fait du ski?** *How about skiing?* 5; **On joue au base-ball?** *How about playing baseball?* 5; **On peut...** *We can . . . ,* 6; **On va au café?** *Shall we go to the café?* 5; **On... ?** *How about . . . ?* 4
l' **oncle** (m.) *uncle,* 7
opulent(e) *rich,* 7
l' **or** (m.) *gold,* 12
orange (inv.) *orange (color),* 3
l' **orange** (f.) *orange,* 8; **le jus d'orange** *orange juice*
l' **ordinateur** (m.) *computer,* 3
l' **otarie** (f.) *sea lion,* 6
ôter *to cut out,* 8
ou *or,* 1
où *where,* 6; **Où (ça)?** *Where?* 6; **Où est-ce que tu vas aller... ?** *Where are you going to go . . . ?* 11; **Tu es allé(e) où?** *Where did you go?* 9
oublier *to forget,* 9; **Je n'ai rien oublié.** *I didn't forget anything.* 11; **Oublie-le/-la/-les!** *Forget him/her/them!* 9; **J'ai oublié.** *I forgot.* 3; **N'oublie pas de...** *Don't forget . . . ,* 8; **Tu n'as pas oublié... ?** *You didn't forget . . . ?* 11
oui *yes,* 1; **Oui, c'est...** *Yes it's . . . ,* 4; **Oui, s'il te/vous plaît.** *Yes, please.* 8
ouvert(e) *open,* 6
l' **ouverture** (f.) *opening,* 6
ouvrez : Ouvrez vos livres à la page... *Open your books to page . . . ,* 0

P

la **page** *page,* 0
la **pagne** *a piece of dyed African cloth,* 10
le **pain** *bread,* 8

le **palais** *palace,* 1; **le palais de justice** *court, courthouse,* 1
le **pamplemousse** *grapefruit,* 5
le **panier** *basket,* 3
le **pantalon** *pair of pants,* 10
la **papaye** *papaya,* 8
la **papeterie** *stationery store,* 12; **librairie-papeterie** *bookstore/stationery store,* 3
le **papier** *paper,* 0; **des feuilles** (f.) **de papier** *sheets of paper,* 3
le **paquet** *package, box,* 8; **un paquet de** *a package/box of,* 8
par *by,* 12; *per,* 6; **par hasard** *by chance,* 12; **prix par personne** *price per person,* 6
le **parachute** *parachute,* 0
paraître *to appear; seem,* 12
le **parapluie** *umbrella,* 11
le **parc** *park,* 6
parce que *because,* 5; **Je ne peux pas parce que...** *I can't because . . . ,* 5
Pardon. *Pardon me.* 3; **Pardon, madame... , s'il vous plaît?** *Excuse me, ma'am . . . , please?* 12; **Pardon, monsieur. Je cherche... , s'il vous plaît.** *Excuse me, sir. I'm looking for. . . , please.* 12
le **parent** *parent; relative,* 7
paresseux (-euse) *lazy,* 2
parfait(e) *perfect,* 3; **C'est parfait.** *It's perfect.* 10
parfois *sometimes,* 4
parfumer *to flavor,* 8
parlé (pp. of parler) *talked, spoke,* 9; **Nous avons parlé.** *We talked.* 9
parler *to talk,* 1; *to speak,* 9; **(Est-ce que) je peux parler à... ?** *Could I speak to. . . ?* 9; **Je peux te parler?** *Can I talk to you?* 9; **parler au téléphone** *to talk on the phone,* 1; **Parlons!** *Let's talk!* 2
partagé(e) *split, shared,* 6
partir *to leave,* 11; **Tu ne peux pas partir sans...** *You can't leave without . . . ,* 11
pas *not,* 1; **pas bon** *not good,* 5; **Pas ce soir.** *Not tonight.* 7; **pas content du tout** *not happy at all,* 2; **Il/Elle ne va pas du tout avec...** *It doesn't go at all with . . . ,* 10; **Pas grand-chose.** *Not much.* 6; **Pas mal.** *Not bad.* 1; **pas mauvais** *not bad,* 9; **Pas question!** *Out of the question!* 7; **pas super** *not so hot,* 2; **Pas terrible.** *Not so great.* 1

les **passe-temps** (m. pl.) *pastimes,* 4
passé : Ça s'est bien passé? *Did it go well?* 11; **Qu'est-ce qui s'est passé?** *What happened?* 9; **Tu as passé un bon week-end?** *Did you have a good weekend?* 9
le **passeport** *passport,* 11
passé (pp. of passer) : **Qu'est-ce qui s'est passé?** *What happened?* 9; **Tu as passé un bon week-end?** *Did you have a good weekend?* 9
passer *to pass,* 12; *to go by,* 12; **Tu pourrais passer à... ?** *Could you go by . . . ?* 12; **Vous passez...** *You'll pass . . . ,* 12; **passer l'aspirateur** *to vacuum,* 7; **passer un examen** *to take a test,* 9
passerais : je passerais le bac... *I would take bac . . . ,* 2
passionnant(e) *fascinating,* 2
la **pastille** *tablet,* 3
la **pâte** *dough,* 8; **la pâte d'arachide** *peanut butter,* 8; **la pâte de tomates** *tomato paste,* 8
le **pâté** *pâté,* 0
les **pâtes** (f. pl.) *pasta,* 11
le **patin** *skating,* 1; **faire du patin à glace** *to ice skate,* 4
le **patin à roulettes** *rollerskating,* 4
le **patinage** *skating,* 4
patiner *to skate,* 4
la **patinoire** *skating rink,* 6
la **pâtisserie** *pastry shop, pastry,* 12
le **patrimoine** *heritage,* 6
patronal(e) *having to do with saints;* **la fête patronale** *patron saint's holiday,* 12
les **pattes d'eph** (f. pl.) *bell-bottoms,* 10
pauvre *poor,* 7
le **pays** *country,* 6
le **paysage** *landscape,* 11
la **pêche** *peach,* 8
la **peinture** *painting,* 6
pendant *during,* 1
pénible *annoying,* 7
penser *to think;* **J'ai pensé à tout.** *I've thought of everything.* 11; **Qu'en penses-tu?** *What do you think (about it)?* 1
perdre *to lose,* 9
le **père** *father,* 7
permettre *to allow,* 9
le **permis de conduire** *driver's license,* 12; **le permis accompagné** *learner's permit (driving),* 12; **le permis probatoire** *learner's permit (driving),* 12
le **personnage** *individual, character,* 9

personnel(le) *personal*, 4

le petit copain *boyfriend*, 2

le petit déjeuner *breakfast*, 8

petit(e) *short (height)*, 7; *small (size)*, 10; petites annonces *classified ads*, 1

le petit-fils *grandson*, 7

la petite copine *girlfriend*, 2

la petite-fille *granddaughter*, 7

les petits pois (m.) *peas*, 8

les petits-enfants (m.) *grandchildren*, 7

peu *not very*, 2; à peu près *about, approximately*, 9; peu content *not very happy*, 2; un peu *a little*, 6

peut : On peut... *We can . . .*, 6

peut-être *maybe; perhaps*, 11

peux : Désolé(e), mais je ne peux pas. *Sorry, but I can't.* 4; **Tu peux... ?** *Can you . . . ?* 8

la pharmacie *drugstore*, 12

la philosophie *philosophy*, 2

le phoque *seal*, 6

la photo *picture, photo*, 4; **faire de la photo** *to do photography*, 4; **faire des photos** *to take pictures*, 4

la photographie *photography*, 1

les photographies (f. pl.) *photographs*, 6

la phrase *sentence*, 4

la physique *physics*, 2

la pièce *play*, 6; **voir une pièce** *to see a play*, 6

le pied *foot*, 12; **à pied** *on foot*, 12

le pinceau *paintbrush*, 3

la pince : des pantalons à pinces *pleated pants*, 10

le pingouin *penguin*, 0

le pique-nique *picnic*, 6; **faire un pique-nique** *to have a picnic*, 6

la piscine *swimming pool*, 6

la pizza *pizza*, 1

la plage *beach*, 1

le plaisir *pleasure, enjoyment*, 4; **Oui, avec plaisir.** *Yes, with pleasure.* 8

plaît : Il/Elle me plaît, mais il/elle est cher/chère. *I like it, but it's expensive.* 10; Il/Elle te/vous plaît? *Do you like it?* 10; Ça te plaît? *Do you like it?* 2; s'il vous/te plaît *please*, 3

la planche *board;* **faire de la planche à voile** *to go windsurfing*, 11

la plaque *plate (of metal or glass);* la plaque d'immatriculation *license plate*, 0

les plats à emporter (m.) *food to go*, 11

pleut : Il pleut. *It's raining.* 4

la plongée *diving;* **faire de la plongée** *to go scuba diving*, 11

plus *plus (math)*, 2; *(with numbers) higher*, 0; **Je n'en veux plus.** *I don't want any more*, 8; **Moi non plus.** *Neither do I.* 2; **Non, merci. Je n'ai plus faim.** *No thanks. I'm not hungry anymore.* 8

la poche *pocket*, 10

le poème *poem*, 0

la poire *pear*, 8

le poisson *fish*, 7

la poissonnerie *fish shop*, 12

la poitrine *chest*, 10

le poivre *pepper*, 8

le poivron *green or red pepper*, 5

la pollution *pollution*, 1

la pomme *apple*, 8; **jus de pomme** *apple juice*, 5

la pomme de terre (f.) *potato*, 8

le pompiste *gas pump attendant*, 11

le porc *pork*, 8

la porte *door*, 0

le porte-monnaie *change purse*, 5

le portefeuille *wallet*, 3

porter *to wear*, 10

le portugais *Portuguese (language)*, 2

la poste *post office*, 12

le poster *poster*, 0

le pot de colle *container of glue*, 3

la poubelle *trashcan*, 7; **sortir la poubelle** *to take out the trash*, 7

la poudre *powder*, 8

la poule *(animal) chicken* 8

le poulet *chicken (meat)*, 8

pour *for*, 2; **Qu'est-ce qu'il te faut pour...** *What do you need for . . . ? (informal)*, 3; **Qu'est-ce que tu fais pour t'amuser?** *What do you do to have fun?* 4

pourquoi *why*, 0; **Pourquoi est-ce que tu ne mets pas... ?** *Why don't you wear . . . ?* 10; **Pourquoi pas?** *Why not?* 6; **Pourquoi tu ne... pas?** *Why don't you . . . ?* 9

pourtant *yet; nevertheless*, 9

pourrais : Tu pourrais passer à ...? *Could you go by . . . ?* 12

pouvoir *to be able to, can*, 8; **(Est-ce que) je peux... ?** *May I . . . ?* 7; **Tu peux... ?** *Can you . . . ?* 8; **Je ne peux pas maintenant.** *I can't right now.* 8; **Je peux te parler?** *Can I talk to you?*, 9; **Non, je ne peux pas.** *No, I can't.* 12; **On peut...** *We can . . .*, 6; **Qu'est-ce que je peux faire?** *What can I do?* 9; **(Est-ce que) tu pourrais me rendre un petit service?** *Could you do me a favor?* 12; **Tu pourrais passer à... ?** *Could you go by . . . ?*, 12

précieusement *carefully*, 2

précisant : en précisant *specifying*, 1

préféré(e) *favorite*, 4

la préférence *preference*, 3

préférer *to prefer*, 1; **Je préfère...** *I prefer . . .*, 1

premier (-ière) *first*, 1

prendre *to take or to have (food or drink)*, 5; **Je vais prendre... , s'il vous plaît.** *I'm going to have . . . , please.* 5; **On peut prendre...** *We can take . . .*, 12; **Prends...** *Get . . .*, 8; *Have . . .*, 5; **Je le/la/les prends.** *I'll take it/them.* 10; **Tu prends... ?** *Will you have . . . ?*, 8; *Are you taking. . . ?*, 11; **Prenez une feuille de papier.** *Take out a sheet of paper.* 0; **Vous prenez... ?** *What are you having?* 5; *Will you have . . . ?*, 8; **Prenez la rue... puis traversez la rue...** *You take . . . Street, then cross . . . Street*, 12; **Vous avez décidé de prendre... ?** *Have you decided to take . . . ?* 10; **Vous le/la/les prenez?** *Are you going to take it/them?* 10

le prénom *first name*, 1

près *close*, 12; **près de** *close to*, 12

présenter: *to introduce;* **Je te (vous) présente...** *I'd like you to meet . . .*, 7; **Présente-toi!** *Introduce yourself!* 0

prévoir *to anticipate*, 4

prévu(e) (pp. of prévoir) *planned;* **Je n'ai rien de prévu.** *I don't have any plans.* 11

principal(e) *main;* la ville principale *main city*, 12

le printemps *spring*, 4; **au printemps** *in the spring*, 4

pris (pp. of prendre) *took, taken*, 9

le prisonnier *prisoner*, 4

le prix *price*, 6

le problème *problem*, 9; **J'ai un petit problème.** *I've got a little problem.* 9

prochain(e) *next*, 12; **Vous continuez jusqu'au prochain feu rouge.** *You keep going until the next light.* 12

les produits laitiers (m.) *dairy products*, 8

le prof(esseur) *teacher*, 0

les progrès (m.) *progress*, 11

la promenade *walk*, 6; **faire une promenade** *to go for a walk*, 6

promener *to walk*, 6; **promener le chien** *to walk the dog*, 7

promets (promettre) *to promise*, 1

prononcer *to pronounce*, 1; **prononcent : ne se prononcent pas** *no response*, 2

la prononciation *pronunciation*, 2

la protéine *protein*, 8

le publiphone à cartes *card-operated telephone*, 9

puis *then*, 12; **Prenez la rue... puis traversez la rue...** *Take . . . Street, then cross . . . Street*, 12

le pull(-over) *pullover sweater*, 3

la punition *punishment*, 9

Q

qu'est-ce que *what*, 1; **Qu'est-ce qu'il te faut pour... ?** *What do you need for . . . ?* (informal), 3; **Qu'est-ce qu'il vous faut pour... ?** *What do you need for . . . ?* (formal), 3; **Qu'est-ce qu'il y a dans...?** *What's in the . . . ?* 3; **Qu'est-ce qu'il y a?** *What's wrong?* 2; **Qu'est-ce qu'on fait?** *What are we/they doing?* 4; **Qu'est-ce que je peux faire?** *What can I do?* 9; **Qu'est-ce que tu as fait... ?** *What did you do . . . ?* 9; **Qu'est-ce que tu fais... ?** *What do you do . . . ?* 4; **Qu'est-ce que tu vas faire... ?** *What are you going to do . . . ?* 6; **Qu'est-ce que vous avez comme boissons?** *What do you have to drink?* 5; **Qu'est-ce qu'il y a à boire?** *What is there to drink?* 5; **Qu'est-ce qui manque?** *What's missing?* 2

qu'est-ce qui *what* (subj.), 9; **Qu'est-ce qui s'est passé?** *What happened?* 9

quand *when*, 6; **Quand (ça)?** *When?* 6

le quart *quarter*, 6; **et quart** *quarter past*, 6; **moins le quart** *quarter to*, 6

que *that; what*, 1; **Que sais-je?** *Self-check (What do I know?)*, 1

le Québec *Quebec*, 0

québécois(e) *from Quebec*, 1

quel(le) *what, which*, 1; **Ils ont quels cours?** *What classes do they have?* 2; **Tu as quel âge?** *How old are you?* 1; **Tu as quels cours... ?** *What classes do you have . . . ?* 2; **Tu as... à quelle heure?** *At what time do you have . . . ?* 2; **Quelle heure est-il?** *What time is it?* 6; **Quel temps fait-il?** *What's the weather like?* 4

quelqu'un *someone*, 1

quelque chose *something*, 6; **Je cherche quelque chose pour...** *I'm looking for something for . . .* , 10

quelquefois *sometimes*, 4

la question *question*, 0

le questionnaire *questionnaire, survey*, 4

qui *who*, 0; **Avec qui?** *With whom?* 6; **C'est qui?** *Who is it?* 2; **Qui suis-je?** *Who am I?* 0

la quiche *quiche: a type of custard pie with a filling, such as ham, bacon, cheese, or spinach*, 5

quittez : Ne quittez pas. *Hold on.* 9

quoi *what*, 10; **De quoi est-ce que tu as besoin?** *What do you need?* 5; **Je ne sais pas quoi mettre pour...** *I don't know what to wear for/to . . .* , 10; **Tu as quoi... ?** *What do you have. . .?* 2 **Tu vas faire quoi?** *What are you going to do?* 6

quotidien(ne) *everyday*, 6

R

le rabat *flap*, 3

le raccourci *short cut*, 2

raconter *to tell*, 9

la radio *radio*, 3

le radis *radish*, 8

le raisin *grapes*, 8

la randonnée *hike*, 11; **faire de la randonnée** *to go hiking*, 11

ranger *to arrange, straighten*; **ranger ta chambre** *to pick up your room*, 7

le rap *rap music*, 1

râpé(e) (pp. of râper) *grated*, 8

rappeler *to call back*, 9; **Vous pouvez rappeler plus tard?** *Can you call back later?* 9; **Tu te rappelles?** *Do you remember?* 3

rapporter *to bring back*, 8; **Rapporte-moi...** *Bring me back . . .* , 8; **Tu me rapportes... ?** *Will you bring me . . . ?* 8

rarement *rarely*, 4

rater *to fail*, 9; *to miss*, 9; **rater le bus** *to miss the bus*, 9; **rater une interro** *to fail a quiz*, 9

le rayon *department*, 3; **au rayon de musique** *in the music department*, 3

la rayonne *rayon*, 10

la réalité *reality*, 11

la recette *recipe*, 8

recevoir *to receive*, 1

la récréation *break*, 2

recueilli (pp. of recueillir) *to take in*, 7

refaire *to redo, remake*, 8

réfléchir *to think about*, 2; *to reflect*; **Réfléchissez.** *Think about it.* 2

le reflet *reflection*, 10

le refuge *animal shelter*, 7

le réfugié *refugee*, 1

le refus *refusal*, 6

le regard *look*, 7

regarder *to look*, 10; *to watch*, 1; **Non, merci, je regarde.** *No, thanks, I'm just looking.* 10; **Regarde, voilà...** *Look, here's/there's/it's . . .* , 12; **regarder la télé** *to watch TV*, 1; **regarder un match** *to watch a game (on TV)*, 6; **Regardez la carte!** *Look at the map!* 0

la règle *ruler*, 3

regrette : Je regrette. *Sorry.* 3; **Je regrette, mais je n'ai pas le temps.** *I'm sorry, but I don't have time.* 8

regroupé(e) *rearranged*, 6

rejoint (pp. of rejoindre) *rejoined*, 7

relier *to connect*, 9

le remboursement *repayment*, 9

la rencontre *encounter*, 1

rencontrer *to meet*, 9

rendre *to return something*, 12; **Rendez-vous...** *We'll meet . . .* , 6; **pour les rendre plus originales** *to make them more original*, 10

le renfort *reinforcement*; **renforts aux épaules** *reinforced shoulder seams*, 10 les renseignements (m.) *information*, 9

la rentrée *back to school*, 2

le repas *meal*, 8

le répertoire *index*, 9

répéter *to rehearse, practice*, 9; **Répétez!** *Repeat!* 0

le répondant *respondent*, 4

le répondeur *answering machine*, 9

répondre *to answer*, 9; **Ça ne répond pas.** *There's no answer*. 9

la réponse *response, answer*, 2

reposer *to rest; to relax;* laisser reposer *to let stand*, 8; se reposer *to relax*, 11

la République de Côte d'Ivoire *the Republic of Côte d'Ivoire*, 0

respectueux (-euse) *respectful*, 2

ressemblez : si vous me ressemblez *if you're like me*, 1

le restaurant *restaurant*, 6

la restauration *dining*, 6

le resto *restaurant*, 11

retard : en retard *late*, 2

retirer *to take out, to remove;* **retirer de l'argent** *to withdraw money*, 12

le retour *return*, 6

rétro (inv.) *retro*, 10

retrouve : Bon, on se retrouve... *OK, we'll meet . . .* , 6

retrouver *to find again*, 6

la Réunion *the island of Réunion*, 0

rêvait (imp. of rêver) *to dream*, 7

le rêve *dream*, 11

revenir *to come back*, 5

ridicule *ridiculous*, 10

rien *nothing*, 6; *anything*, 11; **Ça ne me dit rien.** *I don't feel like it.* 4; **Je n'ai rien oublié.** *I didn't forget anything.* 11; **Rien de spécial.** *Nothing special.* 6

rigoler *to laugh*, 10

le riz *rice*, 8

la robe *dress*, 10

le rock *rock (music)*, 4

le roller *skate;* **faire du roller en ligne** *to in-line skate*, 4

romain(e) *Roman (adj.)*, 9

le roman *novel*, 3

rond(e) *round*, 12

ronronner *to purr*, 7

le rosbif *roast beef*, 5

rose *pink*, 3

la rose *rose*, 0

le rôti *roast*, 5

rouge *red*, 3

le rouleau *roll*, 3; un rouleau protège-livres *a roll of plastic material to protect books*, 3

rouspètent (rouspéter) *to complain*, 9

roux (rousse) *redheaded*, 7

le ruban *ribbon; tape;* ruban adhésif transparent *transparent adhesive tape*, 3

la rue *street*, 12

s'il te plaît (informal) *please*, 3; **Oui, s'il te plaît.** *Yes, please.* (informal), 8

s'il vous plaît *please*, 3 (formal); **Oui, s'il vous plaît.** *Yes, please.* (formal), 8

sa *his, her*, 7

le sac *bag;* **le sac à dos** *backpack*, 3

sage *wise*, 12

sais : Je n'en sais rien. *I have no idea.* 11; **Je ne sais pas.** *I don't know.* 10; **Que sais-je?** *Self-check (What do I know?)*, 1

la saison *season*, 4; la basse saison *off season*, 12; la haute saison *tourist season*, 12

la salade *salad*, 8

les salades (f.) *heads of lettuce*, 8

saler *to salt*, 8

la salle *room*, 2; la salle de classe *classroom*, 2

Salut *Hi! or Goodbye!* 1

samedi *Saturday*, 2; **le samedi** *on Saturdays*, 2

les sandales (f.) *sandals*, 10

le sandwich *sandwich*, 5; **un sandwich au fromage** *cheese sandwich*, 5; **un sandwich au jambon** *ham sandwich*, 5; **un sandwich au saucisson** *salami sandwich*, 5;

sans *without*, 3; sans doute *probably*, 10

la sauce arachide *sauce made of peanut butter with beef chicken, or fish, hot peppers, peanut oil, garlic, onions, tomato paste, tomatoes, and other vegetables*, 8

la sauce pimentée *spicy sauce*, 8

le saucisson *salami*, 5

savais : Savais-tu que... ? *Did you know . . . ?* 2

savoir *to know*, 1

scellé(e) (pp. of sceller) *sealed*, 9

la science-fiction *science fiction*, 1

les sciences naturelles (f. pl.) *natural science*, 2

scolaire *having to do with school*, 2; la vie scolaire *school life*, 2

la séance *showing (at the movies)*, 6

la seconde *second*, 9; **Une seconde, s'il vous plaît.** *One second, please.* 9

le secours *aid, help;* le poste de secours *first-aid station*, 6

le séjour *stay, residence*, 7

le sel *salt*, 8

selon *according to*, 8

la semaine *week*, 4; **une fois par semaine** *once a week*, 4

le Sénégal *Senegal*, 0

sensas (sensationnel) *fantastic*, 10

septembre *September*, 4; **en septembre** *in September*, 4

sera : ce sera *it will be*, 6

le serpent *snake*, 0

serré(e) *tight*, 10

service compris *tip included*, 5

le service *service*, 3; **A votre service.** *At your service; You're welcome*, 3

ses *his, her*, 7

le sésame *sesame*, 8

sévère *severe, harsh*, 0

le short *(pair of) shorts*, 3

si *yes (to contradict a negative question)*, 2; **Moi, si.** *I do.* 2; **Oui, si tu veux.** *Yes, if you want to.* 7

le siècle *century*, 6

le signe *sign*, 12

sinon *otherwise; other than that*, 9

le sirop de fraise (à l'eau) *water with strawberry syrup*, 5

le ski *skiing*, 1; **faire du ski** *to ski*, 4; **faire du ski nautique** *to water-ski*, 4

la sœur *sister*, 7

la soie *silk*, 10

la soif *thirst;* **avoir soif** *to be thirsty*, 5

soigné(e) *with attention to detail*, 10

soigneusement *carefully*, 11

le soir *evening; in the evening*, 4; **Pas ce soir.** *Not tonight.* 7

sois (command form of être) : Ne sois pas découragée! *Don't be discouraged!* 9

soit *either;* soit chez moi, ou bien chez eux *whether at my house or at theirs*, 5

les soldes (m.) *sales*, 6

le soleil *sun, sunshine*, 4

le solfège *music theory*, 4

le sommet *top; summit*, 6

son *his, her*, 7

le sondage *poll*, 1

la sonnerie *ringing (of the telephone)*, 9

sont : Ce sont... *These/Those are . . .* , 7; **Ils/Elles sont...** *They are . . .* , 7; **Ils/Elles sont**

comment? *What are they like?* 7

sorti(e) (pp. of sortir) *went out,* 9; **Après, je suis sorti(e).** *Afterwards, I went out.* 9

la **sortie** *dismissal (when school gets out),* 2

sortir *to go out,* 1; *to take out,* 7; **sortir avec les copains** *to go out with friends,* 1; **sortir la poubelle** *to take out the trash,* 7

souterrain(e) *underground,* 11

souvent *often,* 4

spécial(e) *special,* 6; **Rien de spécial.** *Nothing special.* 6

le **spectacle** *show,* 11

le **sport** *gym,* 2; *sports,* 1; **faire du sport** *to play sports,* 1; **Qu'est-ce que tu fais comme sport?** *What sports do you play?* 4

le **sportif** (la **sportive**) *sportsman (sportswoman),* 4

le **stade** *stadium,* 6

la **stalactite** *stalactite,* 11

la **station-service** *service station, gas station,* 11

le **steak-frites** *steak and French fries,* 5

le **style** *style;* **C'est tout à fait ton style.** *It looks great on you!* 10

le **stylo** *pen,* 0; **un stylo plume** *fountain pen,* 3

la **subvention** *subsidy,* 7

le **sucre** *sugar,* 8

sucré(e) *sweet,* 8

suis : Qui suis-je? *Who am I?* 0; **Désolé(e), je suis occupé(e).** *Sorry, I'm busy.* 6; **Je suis bien chez . . . ?** *Is this . . . .'s house?* 9

suisse *Swiss* (adj.), 1; **la Suisse** *Switzerland,* 0

suivre *to follow,* 9

super *super,* 2; **Super!** *Great!* 1; **pas super** *not so hot,* 2

le **supermarché** *supermarket,* 8

supportez (supporter) *to put up with,* 2

sur *on;* **sur place** *on-site,* 4; **sur un total de** *out of a total of,* 4

le **surligneur** *highlighting marker,* 3

surtout *especially,* 1

le **sweat-shirt** *sweatshirt,* 3

sympa (inv.; abbrev. of **sympathique**) *nice,* 7

T

ta *your,* 7

le **tableau** *blackboard,* 0

la **tache** *spot,* 7

la **taille** *size,* 10; **taille unique** *one size fits all,* 10; **en taille... in size. . . ,** 10

la **taille élastiquée** *elastic waist,* 10

le **taille-crayon** *pencil sharpener,* 3

tant : tant privée que professionelle *private as well as professional,* 9

la **tante** *aunt,* 7

le **tarif : tarif réduit** *reduced fee,* 6

la **tarte** *pie,* 8

le **tas** *pile, heap;* **J'ai des tas de choses à faire.** *I have lots of things to do.* 5

le **taux de réussite** *rate of success,* 2

le **taxi** *taxi,* 12; **en taxi** *by taxi,* 12

le **Tchad** *Chad,* 0

Tchao! *Bye!* 1

la **techno** *techno music,* 1

le **tee-shirt** *T-shirt,* 3

la **télécarte** *phone card,* 9

le **télécopieur** *fax machine,* 9

le **téléphone** *telephone,* 0; **parler au téléphone** *to talk on the phone,* 1; **le téléphone à pièces** *coin-operated telephone,* 9; **le téléphone sans fil** *cordless telephone,* 9

téléphoné (pp. of téléphoner) *called, phoned,* 9; **Vous pouvez lui dire que j'ai téléphoné?** *Can you tell him/her that I called?* 9

téléphoner *to call, to phone,* 9; **Téléphone-lui/-leur!** *Call him/her/them!* 9

la **télévision** *television,* 0; **regarder la télé(vision)** *to watch TV,* 1

tellement *so; so much;* **Pas tellement.** *Not too much.* 4

le **temps** *time,* 4; *weather,* 4; **de temps en temps** *from time to time,* 4; **Je regrette, mais je n'ai pas le temps.** *I'm sorry, but I don't have time.* 8; **Quel temps est-ce qu'il fait à... ?** *How's the weather in . . . ?* 4; **Quel temps fait-il?** *What's the weather like?* 4

le **tennis** *tennis,* 4; **jouer au tennis** *to play tennis,* 4

la **tenue** *outfit;* **une tenue de gymnastique** *gym suit,* 3

la **terminale** *final year of French high school, usually spent preparing for the bac,* 2

termine (terminer) *to finish,* 2

terrible *terrible, awful;* **Pas terrible.** *Not so great.* 1

le **territoire d'outre-mer** *overseas territory,* 12

tes *your,* 7

le **théâtre** *theater,* 6; **faire du théâtre** *to do drama,* 4

théorique *theoretical,* 12

le **thon** *tuna,* 5

Tiens! *Hey!* 3

tient (tenir) *to hold,* 12

le **tilleul** *lime green,* 10

le **timbre** *stamp,* 12

timide *shy,* 7

le **tissue** *cloth, fabric,* 10

toi *you,* 1; **Et toi?** *And you?* 1

le **tollé** *outcry,* 12

la **tomate** *tomato,* 8

tomber *to fall,* 10

ton *your,* 7

tondre *to mow,* 7; **tondre le gazon** *to mow the lawn,* 7

le **tour** *measurement;* **tour de poitrine** *chest size,* 10

tournez : Vous tournez... *You turn . . . ,* 12

le **tournoi** *tournament,* 4

tous *all,* 2

tout(e) *all,* 2; **A tout à l'heure!** *See you later!* 1; **J'ai pensé à tout.** *I've thought of everything.* 11; **pas du tout** *not at all,* 2; **Il/Elle ne va pas du tout avec...** *It doesn't go at all with . . . ,* 10; **C'est tout à fait ton style.** *It looks great on you!* 10; **tout de suite** *right away,* 6; **C'est tout de suite à...** *It's right there on the . . . ,* 12; **J'y vais tout de suite.** *I'll go right away.* 8; **Vous allez tout droit jusqu'à...** *You go straight ahead until you get to . . . ,* 12; **tout(e) seul(e)** *all alone,* 12

le **train** *train,* 12; **en train** *by train,* 12; **un billet de train** *train ticket,* 11

traité : être traité comme une gosse *to be treated like a kid,* 2

le **trajet** *route,* 12

la **tranche** *slice,* 8; **une tranche de** *a slice of,* 8

le **travail scolaire** *school work,* 2

travailler *to work,* 9; **travailler la pâte** *to knead the dough,* 8

les **travaux pratiques** (m. pl.) *lab,* 2

traverser *to cross,* 12

très *very,* 1; **Très bien.** *Very well.* 1; **Très heureux (heureuse).** *Pleased to meet you.* 7

le **trésor** *treasure,* 3; **chasse au trésor** *treasure hunt,* 3

la trompette *trumpet*, 0
trop *too (much)*, 10; **Il/Elle est trop cher/chère.** *It's too expensive.* 10; **Non, pas trop.** *No, not too much.* 2
la **trousse** *pencil case*, 3
trouver *to find*, 9; **Comment tu trouves ça?** *What do you think of that/it?* 2; **Comment tu trouves... ?** *What do you think of . . . ?* 2; **Je le/la/les trouve...** *I think it's/ they're . . .* , 10; **Tu trouves?** *Do you think so?* 10
le **truc** *thing*, 5; **J'ai des trucs à faire.** *I have some things to do.* 5
tu *you*, 0
la **Tunisie** *Tunisia*, 0

un (m.) *a, an*, 3
une (f.) *a, an*, 3
l' **uniforme** (m.) *uniform*, 0
utiliser *to use*, 10

va : Ça va. *Fine.* 1; **(Comment) ça va?** *How's it going?* 1; **Comment est-ce qu'on y va?** *How can we get there?* 12; **Il/Elle me va?** *Does it suit me?* 10; **Il/Elle ne te/vous va pas du tout.** *It doesn't look good on you at all.* 10; **Il/Elle ne va pas du tout avec...** *It doesn't go at all with . . .* , 10
les **vacances** (f. pl.) *vacation*, 1; **Bonnes vacances!** *Have a good vacation!* 11; **en colonie de vacances** *to/at a summer camp*, 11; **en vacances** *on vacation*, 4
vais : Je vais... *I'm going . . .* , 6; *I'm going (to) . . .* , 11; **J'y vais tout de suite.** *I'll go right away.* 8
la **vaisselle** *dishes*, 7; **faire la vaisselle** *to do the dishes*, 7
valable *valid*, 6
la **valise** *suitcase*, 11
la **vanille** *vanilla*, 8
vas : Qu'est-ce que tu vas faire? *What are you going to do?* 6
la **vedette** *celebrity*, 1
le **vélo** *biking*, 1; **à vélo** *by bike*, 12; **faire du vélo** *to bike*, 4
le **vendeur** *salesperson*, 3
la **vendeuse** *salesperson*, 3
vendre *to sell*, 9

vendredi *Friday*, 2; **le vendredi** *on Fridays*, 2
la **vente** *sales*, 6
la **verdure** *vegetation*, 11
véritable *real*, 11; **C'était un véritable cauchemar!** *It was a real nightmare!* 11
le **verre** *glass*, 6
vers *about*, 6
vert(e) *green*, 3
la **veste** *suit jacket, blazer*, 10
le **vêtement** *clothing item*, 10
veux : Je veux bien. *I'd really like to.* 6; **Tu veux... avec moi?** *Do you want . . . with me?* 6
la **viande** *meat*, 8
vide *empty*, 12
la **vidéo** *video*, 4; **faire de la vidéo** *to make videos*, 4; **des jeux vidéo** *video games*, 4
la **vidéocassette** *videotape*, 3
la **vie scolaire** *school life*, 2
viennois(e) *Viennese* (adj.), 5
viens : Tu viens? *Will you come?* 6
vietnamien(ne) *Vietnamese* (adj.), 1
vieux *old*, 4
la **ville** *city*, 12
le **vinaigre** *vinegar*, 8
la **violence** *violence*, 1
violet(te) *purple*, 3
la **virgule** *comma*, 3
visiter *to visit (a place)*, 9
le **visiteur** *visitor*, 9
vite *fast, quickly*, 2
la **vitrine** *window (of a shop)*; **faire les vitrines** *to window-shop*, 6
vivant *lively, living*, 7
Vive... ! *Hurray for . . . !* 3
vivre *to live*, 2
le **vocabulaire** *vocabulary*, 1
Voici... *Here's . . .* , 7
Voilà. *Here.* 3; **Voilà...** *There's . . .* , 7
la **voile** *sailing*, 11; **faire de la planche à voile** *to go wind-surfing*, 11; **faire de la voile** *to go sailing*, 11
voir *to see*, 6; **voir un film** *to see a movie*, 6; **aller voir un match** *to go see a game*, 6; **voir une pièce** *to see a play*, 6
le **voisin (la voisine)** *neighbor*, 1
la **voiture** *car*, 7; **en voiture** *by car*, 12; **laver la voiture** *to wash the car*, 7
la **voix** *voice*, 3

le **volley (-ball)** *volleyball*, 4; **jouer au volley (-ball)** *to play volleyball*, 4
volontiers *with pleasure; gladly*, 8
vos *your*, 7
votre *your*, 7
voudrais : Je voudrais... *I'd like . . .* 3
vouloir *to want*, 6; **Je n'en veux plus.** *I don't want any-more.* 8; **Je veux bien.** *I'd really like to.* 6; *Gladly.* 8; **Oui, j'en veux bien.** *Yes, I'd like some.* 8; **Oui, si tu veux.** *Yes, if you want to.* 7; **Tu veux... ?** *Do you want . . . ?* 6; **voulez : Vous voulez... ?** *Do you want . . . ?* 8
vous *you*, 1
le **voyage** *voyage, trip*, 0
voyager *to travel*, 1; **Bon voyage!** *Have a good trip!* 11
vrai(e) *true*, 2
vraiment *really*, 11; **Non, pas vraiment.** *No, not really.* 11
vu (pp. of voir) *seen, saw*, 9
la **vue** *view*, 6

le **week-end** *on weekends*, 4; *weekend*, 6
le **western** *western (movie)*, 0

le **xylophone** *xylophone*, 0

y *there*, 12; **Allons-y!** *Let's go!* 4; **Comment est-ce qu'on y va?** *How can we get there?* 12; **J'y vais tout de suite.** *I'll go right away.* 8; **On peut y aller...** *We can go there . . .* , 12
les **yaourts** (m.) *yogurt*, 8
les **yeux** (m. pl.) *eyes*, 8
le **yo-yo** *yo-yo*, 0
la **yole** *skiff (a type of boat)*, 12

le **zèbre** *zebra*, 0
zéro *a waste of time*, 2
le **zoo** *zoo*, 6
Zut! *Darn!* 3

ENGLISH-FRENCH VOCABULARY

In this vocabulary, the English definitions of all active French words in the book have been listed, followed by the French. The number after each entry refers to the chapter in which the entry is introduced. It is important to use a French word in its correct context. The use of a word can be checked easily by referring to the chapter where it appears.

French words and phrases are presented in the same way as in the French-English vocabulary.

a *un, une,* 3
able: to be able to *pouvoir,* 8
about *vers,* 6
across from *en face de,* 12
adore *adorer,* 1; **I adore . . .** *J'adore... ,* 1
advise *conseiller;* **What do you advise me to do?** *Qu'est-ce que tu me conseilles?* 9
aerobics *l'aérobic* (f.), 4; **to do aerobics** *faire de l'aérobic,* 4
after *après,* 9; **And after that, . . .** *Et après ça...,* 9
afternoon *l'après-midi* (m.), 2; **afternoon off** *l'après-midi libre,* 2; **in the afternoon** *l'après-midi,* 2
afterwards *après,* 9; **Afterwards, I went out.** *Après, je suis sorti(e).* 9; **And afterwards?** *Et après?* 9
Agreed. *Entendu.* 6
algebra *l'algèbre* (f.), 2
all *tout(e):* **Not at all.** *Pas du tout.* 4
already *déjà,* 9
also *aussi,* 1
am: I am . . . years old. *J'ai... ans.* 1
an *un, une,* 3
and *et,* 1
annoying *embêtant(e),* 7; *pénible,* 7
answer *répondre,* 9; **There's no answer.** *Ça ne répond pas.* 9
any (of it) *en,* 8; **any more: I don't want any more.** *Je n'en veux plus.* 8
anything: I didn't forget anything. *Je n'ai rien oublié.* 11
apple *la pomme,* 8
apple juice *le jus de pomme,* 5
April *avril,* 4
are: These/those are . . . *Ce sont... ,* 7; **They're . . .** *Ils/Elles sont... ,* 7
art class *les arts plastiques* (m. pl.), 2
at *à la, au, a l', aux,* 6; **at . . . fifteen** *à... heure(s) quinze,* 2; **at . . . forty-five** *à... heure(s) quarante-cinq,* 2; **at . . . thirty** *à... heure(s) trente,* 2; **at . . . ('s) house** *chez... ,* 6; **at the record store** *chez le*

disquaire, 12; **At what time?** *A quelle heure?* 6
August *août,* 4
autumn *l'automne* (m.), 4
aunt *la tante,* 7
avocado *l'avocat* (m.), 8

backpack *le sac à dos,* 3
bad *mauvais(e),* 5; **Not bad.** *Pas mal.* 1; **Oh, pas mauvais.** *Oh, not bad.* 9; **Very bad.** *Très mauvais.* 9
bag *le sac,* 3
baggy *large,* 10
bakery *la boulangerie,* 12
banana *la banane,* 8
bank *la banque,* 12
baseball *le base-ball,* 4; **to play baseball** *jouer au base-ball,* 4
basketball *le basket(-ball),* 4; **to play basketball** *jouer au basket (-ball),* 4
bathing suit *le maillot de bain,* 10
be *être,* 7
be able to, can *pouvoir,* 8; **Can you . . . ?** *Tu peux... ?* 12
beach *la plage,* 1
beans *les haricots* (m.), 8; **green beans** *les haricots verts* (m.), 8
because *parce que,* 5
beef *le bœuf,* 8
begin *commencer,* 9
behind *derrière,* 12
belt *la ceinture,* 10
better *mieux,* 9; **It's going to get better!** *Ça va aller mieux!* 9
between *entre,* 12
big *grand(e),* 10
bike *le vélo; faire du vélo,* 4; **by bike** *à vélo,* 12
biking *le vélo,* 1
binder: loose-leaf binder *le classeur,* 3
biology *la biologie,* 2
black *noir(e),* 3
blackboard *le tableau,* 0; **Go to the blackboard!** *Allez au tableau!* 0
blazer *la veste,* 10
blond *blond(e),* 7

blue *bleu(e),* 3
boat *le bateau,* 11; **by boat** *en bateau,* 12; **to go boating** *faire du bateau,* 11
book *le livre,* 0
bookstore *la librairie,* 12
boots *les bottes* (f.), 10
boring *barbant(e),* 2; **It was boring.** *C'était ennuyeux.* 11; *C'était barbant!* 11
borrow *emprunter,* 12
bottle *la bouteille,* 8; **a bottle of** *une bouteille de,* 8
box *le paquet,* 8; **a package/box of** *un paquet de,* 8
boy *le garçon,* 8
bracelet *le bracelet,* 3
bread *le pain,* 8; **long, thin loaf of bread** *la baguette,* 12
break *la récréation,* 2
breakfast *le petit déjeuner,* 8
bring *apporter,* 9; **Bring me back . . .** *Rapporte-moi... ,* 8; **Please bring me . . .** *Apportez-moi... , s'il vous plaît.* 5; **Will you bring me . . . ?** *Tu me rapportes... ?* 8
brother *le frère,* 7
brown *marron* (inv.), 3
brunette *brun(e),* 7
bus *le bus,* 12; **by bus** *en bus,* 12; **to miss the bus** *rater le bus,* 9
busy *occupé(e),* 6; **It's busy.** *C'est occupé.* 9; **Sorry, I'm busy.** *Désolé(e), je suis occupé(e).* 6
but *mais,* 1
butter *le beurre,* 8
buy *acheter,* 9; **Buy (me) . . .** *Achète(-moi)... ,* 8
Bye! *Tchao!* 1

C

cafeteria *la cantine,* 9; **at the school cafeteria** *à la cantine,* 9
cake *le gâteau,* 8
calculator *la calculatrice,* 3
call *téléphoner,* 9; **Call him/her/them!** *Téléphone-lui/-leur!* 9; **Can you call back later?** *Vous pouvez rappeler plus*

R72

tard? 9; **Who's calling?** *Qui est à l'appareil?* 9
camera *l'appareil-photo* (m.), 11
camp *la colonie de vacances,* 11; **to/at a summer camp** *en colonie de vacances,* 11
camping *le camping,* 11; **to go camping** *faire du camping,* 11
can: to be able to, can *pouvoir,* 8; **Can I talk to you?** *Je peux te parler?* 9; **Can you . . . ?** *Est-ce que tu peux... ?* 12; **Can you . . . ?** *Tu peux... ?* 8; **Can I try on . . . ?** *Je peux essayer... ?* 10; **We can . . . On peut... ,** 6; **What can I do?** *Qu'est-ce que je peux faire?* 9
can *la boîte,* 8; **a can of** *une boîte de,* 8
can't: I can't right now. *Je ne peux pas maintenant.* 8; **No, I can't.** *Non, je ne peux pas.* 12
canary *le canari,* 7
cap *la casquette,* 10
car *la voiture,* 7; **by car** *en voiture,* 12; **to wash the car** *laver la voiture,* 7
cards *les cartes* (f.), 4; **to play cards** *jouer aux cartes,* 4
carrot *la carotte,* 8
cassette tape *la cassette,* 3
cat *le chat,* 7
CD/compact disc *le disque compact/le CD,* 3
Certainly. *Bien sûr.* 9
chair *la chaise,* 0
check *l'addition* (f.), 5; **The check, please.** *L'addition, s'il vous plaît.* 5
cheese *le fromage,* 5; **toasted cheese and ham sandwich** *le croque-monsieur,* 5
chemistry *la chimie,* 2
chic *chic* (inv.), 10
chicken (animal) *la poule,* 8; **chicken meat** *le poulet,* 8
child *l'enfant* (m./f.), 7; **children** *les enfants,* 7
chocolate *le chocolat,* 1; **hot chocolate** *un chocolat,* 5
choir *la chorale,* 2
choose *choisir,* 10; **Have you chosen?** *Vous avez choisi?* 5
class *le cours,* 2; **What classes do you have . . . ?** *Tu as quels cours... ?* 2
clean: to clean house *faire le ménage,* 7
clear: to clear the table *débarrasser la table,* 7
close: Close the door! *Fermez la porte!* 0
close to *près de,* 12
clothing *les vêtements,* 10

coast *le bord,* 11; **to/on the coast** *au bord de la mer,* 11
coat *le manteau,* 10
coconut *la noix de coco,* 8
coffee *le café,* 5
cola *le coca,* 5
cold *froid,(e)* 4; **It's cold.** *Il fait froid.* 4
color *la couleur,* 3; **What color is . .?** *De quelle couleur est... ?* 3
come: Will you come? *Tu viens?* 6
compact disc/CD *le disque compact/le CD,* 3
computer *l'ordinateur* (m.), 3
computer science *l'informatique* (f.), 2
concert *le concert,* 1
continue *continuer,* 12
cool *cool,* 2; **It's cool out.** *Il fait frais.* 4; **Very cool (great).** *Très chouette.* 9
corn *le maïs,* 8
corner *le coin,* 12; **on the corner of** *au coin de,* 12
cotton (adj.) *en coton,* 10
could: Could you do me a favor? *(Est-ce que) tu peux me rendre un petit service?* 12; **Could you go by . . . ?** *Tu pourrais passer à... ?* 12
countryside *la campagne,* 11; **to/in the countryside** *à la campagne,* 11
course *le cours,* 2
course: Of course. *Bien sûr.* 3
cousin *le cousin (la cousine),* 7
cross *traverser,* 12
cute *mignon(ne),* 7

dairy products *les produits* (m.) *laitiers,* 8
dance *danser,* 1
dance *la danse,* 2
Darn! *Zut!* 3
daughter *la fille,* 7
day *le jour,* 2
December *décembre,* 4; **in December** *en décembre,* 4
decided: Have you decided? *Vous avez choisi?* 5; **Have you decided to take . . . ?** *Vous avez décidé de prendre... ?* 10
delicious *délicieux(-euse),* 5
denim *le jean,* 10; **in denim** *en jean,* 10
deposit *déposer,* 12; **to deposit money** *déposer de l'argent,* 12
dictionary *le dictionnaire,* 3
difficult *difficile,* 2
dinner *le dîner,* 8; **to have dinner** *dîner,* 9
dishes *la vaisselle,* 7; **to do the dishes** *faire la vaisselle,* 7

dismissal (when school gets out) *la sortie,* 2
do *faire,* 4; **Do you play/do . . . ?** *Est-ce que tu fais... ?* 4; **I do.** *Moi, si.* 2; **to do homework** *faire les devoirs,* 7; **to do the dishes** *faire la vaisselle,* 7; **I don't play/do . . .** *Je ne fais pas de... ,* 4; **I have errands to do.** *J'ai des courses à faire.* 5; **I play/do . . .** *Je fais... ,* 4; **In your opinion, what do I do?** *A ton avis, qu'est-ce que je fais?* 9; **Sorry. I have homework to do.** *Désolé(e). J'ai des devoirs à faire.* 5; **What are you going to do . . . ?** *Qu'est-ce que tu vas faire... ?* 6; *Tu vas faire quoi... ?* 6; **What can I do?** *Qu'est-ce que je peux faire?* 9; **What did you do . . . ?** *Qu'est-ce que tu as fait... ?* 9; **What do you advise me to do?** *Qu'est-ce que tu me conseilles?* 9; **What do you do . . . ?** *Qu'est-ce que tu fais... ?* 4; **What do you do when . . . ?** *Qu'est-ce que tu fais quand... ?* 4
dog *le chien,* 7; **to walk the dog** *promener le chien,* 7
done, made *fait* (pp. of faire), 9
door *la porte,* 0
down: You go down this street to the next light. *Vous continuez jusqu'au prochain feu rouge.* 12
dozen *la douzaine,* 8; **a dozen** *une douzaine de,* 8
drama *le théâtre,* 4; **to do drama** *faire du théâtre,* 4
dress *la robe,* 10
drink *la boisson,* 5; **What do you have to drink?** *Qu'est-ce que vous avez comme boissons?* 5; **What is there to drink?** *Qu'est-ce qu'il y a à boire?* 5
drugstore *la pharmacie,* 12

earn *gagner,* 9
earrings *les boucles d'oreilles* (f.), 10
easy *facile,* 2
eat *manger,* 6
egg *l'œuf* (m.), 8
English (language) *l'anglais* (m.), 1
envelope *l'enveloppe* (f.), 12
eraser *la gomme,* 3
errands *les courses* (f.), 7; **I have errands to do.** *J'ai des courses à faire.* 5
especially *surtout,* 1
evening *le soir,* 4; **in the evening** *le soir,* 4
everything *tout,* 11; **I've thought of everything.** *J'ai pensé à tout.* 11

ENGLISH-FRENCH VOCABULARY

exam *l'examen* (m.), 1
excellent *excellent(e)*, 5; **Yes, excellent.** *Oui, excellent.* 9
excuse: **Excuse me.** *Excusez-moi.* 3; **Excuse me, . . . , please?** *Pardon, ... s'il vous plaît?* 12; **Excuse me. Where is . . . , please?** *Pardon. Où est... , s'il vous plaît?* 12; **Excuse me. I'm looking for . . . , please.** *Pardon. Je cherche... , s'il vous plaît.* 12
expensive *cher (chère),* 10; **It's too expensive.** *C'est trop cher.* 10

F

fail *rater,* 9; **to fail a test** *rater un examen,* 9; **to fail a quiz** *rater une interro,* 9
fall *l'automne* (m.), 4; **in the fall** *en automne,* 4
fantastic *sensas (sensationnel),* 10
far from *loin de,* 12
fascinating *passionnant(e),* 2
fat *gros (-se),* 7
father *le père,* 7
February *février,* 4; **in February** *en février,* 4
feel: **I feel like . . .** *J'ai envie de... ,* 11; **I don't feel like it.** *Ça ne me dit rien.* 6
finally *enfin,* 9; *finalement,* 9
find *trouver,* 9
Fine. *Ça va.* 1; **Yes, it was fine.** *Oui, ça a été.* 9
first *d'abord,* 7; **OK, if you . . . first.** *D'accord, si tu... d'abord.* 7
fish *le poisson,* 7
flour *la farine,* 8
foot *le pied,* 12; **on foot** *à pied,* 12
football *le football américain,* 4; **to play football** *jouer au football américain,* 4
for *pour,* 3; **What do you need for . . . ?** (informal) *Qu'est qu'il te faut pour... ?* 3
forest *la forêt,* 11; **to/in the forest** *en forêt,* 11
forget *oublier,* 9; **Don't forget . . .** *N'oublie pas de... ,* 8; **Forget him/her/them!** *Oublie-le/-la/-les!* 9; **I didn't forget anything.** *Je n'ai rien oublié.* 11; **You didn't forget . . . ?** *Tu n'as pas oublié... ?* 11
franc (the French monetary unit) *le franc,* 3; **It's . . . francs.** *C'est/Ça fait...francs.* 5
French (language) *le français,* 1; **French fries** *les frites* (f.), 1
Friday *vendredi,* 2; **on Fridays** *le vendredi,* 2

friend *l'ami(e)* (m./f.), 1; **to go out with friends** *sortir avec les copains,* 1
from *de,* 0
front: **in front of** *devant,* 6
fruit *le fruit,* 8
fun: **Did you have fun?** *Tu t'es bien amusé(e)?* 11; **Have fun!** *Amuse-toi bien!* 11; **What do you do to have fun?** *Qu'est-ce que tu fais pour t'amuser?* 4
funny *amusant(e),* 7

G

gain: **to gain weight** *grossir,* 10
game *le match,* 6; **to play video games** *jouer à des jeux vidéo,* 4; **to watch a game (on TV)** *regarder un match,* 6; **to go see a game** *aller voir un match,* 6
geography *la géographie,* 2
geometry *la géométrie,* 2
German (language) *l'allemand* (m.), 2
get: **Get . . .** *Prends... ,* 8; **How can we get there?** *Comment est-ce qu'on y va?* 12
gift *le cadeau,* 11
girl *la fille,* 0
give *donner,* 5; **Please give me . . .** *Donnez-moi... , s'il vous plaît.* 5
Gladly. *Je veux bien.* 8
go *aller,* 6; **Go to the blackboard!** *Allez au tableau!* 0; **I'm going . . .** *Je vais... ,* 6; **What are you going to do . . . ?** *Tu vas faire quoi... ?* 6; **It doesn't go at all with . . .** *Il/Elle ne va pas du tout avec... ,* 10; **It goes very well with . . .** *Il/Elle va très bien avec... ,* 10; **to go out with friends** *sortir avec les copains,* 1; **I'd like . . . to go with . . .** *J'aimerais... pour aller avec... ,* 10; **Afterwards, I went out.** *Après, je suis sorti(e).* 9; **Could you go by . . . ?** *Tu pourrais passer à... ?* 12; **Did it go well?** *Ça s'est bien passé?* 11; **I'm going to have . . . , please.** *Je vais prendre... , s'il vous plaît.* 5; **What are you going to do . . . ?** *Qu'est-ce que tu vas faire... ?* 6; **I went . . .** *Je suis allé(e)... ,* 9; **I'm going to . . .** *Je vais... ,* 11; **Let's go . . .** *Allons... ,* 6; **to go for a walk** *faire une promenade,* 6; **We can go there . . .** *On peut y aller... ,* 12; **Where are you going to go . . . ?** *Où est-ce que tu vas aller... ?* 11; **Where did you go?** *Tu es allé(e) où?* 9; **You keep going until the next light.**

Vous continuez jusqu'au prochain feu rouge. 12; **How's it going? (Comment)** *ça va?* 1
golf *le golf,* 4; **to play golf** *jouer au golf,* 4
good *bon(ne),* 5; **Have a good trip!** *Bon voyage!* 11; **Did you have a good . . . ?** *Tu as passé un bon... ?* 11; **It doesn't look good on you at all.** *Il/Elle ne te/vous va pas du tout.* 10; **It's pretty good!** *C'est pas mauvais!* 5; **not good** *pas bon,* 5; **Yes, very good.** *Oui, très bon.* 9
Goodbye! *Au revoir!* 1; *Salut!* 1
got: **No, you've got to . . .** *Non, tu dois... ,* 7
grandfather *le grand-père,* 7
grandmother *la grand-mère,* 7
grapes *le raisin,* 8
great *génial(e),* 2; **Great!** *Super!* 1; **It looks great on you!** *C'est tout à fait ton style!* 10; **It was great!** *C'était formidable!* 11; **Not so great.** *Pas terrible,* 1
green *vert(e),* 3
green beans *les *haricots verts* (m.), 8
grey *gris(e),* 3
grocery store (small) *l'épicerie* (f.), 12
gross *dégoûtant(e),* 5
grow *grandir,* 10
guava *la goyave,* 8
gym *le sport,* 2

H

half *demi(e),* 6; **half past** *et demie,* 6; **half past** (after *midi* and *minuit*) *et demi,* 6
ham *le jambon,* 5; **toasted cheese and ham sandwich** *le croque-monsieur,* 5
hamburger *le hamburger,* 1
hand *la main,* 0
happened: **What happened?** *Qu'est-ce qui s'est passé?* 9
happy *content (e),* 7
hard *difficile,* 2
hat *le chapeau,* 10
have *avoir,* 2; **At what time do you have . . . ?** *Tu as... à quelle heure?* 2; **Did you have a good weekend?** *Tu as passé un bon week-end?* 9; **Do you have . . . ?** *Vous avez... ?* 2; *Tu as... ?* 3; **Do you have that in . . . ?** (size, fabric, color) *Vous avez ça en... ?* 10; **Have . . .** *Prends/Prenez... ,* 5; **What are you having?** *Vous prenez?* 5; **I don't have . . .** *Je n'ai pas de... ,* 3; **I have some things to do.** *J'ai des trucs à faire.* 5; **I have . . .** *J'ai... ,*

R74

ENGLISH-FRENCH VOCABULARY

2; **I'll have . . . , please.** *Je vais prendre... , s'il vous plaît.* 5; **to take or to have (food or drink)** *prendre,* 5; **We have . . .** *Nous avons...,* 2; **What classes do you have . . . ?** *Tu as quels cours... ?* 2; **What do you have . . . ?** *Tu as quoi... ?* 2; **What kind of . . . do you have?** *Qu'est-ce que vous avez comme... ?* 5; **Will you have . . . ?** *Tu prends/Vous prenez... ?* 8;
health *le cours de développement personnel et social (DPS),* 2
Hello. *Bonjour.* 1; **Hello? (on the phone)** *Allô?* 9
help: May I help you? *(Est-ce que) je peux vous aider?* 10
her *la,* 9; *son/sa/ses,* 7; **to her** *lui,* 9
Here. *Voilà.* 3; **Here's . . .** *Voici... ,* 7
Hi! *Salut!* 1
hiking *la randonnée,* 11; **to go hiking** *faire de la randonnée,* 11
him *le,* 9; **to him** *lui,* 9
his *son/sa/ses,* 7
history *l'histoire* (f.), 2
hockey *le* hockey, 4; **to play hockey** *jouer au hockey,* 4
Hold on. *Ne quittez pas.* 9
homework *les devoirs* (m.), 2; **I've got homework to do.** *J'ai des devoirs à faire.* 5; **to do homework** *faire les devoirs,* 7
horrible *épouvantable,* 9; **It was horrible.** *C'était épouvantable.* 9
horseback riding *l'équitation* (f.), 1; **to go horseback riding** *faire de l'équitation,* 1
hose *le collant,* 10
hot chocolate *le chocolat,* 5
hot dog *le* hot-dog, 5
hot *chaud,* 4; **It's hot.** *Il fait chaud.* 4; **not so hot** *pas super,* 2
house: at my house *chez moi,* 6; **Is this . . . 's house?** *Je suis bien chez... ?* 9; **to/at . . . 's house** *chez... ,* 6;
housework *le ménage,* 1; **to do housework** *faire le ménage,* 1
how: How old are you? *Tu as quel âge?* 1; **How about . . . ?** *On... ? 4;* **How do you like it?** *Comment tu trouves ça?* 5; **How much is . . . ?** *C'est combien... ?* 5; **How much is it?** *C'est combien?* 3; **How much is it, please? (total)** *Ça fait combien, s'il vous plaît?* 5; **How's it going?** *(Comment) ça va?* 1
how much *combien,* 3; **How much is . . . ?** *C'est combien,... ?* 3; **How much is it? (total)** *Ça fait combien, s'il vous plaît?* 5
hundred *cent,* 3; **two hundred**

deux cents, 3
hungry: to be hungry *avoir faim,* 5; **No thanks. I'm not hungry anymore.** *Non, merci. Je n'ai plus faim.* 8
husband *le mari,* 7

I *je,* 1; **I do.** *Moi, si.* 2; **I don't.** *Moi, non.* 2
ice cream *la glace,* 1
ice-skate *faire du patin à glace,* 4
idea *l'idée* (f.), 4; **Good idea.** *Bonne idée.* 4; **I have no idea.** *Je n'en sais rien.* 11
if *si,* 7; **OK, if you . . . first.** *D'accord, si tu... d'abord...* 7
impossible *impossible,* 7; **No, that's impossible.** *Non, c'est impossible.* 7
in *dans,* 6; **in (a city or place)** *à,* 11; **in (before a feminine country)** *en,* 11; **in (before a masculine noun)** *au,* 11; **in (before a plural country)** *aux,* 11; **in front of** *devant,* 6; **in the afternoon** *l'après-midi,* 2; **in the evening** *le soir,* 4; **in the morning** *le matin,* 2
in-line skate *le roller en ligne,* 4; **to in-line skate** *faire du roller en ligne,* 4
indifference: (expression of indifference) *Bof!* 1
intend: I intend to . . . *J'ai l'intention de... ,* 11
interest: That doesn't interest me. *Ça ne me dit rien.* 4
interesting *intéressant(e),* 2
is: He is . . . *Il est... ,* 7; **It's . . .** *C'est... ,* 2; **She is . . .** *Elle est... ,* 7; **There's . . .** *Voilà... ,* 7; **This is . . .** *C'est... ; Voici... ,* 7
it *le, la,* 9
It's . . . *C'est... ,* 2; **It's . . .** *Il est...* (time), 6; **It's . . . francs.** *C'est... francs.* 5; *Ça fait... francs.* 5; **No, it's . . .** *Non, c'est... ,* 4; **Yes, it's . . .** *Oui, c'est... ,* 4

jacket *le blouson,* 10; **suit jacket** *la veste,* 10
jam *la confiture,* 8
January *janvier,* 4; **in January** *en janvier,* 4
jeans *le jean,* 3
jog *faire du jogging,* 4
jogging *le jogging,* 4
juice *le jus,* 5; **orange juice** *le jus d'orange,* 5; **apple juice** *le jus de pomme,* 5

July *juillet,* 4; **in July** *en juillet,* 4
June *juin,* 4; **in june** *en juin,* 4

kilogram *le kilo(kilogramme),* 8; **a kilogram of** *un kilo de,* 8
kind: What kind of . . . do you have? *Qu'est-ce que vous avez comme... ?* 5
know: I don't know. *Je ne sais pas.* 10

lab *les travaux pratiques* (m. pl.), 2
later: Can you call back later? *Vous pouvez rappeler plus tard?* 9; **See you later!** *A tout à l'heure!* 1
Latin (language) *le latin,* 2
lawn *le gazon,* 7; **to mow the lawn** *tondre le gazon,* 7
learn *apprendre,* 0
leather *le cuir,* 10; **in leather** *en cuir,* 10
leave *partir,* 11; **Can I leave a message?** *Je peux laisser un message?* 9; **You can't leave without . . .** *Tu ne peux pas partir sans... ,* 11
left *la gauche,* 12; **to the left** *à gauche (de),* 12
lemon *le citron,* 8
lemon soda *la limonade,* 5
lemonade *le citron pressé,* 5
let's: Let's go . . . *Allons... ,* 6; **Let's go!** *Allons-y!* 4
letter *la lettre,* 12; **to send letters** *envoyer des lettres,* 12
lettuce *la salade* (f.), 8
library *la bibliothèque,* 6
like *aimer,* 1; **I'd really like . . .** *Je voudrais bien... ,* 11; **Do you like . . . ?** *Tu aimes... ?* 1; **Do you like it?** *Il/Elle te (vous) plaît?* 10; **How do you like . . . ?** *Comment tu trouves... ?* 10; **How do you like it?** *Comment tu trouves ça?* 5; **I (really) like . . .** *Moi, j'aime (bien)... ,* 1; **I don't like . . .** *Je n'aime pas... ,* 1; **I like it, but it's expensive.** *Il/Elle me plaît, mais il/elle est cher (chère).* 10; **I'd like. . .** *Je voudrais... ,* 3; **I'd like . . . to go with . . .** *J'aimerais... pour aller avec... ,* 10; **I'd really like to.** *Je veux bien.* 6; **I'd like to buy . . .** *Je voudrais acheter... ,* 3; **What would you like?** *Vous désirez?* 10
like: What are they like? *Ils/Elles sont comment?* 7; **What is he like?** *Il est comment?* 7; **What is she**

ENGLISH-FRENCH VOCABULARY

R75

R75

like? *Elle est comment?* 7

listen *écouter*, 1; **Listen!** *Ecoutez!* 0; **I'm listening.** *Je t'écoute.* 9; **to listen to music** *écouter de la musique*, 1

liter *le litre*, 8; **a liter of** *un litre de*, 8

long *long (ue)*, 10

look after: to look after . . . *garder...* , 7

look: Look at the map! *Regardez la carte!* 0; **It doesn't look good on you at all.** *Il/Elle ne te/vous va pas du tout.* 10; **I'm looking for something for . . .** *Je cherche quelque chose pour...* , 10; **It looks great on you!** *C'est tout à fait ton style!* 10; **Look, here's/there's/ it's . . .** *Regarde, voilà...* , 12; **No, thanks, I'm just looking.** *Non, merci, je regarde.* 10; **to look for** *chercher*, 9;

loose-leaf binder *le classeur*, 3

looks: It looks great on you! *C'est tout à fait ton style!* 10

lose *perdre*, 9; **to lose weight** *maigrir*, 10

lot: A lot. *Beaucoup.* 4

lots: I have lots of things to do. *J'ai des tas de choses à faire.* 5

lower (number) *moins*, 0

luck *la chance*, 11; **Good luck!** *Bon courage!* 2; *Bonne chance!* 11

lunch *le déjeuner*, 2; **to have lunch** *déjeuner*, 9

ma'am *madame (Mme)*, 1

made *fait* (pp of *faire*), 9

magazine *le magazine*, 3

make *faire*, 4

mall *le centre commercial*, 6

mango *la mangue*, 8

map *la carte*, 0

March *mars*, 4; **in March** *en mars*, 4

market *le marché*, 8

math *les maths* (f. pl.), *les mathématiques*, 1

May *mai*, 4; **in May** *en mai*, 4

may: May I . . . ? *(Est-ce que) je peux...* ? 7; **May I help you?** *(Est-ce que) je peux vous aider?* 10

me *moi*, 2; **Me, too.** *Moi aussi.* 2; **Not me.** *Pas moi.* 2

mean *méchant(e)*, 7

meat *la viande*, 8

medicine *les médicaments* (m.), 12

meet *retrouver*, 6; *rencontrer*, 9; **I'd like you to meet . . .** *Je te (vous) présente...* , 7; **Pleased to meet you.** *Très heureux (heureuse).* 7; **OK,**

we'll meet . . . *Bon, on se retrouve...* , 6; **We'll meet. . .** *Rendez-vous...* , 6

menu *la carte*, 5; **The menu, please.** *La carte, s'il vous plaît.* 5

message *le message*, 9; **Can I leave a message?** *Je peux laisser un message?* 9

metro *le métro*, 12; **at the . . . metro stop** *au métro...* , 6

midnight *minuit*, 6; **It's midnight.** *Il est minuit.* 6; **It's half past midnight.** *Il est minuit et demi.* 6

milk *le lait*, 8

mineral water *l'eau minérale* (f.), 5

minute *la minute*, 9; **Do you have a minute?** *Tu as une minute?* 9

miss, Miss *mademoiselle (Mlle)*, 1

miss *rater*, 9; **to miss the bus** *rater le bus*, 9

moment *le moment*, 5; **One moment, please.** *Un moment, s'il vous plaît.* 5

Monday *lundi*, 2; **on Mondays** *le lundi*, 2

money *l'argent* (m.), 11

More . . . ? *Encore de... ?* 8; **I don't want any more.** *Je n'en veux plus.* 8

morning *le matin*, 2; **in the morning** *le matin*, 2

mother *la mère*, 7

mountain *la montagne*, 11; **to/in the mountains** *à la montagne*, 11

movie *le film*, 6; **to see a movie** *voir un film*, 6

movie theater *le cinéma*, 6; **the movies** *le cinéma*, 1

mow: to mow the lawn *tondre le gazon*, 7

Mr. *monsieur (M.)*, 1

Mrs. *madame (Mme)*, 1

much: How much is . . . ? *C'est combien,... ?* 5; **How much is it, please?** *Ça fait combien, s'il vous plaît?* 5; **How much is it?** *C'est combien?* 3; **No, not too much.** *Non, pas trop.* 2; **Not much.** *Pas grand-chose.* 6; **Not too much.** *Pas tellement.* 4; **Not very much.** *Pas beaucoup.* 4; **Yes, very much.** *Oui, beaucoup.* 2

museum *le musée*, 6

mushroom *le champignon*, 8

music *la musique*, 2

my *mon/ma/mes*, 7

name: His/Her name is . . . *Il/Elle s'appelle...* , 1; **My name is . . .** *Je m'appelle...* , 0; **What is your name?** *Tu t'appelles comment?* 0

natural science *les sciences naturelles* (f.), 2

need: I need . . . *Il me faut...* , 3; **I need . . .** *J'ai besoin de...* , 8; **What do you need for . . . ?** (formal) *Qu'est-ce qu'il vous faut pour... ?* 3; **What do you need for . . . ?** (informal) *Qu'est-ce qu'il te faut pour... ?* 3; **What do you need?** *De quoi est-ce que tu as besoin?* 8

neither: Neither do I. *Moi non plus.* 2; **neither tall nor short** *ne... ni grand(e) ni petit(e)*, 7

never *ne... jamais*, 4

next *prochain(e)*, 12; **You go down this street to the next light.** *Vous continuez jusqu'au prochain feu rouge.* 12

next to *à côté de*, 12

nice *gentil (gentille)*, 7; *sympa (sympathique)*, 7; **It's nice weather.** *Il fait beau.* 4

nightmare *le cauchemar*, 11; **It was a real nightmare!** *C'était un véritable cauchemar!* 11

no *non*, 1

noon *midi*, 6; **It's noon.** *Il est midi.* 6; **It's half past noon.** *Il est midi et demi.* 6

not: Oh, not bad. *Oh, pas mal/mauvais.* 9; **not yet** *ne... pas encore*, 9; **Not at all.** *Pas du tout.* 4; **Not me.** *Pas moi.* 2; **Not so great.** *Pas terrible.* 1; **not very good** *pas bon*, 5; **No, not really.** *Non, pas vraiment.* 11; **No, not too much.** *Non, pas trop.* 2

notebook *le cahier*, 0, 3

nothing *rien*, 6; **Nothing special.** *Rien de spécial.* 6

novel *le roman*, 3

November *novembre*, 4; **in November** *en novembre*, 4

now *maintenant*, 2; **I can't right now.** *Je ne peux pas maintenant.* 8

o'clock *...heures*, 2; **at . . . o'clock** *à... heure(s)*, 2

October *octobre*, 4; **in October** *en octobre*, 4

of *de*, 0; **of course** *bien sûr*, 3; **of it** *en*, 8; **of them** *en*, 8

often *souvent*, 4

OK. *D'accord.* 4; **Is that OK with you?** *Tu es d'accord?* 7; **Well, OK.** *Bon, d'accord.* 8; **Yes, it was OK.** *Oui, ça a été.*

okra *les gombos* (m.), 8

old: How old are you? *Tu as quel*

age? 1; **I am . . . years old.** *J'ai...
ans.* 1; **older** *âgé(e)*, 7
omelette *l'omelette* (f.), 5
on: Can I try on . . . ? *Je peux
essayer le/la/les... ?* 10; **on foot** *à
pied*, 12; **on Fridays** *le vendredi*, 2;
on Mondays *le lundi*, 2; **on
Saturdays** *le samedi*, 2; **on
Sundays** *le dimanche*, 2; **on
Thursdays** *le jeudi*, 2; **on
Tuesdays** *le mardi*, 2; **on
Wednesdays** *le mercredi*, 2;
once: once a week *une fois par
semaine*, 4
onion *l'oignon* (m.), 8
open: Open your books to page . . .
Ouvrez vos livres à la page... , 0
opinion *l'avis* (m.), 9; **In your opinion, what do I do?** *A ton avis,
qu'est-ce que je fais?* 9
or *ou*, 1
orange (color) *orange* (inv.), 3
orange *l'orange* (f.), 8
orange juice *le jus d'orange*, 5;
our *notre/nos*, 7
out: Out of the question! *Pas question!* 7; **out of style**, *démodé(e)*, 10

package *le paquet*, 8; **a
package/box of** *un paquet de*, 8
page *la page*, 0
pancake: a very thin pancake *la
crêpe*, 5
pants *le pantalon*, 10
papaya *la papaye*, 8
paper *le papier*, 0; **sheets of paper**
les feuilles de papier (f.), 3
pardon: Pardon me. *Pardon.* 3
parent *le parent*, 7
park *le parc*, 6
party *la boum*, 6; **to go to a party**
aller à une boum, 6
pass: You'll pass . . . *Vous passez...* ,
12
passport *le passeport*, 11
pastry *la pâtisserie*, 12; **pastry shop**
la pâtisserie, 12
peach *la pêche*, 8
pear *la poire*, 8
peas *les petits pois* (m.), 8
pen *le stylo*, 0
pencil *le crayon*, 3; **pencil case** *la
trousse*, 3; **pencil sharpener** *le
taille-crayon*, 3
perfect *parfait(e)*, 10; **It's perfect.**
C'est parfait. 10
phone *le téléphone*, 1; **to talk on the
phone** *parler au téléphone*, 1
photography: to do photography
faire de la photo, 4

physical education *l'éducation
physique et sportive (EPS)* (f.), 2
physics *la physique*, 2
pick *choisir*, 10; **to pick up your
room** *ranger ta chambre*, 7
picnic *le pique-nique*, 6; **to have a
picnic** *faire un pique-nique*, 6
picture *la photo*, 4; **to take pictures**
faire des photos, 4
pie *la tarte*, 8
piece *le morceau*, 8; **a piece of** *un
morceau de*, 8
pineapple *l'ananas* (m.), 8
pink *rose*, 3
pizza *la pizza*, 1
place *l'endroit* (m.), 12
plane *l'avion* (m.), 12; **by plane** *en
avion*, 12
plane ticket *le billet d'avion*, 11
plans: I don't have any plans. *Je
n'ai rien de prévu.* 11
plate *l'assiette* (f.), 5
play *la pièce*, 6; **to see a play** *voir
une pièce*, 6
play *jouer*, 4; *faire*, 4; **I don't
play/do . . .** *Je ne fais pas de...* ,
4; **I play . . .** *Je joue...* , 4; **I
play/do. . .** *Je fais...* , 4; **to play
baseball** *jouer au base-ball*, 4; **to
play basketball** *jouer au basket
(-ball)*, 4; **to play football** *jouer
au football américain*, 4; **to play
golf** *jouer au golf*, 4; **to play
hockey** *jouer au hockey*, 4; **to play
soccer** *jouer au foot(ball)*, 4; **to
play sports** *faire du sport*, 1; **to
play tennis** *jouer au tennis*, 4; **to
play video games** *jouer à des jeux
vidéo*, 4; **to play volleyball** *jouer
au volley(-ball)*, 4; **What sports do
you play?** *Qu'est-ce que tu fais
comme sport?* 4
please *s'il te/vous plaît*, 3; **Yes,
please.** *Oui, s'il te/vous plaît.* 8
pleased: Pleased to meet you. *Très
heureux (euse).* 7
pleasure *le plaisir*, 8; **Yes, with
pleasure.** *Oui, avec plaisir.* 8
pork *le porc*, 8
post office *la poste*, 12
poster *le poster*, 0
potato *la pomme de terre*, 8
pound *la livre*, 8; **a pound of** *une
livre de*, 8
practice *répéter*, 9
prefer *préférer*, 1; **I prefer . . .** *Je
préfère...* , 1; *J'aime mieux...* , 1
problem *le problème*, 9; **I've got a
little problem.** *J'ai un petit problème.* 9
pullover (sweater) *le pull-over*, 3
purple *violet(te)*, 3
put *mettre*, 10; **to put on** *mettre*, 10

quarter *le quart*, 6; **quarter past** *et
quart*, 6; **quarter to** *moins le
quart*, 6
question: Out of the question! *Pas
question!* 7
quiche *la quiche*, 5
quiz *l'interro(gation)* (f.), 9

R

radio *la radio*, 3
rain: It's raining. *Il pleut.* 4
raise: Raise your hand! *Levez la
main!* 0
rarely *rarement*, 4
read *lire*, 1; **read (pp.)** *lu* (pp. of
lire), 9
really *vraiment*, 11; **I (really) like
. . .** *Moi, j'aime (bien)...* , 1; **I'd
really like . . .** *Je voudrais
bien...* , 11; **I'd really like to.** *Je
veux bien.* 6; **No, not really.**
Non, pas vraiment. 11
record store *le disquaire*, 12; **at the
record store** *chez le disquaire*, 12
recreation center *la Maison des
jeunes et de la culture (MJC)*, 6
red *rouge*, 3; **redheaded** *roux
(rousse)*, 7
rehearse *répéter*, 9
relative *le parent*, 7
Repeat! *Répétez!* 0
restaurant *le restaurant*, 6
retro (style) *rétro* (inv.), 10
return: to return something *rendre*,
12
rice *le riz*, 8
ride: to go horseback riding *faire de
l'équitation*, 1
right *la droite*, 12; **to the right** *à
droite (de)*, 12
right away *tout de suite*, 6; **Yes,
right away.** *Oui, tout de suite.* 5;
I'll go right away. *J'y vais tout de
suite.* 8
right now *maintenant*, 8; **I can't
right now.** *Je ne peux pas maintenant.* 8
**right there: It's right there on
the . . .** *C'est tout de suite à...* , 12
room *la chambre*, 7; **to pick up your
room** *ranger ta chambre*, 7
ruler *la règle*, 3

S

sailing *la voile*, 11; **to go sailing**
faire de la voile, 11; *faire du bateau*,
11
salad *la salade*, 8

salami *le saucisson*, 5
sandals *les sandales* (f.), 10
sandwich *un sandwich*, 5; **cheese sandwich** *un sandwich au fromage*, 5; **ham sandwich** *un sandwich au jambon*, 5; **salami sandwich** *un sandwich au saucisson*, 5; **toasted cheese and ham sandwich** *le croque-monsieur*, 5
Saturday *samedi*, 2; **on Saturdays** *le samedi*, 2
saw *vu* (pp of *voir*), 9
scarf *l'écharpe* (f.), 10
school *l'école* (f.), 1
science class *les sciences naturelles*, 2
scuba diving *la plongée*, 11; **to go scuba diving** *faire de la plongée*, 11
sea *la mer*, 11
second *la seconde*, 9; **One second, please.** *Une seconde, s'il vous plaît.* 9
see *voir*, 6; **See you later!** *A tout à l'heure!* 1; **See you soon.** *A bientôt.* 1; **See you tomorrow.** *A demain.* 1; **to go see a game** *aller voir un match*, 6; **to see a movie** *voir un film*, 6; **to see a play** *voir une pièce*, 6
seen *vu* (pp. of *voir*), 9
sell *vendre*, 9
send *envoyer*, 12; **to send letters** *envoyer des lettres*, 12
sensational *sensas*, 10
September *septembre*, 4; **in September** *en septembre*, 4
service: **At your service; You're welcome.** *A votre service.* 3
shall: **Shall we go to the café?** *On va au café?* 5
sheet *la feuille*, 0; **a sheet of paper** *une feuille de papier*, 0
shirt (man's) *la chemise*, 10; (woman's) *le chemisier*, 10
shoes *les chaussures* (f.), 10
shop: **to go shopping** *faire les magasins*, 1; **to window-shop** *faire les vitrines*, 6; **Can you do the shopping?** *Tu peux aller faire les courses?* 8
shopping *les courses* (f.), 7; **to do the shopping** *faire les courses*, 7
short (height) *petit(e)*, 7; (length) *court(e)*, 10
shorts: **(pair of) shorts** *le short*, 3
should: **You should . . .** *Tu devrais... ,* 9; **You should talk to him/her/ them.** *Tu devrais lui/leur parler.* 9
show *montrer*, 9
shy *timide*, 7
sing *chanter*, 9
sir *monsieur (M.)*, 1
sister *la sœur*, 7

Sit down! *Asseyez-vous!* 0
size *la taille*, 10
skate: **to ice-skate** *faire du patin à glace*, 4; **to in-line skate** *faire du roller en ligne*, 4
ski *faire du ski*, 4; **How about skiing?** *On fait du ski?* 5; **to water-ski** *faire du ski nautique*, 4; **skiing** *le ski*, 1
skirt *la jupe*, 10
sleep *dormir*, 1
slender *mince*, 7
slice *la tranche*, 8; **a slice of** *une tranche de*, 8
small *petit(e)*, 10
smart *intelligent(e)*, 7
snack: **afternoon snack** *le goûter*, 8
snails *les escargots* (m.), 1
sneakers *les baskets* (f. pl.), 3
snow: **It's snowing.** *Il neige.* 4
So-so. *Comme ci, comme ça.* 1
so: **not so great** *pas terrible*, 5
soccer *le football*, 1; *le foot*, 4; **to play soccer** *jouer au foot(ball)*, 4
socks *les chaussettes* (f.), 10
soda: **lemon soda** *la limonade*, 5
some *des*, 3; **some** *du, de la, de l', des*, 8; **some (of it)** *en*, 8; **Yes, I'd like some.** *Oui, j'en veux bien.* 8
something *quelque chose*, 6; **I'm looking for something for . . . ,** *Je cherche quelque chose pour... ,* 10
sometimes *quelquefois*, 4
son *le fils*, 7
soon: **See you soon.** *A bientôt.* 1
Sorry. *Je regrette.* 3; *Désolé(e).* 5; **Sorry, but I can't.** *Désolé(e), mais je ne peux pas.* 4; **I'm sorry, but I don't have time.** *Je regrette, mais je n'ai pas le temps.* 8; **Sorry, I'm busy.** *Désolé(e), je suis occupé(e).* 6
Spanish (language) *l'espagnol* (m.), 2
speak *parler*, 9; **Could I speak to . . . ?** *(Est-ce que) je peux parler à... ?* 9
special *spécial(e)*, 6; **Nothing special.** *Rien de spécial.* 6
sports *le sport*, 1; **to play sports** *faire du sport*, 1; **What sports do you play?** *Qu'est-ce que tu fais comme sport?* 4
spring *le printemps*, 4; **in the spring** *au printemps*, 4
stadium *le stade*, 6
stamp *le timbre*, 12
stand: **Stand up!** *Levez-vous!* 0
start *commencer*, 9
stationery store *la papeterie*, 12
steak *le bifteck*, 8; **steak and French fries** *le steak-frites*, 5
stop: **at the . . . metro stop** *au métro ... ,* 6

store *le magasin*, 1
straight ahead *tout droit*, 12; **You go straight ahead until you get to . . .** *Vous allez tout droit jusqu'à... ,* 12
strawberry *la fraise*, 8; **water with strawberry syrup** *le sirop de fraises (à l'eau)*, 5
street *la rue*, 12; **Take . . . Street, then cross . . . Street.** *Prenez la rue... , puis traversez la rue... ,* 12
strong *fort(e)*, 7
student *l'élève* (m./f.), 2
study *étudier*, 1
study hall *l'étude* (f.), 2
style *la mode*, 10; **in style** *à la mode*, 10; **out of style** *démodé(e)*, 10
subway *le métro*, 12; **by subway** *en métro*, 12
sugar *le sucre*, 7
suit jacket *la veste*, 10
suit: **Does it suit me?** *Il/Elle me va?* 10; **It suits you really well.** *Il/Elle te/vous va très bien.* 10
suitcase *la valise*, 11
summer *l'été* (m.), 4; **in the summer** *en été*, 4
summer camp *la colonie de vacances*, 11; **to/at a summer camp** *en colonie de vacances*, 11
Sunday *dimanche*, 2; **on Sundays** *le dimanche*, 2
sunglasses *les lunettes de soleil* (f. pl.), 10
super *super*, 2
supermarket *le supermarché*, 8
sure: **I'm not sure.** *J'hésite.* 10
sweater *le cardigan*, 10
sweatshirt *le sweat-shirt*, 3
swim *nager*, 1; *faire de la natation*, 4
swimming *la natation*, 4
swimming pool *la piscine*, 6
syrup: **water with strawberry syrup** *le sirop de fraises (à l'eau)*, 5

T-shirt *le tee-shirt*, 3
table *la table*, 7; **to clear the table** *débarrasser la table*, 7
tacky *moche*, 10; **I think it's (they're) really tacky.** *Je le/la/les trouve moche(s).* 10
take or have (food or drink) *prendre*, 5; **Are you taking it/them?** *Vous le/la/les prenez?* 10; **Are you taking . . . ?** *Tu prends... ?* 11; **Have you decided to take . . . ?** *Vous avez décidé de prendre... ?* 10; **I'll take it/them.** *Je le/la/les prends.* 10; **to take a test** *passer un examen*, 9; **to take pictures**

faire des photos, 4; **We can take . . .** *On peut prendre...* , 12; **Take . . . Street, then . . . Street.** *Prenez la rue... , puis la rue...* , 12

take out: Take out a sheet of paper. *Prenez une feuille de papier.* 0; **to take out the trash** *sortir la poubelle,* 7

taken *pris* (pp. of prendre), 9

talk *parler,* 1; **Can I talk to you?** *Je peux te parler?* 9; **to talk on the phone** *parler au téléphone,* 1; **We talked.** *Nous avons parlé.* 9

tall *grand(e),* 7

taxi *le taxi,* 12; **by taxi** *en taxi,* 12

teacher *le professeur,* 0

telephone *le téléphone,* 0

television *la télévision,* 0

tell *dire,* 9; **Can you tell her/him that I called?** *Vous pouvez lui dire que j'ai téléphoné?* 9

tennis *le tennis,* 4; **to play tennis** *jouer au tennis,* 4

terrible *horrible,* 10

test *l'examen* (m.), 1

Thank you. *Merci.* 3; **No thanks. I'm not hungry anymore.** *Non, merci. Je n'ai plus faim.* 8

that *ce, cet, cette,* 3; **This/That is . . .** *Ça, c'est...* , 12

theater *le théâtre,* 6

their *leur/leurs,* 7

them *les,* 9; **to them** *leur,* 9

then *ensuite,* 9

there *-là* (noun suffix), 3; **there** *il y a,* 5; **there** *y, là,* 12; **Is . . . there, please?** *(Est-ce que)... est là, s'il vous plaît?* 9; **There's . . .** *Voilà...* , 7; **There is/There are . . .** *Il y a...* , 5; **What is there to drink?** *Qu'est-ce qu'il y a à boire?* 5

these *ces,* 3; **These/those are . . .** *Ce sont...* , 7

thing *la chose,* 5; *le truc,* 5; **I have lots of things to do.** *J'ai des tas de choses à faire.* 5; **I have some things to do.** *J'ai des trucs à faire.* 5

think *penser,* 11; **I think it's/they're . . .** *Je le/la/les trouve...* , 10; **I've thought of everything.** *J'ai pensé à tout.* 11; **What do you think of . . . ?** *Comment tu trouves... ?* 2; **What do you think of that/it?** *Comment tu trouves ça?* 2

thirsty: to be thirsty *avoir soif,* 5

this *ce, cet, cette,* 3; **This is . . .** *C'est...* , 7; **This is . . .** *Voilà/Voici...* , 7; **This/That is . . .** *Ça, c'est...* , 12

those *ces,* 3; **These/Those are . . .** *Ce sont...* , 7

Thursday *jeudi,* 4; **on Thursdays** *le jeudi,* 2

ticket *le billet,* 11; **plane ticket** *le billet d'avion,* 11; **train ticket** *le billet de train,* 11

tie *la cravate,* 10

tight *serré(e),* 10

time *le temps,* 8; **a waste of time** *zéro,* 2; **at the time of** *à l'heure de,* 1; **At what time do you have . . . ?** *Tu as... à quelle heure?* 2; **At what time?** *A quelle heure?* 6; **from time to time** *de temps en temps,* 4; **I'm sorry, but I don't have time.** *Je regrette, mais je n'ai pas le temps.* 8; *Je suis désolé(e), mais je n'ai pas le temps.* 12; **What time is it?** *Quelle heure est-il?* 6

to *à la, au, a l', aux,* 6; **to (a city or place)** *à,* 11; **to (before a feminine country)** *en,* 11; **to (before a masculine noun)** *au,* 11; **to (before a plural noun)** *aux,* 11; **to her** *lui,* 9; **to him** *lui,* 9; **to them** *leur,* 9; **five to . . .** *moins cinq,* 6

today *aujourd'hui,* 2

tomato *la tomate,* 8

tomorrow *demain,* 2; **See you tomorrow.** *A demain.* 1

tonight *ce soir,* 7; **Not tonight.** *Pas ce soir.* 7

too (much) *trop,* 10; **It's/They're too . . .** *Il/Elle est (Ils/Elles sont) trop...* , 10; **Me too.** *Moi aussi.* 2; **No, it's too expensive.** *Non, c'est trop cher.* 10; **No, not too much.** *Non, pas trop.* 2; **Not too much.** *Pas tellement.* 4

track *l'athlétisme* (m.), 4; **to do track and field** *faire de l'athlétisme,* 4

train *le train,* 12; **by train** *en train,* 12; **train ticket** *le billet de train,* 11

trash(can) *la poubelle,* 7; **to take out the trash** *sortir la poubelle,* 7

travel *voyager,* 1

trip *le voyage,* 11; **Have a good trip!** *Bon voyage!* 11

true *vrai,* 2

try: Can I try on . . . ? *Je peux essayer... ?* 10; **Can I try it (them) on ?** *Je peux l'/les essayer?* 10

Tuesday *mardi,* 2; **on Tuesdays** *le mardi,* 2

turn *tourner,* 12; **You turn . . .** *Vous tournez...* , 12

TV *la télé(vision),* 1; **to watch TV** *regarder la télé(vision),* 1

umbrella *le parapluie,* 11

uncle *l'oncle* (m.), 7

uncooked *cru(e),* 5

until *jusqu'à,* 12; **You go straight ahead until you get to . . .** *Vous allez tout droit jusqu'à ...* , 12

useless *nul(le),* 2

usually *d'habitude,* 4

vacation *les vacances* (f. pl.), 1; **Have a good vacation!** *Bonnes vacances!* 11; **on vacation** *en vacances,* 4

vacuum (verb) *passer l'aspirateur,* 7

VCR (videocassette recorder) *le magnétoscope,* 0

vegetables *les légumes* (m.), 8

very *très,* 1; **Very well.** *Très bien.* 1; **Yes, very much.** *Oui, beaucoup.* 2

video *la vidéo,* 4; **to make videos** *faire de la vidéo,* 4; **video games** *des jeux vidéo,* 4

videocassette recorder, VCR *le magnétoscope,* 0

videotape *la vidéocassette,* 3

visit (a place) *visiter,* 9

volleyball *le volley(-ball),* 4; **to play volleyball** *jouer au volley(-ball),* 4

W

wait for *attendre,* 9

Waiter! *Monsieur!* 5

Waitress! *Madame!* 5; *Mademoiselle!* 5

walk: to go for a walk *faire une promenade,* 6; **to walk the dog** *promener le chien,* 7

wallet *le portefeuille,* 3

want *vouloir,* 6; **Do you want . . . ?** *Tu veux... ?* 6; **Do you want . . . ?** *Vous voulez... ?* 8; **I don't want any more.** *Je n'en veux plus.* 8; **Yes, if you want to.** *Oui, si tu veux.* 7

wash *laver,* 7; **to wash the car** *laver la voiture,* 7

waste: a waste of time *zéro,* 2

watch *la montre,* 3

watch *regarder,* 1; **to watch a game (on TV)** *regarder un match,* 6; **to watch TV** *regarder la télé(vision),* 1

water *l'eau* (f.), 5; **mineral water** *l'eau minérale,* 5; **water with strawberry syrup** *le sirop de fraises (à l'eau),* 5

water ski *le ski nautique,* 4; **to water ski** *faire du ski nautique,* 4

wear *mettre, porter,* 10; **I don't know what to wear for . . .** *Je ne sais pas quoi mettre pour...* , 10;

Wear . . . *Mets... ,* 10; **What shall I wear?** *Qu'est-ce que je mets?* 10; **Why don't you wear . . . ?** *Pourquoi est-ce que tu ne mets pas... ?* 10

weather *le temps,* 4; **What's the weather like?** *Quel temps fait-il?* 4

Wednesday *mercredi,* 2; **on Wednesdays** *le mercredi,* 2

week *la semaine,* 4; **once a week** *une fois par semaine,* 4

weekend *le week-end,* 6; **Did you have a good weekend?** *Tu as passé un bon week-end?* 9; **on weekends** *le week-end,* 4; **this weekend** *ce week-end,* 6

welcome: **At your service; You're welcome.** *A votre service.* 3

well *bien,* 1; **Did it go well?** *Ça s'est bien passé?* 11; **Very well.** *Très bien.* 1

went: **Afterwards, I went out.** *Après, je suis sorti(e).* 9; **I went . . .** *Je suis allé(e)... ,* 9

what *comment,* 0; **What is your name?** *Tu t'appelles comment?* 0; **What do you think of. . . ?** *Comment tu trouves... ?* 2; **What do you think of that/it?** *Comment tu trouves ça?* 2; **What's his/her name?** *Il/Elle s'appelle comment?* 1

what *qu'est-ce que,* 1; **What are you going to do . . . ?** *Qu'est-ce que tu vas faire... ?* 6; **What do you do to have fun?** *Qu'est-ce que tu fais pour t'amuser?* 4; **What do you have to drink?** *Qu'est-ce que vous avez comme boissons?* 5; **What do you need for . . . ? (formal)** *Qu'est-ce qu'il vous faut pour... ?* 3; **What happened?** *Qu'est-ce qui s'est passé?* 9; **What kind of . . . do you have?** *Qu'est-ce que vous avez comme... ?* 5;

what *quoi,* 2; **I don't know what to wear for . . .** *Je ne sais pas quoi mettre pour... ,* 10; **What are you going to do . . . ?** *Tu vas faire quoi... ?* 6; **What do you have . . . ?** *Tu as quoi... ?* 2; **What do you need?** *De quoi est-ce que tu as besoin?* 5

When? *Quand (ça)?* 6

where *où,* 6; **Where?** *Où (ça)?* 6; **Where are you going to go . . . ?** *Où est-ce que tu vas aller... ?* 11; **Where did you go?** *Tu es allé(e) où?* 9

which *quel(le),* 1

white *blanc(he),* 3

who *qui,* 0; **Who's calling?** *Qui est à l'appareil?* 9

whom *qui,* 6; **With whom?** *Avec qui?* 6

why *pourquoi,* 0; **Why don't you . . . ?** *Pourquoi tu ne... pas?* 9; **Why not?** *Pourquoi pas?* 6

wife *la femme,* 7

win *gagner,* 9

window *la fenêtre,* 0; **to window-shop** *faire les vitrines,* 6

windsurfing *la planche à voile,* 11; **to go windsurfing** *faire de la planche à voile,* 11

winter *l'hiver* (m.), 4; **in the winter** *en hiver,* 4

with *avec,* 6; **with me** *avec moi,* 6; **With whom?** *Avec qui?* 6

withdraw *retirer,* 12; **withdraw money** *retirer de l'argent,* 12

without *sans,* 11; **You can't leave without . . .** *Tu ne peux pas partir sans... ,* 11

work *travailler,* 9

worry: **Don't worry!** *Ne t'en fais pas!* 9

would like: **I'd like to buy . . .** *Je voudrais acheter... ,* 3

year *l'an* (m.); **I am . . . years old.** *J'ai...ans.* 1

yellow *jaune,* 3

yes *oui,* 1; **Yes, please.** *Oui, s'il te/vous plaît.* 8

yesterday *hier,* 9

yet: **not yet** *ne... pas encore,* 9

yogurt *les yaourts* (m.), 8

you *tu, vous,* 0; **And you?** *Et toi?* 1

young *jeune,* 7

your *ton/ta/tes,* 7; *votre/vos,* 7

zoo *le zoo,* 6

GRAMMAR INDEX

Page numbers in boldface type refer to the **Grammaire** and **Note de grammaire** presentations. Other page numbers refer to grammar structures presented in the **Comment dit-on... ?**, **Tu te rappelles?**, **Vocabulaire**, and **A la française** sections. Page numbers beginning with **R** refer to the Grammar Summary in this Reference Section.

A

à: expressions with **jouer 101;** contractions with **le, la, l',** and **les 101,** 157, 316, R18; with cities and countries **290,** R18

adjectives: demonstrative adjectives **77,** R14; adjective agreement and placement 78, **79, 186,** R12–R15; possessive adjectives 179, **181,** R15; adjectives as nouns **265,** R15

à quelle heure: 54, 163, **165,** R17

adverbs: adverbs of frequency **110;** adverb placement with the **passé composé 240,** R15

agreement of adjectives: **79, 186,** R12–R15

aller: 135, 153, **154,** 288, 289, R23; **aller** in the **passé composé 238,** 298, R25

articles: definite articles **le, la, l',** and **les 28,** R16; definite articles with days of the week **153;** indefinite articles **un, une,** and **des** 71, **73,** R16; partitive articles **du, de la,** and **de l'** 207, **208,** 320, R16

avec qui: 163, **165,** R17

avoir: 51, R23; **avoir besoin de 210; avoir envie de** 289; with **passé composé** 237, **239,** 241, **245,** 267, 298, R25

C

ce, cet, cette, and **ces: 77,** R14

c'est: versus **il/elle est** + adjective **274**

cognates: 6–7, 27, 76, 100

commands: 11, 132, 135, **136,** 212, 293, R25; commands with object pronouns 135, 212, **247,** 296, R19–R20

contractions: See **à** or **de.**

countries: prepositions with countries **290,** R18

D

de: expressions with **faire 101;** contractions **104, 325,** R18; indefinite articles (negative) **73;** indicating relationship or ownership **180;** partitive article **208,** R16; with expressions of quantity **214**

definite articles: **28,** R16

demonstrative adjectives: **77,** R14

devoir: 189, R24; **devrais** 247, 290

dire: 244, R24

direct object pronouns: **247, 273,** 296, R19

dormir: 294, R23

E

elle(s): See pronouns.

en: pronoun 214, 219, **220,** 293, R20; preposition before geographic names **290,** R18

-er verbs: 26, 31, 32, **33,** 107, R21; with **passé composé 239,** 241, 298, R25

est-ce que: 103, 165, R17

être: 57, 159, 163, 179, 185, 186, **187,** R23; with **passé composé** 238, 297, 298, R25

F

faire: with **de** + activity **101, 104;** weather 106, R23

falloir: il me/te faut 74, 210, 265, 321, R19

future (near): **aller** + infinitive 76, 135, 153, 288, 289, R24; with the present tense 155, 294

I

il(s): See pronouns.

il est/ils sont: + adjective: 185; versus **c'est** + adjective 274

imperatives: 11, 132, 135, **136,** 212, 293, R25

indefinite articles: 71, **73,** R16

indirect object pronouns: 244, **247,** 296, R20

interrogatives: 54, 163, **165,** 289, R17; **quel** 25; **quels** 51; **pourquoi** 159, 212, 247, 264, 290

-ir verbs: **267,** R21; with **passé composé 267,** R25

For permission to reprint copyrighted material, grateful acknowledgment is made to the following sources:

Agence Vu: Two photographs from "Je passe ma vie au téléphone" by Anne Vaisman, photographs by Claudine Doury, from *Phosphore,* no. 190, February 1997. Copyright © 1997 by Agence Vu.

Air France: Front of Air France boarding pass, "Carte d'accès à bord."

Bayard Presse International: From "Allez, c'est à vous de choisir," text by Florence Farcouli, illustrations by Olivier Tossan, from *Okapi,* no. 568–9, September 1995. Copyright © 1995 by Bayard Presse International. Text and illustrations from "Sondage: les lycéens ont–ils le moral?" from *Phosphore,* no. 160, September 1989. Copyright © 1989 by Bayard Presse International. From "Je passe ma vie au téléphone" by Anne Vaisman from *Phosphore,* no. 190, February 1997. Copyright © 1997 by Bayard Presse International.

C'Rock Radio, Vienne: Logo for C'Rock Radio, 89.5 MHz.

Cacharel: Four adapted photographs with captions of Cacharel products from *Rentrée très classe à prix petits: Nouvelles Galeries Lafayette.*

Caisse Nationale des Monuments Historiques et des Sites: Admission ticket, "Ministère de la Culture, C.N.M.H.S."

Canal B, Bruz: Logo for Canal B Radio, 94 MHz.

Cathédrale d'images: Advertisement, "Cathédrale d'images," from *Évasion Plus.*

Comité Français d'Éducation pour la Santé, 2, rue Auguste Comte-92170 Vanves: From "Les groupes d'aliments" from the brochure *Comment équilibrer votre alimentation,* published and edited by the Comité Français d'Éducation pour la Santé.

Éditions Leconte: Cover of brochure, *Paris Monumental.*

Éditions S.A.E.P.: Recipe and photograph for "Croissants au coco et au sésame," recipe and photograph for "Mousseline africaine de petits légumes," "Signification des symboles accompagnant les recettes," and jacket cover from *La Cuisine Africaine* by Pierrette Chalendar. Copyright © 1993 by S.A.E.P.

EF Foundation: From "Le rêve américain devient réalité, en séjour Immersion avec EF: Vivre à l'américaine," photograph, and "Vacances de Printemps" from "Les U.S.A. en cours Principal: le séjour EF idéal" from *EF Voyages Linguistiques: Hiver, Printemps, et Eté 1993.*

Femme Actuelle: Text from "En direct des refuges: Poupette, 3 ans" by Nicole Lauroy from *Femme Actuelle,* no. 414, August 31–September 6, 1992. Copyright © 1992 by Femme Actuelle. Text from "En direct des refuges: Jupiter, 7 mois" by Nicole Lauroy from *Femme Actuelle,* no. 436, February 1993. Copyright © 1993 by Femme Actuelle. Text from "En direct des refuges: Flora, 3 ans" by Nicole Lauroy from *Femme Actuelle,* no. 457, July 1993. Copyright © 1993 by Femme Actuelle. Text from "En direct des refuges: Dady, 2 ans" and from "Mayo a trouvé une famille" by Nicole Lauroy from *Femme Actuelle,* no. 466, August 30–September 5, 1993. Copyright © 1993 by Femme Actuelle. Text from "En direct des refuges: Camel, 5 ans" by Nicole Lauroy from *Femme Actuelle,* no. 472, October 11–17, 1993. Copyright © 1993 by Femme Actuelle.

France Miniature: Cover, illustration and adapted text from brochure, *Le Pays France Miniature.*

France Telecom: Front and back of the Télécarte.

Galeries Lafayette: Four adapted photographs with captions of Cacharel products and two photographs with captions of NAF NAF products from *Rentrée très classe à prix petits: Nouvelles Galeries Lafayette.*

Grands Bateaux de Provence: Advertisement, "Bateaux 'Mireio'," from *Évasion Plus.*

Grottes de Thouzon: Advertisement, "Grottes de Thouzon," photograph by M. Crotet, from *Évasion Plus,* Provence, Imprimerie Vincent, 1994.

Groupe Filipacchi: Advertisement, "Casablanca," from *7 à Paris,* no. 534, February 12–18, 1992, p. 43.

Hachette Livre (Hachette Tourisme): From "Où dormir?" and "Où manger?" from "Arles (13200)" from *Le Guide du Routard: Provence-Côte d'Azur, 1997/1998.* Copyright © 1997 by Hachette Livre (Hachette Tourisme).

L'Harmattan: Excerpts from French text and six illustrations from *Cheval de bois/Chouval bwa* by Isabelle and Henri Cadoré, illustrated by Bernadette Coléno. Copyright © 1993 by L'Harmattan.

Le Monde: From "Baccalauréat 1996. Les hauts et les bas: Taux de réussite par série" from *Le Monde de l'Éducation,* no. 240, September 1996. Copyright © 1996 by Le Monde.

Loca Center: Advertisement, "Loca Center," from *Guide des Services: La Martinique à domicile.*

Ministère de la Culture: From "Les jeunes aiment sortir" (retitled "Les loisirs préférés") from *Francoscopie: Comment vivent les Français, 1997* by Gérard Mermet.

Musée de l'Empéri: Adapted advertisement, "Musée de l'Empéri," from *Évasion Plus.*

Musée du Louvre: Admission ticket for the Louvre.

NAF NAF: Two photographs with captions of NAF NAF products from *Rentrée très classe à prix petits: Nouvelles Galeries Lafayette.*

NRJ, Paris: Adaptation of logo for NRJ Radio, 100.3 MHz.

OUÏ FM, Paris: Logo for OUÏ FM Radio, 102.3 MHz.

Parc Astérix S.A.: Cover of brochure, *Parc Astérix,* 1992. Advertisement for Parc Astérix from *Paris Vision,* 1993, p. 29.

Parc Zoologique de Paris: Cover and map from brochure, *Parc Zoologique de Paris.*

RATP: Ticket, "Section Urbaine."

RCV: La Radio Rock, Lille: Logo for RCV: La Radio Rock, 99 MHz.

Anne Vaisman: From "Je passe ma vie au téléphone" by Anne Vaisman from *Phosphore,* no. 190, February 1997. Copyright © 1997 by Bayard Presse International.

Village des Sports: Advertisement, "Village des Sports: c'est l'fun, fun, fun!," from *Région de Québec.*

PHOTOGRAPHY CREDITS

Abbreviations used: (t)top, (c) center, (b) bottom, (l) left, (r) right, (bckgd) background, (bdr) border.

CHAPTER OPENER: Background Photographs: HRW Photo by Scott Van Osdol.

TABLE OF CONTENTS: Page vii, HRW Photo/Sam Dudgeon; viii(tl), (bl), HRW Photo/Marty Granger/Edge Productions; viii(all remaining), HRW Photo/Scott Van Osdol; ix(tl), (tc), HRW Photo/Marty Granger/Edge Productions; ix(all remaining), HRW Photo/Scott Van Osdol; x(tl), (br), HRW Photo/Marty Granger/Edge Productions; x(bl), HRW Photo/Sam Dudgeon; x(all remaining), HRW Photo/Scott Van Osdol; xi(tr), (bl), HRW Photo/Marty Granger/Edge Productions; xi(cr), (bc), (br), HRW Photo/Scott Van Osdol; xi(all remaining), HRW Photo/Sam Dudgeon; xii(tl), (br), HRW Photo/Marty Granger/Edge Productions; xii(tr), (cr), (bl), HRW Photo/Sam Dudgeon; xii(all remaining), HRW Photo/Scott Van Osdol; xiii(tc), (tr), HRW Photo/Marty Granger/Edge Productions; xiii(cr), HRW Photo/Sam Dudgeon; xiii(all remaining), HRW Photo/Scott Van Osdol; xiv(tr), (bl), HRW Photo/Marty Granger/Edge Productions; xiv(all remaining), Marion Bermondy; xv(tr), HRW Photo/Louis Boireau/Edge Productions; xv(all remaining), HRW Photo/Scott Van Osdol; xvi(tl), (bl), HRW Photo/Marty Granger/Edge Productions; xvi(all remaining), HRW Photo/Scott Van Osdol; xvii(tc), (br), HRW Photo/Marty Granger/Edge Productions; xvii(all remaining), HRW Photo/Scott Van Osdol; xviii(tl), (br), HRW Photo/Marty Granger/Edge Productions; xviii(all remaining), HRW Photo Scott Van Osdol; xix(tr), (cl), HRW Photo/Marty Granger/Edge Productions; xix(bc), HRW Photo/Sam Dudgeon; xix(all remaining), HRW Photo/Scott Van Osdol.

PRELIMINARY CHAPTER: Page xxvi–1(tc), HRW Photo/Mark Antman; 1(bc),(tr), HRW Photo/Marty Granger/Edge Productions; 1(br), SuperStock; 2(tl), Sipa Press; 2(tr), Duomo Photography, Inc.; 2(c), Archive Photos; 2(b), Vedat Acickalin/Sipa Press; 3(t), Gastaud/Sipa Press; 3(cl), Ron Davis/Shooting Star; 3(cr), Kathy Willens/Wide World Photos, Inc.; 3(b), Archive Photos; 4(tl), HRW Photo/Sam Dudgeon; 4(tc), Barthelemy/Sipa Press; 4(tr), Arianespace/Sipa Press; 4(cl),(c),(cr), HRW Photo/Marty Granger/Edge Productions; 4(bl), Robert Frerck/Odyssey Productions; 4(bc), David R. Frazier/David R. Frazier Photolibrary; 4(br), Derek Berwin/The Image Bank; 5(both), HRW Photo/Marty Granger/Edge Productions; 7(tl), Clay Myers/The Wildlife Collection; 7(tc), Leonard Lee Rue/FPG International, Inc.; 7(tr), (bc), Tim Laman/The Wildlife Collection; 7(bl), Jack Swenson/The Wildlife Collection; 7(br), Martin Harvey/The Wildlife Collection; 10(tl), HRW Photo/Daniel Aubry; 10(tr), HRW Photo/Ken Lax; 10(br), HRW Photo/Louis Boireau/Edge Productions; 10(bl), David Frazier PhotoLibrary; 10(all remaining), HRW Photo/Marty Granger/Edge Productions.

LOCATION: POITIERS: Page 12–13, HRW Photo/Marty Granger/Edge Productions; 14–15(bckgd), Terry Qing/FPG International, Inc.; 14(tr), Tom Craig/FPG International, Inc.; 14(cl), (br), 15(all), HRW Photo/Marty Granger/Edge Productions.

Chapter One: Page 16–17(all), HRW Photo/Marty Granger/Edge Productions; 18(tr),(tr), HRW Photo Louis Boireau/Edge Productions; 18(all remaining), 19(all), HRW Photo/Marty Granger/Edge Productions; 21(tc), HRW Photo/Sam Dudgeon; 21(br), HRW Photo/Alan Oddie; 21(all remaining), HRW Photo/Marty Granger/Edge Productions; 22(l), HRW Photo/John Langford; 22(r), HRW Photo/Marty Granger/Edge Productions; 22(cl), HBJ Photo/Mark Antman; 22(c), HRW Photo; 22(cr), IPA/The Image Works;

23–24(all), HRW Photo/Marty Granger/Edge Productions; 25(tr), Toussaint/Sipa Press; 30(all), HRW Photo/Marty Granger/Edge Productions; 34(tl), HRW Photo/Sam Dudgeon; 34(tc), HRW Photo/Marty Granger/Edge Productions; 34(tr), Robert Brenner/PhotoEdit; 34(cl), HRW Photo/David R. Frazier; 34(c), HBJ Photo/Pierre Capretz; 34(cr), Mark Antman/The Image Works; 34(bl), Lawrence Migdale/Stock Boston; 34(bc), HRW Photo/Ken Karp; 34(br), HBJ Photo/Mark Antman; 34(b), R. Lucas/The Image Works; 36(t), Frank Siteman/The Picture Cube; 36(tc), Richard Hutchings/PhotoEdit; 36(bc), David C. Bitters/The Picture Cube; 36(b), R. Lucas/The Image Works; 37(t),(b), HRW Photo/Russell Dian; 37(tc), HRW Photo/May Polycarpe; 37(bc), R. Lucas/The Image Works; 38(cl), David Young-Wolff/PhotoEdit; 38(all remaining), HRW Photo/Marty Granger/Edge Productions. **Chapter Two:** Page 42–45(all), HRW Photo/Marty Granger/Edge Productions; 56(l) HRW Photo/Louis Boireau/Edge Productions; 56(c),(r), HRW Photo/Marty Granger/Edge Productions. **Chapter Three:** Page 66–69(all), HRW Photo/Marty Granger/Edge Productions; 71(all remaining), 72(t), HRW Photo/Eric Beggs; 72–73(all remaining) HRW Photo/Sam Dudgeon; 75(r), HRW Photo/Louis Boireau/Edge Productions; 75(l), (r), HRW Photo/Marty Granger/Edge Productions; 78(all), 80–81(all), HRW Photo/Michelle Bridwell; 88(all), HRW Photo/Sam Dudgeon.

LOCATION: QUEBEC: Page 90–91, J.A. Kraulis/Masterfile; 92(all), 93(t), (b), HRW Photo/Marty Granger/Edge Productions; 93(cl), Wolfgang Kaehler; 93(cr), Jean-Guy Kérouac/Hervey Smuth, Vue de la Prise de Québec, le 13 septembre 1759, 35.9 x 47.8 cm. Musée du Québec. 78.375. **Chapter Four:** Page 94–95(all), HRW Photo/Marty Granger/ Edge Productions; 96(tr), HRW Photo/Edge Productions 97(all), 99(all),HRW Photo/Marty Granger/Edge Productions; 100(tc), David Young-Wolff/PhotoEdit; 100(tr), HRW Photo/Sam Dudgeon; 100(cl), PhotoEdit; 100(bl), David Lissy/Leo de Wys; 100(bc)HRW Photo/Marty Granger/Edge Productions, 100(br), HRW Photo; 100(all remaining), HRW Photo/Marty Granger/Edge Productions; 103(l), (r), Mat Jacob/The Image Works, 103(cl), Robert Fried/Robert Fried Photography; 103(c), R. Lucas/The Image Works; 103(cr), Mat Jacob/The Image Works;105(l), Robert Fried/Robert Fried Photography; 105(r), (cl), HRW Photo/Sam Dudgeon; 105(c), HBJ Photo/May Polycarpe; 105(cr), HRW Photo/Marty Granger/Edge Productions; 109(l), HRW Photo/Louis Boireau/Edge Productions; 109(r), (c), HRW Photo/Marty Granger/Edge Productions.

LOCATION: PARIS: Page 120–121, Paul/The Stock Market; 122(tr), (c), (b), HRW Photo/Marty Granger/Edge Productions; 123(bl), Peter Menzel/Stock Boston; 123(tr), Bob Handelman/Tony Stone Images; 123(tl), (br), HRW Photo/Marty Granger/Edge Productions. **Chapter Five:** Page 124–127(all), 134(l), (c), HRW Photo/Marty Granger/Edge Productions; 134(r) HRW Photo/Louis Boireau/Edge Productions; 138(cr), HRW Photo/Michelle Bridwell; 138 (all remaining) HRW Photo/Sam Dudgeon; 142(t), HRW Photo/Stuart Cohen; 143(t) HRW Photo/Helena Kolda; 143(c), (b), Pomme de Pain; 143(br), Steven Mark Needhan/Envision. **Chapter Six:** Page 148–149(all), HRW Photo/Marty Granger/Edge Productions; 150(tr), Sevastien Raymond/Sipa Press; 150–151(all remaining), HRW Photo/Marty Granger/Edge Productions; 154(bl), HRW Photo/Sam Dudgeon; 154(bc), David Frazier Photo Library; 154(all remaining), HRW Photo/Marty Granger/Edge Productions; 156(Row 1): (1–3), HRW Photo/Marty Granger/Edge Productions; (4), Tabuteau/The Image Works; (Row 2): (1), Jean Paul Nacivet/Leo de Wys; (2), Greg Meadors/Stock Boston; (3–4), HRW Photo/Marty Granger/Edge Productions; (Row 3): (1), Robert Fried/Stock

R84

Boston; (2), Eva Breckmann; (3), HBJ Photo/Mark Antman; (4), R.Lucas/The Image Works; 158(l), HRW Photo/Louis Boireau/Edge Productions; 158(c),(r), HRW Photo/Marty Granger/Edge Productions; 162(tl), Ulrike Welsch/PhotoEdit; 162(c), HBJ Photo/Mark Antman; 162(tr), HRW Photo/Marty Granger/Edge Productions;170(tr), (bl), SuperStock; 170(tl), HRW Photo. **Chapter Seven**: Pages 174–175(all), 176(t), (cl), (cr) HRW Photo/Marty Granger/Edge Productions; 176(b), HRW Photo/Russell Dian; 177(b), HRW Photo/Marty Granger/Edge Productions; 177(all remaining), HRW Photo/Edge Productions; 178, (l), (lc); HRW Photo/Russell Dian; 178 (rc), (r), HRW Photo/Edge Productions; 179(b), HRW Photo/Russell Dian; 180(Row 1–2(1),(2),(3)) HRW Photo/Edge Productions; 180(Row 2), (4),(5), HRW Photo/Russel Dian; 180(Row 3): (1), HRW Photo/Edge Production; (2), HRW Photo/Marty Granger/Edge Productions; (3–5), HRW Photo/Russell Dian; 180(Row 4): (1), Cherie Mitschke; (2), Marion Bermondy; (3), David Austen/Stock Boston; (4), John Lei/Stock Boston; 181(l to r), HRW Photo/Daniel Aubry; David Young-Wolff/PhotoEdit; HRW Photo/May Polycarpe; Tony Freeman/PhotoEdit; HRW Photo/Sam Dudgeon; 185(bc), Firooz Zahedi/The Kobal Collection; 185(br), TM © 20th Century Fox Film Corp.,1992; 188(all), HRW Photo/Marty Granger/Edge Productions; 192(t),(b), Walter Chandoha; 192(c), HRW Photo; 193(t), (c), Walter Chandoha; 193(b), Gerard Lacz/Peter Arnold, Inc.

LOCATION: ABIDJAN: Page 198–199, Cliché; 200(l), John Elk III/Bruce Coleman, Inc.; 200(tr), Nabil Zorkot/Pro Foto; 200(c), M.& E. Bernheim/Woodfin & Camp & Associates; 201(all), Nabil Zorkot/Pro Foto. **Chapter Eight**: Page 202–205(all), HRW Photo/Louis Boireau/Edge Productions; 206(l), HRW Photo; 206(c), HRW Photo/Sam Dudgeon; 206(cl), (cr), (r), 211(c), HRW Photo/Louis Boireau/Edge Productions; 211(l), (r), HRW Photo/Marty Granger/Edge Productions; 215–216(all), HRW Photo/Louis Boireau/Edge Productions; 217(tl), HRW Photo/Lance Shriner; 217(tr), HRW Photo/Louis Boireau/Edge Productions; 217(bl), HRW Photo/Sam Dudgeon; 217(br), HRW Photo/Eric Beggs.

LOCATION: ARLES: Page 228–229(all), HRW Photo/Marty Granger/Edge Productions; 230(tr), Cherie Mitschke; 230(cr), Erich Lessing/Art Resource; 230(bl), HRW Photo/Marty Granger/Edge Productions. **Chapter Nine**: Page 231(t), W. Gontscharoff/SuperStock; 231(cl), G. Carde/SuperStock; 231(b), 232–235(all), 236(l), (cl), (cr),HRW Photo/Marty Granger/Edge Productions; 236(r), Ermakoff/The Image Works; 242(l),(r), HRW Photo/Marty Granger/Edge Productions; 242(c), Owen Franken/Stock Boston; 246(all), HRW Photo/Marty Granger/Edge Productions. **Chapter Ten**: Page 256–259(all), HRW Photo/Marty Granger/Edge Productions; 261(all), HRW Photo/Sam Dudgeon; 266, HRW Photo/Michelle Bridwell; 269(l), (c), HRW Photo/Marty Granger/Edge Productions; 269(r), HRW Photo/Louis Boireau/Edge Productions; 273, 276(all), 277(l) HRW Photo/Sam Dudgeon; 277(r), HRW Photo/Michelle Bridwell; 278(l), (r), Don Iron/Sipa Press; 278(c), Barthelemy/Sipa Press; 279(t), HRW Photo/Michelle Bridwell; 280(l), (r), HRW Photo/Sam Dudgeon. **Chapter Eleven**: Page 282–283(all), HRW Photo/Marty Granger/Edge Productions; 284(tl), HRW Photo/May Polycarpe; 284(bcl), David Florenz/Option Photo; 284(tr), Same Films/Edge Productions; 284(all remaining), 285–286(all), 292(c), HRW Photo/Marty Granger/Edge Productions; 292(l), HRW Photo/Louis Boireau/Edge Productions; 295 (l), (c), (r), HRW Photo/Marty Granger/Edge Productions; 295(b), Pierre Jaques/FOC Photo; 297(both), 298(cl), HRW Photo/Marty Granger/Edge Productions; 298(cr), Robert Fried/Stock Boston; 298(br), J. Messerschmidt/Leo de Wys;

298(bl), Francis De Richem/The Image Works; 298(bc), Joachim Messer/Leo de Wys; 300(bckgd), HRW Photo/Sam Dudgeon; 303(all), HRW Photo/Marty Granger/Edge Productions.

LOCATION: FORT-DE-FRANCE: Page 306–309(all), HRW Photo/Marty Granger/Edge Productions. **Chapter Twelve**: Page 310–314(all), HRW Photo/Marty Granger/Edge Productions; 315(tl), Tony Freeman/PhotoEdit; 315(c), HBJ Photo/Pierre Capretz; 315(cr), IPA/The Image Works; 315(bc), Robert Fried/Stock Boston; 315(all remaining), HRW Photo/Marty Granger/Edge Productions; 318(tl), (br), Chris Huxley/Leo de Wys; 318(all remaining), HRW Photo/Marty Granger/Edge Productions;321(cl), HRW Photo/Helen Kolda; 321(cr), HRW Photo/Sam Dudgeon (Duly authorized by CASTERMAN, Belgium); 321(bc), HRW Photo/Russell Dian; 321(all remaining) HRW Photo/Sam Dudgeon; 322(tl), Elizabeth Zuckerman/PhotoEdit; 322(tr), Amy Etra/PhotoEdit; 322(c), HRW Photo/Louis Boireau/Edge Productions; 322(bl), Robert Rathe/Stock Boston; 322(br), Mark Antman/The Image Works; 322(tc), (cl), (cr), 324(all), HRW Photo/Marty Granger/Edge Productions; 328(tl), Chris Huxley/Leo de Wys; 328(tr), HRW Photo/Marty Granger/Edge Productions; 331(bckgd), HRW Photo/Mark Antman; 332(l), (cl), (cr), HRW Photo/Marty Granger/Edge Productions; 332(r), Chris Huxley/Leo de Wys.

ILLUSTRATION AND CARTOGRAPHY CREDITS

Abbreviated as follows: (t) top, (b) bottom, (l) left, (r) right, (c) center.

All art, unless otherwise noted, by Holt, Rinehart and Winston.

PRELIMINARY CHAPTER: Page i, Holly Cooper; vi, Holly Cooper; ix, Holly Cooper; xiii, Holly Cooper; xviii, Holly Cooper; xxi, GeoSystems; xxii, GeoSystems; xxiii, GeoSystems.

LOCATION: POITIERS
Chapter One: Page 6, Bruce Roberts; 9, Ellen Beier; 11, Jocelyne Bouchard; 13, GeoSystems; 22, Vincent Rio; 23, Jocelyne Bouchard; 26, Jocelyne Bouchard; 27, Yves Larvor; 28, Camille Meyer; 29, Yves Larvor; 31, Yves Larvor; 33, Vincent Rio; 40, Yves Larvor. **Chapter Two:** Page 47, Yves Larvor; 48 (t), Bruce Roberts; 48 (b), Brian Stevens; 50, Bruce Roberts; 52, Pascal Garnier; 54, Keith Petrus; 55, Guy Maestracci; 58, Brian Stevens; 64, Bruce Roberts. **Chapter Three:** Page 71, Yves Larvor; 72, Vincent Rio; 73, Michel Loppé; 74, Brian Stevens; 76, Brian Stevens; 79, Vincent Rio; 81, Michel Loppé; 82, Jean-Pierre Foissy; 83, Michel Loppé; 88, Bruce Roberts.

LOCATION: QUEBEC
Chapter Four: Page 91, GeoSystems; 101, Michel Loppé; 102, Jocelyne Bouchard; 103, Yves Larvor; 105, Jocelyne Bouchard; 106, Brian Stevens; 107, Jocelyne Bouchard; 108, Michel Loppé; 118, Jocelyne Bouchard.

LOCATION: PARIS
Chapter Five: Page 121, GeoSystems; 129, Andrew Bylo; 130, Vincent Rio; 131, Jocelyne Bouchard; 132, Vincent Rio; 133, Camille Meyer; 139, Guy Maestracci; 140, Jean-Pierre Foissy; 146, Yves Larvor. **Chapter Six:** Page 155, Jocelyne Bouchard; 157 (c), Guy Maestracci; 157 (t), Yves Larvor; 159, Jean-Pierre Foissy; 160, Brian Stevens; 161, Jean-Pierre Foissy; 163, Jean-Pierre Foissy; 164, Jocelyne Bouchard; 172 (t), Jocelyne Bouchard, 172 (b), Guy Maestracci. **Chapter Seven:** Page 179, Vincent Rio; 182 (cr), Guy Maestracci; 182 (b), Jocelyne Bouchard; 183, Vincent Rio; 184, Pascal

Garnier; 185, Brian Stevens; 186, Jean-Pierre Foissy; 187, Vincent Rio; 189 (br), Guy Maestracci; 189 (tr), Pascal Garnier; 190 (t), Vincent Rio; 190 (b), Pascal Garnier; 195, Guy Maestracci; 196, Pascal Garnier.

LOCATION: ABIDJAN
Chapter Eight: Page 199, GeoSystems; 207, Yves Larvor; 208, Camille Meyer; 209, George Kimani; 212, Andrew Bylo; 214, Yves Larvor; 218 (t), Michel Loppé; 218 (b), Jocelyne Bouchard; 219, Michel Loppé; 220 (bl), George Kimani; 220 (tr), Jocelyne Bouchard; 226, Yves Larvor.

LOCATION: ARLES
Chapter Nine: Page 229, GeoSystems; 237, Jean-Pierre Foissy; 238, Jean-Pierre Foissy; 239, Camille Meyer; 241, Guy Maestracci; 242, Jocelyne Bouchard; 243, Michel Loppé; 245, Andrew Bylo; 248, Brian Stevens; 254; Jocelyne Bouchard. **Chapter Ten:** Page 261, Jocelyne Bouchard; 262

(c), Michel Loppé; 262 (t), Yves Larvor; 263, Vincent Rio; 264, Jean-Pierre Foissy; 265, Jean-Pierre Foissy; 268 (t), Brian Stevens; 268 (c), Jocelyne Bouchard; 270, Jean-Pierre Foissy; 271, Michel Loppé; 272, Guy Maestracci; 274, Jean-Pierre Foissy; 280, Yves Larvor. **Chapter Eleven:** Page 287 (c), Brian Stevens; 287 (b), Russell Moore; 288, Guy Maestracci; 289, Camille Meyer; 291, Bruce Roberts; 293, Michel Loppé; 294, Yves Larvor; 296, Jean-Pierre Foissy; 304, Yves Larvor.

LOCATION: FORT-DE-FRANCE
Chapter Twelve: Page 307, GeoSystems; 317, Anne de Masson; 319, Anne de Masson; 320, Anne de Masson; 321, Jean-Pierre Foissy; 323, Brian Stevens; 325, Anne Stanley; 326, Anne de Masson; 327, Anne de Masson; 328, Anne Stanley; 332, Anne de Masson; 334, Anne de Masson.